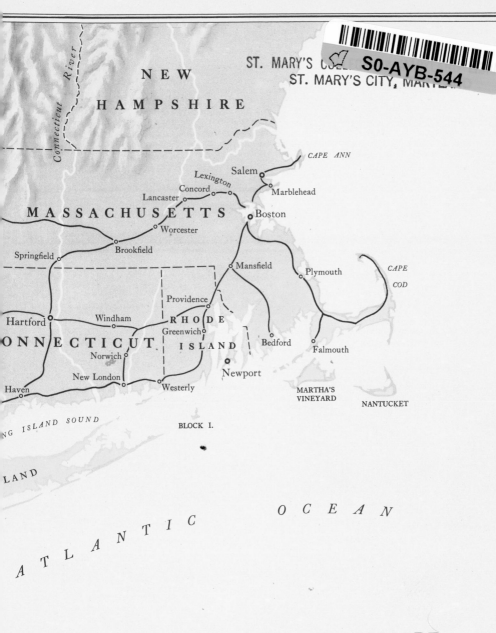

NEW HAMPSHIRE

Connecticut River

MASSACHUSETTS

CAPE ANN

Salem
Lexington
Concord
Marblehead
Lancaster
Boston
Worcester
Springfield
Brookfield
Mansfield
Plymouth
CAPE COD
Providence
Hartford
Windham
R H O D E
Greenwich
Bedford
ONNECTICUT
ISLAND
Norwich
Falmouth
Haven
New London
Westerly
Newport
MARTHA'S VINEYARD
NANTUCKET

NG ISLAND SOUND

BLOCK I.

LAND

ATLANTIC OCEAN

CAPE ANN to BALTIMORE

Principal Towns and some of the Highways

1759-1778

Statute Miles

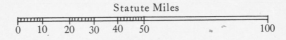

0   10   20   30   40   50   100

GEORGE WASHINGTON

BOOKS BY DOUGLAS SOUTHALL FREEMAN

GEORGE WASHINGTON

LEE'S LIEUTENANTS

THE SOUTH TO POSTERITY

R. E. LEE

CHARLES SCRIBNER'S SONS

WASHINGTON AFTER THE TRENTON-PRINCETON CAMPAIGN

The original, in the gallery of the Pennsylvania Academy of Fine Arts, was the first of numerous large pictures of Washington that Charles Willson Peale made, according to the same general design, in 1778 and later. Details of background vary, also, in Peale's successive copies of this famous portrait, which was ordered by the Executive Council of Pennsylvania.

GEORGE WASHINGTON

A BIOGRAPHY

By

Douglas Southall Freeman

VOLUME FOUR

LEADER OF
THE REVOLUTION

NEW YORK
CHARLES SCRIBNER'S SONS

15895

CONTENTS

v

CONTENTS

APPENDICES

ILLUSTRATIONS

MAPS

GEORGE WASHINGTON

CHAPTER I

How Can Boston Be Recovered?

(January–February, 1776)

THE NEW YEAR, 1776, began with a chill, discouraging wind that died away after darkness.[1] So few were the troops in the redoubts and in the barracks that the lines at some points were bare of defenders;[2] but the British did not stir, and Washington issued a long appeal for "order, regularity and discipline," as if he were sure of "the new army, which," he said, "in every point of view is entirely continental."[3] All offenses of the old establishment were pardoned; the guardhouse doors were opened for all imprisoned American soldiers;[4] the British union flag was raised as if to honor the birthday of the Army.[5] This was done with an air of confidence, almost of bravado; at heart Washington was far less sure of the morrow than he appeared to be. He told Joseph Reed, "We are now left with a good deal less than half raised Regiments, and about 5000 militia who only stand engaged to the middle of this month, when, according to custom, they will depart, let the necessity of their stay be never so urgent. Thus it is that for more than two months past I have scarcely emerged from one difficulty before I have plunged into another. How it will end, God in his great goodness will direct. I am thankful for his protection to this time. We are told that we shall soon get the army completed, but I have been told so many things which have never come to pass that I distrust everything."[6]

Misgiving did not stay the arm of discipline. Washington renewed all the orders he previously had issued to make fighters of farmers and he added a few requirements he had not thought it worth while, apparently, to introduce in the last days of troops about to scatter.[7] As if he felt that sound organization could defy adversity,[8] he announced that

[1] *McCurtin's Journal*, 30.   [2] *J. Baldwin's Journal*, Jan. 1 *et post*, 1777.
[3] 4 *G. W.*, 202.   [4] Cf. *ibid.*, 204.
[5] *Ibid.*, 210.   [6] Letter of Jan. 4, 1776; 4 *G. W.*, 211–12.
[7] Cf. *ibid.*, 202–03, 206 ff, 214, 246.
[8] Cf. *Diary of Ezekiel Price*, Jan. 1, 1776, p. 225: "This day begins a new year, which there is the greatest reason to suppose will be by far the most important year that ever happened

the Regiments of the new establishment were to consist of eight Companies each, and that each Company was to have "seventy-six privates, and no more, under any pretence, or plea whatsoever." [9] If informed officers had to conceal an amused smile, as they heard that order read, they had one incident over which they could laugh unhindered and unabashed. Two days after Washington had hoisted the union flag "in honor of the United Colonies," the camps received the long-delayed text of the King's speech from the throne to both Houses of Parliament on the 26th of October. George III then had announced his intention of putting "a speedy end" to what he described as a "rebellious war . . . manifestly carried on for the purpose of establishing an independent empire." He informed Parliament that he had increased his army and navy and had "received the most friendly offers of foreign assistance," by which he meant, of course, that he had hired troops from German States. The Monarch went on to say, in the spirit of Lord North's "compromise," that he would give "authority to certain persons upon the spot to grant general or particular pardons and indemnities . . . as they shall think fit, and to receive the submission of any Province or Colony which shall be disposed to return to its allegiance." There followed a hint that any such Colony would be restored "to the free exercise of its trade and commerce, and to the same protection and security as if such Province or Colony had never revolted." [10] This speech evoked nothing but ridicule from Chelsea to Dorchester Neck, but when Boston Tories saw the union flag lifted on the first day of the New Year, they assumed that the Americans already had read the King's speech and had put up the flag as a symbol of submission. News of this feeling in the occupied city amused even Washington. "By this time," he wrote on the 4th, "I presume they begin to think it strange that we have not made a formal surrender of our lines." [11]

Relief came with laughter. By the evening of that same 4th of January, a sufficient number of militia had arrived for the Brigadiers to reoccupy thinly those parts of the line that had been undefended for three days. Nathanael Greene confided that on the night the old troops went away, he could not have mustered 700 men on his front, though

in America. It is probable that in this year it will be determined whether America will be tributary to venal and arbitrary administration, or that her sons be freemen."

[9] 4 *G. W.,* 205.
[10] Text conveniently in *Dodsley's Annual Register,* 1775, p. 269 ff.
[11] 4 *G. W.,* 211.

the returns credited him with more than 1900. Now, he said confidently, he was "strong enough to defend [himself] against all the force in Boston." [12] In another four days, the number of men present for duty, fit, was to rise to 10,209,[13] but that was less than half the authorized strength of the Army,[14] and even that figure now might face subtraction because of new developments to which Charles Lee insistently called attention.

Lee had indulged himself at the beginning of December in another argumentative letter to Burgoyne.[15] Then, during the third week of the month, he had gone to Rhode Island to advise Governor Cooke concerning the defence of the Colony, and while there had rounded up eight of the leading Tories to whom he had undertaken to administer a stern oath of allegiance to the Continental Congress.[16] Upon his return shortly before the beginning of January, Lee justified his severity by pointing to Washington's intelligence reports which indicated that the British in Boston were fitting out a fleet. The objective of this force might be New York [17] and its aim might be not only to seize the most valuable point strategically on the coast but also to rally and recruit Tories, who had made that city their stronghold. New York must be occupied and the Tories curbed—that became Lee's temporary creed. "For Heaven's sake," he hurriedly wrote Robert Morris, "why have you not fortified and garrisoned that city with a strong force from Connecticut, Jersey and Pennsylvania? for if the enemy once takes post there, we cannot paint to our imagination the magnitude of the calamities which must flow to the continent from our amazing negligence . . ." [18]

Like views Lee urged on Washington, who as long previously as October, 1775, had considered the possibility of a British descent on

---

[12] Letter of Jan. 4, 1776, to Samuel Ward; 4 *Force* (4) p. 573.

[13] 4 *Force* (4) p. 631–32; James Warren to Samuel Adams, Jan. 14, 1776, 2 *Warren-Adams Letters*, 431.

[14] 4 *G. W.*, 223, 225. The second of these references is to a rebuke administered Gen. Sullivan for making inadequate returns.

[15] Lee's professed reason was a report that Burgoyne was returning to England. For the letter, dated Dec. 1, 1775, see 1 *Lee Papers*, 222. Washington's order to Ward for the transmission of the letter, unopened, by flag, is in the *Artemas Ward Papers*, Dec. 3, 1775, p. 50, MHS.

[16] *Penn. Gazette*, Jan. 17, 1776; 1 *Lee Papers*, 233; 1 Ezra Stiles's *Literary Diary*, 646. According to Stiles, five of the eight took the oath. The others were imprisoned. 4 *Force* (4) p. 488. In 1 *Moore*, 183–84, the full oath is reprinted. For Lee's acknowledgment of a gift from the Rhode Island authorities see his letter of Jan. 9, 1776; *AASP.*, October, 1926, p. 300.

[17] 4 *G. W.*, 218.

[18] Letter of Jan. 3, 1776; 1 *Lee Papers*, 233.

New York and had asked whether, in such an event, he should detach troops, should await instructions, or should rely on the men of that and nearby Colonies to defend the city.[19] In answer, no decision by Congress had been communicated to him. Now that a British movement from Boston was in the making, Washington shared Lee's view that immediate action should be taken at the mouth of the Hudson, and he urged forthwith that New Jersey troops be thrown into the city, on which he asked the Continental Congress to keep a watchful eye.[20] More than this he did not think he should urge, because of his lack of familiarity with conditions in New York. Distance and circumstance had made his position as Commander-in-Chief more nominal than directional. He held the inclusive title; he was not sure he should exercise all the powers his title seemed to confer.[21] Learning this, Lee at once argued: "I have the greatest reason to believe, from the most authentic intelligence, that the best members of Congress expect that you would take much upon yourself, as referring everything to them is, in fact, defeating the project . . . To you they look up for decision; by your conduct they are to be inspired by decision." Lee then made a detailed proposal for the occupation of New York City and of the nearby country.[22] The plan, in its fundamental strategy, appealed to Washington; but he remained in some doubt concerning his authority, and, as John Adams happened fortunately to be near at hand, Washington consulted the

[19] 4 *G. W.*, 24–25.
[20] *Ibid.*, 209, 212.
[21] No deliberate action had been taken by Congress to limit the command of Washington, nor had any opposition to him developed among members. The two influences that had operated to curtail his command had been, first, the organization of the staff departments and, second, the necessity of communicating directly from Philadelphia with the officers in charge of the operations against the British in Canada. When Congress on July 19, 1775, named Joseph Trumbull as Commissary General, it authorized Washington to select various other officers of what now would be termed the General Staff (2 *JCC.*, 190). John Adams thought this a major mistake because, said he, these officers would be a check on the Commander-in-Chief and vice versa (1 *Warren-Adams Letters*, 86, cited in 1 *Burnett*, 177–78). It doubtless was in this spirit that Congress itself named James Warren Paymaster General, July 27, 1775 (2 *JCC.*, 211). The half-severance of Schuyler's command and of the greater part of the Canadian expedition from Washington's care was entirely circumstantial. At the time Congress made Schuyler responsible for New York, July 20, 1775, it stipulated he was to pursue, "if in his power" its former orders and was to be subject to those given in the future by the Commander-in-Chief (2 *JCC.*, 194); but by September 20, the President of Congress was giving instructions to Schuyler, without reference to Washington (1 *Burnett*, 202). The President opened in October similar direct communication with Brig. Gen. David Wooster, who manifestly did not consider that his troops were under Montgomery's or Schuyler's or even Washington's orders (1 *Burnett*, 224; 3 *Force* (4) p. 1107–08). Still again, in December, President Hancock, without "clearing" through Washington, had called on Governor Trumbull to recruit for Schuyler's Army (1 *Burnett*, 268).
[22] 1 *Lee Papers*, 234; a slightly different and more grammatical version in 1 *LTW.*, 106 and in 4 *Force* (4) p. 582–83.

Congressman.[23] His long experience as a legislator had taught the General that the time to avoid criticism was in advance of action and that the way to do this was to consult and convince those who might be critical later. In this instance, Washington told Adams that if the plan was to be executed, it should be undertaken at once and by Lee. Might not "such a step, though right in itself," be "looked upon as beyond my line . . ."?[24] Adams's reply was immediate and unequivocal: Washington should seize New York; it was entirely within his authority to do so. Specifically, said the Massachusetts leader, "your commission constitutes you commander of all the forces . . . and you are vested with full power and authority to act as you shall think for the good and welfare of the service."[25]

This satisfied Washington. He wrote Governor Trumbull of Connecticut about the fleet that was being prepared at Boston and he explained that if the British did not design to take New York immediately, they certainly intended to occupy Long Island. "It is of the utmost importance," he said, "to prevent the enemy from possessing themselves of the City of New York and the North River, which would give them command of the country and the communication with Canada . . ."[26] Lee's instructions were drafted forthwith. As it was impossible to detach any troops from the lines in front of Boston,[27] Lee was to raise volunteers in Connecticut, was then to proceed to New York, was to get assistance from New Jersey, was to curb the disaffected element on Long Island and elsewhere, and was to put New York City "into the best posture of defence which the season and circumstances will admit of."[28] Nothing in Washington's instructions and nothing in Lee's attitude suggested there was a desire on one side to be rid of an over-active lieutenant or, on the other, a secret wish to be free of subordination. Instead, the final admonition in the orders to Lee was, "that you endeavor as much as possible, at all times, to be in readiness to join the Army if the exigency of our affairs here should call for it."[29]

The day after he gave Lee this paper, Washington received the first detailed returns of the new Army, the returns he had insisted his sub-

---

[23] Cf. 4 *G. W.*, 219–20.　　　　　　[24] *Ibid.*, 220.

[25] Letter of Jan. 6, 1776; 1 *LTW.*, 112; 4 *Force* (4) p. 604.

[26] In the original (4 *G. W.*, 218), this sentence begins with "as" and is prefatory to an announcement that Lee is to be sent to New York. The notice to the New York Committee of Safety was to the same effect, with the reminder that it would be a "fatal stab . . . to the interests of America to suffer the City of New York to fall into the hands of our enemies" (letter of Jan. 8, 1776; *ibid.*, 221).

[27] *Ibid.*, 218.　　　　　[28] *Ibid.*, 220–21.　　　　　[29] *Ibid.*, 223.

ordinates make with promptness and care. He had estimated from incomplete weekly figures that the total would be 10,500, or about 45 per cent of the authorized strength. Now he was appalled to find that actual enlistments were 8212, and that the number of men present for duty, fit, was 5582 only.[30] If these calculations were correct—and there was good reason to fear no material error had been made—then the most slovenly negligence had been shown in the totals previously reported. Recruiting had been a failure, particularly when attempted, contrary to Washington's judgment, by individuals who hoped in this manner to get a commission.[31] It was manifest, too, that many men who should have reenlisted for continental service were joining provincial military organizations in which they expected easier duty nearer home.[32] Two weeks' further effort, Washington soon was to learn, had added scarcely more than 1000 names to the rolls.[33]

In the light of these unhappy facts, he was so discouraged that he doubted whether the Army ever could be completed by voluntary enlistment. He said so without advocating immediately an alternative policy,[34] though he believed a draft or a bounty for long-term enlistment would be necessary.[35] In the developing new emergency, he had once again to look to the militia. The time of those called to the lines in December at continental cost would expire Jan. 15, 1776. Although Washington's anxiety prompted him to ask the Massachusetts Legislature to keep these men with the Army until February,[36] his experience admonished him of the old, ugly, mocking fact he had set down not long previously: a great part of the militia would not extend their service even for two weeks.[37] In spite of everything John Sullivan could do, 350 of the New Hampshire contingent—"worthless scoundrels" Sullivan styled them—bluntly refused to stay and, as they went away, protested angrily that Washington's inability to pay them from a depleted war chest was, in reality, nothing "less than a contrivance to cheat them of their wages." [38]

Weakened in this way, Washington felt that he should call a council of war to consider how he could get the men with whom to carry out the plan to which he always returned from every wrestle with adverse

30 *Ibid.*, 225.
31 Cf. *ibid.*, 228.
32 *Ibid.*, 227.
33 *Ibid.*, 241, as of January 14.
34 *Ibid.*, 227, 239, 252.
35 *Ibid.*, 246, 300.
36 *Ibid.*, 227.
37 Huntington in 20 *CHS Cols.*, 28; *E. Price's Diary*, 229; 4 *G. W.*, 242, 255.
38 The words again are Sullivan's. See his letter of Jan. 17, 1776; 1 *Sullivan Papers*, 167.

circumstance, the plan of attacking Boston or of inducing Howe to come out and fight. Washington asked John Adams and James Warren to attend, along with his general officers, and on January 16,[39] he laid before them "a state of the Regiments in the Continental army, the consequent weakness of his lines, and, in his judgment, the indispensable necessity of making a bold attempt to conquer the ministerial troops in Boston, before they can be reenforced in the spring, if the means can be provided, and a favorable opportunity offered, and then [he] desired the opinion of the council thereon." [40] This time, all the doubters were convinced: the attack should be made as soon as practicable; to facilitate it, Washington should call for thirteen militia Regiments to serve from February 1 to the end of March; these Regiments should have the same number of officers and men as were authorized for the Continental Regiments. Massachusetts must be asked for seven, Connecticut for four, and New Hampshire for two.[41]

The call went out accordingly.[42] What the result of this new application might be, Washington could not foresee; but in the acuteness of his anxiety he opened his heart to his friend Joseph Reed: "The reflection on my situation and that of this Army produces many an unhappy hour when all around me are wrapped in sleep. Few people know the predicament we are in on a thousand accounts; still fewer will believe, if any disaster happens to these lines, from what cause it flows. I have often thought how much happier I should have been, if, instead of accepting a command under such circumstances, I had taken my musket on my shoulder and entered the ranks, or if I could have justified the measure to posterity and my own conscience, had retired to the back country, and lived in a wigwam. If I shall be able to rise superior to these and many other difficulties which might be enumerated, I shall most religiously believe that the finger of Providence is in it, to blind the eyes of our enemies; for surely if we get well through this month, it must be for want of their knowing the disadvantages we labor under. Could I have foreseen the difficulties which have come upon us; could

---

[39] The minutes of this conference appear in 4 *Force* (4) p. 774–75 immediately after other minutes, presently to be mentioned, that wrongly bear the same date. In 152 *Papers of the Continental Congress*, pt. 1, p. 423, LC, both the proceedings discussed in the text are marked January 18, though wrongly endorsed January 16 by Washington himself; but in 4 *Force* (4) p. 1193, the minutes of a later meeting stated that the councils were held January 16 and 18. Internal evidence confirms those dates.

[40] 4 *Force* (4) p. 774–75.

[41] *Ibid*. Rhode Island was excepted from this appeal for the reason given in n. 62, *infra*.

[42] 4 *G. W.*, 247, 248, 250.

I have known that such a backwardness would have been discovered in the old soldiers to the service, all the Generals upon earth should not have convinced me of the propriety of delaying an attack upon Boston till this time. When it can now be attempted, I will not undertake to say; but this much I will answer for, that no opportunity can present itself earlier than my wishes." [43]

Opportunity! The word seemed to be mocked by papers that lay in Washington's headquarters as he wrote. A return of small arms taken from departing soldiers in December had been made about the time Washington learned that he had on the lines, fit for duty, no more than 5582 men. He discovered now that, if such a thing was possible, he was even worse off for arms than for soldiers. Virtually all the muskets taken aboard *Nancy* had been distributed.[44] From the troops who had gone home after their refusal to reenlist, barely 1620 arms had been appraised and taken for reasons with which Washington was familiar—the badness of most of the guns and the success of many of the men in carrying off those that were good.[45] Those purchased muskets that were fit for use had been issued one by one to recruits who had none, until the store had been reduced on the 14th of January to less than 100.[46] Recruiting officers reported, moreover, that few of the men who were willing to enter the ranks had muskets of any sort. "They are reduced," Washington said grimly of these officers, "to the alternative of either getting no men, or men without arms." [47] He appealed as usual to the New England Governors and lawmakers[48] and he half-despairingly asked John Hancock: "I hope it is in the power of Congress to afford us relief; if it is not, what must, what can be done?" [49] This quest was to yield so few that Washington was doomed to report on the 9th of February that nearly 2000 men in the camps were without firearms.[50]

[43] Letter of Jan. 14, 1776; *ibid.*, 243.
[44] 4 *G. W.*, 242.
[45] *Ibid.*, 235, 238. The use of the word "gun" to describe small arms was permissible, though not common, in 1776. "Gun" was used principally with reference to cannon.
[46] *Ibid.*, 242.
[47] Letter of Jan. 13, 1776, to the Massachusetts Legislature; *ibid.*, 235.
[48] *Ibid.*, 235, 236–37, 249–50.
[49] Letter of Jan. 14, 1776; *ibid.*, 238. His immediate decision was to send out officers to purchase private arms (*ibid.*, 264).
[50] *Ibid.*, 314. For the inability of nearby Colonies to render assistance, see *ibid.*, 276, 290–91, 325, 326; 5 *Force* (4) p. 289. Benjamin Franklin's familiar proposal of Feb. 11, 1776 that the troops fight with pikes and with bows and arrows will be found in 6 *Smyth's Franklin*, 439. Washington was to continue his efforts to purchase arms (4 *G. W.*, 344), and to procure them from Schuyler (*ibid.*, 346–47); but, on February 12, he was to be compelled to order the discharge of militia who came to camp without arms (*ibid.*, 328–29). In 23 *Papers of G. W.*, 19, LC, is a letter of inquiry from Stephen Moylan to John Sullivan, Jan. 27, 1776.

A dangerous shortage of men and a desperate scarcity of arms were not the full measure of Washington's concern in those bleak January days, when the scolding wind of the frowning dawn of the morrow might bring the sound of British attack. His months-long anxiety over the outcome of the advance of Montgomery and Arnold to Quebec was more and more acute. No confirmation came of the gloomy interpretation Henry Knox had said the timid were putting on a rumor that Arnold had made a slight withdrawal.[51] Philip Schuyler had written under date of January 5 that Arnold and Montgomery had formed a junction, "but," the New Yorker had said, "their force is so small and the weather has been so severe that I fear they have not been able to possess themselves of Quebec." Unhappy and in ill-health, Schuyler had added: "Should an attempt have been made to storm it, and accidents have happened to Montgomery and Arnold, I tremble lest Canada should be lost." [52] Receipt of this letter deepened Washington's dread of disaster in Canada but it also had the effect on his mind that bad news usually did: It stiffened his resolution. He had written on the 12th to Montgomery and to Arnold on the supposition that they soon would enter Quebec if they were not already there, and he had asked that they send him, if they could, some of the arms, blankets and stores he assumed they had taken from the British.[53] Now he replied to Schuyler: "I confess I am much concerned for General Montgomery and Colonel Arnold; and the consequences which will result from their miscarriage, should it happen, will be very alarming. I fear no less fatal than you mention. However, I trust that their distinguished conduct, bravery and perseverance will meet with the Smile of Fortune and put them in possession of this important fortress. I wish their force was greater; the reduction would then be certain." [54]

He did not have to wait long this time. On the evening of the 17th [55]

In this Moylan stated: "His Excellency is informed that you had ordered 215 stand of arms from Newbury to Portsmouth. He would be glad to know what is become of them and how he may procure them for this camp"—a somewhat serious admission that as Mustermaster, Moylan was not always diligent in caring for the arms in his custody. For possible preoccupation of other sorts on Moylan's part, see Charles Lee to Robert Morris, July 27, 1775; 1 *Lee Papers*, 200.

[51] See *supra*, Vol. III, p. 584.   [52] 1 *LTW.*, 110.
[53] 4 *G. W.*, 231, 232.   [54] Letter of Jan. 16, 1776; *ibid.*, 252.

[55] See *supra*, n. 39 with reference to the error in dating the conferences of January 16 and 18. The news presently to be mentioned in the text does not seem to have been known in the camps until the 18th. See *J. Baldwin's Journal*, Jan. 18, 1776. For the circumstances of the receipt of the news in Philadelphia during the sitting of Congress on the 17th, see 1 *Burnett*, 316–17, in which sterling work appears a comprehensive note on the subsidiary correspondence.

when Washington broke the seal of a dispatch written by Schuyler from Albany on the 13th, these opening words were so many blows in the face: "I wish I had no occasion to send my dear General this melancholy account. My amiable friend, the gallant Montgomery, is no more; the brave Arnold is wounded; and we have met with a severe check in an unsuccessful attempt on Quebec." The situation, Schuyler wrote Washington, called for "an immediate reenforcement that is nowhere to be had but from you." Schuyler added that he would remain on duty, though he had asked previously to be permitted to retire.[56] Among the enclosures in Schuyler's communication was a somewhat lengthy but uninformative report by the surviving, unwounded senior officer, Col. Donald Campbell, December 31. Another paper forwarded to Washington was one that Arnold had written Wooster from the hospital before he knew definitely what had been the fate of his own detachment, which had sustained casualties he reckoned at 200.[57]

This news stunned. The invasion of Canada had been ordered by Congress[58] but the cooperation of Arnold through an advance on Quebec had been Washington's own design, his first adventure in strategy on a scale of any magnitude. It had failed, with heavy loss and with dark potential consequences: If Canada were lost to the Americans, that country would be a secure base for the confident planning of an offensive down the Lakes and down the Hudson simultaneously with an attack on New York City by the British fleet and perhaps by Howe's army. Were this joint operation to succeed, then the Colonies would be divided and might be subdued.

[56] 1 LTW., 114–15. Arnold's first known letter to Washington after the defeat was that of January 14, in 1 LTW., 116–18. This told of a double assault on the lower town at Quebec, Dec. 31, 1775, during the first phase of which Montgomery was killed. Soon Arnold was wounded. Then, the retreat of some of the Americans being cut off, panic seized most of the survivors. With difficulty the men were rallied later and were placed where they could hope, when they had rested, to maintain the semblance of a blockade of the city. In 2 Justin Smith, Struggle, 111–47 is a highly detailed account of the assault, with many references to the source material. A simpler, clearer narrative will be found in Dodsley's Annual Register for 1776, p. 12–15.

[57] In his dispatch to Washington, January 13, Schuyler (1 LTW., 114–15), did not mention any enclosures, but Washington's reply of January 18 (4 G. W., 254), referred to them. They must certainly have included Campbell to Wooster, and Arnold to Wooster, December 31, (4 Force (4) p. 480–82); but it is proper to point out that these are not accompanied by any covering letter of Wooster. That officer's first reference to enclosures from Arnold and Campbell was in Wooster to Schuyler, January 5, which appears in 4 Force (4) p. 668. This is followed in Force by letters from Arnold and Campbell to Wooster, written in front of Quebec, January 2. The content of John Sullivan's letter of Jan. 18, 1776, to the New Hampshire Assembly (4 Force (4) p. 768), makes it plain that most of the essential facts of the reverse in front of Quebec were known by that date in Cambridge.

[58] See 2 JCC., 109 and 1 Burnett, 146, 147.

Such was the first reflection of every soldier. Washington saw the full picture in all its blackness and felt grief for Montgomery, whom he had never met but had respected as man and soldier.[59] There was in Washington's heart, of course, a sharper concern for the wounded Arnold. Individual grief apart, "this well intended but unfortunate attempt," [60] as Washington termed it, must be redeemed, if that was within reach of the continental army. At the same time, Washington dissented instantly from Schuyler's statement, "an immediate reenforcement . . . is nowhere to be had but from you." [61] As Washington saw it, the question was not one of detaching troops from his command to reenforce Arnold; it was, instead, how could additional soldiers be found elsewhere for the relief of a gallant man and the capture of the enemy's northern base?

Question and first conclusion were almost instinctive on the evening of January 17 but Washington felt they should be confirmed by the best judgment he could command. He summoned an immediate council of war, to which John Adams accepted an invitation, and when he had the Generals and the Delegate together in a private room, Washington inquired "whether it be proper, in the present circumstances of the lines, to detach a reenforcement from hence to the succor of the troops in Canada?" The senior officers were convinced that in the "present feeble state of the Regiments" this was "improper," but there was unanimous assent to a proposal Washington made that the New England Colonies be requested to supply men to aid Arnold. The advice of the council was that Massachusetts, Connecticut and New Hampshire each be urged with utmost emphasis to supply a Regiment of 728 men for service in Canada to Jan. 1, 1777 at continental cost. It was recommended, also, that the numerical equivalent of these troops be deducted from the thirteen militia Regiments the Colonies had been requested on the 16th to supply the Army in front of Boston for service until April 1, 1776.[62] Washington was not sure he had authority to raise three Regiments and to put them on the regular establishment, and he was careful, in notifying Congress, to say that if his action vio-

---

[59] A fine sketch of Montgomery's character will be found in Robert Livingston to Thomas Livingston, Feb. n.d., 1776; *Livingston Papers,* 132; NYPL. See also Donald Campbell to Robert Livingston, Jan. 12, 1776; *ibid.,* 107.

[60] 4 *G. W.,* 254–55.   [61] Cf. *ibid.,* 259.

[62] 4 *Force* (4) p. 774. The council was of opinion that it was "neither prudent nor reasonable to demand" any more men from Rhode Island because of its continued exposure to attack by "the ministerial fleet and detached bodies of troops" (*Ibid.*).

lated any resolution, he would expect it to be countermanded at once.[63] Meantime, he proceeded to expedite the enlistment of these volunteers [64] and he wrote to encourage Schuyler, Arnold and Wooster,[65] though he had little hope he would be able to arouse Wooster.[66] When Washington later was to have report of Congress' endorsement of his course he was to learn, also, that other new levies were to be raised for service in Canada and that he was to contribute a Battalion from his Army if possible [67]—to which he was to reply, that it was *not* possible.[68] This renewed insistence on concentration of force implied no change in his belief in the importance of Canada to the United Colonies. In his judgment, as Canada went, the balance might turn; the winter of 1775–76 would be decisive there because, when spring came, the enemy most certainly would send large reenforcements to the St. Lawrence. Washington had more confidence than ever in Arnold,[69] and he hoped that officer, recovering promptly, would add, as he wrote him, "the only link wanting in the great chain of continental union." Arnold thus would "render the freedom of your country secure." [70]

Scarcely had this exhortation been written than Washington found affairs in Canada involved anew and differently with those of New York. Hampered by bad weather, Charles Lee had proceeded in no great haste toward his temporary post at the mouth of the Hudson and, as he had gone westward through Connecticut, transmitting regular reports to Washington, he had undertaken with professed success to interest the young men of the Colony in protecting New York against British attack and Tory machination. "I believe," he soon was to say, "I might have collected 10,000 volunteers." [71]

During the last week in January, Washington learned that Lee had been halted at Stamford, Connecticut, by an attack of gout and—what was equally bad—had been confronted there by a strange and disconcerting letter from the Committee of Safety in New York City. The committee told of reports it had received that Lee was about to enter the

---

[63] 4 *G. W.*, 259–60.

[64] *Ibid.*, 257, 260, 267, 302. For the manner in which Governor Trumbull anticipated Washington's request, on receipt of a dispatch from General Wooster (4 *Force* (4) p. 766) see *ibid.*, 765 and the grateful acknowledgment of Washington (4 *G. W.*, 263). Trumbull's optimistic view of his Colony's prospective aid is recorded in 4 *Force* (4) p. 918, 930 ff.

[65] 4 *G. W.*, 279, 281, 283.

[66] *Ibid.*, 278. For Wooster's view of his own lack of means with which to accomplish anything, see 1 *LTW.*, 133.

[67] 1 *LTW.*, 129–30, 138.   [68] 4 *G. W.*, 286.

[69] *Ibid.*, 298.   [70] *Ibid.*, 282–83.

[71] Letter of Jan. 24, 1776; 1 *Lee Papers*, 259.

city with a considerable body of troops; and, after various disclaimers and avowals, it informed him that it had little powder and no defensive works. Because of this situation, members felt that hostilities in New York City should not be provoked before March 1, if then. Lee was requested to halt his troops on the western confines of Connecticut, "till," the committee wrote, "we shall have been honored by you with such an explanation on this important subject as you may conceive your duty may permit you to enter into with us . . ." [72] Lee's letter to Washington enclosed this document and his reply, the substance of which was that his object in planning to enter New York was to keep the British from taking post in the city or from effecting lodgment on Long Island. ". . . I give you my word," Lee had written the committee, "that no active service is proposed as you seem to apprehend." He specified: "If the ships of war are quiet, I shall be quiet; but I declare solemnly that if they make a pretext of my presence to fire on the town the first house set in flames by their guns shall be the funeral pile of some of their best friends—but I believe, sir, the inhabitants may rest in security on this subject." [73] Further, Lee wrote his chief, he had concluded he would receive instructions from Congress, to which he had written on the subject. Otherwise he would not venture to march into the Province. The reason was a resolution of that body to the effect that when detached continental troops went into a Colony to assist in suppressing Tories, they passed under the control of the patriotic authorities of the State. [74] In due time Washington learned that the response of Congress, at the instance of the New York delegation, was to send

[72] Letter of Jan. 21, 1776; 4 *Force* (4), p. 807–08.

[73] 1 *Lee Papers*, 256–57. This was no new idea to Lee. On Nov. 5, 1775, writing Dr. Palfrey of the threatened attacks on coastal towns, he had said: ". . . it should be made known to these piratical assassins that the first house set on fire by the ships shall be the funeral pile of a bunch of these their worthy associates" (*Emmett Col.*, 8678, NYPL). Attention of the students of Charles Lee's life is called to the fact that this somewhat important letter is not in the *Lee Papers*.

[74] This legislation originated, partially, in an incursion Connecticut men had made November 27 into New York City, where they had destroyed the press, overturned some of the cases and carried off the remainder of the type of the loyalist printer, James Rivington, an unusual man of enterprise, who earlier had distinguished himself as a book publisher (see 1 Jones, *History N. Y.*, 66). Governor Trumbull apologized, recovered some of the mob's loot, and returned it (4 *Force* (4) p. 401); but New York City petitioned the Congress of the Colony to prevent future interference of this irresponsible sort. Members of the New York Congress sensed the dangers that might be stirred by scolding a neighbor whose help might some day be needed, and they hesitated before they came to a conclusion. Their final action was in the form of a request to New York Delegates to have Congress regulate the entry of troops from one Colony into another (4 *Force* (4) p. 400–01). Congress took up the application at a time when plans were afoot for the dispatch of New Jersey reenforcements to the vicinity of New York, if not to the city itself. From these deliberations there came, in a long series of resolves on January 2, a provision that when a detachment of continental troops went into a Colony to

to that Colony a committee of three members—Benjamin Harrison, Thomas Lynch and Andrew Allen—to reconcile differences and to decide what should be done for the defence of New York.[75]

Even before Lee had recovered sufficiently from the gout to proceed on his way and to test the judgment of Congressmen, the temper of patriots and the stomach of Loyalists in New York, his direction of defence there for any length of time was put in doubt. At Cambridge headquarters, as early as January 22, it was surmised by some on the basis of what Henry Knox had observed, that Philip Schuyler did not wish to exercise general command in Canada, but Washington was not long of this mind. Schuyler, he thought, might be prevailed upon to accept the responsibility. If the New Yorker did not, then all were agreed that David Wooster was too infirm in body and too inactive in spirit to lead so difficult an enterprise.[76] By elimination as well as by the ability credited to him, Charles Lee manifestly would be the logical man to head the operation, and he was so notified unofficially by the Adjutant General.[77] Washington's precise regard for all the amenities kept him, of course, from making any suggestions until inquiry was addressed him by Congress. When, on January 29, he received a request from Hancock that he designate one of his Generals for the Canadian command, he replied cautiously that Lee was in New York [78] and would be ready to obey any orders Congress sent him; "but," the General added immediately, "if I am not greatly deceived, he or some other spirited, able officer will be wanted there in the spring, as we have undoubted intelligence that General Clinton has sailed with some troops . . ." [79] More than this Washington did not attempt to state on the employment of Lee, and regarding other possible

---

assist in dealing with Tories, these soldiers would be subject to the control of the patriotic representatives of that Colony (4 *JCC.*, 20). To judge from references in later debate (1 *Burnett*, 339), it seems probable that some of the members of Congress did not realize what complications might develop from his early assertion of "colonial States' rights."

[75] 4 *JCC.*, 92–94; 1 *Burnett*, 330; 4 *Force* (4) p. 1100.

[76] 1 *Lee Papers*, 251; 4 *G. W.*, 270. Washington had been convinced for months that Wooster was neither aggressive as a commander nor disciplined as a subordinate. See 4 *G. W.*, 18, 65.

[77] 1 *Lee Papers*, 251.

[78] Actually, Lee did not arrive until February 4 (*ibid.*, 271).

[79] 4 *G. W.*, 289. Washington's first intelligence reports concerning the departure of Gen. Sir Henry Clinton from Boston had been received about January 20 but they were not in agreement regarding the strength of the force Clinton had taken with him (*ibid.*, 267, 273). It was any man's guess where Clinton might be headed (cf. *ibid.*, 271). All the American leaders around Boston accepted the reports of his departure as authentic and assumed he was bound southward. Some said he was sailing for New York; others believed his destination was Virginia or a port still farther down the Atlantic coast.

appointees he said only: "General Putnam is a most valuable man and a fine executive officer but I do not know how he would conduct in a separate department. He is a younger Major General than Mr. Schuyler who . . . having determined to continue in service will, I expect, repair into Canada." [80] In writing this, Washington obeyed once again his impulse to defer to Congress—a disciplined impulse sharpened by his years of service as a legislator—and he may not have realized that he perhaps was leaving the members in doubt concerning his recommendation. Committeemen, reading his letter, might have to weigh the clauses carefully before concluding he meant to suggest that Lee be left temporarily in New York, for ultimate return to the Boston front, and that Schuyler be entrusted with the Canadian command.

Events did not take that easy twist. Lee professed pleasure at learning that the committee of three members of Congress was coming to New York, because, he said, without the intervention of some such body, compliance with the resolution on colonial control of continental troops would "have made [him] a most ridiculous figure besides bringing upon [him] the enmity of the whole Province." [81] The committee, Lee went on, had conferred with him twice and had agreed that New York City could not be fortified against naval attack but that "lodgments" to shelter 2000 defenders should be constructed at commanding points in the town. [82] From Thomas Lynch, one of the trio sent by Congress, Washington had a more discouraged view of conditions in New York: "Everything is wanting. The strong apathy that holds Congress in fetters is still more forcible here" [83]—a statement that would have represented the very nadir of futility had Washington known at the moment how deeply Congress itself was bogged in a slough of clinging detail. [84] If there was in these letters to Washington any salt for the acid of bad news, it was that Clinton's disappearance was explained: he had turned up in New York, without troops, and with assurances of good will and pacific intent. [85] Soon the papers that came to headquarters in Cambridge told of plans for the dispatch of

---

[80] Letter of Jan. 30, 1776; *ibid.*, 289–90.

[81] Letter of Feb. 5, 1776, to Washington; 1 *Lee Papers*, 271.

[82] *Ibid.*, 272. As of the date when Lee wrote, "lodgment" was used in two different military senses, first, as quarters for troops and, second, as temporary defences on captured positions. It is not clear in which of these two senses Lee was speaking.

[83] Letter of Feb. 5, 1776; 4 *Force* (4) p. 943.

[84] Two almost incredible examples are presented in Richard Smith's entries in his Diary, February 8 and 9, for which see 1 *Burnett*, 342.

[85] Lee's and Lynch's letters, as *supra*.

Lee, rather than of Schuyler, to Canada. Lee continued willing, though his recovery from the gout was slow,[86] and he was insistent only in asking for three of the essentials of war most difficult to get in America —trained subordinates, cannon and ammunition.[87] He wished, in particular, to have either Nathanael Greene or John Sullivan assigned him,[88] but the soldierly qualities of these Brigadiers that made him desire the services of one or the other of them were the very excellencies, among others, that led Washington to want both men to remain with the Army in front of Boston. Lee did not insist. In spite of the pain of his malady, he was in good spirits; and well he might have been, because his proposal to occupy New York brought him much praise.[89] This aroused no jealousy in Washington's heart. He wanted Canada;[90] he would part with his most experienced if erratic lieutenant were that necessary to get it; he regretted that he could spare no troops to help win the northern province, but he was as convinced as ever that he could not afford to detach even a Battalion, and he was resolved not to do so otherwise than under peremptory orders.

This firm, unyielding insistence by Washington on concentration of force accorded with the answer he had given to all previous appeals for detachments: If Howe did not attack, he would, and to do so he required every man who held a musket anywhere between Chelsea and Dorchester Neck. He needed, too, more powder than ever, and he had relatively less,[91] both because of wastage[92] and because he now had more heavy guns. Henry Knox had arrived at Framingham with fifty-

---

[86] 1 *Lee Papers*, 297.

[87] 1 *Burnett*, 345; 1 *LTW.*, 156 ff; 1 *Lee Papers*, 297, 300, 340.

[88] 1 *LTW.*, 152.

[89] Cf. John Adams to James Warren, Feb. 18, 1776: "[Lee's] address, his fluency in French, his great experience and skill, we hope will succeed. . . . It is true that we want Lee both at Cambridge and New York! But we cannot have him in three armies at once, and Canada seems to me the most dangerous post, and that there is the greatest necessity for him there" (1 *Burnett*, 354–55). See also John Adams to Charles Lee, Feb. 19, 1776: "A luckier, a happier expedition than yours to N[ew] York never was projected. The whole Whig world is blessing you for it . . ." (1 *Lee Papers*, 312).

[90] 4 *G. W.*, 357.

[91] On Jan. 12, 1776, he had put powder first among his needs: "After powder, the principal deficiency is of arms" (4 *G. W.*, 231). Again, January 23: "If Congress mean that we should do anything this winter, no time should be lost in forwarding powder" (*ibid.*, 271). The history of shortage and of shipment to February 15 may be traced in *ibid.*, 234, 273, 283, 307, 308, 333; 1 *LTW.*, 104, 122, 144; 1 *Burnett*, 300, 303; 1 *Lee Papers*, 243, 277, 285. In 23 *Papers G. W.*, 30, LC, is a return of powder by E. Cheever, Commissary of Artillery, for the period July 1, 1775–Jan. 30, 1776. The total received during those six months was 443 barrels.

[92] See Washington to the President of Congress, Jan. 30, 1776 (4 *G. W.*, 288), for mention of special channels of waste.

two cannon,[93] nine large mortars and five cohorns, which he had hauled over the snow from Fort Ticonderoga.[94] Had Washington gone out to Framingham[95] to see this ordnance for himself, he would have been encouraged vastly by the difference between his enlarged park of artillery and the cannon and mortars he had even three months previously. At the earlier date, he could employ no more than five twenty-four pounders, six eighteen-pounders, and twenty-five lighter pieces, with seven mortars and eight howitzers—a total of fifty-one.[96] Now, by the occupation of the best position on Dorchester Heights, he might be able to plant there the "Old Sow," the two other thirteen-inch mortars from Ticonderoga, and the "Congress," brass mortar from the *Nancy*. With these, the twenty-four pounders and the eighteen-pounders, he might hope to drive the British from the wharves of Boston if ever he had in store sufficient powder for a long bombardment.

Preparation of this artillery was young Harry Knox's assignment and was well handled; transaction of much of the other public business was

[93] Included were one brass twenty-four pounder, nine iron and one brass eighteen-pounders, and ten iron twelve-pounders.

[94] The story of this remarkable achievement does not appear to have been told in its entirety. Knox had left Cambridge shortly after November 16 (4 *G. W.*, 93; Knox to Mrs. Knox, Nov. 16, 1775; 1 *Knox Papers*, MHS, p. 172), had reached Hartford November 25, and thence, via New York City and Albany, had arrived at Ticonderoga, December 5 (see the fragments of his Journal in 30 *NEH & GR*, 322). The ice had been so thin and sleds so few (*ibid.* and Schuyler in 1 *LTW.*, 111) that it was January 7 before the last of the cannon and mortars were across Lake Champlain. After that, even the impatient and ambitious Knox was surprised at the speed with which the heavy cannon were moved over the steep grades (Journal, *loc. cit.*). According to General Heath (*Memoirs*, 45–46), the date of Knox's return to Cambridge was January 18. Knox was ordered to leave his guns for the time at Framingham, where John Adams saw and listed them on January 25 (see 2 *John Adams*, 431–32). Among them, the one that created the largest interest was the "Old Sow," the heaviest of three 13-inch mortars (Huntington Letters in 20 *CHS Cols.*, 30). For a list of the cannon, etc., that Knox had been expected to bring from Ticonderoga, see 4 *Force* (4), p. 188. A return of cannon captured at "the several Northern posts," from May 1 to Nov. 13, 1775, will be found in *ibid.*, 534–35. Readers who desire to pursue in the original sources the story of Knox's adventure may find the following supplementary references useful: 4 *Force* (4) p. 1140, 1676; 1 *LTW.*, 85, 94, 111; 4 *G. W.*, 139, 179, 182, 234, 253; 1 *Burnett*, 338; 1 *Lee Papers*, 260; E. Price's Diary in *MHSP.*, 1863–64, p. 228; *Schuyler Letter Book* 1775–76, p. 251, NYPL. Numerous unpublished Knox letters, including some of special charm, addressed to his wife, are in the records of MHS. Of particular historical interest are: Knox to Mrs. Knox, Nov. 16, 1775, Jan. 3, 1776, 1 *Knox Papers*, 172; 2 *ibid.*, 21; Henry Knox to William Knox, Dec. 14, 1775, 2 *ibid.*, 2; Knox to Philip Schuyler, Dec. 17, 1775, 2 *ibid.*, 3; [George] Palmer to Knox, Dec. 25, 1775, 2 *ibid.*, 7; Philip Schuyler to Knox, Dec. 18, 1775, 2 *ibid.*, 6. The basic document is the incomplete journal, already cited, in 30 *NEH & GR*.

[95] It was a ride of almost twenty miles.

[96] 4 *Force* (4) p. 494, as of Oct. 20, 1775. The position of the army's cannon, Feb. 19, 1776, is given in 4 *Force* (4) p. 1194 and is of interest chiefly as showing, properly enough, that all seven of the twenty-four pounders then in service were either on the Roxbury front or on Winter and Prospect Hills. Four eighteen-pounders guarded the Roxbury-Dorchester defences; two were at Cobble Hill. Nowhere else on the front were there any mounted cannon heavier than nine-pounders. The location of the mortars is not stated. They probably were in reserve for the use to which they were put in March.

more difficult now because of changes in Washington's personal staff. Edmund Randolph, after a fine beginning, had been compelled to start back to Virginia early in November to look after the estate of his uncle, Peyton Randolph, who had died suddenly in Philadelphia on the 22nd of October.[97] A few weeks later, to Washington's annoyance and distress, Joseph Reed had succumbed to a long bombardment of family and friends[98] and on October 29 had set out for Philadelphia to look after certain cases pending in his law practice. Although Reed had started from that city the previous June with no intention of staying any longer than a few days, he had become interested and had proved himself so nearly indispensable that Washington had written Richard Henry Lee to endeavor to prevail upon opposing counsel to agree to postpone trials in order that when Reed had attended to imperative business, he might return promptly to Cambridge.[99] For the discharge of the less important if necessary duties of aide, Washington sought and procured the services of a native of Maryland, Robert Hanson Harrison, aged 30.[100] A fortnight sufficed to show that these arrangements would not be satisfactory for some time to come.[101] Stephen Moylan, who was entirely qualified, gave such help as he could but he had his own regular work to do as Mustermaster General.[102] Thus shorthanded, Washington repeatedly but vainly called on Reed to hasten back, which the Philadelphian seemed in no hurry to do.[103] By the third week in January, 1776, it looked as if Washington might have to dispense for a time with the service of Harrison, who then was beginning to measure up to his duties. Harrison obligingly undertook to arrange his affairs so that he could remain, but Washington turned again to Reed and

[97] 4 *G. W.*, 58. For reports of Randolph's death, see 1 *LTW.*, 67; 1 *Burnett*, 240; 4 *Jefferson*, 41; 3 *JCC.*, 302 and 303 n.

[98] This diverting correspondence is preserved chiefly in vol. 3 of the MS *Papers of Joseph Reed*, NYHS. Of particular interest are: Charles Pettit to Joseph Reed, July 22; Pettit to Mrs. Joseph Reed, July 24; Joseph Reed to his wife, July 26; John Cox to Joseph Reed, July 26; Mrs. Joseph Reed to Charles Pettit, Oct. 24, 1775. A fine letter from Reed, probably to Pettit, n.d., but in all likelihood of November, 1775, will be found in these *Papers*.

[99] 4 *G. W.*, 52. Reed left Cambridge Oct. 29, 1775 (*ibid.*, 62).

[100] *Ibid.*, 68; the appointment was announced November 6. Washington had invited Harrison on Aug. 26, 1775, through Lund Washington, to become his aide (Lund Washington to Washington, Oct. 5, 1775; *Thom Cols.*, Mount Vernon MSS.).

[101] Cf. Washington to Joseph Reed, Nov. 20, 1775: ". . . Mr. Baylor, contrary to my expectation, is not in the slightest degree a penman, though spirited and willing; and . . . Mr. Harrison, though sensible, clever and perfectly confidential, has never yet moved upon so large a scale as to comprehend at one view the diversity of matter which comes before me, so as to afford me that ready assistance which every man in my situation must stand more or less in need of" (4 *G. W.*, 104).

[102] *Ibid.*

[103] *Ibid.*, 104, 123, 127, 166; 1 *LTW.*, 82.

explained: "At present, my time is so much taken up at my desk that I am obliged to neglect many other essential parts of my duty. It is absolutely necessary, therefore, for me to have persons that can think for me, as well as execute orders." [104] It was in vain the General appealed. Reed undertook a brief tour of duty as Lieutenant Colonel of a Pennsylvania Regiment sent to New York, though, early in March, he was to write that he hoped to join Washington in the summer. [105] Fortunately, Harrison continued to improve and thereby lessened the inconvenience and loss of time Washington suffered.

The best effort of the new aide could not compensate for the absence of the facile, quick-witted Reed, as February crept on, and "if, if, if," kept snapping at the heels of every dragging day. "If we had powder," Stephen Moylan had written two weeks previously, "I do believe Boston would fall into our hands." [106]

Washington heard this talk around him and knew that many persons lacked Moylan's understanding of the reasons why an attack had not been made. These individuals, who included some of the best and most patriotic, might be saying that the commanding General was slow or timid or of uncertain mind. It was impossible to tell them the truth —that he did not take the offensive because he might exhaust his supply of powder before he could blast the British from their redoubts. [107] Reconnaissance on the 11th and 12th of February [108] showed more clearly than ever that good artillery positions might be taken on the hills of Dorchester Neck—an opinion the British evidently shared, because, on the night of the 13th they landed there and burned some houses, but they withdrew before they could be challenged, and they did not return the next day. [109]

That day, February 13, Washington went to Lechmere Point. He found the ice there frozen solidly all the way across the channel to Boston—so heavily frozen in fact that some soldiers at the fort on the point were making it a business to go out on the ice and pick up the

[104] Letter of Jan. 23, 1776; 4 *G. W.*, 269.

[105] 4 *G. W.*, 323; 1 *Burnett*, 349, 371; 1 *LTW.*, 162.

[106] Letter of Jan. 30, 1776, to Joseph Reed; 1 *Reed*, 160.

[107] See *infra*, p. 21, 28.

[108] *Martyn's Ward*, 191 and n. 2, with quotation from letter of Capt. John Chester, Feb. 13, 1776. Chester said only that "the Generals" went to Dorchester and he mentioned the name of no general officer except Putnam; but if Putnam was there, on Ward's front, it is almost certain that he was in the company of Washington and of Ward, commander of the right "Grand Division."

[109] 4 *G. W.*, 331.

spent balls British troops had fired in their direction. One American boasted that he had recovered eighty bullets.[110] Washington looked carefully at this new bridge to Boston and reflected once again that he did not have the powder with which to drive the enemy from the town. The key position to the northward, Bunker Hill, was so strongly fortified the Americans could not hope to recover it otherwise than by a lucky surprise.[111] As an alternative, would it be practicable to attack across the ice and to rely primarily on the fire of small arms? Granting that so exposed an advance would involve considerable losses, would not a swift assault of this nature be more economical than an assault by water or one by land, up Boston Neck? [112]

If this bold move was to be undertaken at all, it should be attempted at once. Washington could not even wait for the arrival of all the militia, because the ice might break up and British reenforcements might sail into Boston before the last Company of "Long Faces" arrived. So, on the 16th of February—precisely one month after the first of the two January councils—Washington called his Generals together again and laid the facts before them. He had 7280 militia, he said, and 8797 Continentals fit for duty, in addition to their officers. "On command," that is to say, on detached service were 1405 men.[113] To these troops, he estimated, the British in Boston could not oppose many more than 5000 foot soldiers. Then he put the question he already had answered in his own mind: Was it not better to deliver a general assault over the ice, employing musketry, than to wait until the enemy was stronger and was able to penetrate into the country? Washington reviewed briefly in their proper place all the other arguments he had been revolving in his mind and, with no waste of words, submitted his plan to his Generals.[114]

Every man of them was against it. They thought that Washington greatly underestimated the strength of the British and much exaggerated the offensive power of his own force, which, the Generals said, was not more than sufficient to maintain the blockade and to defend the lines. Besides, the field officers, who had talked of this, as of every

[110] *J. Baldwin's Journal*, 25–26, February 11–13.

[111] 4 *G. W.*, 322.

[112] 4 *G. W.*, 335; 4 *Force* (4) p. 1193.

[113] Washington said "on command" (4 *Force* (4) p. 1193), which words were, of course, then "standard," but this is one of the instances in which eighteenth-century military language was so different from later phrases that in the first use of the term, the insertion of the modern equivalent along with the original seems justified.

[114] 4 *Force* (4) p. 1193.

other proposal, thought success "exceedingly doubtful." [115] At the very least, if an assault was to be undertaken then or thereafter, it should be preceded by a bombardment of several days.

Would it be advisable, Washington asked, to begin a bombardment with the small stock of powder the Army then had? The reply was: Bombardment should begin as soon as the supply of powder was adequate, but it should not be attempted till then. Meanwhile, an effort should be made to draw out the enemy. The British had shown some concern over Dorchester Neck: If the Americans seized the high ground there, the enemy might be tempted to sortie. Repulse of Howe's attack on fortified positions might be a cheap victory. The same result might attend American occupation of Noodle's Island, if that was practicable.[116]

Washington was set back by this counsel. As far as he could he had reckoned the cost of the long assault over the ice, and he had agreed that success would depend on the good behavior of the troops, but he had been willing to take the risk because this seemed the one feasible operation for an army that lacked powder for a sustained bombardment.[117] When his Generals were decidedly of opinion [118] that he was wrong, he could not persist in asserting himself right. He did not change his mind but, he admitted subsequently, "the irksomeness of my situation . . . might have inclined me to put more to the hazard than was consistent with prudence." Candidly he continued: "If it had, I am not sensible of it, as I endeavored to give it all the consideration that a matter of such importance required. True it is, and I cannot help acknowledging that I have many disagreeable sensations on account of my situation; for to have the eyes of the whole continent fixed, with anxious expectation of hearing of some great event, and to be restrained in every military operation for want of the necessary means of carrying it on, is not very pleasing, especially as the means used to conceal my weakness from the enemy conceals it also from our friends and adds to their wonder." [119] A little later his humbleminded acceptance of the decision of the council of war was to be tinged with disgust over the readiness of his Generals to shake their heads on the day of opportunity

[115] *Ibid.*

[116] *Ibid.*, 1194.

[117] 4 *G. W.*, 321–22, 336, 338–39.

[118] Washington said "almost unanimous" (*ibid.*, 336); the minutes (4 *Force* (4) p. 1193–94) do not disclose the vote or the view of any participant besides Washington.

[119] Letter of Feb. 18, 1776, to the President of Congress; 4 *G. W.*, 336.

JOSEPH REED, FIRST SECRETARY

The portrait of Joseph Reed on the opposite page is reproduced from one of two originals by Charles Willson Peale; but the other, though most attractive as the frontispiece of William B. Reed's biography of his grandfather, is second in historical interest to the canvas that here portrays in continental uniform the handsome and intelligent young Colonel.

Nine years Washington's junior, Reed was born at Trenton, New Jersey, and was sent by his well-to-do father, a successful merchant, to the Philadelphia Academy and then to the College of New Jersey, which at that time was completing proudly the largest academic building in the Colonies. After graduation at Princeton, Reed studied law, won admission to the Jersey bar in 1763 and then went to England, where two years of life in Middle Temple were not so zealously devoted to his profession that he had a mind only for the printed book before him. He visited frequently the House of Commons, from the gallery of which he heard the debates of 1764 and early 1765. On his return to America, Reed was about as well schooled for public service as a Colonial of his day could be. He soon added varied business enterprises to the practice of the law at Trenton and afterward in Philadelphia, where he became active in politics. By the time Washington prevailed on him to serve as military secretary at headquarters, Reed had distinction as President of the Second Provincial Congress of Pennsylvania.

Reed cherished unfeigned affection and admiration for Washington and he held the esteem of the General even after the unpleasant episode of the letter from Charles Lee that Washington opened in the belief it was an official communication to Reed (Vol. IV, p. 269–70). Other friends Reed had in opulent number, and he preserved their correspondence with a care for which students of American history are grateful. He could hate as heartily as he loved; and if he had his champions, he repeatedly faced detractors, some of whom were not discriminating in their choice of weapons. Whatever of justice there may have been in the charges against Reed—and he was far more often right than wrong—his relations with Washington always exemplified the fine qualities that shine in his friendly face.

(After the original by C. W. Peale, Independence Hall, Philadelphia.)

THOMAS MIFFLIN, PROGRESSIVELY A PUZZLE

The likeness of Thomas Mifflin on the adjoining page is only a part of the picture. In the original, he is looking at Mrs. Mifflin, who is using a little loom on a table and appears to be making a fringe of white silk. She is lovely and she is happy. Life for her and for her able husband is just beginning. If, as many think, that portrait by Copley (1773) is the richest treasure in the collection of the Historical Society of Pennsylvania, reproduction here of a "part of the picture" is fortuitously typical of Mifflin's place in the biography of Washington during the Revolution. From the time Mifflin appears at age of 31, in Chapter XIX of Volume III, as aide to the newly elected Commander-in-Chief, the face of the Pennsylvanian was in the scene, but after Mifflin was alienated from Washington, in the summer of 1777, his part was not discoverable in certain political occurrences with which he was believed to be connected. To this day, it is impossible to say how large a share he had in the Conway Cabal, or why he participated at all, unless he was jealous of Washington's fame and thought he could advance himself by supporting Gates.

Mifflin, said Benjamin Rush, "possessed genius, knowledge, eloquence, patriotism, courage, self-government and an independent spirit in the first years of the war." Rush continued: "He was extremely useful in the gloomy winter of 1776 by rallying the drooping courage of the militia of his native State. . . . His influence was much promoted by an elegant person, an animated countenance and popular manners. Had he fallen in battle, or died in the year 1778, he would have ranked with Warren and the first patriots of the Revolution."

Rush prefaced his sketch with the statement: "Those who knew this man in the close of the Revolution and in the evening of life will scarcely believe" that Mifflin had the qualities the physician credited to him. The decline in Mifflin's standards was rapid and progressive. When Rush recorded the election of Mifflin as Governor in October, 1790, he had to say, "His popularity was acquired by the basest acts of familiarity with the meanest of the people." Rush may have been correct in his observations, but when both Mifflin and the Revolution were young, the Philadelphia aide of Washington seemed full of promise and of faith.

(After the original by Copley in the gallery of The Historical Society of Pennsylvania.)

for which "we had been waiting all the year." [120] At the moment,
Washington swallowed his disappointment.

The hard freeze ended quickly; [121] by February 20, the snow had
almost disappeared in Boston.[122] Washington had to turn again to what
appeared to be the almost hopeless task of building up a reserve of
powder, and to the enterprise the council had recommended, that of
occupying some of the hills of Dorchester Neck in the hope the enemy
would resent this and would attempt to drive the Americans from the
high ground. The previous year, a similar effort on Breed's Hill had
brought out the British from Boston; [123] this time, fortification would
be exceedingly difficult because the ground was frozen hard to a depth
of two feet or more.[124] As for "the needful," Washington continued to
receive small quantities but he estimated that if he got every pound
that seemed within his reach,[125] the issue of twenty-four rounds per
man, militia included,[126] would reduce the Army's store to approximately 100 barrels, or about five tons—a dangerously small reserve for
such a throw as he was to make on the table of fate.[127]

In spite of ice, platforms were prepared at Lechmere Point; [128] numerous preliminaries of the occupation of Dorchester Heights were taken
in hand; everything seemed to be proceeding well. Then, about four
days after the council of war, secret reports from Boston were to the
effect that the British were putting several of their heavy guns and a
quantity of bedding aboard ship. Numerous vessels were taking on
water; biscuit in vast number were being baked.[129] On the 25th, a
patriot [130] brought Washington news that the British had taken up every
ship in the harbor for government service and had paid in advance for
two months' use of them.[131] Townsfolk, said this informant, believed
Howe was preparing to move either to New York or to Virginia.[132]
Sails were bent; [133] everything seemed to forecast departure.

[120] Letter of Feb. 26, 1776, to Joseph Reed; *ibid.*, 348.

[121] Cf. Washington to Jonathan Trumbull, Feb. 19, 1776: "A golden opportunity has been
lost, perhaps not to be acquired again this year. The late freezing weather had formed some
pretty strong ice . . ." (*ibid.*, 338–39).

[122] *Carter, Letters to a Friend*, 23. *Dodsley's Annual Register* of 1776, p. 147, noted that
"the winter was uncommonly mild and the frosts had none of the effects [the Americans]
had expected" in providing ice for an easy attack.

[123] 4 *G. W.*, 350–51.

[124] It had been frozen "very hard" as far down as twenty-eight inches, according to the
entry in Jeduthan Baldwin's Journal.   [125] 1 *LTW.*, 143; 4 *G. W.*, 333, 338, 343.

[126] 4 *G. W.*, 334, 337.   [127] *Ibid.*, 339.

[128] *Ibid.*, 348.   [129] *Ibid.*, 349.

[130] Identified by Washington simply as a Mr. Ides.

[131] 4 *G. W.*, 349.   [132] *Ibid.*   [133] *Ibid.*, 352.

Washington, analyzing this intelligence, reasoned that Howe might be fashioning a ruse, or might actually be about to leave Boston, or might be making ready in anticipation of orders to evacuate the city.[134] If the British commander were trying to deceive the Americans, he must be outwitted; but if he was preparing to make sail for New York, Lee must be notified and must be assured that on Howe's departure from Boston, Washington would do immediately what previously he always had refused to consider: He would make a heavy detachment of force, and if Howe actually proceeded to New York, Washington at once would send the greater part, or even the whole of the Army to the mouth of the Hudson. Dispersion of force in the presence of the enemy was madness; the speed of transfer when the enemy moved to a new theatre of war was a test of military wisdom. "I shall keep a good watch on their motions," Washington wrote Lee with reference to the British, "and give you the speediest information possible." [135]

Speculation on Howe's designs was not permitted to slow the preparations for the seizure of high ground on Dorchester Neck. As Washington developed his plans for this operation, he gained faith in it. "If anything will induce General Howe to risk an engagement, it will be this," he said when he described the fortification of Dorchester Heights and the placing of heavy guns in the fort at Lechmere Point. He added: "I am determined to do everything in my power to bring on [an engagement], and that as soon as possible. How far my views may be answered, time must determine." [136]

Time seemed now to run swiftly toward a decision. At all the batteries within easy range of Boston, solid shot and shell were brought forward, and the precious kegs of powder were placed where no moisture could reach them. Nurses were sought; [137] fully 2000 bandages were prepared.[138] From February 21 onward, every effort was made to get full information of the enemy [139] and to stop passage from all parts of the American lines to Boston,[140] but this last precaution did not suffice. On the 27th of February, Washington learned of the desertion of a rifleman who of course would disclose to the enemy as much as he

---

134 Ibid., 352, 360.
135 Letter of Feb. 26, 1776; 4 G. W., 352.
136 Letter of Feb. 27, 1776, to Philip Schuyler; 4 G. W., 358.
137 N. E. Chronicle and Essex Gazette, Feb. 29, 1776.
138 2 Gordon, 25.
139 See Joseph Reed (of Boston) to Artemas Ward, Feb. 26, 1776; 2 Knox Papers, 37, MHS.
140 Gates to Ward, Feb. 21, 1776; LC Photostat.

knew of American plans. In addition, a report spread that British troops were being sent in boats to Dorchester Heights from the "Castle" in the harbor. Washington was quick to dispatch one of his own aides to ascertain the facts, and he was relieved to hear that the report was false, but he was careful to have Ward put out trusty men to watch the approaches. "[Order] particular Regiments," he told the Major General on the right, "to be ready to march at a moment's warning to the heights of Dorchester; for should the enemy get possession of those hills before us, they would render it a difficult task to dispossess them; better it is, therefore, to prevent than to remedy an evil." [141] General orders that day were in the same spirit: "As the season is now fast approaching when every man must expect to be drawn into the field of action, it is highly necessary that he should prepare his mind as well as everything necessary for it. It is a noble cause we are engaged in; it is the cause of virtue and mankind. Every temporal advantage and comfort to us and our posterity depends upon the vigor of our exertions. In short, freedom or slavery must be the result of our conduct. There can, therefore, be no greater inducement to men to behave well. But it may not be amiss for the troops to know that if any man in action shall presume to skulk, hide himself, or retreat from the enemy, without the orders of his commanding officer, he will be *instantly shot down,* as an example of cowardice—cowards having too frequently disconcerted the best formed troops by their dastardly behavior." [142]

Washington "prepared his mind," as the time for the attack drew near, precisely as he admonished his men to do, and with his usual diligence he cleared as much correspondence as he could [143] and did so in the knowledge that if he lost the struggle that lay ahead, the American cause might be in ruins and he might be hunted by British patrols. He wrote his wife's brother-in-law, Burwell Bassett, who was looking after those parts of his business that had to be transacted in Williamsburg: "I thank you heartily for the attention you have kindly paid to my landed affairs on the Ohio,"—and he went on in serious

[141] 4 *G. W.,* 354.

[142] 4 *G. W.,* 355, with the punctuation sharply revised.

[143] Not long previously, in going over some papers in order to destroy those which were valueless, he had found a poem the young Negress, Phillis Wheatley, had written in his honor. He had put it aside after reading it in December, because he thought that publication of it might seem an act of vanity. When he rediscovered it, he sent Joseph Reed a copy (*ibid.,* 323) and now he wrote her a formal acknowledgment with a tribute to her "great poetical talents" and an invitation to call at headquarters if she should come to Cambridge or be nearby (*ibid.,* 360–61).

candor—"my interest in which I shall be more careful of, as in the worst event they will serve for an asylum." [144] He had penned nothing like that previously, but from the manner in which it was set down now, it read as if it was a conclusion he had reached months before in full realization of the possible adverse outcome of the contest to which he had pledged his fortune and his fate. War had changed values. Washington had acquired those lands along the Ohio as a means of increasing his fortune when settlement was extended and the demand for farms was multiplied. In the outworking, those distant meadows might yield a living if all else was snatched from him.

Nothing should be lost if effort could save it! On that he was resolved. As the extra day of the Leap Year gave place to a very cold, clear 1st of March,[145] it was known in the camps, by the soldiers' own strangely accurate intelligence system, that the Dorchester Heights were to be occupied,[146] and it was reported that General Howe had said he would attack, regardless of loss, if the Americans so much as "broke ground." [147] Washington, for his part, had arranged that if the ground remained too hard-frozen for entrenching tools to penetrate, he would make shift with devices on which some of his men had been working for weeks.[148] By the 2nd, moreover, his engineers had placed a thirteen-inch mortar and a ten-inch at Lechmere Point, and a thirteen-inch companion at Lamb's Dam in Roxbury.[149] The Massachusetts Legislature was sending up, in support, militia [150] Washington had asked from the Dorchester area.[151] If there was to be a prolonged nighttime bombardment and then an effort to fortify Dorchester Heights under cover of darkness, the time was at hand because the British soon might discover the plan and might move out from Boston Neck and block the route to Dorchester Peninsula. The bombardment might most advantageously be started on the night of March 2. For the rest:

144 Letter of Feb. 28, 1776; *ibid.*, 359.
145 *Deacon Tudor's Diary*, 60; E. Price's Diary in *MHSP.*, 1863–64, p. 239. Stephen Kemble noted, February 29, that the weather was so cold the British could not complete a battery on which they were at work (1 *Kemble*, p. 69, 70).
146 McCurtin's Journal, *loc. cit.*, 32.
147 1 *Webb*, 131.   148 *Ibid.*, 366.
149 1 *Webb*, 132. Built "to keep the tide from overflowing the marshes," the dam "extended from about the junction of Hampden and Albany Streets to a point near the present Walnut Place." See 4 *G. W.*, 370 n, and supra, Vol. III, p. 485.
150 4 *G. W.*, 350–51, 374. See an informative note, 21, in *French's First Year*, 658.
151 A certain probable if undemonstrable verity seems to lie behind the tradition, cited in 2 *Gordon*, 25, that the date was chosen in order that if the British attempted to storm the heights the Americans fortified, the fighting would be on the 5th of March, the anniversary of the "Boston Massacre."

Cambridge, March 2, 1776

[General Ward, Roxbury]

Sir: After weighing all circumstances of tide, &c, and considering the hazard of having the posts on Dorchester Neck taken by the enemy, and the evil consequences which would result from it, the gentlemen here are of opinion that we should go on there Monday night [March 4]. I give you this early notice of it, that you may delay no time in preparing for it, as everything here will be got in readiness to cooperate. In haste I am, sir, etc

George Washington.[152]

[152] 4 G. W., 363.

CHAPTER II

THE OPERATIONS ON DORCHESTER HEIGHTS
(March 2–27, 1776)

FOR THE operation he now was to undertake, Washington had present approximately 14,000 foot soldiers, of whom about 9000 were continental troops, veterans or new recruits, and 5000 militia.[1] In addition, the militia of the area around Roxbury and Dorchester were beginning to arrive [2] at the front and could man part of the lines in event the regular defenders of the works had to be moved. Artillerists under Henry Knox were counted at 635.[3] The supply of powder probably amounted to 174 barrels, exclusive of what had been issued for small arms.[4]

With these men and ammunition, the Commander-in-Chief planned to do much more than had been suggested in the initial discussion of a substitute for the unacceptable scheme to deliver an assault across the ice. First, as a feint, Washington would conduct from Cobble Hill, Lechmere Point and Lamb's Dam as extensive a bombardment of the British works in and adjacent to Boston as he could afford; second, on the third night of this bombardment, he would undertake to seize and to fortify on Dorchester Peninsula two hills [5] that were relatively far from the city but manifestly near enough to present a challenge he hoped the British would accept by attempting to wrest from his men the high ground he occupied; third, if the British delivered on Dorchester

---

[1] The precise figures (5 *Force* (4) p. 43, 115 ff) were: continentals, 9170; militia, 4970; total, 14,140.

[2] 4 *G. W.*, 384.

[3] 5 *Force* (4) p. 117.

[4] Knox in 5 *Force* (4) p. 114; E. Cheever in 24 *Papers of G. W.*, 73, LC. Records do not show how much powder Washington received from Connecticut and from Philadelphia subsequent to February 17, when he calculated that he had a reserve of 100 barrels only. More than once he mentioned the receipt of a "small supply" (4 *G. W.*, 343, 433, 447). John Hancock wrote March 6 of five and a half tons ordered to Washington "some time ago," but whether that had reached Cambridge, the President of Congress did not know (1 *LTW.*, 166).

[5] As given on the maps of 1775–76, the names of the four hills were, from East to West: Bush Tree (the one farthest to the Northeast), then Signal Tree (lying to the Southwest of Bush Tree), next Forster later dubbed Telegraph (Northwest of Signal Tree) and, finally, Dorchester, which was seldom marked Nook's on the maps but seems generally to have been called by that name. Together, Forster's and Signal Tree Hill were styled "Dorchester Heights," and, by Pelham, a British cartographer, were delineated as the "Twin Hills."

Heights the assault which he believed he could repulse, he would have ready on the Cambridge-Lechmere front a strong force that could undertake, if desirable, to cross in boats to Boston and to capture the city; fourth—the principal development of the basic plan—if the British did not assault the farther elevations of the Peninsula, or sustained no ruinous defeat in doing so, then Washington would try to take Nook's Hill on Dorchester Peninsula. This eminence was within three-quarters of a mile of Boston, and was so commanding that when Americans won it, they could compel the British to quit the town and the inner harbor.[6]

Basically, the design of occupying Dorchester Heights in two stages was dictated by the shortage of powder and by the nature of the ground. The high hills at the greater distance from Boston could be taken, Washington hoped, without the expenditure of too large a part of his meagre store of explosive. Occupation of Nook's Hill at a single thrust would be so manifest a death-sentence on the British in Boston that they would try from the outset to halt American fortification which would be difficult enough in any event because of a marshy approach.[7] In trying to defend the hill, Washington might consume all his powder and still might not retain the crest.

The arrangement—not to say the perfection—of the details of this enterprise manifestly would be a supreme test of so young an organization as Washington commanded. It would not be easy to assure on the American left and left centre the coordination of the artillery on Cobble Hill and at Lechmere Point to bombard British positions in Boston. Reliable troops had to be placed in the redoubts;[8] two columns, totaling 4000 men, under John Sullivan and Nathanael Greene, were to be subject to Putnam's general command.[9] If a predetermined signal were flown at Roxbury, to indicate the British were attacking there, these men were to proceed from the Cambridge front to Boston in boats that had been collected over a period of weeks. Objectives in the

---

[6] As Washington issued no written general order to cover these operations and made no minute of any of his last-hour conferences regarding them, the plan is nowhere set forth explicitly in the commander's own words, but its scope is ascertained easily from his remarks on the various moves. One of the clearest statements of the military relationship of the different hills is that of Stephen Moylan, in a letter of March 9 to the commanding officer in New York: "The possession of these heights are preparatory to our forming a fort upon Nook-Hill, which commands the South of Boston, and to which their shipping will be much exposed" (5 Force (4) p. 166). Washington himself wrote John Hancock, March 7: "Our taking possession of Dorchester Heights is only preparatory to taking post on Nuke Hill and the points opposite the south end of Boston" (4 G. W., 371).

[7] See infra, p. 34 ff.   [8] 4 G. W., 362–63.   [9] Ibid., 455.

besieged town were specified carefully.[10] Three floating batteries—the Washington, the Putnam and the Lee—might be used to cover the crossing of the other boats.[11]

This part of the general operation so manifestly was dangerous that it was not to be undertaken at all unless a heavy British attack, involving most of the redcoats, was launched against the Americans who seized the hills of Dorchester Peninsula. On that prospective battleground, as anticipated, one of the greatest difficulties would be that of entrenching on hills frozen to a depth of two feet. The device for coping with this was supposed to be a secret, but many persons had a hand in the work, which was by no means novel. The only question was whether the British knew what was planned. For two months and more,[12] behind the lines, scores of men had been cutting and binding fascines and had been making chandeliers, which were frames that could be filled with fascines and used as traverses or as cover for men under fire. Other detachments had been collecting hay and had been screwing it into great bundles. All these contrivances were to be carried up the hills at the proper time and were to be placed where the entrenchments were to be run. If earth could be thrown over the fascines and bundles of hay, and the chandeliers could be used as they were intended to be employed, fortifications of some strength could be erected quickly; and if the ground remained unyielding, the improvised parapets would protect the troops. To convey this cover to the hilltops, wagons and carts were being assembled from the districts South and Southeast of Roxbury. Few of these preparations could be hidden completely. The countryside saw that something of magnitude was about to happen, though the time of execution was not known.

On the night of March 2, Abigail Adams at Braintree was writing for all New England women when she shaped these words to her husband in silence by candle-light: "I have been kept in a continual state of anxiety and expectation ever since you left. It has been said, 'tomorrow' and 'tomorrow' for this month, but when the dreadful tomorrow will

10 Sullivan was to land at the Powder House and was to gain "Bacon [Beacon] Hill and Mount Horam" [Mount Whoredom or, more politely, in Drake's words, "the spur of Beacon Hill, known as Mount Vernon"]. Greene was to push ashore "at Barton's Point or a little South of it, and after securing that post, to join the other division and force the enemy's works and gates for letting in the Roxbury troops" (4 *G. W.*, 373).

11 Each of these floating batteries was meant to carry a single twelve-pounder. A return of boats, forty-seven of which were ready for service, will be found in 24 *Papers of G. W.*, 19, LC, over the signature of Jacob Rhoades, Master of Carpenters.

12 *Samuel Haws's Diary*, 86; *Isaac Bangs's Diary*, 9.

be, I know not." At that instant, across the field and water came the sharp sound of an explosion. It was a cannon shot—that was certain. Cambridge and Braintree folk and all their neighbors had heard that sudden b-o-o-m too frequently not to recognize it. The house shook; the wise young wife of John Adams went to the door and listened. Another explosion, another, and another! Word spread mysteriously that this was *it*; all the remaining militia were to repair to the lines by midnight of Monday, March 4–5. Abigail came back to her writing: "No sleep for me tonight. And if I cannot, who have no guilt upon my soul with regard to this cause, how shall the miserable wretches who have been the procurers of this dreadful scene, and those who are to be the actors, lie down with the load of guilt . . . ?" [13]

Except as the bombardment indicated that the Americans had seized the initiative, it was a trifle—only eleven shells and thirteen solid shot from the heavy mortars and the eighteen-pounders.[14] The British reply was prompt and lively but, from the American point of view, was not of a sort to make a quaking militia fearful of instant death: some of the British shells burst in flight; others did not explode at all.[15] Doubtless veterans who had fought at Bunker Hill mocked now the poor night-firing of their adversary. Washington, for his part, said little and of course regarded this first exchange of fire as insignificant. His test and his army's lay ahead. The next week would show how his plans compared in quality with those of his opponents. He would know whether or not he was equipped for the burdensome duty that Congress had imposed on him more than eight months previously. Eight months! It had taken that long to make ready if, indeed, even now, the army was seasoned and its powder sufficient.

Sunday, March 3, brought bad news. The enemy's fire, which ceased at dawn,[16] had inflicted no damage, but two of the Americans' large-bore mortars at Lechmere Point and one at Roxbury had split, either because of defects in the metal or because of inexperience on the part of the artillerists.[17] Washington felt that this loss reduced greatly his

---

[13] *Adams, Fam. Let.,* 137. Abigail wrote with so much maturity of judgment that it is difficult to realize she was at this time 31 only.

[14] Harry M. Lydenberg, ed., *Archibald Robertson . . . His Diaries and Sketches,* 1762–1780 (cited hereafter as *A. Robertson's Diaries*) p. 73. Fire seems to have been opened at different hours from the participating batteries. Robertson (*loc. cit.*) stated that the first shot came about midnight; on the left, the opening gun was fired at 1:30 A.M. See 1 *Webb,* 132.

[15] *Barker's Diary,* 69.

[16] 1 *Webb,* 133; Horatio Gates to John Adams, Mch. 8, 1776; *MHSP.,* 1875–76, p. 281–82

[17] 4 *G. W.,* 370–71; 1 *Webb,* 133; *David How's Diary,* 8; C. I. Bushnell, ed., *Journal of*

chance of bombarding Boston effectively [18] and he began immediately to consider how he might replace these Goliaths of his ordnance. Meantime, he directed that the prize possession of the Army, the thirteen-inch brass mortar "Congress" captured on *Nancy,* should be placed on Cobble Hill.[19]

Nearly all of Washington's other orders of the day were preparatory or precautionary. Troops in supporting positions around Roxbury were brought closer to the front, even though this meant that some of these men would be without barracks.[20] Woodchoppers were recalled from the forests; townsmen of Roxbury were invited to take a hand in the fighting; no absence from post was to be permitted otherwise than on written order of a general officer.[21] Washington's chief concern, shared by some of the other seniors at Cambridge, was that the enemy had intelligence of the impending attack and might seize the Dorchester Heights before the Americans could. Previous orders stood: The occupation of the high ground must not be delayed beyond the night of Monday–Tuesday, March 4–5. General Thomas was to be in immediate charge; General Ward of course was to have supervision of everything on his part of the front and now was assured he would get reenforcement both of infantry and of riflemen. Ward received, also, the headquarters' estimate of the number of men required for each phase of the occupation. Washington's letter of the early morning, covering these details, concluded awkwardly but generously: ". . . You will settle matters with the officers with you, as what I have said here is intended rather to convey my ideas generally than wishing them to be adhered to strictly." [22]

More than once during the French and Indian War, when Washington had completed preparation and was anticipating action, he had

---

Solomon Nash . . . (cited hereafter as *Solomon Nash's Diary*) p. 7. Which of these ruined mortars were of thirteen inches and which of ten inches, the records do not show. All that is known is that, during the course of these operations in March, Washington lost two of the larger and three of the smaller bore (4 *G. W.,* 370). There is, moreover, a conflict of testimony concerning the time these mortars were rendered useless, a conflict typical of many that develop from the diaries of the siege. Often a man who kept a journal was misinformed as to the date of a particular occurrence; sometimes he made his entries after the events and confused the happenings of one day with those of another. A safe working rule is: Never accept a date in a single diary as positive for a particular event, unless the internal evidence shows that the episode was directly under the eye of that particular writer who demonstrably was in the habit of making daily entries. In almost all other instances, a margin of forty-eight hours of possible error in timing will be found not unreasonably conservative when a diary gives the only extant account of an incident.   18 Cf. 4 *G. W.,* 370–71.

19 1 *Webb,* 133.   20 *Isaac Bangs's Diary,* 10.

21 4 *G. W.,* 363.   22 37 *ibid.,* 519–21.

used his waiting hours to catch up with his correspondence. In that same detachment of mind, he sat down this Sunday morning and wrote his friend Joseph Reed his views of the confusion that had followed a recent development elsewhere, Governor Trumbull's formal enlistment of troops for duty in New York at continental expense when the Commander-in-Chief had intended them to be gentlemen volunteers for temporary service. Washington took time, also, to give Reed his ideas concerning a headquarters light wagon he wanted. The desirability of having "a pair of clever horses of the same color" was stressed by the General. His sole reference to his own operations was that he hoped soon to be ready to take post "on Dorchester," even though, as he explained the redoubts had to be of fascines, chandeliers and screwed hay because the ground was so frozen that regular entrenchment was impossible. Washington was calm in writing all this, but he had one touch of bitterness, if one only, and that at the very beginning of his letter. He was obliged to Reed, he said, for informing him that progress was being made in the manufacture of powder and that a prospect of getting arms existed. The General went on sharply: ". . . there is some consolation in knowing that these useful articles will supply the wants of some part of the continental troops, though I feel too sensibly the mortification of having them withheld from me, Congress not even thinking it necessary to take the least notice of my application for these things." [23] That was all, but it was enough to disclose some of the thoughts which, as he had said earlier, had cost him anxious, sleepless hours: Too much of the burden had been put on his shoulders, he thought, by men who then went their way and left him to struggle on. If he had to do so, he would! He never had said that, *literatim,* but he had exemplified it consistently. At this decisive hour, even in writing to a friend who knew his heart, he would not yield to self-pity or think of himself as a martyr to the indifference of Congress.[24]

[23] 4 *ibid.,* 365 ff.

[24] Congress had no intention of ignoring Washington's appeals or of subordinating his requirements to those of other commanders. His prestige still was of the highest; he enjoyed the undiminished confidence of his former colleagues in Philadelphia. As far as the correspondence in *Burnett* discloses, there was no criticism of his conduct of affairs, though he may have been correct in suspecting that some members were becoming impatient and were beginning to wonder why he did not strike a blow. At the same time, it is a fact, clearly discernible between the lines of the letters collected by the diligent Burnett, that by Mch. 1, 1776, Washington was taken for granted by Congress and was assumed to be able to care for himself and for the men entrusted to him, with minimum supervision by Congress. This implied a compliment (Cf. 4 *Force* (4) p. 1144) but it manifestly might lead to neglect of the Boston front when a critical situation in Canada called for much powder and many arms. Southern members of

After a day of diligent preparation, the artillery opened on the night of March 3-4 at 9 P.M.[25] from the same fixed positions—Cobble Hill, Lechmere Point and Lamb's Dam. To save powder, the fire was no faster than the minimum required to keep the enemy in a state of alarm.[26] Bombardment did no damage[27] except to the Americans' pride: On the third shot, the brass "Congress" split as shamelessly as the iron mortars had.[28] The British fire was less bad in the eyes of the critical redcoat foot-soldiers than on the previous night,[29] but it ceased when that of the Americans ended early Monday morning, March 4.

Washington now had come to the day of the first major move, the day on which the occupation of Dorchester Heights was to begin. The auguries were contradictory. "Long Faces" continued to put in their appearance, with genuine alertness,[30] but word came about 10 o'clock that British troops were embarking in boats opposite Lechmere Point. Immediately the alarm was sounded, and the American Regiments in that district were put under arms and were hurried to their posts. Two hours of uncertainty passed. Then Washington heard that some of the British had entered the boats but apparently had discovered that the continentals were waiting for them, and thereupon they had given up whatever design they had.[31]

From that time until nightfall, everything outwardly was quiet. Around Roxbury, teams were assembled, fascines were loaded, the men were made ready to march, the entrenching tools were put into carts, and barrels were filled with stone and sand and were lifted into the stoutest vehicles. These barrels were to be rolled down the hills, in order to bowl over the redcoats who delivered the assault. All officers on the northwestern and western lines were told to watch the flagpole on Prospect Hill and the one at the Laboratory on the Cambridge Common. If the flags were raised there, it was the signal of a general alarm. All troops were then to proceed immediately to their stations. The Surgeons met with the Medical Director and received their assign-

---

Congress, moreover, were fearful of invasion below the Potomac and were apt to forget manifest and continuing need in Massachusetts.

[25] 1 *Webb*, 133.   [26] *Ibid.*

[27] *A. Robertson's Diaries*, 73; cf. 4 *G. W.*, 370.

[28] 1 *Webb*, 133; 4 *G. W.*, 370, 379; *David How's Diary*, 8. This occurred "about midnight." As recorded by one or two of the diarists, the incident appears to have been on the night of the 4th-5th, but the preponderance of evidence favors the date here assigned.

[29] *Barker's Diary*, 69.   [30] 4 *G. W.*, 370-71.

[31] 1 *Webb*, 133-34.

ments, hospitals were cleared for the arrival of the wounded,[32] and so with many other details as the clock ticked the crowded minutes. The next twelve hours might show whether George Washington should continue as a soldier or, failing, would do well to return to Mount Vernon and grind flour to feed fighting men.

At dusk, about 7 P.M., that 4th of March,[33] the bombardment began. The 3000 troops that John Thomas had chosen for a hard night's work started from Roxbury for the hills on Dorchester Peninsula.[34] American fire now was almost ten times as fast as it had been either of the two previous nights. British artillerists answered as if they knew that this time something serious impended.[35] Soon, as many as seven shell could be seen in the air at the same instant,[36] a sight never witnessed previously there.

Fortunately, the sky was clear, the moon was full, the night was mild.[37] About 300 teams started with their allotment of fascines, chandeliers and barrels[38] and as early as 8 P.M. were climbing the nearer hills.[39] The infantry moved in silently;[40] the riflemen spread themselves out along the waterfront and sought such cover as they could find—protection by night and ambush by day.[41] Men who previously had surveyed the ground saw that the dumping was at the proper places; teamsters turned around, drove down the hill and, in many instances, came back with a second load, some with a third.[42] Next was the sad business of cutting down orchards to provide abattis.[43] Washington was there to observe and to encourage[44] and he well might have

---

[32] GO of Mch. 4, 1776; 4 G. W., 368–69.

[33] J. Baldwin's Journal, 28; John Thomas to his wife, Mch. 9, 1776, in Coffin's Thomas, 20–21.

[34] Thomas's letter, loc. cit.; 1 Webb, 133–34.

[35] A. Robertson's Diaries, 73. During the night the Americans fired 144 solid shot and thirteen shell into Boston. See Knox's statement in 5 Force (4) p. 114.

[36] McCurtin's Journal, 33.

[37] 4 G. W., 380; Thacher, 38. Edgar W. Woolard, Acting Director of the Nautical Almanac, United States Naval Observatory, kindly computed, June, 1949, that the moon which rose at approximately 5:20 P.M. on March 4, 1776, was full at 4:30 A.M. on the 5th and set about 6:44 A.M.

[38] Washington gave the number of teams as 300 (4 G. W., 380); J. Baldwin reckoned them at 280 (see his Journal, 29); John Thomas in the letter to his wife (cited supra) put the total at 360. Most of these draft animals were oxen.

[39] Thomas's letter, loc. cit.   [40] Thacher, 38.

[41] Bedinger's Journal, 123. It was 1 A.M. of the 5th, Bedinger stated, when the riflemen took their position.

[42] Letter from New York, March 13, in Lloyd's Evening Post and British Chronicle, May 13–15, 1776, quoted in Willard, 275.

[43] Heath, 49. It probably was the sound of the axes and of the falling trees that gave the British their first notice, about 10 P.M., that the Americans were entrenching on Dorchester Heights (A. Robertson's Diaries, 73).   [44] Thacher, 39.

found satisfaction in the smooth swiftness of all these preliminaries. He scarcely could have asked better performance. The soldiers soon were covered against random night fire. Long before day, they began to break ground that had thawed somewhat on the surface.[45]

Three thousand fresh troops [46] came up about 3 o'clock on the morning of the 5th to take the place of those who had started work early in the night. Riflemen on the flats could not be relieved because no organized marksmen of like skill were available, but on promise of provisions the "shirtmen" agreed to remain at their posts.[47] As the newcomers on the hills took the entrenching tools from the hands of their tired comrades, all the toilers must have looked like an army of ghosts in the moonlight, but they had caught the spirit of an adventure they now understood, and they made every spade count in raising the parapets.

Dawn came at last on the 5th of March, the anniversary, Washington reminded the men, of the "Boston Massacre." Near Cambridge, two Regiments were mustered for an early march to Roxbury, in order to strengthen the lines there.[48] The alert was ordered all the way around the crude arc of the American lines as far as Chelsea.[49] At sunrise, if instructions were followed, the troops on the left centre were to be drawn up near Charles River. If they received the known signal, indicating that the enemy was about to assault the new works beyond Roxbury, they were to begin embarkation on the waiting flatboats and were to force a crossing to Boston.[50] On Dorchester Heights, when it was sufficiently light for the men to see the fortifications beyond those on

[45] Horatio Gates to John Adams, Mch. 8, 1776; *MHSP.*, 1875-76, p. 281-82. Information regarding the condition of the ground on the 4th is meagre. Washington, it will be recalled, wrote Reed on the 3rd of March that the ground was so hard frozen that "we cannot entrench" (4 *G. W.*, 366), but it is not quite certain from the context that he meant this to apply specifically to that date. Isaac Bangs stated (*Diary*, 9) that the deep frost prevented the start of fortification until the 4th. There is, on the other hand, no reference to particular difficulty in entrenching on the night of March 4-5. The assumption in the text consequently seems the reasonable one in the light of Thacher's statement that the night of March 4-5 was "mild and pleasant" (*op. cit.*, 38). Needless to say, it is highly improbable that the ground had been thawed to any considerable depth. The troops probably had to scrape topsoil from a considerable area in order to get enough to throw against the fascines for a parapet sufficiently stout to resist cannon fire. If the fascines were of standard size for the purpose they were to serve, they were, according to Simes, "between two and three feet in thickness, and four feet long."

[46] Accounts vary as much as 500 in stating the size of the first and second contingents, but the difference is not important.

[47] *Bedinger's Journal*, 129.   [48] 4 *G. W.*, 380-81; 37 *ibid.*, 520.

[49] *Baldwin Papers*, Harvard Coll. Lib.

[50] Horatio Gates to John Adams, Mch. 8, 1776, *loc. cit.* Gates's narrative may leave the impression that this was done on the morning of the 4th, but the correct date must have been the 5th, if for no other reason than that the "new works" were not in existence until then.

which each Company had been working, they were surprised and proud to observe how much had been accomplished under the curtain of that single March night.[51] Six fortifications had been laid out on the higher hills and on the tableland. Included in the six was cover for the flank and rear against fire from the British cannon on Boston Neck.[52]

Presently, the Americans on the high ground could glimpse the outlines of the city beyond a fog that hung over the flats of Dorchester Peninsula.[53] All the continentals eagerly tried to see what damage their guns had done. During the night, some of the soldiers had thought they heard the cries of women and children after their projectiles had struck: was Boston now a shambles?[54] The answer was both reassuring and disappointing. Nothing indicated that any perceptible damage had been inflicted. Already on housetops and on the wharves,[55] were many persons who appeared to be looking toward Dorchester Heights, as if they were much more interested in what was happening there than in what had occurred in town. That, in the first hours of day, was all the men in the new defences could descry. There was no sign of any immediate assembly of British troops, no activity in the fleet to suggest that troops were about to be taken aboard. The fire of the batteries in the city and of some of those on Boston Neck soon was brisk but it was delivered ineffectually[56] below the crest of the hills.

Washington was not deceived. He knew that flood tide would be about noon[57] and that nothing except artillery fire could be expected until the water was high enough to permit the landing of a force on Dorchester Peninsula itself. If the British did not attack then, they would have to wait for the next tide, because no commander would be fool enough to order his men to get out of their boats and to wade ashore across the mudflats that were exposed for a long distance at low tide to a raking fire. Everything indicated that the "lobsters" would come in with the tide; the bait was attracting them just as the anglers

---

[51] *Isaac Bangs's Diary*, 11.

[52] *J. Baldwin's Journal*, 29; *A. Robertson's Diaries*, 73–74. No detailed nor even an approximately accurate sketch of these earthworks has been found. Eben. Huntington, who had been writing expectantly about Dorchester Heights from January 12 onward (*Letters*, 26, 27, 29), mentioned "two forts, one on each of the high hills, and two small redoubts just as you pass the Neck, which redoubts were built to play upon the floating batteries that should attempt to annoy our people passing the Neck" (*ibid.*, 31).

[53] For the fog see *Thacher*, 40, where the statement is made that from Boston lookouts the American works loomed vaguely above the fog, and seemed to be more formidable than actually they were.

[54] 1 *Webb*, 134–35.

[56] *Ibid.*

[55] Thomas's letter of March 9, *loc. cit.*

[57] 1 *Webb*, 134–35.

had hoped it would.[58] The Americans awaited confidently and, on the Cambridge arc, were ready now to launch their counterattack on Boston when the British tried to storm Dorchester Heights.[59] Washington realized that he was demanding much of Putnam, of Sullivan, of Greene and of their men [60] in ordering them to cross the open water, but he was willing to take the risk.

About two hours after the British began their cannonade of the new works they suspended it for the manifest reason that they could not elevate their guns to reach the high parapets.[61] This cessation of fire encouraged the men who already were in high spirits and were sure they could repel attack.[62] Almost simultaneously with the halt in the rain from the enemy's cannon, there were signs of commotion and confusion in the town,[63] much as if the British were just arousing themselves from bewilderment. A general alarm was sounded. The town began to buzz like a bee-hive an inquisitive dog had disturbed. Late in the forenoon, troops could be seen embarking, with their artillery, on small boats that carried them to transports. A few of these vessels thereupon dropped down to anchorages off the Castle.[64] By the time this was done, it was manifest that the hours of best opportunity had been lost in slow or disordered preparation.[65] The tide was past the flood. Either, then, the British were preparing for some sort of a surprise maneuver or else they were assembling their ships in the hope of disembarking their men on the next tide, under cover of darkness. Washington's troops meanwhile were planting six 12-pounders and were wheeling probably a larger number of field pieces into their works,[66] and they had continued to pile up earth, but they could do no more than that—

---

58 4 G. W., 380.   59 Ibid., 373.   60 Cf. ibid., 321.

61 John Sullivan to John Adams, Mch. 15, 1776, MHSP., 1875–76, p. 283. Sullivan explained that the British tried to sink the "hinder wheels" of their cannon into the ground in the hope of gaining the required elevation, but it is not certain this was observed in the early morning of the 5th.

62 John Trumbull, Reminiscences, 25.

63 4 G. W., 372.

64 Thomas's letter (loc. cit.) fixed the time at 10:30; J. Baldwin's Journal gave the hour as "about noon"; in A. Robertson's Diaries, 74, which must be accepted as the superior authority, though not always accurate, the embarkation is said to have been ordered at 11:30.

65 4 G. W., 380.

66 John Trumbull in his Reminiscences, 24, thought there were twenty guns. If Solomon Nash (Diary, 8) was correct in saying the armament on the heights included six 12-pounders, then Knox was using some of the guns of that class he had brought from Ticonderoga. As of Oct. 20, 1775, Colonel Gridley had listed two cannon only for projectiles of that weight. Nash's Diary would indicate that this ordnance was placed on Dorchester during the night of March 4–5, but it probably could not have been put into position until the works were advanced and daylight had arrived.

except to eat, to doze and to swear that when the redcoats came, they would "give it to them." The only offensive action was two shots about 6 P.M. at one of the vessels off the Castle,[67] where some of the troops from the transports were disembarking.[68]

Expectation now was drenched. During the late afternoon, the weather had become colder and the wind had shifted. By evening, there was an astonishing change. A furious storm roared in from the South [69] with a high, cruelly cold wind and a lashing rain.[70] Before darkness settled, it was plain that the transports which had not left the inner harbor could not come down to the Castle. Even if good seamanship could have brought them there, the flat-bottomed boats for landing the soldiers on the night tide would have been swamped.[71] Stout ships in the harbor scarcely could endure the assault. Two of them, fighting the sea with anchor and cable and rudder, were driven ashore.[72] In that full gale, man's implements of wrath were feeble and futile. Washington let no powder be wet that night in attempted continuance of the bombardment.[73]

When he awoke the next morning, Wednesday, March 6, the storm was still roaring,[74] but he rode toward the lines, the rain slackened and by 8 o'clock it ceased.[75] The wind remained high [76] and apparently was holding the transports to their anchorage. Perhaps, after Washington mounted the heights,[77] he was told that British troops, estimated

---

[67] *A. Robertson's Diaries*, 75.   [68] 4 *G. W.*, 372.

[69] Webb (*op. cit.*, v. 1, p. 136), gave the direction of the wind as Southeast, but *Deacon Tudor's Diary* (61), E. Price's Diary (*MHSP.*, 1863–64, p. 240) and S. Cooper (6 *A. H. R.*, 336), all agreed that the wind came from the South.

[70] The unhappy McCurtin, acutely sensitive to low temperature, once more wrote: "I never before felt such cold" (*op. cit.*, 33).

[71] 1 *Kemble*, 71. For the storm, see *Carter, Letters to a Friend*, 25, *A. Robertson's Diaries*, 76, and an anonymous British officer in *Morning Chronicle and London Advertiser*, May 15, 1776, quoted in *Willard*, 278. The last named of these authorities spoke of "a wind, more violent than anything I ever heard . . ." If the minor changes in weather during March, 1776, are of interest to any student, they will be found succinctly and carefully set forth in the Diary of Capt. William Bamford, 27 *Md. His. Mag.*, 248 ff. He gave the direction of the wind on the evening of the 5th as Southwest.

[72] 1 *Webb*, 135.   [73] *A. Robertson's Diaries*, 75.

[74] It is not known where Washington spent the night of the 4th–5th or of the 5th–6th. Although Thacher (*op. cit.*, 38), is the sole authority who stated that Washington was on the lines during the night of March 4–5, the probability is strong that Thacher was correct and that Washington could not permit himself to remain at Cambridge during those critical hours of darkness. By the same uncertain logic of probability, it would appear that Washington may well have gone back to Cambridge, and to the comfort of dry clothes and a warm bed, after it was plain that the storm forbade a British attack on the night of the 5th–6th.

[75] 4 *G. W.*, 373.

[76] *E. Price's Diary* in MHSP., 1863–64, p. 240. Cf. 1 *Webb*, 136; Bomford, as *supra*, n. 71.

[77] *J. Baldwin's Journal*, 29, records his presence there.

at two Regiments, who had been on transports, had relanded at one of the Boston wharves.[78]

What did these confused occurrences forecast? Was the attack merely delayed? Normally, Washington could have made a good guess at the answer, because reports of what happened in Boston reached head-quarters through one channel or another almost every day. In addition to the usual lookout at Chelsea, there now was an American signal party on Noodle's Island.[79] Despite this, Boston now was sealed, tightly sealed. In the complaining language of Joseph Trumbull, all officers at headquarters might protest, "We have not had a deserter or prisoner, nor an inhabitant escaped from town to give us any information. . . ."[80] Washington had, consequently, no first-hand intelligence and he had to base his conclusions on what could be observed at a distance and, *a priori,* on what an experienced, though none-too-aggressive adversary should be expected to do.

One thing only remained certain: If there was to be an attack, it could not come by water until the wind dropped. Thus delayed in the harbor, Howe might sally on Boston Neck, in the hope of cutting off the American troops on Dorchester Peninsula. Any such attempt must of course be met with vigilance and prompt fire. In event a sortie in-cluded the greater part of the British garrison, then the counterstroke might be delivered from the side of Cambridge as originally planned. The water there was not so turbulent as to make an American crossing impossible.

Outstanding orders, then, were to continue in force: 4000 men were to be held in readiness to cross the river to Boston should the redcoats stream down Boston Neck.[81] Work on the new fortifications was renewed, mud or no mud;[82] at high water, the American positions on the Peninsula were to be manned.[83] The next duty might be the hard-est—to wait and to wonder what was happening at British headquarters in Boston. This did not involve agonizing and it scarcely stirred anxious doubt. Conditions were better hourly. The defences on the high

---

[78] *A. Robertson's Diaries,* 75. "Perhaps" has to preface this sentence, because it is not certain that this incident was observed from any point on Dorchester Peninsula.

[79] Loammi Baldwin to his wife, Mch. 6, 1776; *Baldwin Papers,* Harvard Coll. Lib.

[80] Letter of Mch. 6, 1776, to William Hopper, 5 *Force* (4) p. 200–01; 4 *G. W.,* 379–80.

[81] 1 *Webb,* 136.

[82] This was not reported from any American source but was observed by the British. See *A. Robertson's Diaries,* 75.

[83] *McCurtin's Journal,* 33–34. According to McCurtin, the defences were manned daily through the 11th.

ground of Dorchester soon would be so strong that if the British assaulted, their troops would be mowed down. If they did not attack, Nook's Hill soon could be occupied by Washington's men. This done, American cannon would be so close to the town that the wharves of Boston would be untenable. What then?

Washington still did not attempt to answer the question, but on the 7th, he felt the situation sufficiently stabilized to justify the dismissal of those militia men who lived at Dorchester and in the adjoining area and had brought with them three days' provisions only.[84] They had done their duty so well that Washington praised and thanked them both in general orders [85] and in the detailed report he wrote that day to the Congress in Philadelphia. It was the first time he had addressed the President since he had explained his plans in a dispatch of February 26 [86] Washington had said then of the proposed occupation of Dorchester Heights as a means of inducing the enemy to attack, "how far our expectations may be answered, time alone can determine." [87] Now he explained that in spite of the loss of the heavy mortars, he believed the cannonade of Boston had facilitated the seizure of the high ground where he hoped the works soon would be complete and strong enough to "enable our troops stationed there to make a vigorous and obstinate stand." [88] He went on to describe how a bombardment might be undertaken from Nook's Hill, and he expressed the belief that if he could get heavy mortars quickly, the British would be "so galled and annoyed that they must either give us battle, or quit their present possessions." Then he added: "I am resolved that nothing on my part shall be wanting to effect the one or the other." [89]

That was the plan—but elaboration of it was not all that a dispatch to the President of Congress should cover. Other matters were pending and they, too, should be included and should be discussed in precise detail, even though an aide might run into the room the next minute and report that the British were attacking like mad savages. So, after announcing to Hancock that the Dorchester militia had been sent home, Washington proceeded to review the need of a third Major General to take the place of the absent Charles Lee. The senior in line of promo-

---

[84] 4 G. W., 374. Cf. ibid., 372.
[85] As of Mch. 8, 1776. He commended their "spirited and alert march to Roxbury" and the "noble ardor they discovered in defence of the cause of liberty and their country" (ibid., 384).
[86] Ibid., 348–49.
[87] Ibid., 349.
[88] Ibid., 371.
[89] Ibid., 372.

tion was Brig. Gen. John Thomas, who had acquitted himself admirably in Dorchester Neck. In fact, it was his organizing industry, his hard sweating in freezing weather, so to say, that was responsible for the smooth preparations on the night of March 3–4. Washington of course had observed this and he esteemed Thomas, but because he knew jealous eyes in Philadelphia might scrutinize and criticize his words, he wrote with a restraint that seemed the meagrest of praise: "General Thomas is the first Brigadier, stands fair in point of reputation and is esteemed a brave and good officer." Then he went on with like economy of approbation to recommend the Colonel of the Rifle Regiment, William Thompson, for advancement to the rank of Brigadier: ". . . as far as I have had an opportunity of judging . . . a good officer and a man of courage. What I have said of these two gentlemen, I conceive to be my duty, at the same time acknowledging whatever promotions are made will be satisfactory to me." [90]

So spake the ex-Burgess, the planter who had buckled on his sword and had pledged the members of the New York Congress that the citizen would not be lost in the soldier. As no interruption occurred during the writing of this letter, Washington indulged himself in another, this one a lengthy epistle to Joseph Reed, to whom, without reticent formality, he could speak of Thomas's appointment. If an outsider were brought to the Boston theatre of war as Major General, Washington said, "Thomas, if no more, would surely quit, and I believe him to be a good man." As for the prospective vacancy among the Brigadiers, "I have heard of one other valiant son of New England waiting promotion, since the advancement of [Joseph] Frye, who has not, and I doubt will not, do much service to the cause; at present he keeps his room and talks learnedly of emetics, cathartics, &c. For my own part, I see nothing but a declining life that matters [to?] him." [91]

It was pleasant to be free to fill four sheets of paper with candid observations in diverting contrast to the stiff regularity of his letters to the President of Congress; perhaps, too, there may have been some pride on Washington's part in being able to concentrate his mind on matters of this sort when some men could have thought of imminent battle only. However all this might be, Washington had to turn from his desk and ascertain what was happening at the front during those early

[90] *Ibid.*, 374.
[91] *Ibid.*, 382. Joseph Frye of Massachusetts had been elected Brigadier Jan. 10, 1776. See 4 *JCC.*, 47. Benedict Arnold had been given like rank the same day.

hours of March 7, the third day of the operation. Work, he was told, was going briskly on. As he had hoped and expected, the fortifications were stronger every hour. One thing only of possible importance had occurred and that was somewhat mysterious: the British most certainly and unmistakably were moving cannon [92] in Boston—and why? Could it be that they were preparing to abandon the city? If not, whither were they shifting their heavy guns, and for what purpose? There were other vague indications, also, that the redcoats might be preparing to leave [93] but nothing definite, nothing more than bustle on shore and stir on ships. It was baffling! Except for the craning of necks and the chatter over the meaning of what was happening in Boston, the men on Dorchester Heights might as well have been at work, untroubled, on defences out of range and beyond dispute. The enemy needed to be prodded—to be baited again—and soon he would be. Probably at that very hour fascines were being conveyed, by paths the British could not see, as close as possible to Nook's Hill, in anticipation of the order to mount that nearest eminence to Boston. This hauling of awkward bundles of small branches was not easy work, because of the swampy ground between the hill and the redoubts already erected, but it was done steadily.[94]

Now it was the 8th and just such a day as the 7th, busy for the men with the shovels but unexciting for them and for all the other troops until 2 P.M. About that hour, a flag of truce was seen at the British advanced post on Boston Neck.[95] A parley was sounded. Col. Ebenezer Learned, commanding on that part of the front, went out to meet the party, which included a man in British uniform and three civilians. The British officer introduced himself as Maj. Henry Bassett of the 10th Regiment. His companions were Thomas and Jonathan Amory and Peter Johonnot, who produced a letter which they begged Colonel Learned to deliver General Washington as soon as possible. It was, they said, from the Selectmen of Boston. Colonel Learned agreed to forward the paper; the ceremonies were completed; the flag went back to the British lines, and the communication was forwarded in haste to Washington.

[92] 1 *Webb*, 137.
[93] 4 *G. W.*, 386.
[94] *Isaac Bangs's Diary*, 12, with the caveat that the date of this stacking of fascines is not established beyond all challenge. The work may have been begun on the 7th or on the 9th, but the 8th seems most reasonably the date.
[95] For the time, see John Thomas's letter of Mch. 9, 1776, *loc. cit.*

There it was. He took it, glanced at the inscription, broke the seal and began to read:

Boston, 8 March, 1776

"As his Excellency General Howe is determined to leave the town with the troops under his command . . ."

What was that? Howe to leave? Driven out already?
Washington read on:

". . . a number of the respectable inhabitants, being very anxious for its preservation and safety, have applied to General Robertson for this purpose, who at their request have communicated the same to his Excellency Genl. Howe, who has assured them that he has no intention of destroying the town, unless the troops under his command are molested during their embarkation or at their departure, by the armed forces without, which declaration he gave Genl. Robertson leave to communicate to the inhabitants; If such an opposition should take place, we have the greatest reason to expect the town will be exposed to entire destruction. As our fears are quieted with regard to Genl. Howe's intentions, we beg we may have some assurances that so dreadful a calamity may not be brought on by any measures without. As a testimony of the truth of the above, we have signed our names to this paper, carried out by Messrs. Thomas and Jonathan Amory and Peter Johonnot, who have at the earnest entreaties of the inhabitants, through the Lt. Governor, solicited a flag of truce for this purpose."

"John Scollay, Timothy Newell, Thomas Marshall, Samuel Austin" [96]

There might be treachery behind this. Howe might be deceiving the Selectmen; but would he have said he intended to leave the town unless he really purposed to do so? If actually he did, his retreat by sea would be an American victory. Washington's first campaign would be a success and at insignificant cost to date, two killed and four or five slightly wounded.[97]

If there was natural exultation over this possible outcome, it was momentary, because Washington had to decide what answer he would make to a paper which, in his own words, appeared "under covert, unauthorized and addressed to nobody." [98] The largest instant question

[96] 4 G. W., 377 n.
[97] As of March 7 (4 G. W., 371). The ultimate total was six killed and not more than that number wounded. See Joseph Ward to John Adams, Mch. 14, 1776; MHSP., 1875–76, p. 282.
[98] 4 G. W., 384.

was whether Howe himself stood behind what was, in effect, a proposal to abandon the city if he were permitted to sail away unmolested and "with the honors of war." The authenticity and bona fides of the communication seemed to Washington so dubious that he sought counsel. Those general officers unoccupied and near at hand were asked to come to headquarters immediately and, when they arrived, were shown the Selectmen's letter.[99] Washington, of course, wanted Boston, and wanted it with the least injury of citizens' property and the heaviest possible losses to Howe in men and in stores; but the American commander had to admit to himself that if the British really had decided to leave Boston, he could do no more than inflict some damage on the outgoing ships by an uncertain cannonade of moving targets.[100] He found his Generals of the same mind,[101] but they were so suspicious of their adversary that they could not believe Howe was disposed to withhold the torch from Boston for reasons of humanity if, by burning it, the British General could embark men and equipment with less loss than otherwise he might. They distrusted any proposal for a bargain. Caution was the first law of conduct where treachery was possible— that was the conclusion of the council. Washington should acknowledge the letter of the Selectmen, should point out that it covered no written pledge by Howe, and should reserve all the rights of war. A letter for the signature of Colonel Learned was drafted, probably by General Gates,[102] to this effect:

"Roxbury, 9 March, 1776

"Sir: Agreeably to a promise made to you at the lines yesterday, I waited upon His Excellency General Washington, and presented to Him the Paper (handed to me by you) from the Select Men of Boston. The Answer I received from Him was to this effect: 'That, as it was an unauthenticated Paper; without an Address, and not Obligatory Upon General Howe; He would take no Notice of it.' I am, with esteem and respect, Gentlemen, your most obedt. Servt,

Ebenezer Learned

"To Messrs. Amorys and Johonnot." [103]

99 *Ibid.*, 376.　　　　100 *Ibid.*, 377.　　　　101 *Ibid.*

102 The copy in 24 *Papers of G. W.*, 35, LC, is in his autograph.

103 4 *G. W.*, 377 n. Webb (*op. cit.*, v. 1, p. 137–38), and many subsequent writers appear to have been of opinion that Washington concluded at this council to accept tacitly the proposal submitted by the Selectmen though publicly declining its terms for the reasons set forth in the paper signed by Learned. All the evidence seems to suggest, on the contrary, that Washington was as suspicious as any of his lieutenants and was disposed to "wait and see."

Until about the time this answer was written, Washington had been feeling his way in the dark, so to speak, because he still lacked information from inside the town. In echo of Joseph Trumbull's complaint, Washington had written Reed on the 7th: ". . . there has not been a creature out of Boston . . ."[104] Now, under Col. Loammi Baldwin's guidance,[105] there arrived at headquarters a Captain Irvine, master of a merchant ship then tied up where the British flag still floated. He and his crew had slipped out on the night of the 7th–8th, and he consequently had fresh intelligence. The British, he said, were preparing to leave Boston and would do so in a day or two. Their transports were being made ready with the utmost haste. Amid much confusion, the troops were moving their artillery and their stores to the wharves. All Tories in the city were to be allowed to leave by sea, on the King's ships or on vessels of their own hire,[106] but the shortage of mariners was so great that many vessels were without crews and probably would be burned. Some townsfolk believed the entire city, like the idle ships, was to be set afire and was to have the fate of Falmouth. Captain Irvine had much more than this to narrate, some of it exaggerated third-hand talk of damage done and bloody toll taken by the American fire; and he repeated, also, a story of reasonable verisimilitude concerning preparations the storm of the night of March 5–6 had set at naught. Had not rain and gale intervened, the British planned, Irvine said, to assault the fortified Dorchester hills at 8 o'clock on the morning of the 6th.[107]

It was a story to stir the pride of American commanders and to stimulate the self-confidence of the men in the ranks. Soldiers could look ahead to the day when, as the deliverers of Boston, they could walk the streets of the town and could see for themselves what the informant described. At the moment, the tall man in the headquarters office at Cambridge had to decide whether Captain Irvine was a courageous patriot, a bold liar, or a calculating spy. Washington, listening, weighing and scrutinizing, felt that the shipmaster was telling the truth as far as it was known to him. All that Irvine said of the situation accorded with what Washington and the other officers had observed through their glasses, and it bore out the statement the Selectmen had made of Howe's intentions.

[104] 4 *G. W.*, 379–80.
[105] Loammi Baldwin to his wife, Mch. 8, 1776; *Baldwin Papers,* Harvard Coll. Lib.
[106] The verb "charter" does not appear to have been used in this sense prior to the nineteenth century.
[107] 4 *G. W.*, 374–76.

Assume, then, that the British were about to leave. Admit, once again, that the troops on Dorchester could not halt the embarkation or inflict any greater damage on the departing vessels than to knock off a rail here and splinter a bit of planking there: what must Washington design for the days when the British would be afloat on the Atlantic and free to strike where they chose? His judgment told him:

1. To proceed with the fortification of Nook's Hill on the first favorable night and thereby to make certain that if Howe changed his mind or lingered overlong he could be blasted out of Boston.

2. To prepare for the more difficult task of defending the Hudson instead of assuming, as many already were, that Howe was sailing to Halifax for slow refit and long leisure. As soon as the British were gone, surely and completely gone, American troops must start for New York.

3. To man all the headlands around Boston in order to meet the possibility that Howe might simply be extricating himself from the narrowing arc of American fire, in order to land somewhere on flank, perhaps for destructive expeditions to the interior.

4. To direct that if the British fleet sailed away, the little American squadron dog its wake, destroy cripples and strays, and ascertain whither the ships were bound.

5. To consider the desirability of building defences at the entrance to Boston harbor, after the British departure, so that a returning hostile fleet might be compelled, at the least, to fight for that haven.[108]

The first of these five decisions was the one to be translated immediately into action. On the morning of the 9th—there being no new development in Boston—the Americans boldly laid out on Nook's Hill, in plain view of the British, the work they proposed to construct that night.[109] They paid for their imprudence! No sooner did they start work after darkness fell [110] than shells fell also, and precisely where the Americans were to put their fascines and raise their parapets. The British evidently had observed carefully what had been done during the day and had calculated the range with precision. In a short time, four men were struck as they stood around a fire; others became uneasy as the projectiles crashed; the undertaking was abandoned for the night—the first instance in which anything had gone seriously amiss

---

108 *Ibid.*, 377–78; Moylan to commanding officer at New York, Mch. 9, 1776; 5 *Force* (4) p. 166–67.
109 See letter of unidentified writer in Cambridge, Mch. 10, 1776, in 5 *Force* (4) p. 177.
110 1 *Webb*, 138.

from the time the heavy mortars had exploded early in the operation.[111] The fire of the British was the heaviest they had directed against any of the new American positions[112] and it might indicate that Howe had resolved to stay in Boston and, in order to do so, had determined to keep the continentals off Nook's Hill. Washington did not so interpret the bombardment. All the shot came from the narrow, near arc of British gun positions, a fact which indicated most strongly that the cannon had been removed from the other redoubts and had been put aboard ship.[113] Besides, there was as much bustle as ever in the town and on the wharves. From this evidence, Washington concluded that the British were not quite ready to leave and that they repelled him because they knew he could force them precipitately to abandon the Massachusetts capital as soon as he secured artillery positions on that height. Further, he reasoned that if the British were delaying their departure solely to carry off all their gear and baggage, he would do well to defer a more vigorous effort to fortify the hill until he had his own Army in condition to move quickly. Then, if Howe sailed out of Massachusetts Bay and headed for New York, the American commander would have only to beat the drums and start his troops down the roads that paralleled the route of the ships.[114]

Events of Sunday, March 10, seemed to vindicate Washington's judgment. A great stir was visible at the landing-places of Boston as if the redcoats were cramming all they could into the holds of vessels that bulged already. Soon, one ship after another raised sail and dropped down the harbor. This, of course, was a signal for Washington's troops to move out from Roxbury and to man their positions on Dorchester Heights, but no boats were lowered from the fleet and no indications of a landing were observed.[115] Nor was there any perceptible change on Monday, March 11. Additional ships left the wharves, in the face of adverse wind, and relied on the tide to wash them down the channel toward Nantasket Road;[116] the field of every glass turned on

111 *J. Baldwin's* Journal, 29; *Solomon Nash's Diary*, 9 and 51 n; *McCurtin's Journal*, 34; return of ammunition used, 24 *Papers of G. W.*, 37, LC; 5 *Force* (4) p. 166, 177, 199–200.

112 *McCurtin's Journal*, loc. cit.; *Deacon Tudor's Diary*, 61–62.

113 1 *Webb*, 138.   114 4 *G. W.*, 392.

115 *A. Robertson's Diaries*, 30; *J. Baldwin's Journal*, 60. Anyone who uses Baldwin's valuable Journal for the second week in March, 1776, should verify the dates given there for occurrences around Boston, because Baldwin appears to have become confused in his chronology. The deviation in one instance is as much as three days from the date given by all other responsible authorities.

116 L. Baldwin to his wife, Mch. 11, 1776; *Baldwin Papers*, Harvard Coll. Lib. For the fact that the vessels went as far as Nantasket Road, see 4 *G. W.*, 390.

Boston yielded the same picture of preparations for general departure of army and of fleet.[117] While expectancy remained and some anxiety lingered in Washington's mind, he was now more confident of the outcome and, at an unhurried dinner, talked with Boston refugees concerning the early occupation of the town as if he were certain of the complete departure of the British.[118] Two brass mortars were sent to Noodle's Island to be used against shipping; [119] the last work on the redoubts atop the Dorchester hills was finished; barracks nearby for 600 men were completed; officers agreed that American cannon now could command the whole of the little peninsula; [120] orders were that "not a moment's time . . . be lost in preparing for the march." [121]

By the 12th—another negative day—the waiting at Cambridge headquarters and on the Dorchester line was exasperating. Within twenty-four hours more, it was enough to infuriate impatient minds. When Washington seated himself on the 13th to review the situation in a letter to the President of Congress, he had to admit "I have been deceived and was rather premature in the opinion I had . . . formed" in letters of the 7th and 9th concerning the imminent departure of the British; but, he added, he had "little reason . . . to doubt the event will take place in a very short time . . ." [122] There still was a possibility, he thought, that the British might be making a feint and that he could not afford to strip his lines of men.[123]

Was Halifax or New York the destination of the fleet? The American General held as tenaciously as ever to the belief that the objective was the mouth of the Hudson,[124] and he brought his general officers together on the 13th to give him their judgment on the number of troops he should send to New York and on the time when it would be safe to start the movement. The advice of his council was that he could begin the transfer of force immediately but that he ought not to dispatch any men besides the rifle Companies and one Brigade until the British actually had left Boston.[125] Plans were made accordingly for the departure of this

117 Cf. S. Cooper's Diary, 6 *A. H. R.*, 336; *Letters and Diary of John Rowe*, 301 ff.
118 S. Cooper's Diary in 6 *A. H. R.*, 336.
119 L. Baldwin to his wife, *loc. cit.*; John Sullivan to L. Baldwin, Mch. 11, 1776, *L. Baldwin Papers*, Clements Library.
120 Horatio Gates to John Adams, Mch. 8, 1776, *MHSP.*, 1775–76, p. 281–82.
121 GO., Mch. 11, 1776; 4 *G. W.*, 387. Cf. Joseph Ward to John Adams, Mch. 14, 1776; *MHSP.*, 1875–76, p. 282.
122 4 *G. W.*, 390.   123 *Ibid.*, 395.
124 *Ibid.*, 391, 395–96.
125 *Ibid.*, 391; minutes of the council of March 13; 5 *Force* (4) p. 206.

advance column.[126] Washington was of opinion, by this time, that the torch would not be applied to the city.[127] Reports were that the British were breaking up their furniture, wagons and carts, a troublesome labor to which they would not have put their men—at least Washington so reasoned—if they intended to start fires that would destroy the town and everything in it.[128]

Washington took into account the badness of the roads over which his men would march to New York and he concluded that canvas might carry the redcoats to their destination more quickly than muscle would transport even the fast-marching "shirtmen." To reduce the risk of having the mouth of the Hudson virtually undefended when the British arrived, Washington appealed to Governor Trumbull to send 2000 men temporarily to New York. From Jersey, 1000 were to be sought.[129] The existence of laboriously constructed lines around Boston, he wrote Hancock in effect, constituted warning that it was better to prevent a lodgment at New York than to have the task of ousting an adversary already entrenched there.[130] Washington found himself justified immediately in these precautions, because bad weather deepened mud and inexperience delayed preparations for the march of an Army that had long been encamped. The rifle Companies got away on the 15th;[131] the five Regiments of Foot and the two artillery Companies that were to follow the "shirtmen" could not take the road at the appointed time.[132]

The 15th of March was the eighth day after the receipt of the Selectmen's announcement of the impending departure of Howe—and the British still held Boston. Although many of the ships had gone to Nantasket Road by this time and were at anchor there, the grip of the redcoats on the town was unbroken. The arrogant roll of distant drums, the change of guard, the flapping of the King's flag from Beacon Hill—all these marked the daily round of occupation. Patient as was the American General, confident as he remained that Howe was in process of evacuating Boston, Washington now had to endure the news that the wind was favorable for the departure of the British but that they

[126] 4 G. W., 390, 394.
[127] Ibid., 389.
[128] 4 G. W., 390–91.
[129] Ibid., 391–92, 395–96.
[130] His somewhat awkward phrasing was: "The lines in Boston and on Boston Neck point out the propriety and suggest the necessity of keeping them from gaining possession [of New York] and making a lodgment" (ibid., 392).
[131] Heath, 52; Bedinger's Journal, op. cit., 132.
[132] 4 G. W., 394, 400, 402.

loitered still. Then before the 15th ended, the wind shifted so adversely that the King's men could not leave if they would.[133] The next day was as bad.[134] Confusion manifestly prevailed in Boston [135] but no important movement there was observable from the hills. Washington's own men still looked glumly from their bleak barracks at the miry road they were to follow when their marching orders could be renewed. As they were ready now and waited only on the skies, Washington felt that he had nothing further to gain by delaying any longer the fortification of Nook's Hill. He would occupy the eminence that night: once the British saw his battery planted there, they must leave Boston or take the risks of a short-range bombardment, which they most certainly would not relish. As between standing fire and making sail, Washington did not think they would hesitate long.[136]

Up the hill, then, the men were ordered to go on the night of the 16th–17th of March. This time they would have no frozen ground to dig in order to throw dirt around their fascines. Their foe was mud, not ice and soon was overcome without excessive toil and tugging. The British artillery challenged the workers as it had on the night of the 9th, but this time the fire, though prolonged, was listless. Not one American had been hurt [137] when, at daylight, the workers could see the fruits of their labor and, vaguely at a distance, the effect on their adversary.

As Irishmen looked at Boston from Nook's Hill and Lechmere Point that fine, clear morning of Sunday, March 17,[138] they did not forget it was St. Patrick's Day,[139] and soon they and all their comrades had reason to believe it would be for America, as traditionally it was for Erin, a day of good fortune. The wind was from the quarter favorable for departure; [140] the wharves were thronged with men in uniform. About 8 o'clock, these troops could be seen to enter boats and to start in great numbers for the vessels that were riding comfortably at anchor below the Castle.[141] As the boats reached the ships, the soldiers climbed

[133] *Barker's Diary*, 71.

[134] Kemble said (*op. cit.*, v. 1, p. 73) that the wind was favorable but the weather cloudy; Barker's comment (*op. cit.*, 71) was that the British army still was detained by the wind.

[135] *A. Robertson's Diaries*, 79.   [136] 4 *G. W.*, 405.

[137] 4 *G. W.*, 403, 405; Kemble, *op. cit.*, p. 72–73; John Sullivan to John Adams, Mch. 19, 1776; *MHSP.*, 1875–76, p. 284; Jed. Huntington to Joshua Huntington, Mch. 17, 1776; 20 *CHS Cols.*, 275; *Isaac Bangs's Diary*, 13.

[138] For the weather, see 1 *Kemble*, 73.   [139] Cf. John Trumbull, *Reminiscences*, 25.

[140] 1 *Kemble*, loc. cit.

[141] Anonymous letter from Cambridge, Mch. 21, 1776, in 5 *Force* (4) p. 422–24. This is one of the best accounts of the day's events.

aboard. To some watchers on the hills, this loading of transports had the appearance of preparation for the long-awaited assault on the Dorchester fortifications; other observers told themselves this was the end! The British must be leaving Boston.[142] About 9 o'clock, word came that troops in large number were marching away from Bunker Hill.[143] Opposite that position [144] and on the Roxbury front, the American Regiments were paraded at once. Continental troops were embarked and were started down Charles River.[145] The batteries on Dorchester Neck were manned. Everything was in readiness for the shouted command that would give the nearer American gunners the fairest, broadest target they ever had seen in front of the muzzles of their cannon, but not one officer cried "Fire!" The British van was unchallenged as it started majestically toward the open sea. One vessel after another spread its canvas and defiantly moved off until the outer harbor was dotted with white above and with a frothy wake below.[146] Americans caught their breath in admiration and almost forgot that every tick of their watches carried their enemy farther and farther toward the point their round shot could not reach.[147]

Had all the British left the town? Was the prize actually now within the uncontested grasp of the continentals? For many minutes, there was doubt. Then, from in front of the outposts on Boston Neck, the scene of so many vigils, sentinels heard the happy shouts of American boys. The British were all gone, the lads cried; Selectmen were on their way to Roxbury. Soon, down the Neck, from the hostile works, came Austin, Scollay, Marshall and others, who were hurried to General Ward's quarters. When their tale was told, Ward gave his orders: [148] Col. Ebenezer Learned was to select 500 men who had experienced smallpox, and with this force and two Companies of artillery, he was to pass through the British defences, and was to enter Boston.[149]

Information of these developments in front of Roxbury and Dorchester was sent at once to Washington but before it arrived, he prob-

---

[142] John Sullivan to John Adams, Mch. 19, 1776; MHSP., 1875–76, p. 284.
[143] 5 Force (4) p. 423.   [144] Ibid.   [145] Ibid.
[146] For an accurate description of the Boston channels at this time, see Mass. Council minutes, Apr. 3, 1776, in ibid., 1260.
[147] John Trumbull, Reminiscences, 25; Thacher, 41. The troops in Boston had been put under arms at 4 A.M., had been ordered to move at 5, and by 8 or 9, according to different authorities, had all been embarked. See Barker's Diary, 71; Kemble, op. cit., v. 1, p. 73; Carter, Letters to a Friend, 27. For Howe's account, in his report to Lord Dartmouth, Mch. 21, 1776, see 5 Force (4) p. 458 ff.
[148] Jed. Huntington to Jabez Huntington, Mch. 17, 1776; 20 CHS Cols., 34.
[149] Ibid., and 5 Force (4) p. 423.

ably had heard of the British departure through General Sullivan,[150] who had shared an odd adventure early in the day. As the Brigadier was going the rounds, about 8 o'clock, he saw the ships underway and the river full of boats. At so great a distance from the harbor, it was impossible to ascertain whether the movement was evacuation or the preliminary of an attack on Dorchester Heights. Sullivan hastened to Plowed Hill and, leveling his glass from the crest, could see that the redcoats from the open boats were clambering up the sides of the ships. This satisfied him that these men were quitting Boston. His next question of course was the one that was being asked at that very time on Roxbury Neck: Were *all* the British leaving or were some remaining in the defences? Troops had left Bunker Hill. Had they constituted the entire garrison? In the proud British stronghold above Charlestown, he could see the sentinels at their accustomed posts, but he observed quickly that not one of them moved and he became suspicious. Focusing his glass on them, he could see that they were mere effigies. "This convinced me," Sullivan said afterward, "that [the British] were actually fled, for if they meant to decoy us, they would have taken away every appearance of man." Attended by his Brigade Major and by Colonel Mifflin, who had now joined him, Sullivan quickly arranged a reconnaissance. With a chuckle, he wrote later: "I sent for a strong party to follow us on to the hill, to assist us in running away (if necessary). We found no person there and bravely took a fortress defended by lifeless sentries." One of these, he might have added, facetiously had a placard that read, "Welcome Brother Jonathan." [151] The New Hampshire General continued, almost laughingly: "I then brought on the party to secure what we had so bravely won, and went down to the other works, where we found all abandoned, but the works not injured in any part. We hailed the ferry boat, which came over and informed us that they had abandoned the town. We then informed the General . . ." [152]

Washington showed no elation over an event he long had anticipated.[153] He ordered Sullivan to occupy Charlestown while Putnam

---

[150] This is inferential but, time and distance considered, seems altogether likely.

[151] Ezra Stiles's *Literary Diary*, 2.

[152] Sullivan to John Adams, Mch. 19, 1776; *MHSP.*, 1875–76, p. 284. Cf. 1 *Lee Papers*, 363; 1 *Ballagh, Lee Letters*, 171. Sullivan at this time was under attack in New Hampshire on the false ground that he was making money from the public service and "took too much on himself" (1 *Sullivan Papers*, 187, 189).

[153] That is to say, there is no known record of any observation by him on the 17th that displayed any pronounced feeling of triumph over the outcome.

collected men who had the scars of smallpox and could enter Boston without fear of contracting and spreading the disease.[154] It was done with enthusiasm and alacrity. Ward's force of 500 proceeded to the British outpost and then to the advanced line, where about 11 o'clock, Colonel Learned ceremoniously unbarred and opened the gates on the main road. With Ensign Richards carrying the standard, the troops marched in, though many of them doubtless damned the British anew when they discovered that the departing enemy had sprinkled the road with iron "crowsfeet" to make the last mile of the way harder than any.[155] Putnam's men, crossing in boats, found easier walking from the landing at Sewell's Point, which they reached about noon.[156] Nowhere did they encounter any British soldiers in uniform, but there was abundant work for "Old Put," who assumed command, in locating and salvaging the public property, the cannon, the small arms and the weapons the British left behind them.[157] Significantly, Putnam took possession in the name of the United Colonies.[158]

Washington did not leave Cambridge that day to indulge himself in a triumphant entry. He had too much to do and, in addition, must set an example, if time permitted, in church attendance. Everything went so smoothly that he was able in the afternoon to go to the meeting house where Rev. Abiel Leonard [159] preached from Exodus xiv, 25: "And took off their chariot wheels that they drove them heavily, so that the Egyptians said, Let us flee from the face of Israel, for the Lord fighteth for them against the Egyptians." [160] If Washington dutifully applied the analogy, he had to ask himself once again—during the discourse or afterward—whither the new "Egyptians" had fled—a question to which he gave the same convinced answer: Howe's objective certainly was southward, Washington thought, and most probably was New York. It was not apt to be Rhode Island, though the danger there was sufficiently strong to warrant a suggestion that the militia be called out to defend the possible landing places. In execution of the larger strategy, the troops that had been delayed in their departure for the mouth of the Hudson could now be dispatched.[161]

---

154 Sullivan to John Adams, *loc. cit.*; 5 *Force* (4) p. 423; 4 *G. W.*, 404.
155 5 *Force* (4) p. 423, 424.   156 *Letters and Diary of John Rowe*, 304.
157 *Ibid.*   158 *Ibid.*
159 He was described in a footnote to *Moore*, 223, cited *infra*, as "Chaplain to General Putnam's command," but actually he had been Chaplain of Putnam's old Regiment, the Third Connecticut, and at this time he held the same office in Knox's Artillery Regiment.
160 *Penn. Evening Post*, Mch. 30, 1776, quoted in 1 *Moore*, 222–23.
161 4 *G. W.*, 401, 402.

Such was the situation at the end of the most encouraging day Washington had spent after he had assumed command at Cambridge eight and a half months previously. He had seen far less of the drama and excitement of that 17th of March than had the young men who had stood on Dorchester Heights and, with flashing eye and fast-beating hearts, had watched the fleet of all-powerful Britain sail out in silent admission of defeat. His was the deeper satisfaction of knowing that he had forced the redcoats to evacuate Boston almost without loss of American life, and, as he soon was to report to Congress, "without endangering the lives and property of the remaining unhappy inhabitants." [162] There was one regret, one doubt only, when night fell and lights began to dance in the harbor: The British fleet had not actually gone to sea. Vessels that had sailed from Boston prior to the 17th doubtless were in Nantasket Road; the transports that had left Boston on St. Patrick's Day were riding now in a long line between the Castle and the Lighthouse. [163] They "make a formidable sight," wrote one officer who added immediately: "We shall keep a sharp look out till they are out of sight at least." [164] Washington agreed.

They were close, dangerously close, and they still were there the next morning, Monday, March 18. As Washington could do nothing against the fleet, he took time to visit Boston and to see for himself the damage that had been wrought. It was a strange experience to ride on streets about which he had heard daily talk since July, though he had trod none of them for twenty years and then only for the few days of his visit to General Shirley during the controversy with Captain Dagworthy. [165] In 1756, he had been a young Virginia Colonel, ambitious for rank and for a place in the regular establishment; now he could observe the results of his long effort to defeat the army in which he had sought to serve. Across the river he had been close enough to Boston to scrutinize daily with his glass the hills, the wharves and the fortifications; this time he could see them from the rear and could ascertain how their strength and armament corresponded to his estimate and to his intelligence reports. In a sense, it was like reading a novel and then seeing its characters come to life—or looking at a picture and, on closer view, finding it animated.

[162] Dispatch of Mch. 19, 1776; 4 *G. W.*, 403. Cf. his letter of March 17 to Governor Cooke: "I have the pleasure to inform you that this morning the ministerial troops evacuated the town of Boston, without destroying it . . ." (*ibid.*, 401).
[163] Jed. Huntington to Jabez Huntington, Mch. 17, 1776; 20 *CHS Cols.*, 34.
[164] *Ibid.*   [165] Vol. II, p. 163 ff.

His first concern was to see what injury had been done by the British soldiery and by the American artillery. Several of the churches had been stripped of their pews and had been turned into riding schools; some of the public resorts and numerous old wooden buildings had been torn down for firewood; the stores around the wharves had been looted of groceries which had been dumped in the filthy streets; salt and molasses, in particular, had been spoiled and wasted in considerable quantity, though far more salt was found in hogsheads than had been thrown away.[166] Strangely, none of the possessions of John Hancock had been disturbed, and some of his property seemed to have received particular care, as if the British had sought to placate the "arch-rebel," President of the Continental Congress.[167] "The town," Washington wrote, "although it has suffered greatly, is not in so bad a state as I expected to find it." [168] If his observations of the residents were similar to those made by other officers, he found the people joyful in their welcome but not yet free of the gloom that the long siege had stamped on their countenances.[169] General Howe, in the last days, had offered a reward of £50 to anyone who convicted another person of cutting or defacing a picture of the King or Queen.[170] Doubtless Washington had not realized how uncertainty of food and fuel, anxiety over absent husbands and sons, and endless alarms and rumors had done precisely that to the visages of patriots—had defaced them.

Washington was much impressed by the fortifications, few parts of which had been damaged either by the fire of the Americans or by the axe of the British. The town, he subsequently wrote, was "amazingly strong . . . almost impregnable, every avenue fortified." [171] On Boston Neck, where the defences were much stronger and better built than elsewhere, the works were complete and of a sort to evoke the admiring praise of the captors.[172] Most of the heavy cannon—John Sullivan alone counted forty of them—had been left in position. All had been spiked but so carelessly that some were quickly cleared again.[173] The final count was to show sixty-nine cannon that probably could be made to

166 *Samuel Richards' Diary*, 28; John Sullivan to John Adams, Mch. 19, 1776; *MHSP.*, 1875–76, p. 284. See the full list of "Stores belonging to the King and left in Boston . . ."; 5 *Force* (4) p. 488–89.
167 4 *G. W.*, 404; John Sullivan to John Adams, *loc. cit.*
168 4 *G. W.*, 404.   169 *Thacher*, 41.
170 1 *Kemble*, Mch. 14, 1776, p. 322.
171 4 *G. W.*, 406. He said of Bunker Hill, "Twenty thousand men could not carry it against 1000, had [it] been well defended" (*ibid.*).   172 *Isaac Bangs's Diary*, 13–14.
173 *Ibid.*; John Sullivan to John Adams, *loc. cit.*; 4 *G. W.*, 405; 5 *Force* (4) p. 423.

fire against their former masters, and thirty-one that were useless. Of the mortars left by the British, one only was of thirteen inches. The others, few in number, were cohorns.[174] Miscellaneous ordnance stores, almost the whole of the British medical supplies,[175] a surprising stock of 3000 blankets and much equipment were found on the wharves.

During his first visit, Washington saw a part only of all this, because he spent little time in town on the 18th and, after looking at the condition of John Hancock's house, he started back to Cambridge.[176] Unlike many of his companions in arms, he did not have to shun the smallpox, which was said to prevail in fourteen homes,[177] but so long as those British ships rode at anchor in Massachusetts waters, he doubtless would have been more concerned about them than about exposure to disease. Moreover, to protect the soldiers from the maladies of the populace and the people from the violence of some of the troops, he issued strict orders concerning the unlawful entry into the town of uniformed men,[178] and he had to direct the drafting of a formal proclamation "for the preservation of peace, good order and discipline." [179] The town was to be retained as well as policed. Washington was resolved on this and, in addition, was so suspicious because of the enemy's continued presence in Nantasket Road that he ordered immediately the construction of a strong work on Fort Hill, a dominant position.[180]

As the parapet rose fast with rapid digging, while the enemy remained close at hand, Washington's state of mind was one of disappointment and misgiving.[181] On the night of the 19th–20th, the British demolished the defences at the Castle and blew up buildings that could not readily be burned.[182] The enemy made some efforts, also, to block the

---

[174] 24 *Papers of G. W.*, 80; 25 *Ibid.*, 59, LC. Washington had an unverified report that another large mortar had been thrown off a wharf (4 *G. W.*, 404), but British reports indicate this particular mortar was tipped over accidentally.

[175] 5 *Force* (4) p. 484.

[176] *Letters and Diary of John Rowe*, 304; John Sullivan to John Adams, *loc. cit.*

[177] As of Mch. 21, 1776; 2 Ezra Stiles's *Literary Diary*, 2.

[178] 4 *G. W.*, 402, 411. In a measure, these orders had been anticipated on March 13. See *ibid.*, 389.

[179] *Ibid.*, 412; a reproduction of the contemporary printed text from MHS appears in *ibid.*, opposite p. 412.

[180] *Ibid.*, 425–26. ". . . it commands the whole harbor and when fortified, if properly supported, will greatly annoy any fleet the enemy may send against the town, and render the landing of their troops exceedingly difficult, if not impracticable."

[181] *Ibid.*, 424: ". . . to my surprise and disappointment the fleet is still [March 24] in Nantasket Road. The purpose inducing their stay is altogether unknown; nor can I suggest any satisfactory reason for it."

[182] Three eighteen-pounders apparently were overlooked and were found intact. All the others were spiked and were rendered temporarily useless by the same methods employed in Boston. See *Carter, Letters to a Friend*, 27; 1 *Kemble*, 74; *Isaac Bangs's Diary*, 18–19.

channels.[183] If, as seems logical, these were the acts of a commander who was abandoning Boston, why did he not proceed to Halifax, as his men had told Boston people he intended to do; and if Howe was going, instead, to New York or Long Island, as Washington still believed,[184] what deterred him from gaining the manifest advantage of early arrival? Washington started Heath and a Brigade of foot for New York on the 20th;[185] but more men than this he did not think he ought to detach until he could ascertain what the British intended to do. If they did not die of old age there in the Road—if *ever* they started for New York—Washington saw clearly his duty. Once again he restated the great fundamental of coastal strategy in dealing with a foe who commanded the sea. New York, he told Governor Cooke, "secures the free and only communication between the Northern and Southern Colonies, which will be entirely cut off by their [the British] possessing it, and give them the command of Hudson's River and an easy pass into Canada . . ." This made it "absolutely and indispensably necessary for the whole of this army, which is but inconsiderable . . . to be marched from hence for [the] defence [of New York] with all possible expedition."[186] Barring direct invasion, no part of the Army could be detached to Rhode Island—that was reiterated—and no more troops would be left in Boston than were required to give the town protection against surprise attack. As much as possible would be done, according to existing plans, to make the fortifications of the place strong enough to hold off a much larger force than the one that defended it.[187]

Repetition, repetition, the same planning, the same promises, the same maddening presence of the British in the outer harbor—this was now the round of Washington's life, and it was enough to wear his patience to nakedness. After all those months of hard effort, the British had been compelled to leave Boston and yet they refused to quit the harbor. It was amusing perhaps to outsiders, as it was to be to posterity, but to the American commander it was inexplicable behavior that took all the sweetness from victory. The British should go to New York if their strategy was intelligent: why did they linger, and why, in particular, on the 22nd, and the 23rd, when the wind was favorable?[188] Six additional American Regiments were made ready for the road,

183 Carter, *loc cit.*
185 *Heath*, 53.
187 *Ibid.*, 414, 416–17, 421–22, 425–26.

184 4 *G. W.*, 407.
186 Letter of Mch. 21, 1776; 4 *G. W.*, 414.
188 *Ibid.*, 423.

under command of John Sullivan,[189] so that they would lose no time if the fleet disappeared; but manifestly this further detachment of troops could not be justified so long as a chance remained that Howe might reland his forces somewhere on the coast of Massachusetts.

Although the wind continued favorable for departure from Nantasket Road on the 24th, the report still was, "No change." Washington had to conclude that the fleet would not wait so long merely to make a raid. If Howe were going to do anything at all, he must be preparing a major blow.[190] "As these favorable winds do not waft the fleet from Nantasket," he wrote General Ward, "my suspicions are more and more aroused." Ward must make ready fire-rafts of a sort Col. Benjamin Tupper had described, and some dark or windy night, Ward must send these against the British fleet. "I think," said Washington, "this would discover their designs if no other good effect resulted from it." [191] Time would be required, of course, to put the rafts in condition to catch fire easily and to burn steadily in rain or in a heavy wash.

Meantime, two more days dragged anxiously on, Monday and Tuesday, March 25 and 26. Washington's first duty now was to see that every outpost was alert and that the men in the camps always were in condition to take the road in any direction. Loammi Baldwin at Chelsea was directed on the morning of the 27th to resume daily reports of all movements discernible from his post; [192] orders to the Army, issued on the 23rd, had commanded Sullivan's men "to be ready at a moment's warning," [193] and orders of the 24th had directed that straggling be prevented, that arms be in order, and that roll-calls be regular, because the British might "have some design of aiming a blow at us before they depart . . ." [194]

If, then, impatience did not make men reckless or careless, Washington might hope for prompt intelligence of anything that might develop on the 27th, a day when the waters of Massachusetts Bay were running high, and a fair wind, with the promise of spring in its breath, was blowing steadily from North-Northwest.[195] Washington had much to do. A tangle over militia pay had to be straightened out, alarm posts for certain Regiments had to be reassigned; two artillery Companies had to be designated for service in Canada; before the day was out

189 *Ibid.*, 420–21.
190 4 *G. W.*, 421, 423, 430.
191 Letter of Mch. 24, 1776; 37 *G. W.*, 523.
192 *Baldwin Papers*, Harvard Coll. Lib.
193 4 *G. W.*, 420.
194 *Ibid.*, 423.
195 1 *Kemble*, 75.

Congress must be told that residents of Nova Scotia wished to know if help against Great Britain would be afforded them.[196] All this business had been transacted, dinner had been eaten, the end of the day was at hand, the twenty-fifth day after the opening gun on Dorchester Heights—when a messenger from that front drew rein at Headquarters. He brought news, *the* news: That morning at 11, the flagship *Fowey* had hoisted signal; at 3 P.M., the fleet had made sail from Nantasket. Now the whole of it, except for three or four vessels, was standing out to sea.[197]

[196] 4 *G. W.*, 436–38.
[197] Kemble, *loc. cit.*; *A. Robertson's Diaries*, 82; 4 *G. W.*, 436. Robertson was two days "off" in his chronology at this point, unless he left Boston before the greater part of the fleet did.

CHAPTER III

THE SIEGE OF BOSTON IN REVIEW
(June, 1775–March, 1776)

"GENERAL HOWE has a grand maneuvre in view or has made an inglorious retreat"—that was Washington's comment,[1] and it was accompanied almost in the same breath by orders for the dispatch of additional troops to New York.[2] Other men might say, as Charles Pettit did, that Halifax was "the only place in America where [Howe] can remain in quiet to refresh his wornout troops" who "have been so harrassed with severe duty and bad living";[3] Washington admitted the possibility but continued to believe the strategic importance of New York so great to the British that he was not justified in delaying for a day the march to that city of all his Army except Regiments manifestly needed to garrison Boston. The artillery were to follow the Regiments.[4] On arrival in New York, by well-known routes,[5] the whole

---

[1] Letter of Mch. 28, 1776 to Joseph Reed; 4 *G. W.*, 439.

[2] John Sullivan and six Regiments left their barracks on the 29th (*ibid.*, 440); Nathanael Greene departed on the 31st with five (*ibid.*, 442), and Joseph Spencer with a like number moved on the 4th of April (*ibid.*, 444). For Washington's original schedule, see *ibid.*, 439.

[3] Letter of Mch. 25, 1776 to Joseph Reed; *Papers of Joseph Reed*, NYHS.

[4] 4 *G. W.*, 462; *Solomon Nash's Diary*, 11; Cf. Ezekiel Cheever to Artemas Ward, Mch. 30, 1776; *Artemas Ward Papers*, 93, MHS. At this period Washington rarely, if ever, used the word "Infantry." He had no Cavalry as yet; the Artillery Regiment always was described with the prefix; all Regiments, unless otherwise noted, were Infantry and were styled simply the "Regiments," usually with the Colonel's name. If it was necessary for any reason to distinguish Infantry from Cavalry, Washington adhered to the standard usage of the time and called them Foot and Horse. A later note will record the earliest employment by him of the term "Infantry." For the subsequent movement of the Artillery, see Cheever to Ward, Mch. 30, 1776, *Artemas Ward Papers*, 93, MHS; Thomas Randall to Knox, April 4; Knox to James Warren, April 5; Knox's orders of April 12; 2 *Knox Papers*, 40, 56, 61, MHS.

[5] Heath, *op. cit.*, 52–53, said only that his route was Roxbury, Mendon, Norwich, New London, transport to Turtle Bay and thence to New York. McCurtin's itinerary (see his *Diary*, 35–36) ran as follows: Cambridge, Grafton, Sutton, Oxford, Dudley, Woodstock, Southard, Bolton, Hartford, Wethersfield, Wallingford, New Haven, Stratford, Fairfield, Stamford, King's Bridge. The line of advance of the column mentioned in the *Diary of Ensign Caleb Clap* (cited hereafter as *Clap's Diary*) was that of John Sullivan, who was ordered to deviate from the regularly used roads and to proceed to Providence, Rhode Island, on receipt of a report that the enemy was landing there. For his "file-off," see 4 *G. W.*, 456, 471; Loammi Baldwin to his wife, Apr. 1, 3, 1776; *Baldwin Papers*, Army Letters, 23, Harvard Coll. Lib. Clap listed these towns and villages on his way: Cambridge, Waltham, Marlboro, Grafton, Bellingham, Providence, Coventry, Plainsfield, Norwich, New London, New York. The march, Washington estimated, normally could be made in eight to 10 days (4 *G. W.*, 443). In *Papers of G. W.*, LC. is this

force was to be under the command of General Putnam [6] till Washington himself moved his headquarters there. To expedite his own departure, Washington transacted all business as soon as he possibly could get it before him, from the day the British fleet sailed away. On the 28th he wrote to inquire of the Massachusetts Legislature whether the furniture which had been added to that originally in the Vassall House when he established himself in Cambridge had been charged to the public, or was a loan, or was rented.[7] He had started two weeks previously to procure new quarters in New York.[8] To these matters of personal comfort and dignity, which Washington never disregarded, were added all the vexatious details [9] of moving 9000 or 10,000 men; [10] and on this were superimposed the ceremonials of congratulation and farewell.

Fortunately for a busy man, a considerable part of the thanksgiving and celebration was compressed into a single day, March 28, the morrow of Howe's disappearance with his fleet. The Massachusetts Assembly presented Washington [11] an address in which it praised his achievements during the siege and, in rounded phrase, voiced the hope: "May the United Colonies be defended from slavery by your victorious arms. May they still see their enemies flying before you." The address proceeded as if the man who had wrought the deliverance of the Massachusetts town was assured a place among the immortals: "And (the

---

"Route from Cambridge to New York." The first numerals indicate the particular days of the march. "1 To Framingham, 18 [miles]; 2 To Sutton, 18; 3 Dudley, 16; 4 Woodstock, 8; 60 miles. 5th Day, Halt. 6 Mansfield, 18; 7 Bolton, 18; 8 Hartford, 12; 108 miles. 9th Day Halt. 10 Kensington, 14; 11 Wallingford, 12; 12 New Haven, 13; 147 miles. 13th Day Halt. 14 Stratford, 14; 15 Norwalk, 20; 16 Greenwich, 13; 194 miles. 17th Day Halt. 18 New Rochelle, 11; 19 Kingsbridge, 10; 20 New York, 15. 230 miles."

6 *G. W.*, 442-43.

7 He was told in answer, that "no charge is to be exhibited against his Excellency or the continent" and that he need do no more than leave the furniture in the hands of someone authorized to deliver it on order of the Court. See Samuel Thacher to unnamed staff officer, Mch. 28, 1776; 24 *Papers of G. W.*, 103, LC.

8 He needed "a large house ready furnished somewhere in or about Bowery Lane." As "his family is large and he has a number of horses," he required "a spacious house with large stables." DeLancey's mansion was suggested. A housekeeper, a cook and a steward were to be employed. See Stephen Moylan to Colonel McDougall; *McDougall Papers*, NYHS.

9 E.g., 4 *G. W.*, 464-65, 471-73.

10 The full return of Mch. n.d., 1776, in 24 *Papers of G. W.*, 128, LC shows all Regiments full—728 men each—to a total of 18,928, but from these figures were to be deducted the Massachusetts militia, to a total of about 6800 (see table in *Frothingham's Siege*, 406), and the troops who were to be left at Boston, a number not then determined but estimated here, for purpose of calculation, at 2500. This would indicate that about 9600 were of the new continental establishment.

11 Presumably in the Council Chamber. See *Penn. Evening Post*, Apr. 9, 1776, quoted in 4 *G. W.*, 440 n.

deliverance of your country being effected) may you, in retirement, enjoy the peace and satisfaction of mind which always attends the good and great. And may future generations, in the peaceful enjoyment of that freedom, the exercise of which your sword shall have established raise the richest and most lasting monuments to the name of Washington." [12]

Washington probably had been shown the text in advance and had been careful to have a reply prepared for him.[13] He read it at once and without disclaiming any of the extravagant homage paid him. In thanking the lawmakers for their approval of his conduct, he said proudly but honestly that he wished "for no other reward than that arising from a conscientious discharge of the important trust, and that my services might contribute to the establishment of freedom and peace upon a permanent foundation and merit the applause of my countrymen and every virtuous citizen." If that had the ring of 1756, the Burgess of Virginia acknowledged the legislators' reference to the attention he had shown the civil "constitution of this Colony." He gave assurance that "a regard to every provincial institution, where not incompatible with the common interest, I hold a principle of duty and of policy, and it shall ever form a part of my conduct." He added: "Had I not learnt this before, the happy experience of the advantages resulting from a friendly intercourse with your honorable body, their ready and willing concurrence to aid and to counsel, whenever called upon in cases of difficulty and emergency, would have taught me the useful lesson." Reverent thanks followed to "that Being, who is powerful to save, and in whose hands is the fate of nations . . ." [14]

These good wishes having been exchanged, Washington listened to the first of the resumed "Thursday lectures" of Dr. Andrew Eliot, who spoke on the text Isaiah xxxiii, 20: "Look upon Zion, the city of our solemnities: Thine eyes shall see Jerusalem a quiet habitation, a tabernacle that shall not be taken down; not one of the stakes thereof

---

[12] 5 *Force* (4) p. 539–40.

[13] It is difficult to say who, at this period, was writing Washington's answers to papers of this character. The pious undertone of the reply to the Massachusetts address and the employment of "New England words" seldom used in Washington's letters suggest the possibility that he elaborated a paper written for him by one or another of the able ministers of Boston.

[14] This, in particular, is the passage that suggests the assistance of some minister in the preparation of the address, the MS of which is not among the papers of Washington in the Library of Congress. Fitzpatrick got his text from Ford (3 *Ford*, 497–500) who took it from Sparks (3 *Sparks*, 336). The original editor capitalized references to Divinity; so did Ford, but Fitzpatrick did not, though he used capitals for He and His in the final paragraph of the address (4 *G. W.*, 440–42).

shall ever be removed, neither shall any of the cords thereof be broken."
After this discourse came a dinner tendered by a committee of the
General Court, with most of the leading men of Boston in attendance.[15]
The meal over, Washington walked to Fort Hill [16] and examined the
work projected there. A few days later he received from the Selectmen
of Boston a brief, laudatory address, which pleased him almost as much
as the paper from the General Court had.[17] He was grateful and polite
in his response, though he fashioned no needless flourishes.[18] Harvard,
in its turn, voted him the honorary degree of Doctor of Laws and
planned to give it to him before his departure, but unhappy delays in
preparing the diploma prevented its delivery.[19]

One pleasant aspect of these relations with the people of Boston was
the opportunity it afforded Washington of ascertaining the truth about
some of the occurrences the lens of his glass never had shown him
during those March days when he had focused it so often and so
anxiously on hills and wharves and streets. Second only to "seeing over
the hill" while the moves were being made, was this privilege of ques-
tioning those who had been in Boston during the siege and had observed
the British response to the American maneuvers. As the story was put
together, then and thereafter,[20] it was this: The British were surprised
to discover on the morning of March 5, the magnitude of the work
done the previous night on the hills of Dorchester. Howe thought
12,000 men must have labored on the fortifications;[21] others put the
figure as high as 15,000 to 20,000;[22] Boston people repeated gleefully
that the British, marvelling at the height and length of the redoubts,
said the devil must help the Yankees.[23] Even junior English officers
realized, in the words of one of them, that "the enemy must be driven
away or we must go." [24] Howe directed at 11:30 A.M. on the 5th [25] that

15 Cooper said (6 *A. H. R.*, 339) that the dinner was at Bunch of Grapes Tavern. In the
Letters and Diary of John Rowe, 305–06, is the statement that the entertainment was "at Captain
Marston's, who now lives in Colonel Ingersoll's house." Doctor Eliot spoke "at Dr. Chauncey's
meeting."

16 Samuel Cooper's Diary, 6 *A. H. R.*, 339. 17 See *infra*, p. 75–76.

18 5 *Force* (4) p. 758–59. This exchange presumably was on April 1.

19 When Dr. Samuel Cooper signed it on April 4 and took it to Washington's headquarters
in Cambridge, he found that the General had left. See Cooper's Diary in 6 *A. H. R.*, 339.

20 Needless to say, it is impossible to be precise regarding the range of the information Washington received immediately after the evacuation of Boston, but his references and those of his
contemporaries show that all the essentials of British plans and attempted operations were ascertained. Uncertainty involves details only.

21 See his report in 5 *Force* (4) p. 458–59.

22 *A. Robertson's Diaries*, 73–74. 23 *Deacon Tudor's Diary*, loc. cit.

24 *Carter, Letters to a Friend*, 26. 25 *A. Robertson's Diaries*, 74.

five Regiments be put on transports which were to proceed to the Castle and were to tow the flatboats [26] for a landing below the Dorchester hills West of the Castle.[27] Two other Regiments were to embark at 7 P.M. to serve as support.[28] Howe said afterward that these troops, numbering about 2500, displayed an ardor that encouraged him.[29] They were to go ashore at night and presumably were to deliver their attack at dawn; but when the storm that broke on the evening of the 5th continued into the morning of the 6th, British seniors shook their heads decisively: the Americans must have used every hour of darkness to make strong works impregnable; an assault on the heights would be suicide.[30] Some of the King's officers were relieved to find it so because they had believed an attack hopeless in any circumstances.[31] About 11 o'clock on the morning of the 6th, Howe called his officers together and announced that he was going to transfer the entire force to Halifax.[32] At the same time he directed that the men be told the operation arranged for the previous evening had been "unavoidably put off by the badness of the weather." [33] After that, the British devoted themselves to loading their ships and took the offensive with their artillery only when, as on the night of the 9th, they apprehended the Americans would seize advance positions and force them to evacuate Boston before they were ready. By the 14th, Howe reported later, he was prepared to leave whenever the wind favored him. Tories who wished to depart under cover of the fleet were given all possible aid.[34]

Howe felt that he had all the disadvantage of a fixed position, against which the Americans could direct a converging fire at steadily reduced range. Moreover, he was short of provisions, which he had been unable to replenish, as expected, from the West Indies. Washington and his naval officers in particular would have been pleased if they could have seen this sentence from Howe's report: "Unless these supplies are sent under convoy, or of force to defend themselves, they will become very precarious, as the Rebels have greatly increased their naval strength; and I fear that many of those now on their voyage will fall into the enemy's

---

[26] *Ibid.*
[27] 1 *Kemble*, 71. Cf. Howe's embarkation order in *ibid.*, 312.
[28] *A. Robertson's Diaries*, 74.
[29] See his report of Mch. 21, 1776; 5 *Force* (4) p. 458–60.
[30] Howe, *loc. cit.*, 459; *Barker's Diary*, 70; 1 *Kemble*, 71.
[31] Cf. the officer quoted in *Morning Chronicle and London Advertiser*, May 15, 1776, cited in *Willard*, 278.
[32] *A. Robertson's Diaries*, 75.   [33] *NYHS Cols.*, 1883, p. 313.
[34] 5 *Force* (4) p. 459, 484, 1082; *Barker's Diary*, 71.

hands, notwithstanding all the efforts which his Majesty's ships (unequal in number to the service they are upon,) can make." [35]

That parenthesis contained the mildest possible statement of a condition that had hampered Howe far more than Washington had realized. The truth had been told bluntly in a Boston letter published in a London newspaper a few days before Washington occupied Dorchester Heights. "[Ours]" said a correspondent in the beleaguered city, "is only a nominal fleet; almost all of them came out short of their lowest peace complement and have had no opportunity of recruiting their numbers; so that from death and desertion, and other accidents, they are reduced to a state of inactivity." [36] The last dispatches received by Howe prior to the evacuation of Boston bore date of Oct. 22, 1775.[37] Publicly and with formal politeness, the General attributed this to the difficulty ships encountered in reaching Boston; [38] some of his subordinates doubtless agreed with one of their number who wrote, "it looked as if we were left destitute to get out of a bad scrape as we liked best." [39] Actually, the Ministry had written Howe before that time to inquire whether he should not leave Boston. His answer had been that he did not have sufficient transports to evacuate all his men and equipment at a single embarkation and that two would be dangerous. He and his Generals were agreed, he reported, that it would be inexpedient to quit Boston before the spring of 1776.[40] Howe did not then restate, though he probably believed, what Gage previously had said—that the shortage of land transports was as serious a barrier to offensive army operations as the lack of tonnage was to movement by sea. "On the supposition of a certainty of in forcing the enemy [from his defences]" Gage had written as long previously as August, 1775, "in which considerable loss must be expected, little would be gained by it, as neither horses, carriages, [n]or other articles for moving forward could be procured." [41]

[35] 5 Force (4) p. 460.

[36] Boston letter of Jan. 20, 1776, in London Public Advertiser, Feb. 27, 1776, cited in Willard, 257. The shortcomings of Admiral Samuel Graves, who continued in command until about the end of December, 1775, are notorious but are not a part of this narrative. For an illuminating extract from Graves's unpublished apologia, see French's First Year, 650. Graves's successor, Admiral Molyneux Shuldham, was of more vigorous nature but, in the early months of 1776, was no better equipped than Graves had been.

[37] 5 Force (4) p. 460.   [38] Ibid.

[39] Letter of anonymous correspondent aboard H. M. S. Chatham, Mch. 27, 1776; 5 Force (4) p. 484. Howe's plans for operations after leaving Boston were outlined in his dispatch of Mch. 21, 1776, loc. cit. He intended to revictual and refit at Halifax for an attack on New York.

[40] Howe to Dartmouth, Nov. 26, 1775; 3 Force (4) p. 1672.

[41] Gage to Dartmouth, Aug. 20, 1775; 1 Gage, 413. Cf. same to same, Oct. 1, 1775, ibid., 418: "On the supposition of a certainty of driving the rebels from their entrenchment, no

Had Washington been able to ascertain in the last days of March all these facts concerning the British, he could have occupied usefully every spare moment of his time in a critical examination of his own intelligence methods and, having ascertained why he had not learned some things he should have discovered, he might well have asked himself what mistakes he had made in dealing with his adversary. If he had carried this still further—as posterity must—and had reviewed his conduct of his command to the end of this first campaign, he would have told himself, as an honest-minded man, that he had somewhat underestimated the effective strength of Howe [42] and had overestimated the mobility of the besieged British forces at sea and on land. It remains doubtful whether a correct understanding of Howe's enchainment to Boston would have made more vigorous operations possible by Washington while the American supply of powder was paralyzingly short and the colonial navy was little more than a dream.

A positive mistake, perhaps the most serious that Washington made, was the dispatch of Arnold's small, ill-equipped and poorly provisioned force over an extremely difficult wilderness route concerning which Washington's information was both inadequate and inaccurate. Washington was correct in maintaining that if a blow was to be struck at feebly defended Quebec that year, the expedition should be started without further delay, because the season already was advanced; but he appears to have exaggerated what 1000 men could do in that savage country, precisely as he had been mistaken twenty-one years previously in his first march for Fort DuQuesne. Daring sometimes could defy men, but it could not disregard nature. Initiative was no substitute for preparation. More than this may not be said about the strategy of the operation, unless one wishes to venture into the realm of the might have been.

It is in that same land, where fact sinks into the sands of supposition, that two other possible mistakes by Washington must be left—his plan to attack Boston across the ice and his long and hazardous delay in

advantage would be gained but reputation; victory could not be improved through want of every necessary to march into the country."

[42] One of the victual returns left behind by the British showed a force of 7579 foot, exclusive of staff, marines and sailors. Americans reasoned, according to Gordon, that Howe "might have been considered as 10,000 strong, had it not been for the mutual jealousies which took place between the army and the navy" (Entry of Mch. 17, 1776 in 2 *Gordon*, (ed. cit.) 30–31). Washington himself, citing this victual return, said of the British, "it appears that their number was greater than we had an idea of" (Letter of Mch. 24, 1776, to the President of Congress; 4 *G. W.*, 426).

occupying the high ground on Dorchester Neck. The proposed advance over the frozen water from Lechmere Point to the nearest firm ground in Boston would have covered slightly more than 1000 yards. Washington left no estimate, though he must have made one, of the direct and enfilading cannon-fire to which this column of attack would be exposed. He planned a surprise that probably would have been set underway at dawn. The slippery footing of the troops, the target they presented against the ice even in half darkness, and their complete inexperience in assault are imponderables it is proper to list but impossible to weigh. Washington admitted that the attempt would be hazardous but, it will be recalled, he could not bring himself to think it beyond the ability of his men if they behaved well under courageous and intelligent leaders. He even believed a crossing in open boats might be practicable under favorable circumstance of high surprise and slight opposition.[43] These plans had been formulated when Washington doubted whether he could procure at an early date the powder needed for the more obvious and effective alternative of closer approach and bombardment. As he saw it, he must make the best plan he could for the fullest employment of what he possessed of men and material and he must shape it, also, to the mold of his limitations. He might have asked critics of his plan to cross the ice or to row men from the Lechmere-Cambridge front while he was engaged at Dorchester, what else could be done? Were the risks of action any worse than those of waiting till the British were reenforced and able to seize the initiative? Beyond that question lay the contingent factor in war, the x that no man can resolve in advance of actual combat.

The other mistake, that of not seizing Dorchester Heights earlier, was it really a mistake? If Howe had not been Howe, or Gage had been a different man, one or the other of them might have taken a chance of securing the high ground of the peninsula and might have forced Washington to buy it in blood or else to deliver his assault under the greatest disadvantage up narrow Boston Neck. When the British failed to occupy the elevations that overlooked the town, then Washington doubtless reasoned that he could not afford to do so prior to

---

[43] Evidently he realized that this secondary aspect of the Dorchester operation was regarded unfavorably. In writing Joseph Reed, April 1, Washington maintained that Putnam "would have had pretty easy work of it," because the movement was to be directed "by signals" which would be based on "appearances"; but he added that Putnam "would not have made the attempt, unless the town had been drained, or very considerably weakened of its force" (4 G. W., 455).

March, because that would have inspired a British attack which he might not be able to beat off with the powder he had, otherwise than by reducing his supply to the point where he would have been helpless in the face of a second onslaught. Thus did the occupation of Dorchester come back, as did nearly all similar issues, offensive and defensive, in Washington's first campaign, to the powder barrel. His apparent lack of aggressiveness was lack of powder.

The same thing probably should be said of a situation Howe took seriously though Washington apparently did not. This was the fortification by the Americans of Lechmere Point, half a mile South and slightly West of Cobble Hill and not quite a mile from Barton's Point, the northwest tip of Boston across the water. Howe had watched with deepest concern the rise of a bomb battery there and then of two redoubts, in one of which a heavy mortar was to be placed.[44] Begun at the end of November, 1775,[45] the work was delayed by severe weather and was not completed until about the middle of February, 1776. Washington remarked of this fort, "It is within as commanding a distance of Boston as Dorchester Hill, though of a different part"—and there he left the subject.[46] Howe did not. In his report on the operations that led to his withdrawal from Boston, the British commander put first among the serious local developments of the winter the construction of the fortifications at Lechmere Point, or Phipps's Farm, as he called it. He said of the construction there, "lying under the cover of their strongest posts, and so situated as to be supported by their whole force from Cambridge [the erection of the defences] was not to be prevented." [47] Howe evidently feared early bombardment from Lechmere Point, but Washington never recorded any plan that contemplated the use of that position as bait for the enemy prior to the general bombardment of March 2-4. When at length he read Howe's report, he may have reflected that he could not have reached the British fleet with fire from Lechmere Point, could not have hoped to tempt Howe there as readily as from the open water East of Boston and, in any event, had not possessed powder for a long cannonade of doubtful result.

[44] 4 *G. W.*, 184.   [45] *Ibid.*, 131.

[46] *Ibid.*, 323. It is possible to interpret two of Washington's letters (*ibid.*, 352, 357) as expressing his opinion that if Howe did not trouble the works at Lechmere Point, it was a certain indication of a British purpose to evacuate Boston; but a careful reading of the two sentences probably will leave the clear impression that Washington was not speaking of Lechmere Point but of Dorchester Heights.

[47] 5 *Force* (4) p. 458.

If Washington's mistakes had been few and explicable, his shortcomings—the negative as set against the positive—had been more numerous. He who personally had been a good recruiting officer and then an awkward and unsuccessful director of recruiting in the French and Indian War had not shown any larger skill in 1775 or, for that matter, any sense of direct responsibility for the enlistment of men. Often he had spent sleepless hours in thinking of what would happen when short-term enlistments ended, but he had left all the details of recruitment to his subordinates and to the authorities of the New England Colonies. Again, in part from habit and in part from assumed necessity, he had devoted too much of his own time to "paper work." A third shortcoming, primarily attributable to distance, was his virtual failure to exercise the full functions of a Commander-in-Chief. Occasionally, in dealing with Schuyler, he mingled good counsel with the grant of discretion and thereby fulfilled in a measure his function; but usually he did not even attempt to supervise what Schuyler was doing, and he manifestly had concluded that it was a waste of time to communicate with Wooster or to expect that veteran to accomplish anything.[48] A well-schooled soldier, thumbing through the headquarters Letter Book, would say unhesitatingly that Washington had a realistic and probably a correct sense of the fundamental strategy of New England and of New York, but that Washington had not demonstrated he could supervise all the plays on the continental chessboard. He might prove a good leader in the field, but he had yet to show that he would be a competent Commander-in-Chief, even with the limits of the central authority that could be exercised prudently in a land of endless distances and of bottomless roads.

That reservation did not cancel what Washington had demonstrated already—that he knew how to make an army out of a congeries of jealous colonial contingents. He had learned while he had been teaching, he who had read few books on war in sixteen years of peaceful life at Mount Vernon. Because he had no experienced artillerist on whom he could rely, he had studied gunnery in the track of the missiles and now he had sufficient acquaintance with that arm to know, in broad terms, what he could and could not expect artillery to do. This self-

[48] If it be objected that Wooster was properly to be reached through the channels of command, it should be recalled that Wooster had admitted himself subordinate to Montgomery, when the issue had been raised, but had insisted that his troops were not subject to his immediate superior's orders (3 *Force* (4) p. 1107–08.)

instruction was acquired while his youthful new chief of artillery, Henry Knox, was getting mastery of the cannon. General and Colonel must have gained knowledge together by conversation and test. It was different with Washington's adherence to the great fundamental of concentration of force, and different, too, with that categorical imperative of American defence—sea power. Much was taught Washington and, through him, his country, by his observation of what a few American ships in the hands of courageous men had done in cutting off supplies from Boston,[49] but, basically, he seemed to have from the beginning of the campaign a correct understanding of the larger principles of naval warfare and, in particular, of American defence. These doctrines, the quintessence of common sense, apparently had been absorbed as matters of course by a man who was the personification of that same quality.

It could be written down, moreover, when the British sailed from Boston that Washington daily was learning more and more about men. Fortune had favored him in that he had his introduction to army command through siege operations, when casualties were light and risks— had he known it—were reduced by the condition of his adversary. Thus circumstanced, Washington had shown that he could discharge the business of an army with justice, with diligence and with excellent judgment, and in doing this he had given his subordinates confidence not in him only but also in the cause he represented. His absolute integrity had been demonstrated again and again; his singleminded devotion to his task had been exemplified in his refusal to leave the camps for any social or personal reasons during the whole of the siege;[50] the dignity and dispatch with which he transacted business, and his courteous good humor in dealing with all comers created an aura. In November, James Warren had written of Washington: "His judgment and firmness I hope will carry him through [his many difficulties]. He is certainly the best man for the place he is in, important as it is, that ever lived."[51] Statements almost as strong were made by persons who were not prone to enthusiastic apostrophe, but, on the contrary, were more disposed to use words as rapiers than as caresses.

Washington, in short, had fulfilled the highest expectations of his

---

49 Washington's accumulating sense of sea power is disclosed frequently in Volume IV.

50 Cf. his remark to Joseph Reed concerning alleged slights to Massachusetts lawmakers: ". . . I am acquainted with few of the members, never go out of my own lines, or see any of them in them" (4 G. W., 241).

51 1 Warren-Adams Letters, 186.

admirers and had exceeded by far anything that would have been anticipated by those who realized how vastly out of scale with his experience
as a provincial Colonel were his responsibilities as continental Commander-in-Chief.[52] He had not gained this esteem by genius, in the sense
of specialized ability incomparably greater than that of the average man.
Washington had won this place by the balance of his parts. In nothing
transcendent, he was credited with possessing in ample measure every
quality of character that the administration of the army demanded.
Already he had become a moral rallying-post, the embodiment of the
purpose, the patience and the determination necessary for the triumph
of the revolutionary cause. He had retained the support of Congress
and had won that of New England in like manner and measure, by
directness, by deference, and by manifest dedication to duty.

His own growth in spirit had been remarkable. He doubtless still
was sensitive, because he still was eager to have public approval, but he
realized now that he could not discharge his duties unless he was informed of the evil as well as of the good that was spoken of him. In
January, 1776, he had written Joseph Reed: "I can bear to hear of
imputed or real errors. The man who wishes to stand well in the
opinion of others must do this, because he is thereby enabled to correct
his faults or remove prejudices which are imbibed against him. For this
reason, I shall thank you for giving me the opinions of the world, upon
such points as you know me to be interested in; for as I have but one
capital object in view, I could wish to make my conduct coincide with
the wishes of mankind, as far as I can consistently; I mean, without
departing from that great line of duty, which, though hid under a cloud
for some time, for a peculiarity of circumstance, may nevertheless bear
a scrutiny."[53] He meant this; he tried to practice it. When told by
Reed of complaints in Philadelphia that he had shown lack of consideration for Massachusetts lawmakers, he said humbly: "I cannot charge
myself with incivility, or what in my opinion is tantamount, ceremonious civility, to the gentlemen of this Colony; but if such my conduct
appears, I will endeavor at a reformation, as I assure you, my dear
Reed, that I wish to walk in such a line as will give most general
satisfaction."[54]

[52] Cf. Washington's reference to Sullivan, 5 G. W., 152–53.

[53] 4 G. W., 240. He echoed these sentiments in another letter to Reed, Feb. 10, 1776;
ibid., 319.

[54] Letter of Dec. 15, 1775; 4 G. W., 165.

Because he knew how readily his remarks might be distorted by envious, ambitious men and their jealous friends, he avoided in his dispatches "every expression," as he said, "that could give pain or uneasiness," and after hearing that the sensibilities of the Bay State legislators had been offended, he resolved to be equally careful in his personal letters.[55] Unfailing tact and restraint must be shown at headquarters also. Among the first recommendations of men who served as his aides was their absolute regard for his confidences.[56] One reason why he wrote so many of his own letters, during a time when he had few aides, was this same caution against subjecting himself to tattlers. He told Reed: "I know no persons able to supply your places (in this part of the world) with whom I would choose to live in unbounded confidence."[57]

He was building up, of necessity, a reserve against misrepresentation, and he never permitted himself to write freely to any persons except Reed and his brother "Jack," now addressed by his formal name, John Augustine Washington. In letters to these two, he now was free of all the awkward self-consciousness that sometimes had distorted and obscured his meaning when he was a young man. If he talked as he wrote to those whose discretion he trusted, he conversed with confidence, with vigor, with candor, and even with some of the quality he most had lacked, humor. When he had to face the prospect of having a second aide who could not write easily, Washington's observation was, "I shall make a lame hand . . . to have two of this kidney."[58] His operation against Dorchester Heights was "the rumpus which everybody expected to see between the Ministerialists in Boston and our troops."[59]

Nor did Washington hesitate now,[60] when he knew his words would not be repeated, to pass judgment on those who did not do a man's part, unselfishly and actively, for American liberty. "I have no opinion at all of W[ooster]'s enterprising genius," he wrote Reed.[61] Critics who

---

55 *Ibid.* Cf. letter of Nov. 27, 1775 to Joseph Reed (4 *G. W.*, 119) with probable reference to the likelihood that his letters might be opened en route: "The same reasons which restrained you from writing freely also prevent me."

56 Cf. his references to Harrison, *ibid.*, 104.

57 Letter of Jan. 23, 1776; *ibid.*, 269.

58 Letter of Nov. 28, 1775, to Joseph Reed; *ibid.*, 126.

59 Letter of Mch. 31, 1776, to John Augustine Washington; *ibid.*, 449.

60 Correspondence of his earlier years is not sufficient in volume to make possible any accurate statement of how soon this was characteristic of him.

61 Letter of Jan. 23, 1776; *ibid.*, 270.

urged that he attempt the impossible at Boston were "chimney corner heroes." [62] Of Boston Tories he said after the departure of the British Army, "By all accounts, there never existed a more miserable set of beings than these wretched creatures now are." [63] He was as deferential as always to Congress and, in general, to the provincial lawmaking bodies, but he was forthright in criticism of specific blunders, of self-seeking and of injustice. "I think," he confided to Reed, "my [Virginia] countrymen made a capital mistake when they took [Patrick] Henry out of the Senate to place him in the field; and pity it is that he does not see this and remove every difficulty by a voluntary resignation." [64] Washington was equally frank to Reed concerning the promotion of his old comrade, John Armstrong of Pennsylvania, to the rank of Major General in the situation that then existed, though he had no less faith in Armstrong than friendship for that veteran. With like directness Washington privately opposed an excessively responsible assignment for William Thompson, whose seniority seemed to him to be more fortuitously conferred than valiantly earned. [65] This was Washington's stand, also, where his own appointees were involved. Thomas Mifflin had come to Boston as an aide and close friend and he had enjoyed the highest prestige. During the last weeks of operations in front of Boston, whispers had been going the rounds that he was involved in buying and selling provisions, or, in other words, had been dealing with himself after Congress had named him Quartermaster General. Washington told Reed: "I have taken occasion to hint to a certain gentleman in this camp, without introducing names, my apprehensions of his being concerned in trade. He protests most solemnly that he is not, directly or indirectly, and derives no other profit than Congress allows him for defraying the expenses, to wit 5 per cent on the goods purchased." [66] There was no more hesitation on Washington's part in confiding this to Reed than there was in confronting Mifflin with the rumor. Washington tucked away the whole subject in the book of his memory for further candid examination.

He was critical of himself, too, and even of his attitude toward his acknowledged masters, the Congress of the United Colonies. "I am not fond of stretching my powers," he told Reed, a propos of the enlistment

---

[62] Letter of Feb. 10, 1776 to Joseph Reed; *ibid.*, 321.
[63] Letter of Mch. 31, 1776, to John Augustine Washington; *ibid.*, 449.
[64] Letter of Mch. 7, 1776; *ibid.*, 381.
[65] *Ibid.*, 382.   [66] Letter of Mch. 25, 1776; *ibid.*, 432.

of troops for special duty in New York, "and if the Congress will say, 'Thus far and no farther you shall go,' I will promise not to offend whilst I continue in their service." Again, almost humorously, in stating that Congress would authorize payment for some headquarters equipment, he remarked to his Philadelphia confidant, "Congress must be sensible that I cannot take the field without equipage and after I have once got into a tent I shall not soon quit it." [67]

Had the final phase of the siege of Boston developed as he would have desired it? He was not quite sure. Frankly he wrote Reed: "I will not lament or repine at any act of Providence because I am in a great measure a convert to Mr. Pope's opinion that whatever is, is right, but I think everything had the appearance of a successful issue, if we had come to an engagement on that day. It was the 5th of March, which I recalled to their remembrance as a day never to be forgotten; an engagement was fully expected, and I never saw spirits higher or more prevailing." [68]

The issue that lay behind the battle, the campaign and the war was clearer than ever it had been. After the receipt of the text of the King's speech of Oct. 26, 1775, Washington had regarded all attempts at conciliation as futile. [69] No more was said in his letters about any return home when the outcome of the siege of Boston had ended hostilities through submission to England or through recognition of colonial rights. He was puzzled now over reports that peace commissioners were on their way to America and he was doubtful how he should receive them; but even before that rumor was discredited, he was explicit in his statement of the course he thought the American people should take in dealing with the Ministry: "I would not be deceived by artful declarations, nor specious pretences; nor would I be amused by unmeaning propositions; but in open undisguised, and manly terms proclaim our wrongs and our resolution to be redressed. I would tell them that we have borne much, that we had long and ardently sought for reconciliation upon honorable terms, that it had been denied us, that all our attempts after peace had proved abortive, and had been grossly misrepresented, that we had done everything which could be expected from the best of subjects, that the spirit of freedom beat too

[67] Letter of Mch. 3, 1776; *ibid.*, 368.
[68] Letter of Mch. 7, 1776; *ibid.*, 380–81. Much the same sentiment was expressed to Landon Carter in a letter of March 25 (*ibid.*, 433).
[69] Cf. *ibid.*, 209–10, 321.

high in us to submit to slavery, and that, if nothing else could satisfy a tyrant and his diabolical ministry, we are determined to shake off all connections with a state so unjust and unnatural. This I would tell them, not under covert, but in words as clear as the sun in its meridian brightness." [70]

Nowhere, in any of this, was there a hint by Washington that he had surprised himself by his accomplishments in front of Boston. He wrote and acted as if he had been schooled and prepared for the victory that had been won, and he admitted to his brother, if to none of his other close friends, that he was proud of his achievements and of the applause they had drawn. A few days after the British mastheads disappeared over the horizon, Washington wrote John Augustine of the shortage of powder that had crippled the Army to the very last, and then he asserted: "Another thing has been done which, added to the above, will put it in the power of this Army to say what perhaps none other with justice ever could. We have maintained our ground against the enemy, under the above want of powder, and we have disbanded one Army and recruited another, while within musket shot of two and twenty Regiments, the flower of the British Army, when our strength have been little if any superior to theirs; and, at last, have beat them in a shameful and precipitate manner out of a place the strongest by nature on this continent, and strengthened and fortified in the best manner and at enormous expense." [71] Washington traced in some detail the course of operations and then added this paragraph: "I believe I may with great truth affirm that no man perhaps since the first institution of armies ever commanded one under more difficult circumstances, than I have done. To enumerate the particulars would fill a volume. Many of my difficulties and distresses were of so peculiar a cast that in order to conceal them from the enemy, I was obliged to conceal them from my friends, indeed from my own Army, thereby subjecting my conduct to interpretations unfavorable to my character, especially by those at a distance, who could not in the smallest degree be acquainted with the springs that governed it. I am happy, however, to find and to hear from different quarters that my reputation stands fair, that my conduct hitherto has given universal satisfaction. The addresses which I have received, and which I suppose will be published, from the General Court of the Colony—the same as our General Assembly—and

[70] Letter of Feb. 10, 1776; *ibid.*, 321.   [71] Letter of Mch. 31, 1776; *ibid.*, 446.

from the selectmen of Boston upon the evacuation of the town and my approaching departure from the Colony, exhibits a pleasing testimony of their approbation of my conduct and of their personal regard, which I have found in various other instances, and which, in retirement, will afford many comfortable reflections." [72]

In this spirit, on April 4, he left Boston [73] for New York, a prouder man by far, and more self confident, than when he had arrived, nine months previously, to undertake his first campaign. He had won; he believed he could do it again.

[72] *Ibid.,* 450, heavily repunctuated.
[73] S. Cooper's Diary in 6 *A. H. R.,* 339; 4 *G. W.,* 473; *Letters and Diary of John Rowe,* 306.

CHAPTER IV

THE PROBLEM OF DEFENDING NEW YORK
(April 13–June 21, 1776)

WASHINGTON'S ROUTE was to be by way of Providence and the Connecticut towns near Long Island Sound, in order that he might observe and expedite the march of his troops;[1] Martha and her entourage proceeded via Hartford, a somewhat easier but not perceptibly a shorter route.[2] She had made a good, if not a dazzling impression on Massachusetts society. "Mrs. Washington," said Mercy Warren, "is amiable in her deportment and sweet in her manner and I am very glad [the General] has had her companionship so well qualified to soften the cares and toils of war."[3] Martha herself left no record of her impressions but, doubtless, she was discreet as she always was, and, if she did not captivate, she did not aggravate.[4] In the expectation of rejoining her in New York, Washington duly proceeded to Providence, and received warm welcome in a parade and at a generous entertainment by Governor Cooke and some of the gentlemen of the town on the 6th.[5] Then he went on to Norwich[6] and thence to New London,[7] in which now familiar town he found Nathanael Greene, whose march had been much delayed by bad roads and by trouble in procuring teams.[8] As Greene had transports waiting,[9] Washington hastened on to New Haven, where he spent part of the 11th.[10] By the afternoon of the 13th[11] he was in New York.[12]

---

[1] 4 G. W., 479. [2] *Ibid.*, 482.

[3] Letter of Apr. [5], 1776 to Mrs. Hancock; *Mercy Warren Letter Book,* 109, MHS.

[4] No record has been found of "Jack" Custis's introduction to Massachusetts society, or of his wife's relations with the ladies of the Bay Colony.

[5] 4 G. W., 475; *Providence Gazette,* Apr. 6, 1776.

[6] 4 G. W., 504–05; 37 *ibid.*, 523; *Norwich* (Conn.) *Packet,* Apr. 1–8, 1776. Loammi Baldwin, arriving two days previously, wrote his wife, April 6 that, "considering the weather and going," his march had been "tolerably pleasant." (*Baldwin Papers,* Harvard Coll. Lib.)

[7] Apr. 9, 1776; Caulkins, *History of New London,* 599.

[8] 4 G. W., 479–80.

[9] The number of vessels available as transports was considerable. Sullivan used twenty-three vessels to bring his troops down Long Island Sound (*Penn. Evening Post,* Apr. 11, 1776).

[10] 4 G. W., 475. In Lamb's *New York City,* v. 2, p. 70, the statement is made that Washington spent a night in Lyme, Conn., at the home of John McCurdy.

[11] *Heath,* 54; 4 G. W., 479; *Penn. Gazette,* Apr. 17, 1776.

[12] The expenses of his party on the road, £53 odd money, included "at Baptist meeting, 4s: 6." See 25 *Papers of G. W.,* LC. His precise route can be traced, in part, by this account.

The city on the island between North and East Rivers offered a well-nigh bewildering contrast to Boston. Mercy Warren had said of the delivered town: "Instead of the bustle of the camp and the busy preparations for attack and defence, a dead silence reigns through the long, extended lines. The total stagnation of business within, and the still calm without the walls of Boston resemble that serenity which often succeeds the most violent concussion in the world of nature." [13] Col. Loammi Baldwin, who had watched so long at Chelsea, described in these terms the scene on which Washington now looked: "The city is grand, the buildings lofty and elegant. The streets are not so fine, I think, as those in Boston, but the buildings exceed . . . The manners of the people differ something from the natural inhabitants of Boston, having Jewish, Dutch and Irish customs." [14] Tories were diminishing in number [15] but still were strong, and were not lacking in confidence, because they had the protection of British men-of-war that could set the town afire at any hour.[16] The "Sons of Liberty" were not cowed by the cannon of the ships and were not disposed to let the Loyalists plot mischief. On the 12th, the Committee of Safety had received and had put aside the protest of a printer who had complained that a mob had entered his building and had seized, carried off and burned the entire edition of an answer to *Common Sense*,[17] though the reply was entirely decent in tone.[18] Feeling, already tense, was rising daily. Some defensive works had been completed by militia who had just been discharged; [19] other fortification was in progress.[20] Putnam was in general command with Heath under him; [21] troops were fewer than Washington had expected to find and they were rashly dispersed.[22]

The entire situation was disorganized and confused because it lacked the experienced direction of Charles Lee who had designated sites but had left execution in its first stage when he had received command

[13] Letter to Mrs. Hancock, *supra*.

[14] Letter of Apr. 19, 1776 to his wife; *Baldwin Papers*, Army Letters, 29; Harvard Coll. Lib.

[15] Alexander Scammel thought the town "deserted by the Tories." See his letter of Apr. 10, 1776, to his brother, Doctor Scammel; *Anderson Gallery Cat.*, April, 1915.

[16] Cf. *Heath*, 54; 4 *G. W.*, 480.

[17] The more the correspondence and fugitive publications of these months are examined, the more widespread does the influence of Thomas Paine's renowned pamphlet appear to have been.

[18] 5 *Force* (4) p. 1441.

[19] 4 *G. W.*, 476, 480. For the detailed fortification of Bayard's Hill, see Nicholas Fish to Richard Varick, Apr. 2, 1776; 5 *His. Mag.* (2), p. 203.

[20] 4 *G. W.*, 480.   [21] Cf. 1 *Moore*, 229–30.

[22] 4 *G. W.*, 480, 521. Locally, the strength of the defending force was exaggerated. As of April 10, Peter Elting estimated it at 12,000. See his letter of that date to Captain Varick; *Tomlinson MSS*, NYPL.

of a newly created Southern Department.[23] Lee had thought it "more prudent" that he be dispatched to Canada, because of his knowledge of French,[24] and he had regarded that appointment as "very flattering to my ambition," [25] but he wrote of the Southern command, "I shall obey with alacrity and hope with success." [26] He was glad, too, to receive semi-independent command, though he had protested loyally enough, when seemingly laggard in some of his later reports to Washington, "my first business is to be attentive to my General." [27] The transfer had been regarded by admiring New Englanders [28] as scarcely less than a calamity; [29] John Hancock had written Lee of the "warm contest" for the General's service, occasioned by "the high estimation the members of Congress have of your worth and abilities"; [30] Washington had said: "As a Virginian, I must rejoice at the change; but, as an American, I think you would have done more essential service to the common cause in Canada." [31]

Emboldened by this praise or impelled by what he considered necessity, Lee had proceeded to cut himself a wide swath as he went southward. In Baltimore, he had hired an engineer without asking the leave of a Congress that had frowned on so expensive a precedent; [32] and when he had reached Williamsburg he had established himself in the Governor's Palace which, Robert Morris wrote General Gates, "I fancy will be not much approved of by the gentlemen of that country." [33] Lee was commended by his friend Richard Henry of the same patronymic to Robert Carter Nicholas, who still was a dominant figure in Virginia life; but the new Chief of Department had not approved the arrangements made by Nicholas's compatriots for the defence of the Colony. Said Lee humorously: "The distribution of their troops is likewise a masterpiece—I wonder they did not carry it still further and post one or two men by way of general security in every individual

[23] 4 *JCC.*, 174, 175, 180–81. Lee was named by Congress to this new post March 1. The Department was to consist of Virginia, North Carolina, South Carolina and Georgia. Three Brigadier Generals were to serve under him (*ibid.*, 174).

[24] 1 *LTW.*, 161. Cf. Alexander McDougall, Mch. 7, 1776; 1 *John Jay*, 46.

[25] 1 *Lee Papers*, 280.   [26] 1 *LTW.*, 161.

[27] 1 *Lee Papers*, 336.

[28] Cf. his letter of thanks to Governor Cooke, Jan. 9, 1776, *AASP*, October, 1926, p. 300.

[29] See Abigail Adams to John Adams, Mch. 7, 1776 (*Adams, Fam. Let.*, 139): ". . . How can we spare him from here? Can you make his place good? Can you supply it with a man equally qualified to save us?"

[30] Letter of Mch. 1, 1776; 1 *Lee Papers*, 342.

[31] Letter of Mch. 14, 1776; 4 *G. W.*, 397.

[32] 1 *Lee Papers*, 360; 1 *Ballagh, Lee Letters*, 171.

[33] Letter of Apr. 6, 1776; 1 *Lee Papers*, 388.

gentleman's house." [34] To Washington he wrote: "My situation is just as I expected. I am afraid that I shall make a shabby figure without any real demerits of my own. I am like a dog in a dancing school—I know not where to turn myself, where to fix myself. The circumstances of the country, intersected by navigable rivers, the uncertainty of the enemy's designs and motions, who can fly in an instant to any spot where they chose with their canvass wings, throw me or would have thrown Julius Caesar into this inevitable dilemma . . . I can only act from surmise and have a very good chance of surmising wrong. I am sorry to grate your ears with a truth, but must at all events assure you that the Provincial Congress of New York are angels of decision when compared with your countrymen—the Committee of Safety assembled at Williamsburg. Page, Lee, Mercer and Payne are indeed exceptions; but from Pendleton, Bland, the Treasurer & Co—libera nos, Domine." [35]

Washington already had written to his brother "Jack" his confidential opinion of the critic. Slow to judge, lest haste work injustice, Washington had begun to doubt the stability, perhaps the dependability, of his senior lieutenant. "He is," Washington wrote, "the first officer in military knowledge and experience we have in the whole Army. He is zealously attached to the cause, honest and well-meaning but rather fickle and violent I fear in his temper.[36] However, as he possesses an uncommon share of good sense and spirit, I congratulate my countrymen upon his appointment to that Department." [37] That "however" was not written merely to bridge two sentences. It was intended to balance good and bad and not to erase the warning of "fickle," which was a word Washington seldom had used in his letters.

Before Washington could master the details of the fortifications Lee had left unfinished in New York,[38] the Commander-in-Chief was compelled to deal with a dismal situation in Canada. This already had so

[34] Letter of Apr. 5, 1776 to Brig. Gen. Robert Howe; 1 *Lee Papers*, 376.
[35] Letter of Apr. 5, 1776; *ibid.*, 376–77.
[36] The punctuation of this sentence has been preserved.
[37] Letter of Mch. 31, 1776; 4 *G. W.*, 451.
[38] The defensive system Lee recommended at New York is sketched *infra*, p. 87, on the basis of 4 *JCC.*, 201. Knox, writing his wife, Apr. 24, 1776, remarked that he was examining the harbor, at Washington's instance, in order to make it a rendezvous or retreat for "our ships of the American Navy." (2 *Knox Papers*, 66, MHS.) Names and locations of some of the principal batteries are given in 5 *G. W.*, 73. The guard posts and the number of men at each of them are listed in *Clap's Diary*, 134, as of May 18, 1776. Jeduthan Baldwin's Journal contains numerous references to the construction of the New York defences, in the design of which so many men had a hand that it would be difficult, were it worthwhile, to attempt to trace individual responsibility for particular fortifications.

alarmed Congress that the members had decided on February 15 to name three commissioners to proceed to Canada for the execution of any policy that might subsequently be formulated.[39] In addition, Congress had determined to send to the St. Lawrence an officer of high rank and recognized ability. As Philip Schuyler was needed to forward supplies and was physically unfit to take the field, Congress on March 6 had chosen John Thomas for this mission and had made him a Major General.[40] Washington had acquiesced uncomplainingly in the transfer of Thomas, because he yielded now as almost always to the will of Congress and, secondly, because he doubtless realized what Joseph Reed affirmed in a letter from Philadelphia, "your camp is considered a school."[41] Thomas had left Roxbury on the 22nd[42] of March and on the 28th had reached Albany[43] where he had caught the echo of much doubt and misery voiced by officers and men in Canada.[44] Schuyler had never been able to procure from Gen. David Wooster, the surviving senior officer in Canada, any return of the troops there.[45] Neither Schuyler nor Washington knew how many of Montgomery's former command and of Arnold's column had survived the bullets of Quebec and the rigors of the winter. When successive fragmentary reports could be pieced together during April, they showed many discouragements. Wooster had transferred his headquarters[46] to the camp of the small American force that still was keeping up the pretence of a siege of Quebec; Arnold, trading places, had gone to Montreal, which was still in the hands of continental troops. Before Arnold had left Quebec, he had undertaken to erect several batteries but had been hampered by the sullenness of discontented men in his command and by the presence of

---

[39] 4 *JCC.*, 151–52.

[40] 4 *JCC.*, 186; Hancock to Washington, Mch. 6, 1776; 1 *LTW.*, 165; Hancock to Schuyler, Mch. 7, 1776, 1 *Burnett*, 381.

[41] Letter of Mch. 15, 1776; 1 *Reed*, 171, quoted in 4 *G. W.*, 453 n.

[42] Letter of Apr. 8, 1776, to John Hancock, 5 *Force* (4) p. 822.

[43] *Ibid.*

[44] In his dispatch of April 7 to Washington, written in Albany, 5 *Force* (4) p. 813, Thomas stated that the most recent news from Canada was that of approximately March 25, but he did not record when letters of that date were received in Albany. The same lack of exact dating in other letters makes difficult the task of ascertaining precisely when information of the state of affairs in Canada at a particular time became known in Albany and in New York City. Fortunately, in this instance, uncertainty creates no historical pitfalls because the unhappy situation along the St. Lawrence was static. A margin of as much as a week in the assumed date of the arrival in Albany of dispatches from Montreal or Point Levis, during March and April, involves no danger of crediting Schuyler, Thomas or Washington with information none of the three could have possessed at a given time.

[45] Cf. Schuyler to Washington, Apr. 12, 1776, 1 *LTW.*, 186.

[46] He left Montreal Mch. 27, 1776. See 5 *Force* (4) p. 869.

no less than five feet of snow. "We labor," he had written grimly, "under almost as many difficulties as the Israelites did of old, obliged to make brick without straw." He had 400 sick and wounded on his hands, though, mercifully, he himself had almost recovered. Less than 1000 of the promised reenforcement had been received.[47] After Wooster reached the lines across the St. Lawrence from Quebec, he had an even gloomier tale to tell. The American forces on that front, he said,[48] numbered between 2000 and 3000, of whom not more than half were fit for duty. Many of these were determined to leave April 15, when their enlistment expired. New troops were arriving slowly and were of small use because of the prevalence of smallpox. Powder and artillery stores, Wooster reported, were "so trifling" that "no great results ought to be expected from them." [49] During the time between Wooster's departure and Arnold's arrival, the acting commander, Col. Moses Hazen, had sent Schuyler a discouraging report. The French natives, he said, had been alienated by the failure of the Americans to pay in hard money for purchases; the clergy had been neglected; the Indians were cold. "We have brought on ourselves by mismanagement," Hazen wrote bluntly, "what Governor Carleton himself never could effect." [50]

Weeks before the worst of this was known, Congress had reaffirmed, in effect, its resolution to add Canada to the United Colonies and to retrieve with new troops the defeat Montgomery had sustained.[51] "The Congress being of opinion"—so read a paper adopted in March 25— "that the reduction of Quebec and the general security of the province of Canada are objects of great concern," Washington had been directed to detach four Battalions to Canada from his Army "as soon as he shall be of opinion that the safety of New York and the eastern service will permit." [52] In addition, three able commissioners of Congress—Benjamin Franklin, Samuel Chase and Charles Carroll—had been given

---

[47] Arnold to unnamed correspondent, Mch. 26–28, 1776; 5 *Force* (4) p. 512.

[48] His actual language was: "By a return of the state of the Army, which General Arnold sent about ten days ago to Mr. Deane . . . ," but by "the Army," Wooster manifestly meant the troops under Arnold's command and not the whole force in Canada.

[49] Dispatch of Apr. 10, 1776 to the President of Congress; 5 *Force* (4) p. 845–46. Wooster had written from Montreal, March 16, that the American supply of powder "in this country" did not exceed "sixty rounds for 6000 men, supposing we had no use for cannon" (*ibid.*, 868). He did not elaborate on the possibility of success without artillery.

[50] Letter of April 1, 1776; 5 *Force* (4) p. 869–70. Washington forwarded this letter to Hancock April 19. See 4 *G. W.*, 492.

[51] 1 *Burnett*, 302, 319.

[52] 4 *JCC.*, 236. This resolution had been introduced and urged by Richard Henry Lee. See his letter of Mch. 25, 1776, to Charles Lee, 1 *Lee Papers*, 363.

instructions,[53] had been vested with discretionary power to raise Independent Companies,[54] and had been started on their way.[55]

It now was time for Washington to do his part in this effort to win Canada to the colonial cause. Thomas, Wooster and Schuyler were calling for troops with whom to combat Carleton and the reenforcements the Americans expected he soon would receive;[56] Washington alone could supply trained men in sufficient strength to shift the balance again. Hancock's conditional instructions[57] to dispatch four Battalions from the main Army had been received April 2, two days before the Commander-in-Chief had left Boston.[58] Washington's deep, continuing desire to destroy the enemy's strongholds in Canada[59] disposed him to relax somewhat his insistence on concentration of force and to comply vigorously with orders he would in any event have obeyed. He was inclined, also, to give more credit than formerly to the reports picked up in Boston before the evacuation, to the effect that Howe's fleet was bound for Halifax, whence, of course, it would be easy for the enemy to detach men and transport around Cape Breton and up the St. Lawrence to Quebec.[60] Washington consequently had given Hancock assurance that the four Battalions would be dispatched after the Army reached New York;[61] Schuyler was told the troop movement would begin as soon as Howe's destination was known.[62] Now that Washington had made his first survey of affairs at the mouth of the Hudson, he felt confident that New York was too rich a prize strategically for a competent British commander to ignore. In precisely the same way, he regarded Canada as a base so convenient and so valuable for the British that the Americans were justified in taking risks and in making sacrifices to wrest the northern province from the enemy.

Thus was the strategy of the struggle changing. Instead of being a campaign to deny the British a base in New England, it was becoming a contest for the control of the Hudson: If Howe could seize and occupy the mouth of the river, he might be able to dominate the whole of that noble waterway, as well as the Northern Lakes, and thereby might sever

---

[53] March 20; 4 *JCC.*, 215 ff.   [54] *Ibid.*, 233.

[55] They reached Albany April 7. See 1 *LTW.*, 185. The Diary of Charles Carroll, which is the prime authority on the activities of this commission, begins Apr. 2, 1776. See 1 *Rowland, Carroll*, 363 ff.

[56] 5 *Force* (4) p. 822, 846, 872; 1 *LTW.*, 185, 187.

[57] Mch. 25, 1776; 1 *LTW.*, 175–77.   [58] Cf. 4 *G. W.*, 470.

[59] *Ibid.*, 278–81, 357.   [60] *Ibid.*, 459–60, 461.

[61] *Ibid.*, 471.   [62] *Ibid.*, 459.

the eastern Colonies from the others. Conversely, if Washington could close the St. Lawrence between Quebec and Montreal, he could prevent the use of that river and its towns as a convenient and secure starting-point for operations against the Hudson. It was a dramatic race—Washington to Quebec, Howe to New York.

The American commander was resolved not to lose the contest if he could win it by a prompt beginning and by the utmost use of the feeble resources he commanded. The four Battalions [63] were made ready to proceed up the Hudson under the command of William Thompson, who had been advanced to the rank of Brigadier even before Washington's privately qualified endorsement of him had reached Congress; [64] but it was April 21 when the men had a favoring wind. [65] They were supplied with 500 barrels of provisions [66] and were to be followed by a Company of riflemen, a Company of artificers, and two engineers. [67]

By the time Washington received word on the 27th of the arrival of the main body of these troops in Albany, [68] he had new orders from Philadelphia: He was to send six additional Regiments to Canada, in order to assure the capture of Quebec, and if he thought this force insufficient, he was to advise Congress and was to indicate whether still more men could be spared from the Army in New York. [69] Washington immediately designated the half-dozen Regiments that were to go and he named John Sullivan to the command. [70] On the question of still larger assistance for the Canadian expedition, he advanced somewhat further the strategical argument of Hudson vs. St. Lawrence. He said: ". . . I am really at a loss what to advise, as it is impossible at present to know the designs of the enemy. Should they send the whole force under General Howe up the River St. Lawrence to relieve Quebec and recover Canada, the [American] troops gone and now going will be insufficient to stop their progress, and should they think proper to send that or an equal force this way from Great Britain, for the purpose of possessing this city and securing the navigation of Hudson River, the

---

[63] Washington at this time used "Battalion" (*ibid.*, 480) and "Regiment" (*ibid.*, 478) as synonyms.

[64] *Ibid.*, 479, 480, 481. For Thompson, see 4 *JCC.*, 181 and *supra*, p. 73.

[65] 4 *G. W.*, 492–93, 500.   [66] *Ibid.*, 495.

[67] *Ibid.*, 497.   [68] On the 24th of April; 5 *ibid.*, 2.

[69] Letter of John Hancock, Apr. 23, 1776; 1 *LTW.*, 188. The resolution of Congress, (4 *JCC.*, 302) originally had directed that Washington send "as many Regiments as he may think the security of the city will admit of."

[70] 4 *G. W.*, 526, 537. Two of these Regiments belonged to Sullivan's own Brigade, two to Greene's, and two to Lord Stirling's command, which Washington had found in New York on arrival there.

troops left here will not be sufficient to oppose them, and yet for any-thing we know, I think it not improbable they may attempt both, both being of the greatest importance to them if they have men. I should wish indeed that the army in Canada should be more powerfully reenforced; at the same time I am conscious that the trusting this impor-tant post (which is now become the Grand Magazine of America) to the handful of men remaining here is running too great a risk: The securing this post and Hudsons River is to us also of so great importance that I cannot at present advise the sending any more troops from hence." Then he went on to explain that his officers thought a garrison of 10,000 necessary for New York.[71]

Hence, for a few days, the issue of further reenforcement for Canada was left, while Washington devoted more of his time to disciplining his men. In restless, divided New York, the young soldiers and some of the officers were subjected to temptations different from those they had faced in small New England villages and in camps from which women were excluded. The neighborhood known satirically as "the holy ground" was shocking to some of the men of Puritan descent. Col. Loammi Baldwin soon was to tell his wife in uncloaked words: "The whores (by information) continue their employ which is become very lucrative. Their unparalleled conduct is a sufficient antidote against any desires that a person can have that has one spark of modesty or virtue left in him . . . Perhaps you will call me censorious and exclaim too much upon bare reports when I say that I was never within the doors of nor 'changed a word with any of them except in the execution of my duty as officer of the day in going the grand round with my guard of escort, have broke up the knots of men and women fighting, pulling caps, swearing, crying 'Murder' & c—hurried them off to the Provost Dungeon by half dozens, there let them lay mixed till next day. Then some are punished and some get off clear—hell's work . . ."[72] Wild tales were told of what was done by denizens of these dark places. Pain-fully but precisely Solomon Nash wrote in his diary how his Company worked to place cannon. Then he recorded: "Several limbs and heads of men ware found at the Holey ground which was supposed to be ciled by the hoars. The rifed men tore down a hous. No man is suf-fered to be there after Nine o'clock at night."[73] Many of the soldiers

---

[71] *Ibid.*, 519–20.
[72] Letter of June 17, 1776; *Baldwin Papers*, Harvard Coll. Lib.
[73] *Solomon Nash's Diary*, 13.

went to the dives, in defiance of guard and of hours, with the result that venereal disease was widely prevalent in some commands.[74]

There were, too, numerous cases of desertion [75] and some instances of drunkenness, combined with so much disorder that the offenders had to be brought before general courtmartial.[76] At least one outbreak of violence was denounced by Washington with a threat that if the rioters resisted arrest, they would be treated "as common enemy." [77] A considerable part of the Commander-in-Chief's orders on disciplinary matters dealt with camp sanitation and with the protection of the houses, the trees and the gardens of citizens.[78] Some of those same New Yorkers proved refractory in their dealings with the British on the ships below the city. Washington first requested the Committee of Safety to put an end to this trading with the enemy [79] and, when that did not suffice, he served notice that traffickers would be punished.[80]

The strangest infringement of discipline, one that posed for Washington a succession of tangled alternatives, involved Lieut. Thomas Grover of the Second Regiment. When the command of his Company became vacant, Grover considered himself automatically advanced to the rank of Captain, and after the Company was placed in charge of another man, Grover refused to obey his new Captain's orders and abused the officer with hearty vehemence. For this, of course, the Captain ordered Grover put under arrest. Charges were preferred; the Lieutenant was brought before a courtmartial and was convicted; but, probably because the members of the court sympathized with his contention, he was given no further punishment than the loss of a half-month's pay.[81] This alarmed Washington. He saw in it a possible precedent of automatic succession to command that might give higher rank to incompetents. At the same time, if promotion by seniority was denied in many instances, junior officers might become discontented and might conclude they never would be advanced. The case was referred to Congress with the recommendation that action be taken to make it plain that "no succession or promotion can take place in case of vacancies, without a continental commission giving and authorizing it." Washington added deferentially, as always, that if the contrary

---

[74] Cf. 4 Force (4) p. 990; Isaac Bangs's Diary, 29.
[75] Usually punished with thirty-nine lashes "on the bare back." Cf. 5 G. W., 6–7.
[76] Cf. ibid., 515.
[77] Ibid., 526.
[78] Ibid., 485, 514; ibid., 11, 13.
[79] 4 ibid., 486–87.
[80] Ibid., 533.
[81] 5 ibid., 17, 55.

view prevailed, it might be made known and the point settled, but he left no doubt of his own views.[82] While waiting for the decision of Congress, he saw to it that Lieutenant Grover was brought to an understanding of the seriousness of the offence. When this was done and Grover was repentant and apologetic, Washington released the young man from arrest.[83]

The General notified Congress of this and explained frankly his attitude toward disciplinary cases of this type: While he had endeavored, he said, to support Congress and to keep the Army in due subordination, "I have found it of importance and expedient to yield many points, in fact, without seeming to have done it, and this to avoid bringing on a too-frequent discussion of matters which, in a political view, ought to be kept a little behind the curtain, and not be made too much the subjects of disquisition." [84] In other words, discipline was necessary but it must be administered within the army organization itself and must not raise issues that would become political to the possible injury of the larger cause of liberty.

The defences of New York were strengthened while Washington sought to administer this patiently cautious discipline. Along with his scheme of fortification,[85] Charles Lee had given Congress his analysis of the tactical possibilities of coping with an adversary who commanded the waters around New York City. Lee's theory was that the town itself scarcely could be made a tenable fortress, but that, in his own words, it could be "made a most advantageous field of battle, so advantageous, indeed, that if our people behave with common spirit, and the commanders are men of discretion, it might cost the enemy many thousands of men to get possession of it." [86]

Long Island Sound, Lee reasoned, must and could be dominated by the Americans; Long Island itself could be defended by 4000 to 5000 men if properly supplied with redoubts at its western end. Cross fire from these fortifications and those of New York would make it almost certain, Lee thought, that East River could be closed to the British. North River, on the other hand, was "so extremely wide and deep" that the enemy certainly could navigate it but might have less power to do mischief than had been assumed. The ground offered some protection from naval ordnance; batteries well situated on New York Island could

[82] 5 *ibid.*, 17–18.   [83] 6 *Force* (4) p. 426; 5 *G. W.*, 55.
[84] 5 *G. W.*, 33.   [85] See *supra.*, p. 80.
[86] 4 *JCC.*, 203.

keep the British men-of-war at a distance. Barriers and redoubts must be erected; King's Bridge must be so fortified that communication would be "free and open" with Connecticut, to which New York would have to look for reenforcements. New Jersey could not be relied upon for immediate help in an hour of sudden danger because the breadth and depth of North River made easy contact precarious.[87]

Thus Lee had written, and so convincingly that Congress forthwith had voted to raise the garrison of New York and Long Island to 8000, the number the General had set as the required total;[88] but he had been able to interpret a small part only of his program in terms of parapets and ditches before he had been sent to the South. Washington had to complete what Lee merely had begun.[89] That was half only and, though vexatious, was the easier part of the task. More troops had to be made available for service, whenever the lookouts signalled that the King's canvas was visible on the horizon. Washington had barely 8300 men fit for duty as of April 23[90] and, though he did not say so in plain words, he lacked Lee's confidence that this force could stand off the troops Howe would bring.

With patient deference Washington appealed to the New York Committee of Safety to provide 2000 to 2500 militia for assembly in an emergency[91] and, while setting no figure, he made a like request of New Jersey, in which Colony the situation was so much confused that he did not know whether the governing body was a Legislature or a Committee of Safety.[92] Connecticut, too, was enjoined to have men ready for the instant succor of their comrades in New York in the day of threat.[93] Whenever two flags were flown one under the other on the middle flagstaff of Staten Island heights, that signified the British fleet was approaching or was sending boats toward Amboy. Three flags from the same staff indicated in the same way that the objective was New York.[94] As always, much had to be done in establishing camps in

---

[87] *Ibid.*, 201–04. The British took pains to observe the progress of all parts of this work and, by June 6, 1776, they had a full and probably accurate description of the "state of the forts and batteries and breastworks erected about the city of New York and Hudson River." This report is in the *Clinton Papers*, Clements Lib.

[88] *Ibid.*, 203, 204.

[89] Henry Knox did not think this an impossible task. On the contrary, soon after reaching New York, he wrote his wife, May 2, 1776: "Affairs here have an aspect very formidable—the works are strong and well constructed so that this place will be much more secure from an attack of the shipping than almost any other harbor known . . ." (2 *Knox Papers*, 66; MHS).

[90] 6 *Force* (4) p. 1070.   [91] 4 *G. W.*, 498.

[92] *Ibid.*, 509.   [93] *Ibid.*, 524.

[94] *Ibid.*, 524 n.

the city and on Long Island,[95] in placating sensitive provincial law-makers,[96] and in reorganizing the continental forces. Lord Stirling's four Regiments became the Fifth Brigade.[97] Sullivan's command was continued as the Third Brigade,[98] though two of its five Regiments had been detached for service in Canada.[99]

When Washington had discharged these first tasks of discipline, defence and organization, he had from about the 6th of May a fort-night when the industrious sound of pick and spade was heard on many a New York street, and the anxious question, "What next?" was asked in every tavern. Bickering and argument between Whig and Tory became more violent. If the Loyalist looked down the harbor toward the masts of the *Asia*[100] and prayed for the arrival of a delivering fleet, the Americans talked increasingly of proclaiming independence[101] and of jailing spies and traitors. From its pedestal on the Bowling Green, the gilded leaden image of the King looked down in majestic benevolence on the busy, shuffling, ever-shifting throng of his former subjects, but those who lifted hat or even eyes in homage were fewer and fewer. The anniversary of Concord and Lexington was past; in a few weeks the dead of Bunker Hill would have been for twelve months in their bivouac. Uncertainty had prevailed for a year: there soon must be a decision.

Washington sensed or saw it all. On arrival in New York from Boston, he had opened headquarters at the residence of William Smith,[102] but he moved to Mortier's when Martha joined him on the 17th of

---

[95] *Ibid.*, 514, 535–36; 5 *ibid.*, 5, 11, 21.

[96] 4 *ibid.*, 534–35, 538.

[97] There had been some muttering among New Yorkers over this appointment. See Alexander McDougall to Philip Schuyler, Mch. 14, Apr. 26, 1776; *McDougall Papers*, NYHS. Stirling had some administrative experience of value in New York before Washington arrived from Boston. See, as typical, Stirling to Hancock, Mch. 19, 1776; *Alexander Papers*, 1770–79, NYHS.

[98] The First was Heath's, the Second was Spencer's, the Fourth was Greene's (4 *G. W.*, 512–13).

[99] *Ibid.*, 519, 526, 531, 537.

[100] As of early May, she was five miles below the Narrows; the other warships had gone down to the Hook (5 *ibid.*, 7).

[101] Cf. *McCurtin's Journal*, 38: ". . . a great noise about independency. The people seem to quiver at the word, I mean on this island [of New York]" (Apr. 22, 1776).

[102] 1 Jones, *History of N. Y.*, 85. The house, which at this time was called Montier's, stood at what now is the corner of Varick and Charlton Streets (T. E. V. Smith, *New York City*, 217; Ulmann, *Landmark History of New York*, 107). The fullest description of the house as it was thirteen years later is given in *New Letters of Abigail Adams*, 17. Mrs. Adams noted, "The house is convenient for one family, but too small for more." Whether Washington had a "downtown" office in the late summer of 1776 is an historical riddle of amusing and almost of baffling character. Traditions are numerous but facts are few. The evidence is reviewed at length in Appendix IV-1, p. 635–37.

April.[103] They had proceeded to purchase a feather bed, bolster, pillows, bed curtains, and some crockery and glassware,[104] while Washington took advantage of the New York market to procure at continental expense a chamber marquee with an ante-room, a large dining marquee, eighteen walnut camp stools, three walnut camp tables, and the necessary packing cases.[105] These things gave the General the assurance that when he took the field, he would have a dignified and appropriate abode, but for the moment there was little social activity. Life in New York was too tense; Washington was so busy that he allowed himself no time for amusement.[106]

Of honor, there was as much as he who loved the approval of his fellowmen could ask. Although he had informed Congress promptly of the occupation of Boston and later of the final British withdrawal from Nantasket,[107] he had received no notice, when he left Boston, of any action by Congress on his announcement that "the forces of the United Colonies are now in actual possession" of Boston.[108] Doubtless Washington had seen articles in the newspapers on the proceedings, and he had, through a private hand, a letter in which John Adams had informed him that Congress had voted thanks and a gold medal. As author of this motion and chairman of the committee on the design of a medal, Adams had wished Washington's "sentiments concerning a proper" device.[109] Washington, in reply, had expressed his gratitude and had added, "whatever device may be determined upon by the respectable committee [Congress has] chosen for that purpose will be highly agreeable to me." [110] Hancock, too, had written personally on March 25 to congratulate him on the "partial victory," which the President wrote, "I hope will turn out a happy presage of a more general one." [111] Formal notification, prepared by Adams's committee, approved by Congress on April 2, and duly signed by John Hancock,[112]

---

[103] N. Y. Gazette and Weekly Mercury, Apr. 22, 1776. Nathanael Greene's Brigade is said on the same authority to have landed that day from New London, Conn. Mrs. Washington was delayed en route because "Jack" fell sick (4 G. W., 483).

[104] 26 Papers of G. W., 7, 77; 27 ibid., 124; 28 ibid., 65, LC.

[105] This order, filled by Plunket Fleason, amounted to £64 odd money (26 Papers of G. W., 77, LC).

[106] Cf. Washington to the President of Congress, Apr. 23, 1776: "I give into no kind of amusements myself . . ." (4 G. W., 506).

[107] 4 ibid., 403, 436.

[108] 4 ibid., 403.

[109] 1 LTW., 177; 1 Burnett, 413; 3 John Adams, 38.

[110] Letter of Apr. 15, 1776; 4 G. W., 484.

[111] 1 LTW., 175.

[112] 4 JCC., 234, 248.

overtook Washington, at last, on the 17th. It contained this high language:

The disinterested and patriotic principles which led you to the field, have also led you to glory: and it affords no little consolation to your countrymen to reflect that, as a peculiar greatness of mind induced you to decline any compensation for serving them, except the pleasure of promoting their happiness, they may, without your permission, bestow upon you the largest share of their affections and esteem.

Those pages in the annals of America will record your title to a conspicuous place in the Temple of Fame, which shall inform posterity that under your directions an undisciplined hand of husbandmen, in the course of a few months became soldiers . . .

and so into a brief but highly eulogistic review of the campaign. Then followed official thanks which Washington was to communicate to the Army.[113] The General's reply was, in part, an assurance "that it will ever be my highest ambition to approve myself a faithful servant of the public; and that to be in any degree instrumental in procuring to my American brethren a restitution of their just rights and privileges will constitute my chief happiness." Then, in justice to his men, Washington said: "They were indeed at first 'a band of undisciplined husbandmen' but it is (under God) to their bravery and attention to their duty that I am indebted for that success which procured for me the only reward I wish to receive, the affection and esteem of my countrymen." [114]

He might have admitted, had it been in order, that this had been true ever since his first introduction to public service twenty-three years previously: always the approval and applause of his fellow-men had been the supreme goal of life, next that of acquiring a fortune. It had been to deserve this approval that he had shaped his life and disciplined his spirit. Now, in larger measure than ever, he had "honor" and something already approaching veneration. That was as pleasing as it was embarrassing, but it was bought at the price of hourly effort, concentration of thought, vexation of mind and, on occasion, anguish of soul. There were so few fellow-laborers who had dedicated their spirit to America, and so many in whom war, as in every age and land, was bringing out the worst of selfish ambition and grasping venality. Washington scarcely would have been blasphemous or even blameworthy

113 *Ibid.,* 248–49; 4 *G. W.,* 488–89.   114 4 *G. W.,* 489.

had he said despairingly that sometimes he had to tread the wine-press alone.

Now, for example, he had to contend with an acute shortage of small arms,[115] with the slow progress of recruiting in New York,[116] with the termination of July 1 of the enlistment of the riflemen,[117] and with the possibility that neglect of the refortification of Boston might invite a return of the British. Artemas Ward had presented his resignation as Major General on the grounds of ill-health, immediately after the occupation of the city by the Americans.[118] Then he had withdrawn the paper, ostensibly at the instance of his officers [119]—only to resign again within a few weeks.[120] This time Congress had acquiesced,[121] with moderate praise by Hancock in transmitting notice to that effect; [122] but Congress had failed to name a successor, and Washington could not spare a competent officer of rank and experience. New Brigadiers were needed and not named promptly: [123] Ward remained though he still asked to be relieved; [124] the construction of defences in Boston harbor lagged. Washington had been compelled to write Col. Richard Gridley with some sharpness concerning reports that the works had not been advanced: "Who am I to blame for this shameful neglect but you, sir, who was to have them executed? It is not an agreeable task to be under the necessity of putting any gentleman in mind of his duty, but it is what I owe to the public. I expect and desire, sir, that you will exert yourself in completing the works with all possible dispatch, and do not lay me under the disagreeable necessity of writing you again upon this subject." [125]

Washington had been informed, also, that Ward was under the impression that troops guarding Bunker Hill and Dorchester Neck were exempt from fatigue duty on the fortifications; and as this was not the fact, he so notified the commander at Boston.[126] General Ward indignantly denounced the information as "injurious falsehood" . . . He asserted in round terms: "I believe I can truly affirm that more work

---

115 *Ibid.*, 500, 504, 531, 534-35, 538; 5 *ibid.*, 18.

116 McDougall to Schuyler, April 26; Richard Varick to McDougall, May 12, 1776; *McDougall Papers*, NYHS.

117 4 *G. W.*, 501–02.   118 5 *Force* (4) p. 467.

119 4 *G. W.*, 452. Ward's orderly book for this tour of duty, beginning Mch. 31, 1776, is in *MHSP.*, 1878, p. 337.

120 Apr. 12, 1776; 5 *Force* (4) p. 872.   121 4 *JCC.*, 300.

122 1 *Burnett*, 430.   123 5 *G. W.*, 36-37.

124 1 *LTW.*, 191.

125 Letter of Apr. 28, 1776; 4 *G. W.*, 528-29.

126 *Ibid.*, 529; 5 *Force* (4) p. 1174.

has never been done in the American army by an equal number of troops than has been performed by the troops which are stationed here, in the same space of time; but because 1500 men could not throw up the works as fast as 6000 or 7000 had done in time past, there appeared to some an unaccountable delay."

Washington had no high opinion of Ward and when he heard that the commander in Massachusetts had withdrawn the resignation, he wrote Charles Lee that Ward first had proposed to quit the service from a probability of having to remove "from the smoke of his own chimney." [127] At the same time, Washington did not wish to engage in a controversy, and when the matter was taken up by Rev. William Gordon, who reported some dissatisfaction in the Bay Colony with Ward, the Commander-in-Chief contented himself with asking, "If General W[ard] is judged an improper person to command five Regiments in a peaceable camp or garrison . . . why was he appointed to the first military command in the Massachusetts government? By whom was he appointed in the first instance, and by whom supported in the next?" Washington felt that he had acted justly, from any point of view in dealing with Ward, but he realized New Englanders were of two minds on this; and he added, "free people will judge freely, and I do not condemn them for it; it is the only way to bring matters to a fair discussion." [128] Ward himself was reassured that the reports of exemption from work on the forts had been circulated generally in New York, not as a reflection on him but as the result of a misunderstanding.[129] He was told further that his statement of the progress made on the Boston defences was "very agreeable"; but in this, Washington said nothing to indicate his regret at the news that Ward had decided again to leave the Army. The language of the Commander-in-Chief was polite and adequate and no more than that: "I have had no advice from Congress relative to your resignation. I shall write them this day to know whom they may think proper to appoint to the command in your State. When I receive their answer, you shall be informed thereof." [130]

[127] Letter of May [1], 1776; 5 G. W., 3.

[128] Letter of May 13, 1776; 37 ibid., 525. This part of the episode is obscure because a part only of the letter is published, on the basis, principally, of a facsimile in a dealer's catalogue of 1937. The present ownership of the letter is not known.

[129] Robert H. Harrison to Ward, May 16, 1776; 6 Force (4) p. 478.

[130] Letter of May 13, 1776; 5 G. W., 41. Martyn reviewed in his Artemas Ward, 216 ff the tradition that this affair deepened the differences between Ward and Washington, who never had been friendly.

The possibility of an attack on Boston seemed at times to Washington to be remote [131] and, in other circumstances, to be not unlikely; [132] but as of May 5, he had to admit, "The designs of the enemy are too much behind the curtain for me to form any accurate opinion of their plan of operations for the summer's campaign." He still thought that no place was of more importance to the British than the mouth of the Hudson, and it was for that reason, he told Congress, that he had brought the Army to New York. He added: ". . . if the Congress from their knowledge, information or belief [133] think it best for the general good of the service that I should go to the northward, or elsewhere, they are convinced, I hope, that they have nothing more to do than signify their commands." [134]

He and the members of Congress soon had information that the British might be strong enough to reenforce their troops in Canada, to send Howe to New York, and, perhaps, to strike simultaneously at some other point. By the second week in May, American leaders came to believe there was truth to reports in circulation that the King had hired German troops from continental princes. [135] Regiments were known to have been dispatched from Ireland, also. [136] A stronger Britain would confront an America weakened by dispersion of force, by losses of many sorts, and by the ravages of smallpox. Bad conditions must not be permitted to get worse. As Washington now had in New York only 6717 men fit for duty [137]—the militia having been dismissed by order of Congress [138]—he was resolved that he would not send any of these to Boston otherwise than on orders from Congress. [139] To reduce attrition by smallpox, Washington provided for prompt isolation of suspects [140] and he sternly prohibited the ignorant and imprudent inoculation of soldiers in the ranks. [141]

[131] 37 ibid., 525.   [132] 5 ibid., 25.

[133] In the original, this word is "believe."

[134] Letter to the President of Congress; 5 ibid., 19–20.

[135] Washington's first printed reference to the reports was on May 9 (see 5 ibid., 25), but as early as March 11, Lord Stirling had forwarded from New York information supplied the previous evening by "three gentlemen landed here from on board a packet, nine weeks out from Falmouth" (1 LTW., 172). Their report was that seven Regiments of Foot were embarked and ready to sail from Cork, about January 6, for the Southern Colonies. Four thousand Hanoverians and 6000 Hessians were said to have been engaged for service in America. Negotiations were reported to be in progress for 10,000 Russians.

[136] Cf. Dodsley's Annual Register, 1776, p. 124. These forces numbered 4000.

[137] 6 Force (4) p. 527–28.

[138] May 16. See 5 G. W., 50 and 4 JCC., 272.

[139] 5 G. W., 27.   [140] 5 ibid., 25; Heath, 55.

[141] 5 ibid., 63, 82, 84. See 2 Gordon, 63, for a report that smallpox was brought to the American troops in Canada by "a girl who had been a nurse in the city hospital and came out

The worst nightmare was not disease and not dispersion but disaster, disaster in Canada. John Thomas, the new Major General, had arrived in front of Quebec on the 1st of May and had taken general command; [142] William Thompson, promoted Brigadier, was known to have reached Fort George, at the southern end of the lake of that name; [143] Sullivan and his command, a total of 5040 fit men,[144] were supposed to be proceeding northward from Albany; [145] Schuyler was doing his utmost, at Albany and at Saratoga, to forward supplies.[146] The commissioners to Canada had reported from Montreal on the 6th of May that a supply of gold and silver coin for use in Canada was necessary and that the lack of it was responsible, along with "other arbitrary proceedings," for many of the difficulties the troops were encountering. The commissioners served notice: "If hard money cannot be procured and forwarded with dispatch to Canada, it would be advisable, in our opinion, to withdraw our Army and fortify the passes on the Lakes . . ." [147] By the 15th of May, the papers that passed through Washington's hands led him to conclude: "nothing less than the most wise and vigorous exertions of Congress and the Army there can promise success . . . in that quarter." Then he added, "What might have been effected last year without much difficulty has become an arduous and important work. However, I hope, all things will yet go well." [148]

It did not so befall. Two days after writing this letter, Washington received from Philip Schuyler a report that covered a tale of calamity.[149] Smallpox, paper money, poor transport and divided leadership had weakened the Americans hopelessly in the face of a strengthened

---

among them." He continued: "The distemper spread, and the soldiers inoculated themselves for their own safety, regardless of all orders to the contrary." There had been fear of the spread of smallpox in the Army around Boston because of refugees from the city, where the disease was known to exist (4 *G. W.*, 78, 154, 162; Harrison to Baldwin, Dec. 13, 1776; *Baldwin Papers*, Harvard Coll. Lib.); and a diarist later had mentioned a case as if its occurrence was in no sense unusual (see *David How's Diary*, 6), but no epidemic had occurred.

142 1 *LTW.*, 196.

143 Thompson to Washington, May 6, 1776; *Washington MSS*, Huntington Lib.

144 6 *Force* (4) p. 411–12.

145 Cf. 1 *Sullivan Papers*, 199; 5 *G. W.*, 54.

146 *Ibid.*, and Thompson to Washington, *supra*.

147 5 *Force* (4) p. 1214.

148 Letter to Philip Schuyler, May 15, 1776; 5 *G. W.*, 47.

149 Washington did not specify, in his acknowledgment of May 17 (*ibid.*, 52), the nature of the enclosures in Schuyler's communication of May 13, but that paper (6 *Force* (4) p. 449), referred, first, to the commissioners' letters, which manifestly were those of May 10 (*ibid.*, 449–51), and, second, to a dispatch of Arnold's which must have been that of the same date (*ibid.*, 452–53). In *Force*, along with these documents are the more essential underlying reports and correspondence. Receipt of "bad news from Quebec" seems to have been known by many officers. Cf. Loammi Baldwin to his wife, May 21, 1776 (*Baldwin Papers*, Harvard Coll. Lib.).

adversary. On the 6th of May, a British squadron of five vessels had reached Quebec, at the very time the British commander had intimation the Americans were about to abandon their perfunctory siege of the staunch city. Sir Guy Carleton had determined immediately to ascertain the truth of this report and, to that end, had moved out a battery of field artillery and a column of Foot. There followed an affair thus summarized in the American commissioners' letter to Schuyler, which was the paper Washington read: "The enemy made a sally . . . in a body supposed not to be less than a thousand: Our forces were so dispersed that not more than two hundred could be collected at headquarters. In this situation, a retreat was inevitable, and made in the utmost precipitation and confusion, with the loss of our cannon on the batteries, provisions, five hundred stands of small arms and a batteau load of powder . . ." About 200 sick men, too ill to be moved, were left to the mercy of the victors.[150] The rout of the Americans was halted by General Thomas at Deschambault, forty miles up the St. Lawrence from Quebec and slightly more than half way to Three Rivers,[151] but a council of war decided to withdraw what was left of the army to Sorel, on the south shore of the St. Lawrence and at the mouth of the Richelieu River.[152] To that strategic point, Benedict Arnold was to proceed in the dim hope that if the British force was found to be small, a return to Deschambault might be possible.[153]

In reporting this disaster, the commissioners of Congress wrote Schuyler: "A further reenforcement will only increase our distress. An immediate supply of provisions from over the Lakes is absolutely necessary for the preservation of the troops already in this Province [of Montreal], as we shall be obliged to evacuate all this country except [the district around Fort St. John].[154] No provisions can be drawn from Canada; the subsistence, therefore, of our Army will entirely depend on the supplies it can receive, and that immediately, from Ticonder-

[150] 6 Force (4) p. 449–50.

[151] A map will be found conveniently in 2 Justin Smith, Struggle, 311.

[152] See the map in Atlas of American History, Plate 67. Again it may be permissible to note that Americans frequently styled this river the Sorel. The most detailed narrative of the retreat is in Justin Smith, op. cit., v. 2, p. 320 ff.

[153] Commissioners in Canada to the President of Congress, May 10, 1776 (6 Force (4) p. 450).

[154] The original reads: "except that part of it already mentioned," (6 Force (4) p. 450), but in the preceding paragraph the commissioners said: ". . . it is very probable we shall lie under the necessity of abandoning Canada, at least all except that part which lies on the Sorel. We may certainly keep possession of St. Johns until the enemy can bring up against that post a superior force and an artillery to besiege it."

oga." [155] Thus implored, General Schuyler gave Washington such assurance as he could: ". . . I shall do everything in my power," he wrote, "to prevent the disaster a scarcity of provisions would occasion in Canada." Sullivan's advance and that of Thompson's column would be halted, Schuyler said. [156]

Washington had hoped that the besiegers of Quebec could remain in front of the city until the reenforcement of ten Regiments from his own Army arrived, [157] but he did not interpret the bad news to mean that the major effort of the British was certain to be directed southward from that stronghold. On the contrary, his office was at that very time preparing to draft orders for a continuing general alert in New York. [158] He had, in short, to face the possibility that the vital line of the Hudson might be assailed from the North and from the South; but he felt that the response to this should not be vain regret but active resolution. He wrote Schuyler at once: ". . . I am not without my fears, I confess, that the prospect we had of possessing [Canada], of so much importance in the present controversy, is almost over, or at least, that it will be effected with much more difficulty and effusion of blood than were necessary, had our exertions been timely applied. However, we must not despair. A manly and spirited opposition can only ensure success and prevent the enemy from improving the advantage they have obtained." Washington went on to say, in a single sentence, that he was forwarding the papers to Congress and would transmit such answers as that body made. Then he encouraged and exhorted Schuyler, and, in another letter, undertook to rally John Sullivan in the same way. [159]

All this was on the 17th of May. The next two days were scarcely less exciting. Washington received on the 18th from an escaped prisoner of war, George Merchant, [160] a number of papers, among which were copies of the treaties England had made in January and February for the employment of approximately 17,000 German troops. [161] These

---

155 6 *Force* (4) p. 450.

156 His language was: "I must of necessity comply with [the commissioners'] request of halting the troops . . ." *ibid.*, 449.

157 5 *G. W.*, 64.

158 GO of May 19, 1776; *ibid.*, 59–60, and, for the artillery, GO of May 20, 1776; *ibid.*, 62–63.

159 *Ibid.*, 52–53.   160 See *ibid.*, 57 n, *Clap's Diary*, 134.

161 Treaty of Jan. 9, 1776, with the Duke of Brunswick; that of Jan. 15, 1776, with the Landgrave of Hesse Cassel; and that of Feb. 5, 1776, with the Prince of Hesse Cassel, Count of Hanau. Text of all three is in 6 *Force* (4) p. 271–77.

soldiers manifestly were intended for use in America, precisely as had been rumored. To colonials, it appeared that Britain was guilty in this of an incredible offence, the hiring of mercenaries to subdue free-born men who had inherited all the rights their ancestors had wrung by like "rebellion" from earlier Kings. This action of Lord North's Ministry was enough to give momentum to the quickened demand for a final break with the mother country, and, so far as Washington's military problem was concerned, it meant also that the enemy with more troops, could strike heavier blows in more places—and speedily. George Merchant brought with him a letter, addressed to Dr. Franklin, that covered one written ostensibly to Lieutenant Governor Cadwallader Colden, a New York Royalist. This indicated that fifteen British Regiments probably were at sea in May or soon would be bound for America. The Germans, it was said, could not sail before April. "Upon the whole," the letter read, "the Ministry, if everything favors them, may have about 30,000 men in America by the latter end of June." [162]

Valuable and alarming as was this information, if true, it was accompanied by some embittered and partisan references. "From experience," ran one sentence in the covering letter to Franklin, "I can say (though without any connection or commerce with them) the New England men are fittest to be trusted in any dangerous or important enterprise." [163] Again, in the longer paper addressed to Colden, the writer said he could not trust two of the members of the secret committee, and by mentioning their places on the roster of five members, he made it plain that he referred to Benjamin Franklin and to John Jay. [164] Still another slur apparently was on Washington. The writer of the letter to Colden observed near the end of the communication: "A general of the first abilities and experience would go over if he could have any assurance from Congress of keeping his rank; but that being very high, he would not submit to have anyone but an American his superior, and that only in consideration of the confidence due to an American in a question so peculiarly American." Another letter of like purport, dated one day later [165] had as its final sentences: "A general of the first rank and abilities would go over, if the Congress would authorize anyone to

---

[162] Francis Wharton, *The Revolutionary Diplomatic Correspondence of the United States* (cited hereafter as *Wharton*), v. 2, p. 71 ff. The circumstances of the transmission of this correspondence to Washington are set forth in *ibid.*, 74 ff, n.
[163] *Ibid.*, 72.   [164] *Ibid.*
[165] The two were Feb. 13 and 14, 1776.

promise him a proper reception. This I had from Mr. Lee, agent for Massachusetts, but it must be secret with you, as I was not to mention it." [166]

There was, of course, no mystery about "Mr. Lee, agent for Massachusetts." He was Arthur Lee, London agent for Bay Colony and a younger brother of Washington's friend and long-time legislative colleague, Richard Henry Lee. In fact, it was not unreasonable for Washington to guess that Arthur was the man who addressed Colden and sent the information under cover to Franklin with a request that the Pennsylvania member of Congress forward the papers to "R. H. L." Did this mean that Arthur Lee and perhaps some of his friends thought it desirable to pass the real, if not the nominal command of the Army to a foreign soldier of "first abilities," with the plain implication that Washington's abilities were not of that order?

If Washington asked himself that question, he once more overcame his sensitiveness and pondered another: How should he communicate these documents, which were certain to create irritations? His first thought was to conform to the expressed wish of the anonymous writer and to forward all the papers to Richard Henry Lee, who might use his discretion in eliminating the offensive passages, but, on remembering that Franklin was in Canada, Washington decided to send "Poor Richard" the original of the letter addressed to that gentleman and to forward to Lee a copy of it, along with the other documents. Washington's only comment to Lee was, "I have no time to add the necessity of vigorous exertions; they are too obvious to need any stimulus from me." [167]

In order that Congress might act without loss of time and in full understanding of everything known at headquarters, Washington concluded that either he or the Adjutant General, Horatio Gates, should go at once to Philadelphia. On reflection, he did not feel that he should leave New York when there was a prospect the British fleet might descend on that city at any time; consequently he turned over to Gates the copies George Merchant had brought of the German treaties, and, in a communication to Hancock he let it be understood that Gates had

---

[166] 2 *Wharton*, 74, 78. See 1 *ibid.*, 391 ff for the evidence, which is almost conclusive, that this General was Count Charles Francis Broglie, brother of Victor François, Duc de Broglie and Marshal of France. Cf. André Lasseray, *Les Français sous les Treize Étoiles*, 19 ff., 573 ff.; Henri Doniol, *Histoire de la Participation de la France à l'établissement des États-Unis d'Amérique*, v. 1, p. 636.

[167] 5 *G. W.*, 57. For the letter to Franklin, May 20, see *ibid.*, 64–65.

the largest latitude to make suggestions. "His military experience and intimate acquaintance with the situation of our affairs," Washington told the President of Congress with reference to Gates, "will enable him to give Congress the fullest satisfaction about the measures necessary to be adopted at this alarming crisis, and with his zeal and attachment to the cause of America, have a claim to their notice and favors." [168] This was almost the language military etiquette prescribed for the introduction of an officer who carried "victory dispatches," and it proved language particularly suited to the occasion. On the evening of the day when Washington wrote this letter, there arrived from Philadelphia over Hancock's signature an invitation for Washington himself to visit that city for his health and for consultation with Congress.[169] Along with this came highly interesting army news: Horatio Gates had been promoted Major General, and Thomas Mifflin, Washington's former aide and at this time Quartermaster General had been made a Brigadier.[170]

This advancement of Gates had behind it an accumulation of good will gained by hard work, intelligently performed, and by assiduous correspondence with public men. "Pray continue to write me," John Adams had told him, "for a letter from you cures me of all anxiety and ill humor for two or three days at least, and besides that, leaves me better informed in many things, and confirmed in my good resolution, for my whole life." [171] In like appreciation, John Hancock, notifying Gates of his new honor, said formally that Congress had been led to act because of "the very great service you have performed for America, by introducing order and discipline into the Army of the United Colonies, as well as your zeal and ardor in the American cause." [172]

With this praise of his Adjutant General, Washington was heartily in accord. The one disturbing note was in a request from Hancock that

168 *Ibid.,* 58.

169 6 *Force* (4) p. 473. Reference to Washington's health has been construed to mean that he was suffering at this time from some illness of an alarming sort. If this is true, the instance is one in which no mention of a malady occurs in Washington's own correspondence. This was not usual with him. When ill, he normally mentioned it without hesitation and in complete avoidance of any impulse to play the rôle of the man of iron. Probability is, therefore, that Hancock spoke of Washington's "health" in the sense, which was wholly natural, that Washington was weary from ten months of constant attention to duty and was, for that reason, in need of relaxation and refreshment and, perhaps, of some review of the organization of his office in order that he might not be compelled to bear an excessive part of the load of army business. Washington's acknowledgment to Hancock simply was of thanks to Congress "for their kind attention to the means which they may think conducive to my health" (5 *G. W.,* 62).

170 1 *Burnett,* 449–50; 4 *JCC.,* 359. Although the letter that conveyed this information bore date of May 16, Washington noted (5 *G. W.,* 62) that he did not receive it till the night of the 19th.

171 1 *Burnett,* 433.   172 6 *Force* (4) p. 473.

both Gates and Mifflin be assigned to duty in Massachusetts,[173] where Washington did not believe there was material danger of a British landing. Thomas and Sullivan already had been detached; Charles Lee was in command of the Southern Department: it was too much to lose Gates as Adjutant General and to have him shelved on Beacon Hill.[174] Particularly was that true when Washington, at this very time, was receiving complaints from the back country of New England against Philip Schuyler, in whose patriotism and integrity he had confidence most absolute. In forwarding the New York commander copies of some "information" [175] that voiced distrust of Schuyler's ability and devotion, Washington wrote him indignantly: "From these [papers] you will readily discover the diabolical arts and schemes carrying on by the Tories and friends to government, to raise distrust, dissensions and divisions among us." He would ignore the charges, Washington went on, had he not been assured that they were widely circulated and that if he failed to mention them, Schuyler might think his silence due to belief that the tales were true.[176] It was ugly slander.[177] Troubles were multiplying in a command that contained few men of abilities and experience. There was no denying that!

Washington drew up careful instructions for General Putnam to press the fortification of the district around New York and to demand the utmost vigilance of the troops, and then, on the 21st of May, the Commander-in-Chief set out for Philadelphia.[178] He stopped at Perth Amboy on the 22nd to examine defensive positions there, as well as on Staten Island,[179] and the next day pressed on to Philadelphia,[180] where he

173 1 Burnett, 449–50.

174 Abigail Adams (Adams, Fam. Letters, 180) wrote her husband, May 27, of a rumor that Gates was coming to Boston with three Regiments. "I think," she said, "he is the man we want." See also Samuel Adams to Gates, June 10, 1776; 1 Burnett, 479. Announcement of Gates's promotion was made in GO of June 7 (5 G. W., 105).

175 Cf. 6 Force (4) p. 504, 582, and, as of June 7, ibid., 744–46.

176 Washington's words were: ". . . that you . . . would consider my suppressing them as an evidence of my belief, or at best of my doubts of the charges" (5 G. W., 66).

177 The general scope of the charges against Schuyler was outlined in 3 Sparks, 536. A long note on the subject in 4 Ford, 91–94 is merely a restatement of Sparks's observations.

178 5 G. W., 67 ff; Henry Knox, writing his brother William, May 23, 1776, wrongly gave the date of Washington's departure as May 22. (2 Knox Papers, 101; MHS)

179 5 G. W., 74.

180 C. Marshall's Diary, 73. Martha preceded her husband in order that she might undergo inoculation for smallpox (ibid., 4 G. W., 531; 5 G. W., 93), but Marshall was mistaken in saying that Martha reached Philadelphia on the 22nd. She arrived not later than the 18th, because May 31 was the thirteenth day of her inoculation (5 ibid., 93). Although John Hancock had invited the General and Mrs. Washington to stay at his residence while they were in Philadelphia, and to have Martha inoculated there (1 LTW., 205) Washington had been unwilling to subject a host to inconvenience and to possible risk. The location of the General's quarters in Philadelphia at this time has not been ascertained.

found a great diversity of business to be transacted [181] in an atmosphere of excitement over independence and of depression over the "most shocking and unaccountable misconduct"—to use Josiah Bartlett's words—"of the whole affair" in Canada.[182] John Hancock doubtless spoke for most of his colleagues when he wrote General Thomas: "Should our troops retire before the enemy, and entirely evacuate that Province, it is not in human wisdom to foretell the consequences. In this case, the loss of Canada will not be all; the whole frontiers of the New England and New York governments will be exposed not only to the ravages of the Indians, but also of the British forces, not less savage and barbarous in the prosecution of the present war." [183] When the Commissioners prepared their report, four days after Washington dismounted in Philadelphia, they listed a score of circumstances any one of which was enough to humiliate the continent: "General Wooster is, in our opinion unfit, totally unfit, to command your Army . . . His stay in this Colony is unnecessary and even prejudicial to our affairs; we would therefore humbly advise his recall . . . Your army is badly paid; and so exhausted is your credit that even a cart cannot be procured without ready money or force . . . Your army in Canada do not exceed 4000; above 400 are sick with different disorders; three-fourths of the Army have not had the smallpox . . . We cannot conceal our concern that 6000 men should be ordered to Canada, without taking care to have magazines formed for their subsistence, cash to pay them, or to pay the inhabitants for their labor in transporting the baggage, stores and provisions of the Army. We cannot find words to describe our miserable situation . . ." [184] Washington listened to what Congressmen said, and he told himself that America must expect a "bloody summer" for which she was not prepared; [185] but as a soldier he always had fought with poor equipment, and with adversity as his daily companion, and he could not believe the situation in Canada beyond re-

---

[181] 5 G. W., 85.

[182] Bartlett, in Philadelphia, to John Langdon, May 19, 1776; 6 Force (4) p. 1021.

[183] Letter of May 24, 1776; 1 Burnett, 463. Almost simultaneously—and unknown as yet to members of Congress—some of the men close to the scene of calamity in Canada were appalled by what they saw. At the mouth of the Richelieu (Sorel) River, Charles Carroll was writing: "We found the discipline of the camp very remiss, and everything in confusion . . ." (1 Rowland, Carroll, 395). John Sullivan soon was to echo the words: "everything is in the utmost confusion and almost everyone frightened at they know not what." (Letter of June 1, 1776, from St. John's, to John Hancock; 1 Sullivan Papers, 212.)

[184] 6 Force (4) p. 589–90. Benjamin Franklin had left the other Commissioners by this date, May 27. The signers consequently were Samuel Chase and Charles Carroll of Carrollton.

[185] 5 G. W., 93.

demption by courage and effort. Thomas must take post as far down the St. Lawrence as possible in the direction of Quebec: "This misfortune must be repaired, if possible," he said, "by our more vigorous exertions . . ." [186] The force in Canada must be augmented, but not at the expense of the Army that was to defend New York against the almost certain attack of the most powerful British force.[187] That was the major premise of his recommendations to Congress.

Discussions began immediately after Washington's arrival in Philadelphia. On the 24th and the 25th he appeared in person before Congress to answer the inquiries of members,[188] an experience in strange contrast to his previous quiet participation in the deliberations of that assembly. When this proved an awkward arrangement, he, Gates and Mifflin held long and frequent conferences with a committee of twelve, named for that purpose.[189] The findings of this committee were based largely on Washington's advice and, though they were modified slightly by Congress,[190] they conformed to his views of the extent to which military requirements could be squared with the limited resources of the Colonies. The broad conclusion was to contest "every foot of ground" [191] occupied by the Americans in Canada and to do the utmost to hold a position below the mouth of the Richelieu (Sorel) River. Entry of the British into the upper country of the United Colonies was to be prevented by American operations on the St. Lawrence; efforts were to be made to prevail on the Indians to attack Niagara and Detroit; New York and the mouth of the Hudson were of course to be defended. To deal with an adversary so well disciplined and equipped, a two-to-one superiority of force was desired and was to be had, substantially, by enlisting until Dec. 1, 1776, a total of approximately 20,000 militia, who were to be apportioned among the Colonies from New Jersey northward.[192] Indians not exceeding 2000 were to be hired in Canada.[193] In addition, the Middle Colonies of Delaware, Pennsylvania and Maryland were to provide until December, 1776, a total of 10,000 militia who were to constitute a "Flying Camp," [194] which was to

---

186 Letter of May 24, 1776, to John Thomas; *ibid.*, 79.
187 *Ibid.*, 96.   188 4 *JCC.*, 389, 391.
189 *Ibid.*, 391, 399.   190 *Ibid.*, 399–401; 412–13.
191 *Ibid.*, 388.   192 *Ibid.*, 399–401, 412–13.
193 *Ibid.*, 412.
194 Strictly speaking, a Flying Camp or Camp Volant was a small army of Horse and Foot that was supposed to be continuously in motion and without fixed station. Actually, as the term was used by Washington and his contemporaries, it was a synonym for the modern "mobile reserve."

be under "such continental general officers as the Commander-in-Chief shall direct." [195] All this was agreed upon readily. If any Delegate questioned whether the Colonies would supply 30,000 militia, and whether it would be safe to enlist these men for so brief a term as that to December 1, no echo of doubt found its way into the letters of members.[196] Washington himself believed short-term enlistment responsible for much of the woe of the Army in Canada and he urged on Congress the grant of a bounty to men already in the Army who would enlist for a term of years or for the "continuance of the war." Apparently he did not advocate a call on the Colonies for militia to serve beyond Dec. 31, 1776, because he must have reasoned that any such proposal would defeat its own ends. He found Congress not yet willing to vote the bounty or provide for the enlargement of the "regular establishment"—the Continental Line—on the basis of two or three years' service. Reliance still was on the militia for emergencies. Washington acquiesced.[197]

While this discussion of "survive or perish," recruit or hang, necessarily called for Washington's full participation, the other subject of talk at every table—whether and when the Colonies should declare their independence—was one with which he scarcely had patience. Some members of Congress still maintained that Peace Commissioners were coming to America and that reconciliation still was possible. This angered Washington. He wrote his brother: ". . . things have come to that pass now as to convince us that we have nothing more to expect from the justice of Great Britain; also, that she is capable of the most delusive arts, for I am satisfied that no Commissioners ever were designed, except Hessians and other foreigners, and that the idea was only to deceive and throw us off our guard . . . for no man that entertains a hope of seeing this dispute speedily and equitably adjusted by Commissioners will go to the same expense and run the same hazards to prepare for the worst event as he who believes that we must conquer or submit to unconditional terms and its concomitants, such as confiscation, hangings, &c., &c." [198]

[195] 5 JCC., 418.
[196] That is to say, into letters that have been preserved, though there is no reason to assume that lost letters contained any challenge of short-term enlistments, which were taken as a matter of course at this time.   [197] 5 G. W., 112.
[198] Ibid., 92. Correspondence from February, 1776, onward, is studded with references to the prospect of an early declaration of independence. A ready guide to many of these is presented in Burnett. The entries in 6 Force (4), index heading "Independence," are equally informative and perhaps more representative.

Washington found this the view of virtually all those members of Congress with whom he had been on closest terms during the months he had belonged to the Virginia delegation. On the 10th of May, Congress had passed a resolution in which it "was recommended to the respective assemblies and conventions of the United Colonies, where no government sufficient to the exigencies of their affairs have been hitherto established, to adopt such government as shall, in the opinion of the representatives of the people, best conduce to the happiness and safety of their constituents in particular, and America in general." [199] To this resolution a preamble was added on the 15th in terms that approached a full renunciation of any oath of allegiance to Great Britain.[200] The effect of all this on the minds of some doubters was that of burning the bridges behind them. Having gone so far, they felt they now might as well go all the way.[201] Most of New England was known to be impatient over the long delay.[202] As the end of May approached, Virginia and North Carolina were believed to be ready for action.[203] It was understood that the Middle Colonies and some of those in the South would be the last to assent,[204] but there was a disposition to wait for a few weeks in the belief that unanimity might be achieved. Soon, it seemed, an answer was to be made to the wrathful warning of Charles Lee: "If you do not declare immediately for positive independence, we are all ruined. There is a poorness of spirit and languor in the late proceedings of Congress that I confess frightens me so much that at times I regret having embarked my all, fortune, life and reputation, in their bottom." [205]

Washington, having no regrets and no new argument, presented an example of complete resolution. His immediate task was to counsel regarding the means by which the evil day in Canada could be redeemed, and his, too, was the duty of advising quietly on the choice of men to take the place of Gates as Adjutant General and of Mifflin as Quartermaster General. One proposal of his concerning these offices was a surprise. Although Joseph Reed had left Cambridge Headquarters as long previously as Oct. 29, 1775,[206] Washington had not

<hr/>

[199] 4 JCC., 342.

[200] Ibid., 358; John Adams to his wife, May 17, 1776; 6 Force (4) p. 488.

[201] 1 Burnett, 429, 445, 453, 460; 3 Samuel Adams, 281.

[202] Cf. 1 Burnett, 438.   [203] Ibid., 438, 467, 468.   [204] Ibid., 460, 467.

[205] 2 Lee Papers 20; 6 Force (4) p. 407. Charles Lee had written this May 10 and had added: "I sometimes wish I had settled in some country of slaves, where the most lenient master governs."

[206] See Washington to Reed, Oct. 30, 1775; 1 Reed, 125.

ceased to miss him and, indeed, had found nobody to fill completely the place Reed had occupied. Stephen Moylan and William Palfrey had been accepted formally as aides early in March, 1776;[207] Robert H. Harrison, who still was growing in usefulness though not yet wholly adequate, was made official Secretary to the Commander-in-Chief on May 16. Washington then had to announce in general orders that Reed's "private concerns will not permit him to continue in that office."[208] Now it was possible to offer Reed the post of Adjutant General and to invoke the aid of some members of Congress in prevailing on him to accept. Reed's lack of precise knowledge of the Adjutant's functions and duties did not weigh decisively, in Washington's mind, when set against the quick perception and social skill of the Philadelphian. Washington had voiced one particular need of Reed's special qualities of suavity and accommodation when he had written in April of the division among the Colonies over independence. He had said: "These are the shelves we have to avoid, or our bark will split and tumble to pieces. Here lies our danger, and I almost tremble when I think of this rock. Nothing but disunion can hurt our cause. This will ruin it, if great prudence, temper and moderation is not mixed in our counsels and made the governing principles of the contending parties."

Then Washington had asked, half-anxiously: "When, my good sir, will you be with me? I fear I shall have a difficult card to play in this government [of New York] and could wish for your assistance and advice to manage it."[209]

That was both confession and tribute: Divided New York called for the finesse Reed could display. Washington had been showing the greatest deference for the sensitive feelings of New York, but he wanted to have at his command the diplomatic address and diversified knowledge of men and of law that Reed possessed. With some difficulty, he prevailed.[210] Washington did not see, of course, the letter Reed wrote his wife and consequently the General did not know all the considerations that lay behind the decision of the new Adjutant General. Reed told his lady the "appointments of the office" were equivalent to £700 a year, "which will help to support us till these calamitous times are at an end." Then he went on: "Besides, this post is honorable, and if the

---

[207] 4 *G. W.*, 369. The exact date of the announcement in GO was March 6.
[208] 5 *ibid.*, 50.
[209] Letter of Apr. 15, 1776; 4 *ibid.*, 482–83.
[210] 1 *Reed*, 190–91.

issue is favorable to America, must put me on a respectable scale. Should it be otherwise, I have done enough to expose myself to ruin." [211]

For Mifflin's successor as Quartermaster General, Washington turned to another member of his military "family," his recently appointed aide Stephen Moylan, 39 years of age, who previously had been Mustermaster General. Moylan was an Irish Catholic who had come to Philadelphia in 1768 and had won for himself a seat at the best tables. He had energy and a ready tongue and at the moment he gave promise of as good an administration as could be expected where almost everything a Quartermaster sought was crude and costly or unprocurable. [212]

Throughout these protracted consultations with Congress, Washington had felt heightened concern for the safety of New York. Five days after his arrival in Philadelphia he had directed General Putnam to inform him at the earliest possible moment of the arrival or approach of the enemy's fleet. Horses were to be procured and kept ready at the different stopping-places on the road, [213] so that Washington and his staff could return to New York, as he phrased it, "with the utmost expedition." [214] Thanks to hidden circumstances, no weary express knocked at Washington's door with the anticipated news from North River. All imperative business in Philadelphia could be concluded unhurriedly and in comparative calm. On the 3rd of June, John Hancock, who temporarily was crippled by gout, expressed to Washington the thanks of Congress for "unremitted attention" to his trust and especially for assistance in making plans for the defence of the Colonies. The General was free, Hancock wrote, to return to headquarters when he saw fit. [215] Washington waited only to get copies of the various resolves of Congress that concerned his duties, and then, leaving Martha in the Quaker City on the 4th, [216] he was off for New York, where he arrived at 1 P.M. on the 6th. [217]

---

[211] *Ibid.*, 190. There is conflict of evidence involving one or perhaps two days in the chronology of the offer to Reed and of his acceptance, but it is not important.

[212] Washington's responsibility for Moylan's election by Congress is not established by the record. The election, in fact, did not occur until June 5 (see 4 *JCC.*, 419), after Washington had left Philadelphia, but it is certain that Congress would not have named a member of Washington's staff to this position otherwise than at the General's instance or with his approval. Perhaps, also, Washington may have advised Congress regarding the election of his friend, Dr. Hugh Mercer, as one of the new Brigadiers. This seems the more likely because of Congress' specific vote to have Mercer repair immediately to New York headquarters (*ibid.*, 420, 424; 6 *Force* (4) p. 723).

[213] Washington used the then-familiar phrase "necessary stages on the road."

[214] Letter of June 28, 1776; 5 *G. W.*, 87–88.   [215] 1 *Burnett*, 471–72.

[216] 1 *LTW.*, 221.   [217] 5 *G. W.*, 103.

Good news and bad awaited him. It was good because all was quiet and because visible progress had been made on the defences; [218] it was bad in that letters from Canada gave alarming if vague [219] details of a new defeat at a place styled The Cedars, about thirty miles up the St. Lawrence from Montreal.[220] So little about the engagement was set forth explicitly in Schuyler's dispatches [221] and in a letter from Capt. James Wilkinson to General Greene [222] that it was impossible to determine precisely what had happened,[223] but the desperate tone of Wilkinson led Washington to fear that the next intelligence would be of the loss of Montreal.[224] From other sources, Washington heard that General Thomas had the smallpox [225] and, on the 8th, he had the shocking announcement that the vigorous New Englander was dead.[226] Deeply distressed, Washington, as always, was rallied by disaster to firmer resolution. He reiterated to Schuyler what he had said to more than one correspondent: "The most vigorous exertions will be necessary to retrieve our circumstances there, and I hope you will strain every nerve for that purpose. Unless it can be done now, Canada will be lost forever, the fatal consequences of which everyone must feel." [227] Without a day's delay he began, too, to urge the muster of militia in New York to meet the quota set during the conferences in Philadelphia.[228]

Thomas's death would have meant normally that Brig. Gen. David Wooster, as senior officer of that rank in Canada, would have assumed temporary command; but on the very day that Washington learned that Thomas had succumbed to smallpox, notice was received from Hancock that Congress had ordered on the 6th that Wooster "be directed immediately to repair to headquarters at New York" [229]—in short, that Wooster had been relieved of command. Next in rank to

[218] *Ibid.*, 103–04. For the beginning of the fortification of Powles Hook, see Loammi Baldwin to his wife, May 25, 1776; *Baldwin Papers*, Harvard Coll. Lib.

[219] Cf. Baldwin to his wife, *loc. cit.*, May 30, 1776: "Bad news from Quebec. We have had no particular account from there that we can depend on, which seems strange to me."

[220] The location is described in 2 *Justin Smith, Struggle*, 365, and is included on Faden's map reproduced on small scale in *ibid.*, 359.

[221] These are not mentioned by date in Washington's acknowledgment (5 *G. W.*, 101–02), but as Schuyler was at Fort George on the 3rd and there answered Putnam's letter of June 1, (see 6 *Force* (4) p. 692), Schuyler's dispatch of that date may have been one of those to which Washington referred.

[222] *Ibid.*, 741.   [223] 5 *G. W.*, 108.

[224] *Ibid.*, 102.   [225] *Ibid.*, 102.

[226] *Heath*, 55; 5 *G. W.*, 136. Death came June 2 after an attack so violent that Thomas was blinded. *MHSP.*, 1903–04, p. 431; 1 *LTW.*, 211.

[227] 5 *G. W.*, 102.

[228] *Ibid.*, 103. On the 10th of June he made a similar appeal to Connecticut (*ibid.*, 123).

[229] 5 *JCC.*, 421; 6 *Force* (4) p. 740.

him in Canada stood John Sullivan. As the New Hampshire Brigadier and all the other general officers had been studied carefully by Washington during the siege of Boston, this estimate of Sullivan now was ready: "I think it my duty to observe, as of my own knowledge, that he is active, spirited and zealously attached to the cause; that he does not want abilities, many members of Congress, as well as myself can testify. But he has his wants, and he has his foibles. The latter are manifested in a little tincture of vanity and in an overdesire of being popular, which now and then leads him into some embarassments. His wants are common to us all; the want of experience to move upon a large scale; for the contracted knowledge which any of us have in military matters stands in very little stead, and is greatly overbalanced by sound judgment and some knowledge of men and books; especially when accompanied by an enterprising genius, which I must do General Sullivan the justice to say, I think he possesses but as the security of Canada is of the last importance to the well being of these Colonies, I should like to know the sentiments of Congress, respecting the nomination of any officer to that command." The main consideration, Washington said in complete candor, was whether Sullivan merited the command or not.[230]

While Congress deliberated on that, and the lookouts on Staten Island strained their eyes for a mass of white sails on the horizon, Charles Carroll and Samuel Chase, two of the three Canadian Commissioners of Congress, reached New York and reported to Washington at Montier's.[231] They probably added little to what Washington knew already about the bewildered plight of quartermasters and commissaries whose transport had collapsed;[232] but they touched with red and with black many details that had been obscure. The particular individual object of the wrath of the Commissioners was General Wooster, who soon would be on his way to New York. "I wish to know what I am to do with him," Washington asked Congress, "when he comes."[233]

Supplies for Canada had to be hurried up the Hudson whenever the south wind permitted; the fortification of New York was continued, that of Powles Hook on the Jersey side of North River was pressed,[234] and the task of guarding the New York highlands was entrusted to

---

[230] 5 *G. W.*, 152–53.
[232] 5 *G. W.*, 119, 120.
[233] Letter of June 9, 1776; *ibid.*, 114.
[234] June 19, 1776. See *ibid.*, 158–59.

[231] 1 *Rowland, Carroll*, 399.

Col. James Clinton.[235] Discipline was enforced with even more vigor than previously;[236] four "able bodied, active men" of each Company of Foot were added to the Artillery Regiment in order that all the defences might be served.[237] These and kindred tasks were discharged in an atmosphere of expectancy that contrasted strangely with the social life of the town. On his return from Philadelphia, Washington had received the formal thanks of the Provincial Congress of New York and the assurance of its support, which he acknowledged in a few words,[238] and later he, his Generals and staff and the commanding officers of the Regiments were the guests of the Congress at "an elegant entertainment" in Fraunces's Tavern[239]—an occasion of much jollity, marred only by the sudden sickness of General Putnam, who was compelled to leave the table before the dinner was over.[240] Officers light-heartedly applauded "Little Phil" of Washington's Guard, as he sang a "new campaign song," but then and thereafter, hour by hour, their suspense was heightened.

As early as June 10, Governor Tryon was credited with saying that a frigate from Halifax had brought news of the embarkation of Howe's army for New York.[241] In the camps, it was predicted confidently that the enemy would attack within ten days.[242] Washington felt that this information originated with Loyalists who were reporting all American activities to the *Asia* or to the ships off Sandy Hook and were supplying them with fresh provisions. When he had gone to Philadelphia he had been hopeful that the New York authorities would continue the activity they then were displaying[243] and would arrest the men most apt to aid the King. Orders had been given at that time for the con-

---

[235] *Ibid.*, 138. The feebleness of defences there is described in some detail in Henry Livingston to Robert Livingston, May 29, 1776; *Livingston Papers*, 177, NYPL. For an excellent sketch of this region, prepared under the supervision of Col. Herman Beukema of West Point, see *Atlas of American History*, Plate 73.

[236] See the daily GO of June 8 and after, 5 *G. W.*, 106 ff.

[237] June 14, 1776; *ibid.*, 134. The march of Knox's artillery to New York had necessarily been slow but had been completed without accident. For his views on the reenforcement and opportunities of the artillery arm, see his letter of July 1 to William Knox and his report of July 9, 1776; 2 *Knox Papers*, 141, 149; MHS.

[238] June 8–9, 1776; 6 *Force* (4) p. 1386.

[239] Incidentally, the name is spelled Frances's in the formal invitation preserved in the *Baldwin Papers*, Army Letters, 41, Harvard Coll. Lib.

[240] Letter of Capt. Caleb Gibbs, Washington's Guard; 1 *Moore*, 114.

[241] 5 *G. W.*, 121.

[242] *Clap's Diary*, 135; entry of June 13. Washington himself believed the Tories of New York looked for the arrival of the British fleet at any hour (5 *G. W.*, 121).

[243] Loammi Baldwin wrote his wife, May 15, 1776, *loc. cit.*: "The City Committee have been disarming the Tories. Some have been confined but we meet with little difficulty with them at present."

tinental forces to render New York officials all the assistance the officers
of the law might require. On his return, Washington had been compelled to write the President of Congress regarding the attitude of the
provincial leaders: ". . . the subject is delicate, and nothing is done in
it: we may therefore have internal as well as external enemies to contend with." [244] Now a vigorous policy again was pursued by the New
York patriots; a general search for disaffected persons was begun.[245]

During the first stages of this hunt for Tories who did not resist and
for traitors who evaded the fowler, Washington had no concern over
the prospective vote on independence. He doubtless was informed
promptly that Congress had decided on the 10th of June to postpone
further discussion of the issue for three weeks in the hope that the
Delegates of the most hesitant Colonies would receive by that time
authority to vote for separation from England.[246] Concerning this, John
Adams was both reporter and prophet when he wrote: ". . . Objects of
the most stupendous magnitude, and measures in which the lives and
liberties of millions yet unborn are intimately interested, are now before
us. We are in the midst of a revolution, the most complete, unexpected
and remarkable, of any in the history of nations." [247]

Even if nothing of consequence was to come from Philadelphia before
the 1st of July, news might be expected at any time from Canada, news
so grim that Washington almost dreaded its arrival.[248] When the first
additional budget reached him in the form of two dispatches from John
Sullivan,[249] he felt distinct relief. Sullivan wrote from Sorel and described enthusiastically what he pronounced a "strange turn" in the
American cause. "The Canadians," he said, "are flocking by hundreds
to take a part with us." He had ordered General Thompson with 2000
troops to proceed to Three Rivers and, if that officer did not find the
enemy greatly superior in numbers, to attack and to open the way, as
Sullivan put it, "for our recovering that ground which former troops
have so shamefully lost." [250] This was precisely what Washington had
been advocating—a renewal of the offensive and the reestablishment of

---

[244] Letter of June 10, 1776; 5 G. W., 122.

[245] 6 Force (4) p. 1152, 1183; 5 G. W., 122–23.

[246] A committee of five was meantime to draft a declaration (5 JCC., 428–29, 431; 1
Burnett, 484–85; 1 Jefferson, 18 ff).

[247] Letter of June 9, 1776, to William Cushing, quoted in 1 Burnett, 478, from 9 John
Adams, 391.

[248] 5 G. W., 148.

[249] June 5 and 6, 1776; 1 Sullivan Papers, 217.

[250] Ibid., 219–22.

the American front as far as possible in the direction of Quebec.[251] He consequently approved Sullivan's plan with heartiness and, at the same time, with cautious understanding of the difficulties that had to be overcome. Washington wrote the commander in Canada: "The farther down we can take and maintain posts, the greater will our possession of the country be; observing at the same time the necessity of having a safe retreat left, if you should be obliged to abandon them by a superior force . . . It will be of material consequence, in your advances down the country, to secure the several important posts as you go; at which you may, in case you should be obliged to decline the main object you have in view, make a vigorous and successful stand in your retreat." [252]

There was quite enough in different strain to avoid the creation in Sullivan's mind of an impression that he was expected to fail, but the undertone was different from that of previous weeks and was pitched by experience: not since the occupation of Montreal had the Americans gained a victory in Canada. Washington in no wise renounced the plan to win the province for the United Colonies but he was more anxiously conscious now of the lateness of the hour and the increasing power of the British.

He perceived, too, from the content of the dispatches, that the ambitions of Sullivan had been stirred, and he read confirmation of this in a private letter the New Hampshire Brigadier forwarded.[253] This contained an appeal that Washington or Charles Lee come to Canada and assume command, and then this sentence: "Though I suppose General Lee cannot be spared where he is, I am well persuaded that Canada would be ours from the moment of your Excellency's arrival; but in case neither of you can come to take the command, I beg that if any other officer is sent to take it, that I may have leave to return, as I am well convinced that the same disorder and confusion which has almost ruined our army here would again take place and complete its destruction, which I do not wish to see." In short, Sullivan manifestly was "aiming at the command in Canada." [254] Washington accordingly decided to transmit the letter to John Hancock and, after presenting as

251 Washington, it will be remembered, previously had named Deschambault, twenty miles down stream from Three Rivers, as a proper advanced position.

252 5 G. W., 149–50.

253 This letter of June 7 probably was sent with those dated June 5 and 6. Such a construction seemed to be justified by the opening sentences of the communication of the 7th, (1 Sullivan Papers, 226) but positive proof is lacking.

254 5 G. W., 152.

fair a sketch as he could of the character of Sullivan,[255] to say nothing to influence the decision of Congress whether the New Hampshire General should be placed at the head of the little Army in Canada.[256]

All embarrassment was escaped by prompt action in Philadelphia. The very day Washington's letter to the President was written, Congress decided to vest in Horatio Gates the Canadian command and to direct Washington to expedite the departure of the new Major General, who was given both the authority to fill vacancies and the temporary power to suspend officers.[257] Whether Gates would be acceptable to Sullivan, it was impossible for Washington to say.[258] Nor was it certain that Gates would go there in the most cooperative state of mind. He had coveted the highly honorific command at Boston for his friend Thomas Mifflin and in his confidential letters to his New England friends, he was becoming critical of Washington. As Gates wrote Samuel Adams, the Commander-in-Chief declined to send Mifflin to Boston on the ground that the British did not intend to return to that city. Gates commented: ". . . to say where the enemy will not come is too mighty for my judgment." He had argued in opposition, also, on the perennial question of the enemy's willingness to negotiate. "If," he said with reference to some previous discussion of the subject; "the Dutch thought it was necessary to send Field Deputies [259] to assist, or as was said, to watch the Duke of Marlborough, surely when the freedom of this continent is at stake we can't have too much wisdom nor too many arms employed to save it." [260]

Washington probably knew nothing of this correspondence, but he doubtless felt that he had good fortune in avoiding a disagreeable encounter with General Wooster, who arrived in New York on the 17th of June.[261] No high officer of the Army was held in such low opinion by most of those whose opinion was of value. Some had wished to seize him as a Tory,[262] because they thought his do-nothing policy and his contempt for standard disciplinary methods were a contribution to the King's cause.[263] Perhaps Wooster's singularity had been illustrated

---

255 This is the sketch quoted *supra*, p. 109.   256 5 *G. W.*, 152–53.
257 5 *JCC.*, 448; 1 *LTW.*, 225.   258 5 *G. W.*, 153.
259 This word is obscure in the original.
260 Letter of June 8, 1776; *Samuel Adams Papers*, NYPL.
261 *Heath*, 56.   262 5 *G. W.*, 114.
263 Cf. Schuyler to Robert R. Livingston, May 12, 1776: "General Thomas will have a disagreeable task to introduce order into an army many of whom have been spoiled by the indulgence given them by Wooster. I wish he had been ordered from Canada long ago" (*Livingston Papers*, 175; NYPL).

in a story circulated during the previous September. It was said that
when a strumpet had been brought into the Camp by one of the men
and had been caught, Wooster had ordered her stripped to the waist
and tarred and feathered, and then he had directed that she be placed on
a cart and be driven about while the offending soldier was made to hug
and kiss her.[264] The doubtful truth of this tale scarcely was as important as the fact that it was repeated and apparently was credited.

Washington had felt for months that Wooster would give no help to
the other commanders, but whether this had been from perversity or
necessity, Washington had not attempted to say.[265] When Wooster
arrived, the Commander-in-Chief had received from Congress no
answer to his inquiry concerning what he should do with the Connecticut officer, but he heard with some satisfaction that Wooster desired to go home for a visit; so, in renewing his question about the
employment of the veteran, Washington told Congress of the General's
wish.[266] Again patience paid its practitioner. Wooster announced that
he wished to proceed to Philadelphia and to talk with Congressmen
before going home. Gladly and promptly Washington assented.[267]

Thus stood matters—the situation in Canada apparently somewhat
less desperate, the defences of New York and of the Hudson rising, the
arrival of Howe's fleet daily expected—when on the afternoon of
June 21, Washington received from a committee of the Provincial Congress a letter for which he was not unprepared: David Matthews, Mayor
of New York, was "charged with dangerous designs and treasonable
conspiracies against the rights and liberties of the United Colonies of
America"; Washington was authorized and requested to apprehend
and secure the Mayor and all his papers. Without hesitation, Washington immediately ordered General Greene to have the warrant
executed the next morning precisely at 1 o'clock.[268]

[264] *Anon. New York Journal*, Sept. 27, 1775, MS., LC.
[265] Cf. 4 *G. W.*, 278.   [266] 5 *ibid.*, 153.
[267] *Ibid.*, 160.   [268] 6 *Force* (4) p. 1158.

CHAPTER V

FLAGS FLY, NEWS COMES, A KING FALLS
(June 22–July 9, 1776)

DAVID MATTHEWS had been listed a few weeks previously by the Provincial Congress of New York as one of those whom the people were "naturally led to consider . . . as their enemies" because of failure to aid the American cause,[1] but no action had been taken against him prior to June 15, when the committee of that body was organized "for the hearing and trying disaffected persons and those of equivocal characters." [2] On the 17th, a man named Isaac Ketcham, who was confined in jail for complicity in an attempt at counterfeiting, informed the Provincial Congress that he believed two fellow prisoners, continental soldiers, Thomas Hickey and Michael Lynch, belonged to some "corps" that was receiving money from the British fleet. These culprits and persons who came to see them in prison talked of cutting down King's Bridge and of going over to the enemy when the British fleet came.[3] The Provincial Congress listened in some alarm to Ketcham and, after a meeting between Washington and one of its spokesmen that day, named a committee of three to confer with the General.[4]

As a result of this or of other circumstances, John Jay and Gouverneur Morris, of the special secret committee, examined William Leary who had come to town from Orange County on the 17th in search of a runaway servant of Erskine's Bigwood Ironworks. Leary readily found the absconder but lost him at the Powles Hook Ferry to a Sergeant who immediately enlisted the man in Captain Roosevelt's Company. While waiting at the ferry, Leary chanced upon one James Mason, who previously had been in the employ of the operator of the ironworks but had been discharged. Mason, after an exchange of greetings, asked if Leary would like to see certain men known to both of them. Leary, being of inquisitive mind, was agreeable to this, but

---

[1] Proceedings N. Y. Provincial Congress, June 5, 1776; 6 Force (4) p. 1368–69.
[2] Ibid., 1152.   [3] Ibid., 1411.   [4] Ibid., 1412.

Mason said that before visiting these acquaintances, Leary must swear that he had not come to apprehend them. Leary refused to make oath but repeated that he wished to meet the men and he pretended that he, too, was a runaway. After a bit more of cautious fencing, Mason confided that he and several companions had sworn to quit New York and to go on board a British man-of-war. Until they could be carried out safely to the ship, they were receiving wages and provisions, he said, from a man who represented the Mayor of the city or the Governor of the Colony. Leary then went with Mason to visit their friends, and later he made an attempt to lure them to one of the American camps, but they became suspicious of him and scattered. The substance of Leary's testimony to the committee thus was that enlistment for service aboard a British ship was in progress and that the Mayor or the Governor was alleged to be paying the costs.[5] Leary believed the money came from Mayor Matthews but he was not certain.

Thanks to the information supplied by Leary, who probably was used further,[6] the secret committee found and arrested Mason. He, in turn, told how a man called William Forbes had informed him that Governor Tryon would pay five guineas and make a liberal land grant to any man who would enlist in His Majesty's service. These recruits were not to go aboard ship, Mason explained, because the vessels were crowded and food was scarce. All who enlisted for the King were to remain on shore where they "could do more good." Later, Mason said, he had been "qualified" by a gunsmith, Gilbert Forbes, who promised him ten shillings a week for subsistence, and paid him, first and last, twenty-six shillings, eight pence. On one occasion, Mason testified, this man Gilbert Forbes had said he would go to the Mayor's and get £100, which he must have. Mason professed, indeed, to have been with Forbes when that individual called at a fine house which Forbes told him was that of a brother of the Mayor's.

In the course of this examination, Mason gave the names of various men alleged to be connected in one way or another with recruiting for the King. A former schoolmaster from the vicinity of Goshen in Orange County—Mason knew him only as "Clarke"—was alleged to have boasted that he had prevailed upon sixty men to join. Mason went on to say that he believed "one Hickey of the General's Guards" was

[5] *Ibid.*, 1154–55.
[6] The Provincial Congress paid him £3, 6s. See *ibid.*, 1428.

involved, and he was certain a drummer of the same command, Greene by name, also was concerned in the affair, because he had seen Greene in conversation with Gilbert Forbes. Besides, Greene was the man who had administered the oath to Hickey and to some others of Washington's Guards—among them a fellow named Barnes and one called Johnson, a fifer.[7]

It was on the basis of the testimony of Mason and of Leary that the committee asked Washington to take David Matthews into custody and to seize his papers. Matthews surrendered without resistance when arrested at his residence in Flatbush, but no incriminating written evidence was found there.[8] Gilbert Forbes, the gunsmith, "a short, thick man who wears a white coat," was not unknown, because his shop was on Broadway, opposite Hull's Tavern. He was apprehended on the night of David Matthews's arrest and was taken before the committee of the Provincial Congress, but he was unwilling to say anything. The next morning, a young minister, Robert Livingston, visited him and sympathetically exhorted him to tell the truth as he probably had only a few days of life.[9] This stirred Forbes either to clear his conscience or to try to save his neck. With no more ado he offered to go before the committee and to confess everything.[10] The net thereupon was carefully and widely spread. Those of the suspects who belonged to Washington's Guard apparently had no warning of danger until they were confronted with the bayonets of the Provost Marshal's men. William Forbes, too, was found and was locked up.[11]

On the 23rd, David Matthews was examined before Philip Livingston, John Jay and Gouverneur Morris. The Mayor stated with apparent candor that in May he had gone aboard the *Duchess of Gordon,* by permission of General Putnam, to arrange passage to Bermuda for Lord Drummond, a self-appointed peace commissioner who had been ineptly active in the Middle Colonies. As he was about to leave the vessel, Matthews said, Governor Tryon put a bundle of· paper money into his hand and told him to give £5 to the prisoners in the jail and to pay the balance to Gilbert Forbes for some rifles and

---

[7] *Ibid.,* 1155–57.

[8] Nathanael Greene's statement of June 22, 1776; *ibid.,* 1158.

[9] *Ibid.,* 1054; *Penn. Journal,* June 26; *Penn. Gazette,* July 3, 1776.

[10] Some contemporary accounts state that Forbes appeared before the Provincial Congress, but that body was not in session on the 22nd or the 23rd. He must have presented himself to the committee.

[11] 6 *Force* (4) p. 1166.

smooth-bore guns Forbes had made for the Governor. Forbes was to be told, also, that the Governor did not want any more rifles. Matthews said he had hesitated to take the money and had hesitated still more to deliver it to Forbes but at length had done so. After that, the Mayor testified, numbers of men had come to him to enlist or to get aboard the King's ships, but he had given no help or encouragement to any of them and had told all of them to go home and keep quiet. During this time of reluctant association, Forbes had broached to the Mayor a scheme for taking one of the New York batteries when the fleet arrived, and he had disclosed another plan to cut down King's Bridge. Matthews asserted that he sent word to Forbes to abandon these ideas.[12] The Mayor had received no additional funds from Governor Tryon, he said, and he had no knowledge, other than that he had related, concerning communication with the fleet or enlistment for the King. There were some denials and partial contradictions of Matthews's testimony [13] but no positive evidence of any service by him to the royalist cause except that of his confessed payment of money to Forbes.

Along with many other Americans, Washington believed that Matthews was guilty [14] and that the conspiracy originated with Governor Tryon, but, of course, he concerned himself first with the allegation that soldiers of his Army, of his own Headquarters Guard, even, had been charged with crimes that ranged from threats of desertion to treasonable communication with the enemy. The men who had been plotting together apparently had considered little that was definite, but they, too, had talked vaguely of destroying King's Bridge to cut off reenforcements and also of seizing a battery when the fleet attacked. More elaborate designs were sketched by a retired Sergeant of Royal Artillery, who told how New York was to be captured.[15] If any officers of rank reviewed the details of what the Sergeant had to say, they were apt to be impressed by it and perhaps were puzzled to know how he acquired familiarity with so sound a plan of campaign. However that

---

[12] *Ibid.,* 1164–66.

[13] Particularly that of William Forbes (*ibid.,* 1166) and that of George Brewerton (*ibid.,* 1174–75).

[14] 5 *G. W.,* 193.

[15] 6 *Force* (4) p. 1178. This Sergeant Graham, may have been the "man without an arm" whom James Mason believed "to be an old pensioner" (*ibid.,* 1156). Graham's schemes were not of record until Gilbert Forbes testified before the New York Committee on June 29 (*ibid.,* 1177), but as Forbes was examined informally before that date, there is every reason to assume that Washington had been acquainted with substantially everything that Gilbert Forbes subsequently affirmed on the stand.

might be explained, there manifestly was disaffection and perhaps conspiracy in the American Army and it must be dealt with immediately. Drummer William Greene of the General's Guard, though among those most criminally involved, was willing to confess and to throw himself on the mercy of the court; Forbes, too, would turn on his fellow-conspirators. The most obdurate suspect was a man Isaac Ketcham had mentioned, namely, Thomas Hickey, one of two continental soldiers jailed for an alleged attempt to pass a counterfeit bill of credit.[16] Hickey was believed to be a former deserter from the royal army who had resided in Wethersfield, Connecticut, for a number of years. After his arrest for trafficking in bad money, he and his companion, Michael Lynch, were said by one witness to have sworn they never would fight any more for America. Later, when they heard of the discovery of the plot of enlistment, they had expressed relief that their signatures would not be found on the list of those who had agreed to go to the British men-of-war.[17] Hickey and Lynch had boasted, moreover, that almost 700 men had promised to stand by the King,[18] and the two culprits confided to other inmates of the jail that the American Army had become damnably corrupted, that the fleet was soon to arrive, and that a band was to turn against the Americans then. Eight of the General's Guard, Hickey had said, were participants in the plan.[19]

In these circumstances, it seemed best to make an example of Hickey. He was arraigned before a courtmartial on the 26th, when Greene, Gilbert Forbes and other witnesses adhered to their previous statements, though Greene said all he could to extenuate Hickey's offence. The evidence demonstrated that Hickey had signed the list of those who would help the King when the fleet came, that he had received half a dollar, and that he had undertaken to induce one William Welch to join other "old countrymen" in making their peace before the British came. In his own behalf, Hickey produced no witnesses and said only that he had engaged in the plan at first to cheat the Tories and to get some money from them, and that he later had consented to have his name forwarded to the ship in order that he might be safe in event

16 Cf. 6 Force (4) p. 1406, 1410. In addition to a known effort to make fraudulent paper money in New York, there was some testimony that counterfeit notes were being printed on one of the vessels of the Royal Navy blockading the city. See ibid., p. 1177.
17 Testimony of Israel Youngs, June 26, 1776; 6 Force (4) p. 1178.
18 Ibid.
19 Courtmartial testimony of Isaac Ketcham, June 26, 1776; ibid., 1085–86.

the British came, defeated the American Army and made him prisoner. It was a pathetically feeble defence.

The verdict was immediate and unanimous, death by hanging,[20] a sentence which Washington confirmed the next day and put in execution a little before noon, June 28. Almost 20,000 gathered to see the man swing to his death. He was said to have declined the services of chaplains on the ground all of them were cut-throats, but, it was reported, he had wept at the last and then, wiping away the tears in wrath, had warned that "unless Greene was very cautious, the design would as yet be executed on him." [21] According to gossip, Hickey confessed, also, that dealing with lewd women had been the beginning of his downfall, an observation Washington duly incorporated in general orders for the admonition of his men.[22] The day after Hickey was executed, Gilbert Forbes was examined by the committee of the New York Provincial Congress. He rounded out some of the evidence and added without abashment that the nine rifles he sold Governor Tryon and sent aboard the warship were "bad and would not shoot straight." [23] As far as the records show, neither Forbes nor any of the others was punished, though Greene had been more active in the conspiracy than Hickey was. As for Mayor Matthews, he was held in jail and was allowed to communicate with outsiders on order of the Provincial Council only and then in the presence of a designated person.[24]

At headquarters, the feeling doubtless persisted that Mayor Matthews and Governor Tryon were behind the conspiracy, for conspiracy it was believed to be, however awkward in design and clumsy in execution. Even if the scheme had no larger aim than the difficult one of seizing a battery and of trying to destroy King's Bridge, the Americans took it seriously. Joseph Reed, who was close to the details, thought at the

---

[20] The specific accusation was that of "exciting and joining in a mutiny and sedition, and of treacherously corresponding with, enlisting among and receiving pay from the enemies of the United American Colonies," in violation of "the fifth and thirtieth articles of the rules and regulations for the government of the Continental Forces." The minutes of the courtmartial, with abstracts of the testimony, are in *ibid.*, 1084–86.

[21] In the original version of this, a letter of Surgeon William Eustis, June 28, 1776, 23 *NEH & GR.*, 208, quoted in Godfrey, *The Commander-in-Chief's Guard*, 29 ff, the name is "General Greene," which may be correct if Hickey was speaking of the "design" of campaign mentioned by Graham; but in view of the fact that William Greene, the comrade and fellow-conspirator of Hickey, was one of the witnesses against him, it seems possible that Hickey's last remark should be addressed to him, not to "General Greene."

[22] 5 *G. W.*, 195. See *ibid.*, 182, 193, and 6 *Force* (4) p. 1119–20 for the final warrant and certificate of execution. In the Diary of Caleb Clap, who was much interested in the case, it was stated (p. 136), that Hickey said little but "left something in writing."

[23] 6 *Force* (4) p. 1178–79.   [24] Cf. *ibid.*, 1440.

outset that the plan extended to the destruction of the magazine and artillery and a rising of the Tories when the fleet came.[25] This was not enough for the gullible, the imaginative and the rumor-mongers. They had it that the conspiracy had been known for more than a fortnight.[26] Washington was to be assassinated,[27] stabbed, in fact, by Drummer Greene;[28] the other general officers were to have the same bloody end; the arrival of the fleet was to be the signal for the uprising unless earlier opportunity challenged;[29] the cannon were to be turned on the troops;[30] the town was to be set afire in nine places; 200 Tories already were under arms in woods and swamps not far from the city;[31] and so to endless absurdities.

Washington believed some of the Tories capable of almost any crime to defeat the American cause, but he knew, of course, that rumor had far outlied the most mendacious witness and, in reporting the circumstances to Congress, he said of Hickey's execution, "I am hopeful this example will produce many salutary consequences and deter others from entering into like traitorous practices."[32] That was written with characteristic restraint and at a time when events more serious, by far, than a scotched conspiracy, called for Washington's attention.

On the day Matthews and several of the other suspects had been arrested, June 22, an express from General Schuyler had reached Washington with news that contradicted all the high hopes voiced in the letters last received from John Sullivan. In accordance with orders, Brig. Gen. William Thompson had proceeded to Three Rivers on the St. Lawrence, had attacked the British there, and had sustained a reverse on the 8th of June. Thrown back into woods and mire where, as one of his officers wrote, "nature perhaps never formed a place better calculated for the destruction of an army,"[33] Thompson and a consid-

[25] 1 *Reed*, 192. Loammi Baldwin to his wife, June 22, 24, 1776; *Baldwin Papers*, Harvard Coll. Lib.

[26] Bedinger's Journal, *op. cit.*, 144; Curtenius to unnamed correspondent, June 22, 1776; Misc. MSS, PHS.

[27] *Solomon Nash's Diary*, 21.

[28] Solomon Drowne to his sister, June 24, 1776, *Tomlinson Papers*, NYPL, partly quoted in Dawson, *New York City*, 76.

[29] 1 *Webb*, 148.

[30] *Clap's Diary*, 135, 136.

[31] Drowne's letter, *loc. cit.*; cf. 5 *G. W.*, 194. For the later, familiar and entirely groundless traditions that an inn-waiter, William Collier, uncovered the plot, and that "Mrs. Fraunces" or "Young Peggy Fraunces," or some other "housekeeper" pretended to conspire with Hickey to poison Washington, see B. J. Lossing, *Life of Washington*, v. 2, p. 177; summarized in 2 *Hughes*, 397.

[32] Letter of June 28, 1776; 5 *G. W.*, 193.

[33] Col. William Irvine, 6 *His. Mag.* (1862), p. 116, quoted in 2 *Justin Smith, Struggle*, 414.

erable number of his officers and men surrendered.[34] The remainder
of the original force of approximately 2000 counted themselves lucky
in getting back to Sorel,[35] which it now was manifest the Americans
could not hold. By the evening of the 23rd,[36] Washington had dispatches which indicated that the only question in dispute among the
officers immediately responsible for operations in Canada was that of
the depth of their withdrawal. They had to quit the province: how far
South should they retreat before attempting to make a stand with a
force that smallpox and flux had afflicted and almost had destroyed?[37]
Some of those who should have best judgment on the issue thought the
Army should not attempt to hold a position North of Crown Point, 150
miles South of Sorel.[38] Arnold, meantime, on the night of June 15 had
evacuated Montreal with his force of 300 and had proceeded to Ile aux
Noix, where he arrived on the 18th.[39] As reunited at that point, the
American forces numbered approximately 7000 men, about half of
whom, according to Arnold's estimate, were sick and unfit for duty,
though many were recovering.[40]

Washington was profoundly alarmed by this reverse and, in particular, by the distressed spirit of the men, which was manifest from
the first news of Thompson's defeat.[41] Gen. John Burgoyne apparently
had reached Canada with a considerable force to strengthen Sir Guy
Carleton; the Americans were outnumbered, if not outgeneraled, and
had no alternative to retreat; Canada was lost; Sullivan would be
fortunate if he could escape and, with Schuyler's help, fortify and hold
the passes of the Northern New York Lakes and prevent incursions.

[34] The number was not known as late as June 19, 1776, when Sullivan estimated the total
loss as "about 150." See 1 *Sullivan Papers*, 250. Actually, the British listed 236 prisoners and
counted "upwards of fifty" dead in the woods. Justin Smith concluded that casualties were "not
under 400." British losses were less than twenty (2 *Justin Smith, Struggle*, 416, 598).

[35] It will be understood that few of these details were given in the first dispatches to Washington. Emotional excitement, as well as confusion, prevailed at the headquarters of Sullivan.
In a dispatch of June 12 to Schuyler he wrote: "I now think only of a glorious death or a
victory obtained against superior numbers" (1 *Sullivan Papers*, 234).

[36] 5 *G. W.*, 170–71.

[37] 1 *LTW.*, 231, 233, 237, 239: 1 *Sullivan Papers*, 232, 237–38, 261 ff; 6 *Force* (4)
p. 975–76. Cf. *Adams, Fam. Let.*, 189, June 26, 1776: "The smallpox is ten times more terrible
than Britons, Canadians and Indians together."

[38] Ile aux Noix, where Sullivan halted until nearly the end of June, was sixty-five miles
South of Sorel. His hesitation to go farther southward was due to his belief that he was not
authorized to do so, unless he had new orders from Washington or from Schuyler. See
Sullivan to Schuyler, June 19, 1776; 1 *Sullivan Papers*, 253; Schuyler to Washington, June 25,
1776; 1 *LTW.*, 240.

[39] Letter to Washington, June 25, 1776; *ibid.*, 237.

[40] *Ibid.*, 239.

[41] 5 *G. W.*, 167.

Such were Washington's conclusions.[42] In the face of them, there was no comfort and small prospect of gain in the receipt of a resolution of Congress that directed him to investigate the conduct of officers in Canada and to bring before courtmartial those accused of specified military offences, even though the individuals had resigned from the service.[43]

Horatio Gates had, of course, to proceed northward at once and take command [44] of the troops under the discouraged but still ambitious Sullivan.[45] No detailed orders, covering anything beyond administrative matters, could be given the new Major General. Washington at the end of his letter could say no more than this: "The distance of the scene, and the frequent changes which have happened in the state of our affairs in Canada do not allow me to be more particular in my instructions. The command is important, the service difficult but honorable; and I most devoutly pray that Providence may crown your arms with abundant success." [46]

Left to devise his own plans with the resources that could be assigned him, Gates could hope to accomplish little unless there was early attainment of the goal set in Congress' resolution of June 25 that "the number of men destined for the Northern Department be augmented to 4000." [47] To provide reenforcement, Congress at length had heeded Washington's plea for a bounty and had offered ten dollars to every Sergeant, Corporal and private soldier who would enlist for three years—the first real hope Congress yet had held out of escape from the recurring danger of such a crisis as Washington had faced during December, 1775.[48] Washington himself had not asked long-term enlistments early in the war, because he had hoped that a single campaign would bring a settlement, and when the organization of two Battalions of Marines had been proposed, he had reported the feeling of officers that "it will be impossible to get the men to enlist for the continuance of the war"; [49] but his

[42] *Ibid.*, 167, 170 ff, 183, 189.

[43] Hancock to Washington, June 21, 1776; 1 *LTW.*, 227–28; 5 *JCC.*, 472.

[44] He left New York June 25. See 5 *G. W.*, 168, 172, 173, 194.

[45] For Sullivan's state of mind, see his letters of June 8–24, in 1 *Sullivan Papers*, 226–264, and particularly 234, 241 and 257.

[46] June 24, 1776; 5 *G. W.*, 175.

[47] Two new continental Regiments were to be raised. Massachusettts, Connecticut and New Hampshire among them, were asked to supply four Regiments of their militia for the Northern Department (5 *JCC.*, 471, 479).

[48] *Ibid.*, 483; June 26, 1776.

[49] Letter of Nov. 28, 1775, quoted in Bernhard Knollenberg, *Washington and the Revolution*, 125. The full text will be found in 4 *G. W.*, 121.

experience after that time had confirmed all he had learned in Virginia during the struggle with the French and Indians: Brief service hobbled an Army [50] and might ruin a cause.

Gates, therefore, had to do what he could in reorganizing the broken forces that had survived the campaign and he had to see, further, how soon and in what numbers the bounty would bring men to his camp. Washington, for his part, had to face the high probability that soon the British would be hammering at both ends of the waterline and portages that linked the St. Lawrence with Sandy Hook. If Burgoyne already had begun the ascent of the Richelieu, it could not be long before Howe would be pointing the bows of his ships up the Hudson. While giving all possible assistance to Gates's expedition, Washington had to struggle hourly with the supreme vexation of command, that of trying to achieve quickly and securely what ignorant men with rude implements and feeble equipment were apt to do slowly, awkwardly, and in slovenly style. Actually, the troops around New York were in good spirits,[51] but, as always, emergency seemed greater to the General than to the soldier with the shovel. If the officer cried, "Today," the man in the ranks answered, "Tomorrow." Washington had, also, to entrust some of this work to officers of little experience—to Joseph Reed in the place of Gates and to new, if competent aides, Samuel Webb and Richard Cary.[52] Fortunately, brigade and regimental organization now was familiar with its duties and was able to take some of the detail off the hands of the commanding General.

So much had to be done! The establishment of a Troop of Light Horse [53] had to be approved and encouraged; [54] fortification had to be

[50] For a review of the subject, see Knollenberg, *op. cit.*, 122–128.

[51] 1 *Reed*, 191.

[52] Richard Cary was from Peartree, in Warwick Co., Virginia, and was approximately of the age of his distant kinswoman, Sally Cary Fairfax. For these appointments and that of Alexander Contee Hanson as assistant secretary to Washington, see 5 *G. W.*, 165, GO of June 21, 1776; 1 *Reed*, 191; 1 *Webb*, 148. Reed wrote, June 21: "The office I am in has not much severe duty, but it is so entirely out of my line that I do not feel myself so easy with it as one of a different kind. Perhaps a little time will reconcile me better to it" (*loc. cit.*). Reed's office was moved, June 25, "to a small brick house, one of the offices belonging to headquarters" (5 *G. W.*, 176).

[53] These mounted troops derived their odd name from the fact that when first established they were distinguished from men at arms in that they wore no armor. In most European armies, and in that of England, a few commands still wore ornamental armor and had usually the designation of Guards. Dragoons at this period were defined as mounted musketeers. In theory, a Regiment of Light Horse consisted of six Troops, with a Colonel, Lieutenant Colonel, Major and the usual company officers. The subalterns were termed cornets, but the word "Subaltern" was itself changing in application and was being applied to n.c.o's as well as to the lowest rank of commissioned officers who often were "gentlemen volunteers" hopeful of winning a lieutenancy.   [54] 5 *G. W.*, 163.

pressed;[55] obstructions were placed in North River to discourage a naval commander who might feel confident he could pass the batteries;[56] arrangement had to be made for the prompt summons of the militia from other Colonies, when the fleet hove in sight, and for the service of these contingents with troops from their own native soil;[57] the New York Legislature was asked to remove the cattle from all coastal areas where the enemy was apt to make incursion;[58] greater vigilance in the patrol of nearby waters was ordered to prevent communication between ship and shore;[59] additional arms, though distressingly few in number, were sought from captured stores in Boston;[60] snarls in the negotiations of Schuyler with the Indians had to be untangled.[61] In nearly all the defensive measures there was, of course, a degree of danger that something would go amiss, and even more danger that the best use of the frail resources of the Colonies would not suffice to balk the British. Washington had under his command scarcely more than 10,000 Foot, because the militia then in camp did not exceed 1000.[62] Of this total force, those present and able to perform duty were reported to be about 7400. Knox had something less than 400 fit artillerists; a young New York Captain, Alexander Hamilton by name, had a provincial Company of 93 gunners.[63] The Army's greatest need continued to be that of small arms.[64] Fortunately, sufficient powder was available,[65] though Washington still enjoined unyielding economy[66] and lamented the capture by the British near New York of a vessel from France laden with twelve tons of explosive and 500 small arms.[67] Almost the only advantage of the troops was in their

[55] *Ibid.*, 165, and in almost daily references of one form and another in GO.

[56] These obstructions are described briefly in *Heath*, 57. It will be remembered that Charles Lee did not think the Americans could close to the British so wide and deep a watercourse as North River, though he believed that if an attacking fleet in the stream were challenged vigorously by the batteries, it would not be able "to annoy dangerously . . . , much less to destroy" New York (4 *JCC.*, 202 and *supra*, p. 87).

[57] 5 *G. W.*, 176, 186.   [58] *Ibid.*, 187.

[59] *Ibid.*, 179.   [60] *Ibid.*, 179.

[61] *Ibid.*, 184, 185–86; 1 *LTW.*, 235. Numerous earlier references will be found in 5 *G. W.*, and in 6 *Force* (4).

[62] 5 *G. W.*, 190, 194.

[63] All these figures are of June 28, 1776. Details are given in 6 *Force* (4) p. 1119–20. A convenient tabulation of returns of Washington's Army, July 19, 1775 to Dec. 22, 1776, will be found in 3 *Sparks*, 493.

[64] 5 *G. W.*, 179. As late as June 14, Washington had reported that he had some troops without arms (*ibid.*, 136).

[65] 1 *Reed*, 192.   [66] 5 *G. W.*, 50.

[67] 1 *Webb*, 142. For the vicissitudes in the importation, manufacture and supply of powder for the continental forces in April–June, 1776, see 4 *G. W.*, 471–72; 5 *ibid.*, 4, 16, 85; 1 *Lee Papers*, 388; 1 *Ballagh, Lee Letters*, 188, 192; 1 *Burnett*, 459. These references do

food. "Few armies, if any," Washington was able to affirm, "have been better and more plentifully supplied . . ." [68]

In these activities, Washington passed the first anniversary of his arrival in New York and of his start through Connecticut on the way to Cambridge. The 28th of June, 1776, for instance, was twelve months from the day on which he had reached New Haven as he hurried toward the town the improvised and undisciplined New England army was besieging. Since that date he had . . . but there was no time for reminiscence, because information that appeared to be positive and indisputable was laid before the busy General at headquarters. It was intelligence of a sort that would have prompted a nervous commander to order the tocsin from every steeple in New York: General Howe had left Halifax for New York on the 9th of June with 130 sail. It even was reported that his flagship already was at Sandy Hook.[69] The probability of the truth of these reports was so great that Washington at once called on the authorities of Massachusetts and Connecticut to "lose not a moment's time in sending forward the militia of your province as the enemy will undoubtedly attack us in our weak state as soon as a sufficient force arrives to enable them to attempt it with the least probability of success . . ." [70] This was the supreme concern of the Commander-in-Chief, but in the minds of most of the 20,000 who went out to the field between Spencer's and Lord Stirling's camps to witness the hanging of Thomas Hickey that day, the nearer interest may have been the greater.

The night of the 28th–29th passed quietly, except where men sat and talked of every detail of the execution of Hickey. About 9 o'clock the

---

not include any of the false reports, less numerous than in earlier months, of the capture of large consignments of powder. There scarcely could have been a stronger evidence of the changed situation of the army, as respects powder, than the order Washington soon was to issue Ward to send to Norwich, for storage in event an emergency developed, "from three to four hundred barrels" (July 7, 1776; 5 G. W., 231). Not many months previously the difference between 300 and 400 barrels might have meant all the difference between a reluctant defensive and an attack on Boston.

[68] 5 G. W., 192. This was a propos of a move in Congress to change the commissary arrangements in the Colony of New York.

[69] Ibid., 187; 1 Webb, 150. The information concerning Howe's reported departure from Halifax was supplied by Lieut. Joseph Davison, armed sloop Schuyler, who had it from a prisoner taken on a recovered prize vessel. See Davison to Washington, June 27, 1776; 6 Force (4) p. 1111. On the 7th of June, Howe had written Lord Germaine from Halifax: "I have suffered the most sensible mortification by being so long detained at this place; but the late arrivals of the provision ships and the repairing of those included in the number requisite for transporting the troops . . . have made an earlier removal impracticable. The troops, however, are at length embarked, waiting only for favorable weather to proceed to Sandy Hook" (ibid., p. 728).

[70] 5 G. W., 187–88.

next morning, Saturday, June 29, as officers looked through the Narrows to the high ground on Staten Island, where three tall flag-staffs rose, they saw with their glasses what they long had been looking for, a changing glint of color. The flags were up—the agreed signal that the British fleet was in sight.[71] An humble observer saw and wrote: "I was upstairs in an outhouse and spied as I peeped out the Bay something resembling a wood of pine trees trimmed. I declare, at my noticing this, that I could not believe my eyes, but keeping my eyes fixed at the very spot, judge you of my surprise when in about ten minutes, the whole Bay was full of shipping as ever it could be. I declare that I thought all London was afloat." [72] It was true. By the time Washington sat down to write a dispatch to the President of Congress, forty-five ships had come in; [73] when an express arrived from the lower bay about 2 P.M., he reported that almost 100 rigged vessels had arrived and had anchored in the Hook.[74] Washington speeded additional messengers to inform the Colonies of his need of militia; [75] he called a council to review plans for defence; [76] and he wrote briefly and grimly to Hancock without any attempt at literary finish or rhetorical flourish: "I am hopeful before [the British] are prepared to attack that I shall get some reenforcements, but be that as it may, I shall attempt to make the best disposition I can for our troops, in order to give them a proper reception, and to prevent the ruin and destruction they are meditating against us." [77] There was no blinking the desperate nature of the task ahead of him and no disposition to ignore the possibility that the enemy's men-of-war might slip past the batteries on the shores of the North River and might pass upstream to a junction with Burgoyne. "Make all possible preparation" was Washington's word to Col. James

---

[71] 1 Webb, 150–51. Webb stated specifically that this was on Staten Island, where the principal signal was located. Incidentally, Henry Knox wrote his brother William that Sandy Hook was "in sight about twenty-four miles distant" (Letter of July 1, 1776; 2 Knox Papers, 141, MHS). Unfortunately for precise narration, it is impossible to state how many flags were flying, one under the other, on the middle flag staff at Staten Island. It will be remembered that the agreed signals were, two flags in event the British ships or their boats, were moving toward Amboy, and three flags if the objective was New York. See 4 G. W., 524 n.

[72] McCurtin's Journal, 40. McCurtin added: "Just about five minutes before I see this sight, I got my discharge"—to the loss of history and to the distress of all those who afterward read his crude but most informative diary.

[73] 5 G. W., 203.

[74] 1 Webb, 150–51; Heath, 57. The fleet had sighted land near Sandy Hook at 6 A.M. and had anchored "behind the Hook" by 3 P.M. (A. Robertson's Diaries, 85–86).

[75] 1 Webb, 151.

[76] Heath, 57.

[77] 5 G. W., 200.

Clinton who was in charge of the forts being erected in the Highlands to command the Hudson.[78]

Preparation at New York was hampered by the shortage of senior officers. Now that Thomas had died and Gates had followed Charles Lee away from headquarters that still were the Colonies' one military training school, Washington had a single Major General at New York, "Old Put." All the Brigadiers were occupied. Before Hugh Mercer, the new Virginia officer of that rank, could reach New York, he had to stop on the way and assist in the defence of Jersey.[79] Washington also was encumbered by a mass of "paper work" he could not pass on readily to the inexperienced men who had joined his small staff.[80] As always, he sought by hard effort to remedy the unescapable defects of immature organization, and day after day he undertook in general orders to make ready, in state of mind as in physical defences, for the coming ordeal of fire. The principal object of most of these orders was a dual one—to complete the fortifications and to prevent surprise attack.[81]

The American force at Washington's command was being increased slowly, and some days scarcely at all, by the militia for whom Washington continued to call anxiously and urgently.[82] All gain seemed to be doubtful and temporary. There was, for example, earnest correspondence and manifest lack of understanding about Connecticut light horse militia. Washington wanted the men and wished to encourage the organization of mounted troops but he did not think he could provide in New York for the mounts.[83] Next, an old problem was applied to different troops: The term of the rifle Companies was expiring; few of these men were willing to reenlist.[84] Then, as the militia of Massa-

---

[78] *Ibid.*, 201.

[79] *Ibid.*, 210. Mercer arrived July 3. See 1 *Webb*, 152, and see, also, 5 *G. W.*, 240, for Washington's refusal to send Mercer to Rhode Island, where a competent general officer was sought by Governor Cooke.

[80] He had, for example, at this difficult time, to handle troublesome questions connected with naval prizes. See 5 *G. W.*, 233.

[81] For his orders concerning work on the defences, see *ibid.*, 208, 213, 229. The orders for vigilance and proper care of small arms appear in *ibid.*, 197, 209, 211, 214, 230. See *ibid.*, 197 for the provisioning of outposts, and *ibid.*, 215, for the removal of cattle from Staten Island.

[82] *Ibid.*, 199, 214, 234. Joseph Reed was more optimistic than his chief. On the 1st of July, Reed wrote his wife: "Troops are coming in fast, and if they defer an attack any time, we shall have a number sufficient to cope with them" (1 *Reed*, 194). Henry Knox, too, was not alarmed. He predicted to his brother July 1: "If [Howe] comes up like a man and brings his ships to before our batteries, there must the finest fight ensue that ever was seen. We shall be able in that case to bring a great number of cannon and mortars to bear on the ships at once . . ." (2 *Knox Papers*, 141; MHS).

[83] 5 *G. W.*, 228, 238, 242.

[84] 5 *G. W.*, 216.

chusetts seemed loath to assemble and to start a march for the relief of
New York, Washington had to arrange, after vexing negotiation, for
the transfer to the lower Hudson of three of the five Regiments of
continental troops he had left in the Bay Colony.[85] Before a date for
the start of these "regulars" could even be set, Washington had to make
subtraction from the New Jersey militia who had been arriving in
appreciable number.[86] All except 500 of them had to be sent back in
order that they might defend Bergen Neck and nearby territory, where
the fortifications were feeble and poorly constructed.[87] The exposed
situation in Jersey made Washington all the more anxious to see Congress organize the Flying Camp of 10,000 that had been authorized
June 3.[88]

In dealing with these matters, Washington did not have the boon
of concentrated thought to the exclusion of everything else. He had to
get Martha started homeward, because New York under hourly threat
of bombardment and attack manifestly was no place for her,[89] and he
had as much vexation and anxiety as he would permit himself concerning developments in Northern New York. Sullivan had overcome his
doubts concerning his right to retire farther southward without specific
orders and, on July 1, he reached Crown Point with all his troops except
600 whom he had left to assist the armed vessels on Lake Champlain.[90]
He was somewhat apologetic to Washington for having to make so
many decisions on his own account;[91] but he was in better spirits and
manifestly felt as strongly as ever the stirring of ambition to command.[92]

[85] This first was proposed to Washington by Joseph Hawley (see 1 *LTW.*, 229–31). The
principal correspondence regarding the transfer is included or mentioned in 5 *G. W.*, 203, 219,
231, 242.

[86] 1 *Webb*, 152.

[87] For the works, see *A. Robertson's Diaries*, 88. The return of the militia and the organization of the defence are described in Mercer to William Livingston, July 3, 1776; *Emmet Col.*,
8263, NYPL; 5 *G. W.*, 217, 224, 226; 37 *ibid.*, 527. An interesting letter of William Franklin
on conditions in Jersey at this time is that of June 23, 1776 to "the Council and Assembly of
New Jersey," MS, HE 11: 14½ NJHS. Cols.

[88] See *supra*, p. 103 and 4 *JCC.*, 412–13. Washington's appeal for action appears in 5 *G. W.*,
214, 219. He thought the force should be established near Amboy, the present Perth Amboy,
opposite the southern end of Staten Island.

[89] She had recovered completely from inoculation and had returned to New York from
Philadelphia, probably during the week of June 16 (Hancock to Washington, June 11, 1776;
1 *LTW.*, 222). If Heath was correct in his chronology—and he was not always so—she left
New York for Virginia on the 30th of June (*Heath*, 58; 1 *Reed*, 194). "Jack" Custis and his
wife had gone home soon after May 13, when Washington took the young man's receipt for
£250 to be delivered to Lund Washington (26 *Papers of G. W.*, 83, LC). Mrs. Nathanael
Greene created some talk by returning to New York when the wives of other officers were
leaving (Henry Knox to Mrs. Knox, July 8, 1776; 2 *Knox Papers*, 146, MHS).

[90] 1 *Sullivan Papers*, 271 ff.   [91] *Ibid.*, 277.

[92] Cf. *ibid.*, 272.

Within a few days Sullivan learned that Gates had been sent North to take charge of operations, and he blazed instantly with resentment and humiliation. He asked Schuyler to permit him to leave the department, with the intimation that he would resign.[93] Schuyler, smoothing him down, gave permission for him to go to see Washington;[94] but Schuyler himself was engaged already in controversy with Gates over their respective authority. Schuyler maintained that Gates had no control of the Northern troops except in Canada; Gates contended that he had command of the little army wherever it was.[95] Both men displayed candor and good temper,[96] but neither yielded anything to the other. Washington read with regret of their clash and referred it to Congress with a request for a prompt decision. He said: ". . . although I do not presume to advise in a matter now of this delicacy, yet as it appears evident that the Northern Army has retreated to Crown Point and mean to act upon the defensive only, I cannot help giving it as my opinion that one of the Major Generals in that quarter would be more usefully employed here, or in the Flying Camp than there . . ."[97] His moderation and realism were not welcome to partisans of the rivals. With singular venom Joseph Trumbull wrote Gates: "Your authority at an end, commanded by a person who will be willing to have you knocked in the head as General Montgomery was, if he can have the money chest go in his power, I expect to see you soon and your lieutenants back here again . . ."[98] With this situation, Washington might have to deal in time. At the moment, when there was a veritable palisade of British masts down the harbor, Washington felt he could leave the dispute to the gentlemen in Philadelphia. Additional New Jersey and Connecticut levies were beginning to arrive now[99] and would strengthen somewhat the weak forces at the mouth of the Hudson. They would help, but their presence most certainly did not make possible any further detachment of troops to aid Gates. One thing on which Washington was most insistent, he put in clear and simple

[93] *Ibid.*, 281; 30 *Papers of G. W.*, 8, LC.
[94] 1 *Sullivan Papers*, 281–82.
[95] Schuyler to Washington, July 1, 1776; 1 *LTW.*, 247 ff.
[96] *Ibid.*, 250–51.
[97] 5 *G. W.*, 223. In further emphasis upon the scarcity of trained leaders, Washington added: "If another experienced officer is taken from here in order to command the Flying Camp . . . your Grand Army will be entirely stripped of Generals who have seen service, being in a manner already destitute of such."
[98] This seems to be the sense of a passage punctuated in a baffling manner; Joseph Trumbull to Gates, July 5, 1776; *Gates Papers*, NYHS.
[99] July 8; 5 *G. W.*, 236.

words: "The situation of the Northern Army is certainly distressing, but no relief can be afforded by me . . ." [100]

A few days earlier Washington might, indeed, have asked for the return of some of his Regiments from Lake Champlain because the movements of the British fleet had indicated that Howe was about to attack one part or another of the district around the city of New York. On the 1st of July many vessels raised sail, came closer to the Narrows and anchored off Gravesend, Long Island,[101] whereupon Washington sent 500 men to strengthen the small force which was stationed there under Nathanael Greene.[102] The next day some of the British men-of-war were within 700 or 800 yards of Long Island; before nightfall approximately fifty-five vessels had maneuvered close to Staten Island and had anchored there.[103]

By this time, Washington believed that the entire fleet from Halifax was off New York, and he began to wonder if Howe intended to surround the city [104] where daily the troops now were at their alarm posts before dawn.[105] A heavy British landing on Staten Island, July 3, deepened concern for a day; [106] but when the enemy began throwing up works there, July 5, Washington concluded that his adversaries had no more serious immediate design than to make themselves masters of the island, which was known as a stronghold of Tory feeling.[107] Deserters' reports [108] and other information suggested that the British might be planning an advance in Jersey simultaneously with an attack on New York by another column, which would have the support of the fleet. This operation, it was thought, the British would not undertake prior to an event for which they were known to be waiting with much eagerness—the arrival of Gen. William Howe's brother, Richard, Admiral Viscount Howe, newly appointed to the command of the North American station. Prediction was that he soon would reach Sandy Hook with 150 sail and more troops.[109]

---

[100] Letter of July 7, 1776, to Jonathan Trumbull; *ibid.*, 235.

[101] *A. Robertson's Diaries*, 86.   [102] 1 *Reed*, 181.

[103] *A. Robertson's Diaries*, 86; 1 *Reed*, 151; Clap, who here made a mistake of one day in his chronology, *op. cit.*, 137.

[104] Alexander McDougall had somewhat similar apprehension. The fundamental American error, he thought, was in Putnam's assumption that the British would not attempt to pass the batteries that overlooked North River (McDougall to Schuyler, June 11, 1776; *Schuyler Papers*, NYPL).   [105] 5 *G. W.*, 214; 1 *Webb*, 151.

[106] *A. Robertson's Diaries*, 87; 5 *G. W.*, 220; *Clap's Diary*, 137.

[107] 5 *G. W.*, 222, 226; Loammi Baldwin to his wife, July 5, 1776; *Baldwin Papers*, Army Letters, 46; Harvard Coll. Lib.; *Clap's Diary*, 137.

[108] 30 *Papers of G. W.*, 13, LC.   [109] 5 *G. W.*, 228.

FORMAL NOTICE OF THE "DECLARATION"

Was it their enthusiasm, or was it clear vision that gave some American revolutionary leaders the ability to put their struggle in justified relationship to great political principles? "Clear vision" may seem a vague term with which to describe one explanation of the manner in which John Adams, Thomas Jefferson, George Mason, John Hancock and their compatriots squared their policy with their philosophy, but perhaps the two words are accurate for the very reason that they are not precise. A few only of the Americans had read deeply of what was being written in their day on political philosophy. Rousseau had made little impression on America at that time; the prospectus of the French *Encyclopédie* of Diderot had few subscribers in America; the prospectus of Panckoucke's revision did not appear until the year after the victory at Yorktown. In one edition of Jefferson's *Works,* the first indexed reference to John Locke bears date of 1790, but Malone remarks significantly, "If [Jefferson] did not draw on Locke in the first place, but got the ideas of that noted writer second hand he certainly had his very phraseology by heart in 1776." The revolutionists absorbed more than they read.

Becker and Chinard and Malone and Boyd may be trusted for the correct, detailed answer to the question of how the Americans of 1776 reared their structure squarely on the true lines of old political foundations. The famous letter on the facing page illustrates how John Hancock had "eyes to see" the widest historical significance of what Congress had done two days previously. The Delegates, he informed Washington, "for some Time past, have had their Attention occupied by one of the most interesting and important Subjects that could possably come before them or any other Assembly of Men." The President of Congress continued: "Altho it is not possible to foresee the Consequences of Human Actions, yet it is nevertheless a Duty we owe ourselves and Posterity, in all our public Counsels, to decide in the best Manner we are able, and to leave the Event to that Being who controls both Causes and Events to bring about his own Determination." When Washington received this, he already had been informed unofficially of the action of Congress; so, in General Orders of July 9, he directed that the paper adopted on the 4th of July be read to all the troops. That evening for the first time they heard, "When in the course of human events . . ."

(After the original manuscript in the Library of Congress.)

Philadelphia July 6th. 1776.

Sir,

The Congress, for some Time past, have had their Attention occupied by one of the most interesting and important Subjects, that could possibly come before them, or any other Assembly of Men.

Altho, it is not possible to foresee the Consequences of Human Actions, yet it is nevertheless a Duty we owe ourselves and Posterity, in all our public Councils, to decide in the best Manner we are able, and to leave the Event to that Being who controuls both Causes and Events to bring about

I have the Honour to be.

Sir,

with perfect Esteem

your most Obed. &
very hble Servt

John Hancock Prest.

Vis Excellency Genl. Washington

HENRY KNOX, A MODEL ADMINISTRATOR

From the time Washington met Henry Knox on the road between Cambridge and Roxbury, July 5, 1775 (Vol. III, p. 484), the Commander-in-Chief had constant and highly proficient service from the bulky young Bostonian, whom he made his Chief of Artillery, in December, 1776, at the age of 26. Knox was almost completely self-taught in the military arts. Because he had little opportunity of acquiring experience in the field, he studied gunnery and tactics in his own bookstore, and as late as 1777, he seemed to at least one French professional soldier neither to know how to take cannon into action nor how to withdraw them; but if he acquired slowly the fine points of the employment of artillery, he quickly developed high skill in dealing with men. His administration of his arm of the service was quiet and was marred by few jealousies on the part of his subordinates. Plans and problems usually were set down on paper; for their solution, he elicited the best judgment of his ablest comrades.

The artillery companies at the outset were equipped feebly with guns from old forts or from warehouses and wharves where vessels had left their armament after the peace of 1763. More cannon and mortars were brought by Knox himself from Ticonderoga in the winter of 1775–76. Others were taken from prizes captured at sea. By the end of the period covered by this volume, the artillery of the continental Army met nearly all of Washington's requirements. While this achievement was vastly to Knox's honor, he deserved equal credit for his unwavering loyalty to his chief and for his willingness to spare Washington the performance of any task he could discharge himself. Along with Lafayette, "Light Horse Harry" Lee, Benjamin Tallmadge and a few others, Knox represented the competence as well as the daring of the best type of young soldier. There is no portrait of him as he appeared during the Revolution, but the one here reproduced from the original by Edward Savage at Philipse Manor Hall, Yonkers, N. Y., probably is the earliest of several painted after the war.

(Reproduced by courtesy of the American Scenic and Historic Preservation Society, New York City.)

When the attack would be delivered, Washington of course could not foresee, but he expected the British to waste no time, and he felt sure they would direct their main effort of 1776 against New York.[110] He was of this mind on July 9, a date of some interest. Exactly a year before, as Commander-in-Chief, he had held at Cambridge his first council of war, which had fixed a rendezvous in the country behind Roxbury and Cambridge, in event the Army was dissolved or was forced to retreat.[111] Neither of those eventualities had been realized, but, incredibly, in the twelve months that had elapsed, Washington had fought no battle. There had been a few skirmishes and several days of cannonading, but not once had lines been drawn in the open field where Americans and British exchanged volleys. Washington had demonstrated that he could organize, train, discipline and administer an Army and that he could prevail upon most officers to subordinate personal ambition to the needs of a common cause. By complete devotion to duty, by justice to his men, by moderation of judgment and by unchallengeable integrity he had become the symbol of what the best of the Americans wished their cause to represent. Many thought what the Massachusetts lawmakers had said of him in their final address,[112] but the stubborn fact remained: he had fame without fight. In a year he had lost no more men in combat than had been killed in one of the Indian raids on the Virginia frontier twenty years previously.

Now it would be different. It had to be. Howe, not he, had the initiative. A battle, perhaps a long campaign must be faced, without hope of any such maneuver as that by which Boston had been recovered. Washington and the Army had to meet the test of battle—and meet it now with the assurance that if they failed, nobody would plead in Parliament or at the foot of the throne for mercy on devoted, if errant subjects of the King. The Delegates in Philadelphia had renounced that allegiance. On the evening of the 4th, the rumor spread among the coffee houses that the Congress in Philadelphia had declared the Colonies independent.[113] Two days later, confirmation of this report had sent many officers to the public houses, "to testify our joy," as one young man wrote.[114] It was not until the 9th that official notice was

---

[110] *Ibid.*, 231. [111] Cf. *ibid.*, 320 and *supra*, Vol. III, p. 494.
[112] See *supra*, p. 61–62.
[113] Ebenezer Hazard to Horatio Gates, July 5, 1776; *Gates Papers*, NYHS.
[114] *Isaac Bangs's Diary*, 56. The author of the useful Journal, cited as *Anon. New York Journal*, LC, gave the date of the arrival of the Declaration as July 7.

at hand in form for Washington to include the intelligence in general orders. He had the Adjutant General write of deserters whose court-martial sentence of thirty-nine lashes was confirmed; then regulations concerning passes and chaplains were explained. When all these matters were set forth, the General announced:

> The Hon. The Continental Congress, impelled by the dictates of duty, policy and necessity, having been pleased to dissolve the Connection which subsisted between this Country, and Great Britain, and to declare the United Colonies of North America, free and independent States: The several brigades are to be drawn up this evening on their respective Parades, at Six OClock, when the declaration of Congress, shewing the grounds and reasons of this measure, is to be read with an audible voice.
>
> The General hopes this important Event will serve as a fresh incentive to every officer, and soldier, to act with Fidelity and Courage, as knowing that now the peace and safety of his Country depends (under God) solely on the success of our arms: And that he is now in the service of a State, possessed of sufficient power to reward his merit, and advance him to the highest Honors of a free Country.
>
> The Brigade Majors are to receive, at the Adjutant Generals Office, several of the Declarations to be delivered to the Brigadiers General, and the Colonels of Regiments.[115]

The last clauses of the long sentence that constituted the first paragraph meant uniforms spruced up, and bayonets fixed to heavy muskets, and perhaps a long wait under a slanting sun; but after that there might be a frolic. So, as 6 o'clock approached, all the men not on pressing active duty marched out and took their places. Then, ere long, from the front of each Brigade, at different moments and in varying tones, loud voices proclaimed: "When, in the course of human events . . . " Those who could hear doubtless listened to the new, strange words and agreed with the indictment of the King for all the misdeeds that previously had been charged against him. At the end came: "And for the support of this Declaration, with a firm reliance on the protection of Divine Providence, we mutually pledge to each other our Lives, our Fortunes, and our sacred Honor." There was a pause and then, in some commands, three cheers and in others, a great shout.[116]

---

[115] 5 *G. W.*, 245, verbatim.

[116] *Solomon Nash's Diary*, 24; *Heath*, 58; 1 *Webb*, 153. No basis has been found for the familiar tradition that Washington heard the declaration read as he sat astride his horse, with the troops around him in a hollow square.

The troops moved off; the parade was dismissed. Most of the men were held in camps because the alarm might be sounded at any moment, but in the early evening hours there was nothing to keep New York from sauntering and cheering and gathering around the equestrian statue of George III on the Bowling Green. A handsome statue it was —the King in the garb of a Roman Emperor, horse and rider about one-third larger than life, cast in lead, and gilded all over. The pedestal, which was of white marble, stood full fifteen feet high as if the Monarch were looking, over the heads of groundlings, to the remoter riches of his realm. To hedge His Majesty, the grass-seeded oval was surrounded by a ten-foot fence, the upper eight feet of which were of open iron-work.[117] The crowd gazed upward now, scornfully, triumphantly; perhaps the nightwatchmen thought it well to turn their eyes the other way. Over the fence, up the pedestal, to the belly of the horse, incredibly, climbed some agile young Sons of Liberty, who long had wished to rid the town of the statue. Soon they had ropes and bars and were tugging and battering, and then—down crashed the King, off went his head.[118]

[117] Posterity is indebted to Lieut. Isaac Bangs (*Diary*, 25), for this full and useful description of the statue which was erected in 1770 and, he noted carefully, was in a plot of about a quarter of an acre. T. E. V. Smith (*New York, 1789*, p. 20) reported that the statue stood about fifty feet from the lower edge of Bowling Green.

[118] *Isaac Bangs's Diary*, 56; 1 *Webb*, 153. What is believed to be part of the tail of the horse from this statue is in the museum of NYHS. See *NYHS Quarterly*, July, 1920, p. 54.

CHAPTER VI

A CONTEST OF BEGINNERS WITH VETERANS
(July 10–August 29, 1776)

WASHINGTON officially frowned on the destruction of the statue of George III in New York on the night of July 9, 1776,[1] but as a thrifty man of war, he could not disdain the report that the overthrown monarch and mount contained 4000 lbs. of lead that might most usefully be molded into bullets.[2] Besides, Washington's contention with the King's subjects left him little time in which to think of the King's effigy. There was a report on the 10th of July that British regulars in large number were drawn up at the Staten Island Ferry: they would bear watching.[3] Before Washington could be certain whether this forecast an incursion of the Jersey shore, he had dramatic and alarming proof that General Howe was preparing for the long-dreaded move to open the Hudson to the British and to close it to the Americans. A deserter had reported that ships of the fleet were about to ascend North River and cut communications with Jersey, but the date passed for which, as he understood it, the operation had been set.[4] Then, on the afternoon of July 12, when a strong and steady breeze was blowing from the South and the incoming tide was flowing fast, forty-gun *Phoenix* and *Rose*, twenty guns, with the accompanying schooner *Tryal* and two tenders,[5] were seen to leave their berths and to move toward North River. The alarm was sounded; within twenty-five minutes the vessels were close enough

---

[1] GOs of July 10, 1776; 5 *G. W.*, 246.

[2] *Penn. Gazette*, July 17, 1776; *Isaac Bangs' Diary*, 57. Bangs added that "a man undertook to take 10 ounces of gold from the superfices, as both man and horse were covered with gold leaf." In a note to 5 *G. W.*, 246, Fitzpatrick wrote: "Col. John Montresor secured the head after the British took New York and sent it to Lord Townshend. Most of the statue was carried to Litchfield, Conn., and melted into bullets for the American troops." Demolition of the King's arms in the City Hall, reported by Governor Tryon (1 *Force* (5), p. 949) occurred after the formal proclamation there, July 18, of the Declaration of Independence. (*Clap's Diary*, 248; *Anon. N. Y. Journal*, LC). Royal arms were removed about the same time from the churches (*Ibid.*).

[3] 30 *Papers of G. W.*, 37, LC.

[4] 5 *G. W.*, 254.

[5] The correct number of auxiliaries, a subject of some conflict of testimony, is given in 1 *Kemble*, 80.

to the town for the American batteries on both shores to open. In comparison with the days of stinted artillery fire at Boston, there was a veritable avalanche of round shots and even a few shells—to the total of no less than 196 [6]—but few of these projectiles hulled the British oak. In a short time the two men-of-war, the schooner and the tenders were up the river, almost intact, and ere long were casting anchor confidently in the Tappan Sea.[7] What they expected to do there, Washington could not predict otherwise than in terms of the British general strategy of establishing contact between Howe and Burgoyne. The vessels, in the judgment of the American commander, either were to be employed to stop the shipment of supplies between New York and Albany by land as well as by water, or else the crews were to put arms ashore for the Tories of the region.[8] Washington was prompt to urge the vigilant defence of the Highland passes,[9] and he was relieved, in a measure, to hear from the Commissary General that interruption of the flow of supplies would not hamper operations in Northern New York. Sufficient food was stored there, Washington was told, to provide for 10,000 men over a period of four months.[10]

One serious aspect of this affair of *Phoenix* and *Rose* was the misbehavior of many of the American soldiers, who, at the sounding of the alarm, should have hurried to their posts. They did almost everything except that. Not more than half the artillerists even went to the guns. Hundreds of the troops appeared to forget their duty in watching the race of the ships up the stream.[11] Several men were killed and two or three were wounded because they carelessly failed to sponge their guns. Some of their comrades attributed this to drunkenness; the absence of still others was due, in the language of one disgusted diarist, to the fact that they "were at their cups or whoring." [12] That, surely, was not the disciplinary standard necessary in service of the sort that manifestly lay ahead. "Such unsoldierly conduct," Washington said the next day in General Orders, "must grieve every good officer, and give the enemy a

---

[6] *A. Robertson's Diaries*, 89.

[7] 5 *G. W.*, 264, 272; 1 *Webb*, 154; Henry Knox to William Knox, July 11; Henry Knox to Mrs. Knox, July 17, 1776; *Knox Papers*, MHS. The Tappan Sea is, speaking generally, the wide stretch of the Hudson opposite Tarrytown and vicinity.

[8] 5 *G. W.*, 275.   [9] *Ibid.*, 265–66.

[10] *Ibid.*, 276, 277.   [11] 5 *G. W.*, 268–69.

[12] *Isaac Bangs's Diary*, 58–59. See also *Clap's Diary*, 247 and *Anon. N. Y. Journal*, LC. The marvel of the affair was that a shot from one of the British ships entered an embrasure of a small redoubt, passed between the legs of two soldiers, without injuring them, and struck the banquette or step under the parapet on the opposite side (*Heath*, 58).

mean opinion of the Army, as nothing shows the brave and good soldier more than in case of alarms, cooly and calmly repairing to his post and there waiting his orders, whereas a weak curiosity at such a time makes a man look mean and contemptible." [13] Henry Knox was philosophical: "The affair will be of service to my people," he wrote his wife, "it will teach them to moderate their fiery courage. . . ." [14]

While the ill-disciplined American troops were running up the east bank of the Hudson, like boys following a band in a parade, something potentially more serious was happening in the lower harbor: a tall ship flying St. George's flag at her fore topmast head was making her way to her anchorage. Experienced seafaring men identified her as *Eagle* and of course knew from the position of her flag that she had a Vice Admiral aboard. When she was saluted forthwith by every British ship-of-war, the universal guess was confirmed: Vice Admiral Lord Howe had arrived; behind him would come transports and escorts that were supposed to number 150 sail, with a reenforcement of 15,000 men. [15]

This was a prospect of adverse odds for the American commander of Continentals and militia, good or bad, who did not reach a higher aggregate than that of the hostile reenforcement. [16] Even this American figure was subject to deduction, because approximately 500 Connecticut horse militia, who had been willing to pay temporarily for the pasturage of their mounts, declined to perform the ordinary duties of a soldier. If they persisted in that state of mind, they could be of no use in New York and might as well be dismissed. Washington told their officers precisely that. [17] To strengthen the small American force, New England was to be stripped of Continentals who were to be brought to the mouth of the Hudson or were to be sent to Gates as soon as they were free of smallpox. [18] Indians were to be enlisted; [19] the artillerymen were

---

[13] 5 *G. W.*, 269.

[14] Henry Knox to Mrs. Knox, July 17, 1776; *Knox Papers*, MHS.

[15] *Eagle* cast anchor at 7 P.M. *A. Robertson's Diaries*, 89–90. For the arrival of the ship and speculation over the convoy, see 5 *G. W.*, 240, 250, 262, 264, 281; *Penn. Gazette*, July 10, 17, 1776; 2 *Burnett*, 17. The log of *Eagle* from the time of her arrival is printed in 38 *Penn. Mag.*, 211. It contains much information on British ship movements. Cf. Captain Hall: "[Lord Howe's] conduct in the late war has secured him a reputation that cannot be exalted; at the same time a hauteur, contracted from early command, joined to a natural and frigid reserve, sometimes gives umbrage to those about him, and throws a passing gloom over those qualities which have gained him the admiration of the world" (*Civil War in America*, 176).

[16] As of July 20, 1776, the return of Continentals and militia, sick and fit, present and absent, was 14,866 (1 *Force* (5), p. 507), but this included the Connecticut Horse.

[17] 5 *G. W.*, 286, 295. For the antecedent circumstances, see *ibid.*, 240, 242, 260.

[18] 5 *JCC.*, 527; 5 *G. W.*, 251, 256.

[19] 5 *G. W.*, 261, 386; 5 *JCC.*, 527.

to be recruited; [20] troops already in service were to receive the bounty of ten dollars, if they, like the recruits, enlisted for three years; [21] further militia drafts were to be expected.[22] If, meantime, Lord Howe's expected troops arrived and joined with his brother's Regiments in attacking by any of the several approaches to New York, the danger that confronted Washington would be instant and might be fatal to the American cause.

Suddenly, there was an entirely new development. About 3 o'clock on the afternoon of the 12th of July a messenger from the waterfront brought word to headquarters that a British naval officer had come up the harbor with a flag of truce and a letter which he desired to deliver to Washington. Some intimation was given that the paper might not be addressed acceptably,[23] for which reason Washington immediately called into council the Generals who happened to be close at hand. They agreed with him that he should give safe conduct to any officer who brought an official message to him as American commander but that he should not receive any communication that did not recognize his position as head of an organized force. Adjutant General Reed accordingly was directed to meet the British officer in the harbor and to ascertain how the letter was addressed.[24] With Reed went Henry Knox and Samuel Webb.

When Reed returned in the course of a few hours, he reported that he had met Lieutenant Brown of *Eagle* who had risen with bared head and had bowed ceremoniously.

"I have a letter, sir, from Lord Howe to Mr. Washington."

"Sir," Colonel Reed had replied, "we have no person here in our Army with that address."

"Sir," the British officer had continued, "will you look at that address?"

Thereupon he had taken the letter from his pocket. The cover read:

George Washington, Esq.

Howe   New York

[20] 1 *Force* (5), p. 502, with return of July 20, *ibid.*, 507. See also 5 *G. W.*, 322–23.
[21] 5 *G. W.*, 249; 5 *JCC.*, 565.
[22] Cf. 5 *G. W.*, 307, 317, 318.
[23] Clap stated in his Diary, *loc. cit.*, 247, that the flag first reached Col. Benjamin Tupper, who observed the improper address and said he would send ashore and see if there was any such person as the one to whom the letter was supposed to be delivered.
[24] 5 *G. W.*, 273.

"No, sir," Colonel Reed had answered, after he had glanced at the paper, "I cannot receive that letter."

"I am very sorry and so will be Lord Howe that any error in superscription should prevent the letter being received by General Washington."

Reed had been content to say: "Why, sir, I must obey orders."

"Oh, yes, sir, you must obey orders, to be sure."

The American then had given the Lieutenant some letters from prisoners in New York, and, after bowing and saluting, had pulled away.

In a minute or so, the British officer put about and asked by what particular title Washington chose to be addressed.

"You are sensible, sir," Reed had replied, "of the rank of General Washington in our Army."

"Yes, sir, we are. I am sure Lord Howe will lament exceedingly this affair, as the letter is quite of a civil nature and not a military one. He laments exceedingly that he was not here a little sooner."

That had ended it, except as the Americans had wondered whether the final remark of the British officer meant that Lord Howe regretted he had not reached New York before the Declaration of Independence.[25]

Washington immediately decided that on a matter of so much importance he should submit his action for the approval of Congress and he wrote at once for further instruction. The significant fact, as he saw it, was the manifest anxiety of Lieutenant Brown to deliver the letter. Evidently, Lord Howe wished to negotiate and, while endeavoring to do so, might not strike a blow. This judgment was confirmed on the evening of the 16th of July by the tender, which again was declined, of a letter sent under flag of truce to "George Washington, Esq., &ca, &ca." [26] On the 17th there came a third flag with an inquiry whether His Excellency, General Washington, would receive the Adjutant General of General Howe. Immediate assurance of the American commander's willingness to do this was given,[27] with the result that an appointment for noon on the 20th was made.

Washington dressed the occasion with much care. Shortly before mid-day, he went to the handsome quarters of Col. Henry Knox, not far from the landing near the Grand Battery, and outside the house

---

[25] Henry Knox to Mrs. Knox, July 15, 1776; *Knox Papers*, MHS; 1 *Reed*, 204; 1 *Webb*, 155.
[26] 5 *G. W.*, 297; 1 *Webb*, 156.   [27] 1 *Webb*, 156.

he had his guard placed, under orders to open ranks when the British officer appeared. Everything went according to arrangements. The visitor proved to be Lieut. Col. James Patterson, a suave and experienced officer who behaved as deferentially as if he had been addressing his Most Christian Majesty or had been at Sans Souci in the presence of Frederick II. After some finessing, Colonel Patterson discussed an exchange of prisoners and then proceeded to explain that Lord Howe and his brother the General had large powers as the King's commissioners to settle the unhappy differences with America. Patterson wished his visit to be considered as the first advances to that end. Washington was prepared for this approach, which he met with the statement that he had no authority to treat on that subject. He added in plain words that he thought the Howe brothers were empowered only to grant written pardons. These papers, said the General, were not desired by Americans who felt they had committed no fault but, instead, were defending their indisputable rights. This discouraged Colonel Patterson who brought the conversation back to the exchange of specific prisoners. After a short time, the British officer left. He declined a collation, with the excuse that he had eaten a late breakfast, but he chatted freely and showed manifest gratitude for the considerate restraint of the Americans in not blindfolding him when he passed the defences.[28] The alleged "offer" of the Howes was destined to provoke discussion and some cleavage of opinion in Congress;[29] but Washington had no faith whatever in these particular peace negotiations and he reasoned that the Howe brothers, conscious at last of the temper of the American people, now would delay their attack only until the expected British reenforcements arrived.[30]

[28] Perhaps the most conveniently accessible text of the official report of this interview, as made public by Congress, is in 5 G. W., 321–23 n. Another text will be found in 1 Force (5), p. 500 and still another in Va. Gazette, Aug. 16, 1776. Washington's own account is in 5 G. W., 321; Reed's is in 1 Reed, 205; Webb's is in 1 Webb, 156. In his Diary, loc. cit., 248, Clap described briefly the ceremonies outside Knox's house. Knox wrote his wife that Washington's servants "did" the collation "tolerably well, though the Adjutant General disappointed us." The quarters of Knox were at the Kennedy House, No. 1 Broadway, a site with a commanding view. The Chief of Artillery explained: "As it grew late [Colonel Patterson] even excused himself from drinking one glass of wine. He said Lord Howe and General Howe would wait for him as they were to dine on board Eagle man of war . . ." (Letter of July 23, 1776, Knox Papers, MHS.)
[29] Cf. Robert Morris to Joseph Reed, July 20, 1776; 1 Reed, 202, and John Adams's comment, 3 John Adams, 83 ff; 9 ibid., 438. These references to Adams have to do specifically with the negotiations that were renewed through another American at the end of August. See infra, p. 176.
[30] 5 G. W., 303–04. Cf. ibid., 288, as of July 17 and 19. Patterson's visit merely confirmed Washington's opinion.

Definite encouragement was found in news received a few hours after Patterson's departure to the effect that Charles Lee and the South Carolinians had beaten off Sir Henry Clinton's attack on Charleston.[31] Along the front for which Washington personally was responsible, everything indicated a desperate contest of doubtful issue as soon as the last of the incoming ships brought the final contingent of Howe's army. In no illusion of the easy triumph of a righteous cause, Washington wrote one of his brothers two days after the interview with Patterson: "When this [British reenforcement] arrives, if the report of deserters, prisoners and Tories are [sic] to be depended upon, the enemy's number will amount at least to 25,000 men; ours to about 15,000. More indeed are expected, but there is no certainty of their arrival, as harvest and a thousand other excuses are urged for the reasons of delay. What kind of opposition we shall be able to make, time only can show. I can only say that the men appear to be in good spirits, and that if they stand by me, the place shall not be carried without some loss, notwithstanding we are not yet in such a posture of defence as I could wish." [32]

There were so many other discouragements! In Washington's own Army, fatigue duty, hot weather and bad water in a dry season were causing much sickness; [33] desertion was daily on the increase,[34] and with it a trick of some rascally soldiers in leaving one command and enlisting in another to get the bounty of ten dollars.[35] A somewhat disquieting case arose over Col. Rudolphus Ritzema, who wished to resign while under charges that included discourtesy to a general officer.[36] Provincial jealousies showed themselves ominously.[37] A multitude of obstacles stood in the way of attaining one ideal that Washington doubtless would have approved substantially in the words John Adams employed: "The practice we have hitherto been in, of ditching round about our enemies, will not always do. We must learn to use other

---

[31] 1 *Webb*, 156–57. Washington's announcement of this victory was in GOs of July 21, 1776; 5 *G. W.*, 314–15. His congratulatory letter of August 12 to Lee is in 2 *Lee Papers*, 208–211, but is not to be found in *G. W.*

[32] Letter to John Augustine Washington, July 22, 1776; 5 *G. W.*, 325, drastically repunctuated.

[33] 5 *G. W.*, 263, 299, 353; 1 *Reed*, 211, 215.

[34] Almost daily sentences to the usual punishment of thirty-nine lashes appear in GOs of this period. Cf. 5 *G. W.*, 244 ff.

[35] 5 *G. W.*, 327.

[36] 1 *Force* (5), p. 333; 5 *G. W.*, 270, 278–79, 287. Earlier, Ritzema, who finally went over to the British, had professed much zeal for the American cause. Cf. his letter of Nov. 19, 1775, to Alexander McDougall in *McDougall Papers*, NYHS.

[37] 5 *G. W.*, 361.

weapons than the pick and the spade. Our armies must be disciplined and learn to fight." [38]

A special test of patience was presented in Northern New York. There and in Canada, Washington had "more trouble and concern," according to his Adjutant General, than in front of Howe.[39] First among the new difficulties of the American commander was that of placating John Sullivan, who was returning to New York in dissatisfaction over the appointment of Gates to succeed him as senior officer in the operations on the Lakes. "I shall try to settle the affair and prevail on him to continue," Washington said of Sullivan, "as I think his resignation will take from the service a useful and good officer." [40] Before Sullivan arrived on the 21st of July,[41] Washington learned that the Generals of the Northern Department had decided on the evacuation of Crown Point and a withdrawal to Ticonderoga. This had seemed to some of the field officers so dangerous a move that twenty-one of them had joined in a formal protest.[42] Washington himself had never been on the Northern Lakes but some of the Generals and senior Colonels in New York were familiar with that militarily fascinating country. Their description and the argument advanced in the protest almost convinced Washington that a mistake had been made in the abandonment of Crown Point in favor of Ticonderoga as the forward base of the Northern Army. In plain words Washington stated this to Gates, with the opening reminder that Gates had not written him since taking command on the Lakes. Washington said in later sentences: "Nothing but a belief that you have actually removed the Army from [Crown Point] to Ticonderoga and demolished the works at the former; and the fear of creating dissensions, and encouraging a spirit of remonstrating against the conduct of superior officers by inferiors, have prevented me, by advice of the general officers here, from directing the post at Crown Point to be held till Congress should decide upon the propriety of its evacuation." [43]

A sense of danger sharpened these words and probably made Washington less careful than otherwise he would have been in addressing even so close a comrade as Gates. Certainly Washington was negligent

[38] Letter of July 7, 1776 to Mrs. Adams; *Adams, Fam. Let.*, 195.
[39] Reed to Robert Morris, July 18, 1776; 1 *Reed*, 200.
[40] 5 *G. W.*, 296.   [41] *Heath*, 60; *Clap's Diary*, 248.
[42] The minute of the council of war and the protest of the field officers are in 1 *Force* (5), p. 233–34.
[43] Letter of July 19, 1776, with the odd punctuation preserved; 5 *G. W.*, 303.

in not explaining more precisely that he merely had discussed with some officers in New York the unwisdom of leaving Crown Point to be occupied at pleasure by the British. As soon as letters could be exchanged, he learned that Gates and Schuyler, forgetting their own rivalries, made common cause in denouncing what they took to be the judgment of a council of war in New York on their strategy. Washington's reference to "advice of the general officers here" had been construed to mean nothing less than formal council and trial and condemnation in absentia. It was to be a task of much time and diplomacy to explain that nothing official had occurred, and that friends simply had talked together. Before he could restore complete understanding, Washington had, in fact, to withdraw somewhat from his criticism of the decision to quit Crown Point.[44]

This was a humiliating incident of a tediously inglorious story. "An unaccountable kind of fatality," said Washington, "seems to have attended all our movements in Canada since the death of poor Montgomery."[45] Joseph Reed was blunter: ". . . we dare not even hope for good news from Canada:—A sickly, beaten, dispirited army,—quarreling generals,—provincial jealousies,—and disputes added to a most incredible waste or embezzlement of all stores and provisions, leave us so little chance of success, that we dread the sight of a letter or express from thence."[46]

During the third week of July, while these vexations were multiplying and the new drafts of militia were reporting with intolerable slowness,[47] the number of British sail off Staten Island was rising ominously. Almost daily the lookout reported ships in the offing,[48] though the very fact that they came in small squadrons led Washington to believe that the fleet probably had been scattered by a storm.[49] The 1st of August brought a large augmentation of approximately forty vessels,[50] which

---

[44] 5 *G. W.*, 302–03, 304, 354, 359, 430; 1 *Force* (5), p. 562, 650–51, 714, 747, 794. It is quite likely that Gates and Schuyler blamed Sullivan for the view taken in New York of the evacuation of Crown Point, though actually, as stated in the text, Washington had formed his opinion before the arrival of the New Hampshire General.

[45] Letter of July 20, 1776, to Adam Stephen; 5 *G. W.*, 312.

[46] Letter of July 26, 1776, to Mrs. Reed; 1 *Reed*, 210, verbatim.

[47] 5 *G. W.*, 307, 317, 318.

[48] 5 *G. W.*, 312–13, 316, 329, 343, 347. The nearest American approach to an accurate day-by-day count of the new arrivals is in Webb's Diary, 1 *Webb*, 157. See "A Detail of the Particular Services in America, 1776 . . . by Commodore Sir George Collier . . ." in 32 *Naval Chronicle*. On. p. 269 is an amusing account of the impatience of the Hessian General and of the measures taken by Commodore Cooper to mollify the soldier.

[49] 5 *G. W.*, 352.

[50] 1 *Force* (5), p. 713; 5 *G. W.*, 363.

Washington took to be the transports of part of the expected Hessian force.[51] For a short time after that, attention was shifted from the fleet in the lower harbor to the vessels and tenders in the Tappan Sea. *Phoenix* and *Rose* had severed water communication between New York and Albany as completely as had been apprehended,[52] and temporarily they had created a fear of a shortage of provisions on the Lakes in spite of the Commissary's belief that supplies there were ample.[53] Authorities of the nascent State of New York had been vigilant and had been given all possible help by Washington,[54] who now directed that the British vessels be attacked by a few gondolas and row galleys that had been built and collected with much labor and difficulty.[55] On the 3rd of August five of these little craft went up North River under Lt. Col. Benjamin Tupper, the intrepid officer who had conducted the successful raid on the Boston lighthouse in the summer of 1775.[56] Tupper boldly assailed the British ships, but tide and weight of metal both were against him and his tough-fibred crew. The American boats, making a gallant if futile fight, had at length to withdraw, badly mauled, to Dobbs Ferry.[57]

Then interest again was turned to the British fleet off New York, those ships that proclaimed the presence and power of the enemy but never gave a hint of what choice the British commander would make among the strategical alternatives so abundantly open to him. Had not Washington encountered it previously at Boston, sea power might have baffled his planning and paralyzed his initiative. Regularly he would receive from faithful Col. Edward Hand, at the lookout on Long Island, a report of arriving and departing vessels and of boats that passed from ship to shore. Washington even might be told of the uniforms debarking troops wore,[58] but unless some deserter got to him, the American commander could not learn anything specific about the men those dark hulls hid. He could go to sleep at night knowing that every ship of the British fleet was in its place, but he had to admonish himself that the

---

[51] 5 *G. W.*, 364.   [52] *Ibid.*, 313.
[53] *Ibid.*, 276, 290, 291.
[54] 1 *LTW.*, 260; 5 *G. W.*, 288, 297, 310–11, 318, 326.
[55] 5 *G. W.*, 282–83, 335, 343, 347; *Clap's Diary*, 249; *Penn. Gazette*, July 23, 1776. For the procurement of these craft, see also Israel Putnam to Washington, July 13, 1776, Washington Papers, Huntington Lib., and Stephen Moylan to "Mr. Wadsworth" July 28, 1776, *L. W. Smith Coll.*
[56] July 31–Aug. 1, 1775; See Vol. III, p. 508.
[57] Tupper's report is in 1 *Force* (5), p. 766–77; Washington's brief accounts are in 5 *G. W.*, 370–71, 373. See also 1 *Moore*, 292–93; *Anon. New York Journal*, LC., and *Clap's Diary*, 249.
[58] Cf. 5 *G. W.*, 329, 363.

next morning he might find all of them riding near the shore of Long Island, or in line off the Grand Battery, or preparing to ascend East or North River and to land troops in his rear. Men aboard the ships were said to be talking much of Long Island and of the rich provisions awaiting any soldier who would brain a sheep or rob a hen-roost;[59] but how was the American General to know whether this echoed what the soldiers had overheard their officers say, or whether it merely mirrored the dreams they had fashioned as they had turned from their mess of salt pork and had looked at the summer abundance of the lush island? It was enough to drive a weak commander mad—to see so much of what an adversary was doing and yet to be able to make no more than a rough guess of the strength and design of the foe!

The guess might be wrong; in fact, it was wrong. On the 7th of August, Washington had finished a careful letter to Congress concerning a delicate subject when he was informed that two men who had deserted the previous evening from *Solebay*, one of the vessels of the fleet, had told an almost incredible tale: Their ship was among those that had arrived on the 1st of August, but they did not belong to Hessian reenforcement and they had not come directly from "home." They were part of the army of Sir Henry Clinton; they had been sent to South Carolina and, having been repulsed there, had joined General Howe in order to share in the capture of New York and the occupation of New Jersey.[60]

Clinton! He had been left out of all calculations regarding New York after he had left that city and had gone South. Now he was back. Washington had to admit that this had not been anticipated;[61] Joseph Reed said more dramatically, "Clinton's coming was as unexpected to us as if he had dropped from the clouds, and was what I could never have believed if we had it not confirmed to us by such proofs as to put it beyond all doubt."[62] Among those proofs were statements by the deserters that conformed to everything Charles Lee already had written of operations in Carolina. Much that the men told of occurrences at Charleston was so specific and had such verisimilitude that it could not possibly be imaginary.[63]

[59] *Ibid.*, 335.
[60] 5 *G. W.*, 382, 389–90. Governor Tryon on June 7 had written Clinton confidentially of the receipt of a dispatch, dated May 22, in which Howe informed him that Clinton had been ordered to New York. *Clinton Papers*, Clements Lib.
[61] 5 *G. W.*, 396.   [62] Letter of Aug. 9, 1776, to Mrs. Reed; 1 *Reed*, 215.
[63] 5 *G. W.*, 401. Cf. Sir George Collier (in 32 *Naval Chronicle*, 270): "The arrival of a

Washington, then, had to face the 3000 men, more or less, who belonged to Clinton's command,[64] in addition to the Regiments Howe had brought from Halifax [65] and the Germans who were to come from across the Atlantic. The anticipated worst was foreshadowed in the intelligence reports. A letter from Boston covered a statement by a merchant Captain who had been a prisoner of war in one of the convoys.[66] He made it plain that the vessel was southward bound from the port in Nova Scotia. Two Virginia travelers who were allowed to leave Staten Island on the 8th of August estimated the forces already there at 15,000. British officers, they reported, were becoming impatient for the arrival of the foreign contingents, a few of whom only had reached the western shores of the Atlantic. "They say," Washington wrote of his Virginian informants, "from what they could collect from the conversation of officers &c, [the British] mean to hem us in by getting above us and cutting off all communication with the country." The General added somewhat awkwardly: "That this is their plan seems to be corroborated and confirmed by the circumstances of some ships of war going out at different times within a few days past and other vessels" [67] [sic].

Washington had not asked and Congress on its own initiative had done nothing for an increase in the number of continental Regiments in the Army directly under his command.[68] Besides, it was now too late to recruit on a large scale for a campaign that might develop furiously within a week.[69] If, then, help was forthcoming at all, it must be from the Flying Camp that was being set up in New Jersey and, on a still larger scale, from the militia. These two sources were in reality one, because the 10,000 men proposed as a Flying Camp were to be militia from the Middle Colonies of Pennsylvania, Delaware and Maryland; [70] and all of the additional 15,000 Congress had asked of Massachusetts,

---

crippled ship and a defeated officer at this time was very unwelcome; for it infused fresh spirits into the rebels and showed them that ships were sometimes obliged to retreat from batteries."

64 *A. Robertson's Diaries*, 92; 1 *Kemble*, 83.

65 It was reported in England that Howe put on ship 6155 effectives (*Kentish Gazette* (Canterbury), quoted in 5 *Stokes, Iconography*, 990).

66 5 *G. W.*, 403. The documents mentioned by Washington are in 1 *Force* (5), p. 836.

67 Letter of Aug. 8–9, 1776, to the President of Congress; 5 *G. W.*, 406. For Washington's conclusion that the odds against him would be approximately two to one, unless he was reenforced strongly and at once, see *ibid.*, 383, 387, 389.

68 Cf. 4 *JCC.*, 399–400.

69 For Washington's belief that the blow might fall "in the course of a week," see his letter of Aug. 7, 1776, to Jonathan Trumbull; 5 *G. W.*, 389.

70 See 4 *JCC.*, 400.

Connecticut, New York, New Jersey and Pennsylvania [71] were of the same category. Both forces were to be employed to Dec. 1, 1776, unless sooner discharged. [72] The principal difference among these contingents would lie in the possibility that some of the more populous and patriotic States would forward their quotas with less than the normal delay. Washington resolved that he would do his utmost to speed the militia of the nearest Colonies, in the spirit of a letter he addressed to a Connecticut Colonel, who was reminded of authority granted under the law of that State for the senior officer of a Regiment to call it out on his own initiative in time of alarm. "Since the settlement of these Colonies," said Washington, "there has never been such just occasion of alarm or such an appearance of an enemy, both by sea and land." [73]

This sort of recruiting was enough to drive a General mad, because it brought to light so much ugly selfishness and lack of public spirit. For example, a considerable body of Pennsylvania militia, calling themselves "Associators," might be made available, but they had established their camp at Trenton, from which village it was not certain they could be prevailed upon to advance. [74] Again, George Clinton, whom Washington somewhat hesitantly had recommended to command the New York temporary troops, [75] reported that 300 New England militia had marched off from Peekskill without so much as giving notice. [76] Col. Jonathan Fitch did his best to assemble his Regiment but, he said, the men had many excuses. In particular, they averred that the males left at home to look after the crops [77] were too few to tend and to harvest what had been planted. Still again, Brig. Gen. Hugh Mercer had taken command of the Flying Camp with much energy [78] and he acted in full accord with a resolution of Congress that sanctioned the dispatch to New York of 2000 men from the camp if Washington called for them. [79] The difficulty was in finding that number of militia who

[71] Ibid. Pennsylvania's contingent of the New York army was to consist of two full Battalions of the State "establishment."
[72] Ibid.
[73] Letter of Aug. 7, 1776; 5 G. W., 387. Cf. other calls in ibid., 388–89, 391, 396–97, 397–98, 400–01.
[74] 5 G. W., 247–48, 278, 295, 393 ff.
[75] Ibid., 398–99.
[76] 1 Force (5), p. 728. Clinton explained that he thought they had the consent of a committee of the State Congress.
[77] Ibid., 938. Washington tried to make it plain that all these militia were to be in continental pay (5 G. W., 413).
[78] He had reported in New York on the 3rd of July (1 Webb, 152) and for a time he hoped to launch a local offensive (1 Force (5), p. 369, 413, 443).
[79] 5 JCC., 565. Cf. ibid., 559.

would obey orders to proceed across North River from Amboy.[80] Some organizations of Pennsylvania "Associators," said Mercer, were deserting *en masse*;[81] men of other Battalions were in ugly humor and were abusing their officers.[82] It was dangerous, Mercer thought, to call on these malcontents to build defences when it was all he could do to keep them from deserting their posts.[83]

Such was the outlook for reenforcement of Washington's Army before the steadily increasing British Regiments were hurled against the feeble American lines: there was no certainty regarding the number of militiamen who would be available, the time when they would arrive, or the spirit in which they would fight. Washington's experience in Virginia during the French and Indian War had admonished him that the militia would arrive late and would desert in large part at first opportunity. Subsequent operations in the Old Dominion under Andrew Lewis had indicated that the militia had improved in loyalty and tenacity. Much the same thing could be said of the fighting in front of Boston during 1775–76. It was true that militiamen had shown complete unwillingness to remain on duty an hour beyond their designated period of compulsory service. Could Washington ever forget the anxious days at the end of November and during the last week of December? Those times of trial excepted, Washington had found New England militia prompt, diligent and, for the type of duty assigned them, sufficiently intelligent and courageous. Would it be so now? Was he doomed to duplicate that dreadful period of militia desertion in May, 1756,[84] or were the militia of Connecticut, New York, the Jerseys and Pennsylvania to show themselves punctual and reliable as the men of Roxbury and of Dorchester had proven in March, 1776? While Washington, half in hope and half in fear,[85] sought reenforcement wherever it possibly could be mustered, he had immediately at his disposal no more than 10,000 effectives in a total of 17,225,[86] with whom, as he put it, he had "to oppose an army of 30,000 experienced veterans" on a front of approximately fifteen miles.[87]

---

[80] For the slow increase in numbers at Flying Camp, see 1 *Force* (5), p. 574, 5 *G. W.*, 344. The figures in 1 *Force* (5), p. 762 manifestly refer to the new levies, not to the total. See 5 *G. W.*, 404.

[81] 1 *Force* (5), p. 885. Cf. *ibid.*, 895, 962.   [82] *Ibid.*, 886.

[83] *Ibid.*, 834.   [84] See Vol. II, p. 179 ff.   [85] Cf. 5 *G. W.*, 408–09.

[86] Plus the unreported strength of Col. William Smallwood's Battalion, then in transit from New Jersey (5 *G. W.*, 404).

[87] 5 *G. W.*, 390, 404. Actually, Howe had 20,121 rank and file, of whom 1677 were sick. See his *Observations*, 45, in the pagination of his *Narrative*.

These perplexities of adverse odds were presented at a time when Washington's staff scarcely was able to cope with the day-by-day problem of directing the Army's business. Transfer of Gates to the Canadian command had been so recent [88] that the new Adjutant General, Joseph Reed, could not be expected in an acute crisis to discharge all the duties of that office. Reed was brilliant; he would not himself have asserted that he was experienced in applying the regulations and the practices of army routine.[89] Besides this untrained administrative officer, Washington had two new aides, it will be remembered, and an assistant secretary, Alexander Contee Hanson, who was unfamiliar with the office. All these men had assumed their tasks barely a fortnight before Washington learned of the presence of Sir Henry Clinton's forces with Howe's Army in the harbor; [90] and as Stephen Moylan had left headquarters to undertake his new labors as Quartermaster General,[91] the Commander-in-Chief was dismally burdened and still was over-conscientious in thinking that certain matters of correspondence called for his personal attention.[92] Occasionally he would seek to have others transact business that came to his desk,[93] and he realized that he was excessively busy,[94] but he was loath to call for more assistance in his office. It was July 25 when he brought himself to explain his circumstances and to ask of Congress "an increase of my Aid de Camps" [95]— a request the Delegates answered in the singular. "I have the pleasure

[88] GO of June 7, 1776; 5 G. W., 105.

[89] Cf. his letter of June 21, 1776, to Mrs. Reed: "The office I am in has not much severe duty, but it is so entirely out of my line that I do not feel myself so easy with it as one of a different kind. Perhaps a little time will reconcile me better to it" (1 Reed, 191).

[90] The appointments were announced in GOs of June 21, 1776. See 5 G. W., 165, and 1 Webb, 148.

[91] June 7, 1776; 5 G. W., 105.

[92] An example of this weakness was represented in the summer of 1776 by his personal handling of the parole of the persistent prisoner of war, Maj. Christopher French (5 G. W., 342, 378–79, 390–91, 448–49). Further instances of the performance of tasks that should have been delegated to others are glimpsed in a letter of July 17 to Schuyler (ibid., 289–93) and in one of July 26 to George Clinton (ibid., 340–41). A letter of August 19 to Lund Washington on public affairs and on personal business ran to about 1400 words, all in Washington's autograph (ibid., 457).

[93] Cf. 5 G. W., 284.

[94] "For me, whose time is employed from the hour of my rising 'till I retire to bed again . . ." (ibid., 253).

[95] Ibid., 337. Nathanael Greene and Hugh Mercer were complaining simultaneously of the amount of office work they had to do (1 LTW., 264; 1 Force (5), p. 371). Greene's observation could most aptly have been repeated by his chief : "The science or art of war requires a freedom of thought, and leisure to reflect upon the various incidents that daily occur, which cannot be had where the whole of one's time is engrossed in clerical employments. The time devoted to this employment is not the only injury that I feel; but it confines my thoughts as well as engrosses my time. It is like a merchandise of small wares." (Text in 1 LTW., 264, differs slightly from that cited by Fitzpatrick in 5 G. W., 338 n).

to inform you," Hancock wrote, "the Congress readily agrees to your having another Aid-de-Camp." [96]

Besides more secretaries, Washington had needed additional senior officers, had needed them desperately, and had written Congress on the subject August 7, the day the two deserters from *Solebay* told of the arrival of Clinton.[97] The argument of Washington was, in effect, that he had one Major General only in the person of Israel Putnam, though three were the minimum to discharge essential duty. Three Brigadiers were desired in New York, also, and an equal number, or more, were required elsewhere.[98] Congress was quick to respond with the promotion of William Heath, Joseph Spencer, John Sullivan and Nathanael Greene to the rank of Major General, and of six Colonels to brigade command.[99] Although there had been some muttering over the failure of New England Colonels to receive higher commission,[100] three of the six new Brigadiers were from that region [101] and were acceptable to the Commander-in-Chief. These new appointments meant the shift of Regiments and all the uncertainty that attends dealing with strange officers through unfamiliar channels.[102] Even if changed commanders and different associations did not heighten the dangers that seemed to lie immediately ahead, they suggested comparisons. Said Joseph Reed: ". . . we have neither such an army nor such a council as last year, and yet we want it more." [103]

[96] 1 *Force* (5), p. 636.   [97] Cf. 5 *G. W.*, 379–82 and *supra*, p. 145.
[98] 5 *G. W.*, 380. Cf. *ibid.*, 372.

[99] 5 *G. W.*, 421. For the vote in Congress, see 5 *JCC.*, 641, and 2 *Burnett*, 45–46, 55. Wooster had surprising support in the balloting for Major Generals.

[100] Cf. Nathanael Greene to John Adams, July 14, 1776: "I wish the officers in general were as studious to deserve promotion as they are anxious to obtain it." (G. W. Greene, *The Life of Nathanael Greene*, cited hereafter as *Greene's Greene*, v. 1, p. 181). John Adams' comment now was: "I am ashamed and grieved to my inmost soul for the disgrace brought upon the Massachusetts [sic] in not having half its proportions of general officers. But there is not a single man among all our Colonels that I dare to recommend for a general officer except [Henry] Knox and [Elisha?] Porter and these are so low down in the list, that it is dangerous promoting them over the heads of so many." Letter of Aug. 25, 1776, to James Hawley, 9 *John Adams*, 434–35. It is possible that "Porter" is a misreading of some other name because Elisha Porter, according to *Heitman*, was a Colonel of militia, not of the continental establishment.

[101] James Reed of New Hampshire, John Nixon of Massachusetts and Samuel Holden Parsons of Connecticut. Two, Alexander McDougall and James Clinton, were from New York. Arthur St. Clair, a native of Scotland, was owner of much Pennsylvania land and had commanded the Second Pennsylvania Battalion.

[102] For the changes, see 5 *G. W.*, 421, 423. Cf. Washington's statement, August 23, that returns were unsatisfactory because of the "shifting and changing the Regiments have undergone of late" (5 *G. W.*, 491).

[103] Letter of July 22, 1776, to Mrs. Reed; 1 *Reed*, 209. See 5 *G. W.*, 253, for Washington's appeal for an office of audit, and 5 *G. W.*, 347–49, for his suggestion of a system of inspection to fill vacancies.

The "want" was manifested daily. On the 12th and 13th of August, at the very time of extensive reorganization, ninety-six ships or more came into the lower harbor. Approximately twenty others dropped anchor on the 14th. These, surely, must be bringing the Hessians and must be the last of the tremendous fleet. If they were, then the onslaught would come in a few days; it could not be long delayed.[104] On the 14th, there was much stir of small boats and indications both of landing and of embarking troops, but Washington's last reports of the day were that the newly arrived Hessians were being put ashore on Staten Island.[105] As it chanced, a heavy rain that day disrupted movement, broke a long drought [106] and ushered in a brief, blusterous period of sickness and uncertainty. "The badness of the weather," Washington told his men, "has undoubtedly prevented an attack," and he admonished them to keep their canteens filled and to have two days' dressed rations on hand.[107]

There was some good news along with the bad in this period of strain and suspense. Militiamen arrived in such numbers that by the 19th of August they had raised Washington's total strength to 23,000.[108] Another gratifying item was an attack, August 16, of fire-rafts on *Phoenix* and *Rose*. This failed after threatening for a time to set the larger ship aflame; but the daring move so alarmed the British commander that he abandoned his station, ran the gauntlet of the forts on North River and, August 18, rejoined the fleet. For the moment, at least, the Hudson again was open to the Americans,[109] but they had woes enough. The long dry weather polluted the water supply; the subsequent chill days of heavy rain were attended by much sickness. In some Regiments, all the field officers were incapacitated.[110] Foremost among the temporary victims was the man in command of what might be the battleground—Nathanael Greene on Long Island. His

104 5 *G. W.*, 424, 427, 431, 433, 435; the brief British reports are in 1 *Force* (5), p. 949, 963.
105 5 *G. W.*, 439; 1 *Force* (5), p. 967.
106 Clap asserted in his Diary, *loc. cit.*, 250, that more rain fell on the 14th than during the previous three or four months.
107 5 *G. W.*, 442.
108 5 *G. W.*, 457–58.
109 Heath's brief account as an eye-witness probably is the most informative (*Heath*, 62). See also his letters in 1 *LTW.*, 276, 277, and the details given in 1 *Reed*, 213. Washington's report is in 5 *G. W.*, 458. Cf. *ibid.*, 457. The return of the ships to the fleet is reported in *Heath*, 64, 1 *LTW.*, 277, 5 *G. W.*, 452, 458, and in 1 *Kemble*, 84. Somewhat detailed accounts of preparations for this foray will be found in *Md. Gazette*, Aug. 8, and *Va. Gazette*, Aug. 16, 30, 1776.
110 5 *G. W.*, 439–40.

had been the duty of watching the enemy's movements and of guarding an estimated 100,000 pastured cattle and an even larger number of
sheep. This livestock could not be removed to the mainland [111] though
it would supply food for months to an adversary whose landing could
not be prevented. For his combined service as guard and shepherd,
Greene had been compelled to rely on what John Sullivan styled "six
broken Regiments" [112] and the Rhode Islander had felt justified in telling his patient Commander-in-Chief that "most of the troops that come
over here are strangers to the ground, undisciplined and badly furnished with arms." [113] In spite of difficulties, Greene had developed
more in Washington's fourteen months of command than had almost
any other subordinate officer. He was of all of them the man who
probably could get the utmost in wholehearted defence from the troops
allotted him; and now—of all inconvenient times!—he had on the 15th
of August to report himself confined to bed with a raging fever. [114]
For two days he was no better; on the 18th he was somewhat improved
and expressed the hope that he would be on his feet shortly, but he
had to confess he was very weak. [115] By the 20th, when intelligence reports indicated that one of the two early landings of the British was
apt to be on Long Island, [116] Washington had to decide whether he
could afford to gamble on Greene's resumption of command before
the attack was delivered if, indeed, predictions of a descent on the
island were borne out. The question was not one to be debated long:
Greene's early discharge of military duty was impossible; [117] someone
had to be assigned in his stead—and who?

Washington's choice fell on John Sullivan. That officer had little or
no acquaintance with the island, [118] because his service in New York
City had been brief—something less than a month in April–May,
1775, [119] and a day or two during the third week in July, 1776, [120] after
his disgruntled return from the Northern Department. [121] He then had
gone to Philadelphia and had tendered his resignation, but at John

[111] 1 Force (5), p. 538; 5 G. W., 400.   [112] 1 Sullivan Papers, 291.
[113] 1 Force (5), p. 967.   [114] Ibid.
[115] Ibid., 998, 1029.   [116] 5 G. W., 467.
[117] Cf. 5 G. W., 477.
[118] Cf. Joseph Reed: "[Sullivan] was wholly unacquainted with the ground or country"
(1 Force (5), p. 1231).
[119] He had arrived shortly before April 15 (4 G. W., 480) and had left May 6 (1 Sullivan
Papers, 197).
[120] It will be remembered that Sullivan arrived from Northern New York, July 21 (see
supra, p. 142), but he was in Philadelphia by July 26 (1 Force (5), p. 594, 637).
[121] See supra, p. 142.

Hancock's instance had withdrawn it, just in time, perhaps, to prevent indignant acceptance of it.[122] Back in New York, he wrote directly to the President of Congress and expressed his ideas on the strategy of the brewing campaign as authoritatively as if he had been in general command.[123] Sullivan, in short, had displayed nearly all the qualities Washington attributed to him when writing about his ambitions to head the army in Canada.[124] To some eyes, he was not prepossessing, either—"a short-set, rough, ill-looking fellow" in the words of a British officer [125]—but in Washington's opinion he was the best available man for a most difficult assignment. Besides, he had specific advantage, from the viewpoint of army headquarters, because he appreciated the importance of Long Island and believed that it had to be held if New York City was to remain in American hands.[126] To Long Island, then, John Sullivan went on August 20, under orders that made plain the fact that the assignment was temporary. Lord Stirling was to command Sullivan's Division during the service of that officer at Greene's post.[127] The one man most displeased by these assignments was the senior Major General present, Israel Putnam. He liked Sullivan well enough and doubtless shared the wide confidence in the New Hampshire commander, but if fighting was to be done, he wanted a hand in it.

The day after Sullivan was named, several ships of the British fleet, crowded with soldiers, dropped down from the anchorage to The Narrows. Whether these vessels were bound on some special mission or were making the first move in an operation all the warships were to share, Washington could not ascertain before darkness. During the

---

122 1 *Force* (5), p. 594, 637, 690; 2 *Burnett*, 28.

123 1 *Sullivan Papers*, 290; 1 *Force* (5), p. 770. Sullivan must have left Philadelphia at the end of July or the beginning of August. See 1 *Force* (5), p. 690.

124 See *supra*, p. 112, 129.

125 1 *Mackenzie*, p. 39. A different view is that of Thacher, *op. cit.*, 456: "He was fond of display, and his personal appearance and dignified deportment commanded respect."

126 Cf. Sullivan to the President of Congress, Oct. 25, 1777: "I have often urged both by word and writing, that, as the enemy had doubtless both these objects in view [the occupation of Long Island and of New York City] they would first try for Long Island, which commanded the other, and then New York (which was completely commanded by it) would fall of course" (*Long Island Historical Society Memoirs*, cited hereafter as *LIHS Mem.*, v. 2, p. 371). This and v. 3 of the same series contain many reprinted and some original documents on Long Island operations to supplement the long and fine introductory narratives by Thomas W. Field (v. 2) and by Henry P. Johnston (v. 3). As some of these documents might have been overlooked in the course of the present inquiry, it has seemed proper to quote from the *Memoirs* and not from the original texts. In citing from v. 3, references are to the separate pagination of the documents and not to the text of Johnston's narrative unless so stated.

127 5 *G. W.*, 469.

early hours of the night, a thunderstorm and squall [128] halted everything. The next morning the word was that more of the 400 transports and thirty-seven men-of-war off Staten Island [129] had gone to
The Narrows. Then came full, ominous intelligence from Sullivan:
British troops were disembarking on the shore of Gravesend Bay,
Long Island; Sir Henry Clinton's Grenadiers and the Light Infantry
formed the van; [130] Colonel Hand's men were withdrawing and were
burning supplies that would be useful to the enemy; the force already
ashore apparently numbered about 8000. [131] Detachments had pushed
on to Flatbush, [132] a village about four miles and a half by road from
the landing place and approximately three miles from the outer American positions, with woods and broken ground between. [133] The first
report to Washington was that the British had undertaken to deliver
a surprise attack on Sullivan's men, who manifestly had to be reenforced
as heavily as this could be done before it was known whether the British simultaneously were to assail New York. [134] Six Battalions were
assembled promptly and were hurried across East River. The men
went off in fine fighting mood, even though some of them were without the prescribed two days' dressed provisions. [135]

Morning reports on the 23rd were, in effect, "No change." The
enemy had extended his front but had delivered no attack during the
night. Washington thought this increased the probability that Long

[128] Washingon termed it (5 G. W., 475) "a most violent gust," but "gust" was used at
that time to describe a squall and even a gale. For a description of the thunderstorm, with
some strange details of the death of three officers by a stroke of lightning, see 1 Force (5),
p. 1112; Penn. Gazette, Aug. 28, 1776; Diary of the Moravian Congregation of New York,
1 Penn. Mag., 145–46.
[129] Sir George Collier in 2 LIHS Mem., 409. Serle (op. cit., 68) wrote Aug. 14, 1776, that
the fleet in New York consisted of 350 sail. See also Lieutenant Hinrick in W. L. Stone,
Revolutionary Letters, 193–94.
[130] 2 LIHS Mem., 411.
[131] 4 G. W., 475. Joseph Reed (1 Reed, 219) put the number at 5000 to 8000; Washington
on the 23rd (5 G. W., 476) estimated the force at 8000 to 9000. All these figures were far
below the actual totals. In seventy-five flatboats, eleven batteaux and two galleys, organized
in ten divisions, the British in two and a half hours landed close to 15,000 men (Kemble
op. cit., 85, gave the specific figure at 14,700) and put ashore, in addition, the horses of their
dragoons, and no less than forty cannon (1 Force (5), p. 1255, 1256)—a most remarkable
achievement. Howe in his Observations, 45, in the pagination of his Narrative, stated that he
landed between 15,000 and 16,000. A note in 1 Kemble, 382, states that Howe's Orderly Book
for June 30 to Oct. 5, 1776, is missing from Kemble's files, but the so-called Glyn Journal in
the Library of Princeton University contains all the orders of general application for the period.
Howe's order of battle, as of Aug. 16, 1776, is included.
[132] For the details of the withdrawal and the first skirmishing at Flatbush, see 2 LIHS
Mem., 400–01. See also Va. Gazette, Sept. 6, 1776.
[133] 5 G. W., 476, 485.   [134] Ibid., 475.
[135] Ibid., 477, 478–79. The stout, terse phrase "cooked rations" was not used in Washington's Army at this time.

Island was to be the sole immediate objective of the British, but he did not feel he should count on it as a reasonable certainty and he did not think he should leave his post on New York Island, even temporarily, until flood tide passed without any indication of attack there. While he awaited the high water, which would come at 11 A.M., he had to deal with a report, widespread in New York, that he intended to sanction the burning of the town if he were compelled to evacuate it. After a prompt denial of this,[136] he had some satisfaction in the rise of a wind adverse to the British.[137] Then, as he could discern no preparations aboard the British fleet for a new landing,[138] he had five more Battalions made ready,[139] and he crossed in person to Long Island.[140] Either his observations there, or the pleas of "Old Put" convinced him it would be well to send that General to the island to supervise the defence. Putnam went accordingly—and to his immense satisfaction.[141] Fortunately for the New England veteran, this second transfer of command within four days was effected at a time when nothing worse was happening than an exchange of outpost firing on a small scale. Washington observed, studied the ground and the disposition of the forces, and then returned to New York. There late in the day, he received from Sullivan a dispatch that told of an affair in which the British had been worsted.[142] Said Sullivan: "We have driven them half a mile from their former station. These things argue well for us, and I hope are so many preludes to a general victory."[143] Washington read and, knowing Sullivan, doubted whether the attack of the redcoats was on the scale the Major General thought, but as the repulsed advance might be the first move of a larger effort, Washington decided to send four more Regiments to Long Island and to post them where they could be used by Sullivan, if necessary, or could be ferried back to New York in event the main operation were directed against the city.[144]

136 *Ibid.,* 478; for the light operations of the day, see *Penn. Gazette,* Sept. 4, 1776.
137 5 *G. W.,* 481.   138 1 *Reed,* 219.
139 5 *G. W.,* 476.   140 *Ibid.,* 481.
141 1 *Reed,* 220. GOs contain no mention of this assignment to a duty the scope and effect of which have been the subject of some speculation and dispute. Army regulations and usage, of course, would have made Putnam's command inclusive unless there were specific orders or instructions that restricted him. So far as the records show, no paper was issued that curtailed his authority. It must be assumed, therefore, that Putnam's command was real, and not merely titular. How far he exercised it is a different question. So is that of Sullivan's own authority, which is presently to be considered.
142 This was on the Bedford Road, which will be described in a later paragraph.
143 1 *Sullivan Papers,* 299, after 1 *Force* (5), p. 1136. See also *Penn. Gazette,* Sept. 4, 1776.
144 5 *G. W.,* 481.

On the morning of the 24th, the wind still was adverse to the British.[145] Washington reasoned that he could put aside again that day the probability of an attack on New York while the troops on Long Island were being hurled against Sullivan and Putnam, but he could not persuade himself that the danger of a dual offensive was past. It still seemed to the anxious Commander-in-Chief that his powerful adversary would not be content to strike one blow and one only. Washington was deepened, too, in his conviction that with his inferior force of troops, most of them untrained, he could do no more than hold his works and the approaches to them. Offensive operations were precluded unless, indeed, Governor Trumbull of Connecticut could organize a force of perhaps 1000 men to cross the Sound and to harass British who otherwise would be free to ravage and to plunder nearly the whole of Long Island. Washington asked the Governor to do this, though with little faith in the accomplishment of it.[146] Time had to be taken that morning of the 24th, tense though every moment was, to smooth the ruffled sensibilities of Philip Schuyler and to settle the usual number of questions with that harassed officer.[147] Then, once again, Washington went to the island, rode along the front and saw enough to draw from him a firm and reproachful letter to Putnam. The soldiers, Washington wrote, were wasting their shots; riflemen should be placed in a wood near a strategically important fortification at Red Hook; traps and ambuscades must be prepared; a line must be drawn and held.[148] Washington was concerned, among other things, because he feared the useless fire with small arms would keep back Hessians who were being urged to desert. A printed appeal to them had been wrapped about bits of tobacco and had been placed where the Germans would find the little packages and would read a message in their own language.[149] The invitation extended in this manner should not be cancelled, Washington argued, by musket balls. He would have been concerned on still another score had he been acquainted with a condition that Sullivan made the subject of General Orders on the 25th: discipline was so lax that American soldiers were wandering about western Long Island, sometimes miles beyond their

[145] Ibid., 485.
[146] 5 G. W., 485–86.
[147] Ibid., 482–83.
[148] Ibid., 486–89. For Red Hook, see the map, p. 160.
[149] Ibid., 451, 491.

position.[150] If the coming battle was to be a test of discipline, the auguries were not favorable to America.

The 25th of August passed without incident, except for the silent slipping of more and more of the British ships to The Narrows, while great fields of white tents disappeared from Staten Island. A rude and noisy night of thunder and lightning[151] ushered in the 26th, a day of tightened expectancy. Washington now faced somewhat decreased odds, because a total of nine Connecticut militia Regiments, approximately 3000 men,[152] had reported after the British landing on Long Island.[153] Otherwise, there was no great change in the situation. If new intelligence reports contained anything positive it was cumulative to the effect that simultaneous British attacks at two points were not in preparation. The Commander-in-Chief continued to warn his senior subordinate in New York that the occupation of part of the adjacent island might be a feint;[154] but "we are led to think," Washington now wrote Congress, "[the British] mean to land the main force of their army on Long Island, and to make their grand push there."[155] More American troops accordingly were rowed across East River to strengthen Putnam[156] who occupied a position that had some most unusual features. The essential of American strategy on Long Island was that of holding Brooklyn Heights, which commanded East River and the City of New York, much as the hills of Dorchester Peninsula had overlooked Boston. To secure Brooklyn, a line of parapets and a string of forts

---

[150] See the orders in 3 *LIHS Mem.*, 29.

[151] *Doctor Moffat's Diary*, MS, LC.

[152] 5 *G. W.*, 491.

[153] Col. William Douglas stated on August 23 that "almost one half of the grand Army now consists of Connecticut troops" (3 *LIHS Mem.*, 68).

[154] 5 *G. W.*, 493.

[155] *Ibid.*, 491.

[156] It is a singular fact that the effective strength of the American forces on Long Island at this time is nowhere stated authoritatively. Washington wrote, August 26, that the transfer of Regiments from one Brigade to another, because of the appointment of new Brigadiers, had made it impossible to prepare a general return (5 *G. W.*, 491); but even after the action he did not specify in any known document which of his units were on Long Island and which remained in New York, in the Flying Camp at Amboy, and at stations on North River or nearby. To reduce detailed calculations to simplest terms, the average Regiment or Batallion under Washington—the terms were used synonymously—had present, fit for duty, about 350 officers, nco's and privates. Sullivan on August 25 (3 *LIHS Mem.*, 28–29) listed twenty-six Battalions, added one the next day (*ibid.*, 27), and spoke of the arrival of others the number and designation of which he manifestly did not know (*ibid.*, 29–30). If, then, these were average Battalions—and the number suffices to yield a trustworthy average—Putnam had a minimum of 9450 effectives, officers and men. Reenforcement by even five Battalions on the 26th would have given Putnam slightly more than 11,000. Although this is a figure far above that credited to him in uninformed contemporary accounts, no major error will be made if it is assumed that the number of American troops on Long Island, as of August 27, was at least 10,000 effectives.

had been constructed near the western tip of the island, for a distance of about one mile, from the salt marshes overlooking Wallabout Bay to those of Gowanus Creek, which were believed to be impassable.[157] The general direction of these works was from Northeast to Southwest. About a mile and a half from this man-made line was the nearest point of the natural defences of Brooklyn—a long row of hills almost parallel to the fortifications.[158] This elevated ground extended for more than five miles and had a heavy cover of forest, as if designed by the Almighty to protect the defenders of Brooklyn Heights. The strength of this natural position was all the greater because it overlooked a wide and open plain that extended eastward and northeastward from Gravesend Bay. These hills, in a word, were the high natural out-works of Brooklyn and, therefore, of New York.

Travelers had found them as formidable as the continental soldiers hoped they would prove, but, through the years, farmers and carriers had opened four roads northward from the plain and over the hills, like the four fingers of a hand, with the thumb as the western end of the island.[159] Closest to the waters of New York Bay was the Gowanus Road, which nowhere was more than a mile and a half from The Narrows. Then came the Flatbush Road. From this, about half a mile South of Flatbush, diverged to the eastward the road that ran to Bedford and bore the name of that village. Approximately a mile and a half East of the point where the Bedford Road reached the crest of the hills, another road led around the edge of the ridge to the town of Jamaica. From that settlement, along the tips of the fingers, so to say, a cross road led to Brooklyn and to the East River Ferry thus: [160]

Putnam was in general command of all these positions, but he decided to guard in person the main defensive line of Brooklyn and to

[157] Reference is omitted to Smith's barbette on Cobble Hill, to Fort Stirling and to Fort Defiance on Red Hook, three strong positions that were not of any large service in the operations about to be described.

[158] In reality, more nearly from East to West.

[159] Much the best description of the terrain, in fact a model of lucid and simple explanation, is in Gen. Samuel H. Parsons's letter of Oct. 8, 1776, to John Adams, 3 *LIHS Mem.*, 35. This and Parsons's letter of Aug. 29, 1776, to John Adams appear in Charles S. Hall, *Life and Letters of Samuel Holden Parsons*, 54–57. The two are among the clearest brief accounts of the Battle of Long Island. This biography of Parsons is cited as *Hall's Parsons.*

[160] Perhaps the most useful map, on a scale of four inches to a mile, is that of Henry P. Johnston, in 3 *LIHS Mem.* This is executed with the scholarly care that marked all of Professor Johnston's work. In 2 *ibid.*, is Thomas W. Field's somewhat similar map which superimposed Brooklyn streets as they existed about 1868 on the old battleground. Unhappily, Field omitted a scale. Even when positions on his map are reconciled with those on Johnston's, which are on a different scale, there are some deviations of as much as one-fourth of a mile in two miles.

deputize to John Sullivan the management of the battle on the "out-work" of the hills. Sullivan, in turn, followed traditional seniority in his order of battle: he put Lord Stirling in command of the right and of the reserve within the earthworks,[161] which were closer to the right than to any other part of the line. Direct command of the centre and supervision of the left on the hills, covering the Flatbush and Bedford Roads, were under the care of Sullivan himself. His left element was Col. Samuel Miles's Pennsylvania Regiment of Stirling's Brigade, which had its exposed flank in the air. Miles was under orders to patrol in the direction of the road that led around the eastern end of the ridge to Jamaica; but as he had no mounted troops, he did not attempt to place vedettes far in advance, or to maintain them anywhere outside his lines at night.[162] Sullivan seemed to his subordinates to have his mind fixed on the probability of an attack along the road from Flatbush to Bedford, though he maintained later that he had hired horses at his own expense for a patrol of the Jamaica Road. On the evening of the 26th, he said, he arranged to send out five young officers to give him early word of any development there during the night.[163]

Washington observed and doubtless approved the principal dispositions. It is not certain that he knew in detail what was and was not being done to cover the left. Everything he saw and heard of the enemy indicated that the blow was about to fall. Additional troops had been brought ashore by the British;[164] the hostile camps, where visible, were astir. If an attack of magnitude was in the making, it had to be upgrade through the woods, Washington reasoned, and it could be delayed and hampered by the parties that had been posted along each of the three usual routes over the hills.[165] On the assumption that his soldiers behaved well, Washington could hope his main strategical objective would be achieved to the extent, at least, that by holding the

---

[161] On this point, Sullivan's memory later deceived him. In October, 1777, he maintained that "Lord Stirling commanded the main body without the lines; I was to have command under General Putnam within the lines" (2 *LIHS Mem.*, 370), but his own statement of some of the orders he gave (e.g., 3 *LIHS Mem.*, 27–28) and the text of his orders of August 25, concerning Stirling's command (*ibid.*, 30) leave no doubt whatsoever that he was vested with command outside the Brooklyn defences.

[162] Cf. Maj. Daniel Brodhead in 3 *LIHS Mem.*, 64.

[163] This is a moot issue, but the statement in the text appears to be one way, perhaps the only way, of reconciling the positive criticism made by Colonel Miles with Sullivan's common sense as a soldier. See 2 *LIHS Mem.*, 370–71; 3 *ibid.*, 60–61 and text, 176.

[164] On the 25th, two Brigades of Hessians under General von Heister were transferred from Staten Island to Long Island; see Howe's report of Sept. 2, 1776; 1 *Force* (5), p. 1256, and 1 *Kemble*, 85.

[165] See R. H. Harrison to the President of Congress, Aug. 27, 1776; 5 *G. W.*, 494.

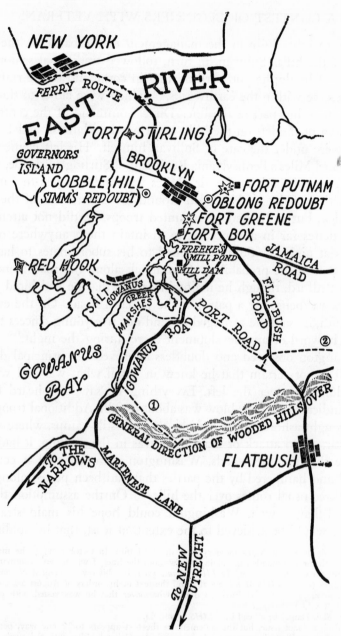

NEW YORK

FERRY ROUTE

EAST RIVER

FORT STIRLING

GOVERNORS ISLAND

BROOKLYN

COBBLE HILL
(SIMM'S REDOUBT)

FORT PUTNAM

OBLONG REDOUBT

FORT GREENE

FORT BOX

FREEKE'S MILL POND

MILL DAM

JAMAICA ROAD

RED HOOK

SALT

GOWANUS

CREEK

MARSHES

FLATBUSH ROAD

PORT ROAD

GOWANUS BAY

GOWANUS ROAD

②

①

GENERAL DIRECTION OF WOODED HILLS OVER

FLATBUSH

TO THE NARROWS

MARTENSE LANE

TO NEW UTRECHT

LONG ISLAND APPROACHES TO

This map is based on that of Thomas W. Field in *Memoirs of the Long Island Historical Society,*
Vol. II, and on that of Henry P. Johnston in Vol. III of the same publication, but the map must
be used with caution, because the two authorities sometimes were at variance by as much as half
a mile in their measurements. Certain positions cannot now be determined with precision;
several stretches of old road are lost beyond all possible identification among modern Brooklyn

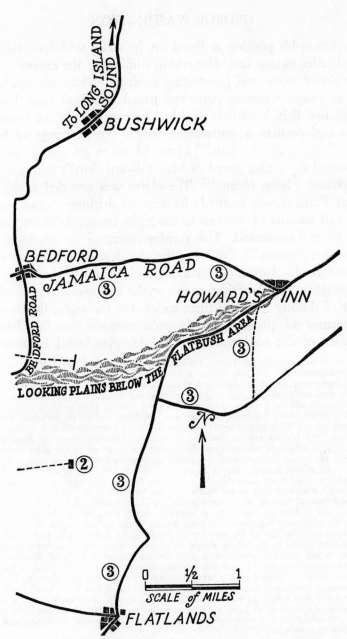

THE BROOKLYN DEFENCES

streets. The course of Schoonmaker's Creek is not known, except for the fact that the British crossed before they reached Howard's Inn. Either of two small streams on old maps, in the area immediately Southwest of the inn, would fit meagre surviving references to the creek. The numerals on the map indicate: (1) Stirling's advanced position on the morning of Aug. 27, 1776; (2) The front and left flank of Sullivan; (3) the direction of the principal British movement.

approaches to his position at Brooklyn, he could withdraw safely and in good order to that line after taking stiff toll of the enemy.

A night of sharp and penetrating coldness [166] had not reached the stroke of twelve when an American patrol near Red Lion Tavern [167] ran into two British soldiers who had been exploring the treasures of no less a place than a watermelon patch. An exchange of fire followed.[168] Next, about 1 A.M.,[169] a force of 200 to 300 men [170] attempted to surround the picket guard of Maj. Edward Burd's Battalion of the Pennsylvania Flying Camp.[171] The alarm was sounded at the front; General Putnam was notified; he aroused Stirling [172] and sent that officer and Samuel H. Parsons to the right front. Sullivan, too, went out in general command. This reenforcement of the advanced guard was about 2300 men.[173] Counting the 400 already in front on each of the three roads—Gowanus, Flatbush and Bedford—there now were approximately 3500 American troops on the high wooded ground along a front of slightly less than three miles. On the right, this reenforcement seemed adequate. The only embarrassment was the absence, at the outset, of the commanders of the Maryland and Delaware Bat-

[166] Journal of Capt. George Harris, Lushington's *Harris,* 76; 3 *LIHS Mem.,* 405–06. As sometimes happens, the literature of the action about to be described in the text is overabundant concerning details of slight importance to any except the participants. At the same time it is deplorably meagre regarding dispositions and maneuvers where the decision was reached. Virtually all the accounts of the battle known prior to 1878 to be in existence appear in 2 and 3 *LIHS Mem.,* but many of these are repetitious and of no historical significance. Washington did not file a formal report but gave in several letters (notably 5 *G. W.,* 496, 506 and 6 *ibid.,* 75) his reticent interpretation of events. Stirling's report of Aug. 29, 1776, (1 *Force* (5), p. 1245–46) was criticized for brevity but is as full as the circumstances of its composition permitted. Sullivan made no report and fathered no written statement that has survived, so far as now known, prior to his letters of Oct. 25 and Nov. 9, 1777, (2 *LIHS Mem.,* 369–71 and, perhaps more accessibly, in 1 *Sullivan Papers,* 549, 575) which contain vague and incidental references only to the Battle of Long Island. For the contest on the American right, under General Stirling, the accounts by Col. William Smallwood (2 *LIHS Mem.,* 387 ff), by Col. Samuel J. Atlee (1 *Force* (5), p. 1251 ff) and by Gen. Samuel H. Parsons (3 *LIHS Mem.,* 33 ff) adequately supplement Stirling's report. From the centre, the best contemporary account, historically, is that of Lt. Col. Daniel Brodhead (3 *LIHS Mem.,* 63 ff). Col. Samuel Miles's defence (*ibid.,* 60 ff), which should be a major document concerning operations on the American left, was not written until after the appearance in 1788 of William Gordon's *History.* Hessian reports are few and unimportant; British reports include those of Lord Howe and General Howe (1 *Force* (5), p. 1255–58), which are condensed but adequate. Useful, also, is the previously cited Journal of Capt. George Harris (included in a letter to his uncle, printed in Lushington's *Harris,* and quoted in 2 *LIHS Mem.,* 405–07). Testimony before a committee of the House of Commons in June, 1779, summarized in 2 *LIHS Mem.,* 460 ff, is singularly infertile. "Standard" British contemporary diaries—those of Kemble, Mackenzie and Robertson—contain little of value.

[167] At the junction of Martenese Lane and the road to The Narrows.

[168] This opening incident is mentioned in a letter of an unidentified Pennsylvania officer, Aug. 27, 1776. See 1 *Force* (5), p. 1183–84.

[169] The column established contact shortly after midnight (General Howe's report, *loc cit.*).

[170] 1 *Force* (5), p. 1183.   [171] *Ibid.,* 1251.

[172] *Ibid.,* 1245.   [173] *Ibid.,* 1251.

talions, who had been detained in New York by service on a court martial.[174] Another absentee was Jed. Huntington, an able Colonel of Connecticut Continentals, now the victim of a slow fever.[175]

Stirling kept his troops well in hand as they moved down the Gowanus Road, and at 7:30, he ordered them to deploy on high ground when he saw a strong British force advancing in his front.[176] This desired position was gained with small loss and was held against an adversary who established his light troops 150 yards from Stirling's right and soon opened a steady cannonade but did not make any general assault.[177] Eight o'clock of a clear, cool and pleasant day found the opposing forces briskly skirmishing.[178]

Sullivan by that hour probably had gone over to the centre of the line, opposite the Flatbush and Bedford roads.[179] He found, or else heard quickly, that the Hessians down the Flatbush Road had been cannonading the front since shortly after daylight[180] but that the enemy seemed to be moving against Stirling.[181] Thereupon Sullivan sent another Battalion to Stirling's support.[182]

It probably was about this time that Washington reached the scene from headquarters in New York.[183] He had directed the movement

---

[174] 2 *LIHS Mem.*, 387. [175] 3 *LIHS Mem.*, 40 and text, 163.

[176] 1 *Force* (5), p. 1145, 1252. [177] *Ibid.*

[178] Detailed accounts exist of the various moves in the occupation of the hill and of a hedge in front, but these were not important. For the weather, see *Serle*, 78.

[179] Maj. John Burnham's *Recollections*, 6. Testimony concerning Sullivan's presence at the centre during the early morning of the 27th depends in part on Burnham's testimony and, oddly, on whether or not there was a misprint in an article in the *South Carolina and American General Gazette* of Oct. 2, 1776, republished in 3 *LIHS Mem.*, 58–60. This article, which mingled fact and hearsay, stated "that about 8 o'clock General Sullivan sent down the Flat[bush] middle [road] and inquired of the guards whether they discovered any movements of the enemy in either of the roads." In recording this, H. P. Johnston inserted "[went?]" after "sent" in the text. Manifestly either word might have been employed, but acceptance of the text, as printed, would indicate that Sullivan, as commanding General outside the Brooklyn defences, may not have visited that part of the line where a surprise might have been expected. In war, the difference between "went" and "sent" often is the difference between vigilance and the lack of it.

[180] 1 *Force* (5), p. 1257.

[181] The account in the Charleston paper, cited *supra*, n. 179, stated that the enemy was moving up the Yellow Hook Road. This apparently was another name for part of the Gowanus Road.

[182] 3 *LIHS Mem.*, 59.

[183] No exact statement of the time of his arrival has been found, but R. H. Harrison's letter of the 27th to the President of Congress (5 *G. W.*, 494) makes it plain that the Commander-in-Chief returned to New York from Brooklyn on the 26th. Said Harrison of Washington: ". . . yesterday [the 26th] he went there [to Long Island] and continued till evening . . ." Further, in 1 *Force* (5), p. 1195, is an extract from a letter said to have been dated, "Headquarters, Long Island, Aug. 28, 1776." This reads as if it were written by some member of Washington's official family, and it begins as follows: "Yesterday General Washington and his suite came over to this place upon receiving intelligence that Generals Howe and Clinton had landed with all their troops, except a few to guard Staten Island." A

to the island of reenforcements, some of whom did not stomach the sight of the bloody wounded brought from the front;[184] and he had watched with anxiety the effort of five British war vessels to enter East River so that they might bombard the rear of American positions in Brooklyn and might sever communications with New York. Mercifully, soon after daybreak, the wind had shifted to the North against the British[185] and had favored the Americans, though the tide was running up East River. The attempt was still in progress. One vessel of the squadron, *Roebuck,* was tacking with conspicuous skill and might get within range of the battery at Red Hook.[186] A battle of uncertain issue thus was underway between wind and British oak and canvas, with the garrison of Red Hook as anxious spectators. It was a warning of what might yet be accomplished by the royal fleet. Washington's troops around Brooklyn might be cut off if the wind shifted to the South when the tide was rising.

On the island, the American commander faced the first pitched battle he ever had directed. Those five years on the Virginia frontier, those long months since he had opened headquarters at Cambridge—all had led to this confused hour and had not involved a single stand-up, field contest, for the outcome of which he would be held responsible. At the moment, there was little that Washington could do. Stirling seemed to be holding his own on the right, which might prove to be the critical position. On the centre and left, though the Hessians persisted in their fire, they had delivered no attack and they gave no indication that they intended to advance within the next hour or so. Every experienced soldier reasoned, of course, that the British would not be demonstrating so widely unless they planned a heavy blow. Even so, if the Americans showed discipline along with a fighting spirit, loss of the woodland

---

measure of suspicion is aroused by this because Howe and Clinton had landed on the 22nd; but the statement will stand up if "with" be omitted from the sentence. It then would state the fact—that all the troops had landed. Included would be those of von Heister, who, it will be remembered, had crossed The Narrows on the 26th. The statement continues: "Immediately on our arrival we heard the noise of a very smart engagement with musketry and field pieces; it proved to be Lord Stirling's Brigade . . ." While this is not historical evidence of the first order, it scarcely can be rejected. If accepted, it can mean only that Washington arrived after Stirling had become engaged vigorously, which was the case by 8 o'clock or approximately that hour.

[184] Cf. 2 *LIHS Mem.,* 508.

[185] Admiral Lord Howe's report in 1 *Force* (5), p. 1255–56.

[186] 5 *G. W.,* 495; Admiral Howe's report, *loc. cit.* Cf. 1 *Force* (5), p. 1249. Howe's report may be interpreted to indicate an early withdrawal of the vessels but at 12:35 P.M., a New York observer wrote: "A man of war coming up, said to be the *Roebuck,* has just lost by a flaw, [i.e., a sudden, brief gust] all she gained last tack" (*ibid.,* 1184).

would be gradual. An orderly withdrawal to the fortified line of Brooklyn should be entirely possible.

At nine o'clock, the clear, distinct sound of a cannon shot was audible, followed immediately by another from the same direction—signal guns, undoubtedly, but from the rear, not from the front of action. Whose guns were they? What did their fire signify? Everyone who heard them asked the same question and soon had the answer: British troops in large number were on the Bedford Road, in rear of Sullivan's men who were facing the Hessians around Flatbush. In an amazingly short time after that, the redcoats were pushing forward along the stretch of the Jamaica Road that led from Bedford to the point where it joined the Flatbush Road to the Brooklyn defences. Soon the British would reach the Gowanus Road and would cut off Stirling's line of retreat to the fortifications. Unseen and unopposed, the enemy had gone around the eastern end of the hills, on the road toward Jamaica, and then had turned to the left and South. A surprise had been executed as complete as that which had overwhelmed Braddock. In two wars, Washington's first major field engagement had that same tragic beginning.[187]

The British quickly covered their left, in the direction of Flatbush, as they faced to the West and pressed furiously onward from Bedford. At the signal, for which they long had been waiting, the Hessians pushed up the wooded ridge from Flatbush. The troops in front of Stirling abandoned their teasing tactics and opened in earnest. Everywhere the command seemed to be the same—to force the American volley and then to close with the bayonet before the Continentals could reload.[188]

Outwitted and outnumbered, the troops on the three roads saw no alternative to destruction except that of immediate retreat. Sullivan's men on the hills above Flatbush had a byway, called the Port Road, along which most of them fled almost on a straight line to the Brooklyn defences at a point near an earthwork called Fort Box. Others of Sullivan's troops, drifting to the left, were caught in the salt marshes of

[187] For the time of the arrival at Bedford, about 8:30 A.M., see Howe's report in 1 *Force* (5), p. 1256. The firing of the signal guns is mentioned in Captain Harris's letter to his uncle, Lushington's *Harris*, 76, reprinted in 2 *LIHS Mem.*, 406. Details of the British turning movement are summarized in the critique, p. 177. Cf. p. 369.

[188] 1 *Force* (5), p. 1259–60. The Hessians had been told that the Americans would kill all they captured. Consequently, when the Germans came to grips, some of the mercenaries impaled or brained those who fell or surrendered, but instances of this sort probably were not as numerous as they were reported at the time to have been.

Gowanus Creek. Stirling found his retreat almost cut off by his pursuers and by British advancing on the Jamaica Road, and he had to send most of his bewildered soldiers through the morass, while the men of Smallwood's Maryland Battalion endeavored to hold off the enemy long enough for their comrades to escape.[189] Washington is said to have watched the Marylanders take this position. In admiration he is reported to have cried, "Good God, what brave fellows I must this day lose!"[190] The price was as high as he feared it would be. At the front and in this last defence, 256 of Smallwood's men were killed, drowned or captured of a total 684.[191] Several other of Stirling's Battalions of Pennsylvania and Delaware troops suffered dismally in making their way back to the Brooklyn line.[192]

By early afternoon,[193] most of the Continentals who had escaped the bayonets of the British or had made their way through the bottomless marsh, had reached the Brooklyn defences, where Washington himself shared the work of rallying them. "Remember what you are contending for," he cried to some of them [194] but he did not have at hand the leaders the men knew best. Stirling was missing. Sullivan had failed to fight his way out. Several promising officers were known to have been killed; Col. Samuel J. Atlee was a prisoner,[195] so was Col. Samuel Miles.[196] One Pennsylvania militia Major was alleged to have fled the island altogether when he heard the alarm sounded on the approach of the enemy.[197] At the moment, in the bewildering confusion, it was

189 2 *LIHS Mem.*, 387 ff. This, the most dramatic and gallant episode of the engagement, was between the Cortelyou and Schoonmaker houses, in the district of Third and Eighth Streets, West of Fifth Avenue, Brooklyn.

190 Narrative of an unnamed soldier, Sept. 1, 1776, in Onderdonk, *Revolutionary Incidents, Suffolk County*, 147, quoted in 2 *LIHS Mem.*, 528.

191 2 *LIHS Mem.*, 390, 404. After reviewing the evidence with careful detachment, Prof. H. P. Johnston concluded (3 *LIHS Mem.*, 188 n) there was no foundation for the charge made by Smallwood (2 *LIHS Mem.*, 388) that the bridge at one end of the milldam below Freeke's Pond was burned by Col. Jonathan Ward. The crossing was covered by continental cannon and would have been available for Stirling's men. In the opinion of Johnston, it was not destroyed until Cornwallis's troops were in position to use it and thereby to cut off Americans. Heath (*op. cit.*, 66) manifestly was mistaken in attributing the American defeat to the burning of this bridge.

192 See Stirling in 1 *Force* (5), p. 1245–46, Atlee in *ibid.*, 1253 ff. Reference to Col. John Haslet and his Delaware command is made in *ibid.*, 1176.

193 This is as close an approximation of the time as seems possible in the absence of specific statement by any of the commanding Generals on either side. Stirling noted (1 *Force* (5), p. 1245) that Howe's troops were discovered in his rear at 11 A.M. Howe (*ibid.*, 1257) said only, "In the evening of the 27th, the army encamped in front of the enemy's works." As will appear presently, the first time definitely fixed in reports is 4 P.M.

194 *Diary of Samuel Richards*, 36.   195 1 *Force* (5), p. 1254.

196 3 *LIHS Mem.*, 63. On the Pennsylvania casualty return (*ibid.*, 1250), Col. [James] Piper is mentioned as a prisoner but he was, in reality, a Lieutenant Colonel, not a Colonel.

197 6 *G. W.*, 26, 41.

impossible to say how many officers had been captured.[198] Casualties among nco's and enlisted men obviously ran into the hundreds,[199] and might rise higher because the British were drawing nearer, as if they were preparing to assault the American line. Some officers, at least, became nervously conscious of the weakness of the defences in front of Brooklyn. Troops were put to work immediately to complete several fortifications, particularly those that were designed to cover the approaches on the Jamaica Road;[200] but in the haste and excitement of the afternoon, hard tasks were slighted, and dangerous duty was dodged.[201] The one immediate relief was the discovery that the last of the British men-of-war that had attempted to come up East River had been able to do no more than to send a few shots in the direction of the fort at Red Hook and then, in the face of an ebbtide, had been compelled to anchor, as others already had, out of range.[202] The royal Regiments in front of Brooklyn might or might not be held off; there was no danger the defences would be bombarded from the rear that evening with the heavy projectiles of the fleet.

Washington and the other officers did all they could to rally the Army, but every quality of leadership was tested. After the action,

[198] Final British figures put the total at eighty-nine. Captured "staff" included two volunteers not counted as officers (1 *Force* (5), p. 1258; 3 *Force* (5), p. 1058.)

[199] British summaries (*ibid.*), list 1006 captured privates in a total of 1097. Washington subsequently reckoned his losses at 700 to 1000 (6 *G. W.*, 10) and still later put the total at about 800, of whom more than three-fourths were prisoners (*ibid.*, 75). As there is no reason to question the honesty of the official return by the British Commissary of Prisoners, the discrepancy is to be explained, probably, on the ground that Washington's headquarters never received returns of some of the temporary units of the Flying Camp or of other militia hurriedly sent to the island. The number of Americans killed in the action cannot be determined, but if fatalities in the entire force were in the same ratio as the known killed and missing among Pennsylvania officers were to those made prisoner from that corps of officers, they were as seven killed or missing to twenty-five prisoners, or roughly 1:3.5. This ratio would indicate the killed and permanently missing were about 312. The resulting total would be 1407 killed, wounded, missing victims of the marshes, and prisoners of war, a figure that may not be an unreasonable median, so to say, between American estimates that manifestly are too low and such exaggeration of casualties as the figure of 3300 in Howe's report (1 *Force* (5), p. 1057), "near 4000" in *Serle*, 88, "about 4000" in Sir George Collier's narrative, *loc. cit.*, 272, and "near 6000" of Gen. Sir Henry Clinton in his letter of Sept. 7, 1776, to Edward Harvey; *Clinton Papers*, Clements Lib. For Prof. H. P. Johnston's different view and for his argument that the figures in Washington's letters are substantially correct, see 3 *LIHS Mem.*, text, 202 n. British casualties were reported officially on September 3 as 339 and those of the Hessians as twenty. Of this total of 367, the reported fatalities were sixty-three (1 *Force* (5), p. 1257) but that figure probably was increased slightly by the subsequent death of some of the wounded. Washington was convinced that British casualties exceeded American (6 *G. W.*, 76).

[200] See John Morin Scott to John Jay, Sept. 6, 1776; 3 *LIHS Mem.*, 37.

[201] Cf. minutes of council of Aug. 29, 1776, 1 *Force* (5), p. 1246: "Though our lines were fortified with some strong redoubts, yet a great part of them were weak, being abbatied with brush and affording no strong cover . . ."

[202] See Admiral Lord Howe's report of Oct. 10, 1776; 1 *Force* (5), p. 1255-56.

many of the soldiers found themselves in the company of strangers; their familiar comrades were lost; their officers were absent;[203] the enemy appeared ready to finish the slaughter. At any minute, timid men told themselves, the red line might form in the fields and might charge straight up to the works and over them. The assault might be irresistible, if it were delivered . . . but it was not. Before the bewildered eyes of the exhausted Americans in the redoubts, the British drew back, out of cannon range, and halted as if they had other plans afoot than those of an assault. It was a respite; it must not be an informal truce. American officers still had sufficient fight left in them to order continental riflemen into a wood near the British front. From that cover, the marksmen opened a steady fire after 4 P.M. This irritated the British and cramped their movement without provoking either a farther withdrawal or an attempt to clear the Americans from among the trees.[204]

Were the British and Hessians being rested for a night attack? Such trained and experienced regulars as those in front of Washington were able to execute that difficult maneuver, even over unfamiliar ground, under the direction of good officers: if an attack were launched under blackened skies, could the Continentals resist? It might be a desperate, murderous issue, but it did not present its full horror to Washington. He had acquired some knowledge of his adversary during those anxious months around Boston, and though he had spent an agonizing day, he had not lost his clear reasoning. Now he began to suspect that, instead of attacking forthwith, Howe might prefer to undertake regular approaches.[205]

Darkness fell, and then the dragging minutes crept to a midnight that threatened never to come. There was no attack. Not a sound of preparation for an assault was audible from the British camp. Silence continued even at the approach of those hours before dawn when fear commands the exhausted mind, and the air is full of whispering, and every rustle of leaves is, in imagination, the movement of those who are forming a line for a surprise attack. Washington had some sleep during the night but by 4 o'clock on the 28th [206] he was astir. The first

---

[203] Minutes of the council of Aug. 29, 1776, 1 *Force* (5), p. 1246.

[204] See letter of Capt. George Harris to his uncle, Lushington's *Harris*, 77; reprinted in 2 *LIHS Mem.*, 406. As intimated *supra*, n. 193, this exposure of the British at 4 P.M. is the first event of the afternoon for which a time may be set with any certainty.

[205] 5 *G. W.*, 494 and n. 215 *infra*.   [206] 1 *Force* (5), p. 1195.

moments of visibility showed him that the British were still in the
position they held the previous evening. They were making no preparations, apparently, to hurl their heavy Battalions at the brittle American
lines. Relieved by this, Washington did what he could to see that the
men found their Regiments, got their food, put their arms in order
and, if wounded, had the attention of a surgeon. Out in East River,
whither the eyes of officers frequently were turned, the wind still
favored the Continentals and kept the British warships so far off that
the Americans' communication between Long Island and New York
could be maintained. The fort at Red Hook was not troubled.

For the defence of the Brooklyn earthworks, additional troops were
brought over to reenforce those of Putnam's men who thus far had
been called on to do nothing more than to stand at their alarm posts.[207]
By these efforts during the early hours of the 28th, Washington was
able to improve somewhat his chances of repulsing Howe's assault,
which was slow in the making and perhaps for that reason might be
the more dangerous. Waiting for it, Washington had to give an answer
to a representative of the New York Convention who sought the detachment of two Long Island militia Regiments, then in the Brooklyn
defences, to help the diligent Brigadier of the militia of the island,
Nathaniel Woodhull, in protecting the live stock around Jamaica.[208]
Washington called together the general officers near at hand and asked
their opinion before he replied to the messenger of the convention,
but he had no doubt what he should say: Although Howe manifestly
was employing on Long Island a considerable part of the entire British
forces, the royal commander might, in Washington's word, have "reserved some to attack New York." To hold that town, Washington had
no more than minimum strength; he needed every firelock he could
command. Not even the Long Island militia could be spared for use
in protecting any part of the island outside the Brooklyn lines.[209]

Anxiously and slowly the morning of the 28th passed without a
British movement against those lines. Afternoon brought a measure
of temporary security at the price of hours of wretched discomfort.
Many of the reenforcements had been hurried to Long Island without

---

[207] A few of the Regiments brought over from New York probably can be identified, but
none of Washington's orders of the day survive. No GOs were issued or, if issued, transcribed.
[208] These two Regiments, Josiah Smith's and Jeronimus Remsen's, had been acting temporarily with Nixon's Brigade. See 3 LIHS Mem., 131 n.
[209] 5 G. W., 495.

their tents; the canvas previously spread there and the houses of the townspeople did not suffice to put a roof of any sort over a large part of the Army. Now a cold rain began to fall on ground already water-soaked. The temperature dropped; chill and moisture pervaded everything; it was impossible for many of the soldiers to keep even their firearms dry.[210] For the relief of these shivering and discouraged men, Washington had tents ferried across East River, and he spent the night seeing that they were raised as soon as they were landed; but it was slow work, though done in the unhappy knowledge that every hour of inevitable delay would add scores, perhaps hundreds, to the sick list.[211]

At 4:30 on the morning of the 29th, Washington found time and shelter in which to write Congress briefly of the rain and distress that had followed what he termed the "engagement between a detachment of our men and the enemy" on the 27th.[212] He had to inform the Delegates, also, that he had heard nothing of Lord Stirling or of General Sullivan, and that he could not give any figures of the losses sustained. Some of the missing, he said hopefully, might come in.[213] The entire night had been so noisy with rain that nothing of what might be happening on the British lines had been audible. At the time Washington drafted his report to Congress, he had received no intelligence of any change in front of the American lines; but when he went out after completing his dispatch, he saw through the downpour the carefully drawn outline of a British redoubt, for which the enemy had broken ground during the night. The earthwork was confidently, arrogantly close—not more than 600 yards from the American left—and on a site well chosen.[214] Washington immediately accepted the rising mudbank as confirmation of what he had suspected since the afternoon of the 27th—that the British were to undertake the capture of the American lines by regular approaches over a stretch of land favorable to that type of operation.[215]

[210] 5 G. W., 497; Col. Moses Little in 3 LIHS Mem., 43. The Diary of the Moravian Congregation, 1 Penn. Mag., 147) mentions a heavy rain in New York City "till toward evening" and on the afternoon of the 29th "such heavy rainfall again as can hardly be remembered." This storm must have been a typical "August nor'easter."

[211] 5 G. W., 497. For his night-long activity, see ibid., 506.

[212] 5 G. W., 496.   [213] Ibid.

[214] Minutes of council of Aug. 29, 1776; 1 Force (5), p. 1246; General Howe's report, ibid., 1257.

[215] 6 G. W., 21. "Regular approaches," in the military language of Washington's day, included all earthworks, whatever their size or nature, erected by a besieger to shorten the distance to a hostile, fortified position, and thereby to facilitate final bombardment or assault.

If Brooklyn was to be besieged, it was imperative, first of all, that the wounded of August 27 be sent across East River to New York and that fresh troops take the place, as far as might be, of those who were weary, wet and disheartened. Washington now thought it probable that the British might attack New York while part of Howe's army held him in Brooklyn, and for this precautionary reason the American commander did not strip New York of its last guards. Instead, he called additional reenforcements from the Flying Camp of General Mercer at Amboy. The number who could be supplied from that quarter was small, and the troops themselves were newly mustered militia, but any help would be an encouragement that drenching day. In orders, therefore, announcement was made of the coming of troops from the Flying Camp that afternoon, with the assurance that this would change the situation.[216]

Regardless of this or of anything else that occurred on land, short of a successful continental sortie, the fate of the American troops on Long Island depended, of course, on the continuance of winds that would keep the British from pitting their navigation against the cunning of the men who had placed the obstructions in East River and had located batteries to sweep that waterway. After what had happened in North River when *Phoenix* and *Rose* had mocked the frown of Knox's guns, there was small reason to hope the American forts would turn back Lord Howe's fleet now, even though the ranges were much shorter than they were opposite the Jersey shore. At the moment, Washington's flatboats were crossing the East River undisturbed. The wind still was from the Northeast and was adverse to the British. Fog and mist obscured the fleet. If any threatening movement was in the making on the part of Admiral Howe, it could not be observed.

The day of the 29th wore on wearily, in unrelenting rain and deepened gloom. Arms could not be put in order; much ammunition was spoiled by dampness; honest-minded commanders had to ask themselves whether their wet and weary men could stay in the flooded trenches if the British delivered a strong attack. An alarming report came in, also, of the presence of British ships at Flushing Bay, about nine miles Northeast of the Brooklyn position. There was intimation, or at least fear, that the British might be moving part of their troops

---

216 Orders of Aug. 29, 1776 "Headquarters Long Island," (3 *LIHS Mem.*, 30–31). This paper is not in the style of Washington's GOs, is not included in the recorded orders, and, as Fitzpatrick suggested, probably was written by one of Putnam's staff.

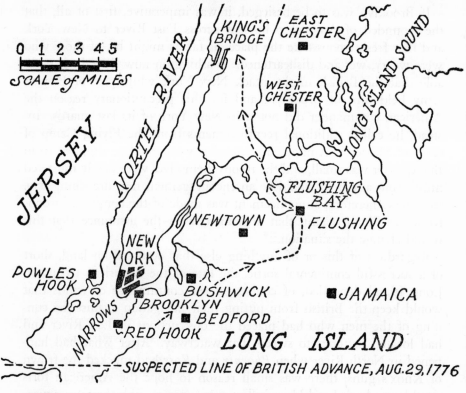

DIRECTION OF SUSPECTED TURNING MOVEMENT, AUG. 29, 1776

When the British did not renew their attack after the success of August 27, some of the American leaders on Long Island thought the enemy might be planning to move, via Flushing, to King's Bridge and thereby to cut off American retreat from New York Island.

over Long Island behind their lines to Flushing, perhaps to cross thence to the mainland and to assail Kings Bridge as shown above.[217] Added to these depressing circumstances during the day was the regretful assurance informed Brooklyn citizens gave that even if the obstructions in the main channel stopped the British men-of-war, armed ships of light draft could pass between Long Island and Governor's Island. No obstruction had been placed on that stretch because the water had been regarded as so shallow that no vessel could nagivate there.[218] This and almost every other strategical aspect of the operation

[217] See minutes of council, Aug. 29, 1776, 1 *Force* (5), p. 1246. The information of Maj. Gen. William Heath, commanding officer at King's Bridge, was to the effect that approximately 100 of the British Light Horse were pillaging at Flushing. See *ibid.*, 1216.

[218] See minutes of council, Aug. 29, 1776, as *supra*. It is to the loss of drama in American

were a reminder Washington scarcely needed—that he continued to keep his small Army dangerously divided in the face of an adversary who controlled the waterways and therefore could concentrate in force wherever desired, whenever the wind and tide permitted.

These adversities combined so manifestly to threaten the destruction of the dispersed American Army that Washington felt he should consult his council of war. That afternoon, at Philip Livingston's country house,[219] he asked the seven Generals then in the Brooklyn defences [220] whether, in the words of the minutes of the council, "under all circumstances, it would not be eligible to leave Long Island and its dependencies, and remove the Army to New York." [221] No less than eight reasons for an affirmative answer were marshalled, doubtless by Washington himself, weary though he was; but the seventh reason was the one most ominously phrased: "The divided state of the troops render our defence very precarious, and the duty of defending long and extensive lines at so many different places, without proper conveniences and covering, so very fatiguing that the troops had become dispirited by their incessant duty and watching." [222] Gen. John Morin Scott, a

---

history that no place can be given the tradition of the manner in which Col. Joseph Reed and Col. William Grayson are alleged to have looked from the fog-covered shore on the 29th and to have seen plainly, the wind having shifted, that boats were hurrying to and from the flagship in manifest preparation for a movement which the observers took to be the attempted passage of East River. Reed is supposed to have informed Washington of this activity, whereupon a council of war was called with the resulting decision presently to be described. Behind this was a story that Colonel Reed made this reconnaissance at the instance of Col. John Shee of the Third Pennsylvania Battalion who was inspired by Capt. Alexander Graydon as duly set forth in the *Memoirs* of that worthy (p. 166). The reasons for rejecting the tradition are: First, the wind did not shift sufficiently that day, if at all, to justify preparations for the ascent of the river. Kemble, (*loc. cit.,* 86) said the wind on the 29th was adverse. Reed himself in a letter of August 30 to Gen. William Livingston stated that every day the enemy was attempting, "with the wind ahead," to come up East River (2 *LIHS Mem.,* 398). Moreover, in the minutes of the council of August 29, there is reference to the fact that the wind was Northeast. While the tense of the verbs in these council minutes was a bit unusual, there is every reason to think the reference was to a continuing wind from that quarter. Second, no reference to the immediate prospect of any movement up the East River occurs in the minutes of the council of war, which took into account all ascertained facts in the situation. In the third place, Colonel Reed mentioned no such incident in any known letter of this period, though he wrote frequently and with candor. Fourth, the story of what Grayson and Reed are alleged to have seen from the shore is said to have been told in 1789 or in 1790 by William Grayson to Gen. John Armstrong who, at the age of 84, in March, 1843, wrote of it to William B. Reed. The time-gap between the occurrence and the printed narration thus was almost sixty-seven years— and second hand at that. It is too bad that so charming a story will not stand the tests of historical criticism!

219 John Morin Scott in 3 *LIHS Mem.,* 37; Reed (*op. cit.,* v. 1, p. 227) is authority for the statement that the council was held in the afternoon.

220 They were Major Generals Putnam and Spencer, and Brigadiers Mifflin, McDougall, Parsons, John Morin Scott and James Wadsworth. The last two on this list were commanding militia.

221 Minutes of council, Aug. 29, 1776; 1 *Force* (5), p. 1246.

222 *Ibid.*

militia officer of little experience, argued for a time against the evacuation of Long Island on the fundamental that every inch of ground should be contested, but he was won over by the other considerations and, in particular, by the endorsement Alexander McDougall gave the statement of Brooklyn citizens that the enemy could penetrate readily the unobstructed waters East of Governor's Island.[223] As McDougall had been a mariner as well as a New York merchant, his knowledge of the waterfront was accepted. The decision of the council was unanimous for evacuation and was affirmed in a brief paper to which all members of the council subscribed.[224] Washington himself reduced the decision to its simplest terms when he said the decisive facts were the regular approaches of Howe over favorable ground and the prospect of being cut off by the fleet. As Washington put it in a letter to Governor Trumbull, the British could keep the American Army divided and therefore unable to oppose the enemy at any point.[225]

Preparation had to be started at once for so complicated a movement as the transfer of 10,000 or perhaps 12,000 men across East River in the darkness. The ten flat-bottomed boats that had been set aside for the use of Greene's troops [226] had to be supplemented by all that could be assembled on East River and then could be ferried to Long Island after darkness.[227] In a short time the activity of officers, the whispered exchanges, the arrival and dispatch of messengers made it plain to the troops that something of magnitude was afoot. As the men speculated, many concluded they were to be called on to attack the British, and they talked of this and of other possibilities with so much earnestness that the mutter of many voices could be heard,[228] but providentially, as some thought, the fog settled heavily ere long and blanketed all sound.[229] As quickly as possible after nightfall, men and moveables were sent to

[223] A British intelligence report of Apr. 6, 1776, had included a statement, almost casually, that a ship or sloop could get between Governor's Island and Long Island and could assail the batteries of both positions. (*Clinton Papers*, loc. cit.).

[224] Except Washington, whom, in a technical sense, the council was advising. The original document, with the seven signatures, is reproduced in 5 *G. W.*, opposite p. 496. It is interesting to note how firmly some of the names are written, in spite of the excitement and the strain of sleepless hours.

[225] Letter of Sept. 6, 1776 (6 *G. W.*, 21–22); Cf. to the New York Legislature, August 30, 1776: "Circumstanced as this Army was, in respect to situation, strength, &c, it was the unanimous advice of a council of general officers to give up Long Island; and not, by dividing our force, be unable to resist the enemy in any one point of attack" (5 *ibid.*, 498–99).

[226] Aug. 13, 1776; 5 *G. W.*, 425.

[227] Cf. Thomas Mifflin to William Heath, Aug. 29, 1776; 3 *LIHS Mem.*, 218.

[228] *Graydon*, 165–66.

[229] 1 *Force* (5), p. 1233; the same account is in 2 *LIHS Mem.*, 523.

the ferry landing whence, with surprising speed, they were rowed to New York. Again and again, the boats came back and took their loads and disappeared but did not lose direction. Some troops were brought to the waterfront before it was their turn to embark and they had to be marched to their former stations and held there. Men said afterwards that they had seen no finer display of discipline than that of the Battalions who marched, unmurmuring, away from the boats that would have conveyed them to shelter and to safety.[230]

The night hours seemed agonizingly long for those who had to wait, and not long enough for officers charged with the duty of getting all the troops and all the equipment to New York. Every tick of a watch seemed as slow as the words of a judge passing sentence that might mean either life or death. Effort tipped the scale. Before the late August dawn, all the men except a few sentinels had been put aboard. The heavy guns only had to be left behind, because they sank hub-deep in mud from which they could not be pulled by all the men who could put hand to rope.[231] One of the last to leave the island, Lieut. Benjamin Tallmadge,[232] saw a tall figure on the ferry stairs as he went down and, though he was not sure, he thought it was General Washington.[233] The next time most of the soldiers heard anything from their Commander-in-Chief, he was explaining in General Orders that no doubt concerning the courage of the Army had entered into the decision to retreat from Long Island, that the situation now was reversed, that the British could receive little help from their ships, and that the Americans could act together against dispersed adversaries. "They must effect a landing under so many disadvantages that if officers and soldiers are vigilant and alert, to prevent surprise and add spirit when they approach, there is no doubt of our success." [234]

The battle had been lost; the campaign must not be!

230 1 *Reed*, 228–29; *Heath*, 67; 1 *Force* (5), p. 1233.
231 5 *G. W.*, 506; 3 *LIHS Mem.*, 38.
232 Then Adjutant of Col. John Chester's Connecticut State Regiment.
233 *Memoir of Col. Benjamin Tallmadge*, (ed. 1904) p. 13; the same incident is mentioned in 3 *LIHS Mem.*, 79.
234 GO of Aug. 31, 1776; 5 *G. W.*, 502.

CHAPTER VII

Doubtful Balance of Loss and Gain

(August 30–September 16, 1776)

ON THE evening of the 30th and the morning of the 31st of August, the small garrison of Governor's Island was transported to New York under the very eyes of British naval officers who still encountered, out of range, that persistent northeast wind, a strong if temporary American ally.[1] While this removal was making red faces match their owners' coats, Washington ruefully was reckoning the number of good leaders he had lost on Long Island. Word had been received during the exciting hours of the 29th that General Sullivan, Lord Stirling and several others were prisoners of war.[2] Stirling, cut off, had surrendered in person to General von Heister;[3] the New Hampshire General had been caught on the 27th in a cornfield about a hundred yards from the post of one of the Hessian commanders.[4] Now, on the 30th, Sullivan came over to New York from the Long Island lines on parole,[5] and in a new capacity: he was sent by Lord Howe to give notice that the British Admiral wanted to see some members of Congress in order that he might explain to them the nature of the peace mission with which he and his brother, the General, were entrusted. Washington was busy with all the sombre details of salvage and reorganization, but he was of opinion that in a matter important in form, even if deceptive and fragile in substance, he should not deny Sullivan the privilege that officer sought of going to Philadelphia and of repeating to the Delegates what Howe had told him.[6] Off, then, Sullivan rode—to put the match to a controversy so hot and furious that the defeat of Long Island ceased to be the exclusive subject of conversation.[7]

---

[1] 5 G. W., 507; 1 Kemble, 86.

[2] Joseph Reed to William Livingston, Aug. 30, 1776; 1 Force (5), p. 1231. Stirling's report, written aboard Eagle, was dated August 29 (ibid., 1245–46; also in 4 Sparks, 516–17), and was delivered to Washington the next day by Sullivan (5 G. W., 507).

[3] 1 Force (5), p. 1246.   [4] 2 LIHS Mem., 436, text.

[5] 1 Force (5), p. 1250; 1 Sullivan Papers, 299.

[6] 5 G. W., 507; 1 Sullivan Papers, 299–300.

[7] Cf. 2 Burnett, 66, 69, 74. Congress divided squarely on the question of creating a committee to confer in a private capacity with the Howes, as those gentlemen desired, but in

This was not the case in New York. Men who had found both hardship and humiliation on Long Island talked almost endlessly of what had happened and of why they had lost. Washington did not feel that Stirling's report was sufficiently explicit and detailed to account for some of the occurrences of August 27,[8] but he concluded that the defeat was chargeable primarily against "two detachments of our people, who," as he told the Massachusetts Legislature, "were posted in two roads leading through a wood in order to intercept the enemy in their march, suffering a surprise and making a precipitate retreat, which enabled the enemy to lead a great part of their force against the troops commanded by Lord Stirling . . ."[9] In short, the success of the British operation, as Washington saw it at the time, was due to lack of vigilance on the part of Sullivan's men, who guarded the Flatbush and Bedford Roads but failed to prevent surprise along the Jamaica Road.

Washington was justified in this judgment, to the extent at least that the field officers on the left had neither the force nor the experienced direction required to thwart a flank march that was conceived soundly and was executed with brilliant precision. British dispositions had been made with care;[10] the march from New Utrecht through Flatlands and thence over Schoonmaker's Creek to Howard's Inn[11] was smooth and swift without being fast enough to exhaust the troops.[12] At every stage of their advance the British had good luck: They found the creek undefended; the only patrol encountered by the van was that of the five young officers sent out by Sullivan; these men not only were captured but also were induced to disclose that the road ahead was unoccupied by American troops.[13] Bedford had been reached about 8:30; the

---

the end Congress voted to name a committee of three—Benjamin Franklin, John Adams and Edward Rutledge (5 *JCC.*, 737, 738, 743). The abortive conferences that followed this action are traced in John Adams' correspondence and in Troyer S. Anderson, *The Command of the Howe Brothers during the American Revolution,* 157 ff. Sullivan's departure from Philadelphia, September 7, is mentioned in *Marshall Diary,* 91.

[8] 5 *G. W.,* 507.

[9] Letter of Sept. 19, 1776; 6 *G. W.,* 75–76.

[10] See the details in 1 *Kemble,* 85. Cf. Gen. Sir Henry Clinton to Edward Harvey, Sept. 1. 1776: ". . . we landed here without opposition, at which I was much astonished, as they might have plagued us much . . ." *Clinton Papers,* Clements Lib.

[11] See the map, p. 161. To repeat, Schoonmaker's Creek has not been located, nor is its course described in any account unearthed during this research.

[12] Cf. *Percy Letters,* 67; General Howe's report, 1 *Force* (5), p. 1256. The order of march is in 1 *Kemble,* 85.

[13] 1 *Force* (5), p. 1256; 3 *LIHS Mem.,* 178 n. See 1 *Mackenzie,* 37, for the picturesque detail of the arrival at Howard's Inn of a loyalist volunteer contingent of forty-nine men from the district of Oyster Bay. They carried "before them on a long pole," said Mackenzie, "a white shirt by way of a flag of truce."

attack had been launched thereafter as soon as Cornwallis's and Clinton's men had arrived, and before Lord Percy's Guards had closed the column.[14] The fullest advantages of a complete surprise then awaited the British.

In plain words, the redcoats had outclassed the Continentals. The American Commander-in-Chief had appeared to be a tiro, a bungler as well as a beginner, in comparison with the English General.[15] Washington himself did not attempt to review the details and to set down in full the reasons for the defeat. The longest of the accounts he wrote of the battle did not exceed 500 words,[16] but in a succession of letters he soon shaped what might be termed the "official version" of the operations. This was, in effect, that an American "detachment" had received a "check." [17] Troops on two roads had been surprised, though the forces of Lord Stirling on the right had stood with "great bravery and resolution," [18] against a numerically superior adversary who had sustained heavy losses.[19] The British were so numerous and their fleet so powerful that it later had become necessary to evacuate Long Island and to reunite the American Regiments. This was the story, according to Washington. More than this it was not proper to set down on paper or to discuss publicly,[20] except as the recountal of the retreat might

---

[14] *Percy Letters*, 67.

[15] Perhaps the coldest, most realistic analysis of the poor showing of Washington and of his lieutenants in this action is presented in Charles Francis Adams, *Studies Military and Diplomatic*, 22 ff. In his letter to Edward Harvey, cited *supra*, Gen. Sir Henry Clinton wrote: ". . . whether we shall ever have it in our power to do the same thing I will not say, but if they ever place themselves so absurdly, the same will probably happen . . ."

[16] This was his dispatch of Aug. 31, 1776 to Congress (5 *G. W.*, 506–08). Washington appended to it the reasons advanced at the council of war for the evacuation of the Long Island defences. His other principal accounts of the battle of August 27 were in his letter of Sept. 6, 1776, to Gov. Jonathan Trumbull (6 G. W., 20–22); to the Massachusetts Legislature, Sept. 19, 1776 (*ibid.*, 75–76), and to John Augustine Washington, Sept. 22, 1776 (*ibid.*, 93).

[17] 6 *G. W.*, 4.

[18] 6 G. W., 93. In one letter, Washington's tribute to the men had been inclusive: The engagement, he said, "was warm and [was] conducted with great resolution and bravery on the part of our troops" (To Gov. Jonathan Trumbull, Sept. 6, 1776; 6 G. W., 21).

[19] *Ibid.*

[20] Contemporary letters and subsequent study laid varying emphasis on these considerations: (1) A prime cause of the disaster was the necessary substitution of Sullivan, who did not know the ground, for Greene, who was familiar with it; (2) Putnam's presence confused the situation because it divided authority and raised a doubt, at the last, whether the troops were wisely apportioned between the outworks and the Brooklyn defences, concerning which see Stephen Olney's Diary in C. R. A. Williams, *Biography of Revolutionary Heroes*, 172; (3) Washington erred in anticipating a probable attack on New York simultaneously with the operations on Long Island, and either he should have sought to defend only the Brooklyn lines or else he should have accepted battle on Brooklyn Heights with all his forces; (4) Sullivan's expectation of the main attack on the centre and his inattention personally to the Jamaica Road were the immediate reason for the rout of the left and centre; (5) the Americans were deceived on their right, where the British did no more than make a reconnaissance

salve American pride. Washington was not alone in thinking it to his credit and the Army's that he escaped from Long Island with no other loss than that of the heavy artillery. "In the morning," Stephen Kemble wrote, "to our great astonishment [we] found they had evacuated all their works on Brookland and Red Hook, without a shot being fired at them . . ."[21] Later, in *Dodsley's Annual Register*, a British critic was to write of the evacuation of Long Island, "Those who are best acquainted with the difficulty, embarrassment, noise and tumult which attend even by day, and no enemy at hand, a movement of this nature with several thousand men, will be the first to acknowledge that this retreat should hold a high place among military transactions."[22]

The decision to evacuate Long Island was sound and militarily economical. A very different story might have been written had Washington attempted to escape the night after the battle or under cover of darkness even on the 28th–29th. He had been the more willing to take the risk of remaining until he could leave without heavy loss because he was inclined to think, as early as the evening of the 27th, that Howe was going to undertake regular approaches.[23] In this, Washington was correct. Despite opposition and almost open protest by some of his subordinates, the British commander had refused to press home his attack on the evening of the day he turned the American left. "Had they been permitted to go on," Howe said of his troops in his report, "it is my opinion they would have carried the redoubt; but as it was apparent that the lines must have been ours at a very cheap rate by regular approaches, I would not risk the loss that might have been sustained in the assault . . ."[24]

It was to the credit of the American commander that he put the cor-

---

in force, opposite Stirling, until the turning movement had been completed; (6) in general, the American defence was incompetently directed by officers who did not have a correct understanding of what the enemy was doing at any time prior to the arrival of the British van on the Bedford Road in rear of Sullivan. Typical of the mistaken spirit of the defence was the action of Putnam in walking up and down the lines, after the approach of the enemy, while he repeated over and over his command at Bunker Hill, "Don't fire, boys, until you can see the whites of their eyes" (2 *LIHS. Mem.*, 222, text).

[21] *Op. cit.*, 86.

[22] *Dodsley's Annual Register*, 1776, "History of Europe," 173. Cf. An Officer of the Army ["Captain Hall"], *The History of the Civil War in America*, 194: "This astonishing and daring retreat—the very attempt of which did honor to the enemy—was effected across a river, or rather arm of the sea, almost a mile wide, and in the face of near twenty thousand victorious troops, who merely by being put in motion, must have ensured a success that would have gone near to finish the rebellion, in the destruction of so great a part of the rebel army."

[23] 5 *G. W.*, 494.

[24] 1 *Force* (5), p. 1257; *Howe's Narrative*, 4.

rect interpretation on this movement, but Washington knew that successful evacuation of a strong position never won a war and seldom was a preliminary of a successful campaign. As he faced on September 1 the next phase of the struggle for American independence, he had to ascertain, if he might, whether he could rely on the troops, whether he could entrust their lives to his officers, and whether he himself was competent. Had he been compelled to answer in plain words the critcial question, "Will your men stand up against the British?" he could have said only, "some will." He did not have confidence in the Army as a whole. Much the same answer would have been given an inquiry concerning the qualifications of his commissioned subordinates. The day of test on Long Island had shown him that field and general officers ranged from high promise to absolute worthlessness. As for himself, he penned nothing and he said nothing to indicate doubt in his mind of his own ability. At heart modest, he told himself and his friends that from lack of high ability as well as of experience, he might make mistakes which would be written in the blood of his men, but he did not feel that he was responsible for the losses on Long Island, and he had so positive a sense of his duty that he did not offer to stand aside.

In fact, the defeat on Long Island led immediately to a crisis that absorbed Washington's thought so completely he had no time for retrospect or for self-reproach: Before he could complete the reorganization of the Army necessitated by the death or capture of officers, he found, as he said, that "the check our detachment sustained . . . dispirited too great a proportion of our troops and filled their minds with apprehension and despair." [25] Militia began to melt away like ice in the summer sun. Almost by Regiments, they boldly left their camps and started home [26]—discouraged and unpaid, disillusioned and embittered.[27] Most of these men were part of the levies customarily supplied for brief emergencies; others were so-called "continental militia," who had been drafted by the states for a specified term of months at the expense of all America. Within little more than a week after the Battle of Long Island, the 8000 men in thirteen Connecticut militia Regiments had dwindled to 2000.[28] To what extent they quit because they thought it futile and personally dangerous to take up arms against

25 6 G. W., 4.   26 Ibid., 5.
27 Ibid., 23, 24.   28 Ibid., 32.

the British, Washington could not say, but when he reported to Congress the defection of the militia, he wrote: "if I were called upon to declare upon oath, whether the militia had been most serviceable or hurtful upon the whole, I should subscribe to the latter." [29] Other temporary soldiers were coming from Massachusetts and Connecticut to take the place of those who were going home; but these unwilling recruits had no small arms, tents or even camp-kettles, and, in most instances, they manifestly had no stomach for a fight.[30] Washington knew there would be some conscientious individuals among the "Long Faces," but he did not believe these new militia, *en masse,* would be any better than the old, whose mischief-making did not end with their own disdain of every law of military discipline. They took liberties, Washington protested, "which the soldier is punished for; this creates jealousy; jealousy begets dissatisfaction, and these by degrees ripen into mutiny . . ." Such discipline as the Army ever had possessed, the General said, "is in a manner done away with by having such a mixture of troops . . ." [31] The militiamen's example "infected another part of the Army" which felt that it could defy discipline precisely as the militia did.[32] This contagion showed itself in straggling [33] and in plundering [34] of which there previously had been little. Men of the Army looted even the quarters of Lord Stirling, the imprisoned General.[35] Washington threatened the death penalty unless there was an early end of cowardice, plunder and riot,[36] but, in imposing sentence, the courtsmartial had to be restrained. When one of Colonel Ritzema's men was convicted of a part in rifling Stirling's effects and was sentenced to thirty-nine lashes, Washington thought it prudent to have the culprit's Regiment marched off the parade before the punishment was inflicted.[37]

[29] Letter of Sept. 24, 1776; *ibid.,* 112.

[30] *Ibid.,* 39–40, 74–75, 78, 106; 2 *Force* (5), p. 441. Some of these militiamen represented almost the last man-power their communities could spare without taking the risk that crops might not be harvested for lack of hands. Half the men of arms-bearing age, Abigail Adams wrote her husband, had left her neighborhood for service with the Army (Adams, *Fam. Let.,* 230). In the region known as the Forks of the Brandywine, the women already were in the fields, with the ploughs, and were fallowing the land. They affirmed that if the men were called away, they would put in the crop of wheat (*Va. Gazette,* Sept. 6, 1776).

[31] 6 *G. W.,* 111.   [32] *Ibid.,* 5.   [33] *Ibid.,* 16, 41.

[34] *Ibid.,* 8–9.   [35] *Ibid.,* 18; Cf. *ibid.,* 25.

[36] *Ibid.,* 8–9. See *ibid.,* 37 for warning of immediate courtmartial, and *ibid.,* 41 for an order to have three roll-calls a day to check stragglers. Andrew Hunter wrote Sept. 18, 1777, of a Captain of Connecticut troops convicted of forging a pass to go home and sentenced to be dressed in woman's clothing with wooden sword and musket, and to be ridden from guard to guard until he reached his domicile (*Andrew Hunter's Diary,* MS., Princeton Univ. Lib).

[37] 6 *G. W.,* 42.

The situation would have been affrighting at any stage of the war, because it threatened not mutiny alone but also the dissolution of the Army—in the face of a powerful, confident adversary who was free to maneuver almost at will because of British sea power. It was Washington's good fortune and perhaps the salvation of America that the well-equipped British, with all the élan of victory, were under the command of a man whose innate caution was deepened by the desire of his brother, the Admiral, and by his own ambition, to pursue negotiations for peace before employing to the utmost the bayonets of the soldiers and the cannon of the ships. General Howe's slowness was a boon; it could not be an escape. Sooner or later—the difference might be a matter of no more than a few weeks or even days—the British would strike somewhere, on the front of sixteen to eighteen miles [38] defended by half-demoralized men whom Washington reckoned at less than 20,000 effectives.[39] A fourth of these were believed to be sick,[40] but all figures of this nature were guesses because it was impossible to get accurate returns of scattered troops under changed commanders.[41] The militia continued to slip away in such numbers that General Mercer did not believe Washington could muster among them, at the moment, more than 5000 dependable soldiers.[42] Only the bravest and the most philosophical could say with Joseph Reed, "Our comfort is that the season is far advanced, and if a sacrifice of us can save the cause of America, there will be time to collect another army before spring, and the country be preserved." [43] Even that had in it the warning of a calamity that every day was bringing nearer. "Another army before spring," said Reed, and in the saying set down the fact that always was in the background: Whether militia stood their ground or ran away, whether the surviving veterans were saved or sacrificed, the passage of four months would terminate the service of the New England continental Regiments and would bring a repetition of those dreadful days of December, 1775, when rod on rod of trenches had been undefended and the few reenlisted veterans would have been at the mercy of an aggressive opponent.

Certain defensive arrangements could be made now. The enemy could be confronted with the most vigilant of the officers; [44] reenforce-

---

[38] *Ibid.*, 94.   [39] *Ibid.*, 6.   [40] *Ibid.*, 30, 94.
[41] *Ibid.*, 16, 17.   [42] 2 *Force* (5), p. 158.
[43] Letter of Sept. 2, 1776, to Mrs. Reed; 1 *Reed*, 230–31.
[44] See Washington to Heath, Aug. 31, 1776; 5 *G. W.*, 504–05.

ments from Virginia and Maryland, as well as the incoming militia, could be hurried forward;[45] the sick could be removed from exposed New York;[46] surplus supplies likewise could be hauled beyond the snatch of the British lion;[47] seasoned troops could be taken from the forts and could be replaced by men of the Flying Camp;[48] all the roads that flanked American positions could be blocked;[49] North River could be obstructed more stoutly and could be subjected to a heavier cross fire from batteries;[50] the garrisons of the Highland defences of the Hudson might be strengthened;[51] available troops might be posted where they could be moved quickly to meet any force landed from British transports.[52] Other expedients might suggest themselves after the form of the attack on New York was disclosed; but would they, could they suffice? An American offensive manifestly could not be attempted at the time; would a strong, resourceful defense keep the British out of New York? Nathanael Greene, who was well enough to resume his duties by the 5th of September, was of opinion that no effort should be made to save the town. It should be burned and evacuated, he said; two-thirds of the property there belonged to Tories anyway.[53] General Heath and doubtless others argued that where vast labor had been spent in rearing earthworks, the city should be held, if possible.[54] Rufus Putnam, acting Chief Engineer, considered fortification a waste of energy where so many landing places existed.[55] Washington said, "Till of late I had no doubt in my mind of defending this place, nor should I have yet, if the men would do their duty, but this I despair of."[56] It was for Congress, he thought, and not for himself to say whether the town should be destroyed or left alone. As he phrased it in its least painful form, the question was, "If we should be obliged to abandon the town, ought it to stand as winter quarters for the enemy?"[57] The answer he had given himself was positive and plain: he would apply the torch to the entire city if permitted to do so. By so doing, he would deny the British comfortable winterquarters in

[45] 6 G. W., 32, 33.

[46] Ibid., 36, 49, 51.

[47] Ibid., 15. No report of the stores in New York at this time seems to have survived, but as of June 7, 1776, the Commissary General had in the city 4500 bbls. of flour, 211 bbls. of pork, 105 hogsheads of molasses and relatively small quantities of other provisions (Joseph Trumbull Papers, CHS.).

[48] Cf. Ward's Regiment, 6 G. W., 33.

[49] 2 Force (5), p. 259.

[50] 6 G. W., 10, 17–18, 33.

[51] 2 Force (5), p. 676.

[52] Ibid., 274.

[53] 1 Greene's Greene, 210 ff; 1 Reed, 213.

[54] Cf. Heath, 68.

[55] 2 Force (5), p. 140.

[56] Letter of Sept. 2, 1776, to the President of Congress (6 G. W., 6).

[57] Ibid.

a town they could hold easily thereafter, with their fleet and a small force, while their main army proceeded against the Americans.[58]

Congress had a different view, of which he was informed by the 6th of September: [59] "Resolved, That General Washington be acquainted, that the Congress would have especial care taken, in case he should find it necessary to quit New York, that no damage be done to the said city by his troops, on their leaving it: The Congress having no doubt of being able to recover the same, though the enemy should, for a time, obtain possession of it." [60] Washington read this in the belief that it might represent one of the capital errors of Congress [61] but he determined fully and at once to make the best defence he could of a city [62] located where all the physical advantage was on the side of a foe who commanded the waterways. New York Island was thirteen miles in length from its northern end at Spuyten Duyvil to its southern tip. For the lower eight miles of this long axis, the width of the island was almost uniformly two miles. Above that point the island was narrowed by the course of Harlem River, which ran from Spuyten Duyvil eastward, southward and southeastward to separate the island from Morrisania and Westchester. The town of New York occupied slightly less than the lower three miles of the island. North of the upper suburb of the town was the district called Bloomingdale. Beyond that, the land rose gradually in a rocky formation, known as Harlem Heights [63] that ran Southeast-Northwest to a declivity about eight miles from the lower end of the island.[64] Beyond this stretch the ground rose still higher on the western side of the island and formed a cliff with an elevation of 200 feet and a little more. North of this, above Spuyten Duyvil and the upper stretch of Harlem River, were Fordham Heights. East of this cliff was the same stream and, still farther East, Valentine's Hill and the large estate of Morrisania. South of the eminence was a gradient down to the declivity already mentioned. On the West was North River.[65]

---

[58] Letter of Oct. 6, 1776, to Lund Washington, 37 *G. W.,* 532.

[59] 6 *G. W.,* 23.

[60] Resolution of Sept. 3, 1776; 5 *JCC.,* 733; cf. 2 *Force* (5), p. 135.

[61] 37 *G. W.,* 532.   [62] 6 *G. W.,* 22.

[63] The southern stretch was styled Vandewater's Heights.

[64] That is, from the northeastern end of Central Park Northwest to Morningside Heights and the high ground South of 125th Street.

[65] The impression the geography of New York Island probably made on intelligent soldiers seeing it for the first time may have been similar to that which Andrew Hunter recorded in his *Diary* Sept. 10 and 11, 1776. Harlem was "a sweet little village with one church."

NEW YORK AS A STRATEGICAL PROBLEM, 1776

New York Island and the area immediately adjacent, from Fort Independence, above King's Bridge, to Red Hook, Long Island, 1776, are here outlined, after "A Sketch of the Operations of His Majesty's Fleet and Army . . . Published January, 1777, by J. F. W. Des Barres." A few place names, not on the original map, have been inserted.

There were three main north-and-south roads in the part of New York Island North of the city and South of Harlem. In that village the three came together and mounted the western cliff at an easy grade as one highway. On the heights, the roads again divided. One fork led North to the crossing of Spuyten Duyvil; the other bent to the Northeast and to King's Bridge, which spanned Harlem River close to the point where that stream turned from its easterly to its southern course. King's Bridge, then, was one of the important military positions on New York Island. Whoever held firmly that crossing and its approaches could open or shut at pleasure the city gate, whence the roads led upstate and, easterly, into New England.

To cover King's Bridge, the Americans had constructed Fort Independence at the southern end of the Fordham Heights. On the cliff South of King's Bridge, the Continentals were erecting another large earthwork, which they called Fort Washington.[66] The whole of the adjoining high ground had recently been dubbed Mount Washington. Correctly speaking, Mount Washington was the entire area and Fort Washington the defences on the crest; but the two names were loosely used as synonyms. Almost directly opposite these works was Fort Constitution, soon to be renamed Fort Lee, on the Jersey side of North River. Its fire and that of Fort Washington crossed where obstructions had been placed in the river to keep the British from using the Hudson. Below Mount Washington on New York Island no large work had been erected except in New York city itself, but the high ridge from what was known as McGowan's Pass [67] to the declivity South of Mount Washington was naturally strong and could be used for defence against an adversary who commanded the plains of Harlem. In the city itself, a redoubt of some strength had been erected on Bayard's Hill,[68] and trenches had been dug wherever a landing seemed likely or a field of fire was offered. Most of these works appeared later to a British observer to have been "calculated more to amuse than for use." [69] The key positions on the island were the two already mentioned, King's Bridge and Fort Washington. During the difficult days of early September, Washington suspected that the enemy intended to land near King's Bridge and thereby both to hem him into the area South of Harlem and to sever his communications.[70] Proper disposition to meet such a move

[66] A letter from Thomas Chew to his father, Jeremiah Chew, July 7, 1776 (23 *Penn. Mag.*, 397), told of work on the fort from approximately June 30. The inference is that this was the first labor on the defences at that point, but positive proof is lacking.

[67] Approximately at the northeast corner of Central Park.

[68] Between the present Grand and Mott Streets. Jeduthan Baldwin, who had this position under his care, called it Bunker Hill.

[69] 1 *Kemble*, 89.

[70] 6 *G. W.*, 23. Washington believed, in a word, that the British sought to pen him on the lower part of Manhattan Island.

called for a council of war, which Washington brought together on the 7th of September.[71] Over the vigorous opposition of Greene, a majority of the council of war recommended that an effort be made, as Congress apparently desired, to hold New York. Five thousand men should be assigned for this duty; 9000 should be stationed at King's Bridge; the remainder should be encamped between the town and the bridge. Part of this intermediate force should be placed at Fort Washington. That defence and Fort Constitution, in Jersey, should be the anchors of stronger North River obstructions.[72]

The arguments that led to these conclusions may have been punctuated by the sound of distant guns, because the British by September 7 were feeling their way up East River with a contentious frigate, and were completing a battery on Long Island at a point opposite Horne's Hook.[73] On the 8th, this battery opened but quickly drew the fire of American gunners who were confident of their skill after having had the better of exchanges with the British frigate.[74] Then, on the 10th, the British occupied Montresor's Island, at the mouth of Harlem River. From that well-chosen advance post, they could land either on the plains of Harlem, South of King's Bridge, or on the Morrisania estate, whence they could flank the position at King's Bridge by a march of six or seven miles. A bad situation was getting worse. "How the event will be," Washington wrote Congress, "God only knows; but you may be assured that nothing in my power, circumstanced as I am, shall be wanting to effect a favorable and happy issue." [75] He might well have underscored the reference to the circumstances, because signs multiplied that the enemy's attack was to be both North and South of King's Bridge. One landing-place probably was to be Harlem; the other, in all likelihood, was to be Throg's Point, eight miles on a straight line from

---

[71] *Heath*, 68.

[72] The minutes of this council of war are not believed to be in existence (see 6 *G. W.*, 27 n.), but the principal decisions can be pieced together from the statements in Washington's letter of Sept. 8, 1776, to the President of Congress (6 *G. W.*, 27 ff., particularly p. 30–31).

[73] *Heath*, 68; Benjamin Trumbull's Diary in 7 *CHS Cols.*, 189–90. For the appearance of a man-of-war in the same waters, September 2, see *Eben. Huntington's Letters*, 44. Washington visited Horne's Hook September 5 (*David How's Diary*, 27). While the fact is not of large importance here, it should perhaps be noted that contemporary maps varied in a most confusing manner as respects the location of Horne's Hook, of Kip's Bay, and of the islands in East River. There was conflict, also, concerning the names of the islands. Maps of the seventeen-seventies list Buchanan's, Montresor's and Blackwell's Islands, but they did not agree which was which. Most of these maps correctly placed Horne's Hook or Point slightly Northwest of the upper end of Welfare Island, about at the northern boundary of Carl Schurz Park.

[74] *Heath*, 69; *Penn. Gazette*, Sept. 11, 1776; *Trumbull's Diary*, loc. cit.

[75] 6 *G. W.*, 45.

the north side of King's Bridge.[76] Such a move readily might cut off the retreat of the American Army and force it to surrender or else to fight in New York against the British and against starvation.[77]

The apparent imminence of this two-pronged thrust at the vitals of the Army led Nathanael Greene to draft and to circulate on September 11 a petition to Washington for review of the decision reached on the 7th to defend New York. Washington himself believed it futile and perhaps fatal to attempt to hold the town, and he consequently responded immediately with a call for a new council at McDougall's headquarters [78] September 12.[79] This time all except three of the participants [80] were for the evacuation of the entire area South of Harlem River, with the exception of Fort Washington, as soon as supplies could be withdrawn.[81] Eight thousand men were to be left at the fort, whence they could be removed northward or across the river to Jersey; the remainder were to be brought together as a single fighting force, to be maneuvered as need and opportunity dictated.[82]

Washington reported this decision to Congress with some renewal of hope, but in clear understanding that a race was on from that very hour between the teams hauling supplies out of New York and the British boats that were bringing redcoats closer to their landing. He warned the President of Congress that the council of war regarded the situation as "extremely perilous" [83] and then, telling of the effort to remove supplies and of the unexpected delay in the attack by the enemy, he said: "If [the British offensive] is deferred a while longer, I flatter myself all [supplies] will be got away and our force be more concentrated and of course more likely to resist them with success." [84] To all of this, the proviso should have been added that Washington would fight defensively if his Army was not reduced by militia desertion to impotence. As it was, the "Long Faces" continued to slip away.

---

[76] See Mifflin to Heath, Sept. 10, 1776; 2 Force (5), p. 274-75. Throg's Point often was called Frog's Point, but it appears to have been named after Throgmorton or Throckmorton, the first English settler there (1 Jones, History N. Y., 620).

[77] Cf. 6 G. W., 53-54, 82.

[78] McDougall Papers, NYHS.

[79] 2 Force (5), p. 326-28; 6 G. W., 53-54.

[80] Joseph Spencer, George Clinton and William Heath. These three, years later, Alexander McDougall described as "a fool, a knave and an honest, obstinate man."

[81] Heath, 69; 2 Force (5), p. 329-30.

[82] Strictly speaking, the advice of the council simply was to rescind previous action and to place 8000 men at Fort Washington, but the understanding was that withdrawal from New York would be the next step.

[83] 6 G. W., 53.   [84] Ibid., 54.

A gamble was presented daily, whether the number of militia who left the Army equalled the number who arrived.

September 13 brought more evidence that the onslaught might be close at hand. After dinner, a forty-gun ship started up East River and opened on the batteries, which responded angrily. British guns on Governor's Island went into action. Washington rode over to one of the forts, probably the one at Horne's Hook, to see whether the movement of the enemy had begun, but he found no transports with the man-of-war and no indication of an immediate landing. The reward of his curiosity was ungracious, a cannon ball that struck within six feet of him.[85] An anxious night followed, without the crash of artillery or the roll of drum.[86] On the 14th came assurance from Congress that its resolution against the burning of New York was not to be construed to mean that Washington "should remain in that city a moment longer than he shall think it proper for the public service that the troops be continued there." [87]

The General acknowledged gratefully this expression of confidence in him, but he said of the city, in stern, awkward phrases: "I could wish to maintain it, because it is known to be important, but I am fully convinced that it cannot be done, and that an attempt for that purpose, if persevered in, might and most certainly would be attended with consequences the most fatal and alarming in their nature." [88] To the Generals, his orders carried a reminder that this was "no time for ease and indulgence." The utmost vigilance must be shown in the care of arms and in the detection of malingerers. Unhappily mindful of Long Island, Washington admonished: "We have once found the bad consequences of a surprise; let the utmost care be used to prevent another. For this purpose, the General directs that none be put out at night but picked men; that they be visited every hour, and every motion of the enemy narrowly watched." [89] This he wrote in no confidence that any except the best trained and disciplined of his soldiers would meet the ordeal. Such hope as he cherished was in the element of brave men among the rank and file, and in the comparatively small number of officers who would act with judgment and intelligence.

Washington had a measure of comfort at this time in the arrival of the Third Regiment of Virginia Continentals, under Col. George

[85] Col. Joshua Babcock to Gov. Nicholas Cooke, Sept. 21, 1776; 2 *Force* (5), p. 442.
[86] 6 *G. W.*, 54.   [87] Resolution of Sept. 10, 1776; 5 *JCC.*, 749.
[88] Letter of Sept. 14, 1776; 6 *G. W.*, 53.   [89] GO of September 14; 6 *G. W.*, 55–56.

Weedon, whom he had known as a tavern-keeper in Fredericksburg. Weedon commanded slightly more than 600 enlisted men; he was to be followed to camp by Isaac Read with the Ninth Virginia, nearly 500 rank and file. One of the newcomers wrote home: ". . . great joy was expressed at our arrival and great things are expected from Virginians, and of consequence we must go through great fatigue and danger." [90] It was gratifying to Washington to hear the familiar names of home and to receive nearly 1100 men whose term of service did not end with the year 1776; but, of course the reenforcement was small in terms of the Army's needs. Joseph Reed spoke not for himself only but also for his chief and for every patriot in the Army when he wrote his wife that day: "The enemy are evidently intending to encompass us on this island by a grand military exertion . . . I hope they will fail. It is now a trial of skill whether they shall or shall not, and every night we lie down with the most anxious fears for the fate of tomorrow." [91]

He and his General were not permitted to seek their beds that 14th of September without a new alarm. About sunset, word reached Washington that six ships or more were proceeding to a station in East River, that British troops were being assembled on the islands in Hell Gate, and that widespread movement was observed by scouts and lookouts. Anxiously, Washington took horse and hurried to Harlem in the belief that the blow would fall there or across the mouth of Harlem River at Morrisania. On arrival, he saw what others had reported but he observed no additional preparation. Fire had not been opened; no landing had been attempted. It was manifest that the unhappy, straggling and disheartened troops of the American Army were not to be shaken into their innate manliness that evening, or debased into cowardice by fear and panic. In the belief that these alternatives were to be tried in British fire before many hours elapsed, Washington rode back to new headquarters opened at the home of Roger Morris, near King's Bridge and on Harlem Heights, whence he thought he could proceed more quickly to a threatened position than from his old office.[92]

---

[90] John Chilton to Joseph Blackwell, Sept. 17, 1776 (12 *T* 91). Weedon had brought to headquarters a dispatch from Hugh Mercer on the 11th (6 *G. W.*, 43) and probably had his Regiment close at hand then. Read's Regiment did not appear on the return of September 21 but was on the return of September 30 (2 *Force* (5), p. 451, 607). Because Weedon was alleged to have dispensed rum punch from a gourd, to the patrons of his tavern, he was known to his soldiers as "Joe Gourd" Weedon, or as "Old Joe Gourd."

[91] Letter to Mrs. Reed; 1 *Reed*, 235.

[92] 6 *G. W.*, 95; 1 *Reed*, 235. This is the familiar structure, fortunately preserved, later

The next morning was fine and bright with a breeze from the South-west [93] and was as quiet as fine until about 11 o'clock, when a sound of heavy firing rolled up to King's Bridge. It did not come from the plains of Harlem or from Morrisania, but from a point farther down East River than Washington had expected. In ignorance of what was happening—that very fact an evidence of the disordered condition of the Army—the apprehensive General took horse and, with his aides, started for the scene of the bombardment. Unknown to him, while six transports remained off Bushwick Point,[94] five warships left that temporary station at earliest dawn [95] and anchored broadside along the New York shore from Kip's Bay southward to Watts' house, a distance of about 1100 yards.[96] These vessels were so close that when American sentinels on shore passed on the cry "All is well," British sailors could be heard when they shouted back, "We'll alter your tune before tomorrow night." [97] When it became light enough to see, Americans could read the name of a ship that had swung around until the stern was visible at an angle. She was *Phoenix*,[98] the vessel that twice had run past the batteries along North River. Up that stream, at that very hour, a trio of ships were making their way to Bloomingdale, three and a half miles North of Washington's former headquarters at Montier's. If those men-of-war in North River were intended to cover a landing there, simultaneously with one on East River, then the hour of decision had come, no matter how ill Washington was prepared for it.

About 10 o'clock when both tide and wind were setting strongly upstream, Americans who had a clear view of Newtown Cove on Long

known as the Jumel Mansion. For information concerning this and other changes in Washington's headquarters during the operations around New York, see Appendix IV-1.

[93] *Serle*, 103, 105.

[94] Bushwick Point was between Newtown and Bushwick Creeks on Long Island, East and Southeast of Kip's Bay. The transports arrived there the previous evening under fire (1 *Mackenzie*, 46; Howe's report of Sept. 21, 1776 in 2 *Force* (5), p. 378). These are two of the principal sources of information on the action of September 15. Mackenzie's account, which was not available in printed form until 1930, is much the most detailed from the British point of view. A. Robertson's and Kemble's Diaries also are useful. Washington's letter of Sept. 16, 1776, to the President of Congress (6 *G. W.*, 57) is the nearest approach to an official American report. Narratives by participants in the action are not numerous, but the accounts by Col. William Douglas (3 *LIHS Mem.*, 71) and by Private James S. Martin of Colonel Douglas's Regiment (*ibid.*, 81) are informative. The same may be said of the proceedings of the court of inquiry in the case of Col. John Tyler of the Tenth Continental, 2 *Force* (5), p. 1251–54.

[95] *A. Robertson's Diaries*, 97.

[96] 1 *Mackenzie*, 46. The distance is computed from Thomas Kitchin's map.

[97] James S. Martin, *loc. cit.* Martin apparently was in error concerning the time the vessels dropped anchor. He seemed to think it was before midnight, but Mackenzie, who was in position to know the facts, stated explicitly that the men-of-war took position early in the morning.

[98] James S. Martin, *loc. cit.*

Island,[99] Southeast of Kip's Bay, saw British flatboats move out of the mouth of the creek and take shelter astern the transports. Men from other boats climbed up the sides of the ships, which manifestly were to convey the troops to some landing place [100]—but what place? On the New York shore, under the British guns and in sight of the redcoats embarking on Long Island, were one Regiment of Connecticut "levies" and three "continental militia" Regiments from the same State, under Col. William Douglas.[101] On the right of this Brigade, downstream, were Wadsworth's five Regiments of Connecticut militia. In support were Fellows' small Brigade of Massachusetts militia and Parsons' Brigade of Connecticut Continentals.[102] In addition, General Mifflin had been told to hold his men in reserve at Colonel Morris's, about five miles North of Kip's Bay, so that he could draw troops from Mount Washington and move southward in event of an attack from Harlem Plains.[103] This force seemed adequate to meet at least the first troops that came ashore, provided the Americans would assemble quickly at the point of attack and would stand up to their better trained opponents. At the moment, American troops were marching to right and to left, upstream and down, as individual commanders made their guesses, good or bad, of the enemy's destination.[104]

Eighty British guns began to roar shortly before 11 A.M.,[105] with a fire that seemed to one of the King's officers to be "both terrible and pleasing." [106] American supports did not venture within less than half a mile of the shore; the men who were expected to meet the first landing were pinned to their lines which, as one of them said afterwards, were "nothing more than a ditch dug along on the bank of the river with the dirt thrown out towards the water." [107] This paralyzing fire

99 Newtown Cove was at the mouth of Newtown Creek, the northern boundary of Bushwick Point.

100 1 *Mackenzie*, 47; Howe's report, *loc. cit.*

101 This is nowhere stated specifically by Washington, who mentioned only the supports (6 *G. W.*, 58); but Colonel Douglas's letter of September 18 to Mrs. Douglas (3 *LIHS Mem.*, 71), makes it plain that his Brigade, of known composition (2 *Force* (5), p. 451), was near Turtle Bay.

102 2 *Force* (5), p. 352; 6 *G. W.*, 58. See H. P. Johnston's careful analysis in 3 *LIHS Mem.*, 232 n. and his Map II, at the back of the same volume. A list, in Washington's autograph, of the Brigades of the American Army is in the *Washington Papers*, Huntington Lib. Although it is with documents of 1777, the inclusion of Ritzema's and Thomas's Brigades date it as of the summer of 1776.

103 Mifflin also was in reserve to move to Throg's Point in event of attack there. See Mifflin to Heath, Sept. 10, 1776; 2 *Force* (5), p. 274-75.

104 1 *Mackenzie*, 47; Howe's report, *loc. cit.*

105 The figure is approximate; the five ships carried 164 guns (1 *Mackenzie*, 46, 47).

106 1 *Kemble*, 88.   107 James S. Martin, *loc. cit.*

continued for more than an hour and spread smoke so heavily over East River [108] that the militiamen in the trenches could have seen only a short distance beyond the shore if they had been reckless enough to lift their heads above the low parapet. About 1 P.M.—a hot day it was [109] —the bombardment ceased, the smoke began slowly to drift away, and different sounds became audible, shouted commands, the grinding of bows on the river bank, the dull percussion of heavy feet on boat bottoms, and then—British and Hessians splashing ashore and forming on both sides of Kip's Bay,[110] at one point within forty yards of the breastworks.[111]

It was not long after this landing that Washington rode up at furious pace with his aides [112]—only to find that the militiamen already had abandoned their trenches without firing a shot [113] and now were retreating in mad confusion. General Parsons and General Fellows had arrived with their supports and were doing everything they could to rally the men but their commands were unheard or unheeded. Washington and the young officers with him rode among the scattered troops and tried to form them. It was in vain—men who bore the insignia of rank were hurrying off; soldiers were running without so much as turning around to fire even once. Washington's wrath rose. "Take the wall," he shouted, "take the cornfield," and he pointed to the positions. Some men filed out from the road to do as he said; General Parsons hastened to them and tried to get them into a line,[114] but the panic-stricken outnumbered by far those who kept their heads. Fellows' Brigade broke and scattered. In Watts's orchard, on the right of the assailed front, a few men disputed the advance of Hessians—only to see the Germans shoot down and bayonet some Americans who came forward with uplifted hands to surrender.[115] At another scene of maddened disorder, the troops did not even stop at the King's Bridge Road, which ran North about half a mile from the shore line. They plunged westward, across the fields and through the scattered woods, to the Bloomingdale Road.[116] Nearer the landing place at Kip's Bay, Wash-

---

108 *A. Robertson's Diaries*, 97. 109 *2 Force* (5), p. 1251.
110 1 *Mackenzie*, 47.
111 *A. Robertson's Diaries*, 98; Howe's report, *loc. cit.*; 1 *Mackenzie*, 47.
112 *6 G. W.*, 58.
113 1 *Mackenzie*, 48. Col. George Weedon (letter of Sept. 20, 1776, to John Page, *Chicago HS.* MSS) and Capt. John Chilton (letter to unnamed correspondent, Sept. 20, 1776, 12 *T* 92) agree that the defenders of Kip's Bay did not fire even one volley, but neither of these two writers, though near at hand, was an eye-witness.
114 *2 Force* (5), p. 1252. 115 1 *Mackenzie*, 48. 116 *2 Force* (5), p. 1252.

ington continued his efforts to rally the half-frenzied men, but just when it looked as if he might get some hundreds of them to stand, a body of sixty or seventy British soldiers started towards them. Almost on the instant, the Americans broke, ran away, and left Washington and his aides to face the attacking party without a single musket.[117] Furious at the sight of such behavior,[118] Washington had to give ground himself and, intensely humiliated, had to send orders for the Harlem Heights to be secured.[119] Over on the Bloomingdale Road, about that time, the cry was raised that the British Light Horse were attacking the rear. That completed the panic of some and speeded the retreat of the others.[120] There was no halt, not even a pause, by most of the fugitives. Parsons' Continentals were as bad now as Douglas's and Fellows' militia. All ran away and did not rally until they formed North of McGown's Pass, to which point General Mifflin had proceeded promptly with his troops.[121] The British pursued as far as Murray's Hill,[122] while the advance was pushed towards Harlem Heights and was extended by the left flank across to North River.[123]

This trifling and disgraceful affair fixed the fate of New York. Establishment of the British line across the island put an end to the orderly evacuation of supplies by land, precisely as all water transit had been stopped early that morning by the dispatch of three British warships to Bloomingdale.[124] The defeat was as grievous in losses of property as it was shameful in the cowardice it uncovered. Washington had succeeded in getting the last of his sick to places of safety but he had to leave all the heavy cannon mounted in the town, a "considerable part" of the

[117] 6 *G. W.,* 58.

[118] *Ibid.* Traditions of Washington's behavior on the field are numerous but, as usual, are improbable or unverifiable. Heath included in his *Memoirs,* 70, a story that when Washington saw the troops running away en masse, the Commander-in-Chief, throwing hat to ground, exclaimed, "Are these the men with which I am to defend America?" Weedon, *loc. cit., supra,* n. 113, repeated camp gossip that the General cried, "Good God, have I got such troops as those?" Smallwood, who was not present, stated that Washington, Putnam and Mifflin caned the militiamen from Connecticut in an effort to get them to stand and fight (2 *Force* (5), p. 1013). The presence of Putnam is asserted by Baurmeister (5 *Mag. Am. Hist.,* pt. 1, p. 37) who suggested that the General was identified by his mount, but the author of the anonymous account in 2 *Force* (5), p. 352, stated that Putnam was in New York and that Henry Knox was looking for a boat on which to cross North River. While this may have been true, it is highly probable that Putnam started for the scene as soon as he heard the firing.

[119] *Ibid.*   [120] 2 *Force* (5), p. 1252.   [121] *Ibid.,* 352.

[122] 1 *Mackenzie,* 48. It was styled Ingleberg or Inclenberg, with numerous variants. The location was slightly North of a line drawn directly westward from Kip's Bay.

[123] Howe, in his report (2 *Force* (5), p. 372) said that the line at the close of the day extended from Horne's Hook to a point on North River "near Bloomingdale." Kemble (*op. cit.,* 88), stated more specifically that the advance was to the Black Horse and thence by Apthorpe's House, in Bloomingdale, to North River.

[124] 6 *G. W.,* 57–58.

Army's baggage and tents, and many provisions and stores.[125] In addition, the British reported the capture, at Kip's Bay and elsewhere in the new lines, of twenty officers and about 300 men,[126] a figure that surprised Washington, who did not believe he had lost so many.[127] American dead, though never counted, probably were few. British losses, not known till later, were reported as three killed and sixteen to eighteen wounded.[128] There never had been a more outrageous affair, and seldom so complete a British victory for so small an expenditure of blood and bullets.

As the weary American commander that evening went painstakingly over the lines on Harlem Heights,[129] he might well have asked himself if America could hope to win her independence with such troops as those he had seen in panic that day. He had put them on the high ground beyond Brooklyn and he had found them lacking in vigilance and quick to take flight. Now, when he had called on them a second time to meet an equally desperate threat, they had run away again! He was convinced more than ever of the costly truth he was to repeat before many days, in gray, discouraged words—"the dependence which the Congress has placed upon the militia has already greatly injured and I fear will totally ruin our cause." [130] Neither on Long Island nor on the banks of Kip's Bay had field or even general officers been able to control their troops. Washington already had condemned the leaders who had failed on the Flatbush and Bedford Roads of Long Island; this time he had seen a Colonel, John Tyler of the Tenth Continental, who appeared to have shown the white feather: as soon as conditions permitted, Tyler must be arrested and brought before a court of inquiry.[131]

In this concern over the behavior of officers and men on the 15th of September, Washington was too depressed in spirit and too busy with instant duties to reflect that some of his Generals and perhaps he himself had erred in posting the troops and had failed to give proper instruction to those who had been stationed where the British landed. He had ex-

---

125 *Ibid.*, 59, 63, 98.   126 Howe's report, *loc. cit.*   127 6 *G. W.*, 117.
128 1 *Kemble*, 88. For this attack Howe's GOs of Sept. 13, 1777 recommended "to the troops an entire dependence on their bayonets, with which they will always command that success their bravery so well deserves" (*Glyn Journal*, Princeton Univ. Lib.).
129 2 *Fithian's Journals*, 234.
130 Letter of Sept. 22, 1776, to his brother "Jack" (6 *G. W.*, 96).
131 He was ordered under arrest Sept. 27, 1776; 2 *Force* (5), p. 569, 591. In the index of 2 *ibid.*, this officer is listed as Robert Tyler, but no Robert Tyler of any rank is in *Heitman*. The Colonel could have been none other than John Tyler. The hearing was held Oct. 26, 1776; 2 *Force* (5), p. 1251–54.

pected the enemy to attack on the plains of Harlem [132] and he had made his dispositions accordingly. With so few well-trained men in his small Army he could not have reliable forces both at Harlem and all along East River. The arrangement he made of two militia Brigades on the waterfront, with one militia and one continental Brigade in support,[133] may have been as prudent and as economical as his circumstances permitted. Parsons' and Fellows' Brigades had been in Putnam's Division; Douglas and Wadsworth served in Spencer's command;[134] all four Brigades at this very time were in process of transfer to Heath.[135] The troops might, therefore, have been everybody's and nobody's responsibility on the day of their test. A Chaplain of Connecticut infantry, who was closer to an understanding of the men than were most of the officers, indicted the command when he said: "The men were blamed for retreating and even flying in these circumstances, but I image [sic] the fault was principally in the general officers in not disposing of things so as to give the men a rational prospect of defence and a safe retreat should they engage the enemy. And it is probable many lives were saved, and much to the Army prevented in their coming off as they did though it was not honorable. It is admirable that so few men are lost." [136] General Heath believed the poor behavior of the troops was due to the "wounds of Long Island" and to the knowledge of the officers, and perhaps of the men also, that the town of New York was not to be defended.[137] Washington, normally tolerant, spoke his mind fully when he said that the conduct of participants was "disgraceful and dastardly," [138] and he added nothing and extenuated nothing thereafter, except to confide to one of his brothers that the evacuation of New York, like that of Long Island, would have been effected without loss, "but for a defect in the department of the Quarter Master General's not providing teams enough." [139]

Such was judgment on the action at Kip's Bay, an action that was no more than a skirmish in itself but was of high importance in that it precipitated the evacuation of New York and deepened the anxiety of Washington over the morale of his soldiers and the competence of some

[132] 6 G. W., 95.
[133] Douglas and Wadsworth on the river, Parsons' Continentals and Fellows' militia in support.
[134] 6 G. W., 4.   [135] Ibid., 52.
[136] Benjamin Trumbull's Diary in 7 CHS Cols., 195.
[137] Heath, 70.   [138] 6 G. W., 58.
[139] Letter of Oct. 5, 1776, to Samuel Washington; 6 G. W., 170. Cf. Nathanael Greene to Gov. Nicholas Cooke, Sept. 17, 1776; 2 Force (5), p. 369-70.

of his commanders. He did not lose his faith in himself or in his leadership.

During the early morning of Monday, September 16, the General sent out reconnoitering parties to see what the British were doing [140] and then he sat down with heavy heart to report to Congress on the humiliating events of the preceding day. He related the facts without minimizing in any particular the ugly tale of panic, and at the end he wrote: "We are now encamped with the main body of the Army on the Heights of Harlem, where I should hope the enemy would meet with a defeat in case of an attack if the generality of our troops would behave with tolerable resolution. But experience, to my extreme affliction, has convinced me that this is rather to be wished for than expected. However, I trust that there are many who will act like men and show themselves worthy of the blessings of freedom." [141]

He had not completed the drafting of this letter [142] many minutes when word reached him that the enemy was astir. At 7 o'clock there had been an alarm at the front because, half a mile off, a hostile force had appeared on the plains of Harlem. The American Battalions had been put under arms, but nothing had happened immediately. Most of the troops closest to the line of probable British approach were ordered to stack their muskets and to start work in strengthening and extending the three small redoubts that had been the only man-made defence on that part of the island. [143] Next the report at headquarters was that three large columns had been observed on the low ground at a distance of approximately two miles and a half from headquarters. [144] As false news often was forwarded to the commanding General and might be expected with special frequency when the Army was nervous, Adjutant General Reed asked and gained permission to ride southward from the Morris House and to see if the British appeared to be moving to an attack. [145]

Washington's own apprehension did not permit him to remain in his office until Reed returned or sent a message. If there was even a possibility of an engagement that day, Washington wanted to be on the

---

[140] 6 G. W., 59.

[141] Ibid., with the punctuation simplified somewhat.

[142] See Ibid., 59 n.

[143] Col. G. S. Silliman to his wife, Sept. 17, 1776, in 1 Jones, History N. Y., 606–07. Andrew Hunter in his Diary, loc. cit., noted that on the 16th troops "began to throw up lines" from East River to North River.

[144] 1 Reed, 237; 6 G. W., 67.   [145] 1 Reed, 237.

scene before action opened, in order that he might guard against surprise and make proper disposition of his Regiments. He soon set out [146]
and on his arrival at the advance posts, heard firing to the southward,
occasioned, he was told, by a clash between Lt. Col. Thomas Knowlton's
Rangers, numbering about 150,[147] and a British advance party.[148] The
exchange, though brisk, was not in a volume to indicate anything more
than a skirmish. Washington listened and prepared to receive attack,
but he had no further report of a general advance by the main body of
the British. Some time passed. Then a number of Knowlton's men
began to climb back up the hill to their own positions, where they gave
encouraging news of a stiff encounter still in progress with a body of
redcoats who were concealed in a wood. The Americans had not seen
these troops but the volume of fire from among the trees led the
Rangers to estimate their foes at 300.[149] Reed, returning also, assured
his chief that Knowlton's men had done admirably and deserved support. Would the General approve an advance in some strength to
encourage the men? [150] As Washington pondered, the British came in
sight and sounded their bugles—not with a command to halt or to
deploy but with the call of hunters who have killed the fox and are
ending their chase.[151] "I never felt such a sensation before," said Joseph
Reed, "it seemed to crown our disgrace." [152]

Whether or not this taunt angered him, Washington presently gave
orders—perhaps with some reluctance [153]—for a small demonstration
directly in the enemy's front. Knowlton simultaneously was to take his
men and three Rifle Companies of Weedon's Third Virginia Regiment,

---

[146] 6 *G. W.*, 67. In terms of modern New York streets, the Commander-in-Chief had his
headquarters (see *supra*, n) in the so-called Jumel Mansion, between 161st and 162nd Sts.
and Edgecombe Avenue and Jumel Terrace. Washington's immediate objective was the advance
posts of the American Army, on the north side of West 125th Street, beween Manhattan Avenue
and North River. Before he got to the edge of the declivity, one reconnaissance party had proceeded as far "downtown" as Jones's House, which was close to 106th and Broadway. The
British advance posts were then spread from McGown's Pass, approximately at the northeast
corner of Central Park, westward and southwestward to the river in the vicinity of 105th Street.
An admirable and accurate description of the ground will be found in an article by Reginald P.
Bolton and Edward H. Hall, in 5 *Mag. His.*, 27 ff. This was part of a controversy over the site
of the action of Harlem Heights. Other articles appeared in *ibid.*, v. 4, p. 351 ff., and v. 8,
p. 38 ff.

[147] For a good note on the command see 3 *LIHS Mem.*, text, p. 246–47. Knowlton had been
a faithful and able Connecticut officer from the beginning of the war.

[148] 6 *G. W.*, 67. 　　　[149] *Ibid.*, 68.　　　[150] 1 *Reed*, 237.

[151] This may have been the "whoo-whoop." The length of the blasts on a horn of one key
is given in Joseph B. Thomas, *Hounds and Hunting Through the Ages*, 130.

[152] 1 *Reed*, 237.

[153] Reed, *loc. cit.*, wrote that "the General was prevailed upon to order out a party to
attack them."

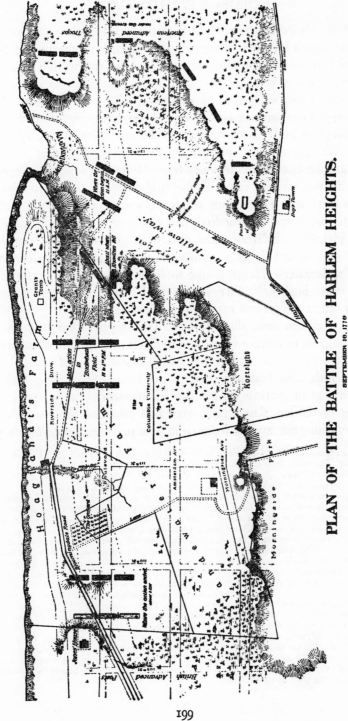

PLAN OF THE BATTLE OF HARLEM HEIGHTS.
SEPTEMBER 16. 1776

The Action on Harlem Heights, Sept. 16, 1776

These are the movements as interpreted by H. P. Johnston, the most careful student of the ground. This sketch, with some of the present-day locations, is reproduced from his *Battle of Harlem Heights.*

under Maj. Andrew Leitch,[154] through the woods and up the rocky side
of Vandewater's Heights [155] to get in rear of these contemptuous British.
As Reed had been to the most advanced line of skirmish, he was to act
as guide, but he was not the only officer outside the participating
organizations who wanted to have a hand in the effort to pen the British
foxhunters. Putnam and and Greene were there, and if they did not
join Knowlton and Leitch, it was not because of any lack of inclination.[156] Washington saw the men start from the left of that part of the
line,[157] and he at once made ready from Nixon's Brigade the force that
was to demonstrate in front of the British.[158] In the early afternoon
Nixon's men were moved out and were sent down into the wide declivity that separated the northern part of Harlem Heights from Vandewater's Heights, which were the next high ground to the South. The
British, regarding this as a challenge, came down into the declivity
from Vandewater's Heights and took position behind a fence and
among some bushes.[159] Fire was opened at once between these contingents but at too great a range to be effective.[160]

Soon, much too soon, there came to Washington's ears the sound of
an exchange of musketry from the left front, on the line of advance of
Knowlton's party, but manifestly this fusillade was not from the rear
of the British who had advanced to the fence. Something had gone
awry: Instead of getting behind the enemy, to cut off his retreat and
force his surrender, Knowlton's men had attacked the enemy's right
flank. Washington waited for a time in some impatience and anxiety

[154] James Monroe, then a Lieutenant, volunteered to go with Knowlton. See *Diary of Samuel Richards*, 39. The three Rifle Companies were those of John Thornton, Charles West and John Ashby (Weedon to John Page, Sept. 20, 1776; *Chicago HS*. MSS).

[155] The modern-day Morningside Heights. Cf. 5 *Mag. His.*, 27.

[156] Vagueness cannot be avoided here, because there is no definite information concerning the position of these men, or of Gen. George Clinton who stated that he was "in the latter part, indeed almost the whole of the action." Rev. Ezra Stiles wrote in his Diary that Putnam and Greene commanded in the action (see 3 *LIHS Mem.*, text 256 n.), but he was not present and probably reported hearsay. Doubtless all these general officers performed service of one sort or another for Washington while they were watching the operation, but if any of them had been in command, Washington almost certainly would have said so in his report to Congress.

[157] A contemporary sketch map appears in John Jay's "Centennial Oration" which, with the appended documents collected by H. P. Johnston, is the standard authority. This map, with two useful additions, was republished in the article of Lucy Leigh Bowie, "Maryland Troops in the Battle of Harlem Heights," *Md. His. Mag.*, v. 43, p. 13.

[158] Some, perhaps all, of these men appear to have been volunteers. See the statement of Capt. John Goode of Barnum's Rhode Island Regiment in 3 *LIHS Mem.*, 88.

[159] 6 *G. W.*, 68; John Chilton to unnamed correspondent, Sept. 17, 1777, 12 *T* 92.

[160] 6 *G. W.*, 68. In other words, the British moved northward from Morningside Heights into the southern part of what was called the Hollow Way, roughly the area South of the present West 124th Street; the Americans came down the hill that runs almost Northwest from 125th Street to the river at 130th Street.

and heard shortly that Major Leitch had been brought out, with three bullets through his body.[161] After him came Colonel Knowlton, mortally wounded. Washington concluded that with both its leaders down, the flanking column, now fighting under Captains, needed further support, and he accordingly dispatched parts of two Maryland Regiments and some New Englanders.[162] The weight of this force and the manifest danger of envelopment led the British to fall back immediately on reserves that were rushed forward to keep open their line of retreat.

Within a few minutes, the enemy's advance party was gone, ingloriously gone. American troops had not previously seen the enemy "on the run" and they could not resist the temptation to pursue; but Washington reasoned that the British would send up heavy reenforcements and he said openly that he did not think his shaken Army should risk a general engagement.[163] He consequently ordered the men to cease their pursuit and to return to their lines. It was encouraging to hear later from Reed that the men abandoned the chase reluctantly.[164]

When the men were back in their camps, and fact had been winnowed from boast, it was ascertained that as Knowlton and Leitch had proceeded around the right flank of the British, "some persons," in Reed's discreet phrase, called to these troops and took them "out of the way [the Adjutant General] intended." [165] Neither he nor Washington

[161] Leitch's subsequent death, after removal to a place of safety, was attributed to lockjaw. George Weedon, in a letter of Oct. 10, 1776, to John Page, described the circumstances and said, "in him America has lost as brave and prudent an officer as ever defended her rights . . ." *Chicago HS. MSS.*

[162] 6 *G. W.*, 68. Washington did not identify these "detachments from Eastern Regiments."

[163] *Ibid.*, 68, 102, 164. Nathanael Greene thought this recall entirely proper and so stated (2 *Force* (5), p. 370). Washington wrote Patrick Henry, Oct. 5, 1776, that "a want of confidence in the generality of the troops" prevented the development of this "and almost every other opportunity which has presented itself" (6 *G. W.*, 165).

[164] 1 *Reed*, 238. This action naturally received much attention at the hands of New York local historians, who brought together at the time of the centennial observance of the event a remarkable collection of eye-witnesses' memoirs and letters. This material was printed in the appendix to John Jay's oration. Other documents supplemented H. P. Johnston's "The Campaign of 1776 around New York and Brooklyn," which was issued in 1878 as Vol. III of the *Memoirs* of the Long Island Society, cited many times in these pages as 3 *LIHS Mem.* The editors of both "source books" were justified, of course, in their inclusion of all material then available, whether primary or secondary. Unfortunately, some of the narratives subsequently based on these documents failed to discriminate among the various papers. The result has been the perpetuation of numerous mistakes, though most of these are not serious. In general, it may be said that few American military engagements, involving such limited numbers of men, have been the subject of so much historical writing. Even the site of the action, which would seem plain from the evidence, has been the subject of a considerable literature. The reader who wishes to ascertain the facts that stood the test of controversy will do well to disregard the earlier publications and to go directly to Henry P. Johnston's final work on this theme, *The Battle of Harlem Heights, Sept. 16, 1776* (New York, 1897).

[165] 1 *Reed*, 237.

indicated who it was who turned the party to the West when it should have proceeded farther southward before moving to the right; but in General Orders congratulating the soldiers, Washington said: "The loss of the enemy yesterday would undoubtedly have been much greater if the orders of the Commander-in-Chief had not in some instances been contradicted by inferior officers who, however well they mean, ought not to presume to direct. It is therefore ordered that no officer, commanding a party, and having received orders from the Commander-in-Chief depart from them without counter orders from the same authority." He then listed those who delivered his orders.[166]

In the opposing camp that day, there was more of relief than of dispute over orders. Washington did not know the facts in detail, but the engagement had its origin in a movement of two Battalions of British Light Infantry, followed by the 42nd Regiment, who were extending their posts to the left when they encountered one of the American reconnaissance parties. As this small force retreated, the redcoats pursued and ventured too far. When their plight was discovered, British commanders hurried additional supports and two field pieces. Headquarters believed that nothing except the quick retreat of the advance force and the speedy forward movement of the supports averted the loss of the two Battalions.[167] Sir Henry Clinton probably expressed the official view years afterward—"The ungovernable impetuosity of the light troops drew us into this scrape."[168] British losses, variously estimated,[169] were set down officially at fourteen killed and eleven officers and 143 n.c.os. and enlisted men wounded.[170] Washington reckoned American casualties at approximately 60.[171]

It was not the disparity of losses that most encouraged the Americans: it was the fact that they had forced British troops to flee before them in the open field. That never had happened before. The British had retreated from Lexington and from Concord, but they had intended to return to Boston anyway. They had quit that city the next March but, again, they had not been worsted in a stand-up battle. The victory won

---

[166] 6 G. W., 65.

[167] Howe's report of Sept. 21, 1776, 2 Force (5), p. 379; 1 Mackenzie, 51; A. Robertson's Diaries, 99. The British commander's congratulatory GOs of Sept. 17, 1776, are in the Glyn Journal, Princeton Lib.

[168] 1 Jones, History N. Y., 606.

[169] Howe in 2 Force (5), p. 379; A. Robertson's Diaries, 99; 6 G. W., 69.

[170] 1 Kemble, 89.

[171] 6 G. W., 96. It was believed by some of the soldiers that Putnam was wounded in this affair. See J. Alsop to Thomas Wharton, Sept. 19, 1776; 29 Penn. Mag., 494.

by Charles Lee in South Carolina, about which the Northern Armies knew little, had been an affair of naval guns. Long Island and Kip's Bay were subjects too sore for mention. This time it was different: The Americans had proved that the British army was *not* invincible. Redcoats had backs! It was a great discovery. Some of the troops almost forgot the events of the previous day in rejoicing over the victory on the heights; some minimized the loss of New York. Said David How in his Diary: "Our people thought best to leave the lower part of the town so that the shipping might not play on us." In the eyes of others, the rout at Kip's Bay gloomily was linked with Long Island. "This joined to our former misfortune was very discouraging"—so wrote Lieut. John Richardson.[172] Washington was pleased but cautious. "The affair," said he in the stiff language of his formal report to Congress, "I am in hopes will be attended with many salutary consequences, as it seems to have greatly inspirited the whole of our troops."[173] Adjutant General Reed echoed the words of his Chief when he wrote his wife: "You can hardly conceive the change it has made in our Army. The men have recovered their spirits and feel a confidence which before they had quite lost." Then he added: "I hope the effects will be lasting."[174]

---

[172] Letter of Sept. 24, 1776, to John Crozier (16 *Penn. Mag.*, 205).

[173] Letter of Sept. 18, 1776; 6 *G. W.*, 69. Later he wrote: "This little advantage has inspirited our troops prodigiously; they find that it only requires resolution and good officers to make an enemy (that they stood in too much dread of) give way" (Letter of Sept. 20, 1776, to Philip Schuyler; 6 *G. W.*, 83). In 2 *Force* (5), p. 371–72, appears an uncredited news report of the battle, with a long "extract of a letter from a general officer who was present at the time of the action." This is, in reality, a rephrasing of part of Washington's report to the President of Congress, Sept. 18, 1776 (6 *G. W.*, 67–69) with this rodomontade addendum: "On the whole, the enemy got completely defeated, which has given great spirits to our army, who are encamped on the heights at Harlem, where they are advantageously posted, and in high spirits, waiting the attack of the enemy."

[174] 1 *Reed*, 238.

CHAPTER VIII

MANEUVER EAST OF THE HUDSON
(September 17–October 28, 1776)

DURING THE ACTION on Harlem Heights, Washington's Adjutant General had an experience that sharpened the implied doubt in the Colonel's remark, "I hope the effects will be lasting." Joseph Reed had observed a private, Ebenezer Liffenwell, of Durkee's Twentieth Continentals, in the act of running away from the fight, with gun in hand. When Reed halted him and told him to go back and do his duty, the man deliberately aimed his musket at the officer, then within about five yards, and pulled the trigger. Fortunately for the Army, the lock merely snapped. Instantly Reed snatched a musket from another private and tried to shoot Liffenwell, but this time, too, the lock failed. Reed then drew his sword, struck Liffenwell over the head and, with another stroke, cut off the man's thumb and thereby subdued the skulker.[1] Liffenwell, of course, was brought before a courtmartial on the charge of cowardice and "misbehavior before the enemy" and also of "presenting his firelock at his superior officer." He was convicted without extenuation and was condemned to death but was pardoned, on Reed's plea, when about to be executed.[2] The great question in the Army—the question on which the independence of America hung in those autumn days of 1776—was whether the spirit of Colonel Knowlton, who gladly gave his life, or the spirit of Private Liffenwell, who would kill an officer to evade a fight, was to dominate the Army. That answer was by no means as clear as the ethics were.

Washington, as always, made the best of what he had and of what he could not change. He promptly extended his new lines across the upper end of Harlem Heights from North River to Harlem River, and he soon felt that if the men would fight, the defences would make any success

---

[1] 1 Reed, 238.
[2] Ibid.; 6 G. W., 90–91, 102–03. Solomon Nash stated in his Diary, 34, that Liffenwell was pardoned after kneeling to be shot. For another case of last-minute reprieve, see 6 G. W., 235, 236, 240.

costly to the British [3] whom he expected to advance at an early date.[4] A great fire that destroyed about a fourth of New York City on the night of September 20–21 and during the forenoon of the 21st [5] seemed to Washington to be an instance in which, as he later wrote Lund, "Providence, or some good honest fellow, has done more for us than we were disposed to do for ourselves," but he had to admit regretfully that "enough of [the city] remains to answer" the purposes of the British.[6] Whether the conflagration was for good or for ill, it was followed on the 23rd by the easy British occupation of Powles Hook, with only three cannon-shot in opposition,[7] but without heavy American loss of artillery or stores.[8] Thereafter, one or two suspicious movements [9] convinced Washington the British would attack during the few remaining weeks of open weather.[10] This prospect, in turn, led Washington to issue another series of orders for strengthening the fortifications [11] and for maintaining a constant and informed alert.[12]

Almost immediately, Washington had evidence that vigilance and discipline and leadership and almost everything else that went into the making of an Army were threatened with ruin. His organization appeared to be collapsing. The militia continued to disappear in such numbers that Washington despaired of getting from them a service that justified their pay. Within a fortnight, one of the thirteen Connecticut militia Regiments was to be reduced to fourteen fit men and no more. All the others slipped away.[13] Another Regiment was to return less than thirty; several were not to muster fifty at roll-call.[14]

[3] Silliman in 1 Jones, History N. Y., 606; 6 G. W., 79, 83–84, 99.
[4] 6 G. W., 73.
[5] For the force, direction and subsequent shift of the wind, see 1 Kemble, 89, and Tryon in 2 Force (5), p. 494. The allegations of American incendiarism are set forth in 1 Moore, 311, in Doctor Moffat's Diary, Sept. 22, MS, LC; and in the elaborate note in 1 Jones, History N. Y., 611 ff. Other accounts will be found in 1 Mackenzie, 58–60, Heath, 73, 2 Force (5), 462 ff., 62 Penn. Mag., 494–95, and in many minor publications. A particularly good account is that of Rev. E. G. Shewkirk, a Moravian Loyalist, in a letter to Bishop Nathaniel Seidel, Dec. 2, 1776; 13 Penn. Mag., 377 ff. The congregational Diary is in 1 ibid., 253 ff. See also Serle, 111–12, and Penn. Gazette, Oct. 2, 1776. This last narrative is specific concerning the cause of the fire and the buildings that escaped destruction in the burned area. Shewkirk will appear again in a Pennsylvania reference, where the name is spelled Schaukirk.
[6] Letter of Oct. 6, 1776; 37 G. W., 533.
[7] 1 Kemble, 90; A. Robertson's Diaries, 100; 6 G. W., 105. Strictly speaking, Powles (or Paulus) Hook was the point of land in Jersey directly on a line drawn West from the southern end of the Island of New York.
[8] Heath, 76.   [9] Ibid., 77; 6 G. W., 140.
[10] 6 G. W., 132, 144. Cf. 2 Force (5), p. 854.
[11] E.g., 6 G. W., 134.
[12] Ibid., 120, 133. In 2 Force (5), p. 853, is an interesting order to officers to acquaint themselves with the ground by systematic reconnaissance.
[13] 6 G. W., 137.   [14] Ibid., 122, 138.

These militia were being replaced, though in most instances as previously with men who had no arms or equipment,[15] and they represented slight numerical net loss; but they escaped with so little punishment for their contempt of discipline that many continental troops followed their evil example. Washington consequently had to issue successive stern but futile General Orders against straggling, plundering,[16] cowardice,[17] malingering[18] and desertion.[19]

In all of this, Washington had to remember that he might be compelled on occasion, however distrustfully, to use the militia and that he might be forced to call for more of them to bridge the gap between the discharge of the old Regiments and the enlistment of the new.[20] He tried to be fair to those temporary soldiers,[21] but his experience with their undependability[22]—experience not singular to him[23]—led him to believe that, if the Army could survive the fall campaign of 1776,[24] it must be reorganized on a basis of long enlistment[25] under sterner articles of war.[26] This was not a new plan, he insisted;[27] it was now one of absolute necessity and it called for attractive bounties of money and of land.[28] Congress had been talking of long-term service[29] and it acceded to most of Washington's requests. On the very day he was directing the action at Harlem Heights, the Delegates passed a series of resolutions for the enlistment of eighty-eight Battalions, by quotas among the several States, "to serve during the present war." Battalions already in service were to be counted in the total if they were recruited

---

[15] *Ibid.*, 106.

[16] September 18 and 19; 6 *G. W.*, 71, 72. Soldiers caught with plunder were to be whipped on the spot (*ibid.*); tents and knapsacks were to be searched (*ibid.*, 88–89); not even the baggage of officers could be assumed free of plunder (*ibid.*, 88–90). Cf. *ibid.*, 104–05, and *ibid.*, 114, for an admission that whipping was not a deterrent.

[17] September 20; *ibid.*, 79.   [18] September 21; *ibid.*, 87–88.

[19] Mackenzie, *op. cit.*, v. 1, p. 64, stated that on a single day close to eighty deserters came into the British lines. Virtual mutiny and mass desertion occurred in September among Pennsylvania troops (5 *JCC.*, 831–32; letter of Lieut. John Richardson to John Crozier, Sept. 24, 1776; 16 *Penn. Mag.*, 205). For the allegation that deserters were sheltered, precisely as men of Washington's command had been during the early years of the French and Indian War, see 2 *Force* (5), p. 352.

[20] 6 *G. W.*, 155.   [21] Cf. *ibid.*, 118.

[22] *Ibid.*, 96, 110 ff., 149–50, 169.

[23] Cf. John Adams, Oct. 8, 1776: "Wherever the men of war have approached, our militia have most manfully turned their backs and run away, officers and men, like sturdy fellows; and their panics have sometimes seized the regular Regiments" (*Adams, Fam. Letters*, 322). Cf. Jonathan Trumbull, Oct. 2, 1776; 2 *Force* (5), p. 847.

[24] 6 *G. W.*, 81.   [25] *Ibid.*, 11, 85, 109.

[26] *Ibid.*, 114 ff.   [27] 6 *G. W.*, 165.

[28] *Ibid.*, 109, 183. Charles Lee noted that the profit and popularity of service on privateers increased the difficulties of recruiting for land duty (1 *Greene's Greene*, 226).

[29] 2 *Burnett*, 83, 85, 89.

for the duration of hostilities.[30] Every private and n.c.o. who enlisted for that service was to receive twenty dollars and 100 acres of land. Officers were to be commissioned by Congress, but "the appointment of all officers, and filling up vacancies (except general officers) [was to] be left to the governments of the several States." Arms and other necessities were to be supplied by the States; clothing was to be charged against the pay of the soldier.[31] New articles of war were adopted, also, for the maintenance of better discipline and for the firm establishment of justice to the individual soldier.[32]

Much of all this, in Washington's opinion, was good as far as it went, but it did not go far enough. The bounty was too small to attract recruits in competition with higher British offers; nothing was done to encourage good officers to remain in the service or to assure the appointment to the new Regiments of leaders of station and intelligence.[33] Elbridge Gerry, Roger Sherman and Francis Lewis, who were named by Congress to visit Washington's camp,[34] arrived there about the 25th of September and held numerous conferences,[35] in which Washington and his Generals disclosed frankly what they had not thought proper to put into official correspondence with Congress—that the corps of officers, taken as a whole, was unworthy of the country, was lacking in competence, and in large measure was responsible for the poor discipline that prevailed. "I have," said Nathanael Greene, "neither seen nor heard of one instance of cowardice among the old troops where they had good officers to lead them . . . I know our men are more than equal to [the enemy's] and were our officers equal to our men, we should have nothing to fear from the best troops in the world." [36] In the same spirit, Greene wrote: "Our men are infinitely better than the officers." [37] Joseph Reed's comment was: "I am sorry to say too many officers from all parts leave the Army when danger approaches." [38] In line with this, and to illustrate the incredible lack of understanding shown by some

---

[30] 2 *Burnett*, 102.

[31] 5 *JCC.*, 762–63. For the transmission of the resolutions on the new Army to the States, see 2 *Burnett*, 98; 2 *Force* (5), p. 953. See also Hancock to Washington, 2 *Force* (5), p. 488.

[32] Sept. 20, 1776, 5 *JCC.*, 788; John Adams to James Warren, 2 *Burnett*, 102. For antecedent action, see *ibid.*, 442, 670, 764, 787. A bibliographical entry on the first publication of the articles, as revised by Congress, appears in 6 *ibid.*, 1125. Washington renewed his main argument for new articles of war, Sept. 22 and 24, 1776 (6 *G. W.*, 91, 114), and he put them into effect as of October 7 (6 *G. W.*, 125, 151).

[33] 6 *G. W.*, 152–53. See also *infra*, p. 210.

[34] 5 *JCC.*, 808.   [35] *Ibid.*, 839; *Heath*, 76.

[36] Letter of Oct. 11, 1776, to Gov. Nicholas Cooke; 2 *Force* (5), p. 996–97.

[37] 1 *Greene's Greene*, 222.   [38] 1 *Reed*, 244.

officers, Reed observed: "It is impossible for anyone to have an idea of the complete equality which exists between the officers and men who compose the greater part of our troops. You may form some notion of it when I tell you that yesterday morning a Captain of Horse, who attends the General, from Connecticut, was seen shaving one of his men on the parade near the house." [39] Reed might have added the satirical case of the Army's Provost Marshal, who was absent without leave when he should have been making arrangements to hang a private condemned to death by a court martial for desertion and mutiny. [40] It developed, in fact, that the Provost Marshal had decamped with some belongings of prisoners. [41] Privately, Washington affirmed that even his continental troops "never had officers, except in a few instances, worth the bread they eat"; [42] officially he was "sensible that the very existence, that the well doing of every army depends upon good officers." [43]

The committee was convinced, as Elbridge Gerry put it, that unless Congress adopted some additional measures concerning the officers to be selected by the State Assemblies, "we shall have such a corps of officers as the Army have been hitherto encumbered with." [44] When the three Congressmen went back to Philadelphia, the understanding probably was that they would make their report in line with Washington's recommendations and that he would write strongly to Congress in support of the policies the committee formulated. [45] It was done accordingly. A mildly phrased committee report [46] was seconded by the strongest, most desperate letter Washington had addressed to the President of Congress. [47] He pleaded for the utmost speed in procuring action by the States on the names of new officers; he insisted on the clothing bounty for soldiers; and he argued almost vehemently for a scale of pay that would make it possible for officers to support their character as gentlemen. [48] His conclusion was startling: ". . . such a cloud of per-

[39] Letter of Oct. 11, 1776, to Mrs. Reed, 1 *Reed*, 243.

[40] 6 *G. W.*, 144–45.

[41] 2 *Force* (5), 869. For the case of a drum major accused of theft, see *David How's Diary*, 30.

[42] Letter of Sept. 30, 1776, to Lund Washington, 6 *G. W.*, 138–39.

[43] 6 *G. W.*, 188.

[44] Letter of Sept. 27, 1776, to Gen. Horatio Gates; 2 *Force* (5), p. 572.

[45] "Probably" has to be inserted in this sentence because there is no positive evidence of agreement, but the circumstances render it almost a certainty.

[46] 5 *JCC.*, 842–44.

[47] Its terms, William Williams wrote Joseph Trumbull, Oct. 10, 1776, were "moving, pathetic, rational and nervous, exceedingly so . . ." (2 *Burnett*, 122).

[48] Cf. 6 *G. W.*, 108.

plexing circumstances appears before me without one flattering hope that I am thoroughly convinced unless the most vigorous and decisive exertions are immediately adopted to remedy these evils, that the certain and absolute loss of our liberties will be the inevitable consequences . . ." One unhappy stroke, he added, would "throw a powerful weight into the scale against us." [49]

This language from a trusted leader was decisive with Congress, which already had acted favorably on some of the committee's recommendations. Members who had balked at the bounty of clothing voted to allow a full year's supply, valued at twenty dollars, to all who entered the service or reenlisted for the entire war.[50] Officers' pay was increased, "as a further encouragement for gentlemen of abilities to engage . . . to serve during the war." [51] The States were urged to complete their levies of new troops by November 10, and were counselled to designate as officers "men of honor and known abilities, without a particular regard to their having before been in the service." [52] As far as they went, these resolves gratified Washington, but a measure simultaneously adopted by Congress alarmed him anew. This was a call on the States that had continental Regiments either in New York or in Pennsylvania to send committees to the Army and to empower them "to appoint all the officers of the Regiments to be raised by their States under the new establishment." The committees were to confer, also, with the Generals and were to promote "such officers as [had] distinguished themselves for their abilities, activity, and vigilance in the service, and especially for their attention to military discipline." [53]

All this was to be done in order that the officers of the new Regiments might "proceed immediately to enlist such men as are now in the service, and incline to reenlist during the war." [54] Washington knew nothing of the origin or sponsorship of this resolution, which certainly did not originate with the committee that had visited the camp; but he had long and vexing experience with the leisurely procedure of State lawmaking bodies and their agents, and he saw what Congress apparently had overlooked: Until the committees arrived and chose the officers, there could be no recruiting for the new Regiments. An ex-

---

[49] Letter of Oct. 4, 1776, 6 G. W., p. 152–56. The quotation is from p. 155–56.
[50] 2 Burnett, 122; 5 JCC., 855.
[51] Proceedings of Oct. 7, 1776; 5 JCC., 853. Cf. William Ellery to Governor Cooke: "The officers of the Army in general are not equal to their appointments, and from thence it is that our soldiery is disorderly and undisciplined" (Letter of Oct. 5, 1776; 2 Burnett, 115).
[52] 5 JCC., 856.   [53] Ibid.   [54] Ibid.

pedient for hastening the induction of leaders might operate to delay the organization of the New Army until after the old one was dissolved.[55]

In the memory of his sleepless nights of December, 1775, he could not be otherwise than apprehensive as December, 1776, approached with the same problem of organization, but as he looked to the future of his forces he had faith in the potentialities of the American soldier. "We have good materials to work upon," he said,[56] and he devoted himself vigorously to the execution of the plan for long enlistment. He wrote those State Governors whom he knew well—Jonathan Trumbull and Patrick Henry, for example—and he exhorted them to see that qualified officers were chosen for the new Battalions. "This is a consideration of exceeding importance," he told the Connecticut executive, "for without good officers, we can never have troops that will be worthy of the name, and with them we may in time have an Army equal to any." [57] In addressing his oldtime fellow Burgess, Governor Henry, the General tactfully asked for care in the selection of officers to head the Virginia troops. "The true criterion to judge by (when past services do not enter into the competition)," he said, "is to consider whether the candidate for [military] office has a just pretention to the character of a gentleman, a proper sense of honor, and some reputation to lose." [58] Washington did not want this vital requirement to wait on words. In a knowledge that the State commissioners were instructed by Congress to "advise with the general officers," [59] Washington instructed some of his principal subordinates to prepare lists of the competent officers in their commands. "I beseech you," he told Heath, "to exhort the officers you consult to lay aside all local prejudices and attachments in their choice." He added solemnly: "The salvation of their country and all we are contending for depends (under Providence) upon a good choice of officers to make this Army formidable to the enemy, and serviceable to the cause we are endeavoring to support. Men who have endeavored to support the character of officers, and who have not placed themselves upon a level with the common soldiery are fit to be preferred. Officers of the latter class will never, in short, they cannot conduct matters with propriety . . ." [60]

[55] 6 *G. W.*, 152, 155–56, 183, 187 ff., 200 ff.
[56] *Ibid.*, 181.
[57] Letter of Oct. 8, 1776, 6 *G. W.*, 181.
[58] Letter of Oct. 5, 1776; 6 *G. W.*, 167.
[59] 5 *JCC.*, 855.
[60] Letter of Oct. 9, 1776; 6 *G. W.*, 186–87.

There he had for the time to leave it. Discipline and morale were no better; [61] the commanding General's barge was hit in North River and three men were killed by a careless mistake; [62] several members of Washington's staff were restive; Joseph Reed was pessimistic [63] and soon was to ask that he be replaced in the new Army because he did not think he was qualified for the sort of duty he was attempting to discharge.[64] The most disquieting failure in staff work with which Washington had to deal at this time of stress was that of his Quarter Master General and former aide, Stephen Moylan. In spite of his devotion to the American cause, Moylan could not handle acceptably the business of procuring teams, tents, and other equipment of the Army. He confessed his failure manfully and accepted advice that he resign. This made clear the way for the reappointment of Thomas Mifflin at the continuing rank of Brigadier; [65] but with the best of fortune, Mifflin could not hope soon to find and to buy the clothing and blankets on which Adjutant General Reed believed the life of the Army in large measure depended during the winter of 1776–77.[66] As a result of the increase in duties without a corresponding improvement in the size and efficiency of his staff, Washington was overloaded. He divested himself, as far as he could, of responsiblity for naval affairs [67] and he reduced or eliminated his detailed reports to State Governors and Legislatures; [68] but he took in hand much of the correspondence regarding a general

---

[61] Cf. GOs of Oct. 7 and 8, 1776.

[62] *Heath*, 80; Benjamin Trumbull's Diary, 7 *CHS Cols.*, 199. Sgt. John Smith stated in his Diary (*Miss. Val. His. Rev.*, v. 20, p. 254) that the boat was fired on because a sail was raised that she was not known to have. The account reaching the ears of Andrew Hunter (Diary, Oct. 11, 1776, *loc. cit.*), was that the craft was hailed but that in the heavy wind the challenge was unheard. She was hit before her crew could hoist the colors.

[63] 1 *Reed*, 244.   [64] 2 *Force* (5), p. 828.

[65] 2 *Burnett*, 114, 116; 2 *Force* (5), p. 570, 998; 6 *G. W.*, 126, 193; 5 *JCC.*, 838; John Jay to Edmund Rutledge, Oct. 11, 1777: "Moylan acted wisely and honorably in resigning. Try no new experiments; you have paid for the last." 1 *Correspondence and Public Papers of John Jay*, ed. H. P. Johnston (cited hereafter as *John Jay*), p. 92.

[66] 1 *Reed*, 243. For Congress' somewhat elaborate plans to procure clothing, see 5 *JCC.*, 820.

[67] 2 *Force* (5), p. 274. The establishment of the Marine and Naval Committees of the Continental Congress is described with characteristic precision in 2 *Burnett*, 216–17 n., 272–73 n. See also C. O. Paullin, *The Navy of the American Revolution*, 35 ff., 79 ff. For a short period, both these Committees operated separately; the Secret Committee was responsible for arming and manning the ships that brought cargoes on "continental account" from Europe to America (4 *JCC.*, 290). John Nixon, John Wharton and Francis Hopkinson were named in November, 1776, to serve, in effect, as executive officers of the Marine Committee (2 *Burnett*, 155 and n.; 6 *JCC.*, 946, 958). The three became known as the Continental Navy Board (Cf. 6 *JCC.*, 592 and G. E. Hastings, *The Life and Works of Francis Hopkinson*, 218–19). Another body, created in April, 1777, to serve in Boston, was termed officially the Navy Commissioners of the Eastern Department (7 *JCC.*, 281). It is to be regretted that Washington could not find time to continue his direction of naval affairs. His early acts showed clear understanding of seapower.

[68] 6 *G. W.*, 62–63, 78.

exchange of prisoners [69] and at times, it would seem, he deliberately turned to letter writing if he wished to keep his mind from bootless reflection on problems he could not solve.[70]

Overwork, strain and the endless vexations of command brought Washington lower in spirits than he had been at any time during the war. To his brother "Jack," he wrote: ". . . it is not in the power of words to describe the task I have to act." He affirmed: "Fifty thousand pounds should not induce me again to undergo what I have done." [71] At the end of a long review of his desperate situation, he told Congress: ". . . the difficulties which have forever surrounded me since I have been in the service, and kept my mind constantly upon the stretch; the wounds which my feelings as an officer have received by a thousand things which have happened, contrary to my expectations and wishes; the effect of my own conduct, and present appearance of things, so little pleasing to myself, as to render it a matter of no great surprise (to me) if I should stand capitally censured by Congress; added to a consciousness of my inability to govern an army composed of such discordant parts, and under such a variety of intricate and perplexing circumstances; induces not only a belief, but a thorough conviction in my mind that it will be impossible unless there is a thorough change in our military systems for me to conduct matters in such a manner as to give satisfaction to the public which is all the recompence I aim at, or ever wished for." [72]

This was set down painfully Sept. 24-25, 1776.[73] Six days later, Washington wrote Lund: ". . . Such is my situation that if I were to wish the bitterest curse to an enemy on this side of the grave, I should put him in my stead with my feelings; and yet I do not know what plan of

---

[69] Ibid., 129 ff.

[70] The period Oct. 4-9, 1776, appears to have been one such time. Frequently as he wrote Congress, he did not do so often enough to satisfy some of the anxious members. Cf. John Adams to his wife, Sept. 22, 1776: "News we have not. Congress seems to have been forgotten by the armies" (Adams, Fam. Let., 228). Less distinguished letter-writers had little news to pass on to friends. Said John Chilton, Oct. 4, 1777: ". . . the enemy have been peaceable but seem vastly busy and we expect something every hour" (Letter to un-named correspondent, 12 T 96). Two days later Chilton wrote: ". . . we are building like moonacks in the ground, nothing has yet happened . . . I begin to think that mankind when engaged in warfare are as wary and timorous of each other as deer are of men, and the boldness of one party increases as they think the other is fearful" (ibid.). Col. George Weedon wrote on the 10th of October: ". . . nothing very material has happened with our Army and that of our enemies; now and then a few shots exchanged by the scouting parties. Except that, we have been very friendly neighbors since the 16th ulto." (Letter to John Page; Chicago HS. MSS.) Both these passages have been repunctuated.

[71] Letter of Sept. 22, 1776; 6 G. W., 96.

[72] 6 G. W., 116.

[73] Ibid., 106 n.

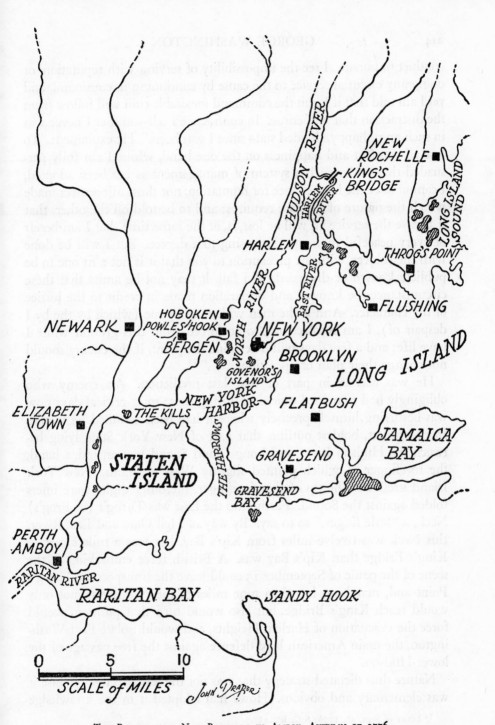

THE REGION FROM NEW ROCHELLE TO AMBOY, AUTUMN OF 1776

The principal scene of the Campaign of 1776, after "The Country Twenty-five Miles Round New York," edition of November, 1776.

conduct to pursue. I see the impossibility of serving with reputation, or doing any essential service to the cause by continuing in command, and yet I am told that if I quit the command inevitable ruin will follow from the distraction that will ensue. In confidence I tell you that I never was in such an unhappy, divided state since I was born." He explained: "To lose all comfort and happiness on the one hand, whilst I am fully persuaded that under such a system of management as has been adopted, I cannot have the least chance for reputation, nor those allowances made which the nature of the case requires; and to be told on the other, that if I leave the service all will be lost, is, at the same time that I am bereft of every peaceful moment, distressing to a degree. But I will be done with the subject, with the precaution to you that it is not a fit one to be publicly known or discussed. If I fall, it may not be amiss that these circumstances be known, and declaration made in credit to the justice of my character. And if the men will stand by me (which by the by I despair of), I am resolved not to be forced from this ground while I have life; and a few days will determine the point, if the enemy should not change their plan of operations . . ."[74]

He was correct in part of that last prediction. An enemy who obligingly had remained quiescent during these most critical days now was bestirring himself precisely where it had been assumed he would. In its crudest, boldest outline, that part of New York State lying between the Hudson River and Long Island Sound was an index hand, the forefinger of which pointed slightly West of South. New York Island itself was the tip of that forefinger, the other digits were inlets folded against the Sound. Farthest to the East was Throg's (or Frog's) Neck, a "little finger," so to say. By way of Hell Gate and East River, this Neck was twelve miles from Kip's Bay, but was a mile closer to King's Bridge than Kip's Bay was. A British force embarking at the scene of the panic of September 15 could leave the transports at Throg's Point and, marching less than nine miles to the Northwest, not only would reach King's Bridge, but also would turn that position, would force the evacuation of Harlem Heights, and would isolate Fort Washington, the main American land defence against the free passage of the lower Hudson.

Nature thus dictated strategy that was not the less effective because it was elementary and obvious. Howe had adopted it in the knowledge

[74] Letter of Sept. 30, 1776; 6 G. W., 138.

that it might save him from having to storm the works on Harlem Heights and at the same time would put him where he could cut the shortest line of Washington's land communications between New York and the lower Connecticut towns.[75] On the 9th of October a squadron of three ships with their tenders passed the obstructions in North River, defied the land batteries and ran up as far, Washington guessed, as Tarrytown, where they of course could stop once again the river shipment of supplies to Washington [76] from Albany. Now, at 9 o'clock on the morning of the 12th,[77] flatboats and small vessels brought ashore at Throg's Point a strong force [78] that had been embarked the previous night at Kip's Bay and had been conveyed successfully through Hell Gate in a thick fog.[79] The landing was unopposed [80] by the detachment of one officer and thirty men on duty at Throg's Point,[81] but the news was transmitted quickly to headquarters, where Washington received it. In continuing doubt of his Army's willingness to fight, he discarded all thought of a general offensive, but he believed that he held defensible ground between the Neck and King's Bridge. It was a district of stone fences that would confine artillery and large bodies of Foot to the main roads.[82] Joseph Reed was most positive. "My opinion," he said, "is that if we cannot fight them here we cannot do it anywhere." [83] Washington's reconnaissance was encouraging; he found the men apparently in good spirits; [84] Nathanael Greene, commanding at Fort Constitution, offered, without so much as a hint from headquarters, to bring three Brigades to help his chief.[85] That of itself was so extraordinary a tender that it made the day notable.

The next day, Washington gave instructions for vigilance and for stronger guards on the lines of probable advance from Throg's Neck.[86] Then, as the enemy remained immobile, Washington made another

[75] Howe hoped, also, to be able to draw Washington into the open and to engage him there. See the British commander's report in 3 *Force* (5), p. 922.

[76] Lord Howe's report, 3 *Force* (5), p. 817; 6 *G. W.*, 193, 196. Oct. 9, 1776: "They bore on without firing more than three or four times, notwithstanding the chevaux de frise and the heaviest fire we could make for an hour and a half."

[77] 3 *Force* (5), p. 922.

[78] 6 *G. W.*, 197; *Heath*, 80. The force initially put ashore was estimated at 4000 (*Penn. Gazette*, Oct. 16, 1776). Glyn noted in his *Journal*, Oct. 12, 1776, that a sloop with artillerymen was "overset," presumably in Hell Gate, and that six were drowned.

[79] Lord Howe in 3 *Force* (5), p. 816.

[80] 1 *Kemble*, 93.   [81] 1 *Mackenzie*, 77.

[82] 6 *G. W.*, 197. Cf. *ibid.*, 202, 208.   [83] 1 *Reed*, 244.

[84] 6 *G. W.*, 197. Cf. Andrew Hunter's Diary, *loc. cit.*, Oct. 14, 1776: "We expect soon a stroke that will decide the victory of this campaign. I feel myself relying on the commander of the universe for success."

[85] 2 *Force* (5), p. 1015–16.   [86] 2 *Force* (5), p. 1027.

reconnaissance on the 14th, this time with some of his Generals,[87] and he reassigned part of his forces, apparently in order to put the best troops under the most experienced commanders and to place the militia where they would have least opportunity either of doing harm or of running away.[88] Tactfully, too, Washington designated Putnam and Spencer to supervise the strengthening of the fortifications [89] and he assigned Heath to command South of King's Bridge where an attack seemed least probable.[90]

The most conspicuous—many would have termed it the most encouraging—aspect of this reorganization was the return of Charles Lee to command. That renowned personage had come to Philadelphia [91] after his victory in Charleston harbor, and he had received a triumphant welcome. He had taken pains that it should be a somewhat profitable appearance, also, because he had prevailed on the Delegates to "advance" him 30,000 dollars to cover losses he had endured or might have to face, in his private fortune.[92] There had been some amused and sarcastic references to the deeds of valor that might be performed by him —"General Lee hourly expected, as if from heaven, with a legion of flaming swordsmen" [93]—but, in the main, the men who carried the burden of their country on their hearts were glad to have him back to share it after nine months of absence from the main Army. Lee had sprinkled Congress with his counsel, while en route from the Schuylkill to the Hudson [94] but privately he professed nothing but contempt for that body: "I do not mean one or two of the cattle," he wrote General Gates, "but the whole stable." Washington, he protested, was "much to blame in not menacing 'em with resignation unless they refrain from unhinging the army by their absurd interference." [95] Ill as was his temper, his knowledge was needed where Washington did not have to count five in order to list all his general officers of intelligence, promptness, decision and courage. Nathanael Greene met most of the qualifications, but he was across the Hudson at Fort Constitution. Sullivan,

---

[87] At least this seems a safe inference from Heath's awkward entry, *op. cit.*, 81.
[88] 6 *G. W.*, 206, 207.   [89] 2 *Force* (5), p. 1027.   [90] *Ibid.*, 1035.
[91] According to *Penn. Gazette* of Oct. 9, 1776, he arrived "last Monday," which was October 7. He reported to Congress that day. See 5 *JCC.*, 850.
[92] 5 *JCC.*, 851. See, also, John Rutledge to Samuel Adams and Stephen Hopkins, July 4, 1777; *Moore's Lee*, p. 33. Cf. John Jay to Rutledge, Oct. 11, 1777; 1 *John Jay*, 92.
[93] William Malcolm writing from New York to John McKesson, Sept. 6, 1776; 2 *Force* (5), p. 197. Cf. Tench Tilghman to William Duer, Oct. 4, 1776; *Ibid.*, 870.
[94] 2 *Force* (5), p. 972, 1008.
[95] Letter of Oct. 14, 1776; 2 *Lee Papers*, 261–62.

too, might be disciplined in spirit to full efficacy. He now was on active duty again, an exchanged prisoner of war,[96] and was assigned a Division.[97] Lord Stirling likewise had been exchanged and was in command of a Brigade [98] because he was not yet ripe for larger command.[99] Brigadier William Thompson, captured at Three Rivers, had been brought to New Jersey but had not been liberated at this time.[100] The new Major General of Massachusetts militia, Benjamin Lincoln, a forty-three-year-old farmer, who had just arrived, was showing unusual promise, but, of course, still was to be tested. Among the other Generals were too many of the "useless old boys, who," in the words of Alexander McDougall, "pride themselves in having been in service, without profiting by it." [101] Eagerly, therefore, Washington received Lee and placed under him immediately all the troops above King's Bridge [102] with the request that he spend a day or two in examining the ground before he undertook active direction of the forces assigned him.[103]

Washington brought Lee and most of the other Generals together on October 16 to counsel him on the broad strategy of his situation. After the retreat from Long Island, he adopted more firmly than ever the basic strategical principle he had to apply: he would rely on the defensive until he built up, at some indeterminable time, the superiority of force necessary to combat successfully a better-trained, better-equipped and better-led adversary. Washington had written Congress: ". . . we should on all occasions avoid a general action, or put anything to the risk, unless compelled by a necessity into which we ought never to be drawn." [104]

When he had said that, he had weighed the arguments on both sides for the defence of New York and he had concluded that it was possible

---

[96] He was exchanged, about September 25, for Gen. Richard Prescott. See 6 G. W., 22, 23, 45, 74, 100 (2 Force (5), p. 463), and was back at headquarters on the 27th (ibid., 569; Heath, 76).

[97] Cf. 6 G. W., 208. [98] Ibid., 179.

[99] His exchange was effected, after much negotiation, on October 7. See 6 G. W., 22, 24, 45, 74, 97, 100, 117, 173, 183. According to George Weedon, in a letter of Oct. 10, 1776, Stirling brought back a story of a meeting inside the British lines with Lord Dunmore, who had been enlisting slaves against their masters in Virginia. When Dunmore accosted Stirling in the presence of other prisoners, the Governor said: "So, how do you do; I am sorry to see you in such damn black company." Stirling "observed to him it was poor consolation to gentlemen officers who the chance of war had put in his power and remarked he had not of late been so familiar with the Black Company as his Lordship" (Chicago HS. MSS).

[100] Heath, 77; 2 Force (5), p. 588.

[101] Letter of Oct. 21, 1776, to Robert Yates; 2 Force (5), p. 1166.

[102] 6 G. W., 208; 2 Force (5), p. 1035, 1100.

[103] Heath, 81.

[104] Letter of Sept. 8, 1776; 6 G. W., 28.

to hold Fort Washington and not only to protect the navigation of the Hudson but also to establish near the fort "an easier and better communication" between the Northern and Southern States.[105] Now he had to review that conclusion: The British repeatedly had run their warships past Fort Washington and over or through the obstructions in North River. This meant that when the brothers Howe so resolved, they could send a squadron up the Hudson with favoring wind and tide, and could land troops in rear of the American Army. Simultaneously, the enemy could move westward from Throg's Point and turn the flank of Washington's unhappy Regiments. The danger manifestly was that the jaws of the trap would be closed suddenly. American forces either might be compelled to abandon their defensive and to fight when and where the enemy pleased, or else the Army might be cut off and starved into surrender. The hour of that capitulation would be the sunset of all hopes of winning independence.

Another consideration had to be taken into account: warnings had come from members of the New York convention that British sympathizers were active in the upper parts of the State and might be preparing to join the King's army. This did not seem improbable; it might prove fatal. Many British sympathizers had been found on Staten Island; royal government was being reestablished on Long Island with the apparent acquiescence of a majority of the householders. Washington himself had so little faith in the patriotism of the average man that when he had pleaded with Congress for a bounty to encourage long-term enlistment, he had argued that the amount paid recruits had to be high because the British were reported to have offered a bounty of £10 and were said to have recruited already at that figure the greater part of a Battalion.[106] In this day of extremity, the service of many men might go to the higher bidder, not to the better cause!

What could be done? Washington read to the council of war on the 16th the reports of Tory stirrings upstate and of deserters' predictions of early attack. After these papers had been discussed, he asked whether the Army could hold its existing position, and, in so doing, could prevent a severance of communication, with consequences apparent to any man capable of sound reasoning.[107] The answer of all the Generals,

---

[105] *Ibid.*, 29.   [106] *Ibid.*, 153.

[107] 2 *Force* (5), p. 1118. The language of the council minute is: "whether (it having appeared that the obstructions in the North River having proved insufficient, and that the enemy's

with the exception of George Clinton, was that the Army could not keep communications open and that, to avoid surrender or a losing battle, new positions had to be occupied.[108] This of course involved the removal northward of all the troops in the works on Harlem Heights, because the Army could not afford to remain divided by Harlem River.

Must Fort Washington be evacuated, also? That earthwork was slightly more than two miles South of King's Bridge and was considered strong. At the beginning of September, when attack on the fortification would of necessity have been from the waterfront, Washington had reasoned that one Regiment plus a vigilant garrison of 300 men would suffice to protect the place against surprise.[109] Manifestly, when the Continental Army abandoned the lines on Harlem Heights, the British were free to undertake formal siege of Fort Washington with as many troops as they could concentrate. In spite of this, General Greene believed the work could be so strengthened and armed, along with Fort Lee on the Jersey side, that the movement of ships over the obstructions in North River could be prevented, in spite of the previous success of the British in running past.[110] Washington was far from being convinced but was hopeful that if more time were available for labor on them, the submerged chevaux de frise would make passage precarious if not impossible.[111] Whether or not he and Greene were correct, Congress wished the effort made to close the river, if it could be done.[112] The contention was, moreover, that if the defenders of Fort Washington were hard pressed by superior force, they always could effect a retreat to the other side of the river, under the guns of Fort Lee.[113] If, finally, Fort Washington were garrisoned by courageous troops, with a competent leader, it would occupy the attention of a considerable British force or else would make General Howe fearful of sorties and therefore cautious in nearby movements

---

whole force is now in our rear on Frog Point), it is now deemed possible in our situation to prevent the enemy cutting off the communication with the country and compelling us to fight them at all disadvantages, or surrender prisoners at discretion?" This awkward sentence has to be read carefully, with proper emphasis on the phrase, "in our situation"; otherwise the language might be taken to mean that surrender or an unequal battle were the sole alternatives.

[108] Here again the language of the minute is clumsy: "Agreed, with but one dissenting voice (viz.: General Clinton), that it is not possible to prevent the communication, and that one of the consequences mentioned in the question must certainly follow" (2 *Force* (5), p. 1118).

[109] 6 *G. W.*, 1.   [110] Cf. 2 *Force* (5), p. 1281.

[111] 6 *G. W.*, 184, 190, 193.   [112] 6 *JCC.*, 866.

[113] Cf. Tench Tilghman in 2 *Force* (5), p. 1311.

of men and supplies. For these reasons, the council of war advised Washington to hold the fort as long as possible.[114]

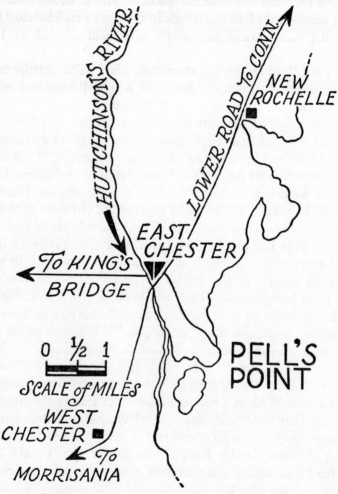

LINES OF ADVANCE FROM PELL'S POINT, OCTOBER, 1776

Sketch of Howe's strategical alternatives, after C. J. Sauthier's "Plan of the Operations of the King's Army under the Command of General Sir William Howe . . . from the 12th of October to the 28th of November, 1776 . . ."

The test of the first of the council's conclusions appeared to be near. Four miles North of Throg's Neck on the coast of Long Island Sound was a better landing-place, Pell's Point, which was East of Hutchinson's

[114] 2 *Force* (5), p. 1118.

River and within easy striking distance of the road from Connecticut, via New Rochelle and East Chester, to King's Bridge. Another road through East Chester led to Morrisania on the eastern side of the mouth of the Harlem River thus: [115]

On the 18th, this logical move was made. Some of the British troops were ferried to Pell's Point and were disembarked there; those on Throg's Neck then were advanced and were moved across the mouth of Hutchinson's River to junction with the men who had landed at Pell's Point.[116] Of his 14,000 effectives, Washington had placed in that quarter about 750 well-schooled troops under Col. John Glover, acting Brigadier.[117] That officer deployed his Regiments in echelon and fell back gradually before the British with negligible loss. Glover was unhappily conscious of his responsibility—"I would have given a thousand worlds," he said afterwards, "to have had General Lee or some other experienced officer present," [118] but, in Washington's opinion, Glover did about all that could have been done and he was commended accordingly.[119] A surgeon in Fellows' Brigade made it plain that his companions did not take the affair even that seriously. In his Diary he wrote: "The hole Brigade had orders to march from Harlem to East Chester but the Regulars were there before us and [Lieut. Col. William] Shephard's [formerly Learned's] and Redes [Joseph Read's Thirteenth Continental] Regiments briskly ingaged them but we was cunning a nurfe not to meddle with the guarrd but bore a way to the North to a town caled Mile Square whare we incamped and left the above named Regiments to box it out with them . . ." [120] Another skirmish occurred on the road from East Chester to New Rochelle, in which direction Howe manifestly was moving his right.[121] At the end of the day, as far as Washington could determine, the British were well secured on a front of about two miles and a half, to the left of the roads that forked at New Rochelle.[122]

115 Needless to say, if this second road had been of particular importance to the British at the time, it could have been cut by a direct march from Throg's Neck, when the tide was favorable, without the trouble of the advance to Pell's Point.

116 Howe explained the six-day wait at Throg's Neck by saying that time was lost because of unfavorable weather, the transportation of supplies, and the transfer of three Battalions of Hessian troops from Staten Island to the scene of the new operation (3 Force (5), p. 817, 922).

117 2 Force (5), p. 908, 909, 1188.   118 Ibid., 1188.

119 6 G. W., 221. The British regarded this as no more than a trivial skirmish (1 Kemble, 94). In the action one of the British casualties was Capt. W. G. Evelyn whose letters, though overconfidently contemptuous of all things American, have definite historical value (Hall, 205).

120 Dr. Stimson's Diary, Oct. 18, 1776; 46 MHSP., 251.   121 3 Force (5), p. 922.

122 One of these roads ran northward to White Plains; the other, bending to the East, ran along the Connecticut coast of the Sound.

Washington had new difficulties in a shortage of cartridges [123] and a temporary lack of flour,[124] but his continuing concern, of course, was the field commander's perennial question, What is the enemy going to do? On the 19th and the 20th, as the British remained where they were, it was reasonable to assume that they intended to attempt one or the other of two things: Either they planned to proceed up the shore of Connecticut and to destroy supplies, stores and property as they advanced, or else they purposed to continue northward in an effort to turn Washington's left.[125] If the British strategy was to confine the American Army between the Sound and North River, then Howe's advance probably would be to White Plains, eighteen miles North of New Rochelle. At White Plains the redcoats would have three advantages: they would command the upper road to Connecticut; they would have the Croton River to cover their rear or, in the improbable event of disaster, to protect a new front, and from White Plains they could proceed with fair ease five miles westward and reach waterborne supplies on the Hudson at Tarrytown. In short, if the British got to the Croton River and the high ground at White Plains before the Americans did, then Washington's Army could be starved or forced to flee, broken and powerless, across the Hudson in small bodies or into Connecticut as mere refugees. This possibility was seen clearly at American headquarters. Washington went to White Plains on the 21st to examine the ground for himself and he resolved both to anticipate a British movement to that strategic position and also to take such measures as he could to withdraw provisions and other stores from exposed towns in southern Connecticut. In this he well knew he would be hampered greatly by the poverty of his transport.[126]

In protecting his Army against the two obvious British alternatives, Washington ran somewhat counter to the dominant opinion at headquarters. In Robert Harrison's words it was "generally conjectured" the British would advance to White Plains and "draw a line to the North River." [127] Washington naturally shaped his main defence to this probability but he did not attempt day-by-day conformation to the movements of the enemy through a gradual shift northward by his left

---

[123] 2 *Force* (5), p. 1136.   [124] *Ibid.*, 217–18, 220.
[125] 6 *G. W.*, 220. His front would change direction from time to time in such a movement and temporarily might assume an east-west direction, in which event the British might move around his right but, in general, his left would be the northern flank and the one to be turned.
[126] See letter of Oct. 21, 1776, to Joseph Trumbull; 6 *G. W.*, 220.
[127] *Ibid.*, 218 n.

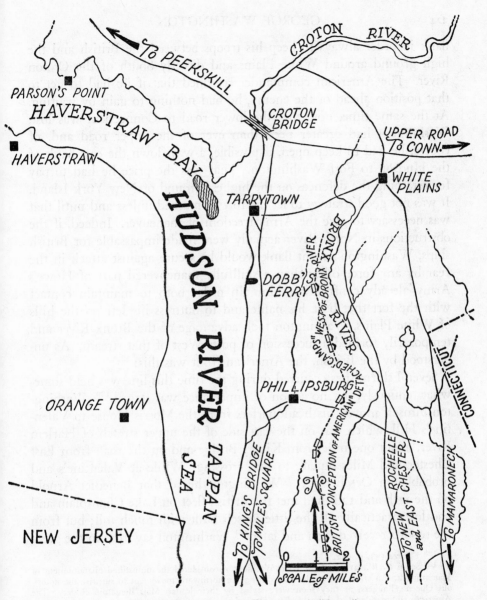

BRITISH MISCONCEPTION OF WASHINGTON'S "CAMPS"

This sketch of the approaches to White Plains, Croton Bridge and the "Upper Road" to Connecticut includes the "Detached Camps" the British assumed Washington was maintaining, late in October, between Valentine's Hill and White Plains. After Sauthier's map, as cited p. 220. It will be observed that some measurements were grossly in error and that the boundaries of Connecticut and New Jersey were placed by Sauthier several miles from their correct location.

223

flank in order always to keep his troops between the British and the high ground around White Plains and directly South of the Croton River. The American commander reasoned that if he had to get to that position ahead of the enemy, he had nothing to gain by waiting. At the same time, now that the lower road to Connecticut was lost, Washington had greater need than ever of the upper road and, of course, he had to keep open, if possible, a way down the east bank of the Hudson to Fort Washington. That was the price he had to pay for retaining the defences on the highest ground of New York Island. It was not good strategy to let the fort be masked unless and until that was necessary to give the Army freedom of maneuver. Indeed, if the obstructions in North River actually were made impassable for British ships, Washington's right flank would be secure against attack in the rear by any force other than a skillfully maneuvered part of Howe's Army already confronting him. In order both to maintain contact with the fort that bore his name and to buttress his left on the hills of White Plains, Washington took advantage of the Bronx River and temporarily formed a succession of posts West of that stream. As understood by the British, the American front was this: [128]

Several skirmishes occurred during the time this line was held somewhat tenuously, but no action of importance was staged.[129] Washington himself moved his headquarters from the Morris House to Valentine's Hill, which was on the east side of the upper stretch of Harlem River, about one mile from King's Bridge and on the road from East Chester and Miles Square to that crossing. While at Valentine's and probably on October 22,[130] Washington heard that Benedict Arnold on the 11th and 12th had met the British fleet on Lake Champlain and had lost practically all the little vessels built with much toil; but from the reports received then and later [131] Washington saw that in the great

[128] 3 *Force* (5), p. 922.

[129] See 6 *G. W.*, 219, 221 for what Washington considered the unjustified abandonment of Mamaroneck. An effort was made, also, during the northward movement to surprise the notorious Queen's Rangers, as they soon were styled by their leader, Maj. Benjamin Rogers. The American commander, Col. John Haslet, described this in 2 *Force* (5), p. 1270. Another account appears in *Heath*, 85, and a third in George Weedon to John Page, Oct. 26, 1776, *Chicago HS.* MSS. Harrison's report, which was virtually that of Washington, covers October 21–25 (2 *Force* (5), p. 1239 and 4 *Sparks*, 524). In 3 *Force* (5), p. 471 ff. is an "Extract of a Letter from a Gentleman in the Army" that contains some details found nowhere else so fully. Most of the statements probably are authentic but some of them demonstrably are mistaken camp gossip and some are not verifiable.

[130] 6 *G. W.*, 223. The news was reported in Newark October 21 (2 *Force* (5), p. 1028) and was known generally in the British camps by October 26. See 1 *Mackenzie*, 88.

[131] Arnold's reports are in 2 *Force* (5), p. 1038, 1079–80, 1116–17. Carleton's account, list-

imperative of stubborn, stand-up fight, Arnold's defeat was a victory of courage over the impulse to run away. There was, in fact, something of the spirit of Sir Richard Grenville in the strange, swarthy Arnold with his light eyes and his biting vigor.[132] It had been Washington's hope that if October and November passed without an American reverse and a British advance down the Northern New York Lakes, nothing need be feared from that quarter until the spring of 1777;[133] now he consoled himself with the reflection that it might be possible for the troops in the Northern Department to hold Ticonderoga, and thereby to block the descent of the enemy to the Hudson, until the severities of winter forced the British to withdraw.[134]

He could give little time to reflection on these dangers upstate because he needed every minute of the day to concentrate his troops for the attacks he expected. It was October 23rd when he opened his headquarters at White Plains in a position which was of some strength but was by no means as formidable as well-drawn lines would be in the higher hills North of the village. He took the less secure position because he wished to hold White Plains itself until the supplies there, which were considerable in bulk and in value, could be removed.[135]

While the Quartermaster's men were doing their best to transport these stores with wagons alarmingly few in number,[136] Washington began to show some confusion of thought on strategy. Sound though his maneuvers had appeared to be, he now questioned their adequacy. Might not the British confine him to the district around White Plains and at their pleasure proceed across the Hudson with part of their troops and ravage Jersey or march, even, on Philadelphia? Could his concentrated Army maintain communication with New England, protect the Highlands of the Hudson, and bar a southward advance of the British and Hessians? Would it not be better to set up two Armies, one to be stationed East of Hudson and supplied from that region, and the other to operate in New Jersey, where it could maneuver freely to

---

ing the United States ships, appears in *ibid.*, 1040–41. See also the report of Captain Thomas Pringle, *ibid.*, 1070.

[132] Washington had known of the plight of Gates's small, sickly force (see Gates's returns and the reports in 2 *Force* (5), p. 479, 618) and he had understood how suspicious, sensitive and unhappy Philip Schuyler had become (*ibid.*, 126, 263, 555; for Schuyler's effort to resign and Congress' vote of confidence in him, see *ibid.*, 864 and 5 *JCC.*, 841), while Arnold had been working, with the full encouragement of Schuyler and of Gates, to build the squadron (2 *Force* (5), p. 223, 352, 440, 481, 530, 591, 834, 982; 6 *G. W.*, 123).

[133] 6 *G. W.*, 193.   [134] *Ibid.*, 224.

[135] Harrison to Hancock, Oct. 29, 1776; 2 *Force* (5), p. 1282, also in 4 *Sparks*, 526.

[136] 2 *Force* (5), p. 1310.

combat any advance from New York in the direction of Philadelphia? Contrary as this question was to everything Washington previously had asserted in opposition to dispersal of force, he directed his Secretary to submit the subject to the consideration of Congress;[137] but he had to defer more detailed personal review of it, because he learned that the enemy undoubtedly was in movement toward White Plains. On the 26th, Adjutant General Reed wrote his wife that the British had advanced about four miles the previous day. "The business of this campaign and possibly the next," he said, "may probably be determined this week."[138] Washington, who was of like mind, saw his elaborate but fragile plans fall apart quickly. He virtually severed land communication for the time being with Fort Washington,[139] called his troops from their posts on the Bronx and, so to say, rolled up his right as if it had been a curtain.[140] Charles Lee, as the most experienced of Washington's lieutenants, was entrusted with the rear of the column that came up Bronx River to the position at White Plains.[141] He arrived October 26 and reported one encouragement: On his march, he had been compelled to halt and to double his teams in order to get his wagons forward, but he had not been troubled by the British, though they were in plain sight.[142] That was a measure of respect for American muskets the redcoats seldom had shown.

During the forenoon of the 27th, while the Regiments waited on the hills above White Plains, the Americans heard the sound of heavy cannonade from the direction of Fort Washington. When sufficient time had elapsed for a messenger to reach headquarters, the weary Commander-in-Chief learned that two frigates had come boldly up North River and had anchored at contemptuously short range, in a manifest determination to halt movement of every sort between Fort Washington and Fort Lee. A British land force simultaneously had presented itself in front of the southern outworks of Fort Washington and had begun demonstrations. The whole undertaking was a quick failure. One of the frigates was mauled remorselessly; the British infantry did not attempt to assault even an isolated redoubt. The com-

---

[137] Harrison to Hancock, Oct. 25, 6 *G. W.*, 228 n.

[138] 1 *Reed*, 246.   [139] Cf. Greene in 2 *Force* (5), p. 1269–70.

[140] *Heath*, 86–87; Howe in 3 *Force* (5), p. 922.

[141] *Heath*, loc. cit. Reservation has to be made as respects Lord Stirling, who was described by Tench Tilghman on October 31 as "keeping pace with the enemy's left flank" (2 *Force* (5), p. 1311–12). While the probability is strong that Stirling had a place in the order of battle on the 28th of October, there is a possibility that he had been detached.

[142] *Heath*, 86–87.

ment at White Plains doubtless was that this affair vindicated the judgment of those officers who had insisted that the North River could be made impassable and Fort Washington impregnable;[143] but, once again, men's emotions were so strained by the situation in their own front that they could not feel concern over the far off fight on North River. Now that Washington might be called upon to defend the position at White Plains, he had undertaken, while the echo from Fort Washington still was swelling, to make a careful reconnaissance in the company of his Generals. His lines, at the moment, were drawn from Northeast to Southwest along and to the North of the road that ran from Tarrytown into the upper Connecticut Road.[144] This front of slightly more than three miles constituted a "tongue of land" so fortified that its natural strength was increased.[145] On either flank long depressions, virtual "hollow ways," led down from the northern hills.

While those elevations offered natural redoubts and long, crude parapets at a distance of about 1000 yards in rear,[146] the position occupied by the Army would have been safe enough but for two circumstances. One was the fact that the defending force was dangerously small for so long a front; the second was the existence of an unusual hill slightly in advance of the right of Washington's Army. This eminence, known as Chatterton's Hill, was separated from the main position by the upper waters of the Bronx, which made a wide convex curve almost around its eastern and southern sides.[147] Although Chatterton's Hill to some extent dominated the American front and enfiladed the direct approaches to that front from the South, it had been

---

[143] The best account of this affair is an extract from an uncredited letter written that day, October 27, at Fort Lee, and printed in 2 *Force* (5), p. 1266. This is republished in 1 *Moore*, 330–31. See also Nathanael Greene's dispatch of Oct. 28, 1776, to Congress; 2 *Force* (5), p. 1269–70, the diary of an unidentified Pennsylvania soldier in *Bul. NYPL*, July 1904, v. 8, no. 7, p. 548, and a letter of Nathanael Greene to Mrs. Greene, Nov. 2, 1776; *Anderson Gal. Cat.*, 1926. Lord Howe gave no account of the affair in his report of Nov. 23, 1776 (3 *Force* (5), p. 816–18). Land operations of the British were described with confessed pride by Lord Percy in a letter of Oct. 30, 1776, to Lord George Germaine (*Percy Letters, 72*).

[144] On this stretch, the upper road went from Croton Bridge to the vicinity of White Plains and eastward to Bedford. The Tarrytown Road, running Northeast from the Hudson, passed through White Plains and joined the upper road about a mile Northeast of the village.

[145] 1 *Kemble*, 95.

[146] *A. Robertson's Diaries*, 107. A map by John Rösch of "White Plains and Environs in 1776," with the present-day streets superimposed, will be found in Mr. Rösch's *Historic White Plains*.

[147] *Heath*, 88, and Howe's report, 3 *Force* (5), p. 923. Students of this phase of the campaign may be able to make some local identifications from Robert Bolton, Jr., *History of the County of Westchester*, v. 2, p. 370; but as often happens, the ownership of property mentioned as matters of common knowledge when the book was written many years ago now is almost as difficult to fix as that of 1776 is.

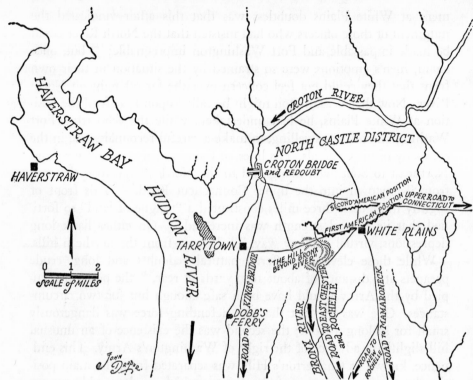

DANGEROUS ERRORS OF DISTANCE AROUND WHITE PLAINS

This sketch of the immediate area of White Plains and Croton Bridge, from Sauthier's map, shows clearly the "Hill beyond Bronx River"; in the centre and to the East lie the two American positions not far from their correct positions, though parts of the lines were run where they took advantage of the ground in a manner Sauthier could not exhibit on the scale he employed. Students who wish to examine the ground in detail should consult the admirable map prepared in 1935 by John Rösch and appended to his *Historic White Plains* (1939). The location of the old sites in relation to modern streets and structures was given unobtrusively and most informatively by that author. Had the battle swung to the North, British misunderstanding of the distances North of White Plains might have proved expensive. It will be noted that Sauthier's map put Croton Bridge less than three miles North of Tarrytown, instead of eight miles, and that it reduced the thirteen miles between White Plains and Croton River to four.

garrisoned with a small force of militia only and had not been fortified. If it had to be used casually in resisting British advance, the hill had stone fences [148] from which well led and courageous men could deliver their volleys in relative safety.[149] All this was plain on reconnaissance, but from the crest of Chatterton's Hill the great security of the heights North of White Plains was even more impressive.

[148] 4 *Sparks*, 528.
[149] The number of stone fences on one part of the line was a question of some importance in the subsequent courtmartial of Col. Morris Graham, for which see 3 *Force* (5), p. 488.

"Yonder," said Lee, pointing, "is the ground we ought to occupy."
"Let us then go and view it," Washington answered.

The officers turned about, touched the flanks of their animals and started northeastward. They were on their way when a member of the Light Horse overtook them at furious pace on a panting mount. The man rode straight to the Commander-in-Chief with a startling message: "The British are on the camp, sir."

Washington turned to his companions. "Gentlemen," he said, "we have now other business than reconnoitring," and with that he put his steed to the gallop. The other Generals followed. When the cavalcade drew rein at headquarters, Adjutant General Reed explained that the advance guards had been driven in and that a general alarm had been sounded. Again Washington looked to his officers. "Gentlemen," he said, "you will repair to your respective posts and do the best you can." [150] As it eventuated, a little time was allowed him, because the British did not pursue the American advance guard. At the end of the day, Howe's main army was reported four miles South of White Plains.[151]

By dawn of the 28th of October, Washington had decided that he must fortify and hold Chatterton's Hill if he was to retain even briefly his position at White Plains. Colonel Reed accordingly was directed to take a designated force to the eminence, to dispose the men, and then to have them entrench. Spencer and Wadsworth were sent out with 500 or 600, mixed militia and Continentals, to delay the expected advance of the British and to collect such information as they could.[152] While the Army waited, Reed went about his task of securing Chatterton's Hill. He started Haslet's Delaware veterans on their way, in order that they might support Brooks's Massachusetts militia, who already were on the high ground, and he gave instructions to the remainder of McDougall's Brigade, with which Brooks's Regiment had been connected, to proceed to the hill and to throw up earthworks.[153]

150 *Heath*, 87–89. This author confused events of the 27th and 28th but, from what he related concerning the sound of fire from Fort Washington, he almost certainly was correct in stating that the reconnaissance was made on the 27th. Known events of October 28 left no time for any such survey of the ground.   151 1 *Kemble*, 95.

152 Letter in the *Penn. Evening Post*, Nov. 14, 1776, reprinted in 1 *Moore*, 335.

153 There is a possibility of error in this. Webb's, Ritzema's, Smallwood's, Haslet's and Brooks's Regiments are listed as McDougall's Brigade in a letter quoted in 2 *Force* (5), p. 1271. This was a somewhat different organization from that of Oct. 5, 1776, reported in *ibid.*, 907. Haslet then was with Mifflin's Brigade, to the command of which Stirling had succeeded. The report of Haslet mentions McDougall's Brigade as if he were not associated with it. Probabilities are that Haslet had left Stirling's Brigade temporarily for the attack of October 20 on Rogers's

Spencer's and Wadsworth's troops meantime—about 9 or 9:30 o'clock [154]—came back to the lines with reports that the British were moving up the East Chester Road [155] in two columns.[156] Soon, from Washington's headquarters, the enemy could be seen plainly [157] in the bright sunlight of the fine autumn day [158] as the long files turned to East and to West at a distance of about one mile from the Americans.[159] In a very short time, the British artillery opened with vigor [160] on widespread targets. Royal gunners seemed merely to be saying, "Here's a taste of our wares for all of your rebels," but the taste was enough on the American right. The second shot directed against the few troops on Chatterton's Hill wounded one of Brooks's militiamen in the thigh, whereupon, said Haslet later, with soldierly restraint of speech, "the whole Regiment broke and fled immediately and were not rallied without much difficulty." [161]

The cannonade continued. Presently, across Bronx River, the Brigade of McDougall climbed the side of Chatterton's Hill and took station behind Haslet and the militia. That disposition did not please the temporary soldiers or even the veterans from Delaware. They saw themselves killed from the rear by careless American fire if they escaped British round shot and shell. At Haslet's request, McDougall extended the line and had his own command file in to the left. In this deployment, Brooks's scared militia were put on the extreme right, whence Haslet felt certain they would run as soon as they were attacked. McDougall agreed to change this, when Haslet warned him, and put Smallwood's men in advance of the militia on the right.[162]

Rangers and had won a reputation for competence in detached service. Reed may have selected the Regiment for that reason.

[154] Benjamin Trumbull in his Diary gave the hour as 9; the unidentified writer in 3 *Force* (5), p. 473 said it was half an hour later.

[155] Cf. *A. Robertson's Diaries,* 105, and Diary of Lieut. James McMichael in *15 Penn. Arc.* (2), p. 201. McMichael wrote that Spencer's troops had instructions to bring on the action but not to take a chance of being captured. The Americans encountered the enemy within two miles of White Plains, skirmished for an hour, and then retreated on news from a flanking party that the British Light Horse were encircling the force.

[156] Ibid., *Penn. Evening Post,* Nov. 14, 1776, as quoted in 1 *Moore,* 335. Sir George Clinton's troops were leading on the right, and Heister's Germans were in front on the left, according to Howe's report 3 *Force* (5), p. 922.

[157] *Penn. Evening Post,* Nov. 14, 1776, as cited.   [158] *Heath,* 89.

[159] Howe's report, as cited. Glyn noted in his Journal, Princeton Lib.: "The rebel Army were found to be very advantageously posted in an entrenched camp across the upper Connecticut Road . . ."

[160] Benjamin Trumbull's Diary, *loc. cit.,* 204.

[161] Letter to Caesar Rodney, Nov. 12, 1776; 4 *Sparks,* 528. This is the most informative single document concerning events on Chatterton's Hill.

[162] *Ibid.* Haslet's use of "onward" and "forward" in the same sentence leave doubt whether

This movement of troops on Chatterton's Hill was visible from the British front[163] and, if seen by Washington, was understood as mere execution of orders given through Reed. Elsewhere along the lines, there was artillery fire and, ere long, some activity in front of Wadsworth's Brigade.[164] This almost was forgotten in a few minutes, because the enemy increased his bombardment of Chatterton's Hill. Then troops began to move from the British left and to form for a crossing of Bronx River. Ere long, smoke was seen to be rising from an eminence almost directly South of Chatterton's Hill. Evidently the enemy had climbed the ridges and was firing across[165] to the right flank of McDougall, but soon the side of Chatterton's Hill was covered with smoke, and the artillery ceased fire on that part of the line. The demonstration against Wadsworth was launched; the crackle of small arms was almost continuous. Then came silence on the extreme right and a humiliating message to Washington: Hessians and British had stormed Chatterton's Hill; the militia had run away again; Smallwood's men had stood for no longer than a quarter of an hour; Webb's Regiment[166] and part of Haslet's command had held their ground but had to retreat when left alone; some of McDougall's men had not pulled trigger.

Chatterton's Hill was lost, and so was the day. The right of the American lines at White Plains no longer was tenable.[167]

---

he meant to say that Smallwood became the left element in advance, with Brooks's militia in support, or whether Smallwood extended the flank; but Haslet's later reference to the fence in front of the militia makes it plain that Smallwood was in advance.

[163] See 1 Kemble, 95.

[164] While it nowhere is so stated, Wadsworth almost certainly was the right Brigade on the main line East of the Bronx River—another example of singular failure on the part of American commanders to perceive that Howe thus far had conducted flanking operations and nowhere had assaulted heavy works. An experienced continental Regiment should have been the flank element.

[165] A fork of the road from East Chester and New Rochelle ran between these hills to Croton Bridge.

[166] 6 G. W., 232.

[167] Haslet's account (loc. cit.) is the only first-hand American narrative and it most certainly does not depreciate its author or the troops he commanded. Howe's report (3 Force (5), p. 924–25), is little more than a matter-of-fact summary of an easy assault on a flank position. Kemble (op. cit., 95), stated that the movement was undertaken because the British observed the arrival of additional troops on Chatterton's Hill and reasoned they had better take that strategically located eminence before it was strengthened. Casualties among the British and Hessians included "several" officers and 180 enlisted men (ibid., 96). American losses were said by Harrison the next day "from conjecture" to be "between 400 and 500" (2 Force (5), p. 1282). By the 6th of November, the General's secretary was able to report the killed, wounded and missing by no means as numerous as had been thought at first (3 Force (5), p. 546–47). Many who were supposed to have been captured by the British simply went home. As of November 19, Washington believed the British loss to have been about 300 and the American total to have been "little more than half" that number (6 G. W., 243).

CHAPTER IX

"HE WHO HESITATES IS . . ."
(October 28–November 24, 1776)

FORTUNATELY for Washington's Army and for the future of the United States, capture of Chatterton's Hill did not expose immediately the whole of the continental lines to British fire. The ground so abounded in natural defences that the American right could be drawn in and the remainder of the front held. Howe himself contributed to this by failing to press the advance. Washington shifted some of his troops to better positions on high ground October 28 and 29, and, all the while, he removed as many supplies from White Plains as the wagons could carry. Howe kept his men under cover but, by the 31st, it was apparent that he was working on four or five batteries that could sweep most of the American positions. Washington accordingly withdrew that night to North Castle, a more rugged country directly North of the town,[1] where assault by the redcoats would be expensive.[2] He moved just in time. The British had planned a general assault on the 31st and they deferred it twenty-four hours because of a heavy, if warm rain.[3] When Howe found the former defences abandoned on the 1st, caution dictated farther reconnaissance before pursuit was ordered.[4]

[1] Robt. Bolton, Jr., *History of the County of Westchester*, v. 2, p. 370, with note on Washington's headquarters.

[2] *Heath*, 89–91; Tench Tilghman in 3 *Force* (5), p. 486; Howe's report in 3 *Force* (5), p. 923; Diary of Sgt. John Smith, *Miss. Val. His. Soc. Rev.*, v. 20, p. 260; *Penn. Evening Post*, Nov. 14, 1776, cited in 1 *Moore*, 336–37. It has been assumed by some writers that Washington withdrew his entire line on the night of October 28–29, but all the evidence indicates that the retirement was gradual. Capt. George Harris complained that "the Americans behaved in the most dastardly manner." They "gave way with such precipitation that they escaped to the heights before our men could reach them" (undated letter to his uncle; Lushington's *Harris*, 82). General Howe, on examination before the House of Commons, subsequently stated that he had "political reasons, and no other, for declining to state" why he did not assault the whole of the American front on the 28th. In his *Narrative*, 4, he explained that by attacking he would have gained " a more brilliant advantage" and would have captured some baggage and provisions, but that he had no reason to assume the American Army would have been destroyed. It could readily have withdrawn. The positions to be carried, he maintained, were not worth the lives they would have cost.

[3] *A. Robertson's Diaries*, 106; Benjamin Trumbull's Diary, *loc. cit.*, 206.

[4] British authorities, for example, 1 *Kemble*, 96; *A. Robertson's Diaries*, 107, stated that the royal troops entered the deserted works during the morning of the 1st. Heath asserted, on the

That opening day of November proved a hard one for Washington. About 6 A.M., while the men were occupying their new citadel, a messenger brought word that Lord Stirling thought two columns were advancing against the station he had taken two or three miles on the right of Washington's line to delay a possible turning movement. During the night Washington had put reenforcements in the road toward Stirling's post, and he now reasoned that the troops seen by the pickets might consist of friends, not of enemies; but, of course, if the detachments actually were British, the entire America Army would have to move farther northward. Off, then, Washington had to ride with his aides, splashing mud everywhere, to see for himself the developments Stirling reported.

The marching men proved to be the American reenforcement.[5] Washington turned back, in some relief of spirit, but, at the same time, he had to recognize that what proved to be a false alarm might have been the beginning of the end. The British now commanded the waterways on both flanks; the upper road to Connecticut was in their hands; supplies, particularly of flour, were low. Suppose Howe moved swiftly northward around the American right and brushed Stirling aside: the way would be open to Croton River, thirteen miles in rear of Washington's position. Across that stream was one bridge only.[6] If that were destroyed, supplies would be cut off. The one alternative to starvation would be for the Army to cut its way through the ranks of an adversary who might surround Washington's weak-spirited Regiments. American troops must go at once to the bridge and must hold it![7] The necessity was part of the problem with which Washington had to deal whenever he was maneuvering where the British Navy could cooperate with the King's army.[8] Now, as soon as the continental leader made his dispositions to cope with a possible attempt by his foe to seize the crossing of the Croton River, he had to face the perplexities of finding provisions for his hungry men.[9]

---

other hand (*op. cit.*, 90–92) that vigorous action occurred on his front that day, but he so confused his account of the events of the first two days of the month that it is difficult to ascertain when he meant to say the withdrawal took place.

[5] 3 *Force* (5), p. 464.

[6] Approximately eight miles directly North of Tarrytown, though the defective contemporary British maps, even the best of them, reduce the distance to less than three miles.

[7] Beall's Maryland Brigade was ordered there (3 *Force* (5), p. 485).

[8] Cf. his observation of Oct. 5, 1776: "[The British] were not only superior in numbers but could bring their whole force to any one point . . ." (6 *G. W.*, 170).

[9] See Harrison in 3 *Force* (5), p. 484.

So far as rock and grade in themselves gave his Army protection, Washington felt he would be secure in the hills North of White Plains as soon as he could add art to nature's bulwarks. Open field combat was impossible at the time. He explained later: "had we ever hazarded a general action . . . unless it had been in our works at New York, or Harlem Heights, we undoubtedly should have risked a good cause upon a very unfavorable issue . . ." So, he added, the Americans had tried to outflank the British Army, and "by degrees" had become "strongly posted on advantageous grounds at this place."[10] That was all he could say with any cheer because, even in the presence of the enemy, he was facing the immediate possibility that his Army might be destroyed by desertion, poor regimental leadership, reliance on militia, and blind adherence to a policy of short-term enlistment. On the 31st of October, Washington's secretary, Robert Harrison, had written Congress: "Our Army is decreasing fast: several gentlemen who have come to camp within a few days have observed large numbers of militia returning home on the different roads, nor are any measures taken as yet to raise the new Army, no committees having come from the States to appoint or signify the nominations of their officers. If this was done perhaps many who are now here might be induced to engage, but at present there are none authorized to recruit."[11] George Clinton, who commanded a thin Brigade of New York militia,[12] saw the larger and worse effects of desertion and he unburdened himself thus: ". . . the enemy are daily increasing their Army by new recruits in those parts of the country they have already acquired, whilst ours are daily decreasing by sickness, deaths and desertions; add to this, one month more disbands a very considerable part of our Army.[13] How a new one will be recruited, God only knows. This I know, many are disgusted with the service. Those will not reenter; and, what is worse, will prevent others, by representing on their return home, the hardships they have endured."[14]

Washington scarcely knew where to look for new soldiers or how to keep the veterans. On the 5th of November he appealed to the militia to remain with the Army, at so critical a time, beyond the expiration

[10] Letter of Nov. 6, 1776, to his brother "Jack"; 6 G. W., 243.
[11] 2 Force (5), p. 1310.
[12] Its five Regiments on Oct. 5, 1776, returned 1061 rank and file, present, fit; (ibid., 907).
[13] See infra, p. 254.
[14] Letter of Oct. 31, 1776, to John McKesson; 2 Force (5), p. 1312.

of their term of service,[15] but he might as well have asked them to scale high heaven. In the attempted enforcement of discipline, he threatened, he exhorted, he admonished.[16] General Orders of November 3 read, in part, to this effect: "The General is sorry to find that there are some soldiers so lost to all sense of honor and honesty as to leave the Army when there is the greatest necessity for their services: He calls upon the officers of every rank to exert themselves in putting a stop to it, and absolutely forbids any officer, under the rank of a Brigadier General, discharging any officer or soldier or giving any permission to leave the camp on any pretence whatsoever." [17]

Such was the plight of the Army when, on the morning of November 5, Washington received news that startled and puzzled: The British had abandoned their camps and had started westward and apparently to the Southwest, also, in the direction of King's Bridge.[18] Headquarters buzzed with interpretation. Washington thought the move might possibly be a feint, and he did not believe Howe could be preparing to go into winter quarters with so little accomplished. It was much more likely, Washington reasoned, that the British intended to besiege Fort Washington, to attempt the subjugation of New Jersey, and perhaps to send an expedition to one or another of the Southern States.[19] Joseph Reed canvassed the possibilities and concluded, with the majority, that a descent on the country West and South of the Hudson was most probable; [20] Charles Lee's pronouncement was, "We have by proper positions brought Mr. Howe to his *ne plus ultra*." [21]

A council of war on the 6th agreed that if the British retreat were toward New York, Howe might be planning to invade New Jersey and that additional American troops consequently should be moved thither. It was suggested, too, that the Regiments for this service be those of States below the Hudson and that men from the Eastern States be returned to that region if circumstances permitted. Three thousand soldiers, the council decided, would be an appropriate guard for the New York Highlands.[22] This advice looked to the creation of two

15 6 *G. W.*, 241.
16 Cf. GOs of Oct. 30, Oct. 31, Nov. 1, 1776; *ibid.*, 233.
17 *Ibid.*, 238; the punctuation, which is somewhat revised here, suggests that this paragraph was written by Robert Harrison.
18 *Ibid.*, 248; *Heath*, 93–94; *Va. Gazette*, Nov. 29, 1776.
19 6 *G. W.*, 249, 255.
20 Letter of Nov. 6, 1776, to Mrs. Reed; 1 *Reed*, 248.
21 3 *Force* (5), p. 541.
22 Minutes in 3 *Force* (5), p. 543–44.

Armies, in accordance with the suggestion previously submitted to
Congress by Washington,[23] and it reflected the weary confusion of mind
to which he was coming in his consideration of strategical plans. Too
weak to take the offensive with one Army, he was in a fair way of
destroying even its defensive power by dividing it in circumstances that
would increase his dependence on militia. At the moment, all the General could do to make this dangerous proposal an experimental reality
was to apportion troops, to provide supplies, and to make preliminary
arrangements for the march and for the crossing of the Hudson. He
postulated, of course, the reunion of his forces West of the river if the
whole or even the greater part of the enemy's army moved into New
Jersey, and, meantime, he kept a close watch on the British, but they
made that an easy task by encamping the greater part of their infantry
at Dobbs Ferry. Hessian troops on this march and in subsequent raids
stripped friend and foe of everything they thought they could use,
barter or sell.[24] More decently, the royal artillery was moved, without
any effort at concealment, to King's Bridge.[25]

While these dispositions manifestly threatened Fort Washington as
well as New Jersey, the British withdrawal from White Plains gave the
American commander almost a week in which to struggle with plundering, half-mutiny, widespread desertion and some obstacles of a sort
that had not been put in his way when he had striven to replace the
Army at the end of 1775. To have called his situation desperate would
have been to brighten the picture. The danger of a complete dissolution of the Army was, in fact, so imminent that while Washington did
what he could to relieve the misery of his men, he could not afford to
admit the justice of some of the soldiers' complaints. Scores of tents
had been lost in the evacuation of New York;[26] incoming militia, as
usual, brought none with them.[27] Compelled to sleep on the ground,
where ice was formed as early as November 2,[28] many of the recruits

---

[23] See *supra*, p. 225-26.

[24] 1 *Kemble*, 97–98; cf. *ibid.*, 91. Americans denounced these outrages and asserted that
rape was added to the other crimes, though Howe insisted afterwards (*Observations*, 59–60) that
one case only was reported to him and that in this instance the victim refused to prosecute.
Continental soldiers themselves did not pretend always to respect private property, food in particular, if they honorably refrained from attacking women. Sergeant John Smith's Diary (*Miss.
Val. HS Rev.*, vol. 20, p. 265 ff.) included the unabashed recountal of much small thievery and
plundering by the Rhode Island command to which he belonged. On the 21st of December he
noted that the men stole "twenty-nine fowls that had not got the countersign." Soldiers even
carried off the farmers' beehives.

[25] General Howe's report in 3 *Force* (5), p. 924.

[26] 6 *G. W.*, 78–79.   [27] *Ibid.*, 86–87.   [28] *Serle*, 136.

fell sick and went to hospitals which were worse, if possible, than the camps.[29] Some of the troops had no cooking utensils;[30] others had to man the works all night when they were weary and were shivering[31] for lack of clothing. "There are few coats among them," a British officer said of the Americans, "but what are out at elbows, and in a whole Regiment there is scarce a pair of breeches."[32] Homesickness afflicted hundreds of newcomers to the Army.[33] Before a month passed, a column of captured Americans was to provoke the laughter of the British because "a great many of them were lads under 15, and old men, and few of them had the appearance of soldiers."[34] In September, when tents were not available for all, Washington's recourse had been to direct that the troops be "stored thicker."[35] That would not now suffice. "The men," said a Connecticut Chaplain of patriotic stock, "are worried in a manner to death and are treated with great hardship and severity, and in my opinion are put to much unnecessary hardship and fatigue."[36] For lack of good officers, they soon would not, and perhaps could not, fight.[37]

Certain it was that they could not be expected to respond with huzzas to the plea that they reenlist for the duration of the war. They saw three Regiments arrive from Virginia and one from Rhode Island to reenforce the Army[38] and doubtless they reasoned there were others where these came from, others who should suffer in their stead and keep the vigil of the freezing dawn. To Washington, the attitude of the men could not have seemed unreasonable, but he believed that if vigorous, persuasive officers were authorized to recruit on the terms Congress had allowed, some of the veterans could be induced to continue in service.[39]

The obstacle to this was a new one: no officer of a Regiment due to

29 Cf. 2 Force (5), p. 1312.   30 Benjamin Trumbull's Diary, op. cit., 202.

31 Cf. George Clinton in 2 Force (5), p. 1312.

32 2 Force (5), p. 1293-94.

33 See, for example, in ibid., 1296, the case of a deserter whose plea was that he wanted to go home to his wife. Cf. Nathanael Greene in a letter of Sept. 28, 1776: "People coming from home with all the tender feelings of domestic life are not sufficiently fortified with natural courage to stand the shocking scenes of war" (1 Greene's Greene, 221).

34 1 Mackenzie, 112.   35 6 G. W., 19.

36 Benjamin Trumbull's Diary, loc. cit., 202.

37 Cf. Greene to Washington concerning the refusal of Col. A. Hawkes Hay's men to discharge their duty. "They say that General Howe had promised them peace, liberty and safety, and that is all they want" (Letter of Nov. 5, 1776; 3 Force (5), p. 523).

38 For the call for the Virginia troops and their response and report, see 5 JCC., 732, 825; 2 Force (5), p. 136, 271; 6 G. W., 43. For the brigading of the Rhode Island Regiment, see 6 G. W., 171.

39 6 G. W., 153-54; cf. 3 Force (5), p. 484.

leave at the end of the year knew whether he was to remain an officer
and whether he had any right to recruit. Under the resolves Congress
recklessly had adopted, nothing could be done in this direction until
the State commissioners journeyed to camp and selected the men who
were to command the Regiments from their States. As of November 6,
not a single officer of a State Regiment had been chosen in this manner
and invested with authority to recruit. Congress had provided, two
days earlier, that if the commissioners had not arrived when Washington received the text of the resolution, he might name the officers who
were to undertake reorganization and recruiting, but this manifestly
might create resentments within the States and might hamper the very
men Washington sought to encourage, the men competent to lead new
Regiments.[40] Another complication—Washington always had to face
at least one—was created by the action of Connecticut, Maryland and
Massachusetts in supplementing the bounty voted by Congress to men
who would enlist for three years or for the continuance of the war.[41]
Washington exposed the dangerous unwisdom of this when he said,
"A different pay cannot exist in the same Army," [42] and he had the
vexation of correspondence and delay before he was past this barrier.
Simultaneously he had to untangle negotiations over Pennsylvania's
appointees to the reorganized Battalions,[43] and he had to await the
pleasure of New York in the selection of her officers,[44] while Congress
debated, before deciding affirmatively, that the bounty of land should
go to those who enlisted for three years as well as to those who accepted
service for the period of the war.[45]

The addition of all these man-made perplexities to the leadership of
a dispirited and feeble army in the presence of a superior foe imposed
on Washington the heaviest load under which he could hope to stagger
on. It did not seem possible for patience to endure another frustration

[40] 6 *JCC.*, 920–21, 973; Hancock in 2 *Burnett*, 139–40; cf. 3 *Force* (5), p. 514–15.

[41] Maryland offered ten dollars as a substitute for the 100 acres of land which her lawmakers mistakenly thought Congress expected the States to provide. As Maryland had no
public lands, she saw no alternative to a grant of funds. The situation in that State is summarized in the resolution of Congress, Oct. 30, 1776 (6 *JCC.*, 912–13). Massachusetts and Connecticut voted 20*s* per man for each month between the time he enlisted and the time his
continental pay began, because the two States believed additional inducements necessary. The
course of this affair, with the protests of Washington, Gates and Schuyler, may be followed in
6 *G. W.*, 270–71, 273; 3 *Force* (5), p. 459, 496, 614–15, 666, 711, 714, 770; 2 *Burnett*, 143,
157; 1 *Warren-Adams Letters*, 276–77.

[42] Letter of Nov. 11, 1776; 6 *G. W.*, 273.

[43] 6 *G. W.*, 251.　　　　　　　　　　　　[44] 6 *G. W.*, 288.

[45] 6 *JCC.*, 944, 971. Final action on this was not taken until Nov. 20, 1776. See also
2 *Burnett*, 161, for the confusion of Maryland over this issue.

or for faith to bear up if disaster came. In bafflement and approaching despair, Washington brought his general officers together in council on the 6th of November, while Howe's plans still were undetermined, and he asked their advice on recruitment: Could anything be done to preserve the Army? The term of enlistment of the Massachusetts "Long Faces" would expire on the 17th of the month; Connecticut militiamen had been called for no specified term and probably could not be held when they decided to go home; [46] two five-months Brigades of the Flying Camp and some of the continental Regiments would complete their service on November 30, and most of the other continentals at the end of December, though not one lawful step could yet be taken to reenlist them on the new terms. Was the situation hopeless? The answer of the council was the old one, perhaps the only one that could be made: As there inevitably would be a gap of some months between the time the Army of '76 disbanded and the Army of '77 was ready for the field, each of the nearby States must be called upon to supply a considerable force of militia—as many as 4000 from Massachusetts for example—to serve until Mch 1, 1777.[47] To this weak and worn expedient was the Commander-in-Chief reduced, he who remembered militiamen's negligence on Long Island, their panic at Kip's Bay, their flight from Chatterton's Hill and their mass desertion when weariness or nostalgia overtook them.

After the council, Washington addressed his appeal to some of the States for these new drafts of militia. He particularly exhorted Gov. William Livingston of New Jersey to put militia in readiness to take the place of men from that State whose term of service was soon to expire. Stock, grain, forage and vehicles should be removed beyond the reach of the enemy; the barracks near Elizabeth Town, Amboy and Brunswick should be repaired because they would be needed.[48] Washington's tone in this was calm if urgent, but when he reported to Congress, which had authorized him to call for militia,[49] he scarcely could conceal his desperation: "The propriety of this application [to the States] I trust will appear when it is known that not a single officer is yet commissioned to recruit,[50] and when it is considered how

---

[46] 6 G. W., 266.
[47] Ibid., 247–48.
[48] 6 G. W., 255–56; cf. ibid., 247–48.
[49] 6 JCC., 921. He called the council before receipt of this new authorization (6 G. W., 272).
[50] Strictly speaking, Washington was in error in this, if the authorization written for Col. Edward Hand, Oct. 11, 1776, actually was delivered to that officer. See ibid., 198–99.

essential it is to keep up some show of force and shadow of an Army." [51]

"Shadow of an Army"—was that all he was to have in the day when Howe manifestly intended to assail Fort Washington and, if successful there, might move against Philadelphia? [52] Washington had to prepare as best he could for these eventualities, but he was wearier than he knew. His judgment increasingly was clouded; his decisions were made more slowly and with hesitation. He still could spur officers to recruit as soon as they were named by the commissioners from their States,[53] and with such men as would "stand by" him,[54] he resolved to confront Howe. Should the British venture into Jersey the American Army must drive them back, if possible, to New York.[55] In his exhausted state of mind, Washington thought the contemplated transfer of American forces across the Hudson was immediately strategic and perhaps was imperative. He would divide the artillery,[56] would leave Heath to guard the New York Highlands,[57] would name Charles Lee to direct operations North of King's Bridge,[58] and would himself proceed to Peekskill on the Hudson, approximately eighteen miles from White Plains on the roads open to him. From that point, he would cross the Hudson with the troops from the Colonies West and South of the river.[59] These men would be few in number, but they could be reenforced, Washington believed, by two Brigades of "five-months" troops from the Flying Camp and by Jersey militia. In failing judgment he estimated that from these two sources he could get at least 5000 troops.[60] With these and his Continentals, he hoped he could hold the British until the development of their offensive made possible the reconcentration of all his troops except, perhaps, those left to garrison the passes of the New York Highlands, the bastion that must be held if it was possible for a small Army to do so.

In this expectation, Washington left the camp above White Plains at 11 A.M. on the 10th of November, pursued his appointed journey,

[51] Ibid., 250.

[52] For Washington's suggestion of this possibility in the last paragraph of his letter of Nov. 6, 1776, to Congress, see 6 G. W., 250.

[53] His GO on this subject bore date of Nov. 10, 1776; ibid., 262–63. Cf. ibid., 274, 289–90, and 3 Force (5), p. 813.

[54] Cf. 6 G. W., 138.   [55] Ibid., 262.

[56] Ibid., 266–67. For Washington's plans to enlarge his artillery, see his letter of Nov. 16, 1776, to the President of Congress (ibid., 280–82).

[57] Ibid., 275.   [58] Ibid., 263 ff.   [59] Ibid., 262, 263, 279.

[60] Ibid., 397. For the "Five Months Brigades" see next chapter.

made a reconnaissance of the Highlands,[61] and by the evening of the 13th reached Nathanael Greene's headquarters at Fort Lee, opposite Fort Washington on New York Island.[62] Nearly all the "Southern" [63] troops then were across the Hudson under the immediate command of Lord Stirling[64]—and were in number less than three full Regiments would have been. With the inclusion of all the militia except those in Fort Washington, the Army East of the Hudson consisted of 13,123 fit, rank and file, on the 3rd of November.[65] Approximately 7000 of these had been left with Lee; [66]Heath had about 4000.[67] Washington reduced his own force to 2000 Virginians and Marylanders, besides artillerists and ambulant sick,[68] and he had no prospect of reenforcement except by Greene's 3500,[69] the men of the Flying Camp and the Jersey militia.

It was incredible but the subtraction spoke for itself: the little Army was split into no less than four fragments—Lee's, Heath's, the forces now in Jersey, and the garrison of Fort Washington. To be sure, Nathanael Greene insisted that the troops on the west bank of North River and those in Fort Washington were in reality one body, because, he maintained, the defenders of the fort could be brought across to Jersey at any time, under cover of the guns of Fort Lee.[70] An optimist might assert, also, that as Lee was not more than three days' march from the Commander-in-Chief, an effective body of fighting men could be reassembled before the British General could make any dangerous new move. However that might be, Washington received information from Greene that was a stunning blow—no less: The Flying Camp did not include anything like as many men as Washington had assumed were there; practically no Jersey militia had rallied to Greene. Instead of the 5000 recruits he had expected,[71] Washington had virtually no

[61] *Heath*, 95.   [62] *Ibid.*

[63] Those who read in the eighteen-thirties Sparks's edition of the *Writings of Washington* must have been amused to find that some revolutionary New Englanders spoke of the Pennsylvanians as "Southerners."

[64] 6 *G. W.*, 272. The only troops that had not yet reached the right bank were those of Smallwood's Maryland Regiment (*ibid.*, 279). For Stirling's advance to Haverstraw and his preparations to pass the Hudson, see 3 *Force* (5), p. 634.

[65] *Ibid.*, 499–502. Stirling, with 1689 effectives, had much the largest Brigade.

[66] Rank and file, present, fit, 5162; on command, 1750; *ibid.*, 709, as of Nov. 16, 1776.

[67] *Ibid.*, 832, as of Nov. 24, 1776.

[68] Washington stated (6 *G. W.*, 244) that he took with him "about 5000 men," but his own returns show this could not have been the total otherwise than by the inclusion of the sick and of officers who were not counted among the effectives.

[69] Present, fit, rank and file, 2667; on command, 870 (3 *Force* (5), p. 663).

[70] *Ibid.*, 740.   [71] 6 *G. W.* 397.

LORD STIRLING, PEER IN A REPUBLIC

To this day, indexers and librarians are perplexed whether the handsome man whose face appears on the opposite page should be listed as William Alexander or as Lord Stirling. The ancient lapsed title had been awarded him by a jury in 1759, but the findings were not approved by the House of Lords. Instead of sitting as a peer at Westminster, the disappointed claimant, son of a staunch Jacobite, returned to America and established himself at Basking Ridge, New Jersey. He was astronomer, landed proprietor, man of affairs and always in his signature, Stirling. There might be a question about the validity of his title but there was none about the loyalty of his service when war came. As Jersey Colonel, as continental Brigadier, and then as a Major General, he was constantly with his troops except when ill health or injury held him captive. Although stories circulated of convivial evenings over a nest of bottles or an unpretending jug, it never was even whispered that he was drunk when Henry Knox's guns were barking, or the rattle of the skirmishers' muskets was heard in the woods.

In 1776, he was regarded as a leader whom experience would ripen; subsequently Lafayette described him as "braver than wise." The Marquis probably was correct. Stirling did not fulfil as a soldier the promise he had shown when, for example, Washington had ridden with him from Philadelphia to Basking Ridge in May, 1773 (Vol. III, p. 321–22). For some reason, a field operation entrusted to Stirling was apt to get snarled. Neither he nor his Chief would know exactly why plans went astray, but they did. If, then, the merciless judgment of the battlefield seldom was in Stirling's favor when night ended the trial of arms, he never had the shame of dishonorable action or of retreat when critical comrades thought he might have stood. They did not consider him incompetent; they liked him and enjoyed his company and admired his social qualities; at the same time they did not expect of him either the strategical sense with which they credited Nathanael Greene, or the fierce, unrelenting combat Benedict Arnold always would offer. The category of Stirling was one of the largest in an army—the comprehensive class of those a Commander-in-Chief never would think of demoting—or of advancing.

(After the original by Bass Otis, Independence Hall, Philadelphia.)

JOSEPH TRUMBULL, WHO FED THE ARMY

What "Lee" implied in Virginia, or "Adams" in Massachusetts, or "Livingston" in New York and Jersey, "Trumbull" signified in the patriotic service of Connecticut. The father of the revolutionary family was Jonathan Trumbull, who gave that spelling in 1766 to the old name Trumble, which had been heard in Massachusetts as early as 1639. At Harvard, where he was graduated in 1727, Jonathan had shown religious impulses that led him to consider the ministry as his calling; but the death of an elder brother compelled him to enter his father's large mercantile business at Lebanon, Connecticut, about twenty-seven miles Southeast of Hartford. Financially, the fortunes of Jonathan Trumbull fluctuated; politically, with a single reverse, he rose steadily to a position of such large influence that he held the office of Governor continuously from 1769 to 1784. He was most picturesque in speech and diligent in duty. Occasional misunderstandings with Washington developed, but Governor Trumbull was the State Executive from whom the Commander-in-Chief always had the best hope of succor in every emergency, whether the desperate need was of men or of meat.

Trumbull was father of three sons distinguished in the years of revolutionary conflict. His namesake was Paymaster General of the Army, then was the mainspring of the Treasury, and in 1781 was to be Washington's Secretary. John Trumbull, the Governor's youngest son, was useful in the American cause as aide and Deputy Adjutant General, but he unhappily was supersensitive about rank and seniority and in February, 1776, he quit the service. Thereafter his interest in painting won for him, after many vicissitudes, the informal title of "Painter of the Revolution," an arduous vocation that was priceless to American history.

Joseph Trumbull, born in 1737, was the Governor's oldest son and from July 19, 1775, was Commissary General of the Army. The story of his hearty labors is an essential part of the biography of Washington; the impatient mistakes of Congress that led to Trumbull's resignation in the spring of 1777 were among the numerous reasons for the miseries of Valley Forge in the winter of '77-'78. He represented the best type of Commissary, in fortunate contrast to the now forgotten staff officers whose lack of success in the vastly more difficult circumstances of 1777-81 brought the continental Army close to disbandment.

(After the painting by John Trumbull in the gallery of the Connecticut Historical Society.)

immediate accession of strength beyond that of the troops Greene had in Fort Lee.

In the face of this dispersion of force, the military situation was more and more bewildering. On the 11th of November, while Washington had been reconnoitring the Highlands, nearly 200 sail had left New York, in the wake, as it were, of twenty-two that had stood out to sea on the 9th.[72] Whither were these vessels bound? Were they going back to England, or were they part of an expedition to the Far South, to Philadelphia, or to Virginia waters? Washington had been thinking for weeks of new operations at a lower latitude [73] and he felt now that the British might be shifting to a warmer clime their winter's effort to subjugate America.[74] He was puzzled, too, by the failure of Howe to cross into Jersey. It was to be assumed that the British commander would undertake to reduce Fort Washington,[75] but did Howe have some other plan, of which the Americans had as yet no information? [76] There might be one more thrust. After that the redcoats might go into winterquarters,[77] but the direction of the probable offensive was put in deeper doubt now by reports Charles Lee sent on November 13 of a British march down North River from Dobbs Ferry in the direction of King's Bridge. Perplexity was increased by Lee's statement that he was not sure his scouts were penetrating far enough into the enemy's lines to get accurate intelligence.[78]

As Washington in hesitant mood read all this and listened to the varying interpretations of the situation by the men about him, he felt that, on the whole, the prudent course for the time being was to leave Heath and Lee where they were and to dispose the troops with him on the various roads leading into New Jersey, unless, indeed, Congress had become anxious for the security of Philadelphia and wished him nearer that city.[79] Never had he been so confused regarding his adver-

[72] 1 *Mackenzie*, 102; 2 *Force* (5), p. 972.   [73] 6 *G. W.*, 120–21.
[74] *Ibid.*, 279.   [75] *Ibid.*, 250.   [76] *Ibid.*, 275.
[77] Washington's instructions of Nov. 10, 1776 to Charles Lee make it plain that the early retirement of Howe to winterquarters was expected. See 6 *G. W.*, 265. Apropos of instructions, it should be noted that if formal orders were drawn at all for some days, the Headquarters Orderly Book for the period from Nov. 10, 1776, to Jan. 12, 1777, is missing from the *Papers of G. W.*, LC. (see 6 *G. W.*, 263 n). Search of minor publications and of the surviving Orderly Books of Washington's subordinates has added a part only (R. C. Powell, ed., *Col. Leven Powell*, cited hereafter as *Leven Powell*, 44) of the GOs of December 27 to the three long known, those, namely, of Dec. 25, 29, 30, 1776. One paragraph of GOs of Jan. 1, 1777, is preserved. See 6 *G. W.*, 453, 466; 37 *ibid.*, 537; *Stryker*, 113.
[78] 3 *Force* (5), p. 653.
[79] 6 *G. W.*, 279. He had not at this date received information of the excitement created in Philadelphia by a report from Long Branch, New Jersey, that many ships had been observed

sary; never had he been so hesitant—and seldom had he been called upon to decide quickly so close a question as that which had been presented for a week and more by Fort Washington: Should it be held or should it be evacuated? Could its garrison beat off attack that seemed certain, or would the place be taken and the officers and men be made prisoners of war unless they could get across the Hudson to Fort Lee? If the defences East of the river were finished as they had been planned, the position was one that would challenge the best of any assailant. At points, the face of Mount Washington was almost precipitous for 100 feet, with a consequent restriction of approaches. Because the climb from Harlem Plains, by the King's Bridge Road, was the least difficult for infantry, three lines of earthworks had been dug South of the fort, though only the middle one of the three was formidable. On the eastern side of the elevation were redoubts that commanded the paths and steep shoulders up which it seemed possible for a storming party to advance. Another chain of redoubts ran along the northern rim of the heights, above Spuyten Duyvil and King's Bridge; but here the main reliance of the Americans was on a triple abattis, behind which it seemed reasonable to suppose that riflemen would be able to beat off an attack. Overlooking North River, on the western side of the position, was a fortified promontory, Jefferys Hook. The main defence, sighted primarily to deal with venturesome British ships in the stream, was Fort Washington.[80] This was a crude pentagon, with an outwork and covert way in front of its entrance, which was on the northern face. The whole work was of earth and lacked a palisade or planking.[81] As the fort rested on rock and was constructed by men with little experience in blowing,[82] there was no ditch.[83] Nor did it have barracks or casements. The outwork was feeble; one of the main redoubts had not been completed;[84] the citadel could be assailed without the digging of parallels; no fuel had been stored in the fort; there was not even a well.[85] Some of these weaknesses were unknown to any except to the garrison. Because the fort stood boldly

there, outward bound from Sandy Hook. Many Philadelphians thought their city the enemy's objective. See 3 *Force* (5), p. 669, 670.

[80] To this point, the description of the defences follows that of E. F. De Lancey in 1 *Mag. Am. His.*, pt. 1, p. 66 ff.

[81] That is to say, a fraise.

[82] The modern word would be "blasting."

[83] 1 *Mackenzie*, 109.

[84] Greene to Henry Knox, Nov. 17, 1776, *loc. cit.*

[85] *Graydon*, 186.

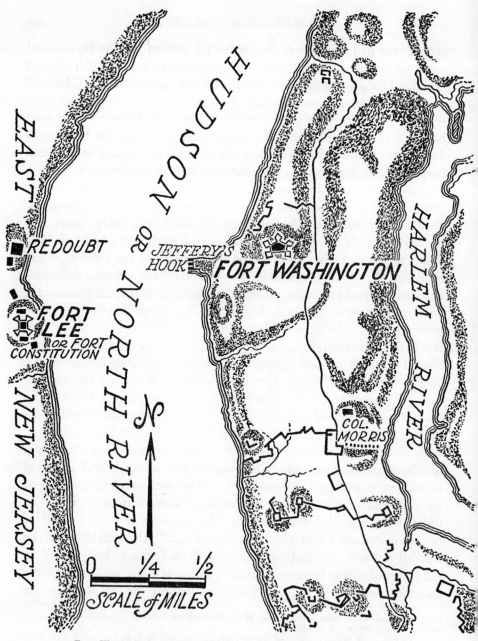

FORT WASHINGTON, ITS OUTER WORKS AND APPROACHES, NOVEMBER, 1776.

A copy of "A Topographical Map of the North. Part of New York Island . . . by Claude Joseph Sauthier," published 1777, is in the Clements Library and is followed in this sketch. The same collection includes a detailed MS "Plan of the Attack of Fort Washington and the Encampment of H. E. General Knyphausen's Corps." The scale is one inch to approximately 880 feet. A detailed "Explication" makes this an invaluable document from the British point of view. See Randolph G. Adams, *British Headquarters Maps and Sketches Used by Sir Henry Clinton . . .* (Ann Arbor, 1928).

on the highest ground of a rough plateau atop the heights—almost 200 feet above North River—it was assumed by all to be strong and by some was proclaimed impregnable. Armament of the fort and of the nearby batteries included thirty-four cannon and a pair of howitzers of calibre five and a half inches.[86] The defenders were Magaw's and Lambert Cadwalader's [87] two Regiments of Pennsylvania State troops, who had been on duty at the fort from July onward, except for brief detachment on Long Island.[88] In the fort or outworks were, also, the remnant of Atlee's Pennsylvania Battalion and what Washington later termed "a handful" of Stephenson's Virginia and Maryland Riflemen, a total of about 1200 men.[89] Nathanael Greene, who had won Washington's confidence,[90] believed the force adequate[91] and perhaps thought this had been demonstrated on the 27th of October in the easy repulse of what he had assumed to be a major effort to capture the fort.[92]

Washington knew little about conditions there. He had lost direct communication with the place about the 22nd of October,[93] and had left its defence to Greene while he himself had been struggling to hold his Army together. On the afternoon of the 5th of November, the frigate *Pearl* and two victual ships had gone up North River, had passed the forts and the obstructions and, when the tide failed, had anchored off Spuyten Duyvil in calm defiance of the "rebels" and the cannon on the heights. Washington had been shaken when he had heard of this exploit.[94] As recently as October 29, Greene had expressed confidence that the forts and the chevaux-de-frise could "prevent any ships from stopping the communication";[95] now again, with no great hurt to

[86] *Ibid.* So far as is known, there is no record of the exact armament of the fort itself.

[87] Cadwalader's was in reality Shee's Third Pennsylvania Battalion, which after October, 1776, was the Fourth Pennsylvania. Col. John Shee, who had been in command, had resigned and had gone home. Lambert Cadwalader was the Lieutenant Colonel.

[88] De Lancey, *loc. cit.*, 69.

[89] See infra, p. 248, and 12 *G. W.*, 347. Among the officers captured at Fort Washington was Lt. Col. Moses Rawlings of this command. See 3 *Force* (5), p. 730.

[90] See 16 *G. W.*, 151; Tench Tilghman in 2 *Force* (5), p. 870 and in 1 *Greene's Greene*, 275. It is entirely probable that the Commander-in-Chief was influenced particularly in Greene's favor at this time by the alertness (cf. 3 *Force* (5), p. 629–30) and the zeal that officer was displaying in the establishment of depots of commissary supplies in New Jersey (2 *Force* (5), p. 1281 and 3 *ibid.*, 493).

[91] Cf. his subsequent statement in 1 *Greene's Greene*, 275.

[92] See supra, p. 226–27 and De Lancey in 1 *Mag. Am. His.*, pt. 1, p. 75.

[93] 6 *G. W.*, 251. The British had considered that all communication between Americans on the island of New York and Washington's Army had been severed after November 3, when six Hessian Battalions had established themselves on the northern end of the heights crowned by Fort Washington. See 1 *Mackenzie*, 94.

[94] Cf. R. H. Harrison to Greene[?], Nov. 7, 1776: "His Excellency apprehends that [the British] have something in view that we have not been apprized of . . ." (*L. W. Smith Coll.*).

[95] 2 *Force* (5), p. 1281.

British hull or crew,[96] ships had ascended the river to carry provisions to Howe's men and at the same time to make all use of the watercourse precarious to Americans. This, Washington had written Greene, "is so plain a proof of the inefficacy of all the obstructions we have thrown into [North River] that I cannot but think it will fully justify a change in the dispositions which has [sic] been made." He had added: "If we cannot prevent vessels passing up, and the enemy are possessed of the surrounding country what valuable purpose can it answer to attempt to hold a post from which the expected benefit cannot be had . . . ?" The Commander-in-Chief then expressed the opinion that it would not be "prudent to hazard the men and the stores at Mount Washington, but," he went on, in apparent hesitation and distrust of his own judgment, "as you are on the spot, [I] leave it to you to give such orders as to evacuating Mount Washington as you judge best and so far revoking the order given Colonel Magaw to defend it to the last." The letter to Greene proceeded to urge that all stores and provisions at the forts or in the adjacent districts be removed or destroyed, except for those immediately needed, because experience had shown that the enemy had "drawn great relief" from supplies found in the area of operations.[97] Washington had meant these instructions to hold until he could visit Greene's headquarters and see the situation for himself.[98]

The order for the removal of excess stores was meant to apply to Fort Washington as well as to Fort Lee, but Joseph Reed, who drafted the letter for the Commander-in-Chief, did not make this as clear as it might have been; nor did Washington, in revising the draft, give precision to the statement.[99] Greene, in answer, had advanced five arguments for retaining Fort Washington: It occupied the attention of a considerable British force; it likewise compelled the enemy to keep troops at King's Bridge to prevent American sorties; it could hold out,

---

[96] 1 *Mackenzie*, 98; 1 *Kemble*, 97. Kemble's reference to the casualties may be confusing because he follows his description of what happened November 5 with a note of his inquiries concerning losses when *Phoenix, Roebuck* and *Tartar* ran up North River on the 9th of October.
[97] 6 *G. W.*, 257–58.　　　　　[98] *Ibid.*, 245.
[99] Besides the quoted language regarding the unwisdom of risking the "men and stores at Mount Washington," the letter referred to the possibility that the enemy "must design a penetration into Jersey and fall down upon your post." The next sentence read: "You will therefore immediately have all the stores &c removed, which you do not deem necessary for your defence . . ." (*ibid.*, 258). It was not unreasonable for Greene to conclude that he was given discretion concerning the withdrawal of surplus supplies as well as of troops from Fort Washington, and that definite orders for sending supplies away applied to Fort Lee and to the nearby districts of Jersey.

according to Colonel Magaw, to the end of the year; giving up the fort would afford the enemy unhampered communication between New York Island and the country to the North; the British assuredly would not attempt to take the post if they did not believe it important. Finally, Greene renewed his assurance that if the situation grew serious, he could remove the garrison of Fort Washington to Fort Lee and then could unite his command with the troops Washington brought over.[100] In submitting these arguments, Greene had said only, concerning the execution of Washington's orders, that an enclosure [101] would show "what measures I took before your favor came to hand," [102]

Now, November 14, at Fort Lee, on hearing Greene's verbal report, Washington met with a disappointment: Greene had begun the re-enforcement of the garrison at Fort Washington [103] and had not removed surplus supplies and equipment from the works on either side of the Hudson. He had as strong conviction as ever that the defences East of the river could be held against an attack that seemed to be in preparation [104] and he had exercised the discretion he thought Washington had given him regarding the fort on New York Island. Washington had to ask himself whether he should let Greene's orders stand, increase the garrison and defend the place to the utmost, or attempt, even at the last hour, to follow his own judgment and to evacuate the garrison and such artillery and supplies as he could. The risk was large, Washington thought, that the garrison and the cannon, which included some of the Army's best, would be lost if the fort were defended. All his experience, all his reasoning told him that. On the other side was the unqualified opinion of Greene and of his senior officers that the position could be held and that, if it were in danger of falling to the enemy, the garrison could escape to the right bank.[105] Besides, the continued abandonment of posts, said Greene, was discouraging to the country.[106] In the next place, Congress in October had "desired" the obstruction of the river "at whatever expense." This manifestly could not be done unless the forts on both sides were in American hands.

---

[100] 3 *Force* (5), p. 618–19.   [101] It appears to have been lost.
[102] Letter of Nov. 9, 1776; 3 *Force* (5), p. 618.
[103] See *infra*, n. 111.
[104] Greene's letter of Nov. 10, 1776, would indicate that he did not send supplies from Fort Lee, to the limit of his resources in transportation, because he did not believe at the time that Howe intended to cross into New Jersey (3 *Force* (5), p. 630).
[105] *Ibid.*, p. 740. For skirmishing close to Fort Washington, Nov. 8–9, 1776, see *ibid.*, 601–02.
[106] 6 *G. W.*, 285.

Again, in the hesitant confusion of a tired mind, the Commander-in-Chief had reasoned that if he continued to occupy Fort Washington, he could preserve easy communication with the troops on the eastern side of the Hudson.[107] Finally, Washington did not feel that he could meet Howe in a general engagement, and, at the same time, he knew he must do his utmost to keep the British from overrunning the country. Anything that tied part of the British to a fixed position was, for these reasons, to be commended.[108]

Such were the considerations for and against the immediate evacuation of Fort Washington. As between them, the weary General could not bring himself to a choice. There was "warfare" in his mind, he confessed later, and with it, hesitation.[109] He did not change Greene's orders, but, leaving the management of affairs to that officer, he went on to Hackensack to study the dispositions that should be made of his forces to resist the anticipated advance of Howe.[110] Greene, as confident as ever, sent across the river to Fort Washington further reenforcement of militia who increased the new defenders of the works to a total of nearly 1700 men. Most of them were Pennsylvanians from the Flying Camp, though their term of enlistment was about to expire. Their coming raised the gross strength of the garrison, Continentals and militia, to a considerably higher figure than the American Commander-in-Chief realized.[111]

[107] On this point, Washington used obscure language when he wrote in August, 1779, of his hesitation over Fort Washington: ". . . I knew that the easy communication between the different parts of the Army then depended on it," that is, on Fort Washington. (16 G. W., 151) Actually, Fort Washington was cut off from the troops under Heath and Lee, East of the river. Washington either had forgotten this or else he reasoned that if Howe held New York with a small force and crossed into Jersey with the main British Army, communication could be restored more easily through Fort Washington than anywhere else, so long as Howe held the City of New York.

[108] Ibid.

[109] Letter of Aug. 22, 1779, to Joseph Reed; 16 G. W., 152. Cf. Reed, in the summer of 1779: ". . . I was extremely anxious that Fort Washington should be evacuated; there was a difference in opinion among those whom the General consulted, and he hesitated more than I ever knew him on any other occasion, and more than I thought the public service admitted." (1 Reed, 262).

[110] Cf. 6 G. W., 285–86.

[111] See infra n. 134. For the expiration of service and the predominance of Pennsylvanians, see ibid., 285, 293. See also Heath, 96–97, and 1 Greene's Greene, 275. From the list of officers taken prisoner at Fort Washington it is possible to identify four Battalions that had been part of the Flying Camp—Michael Swope's, Frederick Watts's, William Montgomery's and Baxter's, but it is impossible to state with absolute certainty that all these were dispatched on the 14th–15th to the defences on the eastern side of North River. Swope himself was there, probably with his Battalion, on the 15th (See the reference to him in Magaw's dispatch, 3 Force (5), p. 700). Another "witness," Ichabod Perry, who belonged to Philip Bradley's Connecticut Regiment, wrote that his command went to Fort Washington about November 10–12. See Ichabod Perry, 5, 10.

At Hackensack, on the 15th, Washington received a brief dispatch from Greene, who enclosed one sent him by Colonel Magaw at Fort Washington. Magaw reported the receipt of a flag of truce from King's Bridge, with the British Adjutant General in the party. The American officer wrote: "The Adjutant General would hardly give two hours for an alternative between surrendering at discretion, or every man being put to the sword." Magaw concluded: "We are determined to defend the post or die," and he appended a copy of his flat rejection of the demand for surrender.[112]

Back, then to Fort Lee the Commander-in-Chief had to ride in the early darkness of a clear evening,[113] to decide—if still there was time for decision—whether an effort should be made to bring the garrison across the North River, or to let Colonel Magaw fight it out with the British.[114] On arrival at Fort Lee, Washington learned that Greene had gone with General Putnam to confer with Colonel Magaw. Washington was told, also, of the reenforcement sent Magaw by Greene. As the original garrison of the fort had consisted of about 1200,[115] it was manifest on the instant that the troops now in the works on the magnificent heights across North River were almost half as numerous as the men, sick and fit, whom Washington had brought with him from White Plains. That was a heavy stake to risk in a blind gamble!

Was it blind? The perplexed and half-despairing commander resolved, as usually he did, to see for himself. With qualified oarsmen, he started across North River, but in the stream, by the most fortunate of chances, he met Nathanael Greene and Israel Putnam, who were returning from the fort. They had favorable information: the garrison was in high spirits; a good defence would be made. As it was late at night, Washington reasoned that he could see no more than the two Generals could tell him, so he had his boat turned about, and he went back to the Jersey shore [116]—to ponder and to debate with his own troubled mind. He reached no new decision.[117]

Shortly before the late dawn of the 16th of November,[118] Washington

112 3 *Force* (5), p. 699–700.

113 Greene's dispatch, *loc. cit.,* dated 4 P.M., should have reached Washington at Hackensack, about six miles distant, by 5:30. For the weather on the 15th, see 1 *Mackenzie,* 104.

114 Washington's movements are described briefly in his letter of Nov. 16, 1776, to the President of Congress; 6 *G. W.,* 285–86.

115 *Ibid.,* 285.   116 *Ibid.,* 286.

117 It is possible that Washington ordered 600 additional troops to cross from Jersey to Fort Washington before daybreak, November 16, but the testimony on this is second-hand. See *infra,* p. 252, n. 134.

118 Sunrise was at approximately 6:48.

started across North River with Putnam, Greene and Hugh Mercer in order to decide, finally and positively, what should be done. Almost at the instant the Generals took their places in the boat, the sound of firing became audible from a part of the ridge where some skirmishing had occurred on the 11th of November.[119] When Washington and his companions climbed to the crest, they learned that the enemy had passed easily the first line across the King's Bridge Road on the southern side of Mount Washington. The second and stronger line was being assailed.[120] Washington was told, also, that British columns had been moving on other approaches, as if they were reconnoitering. Colonel Magaw had made his dispositions, which appeared to be proper. Neither Washington nor his companions saw anything to change, even if it had been possible to shift the troops under the fire of the British and the Hessians.[121]

What, then, should Washington do? He had no orders to give and no suggestions to make to Colonel Magaw. It was awkward for four Generals to stand there as idle observers of what was being done by a Colonel who had his hands full. Embarrassment was eased after a while by the plea of the other senior officers that Washington return to Fort Lee and expose himself no longer. Each of the three, Greene, Putnam and Mercer, offered to remain if Washington thought it neces- sary for a general officer to be available immediately in event Magaw

[119] Nathanael Greene to Henry Knox, Nov. 17, 1776, copy in Clements Library; Herman Wiederhold in 23 Penn. Mag., 95. This account by a Hessian officer is one of the six major British and German narratives of the attack on Fort Washington. Howe's report, the basic document, appears in 3 Force (5), p. 924. Kemble's diary entries are familiar. Two Journals of comparatively recent publication materially supplement the older authorities. These two are Archibald Robertson's, which includes a valuable sketch of the lines of attack, and Frederick Mackenzie's, the contribution of a man who observed Lord Percy's advance and subsequently made inquiry concerning other phases of the operation. A brief, unpublished account of excep- tional clarity is that of Ensign Glyn in the Journal so often cited in these pages (Princeton Lib.). Apparently Glyn was in the column of Brig. Gen. Edward Mathew, which assailed the eastern side of the defences. For the conclusion of E. F. De Lancey that Howe's attack was facilitated by the delivery to the British of plans of the fort, by a deserting American Lieutenant, William Demont, see 1 Mag. Am. His., pt. 1, p. 81 and 1 Jones, History N. Y., 630. On the American side, the "official" or "authoritative" version of the operation, issued by order of Congress, was merely a rephrasing of Washington's inadequate dispatch of November 16 (6 G. W., 284–87). This was published in most newspapers. In Washington's own state, the narrative was printed in the Va. Gazette of Dec. 6, 1776. Neither Col. Robert Magaw nor Col. Lambert Cadwalader ever filed a report. Incidentally, it might be noted that in the index to 3 Force (5), John, and not Lambert Cadwalader mistakenly is said to have commanded one of the Pennsylvania Regiments at Fort Washington. A late account of Col. Lambert Cadwalader appears in Graydon's Memoirs (p. 197–202, ed. of 1846). Graydon himself was at Fort Washington. His is the fullest narrative on the continental side. See also Lambert Cad- walader to Timothy Pickering, May, 1822, in 25 Penn. Mag., 259 ff.

[120] Cf. Graydon, 198.

[121] Greene to Knox, Nov. 17, 1776; loc. cit.

needed counsel. Washington shook his head: No, if he left, the others should, also.

It was agreed; down the heights and back across the river Washington and his party went [122]—to listen, to wonder, and presently to despair. The sound of the firing indicated soon that the British were closing from the South and were within the range of small arms.[123] It was manifest, equally, that stiff resistance was being offered on the northern face of the earthworks.[124] Fighting of indeterminable scope was in progress, also, to the East. Gradually the firing converged; ere long Washington had to conclude that the troops were being driven into the fort itself.[125] If it was possible, the garrison ought to be withdrawn to the Jersey shore; but if that was to be done—as Greene repeatedly had said it could be—the evacuation could not be undertaken till night. Someone must contrive to get into Fort Washington with a message to Magaw. He must be told that if he held out till darkness, the Commander-in-Chief would see to it that the men were brought safely to New Jersey.[126] In his heart, Washington did not think the garrison could resist that long, because all the indications were that the enemy now commanded the approaches to the fort; [127] but the effort should be made. A young officer was found who was willing to cross the river; the message was dispatched. A little later, the tortured Commander-in-Chief sent another volunteer to see if the affairs were as desperate as they appeared to be.[128]

At length, the officer who had taken the first message to Magaw succeeded in getting back to Fort Lee [129] with intelligence to depress the

---

122 *Ibid.*   123 *Ibid.*, and Wiederholt, *op. cit.*, 96.

124 1 *Mackenzie*, 108; *A. Robertson's Diaries*, 101; Howe in 3 *Force* (5), p. 924; 6 *G. W.*, 286.

125 Cf. 1 *Mackenzie*, 106.   126 6 *G. W.*, 286–87.

127 *Ibid.*, 287. Mackenzie said (1 *op. cit.*, 106) that by 1 P.M. "as many Americans as the fort would hold were driven into it, and the remainder into the ditch, and an unfinished outwork"; but as there was no ditch to Fort Washington, the men who could not crowd into the fort or the outwork must have been in the covert way. Magaw had been unable to get his troops to defend this outwork (See *infra*, p. 255, and Greene to Cooke, 3 *Force* (5), p. 1071). By 2 P.M. every other position on Mount Washington was in British hands (1 *Kemble*, 100).

128 6 *G. W.*, 287.

129 Heath stated (*op. cit.*, 97, that this officer was "Captain Gooch of Boston, a brave and daring man [who] ran down to the river, jumped into a small boat, pushed over the river, landed under the bank, ran up to the fort, and delivered the message—came out, ran and jumped over the broken ground, dodging the Hessians, some of whom struck at him with their pieces, and others attempted to thrust him with their bayonets—escaping through them, he got to his boat and returned to Fort Lee." If Heath was correct regarding the name of this gallant soldier, he probably was in error concerning the Captain's State. The only officer mentioned in *Heitman* who fits this description was John Gooch of Rhode Island, a captain of the Ninth Continental Infantry, raised in that State.

stoutest heart: Colonel Magaw sent his thanks to the General but had
to report that he had gone so far with negotiations for surrender that
he could not in honor break them off.[130]

Surrender—Washington had feared that might be the outcome! He
had surrendered once and he knew what it meant, but he had marched
from Fort Necessity that dripping July morning in 1754 with the honors
of war. Were those honors to be allowed the men about to yield themselves to the enemy? The messenger did not know, nor did Washington
learn, that agonizing afternoon, until the second man who had crossed
the river returned to report. He, too, had the worst to tell. Colonel
Cadwalader had informed him that the only terms the British would
allow were those of immediate and absolute surrender as prisoners of
war.[131] While Washington listened to that calamitous news he could
see the great cliff opposite, the heights that seemed so nearly impregnable, and he knew he had to deduct from the rolls of his small Army
the men who might at that very hour be marching from their lost
citadel to some foul prison.[132] They numbered, he thought, about
2000—many of whom, as he sadly wrote Congress, "have been trained
with more than common attention." [133] Actually, the total was 2818
officers and men. Fifty-three fell in the action.[134] These were lost, alto-

[130] 6 G. W., 287. Some of the British authorities contradicted one another in their reports
of the preliminaries of surrender. Mackenzie (op. cit., 108), said that the Americans "beat
their drums, and soon after sent out to desire terms . . ." According to Kemble (1 op. cit., 100),
the Americans had "treated for some time before [4 P.M.] with our officers, particularly the
Hessians . . . [and] desired the honors of war . . ." A. Robertson wrote (Diaries, 112):
"Immediately on the near approach of the Hessians the rebels hung out white flags . . ."
Washington understood (6 G. W., 286) that when the enemy was close to the fort, the troops
were halted and a flag was sent in with a demand for the surrender of the fort. The text of
the "second summons,"—the first presumably being that of November 15—is in Serle, 142.
It called for the immediate surrender of the garrison, as prisoners of war, for the surrender
of all "arms, ammunition and stores of every kind," and for the delivery of two field officers as
hostages for the execution of the terms. The summons concluded: "The General is pleased to
allow the garrison to keep possession of their baggage, and the officers to have their swords."
[131] 6 G. W., 287.
[132] Surrender was at 3 P.M.; the march out began at 4. See 1 Mackenzie, 106. "They were
so thronged in the fort," Kemble wrote in his Diary (v. 1, p. 100), "that they could not have
subsisted there three days" (Cf. 3 Force (5), p. 788). Many of the prisoners were stripped of
their wearing apparel by the Hessians (1 Kemble, 100). Large as was the haul of prisoners,
Glyn probably was echoing the sentiment of his seniors when he wrote in his Journal: "the
works throughout were too extensive for the number of troops, as was generally the case with
the Americans who were indefatigable in constructing redoubts" (Princeton Univ. Lib.).
[133] 6 G. W., 287.
[134] These are the final figures compiled for Howe's report and they are given in 3 Force
(5), p. 1058. If, then, the garrison before reenforcement had numbered 1200, the number sent
over during the few days before the attack must have been close to 1700. Supplementing n. 111,
supra, it is impossible to say when, or in how many detachments these men were ferried over
the river to Fort Washington. Colonel Magaw was quoted by Mackenzie (1 op. cit., 109) as
saying that "there were only 2200 men on the island in the morning, but that a reenforcement,
the numbers of which he was not acquainted with, came over during the attack." While this

gether lost! Perhaps it was by Washington's order—it certainly fitted his mood—that when the fate of the day was manifest, the thirty-two-pounders of Fort Lee were turned on positions across the river visibly in the hands of the enemy. Like almost everything else that concerned those luckless fortifications on Mount Washington, the fire was futile.[135]

The full details of what had happened to Magaw's men and the actual terms of surrender were not yet known on the Jersey side of North River,[136] but criticism did not wait on fact. Those who were wise after the event or were secretly jealous of Nathanael Greene made him their scapegoat and indirectly assailed Washington. "Oh, General," Charles Lee wrote, "why would you be overpersuaded by men of inferior judgment to your own?" Lee added bluntly, "It was a cursed affair" [137] and privately he boasted that he "foresaw, predicted, all that has happened." [138]

---

may be true, no other reference has been found to the movement of troops to Fort Washington on the night of the 15th–16th of November. Probability is against any attempt by Washington to send additional men to Fort Washington during daylight hours on the 16th. It scarcely would have been practicable and it assuredly would have been most hazardous. The one indisputable fact is that Washington's losses by surrender on the 16th were larger than he thought they were. As of Dec. 17, 1776, he was making a vain effort to get a list of the officers and men captured at Fort Washington (6 G. W., 390).

[135] 1 Mackenzie, 109.

[136] Cf. 6 G. W., 293. A few facts were brought Washington on the 19th of November by an artillerist who escaped from the British on the night of the 17th (ibid.). Two days later the General received full information from Colonel Cadwalader, who reported to headquarters after he had been paroled as an acknowledgment of the kindness Cadwalader's father had shown Richard Prescott when that British Brigadier was a prisoner of war. See 6 G. W., 296. Howe employed four separate columns, one of which was instructed originally to make a feint. The main attack was from the North by the German troops in two columns. This progressed slowly because the ground was protected by deep abattis on every path (Glyn's Journal, loc. cit.) and was defended by the riflemen of Magaw's men. On the left of these Germans, a second column, including the Guards Battalions, crossed Harlem Creek on flatboats, suffering no loss, and gained a foothold on the lower reaches of the cliffs. The third column, that of the 42nd Regiment, was the one named to make a demonstration on the left of the Guards, but it was well handled and soon was engaged fully. From the South, with the fourth column, Lord Percy pushed up the easy grade of the King's Bridge Road, took the frail first line without trouble and then assailed the strong, second line of American defences. It was at this stage of the action that the British command decided the 42nd, by changing its demonstration into an assault, might be able to turn the second American line, which Percy was facing. This was done successfully and with a considerable haul of prisoners. Lord Percy then reached the crest of the ridge and, closing in, forced the troops in front of him to take refuge in the defences immediately adjacent to the fort. Thereupon, the Hessians' attack was pressed home. When the Germans were within musket range of the fort, the demand for surrender was made.

[137] Letter of Nov. 19, 1776; 2 Lee Papers, 288. Cf. James Duane to P. Schuyler, Nov. n.d., 1776: "General Washington . . . suffered his better judgment to give way to the zeal and ardor of General Greene, who was positive [the fort] could be defended, or at least could not be taken without a severe conflict and the destruction of a great part of the British army, and that a retreat across the North was practicable at all events. It cannot be said that his opinion has been brought to a test since it appears that the fortress was lost from mere inexperience" (Schuyler Papers, NYPL; cf. H. B. Livingston to P. Schuyler, Nov. 25, 1777; ibid.).

[138] Letter of Nov. 20, 1776, to Benjamin Rush, 2 Lee Papers, 288. Cf. ibid., 283.

Washington realized that the disaster of the 16th was not to be the end of adversity. Tired as he was, he saw clearly, of course, that when Fort Washington was lost, Fort Lee was worthless and, if held, might be another trap. As soon as it was threatened, it must be evacuated. If possible, all the equipment and stores should be removed in advance, but if that was not practicable, the defences and the supplies must be abandoned anyway.[139] This would sharpen the criticism and would deepen public disappointment. Better that than a second Fort Washington at a time when the Army was falling apart hourly! The day after Fort Washington fell, the term of the Massachusetts "Long Faces" with Gen. Charles Lee's troops expired. In his diary, Chaplain Benjamin Trumbull wrote of the disaster at Fort Washington and then set down in a completely matter-of-fact style: "The militia of Massachusetts began to march homeward."[140] That was all there was to it: the militiamen's time had expired; wherefore, though 2800 men from Fort Washington were prisoners, and the life of the country was imperilled, they would go back to their firesides. Nothing had been done by Congress to replace the Flying Camp, from which Washington had been able, on occasion, to draw;[141] the commissioners of some of the States, sent to select officers for the new Regiments, were permitting politics to influence their choice; when Washington went once again to Hackensack in order to resume his preparations for a withdrawal southward,[142] he was appalled to find there scarcely any of the New Jersey militia[143] on whose support he had relied when he crossed the Hudson with his thin shadow of an Army. Although the State was apt to be invaded and property plundered, it appeared as if Jerseymen either were cowed by British victories or at heart were not sympathetic with the American cause.

It scarcely seemed possible that so tremendous a change had come within the ten days that had elapsed since Washington left White Plains, but in cold terms this now was the frightful prospect: By the end of November, as he interpreted the figures, Washington would not have more than 2000 fit soldiers of the continental establishment with whom to oppose Howe in the region West of the Hudson.[144] "Oppose" was his own verb: he knew it was a mockery, but he scarcely could

---

[139] 6 G. W., 293.
[140] Benjamin Trumbull's Diary, loc. cit., 210. Cf. 2 Lee Papers, 288.
[141] 6 G. W., 279.   [142] Ibid., 291.
[143] Cf. ibid., 331.   [144] Ibid., 245.

afford to say so to any of those about him, not even to Joseph Reed, the Adjutant General, whom he loved and trusted. More than normal restraint had to be shown at headquarters, because, in so desperate an hour, the most loyal tongues might loose in dismay some secret that would dishearten soldiers or lawmakers.

The one person to whom the agonized commander of the dissolving Army could unburden himself was his long-time, always prudent confidant, his brother John Augustine. So, at Hackensack, on the 19th, Washington sat down to finish a letter he had started at White Plains, November 6, before the worst of his calamities had overtaken him. The day of Washington's second writing had been made the darker by the receipt of a dispatch in which General Greene reported some facts previously not known to Washington concerning the fall of the fort that bore the name of the Commander-in-Chief. One sentence read: "Colonel Magaw could not get the men to man the lines, otherwise he would not have given up the fort." There had been some display of courage, notably on the part of the Virginia and Maryland riflemen, but if the defence of Fort Washington had been no better than it had been represented to be, then it was a continuation of the story of Long Island and Kip's Bay and White Plains, the story of men who would not stand up and fight for their freedom.

Washington carefully copied Greene's words in the account he wrote his brother of the fall of Fort Washington [145] and then he explained that he had not believed it wise to attempt to hold the position but had given Greene discretion. This led to a paragraph on the slowness of the States in meeting their quotas of troops. When this prompted Washington to review his efforts to build up an Army on the foundations of long-term enlistment, he lost control of his emotions. Indignantly he wrote: ". . . all the year since, I have been pressing [Congress] to delay no time in engaging men upon such terms as would assure success, telling them that the longer it was delayed the more difficult it would grow; but the measure was not set about till it was too late to be effected, and then in such a manner as to bid adieu to every hope of getting an Army from which any services are to be expected; the different States without regard to the merits or qualifications of an officer, quarreling about the appointments, and nominating

145 The *Va. Gazette,* which John Augustine Washington must have read frequently, did not print until Dec. 6, 1776, the authorized version of the action at Fort Washington, issued by Congress.

such as are not fit to be shoe blacks from the local attachments of this or that member of Assembly."

He could not stop even when he had put some of his junior officers lower than shoe blacks. Indignantly he went on: "I am wearied almost to death with the retrograde motions of things, and I solemnly protest that a pecuniary record of £20,000 a year would not induce me to undergo what I do; and, after all, perhaps, to lose my character, as it is impossible under such a variety of distressing circumstances to conduct matters agreeably to public expectation, or even of those who employ me, as they will not make proper allowances for the difficulties their own errors have occasioned." [146]

In this furious disappointment, Washington remained at Hackensack, prepared a second brief candid report for Congress,[147] and resumed his interrupted efforts to dispose his troops for combat or retreat. He felt himself most disadvantageously placed for either, because what remained of his small Army still was divided in four fragments—his own feeble force at Hackensack and Fort Lee, Stirling's eight small Regiments, about 1000 men, at Rahway and Brunswick,[148] Lee at White Plains, and Heath at Peekskill.[149] The last of these separated forces must be left on guard in the Highlands. To keep Howe and Burgoyne from forming a junction and isolating New England remained an imperative of strategy even when the resistance of America had been brought so close to zero. Washington's columns—his own, Lee's and Stirling's—must of course be reunited if Howe made the expected move and, having captured New York, attempted to take Philadelphia, too.

Washington had the multiple phases of this problem before him on the morning of the 20th of November, four days after the loss of Fort Washington, when another of the Army's expresses—those heralds of calamity—brought him a dispatch from Greene: A heavy British force, using 200 boats, had crossed North River that morning below Dobbs Ferry and appeared to be marching rapidly southward over the six miles of road that led to Fort Lee.[150] The dispatch brought Washington to his feet with an instant order for horses. In a few minutes he was

---

[146] 6 G. W., 245-46.

[147] Ibid., 292 ff. His first report (ibid., 284 ff) was written on the 16th.

[148] Washington at this period seldom wrote it "New Brunswick."

[149] This assumes what is highly probable but not altogether certain, namely, that Washington had called to Fort Lee or to Hackensack the few troops that had remained at Amboy, the Flying Camp's former headquarters.

[150] 6 G. W., 295, 298, 302; Thomas Paine's interesting account in 3 Force (5), p. 1291; Serle, 144.

galloping to the ferry and then southeastward toward Fort Lee.[151] Rain had fallen the previous night, but the day was fine [152]—that in itself a boon for the course of action on which Washington already had a fixed resolution. The peninsula between the North River and the Hackensack was the counterpart of New York Island between the North and the East Rivers. Fort Lee corresponded to Fort Washington except that it was on the eastern and Fort Washington on the western side of the two positions. Howe had attempted to encircle the Americans on New York Island; he must not be permitted to do the same thing in Jersey. Fort Washington had been defended and lost; the decision to abandon Fort Lee must be executed at once.

As soon, therefore, as Washington confirmed reports that the British were in greatly superior numbers, he ordered the fort evacuated immediately, even though this meant that pots had to be left boiling and tents standing.[153] For an Army that had no warships to support it and no transports to spare the legs of its men, there was only one avenue of quick escape. That was across the Hackensack, which had a single bridge. This must be secured and used before the British seized it. To lose a minute was to risk an Army—if it still could be styled an Army.

The drums beat; Washington put himself at the head of the column of about 2000; [154] the men fell in, and off they marched. Behind them they left all the cannon that had been in fixed position with the exception of two. The Army abandoned, also, between 200 and 300 tents, about 1000 barrels of flour, all their entrenching tools, and nearly all the baggage of officers and men. "This loss," said Washington, "was inevitable." In justice to the Quartermasters he added: "As many of the stores had been removed as circumstances and time would admit of. The ammunition had been happily got away." [155] The Commanding General did not then know, or else did not see fit to report that a considerable number of soldiers plundered the sutlers' liquor and got so drunk they could not march.[156] It was a high price, but Washington

---

[151] Paine, *loc. cit.*   [152] I *Mackenzie*, 112.

[153] Howe in 3 *Force* (5), p. 925; I *Kemble*, 101.

[154] Greene later said that he had between 2000 and 3000, most of them from the Flying Camp. See 3 *Force* (5), p. 751.

[155] 6 *G. W.*, 295–96, 298. For Greene's difficulties in moving supplies from Fort Lee, see 3 *Force* (5), p. 751. Some 700 cattle had been herded at Fort Lee but they had been fed so poorly that most of them had become unfit for use in rations. See 8 *JCC.*, 499–500.

[156] Journal of an unknown Pennsylvania soldier in *NYPL Bul.*, v. 8, no. 11, p. 549. Greene rode back to the camp, two hours after the evacuation, and collected several hundred stragglers, but he estimated that nearly 100 remained hidden in the woods (Greene to Governor Cooke, Nov. 20, 1776; 3 *Force* (5), p. 1071).

got what he was willing to pay for—access to the bridge and time in
which to use the fords of the Hackensack. Howe's men gained much
booty; they took no more than 105 prisoners.[157]

Once across the stream, Washington found himself for a third time
between rivers, the Hackensack and the Passaic. If he had the men, he
could hold the Hackensack, though there were numerous fords. As it
was, with no Jersey militia to aid him, and Stirling detached to watch
the coastal landings, he was so situated that if the British pushed hard
for the crossings of the second of these watercourses, the Americans
might lose their line of retreat.[158] They scarcely could hope to make a
stand because they now were worse dispirited than ever. The loss of
tents and baggage, following defeats at arms, was more than some of
the men could endure with courage and cheer. Further, the country
was flat and offered no natural strongholds. Even if it had been defensible, there were no picks and shovels for digging trenches. It was
necessary for Washington to order a withdrawal beyond the Passaic
and regretfully to leave a fine country to be ravaged by the Hessians.[159]
On the morning of the 21st, he made the necessary moves and proceeded with his short files to Aquackanock Bridge [160] on the Passaic.

After the crossing he felt he was in a position to watch the enemy
and, at the same time, to avoid the danger of attack from the rear; [161]
but, of course, he wanted now, more than ever, to reunite his scattered
forces. This, he reasoned, would involve a farther withdrawal, probably
to Brunswick, in order to be in touch with Stirling,[162] who had made
ready to join him on receipt of the news that Howe's vanguard, under
Cornwallis, had passed North River. As soon as the full strength of
the British offensive in New Jersey was manifest, the essentials of the
plan adopted in advance by Washington were, of course, to become

[157] 3 *Force* (5), p. 1058. Howe's report (*ibid.,* 925) suggests that the aim of the British
advance, which consisted of about 6000 men under Lord Cornwallis (*Serle,* 144), was to capture
Fort Lee by surprise. Cornwallis was across the river by 8 A.M. (Howe to Sir Henry Clinton,
Nov. 20, 1776, *Clinton Papers,* Clements Lib.). Glyn heard that "had not a countryman early
in the morning apprized [the Americans] of our landing, the whole must have been prisoners"
(*Journal,* loc. cit.). There is nothing to indicate the British contemplated a race for the bridge.
On the contrary, Glyn recorded Nov. 26, 1776, a soldierly but unhurried advance by two
columns, one of which forded the river above Aquackanock and undertook to clear the span
for the other column: ". . . upon our approach to the river, we found the bridge demolished.
The enemy appeared upon the heights above the town but retired upon the approach of the
right column who fortunately seized upon a sloop which enabled us to pass the river." (*loc. cit.*)
[158] 6 *G. W.,* 331.
[159] Washington's fullest explanation of this was in his letter of Nov. 21, 1776, to Charles
Lee; *ibid.,* 297–98.
[160] The modern Passaic, New Jersey; *ibid.,* 301–02.
[161] *Ibid.*   [162] *Ibid.,* 302.

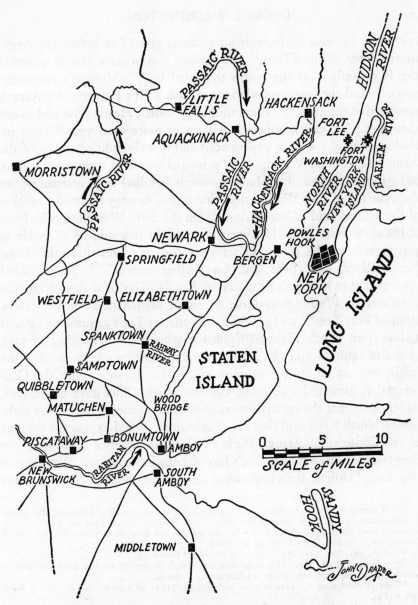

AREA OF THE "JERSEY RETREAT," NOVEMBER–DECEMBER, 1776.

In the country here delineated, the remnant of the "main Army" maneuvered from the fall of
Fort Washington, November 16, to the hurried withdrawal across the Raritan, Dec. 1, 1776.
This sketch is based on one of the earliest detailed surveys by American military topographers,
incorporated in Robert Erskine's "Map of Parts of the States of New York and New Jersey,"
1777. Different sections of this are inconsistent in scale, and errors of distance and orientation
are numerous, but the map was far better than any Washington previously had used. On this
sketch, Erskine's mistakes have been allowed to stand: they are more informative than deceptive.

operative: In accordance with instructions given Lee before the Army moved from White Plains,[163] that officer was to leave Heath to guard the Highlands [164] at the points indicated by Washington's reconnaissance [165] and the recommendations of Col. Rufus Putnam, the Army's most active engineer.[166] With militia included, Heath now had about 4000 men; [167] Lee's numbers had risen to more than 7700 [168] and included some of the most experienced and best disciplined troops of the Army. These were Washington's principal source of strength and were to be moved forthwith to Jersey, though Lee had been asserting, ever since the fall of Fort Washington, that sound strategy dictated retention of the area around White Plains.[169] On the 20th, Washington had one of his aides write Lee: "His Excellency thinks it would be advisable in you to remove the troops under your command on this side of the North River, and there wait for further orders." [170] Joseph Reed reiterated this in a private letter to Lee.[171] The next day, from the Passaic river, Washington wrote his senior lieutenant about the evacuation of Fort Lee [172] and proceeded to answer Lee's arguments against a shift from White Plains. "Upon the whole . . ." Washington said, "I am of opinion and the gentlemen about me concur in it, that the public interest requires your coming over to this side [with the Continental Regiments] . . ." The Commander-in-Chief gave his reasons, which were that the enemy was changing the scene of war to the right side of North River and that the people there would expect the support of the Continental Army. With an alarmed sentence or two on the dangerous effects of the public's loss of faith in the Army, Washington told Lee: "Unless, therefore, some new event should occur, or some

---

[163] Washington to Charles Lee, Nov. 10, 1776: "If the enemy should remove the whole, or the greatest part of their force, to the west side of Hudson river, I have no doubt of your following with all possible dispatch, leaving the militia and invalids to cover the frontiers of Connecticut &c in case of need" (6 G. W., 266).

[164] Ibid., 263, 269, 275, 277.　　　　　　　[165] Heath, 95.

[166] 3 Force (5), p. 768. This document was dated November 19 but doubtless was in accord with advice previously given Washington by Putnam.

[167] As of November 24, present rank and file, fit, 3195; on command, 821. See 3 Force (5), p. 834.

[168] His rank and file, present fit, on November 24, were 5589; on command were 2235 (ibid., 831).

[169] 2 Lee Papers, 285, 287–88; 6 G. W., 290, 299.

[170] 2 Lee Papers, 289; also in 3 Force (5), p. 779.

[171] Sent by Cornelius Cooper and no longer in existence. See 2 Lee Papers, 290. Some confused echo of it may be heard in an improbable tale Heath printed (op. cit., 98–99).

[172] The British decided at this time or a little later to render the fort useless for the future. On Dec. 21, 1776, Gen. George Clinton wrote the New York Convention, "I forgot to mention that Fort Lee is demolished—we were five miles below it" (3 Force (5), p. 1347).

more cogent reason present itself, I would have you move over by the easiest and best passage." [173]

Lee's coming was in reality a matter of life and death in the sternest, most realistic addition and subtraction. If he brought 5000,[174] and Stirling could count 1000 bayonets,[175] these could be added to the fragments of continental Regiments, to Greene's men from Fort Lee, to the militia and to the survivors of the Flying Camp, all of whom had now been assembled under Washington to an unstable aggregate of 4400.[176] On paper, then, the arrival of Lee and Stirling would give the reconcentrated Army a temporary strength of 10,400, but that figure, if attained at all, would be illusory. Within less than ten days the Army would be reduced by slightly over 2000, on the expiration of the service of the Maryland and New Jersey Regiments of the Flying Camp.[177] Eight hundred and fifty more would be free to go home on the 1st of January.[178] That would leave slightly over 7500, of whom 5000 represented Brigades with Lee. Continuance of resistance, in any serious sense, thus depended on that officer's prompt compliance with the instructions sent him. Those instructions were positive but, of course, were phrased considerately. When Washington wrote to Congress of his plan to have Lee join the Army in Jersey, he struck out the words "and ordered him" to come, but the intent was clear.[179]

The weather, which had been unusually fine,[180] now grew bad. Rain poured down on the 22nd and the 23rd [181] of November. The British seemed willing to wait on the elements. At Newark, where Washington established temporary headquarters,[182] there was much work and planning for the commander while the dripping men awaited the next move. Washington decided the eloquent Thomas Mifflin should visit Philadelphia and explain to Congress the weakness of the Army and the unqualified necessity of immediate help.[183] Joseph Reed was dispatched on a similar mission to Gov. William Livingston of New Jersey.[184] Congress was besought, also, to forward money for the pay-

[173] 6 G. W., 299.
[174] Nixon's, McDougall's, Glover's and Sargent's Brigades, 3 Force (5), p. 710.
[175] This was the estimate of Washington, Nov. 23, 1776; 3 Force (5), p. 822.
[176] Ibid. [177] 6 G. W., 311.
[178] 3 Force (5), p. 822. [179] Letter of Nov. 23, 1776; 6 G. W., 303.
[180] 1 Kemble, 101.
[181] 1 Mackenzie, 114; Serle, 145; David How's Diary, 37. At New York, the rain continued through the 24th.
[182] November 23 to the forenoon of November 28.
[183] 6 G. W., 303. [184] Ibid., 304–05

ment of the soldiers of the Flying Camp. If compensated, some of these men, said Washington, might reenlist after visiting their homes [185]—a feeble buttress for a collapsing Army.

Had Washington known what was happening at that time in the Quaker City, he would have reflected that the crisis was shaking the revolutionary leaders out of their strange addiction to defer that which was pressing and to consider promptly that which might be postponed.[186] Congress, city authorities and Council of Safety were almost frantic as they heard one report after another of British plans for marching on Philadelphia.[187] A committee was named by Congress to visit Washington, and another was chosen to devise means of reenforcing him and of obstructing the advance of the enemy.[188] The Commander-in-Chief was authorized, also, to recall the New Jersey and Pennsylvania Regiments then in the Northern Department. To replace them, Schuyler was to apply to New England.[189]

From all of this and from recruits the bounty would attract, there might rise in 1777 a new and more stable Army if, meantime, the frail remnant of the Army of 1776 could survive the bite of the British and the nibble of winter. For the next few weeks, everything would depend upon the activity of Howe, the unpredictable contingencies of war, and the prompt arrival of Charles Lee with his veteran Brigades. Rain or hesitation or both appeared to be holding back the royal army; [190] Lee's coming was taken for granted; the adverse new developments at the beginning of the last week of November were a spread of desertion and the report of a Tory uprising in Monmouth County, New Jersey.[191]

As nothing worse was apparent, a few of the courageous and philosophical men in the Army began to reknit their ravelled hope. Samuel Webb wrote Joseph Trumbull: "You ask me a true account of our situation: 'tis next to impossible to give it to you; I can only say that no lads ever shew greater activity in retreating than we have since we left you. Our soldiers are the best fellows in the world at this business. . . . Our whole body did not amount to 2000 at the time the enemy landed

---

[185] *Ibid.*, 304.   [186] Cf. Rutledge in 3 *Force* (5), p. 826.
[187] *Ibid.*, 820; 2 *Burnett*, 156, 157; circular letter of Penn. Council of Safety, November 24; *Penn. Gazette*, Nov. 27, 1776.
[188] 6 *JCC.*, 975; 3 *Force* (5), p. 825.   [189] 6 *JCC.*, 977.
[190] Cf. George Harris to his uncle, in an undated letter of approximately this period: "We now pursued the enemy, much too slowly for our wishes, but it is not for us subordinates to comment on the movements of our commanders, of which we are in general very incompetent judges" (Lushington's *Harris*, 83).
[191] 6 *G. W.*, 307.

in the Jerseys, of consequence we had it not in our power to make a stand till we arrived at [Newark], where we have collected our force and are not only ready, but willing to meet the lads in blue and red as soon as they think proper. . . . If they come on soon we shall, I trust, give a good account to our country. This must be before the 1st of December, as most of the troops on this side are then their own masters." [192] He would have been even more realistic if he had said the Army would not be strong enough to give battle with any reasonable prospect of success until Lee arrived.

That very day, November 24, Washington opened a letter addressed by Lee to Adjutant General Joseph Reed, who still was absent in consultation with Governor Livingston. It was an astonishing document to this effect:

Camp, Nov. 21, 1776

DEAR SIR—

I have just received your letter dated Hackensack by Cornelius Cooper. His Excellency recommends it to me to move with the troops under my command to the other side of the river. I apprehend that this advice is founded on the presumption either that we have the means of crossing at or nearer Dobbs Ferry, or that my Corps is moved up the country near to King's Ferry. There are no means of passing Dobbs Ferry, and as we remain where he left us, the round by King's Ferry would be so great that we could not be there in time to answer any purpose. I have therefore ordered General Heath who is close to the only ferry which can be passed to detach two thousand men, to apprize his Excellency and wait his further orders, a mode which I flatter myself will answer better what I conceive to be the spirit of the orders than should I move the corps from hence. Withdrawing our troops from hence would be attended with some very serious consequences which at present would be tedious to enumerate. As to myself, I hope to set out tomorrow.

I am, my dear sir, Yours

CHARLES LEE [193]

Washington read with dismay. He had not meant to give Lee discretion; politeness had not been intended to modify orders; the one thing

[192] Letter of Nov. 24, 1776; 1 *Webb*, 172–73, with slight revision of the punctuation. It scarcely need be pointed out that Webb was mistaken about the number of men whose term expired December 1.

[193] 2 *Lee Papers*, 301, with the punctuation modernized and elisions and capitalization conformed to current usage. Although Lee did not state to which of Reed's letters he was replying, there can be no doubt it was the communication of November 20 (see *supra*, p. 260) no copy of which is known to exist. At the date Reed wrote Lee from Hackensack, the express time between Washington's Army and Lee's force was one day only.

about which he had been most explicit before leaving White Plains had
been that Heath should remain to guard the Highlands; now Lee was
taking 2000 of Heath's men and was leaving at White Plains the very
troops Washington most needed, and needed without an hour's avoid-
able delay! There might be several interpretations of Lee's action. Anyone who regarded him as an ambitious adventurer might scrutinize that
letter to Reed and might consider some of the language suspicious, arrogant even—"His Excellency recommends," "some very serious consequences which at present would be tedious to enumerate." Had a critic,
moreover, read this letter in the correspondence book at White Plains, he
would have seen other communications that would have puzzled him.
The day before Lee wrote Reed, he had scratched off to his friend Benjamin Rush the letter in which he had boasted "I foresaw, predicted, all
that has happened" at Fort Washington.[194] Lee had concluded: "I
could say many things—let me talk vainly—had I the powers I could
do you much good, might I but dictate one week; but I am sure you will
never give any man the necessary power . . ."[195] There was much
more in Lee's letter book almost as vainglorious as that [196]—for example, a paper addressed Governor James Bowdoin on the 21st concerning separate armies on either side of the Hudson, with the assurance
that if the enemy attempted to enter New England or force the passes
of the Highlands, "I should never entertain a thought of being suc-
coured from the Western Army" [197]—and much was yet to be written
boastfully in like strain,[198] along with no little that was sound, soldierly
and sensible.[199]

Washington had not seen these letters, of course, nor had he observed
anything to change his opinion that Lee was fickle; [200] but now he took
the view that Lee merely had misunderstood or had misinterpreted
orders, and he wrote immediately to leave no doubt of his wishes:
"From your letter to Colonel Reed, you seem to have mistaken my views
entirely, in ordering troops from General Heath to cross Hudson's
River to this side. The importance of the posts and passes through the
Highlands is so infinitely great that I never thought there should be the

---

[194] See *supra*, p. 253.   [195] 2 *Lee Papers*, 288–89.
[196] Cf. *ibid.*, 118, 256.   [197] 2 *Lee Papers*, 291–92.
[198] Cf. his letter of Nov. 24, 1776 to the Massachusetts Commissioners: "As I flatter myself
that I have given reasons to the continent of America that I am above all jobs and partiality . . ." (*ibid.*, 308).
[199] See *ibid.*, and Lee's orders of Oct. 19 and 21, 1776; *Baldwin Papers*, Harvard Coll. Lib.
[200] See *supra*, Vol. III, p. 80.

last possible risk of losing them. Colonel Reed's second letter [201] will have sufficiently explained my intention upon this subject, and pointed out to you that it was your Division I want to have over." He proceeded then to give such instructions about the march as seemed to be necessary, because of the reported capture of an express who included dispatches to him from Lee.[202]

The consequence of Lee's delay—whatever the reasons for it—could not be blinked. Instead of being en route with the reenforcement that might save the Army from ruin, Lee probably had not started from White Plains. One week from the date of Washington's clarifying letter, 2000 men of the Flying Camp were certain to say good-bye. Unless there was the most extraordinary speed on the part of Lee, he would not reach Washington before those men left. Even if junction meantime were formed with Stirling at New Brunswick, there would be several days during which the British might attack in decisively superior force. They probably had withheld their onslaught because the weather had been foul; but the 24th was a "soft, warm day"; the wind was shifting to the South; [203] the critical days of greatest American weakness might be favorable to the enemy.

Happily, there was another quick change. On the 26th rain fell heavily again most of the day [204] and brought momentary relief to the American cause at the same time that it added misery to the lot of the American soldier. By evening, Washington knew more than previously of what had happened when Charles Lee had undertaken to send 2000 of Heath's troops to Jersey instead of passing his own Division over the river. In a letter received late on the 26th,[205] Lee stated that he had received Washington's "orders" [206] and would "try to put 'em in execution," but, he said "[I] question much whether I shall be able to carry with me any considerable number of men, not so much from a want of zeal in the men as from their wretched condition with respect to shoes, stockings &c, which the present bad weather renders more in-

---

[201] The circumstances attending the dispatch of this letter will be described in a later paragraph.

[202] 6 G. W., 306. Serle stated (op. cit., 137) that a Loyalist made the express drunk and then stole the dispatches. Among them may have been a letter of Joseph Trumbull's to William Williams, printed in Hugh Gaine's N. Y. Gazette, Dec. 9, 1776 and republished in 3 Force (5), p. 1497–98. Trumbull violently assailed the alleged incompetence and sectionalism of Reed and thereby created ill-will that kept the two men from working together at any time thereafter.

[203] 1 Mackenzie, 114, 115. These observations were made in New York, not in Newark, but there probably was no material variation.

[204] Ibid., 115.   [205] 6 G. W., 309.

[206] He must have meant Washington's letter of the 21st (ibid., 297 ff).

tolerable." Then Lee went blandly on: "I sent Heath orders to transport two thousand men across the river, apprize the General and wait for further orders, but that great man (as I might have expected) entrenched himself within the letter of his instructions and refused to part with a single file, though I undertook to replace 'em with a part of my own." [207]

This was disconcerting in that it showed Lee apparently unfamiliar with Washington's plan to keep Heath in the Highlands, regardless of other moves. Further, at the end of his letter, Lee spoke of an opportunity that had presented itself of cutting off some of the enemy's troops within reach of his camp at White Plains. "If we succeed," he said, "it will have a great effect and amply compensate for two days' delay"—as if two days at the end of November might not mean the difference between surviving and perishing. Heath, in his turn, probably reported the first phase of a correspondence with Lee, whose demand for the dispatch of the 2000 men he steadfastly refused as contrary to his direct orders from the Commander-in-Chief.[208] Washington's secretary promptly gave assurance to Heath: "In respect to the troops intended to come to this quarter, his Excellency never meant that they should be from your Division. He has wrote General Lee since so fully and explicitly upon the subject that any misapprehensions he may have been under at first must be by now done away. He will most probably have reached Peekskill before now with his Division, and be pushing to join us." [209]

That last sentence had voiced Washington's hope on the 25th; Lee's letter of the 24th or 25th received on the evening of the 26th showed that Lee had not even started from White Plains. At so desperate a time, Washington could not conceal his disappointment that Lee lingered, but he wrote of it with unfaltering courtesy and with an iron grip on his temper. He told his senior Lieutenant: "I confess I expected you would have been sooner in motion. The force here, when joined by

---

[207] Letter of Nov. 24, 1776; 2 *Lee Papers*, 307. Washington undoubtedly was acknowledging this communication when he wrote Lee on the 27th (6 *G. W.*, 309), but he there spoke of "your letter of the 25th." No dispatch of that date, addressed to Washington, appears in the *Lee Papers*.

[208] Heath's letter of November 24 to Washington has not been found and may not be in existence, but Harrison's acknowledgment, for Washington, is in 3 *Force* (5), p. 839. The familiar exchange between Heath and Lee appears in 2 *Lee Papers*, 291, 299, 304, 305, 313-14, 326. Most of the letters may be found, also, in 3 *Force* (5), but much the most convenient text is in *Heath*, 99-103.

[209] 3 *Force* (5), p. 839.

yours, will not be adequate to any great opposition; at present it is weak, and it has been more owing to the badness of the weather that the enemy's progress has been checked than any resistance we could make. They are now pushing this way; part of 'em have passed the Passaic. Their plan is not entirely unfolded, but I shall not be surprised if Philadelphia should turn out to be the object of their movement. The distress of the troops for want of clothes, I feel much, but what can I do?" [210]

He was doing his utmost. Heath was invoked to try to prevail upon Scott's New York Brigade to remain ten or fifteen days after their time expired, in order that they might strengthen the front from which Charles Lee was moving.[211] Mifflin continued to advise Congress [212] and doubtless had some responsibility for three resolutions of the 26th—that the Pennsylvania militia be asked to serve six weeks, that the German Battalion be sent to reenforce Washington, and that Gov. Patrick Henry be requested to dispatch to his former colleague the Light Horse who had been organized in Virginia.[213] Joseph Reed, who enjoyed the complete confidence of his chief, was laboring to get four New Jersey Regiments raised to serve until April 1, 1777.[214] It was a contest with catastrophe; the odds were against America.

On the 27th, there still was no news that Lee was marching to help his commander, but all the reports were that more of the British were across the Passaic and that still others would be there had not the weather proved adverse. There were indications, too, that a force to support Cornwallis might land at Amboy.[215] With this situation to confront him, Washington of course said—and his officers agreed—that he could not give battle and must retreat at least as far as Brunswick. The move began on the 28th. As the American rearguard left Newark, the British entered the opposite side but they did not attempt pursuit.[216] At noon, November 29, Washington reached Brunswick and halted the Army,[217] which, in spite of all its freezing and splashing in the

---

[210] 6 G. W., 309.

[211] 3 Force (5), p. 871. Scott was doomed to report, November 30 (ibid., 929), that he had prevailed upon most of his commissioned officers to stay but that not more than thirty of the men in the ranks were willing to do so.

[212] 6 G. W., 314. [213] 6 JCC., 979, 980.

[214] Cf. 6 G. W., 312. [215] Ibid., 310, 314.

[216] Ibid., 310–11, 314. The British advance, stage by stage, is outlined in Glyn's Journal, loc. cit. Nov. 27, 1776 et seq. A somewhat belated but useful account of American maneuvers will be found in Penn. Journal, Jan. 27, 1777.

[217] 6 G. W., 314.

mud, doubtless was interested to hear that some of the rank and file of
a previous garrison contingent had found abundant liquor there. Those
earlier sons of Mars were said to have suffered from an ailment of
Bacchus's, "barrel fever," a malady, one officer explained, "which differs
in its effects from any other fever—its concomitants are black eyes and
bloody noses." [218] If the survivors of Washington's luckless campaign
found rum, after the manner of their predecessors, and fought among
themselves and disturbed the uncertain sleep of an anxious town, who
could blame them unduly? Theirs had been a costly and disheartening
year. Some of them had participated in the easy victory of Dorchester
Heights the previous March and had come hopefully to New York, only
to engage in an ugly campaign which, from Long Island to Fort Lee,
had yielded the single small success on Harlem Heights and had cost
some hundreds of lives and more than 4400 prisoners. [219]

Washington did not have those precise figures before him on the 30th
of November, another rainy day. [220] His Army never had been organized well enough for him even to get accurate returns of his own losses;
but he had a calendar and he had a tabulation prepared for Congress
on the 23rd, while he was at Newark. [221] This was the paper which had
shown that of the 5410 troops in and near the town, including 1000 of
Stirling's Brigade, [222] more than 2000 [223] had the right the next day,
December 1, to start home. [224] They undoubtedly would scatter then.
In addition, it had been reported to Washington that some of the 600
militia of Ewing's Brigade were leaving with the others, though their
time did not expire until January 1. "If those go whose service expires
this day," Washington had to write the President of Congress, "our
force will be reduced to a mere handfull"—when a Division of the
enemy was at Elizabeth Town and the King's Quartermasters were
busy in the choice of shelter five miles farther South. [225] The preceding

[218] Lieut. James McMichael's Diary in 15 Penn. Arc. (2), p. 202.
[219] 3 Force (5), p. 1058.   [220] David How's Diary, 38.   [221] 3 Force (5), p. 822.
[222] As of Nov. 3, 1776, it will be remembered, Stirling had 1689 rank and file, present,
fit, and 191 on command. See ibid., 499–500.
[223] To be precise, and to include Bradley's shadow of a Regiment, 2060 (ibid., 822).
[224] In a letter home, Eben. Huntington wrote Nov. 25, 1776: ". . . those of the militia
who have been sent for our assistance, leave us the minute their times are out, and would not
stay though their eternal salvation was to be forfeited if they went home" (Eben. Huntington's
Letters, 53).
[225] 6 G. W., 315. The wane in the strength of the Army was patent, of course, to every
soldier and it prompted John Chilton to write, Nov. 30, 1776: "We must fight to a disadvantage. They exceed us in numbers greatly. You will wonder what has become of the good
army of Americans you were told we had. I really can't tell, they were in some imaginary."
(To Charles Chilton, 12 T 98).

day, in a letter to Heath, the Commander-in-Chief had said: "If the reenforcements are equal to my expectations, I hope I shall at least be able to prevent a further penetration of the enemy," [226] but that was merely the semblance of cheer. The reality was black. Almost as many soldiers were leaving as were remaining; the number of Jersey militia reporting for duty was outrageously small.[227] Never had the situation been so desperate, not even on the corresponding date of 1775, when the Connecticut militia were about to march off, or on December 31, the last day of the "old Army." It seemed futile to appeal to the common man; only the exceptional individual was patriotic. To most of the privates of the Flying Camp who were trying to make their shoes hold together for the journey homeward on the morrow, the "sacred cause of liberty" meant nothing compared with the shelter of a roof, the comfort of a fire in winter, and a belly full of good food. If liberty was to be won in America, it must be by the patience, the courage, the intelligence, the character of a few leaders. These men must stand together.

An express from General Lee, with a letter addressed to Col. Joseph Reed. In his absence,[228] the express insisted on putting the letter in the hands of the Commander-in-Chief. Bring him in . . . the man . . . a brief exchange of words . . . the letter . . . the express walks out. Yes, to Reed, and sealed, but, as always, if it was official, it was to be opened as a matter of course by Washington. A twist of the sheet, the crackling of the sealing-wax, and then:

Camp, Nov'r the 24th, 1776

MY DR. REED:

I received your most obliging, flattering letter—lament with you that fatal indecision of mind which in war is a much greater disqualification than stupidity or even want of personal courage. Accident may put a decisive blunderer in the right, but eternal defeat and miscarriage must attend the man of the best parts if cursed with indecision.

The General . . .

Then followed an explanation of Lee's reasons for not wishing to march to Jersey, and after that came a summary of what he hoped to do to

---

[226] 6 G. W., 311.

[227] 6 G. W., 315. Eben. Huntington on Nov. 25, 1776 wrote his family from Peekskill of reports there that the British had gone into the Jerseys "only to receive the submission of the whole country, people join them almost in Captain's Companies to take oath of allegiance." (Eben. Huntington's Letters, 53).

[228] Reed was at Burlington. See 1 Reed, 258.

"Ranger" Rogers and nearby British. Next a few words about the prospect of recognition by France, and—

I only wait myself for this business I mention of Rogers & Co. being over— shall then fly to you—for to confess a truth I really think my Chief will do better with me than without me.[229]

There it was on that day of calamity and dissolution: Reed, Adjutant General and trusted friend, had written a "most obliging, flattering letter" in which he had lamented that "fatal indecision of mind"; Lee had agreed; Lee and Reed, senior lieutenant and nearest counsellor, thought him indecisive. . . .

[229] 2 *Lee Papers*, 305–06.

CHAPTER X

THE ARMY AND THE CAUSE DEPEND ON LEE
(November 25–December 15, 1776)

WASHINGTON was more hurt than outraged by the accidental discovery that his Adjutant General and his senior division commander apparently had been exchanging letters critical of him. For months he had been on his guard against the "fickleness" of Lee, as he had termed one of the most pronounced peculiarities of his ambitious lieutenant. Now that Lee's state of mind had been disclosed bluntly, Washington would of course be more careful than ever in dealing with that wandering soldier. Officially, there could be no change of attitude. Lee's professional knowledge must be utilized for the country's sake. It was Reed whose secret correspondence mortified—Reed who had shared the most intimate conversation, Reed who knew all that went on at headquarters. Why had not Reed told him what had been passed on to Lee? If the Adjutant General had observed indecision at a time of desperate risk, why had he not come frankly into the office and said, in effect, "General, you are hesitating too long; make up your mind one way or the other about Fort Washington"?[1] As it was, the circumstances of opening the letter had to be explained to Reed; that was the obligation of a gentleman. Washington sat down on that most miserable of his wretched days, the last day of the Flying Camp, and wrote this:

Brunswick, November 30, 1776

DEAR SIR:

The enclosed was put into my hands by an express from the White Plains. Having no idea of its being a private letter, much less suspecting the tendency of the correspondence, I opened it, as I have done all other letters to you, from the same place and Peekskill, upon the business of your office, as I conceived and found them to be.

[1] This instance is one concerning which Washington left a record of his feelings. In a letter of June 14, 1777 to Reed, the General set forth the sentiments with which he read Lee's communication (8 G. W., 247). In another letter to Reed, Aug. 22, 1779, Washington reviewed the reasons for "that warfare in my mind and hesitation which ended in the loss of the garrison" (16 G. W., 151–52).

This, as it is the truth, must be my excuse for seeing the contents of a letter, which neither inclination or [sic] intention would have prompted me to.

I thank you for the trouble and fatigue you have undergone in your journey to Burlington, and sincerely wish that your labors may be crowned with the desired success. My best respects to Mrs. Reed. I am, Dear Sir, etc.

P.S. The petition referred to I keep.[2]

This letter was to be all, unless Reed himself opened the subject. Washington knew that Reed either had resigned as Adjutant General or intended soon to do so. Whether this was because of dissatisfaction with his administration of the Army, Washington could do no more than guess, but he had nobody to take the place of the able Philadelphian, whose energetic abilities were needed by the country. Reed might be a partisan of Lee's and a critic of the Commander-in-Chief: That must not be permitted to interfere with the plain duty Washington had of retaining Reed as Adjutant General, at least until another well qualified man could be found and elected. Personal relations might not be as close and cordial as before; official dealings had to be easy and unrestrained. That doubtless was the reason for the final reference to the Burlington journey and to Mrs. Reed.[3]

Of his larger problem, Washington wrote on the 30th of November, "I will not despair," [4] but before another sun had set, he needed to summon all the resolution that lay behind his words. On the morning of the 1st, scouts reported the enemy at Bonum, four miles from Woodbridge and about ten miles from Brunswick, where Washington was maintaining his headquarters. Rumor had it that reenforcements from Staten Island had joined Cornwallis, a possibility that Washington could not disregard when he put an estimate of 6000 to 7000 on the force of his adversary.[5] The American Army, on the other hand, continued to dwindle in a manner to make a stout heart stop beating. Among the camps of the two "five-months Brigades" whose time expired at the

---

[2] 6 *G. W.*, 313. The petition, of content now unknown, must have been mentioned on some separate memorandum enclosed in Lee's letter to Reed.

[3] Descendants had a tradition that the withdrawal of Reed's resignation at this time (3 *Force* (5), p. 1033–34) was due to the receipt by Reed of another letter in which Washington besought him to remain in the service at so critical a stage of the war (1 *Reed*, 268). This cannot be ruled out as a possibility but there is no reference to such a communication in *G. W.* or in the *Papers of G. W.*, LC.

[4] 6 *G. W.*, 313. In the original sentence there was a transitional "however" between "not" and "despair."

[5] 6 *G. W.*, 319.

end of November, exhortation, oratory and the tender of the bounty had weighed not at all against fear and cold, homesickness and the professed belief that the other man ought now to do his part. The discharged militia went their several ways, December 1, without apology, though the enemy was said to be advancing and to be distant two hours' march only.[6] With scarcely more than 3400 effectives now under his command,[7] Washington of course had to undertake a new retreat. Orders were issued for every man and every vehicle to cross the Raritan at once. It was done in the early afternoon and without loss, but the margin was so narrow that the whole of the bridge could not be destroyed. Barely enough of it was demolished in the face of fire by Hessian Jägers to prevent pursuit[8] by an enemy convinced that the "rebellion" was about to collapse.[9]

Now that odds were so heavy and the future so black, Washington felt that he should not halt for anything, except for hurried eating and brief rest, until he reached the Delaware and put himself where, if necessary, he could move readily to the Pennsylvania side of that barrier river.[10] Boats were to be assembled for the passage of the stream; all supplies and equipment not necessary for the operations of the Army were to be moved to the south bank.[11] Washington continued to send out earnest calls for reenforcements [12] as he proceeded on his way, via Princeton. At the college town he hoped Charles Lee would meet him, but to Washington's disappointment, neither Lee nor any dispatch from that officer was waiting for him. Washington could not understand why Lee had permitted five full days to elapse without report.[13] At the same time, the troops could not be held in the exposed, unfortified posi-

---

[6] 6 G. W., 320; Greene to Governor Cooke; 3 Force (5), p. 1071.

[7] Actually 3442 rank and file, present, fit and on command (3 Force (5), p. 1035). The Army was so disorganized that this return was not available to Washington. He did not know how many men he had, but he did not err seriously in his estimates.

[8] A. Robertson's Diaries, 115. Howe said in his official report (3 Force (5), p. 1316), that if the bridge had not been damaged, his troops would have cut Washington's Army to pieces; but in his Observations, 65, he quoted the testimony of Lord Cornwallis to the effect that the British column marched twenty miles that day over exceedingly bad roads and had to subsist on flour found in the country. The troops, on arrival at Brunswick, said Cornwallis, were not in condition for another long march. Glyn's Journal, loc. cit., describes, under date of Dec. 2 and 3, 1776, the movements of the Brigade in immediate support of Cornwallis.

[9] Cf. 3 Force (5), p. 1037. Significantly, even such careful men as the editors of Dodsley's Annual Register for 1776 concluded their last item on the situation in America, November 8, with the statement: "Everything seemed to promise a decisive event in favor of the royal arms, and a submission of some of the principal colonies was hourly expected" (p. 181).

[10] 6 G. W., 321–22.   [11] Ibid., and 324–25.   [12] Ibid., 319, 320–21.

[13] 6 G. W., 323, 324–25. Lee's line of advance, day by day, will be found in David How's Diary, 37–38.

tion at Princeton, even for the arrival of a reenforcement Washington believed to be about equal, numerically, to his own Army.[14] Stirling with about 1200 men [15] was left at Princeton to act as a check-rein on a galloping chase by Howe; [16] the remainder of the little Army—with the favor of the elements—passed on to Trenton, which was reached the same day, December 3.

There Washington received a dispatch from Lee,[17] but the content was as depressing as silence had been. Lee's letter was four days old, having been written November 30, and it manifestly was in the mood of a man anxious to do as he pleased in quest of fame. More than once, in the presence of his aides, Lee had been heard to exclaim, "Good God, have I come from gathering laurels in many other parts of the world to lose them in America?" [18] Now Lee justified his delay on the ground that when he entered Jersey he would bring "Four thousand firm and willing troops . . ." If the advance had been begun earlier, said the tardy General, "I should have only led an inferior number of unwilling." Lee concluded: "The day after tomorrow we shall pass the river, when I shall be glad to receive your instructions; but I could wish you would bind me as little as possible, not from any opinion, I do assure you, of my own parts, but from a persuasion that detached Generals cannot have too great latitude, unless they are very incompetent indeed." [19] Neither in this nor in any subsequent dispatch did Lee return to his former contention that Heath could have supplied men to Washington more readily than he himself could, and by a shorter route, but he had done his utmost, before leaving the eastern side of North River, to compel Heath to admit subordination. On the ground that he had to make an exchange of troops between Heath and Spencer,[20] Lee wrung from Heath an order for the detachment of two Regiments to march with Lee's own men into Jersey and, having gained this victory of prestige, he returned the two commands to the Highlands. It was

---

[14] 6 *G. W.*, 345, 351-52. These were Washington's estimates of December 10 and 12. There is no reason for assuming that he credited Lee with a lesser force at the time he reached Princeton, especially in view of what is presently to be reported concerning Lee's own informal return.

[15] 6 *G. W.*, 331. It will be observed that the strength of Stirling's command varied by as much as 600 muskets during November and December. The reason probably was the increase or diminution, from time to time, of the militia serving with him.

[16] *Ibid.*, 331.

[17] *Ibid.*, 326.

[18] William Bradford, Jr. so informed Ezra Stiles. See Ezra Stiles's *Lit. Diary*, v. 2, p. 107.

[19] 2 *Lee Papers*, 322.

[20] Cf. 2 *Lee Papers*, 328.

much as if Lee were determined to rub the nose of Heath into the muck of their controversy before marching off.[21]

Washington was to learn of that in due time. At the moment, December 3, in Trenton, he had to adjust himself to the fact that no help could be expected from Lee for several days.[22] Meantime, Howe might advance before militia arrived in number large enough to give hope of a successful defence. Washington had to make the best of the worst, and both for safety and for freedom of maneuver, he executed his plan to pass all his baggage to the Pennsylvania side of the river. He wrote Lee: "You will readily agree that I have sufficient cause for my anxiety and to wish for your arrival as early as possible." Lee was not to take any of Heath's troops, who were needed where they were. The sooner Lee arrived with his own Division, "the sooner the service will be benefited." [23]

Mercifully, as it seemed, Cornwallis lingered at Brunswick, though rumor of what Howe intended to do in Jersey and elsewhere was varied and contradictory.[24] Washington sifted and weighed the reports and concluded that he might be in a better position, strategically, at Princeton, now that he no longer was encumbered by baggage.[25] On the 7th, he started for that town, but en route he heard that the enemy was advancing and he hastened back to Trenton. When the report of a powerful British onmarch was verified, Washington did not delude himself: He could not make a stand otherwise than by risking again what he had escaped narrowly at Brunswick, a hopeless fight with his back to the river. The ghost of the American Army must be transported across the Delaware and, if possible, must be revived. The movement was made that same day, December 7. By nightfall, the troops were in Pennsylvania, opposite Trenton. No public property, other than a few boards, had been left on the Jersey side of the river.[26] Henry Knox bespoke the best spirit that remained in the little Army when he wrote his wife: "You may be surprised at my dating from this place ["Trenton Ferry"], but it is a combination of unlucky circumstances; have been

---

21 *Heath*, 104–107; 2 *Lee Papers*, 326.

22 6 *G. W.*, 328.

23 Letter of Dec. 3, 1776; *ibid.*, 326.

24 *Ibid.*, 326, 328, 331, 333.

25 *Ibid.*, 331.

26 *Ibid.*, 335, 336, 338–39; 1 *Kemble*, 102; Howe's report in 3 *Force* (5), p. 1316–17. If any student cares to make a detailed tactical study of the use of the ferries and fords of the Delaware, he will find of particular value the report of Benedict Arnold to Washington, n.d. [1777], in 169 *Papers Cont. Cong.*, 100.

obliged to retreat from before the enemy. However, we shall soon, I hope, be able to face them." [27]

That seemed a remote prospect on the 8th. The enemy had a part of his column at Maidenhead [28] and at Princeton [29] and he pushed his van to Trenton. One report was that Howe's train included boats in which to ferry those fierce redcoats of his to the open Philadelphia Road.[30] If this were true, then the Americans must be spread, thinly and sparingly, along the Pennsylvania shore, the crossings of which must be fortified. Orders given on the 1st of December for the collection and removal of boats from the left to the right bank of the Delaware were being executed, but these instructions must be enlarged to cover the entire navigable stretch of seventy miles above Philadelphia.[31] If any boats had been overlooked at landings in Jersey, they must be dispatched secretly to the Pennsylvania side or destroyed beyond repair; all the troops must be told what they were to do in event the enemy effected a crossing.[32] The danger of this was greatest, of course, on Washington's right and beyond that flank, because the turn of the river from Southeast to Southwest, below Trenton, put it within the power of the British General to march through unresisting country and to cross in rear of the defending Army.[33] This only was certain: If Howe had any boats in his train, they had not been brought forward, nor had any considerable number thus far been found by his men on the Jersey shore.[34]

Three weeks had now elapsed, November 20–December 11, since Washington had been compelled to abandon Fort Lee and to put the first of the Jersey rivers between him and his adversary. The retreat

---

[27] Letter of Dec. 8, 1776, with the punctuation somewhat revised; *Knox Papers*, MHS.
[28] The present-day Lawrenceville.   [29] 3 *Force* (5), p. 1316–17.
[30] 6 *G. W.*, 349–50.
[31] *Ibid.*, 319, 322, 331 ff.
[32] *Ibid.*, 337, 343, 345, 346.
[33] It is interesting to note that Cornwallis had considered it entirely probable Washington's Army would proceed down the left bank of the Delaware and escape pursuit. Cornwallis had proposed the advance from Brunswick to Trenton and Bordentown for a variety of reasons, the foremost of which was encouragement from the people of Jersey. For ten days, he said, from 300 to 400 came in daily and took the oath (Howe's *Observations*, 68, in the pagination of his *Narrative*). Howe believed that if he held Trenton, he could dominate the whole of the State, East of Princeton.
[34] 6 *G. W.*, 347–48, 349–50, and *infra*, p. 289, 295, 304. Howe later reported: "Lord Cornwallis . . . marched to Corriel's [sic] Ferry, thirteen miles higher up the Delaware, in some expectation of finding boats there, and in the neighborhood, sufficient to pass the river; but in this he was disappointed, the enemy having taken the precaution to destroy, or to secure on the south side, all the boats that could possibly be employed for that purpose. The passage of the Delaware being thus rendered impracticable, his Lordship took post at Pennington," then eight miles North of Trenton (3 *Force* (5), p. 1317).

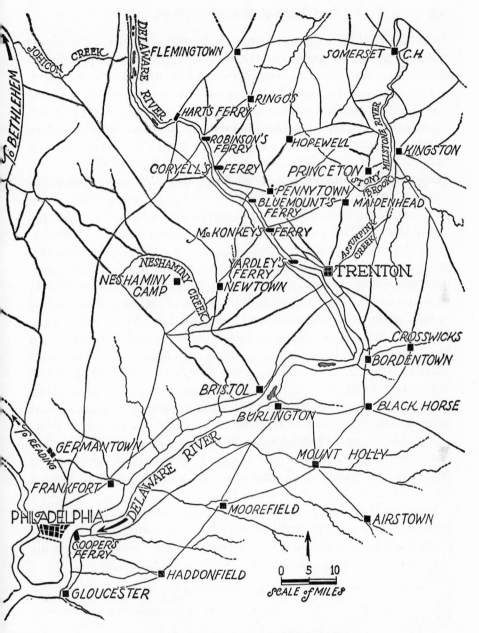

SOUTHERN NEW JERSEY AND EASTERN PENNSYLVANIA.

With Erskine's numerous mistakes preserved, this sketch covers the historic region from Somerset Court House to Philadelphia and shows how troop movements might go astray because of mistakes of distance. Officers soon learned the limitations of their maps and tried to correct them by local inquiry which itself often yielded more of misinformation than of fact.

from the Hudson to the Delaware had covered no less than eighty miles [35] and had witnessed scarcely an exchange of fire, except at Brunswick. An Army that had seemed measurably able to defend itself at White Plains on the 28th of October had scattered so widely and had lost so heavily through capture and expiration of service that it nowhere could offer effective resistance to as many as 5000 British regulars. Washington did not take time to argue the abstract question of the wisdom or imprudence of his dispositions after the fight at White Plains. He believed that the canker of the Army had been short-term enlistment, reliance on militia, and the action of Congress in providing that State commissions should visit the camps and select officers for the Army of 1777. This last requirement had involved not only an intolerable delay in recruiting, but also the choice, in many instances, of officers more acceptable as politicians than competent as leaders.[36] Washington's immediate disappointments had been the small number of men he found in the Flying Camp, and the failure of the New Jersey militia to rally when he moved southward from Fort Lee. At no point on the long road from the Hackensack to the Delaware had as many as 100 Jerseymen reported for duty as a single, organized body.[37] Thomas's Battalion from Essex County was not thought by Brigadier Matthias Williamson to muster more than fifty men; Newark supplied about twenty privates and not a single field officer of militia.[38] The result had been that Washington had received no appreciable addition of force, except that of some Philadelphia militia,[39] to offset the loss of the two "five-months'" Brigades of the Flying Camp.[40] Thus crippled, the American commander had not recovered sufficient power to resist a force as large as the one now pursuing him.[41]

What could be done? Washington and his secretaries covered many folios with their circumstantial answers, but if the commander had been given the time in which to condense the subject, he could have put his

[35] Hackensack, Newark, Elizabeth, Brunswick, Princeton, Trenton, Morrisville.
[36] 6 G. W., 397.
[37] Greene to Governor Cooke, Dec. 21, 1776; 3 Force (5), p. 1342. The language of Greene may be interpreted to mean that the total accession of strength by New Jersey soldiers in the march across part of their State did not exceed 100, but as will appear in a later paragraph, that manifestly was not the fact.
[38] Williamson to Washington, Dec. 8, 1776; 3 Force (5), p. 1120.
[39] See infra, n. 50.
[40] Reference to the five-months' term will be found in Greene to Governor Cooke, Dec. 4, 1776; 3 Force (5), p. 1071.
[41] Cf. G. Johnston to Leven Powell, Dec. 12, 1776: "We are on the south side of the Delaware with about 5000 (militia included) waiting to oppose Gen. Howe's passage and march to Philadelphia with about 12,000" (Leven Powell, 40).

problem into a single sentence: he must concentrate his troops and procure militia reenforcement in order to prevent, if possible, the British capture of Philadelphia before the American Army of 1777 could be recruited and brought into the field.[42] He was not sure this could be done; on the contrary, he did not believe Philadelphia could be saved unless the veteran troops under Lee joined the other Continentals when Howe started the march on the Quaker City.[43] Even with Lee's aid, whatever was done to keep the city from falling into the hands of the enemy must be done quickly, because of the fact—it was ever in mind and often repeated—that Washington could expect no more than three weeks' further service from some of the best of his troops. The time of nearly all the continental Regiments, except those of Virginia and of Maryland, would expire at the end of December. The history of 1775 was being paralleled in a manner that sickened and appalled.

Besides his main hope, which was that of the arrival of Lee's Division, Washington considered again and again the five sources from which, sooner or later, men might come to aid in blocking the road to Philadelphia:

1. New Jersey—was there any prospect Samuel Adams could be proved in error when he said, "Nothing can exceed the lethargy that has seized the people . . .?"[44] Joseph Reed's mission to Burlington had not been successful; the Legislature of the State was about to break up with a *sauve qui peut*;[45] all told, Washington now had collected only about 1000 militia in the State,[46] and he had scant hope of getting appreciably more. As Dr. John Morgan sorrowfully reported, the hurried retreat from Hackensack had "made thousands of Tories."[47]

2. Pennsylvania presented some vexing contradictions, along with good hope. Thomas Mifflin had aroused the Philadelphia militia[48] and, with the Maryland Delegates to Congress, had shaken and shamed the more intelligent men among those who had left the Flying Camp the 1st of December.[49] A tangible reenforcement of the Philadelphia militia already had joined Washington;[50] so had the German Battalion,

---

[42] The closest approach to an epitome of this is in 6 *G. W.*, 339.

[43] *Ibid.*, 341, 345, 351–52.

[44] 1 *Warren-Adams Letters*, 279. Adams included Pennsylvania with New Jersey.

[45] 1 *Reed*, 267.   [46] 6 *G. W.*, 351–52, as of December 12.

[47] 2 *Lee Papers*, 327.

[48] 1 *Reed*, 266–67. Christopher Marshall had thought Mifflin's address to an audience at the State House was "animatedly pleasing" (*Diary*, 106).

[49] 2 *Burnett*, 171.

[50] 6 *G. W.*, 337, 351–52, 357. The exact date of arrival has not been established. It was on or shortly before December 8 (*ibid.*, 337).

which was continental.[51] Together, these numbered about 2000 [52]—the most substantial reenforcements Washington had received since he had crossed the Hudson—and they were not all the men Pennsylvania hoped to send temporarily in answer to fervent and excited appeals by Congress and the State Council of Safety.[53] Gen. John Armstrong, Washington's old friend of the Forbes expedition, was about to start a tour of some of the Pennsylvania Counties to inspirit the militia and to establish magazines.[54] Philadelphia was almost frantic with apprehension; [55] its best element was doing everything possible. As for the rest of Pennsylvania, distances in the State were so formidable in winter that weeks must elapse before any large number of militiamen could be assembled from remote Counties if, indeed, the men were willing to serve.[56]

3. If the enemy remained quiet, Heath's troops in the Highlands, and any other Continentals in the East, could be brought across the Hudson and could be moved southward under authorization already given by Congress.[57] The emergency seemed to Washington on the 7th to justify such a call for Heath, who moved promptly with his one Brigade of men on the "regular establishment." [58] These troops could not be numerous and they might, of necessity, be recalled to their station if even a remote threat developed of a British advance to the Highlands, either from the North or from the South.

4. Schuyler had been directed on November 26 [59] to return from the Northern Department to Washington's immediate command, the New Jersey and Pennsylvania Regiments which Congress three days previously had authorized the Commander-in-Chief to recall.[60] Obediently,

---

[51] 6 JCC., 997. For Washington's effort at this time to recruit other Germans, see 6 G. W., 324.

[52] Ibid., 337.

[53] 3 Force (5), p. 1135, 1215; 6 JCC., 1018–20.

[54] 3 Force (5), p. 1228.

[55] C. Marshall's Diary, 105, 107; 3 Force (5), p. 1046, 1180.

[56] See the letter of D. Griffith to Maj. Leven Powell, dated Philadelphia, Dec. 8, 1776: "No militia has joined us yet from the back counties of Pennsylvania, and I am afraid but very few will. A strange consternation seems to have seized everybody in this country. A universal dissatisfaction prevails, and everybody is furnished with an excuse for declining the public service. Public virtue seems to be quite extinct. The most excessive extortion prevails among the inhabitants, and the greatest peculation and avarice among the servants of the public" (Leven Powell, 70). It is not probable that many of Griffith's contemporaries would subscribe to so extreme a statement.

[57] 3 Force (5), 1026.

[58] This was Parsons' Brigade. Heath's other troops at this time were militia. For his advance to Hackensack, which he reached on the 14th, see 6 G. W., 335; Heath, 110; 3 Force (5), p. 1153, 1169, 1234, 1278; 2 Lee Papers, 340.

[59] See supra, p. 262, and 3 Force (5), p. 854.   [60] 6 JCC., 977.

Schuyler had started southward eight Regiments, under the command of Horatio Gates.[61] The most advanced of the three contingents had reached Peekskill on the 8th of December;[62] but as yet Washington knew little of the composition of this force, or of its progress.[63] If it arrived in time to share at all in the task of keeping the British from Philadelphia, it scarcely would place many additional bayonets across the road that led southward from the Delaware.

5. Clinton's New York Militia Brigade might be placed temporariiy at Washington's disposal;[64] the Eastern and Southern Colonies might send aid when they realized how desperate the situation was; but Philadelphia might be taken meanwhile, and the Army of 1776 might be disbanded, except for the handful of men whose term of enlistment continued beyond December.

Washington did not deceive himself concerning the troops he might get from these five sources. His resolution was inflexible; his hope was waning fast. He remained of the opinion that the enemy would attempt soon to cross the Delaware and to move on Philadelphia. Nothing, he thought, except lack of boats held the British back.[65] Washington continued to take every precaution, both to guard the crossings and to keep boats from falling into the hands of the enemy,[66] but the force he had at the beginning of the retreat across Jersey continued to diminish. Sickness produced by exposure took many who had stood fast against desertion.[67]

All calculations, all argument, came back to the same ugly fact: If any basis of hope remained, it lay in Charles Lee. With his troops, some of them battle-tested, to augment Washington's Continentals and the Philadelphia militia, there was a chance that Howe might be halted, or so discouraged that he would go into winter quarters North of the Delaware. Without Lee, those strong British and Hessian Battalions, with their well-served artillery, almost certainly would destroy with ease the wraith of the Army that lingered after the losses of 1776.[68]

---

61 Cf. Gates to Washington, Dec. 12, 1776; 3 *Force* (5), p. 1190.
62 2 *Lee Papers*, 336.   63 Cf. 3 *Force* (5), p. 1191; 6 *G. W.*, 371.
64 Contingent authorization was voted by the New York Council of Safety on the 10th of December, but, of course, was not known to Washington on the 12th. See 3 *Force* (5), p. 1157–58.
65 6 *G. W.*, 352; cf. Reed, 3 *Force* (5), p. 1181–82.
66 6 *G. W.*, 360–61.   67 *Ibid.*, 378.
68 Warnings of the probable loss of Philadelphia are to be read between the lines of most of Washington's letters to Congress after he had to take refuge on the right bank of the Delaware; the closest approach to an admission of belief that the enemy would capture the city was in the sentence now to be quoted in the text.

Congress must be made to realize this; Lee must be brought to see it. Regard for the feelings of the Delegates must not give any ground for a charge that the Commander-in-Chief concealed danger. Washington wrote Hancock that 12th of December: "Perhaps Congress have some hope and prospect of reenforcements; I have no intelligence of the sort and wish to be informed on the subject. Our little handfull is daily decreasing by sickness and other causes, and without considerable succors and exertions on the part of the people, what can we reasonably look for or expect, but an event that will be severely felt by the common cause and that will wound the heart of every virtuous American, the loss of Philadelphia. The subject is disagreeable, but yet it is true. I will leave it, wishing that our situation may become such as to do away [with] the apprehensions which at this time fill the minds of too many and with too much justice." [69]

This for Congress; what for Lee? Before he started his march, Lee took pains, as one of his Sergeants recorded, to see that ". . . all the lame and lazy and the faint-hearted and all that had no shoes or clothes to keep them warm [were] drafted out . . ." [70] This done, Lee began his crossing on the 2nd of December [71] and proceeded by unhurried marches and with mild grumbling [72] to Morristown, which some of his troops did not reach until the 10th. [73] The previous night [74] Washington received a letter written by Lee on the 8th. On the evening of the 10th, another of the same date arrived. [75] In one of these communications, Lee reported his own troops as 2700 and "our Army," militia included, as 4000. Then Lee said: "If I was not taught to think that your Army was considerably reenforced, I should immediately join you; but as I am assured you are very strong, I should imagine we can make a better impression by hanging on [the enemy's] rear, for which purpose a good post at Chatham seems the best calculated" and he proceeded to explain briefly the advantage of that position. [76]

Washington read this in full appreciation of the advantage of having

---

[69] 6 G. W., 355.
[70] Sgt. John Smith's Diary in *Miss. Val. Hist. Rev.*, v. 20, p. 262. Smith belonged to Lippitt's Regiment of Nixon's Brigade. See also *Heath*, 107.
[71] *Heath*, 107; 3 *Force* (5), p. 1041; *Eben. Huntington's Letters*, 54.
[72] 2 *Lee Papers*, 329.
[73] *David How's Diary*, 40. Lee himself was at Morristown on the 8th. See 2 *Lee Papers*, 336.
[74] 6 G. W., 340.   [75] *Ibid.*, 348.
[76] 2 *Lee Papers*, 337. Chatham, it will be remembered, is seven miles Southeast of Morristown and, in 1776, was eleven miles West of Newark. The city now has crept much closer to the town.

a force in the rear of Howe's army, a strategical possibility of which already Cornwallis was unhappily conscious.[77] Nathanael Greene was of opinion that Lee could achieve more if that officer were on the flank of the British and were proceeding in accordance with the general plans of the Commander-in-Chief;[78] but Washington was not disposed to argue that. Nor did he dwell on the fact that Lee now spoke of 4000 men, though in a previous letter he had mentioned "an army of 5000 good troops in spirits" and, in another communication, had caused Washington to put the strength of the force at 3000.[79] The main issue dominated. Whether with 3000, 4000 or 5000, in the rear or on the flank of the British, Lee could not be left in detached command when Washington did not have sufficient men in front of the British to halt a march on Philadelphia.[80] Lee must be brought to the main Army, but how, how, how? In one of his dispatches of the 8th, Lee had said that he could not believe Philadelphia was the enemy's goal, and he had ended: "It will be difficult I am afraid to join you; but cannot I do you more service by attacking their rear? I shall look about me tomorrow, and inform you further."[81] Additional orders manifestly would be ineffectual in dealing with a man of that mood; a personal appeal was the only recourse. Humiliating as it was to beseech a subordinate to do what was properly to be commanded of him, Washington felt that the cause and the crisis required that meek diplomacy. He gave directions to Stephen Moylan to proceed at once to Morristown and to push forward Lee's troops and Gates's as well.[82] As Lee of course could balk Moylan, the Commander-in-Chief wrote his senior lieutenant that "were it not for the weak and feeble state of the force I have, I should highly approve of your hanging on the rear of the enemy and establishing the post you mention," but in the situation that existed, "I cannot but request and entreat you and this, too, by the advice of all the general officers with me, to march and join me with all your whole [sic] force,

---

[77] See Cornwallis in Howe's *Observations*, 66: "We wanted reenforcement in order to leave troops for the communication between Brunswick and Amboy. It was likewise necessary to pay some attention to a considerable body then passing the North River under General Lee." British headquarters believed this force to number 2500 to 3000 or even 4000 (*ibid.*) and assumed its objective was Philadelphia (1 *Kemble*, 102).

[78] 3 *Force* (5), p. 1107–08.

[79] Letter of Dec. 4, 1776, from Haverstraw; 2 *Lee Papers*, 330; 6 *G. W.*, 346, 351–52.

[80] Washington's letter of Dec. 11, 1776, to Congress; 6 *G. W.*, 350. In this letter, not unnaturally, Washington confused the content of Lee's two dispatches of December 8. This is of no importance except as casual comparison of the letters may be misleading.

[81] 2 *Lee Papers*, 338.

[82] The date of Moylan's departure is not established, but as he was at Morristown after 10 A.M. on the 13th, he probably left the Delaware on the 12th. See 3 *Force* (5), p. 1233.

with all possible expedition." He added solemnly: "The utmost exertions that can be made will not be more than sufficient to save Philadelphia. Without the aid of your force, I think there is but little, if any, prospect of doing so." Washington then wrote briefly of route and of the disposition of British forces, who seemed to be making ready for an attempt to cross the Delaware above Trenton. "Do come on," Washington coaxed, "your arrival may be happy, and if it can be effected without delay, may be the means of preserving a city, whose loss must prove of the most fatal consequences to the cause of America." [83]

The next day, in answer to the second of Lee's letters of the 8th, Washington again humbled himself: ". . . Philadelphia, beyond all question, is the object of the enemy's movements and . . . nothing less than our utmost exertions will be sufficient to prevent General Howe from possessing it. The force I have is weak and entirely incompetent to that end. I must therefore entreat you to push on with every possible succor you can bring. Your aid may give a more favorable complexion to our affairs. You know the importance of the city of Philadelphia and the fatal consequences that must attend the loss of it." [84]

This was the tone of Washington's direct communication to Lee. In reporting to Congress, Washington already had said he did not know how to account for the slowness of Lee's march; [85] now he summarized Lee's letters [86] and said only, "as I have not at present, nor do I see much probability of further reenforcement, I have wrote to him in the most pressing terms to join me with all expedition." [87] From Washington's point of view, that was self-protective because it put on record the fact that Lee had been told to advance his forces, but it was devoid of any hint that Lee was insubordinate—another instance of Washington's desire to keep army disagreements within the Army.

The crisis tightened. Every express had a new sensation to report. On the 13th—a day of melting snow [88]—Washington doubtless heard that Congress had left Philadelphia and had moved to Baltimore, where it was to reassemble not later than the 20th. Before leaving the disturbed Pennsylvania city, the Delegates had voted that, until they should "order otherwise, General Washington [should] be possessed of full

83 Letter of Dec. 10, 1776; 6 G. W., 340–41.
84 Ibid., 348.　　　85 Ibid., 335.
86 See supra, n. 80 on his confusion of the two documents.
87 Letter of Dec. 11, 1776; 6 G. W., 350.　　88 Sgt. John Smith's Diary, loc. cit., 264.

power to order and direct all things relative to the department, and to the operations of war." [89] This manifestly imposed larger responsibility on Washington without giving him the means of discharging it; but he was too busy to point a political moral or to enter a personal disclaimer. Intelligence reports indicated that the enemy might be making dispositions for an attempted crossing; Washington had to place his men, now numbering about 5000 Continentals and militia,[90] where they would have the best chance of holding back the British.[91]

Events seemed to show, also, that the British were so confident of their strength they could afford some dispersion of force in a desirable minor operation. The fleet that had left New York the 1st of December had sailed up the Sound and had discharged near Newport, Rhode Island, on the 8th a force of sufficient magnitude to evoke from State authorities loud and instant calls for assistance.[92] To aid in organizing the defence of the State, Washington ordered Joseph Spencer and Benedict Arnold to proceed there, but he could spare neither Greene nor Gates, whom the Rhode Islanders were anxious to procure,[93] and he had regretfully to inform Governor Cooke that he could not divert to Rhode Island the continental troops previously ordered to the main Army from the Northern Department and from New England.[94]

At the same time it was certain that the presence of a British force in Rhode Island would complicate and perhaps prevent the dispatch of militia from New England to the Middle Colonies. Increasingly, therefore—how tedious the obvious fact had become!—the safety of Philadelphia was a matter of Lee *aut nullus,* and, meantime, a question of whether, somewhere and somehow, the British General could find boats for the crossing, or have the boon of heavy ice on the Delaware. The prospect and the feeling of the Army varied a little from day to

---

[89] This was the resolution of Dec. 12, 1776, the day of adjournment; 6 *JCC.,* 1027. Highly diversified comment on the shift to Baltimore will be found in 3 *Force* (5), p. 1230, 1240, 1241; *Thomas Rodney's Diary,* 13. For some amusing denunciation of the Maryland city as "too dirty and too dear," and a "dirty, boggy hole," see 2 *Burnett,* 187, 196.

[90] 6 *G. W.,* 345.   [91] *Ibid.,* 363–64, 368–69, 372.

[92] For the details of the landing, etc., see Gen. Sir Henry Clinton in 3 *Force* (5), p. 1145–46; 1 *Mackenzie,* 122–23; *Gentleman's Mag.,* 1777, p. 41; 2 Ezra Stiles's *Lit. Diary,* 94–95; Commodore Hopkins in 3 *Force* (5), p. 1162; Governor Cooke in *ibid.,* 1315. Many other references will be found in this volume of *Force,* indexed under "Rhode Island."

[93] 2 *Burnett,* 175.

[94] 6 *G. W.,* 365, 373, 374; 3 *Force* (5), p. 1343, 1717. Washington did not think the British would attempt any deep penetration of New England (6 *G. W.,* 413).

day,[95] but always plans and maneuvers were contingent on Lee's advance.

From him, on the 13th, there came another strange letter, under date of December 11. It began with the statement, "We have three thousand men here at present; but they are so ill-shod that we have been obliged to halt these two days for want of shoes." This was an aggravation of a distress common to the entire Continental Army. Some of Lee's soldiers who had worn out their shoes or had lost them during the summer now were being compelled to lace their feet in the hide of beeves killed the preceding day.[96]

With no elaboration of this reason for delay, Lee's letter proceeded: "Seven Regiments of Gates's corps are on their march, but where they actually are, is not certain." Then, for some reason, the letter was shifted to the third person: "General Lee has sent two officers this day; one to inform him where the Delaware can be crossed above Trenton; the other to examine the road toward Burlington, as General Lee thinks he can, without great risk, cross the great Brunswick post road, and by a forced night's march, make his way to the ferry below Burlington. Boats should be sent from Philadelphia to receive him. But this scheme he only proposes, if the head of the enemy's column actually pass the river. The militia in this part of the province [97] seems sanguine. If they could be sure of an Army remaining amongst 'em"—and here Lee shifted back to the first person, "I believe they would raise a very considerable number." [98]

What did this mean? Why was Lee indulging in this talk of a move across the Brunswick Road, where he would have the British between him and Washington until he passed beyond the left flank of Cornwallis? Was that final reference to an army "amongst 'em" at Morristown a hint that Lee might remain there? Washington did not lose patience in answering: "I am much surprised," he wrote, "that you should be in any doubt respecting the route you should take." With a

---

[95] *Ibid.*, 365, 377, 378; 3 *Force* (5), p. 1231.

[96] Sgt. John Smith's Diary, *loc. cit.*, 264.   [97] Lee still was at Morristown.

[98] 2 *Lee Papers*, 345. To the text of this letter printed in 3 *Force* (5), p. 1167 a note is appended: "The original is endorsed 'From General Lee.'" G. H. Moore took the pains to locate the original of this letter, doubtless in order to ascertain if part of it was written by an aide or secretary. He found it entirely in Lee's autograph (*Moore's Lee*, 54). The natural suspicion is that so strange a letter could not have emanated even from Lee unless he was drunk when he wrote it, but this is not justified by anything known of Lee's behavior during this critical fortnight. There is no suggestion anywhere that he had too close fellowship with the bottle.

brief explanation, once more, of the crossing arranged for Lee, the commanding General proceeded: "I have so frequently mentioned our situation and the necessity of your aid that it is painful to me to add a word upon the subject. Let me once more request and entreat you"— he did not withhold the humiliating verb—"to march immediately for Pittstown, which lies on the route that has been pointed out, and is about eleven miles from Tinnicum Ferry, that is more on the flank of the enemy than where you are.[99] Advise me of the time you will arrive there, that a letter may be sent you, about your future destination and such other movements as may be necessary." Washington added a few paragraphs on army business and public news and dwelt once again on the danger that Philadelphia might fall unless Lee helped to save it.[100]

The tone of this perhaps was firmer and more commanding in a mild way than any of Washington's previous letters to Lee during the retreat across New Jersey, but the difference was not great. Washington had said substantially the same thing to Lee previously and with no observable result. This time he was going to hold out a prospect that he confidently believed no soldier could disregard. Lord Stirling was to follow Stephen Moylan to Lee and was to dispatch other officers to Gates and to Heath. The object of this was to ascertain the condition of the various forces, to learn when the columns could be expected at Pittstown, and to see what proposals Lee, Gates and Heath could make for an attack on the British in concert with Washington's forces.[101]

"Use every possible means without regard to expense," said Washington, "to come with certainty, at the enemy's strength, situation and movements; without this we wander in a wilderness of uncertainties and difficulty, and no plan can be formed upon a rational plan." [102] Stirling well may have gasped at his orders: A General who had declared himself almost certain to fail in the effort to keep the British from Philadelphia without the help of Lee now was hinting that when Lee brought up his 3000, and Gates and Heath added their small contingents, the Army would turn from defensive to offensive. Washington's instructions sketched only in the vaguest way the possibility of recrossing the Delaware and of utilizing all the militia being assem-

---

99 The punctuation of these clauses is that of the original.
100 Letter of Dec. 14, 1776; 6 G. W., 370–71.
101 Ibid., 367–68.　　　　　　　　102 Ibid., 367.

bled at Bristol, but the spirit of the offensive was rising. It might be desperation; it might be military madness; but there would be no more hesitation of the sort that cost Fort Washington and 2811 men. If Lee and the others would come, then in the very teeth of December winds, the American Army would strike.

That day, the 14th, a heavy freeze began.[103] If it continued, the muddy roads would be hard, but the Delaware might be covered with ice. The effect of that might be any man's guess. If the covering soon were thick enough to support men and cannon, then Cornwallis might cross and attack before the American plan of action could be matured. Again, if the river did not freeze heavily enough to present danger of a British advance on too long a front to guard it, the ice might present an obstacle to the Continentals in returning to the north bank for an assault. Washington had to face these possibilities but he refused to permit them to discourage him. Like every other man, he might have better days and worse, might find sunlit hours short and black night long, but he now had rested and had conquered the confusion of mind that had plagued and paralyzed him early in November. "Your worthy General," his old-time comrade Gen. John Armstrong assured the Board of War, "maintains the full possession of himself, is indefatigable by day and night . . ."[104] Said Thomas Paine: "Voltaire has remarked that King William never appeared to full advantage but in difficulties and in action. The same remark may be made on General Washington, for the character fits him." Paine had seen Washington at Fort Lee and in the ghastly retreat across Jersey and he testified as an eye-witness: "There is a natural firmness in some minds which cannot be unlocked by trifles but which, when unlocked, discovers a cabinet of fortitude; and I reckon it among those kind of public blessings which we do not immediately see, that God hath blessed him with uninterrupted health, and given him a mind that can even flourish with care."[105] Washington's planning justified this praise. On the day he once more "entreated" Lee to advance—the day when Stirling was riding fast over treacherous roads toward Morristown—Washington wrote Horatio Gates of the Army's weakness, of the depth of the retreat,

[103] *A. Robertson's Diaries*, 117.
[104] Letter of Dec. 10, 1776; 3 *Force* (5), p. 1151.
[105] "The American Crisis" No. 1, Philadelphia, Dec. 19, 1776, conveniently reprinted in 3 *Force* (5), p. 1294, but available in many forms.

of the great strength the British showed, and of the lack of help from the militia. Then Washington said: "I have heard that you are coming on with seven Regiments, this may have a happy effect, and let me entreat you, not to delay a moment in hastening to Pittstown. You will advise me of your approaches, and of the time you expect to be there, that I may meet you with an express, and inform you of your destination and such further movements as may be necessary," [106] As he penned this, faith rose along with fighting spirit. Washington could not or would not believe that Lee would fail him, and he told Gates: "I expect General Lee will be here this evening or tomorrow, who will be followed by General Heath and his Division. If we can draw our forces together, I trust, under the smiles of providence, we may yet effect an important stroke, or at least prevent General Howe from executing his plans." [107]

Lee did not come that evening; the cold weather continued; the enemy seemed to be hugging the fire in every shelter across the silent Delaware. The forenoon of the 15th brought no change except some unauthenticated reports that the enemy was leaving Trenton and was filing off toward Princeton on the right and Allentown on the left. It was plain from various sources, as Washington wrote later in the day, that the British had "been industrious in their attempts to procure boats and small craft but"—Washington's relief almost drowned the sound of his words—"as yet their efforts [had] not succeeded." [108] Those efforts must not succeed! As soon as Lee arrived, Washington would explore with him the possibilities of an offensive.

Noon and no word from Lee; half an hour past the meridian and still no message from the outposts that the van of the veteran Division was close to the upper crossings of the Delaware, safely beyond the extended right flank of the British. At one o'clock, a spattered horseman drew rein at headquarters; an aide came in to announce him—an express from General Sullivan. So often had expresses brought bad news in recent days and so seldom had they been the bearers of good tidings that Washington had trained himself to expect anything and everything, but he had now something new, something bewildering; Sullivan reported that on the 13th, about 10 o'clock in the morning, at a

[106] Letter of Dec. 14, 1776; 6 G. W., 372.
[107] Ibid.
[108] Ibid., 378.

temporary lodging some three miles from the American lines, General Lee had been captured by a British patrol.[109]

[109] *Ibid.*, 378. Sullivan's dispatch is in 3 *Force* (5), p. 1232. Lee was captured at White's Tavern, in circumstances that are recorded in much detail by a surprising number of witnesses, who explain everything except Lee's reason for going there. The account given by one of Lee's aides, William Bradford, Jr., is in 2 Ezra Stiles's *Lit. Diary*, 106. James Wilkinson, Brigade Major, who had brought Lee a dispatch from Gates to Washington, wrote a full account in his *Memoirs*, v. 1, p. 102–03. Lieut. Col. William Harcourt, later the second Lord Harcourt, the man who made the capture, wrote of it in letters to his father and brother, *The Evelyns in America*, p. 226, 227, 230. General Howe's report is in 3 *Force* (5), p. 1317. As far as is known, neither of the two French officers with Lee wrote any memoir of the incident. Robert Morris's summary of the facts, as he pieced them together, is in 3 *Force* (5), p. 1239, 1333. An inaccurate report from the *Freeman's Journal* is in 1 *Moore*, 360–61. See also 1 *Kemble*, 103; A. Robertson's *Diaries*, 116; Lushington's *Harris*, 84, and a compilation of odd and partisan yarns in *Memoir and Letters of W. G. Evelyn*, 104 ff. A scheme to rescue Lee is mentioned in *Thomas Rodney's Diary*, 28. Wilkinson observed, *op. cit.*, 101, 105, that there were women in the house where Lee was captured, but he noted, also, that one of them screamed and was "in an apparent agony" over some remark or act by one of Lee's aides whom she awakened at Wilkinson's instance (*ibid.*, 101–02). For later reports of the association of Lee with a woman of easy virtue, see *infra*, p. 624, n. 84.

CHAPTER XI

THE GENERAL MAKES HIS DECISION
(December 15–25, 1776)

"UNHAPPY MAN!" Washington wrote when the first shock of the capture of Lee was past. "Taken by his own imprudence, going three or four miles from his own camp and within twenty of the enemy . . ." [1] In a later letter he took pains to set it down that Lee had visited White's Tavern "for the sake of a little better lodging" [2] and, in his first announcement to Congress, he felt it proper to write: "I will not comment upon the melancholy intelligence [conveyed in Sullivan's dispatch], only adding that I sincerely regret General Lee's unhappy fate, and feel much for the loss of my country in his captivity." [3] Comment by others ranged from dismay to puzzlement and to suspicion. The facts were not known in their fullness for days and, when known, scarcely explained Lee's conduct. He had ridden to the tavern with his aides, two Frenchmen and his headquarters guard, and he must have retired at a late hour and must have slept long, because it was 10 o'clock before he had finished breakfasting and bickering. Most of his guards had slipped off to a nearby building and were trying to warm themselves in the sun when a party of four officers and thirty mounted men dashed up the lane, surrounded the tavern and demanded that Lee come out to them. After a few minutes and with scarcely a show of defence, Lee yielded. The British quickly put him on a horse, hatless and not fully clothed, and dashed off with him to Brunswick. It was assumed by the Americans that the expedition had been sent out for the special purpose of capturing the General, but in reality the party had been organized by Lieut. Col. William Harcourt who had volunteered to reconnoitre the position and strength of Lee's forces, when he learned that Lord Cornwallis had no acceptable intelligence of the American column. Accidental capture of an American Light Dragoon

[1] Letter of Dec. 17, 1776, to Lund Washington; 6 *G. W.*, 347.
[2] Letter of Dec. 18, 1776, to Samuel Washington, *ibid.*, 398 and 399 n. See Vol. III, p. 487, for reports of 1775 in Massachusetts that Lee was disdainful of comforts.
[3] 6 *G. W.*, 378.

with a dispatch for Lee had given the clue that prompted Harcourt to sweep down on the inn.[4] Harcourt and his men rode seventy miles on their circuit without loss or accident and they had high welcome when they brought in their prisoner. It was doubtful whether the British or the Americans put the higher valuation on him and on his importance to the continental cause. Congress, much depressed, was anxious to relieve the hardships of Lee's imprisonment and voted him 100 half-joes. Robert Morris was to supply these to Washington, who was requested to forward them through British channels. Washington was to inquire also, by flag of truce, how Lee was being treated and was to remonstrate if the captured General was not having consideration "agreeable to his rank and character."[5] Lee's particular friend, Robert Morris, similarly was fearful that Lee might be subjected to insults because of his previous service in the royal army.[6] Others found consolation in the fact that Horatio Gates was at hand and could be used by Washington for tasks that would have been assigned Lee.[7] Nathanael Greene's generous remark was, "This is a great loss to the American States, as he is a most consummate General."[8] Fear of what the less informed public would make of the affair was voiced by one of Washington's aides, Samuel Webb. ". . . We shall find hard work," he wrote, "to convince many officers and soldiers that [Lee] is not a traitor." Webb hastened to add: "I do not speak of this as though any at headquarters have the most distant thought of his integrity, but it's difficult to convince the common people."[9]

Heath and Gates had recent letters from Lee that would have created suspicions of other and puzzling sorts if the papers had been made public. On the 9th, after having ridiculed Heath to Spencer and even

[4] This is the explanation given in *Glyn's Journal*, Dec. 13, 1776, and it seems the most reasonable. It certainly is more natural and less theatrical than the traditional story of the "treacherous villain" who rode all night to inform the British that Lee was sleeping out (see 3 *Force* (5), p. 1202, 1265). It is interesting to note that Glyn credited the capture to "Cornet Tarleton (who had the advanced guard of this small detachment)." According to *DNB*, Banastre Tarleton was with Howe at the time and may have been the individual mentioned by Glyn, though Tarleton was then a Lieutenant.

[5] 6 *JCC.*, 1029.

[6] 3 *Force* (5), p. 1331. Morris promptly sent Lee bills of exchange for £116 odd money (*ibid.*, 1368, 1374).

[7] 3 *Force* (5), p. 1327.

[8] Letter of Dec. 16, 1776, to Mrs. Greene; 1 *Greene's Greene*, 285.

[9] 1 *Webb*, 174. For other contemporary comment, see *Thomas Rodney's Diary*, 18–19, and 3 *Force* (5), p. 1247. Cf. the reported observation of Sir Joseph Yorke, British Minister to The Hague—that if he were not satisfied the trouble in America would have a happy issue in the course of the summer of 1777, he would be concerned over the capture of Lee, "convinced, from what I have seen and know of him, that he was the worst present which could be made to any army" (quoted in *Moore's Lee*, 81).

to the Commander-in-Chief,[10] Lee confided to Heath that he believed Washington "strong enough" without the troops from the Highlands. Then Lee had added: "I am in hopes here to reconquer (if I may so express myself) the Jerseys. It was really in the hands of the enemy before my arrival." [11] Lee's letter to Gates, as it chanced, was written the morning Lee was captured,[12] and had been snatched up by Gates's messenger as the British troops came thundering up the lane that led to White's Tavern. Had this gossipy document fallen into hostile hands it would have been juicy meat to British teeth and exceedingly hard for Lee to swallow. Said Lee: "The ingenious [sic] maneuver of Fort Washington has unhinged the goodly fabric we have been building—there never was so damned a stroke—*entre nous,* a certain great man is damnably deficient—He has thrown me into a situation where I have my choice of difficulties—if I stay in this Province I risk myself and army and if I do not stay the Province is lost forever." [13] Lee proceeded to list the deficiencies of what he previously had described as "four thousand firm and willing troops, who will make a very important diversion" [14] and he added to Gates: ". . . unless something which I do not expect turns up we are lost—our counsels have been weak to the last degree—as to what relates to yourself if you think you can be in time to aid the General I would have you by all means go. You will at least save your army—it is said that the Whigs are determined to set fire to Philadelphia if they strike this decisive stroke the day will be our own—but unless it is done all chance of liberty in any part of the globe is forever vanished . . ." [15]

Whether or not Washington had sensed any of this, he did not waste words on a situation he could not change. His reply to Sullivan's announcement of the capture of Lee contained two sentences of regret and then—"The event has happened. And I refer you to the several letters which I had wrote him, and to one which now goes to Lord

[10] 2 *Lee Papers,* 307, 328.

[11] Letter of Dec. 9, 1776; 2 *Lee Papers,* 340.

[12] Maj. James Wilkinson, during the night of the 12th–13th, had brought to Lee's headquarters a dispatch from Gates to Washington, the text of which is in 3 *Force* (5), p. 1190. The original is in *Gates Papers,* NYHS. At Wilkinson's instance, Lee had examined the letter, which contained information that, in the Major's opinion, should be divulged to the General in command at Morristown. See 1 *Williamson,* 102.

[13] 2 *Lee Papers,* 348, with the erratic punctuation preserved but the capitalization modernized and a few abbreviated words spelled out.

[14] *Ibid.,* 322; letter of Nov. 30, 1776, to Washington.

[15] *Ibid.,* 348. No definite evidence has been found to justify the statement that Gates did *not* show this letter to Washington but the contents and the circumstances render it highly improbable that Gates would have done so at the time.

Stirling, who I presume is with you, and who was fully possessed of my ideas when he left me, for the measures you and he may judge necessary to adopt." [16] There was neither time nor occasion for more than that, because every hour added new problems and multiplied perplexities. Washington had been seeking to expedite an exchange of prisoners; [17] now he had to deal with like quibbling and stubbornness at a different level, that of millers who refused to grind wheat for the army. The General did not know all the circumstances but he suspected that a new and spreading reluctance to accept continental currency might be one reason. Loss of hope in the success of American resistance was causing the timid and the selfish to shun paper dollars that soon might be worthless.[18] Washington met this state of affairs with his usual practicality, sharpened no doubt by his own experience as a miller: the equities must be established; then the mills or the grain must be seized and used as the circumstances justified.[19] This and similar details of growing need and waning supply must be handled decisively while Washington continued to face those maddening questions on which the life or the death of the Revolution depended: when would Sullivan and Gates arrive; how could the crossing of the Delaware by the British be prevented; was it really possible to forge a counterbolt, or was the situation hopeless?

Judgment and resolution warred hourly over the answer. Every day after the 15th there was hope that Sullivan and perhaps Gates also would arrive; daily—Monday, Tuesday, Wednesday, Thursday—the reunion of the Army failed of attainment.[20] A strange optimism possessed some of the political leaders that large reenforcements would spring up from the ground, so to say,[21] but as every bleak dawn brought tragically nearer the end of the enlistment of most continental troops,[22]

---

[16] 6 G. W., 375–76.

[17] 6 G. W., 319, 322, 324, 348–49, 359, 390, 410–11, 414, 425; 3 Force (5), p. 1193. In ibid., 1233–34 is a heartbreaking account of the miseries American prisoners were forced to endure in their packed New York quarters.

[18] The private advice of John Dickinson in an intercepted letter to his brother, Gen. Philemon Dickinson, was, briefly, "Receive no more Continental money on your bonds and mortgages" (3 Force (5), p. 1255), counsel that outraged leaders of the revolutionary cause. See 6 G. W., 399. The most succinct and informed view of the depreciation of continental currency at this time probably is that of Robert Morris in his letter of Dec. 21, 1776, to the American Commissioners in France (3 Force (5), p. 1334; 2 Wharton, 234).

[19] 6 G. W., 409, 421.

[20] 3 Force (5), p. 1246, 1247; 6 G. W., 347, 396.

[21] See Shippen in 3 Force (5), p. 1258; R. H. Lee in 1 Ballagh, Lee Letters, 229–30; C. Marshall's Diary, 108. Fortunately, at this time, Howe exaggerated Washington's strength. 3 Force (5), 1317.

[22] 6 G. W., 346, 398.

Washington lost one prospect after another of reenforcement. Prudence dictated the return of Heath's 600 [23] to the Highlands; [24] Clinton, too, would be needed there, along with his militia; [25] some consideration had to be given the pleas of Jersey leaders that part of Gates's advancing forces be left on or near the Hackensack River in the hope that the militia would rally to them.[26] Moreover, it became doubtful whether Washington would receive any of the 4000 to 6000 militia that Massachusetts was said to be raising for the protection of the Eastern States, and if any of these were available, they probably would be required in North Jersey and might not be added to the main Army; [27] reports of the reenlistment of New England troops in the continental Regiments marching to Washington's aid proved false.[28] If rumor hopefully had it that Howe was going into winter quarters, Washington told himself that his adversary would stay there so short a time and would emerge with so much strength that the new American army must be organized quickly.[29] Still again, when it seemed likely that the British would undertake to pass the Delaware even at that arduous season,[30] the consolation Washington found in the removal of boats to the right bank [31] was lessened by realization that the river might freeze so deeply the enemy could cross on the ice.[32] Washington had to admit in a confidential letter, "If every nerve is not strained to recruit the New Army with all possible expedition, I think the game is pretty near up . . .";[33] but the deep determination of his spirit, his innate refusal to accept defeat, dictated this sentence in the same letter: ". . . under a full persuasion of the justice of our cause, I cannot entertain an idea that it will finally sink, though it may remain for some time under a cloud."[34] Publicly, he wrote the Massachusetts Legislature: ". . . upon

[23] 3 *Force* (5), p. 1278.
[24] 6 *G. W.*, 366, 373, 383, 385; 3 *Force* (5), p. 1299, 1344.
[25] *Ibid.*, 1261, 1278, 1344, 1347, 1349.
[26] *Ibid.*, 1260, 1296, 1297–98. On the 21st of December, Brig. Gen. William Maxwell was sent to Morristown to take charge of the militia there (6 *G. W.*, 415).
[27] *Ibid.*, 411, 417, 427–28; 3 *Force* (5), p. 1285–86.
[28] 6 *G. W.*, 417. [29] *Ibid.*, 379, 383, 385.
[30] *Ibid.*, 380.
[31] *Ibid.*, 395, 397, 407. Cf. Howe in 3 *Force* (5), p. 1316–17.
[32] Washington to the President of Congress Dec. 20, 1776; 6 *G. W.*, 407. It is possible that Washington did not realize until approximately this date that the Delaware would freeze so heavily it would afford passage for the army. There is an equal possibility, in a bitter pun, that Washington decided he would leave Howe to cross that frozen bridge when the British General came to it. The point to stress is that references by Washington to the freezing of the Delaware became frequent after December 20.
[33] To John Augustine Washington, Dec. 18, 1776; 6 *G. W.*, 398. Cf. *ibid.*, 346.
[34] *Ibid.*, 399.

the whole our affairs are in a much less promising condition than could be wished; yet I trust, under the smiles of Providence and by our own exertions, we shall be happy. Our cause is righteous, and must be supported. Every nerve should be strained to levy the New Army. If we can but procure a respectable one in season, all may be well, and to this end no pains can be too great." [35]

What he enjoined on Massachusetts he was willing to undertake in person. The authority given him by Congress to conduct the department and the operations of war had about it a vagueness that could have been termed benevolent or abdicative, according to the temper of Delegates; [36] the Pennsylvania Council of Safety had given the Commander-in-Chief large powers in compelling service by those who sought to dodge it, but this power was limited of course to the one State.[37] To go beyond the smallest letter of existing "resolves," Washington had to communicate in wintry weather with a Congress sitting in Baltimore [38] and even then to assume that the New Army would be limited to eighty-eight Battalions. Many of these would be commanded by men the State Commissioners had named in accordance with what now appeared to be the suicidal madness of a Congress more intent on honoring political favorites than on winning American freedom.[39] This was the way of ruin. The size of the Army must be increased to 110 Battalions, the artillery must be enlarged, a corps of engineers must be established—half-a-score changes must be made at once if the New Army was to be recruited or to be efficient when created. Deferential as Washington always had been in his attitude toward the men who spoke for America, he felt now that the choice was between country and Congress. On the 20th, in stern and resolute mood, he wrote the Delegates of his need, announced that he would enlist additional artillery, and stated in plain terms that "if any good officers offer to raise men up on continental pay and establishment in this quarter,[40] I shall encourage them to do so, and regiment them when they have done it." Old habit and discipline showed themselves immediately in the next sentence: "If Congress disapprove of this proceeding, they will please to signify it, as I mean it for the best." He could not forbear

---

[35] Letter of Dec. 18, 1776; *ibid.*, 396.   [36] See *supra*, p. 284–85.
[37] 6 *G. W.*, 399.   [38] *Ibid.*, 402.
[39] Cf. ". . . the unfortunate mode adopted by Congress for the appointment of officers under the new establishment has been big with every evil . . ." (*ibid.*, 429).
[40] For his first move to this end, see his letter to Col. Samuel Griffin, Dec. 24, 1776; *ibid.*, 429. The quotation is *ibid.*, 403.

adding: "It may be thought that I am going a good deal out of the line of my duty to adopt these measures, or advise thus freely; a character to lose, an estate to forfeit, the inestimable blessing of liberty at stake, and a life devoted must be my excuse." [41]

As Washington finished this long letter, word came that Sullivan had just arrived with Lee's troops and that Gates, too, had reached camp.[42] From plans for the Army that must somehow be brought into being within twelve dark days, Washington turned once again to the troops who should be kept under discipline to the last day of December and had, meantime, to be put across the Philadelphia Road, as a bar to the advance of Howe, or else had to be thrown offensively against the British. "No man, I believe," Washington had written a brother two days previously, "ever had a greater choice of difficulties and less means to extricate himself from them." [43] He might have been specific: The "5000 good troops in spirits" whom Lee had said as late as December 4 he would bring with him from Haverstraw [44] turned out to number about 2000; Gates's Regiments had no more than 600 rank and file; Washington computed his own force at between 2400 and 2500, plus the militia who had joined since he crossed North River.[45] Formal returns were to show his total effectives to be 7659,[46] far too few and too dispirited, apparently, for the duty to be performed! Gates himself was gloomy and of opinion that the Army should not attempt to reorganize North of the Susquehanna; [47] most of the Brigadier Generals under Sullivan were sick or absent; [48] both Sullivan and Gates reported that few of their men showed any willingness to reenlist for service after the expiration of their term. "If militia do not then come in," Washington said, "the consequences are but too evident." [49] More bluntly Washington reflected that fairweather friends of American freedom were going over to the British and were accepting the pardons Howe was dispensing. Joseph Galloway had joined the enemy and so had three Allen brothers of Philadelphia—Andrew, a former member of Congress, John who had belonged to the Philadelphia Committee, and William, who held a commission as Lieutenant Colonel.[50] Howe,

[41] Letter of Dec. 20, 1776, to the President of Congress; *ibid.*, 402–03. Joseph Reed's letter of Dec. 22, 1776, to Washington contained language most remarkably similar. See 1 *Reed*, 273.
[42] 6 *G. W.*, 409.
[43] *Ibid.*, 398–99.
[44] 2 *Lee Papers*, 330.
[45] 6 *G. W.*, 421.
[46] 3 *Force* (5), p. 1401–02.
[47] 1 *Wilkinson*, 126–27.
[48] 6 *G. W.*, 408.
[49] *Ibid.*, 409.
[50] 3 *Force* (5), p. 1230, 1377, 1397, 1434.

moreover, was gaining strength steadily from arms-bearing American Tories [51] while few recruits joined Washington.[52] It did not help him at the moment to know that politicians continued optimistic, that there was a prospect of more help from Pennsylvania, and that Virginia might give further assistance in a few weeks.[53] Eleventh-hour attempts to offset some of the adverse odds were being made now in all the fever of fear. Old clothing was being sent the shivering soldiers; blankets were collected with hints that if they were not donated, they would be seized; a lucky importation of 856 was forwarded from Philadelphia.[54] Efforts were renewed to procure some of the new militia from Massachusetts; [55] Congress hastily authorized the payment of all such men on the same basis as continental troops; [56] in dealing with Pennsylvania short-term soldiers, Washington invoked the powers of virtual conscription granted him by the State Council of Safety; [57] a start was made toward the establishment of depots of supplies in less exposed towns of the Quaker State.[58] Almost frantically, everything that could be undertaken for the Army was done except as respected the two great imperatives, the supply of soldiers with firelocks in their hands, and the reenlistment of the men who confronted the enemy on the Delaware.

Washington did not withhold a single detail of this tragedy from Congress, which now had named Robert Morris as the head of a committee of three to conduct affairs in Philadelphia [59] that had taken on the look of a plundered town.[60] Two days after the arrival of Sullivan's and Gates's troops, Washington wrote Morris in plainest words: ". . . unless the militia repair to the city of Philadelphia for defence of it, I see no earthly prospect of saving it after the last of this instant;

[51] 6 G. W., 402; Howe's Observations, 18. Governor Tryon reported, Dec. 24, 1776, that on the 10th he had reviewed 820 Loyalist militia in Queen's County, New York, and that on the 12th, near 800 appeared at a review in Suffolk County. The oath of allegiance was administered to all these (3 Force (5), p. 1404). In the Adjutant General's returns of July 1 and 7, 1777 (Clinton Papers, Clements Lib.) will be found the figures on the strength of the loyalist commands at that time.

[52] Cf. 1 Greene's Greene, 284.

[53] Cf. 2 Burnett, 188, Penn. Council of Safety to Washington, Dec. 20, 1776; 3 Force (5), p. 1310; John Trumbull in ibid., 1352; Adam Stephen, ibid., 1314–15, Andrew Lewis to the President of Congress, Dec. 21, 1776; ibid., 1329. See, also, the public appeals of the Penn. Council of Safety and of the Penn. Assembly, ibid., 1375–76; William Whipple, ibid., 1397; William Ellery, ibid., 1418.

[54] 6 JCC., 997–98; 6 G. W., 381, 422; 3 Force (5), p. 1229, 1310, 1331.

[55] 6 G. W., 411, 417, 427–28.   [56] 6 JCC., 1034.

[57] 6 G. W., 423–24.   [58] Ibid., 417.

[59] 6 JCC., 1032. Formal action to this effect was taken on the 21st of December; Morris patriotically was carrying the burden of administration before that time.

[60] Thomas Rodney's Diary, 14, 17.

as that fatal vote of Congress respecting the appointment of new officers has put the recruiting business upon such a footing, and introduced so much confusion into the old Regiments, that I see no chance of raising men out of them; by the first of next month then, we shall be left with five Regiments of Virginia, one of Maryland, General Hands' and the remains of Miles'; reduced so much by sickness, fatigue &ca. as in the whole not to exceed, but fall short of, 1200 men. Upon these and the militia is all our dependence, for you may as well attempt to stop the winds from blowing, or the sun in its diurnal, as the Regiments from going when their term is expired." [61] Then Washington expressed the view that Morris should remain in Philadelphia but should keep there indispensable records only, because, he reiterated "I am satisfied the enemy wait for two events only to begin their operations upon Philadelphia," thick ice on the Delaware and the dissolution "of the poor remains of our debilitated Army." [62]

In spite of this warning, added to all those he had been voicing since the Jersey militia failed to rise,[63] Washington had been hoping against hope—and in contradiction of his words—that after the veterans of Lee's and Gates's commands reached the Delaware and saw the situation there, they would re-enlist in considerable numbers. Christmas Eve brought these men to the last week of their service; sacred hours of expectancy yielded what appeared to be trustworthy intelligence that the British were saying, in effect, Grant us strong ice and we will take Philadelphia within from ten to twenty days after the 16th of December.[64] Reports by some of Washington's officers gave increased probability to the fulfilment of this prediction. In writing the President of Congress on the 24th, Washington said he had been led to hope previously that Gates's and Lee's troops would agree to remain with the Army, but he had to add: ". . . I am authorized to say from the information of their officers that but very few of their men have enlisted. Those who have [done so] are of the troops from Ticonderoga

---

[61] Letter of Dec. 22, 1776; 6 G. W., 420. The punctuation of this historic statement is unchanged except where apostrophes have been added to names. Somewhat similar notice had been sent the previous day to Governor Trumbull; ibid., 411.

[62] Ibid., 421, repeated in substance to the Penn. Council of Safety, ibid., 422–23.

[63] "We have been endeavoring to draw a force together to check General Howe's progress but the militia of New Jersey have been so frightened and the Pennsylvania so disaffected that our endeavors have been ineffectual . . ." (Letter of "William Williams," probably an assumed name of Nathanael Greene, to his wife, Dec. 16, 1776; Anderson Gallery Cat., 1926).

[64] 6 G. W., 433.

and were permitted to visit their friends and homes as part of the terms on which they would reengage." He speculated in a few sentences on the reasons for this unwillingness to continue in the ranks: "Their refusal, I am told, has not proceeded more from an aversion to the service or any fixed determination not to engage again, than from their wishes to return home, the non-appointment of officers in some instances, the turning out of good and putting in of bad in others, and the incomplete or rather no arrangement of them, a work unhappily committed to the management of their States . . ." [65] and then he stated the affrighting truth once more: At the year's end he would have from 1400 to 1500 effectives only. "This handfull, and such militia as may choose to join me, will then compose our Army. When I reflect upon these things, they fill me with much concern, knowing that General Howe has a number of troops cantoned in the towns bordering on and near the Delaware, his intentions to pass as soon as the ice is sufficiently formed, to invade Pennsylvania, and to possess himself of the City of Philadelphia if possible. To guard against his designs and the execution of them shall employ my every exertion, but how is this to be done?" [66]

The gods of the weather appeared to be neutral. A heavy snow on the night of December 19–20 had been followed by a partial thaw on the 21st,[67] with the result that the ice on the Delaware Christmas morning was not heavy enough either to support troops or to prevent the passage of well-handled boats. The ominous condition was the piling up of snow clouds and a shift of wind toward the Northeast. If that meant colder weather and more ice . . . perhaps the prospect found its way into the letter Washington wrote in answer to two from Robert Morris. "I agree with you," the General said, almost bitterly, "that it is vain to ruminate upon, or even reflect upon the authors or causes of our present misfortunes." He proceeded: "We should rather exert ourselves and look forward with hopes that some lucky chance may yet turn up in our favor. Bad as our prospects are, I should not have the least doubts of success in the end, did not the late treachery and defection of those who stood foremost in the opposition, while fortune smiled upon us, make me fearful that many more will follow their

[65] 6 G. W., 432.   [66] Ibid., 432–33.
[67] David How's Diary, 40; Serle, 161; A. Robertson's Diaries, 117.

example, who by using their influence with some and working upon the fears of others, may extend the circle so as to take in whole towns, counties, nay, Provinces. Of this we have a recent instance in Jersey, and I wish many parts of Pennsylvania may not be ready to receive the yoke!" [68]

Washington turned then to the security of the continental warships in the Delaware, and in suggesting that the draft of men to fit them out be delayed, he remarked, "perhaps in a little time hence" the places might be supplied with county militia. He did not elaborate on the phrase, "a little time hence," and he went on with the discussion of other current problems. The closing sentences were as dark as any he had written during those terrible December days of unrelieved suspense: "From an intercepted letter from a person in the secrets of the enemy, I find their intentions are to cross Delaware as soon as the ice is sufficiently strong. I mention this that you may take the necessary steps for the security of such public and private property as ought not to fall into their hands, should they make themselves masters of Philadelphia, of which they do not seem to entertain the least doubt."

Frugal as Washington always was in using paper and reluctant as he sometimes appeared to be in giving a line for a change of subject, he dropped down the sheet and wrote a brief, concluding paragraph: "I hope the next Christmas will prove happier than the present to you and to, dear Sir, etc." [69] A "happier" Christmas in '77—the very hope seemed a mockery, a satire as bitter as that of support by Jersey militia. A "happier Christmas" when the wind was rising more rapidly and many of the men who were hovering around the camp fire doubtless were talking of their departure for home within another week and were commiserating the 1500 who had to remain? "Happier" for the Americans who would have to face the British as soon as the river ice was solid and strong enough to support British and Hessian Battalions? It would have seemed more in order if Washington had run his pen through that line about "happier Christmas" and had repeated what he had written a week previously—"if every nerve is not strained to

[68] 6 *G. W.*, 436–37. Washington's particular reference, needless to say, was to Joseph Galloway and the three Allen brothers. See *supra*, p. 297. Cf. the observations of Samuel Adams, Jan. 9, 1777, on the change that then appeared to be taking place in New Jersey with the rise of a courageous leader, Col. Jacob Ford, Jr. (Letter to John Adams; 9 *John Adams*, 449).

[69] 6 *G. W.*, 438. Washington added a postscript concerning the best location of a depository for army supplies.

recruit the New Army with all expedition, I think the game is pretty nearly up . . ." Washington did not erase the phrase about happier times because, among other reasons, he had on his table that Christmas Day another paper, an order that his troops were to start for McKonkey's Ferry, "as soon as it begins to grow dark . . . and embark on board the boats . . ." [70] Even if he had an Army for only a week more, Washington was going to attack.

[70] *Ibid.*, 439 n.

CHAPTER XII

INCREDIBLE CONTRAST OF NINE DAYS

(December 25-27, 1776)

HE HAD TO attack. The compulsion of road and of watercourse was as positive as that of circumstance. Flowing toward the sea, the Delaware formed a long "nose" to the eastward, between Trenton and Burlington.[1] Along the British side of the river, a road that was serviceable in most weather covered the whole of the "nose." Separate lines of supply led to this river road from South Amboy[2] and from Brunswick. If boats became available, or the river was frozen deeply over, Howe had it in his power to attack directly South from Trenton, on the road to Philadelphia, or else to march around the "nose," to cross in rear of Washington's Army, and to make it impossible for the Continentals to interpose their front between their adversary and Philadelphia. Here were the alternatives:

To protect his position opposite Trenton and his flank across from Burlington, Washington had been compelled to spread his thin Regiments along twenty-five miles of the river—a commitment that made him weak everywhere.[3] He still might hope that the British would go

[1] Bordentown thus is the "tip" of the "nose," the point at which the stream turns from Southeast to Southwest. Warning has to be given that for this area, as around Boston, the maps used by Washington were far from accurate both as to distances and as to compass bearings. No information is available concerning the particular map used in 1776, but it probably was inferior to "A Map of part of the States of New-York and New-Jersey: Laid down, chiefly from Actual Surveys, received from the Right Honble Ld Stirling and others, and Deliniated for the use of His Excely Genl. Washington, by Robt. Erskine F.R.S. 1777." An engraved copy of this map, with some corrections and numerous additions in an autograph believed to be that of Washington, is among the treasures of the Pierpont Morgan Library of New York. A check by modern measurements of known accuracy shows this map of 1777 to be in error at some points by approximately as much as 25 per cent of the distance involved. Mistakes of scale on one part of the map differ substantially from those of other sections. It is not pleasant to be compelled to add that the map of the Trenton-Princeton campaign in Carrington's *Battles of the American Revolution* is grossly out of scale.

[2] Washington usually distinguished between Amboy and South Amboy, but, in general, there was no consistency of usage by American and British authorities regarding the place names Perth Amboy, Amboy and South Amboy. If the reference is to a base of supply, the safest assumption is that Amboy, in any of its three forms, is equivalent to the area of the modern Raritan Bay.

[3] See Henry Knox to Mrs. Knox, Dec. 28, 1776; *Stryker*, 371–72. For Joseph Reed's statement that the task was beyond the resources of the American Army, see his letter of Dec. 12, 1776, to Washington; *ibid.*, 322–23. Washington's apprehension of a turning-operation around the "nose" of the Delaware is reflected in John Cadwalader to the [Penn.] Council of Safety, Dec. 8, 1776 (*ibid.*, 323).

into winterquarters [4] because broken bridges lengthened every march [5] in search of provisions the enemy believed to be abundant,[6] though Americans were of opinion the region had been stripped.[7] Washington's chief reliance had to be on prompt and accurate intelligence of British movements [8] and on the wise use of the boats he had and the enemy lacked. So long as he could cross the Delaware and the British could not—a situation established by the diligence of Col. Humpton and a painstaking detachment [9]—Washington would have the initiative until the ice on the river permitted a British crossing or his Army disintegrated at the year's end. He must use that initiative, use it immediately before the river froze, and use it at a point where his small numbers would count most! [10]

Intelligence reports were being procured with much difficulty from Trenton, because spies were afraid to enter a village where Tories might identify and betray them; [11] but Washington believed the place

---

[4] Tench Tilghman to his father, Dec. 16, 1776; *Memoir of Tench Tilghman,* 148.

[5] Cf. Donop to Grant, Dec. 21, 1776; *Stryker,* 331.

[6] *Ibid.*

[7] Cf. *Thomas Rodney's Diary,* 25: "The whole country . . . appeared one scene of devastation and ruin. Neither hay, straw, grain [n]or any live stock or poultry to be seen."

[8] Cf. Joseph Reed to Washington, Dec. 12, 1776: "The river is not and I believe cannot be sufficiently guarded. We must depend upon intelligence of their motions . . ." (*Stryker,* 322–23). Washington was procuring useful information at this time from David Chambers, who also was engaged in counter-espionage (See his letter of Dec. 16, 1776, to Washington in the *L. W. Smith Coll.*). John Clark, then the most daring and skilful of Washington's agents in dealing with spies, was on duty at Bristol, Penn. at this time (William Grayson to Clark, Dec. 11, 1776, same collection). A detailed sketch of Clark will be found in 1 *PHS Bul.,* separately paged. General McDougall at Morristown was another good source of information, though he was unnecessarily alarmed over the possibility of a British advance on his station. See his letter to Washington, Dec. 22, 1776; 38 *Papers of G. W.,* 5, LC.

[9] Humpton, a native of Yorkshire, England, aged approximately 43, had been a British Captain during the siege of St. Malo. Later, while serving in the West Indies, he had resigned his commission and had come to Pennsylvania, where he had settled on one of the upper branches of the Susquehanna. Named on July 16, 1776, a Lieutenant Colonel of the Flying Camp, he had become Colonel of the Eleventh Pennsylvania, Oct. 25, 1776. For later transfer and promotion, see *Heitman* and 27 *Penn. Mag.,* 387, 403; 48 *ibid.,* 502. A sketch will be found in Appleton's *Cyclopaedia of American Biography.* Perhaps the highest tribute to Humpton was in the *Examination of Joseph Galloway before the House of Commons, June 18, 1779,* p. 42. Galloway, testifying to Howe's mismanagement of the Jersey campaign, could say only, as respected boats, that two had been found by the British on a millpond. His unreasonable intimation was that as each of these boats could have accommodated fifty or sixty men, they should have been used to transport British forces across the river; but Galloway's failure to find any other mention of boats in the testimony of royal officers shows how much thoroughness was credited to Humpton's men. Admirable as was the service of these soldiers, it probably was not as nearly perfect as the enemy later supposed. Besides the two boats on the millpond, a scow and four batteaux may have been in British hands. Cf. 3 *Force* (5), p. 1343. See, also, Donop to Leslie, Dec. 16, 1776, for reports, probably erroneous, of gondolas at Burlington, *Stryker,* 319.

[10] The importance that Washington attached by this time to heavy ice in facilitating a British attack has been disregarded by some writers, but it was set forth plainly and often by the General. See 6 *G. W.,* 413, 421, 423, 433.

[11] 3 *Force* (5), p. 1343–44.

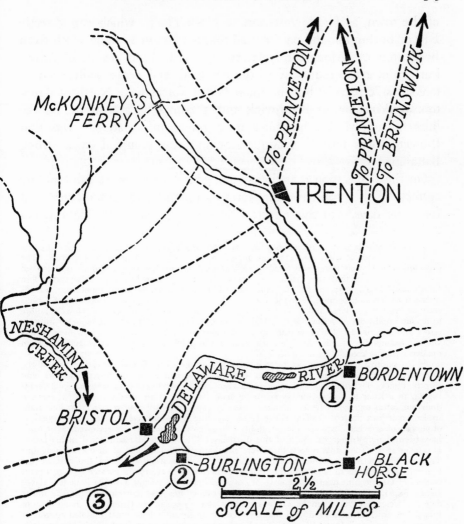

THE "NOSE" OF THE DELAWARE.

Here the fateful "if" of a British advance on Philadelphia concerned boats with which to cross
the broad river. "If" General Howe could find the bottoms, he had a wide choice of maneuver
by which to throw back Washington from the right bank of the Delaware. Howe could cross at
or near (1) Bordentown, (2) Burlington or (3) farther down the Delaware, at Dunk's Ford,
immediately below the edge of this sketch, or even nearer Philadelphia.

was occupied by 2000 to 3000 Hessian troops, who had six field cannon.
So far as was known, no British forces were at Trenton.[12] Hessian
contingents of varying size were encamped to the East and Southeast

[12] Henry Knox to Mrs. Knox, Dec. 28, 1776; *Stryker,* 371–72.

of the town, as far downstream as Black Horse, which was directly East of Burlington and on the road that led almost straight South from Bordentown.[13] Along the Delaware, above Trenton, parties of Americans came over frequently to the left bank and occasionally encountered hostile patrols; but the main British forces were North of Trenton, at Princeton, at Brunswick and, presumably, at Amboy, on the lines of supply. Washington's most recent information[14] was that Princeton was termed headquarters and was occupied by a strong Battalion.

On the assumption that these intelligence reports were substantially correct, Washington gave final form to a plan he had been developing for some days,[15] to this effect: Christmas afternoon, the continental

[13] Cf. Joseph Reed to Washington, Dec. 22, 1776; *ibid.*, 340; 1 *Reed*, 271.

[14] Reed's letter of Dec. 22, 1776, as *supra*. Most of this intelligence was correct. The distribution of Howe's troops was fixed in GOs of Dec. 12, 1776, a copy of which is preserved in *Glyn's Journal* of that date. Howe's report of Dec. 20, 1776, to Germaine was reprinted in *Gentleman's Mag.*, 1777, p. 89. In Howe to Clinton, Dec. 20, is an announcement of his return from Trenton because he found the boats for a crossing destroyed. Howe was conscious then of "rather too large links" in his chain of communication. Apropos of Howe's failure to pursue rapidly across Jersey, Captain Hall wrote (*op. cit.*, 223): "In the catalogue of military errors and misconduct, I will venture to assert this appears so singular that it almost stands without example!—yet this march was extolled in the public papers, and drew applause from the deceived and credulous multitude."

[15] No positive date can be set for the inception of the plan. Before retreating behind the Delaware, Washington had suggested to Charles Lee a succession of forced marches and surprise attacks on Brunswick and other posts (See 2 *Lee Papers*, 337). A reference of December 14, in a letter to Gates, conveys no more than the germ of an offensive plan: "If we can draw our forces together, I trust under the smiles of Providence, we may yet effect an important stroke, or at least prevent General Howe from executing his plans" (*ibid.*, 372). Subsequently, of course, officers had discussed the possibility whenever the situation was reviewed, as it must have been, daily. Rumor was born of this discussion. Christopher Marshall noted in his *Diary*, December 18 (p. 108), that reports then were circulating in Philadelphia of an operation against Trenton. Robert Morris wrote Washington that he had been informed on the 21st of the General's preparations to cross into the Jerseys (Letter of Dec. 21, 1776; 3 *Force* (5), p. 1331). Nathanael Greene hinted simultaneously of plans to "give the enemy a stroke in a few days" (*ibid.*, 1342). The first observed reference in Washington's own correspondence was under date of Dec. 23, 1776, when he expressed regret that Col. Samuel Griffin was not going to Bristol "in order to have conducted matters there in cooperation with what I hinted to you as having in view here" (6 *G. W.*, 428. See *Va. Gazette*, Jan. 10, 1777 for Griffin's movements). John Armstrong stated (*Stryker*, 64), that he heard Washington and Mercer discuss general plans "at least ten days before the attack on Trenton was made"; but Armstrong wrote this down half-a-century after the event, far too late to be acceptable, though he was of course an honest witness. Robert Morris's letter of Dec. 26, 1776, to the President of Congress included what is now a warning to historical writers against any inclination to assign too early a date to a specific plan: "This maneuver of the General," said Morris, "had been determined on some days ago, but he kept it as secret as the nature of the service would permit" (3 *Force* (5), p. 1427). To repeat, the basic idea of an offensive was so obvious that it must have been considered from the very outset, and it can have been debated by courageous men in no other terms than those of ability or lack of ability to muster the required force. Details were worked out "some days" prior to Christmas. Any statement that goes beyond this, in interpretation of the existing evidence, is not history but conjecture. Washington himself remarked in October, 1778: ". . . the success of the enterprise depended too much upon the secrecy of it, not to have used every precaution for concealment" (13 *G. W.*, 108).

Regiments, to a total of about 2400 men [16] were to parade behind the low Pennsylvania hills at McKonkey's Ferry on the Delaware, approximately nine miles upstream from Trenton.[17] That same evening, Brig. Gen. James Ewing was to assemble opposite Trenton his force of New Jersey and Pennsylvania militia, who aggregated 600 to 800.[18] Farther downstream, a Pennsylvania Colonel of militia, John Cadwalader, acting Brigadier, was to bring together Continentals, State troops and Philadelphia "Associators"—all told, about 1800 men [19]—who held the line of the Delaware between Bordentown and Dunk's Ferry, near the mouth of Neshaminy Creek. Cadwalader's point of assembly was to be Bristol.[20] Washington hoped that a column might also be dispatched eastward into New Jersey from Philadelphia, which was under the command of Maj. Gen. Israel Putnam, but of this he had no positive assurance.[21]

The main force of Continentals was to cross at McKonkey's Ferry, in the boats assembled for that purpose, was to make a surprise attack at Trenton,[22] and, if successful there, was to push on to Princeton.[23] The calculation was that the passage of the river could be completed by midnight of December 25–26, and that the blow could be delivered at Trenton by 5 A.M. on the 26th.[24] Ewing, opposite the town, was to time his passage of the stream so that he could land before day dawned, and could seize the bridge over the creek at Trenton and thereby cut off the enemy's easiest line of retreat down the left bank of the Dela-

16 6 *G. W.*, 442. Other and less authoritative estimates range from 2100 (William Hull to Andrew Adams, Jan. 1, 1777; *Stryker*, 375), to "about 2500 to 3000" (Henry Knox to Mrs. Knox, Dec. 28, 1776; *ibid.*, 371).

17 *Memoir of Tench Tilghman*, 148–49. "McKonkey's" was the name of the Pennsylvania end of this ferry; "Johnson's" was the designation of the Jersey side. "John's Ferry," mentioned in Hessian reports, was "Johnson's." Confusion will be avoided if it be remembered that McKonkey's, Johnson's and John's Ferries are the same crossing. See 6 *G. W.*, 440 n.

18 *Stryker*, 82, 346–47. According to Stryker, the command of Ewing extended from Yardley's Ferry, four miles upstream from Trenton, to the ferry opposite Bordentown (*op. cit.*, 82). That is to say, Ewing was in charge of the "nose" of the Delaware to its "tip."

19 The organization of this "Division" is given in *Stryker*, 344–45. Two interesting letters from Samuel C. Morris to the Committee of Safety, from Bristol, Dec. 14 and 24, 1776, describe some of the conditions among the militia on Washington's right (5 *Penn. Arc.*, 109, 132–33). John K. M. Ewing, of Silver Springs, Md., prepared for the Camden County Historical Society an interesting MS narrative of the small action at Mount Holly, Dec. 23, 1776. This included brief extracts from the Journal of George Ewing, cited *infra*.

20 6 *G. W.*, 443.

21 See Washington to Putnam, Dec. 25, 1776; 6 *G. W.*, 440 and 1 *Reed*, 275.

22 Those who wish for the full details of what was done to collect boats and to prepare for the crossing will find them in W. H. H. Davis, "Washington on the West Bank of the Delaware, 1776" in 4 *Penn. Mag.*, 133 ff.

23 Cf. Washington to John Cadwalader, Dec. 24, 1776: ". . . if the like good fortune should attend our enterprize, either at Trenton or Princeton" (6 *G. W.*, 429).

24 *Ibid.*, 442.

ware toward Bordentown and Crosswicks.[25] Instructions to Cadwalader were less specific because Washington had some doubts concerning the cooperation that would be given by the Continentals to a Pennsylvania militia Colonel.[26] Cadwalader merely was told to pass the river, to do the best he could to occupy the enemy and, if possible, to join the main Army.[27] Detailed orders were given the general officers who were to cross with Washington,[28] and careful preparations were made, but almost before the troops were assembled, discouragements developed. From Bristol, Colonel Cadwalader already had sent warning that he could do little with the small number of men under his direct command.[29] Now Joseph Reed reported by letter on a conference he had held, at Washington's instance, with Israel Putnam. The veteran commander in Philadelphia had enlarged on the difficulties he was encountering, and had said that the utmost he could hope to accomplish on the 26th would be to throw 500 militia across the river and, with the aid of a few American troops already there, to demonstrate against the British left outposts.[30] Either Reed's language or Washing-

[25] *Ibid.*, 443.   [26] *Ibid.*, 428.   [27] *Ibid.*, 429; cf. *ibid.*, 438.

[28] Stryker, *op. cit.*, 112, repeated the tradition of a conference at Samuel Merrick's house, General Greene's headquarters, on the evening of December 24th, but he could find no documentary evidence of any formal council. The same industrious author printed (*ibid.*, 113–15), the GOs Washington issued on the 25th, but as Stryker cited no authority, other writers hesitated to print this important document. It is authentic. Parts of it circulated in Virginia. One appears in 12 *T* 106–07, another is in *Leven Powell*, 45.

[29] Cadwalader's letter of December 24 is not in the *Papers of G. W.*, but Washington's answer of Christmas Day, 6 *G. W.*, 438, makes plain the substance of what Cadwalader reported.

[30] Reed's letter to Washington has disappeared, but it probably was later and less hopeful than Reed to John Cadwalader, Dec. 25, 1776, 11 A.M., in 1 *Reed*, 275 n. The optimistic street report in Philadelphia Christmas Day was that Putnam was to proceed into Jersey on the 26th with 3000 men (*C. Marshall's Diary*, 109). Joseph Reed's participation in these events of December 22–26 has been the subject of repeated inquiry and challenge, not to say suspicion. This is to be attributed to (1) Reed's correspondence with Charles Lee, (2) the wholly unjustified accusation of George Bancroft that Reed was in communication with the enemy, for which controversy see *Stryker*, 75–78, and (3) the disposition of some of Colonel Reed's admirers to assert that he had a larger part than actually was his in the planning of the operations of December 25–26 against Trenton. In editing *G. W.*, the late J. C. Fitzpatrick imbibed this prejudice against Reed and excluded from Washington's letters one to Reed under date of Dec. 23, 1776, because, said Fitzpatrick, "it is too evidently compiled from the various authentic letters to Griffin, Cadwalader, Reed and Putnam of December 23, 24, and 25 for the purpose of connecting Reed as closely as possible with the Battle of Trenton" (6 *G. W.*, 427 n). In rejecting this letter, Fitzpatrick dissented from the judgment of Sparks, who said, "it bears the mark of being genuine." Ford did not question it. William B. Reed, grandson and biographer of Joseph Reed stated: "The original of this letter is [1847] in my possession. It was first published several years ago by Wilkinson in his Memoirs" (1 *Reed*, 275 n). As reproduced in facsimile (Smith and Watson's *American Historical and Literary Curiosities*), Washington's letter of December 23 was declared by Fitzpatrick to be "more convincing of forgery than substantiating originality." Fitzpatrick concluded: "The present whereabouts of the alleged original is undivulged" (*loc. cit.*). Other students may be permitted to dissent from the view that the alleged forgery is palpable, but as Fitzpatrick had examined more of Washington's correspondence than anyone else has, his judgment is not to be disregarded. The letter itself contains nothing in the way of historical fact that is not recorded in some form elsewhere;

ton's own interpretation of the report led the Commander-in-Chief
to doubt whether any result of immediate value would attend so contingent an enterprise as that projected from Philadelphia, but Washington did not permit this to deter him. After darkness fell and the
troops began to move toward the Ferry, Washington wrote Cadwalader: "Notwithstanding the discouraging accounts I have received
from Colonel Reed of what might be expected from the operations
below, I am determined, as the night is favorable, to cross the river
and make the attack upon Trenton in the morning." He added: "If
you can do nothing real, at least create as great a diversion as possible." [31]

A dramatic circumstance now underlined the fact that the decision
to deliver the attack without Putnam's aid had to be essentially and
almost exclusively that of Washington himself. He was preparing to
mount at his quarters, near McKonkey's Ferry, when James Wilkinson
came in and presented a paper. "What a time is this to hand me
letters!" Washington exclaimed with more of solemnity, Wilkinson
thought, than of petulance.

The young officer's apologetic answer was that he had been instructed
by General Gates to deliver the document.

"By General Gates? Where is he?"

"I left him this morning in Philadelphia."

"What was he doing there?" Washington inquired.

"I understood him that he was on his way to Congress."

Washington merely echoed, "On his way to Congress!" and then
broke the seal and read the letter.[32]

Gates was gone; Charles Lee was not there to counsel; Putnam had
lost his fighting edge; several of the senior officers who had helped to

---

consequently it has not seemed necessary to subject the document to examination by handwriting experts. It is not quoted in the present work, because it has been challenged, but it is not
repudiated as a proven forgery. Were it part of an experienced lawyer's evidence in a case, it
probably would not be presented and would be labeled "Disputed and unessential."

[31] 6 *G. W.*, 440–441.

[32] 1 *Wilkinson*, 127–28. Prof. Samuel White Patterson, in his *Horatio Gates*, 109, referred
to a letter of Washington's to Gates, Dec. 23, 1776, which letter, if authentic, would throw
doubt on the accuracy of part of this exchange between Washington and Wilkinson, because
the letter would indicate that Washington knew and reluctantly acquiesced in Gates's wish to
go to Philadelphia. No such letter as is described by Professor Patterson, who cited no authority,
is to be found in *G. W.*, in *Ford*, in *Sparks* or in the *Papers of G. W.*, LC; but precisely such
a letter was written Dec. 23, 1776, by Washington to Col. Samuel Griffin. See 6 *G. W.*, 428.
While the alleged communication from the Commander-in-Chief to Gates cannot be accepted,
for these reasons, it is distinctly in order to note that Wilkinson's narrative was written long
after the events by a man who then cherished deep animosity toward Gates.

execute the plan at Dorchester Heights nine months previously were
absent now, most notably John Thomas. In their place were a few
seniors like Hugh Mercer, who was about 52, and Lord Stirling, aged
50; but a majority of Washington's executive officers now were young
men, able and willing to lead, but, with the exception of Nathanael
Greene, not yet sufficiently matured to be of much assistance in formu-
lating sound strategic plans. At a time less tense, someone might have
found significance in the fact that if troops and guns fell into some
disorder as they converged that evening, the voice that bade one Regiment wait and another get aboard was that of a man of 26 years of
age, Henry Knox,[33] whom Washington already had recommended for
promotion to the rank of Brigadier General.[34] Youth was to carry the
American Army across the Delaware in that desperate adventure—
youth and resolution and the patience of Washington.

These qualities and every ounce of courage in the heart of man was
needed, because conditions grew worse as night went on.[35] Blocks of
ice began to float down the river, which was high and was flowing fast;
soon, too, new ice began to form;[36] the wind rose[37] and made the
handling of the long, light-draft "Durham" boats[38] difficult even for
their crews and for the trained seamen of Glover's Marblehead, Massachusetts, Regiment.[39] The loading of eighteen field cannon[40] on the

[33] 1 *Wilkinson*, 128.

[34] 6 *G. W.*, 405; letter of Dec. 20, 1776. Knox was "elected" Brigadier General of Artillery
Dec. 27, 1776. See 6 *JCC.*, 1043.

[35] For the events that follow, the prime source is Washington's brief dispatch of Dec. 27,
1776, to the President of Congress (6 *G. W.*, 441 ff). Second only to this, probably, is Henry
Knox's letter of Dec. 28, 1776, to Mrs. Knox (*Stryker*, 371–72). Stryker collected many indispensable documents and included comparatively little of doubtful authenticity. One only of his
more important papers has to be rejected as a forgery or later compilation. This is the series
of entries from an alleged "Diary of an Officer of Washington's Staff" (*ibid.*, p. 360–364). No
officer could have known as much at the time, or could have seen the relative importance of
events as clearly as this individual set everything forth. It should be said further of General
Stryker, in no derogation of his admirable service, that he accepted various old traditions
uncritically and often failed to cite authority or to state the location of documents from which
he quoted.

[36] 6 *G. W.*, 441.   [37] *Wilkinson*, 128.

[38] Stryker (*op. cit.*, 129), stated that these boats "were like large canoes, some thirty or
forty feet long, usually painted black, pointed at each end, and manned by four or five men."
Alfred H. Bill (*The Campaign of Princeton*, 1776–77, p. 29), gave this slightly different and
more elaborate description: "Ranging from forty to sixty feet in length and eight feet wide,
they drew only twenty inches when fully loaded. The largest of them could carry fifteen tons
and were capable of transporting the whole of some of Washington's little regiments in a
single trip. They had heavy steering sweeps that could be fitted at either end and were
equipped with two masts and sails and with poles to drive them against contrary winds and
currents." These boats were used ordinarily to "carry iron ore and freight between Philadelphia
and the northern counties of New Jersey" (*ibid.*, 28–29).

[39] Stryker (*op. cit.*, 134 n), quoted a tribute Henry Knox paid these men of Marblehead
in a speech delivered before the Legislature of Massachusetts.

[40] The figures are variously given; the number mentioned here is that set down by the

narrow boats was slow, slow work. At midnight, when Washington
had hoped that all his men and guns would be on the Jersey shore, the
task was hours from completion. Not until 3 A.M. on the 26th was the
last of the artillery-pieces out of the boat and safely on Jersey soil,
beyond the reach of the ice.[41] Another hour was required to put all
the Regiments at their stations within an arc that Adam Stephen's
troops had formed around the landing place.

Four o'clock, nine miles of road to cover, sunrise about 7:23, and
light by 7:10 even if the day was dark and tempestuous—in these circumstances Washington reasoned that the advantage of surprise would
certainly be lost. He could not hope that the presence of 2400 men,
eighteen cannon and a considerable number of horses would be unobserved by the Hessians long enough for the columns to reach Trenton. Should the expedition, then, be abandoned? Must the troops be
ordered back to the Pennsylvania shore? Washington asked himself
the question,[42] but he did not hesitate over the answer: His judgment
told him that the loss of the element of surprise scarcely could be worse
than the harassment and casualties involved in a retreat across the
river in the presence of the enemy. The advance must be made, and the
Hessians must be assailed the moment the town was reached.[43]

In that spirit, the Army pressed on. At Birmingham,[44] John Sullivan
took about half the troops and cannon and started down the lower or
River Road which followed, as its name suggested, the general course
of the Delaware. Nathanael Greene, with a like force, filed off to the
left and took the upper or Pennington Road.[45] Washington soon
joined Greene. As closely as the commanding General could estimate
it, the two columns now had nearly the same distance to march—
between four and five miles [46]—to the little town of Trenton.[47] He
consequently had all the officers set their watches by his [48] and he gave
orders that when either column struck the Hessian outposts, it was to
press forward immediately, without waiting to hear from the other

---

man best qualified to know—Henry Knox. See his letter of Dec. 28, 1776, to Mrs. Knox
(*Stryker*, 371; original in MHS.).
    [41] 6 *G. W.*, 442.   [42] *Ibid*.
    [43] *Ibid*.
    [44] According to *Stryker*, 142, with no citation of authority concerning the point at which
the Army was divided.
    [45] On Erskine's map of 1777, Pennington is spelled Pennytown.
    [46] *Stryker*, 143.   [47] 6 *G. W.*, 442.
    [48] Capt. William Hull to Andrew Adams, Jan. 1, 1777; *Stryker*, 375.

column, and was to push into Trenton before the enemy had time to form line of battle.[49]

A light snow had covered the ground when the Army left camp;[50] the wind had risen during the crossing and was roaring angrily down from East Northeast.[51] Now, with the approach of dawn, snow began to descend again.[52] With it was mingled sleet or rain that froze and glazed the road. A more difficult time for a march over an unfamiliar route could not have been devised by the devil himself; it was a night when the indifferent soldier would cover his head with his blanket, and the mercenary would hug the fire.[53] Strong and stern would be the discipline that would carry German patrols over roads on which an icy surface was deeper and more slippery every minute.[54]

Day began to dawn when the column of Greene was still two miles from Trenton.[55] Soon Washington noticed that Greene's advance had halted and he went forward to ascertain the reason. Through the pale light, he saw ahead a narrow stretch of lane and on one side of it, a small Company of men in a field. Before Washington could identify them, word was passed that they were Americans. What were they doing there? Washington must know. Riding on, he called for the commanding officer. A Captain stepped up and introduced himself as Richard Anderson of the Fifth Virginia, Stephen's Brigade. Where had he been? The young man explained that General Stephen had sent him to the left bank Christmas Day to reconnoitre and had told him that, if he could not find the enemy elsewhere, he was to go to Trenton and was to ascertain the location of the enemy's outpost, but that he must exercise care and must not bring on an engagement. Anderson told the commanding General that he had carried out his orders and had just been to the Trenton outpost where his men had encountered and had shot down a sentinel who apparently had not

[49] 6 *G. W.*, 442.

[50] 1 *Wilkinson*, 127. This snow, said Wilkinson, "was tinged here and there with blood from the feet of the men who wore broken shoes."

[51] *Stryker*, 139, with no citation of authority.

[52] So asserted Wilkinson (*op. cit.*, v. 1, p. 128); Thomas Rodney (*Stryker*, 133) stated that the snow began at 11 P.M. where he was.

[53] The storm must have covered a considerable area. Ambrose Serle noted (*Diary*, 163) that the 26th was "a most tempestuous day of rain, frost, wind and snow" in New York.

[54] "Extract of Letter from an Officer of Distinction . . . at Newtown, Bucks County, Pennsylvania, dated December 27, 1776." Stryker, in reprinting this (*op. cit.*, 367–68), stated that it was "generally believed to be by Brigadier General Lord Stirling" and that it was "published by the Council of Safety." This is not the same document as an "Extract of a Letter from an Officer in the American Army, dated Newtown, (in Pennsylvania), December 27, 1776," which will be found in 3 *Force* (5), p. 1442–43

[55] "Officer of Distinction," as above; *Stryker*, 367.

seen them in the storm until the moment they caught sight of the Hessian. Thereupon, said Captain Anderson, he had started back on the road to McKonkey's Ferry.

Adam Stephen was at hand when the Captain reported. Washington turned on the Brigadier in wrath he did not attempt to conceal: How had Stephen dared send a patrol across the river, the day before the expedition started, when he had not asked or received authority to do so? "You, sir," Washington cried, "may have ruined all my plans by having put them on their guard!" It was almost as if Fate had brought Stephen to the Delaware to mock him—Stephen, his one-time political rival who had been suspected, in the old days, of making theatrical moves of no military value.[56] The Brigadier had, of course, no answer. Washington tightened instantly the curb on his temper and spoke quietly to Anderson: The Captain and his men must be fatigued after their hard service; they must proceed with the vanguard so that they would not have the waits the troops farther back on the road had to endure.[57]

This colloquy did not consume many of the precious moments of dawn, but the Pennington Road now was so heavily covered with sleet and frozen rain that the advance became a slow, treacherous slide and stagger. It was half an hour after daylight when Greene's van was at a point the guides reckoned as one mile from the town.[58] As the enemy's advanced guard was believed to be about half-a-mile from Trenton, on either road, Washington had now to halt and to prepare himself and his men for the execution within 800 yards, or thereabouts,

[56] See Vol. III, p. 98; 2 G. W., 404.

[57] The original source of this long-familiar incident was nothing more than a memorandum, written almost a century after the event, by Anderson's son, Gen. Robert Anderson, renowned for his defence of Fort Sumter. The paper is reproduced in Stryker, 373–74; and, late as it is, it has been accepted as essentially valid. It is a young man's recollection of an elder's statement of an incident that was of a sort to have burned itself in the memory of a young, intelligent Captain of 1776. As it happens, some of the main facts, as they relate to Stephen, can be verified in part by a letter from Adam Stephen to his manager, Jonathan Seaman, Jan. 5, 1777 (Adam Stephen Papers, LC). In a careless reference to the advance on Trenton, Stephen said: "The Hessians killed a man of my brigade in a rout—On Christmas day I sent Captain Wall with a party to take revenge. He attacked the enemy's outguard in the evening—killed four and brought off their arms and wounded ten." Stephen's figures are contrary to the German report, which doubtless is authentic, of six wounded and none killed (Stryker, 117–18). Again, it will be noted that Stephen says the commander of this party was "Captain Wall," not Captain Anderson; but so far as Heitman is a safe guide—and he usually is—Stephen had no officer named Wall in his Brigade or, later, in his Division. It is possible Stephen meant to write Wallace, instead of Wall, because there was a Lieut. Adam Wallace in the Seventh Virginia and a Capt. Gustavus Wallace in the Third Virginia, both of which Regiments belonged to Stephen's Brigade. Capt. Richard C. Anderson was of the Fifth Virginia, also of Stephen's Brigade.

[58] Henry Knox to Mrs. Knox, Dec. 28, 1776; Stryker, 371.

of the first of the three phases of his plan.[59] This simple design was based on the geographical position of Trenton and on the configuration of its few streets. The town was a poor place of about 100 houses, the greater part of them abandoned temporarily by their owners,[60] and it was located at the point where the Delaware makes a minor turn from Southeast to South. Across the lower edge of the town, the Assunpink Creek flowed into the river from the Northeast.[61] The depth of the water in this creek varied from time to time and from one part of the stream to another; but, in general, the creek was not safely to be crossed except at the bridge. North from the bridge, Queen Street ran for approximately half a mile to the angle of the road that came down from Pennington, which was to the Northwest.[62] King Street, the other principal driveway of the village, was West of Queen, was parallel to it, and had its northern terminus at the same place, the mouth of the Pennington Road. Washington knew that if he could reach and hold the head of these streets, he could sweep them and probably could drive the enemy from them. If, simultaneously, he could seize the bridge across Assunpink, he might be able to trap the Hessians within the half-mile space between the bridge and the Pennington Road. Then a strong thrust from the West, perpendicular to the two streets, might throw the enemy back to the creek. Thus were the strokes to be one, two, three, and as close together as they could be delivered.

Nothing had been heard of General Ewing, who was to cross directly opposite Trenton and was to seize the Assunpink bridge from its southern end; but there was good news and bad from Sullivan's column. It was good in that it brought assurance Sullivan was moving on steadily and without opposition; it was bad in that the New Hampshire General reported his men's muskets wet and unfit for service. Washington's answer was that Sullivan must "advance and charge." [63] The General himself pushed on in Greene's van, through the unrelenting storm, with the men at a "long trot" [64] and about 8 o'clock he left

---

[59] *Ibid.* In a most informative letter of Dec. 29, 1776, to Leven Powell, the discerning George Johnston, usually quite accurate, said that the halt was within 500 yards of the advanced guard (*Leven Powell*, 41).

[60] Hessian Soldier's Diary, published in *Penn. Evening Post*, July 26, 1777, and reprinted in *Stryker*, 483.

[61] The upper stretches of Assunpink are more nearly from East to West. Several variants of the spelling of the name "Assunpink" occur but modern usage, which is followed here, has as many precedents as the more familiar "Assinpink."

[62] Correctly speaking, NNW.

[63] 1 *Wilkinson*, 129.

[64] George Johnston as cited *supra*, n. 59.

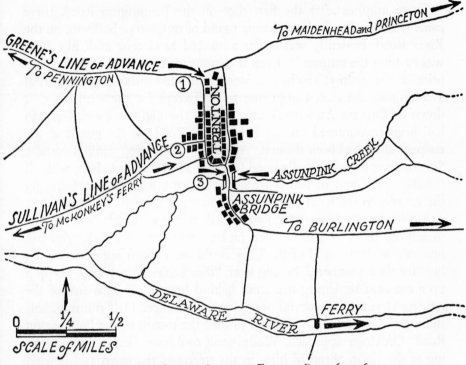

PLAN OF THE SURPRISE ATTACK ON TRENTON, DEC. 26, 1776.

The columns were to deliver the one-two-three blows in succession, to drive the Hessians from the shelter of Trenton houses and to cut off the enemy's retreat by seizing the bridge across the Assunpink. This sketch is adapted from Fischer's map, *infra*, p. 319.

the woods on the Pennington Road at a point about half-a-mile from the village.[65] Ahead was a cooper's shop which, guides said, the Germans were using as an advanced picket post. In a few moments, the Americans were challenged; there were shouts and commands; almost a score of Hessians emerged from the building. The Continentals opened fire at once, though the range was overlong; the officer in charge of the post waited until Washington's men were closer. Then, at the word of command, the Germans delivered a volley which went wild in the roaring storm. Without making any pretence of further resistance at their advanced post, the pickets fell back to the eastward across the fields.[66]

[65] That is to say, about 850 yards from the mouth of the Pennington Road at the head of Queen Street.
[66] Diary of Lieut. Andreas Wiederhold, commander of the picket post, summarized in *Stryker*, 147.

Three minutes after the first shot on the Pennington Road, there came from the South the welcome sound of musketry. Sullivan, on the River Road, evidently was as far advanced as Greene and, like him, was rushing the outpost.[67] Even if there was not to be a complete surprise of the enemy, resolution, storm and circumstance were giving Washington the closest approach to it. Except for the sentinels shot down by Captain Anderson's men during the night, not one German had been encountered on the Pennington Road till the guard at the cooper's shop had been flushed. As far as Washington could ascertain, Sullivan was having equally good fortune. Push forward, then, with all possible speed and in fullest strength; lose not a minute in hurrying the cannon to the head of King and Queen Streets.

As Washington moved down the Pennington Road, he observed something more of the Hessian pickets' withdrawal and he did not underestimate the skill of it. They could offer slight opposition only, but "for their numbers," he said later, "they behaved very well, keeping up a constant retreating fire from behind houses." [68] This fire of the retiring German outpost did not delay the advance. Half running, half sliding, the Americans continued toward the mouth of the Pennington Road. On closer approach, Washington could see the Germans forming to the right, ahead of him, in the streets of the town and beyond to the eastward, but he could not ascertain what they were attempting to do.[69] A few minutes more, and Washington was on high ground whence he could view almost the whole of Trenton.[70] He stopped

[67] 6 *G. W.*, 442. Sullivan encountered the enemy at The Hermitage, Gen. Philemon Dickinson's place on the River Road (*Stryker*, 150). Wilkinson recorded (*op. cit.*, v. 1, p. 128) that Sullivan had been ordered "to halt a few minutes at the cross road, which leads to Howell's Ferry." This was done in order to afford Greene time to catch up. George Johnston wrote Leven Powell (*loc. cit.*) that Greene and Sullivan reached "their respective posts within five minutes of each other, though they had parted four miles from the town and had taken different routes."

[68] 6 *G. W.*, 442.

[69] Cf. Washington to the President of Congress, Dec. 27, 1776: "We presently saw their main body formed, but from their motions they seemed undetermined how to act" (*ibid.*). There follow in the draft of this dispatch two long sentences in which an effort was made to describe what the Germans did and how the Americans balked them. These sentences, like the rest of the draft, are in the autograph of Tench Tilghman; but they were stricken out, as if Washington himself was doubtful of their accuracy (*ibid.*, 442–43 n). This excision and the language of the final text justify the inference that when Washington wrote, the day after the action, he was not certain about some of the details of the engagement.

[70] Stryker (*op. cit.*, 159) identified the site as "on what is now Princeton Avenue, opposite Fountain Avenue . . ." Queen is the present-day Broad Street, Trenton, and King is Warren Street. See A. H. Bill, *op. cit.*, 75. The map on page 319 is one of three drawn by Hessian officers and reproduced by Stryker, *op. cit.*, 124, 126, 128. Although these maps differ in minor typographical detail and in the number of tactical maneuvers entered on them, they are substantially the same map or else are based on a common lost original.

the "long trot" of the infantry and bade them form, in order to give more room to the artillerists of the two leading cannon who were straining to bring the pieces into position. Their comrades with the other advanced guns were scarcely behind hand. From the front of the Second Brigade of Greene's column, three other pieces were being dragged forward as rapidly as the way could be cleared for them.[71] At a time so tense, every movement seemed clumsy and exasperatingly slow; but in reality, the well-drilled and enthusiastic artillerists lost few seconds. Their great moment had come. They knew it. Soon the "b-o-o-m" of the opening gun shook the heavy air. The second shot followed on the instant.[72] Fire itself was a triumph, regardless of target, because vigilance and resourcefulness had been required every minute in order to protect the touch-holes of the cannon from the wet. The Americans had discovered how this could be done. Soon their round shot would be shrieking down King and Queen Streets.

Visibility was so low at times that Washington probably could see nothing of what was happening at the farther end of those streets, where Sullivan was attacking. It was impossible, as yet, to tell whether Ewing had crossed and now commanded the Assunpink Bridge. Nearer at hand, directly West of the buildings that faced East on King Street, Hugh Mercer's men of Greene's command were closing in. Some of them were breaking into houses the enemy held; some were slipping through alleys and walkways and were directing their fire against Germans along the street and beyond it, in the direction of the creek. The Hessians soon undertook to answer the artillery fire by moving cannon into King Street; but these soldiers could be left to the attention of Knox's men and to the care of Stirling's troops who were eager to dash forward and to take the guns. Washington must keep his eye on the larger moves and must ascertain, if he could, what those confused though still powerful mercenaries were going to attempt. For a few minutes it looked as if the enemy might make a bold charge up King Street,[73] but this was broken up easily by the American artil-

---

71 Cf. George Johnston's letter to Leven Powell, *loc. cit.,* and the GOs of Dec. 25, 1776.

72 The anonymous author, presumably Stirling, quoted in *Stryker,* 367, is authority for the statement "we soon got two field-pieces at play, and several others in a short time . . ." Henry Knox said only that his men took possession of the heads of the streets "with cannon and howitzers" (Letter of Dec. 28, 1776, to Mrs. Knox; *ibid.,* 371–72).

73 *Stryker,* 161, on the basis of testimony at the Hessian courtmartial, January, 1782. These proceedings of the military tribunal are the source from which far more has been established regarding the movements of the Hessians in this action than has been preserved concerning the Americans.

HESSIAN GRAPHIC VERSION OF BATTLE
OF TRENTON, DEC. 26, 1776

Three Hessian officers made maps of the scene of
their humiliating defeat on the Delaware. The maps
had a common lost original or else were revised copies
of one or another of the trio. General W. S. Stryker
unearthed the manuscripts and reproduced them in his
Battles of Trenton and Princeton. The one here reprinted from that work, p. 129, was by Lieut. Friedrich
Fischer and was regarded by Stryker as the best of the
series. A non-existent church was placed by Fischer
near the bank of the Assumpink. The Lieutenant's explanation, as translated in Stryker, was as follows:

A. Advance of the provincial troops from John's
[the American force did not cross at Johnson's, but at
McKonkey's] Ferry in two columns. B. Advance on

picket a and Captain von Altenbockum's company **b.**
C. Attack on Trenton after the retreat of the picket
and Captain von Altenbockum's company, and also the
captain's picket c, to Trenton. D. March of the provincial troops in battalion formation. E. March of the
Hessian regiments after leaving Trenton. F. Attack
of the von Lossberg and Rall regiments on Trenton.
G. Provincial troops guarding the bridge. H. Retreat
of the von Knyphausen regiment at the time of the
attack on the von Lossberg and Rall regiments. J. Surrender of the von Lossberg and Rall regiments. K.
Attack on J by the provincial troops. L. Attack on H
after the surrender of the von Lossberg and Rall regiments. M. Provincial artillery. N. Rall cannon which
were at once silenced. R. Von Knyphausen cannon.
S. Von Lossberg cannon. T. Commands which retreated to Burlington. [The church is erased.]

318

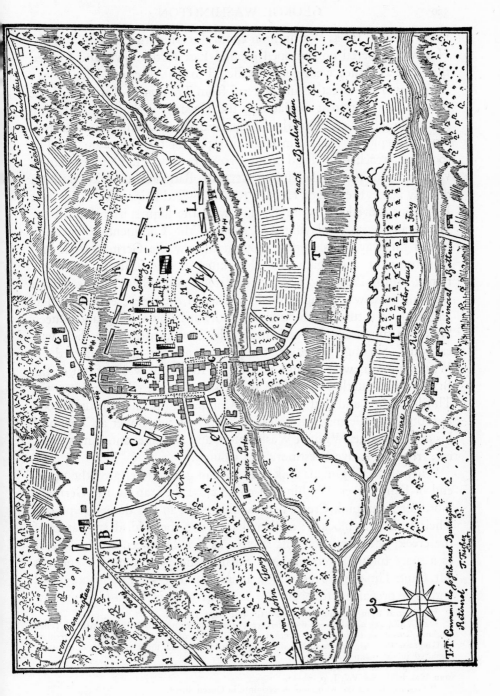

lery. Then, as far as Washington could discern, larger numbers of the Hessians gathered on the open ground East of the town and formed their line as if they were going to file off to the American left.

That was the direction of the road from Trenton to Princeton,[74] the only avenue of retreat available to the Hessians if Sullivan or Ewing by this time had occupied the bridge across the Assunpink. Washington had deployed his left in front of a part of the Princeton Road as soon as he reached the head of the streets; he now sent Colonel Hand's veterans and the Philadelphia German Battalion to take position directly across the line of Hessian retreat toward Princeton.[75] The two Battalions moved out promptly and with the high spirits that all the Americans were displaying. As soon as the Continentals' bayonets barred the way, Washington thought he saw the Germans halt and then begin to shift again as if they knew it was futile to attempt a retreat up the Princeton Road. They stood now where the sleet from the Northeast was flying in their faces, and they were exposing their left flank to a turning movement southward down King and Queen Streets in support of Mercer's men, who continued to fight their way eastward. Stirling's impatient troops were allowed to go forward. If Washington knew at the moment which Regiment was in front of the Brigade, he doubtless had pride in the fact that the command was the Third Virginia and that the leading Company, the one that undertook to capture the German cannon in King Street, was under a Captain of his own surname, William Washington, and a Lieutenant, James Monroe, from his native Westmoreland County.[76]

When these Virginians took the German guns and cleared the upper end of King Street, Washington could close the trap on the Germans North of Assunpink Creek, because they were in this desperate plight: Their front was blocked; at their back were the cold, deep waters of the creek, which ran, on this stretch, as if it had been set by Nature as a snare for molesters. Besides Stirling and Mercer on the enemy's left, Capt. Thomas Forrest was in an advanced position with six guns [77] and was preparing to open fire at shorter range. Washington saw

[74] The road from Pennington led into the one from Trenton.

[75] 6 G. W., 443 n. Although the reference to these two commands is in that part of Tench Tilghman's draft that Washington struck from his dispatch of Dec. 27, 1776, to the President of Congress, there is no reason for doubting that Hand's and the German Battalion were employed in the manner indicated.

[76] Stryker, 164. It will be recalled that the family of President Monroe had resided not far from Wakefield. See Vol. I, p. 51–52.

[77] Presumably, but not with absolute certainty in Queen Street.

the trap shut. Perhaps, too, he observed an American officer ride out to a parley with the German commanders. Then, presently, up the street spurred a young soldier who drew rein and cried rapturously that German Regiments in the field had surrendered.[78]

How numerous they were, Washington did not know; but something the officer said, or else the sound of firing from the vicinity of the bridge led him to believe that Sullivan's column still was fighting. So, wasting neither time nor words, Washington started down King Street, astride his horse, to see for himself what was happening. About half-way to the bridge he came upon some Germans who were assisting a badly wounded officer into a church.[79] Inquiry doubtless brought the explanation that this was Col. Johann Rall, senior officer in the town.[80] At the very moment that the humiliated and suffering Hessian commander was being led away, a prisoner of war, a young American Major came up the street as fast as his horse would venture on so slippery a roadway. He was James Wilkinson, who had brought Washington the previous evening the letter from Gates. This time, Wilkinson represented General Sullivan and carried the best of news: Another Hessian Regiment, the last in the town, had grounded arms. Washington's face shone with satisfaction as he listened. He extended his hand in thanks. "Major Wilkinson," he said, "this is a glorious day for our country."[81]

[78] The anonymous officer, whose letter was published by the Pennsylvania Council of Safety, stated that as he "came in full view of [the Hessians], from the back of the wood, with his Excellency, General Washington, an officer informed [the Commander in-Chief] that the party had grounded their arms and surrendered prisoners" (*Stryker*, 368). General Stryker was of opinion (*op. cit.*, 181–82) that the officer who brought Washington the news of the German surrender was George Baylor. As Washington the next day bestowed on Baylor a special honor which suggested that the young Virginian had distinguished himself, it is entirely possible that Baylor's particular exploit had been that he induced these two German Regiments to surrender when they did, but no positive evidence of this has been found. It should be added that Capt. Thomas Forrest was quoted as saying, long afterward, that Washington was near him during the retreat of the Germans and gave him an order to change to cannister. Forrest answered, "Sir, they have struck." Washington echoed, "Struck?" "Yes," Forrest replied, "their colors are down." Washington said, "So they are" and started immediately toward the enemy's line. Forrest and his men followed. (1 *Wilkinson*, 129–30 n). Unfortunately for a good tale, if Forrest previously "had come down from the head of Queen Street" as Stryker asserted (*op. cit.*, 180), the Captain could not have been at the place where Washington is said to have received word of the two Regiments' surrender. One story or the other has to be discarded. The report that Forrest had moved down the street seems the more probable.

[79] Doubtless under American guard.

[80] 1 *Wilkinson*, 131. The name of the German commander is spelled in many ways, because Americans were not sure of the phonetic value of the broad "a." In his report, Washington wrote it correctly Rall and, a few sentences later, spoke of the wounded man's Regiment as Rohl's (6 *G. W.*, 443). Stryker (*op. cit.*, 41) gave the numerous variants and pointed out that, where it was attached to an official paper, reproduced on p. 24, the name plainly was Rall.

[81] 1 *Wilkinson*, 131.

It was victory! In the most desperate hour of the life of the Army, less than a week from its virtual disbandment, the Continentals had won their greatest success. Ewing had not been able to cross at Trenton ferry because of the ice;[82] at that hour, nothing had been heard from Cadwalader. The troops who had operated under Washington, and they alone, had defeated a force that consisted, prisoners said, of three German Regiments. Some of those Hessians had retreated from their posts near the river bank; still others had escaped by crossing the Assunpink Bridge or by wading, neck high, through the icy waters. These men had gone down the Bordentown Road, presumably to join the Hessian forces there. Residents also told Washington's officers that a troop of twenty British Light Dragoons, on duty at Trenton, had disappeared without striking a blow.[83] How the Hessians had permitted themselves to be surprised, nobody was able as yet to explain,[84] otherwise than by saying that wind and rain and sleet had drowned all sound of firing at the picket posts; but however that might be, American losses had been negligible. Both the young officers, Capt. William Washington and Lieut. James Monroe, had been wounded in leading the charge on the cannon in King Street; one or two privates likewise had been hit, though not fatally so.[85] In the whole engagement, from first contact at 8 A.M. to final surrender before 10 o'clock,[86] not one American life had been lost.[87]

Washington had now to decide whether he could follow up this lucky success. Manifestly, the prisoners must be marched to McKonkey's Ferry, must be rowed to the Pennsylvania side of the Delaware, and then must be placed where they could not be rescued. It would be politic, too, to treat them with consideration and thereby, perhaps, to

[82] Cf. Washington to the President of Congress, Dec. 27, 1776; 6 G. W., 443: ". . . the quantity of ice was so great that, though he did everything in his power to effect it, he could not get over."

[83] Stryker remarked, op. cit., 188: "In no published history of the fight and in no manuscript records can the slightest mention be found of any effort of these men to repel the hostile army."

[84] Von Donop is authority for the statement that the sound of outpost action was inaudible. See 62 Penn. Mag., 495–96. As Washington could not have had time to establish even the main facts until the close of these operations, the critique of Trenton is deferred and is made part of the general review of the campaign, infra, p. 375 ff.

[85] 6 G. W., 443, 446.

[86] See Stryker, 187, for various estimates of the length of time. General Stryker inferred that thirty to forty-five minutes elapsed between the opening gun at the head of the streets and the "cease fire" of Sullivan's command.

[87] Washington wrote Dec. 27, 1776, that a "private or two" had been killed, but on the 28th he returned, in effect, to his first statement that none had been slain (6 G. W., 446, 448).

wean them from the British.[88] Those Hessians who were badly wounded should be paroled and left in the village.[89] Beyond this, what? Manifestly, Ewing and Cadwalader had not been able to traverse the river, though the reasons for their failure to do so were not yet plain. In the absence of these flanking forces, all the Hessians East and Southeast of Trenton could be brought together to challenge any move Washington might make. The number of these Germans he believed to exceed that of his own force. Besides, there had been no contradiction of intelligence reports which indicated that a strong British Battalion was stationed at Princeton. To undertake a new advance with British to the North and Hessians to the East and Southeast obviously involved so many hazards that Washington thought he should consult his general officers.[90] In doing this, he had, of course, to take into account the condition of his troops. They had done all that could have been asked of them, but they were cold, wet and weary. Officers promptly stove in forty hogsheads of rum they found in the town,[91] and in that way they kept the men from getting hopelessly drunk; but some of the soldiers found liquor and drank so heavily that they would not be of any service in an early encounter with the enemy.[92] Still again, the storm was continuing and the temperature was low. If the ice in the river increased, but did not become heavy enough to support troops and wagons, how could the American Regiments be victualled? Hessian provisions at Trenton would not suffice. They and the other stores were, in fact, of no consequence.[93] When all these adverse factors were weighed, the conclusion of the Generals was that of Washington himself: Cannon and small arms and spoils must be sent across the Delaware along with the prisoners; the American Regiments must retrace their steps and,

[88] 6 *G. W.*, 453; Clement Biddle to the Committee of Safety, Dec. 28, 1776; *Stryker*, 369–70; proclamation of the Penn. Council of Safety, Dec. 31, 1776; *ibid*, 395.

[89] The tradition is that Washington and Nathanael Greene visited Rall, who died of his wounds on the evening of the 27th. It would have accorded with Washington's general treatment of captured officers for him to have done what he could for the German commander, but there is no contemporary American evidence to sustain the tradition. If General Stryker uncovered anything on this point in the courtmartial proceedings, he did not cite it specifically.

[90] No minutes of a formal council of war have been found, but both the "notes" subsequently collected by Reed (*Stryker*, 206), and the closing lines of Washington's letter of Dec. 27, 1776, to Robert Morris (6 *G. W.*, 441), are proof that the Commander-in-Chief conferred with his Generals.

[91] 3 *Force* (5), p. 1443.

[92] Cf. Joseph Reed's notes in *Stryker*, 206. It was to this intoxication, no doubt, that Washington referred when he wrote Congress, Dec. 29, 1776 that "another reason . . . might be mentioned" for his decision to withdraw (6 *G. W.*, 452).

[93] The words are Washington's own. See *ibid.*, 444.

for the moment, must not take the chance of losing much by seeking more.[94]

The withdrawal was effected but it was slower and even more painful than the advance had been, both because the men were close to exhaustion and because they had to care for their prisoners and their booty. "We . . . did not get to our tents," one young Captain wrote, "till next morning—two nights and a day in as violent a storm as ever I felt." He hurried on to add, "What can't men do when engaged in so noble a cause?"[95]

Tribute to this spirit was the strongest note in the "victory dispatch" that Washington had Tench Tilghman draft as soon as possible after the General and his staff were back in Pennsylvania on the 27th. "I have the pleasure of congratulating you," the General began, "upon the success of an enterprise which I had formed against a detachment of the enemy lying in Trenton, and which was executed yesterday morning." He described what had happened and expressed belief that the inability of Ewing and Cadwalader to get their men across the river in the prevailing severe weather had been the only reason the British had not been driven "from all their posts below Trenton." Thereupon he explained why he had returned to the southern side of the Delaware, and next he paid homage to the Army: "In justice to the officers and men, I must add that their behavior upon this occasion reflects the highest honor upon them. The difficulty of passing the river in a very severe night, and their march through a violent storm of snow and hail did not in the least abate their ardor. But when they came to the charge, each seemed to vie with the other in pressing forward, and were I to give a preference to any particular Corps, I should do great injustice to the others."[96]

The paper was signed and sealed and doubtless delivered to the waiting messenger by the same hand that had written nine days previously: ". . . if every nerve is not strained to recruit the new Army with all possible expedition, I think the game is pretty near up . . ."[97]

---

[94] Washington's explanation of his withdrawal is given succinctly in Reed's "notes," *loc. cit.*, and in several of Washington's letters of Dec. 27 and 29, 1776. See 6 *G. W.*, 441, 444, 446, 452.

[95] Capt. William Hull to Andrew Adams, Jan. 1, 1777; *Stryker*, 376.

[96] 6 *G. W.*, 444. The honor of delivering this "victory dispatch" was given George Baylor (*ibid.*), who had distinguished himself at Trenton (See *supra*, n. 78).

[97] Letter of Dec. 18, 1776, to John Augustine Washington; 6 *G. W.*, 398 and *supra*, p. 295.

CHAPTER XIII

AUDENTES FORTUNA IUVAT
(December 27, 1776–January 6, 1777)

WHEN ENCAMPED near army headquarters at Newtown, Bucks County,[1] and listed by rank, the well-knit, athletic German prisoners[2] ran to totals the Americans never before had captured—thirty officers, ninety-two nco's, twenty-nine miscellaneous individuals—surgeons' mates, drummers and musicians—740 rank and file, and twenty-five servants —a total of 918.[3] German dead were estimated as "about twenty-five or thirty." [4]

Resolution to exploit those advantages shaped Washington's congratulatory orders, issued the day his "victory dispatch" was written: "The General with the utmost sincerity and affection, thanks the officers and soldiers for their gallant and spirited behavior at Trenton yesterday. It is with inexpressible pleasure that he can declare that he did not see a single instance of bad behavior in either officers or privates; [5] and that if any fault could be found, it proceeded from a too great eagerness to push forward upon the enemy. Much! very much indeed, is it to be lamented that when men are brought to play the part of soldiers thus well, that any of them, for the sake of a little temporary ease, should think of abandoning the cause of liberty and their country at so important a crisis. As a reward to the officers and soldiers for their spirited behavior in such inclement weather, the General will (in behalf of the Continent) have all the field pieces, the arms and accoutrements, horses

[1] Diary of Lieut. James McMichael, 15 *Penn. Arc.* (2), p. 203; Clement Biddle to the Committee of Safety, Dec. 28, 1776; *Stryker*, 369.

[2] Samuel Richards had said in his *Diary*, 42, that the first Hessian prisoners captured in the autumn of 1776 "were well built young men, very athletic."

[3] 6 *G. W.*, 443, 447. In this initial listing, the total was incorrectly given as 919. The figures include the wounded officers and men paroled in Trenton.

[4] *Ibid.*, 447. Actually, according to the Hessian lists summarized in *Stryker*, 195, five officers, including Rall, and seventeen men were killed. Six officers and seventy-eight men were wounded. The total of killed and wounded thus was 106. The Hessian commanding General, Leopold von Heister, later computed at 292 the number who escaped. Stryker's researches led him to give the larger total of 412 (*op. cit.*, 188 n).

[5] Cf. George Weedon to John Page, Dec. 29, 1776: "The behavior of our people in general far exceeded anything seen. It's worth remembering that not one officer or private was known that day to turn his back . . ." (*Chicago HS.* MSS).

and everything else which was taken yesterday, valued and a proportionate distribution of the amount made among the officers (if they choose to partake) and the men who crossed the river. The Commissary is strictly ordered to provide rum for the troops that it may be served out as occasion shall require." [6]

These, surely, were terms on which, as soon as tired, hungry soldiers refreshed themselves, they would contract to deliver the second blow that Congress and the country expected of them.[7] Somehow, too, at the moment, the prospect of reenforcement seemed brighter: the Regiment of Light Horse soon would arrive from Virginia;[8] Benedict Arnold probably would push forward from the Hudson some of those intelligent New England militiamen;[9] perhaps a few would be raised now in New Jersey.[10] The revival of hope in Philadelphia was instant. "This affair," wrote John Nicholson, "has given such amazing spirit to our people that you might do any thing or go any where with them." [11] Immediately on receipt of indirect news of the victory at Trenton, the President of the Pennsylvania Council of Safety wrote to the Congress in Baltimore: "We are sending off reenforcements of militia, in hopes this very important blow may be followed up. The great advantage which will arise to our cause must be apparent. Our militia were turning out by degres, but this will give them a new stimulus . . ." [12] Those who already had assembled on the Delaware, near Bristol, were awaiting the orders of Col. John Cadwalader.

That officer had Joseph Reed and Thomas Mifflin to assist him, but he was displaying on his own account bold and intelligent leadership. On Washington's table, December 27—the day after the fight at Trenton—were two letters, dated the 25th and 26th, that Cadwalader had written him. One gave details of the failure on Christmas Day—how it

[6] GOs of Dec. 27, 1776; *Leven Powell*, 44.

[7] See J. Cadwalader to Washington, Dec. 27, 1776; 1 *Reed*, 281; Comm. of Congress to Washington, Dec. 28, 1776, 3 *Force* (5), p. 1458–60; Stirling to Gov. William Livingston, Dec. 28, 1777, *ibid.*, 1462–63.

[8] 6 *G. W.*, 456–57.

[9] Washington to Heath, Dec. 27, 1776 (*ibid.*, 445), and Heath to Washington, Dec. 28, 1776 (3 *Force* (5), p. 1464–66) are the background of Arnold's letter of that date to Heath (*ibid.*, 1460).

[10] 6 *G. W.*, 449, 450, 455, 460.

[11] Letter of Dec. 27, 1776, to Samuel Purviance, Jr. (3 *Force* (5), p. 1440). The date of this letter may be inaccurate, because it is difficult to believe so much would be known in Philadelphia as is here set forth on the 27th of events of the 26th at Trenton.

[12] Letter of Thomas Wharton, Jr., Dec. 27, 1776; *ibid.* Several other expressions of the same nature might be added, but nearly all of them are dated somewhat later and were colored by events subsequent to Jan. 1, 1777.

had been impossible to land artillery in Jersey after dark, because of the ice. Infantry who had been put ashore on the left bank consequently had been returned to Dunk's Ferry, whence the crossing had been undertaken. Washington already knew the essential facts, but the concluding sentences of the letter had new ideas that displayed a firm spirit: Calwalader proposed that he ferry the Delaware farther downstream and there effect a junction with the troops Putnam was expected to land in Jersey in order to reenforce the militia of that State left at Black Horse by Colonel Griffin. Combined, said Cadwalader, these men "would make a formidable body—this would cause a diversion that would favor any attempt you may design in future and would expose their baggage and stores if they attempt to cross." Cadwalader took care to explain: "It is impossible in our present situation to cooperate with General Putnam. The militia will be easier kept together by being in motion and we shall have some service from Col. Hitchcock's [New England continental] Brigade, whose time of enlistment will be up in a few days. We have procured a considerable number of shoes, stockings and breeches for them. They are in good spirits and enlist very fast." [13]

This was not such a letter as the average Brigadier of militia wrote in an hour of danger and perplexity. Cadwalader's second communication, that of the 26th, was equally bold: He was going to cross on the 27th, he said, and if Washington would send part of the main Army to Crosswicks, "we might perfectly surround the troops at Bordentown, so as to prevent one man escaping." Cadwalader talked, also, of the ease with which a force of 200 at White Hill might be captured. "If possible," the Pennsylvanian went on, "I should be glad to hear from you before we set out." Then he spoke of 1800 Jersey and Pennsylvania militia who were or soon would be in that part of New Jersey, South of Bordentown.[14]

Here was a challenge. Instead of exhorting the militia commander to bestir himself, Washington had to match Cadwalader's offer, but as soon as the General began to consider ways and means of doing this, difficulties eclipsed hopes. The Continentals had lost two nights' sleep and had to be rested before they could be trusted in action again.[15] Bad management and worse weather had so nearly emptied the commissary

---

[13] 38 *Papers of G. W.*, 19, LC.
[14] *Cadwalader Papers*, PHS.
[15] 6 *G. W.*, 447, 449.

that instead of the reward of abundant food, the men had short rations. This, of course, had to be corrected: well-warmed stomachs alone could endure a Jersey January,[16] but, here again, the clock was hostile. Under the best of kitchen generalship, rested men could not be given the contented vigor of strong meat until the 29th or 30th of December—within two days, or even one, of the time when, by every precedent of the Army, the greater number of the soldiers who finished their term of service would stack their arms and start home. If that happened, Washington would be almost as badly crippled as before the victory at Trenton. Only the Pennsylvania militia down the river and the skeleton of the Virginia Regiments would be left to face Howe, his Guards, his Grenadiers and his Hessians.

Had ever a commander, even of a revolutionary army, been tortured in so tight a hair shirt of time? Unable to move before the 29th, and unable to strike after the 31st—that seemed to be Washington's fate, but he did not permit it to discourage, certainly not to deter him. An Army that had survived much adversity would not succumb to this. Bleak as were the skies, light would break through. The puzzle might perplex; it would not baffle! In that unyielding state of mind, Washington wrote Cadwalader on the 27th: "If we could happily beat up the rest of the [enemy's] quarters bordering on and near the river, it would be attended with the most valuable consequence." He had called a council of war, Washington explained, and therefore recommended that Cadwalader and Putnam defer movement till they heard from him again. "Perhaps," Washington said doubtfully, "it may be judged prudent for us to pass here with the force we have, if it is practicable; or, if it is not, that I may come down to you and afford every assistance in my power." [17] If, in other words, he held the men he had, and could cross with them and maneuver against the enemy, he would do so; but if the ranks were thinner, even to a shadow of an Army, he would move to Bristol or Dunk's Ferry and employ his Virginians of unexpired term with the Pennsylvania militia Cadwalader, Mifflin and Putnam had scraped together. After achieving what it had at Trenton, the Army must not, would not perish, even if to all the other contingencies was added the whimsicality of the Delaware. "Please give me," Washington wrote Cadwalader, "frequent information on the state of the river and

---

16 *Ibid.*, 457; 7 *ibid.*, 60.
17 Letter of Dec. 27, 1776; 6 *G. W.*, 446–47, repunctuated.

whether it is to be passed in boats or whether the ice will admit of a passage." [18] There was a third, unmentioned barrier: the ice in the Delaware might be heavy enough to render a crossing excessively hazardous, though the frozen covering of the stream would not bear the weight of men and cannon.

The council of war on the 27th confirmed one possibility of keeping the field if a crossing could be effected—a possibility that was to be for the moment the secret of senior officers,[19] but on the 28th, provisions still were too scanty to restore the fighting spirit of the Army. At the same time, another dispatch from Cadwalader presented a breath-taking opportunity: Although cooperation with troops from Philadelphia had not seemed probable on the 25th,[20] General Mifflin was moving 500 men from that city toward Burlington and would send more.[21] John Cadwalader himself had acted with the greatest boldness: At the head of about 1500 men, he had crossed the Delaware into New Jersey on the morning of the 27th, in the expectation of finding the main Army still there; but even after he learned of its return to Pennsylvania with its prisoners, he had decided to stay on the left bank. More than that, when Cadwalader had learned that the enemy had left the important road junctions of Black Horse and Mount Holly, about six miles East of the river, he had occupied Burlington at the instance of Joseph Reed, who knew that countryside well. To his letter, recounting this maneuver, Cadwalader added: "If you should think it proper to cross over, it may be easily effected [22] at the place where we passed—a pursuit would keep up the panic. They went off with great precipitation, pressed all the wagons in their reach. I am told many of them are gone to South Amboy. If we can drive them from West Jersey, the success will raise an army by next spring and establish the credit of the continental money to support it. I shall write you tomorrow, I hope from Trenton." [23]

The "panic" mentioned by Cadwalader was, of course, the result of defeat of the Hessians on the 26th. Cadwalader was in position to assist in making the most of it if only the Continental Army at Newtown

[18] *Ibid.*, 447.

[19] No minutes of this council were written or, if taken down, were preserved.

[20] See Joseph Reed to John Cadwalader, Dec. 25, 1776, PHS.

[21] 6 *G. W.*, 451–52.

[22] By an understandable *lapsus*, Cadwalader wrote "affected."

[23] Marked "10 o'clock," evidently P.M. The original is in 38 *Papers of G. W.*, 27, LC; a transcript appears in 1 *Reed*, 280–81, though Cadwalader's letters of the 25th and 26th are not printed there. The text above is repunctuated, and its abbreviation is spelled out.

could move! On the 29th, Washington found it would be almost as dangerous to cross the river that day as it would have been on the 28th and for the same maddening reason, the lack of bread and meat;[24] but he ascertained that the commissary wagons would bring up sufficient provisions on the 29th–30th to supply the Army until it was re-established in Jersey.[25] After that, should necessity demand, the men must be fed temporarily on what foraging parties could scrape together. As all could see, the ice that Sunday, the 29th, was too thin to support passage on foot and too heavy to permit the crossing of boats otherwise than by a hard, exhausting struggle;[26] but, somehow, the Army must get across. Orders were issued for the troops to move into Jersey on the 30th.[27] Appeals for diversions on the Hackensack and around Morristown were sent Heath, McDougall and Maxwell;[28] the Philadelphia Light Horse were directed to proceed ahead of the Infantry.[29] "I have taken every precaution in my power for subsisting of the troops," Washington wrote the President of Congress, "and shall without loss of time and as soon as circumstances will admit of, pursue the enemy in their retreat . . ."[30]

When the crossing began on the 30th, it proved altogether as difficult as Washington had anticipated. In some of the nearby villages, the snow was six inches deep;[31] everywhere the cold was cruel. Except for darkness, shivering soldiers underwent all the suffering they had endured Christmas night. So slowly was the battle with the stubborn ice won by each boat's crew that it was manifest some of the troops would not get to the left bank until the 31st.[32] Washington himself went to the Jersey shore on the 30th and proceeded to Trenton.[33] Nowhere on the road was there any opposition, or any evidence of the presence of the enemy after the rout of the 26th. Information was meagre. Cadwalader already had reported Bordentown in his hands and had an-

[24] Cf. Washington to Robert Ogden, Jan. 24, 1777: "I was retarded from crossing the Delaware two days . . ." (7 G. W., 60). As he manifestly could not have considered a return to the left bank on the 27th, this means that the two days must have been the 28th and 29th. Evidence will be presented *infra* that he was speaking of a lack of rations when he said he was "retarded."

[25] 6 G. W., 453; 7 G. W., 60.   [26] 6 G. W., 451.
[27] Ibid., 454.   [28] Ibid., 447–450.
[29] 1 Reed, 281.

[30] He ruined an effective sentence by adding after a comma "try to beat up more of their quarters and, in a word, in every instance adopt such measures as the exigency of our affairs requires and our situation will justify" (6 G. W., 452).

[31] Lieut. James McMichael's Diary, Dec. 29, 1776; 15 Penn. Arc. (2), p. 203.
[32] 6 G. W., 461.   [33] Ibid.

nounced his intention of sending troops to Crosswicks.[34] Apparently there had been a deep retreat by the Hessians in that area. As for the district around Morristown, Alexander McDougall could be trusted to dispatch accurate intelligence.[35] All other reports of the enemy were vague, conflicting or blank.[36] Washington could learn nothing more definite than that Howe probably was effecting a new concentration of force and was fortifying Princeton.[37] To verify or to disprove this, Washington sent a detachment of the Philadelphia Light Horse to reconnoitre in the direction of the college town.[38] Meanwhile Washington posted his troops at Trenton, South of Assunpink Creek, where he felt they would be secure, temporarily, from surprise attack while he considered the possibilities of maneuver.[39]

Then, coldly but apparently with a certain confidence, Washington played his last card, the one that pessimists might have considered decisive, one way or the other, in the gamble of American independence. Before he had left the Pennsylvania side of the river and probably before he held his council of war on the 27th, Washington had resolved to offer a special bounty of ten dollars, besides continuance of pay, to each man who would agree to remain with the Army six weeks after the expiration of service on December 31.[40] This had been the secret, not too well kept, of the Generals who had conferred.[41] As an economical manager, he felt this was a "most extravagant price," but if there was to be a bounty, the figure had been set at ten dollars by Pennsylvania's offer of that sum to militiamen who would bear arms in a brief, winter campaign. Regiments from that State were mustering many youths

34 Cadwalader to Washington, Dec. 28, 1776; 38 *Papers of G. W.*, 42, LC. Crosswicks then was eight miles Southeast of Trenton and three and a half miles East of Bordentown.

35 See his dispatch of the 30th in 3 *Force* (5), p. 1490.

36 For his willingness to pay spies in "hard money" as soon as he could procure it, see 6 *G. W.*, 457. Cf. *ibid.*, 472.

37 *Ibid.*, 462.

38 1 *Reed*, 282–83. The full, connected text of Reed's narrative, which is broken into several sections in the cited biography, will be found in 8 *Penn. Mag.*, 391 ff.

39 It must be pointed out clearly that Washington nowhere spoke of luring the British to Trenton, and he probably did not have specifically that in mind. On the contrary, his first desire was to see the enemy go into winter quarters, but if he could not have that, he wished Howe's forces to be overextended and he placed his own Army where it most certainly could make the most of a British mistake. For directions to the American troops to take position behind the Assunpink, see 37 *G. W.*, 537. This is the crude transcription in the German Battalion's Orderly Book of Washington's GOs of Dec. 30, 1776, but there is no reason to doubt the authenticity of the document.

40 Washington's subsequent references are on occasion to six weeks' and sometimes to four weeks' service. He never cleared the apparent contradiction.

41 See *supra*, p. 329.

who were encouraged by the victory and at the same time were attracted by the State's bounty. Jerseymen, too, were coming in. "A body of firm troops, inured to danger," Washington said later, "were absolutely necessary to lead on the more raw and undisciplined." [42] If the New England Regiments disbanded on the 31st, the Virginians remaining with Washington would not be sufficiently numerous to attract, to hold and to set the pace for the militia. The temporary soldiers would disappear when the greater part of the Continentals did. To keep either volunteers or drafted men of any State after their time had expired, Washington had learned that one appeal only was effective, the appeal of the dollar. Any argument advanced by a recruiting officer in the name of liberty, country and home, would be openly or inferentially met by the soldiers with the statement that they had done their part for the American cause. They demanded that men who had hugged the chimney should now embrace the cold form of winter in the field.

So—sound the drums and put a New England Regiment in line; the Commander-in-Chief wanted to address it. He was no orator, but he had to do this—as he had done a thousand other unpleasant duties—because he had resolved to give himself, his inadequacies along with his abilities, to the cause of American liberty. The line formed; Washington rode forward and drew rein opposite the centre. Then, briefly, as best he could, he described the success of the 26th, and explained why the veterans were needed. They could do more for their country during the next few weeks than ever they could again. He announced the bounty, about which the men previously had heard nothing, and as one Sergeant wrote years afterward, "in the most affectionate manner [he] entreated us to stay." [43]

Washington touched his horse and rode aside; the regimental officers took charge [44] and probably with observations of their own, called on those who would accept the bounty and would remain six weeks to step forward. The drums rolled; Washington ran his eye along the line. Not a man moved, not one.

Was that the humiliating, disgraceful answer? Would it be given by all the Regiments in like silent and sullen refusal, as unanimously as

---

[42] Letter of Jan. 1, 1777, to committee of Congress; 6 *G. W.*, 463–64; cf. *ibid.*, 455–56.
[43] "Sergeant R——" in the Wellsborough (Penn.) *Phenix*, Mch. 24, 1832; reprinted in 20 *Penn. Mag.*, 515.
[44] This seems certain from what followed, but it should be noted that the only reporter, "Sergeant R——" was silent on this point.

if every soldier had shouted "No"? If it was to be that way everywhere, then America . . . but it must not be so! Washington wheeled his horse again and rode back to the centre of the immobile line. He would renew his plea; he must get the men's consent—he must, must, must! Briefly and persuasively he told them of their country's need and of their opportunity. When he had finished and the drums had rolled a second time, either his earnestness or their own reflection made the soldiers look questioningly at one another. Friends exchanged glances; a conscientious veteran muttered that a man could not go home when the Army was in that state. A few stepped boldly out; others followed, and more and more; soon only those who were too feeble to fight or too nearly naked to face the wind remained in the original line. One of the officers, proud and infinitely eased in spirit, asked Washington if those who agreed to remain with the Army should be enrolled. The General shook his head: No; men who had volunteered in that manner, he said, needed no enrolment to keep them to their duty.[45]

It was much the same, Washington soon learned, in the next New England Regiment to which the offer of the bounty was made that day. After that, some of the men of a third Regiment volunteered for longer service; then part of a fourth did. The only large-scale refusal in prospect was—of all Regiments!—in John Glover's famous Marblehead command, whose skill with oars kept the crossing on the 25th from being a failure. These troops, most of them mariners, had caught the fever of privateering, which now was almost an epidemic among seafarers. Washington had been warned to expect "No" when the men were addressed on the 1st of January, but he had been hopeful most of them could be prevailed upon to transfer to the continental frigates.[46] Some of Glover's troops made that choice; others agreed to remain temporarily with their colors.[47] All in all, the response of the forces

---

[45] "Sergeant R——," *op. cit.*, 516. The Sergeant's account was not put in print until more than fifty-five years after the event. Manifestly, then, it is not safe to trust the accuracy of what he quoted as the language of Washington's second brief speech to the soldiers, but merely as a tradition, the words may be set down here: "My brave fellows, you have done all I asked you to do, and more than could be reasonably expected; but your country is at stake, your wives, your houses, and all that you hold dear. You have worn yourselves out with fatigues and hardships, but we know not how to spare you. If you will consent to stay only one month longer, you will render that service to the cause of liberty, and to your country, which you probably never can do under any other circumstances. The present is emphatically the crisis which is to decide our destiny" (*Ibid*).

[46] 6 *G. W.*, 437, 464.

[47] It is possible that the appeal to these men was delayed by design in the hope that they might be prevailed upon to change their minds. No record has been found of the number who accepted the bounty, or of the circumstances in which they did so, but the Brigade, listed

in the village was by no means as emphatic as the Army's needs required, but it took the worst of the gloom from the approaching 1st of January. The Virginians would not be the only Continentals to whom the militia could be asked to rally. New Englanders would be on the next field of battle.

Would Hitchcock's men take their place beside the other troops from East of the Hudson? The three Rhode Island and the two Massachusetts Regiments constituted Nixon's Brigade, and they were with Cadwalader, down the river. Daniel Hitchcock, the temporary commander, was so ill he scarcely could mount a horse—doctors said he had a consumption—but he had some excellent troops in his thin Regiments, and as he held these men in close contact with the Pennsylvania militia the decision of his Brigade might have large effect on what Cadwalader's temporary soldiers would be willing to attempt. The 30th passed without any report to Washington of the answer Hitchcock's stalwarts had made: it must be that they had not yet been addressed.

The next day, the 31st of December, was mild in temperature. Along the Delaware, the snow began to melt,[48] but it still was deep on frozen ground when the men of Hitchcock's Brigade were drawn up in line at Crosswicks. Hitchcock did not attempt to address them; Cadwalader refrained from doing so, not because he lacked either the ability or the confidence of the men, but because he had at hand a distinguished orator, Thomas Mifflin, Quartermaster General. Mounted on a fine horse, wrapped in a rose-colored blanket overcoat and wearing a fur cap, Mifflin rode out in front of the Brigade and spoke with all his skill and in shrewd understanding of the mind of the men in the ranks. He told them of the magnificence of the opportunity. If they would extend their service a month or six weeks, the States would send reenforcements. A strengthened Army would be able to drive the enemy from Jersey. Men who patriotically continued their service to their country would have the thanks and abundant proof of the gratitude of America. Conditions were to be better in the Army. Among other things, troops who captured booty from the British would not be required to give it up; they could divide it among themselves or they could sell it and keep the money. He made various additional promises of a more tolerable

---

then as Sherman's, had an honorable share in the events of January 2–3, presently to be described.

[48] *Life and Recollections of John Howland*, cited hereafter as *John Howland*, p. 71.

life for the men in the ranks and then he directed those who would continue in the service for the designated time to poise their firelocks. Mifflin ended with that and rejoiced instantly: In every platoon, some responded; the imitative followed the zealous. More and more pledged themselves. Lippitt's Regiment, which constituted about one-third of the Brigade, was bound to serve until the 18th of January anyway—a fact the officers seemed to have forgotten—but its members responded with the others.[49] Word could be sent forthwith to General Washington that Hitchcock's veterans would not fail him! One Colonel was so elated at the response of his troops that he called for three huzzas and ordered a gill of rum issued each man who had volunteered for the extended service.[50]

Washington had been so much encouraged by the action of the soldiers at Trenton on the 30th that he had been prompted to ask that a similar appeal be addressed to the four Continental Regiments at Morristown.[51] Now that all the Continental troops along the Delaware had acted, their decision seemed to increase the élan aroused by the success at Trenton the day after Christmas. "Never," wrote one young officer, "were men in higher spirit than our whole Army is." [52]

In offering the bounty that gave him the services of Continentals whom he must have if he was to keep an Army in the field through the winter of 1776–77, Washington had violated one of the fundamentals of his official conduct: he had made an irrevocable pledge of public credit with no authority whatsoever. Eleven months previously when he had ordered the enlistment of three new Regiments to revive the exhausted forces in Canada, he had hastened to write Congress that if it disapproved his action, it could countermand the orders he had issued.[53] Similarly, before he had sent Charles Lee in January, 1776,[54] to assume command in New York, he took superlative pains to inquire of John Adams whether he was exceeding his commission.[55] Now, in

---

[49] *John Howland*, 71; Diary of Stephen Olney in Williams, *Biog. of Rev. Heroes*, 192.

[50] Sgt. John Smith's Diary, 20 *Miss. Val. H.S. Rev.*, 269–70.

[51] 6 *G. W.*, 455. The opening sentence of this letter to "The officer commanding at Morristown" reads as if all the New England Regiments had accepted the bounty on the 30th, but the evidence requires the sequence set forth in the text. As the Regiments at Crosswicks did not agree until the 31st to extend their service, Washington on the 30th manifestly wrote only of the New England Regiments at Trenton.

[52] Thomas Rodney to Caesar Rodney, Dec. 30, 1776; 3 *Force* (5), p. 1487. Cf. Nathanael Greene to Mrs. Greene, Dec. 30, 1776: "God only knows what will be the issue of this campaign, but everything wears a much better prospect than they [sic] have for some weeks past" (1 *Greene's Greene*, 300).   [53] See p. 4–5, and 4 *G. W.*, 259–60.

[54] *Ibid.*, 221.   [55] *Ibid.*, 219–20.

a matter of heavy expense and perhaps of costly precedent, he acted
boldly and without even consulting Robert Morris's committee of three
in Philadelphia to whom Congress had delegated large authority.
Washington's justification was compassed in a foreword of his next
letter to the President of Congress—"What could be done?"[56] It was
a case of pay or perish. His own private credit and that of every responsible and discerning American had to be pledged, if need be, to get
money[57] with which to "push our success" and "to keep up the panic."[58]

Never in Washington's life had boldness been vindicated more dramatically: That last evening of 1776, an express from Philadelphia
brought him a series of resolves adopted in Baltimore by Congress on
the 27th of December. Like Washington, the Delegates had been commanded by that stern General, Necessity, and had been compelled to
approve what, in any other circumstances, they would have shouted
down. The Commander-in-Chief was authorized to establish whatever
system of promotion he and his council thought likely to produce the
widest satisfaction.[59] Another measure empowered Washington to do
the very thing he had done on the 30th—"to use every endeavor, by
giving bounties and otherwise, to prevail upon the troops whose time of
enlistment shall expire at the end of this month to stay with the Army
so long after that period as its situation shall render their stay necessary."[60] A third resolve was in this language:

This Congress, having maturely considered the present crisis; and having
perfect reliance on the wisdom, vigour, and uprightness of General Washington, do, hereby,

Resolve, That General Washington shall be, and he is hereby, vested with
full, ample, and complete powers to raise and collect together, in the most
speedy and effectual manner, from any or all of these United States, sixteen
battallions of infantry, in addition to those already voted by Congress; to
appoint officers for the said battallions; to raise, officer, and equip three thousand light horse; three regiments of artillery, and a corps of engineers, and
to establish their pay; to apply to any of the states for such aid of the militia
as he shall judge necessary; to form such magazines of provisions, and in such
places, as he shall think proper; to displace and appoint all officers under the

---

[56] 6 G. W., 461. He elaborated by another reference to the Pennsylvania bounty of like
amount, and he went on: "The troops feel their importance and would have their price. Indeed,
as their aid is so essential and not to be dispensed with, it is to be wondered they have not
estimated it at a higher rate" (Ibid.).

[57] Ibid., 458.   [58] Ibid.
[59] 6 JCC., 1043.   [60] Ibid.

rank of brigadier general, and to fill up all vacancies in every other department in the American armies; to take, wherever he may be, whatever he may want for the use of the army, if the inhabitants will not sell it, allowing reasonable price for the same; to arrest and confine persons who refuse to take the continental currency, or are otherwise disaffected to the American cause; and return to the states of which they are citizens, their names, and the nature of their offences, together with the witnesses to prove them:

That the foregoing powers be vested in General Washington, for and during the term of six months from the date hereof, unless sooner determined by Congress.[61]

Washington may not have been unprepared for an extension of his authority. He had argued in his long letter of December 20 that a commander at so great a distance from Congress must have discretion [62] and he probably knew that Nathaniel Greene on the 21st had written Congress that "greater powers must be lodged in the hands of the General than he has ever yet exercised." [63] There had been no material opposition to the grant of these powers, nor had any great expectation been aroused. Members of Congress voted "Aye" because they believed the delegation of large authority to Washington was required if the American cause was to be saved from early ruin.[64] The one reservation made by the Delegates was that of time. Pains were taken to have the people understand that the General's new powers were for the period of emergency and would be cancelled at the end of six months.[65] A committee was named, moreover, to prepare a paper that would explain to the States "the reasons which induced Congress to enlarge the powers" of Washington. This committee was also to request the States "to cooperate with him and give him all the aid in their power," [66] a duty the committee discharged promptly. As amended and approved by Congress, the letter to the States gave assurance that authority of such scope would not have been vested "in the Military Department" if the situation "did not require at this crisis a decision and vigor which distance and numbers deny to assemblies far removed from each other and from the immediate seat of war." The remainder of the letter was more hortatory than explanatory and was designed to procure quick action by the States in supplying their quotas of troops.[67]

[61] *Ibid.*, 1045–46, verbatim.
[63] 1 *Greene's Greene*, 290.
[65] Cf. Samuel Adams to James Warren, Jan. 1, 1777; *ibid.*, 202.
[66] 6 *JCC*, 1047.
[62] See *supra*, p. 296–97, and 6 *G. W.*, 402.
[64] See the letters, etc., in 2 *Burnett*, 196 ff.
[67] *Ibid.*, 1053.

The covering letter of the Philadelphia committee to Washington was in the same spirit. Morris and his colleagues wrote: "We find by these resolves your Excellency's hands will be strengthened with very ample powers, and a new reformation of the Army seems to have its origin there. Happy it is for this country that the General of their forces can safely be entrusted with the most unlimited power, and neither personal security, liberty or [sic] property be in the least endangered thereby." [68]

Washington read this, apparently, with none of the pride he would have felt as a younger man at receiving such shining "honor." Responsibility outweighed everything except the cause that created it. He wrote the committee: "Instead of thinking myself freed from all *civil* obligations by this mark of [the Delegates'] confidence, I shall constantly bear in mind that as the sword was the last resort for the preservation of our liberties, so it ought to be the first to be laid aside when those liberties are firmly established." With his usual caution he added: "I shall instantly set about making the most necessary reforms in the Army; but it will not be in my power to make so great a progress as if I had a little leisure time upon my hand." [69]

This was written on the first day of the new year, 1777, and at a time when soldiers who had declined the bounty were turning their backs on their comrades and were starting home. Washington estimated that 2200 or 2300 men had made the second crossing to Jersey with him, and he calculated now that the bounty had been accepted by half, or perhaps more than half of those whose time expired on the 31st. As nearly as he could compute, those who remained, including the Virginians, were between 1500 and 1600.[70] Haslet's Delaware Battalion almost ceased to exist;[71] some Regiments were reduced to 100 men by sickness and by the refusal of soldiers to remain in the ranks.[72] It was manifest that Washington must arrange to use his small veteran force in those phases of his operations that demanded experience and steadiness. For all other duties, he would be compelled to rely on Pennsylvania and New Jersey militia. These restrictions meant, substantially,

[68] Letter of Dec. 31, 1776, 2 *Burnett*, 198, with some repunctuation.
[69] 6 *G. W.*, 464.
[70] 6 *G. W.*, 462–63. He later reckoned that from 1200 to 1400 agreed to stay (7 *ibid.*, 29), but he subsequently reduced that number to a total between 1000 and 1200 (*ibid.*, 53).
[71] See John Haslet to Caesar Rodney, Jan. 1, 1777; *Diary of Thomas Rodney*, 51–52.
[72] 6 *G. W.*, 463.

that in spite of the extension of service, the gamble with ruin was more desperate now than it had been at the end of 1775. When the drums beat before Boston, as '76 was dawning, Washington had at least the protection of redoubts and of far-spreading waters in front of a part of his lines; now, at Trenton, he had no fortifications—and stood deliberately with his back to a wide, deep and unbridged river.[73] He was doing all he could to bestir the militia of Jersey [74] but he could not expect the immediate arrival of any of the promised reenforcements other than perhaps a few more from Pennsylvania, which already had responded largely.

What, then, could be done? As far as Washington understood a situation obscured by the paucity of intelligence, the British in Jersey numbered between 5000 and 6000 men, chiefly at Brunswick and Princeton. These troops were said to be transporting most of their baggage to Brunswick, and were supposed to be raising some earthworks at Princeton. Another report was that General Howe a day or two previously had landed at Amboy an additional 1000 soldiers who were moving forward.[75] Besides this information, Washington had received from Cadwalader a somewhat detailed account of what an American spy had observed in Princeton on the 30th of December. From this agent's description, Cadwalader had drawn and forwarded to Washington a rough sketch of the approaches to the town and of the location of the guns, defences and soldiers' quarters there.[76]

The enemy could concentrate quickly at Princeton or at Brunswick, but was Howe making ready to advance, or was he going into winter quarters? Some of Washington's officers believed that a swift movement by Cadwalader from Crosswicks to Brunswick might result in the capture of the British baggage and in the liberation of Charles Lee. Other advisers thought Washington would gain in advantage if he withdrew from Trenton and moved to Crosswicks, whence he could maneuver freely against the British. Washington put first the defensive concentration of all his Regiments, in the belief that the redcoats were almost certain to attack, because they thought his Army would have been dissolved at the end of the year. He could not repel the assault

---

[73] A critique of the occupation of this ground will be found *infra*, p. 374–75.
[74] 6 *G. W.*, 462.　　　　　　　　[75] *Ibid.*
[76] The original is in LC; a reproduction from A. H. Bill's *Campaign of Princeton*, made with that author's generous consent, appears on page 340.

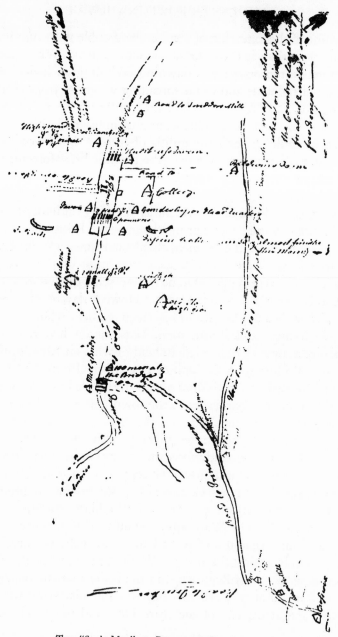

THE "SPY'S MAP" OF PRINCETON, DEC. 30, 1776

Col. John Cadwalader made this sketch on the basis of intelligence supplied by a spy who had visited Princeton. The paper was forwarded by Cadwalader to Washington, Dec. 31, 1776, and was most useful in the operation of Jan. 3, 1777. After the reproduction in Alfred Hoyt Bill, *The Campaign of Princeton, 1776–1777,* p. 100, from the original in the Library of Congress.

with the small force he had at Trenton, but if he retreated he would discourage Jersey militia. On the other hand, if he drew to his position the temporary troops to the East of him, he would expose them to casualties at the same time that he made himself strong enough to accept defensive battle. As between these alternatives, he thought the risk less and the potential gain larger from making Trenton the place of the indispensable concentration of all his men. There they could stand or begin further maneuver as strength and circumstance dictated.

The position there was by no means ideal, but it included a road that led to Princeton as well as the one that followed the course of the river. If the enemy decided to move on Philadelphia by way of Burlington or Bristol, an American force at Trenton would be on the flank of Howe; and if it were maintained that an American army at Crosswicks likewise could threaten the flank of a British column that undertook to cross the Delaware at Trenton, the question resolved itself into one of probability: was it more likely that the adversary would move via Princeton and Trenton or via Crosswicks and, say, Burlington? Washington chose to gamble on the route by way of Trenton. All this had to do with a defensive. If an opportunity were presented of attacking the enemy, Washington would do what he had planned in one form or another ever since he had taken position South of the Delaware: he would try to strike one or more of the enemy's posts in Jersey.

Without hesitation, therefore, Washington on the 31st had ordered Cadwalader to move to Trenton, and he sent similar instructions to General Mifflin who commanded the militia dispatched from Philadelphia to Bordentown.[77] When Cadwalader received his orders to move to Trenton with all the militia, his forces were somewhat scattered. His advance was at Allentown.[78] With the roads deep in mud, Washington knew that many hours would elapse before these troops could take position by the side of the Continentals. Meantime, of course, it was prudent to post a reliable body of veterans on the line of the enemy's most probable advance, the road from Princeton. Fermoy's Brigade, Hand's Regiment, the German Battalion, Scott's Virginia Regiment and a detachment with two cannon of Forrest's battery were

[77] 6 G. W., 467. The entire argument for a concentration at Trenton is nowhere given, though it is inferred easily from this reference, which is to the report Washington addressed on Jan. 5, 1777, to the President of Congress. Some of the considerations are presented in Joseph Reed's Narrative, 1 Reed, 284–85.

[78] 1 Reed, 285. Few of Cadwalader's orders of this period remain in his Papers, PHS. One of Dec. 29, 1777, in the collection is drawn carefully in soldierly spirit.

assigned this duty on the 1st and were stationed on Five Mile Run, about half way between Trenton and Princeton.[79]

New Year's Day brought no other development. During the night of the 1st–2nd, Cadwalader's men began to arrive, though some of them did not reach the encampment until 11 A.M. of the 2nd.[80] Before that time, Washington received word at headquarters that the British were on the march from Princeton to Trenton.[81] The alarm was sounded; the men "fell in." [82] South of the Assunpink, the American artillery position dominated almost the whole of the village,[83] but Joseph Reed pointed out that upstream on Assunpink Creek were fords the British might use. They then might close on Washington's right and cage him in a position of his own choosing. As this was a possibility not to be disregarded, Washington sent Reed to reconnoitre, and on the heels of that officer he forwarded detachments that were to guard the crossings Reed found passable.[84] To retard the advance of the British and to ascertain their strength, Washington directed the troops on Five Mile Run to hold back the enemy as long as possible.[85] In addition, Washington advanced a Brigade to a point one mile from the city,[86] and probably on the eminence at the mouth of the Pennington Road he placed two guns with their muzzles pointing up the Princeton Road.[87]

After that, reports from the front indicated that the delaying action, though brisk, was not costly. For a reason he did not explain, General Fermoy had left his troops and had come back to Trenton,[88] but this

---

[79] *Stryker*, 258, with no citation of authority.

[80] *Thomas Rodney's Diary*, 38. This part of Rodney's Diary was accepted mistakenly by Stryker, *op. cit.*, 376–77, and by various later writers as a letter from Col. John Haslet to Caesar Rodney, "the last letter he wrote."

[81] 1 *Reed*, 285.

[82] Lieut. McMichael stated in his Diary (15 *Penn. Arc.* (2), p. 203), that this was at 10 A.M. An anonymous "officer of distinction" (*Stryker*, 446) gave the hour as 11.

[83] Henry Knox in *Stryker*, 450.

[84] 1 *Reed*, 286. Unfortunately, Reed's useful narrative ends with a description of the fords, one of which might have permitted easy passage. Some reservation has to be made concerning Reed's activity at this time, because his biographer and grandson was inclined to credit to Reed a larger share in the major decisions of this campaign than the record would appear to justify, but, on the other hand, Reed's familiarity with the country around Trenton disposed Washington to consult Reed more than usually he had after the discovery of Reed's critical correspondence with Charles Lee.

[85] 1 *Wilkinson*, 136.

[86] "Officer of Distinction" in *Stryker*, 446; Knox in *ibid.*, 449. In James McMichael's Diary (15 *Penn. Arc.* (2), p. 203), the statement is made that Sullivan's Brigade was sent forward, but this cannot be verified.

[87] Letter "from a Gentleman of Great Worth" to "the printer of the *Maryland Journal*" reprinted in *Stryker*, 466. The gentleman did not state specifically where the guns were put, but the position mentioned in the text is the logical one.

[88] 1 *Wilkinson*, 136. Wilkinson noted, "This man, like De Woedtke, turned out a worthless drunkard, although he wore the croix de St. Louis" (*ibid.*, 135 n).

helped rather than hurt because it put the detachment under Col. Edward Hand. That veteran employed time and cover with much skill. When he had to abandon Five Mile Run, he fell back to a thick wood on the southern side of Shabbakonk Creek and shrewdly deployed his riflemen as if they were engaged in Indian warfare. His fire and a brief pursuit of an incautious advance guard of redcoats were so effective that the British apparently thought the Americans intended to make a stand there. The enemy consequently formed line of battle, brought up artillery and poured fire into the woods, with little injury to Hand's troops. By their stout resistance, his men checked the British for two hours and then withdrew in good order toward Trenton.

North of the town, at a distance of approximately half a mile, a ravine offered a natural defensive line, where the Americans next undertook to face the British. Both sides employed artillery as well as musketry in this clash, which Washington urged the Americans to prolong, because he did not wish to leave the British daylight hours for a general assault on the position South of Assunpink Creek.[89] Obediently, the Continentals held out for a short time [90] until it was manifest the entire weight of the British would be thrown against them; and when they had to give ground, they did so stubbornly. As they withdrew slowly through the village, after 4 o'clock,[91] they fired from behind the houses and at length made their way across the bridge to the lines South of the creek.[92] Washington posted himself astride his horse on the western side of the southern end of the bridge where he could see the withdrawal and could indicate to the various brigade commanders the positions they were to take.[93]

He scarcely could have asked for a better delaying action than now was ending. The only misconduct reported to him was that of the German Battalion, which broke quickly. Its commanding officer, Col. Nicholas Haussegger, surrendered under somewhat suspicious circumstances.[94] In every other Regiment, zeal, discipline and intelligent lead-

---

89 Almost the only detailed account of this fighting North of Trenton on the 2nd of January is in 1 *Wilkinson*, 135 ff. That author's narrative was written approximately forty years after the event, but it was prepared subsequent to an inspection of the scene of action, where he made some measurements and talked to old residents. See *ibid.*, 141, 142 n and 147 n.

90 Cf. Henry Knox in *Stryker*, 449.

91 6 *G. W.*, 468.

92 Letter to the *Maryland Journal* as cited *supra*, n. 87, in *Stryker*, 466.

93 *John Howland*, 73, partly reprinted in C. C. Haven, *Thirty Days in New Jersey*, 38. Howland remembered that "the firm, composed and majestic countenance of the General inspired confidence and assurance . . ."

94 1 *Reed*, 286. Graydon in his *Memoirs*, 237–38, stated that this man, while a prisoner

ership had been shown. When, in the late afternoon, a vigorous cannonade began, Knox's artillerists handled their guns, some thirty or forty in number, with skill and steadfastness.[95] A "feeble and unsupported effort" [96] by British troops to storm the bridge about sunset was beaten off easily.[97]

At nightfall the firing ceased,[98] but to some of Washington's officers and men, his position seemed desperate. His left was on the Delaware; his right was in a wood parallel to the creek.[99] Were the British seeking to turn the left,[100] or was the danger greater on the right? One young Lieutenant wrote: "The most sanguine among us could not flatter himself with any hopes of victory had we waited till morning and been reduced to the necessity of engaging a foe so vastly our superior both in numbers and discipline and who could never have a chance of fighting us on more advantageous terms." [101] Another youthful American had much the same opinion: "It appeared to me then that our army was in the most desperate situation I had ever known it; we had no boats to carry us across the Delaware, and if we had, so powerful an enemy would certainly destroy the better half before we could embark. To cross the enemy's line of march between this and Princeton seemed impracticable; and when we thought of retreating into the south part of Jersey, where there was no support for an army, that was discouraging; notwithstanding all this, the men and officers seemed cheerful and in great spirits; I asked Lieutenant Bridges what he thought now of our independence. He answered cheerfully, 'I don't know, the Lord will help us.' " [102]

In Washington's eyes, the two most controlling realities of the situation were, first, that the British were in greatly superior force and, second, that they planned to surround and to destroy his Army.[103] He did not believe he should risk a battle where he stood,[104] but if he was not to fight on the bank of the Delaware, what was he to do? On that question, which readily might be the issue of life or death for the American cause, Washington almost certainly had reached a decision in his

---

in New York, undertook to persuade other American officers to make terms with the British, whose cause he openly espoused. He was superseded Mch. 19, 1777. See *Heitman*.

[95] Knox in *Stryker*, 450; *Thomas Rodney's Diary*, 31.
[96] *Stryker*, 466.   [97] *Thomas Rodney's Diary*, 31.
[98] *Ibid.*   [99] Knox in *Stryker*, 450.
[100] 1 *Reed*, 286.   [101] Journal of Samuel Shaw; *Stryker*, 482.
[102] Stephen Olney in Williams *Biog. of Rev. Heroes*, 193–94.
[103] 6 *G. W.*, 468.   [104] *Ibid.*, 468, 489.

own mind, but he sought the advice of a council of war, which he assembled at General St. Clair's headquarters early in the evening.[105] The alternative to giving battle was, of course, a retreat, but that could not be completed in a single night directly across the river, if for no other reason than that the boats used by the Army were miles upstream. The line of march would be down the left bank of the Delaware, and that would involve either a later battle or a difficult crossing to Pennsylvania soil. Besides, even if a withdrawal could be completed without excessive danger and loss, the act of quitting the front of the enemy would dampen or destroy all the hopes that had been raised by the defeat of the Hessians on the 26th.

If battle might be ruinous and retreat full of hazards, was there any other alternative? Manifestly there was: The Army might move by its right flank, might cross Assunpink Creek beyond the British left and then might march to Princeton and then to Brunswick,[106] where the enemy was believed to have large supplies. Instead of a defensive at Trenton let the Army take the offensive at Princeton, by using roads more or less familiar to numerous officers and men in various commands. Joseph Reed knew the surrounding country well; a patrol of the Philadelphia Light Horse Troop had been far to the right on an open road and had seen no enemy; Arthur St. Clair had been on the same flank, guarding the fords of Assunpink Creek that day, and had observed the same road, which led to a crossing called the Quaker Bridge. If the Army could reach that point unobserved and unopposed, it then could proceed almost due North to Princeton, distant about six miles from the bridge.[107]

105 It must have been early because Washington stated (*ibid.*, 468) that he ordered the Army's baggage "to be removed silently to Burlington soon after dark." He certainly would not have made that disposition of his wagons had he not decided by that time what the Army was to do. Further, Reed's letter to Putnam, concerning the movement of the wagons and the advance of Putnam's forces, evidently was written after the council and is dated "East side of Trenton Creek, Jan. 2 12 o'clock at night" (*Reed Papers*, NYHS).

106 6 *G. W.*, 470.

107 St. Clair subsequently wrote this account of what happened: "The General summoned a council of the general officers at my quarters, and, after stating the difficulties in his way, the probability of defeat, and the consequences that would necessarily result if it happened, desired advice. I had the good fortune to suggest the idea of turning the left of the enemy in the night, gaining a march upon him, and proceeding with all possible expedition to Brunswick. General Mercer immediately fell in with it, and very forcibly pointed out its practicability and the advantages that would necessarily result from it, and General Washington highly approved it, nor was there one dissenting voice in the council." (St. Clair's Narrative, quoted in *St. Clair Papers*, ed. W. H. Smith, v. 1, p. 36). There is no ground for denying St. Clair a share in the testimony concerning the road on the right, but it does not stand to reason that Washington was ignorant of that road or that he permitted the British to pen him in before he made certain he had a way out. See the critique, *infra*, p. 374-75.

Even if Washington could not get beyond Princeton, his movement might inflict some damage on the enemy, would force the British to withdraw from Trenton, and might add to the prestige of the Army. This last was a consideration of importance at a time when recruits were necessary and militia must be induced to report and to remain in service. Besides, Washington told himself, there might be valuable stores at Princeton and there scarcely could be many troops in the town. Some of the large force across the Assunpink must have been drawn from the camp near the college.[108]

The chief obstacle to an advance on Princeton was the condition of the roads, which the unseasonable thaw had transformed into deep mud[109] that seemed to be almost fluid, mile on mile. The artillery of course must accompany the advance, but no other wagons should go, because they would delay a column that must move rapidly during the night if it was to evade pursuit and surprise the garrison of Princeton. As these vehicles could not be sent across the Delaware at Trenton, they must be moved down the left bank of the river to Burlington and entrusted to Putnam's troops who presumably were marching northward in Jersey, parallel to the course of the stream below the "nose." This disposition of the baggage would be hazardous, but it seemed to be the only way by which the Army could divest itself of a dragging dead weight in a movement the success of which might depend on speed.

When these details had been resolved, Washington sent appropriate orders to Putnam concerning the baggage[110] and adjourned the council with instructions for a start at midnight in complete silence. He had an immediate and pleasant surprise: In the course of a few hours the weather had changed, the wind had shifted to the North,[111] and the roads were beginning to freeze.[112] The men piled higher their fires, kept as warm as they could and, beyond the glare,[113] packed and sent off their baggage.

---

[108] Washington's reference to these considerations, as set forth in his report of Jan. 5, 1777, is among the most confused of all his deliverances. He described the plan for a march to Princeton "where," he said, "I knew they could not have much force left, and might have Stores," and then he continued: "One thing I was sure of, that it would avoid the appearance of a Retreat, which (was of Consequence) or to run the hazard of the whole Army's being cut of was unavoidable whilst we might, by a fortunate stroke, withdraw Genl. Howe from Trenton, give some reputation to our Arms; happily we succeeded." (6 *G. W.*, 468–69, verbatim).

[109] Sgt. William Young's Diary, 8 *Penn. Mag.*, 262.

[110] 1 *Reed*, 287; Reed to Putnam, as *supra*, n. 105.

[111] Thomas Rodney gave the direction as Northwest (*Diary*, 32).

[112] 1 *Reed*, 288; *Thomas Rodney's Diary*, 32.

[113] In prudent contrast to what happened later at Paoli. See *infra*, p. 495.

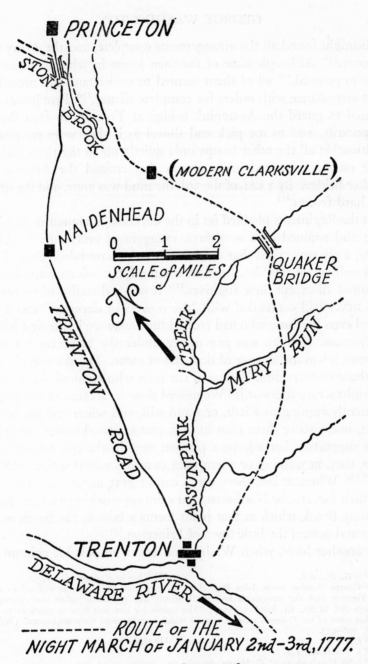

THE NIGHT MARCH ON PRINCETON, Jan. 2–3, 1777

Sketch of the route followed by Washington's Army from its position behind Assunpink Creek, Trenton, to the vicinity of Princeton; after a map prepared in 1894 by Joseph H. West and reproduced in Stryker's *Battles of Trenton and Princeton*, p. 279, with scale added from later surveys.

Midnight found all the arrangements complete, and the Army ready to move.[114] Although none of the men knew in what direction they were to proceed,[115] all of them seemed to understand the necessity of strict compliance with orders for complete silence.[116] Five hundred remained to guard the Assunpink bridge at Trenton, to feed the fires temporarily, and to use pick and shovel as if they were constructing earthworks; all the other troops stole quietly off to the right and soon were moving eastward in a column that crossed the Assunpink at Quaker Bridge. By 2 A.M. of the 3rd, the mud was gone, and the ground was hard frozen.[117]

As the Regiments plodded on in the darkness, imagination fashioned foes; and strained ears, as always, exaggerated every sound. After a while, a cry was raised that the column was surrounded. Some frightened militiamen shuddered and then ran off, but officers controlled and reassured all except these fugitives.[118] It was a dreadful night for men who never had contended with "the powers of darkness" and a cruel ordeal even for those who had crossed the Delaware in the first advance to Trenton. If there was any mercy under the black canopy of the heavens, it was the absence of sleet and of snow. The sky was cloudless, but the stars were dim.[119] One of the men who endured the torture of the night wrote afterward: "We moved slow on account of the artillery, frequently coming to a halt, or stand still, and when ordered forward again, one, two or three men in each platoon would stand, with their arms supported, fast asleep; a platoon next in the rear advancing on them, they, in walking or attempting to move, would strike a stub and fall." [120] When, at last, there was a cast of gray in the East, the troops had their faces to the Northwest, and were approaching a stream known as Stony Brook which at that point forms a bow to the South as if to cover and protect the little town of Princeton.[121]

In another hour, when Washington began to pass his column over

---

[114] 6 *G. W.*, 468.   [115] *Thomas Rodney's Diary*, 32.

[116] George Weedon wrote John Page, Jan. 6, 1777, that the Army moved off so quietly from Trenton that the rearguards and the sentinels did not know when the column left; (*Chicago HS*. MSS). Cf. Stephen Olney: "The orders for our march were given in so low a tone that some of the Colonels were at a stand which way to move their Regiments" (Williams, *op. cit.*, 196–97).

[117] *Ibid.*   [118] *Ibid.*

[119] 1 *Wilkinson*, 140.

[120] John Howland, in C. C. Haven, *op. cit.*, 52.

[121] The line of Washington's march on the night of Jan. 2–3, 1777 cannot be traced with certainty, but it is approximated on the map in *Stryker*, 279. Unfortunately, this map lacks a scale, which is supplied in the sketch on p. 347.

the stream, the sun rose as if in augury.[122] "The morning," in the words of one observer, "was bright, serene, and extremely cold, with a hoar frost which bespangled every object." [123] Ahead was an extension of the Quaker Road, a little more than a mile in length, that followed roughly the course of Stony Brook until it joined the Post Road from Princeton to Trenton. From the turnout near the Quaker Meeting House to the Post Road, this stretch might conveniently be termed the Creek Road. The main Post Road ran nearly Northeast from the creek to Princeton, a distance slightly less than two miles. Another, nameless back road led from the vicinity of the Quaker Meeting House to the town. This route was shown on the sketch Cadwalader had given Washington [124] and it could be used most advantageously in the execution of the simple plan Washington had formulated to rout the British in Princeton while holding off any troops that might be hurried from Trenton to succor the redcoats in the college town. The greater part of the American force was to pass from the Quaker Road into the back road and was to advance immediately into Princeton. If Cadwalader's drawing showed correctly the location of the defences of the town, these small works—scarcely more than trenches—were designed to resist attack up the Post Road and they could be turned almost completely from the back road. While the main body of Washington's troops was undertaking this, a second American column of approximately 350 men was to proceed under Gen. Hugh Mercer up the stretch along the creek to the junction with the Post Road. At that point, close by on Mercer's left, would be Worth's Mill and the Post Road bridge over Stony Brook. Mercer was to destroy this crossing and thereby was to make it impossible for any British from Trenton to reach Princeton quickly by the main highway or for any fugitives from Princeton to retreat down the Post Road.[125]

---

[122] *Thomas Rodney's Diary*, 33.　　　　[123] 1 *Wilkinson*, 141.
[124] See *supra*, 339, 340.
[125] Washington never described in detail his plan of operations; his report of Jan. 5, 1777, to the President of Congress (6 *G. W.*, 467 ff), is singularly uninformative; contemporary personal narratives are few; later accounts are contradictory in part. It is not likely that any review of the brief action will ever be accurate in all particulars. At the outset, there is difference of opinion regarding the mission of Mercer. For example, Capt. Thomas Rodney asserted in his *Diary*, which is one of the principal sources of information, that the advance was to be in three columns to surround the town. See *Stryker*, 438. Actually, there is no record of any other "columns" than Sullivan's main force, and the small contingent under Mercer. If the Virginian had been expected to participate materially in "surrounding" the town, he assuredly would have been given more than the 350 men, or thereabouts, whom he commanded.

All the preliminaries accorded with the plan. Shortly before 8 o'clock,[126] Sullivan's Division, consisting of St. Clair's and Sherman's Brigades [127] filed off to the right from the Creek Road and passed the Quaker Meeting House on the back road shown on Cadwalader's sketch. Mercer proceeded along the Creek side toward Worth's Mill. Farther back on the same road, Cadwalader was advancing with the militia.[128] Hitchcock's Brigade closed the rear.[129]

Washington himself probably was near the turnout to the back road. Everything was moving smoothly when Washington received unexpected news: The British had been found on the Post Road, down which their troops apparently had been marching in considerable number past the Stony Brook bridge, on the way to Trenton.[130] In a few minutes these redcoats turned around in the Post Road, recrossed the brook and started back at a rapid pace toward Princeton. Almost before Washington could grasp the situation or ask himself what he should do, Mercer's men began to run from the road along the creek. They climbed a little hill in the direction of Princeton and then descended on the opposite slope and started northeastward as if they were making their way toward St. Clair and Sherman on the back road.[131] A few minutes later Washington heard challenging musketry and then an an-

---

[126] The time is fixed oddly enough by British officers who heard in Trenton the sound of the cannon and even of the small arms in the action near Princeton. See *A. Robertson's Diaries*, 120. Putnam wrote Congress at 11 A.M. that day from Philadelphia, "A cannonade began about sunrise this morning and still continues" (159 *Papers Cont. Cong.*, 25, LC. Sunrise on January 3 at Princeton was at approximately 7:25.

[127] Sherman's Brigade was in reality Glover's. The shortage of officers—some sick, some on furlough and some pretending to have imperative private business—scarcely could be better illustrated than by the fact that Lt. Col. Isaac Sherman, just promoted to that rank and assigned to the Second Connecticut, should have been the senior officer of the Brigade present January 3.

[128] This is the conclusion reached by T. J. Wertenbaker in the article on "The Battle of Princeton" cited hereafter as *Wertenbaker*, that he contributed to *The Princeton Battle Monument* (1922). Attention is directed to this article because it is the work of a trained historian, is based on a careful study of the ground, and is illustrated with contour maps. The reader should be warned that Maps 3 and 4 are reversed. Map 3 appears on p. 98 and should be on p. 92; Map 4, on p. 92, belongs on p. 98. The underlines of the two maps are in their proper place.

[129] *Wertenbaker*, 71.

[130] Wilkinson stated (1 *Memoirs*, 142) that he saw the glint on British arms and called out to Washington's secretary, Col. R. H. Harrison, who happened to be close by. Harrison probably waited long enough to see two mounted men emerge from the road, and then he hurried to Washington or else sent a messenger to the General.

[131] This is essentially Wertenbaker's interpretation of the preliminary movements, (*op. cit.*, 81 ff). He insisted that the British column, surprised by the approach of the Americans, was seeking to reach the high ground now known as Mercer Heights. Mercer's first move, in the judgment of Doctor Wertenbaker, was an advance to intercept the retreat of the British. When Mercer perceived from the crest of the hill near the junction of the roads that he could not head off the British, he determined to cut across the fields to the column on the back road. There was no point, Wertenbaker maintained, in a race for the orchard of William Clark, because the ground there was not commanding.

swering volley. As Mercer's men were passing through an orchard, a small British force had fired on them, whereupon the Americans had changed front and had pushed to the northern side of the orchard. In

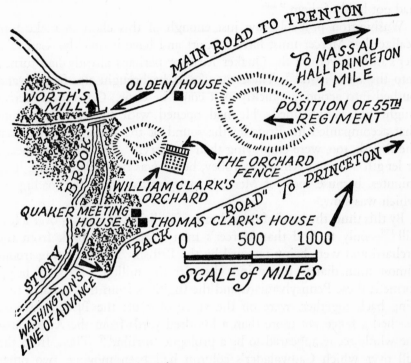

SCENE OF THE MEETING ENGAGEMENT AT PRINCETON

This sketch of the battleground of Jan. 3, 1776, is based on T. J. Wertenbaker, "Battle of Princeton" in *The Princeton Battle Monument*, p. 75, with the scale and the location of the Quaker Meeting House adapted from Alfred Hoyt Bill, *The Campaign of Princeton, 1776–1777*, p. 102. A large-scale contour map is appended to Alfred A. Woodhull, *The Battle of Princeton, A Preliminary Study*.

doing this, they dislodged the British who delivered the first fire from the shelter of a fence. Mercer formed his line along this fence, with his two cannon on his left, and now he was preparing to contest the advance of the British, who quickly left the Post Road in considerable numbers and turned on him.[132] Close to the enemy, Capt. John Flem-

132 *Wertenbaker*, 90–91. It will be noted that the essential differences between Wertenbaker's version and the traditional account is that Wertenbaker considered the fighting in the orchard as a chance meeting, while earlier writers assumed the battleground there had been chosen by both sides because the ground was of tactical and perhaps strategical importance.

ing of the First Virginia shouted, "Gentlemen, dress before you make ready." The British heard him, and answered, "Damn you, we will dress you," and opened fire. The Virginians stood the blast and delivered so effective a volley "that the enemy screamed as if many devils had got hold of them." [133]

Washington probably saw just enough of this clash to make him realize that Mercer must have support and have it quickly. Cadwalader's militia were in the Quaker Road or perhaps already had turned into the back road. [134] These men must be brought up, formed and pushed into action as quickly as it could be done. Otherwise, Mercer might be overwhelmed. He had opened with the two field guns that accompanied his Brigade; the sound of the firing indicated that the British, too, were employing their artillery. [135] Listening ears heard at length a second American volley, but it was delayed for long, long minutes, because most of Mercer's men carried rifles, the loading of which was slow.

By this time, the head of the column of militia was coming over a low hill [136]—only to find that Mercer's men were falling back from the orchard and were being pursued by the British. The retreating troops almost immediately threw into disorder the militia who were being formed; these Pennsylvanians and the fugitives from the orchard, running back together, were on the verge of rout; the British advance reached a fence not more than a hundred yards from the Americans; the whole scene appeared to be a prologue to ruin. [137] Then, from the hill over which Cadwalader's column had been moving, two other American field pieces began to bark as if they had been awaiting a rescue signal. Their fire forced the British behind the fence to run back to the main body. A little later these two guns were used to break up what appeared to be an attempt by a small body of horsemen to turn the right flank of the Americans. [138] The British answered with their brace of field cannon and brought into play, also, the pair Mercer had

---

[133] Baltimore dispatch of January 9 in *Va. Gazette,* Jan. 14, 1777.

[134] Because it was difficult to keep the column closed on a night march, there almost certainly was a stretch of unoccupied road between the rear of the Continentals and the van of the militia under Cadwalader. Had the militia been directly in rear of the Continentals, they would have been in position to support Mercer as soon as he engaged the British. See *Wertenbaker,* 96–97.

[135] "Officer of Distinction," *Stryker,* 447.

[136] This was the hill near the residence of Thomas Clark.

[137] "Officer of Distinction," *Stryker,* 447.

[138] *Ibid.*

been forced to abandon; but these did not silence the guns on the hill. Exposed to this well-directed, defensive fire, the British hesitated to attack. While they waited, Washington was riding, as were Greene, Cadwalader and other officers, among the bewildered troops, who still were sagging back. Mercer was not there to help; neither was Col. John Haslet who commanded what was left of the Delaware contingent. Whether these officers had been killed, wounded or captured, Washington did not know; but he and his companions did their utmost both to rally the survivors of the fight in the orchard and to halt the retreat of the Pennsylvania militia.

It was desperate work and it had to be done in short minutes, but now, for the first time, there was encouragement. Col. Daniel Hitchcock's New England Brigade of Continentals, the rearguard on the march from Trenton, was coming up. Its veterans could be trusted to deliver hard blows. In this assurance, Washington reasoned that if the Pennsylvanians were formed again and put on the flank of Hitchcock, a charge could be delivered that might drive back an enemy whose volume of fire did not indicate great strength. Washington ordered Hitchcock to the right and placed Hand's riflemen beyond the right of Hitchcock. Then Washington rode among the militia, whom Cadwalader was striving to put into line in rear of their former position. "Parade with us, my brave fellows," Washington cried to some of them, "there is but a handful of the enemy, and we will have them directly!" [139]

He did not appeal in vain. The Pennsylvanians were recovering from the first fright of their contact with the enemy and now that they probably were out of range, they stopped running and began to heed what was said to them.[140] In a surprisingly short time, they were ready. Washington placed himself at their head, to the left of Hitchcock, and ordered a general advance. Forward the men moved on a front much wider than that of the British, who had shifted their line somewhat to their left. By Washington's order, the Continentals and militia withheld their fire even when British bullets began to whine. The line did not break or even hesitate.

Steadily the Americans approached the unflinching redcoats. At thirty yards, Washington, astride his horse, drew rein, shouted "Halt,"

[139] "Sergeant R——," op. cit., 517; mentioned also in Wertenbaker, 102.
[140] It is almost certainly true that they were beyond the reach of the British, but no definite testimony to this effect has been found.

and then gave the command to fire. John Fitzgerald, one of Washington's new staff officers, seeing the tall target, covered his face with his hat because he could not bear to see the General fall. The volley was delivered and was answered in an instant; smoke enveloped everything; when it cleared, Washington still was on his horse, unscathed. Fitzgerald spurred to him, cried, "Thank God, your Excellency is safe," and then broke into excited tears.

Washington took him reassuringly by the hand: "Away, my dear Colonel," he said, "and bring up the troops; the day is our own." [141]

He was correct. The British realized now that they must quit the field, though they gallantly if vainly tried to save their guns and the two they had taken from Mercer. As the red line broke and fell back, officers undertook to rally it and to check the advance of the Americans. It could not be done. The men would not stand and load and fire. Most of the bullets the scattered British soldiers sent toward the Americans went wild. Then musketry ceased. A few minutes later, the enemy was across the Post Road and in flight.[142] Washington gave orders that the baggage left on the field by the enemy be guarded[143] and he directed that the bridge across Stony Brook be destroyed,[144] but beyond that, at the moment, he did not exercise his general command. He had for the first time in the war—indeed for the first time in his life—an opportunity of chasing an adversary across an open field, and he could not, would not, restrain himself. Off he spurred, and left to his lieutenants the task of taking the town. "It is a fine fox chase, my boys," he shouted as he raced after an "old red" of a different genus.[145]

When he returned, he found his men in high spirits. Some of the happy warriors, in the words of a resident of the field of battle, were "laughing outright, others smiling, and not a man among them but

---

[141] *Custis*, 191–92. This traditional account is printed with some reservation, because it was set down late in life by G. W. P. Custis, on the strength of what was told him by Colonel Fitzgerald when the former aide was an old man. Custis was prone to be theatrical, and the language he put in Washington's mouth was too formal even for an eighteenth-century leader, in the heat of action, but there probably was some foundation for the story.

[142] George Weedon to John Page, Jan. 6, 1777, *loc. cit.*; "Sergeant R——," *op. cit.*, 517; *Thomas Rodney's Diary*, 36; "Officer of Distinction" in *Stryker*, 447–48; 1 *Wilkinson*, 145; John Chilton's Diary, 12 *T* 283. These sources are not as informative as the list is formidable. Few details have been preserved of what happened during the last quarter of an hour on the field.

[143] *Thomas Rodney's Diary*, 36.

[144] At least, this appears to be the only time at which he could have renewed the order. See 6 *G. W.*, 469.

[145] 1 *Wilkinson*, 145. Wilkinson got the story from David Harris, a Captain of riflemen.

showed joy in his countenance." [146] Washington sought out Daniel
Hitchcock, as soon as he could, and gratefully shook the Rhode
Islander's hand: The Colonel must thank his officers and men, in the
General's name, for their advance.[147] Near a spot on which Washington drew rein, as he passed over the bloody stage of the day's red drama,
he saw a wounded British soldier on the ground, and he paused to praise
a gallant defence and to assure the man that everything the camp could
give the victims of the action would be issued. As Washington turned
away, a ghoul sneaked up and undertook to rob the helpless redcoat.
The General, glancing back, saw the beastly act, returned, sent the thief
scampering, and then posted a guard, with orders to remain till the
wounded soldier could be moved.[148]

By this time, Washington found that his Generals had become
alarmed by his absence. Some feared he might have been killed or
captured.[149] His reappearance was occasion for a double rejoicing, first
because he was safe and, second, because his men had occupied Princeton with much ease and little loss. While Washington had been trying
to rally Mercer's and Cadwalader's troops, Sullivan had been forced
to remain inactive because a British force of undetermined size had been
visible on a high hill [150] between the Post Road and the back road.
After the troops in front of Washington had been defeated, the King's
men on the hill had hurried to Princeton and had joined a Regiment
left there as a garrison. Together, these soldiers had moved out to the
edge of a ravine South of the town,[151] but apparently they had lost heart
after they realized their comrades had been swept away in Washington's attack. They offered no more than perfunctory resistance at the
ravine, and then some of them fled to the college building, which they
had hoped to defend. When the Americans brought up artillery and
prepared to batter down the edifice, those who had taken shelter in the
college surrendered. The remainder of the British disappeared in the
direction of New Brunswick.[152]

Prisoners and townsmen explained that the troops in Princeton had

[146] Anon., *A Brief Narrative of the Ravages*, etc., sometimes cited as the "Old Man's Narrative," p. 38.
[147] *John Howland*, 76.
[148] *Penn. Packet*, Jan. 22, 1777, cited in I *N. J. Arc.* (2), p. 268.
[149] I *Wilkinson*, 148.   [150] Mercer Heights.
[151] The present-day Frog Hollow.
[152] I *Wilkinson*, 148; I *Sullivan Papers*, 320; *Wertenbaker*, 110, with several references to
Princeton records.

consisted of the 17th, the 40th and the 55th Regiments, which formed the 4th Brigade of Howe's army. The commanding officer had been Lt. Col. Charles Mawhood, who had been leading the 17th and 55th on the Post Road, en route to Trenton, when contact had been established. Mawhood had used the 17th and part of the 55th in the fight with Mercer, and had sent the remainder of the 55th to the high hill North of Sullivan's position on the back road. The 40th had remained in Princeton. What the casualties among these troops had been, Washington could not ascertain, nor did he know how many prisoners had been taken.[153] His own losses had not been numerically heavy, but in officers, they had been grievous. Mercer had been killed, Washington was told, and Col. John Haslet had dropped in his tracks with a bullet through his brain. Several other men of promise had been slain.[154] Among them was Captain Fleming, who had called to his men to "dress before you make ready." In Washington's eyes, a shining victory had been darkened by the death of these men.[155]

First examination failed to show any considerable stores in Princeton or on the road. The two guns taken from Mawhood were fine brass field pieces, but Washington was not sure he could procure horses with which to take them away.[156] Included in the booty were a supply of flour [157] and "blankets, shoes and a few other trifling articles," according to Washington.[158] If supplies of value were hidden anywhere in the town, Washington did not have time to search for them. Soldiers close to the bales of new blankets were told to throw away their old covering, if worn, and to take new.[159]

Within two hours after Princeton was occupied, Washington received word that a British column from the direction of Trenton was advancing up the Post Road and already was close to the bridge at Worth's Mill.[160] Experienced men had been at work on the demolition of that crossing, and well-placed artillery were covering them; but if the British on the road were the troops who had occupied Trenton on the 2nd, no time

---

[153] British missing numbered 200 (*Stryker*, 486). See *infra*, p. 361.
[154] 6 *G. W.*, 469.   [155] *Ibid.*   [156] Cf. *ibid.*, 469–70.
[157] Sergeant White's *Narrative*, 24–25; omitted from the extracts printed in *Stryker*, 478.
[158] 6 *G. W.*, 470. It has been assumed by some writers that Washington deliberately minimized his captures in the belief that if he reported all that he took at Princeton, Congress would reduce proportionately the supplies allowed his Army. This would seem to be excluded by the language of Washington's report. Had he said nothing about his booty, his silence might have been designed to conceal his acquisitions, but his words should be accepted at face value.
[159] Sergeant White's *Narrative*, 24–25.
[160] Henry Knox to Mrs. Knox, Jan. 7, 1777; *Stryker*, 451.

should be lost in eluding so strong a force. Washington's Army was too weary to give battle even if the General had been willing to do so. As it was, he had no intention of hazarding a general engagement and, besides, he hoped he might seize some other British post that was not held by a garrison too large to be challenged.[161] Of course, Brunswick would be the great prize; but now that the British were near Princeton, was there any prospect that the American troops would get the rest and refreshment they would need for a swift advance to the base on the Raritan?[162] Perhaps the most that Washington could hope to do with his weary men would be to seize Somerset Court House, where 1300 hostile troops were supposed to be stationed.[163] The long roll was beaten;[164] the men fell in; the captured guns were left behind; the column got underway and cleared the town completely before the van of the British crossed Stony Brook and reached Princeton.[165] It delighted the Americans to hear later—the words were Henry Knox's—that the enemy arrived "in a most infernal sweat—running, puffing, and blowing, and swearing at being so outwitted."[166]

From Princeton, Washington's route was Northeast to Millstone River and then over that stream to Kingston, where the right fork of the road led to Brunswick and the left followed downstream toward Somerset Court House.[167] At the crossroads the final decision had to be made on the cherished plan of capturing New Brunswick. Snow had been encountered North of Princeton;[168] travel would be harder. "The commander and several general officers," Wilkinson wrote afterward, "halted at the forks . . . whilst our troops were filing off to Rocky Hill, when the exclamation was general, 'O that we had 500 fresh men to beat up their quarters at Brunswick.'"[169] Washington was regretful but convinced: ". . . the harassed state of our own troops," he wrote, "(many of them having had no rest for two nights and a day) and the danger of losing the advantage we had gained by aiming at too much, induced me, by the advice of my officers, to relinquish the attempt . . ."; but he set it down as his further conviction that "six or eight hundred fresh troops upon a forced march" could

[161] *Ibid.* [162] 6 *G. W.*, 481.
[163] Knox, as *supra*, n. 160.
[164] See an interesting note on neglect of the long roll by militia (*Stryker*, 432).
[165] 6 *G. W.*, 469–70. [166] *Ibid.*
[167] Cf. Joshua Doughty, Jr. "Washington's March from Princeton to Morristown," *NJHSP*, new ser. v. 5, p. 240 ff.
[168] *Glyn's Journal*, Princeton Lib. [169] 1 *Wilkinson*, 148.

have taken Brunswick, its stores and military chest, and could have "put an end to the war." [170]

From Kingston, then, the exhausted Army staggered on to Rocky Hill and thence to Somerset Court House,[171] with no other hindrance than the presence across the Millstone of a body of horse that finally disappeared.[172] Some of the American troops reached the Court House at dusk; [173] the rear Regiments did not arrive until 8 P.M. or later [174] and then had to bivouac.[175] The Pennsylvania militia suffered most cruelly because their blankets, through someone's blunder, had been sent to Burlington with the other baggage.[176] There was further disappointment in the report by natives that the belongings of the British troops encountered at Princeton had left the Court House under a small escort a bare hour previously. Not one command in Washington's Army had strength left in it to organize pursuit.[177] The next day, January 4, the troops moved to Pluckamin, whence Washington dispatched his report to Congress.[178] To the men, the village was a paradise, because there, in the language of one young Captain's diary, "we got plenty of beef, pork, &c., which we had been starving for a day or two, not having time to draw and dress victuals." [179] On the 5th and 6th, the march was to Morristown where Washington hoped to get shelter and to assure rest for his men.[180]

All his intelligence was that the British had abandoned both Trenton and Princeton and had fallen back to Brunswick [181]—an incredible reversal of the situation that had existed Christmas Day. Henry Knox was writing of demonstrated fact when he told his wife: "The enemy were within nineteen miles of Philadelphia, they are now sixty miles. We have driven them from almost the whole of West Jersey." [182] For this achievement, Washington received congratulations he doubtless

---

[170] Letter of Jan. 5, 1777, to the President of Congress; 6 *G. W.*, 470; cf. *Thomas Rodney's Diary*, 38, and Stirling in *Stryker*, 452.
[171] The present-day Millstone.   [172] See *Thomas Rodney's Diary*, 38–39.
[173] *Ibid.*
[174] McMichael's Diary in 15 *Penn. Arc.* (2), p. 203.
[175] *Thomas Rodney's Diary*, 38.   [176] 6 *G. W.*, 470.
[177] All the relevant facts are summarized admirably in *Wertenbaker*, 116–17.
[178] It is dated Jan. 5, 1777 and will be found in 6 *G. W.*, 467–71.
[179] Diary of John Chilton, 12 *T* 283.   [180] 1 *Wilkinson*, 149.
[181] 6 *G. W.*, 470.
[182] Letter of Jan. 7, 1777 to Mrs. Knox; *Stryker*, 451. Cf. Eben. Huntington to Andrew Huntington, Peekskill, Jan. 5, 1777: ". . . the enemy are pounded and harrested and I think that by the latter end of this week I may inform you that they are drive to the extremity if not entirely from the State of New Jersey . . ." (*Eben. Huntington Letters*, 57, with some modernization of capitals and abbreviated terms.

would have wished the country had expressed earlier in terms of men and supplies. John Hancock wrote in acknowledgment of the arrival of George Baylor with news of the first victory at Trenton, ". . . As it is entirely due to your wisdom and conduct, the United States are indebted for the late success of their arms, the pleasure you must naturally feel on the occasion will be pure and unmixed. May you still proceed" —and with that he shaped his encomium in much the terms the Massachusetts lawmakers had employed after the British evacuated Boston.[183] The *Pennsylvania Journal* went beyond even this: "Washington retreats like a General and acts like a hero. If there are spots in his character, they are like the spots in the sun, only discernible by the magnifying powers of a telescope. Had he lived in the days of idolatry, he had been worshipped as a god. One age cannot do justice to his merit, but the united voices of a grateful posterity shall pay a cheerful tribute of undissembled praise to the great asserter of their country's freedom." [184] That was vastly more than could be desired by a modest soldier, and it was a generous tribute after Long Island and Kip's Bay and Fort Washington . . . but independence could not be built on praise of a leader.

[183] Letter of Jan. 1, 1777; 1 *LTW.*, 218.
[184] Issue of Feb. 19, 1777; reprinted in 1 *Moore,* 397.

CHAPTER XIV

LONG ISLAND TO PRINCETON IN RETROSPECT
(August 22, 1776–January 6, 1777)

To MORRISTOWN, sooner or later, came reports of almost everything that was happening and of much that had occurred, unknown to Washington, during the ten-days' campaign of Trenton and Princeton. When Washington left the college town on the 3rd of January, his information was that Mercer had been killed in the fighting at the orchard.[1] Now it developed that the General had been shot and then, on his refusal to surrender, had been bayoneted five times by British soldiers who had left him for dead on the field. Later he was found to be breathing and was removed to a nearby house, where he was nursed by the women of the family. Washington immediately asked the nearest British senior commander, who proved to be Lord Cornwallis, for permission to send an aide to Mercer. Readily enough, Cornwallis consented; Capt. George Lewis went inside the lines to the quarters of the General. The next information that reached Washington was half-cheerful, half-gloomy: Mercer was desperately wounded but there was at least a chance he would recover. Washington and other sympathetic officers would not despair of a good soldier's life so long as he breathed, yet they scarcely hoped he again would ride at the head of his excellent Brigade. Mercer had not given up his Virginia command until June, 1776, and after he had joined Washington, he had been in command of the Flying Camp for some months, with no chance to distinguish himself in the field. When opportunity had come to him, he had made the utmost of it. The Army would lose one of its most promising general officers if he succumbed.[2]

Later reports confirmed belief that losses were not excessive. In the confusion of records of Brigades, exact returns could not be prepared; but as far as Washington could ascertain, the dead numbered six or seven officers and twenty-five to thirty rank and file. He did not even

[1] 6 G. W., 477.
[2] 6 G. W., 471, 477; G.W.P. Custis, 183; 1 Wilkinson, 147; Dr. Jonathan Potts to Owen Biddle, Jan. 5, 1776; Stryker, 445.

estimate the wounded.[3] British casualties, in Washington's opinion, would run to 500,[4] and, when added to the Hessian losses at Trenton on the 26th of December, would cut deeply into the strength of the enemy. Nathanael Greene, more exuberant than his chief, asserted "within a fortnight past we have taken and killed of Howe's army between two and three thousand men . . ."[5] Mistaken though such loose computations might be, it scarcely was possible to exaggerate the effect of the operations at Trenton and Princeton on the self-confidence of the Army, on the spirit of New Jersey, on the policy of Congress, and on the faith of all the States in the attainment of independence. A dying cause was revivified; timid men who had been afraid to participate in what the British termed "rebellion" now came cheerfully to camp.[6] Metaphorically, the situation might have been described with accuracy in an entry Capt. Thomas Rodney had made in his Diary: ". . . the sun rose as we passed over Stony Brook."[7]

The prospect was not without its shadows. Pennsylvania militia who were praised by Washington for their substantial part in the victory, were becoming restive and anxious to go home.[8] Washington had once more to contemplate the possibility that the militia would leave him, no matter how dire his distress; but even with that to cloud the horizon, he had transformed the military scene. The British did not regard Mawhood's fight at Princeton as a defeat,[9] though they conceded that Washington had outwitted them in leaving Trenton. Until the sound of firing was heard from the direction of Princeton, the British com-

---

[3] 6 G. W., 481.
[4] Ibid. Actually, they were about 286. See Stryker, 458 and Sgt. Thomas Sullivan's MS "Account of the Battle of Princeton," PHS.
[5] Letter of Jan. 9, 1777 to a "Gentleman in Philadelphia"; Stryker, 472.
[6] John Armstrong to unnamed correspondent, Jan. 5, 1777: "If the whole I have seen were joined to General Washington, I should hope his Army will at least consist of 20,000 exclusive of what we may now expect will join him in the Jerseys . . ." (Henkel's Cat. 683, No. 148). See also John Cropper to his wife, Jan. 12, 1777: "Soldiers are flocking from every part which I hope will put an end to the war this winter if our people behave as well as they have." (11 VHS. Cols. n. s., 278). In the same spirit, Gates wrote Washington from Philadelphia, Jan. 24, 1777: "Mr. Morris [et. als.] have desired I remain here to expedite the march of the militia daily arriving in this city . . ." (Gates Papers, NYHS). In addition, see 6 G. W., 489; Stryker, 445, 465, 472; 1 Ballagh, Lee Letters, 248. For Congress' new zeal in seeking alliances with France and Spain, see 3 Force (5), p. 1481.
[7] Diary, 33.
[8] 6 G. W., 470, 504. See Timothy Matlack to John Cadwalader, Jan. 21, 1777: ". . . upon the alarm today, five only agreed to stay" (Cadwalader Papers, PHS); John Cadwalader's address to the Council of Safety, Jan. 15, 1777 (ibid.); Cadwalader's GO on the discharge of his Brigade, n. d. (Ibid.).
[9] See Howe's GO of Jan. 9, 1777; Glyn's Journal, Princeton Lib.; Howe to Germaine Gentleman's Mag., 1777, p. 90.

manders at Trenton had thought that Washington had moved to Bordentown,[10] and they had more respect for him and for his Army when they realized how quickly he had marched to their most vulnerable post. Care was taken at Brunswick and nearby stations to build redoubts that would prevent such surprises in the future;[11] admission was made that a small British army had been imprudently divided.[12] Howe himself felt called upon to explain that he had made a wide extension of his cantonments because he wished to "afford protection to the inhabitants that they might experience the difference between His Majesty's government and that to which they were subject from the rebel leaders."[13]

Beyond this, none of the British commanders would accept responsibility for the reverses; the blame, they maintained, was on the Hessians at Trenton, December 26, and not on them, either in that village on the 2nd of January or at Princeton the next day. They belabored the scapegoat. General Howe wrote Lord George Germaine: ". . . the unfortunate and untimely defeat at Trenton has thrown us further back than was at first apprehended, from the great encouragement it has given to the rebels. I do not now see a prospect of terminating the war but by a general action, and I am aware of the difficulties in our way to obtain it, as the enemy moves with so much more celerity than we possibly can."[14] Governor Tryon fairly wailed: "The rebels carrying off the Hessian Brigade under Colonel Rall at Trenton has given me more real chagrin than any other circumstance this war: the moment was critical, and I believe the rebel chiefs were conscious if some stroke was not struck that would give life to their sinking cause, they should not raise another army."[15] Subsequently, under examination before the House of Commons, Joseph Galloway insisted that the capture of the Hessians "removed the panic with which the new States of the Middle Colonies were struck." The disaster, said he, "contributed in a great measure to the raising of the army which Washington commanded the next campaign."[16] That there should be another campaign because of

[10] *A. Robertson's Diaries,* 120.   [11] *Ibid.,* 121.
[12] *Ibid.,* 121.
[13] His testimony before the House of Commons, December, 1778, conveniently reprinted in Bellamy Partridge, *Sir Billy Howe,* appendix, p. 267.
[14] Dispatch of Jan. 20, 1777; reprinted in *Stryker,* 482.
[15] Letter of Dec. 31, 1776; 3 *Force* (5), p. 1514.
[16] *Examination of Joseph Galloway before the House of Commons, June 16, 1779,* p. 17. Cf. *Glyn's Journal* (loc. cit.), Jan. 9, 1777. See also *Dodsley's Annual Register,* for 1777, p. 20: "These actions, and the sudden recovery from the lowest state of weakness and distress,

the Hessians' blunder was resented by those Britishers who had thought the war so near a victorious termination that they were hoping soon to go home.[17] The Hessian commanders, for their part, instituted a court martial to place the responsibility for the surprise.[18] At the moment, Colonel Donop could think of no excuse other than to pass on to his superior a report that the Americans who had descended on Trenton were 10,000 to 12,000 strong.[19]

Washington, of course, heard little of this immediately, and some of it he never knew, but he appraised the operations realistically. While giving the fullest credit to his general officers and to his troops,[20] he felt that he owed much of his success to circumstance. In writing Robert Morris, he spoke of the first affair at Trenton as "our late lucky blow," [21] and while he was in that village, after his second crossing, he told Heath that he hoped, "with a moderate share of fortune, to give our affairs a more promising aspect than they had worn of late." [22] Again, when he sat down to report to Congress on the move to Princeton, he spoke of the outcome of the fight as "this piece of good fortune" [23] and in sending the news to General Putnam, he began, "Fortune has favored us in an attack on Princeton." [24]

In none of this did Washington exaggerate the part that chance had played throughout the two operations.[25] Now that he was at Morristown, disentangled, Washington could not expect the continued favor of circumstance, but he could and did hope that after he had refreshed his men, he could renew his effort to drive the British out of Jersey.[26] In this he sought the aid of General Heath, whom he urged to make feints against the enemy on New York Island,[27] and soon he faced discouragements of a familiar sort. By the 7th he had to write the Presi-

---

to become a formidable enemy in the field, raised the character of General Washington as a commander, very high, both in Europe and America; and with his preceding and subsequent conduct serve, altogether, to give a sanction to that appelation which is now pretty generally applied to him, of the American Fabius."

[17] Serle, 163.

[18] It did not hand in its verdict until Jan. 11, 1782 and then it acquitted the troops and the surviving officers. The "findings" of the different classes of officers composing the court pronounced Rall rash and negligent (Stryker, 409 ff).

[19] Donop to Knyphausen, Dec. 27, 1776. Stryker, 399.

[20] 6 G. W., 444, 463, 470–71.   [21] Letter of Dec. 30, 1776; ibid., 457.

[22] Letter of Dec. 31, 1776; ibid., 459.   [23] Letter of Jan. 5, 1777; 6 G. W., 469.

[24] Letter of Jan. 5, 1777; ibid., 471. See, also, Washington to Jonathan Trumbull, Jan. 10, 1777: "Our success at Trenton has been followed by another lucky blow at Princeton on the 3rd inst." (ibid., 489).

[25] These contingent factors are reviewed as part of the general critique of the campaign, infra, p. 376 ff.

[26] 6 G. W., 471.   [27] Ibid., 472–73, 475.

dent of Congress: "The severity of the season has made our troops, especially the militia, extremely impatient, and has reduced the number very considerably. Every day more or less leave us. Their complaints and the great fatigues they have undergone induced me to come to this place, as the best calculated of any in this quarter to accomodate and refresh them. The situation is by no means favorable to our views, and as soon as the purposes are answered for which we came, I think to remove, though I confess I do not know how we shall procure covering for our men elsewhere." [28]

If the defection of the militia continued, and Washington neither could find better winter quarters nor had to defend Morristown against the British, then he at last was ending the painful campaign that had opened on Long Island, August 22, when the British had landed at Gravesend Bay. Its first and longer phase had witnessed a succession of defeats, large and small, for the American Army under Washington. The defence of Long Island had been worse than futile; Kip's Bay had been a disgrace, and October 28 at White Plains a humiliation; the surrender of Fort Washington had been a major disaster; the retreat through Jersey had involved a threat to Philadelphia and, indeed, to the very life of the United States. Until that lucky 26th of December, Washington's sole success of any magnitude in field operations had been that of Harlem Heights, Sept. 16, 1776. Even then Washington had called a halt in the pursuit because he did not have confidence in his Army. That same lack of faith in the ability of his men to stand up against the British and their German allies had compelled Washington to conduct a campaign of maneuver and to avoid a general engagement. It had been costly maneuver, too, that had yielded the invaluable base of New York Island to the British, and then had exposed almost the whole of New Jersey to the plundering advance of an enemy who had robbed both friend and foe.

Why had it been so? To what errors of military judgment, to what mistakes of policy, and to what weakness of resources was so long and so sad a record of failure to be attributed? The first of the three answers to these questions had been set down again and again in Washington's dispatches to Congress: primarily because of the short-term enlistment of an Army that always was too small, he never commanded a disci-

[28] 6 G. W., 477–78. The draft of this letter, in the autograph of R. H. Harrison, included a statement that the militia had been reduced "to one third less than it was when we first crossed the Delaware" (ibid., 478 n).

plined force of sufficient size to overpower his adversary. When marked numerical superiority had been his—and that was rarely—the margin had consisted of untrained militia, whose presence in the ranks usually was of such brief duration that the men could not be brought under strict regulation or inured to camp life. From the first clash at Concord and Lexington until almost the end of 1775, Congress had believed, as had Washington, that the outcome of the siege of Boston would fix a peace, advantageous or adverse to the Colonies. One campaign was to end the war. In that belief, the term of enlistment, the volume of supplies and everything else had been limited, essentially, to the year that witnessed the opening of hostilities. By the time it had become apparent that the war was to be of long duration, the prescribed service of enlisted men terminated and the first zeal of most of them had evaporated. Thereafter, nearly all the Regiments of the continental establishment had to be reorganized. Efforts to recruit them to full strength seldom were successful. Each British victory increased the number of those who believed that the King's arms were invincible and that resistance, vain in itself, might put the volunteer in prison if not on the gallows. Popular enthusiasm for the American cause may never have been general and it certainly was on the decline through the later months of 1776.

Even from those Regiments that somehow contrived to have substantial nominal strength, there had been harsh and unrelieved subtraction. Courageous as Washington always was in facing reality, he never set down on paper, so far as is known, any computation of his total losses during the four and a half months from the landing on Long Island to the occupation of Morristown. The number must have been between 4000 and 4500, exclusive of deserters and of deaths from disease. Hospitals were so poorly operated and so feebly supplied that they were a constant scandal. Quite often, soldiers had not even the poor comfort of these wretched places. Late in December, 1776, the New York Convention felt compelled to inform Congress that sick soldiers were dying at Fishkill "for want of the commonest attentions." The President of the Convention wrote: "Without blankets, medicines and the proper care of physicians, they are reduced to the lowest ebb of human wretchedness; and what astonishes us still more—what, indeed, hardly any evidence would make a man of sense believe, is that between two and three hundred men are now here, returned unfit for duty, because there is not sulphur to cure them of the itch." [29] Conditions scarcely less bad existed almost from the beginning of the war. They had been reported to Washington but he had been burdened with so many duties that he could not find time to provide decent, not to say adequate care of the sick. Congress now was of a temper to act summarily. It voted the dismissal of Dr. John Morgan, Director General and Chief Physician of Hospitals, and it took the same action concerning Dr. Samuel Stringer, who held the corresponding, subordinate position in the Northern Department.[30] Almost simultaneously, Washington undertook to have the men of his Army inoculated so that he would not have his troops menaced, as the Canadian expedition had been, by devastating smallpox.[31] Ultimately, these measures might improve conditions and reduce the number of those who had to battle with disease when they had bargained to fight the British only. At the moment, flux and pneumonia were slaying far more men than were being shot down. As of Dec. 22, 1776, seven of the rank and file were sick, for every ten who were present for duty, fit.[32] Those figures explained much of the Army's weakness and failure.

The second reason for Washington's poor showing during nearly the whole of the campaign in New York and Jersey was the inability of Congress to find in America adequate supplies, equipment, clothing and shoes for the Army. Powder now was being manufactured in quantity; the artillery possessed nearly as many cannon as Henry Knox could use, though some of the guns were poor; there was no great shortage of flints; so long as the Army had few mounted troops, horses still could be bought; provisions had been forthcoming during most of the operations. When these five items were listed, they represented the pitiful sum of the Army's sufficiency. Every other essential of war was in short supply or was lacking altogether. Many of the troops were in tatters, and hundreds had shoes that scarcely held together. Some were barefooted even in December. Others had no blankets. The wonder was not in the retreat of such an Army across Jersey. Rather was it that the Army survived to reach the Delaware and then to assume the offensive.

The third reason for the unflattering record of the Army prior to the operations against Trenton and Princeton was the paucity of com-

[29] Letter of Dec. 28, 1776; 3 *Force* (5), p. 1467.
[30] 7 *JCC.*, 24.   [31] 6 *G. W.*, 473.
[32] Present fit, rank and file, 4707; present sick, 680; absent sick, 2590; 3 *Force* (5), p. 1402.

petent leaders of every rank from company Lieutenant to division commander. Few of his military disasters had been as bad, in Washington's judgment, as the action of Congress Oct. 8, 1776, in providing that every State represented in the Army could send commissioners to headquarters and select all the officers for the Regiments that were to be reorganized.[33] Washington had felt that many of the original officers had been incompetent and he feared the commissioners would make bad conditions dangerously worse by permitting politics or friendship to control their choice. There would be scant prospect, he thought, that commissioners would retain or promote the men who had shown themselves qualified to enforce discipline and to fight with courage and clear heads.[34]

At the higher levels of command, the campaigns of 1776 wrought costly revolution. Few of the men commissioned as general officers in June and July, 1775, had shown the requisite ability or, if able, had survived the bloody tests of battle. Two of those who had displayed the intelligent qualities of virile leadership were dead, Richard Montgomery and John Thomas. The General with the highest reputation, Charles Lee, was a prisoner of war. In their field operations, Gates and Schuyler had not been under Washington's immediate command. Although Gates had rejoined the main Army, he had hurried away to Baltimore, presumably to solicit larger support of his forces in upper New York.[35] Schuyler continued to collect and to forward supplies but he was showing himself to be more a Quartermaster than a field commander. He, moreover, was increasingly sensitive to criticism and, generally, had become a difficult person with whom to deal. William Heath and Joseph Spencer still had Divisions, but neither of them had done anything more than discharge routine duties without displaying such scandalous incompetence or sloth as to make their removal a public necessity. Not one flash of shining leadership had come from either of them.

Perhaps the greatest disappointment of all had been the failure of Israel Putnam to add in the least to the reputation he had gained at Bunker Hill. Washington had regarded him as an able executive officer [36] and had made no criticism of his conduct on Long Island in August, but afterward Washington had not employed him extensively

---

[33] 5 *JCC.*, 855.   [34] See *supra*, p. 254, 255–56.   [35] See *supra*, p. 309.
[36] See Washington to Hancock, Jan. 30, 1776; 4 *G. W.*, 290.

DID GREENE DOMINATE WASHINGTON?

No, said the men of the Rhode Island Kentish Guards in Octover, 1774, they would not have an officer who had to hobble about. He was not crippled, in the strict sense of the word, but he had a stiff knee. Who would want to belong to a volunteer Company in which the Captain or one of the Lieutenants had to limp across the parade? It would not be soldierly. Nathanael Greene was sensitive about the stiffness of that knee, and was ambitious besides, but there was nothing he could do except to acquiesce in the verdict of his Rhode Island neighbors and offer to serve as a private. In spite of his 32 years and his position as the able son of a successful iron foundryman, he told his comrades he was completely willing to carry a musket in the cause of America.

It may have been the decision that shaped his career. In May of the next year, when Rhode Island legislators decided to raise 1500 troops and to defy the royal Governor, they remembered Greene's willingness to serve in the ranks and, as they looked about, they could find nobody who seemed to have so many qualifications of leadership. They named him to command the force. Another month and a little more brought him a continental commission as Brigadier; as of the 9th of August, 1776, the man whom the Kentish Guard had rejected as company officer had become the head of a Division.

Then Fortune tricked him for a time. Before the retreat across Jersey had ended, the jealous and the disappointed were saying that the Commander-in-Chief listened too readily to Major General Greene, who was blamed for the loss of Fort Washington and its 2800 defenders. He suffered in consequence, but all his prestige was recovered at Trenton and at Princeton, after which actions, Greene was accepted almost everywhere as second only to Washington in the main Army. Outside that Army, Gates was Greene's only possible rival.

Ability and a sense of military values were credited to Greene by all except a few who were enviously irreconcilable; his defects were of his own making—a haste in decision, an overconfidence in his judgment, an insistence that his integrity be acknowledged formally whenever any act of his was criticized. The less reason he had for heeding carpers, the more sensitive he became.

(After the original by C. W. Peale, Independence Hall, Philadelphia.)

PHILIP SCHUYLER, "DIFFICULT" PATRIOT

Two adjectives, perhaps three, would have been accepted by Philip Schuyler's friends and by his foes as applicable to him: he was patriotic and he was difficult. Most continentals would have admitted, also, that he was able, though some of his critics would have said his mind was more manorial than martial—more suited to collecting supplies than to leading men. In this, he was not unlike a considerable number of successful eighteenth-century Americans, who found to their surprise that war called for rarer qualities than business and commerce demanded.

The complex personality implied by the word "difficult" makes Schuyler one of the most interesting figures of the Revolution. To encounter him in the flesh may have been provoking; to study him in retrospect is fascinating. With men whom he regarded as his appreciative peers, his manners were flawless. Consideration of him always elicited the most generous courtesy. Between him and Washington, there usually was understanding so complete that it seemed literally intuitive. This was so at the beginning of their military relations and, except for a few brief and easily resolved incidents, it so remained.

If noblesse oblige was involved, no man could be more responsive than Schuyler. His hospitality overflowed; his aid always was bountiful if the circumstances imposed an obligation. While he never was facile in dispositions for actual combat, he had sound strategical judgment, Washington thought, and he would work patiently, through any maze of detail, when he thought the duty aided the cause and became a gentleman. These two conditions were almost of equal importance with him. Some labors, even in Congress, were beneath his dignity; he would have no hand in them.

Any criticism of his acts was a challenge of his integrity; any assumption of authority that infringed in the slightest on his prerogative must be renounced at once or he would himself resign. He could be ingratiating and he could be lofty, too. New Englanders resented his air of superiority; he returned disfavor with contempt—but all the while, in his own fortune as in his daily comfort, no man was readier to sacrifice for American freedom.

(After the painting by Trumbull in the New-York Historical Society.)

where risks had to be taken. The impression left by Washington's letters to Putnam is that the Commander-in-Chief had concluded Putnam no longer possessed initiative and served his country best when in command of some such post as that of Philadelphia. In those instances where Washington sent Putnam into the field, he gave the "old hero" explicit instruction.[37] In the eyes of young soldiers, Putnam stood even lower, as the exemplar of an outdated type of warfare.

Of the other men who had been made general officers early in the war, Washington had few on whom he could rely with full confidence. The Commander-in-Chief could not say that Stirling was brilliant but he knew the Jersey soldier to be devoted and courageous, though perhaps too fond of the bottle. Sullivan was able and diligent but he had not shaken off the self-consciousness that Washington had described in a letter to President Hancock when Sullivan had been under consideration for the command in Canada. The New Hampshire General probably had been more responsible than anyone else for failure to guard the Jamaica Road on the American left flank during the fighting on Long Island in August, but, at his worst, Sullivan was a better soldier than most of those to whom Washington had to entrust the lives of his men.

As it was with Sullivan for Long Island, so it was with Nathanael Greene concerning the capture of Fort Washington. Greene had been the man who insisted that the fort be held in strength, and he it was who had given assurance that the high ground overlooking North River could be so fortified that the British would challenge its bastions in vain. The Rhode Islander had been mistaken; the fort had capitulated; Charles Lee, Joseph Reed and doubtless others had put the blame for this directly on Greene and indirectly on Washington for yielding to him. In spite of this criticism, Greene had kept straight on and had become potentially the ablest of Washington's lieutenants. Hugh Mercer might have been his peer and possibly his superior, but word came within a few days that Mercer had lost his last battle. On the 12th of January, he died of the wounds received on the 3rd.

Denied the counsel and the courage of Mercer, the Commander-in-Chief could look hopefully to Henry Knox, to the newcomer Arthur St. Clair, to Benjamin Lincoln who was just arriving at Peekskill,[38]

---

[37] See, for example, Washington's letter of Jan. 5, 1777, concerning an advance by Putnam to Crosswicks; 6 G. W., 471.
[38] Heath, 116; 1 LTW., 320–21.

and to John Cadwalader, the Pennsylvanian of first-rate abilities who had cooperated admirably in the Trenton-Princeton operations. It was distress to Washington and loss to the Army when Cadwalader declined commission as Brigadier. An occasional officer who had served briefly, or not at all with Washington—such a man as Benedict Arnold for example—might display eminent leadership in a desperate hour. Until that happened, Washington would have too small a company of thoroughly qualified officers—Greene, Knox, Sullivan and perhaps St. Clair and Benjamin Lincoln. It could not be said of any of the other Generals that they had been responsible for defeats that threatened ruin to the American cause. Their worst failures had been negative, failures in building up their commands and in keeping their men fit.

If the campaign of 1776 now was ending, what could be said of Washington's own leadership? Had he met the requirements of his post? What had he learned, and what should be unlearn? Did he make mistakes another man might have avoided, with reduced loss of life and of territory?

His basic strategy at the beginning of the campaign scarcely can be challenged. New York had to be defended; otherwise the British probably would have been able to ascend the Hudson and to sever New England. Had that been accomplished, any commander, even one of the very front rank, would have found it exceedingly difficult to keep the American cause alive. Once Washington was committed to this essential strategic operation, he was compelled to protect a large and geographically difficult area against attack by an adversary who possessed the immense advantage of sea power. Howe had almost complete freedom to operate when, where and as he pleased. The American commander had the duty of closing North River to the enemy's fleet, if that was possible; and he had simultaneously to keep the enemy from landing either in Jersey or on New York Island itself as a means of outflanking the forts that defended North River. Virtually the same situation existed on East River. If the high ground of Brooklyn were lost, the British would dominate the channel of East River and, at the same time would have part of the lower end of New York under their guns. This, in turn, called for the fortification of Brooklyn in such a manner that it could not be taken in rear. Again, if Brooklyn had to be protected, then it seemed logical to retain on Long Island a force large enough to keep the enemy at bay; but in attempting this, the

American commander dispersed force and ran the risk of having the garrison of Long Island isolated by the employment of British warships to close East River. Perhaps the best solution of this problem would have been the erection at Brooklyn of strong defences, which could have been held by a relatively small garrison, victualled to stand a protracted siege. Unfortunately, the Americans lacked the engineers, the provisions and the time required for this. It seems entirely probable, also, that the defence of New York Island so nearly absorbed the attention of Washington that he gave little thought to Long Island. Nathanael Greene was left to do what he thought necessary there, and when he was stricken with illness, just prior to the British attack, no other officer knew enough about the situation to conduct a sound defence.

When the attack on Long Island was begun, Sullivan was in command as a substitute for Greene, but Putnam, it will be remembered, was importunate in his appeal that he be given a hand in the battle. Washington acquiesced, but for so doing he scarcely is to be condemned, because Putnam had not then been charged with any lack of initiative. "Old Put" still enjoyed his full reputation and had the confidence of the country and of the Army. Once on Long Island, as senior Major General, he had authority, of course, to direct Sullivan under any general instructions given him by Washington. As far as records show, the Commander-in-Chief gave Putnam a free hand; but in what manner Putnam exercised his command, it is impossible to say. Apparently he retained direct control inside the Brooklyn defences and placed under Sullivan all the troops outside the works, though Sullivan said later he "was to have commanded, under General Putnam, within the lines." [39] The significant fact is the existence of the doubt concerning the relative responsibility of the two men. This of itself may account for some of the mishandling of the defence. Needless to say, blame for failure to protect or at least to patrol the Jamaica Road must be charged against Sullivan, with no extenuation beyond that of his lack of mounted men. Nothing positive is known of Putnam's dispatch or failure to send troops from the defences to support Sullivan and Stirling, though it is proper to add that this question can be raised only as it applies to Putnam's disposition of troops prior to August 27, the day of the battle. After the attack began, the climax

[39] Letter of Oct. 25, 1777; 1 *Sullivan Papers*, 549.

came so quickly that reenforcements scarcely could have been moved from the fortifications in time to be of any assistance.

Whether Washington should have assumed personal command on Long Island does not appear to have been considered in any subsequent discussion of the action. His contemporaries evidently were of opinion that he had to maintain headquarters where he could have a view of every move the enemy might make, because an attempted landing on New York Island, simultaneously with the offensive in front of Brooklyn, did not seem to be beyond the resources of the British. With that possibility before him—some considered it a high probability—Washington could not afford to let himself become absorbed in an engagement at a point where communication with him would be slow. He went to Long Island and directed the withdrawal: that probably was all he should have undertaken to do personally. In assembling the boats and in assuring a steady, unhurried flow of troops to the ferry landing in Brooklyn, he displayed so much skill that many persons almost forgot the defeat in their admiration of the retreat.

During the next stage of the campaign, Washington lost New York Island and a ponderable store of supplies and equipment, tents in particular. He manifestly could have saved these if he had begun the evacuation of the lower end of the island immediately after the abandonment of the Brooklyn defences, but if he had started this sooner than he did, he might have created fears that would have spread to his troops. The militia might have disappeared almost overnight. He had to restore some of the Army's self-confidence, if this was possible, before he quit a town he could not hope to defend against the Howe brothers. Considered in another way, Washington's failure to save all his stores was not the result of poor planning but was due first to the necessity of removing his sick and wounded and, second, to the inexperience of Stephen Moylan, who then was Quartermaster General. Although Moylan was devoted to the American cause, he was not suited to the exacting duties of his indispensable but unappreciated post. The resignation of Moylan, under pressure, before the end of December was, in a sense, his admission of failure.

When Washington withdrew to the northern end of New York Island and disposed his troops to meet any flanking operation directed against King's Bridge, he made no move that any reasonable observer could criticize. He used his limited forces economically and he checkmated Howe all the way to White Plains. Then the situation changed. From the day Washington decided the British might enter Jersey, he showed hesitation that might almost have been described as bewilderment and he began a dispersal of force that mocked all he had said previously about concentration.[40] At the same time he undertook to carry out the expressed will of Congress that the Hudson be closed to the British, though the Continentals did not possess either the skill or the materials for making effective underwater obstructions. It was not certain that the river could be rendered impassable by the retention of Fort Washington and Fort Lee, but obstructions in the river could be removed or avoided easily if the two forts were abandoned.[41] Whether he retained or evacuated these defences, Washington felt that he must keep farther up the stream a force sufficient to guard the Highlands and thereby to make it as difficult as possible for Howe to establish contact with Burgoyne or to take Schuyler's and Gates's troops in rear.

This attempt simultaneously to maneuver against Howe in Jersey, to cling to Fort Washington, and to defend the Highlands produced an extraordinary result. Washington made his division of force by assigning to Lee and to Heath the Regiments that came from States East of the Hudson, while he personally commanded those of the States below that river.[42] This gave him so few men after he crossed on the 13th of November that he was powerless to confront the British. A visitor to the camps in Jersey might have asked in dismay, What has become of the Army; has it been destroyed?

Three days later, the bitter subtraction of the garrison of Fort Washington had to be made. In retrospect, it was easy to affirm that the place should have been evacuated before it was attacked. At the time, the arguments for defending Fort Washington were understood and

---

[40] Charles Lee may have been responsible for the theory that separate armies should be employed on either side of the Hudson, but the evidence is by no means adequate to justify a statement that Lee's advocacy antedated Washington's, or that the proposal was made by Lee as a means of procuring the separate command he undoubtedly desired for himself. Lee wrote Congress Oct. 12, 1776 (2 *Lee Papers,* 261) that a force of 10,000 men should be collected in the Trenton area to deal with British troops Lee expected Howe to throw into Jersey. This suggestion Washington himself would have endorsed as desirable if practicable; in fact, it simply was an extension of the idea of a Flying Camp and it did not imply the organization of a separate Army. Washington advanced the plan for two Armies, in a letter written by Robert Harrison, Oct. 25, 1776 (6 *G. W.,* 228 n); Lee's first observed direct reference was in a letter to James Bowdoin, Nov. 21, 1776 (2 *Lee Papers,* 291).

[41] By January, 1777, Washington had concluded that the Hudson could not be obstructed below the Highlands, but that it could be closed there to shipping (7 *G. W.,* 64–65).

[42] His own term was "South of Hudson's River" (6 *ibid.,* 279).

were admitted to have some validity. The worst blunder was in design-
ing outworks that called for a very large garrison, and then in failing
to give the fort the size required to shelter all the men who might be
compelled to retreat from the trenches and redoubts. Some of these
troops had never been under fire. Their commander, Col. Robert
Magaw, was a competent field officer but he had not handled any
body of men larger than the Fifth Pennsylvania Battalion. Manifestly,
then, the importance of the fort and the size of the garrison called for
the service of a general officer, and preferably of one who had been
schooled in the earthworks around Boston. Nathanael Greene was
directly to blame for employing fewer troops than the outworks required and more men than could find room to fight within the fort
itself; but Washington was not guiltless. He had not given to the problems at Fort Washington the concentrated thought and the day-by-day
attention they required. Neither he nor Greene had experience of the
sort a shrewd and economical defence of such a position demanded.

More fundamentally, Washington's star was in a long eclipse from
the time Howe left the vicinity of White Plains until the remnant of
the American Army drew breath, December 8, on the right bank of
the Delaware. This period of approximately one month brought the
American cause close to utter ruin. Had it collapsed, Washington would
in large degree, and not unjustly, have been adjudged responsible. He
was mentally exhausted and incapable of swift and sound decision.

Washington's weakness early in December was due in part to Charles
Lee's manifest unwillingness to join forces with him in Jersey. The
patience of the Commander-in-Chief in dealing with Lee and the humble tone of his frequent entreaties raise a question: Could Washington
have been timid about entering into a possible controversy with Lee,
or was he merely making allowance for the difficulties a comrade was
encountering? There is some evidence on both sides, and still more
evidence, particularly in public lament of his capture, that Lee enjoyed
a reputation equal and perhaps in some ways superior to Washington's.
For a time, Congress seemed more concerned over the relief of the
prisoner than over any other current business [43] and it proposed to return so many British officers in exchange for him [44] that Robert Morris,
a firm friend of Lee's, had to say he thought Congress overgenerous.[45]

[43] Cf. 2 *Burnett,* 206 ff.
[44] 7 *JCC.,* 10, 15–16, 18; 6 *G. W.,* 501. Cf. Samuel Adams to James Warren, Jan. 1, 1777;
1 *Warren-Adams Letters,* 282.   [45] 2 *Burnett,* 212.

Prior to this, many Americans doubtless had believed that if Lee did not move to Washington's support, he had good military reasons for not doing so. Washington could have given the affair a different color, but he said nothing and joined unreservedly in efforts to alleviate the captivity of his senior lieutenant. The significant fact that apparently evoked no comment from Lee's admirers was this: Lee was absent and a prisoner of war when Washington fashioned and conducted the best campaign the Army had to its credit. The Commander-in-Chief had shown himself able then to devise his own strategy without the counsel of the man whom some may have regarded as his *alter ego*. It might have been maintained that Washington did better in the absence of Lee—witness Dorchester Heights as well as Trenton-Princeton—than when Lee was at his elbow to illustrate a lecture on strategy with personal reminiscences.

During the whole of the Jersey campaign, two events only raised any question of Washington's sound military reasoning from existing facts. One of these was his belief that the Jersey militia would rally to his standard when he entered their State. Where he expected thousands, he never received many more in a single body than the equivalent of a full Company.[46] Washington's mistaken assumption of support from Jersey might have involved the destruction of his Army had Howe overtaken him, because for a fortnight after he crossed the Hackensack, the American commander scarcely had men enough to oppose a single well-handled Brigade. Before entering the State, he must have been misled by advisers who were themselves misinformed. Southwest of New York Island, loyalism had been pronounced from the beginning of the war; defeat on Long Island and the loss of Fort Washington disposed the timid and the lazy to think the Revolution was dying. Others doubtless were cowed by neighbors on the side of the King.

Washington's other debatable act of this period was his choice of ground at Trenton after his second crossing into Jersey. One of the few surviving General Orders of this period shows that he put his Army South of Assunpink Creek on the 30th of December. In doing this he stated that he expected to march "very soon" and that he desired "officers and soldiers to hold themselves in complete readiness to advance at a moment's warning." [47] He manifestly intended his

---

[46] See *supra*, p. 278.

[47] 37 *G. W.*, 538. This is a crude copy, found in an Orderly Book of the German Battalion, but there is no reason to suspect its authenticity.

position South of the Creek to be merely a bivouac until he was ready to resume maneuver, but he was too careful a soldier not to take into account the possibility of an attack by the British, of whose movements he kept himself informed. The question is, therefore, one of the actual weakness of this position, both for temporary defences and for ready egress in event the British came again to Trenton and confronted him across the creek. James Wilkinson wrote years later that Washington permitted himself to be caught in a cul-de-sac from which the Army was extricated by the grace of God and by the advice of Arthur St. Clair; [48] but a competent British army engineer, who was present at the time, said that Cornwallis dared not attack there: the ground was that to which Rall should have withdrawn for a proper defence on the 26th of December.[49] However opinion may differ, hereafter as in the past, on this point, it may be said that the weakness of the ground, in terms of the ranges of 1776, was by no means as definite, and certainly not so serious, as has been supposed. Nor is it likely that Washington owed his deliverance primarily to St. Clair's discovery of a road of escape. With him—it must be repeated[50]—the Commander-in-Chief had a number of men, Joseph Reed among them, who had lived at or near Trenton and knew the surrounding district thoroughly. These officers certainly must have satisfied Washington that he easily could move by his right flank into open country, either to "beat up the enemy's post"—that is, to undertake a new succession of maneuvers— or else to join any force Putnam might dispatch from Philadelphia. To assume that Washington put his Army behind the Assunpink on the 30th of December and that he did not know on the evening of the 2nd of January how he could leave that position is to charge him with complete stupidity at a time when all his other moves were brilliant.[51]

That last fact was not to be disputed. In the most critical test to

---

[48] 1 *Wilkinson*, 133.   [49] *A. Robertson's Diaries*, 119.
[50] See *supra*, p. 345.
[51] General Stryker's article on "The Princeton Surprise, 1777" (in 8 *Mag. Am. His.*, pt. 2., p. 553 ff) lists several persons from whom Washington readily could have procured information concerning the roads on the right of the Assunpink position. In his larger work, the same author called attention to a letter written July 31, 1824, by John Lardner to Capt. J. R. C. Smith of the Philadelphia Light Horse Troop. Lardner stated that he and other members of the troop patrolled the Quaker Road on the night of Jan. 1, 1777 and went as far as the Quaker Bridge. "We found," Lardner wrote, "that the enemy had no patrols there, and that apparently they had no knowledge of it [the road]" (*Stryker*, 273 n and 442). While this is late evidence, it has verisimilitude. Further, it seems to have been admitted by the British that the failure of their Light Dragoons to patrol the Allentown Road on the night of January 2–3 was one reason for Washington's success. Glyn remarked in his Journal, *loc. cit.*, that if the Dragoons had been over the road they certainly would have discovered the American advance.

which Washington had been subjected as a soldier, he had acquitted himself with greater distinction than ever had been his. In this, the American commander had been favored by no less than five contingencies—the seizure of the Delaware boats, the temper and personalities of the hostile commanders, the advanced position of the Hessians, the weather, and the conduct of Major von Dechow. Every one of these was a remarkable stroke of good fortune.

First and weightiest was the American's luck—in reality the fruit of taking pains—in having so many of the boats removed from the left bank of the Delaware that he discouraged all British effort to cross the river and to advance on Philadelphia. Washington was equally fortunate in his adversaries, from Howe at headquarters to Rall at Trenton. On the 30th of November, the Howe brothers had issued a proclamation in which they had called on all bodies of armed men to disperse, and on all congresses and conventions to desist from treasonable acts. Assurance was given that those who reported to designated officials, civil and military, within sixty days and took a simple oath of obedience to the King would receive full pardon for treason or misprison of treason. The inference was that after sixty days no further pardons would be granted, and that traitors would be condemned to the punishment they deserved.[52] This had induced some weak-kneed persons to take the oath and, at the same time, it had led Americans to wonder if General Howe was restraining himself deliberately in his operations. Some officers at Washington's headquarters—Joseph Reed among them—were of opinion that Howe was marking time and was waiting for the end of December, when the term of enlistment of the greater part of Washington's Army would expire.[53] In reality, so far as that particular region was concerned, Howe had contemplated nothing more for the winter of 1776–77 than the occupation of East Jersey, and even for the campaign of 1777 he had looked to a defensive in New Jersey while he subdued New England and opened communications with Canada by way of the Hudson and the Northern New York Lakes. Philadelphia was to be threatened but was not to be the objective of an active campaign until the autumn of that year.[54] Subsequent to the drafting of this plan, the retreat of Washington across New Jersey

---

[52] The proclamation has been printed many times. A convenient text will be found in 3 *Force* (5), 927–28 or in *Stryker,* 314–16.

[53] Cf. 1 *Reed,* 272.

[54] Howe to Germaine, Nov. 30, 1776; 3 *Force* (5), p. 926.

led General Howe to believe that he could advance his line to the Delaware and that he even might occupy Philadelphia. In execution of this amended design, Lord Cornwallis had proceeded to Trenton; but when that officer found all the boats removed or destroyed, and the weather bitterly cold, Howe had abandoned hope of reaching Philadelphia during the winter and had ordered the troops to their designated cantonments. Howe had written on the 20th of December: "The chain [of posts], I own, is rather too extensive, but I was induced to occupy Burlington to cover the County of Monmouth, in which there are many loyal inhabitants; and trusting to the almost general submission of the County to the southward of this chain, and to the strength of the corps placed in the advanced posts, I conclude the troops will be in perfect security." [55] Thus had it come about that Washington had begun his offensive at a time when British and Hessians were in a winter quarters mood.

That good fortune was increased by the departure from the front of Lord Cornwallis, who then hoped to go to England.[56] The American commander could have asked for nothing better than that the diligent Cornwallis should have been succeeded temporarily by Maj. Gen. James Grant, probably of all British officers of high rank the one who had the most vindictive contempt for his foes. He was the same Grant who had conducted the absurd reconnaissance of Fort DuQuesne in September, 1758, and he was, if possible, more vehemently anti-American after almost two decades than he had been during the French and Indian War.[57] In the House of Commons, Feb. 2, 1775, Grant had proclaimed "that the Americans could not fight, and that he would undertake to march from one end of the continent to the other with 5000 men." [58] Grant's prejudices worked all the more to the advantage of the Americans because General Howe most imprudently had sent to the post of greatest danger, the very front of the occupied part of New Jersey, German officers who spoke no English and had few interpreters.[59] By chance, also, Col. Johann Rall, the commander

[55] To Lord George Germaine, *ibid.*, 1317.   [56] *Ibid.*
[57] See Vol. II, p. 341 ff.
[58] Lord Stirling, the American General, had heard Grant make this statement (*Stryker*, 48 n). Cf. Vol. III, p. 315, n. 58.
[59] Kemble remarked in his Diary (*loc. cit.*, v. 1, p. 104), that he thought it a mistake to put the Hessians in front. See also Donop to Grant, Dec. 29, 1776: "[Colonel Sterling] was a reliable man and one able to interpret for me. I am now obliged to guess the meaning of your letters by the sense of the paragraphs, not being able to understand your language fully. Thus I am obliged to exercise much ingenuity in deciphering your orders" (*Stryker*, 426).

sent to Trenton, the most exposed of all the advanced stations, was careless, overconfident and scornful in his attitude toward his opponent. Rall and Grant carried on a correspondence that covered various subjects and, in particular, Colonel Rall's appeals for a wider, more vigilant patrol and for the establishment of a post at Maidenhead.[60] "You may be assured," Grant wrote Rall five days before the attack on Trenton, "that the rebel army in Pennsylvania which has been joined by Lee's corps, Gates' and Arnold's does not exceed 8000 men who have neither shoes nor stockings, are in fact almost naked, dying of cold, without blankets and very ill supplied with provisions." [61] Rall was not convinced but, being more adept in attack than in defence,[62] he took no active precautions at his own station. He even reported to his immediate superior, "I have not made any redoubts or any kind of fortifications because I have the enemy in all directions." [63]

The night before the surprise assault Grant wrote the German: "Washington has been informed that our troops have marched into winter quarters and have [sic] been told that we are weak at Trenton and Princeton and Lord Stirling has expressed a wish to make an attack upon these two places. I don't believe he will attempt it, but be assured that my information is undoubtedly true, so I need not advise you to be upon your guard against an unexpected attack at Trenton." [64] That was both warning and reassurance: Another man than Rall might have wondered which was uppermost in the mind of his British senior, but Rall himself was not inclined to believe the Americans capable of learning the art of war. Almost at the climax of the campaign, when he was informed that a continental detachment had assailed the outpost on the Pennington Road and had wounded six men,[65] he was urged to pack his baggage as a precaution. Rall was disdainful. "Fudge!" he said. "These country clowns cannot

60 See the exchange of letters in *Stryker,* 330 ff.

61 *Stryker,* 334–35.

62 This was von Heister's judgment of him. See his letter of Jan. 5, 1777, to the Prince of Hesse, *Stryker,* 402.

63 Rall to Donop, Dec. 21, 1776 (*Stryker,* 332).

64 *Stryker,* 116.

65 Glyn wrote in his Journal under date of December 26, but in the light of later events: "[Rall] who had information on the 25th of the enemy's being in motion, took no precaution to reenforce his out-picquet, assemble his men at their alarmposts, or send to Conol Donop, who was at Bordentown only six miles distant, but allowed his troops to be taken without effective resistance." (*loc. cit*). In view of what is known of the movements of Captain Anderson's patrol (see *supra,* p. 313), it is almost certain that the news of this affair could not have reached Rall until late in the day, probably not until evening. Anderson and his men doubtless remained in hiding part of the night of December 25–26.

whip us!" [66] He paid with his life for his incredulity, but his British correspondent did not change with changing fortune. When Rall was dying and his troops were being marched off to the prison camps, Grant wrote Donop a letter that disclosed the same singular combination of caution and contempt: "I did not think that all the rebels in America would have taken that Brigade prisoners . . . After all that has happened, if I was with you, your Grenadiers and Jägers, I should not be afraid of an attack from Washington's Army," and then Grant repeated what he previously had said concerning the numbers and the nakedness of the American forces.[67] Had the commander of those troops been privileged to read that letter, he might well have added the temper of this foe to the elements of good fortune that had favored him.

The crowning gift of chance was not the arrogance of General Grant or the negligence of Colonel Rall but the weather and the indulgence of Maj. Friedrich von Dechow, of the Knyphausen Regiment, the officer who urged Rall on Christmas Day to pack the baggage. Von Dechow was on duty the morning of the 26th and was responsible for seeing that the regular patrol, with a pair of cannon, made the rounds two hours before daylight. Because of the severity of the morning, von Dechow excused his men.[68] Had all the other circumstances existed to favor Washington's bold stroke, a vigilant patrol almost certainly would have discovered and challenged the American van and would have sounded the alarm in time to prevent a surprise at Trenton. There probably was not another night during the Hessian occupation of the village that the patrol did not cover the nearer ground over which Washington had to pass before he could attack the village. In nothing, then, had Washington been so fortunate as in his adversaries and in the weather. If he had employed the biblical metaphors in which his friend Governor Trumbull of Connecticut delighted, he could have said that the sleet and the snow of December 26 had been his shield and buckler.

---

[66] Report of the Hessian War Commission, Cassel, Apr. 15, 1782; *Stryker*, 420.
[67] Letter of Dec. 27, 1776; *Stryker*, 400–01.
[68] Report of the Hessian War Commission; *Stryker*, 420–21.

CHAPTER XV

Languor and Danger at Morristown

(January 6–March 31, 1777)

An army that had thrown the winning card in the last hours of a months-long adverse gamble could not be blamed if, by the fire in winter quarters, it spoke pridefully, or even boastfully of the manner in which it had worsted a wily opponent at Trenton and at Princeton. Nor was it unnatural that British who had driven the Americans on Long Island and had herded hundreds of prisoners at Fort Washington should make the utmost of the fact that before the 3rd of January ended, Princeton again was in the keeping of the King's men.[1]

When, later in January, soldiers began to yawn at the mention of the two battles near the Delaware, they had a new subject of debate: How far should the United States go in reprisal if it were true, as reported, that Gen. Charles Lee had been imprisoned and would be tried as a British deserter.[2] Next, in the narrower circle of the better informed,

---

[1] Cf. William Sutherland to Henry Clinton, Feb. 2, 1777, *Clinton Papers,* Clements Lib.; *Leven Powell,* 46; *Journal of Margaret Morris,* ed. Jackson, 63; *Memoir Tench Tilghman,* 150; *Va. Gazette,* Jan. 17, 24, 1777; *N. Y. Mercury,* Jan. 20, 1777. As suggested, *supra* p. 363, the chief lament of some British officers was that the actions at Trenton and Princeton would prolong a struggle they had hoped to end early in the winter of 1776–77. The changed situation might keep them in the field when they had expected to be in New York, or with good luck, in London. Besides George Harris to his uncle, Jan. 16, 1777, Lushington's *Harris,* 86, see William Harcourt to Earl Harcourt, Jan. 13, 1777; *The Evelyns in America,* 228–29. By Mch. 17, 1777, Harcourt had overcome some of his disappointment and wrote manfully of the Americans: ". . . 'though they seem to be ignorant of the precision, order and even of the principles by which large bodies are moved, yet they possess some of the requisites for making good troops, such as extreme cunning, great industry in moving ground and felling of wood, activity and a spirit of enterprise upon any advantage. Having said thus much, I have no occasion to add that though it was once the ton of this army to treat them in the most contemptible light, they are now become a formidable enemy . . ." (*ibid.,* 232–33). Many of the misconceptions of the British were attributable to the singular badness of their intelligence reports at this period. All minor successes were exaggerated and reverses were minimized. Examples will be found in *Serle,* 168 ff, 191, 192, 193, 200, 201.

[2] The *New York Mercury* announced on Jan. 20, 1777, that "Mr. Charles Lee" had been brought to the city from Brunswick and had been put in the custody of a strong guard. It was true, as reported, that Howe thought Lee should be regarded as a deserter from the British service. (Howe to Clinton, Dec. 21, 1776; *Clinton Papers,* Clements Lib.), and as this view soon became public (7 *G. W.,* 1), it led to exaggerated reports of the hardships to which Lee was being subjected. Congress ordered retaliation on Lt. Col. Archibald Campbell and on five Hessian officers in American hands. (See 1 *LTW.,* 356, 358 and 7 *JCC.,* 135, for references to previous correspondence.) Washington did not favor punishment of that sort when it could be avoided, and least of all when the British had captured and then held six times as many

the argument was whether Congress was right in twice deciding it
would not comply with Lee's repeated application for the appointment
of a committee to confer with him on an undisclosed question of importance.[3]

Washington conducted the correspondence on reprisal and confessed he could see no valid reason for denying Lee a conference with
members of Congress;[4] but to these and to numbers of other developments of the wintry months he could give no more of his hurrying
minutes than duty and its cousin, courtesy, exacted. Most of the dangers that had threatened his army continued into 1777. Some of them
grew worse.

Incredibly, too, an Army that had thought it had endured all the
woes of a military existence and all the plagues of politics found itself
beset by new miseries and challenged by unfamiliar perplexities. Early
in the new year, 1777, Washington had the task of holding a sufficient
number of militia to give the semblance of an Army to a force of Continentals that once again was vanishing. Of the 1000 to 1200 who had
agreed to stay in return for a bounty of ten dollars offered on Dec.
30–31, 1776,[5] only about 800 remained on the 19th of January.[6] Although the "return" of the main Army showed a paper strength, pres-

---

American officers as Continentals had British officers their prisoners, or 600 to fifty. He presented that fact to Congress (7 *G. W.*, 211, 253) and argued against retaliation, (*ibid.*, 224-
25) which he intended in no circumstances to be more severe than British treatment of Lee
(*ibid.*, 207–08, 375). Later, when Congress ascertained that Lee was having all consideration,
it directed that its new restrictions be lifted (8 *JCC.*, 411), and subsequently it admitted the
British and Hessian officers to parole, (8 *JCC.*, 653) though it had given warning of further
retaliation in event American prisoners were sent to Great Britain (1 *LTW.*, 381). Simultaneously Washington had been negotiating with Howe for a general exchange of prisoners but
in this for some months the American commander made little progress (See 7 *G. W.*, 10 ff,
41, 84–85, 87, 141, 155, 311, 313–14, 343; 8 *ibid.*, 131, 182, 183, 215, 239, 242; 8 *JCC.*,
421, 430–31, 495). He asked Congress to provide hard money or bills of exchange, if possible,
to relieve the distress of American prisoners in British hands (7 *G. W.*, 435), and in wriitng
General von Heister concerning arrangements for supplying Hessian prisoners, he said, "I
enjoy too much pleasure in softening the hardships of captivity to withhold any comfort from
prisoners." (8 *ibid.*, 58. See *ibid.*, 167 for the dispatch to Cornwallis's lines of a flag of truce
and the body of an officer brutally mutilated by the British. Cornwallis maintained that the
man was bayonetted because he refused to surrender). In his *Memoirs*, 74–75, Elias Boudinot
referred to an interview with Lee in captivity. The General tried to convince him, he said,
that the Americans could not stand up against the British in the field.

[3] His first request was dated Feb. 10, 1777 (2 *Lee Papers*, 358–59); his second was March
19 (*ibid.*, 360) or ten days only before the submission to the Howe brothers of the notorious
paper, "Mr. Lee's Scheme," of which Washington never had information. See 2 *Lee Papers*,
361 ff and Strachey's note. Congress' refusal to send a committee to Lee was voted Feb. 21,
1777 (7 *JCC.*, 141), and was reiterated March 29 (*ibid.*, 207). In 2 *Burnett*, 263 ff, is an abstract
of the debate in Congress, where members spoke plainly of Lee's conceit in making such a
request.

[4] 7 *G. W.*, 224. [5] *Ibid.*, 53 and *supra*, p. 331 ff.

[6] *Ibid.*, 29. By March 2, Washington was to describe his Army as "raw militia, badly
officered and under no government" (*ibid.*, 222).

ent and absent, of 17,812, Washington's actual numbers were so few he confessed to "Jack" Custis his doubts concerning the future. "How we shall be able to rub along till the new Army is raised, I know not," the General said, and added: "Providence has heretofore saved us in a remarkable manner, and on this we must principally rely." [7] Weeks later Nathanael Greene was to confide, "We have but a shadow of force; and are more indebted to the weather for security than to our own strength." [8] This feebleness had of course to be concealed from friends as well as from foes,[9] even if silence or inaction led men to lose their confidence in the vigor of Washington.[10] A surprise or defeat at this time would dishearten Jersey folk who had been brought to believe, after Trenton and Princeton, that American troops were superior to the invaders.[11]

Washington thus was in a position that both humiliated and crippled him: His troops were too few to attack or even to accept battle in open country, so long as Howe's toughened Battalions remained in undiminished strength at Brunswick and Amboy.[12] At a time of year when the American General could not maneuver freely, he had to confine the British, or induce them to disperse force,[13] or do both, until a slow recruitment and the return of spring permitted him, if fortune favored, to shift from defensive to offensive. The Commander-in-Chief reasoned that the best practicable services by his shadow Regiments in tying down the redcoats were these two: first, to destroy or remove the grain, provender and livestock near the hostile camps [14] and, second, to harass constantly the parties sent farther afield to get supplies that could not readily be brought to Brunswick by ship. It was the veriest A-B-C of war to do everything possible to keep oats, corn and fodder

---

[7] *Ibid.,* 53. The "return" of the Army for Jan. 24, 1777, is in the National Archives, War Dept., Rev. Recs. The artillery, reported separately, had 566 men (*ibid*).

[8] Letter of Mch. 3, 1777, to John Adams; 1 *Greene's Greene,* 339.

[9] See 7 *G. W.,* 198.

[10] Cf. John Adams to Sullivan, Feb. 22, 1777: "Are we to go on forever this way, maintaining vast armies in idleness, and losing completely the fairest opportunity that ever was offered of destroying an enemy completely in our power. We have no returns of any army. We know not what is on foot anywhere" (1 *Sullivan Papers,* 325).

[11] Washington to Sullivan, Jan. 28, 1777; 7 *G. W.,* 74–75.

[12] At those places they had no large magazines. Instead, believing in the autumn that their troops would be occupying many small cantonments, the British had established numerous magazines in the small towns and villages of East Jersey (*Memoir Tench Tilghman,* 150).

[13] The distribution of Howe's army of almost 23,000 is set down as of Jan. 8, 1777, in 1 *Kemble,* 107. Howe had 13,799 men in Jersey. About 12,000 of these were Infantry. Washington would have given much to have been informed correctly of those totals.

[14] For the resolution of Congress authorizing impressment of these supplies, see 8 *JCC.,* 498–99, and for the execution see 7 *G. W.,* 97, 119.

from a foe whose mobility depended on his horses.[15] To make feed unavailable was to paralyze the royal army.

Attacks on the British foraging parties had to be made persistently by courageous soldiers under skillful, cool-headed leaders, but these affairs must never be pushed so far that an inferior American force would be compelled to fight. Nathanael Greene described the situation neatly when he said: "General Howe has invariably pursued the maxims of an invader, this campaign, endeavoring to bring us to a general action and avoid skirmishing. General Washington, as every defender ought, has followed directly the contrary conduct by endeavoring to skirmish with the enemy at all times and avoid a general engagement."[16] Alexander Hamilton, he of the New York Artillery, had made an interesting shift, presently to be described, from line to staff, and he considered these persistent forays against wagons and guards "of great service in the general scale, as they serve to harass and distress the enemy, and, by keeping them from forage, will put them under difficulties as to the transportation of their baggage and cannon whenever they think of making any capital movement."[17] He did not exaggerate. The perseverance of the American advance parties compelled the British to employ more and more men in these foraging parties. Thereby the ill-fed horses were worn down progressively.[18]

[15] *Ibid.*, 9–10, 26, 27.

[16] Letter to John Adams, Mch. 3, 1777; 1 *Greene's Greene*, 336.

[17] Letter of Mch. 20, 1777, to Gouverneur Morris; 9 *A. Hamilton*, 45. These counter-raids, which generally were conducted by 400 or 500 Americans, (cf. 7 *G. W.*, 95) were not costly, as a rule, and sometimes they led to the recovery of valuable provisions the British were carrying off. Unhappily, in two of these skirmishes the courage of commanding officers—one of them a Colonel from Washington's own State—was challenged by their comrades. Operations in New Jersey during January–March, 1777, might have some tactical interest historically, were the details preserved, but most of them are reported in terms of captures, losses, booty and the conduct, good or bad, of the opposing forces. The largest encounter appears to have been that of Feb. 23, 1777, for which see 7 *G. W.*, 205, 228; 1 *Greene's Greene*, 331; *N. Y. Gazette*, Mch. 3, 1777. Other brushes and the general situation on the American front are reported by Archibald Robertson in his *Diaries*, 122 ff, by Joseph Reed in a letter of Jan. 24, 1777 to T. Bradford (*Reed Papers*, NYHS) and by Washington in 7 *G. W.*, 48, 100, 115, 146. A letter of Israel Putnam's, dated Princeton, Jan. 21, 1777 and quoted in *Henkel's Cat.*, 683, item 597, describes an advance to Somerset Court House January 20 by the British. Rumor on occasion blew to absurd digits the number of troops and wagons involved in these raids. Cf. 47 *Gentleman's Mag.*, 141, and *Journal of Margaret Morris*, ed. Jackson, 66–67. The charge of cowardice against Col. Mordecai Buckner of the Sixth Virginia and the sentence that he be cashiered from the Army may be traced in 7 *G. W.*, 66, 76, 105, 122, and in the letter of Josiah Parker to George Weedon, Jan. 24, 1777; MS. *Am. Phil. Soc.* Some of the more intimate details appear in John Chilton to his brother, Feb. 11, 1777; 12 *T* 111. The other officer whose conduct was brought into question was Col. Andrew Ward of Connecticut (7 *G. W.*, 95–96, 105). No final report on his case has been found. His Connecticut State Regiment ended its service during the spring of 1777 (cf. *ibid.*, 431); but Ward became a Brigadier General of militia and continued in that position to the end of the war.

[18] Interesting evidences of this are to be found in *A. Robertson's Diaries*, 122 ff.

Washington's judgment of the results of these small raids changed from time to time. He could not believe the British were ignorant of his numerical weakness [19] and he undertook to reduce the adverse odds by prevailing on General Heath to make so heavy a demonstration against the British around King's Bridge that Howe would send reenforcements from Jersey to New York and perhaps give the troops at Morristown the opportunity of striking the redcoats left at Brunswick. Washington's hope rose the day he heard at headquarters the sound of firing from the direction of King's Bridge [20] but Heath did no more than move close to Fort Independence,[21] demand its surrender, waste some gunpowder, and march away again, to the chagrin of his commander and to the accompaniment of mocking British laughter.[22] This failure deepened the apprehension of leaders at Morristown that Howe was gaining, not losing strength, and, when his preparations were complete, probably would advance overland toward Philadelphia.[23] Washington accordingly directed officers commanding on the

[19] See 7 G. W., 32, 35. In the N. Y. Gazette, Jan. 27, 1777, this confident statement was made: "Mr. Washington is now at Morristown with three Battalions of Pennsylvania militia and some troops from other provinces, in the whole about 5000 men." This estimate was slightly above the actual figures. As of February 20, Washington reported that he could not get exact returns but he computed his force at 4000 (7 G. W., 168), predominantly militia. He thought the British in Jersey numbered 7000 to 8000, (ibid). For the return of the 2543 Continentals and the 976 militia at the different posts in New Jersey, Mch. 15, 1777, see 152 Papers Cont. Cong., pt. IV, 15, 17 LC. Typical American intelligence reports on British strength in New Jersey are Thomas Lowry to Washington, and P. Dickinson to Washington, both Feb. 19, 1777; Gates Papers, NYHS.

[20] 7 G. W., 29, 35, 43–44, 59, 74–75.

[21] British writers complained of the frequency with which Americans gave that name to their forts. In this instance, the fort was the one in the Fordham area, directly North of Spuyten Duyvil.

[22] One is tempted to relate in detail the story of this serio-comical affair, but it is not, strictly speaking, a part of the biography of Washington. The history of the operation may be traced in O. Pickering and C. W. Upham, Life of Timothy Pickering, cited hereafter as Pickering, v. 1, p. 97–103, 109; 6 G. W., 472–73, 475, 476, 497–98; 7 Ibid., 29, 31, 70–71, 94, 95, 96 n, 99–100, 104, 107, 125; Heath, 119–25; 1 LTW., 328, 331, 333, 336. Timothy Pickering (op. cit., v. 1, p. 109), said bluntly, "[Heath] has, in the estimation of every discerning man, acquired nought but disgrace." On the British side, Serle's comment was: "One Heath, once a butcher, now a rebel General, has left the Army in disgust, on acount of some reflections thrown upon him by Washington for not attacking Fort Independence. He blamed his men, and his men, him; villains and cowards altogether!" (op. cit., 194). Washington in a private letter told Heath: ". . . your conduct is censured (and by men of sense and judgment who were with you on the expedition to Fort Independence) as being fraught with too much caution by which the Army has been disappointed, and in some degree disgraced. Your summons, as you did not attempt to fulfil your threats, was not only idle but farcical, and will not fail of turning the laugh exceedingly upon us . . ." (7 G. W., 99–100). In reporting to Congress, Washington announced that Heath had decamped, and beyond that he merely cited the reasons Heath gave for return towards White Plains (ibid., 103–04). Washington's encouragement of a simultaneous raid on Long Island will be found in ibid., 23–24, 25–26. Later suggestions are in ibid., 90, 120. See also Tryon to Germaine, Feb. 11, 1777; 47 Gentleman's Mag., p. 141. Two American intelligence reports of Feb. 25, 1777, are in 42 Papers of G. W., 20, LC.

[23] 7 G. W., 32. From day to day, as his intelligence reports varied, Washington was more

Delaware to secure all boats the British might use for a crossing.[24] At the end of the month he told "Jack" Custis, with his usual care for restraint of statement: "If [General Howe] does not [begin an offensive operation], there can be no impropriety, I conceive, [in] pronouncing him a man of no enterprise, as circumstances never will, I hope, favor him so much as at present." [25] In different spirit, Washington wrote Joseph Reed: "I think we are now in one of the most critical periods which America ever saw, and because the enemy are not in actual motion (by the by, I believe they are not far from it) everybody seems to be lulled into ease and security." [26]

The reverse of this was what Washington most desired and daily sought—that the British prolong their fireside sleep and that Americans hurry to the nearest recruiting station in the thirteen States.[27] Until this New Army of 1777 was at his command, Washington would continue to harass the British in Jersey, to confine them as far as he could, and to tempt them to disperse their forces. Besides the futile effort to create a diversion at Fort Independence and another on Long Island, Washington suggested on the 17th of March to the senior officer in Georgia an expedition against St. Augustine, Fla.[28] and he consented, though doubtfully, to proposals for an offensive by General Spencer in Rhode Island,[29] where the Commander-in-Chief himself had been under some criticism; [30] but he put first in all his planning and correspondence the completion of recruiting for his Army and, in particular, for sixteen new Regiments authorized by Congress. "If," he wrote Benedict Arnold, "the enemy will give us time to collect an Army levied for the war, I hope we shall set all our former errors to rights." [31]

---

or less in doubt (cf. *ibid.*, 172) of the objective of the British main army, but after approximately February 18–20, he was so nearly convinced Howe intended to march on the Pennsylvania metropolis that he ordered supplies removed from a magazine almost a day's march West of the city (*ibid.*, 182–83).

[24] *Ibid.*, 158, 164, 168, 172, 175, 176, 185, 187–88, 196.

[25] Letter of Feb. 27, 1777; *ibid*, 198.

[26] *Ibid.*, 192. In Washington to Robert Morris, Mch. 2, 1777 (*ibid.*, 222–23), is a detailed statement of the reasons why the General was surprised that Howe had not begun an advance before that time.

[27] The independent State of "New Connecticut," as Vermont was styled at first, had been set up in January and is here included, but it had not yet been "recognized" by neighbors that asserted title to its territory.

[28] 7 *G. W.*, 297–98.   [29] 1 *LTW.*, 334–36; 7 *G. W.*, 114–15.

[30] Nathanael Greene remarked that "strictures were made on Washington's military conduct by some of the inhabitants of Providence" (1 *Greene's Greene*, 322). For discussion of British removal of troops from Rhode Island, see Stirling to Washington, Feb. 26, 1777; 42 *Papers of G. W.*, 21, LC, and 47 *Gentleman's Mag.*, 141.

[31] Letter of Mch. 2, 1777; 7 *G. W.*, 179. Cf. letter to John Augustine Washington, Feb. 24, 1777; *ibid.*, 199.

Congress favored emphatically a sharp offensive as early as possible, and it assured Washington by formal resolution of its desire to make his Army strong enough "not only to curb and confine the enemy within their present quarters, and prevent them from drawing support of any kind from the country, but [also] by the divine blessing totally to subdue them before they can be reenforced."[32] This language was regarded by some Delegates as an expression of dissatisfaction with Washington's defensive policy.

Had the authors of the motion searched the files of Congress they would have found a letter, written about a month previously, in which Washington had described in these plain words a condition that represented one of the worst barriers to vigorous action: "The Treasury has been for some time empty . . . the recruiting service is particularly injured by this, as many officers are now waiting only for bounty money. . . . If we are not supplied with that necessary article, all matters must be at a stand."[33] Lack of money hampered everything. One commissary of purchases wrote Congress from Allentown: "I have agreeable to his Excellency General Washington's orders to me, made a considerable progress in the purchasing and securing of pork for the use of the Army but have not as yet been so fortunate as to obtain one shilling to pay the people for it . . . I may wait perhaps a considerable time longer, which causes a general murmuring among the people that I have had provisions from . . ."[34] A few weeks later, the same official's protest was: "I have to deal with a set of the most discontented, disaffected wretches that ever existed; they are as hungry after the late despised Continentals as were they ever after half joes or General Howe's protection . . . They now want the prices going at present for the articles bought and agreed with them for, several weeks ago . . . this trouble is chiefly owing to the want of cash and the commissioners going about this quarter, bidding over one another . . ."[35] All this was a familiar tale, but it was becoming a tragedy.

Washington might have used that same word, tragedy, in describing the drama of continued loss of men and the slow, discouraging replacement of those who died or went home. Recruiting an Army in the

[32] 7 JCC., 150; 2 Burnett, 274–75; 1 Greene's Greene, 342.
[33] Letter of Jan. 22, 1777; 7 G. W., 51–52.
[34] Francis Wade to "The Hon. Comm. of Congress," Feb. 16, 1777, considerably repunctuated (78 Papers Cont. Cong., pt. XXIII, p. 367), LC.
[35] Same to same, Allentown, Mch. 4, 1777; ibid., 383. The larger aspects of this problem of scarcity of provisions and rises in price are discussed, infra.

presence of the enemy never was easy, and now it might be harder than ever. About the date of the departure of some of the New England troops who had accepted the bounty at Trenton, the time of a large part of the Pennsylvania militia expired. The Cavalry of Morris County, New Jersey, were decamping before January was half spent. Two infantry Regiments from that State could not be held beyond February.[36]

It was to make the Army independent of militia—this "mixed, motley crew," as Washington termed them, who were "here today, gone tomorrow," [37] that the General had been authorized to recruit sixteen new Battalions of Infantry,[38] four Regiments of Artillery,[39] and a similar number of Regiments of Light Horse, approximately 3000 men. All these, it should be repeated, were in addition to the eighty-eight "old" Battalions, which likewise were to be strengthened.[40] Several months would pass before the most diligent recruiting, under the most favorable conditions, would yield so many men—if ever they were to be had. Some reports of the new enlistments that reached Washington at this time were deceptive in their exaggeration of the numbers enrolled.[41] While scattered fragments of Battalions and even the guards from the frontier of Western Pennsylvania were called to New Jersey, along with organizations approaching their authorized strength,[42] Washington had to adjust the terms of raising the new Regiments to the fitness of recruiting officers and to the characteristics of the people who were sought for the service.[43] Whether officers had fresh enthusi-

---

[36] 7 G. W., 29, 35, 37, 159.   [37] Ibid., 53.

[38] So far as has been ascertained, Washington's occasional use of this word instead of Foot dated from February, 1777 (ibid., 136).

[39] Students of the early history of the Artillery of the United States will find some interesting documents of the winter 1776–77, on equipment, lack of men, etc., in the Knox Papers, MHS.

[40] 7 G. W., 136.   [41] Ibid., 258.

[42] 7 JCC., 15, 90; 2 Burnett, 235–36; 7 G. W., 264–66, 276 ff. Orders were to forward troops as soon as fifty men or other sizeable "batches" were assembled, ibid., 6, 110, 194; 1 LTW., 347.

[43] He made these distinct types of agreement: (1) some newly-selected Colonels were authorized to name subordinate field officers, 6 G. W., 478–79, 483, 487; (2) in other instances explicitly and in still others implicitly Washington stipulated that these officers select as subalterns those who were gentlemen and were not holding commissions in existing organizations of continental troops, e.g., 7 G. W., 33; (3) occasionally Washington himself designated the Lieutenant Colonel and the Major, 6 G. W., 494; (4) frequently he reserved a veto on appointments as in ibid., 494–95; (5) he sometimes permitted recruiting of Ranger Companies by men who were authorized to choose their junior officers, subject to specified qualifications, 7 G. W., 14; (6) in one instance, Washington picked out a Colonel, permitted him to name the officers of four Ranger Companies, sent these men recruiting and then had them undertake to fill the ranks by enlisting 500 Cherokees or other friendly Indians, ibid., 11–12; (7) somewhat skeptically, Washington authorized a French-speaking officer to seek recruits in Canada.

asm or the disillusionment of experience, they encountered still other obstacles of many sorts—rival enlistment for State forces,[44] State and even local bounties for men who would enter the old Regiments,[45] the unanticipated shortage of arms,[46] the paucity of funds,[47] discontent on the part of enlisted men who were not to receive the bounty,[48] fear of sickness that would take men to the notoriously bad army hospitals,[49] and the suspicion that some venal officers were putting on the rolls the names of fictitious recruits, were pocketing the bounty, and then were pretending that these non-existent volunteers had deserted.[50]

After surveying these maddening difficulties Washington had to reconcile himself once again to seeking from nearby States militia who would take the place, numerically, of the departing troops and would remain until the recruits for the Army of 1777 arrived.[51] He did not lose patience but neither did he withhold plain speech, as for example, when he said that militia officers of New Jersey were "generally of the lowest class of people . . ."[52] Again, "my situation with respect to numbers," said Washington on the 20th of January, "is more distressing than it has ever been yet . . ."[53] and it was rendered still worse by an extensive renewal of desertion. Unless the people gave notice of the presence of deserters in their neighborhood, "we shall be obliged," Washington warned Congress, "to detach one half of the Army to bring back the other."[54]

Part of this loss might be reduced by saving the lives of some of the sick and wounded sent to hospitals and thereby condemned, all too frequently, to death in those wretched charnel houses. The main contribution that Congress could make to the welfare of the Army in the

---

[44] 7 *G. W.*, 42–43, 88–90.

[45] Some interesting data on the Connecticut bounty of thirty-three dollars will be found in 1 *Webb*, 185–87. The terms of the New England state bounties are noted in 1 *LTW.*, 344. Local bounties are described in H. Jackson to Henry Knox, Mch. 16, 1777, *Knox Papers*, MHS. Indictment and defence of this system of additional bounties will be found in 7 *G. W.*, 58–60, 85–86, 86–87, 91, 133, 229; 1 *Greene's Greene*, 315; 1 *LTW.*, 342 ff.

[46] 7 *JCC.*, 68, 98; 7 *G. W.*, 49.   [47] *Ibid.*, 81.

[48] *Ibid.*, 103, 195.   [49] *Ibid.*, 150.

[50] *Ibid.*, 251, 257. For a description of the manner in which "harpies" preyed on those who received bounties, see 1 *LTW.*, 348.

[51] 7 *G. W.*, 30, 35, 45–46.

[52] *Ibid.*, 56–57. Washington was philosophical at the same time that he was ashamed of the conduct of some of these men. He wrote Stirling: ". . . a people unused to restraint must be led, they will not be drove, even those who are ingaged for the War, must be disciplin'd by degrees, we must not expect the same ready obedience therefore from New, as from old Troops accustomed to obey" (*ibid.*, 33, letter of Jan. 19, 1777, verbatim).

[53] *Ibid.*, 38.

[54] Letter of Jan. 31, 1777; *ibid.*, 81. See also a request to Joseph Reed to draw up a plan to prevent desertion (*ibid.*, 191–92).

winter of 1776–77 was the promise of a better system. In recognition of many protests against the hardships the patients had been called upon to endure needlessly, the Delegates on the 9th of January voted to dismiss from the service Dr. John Morgan, who was Director General of the Hospitals, and Dr. Samuel Stringer, Director of the Northern Department.[55] As the Commander-in-Chief did not know the specific grounds on which the two Surgeons had been displaced, he so advised them and left them to protest or to retire. Schuyler, being of different temper, took offence at the failure of Congress to notify him of its action against Stringer and he filed a complaint which made Delegates angry.[56] Doctor Morgan undertook to vindicate his administration through a later, long controversy that was not conducted in the best of spirit.[57] Demand for the immediate inclusive reform of the hospitals was another display of the lack of understanding, as Washington later wrote Robert Morris, that led Congress to "think it is but to say Presto, begone, and everything is done." [58] At Washington's request,[59] Dr. William Shippen, Jr. and Dr. John Cochran drew up a plan of reorganization which the General forwarded to Congress, with the reminder, among others, that while the expense of establishing and operating of the proposed hospitals would be "very great," ultimately the new arrangement would "not only be a saving to the public, but the only possible method of keeping an Army afoot." [60]

Another device that Washington selected as a means of strengthening his shadowy forces, while waiting on the doubtful outcome of slow recruiting, was to publish, January 25, a proclamation in which he called on all those who had accepted the Howe brothers' offer of "protection" to surrender it and to take the oath of allegiance to the United States. Otherwise, within thirty days, they must go into the British lines, under penalty of being "deemed adherents to the King of Great Britain and treated as common enemies of the American States." [61] Issuance of this proclamation was one of the rare instances in which Washington

---

[55] 7 *JCC.*, 24; 7 *G. W.*, 23. The original of Washington's notification of Doctor Stringer is among the *Washington MSS* of the Huntington Library.

[56] 7 *JCC.*, 180.

[57] Cf. 7 *G. W.*, 150–51; 8 *JCC.*, 626. See Vol. V.

[58] Letter of Mch. 2, 1777; 7 *G. W.*, 225.   [59] *Ibid.*, 44–45.

[60] 7 *G. W.*, 149. Washington had to prod Congress several times (*ibid.*, 206, 287, 319, 320, 381, 387), before he could procure action, April 8 (7 *JCC.*, 161, 197, 219, 231–37, 244–45), under Doctor Shippen as Director General (*ibid.*, 253). Announcement of the new system was made in GOs of May 5, 8 *G. W.*, 19–20; progress thereafter was slow.

[61] 7 *ibid.*, 61, 62, 109.

made use of the emergency powers granted him by Congress in December, 1776,[62] and it did not fail to raise an immediate question, which two of the New Jersey Delegates, Abraham Clark and Jonathan Sergeant, presented to Congress on the 6th of February in a resolution to this effect: the proclamation might in some States "interrupt the due course of the laws made therein for the trial and punishment of traitors and other offenders against peace and liberty"; wherefore it was set forth that the proclamation was not to prevent the operation of the statutes or to exempt any person from them.[63]

This was a fine bone over which to growl. A committee was named at once to examine the proclamation, and to give its opinion whether the contention of the Jerseymen had meat and marrow. Although the resolve contained no direct reference to any previous action by Congress, Clark maintained that Washington's proclamation disregarded the resolve of Mch. 9, 1776, which provided "that no oath by way of test" should be required of any inhabitant, as Charles Lee had exacted it of Long Island residents.[64] Clark was much alarmed. "I hope our Legislature will take proper notice . . . and not tamely submit their authority to the control of a power unknown in our constitution"—thus he wrote the Speaker of the New Jersey Assembly and added, as if he had his eyes on Morristown headquarters, "We are set out to oppose tyranny in all its strides, and I hope we shall persevere."[65] The committee that studied the proclamation did not share Clark's fears. On February 27, it presented a report that probably was drafted by John Adams: ". . . General Washington's proclamation . . . does not interfere with the laws or civil government of any State; but considering the situation of the Army was prudent and necessary."[66] The report was

---

[62] The New York Gazette of Feb. 3, 1777, reporting the "dictatorship," disposed of it with the statement that Congressmen found themselves in "a slippery situation" and shoved their burdens on "the first simpleton of consequence" who would carry the load. John Adams (Adams, Fam. Let., 255; 2 Burnett, 317) heard rumblings and took pains to explain what had been done. He asserted, "Congress never thought of making [Washington] a dictator or giving him a sovereignty." Washington acted precisely as if he himself had written Adams's words, and he continued to exercise his enlarged powers primarily to provide good officers for the sixteen new Regiments. Undramatic examples will be found in 7 G. W., 243, 383, 431–32 and, particularly 419, in response to a resolve of Congress (7 JCC., 251–52). Although Washington ran counter to the declared policy of Congress in choosing two sites for "elaboratories," (7 G. W., 139, 146) he carefully referred to Congress the detailed proposal of Dr. William Shippen, Jr., for the establishment of a new system of hospitals (ibid., 71).

[63] 7 JCC., 95, resolve of Feb. 6, 1777. Two days later, Washington sent General Parsons a copy of the proclamation and told him to follow its terms on Long Island (7 G. W., 120).

[64] 2 Burnett, 292; 4 JCC., 195.

[65] Letter of Feb. 8, 1777; 2 Burnett, 243.

[66] 7 JCC., 165–66. The original text of the resolution is in the autograph of John Adams.

laid on the table where, to the disgust of Clark, it doubtless soon was buried under other papers. "In many instances," he protested, "the proclamation is exceptionable and very improper and I believe was the production or at least set on foot by some too much in General's good grace, he is too much encumbered to attend to everything, and though I believe him honest, I think him fallible." [67]

Those who most resented this criticism of Washington would have agreed with Clark in saying that Washington was "much encumbered," but one gain of the spring was in the strengthening of the staff at Headquarters. Tench Tilghman of Pennsylvania, a former Captain of the Flying Camp, had joined the headquarters staff as an unpaid volunteer in August, 1776, and had performed usefully many score difficult tasks. John Fitzgerald, a Major of the Third Virginia, had become Aide-de-Camp in October, 1776.[68] George Baylor, Samuel Webb and William Grayson had left Washington's "family" at the beginning of 1777 or early in January to accept regimental command [69]—a trio of transfers that hampered the work of the office, particularly at a time when the post of Adjutant General was unoccupied. George Johnston joined the staff as aide about Jan. 20, 1777; [70] John Walker took a like position in February,[71] and on March 1, young Capt. Alexander Hamilton, who already had distinguished himself as an officer of the New York Artillery, reported as aide; [72] Richard K. Meade took a like position later that month.[73] An unexpected result of this enlargement of staff was a rise in the number and a lamentable increase in the length of letters sent from headquarters over Washington's signature.[74] In the

[67] Letter of Mch. 7, 1777, to Elias Dayton; 2 Burnett, 292.

[68] For Tilghman, see infra, p. 413, and 22 G. W., 71. Heitman gave an undetermined date in November as the beginning of Fitzgerald's service at headquarters, but in 6 G. W., 199, is a note that Fitzgerald wrote for Washington on Oct. 11, 1776. Presumably, Fitzgerald then was admitted to Washington's "family" with the rank of Lieutenant Colonel, though he is not mentioned in G. W. again until December 2 (ibid., 324).

[69] Heitman, 13, gives Webb's last date with Washington as Jan. 1, 1777, Baylor's as January 9 and Grayson's as January 11; but the Papers of G. W., LC., are said by Fitzpatrick to include a draft letter of Washington's in the autograph of Colonel Webb, dated Jan. 11, 1777. See 6 G. W., 493 n.

[70] Ibid., 487; 7 ibid., 38, 41. Heitman consistently spelled the name Johnson.

[71] 7 G. W., 161, 199–200.   [72] Ibid., 218.

[73] Ibid., 280. No further additions were made to the staff until Sept. 6, 1777, when John Laurens and Presley P. Thornton were named. This was the date of formal announcement in GO, (9 G. W., 189), but both young men were chosen in August (ibid., 23, 25; 37 ibid., 539). They began as extra aides—Thornton apparently for a brief time only, as he preferred line service. Laurens was announced on October 6 as a regular aide (9 G. W., 313) and soon was recognized as one of the most brilliant young men of the Army.

[74] For July, 1777, Fitzpatrick found 133 letters, of which eleven were written on a single day, the 25th. Correspondence and GOs for the month fill 183 pages of 8 G. W. June letters

Adjutant General's office the vacancy created at the beginning of the
year was continued for almost five months, in part because Washington
could find no suitable man, and in part because he hoped Congress
might prevail on Horatio Gates to resume the duties.[75] Gates was serving at the time as senior officer in Philadelphia and, so long as militia
continued to arrive in considerable number, he had the temporary
direction of what was, in effect, Washington's general reserve.[76] In
expressed willingness to do what was desired of him, Gates took a position militarily correct and personally natural. He wrote the President
of Congress that he had received no request from the Commander-in-
Chief to resume the duties of Adjutant General and that for him to
"dwindle again into the Adjutant General" after having had the honor
"to command in the second post in America" called for "some philosophy on my side and something more than words upon yours." He
would have to stipulate that Washington should signify a wish to have
him return, and that his rank, pay and staff be not reduced.[77] Washington, for his part, wanted Gates's skilled service at headquarters, and
said so in warm personal letters but he felt that the choice should be
left to Gates. His own wishes and convenience should not be put above
those of the former head of the Northern Department, who might,
said Washington, regard the place as in some sense a "degredation." [78]
There the matter stood until circumstance called for Gates's employment elsewhere.[79] The only other man considered as qualified for
immediate assignment as Adjutant General was Maj. Appolos Morris,
but he was suspected of hesitating in allegiance to America. He was
eager, also, to negotiate for the sort of reconcilation offered in the Howe
brothers' proclamation.[80] When Morris was eliminated as a possible
Adjutant General, Congress was favorable to Col. William Raymond
Lee.[81] That officer generously stood aside for Col. Timothy Pickering,
who was prevailed upon to accept.[82]

---

were almost as bulky, 169 pages. A proposal was made, at his instance, in July, 1777, to provide
Washington with a portable press (8 *JCC.*, 581); but as late as December, Washington, heavily
burdened, wrote a friend in Congress that at times "the multiplicity of writing and other business" were "too great" for the aides he had (10 *G. W.*, 201).

[75] 7 *JCC.*, 136; 7 *G. W.*, 67, 231, 267; 8 *ibid.*, 166, 191–93; 2 *Burnett*, 273.
[76] Gates to Washington, Jan. 24, Feb. 28, 1777, and Gates to "Colonel Shaw," Mch. 4,
1777; *Gates Papers*, NYHS.
[77] 154 *Papers of Cont. Cong.*, 135, LC.   [78] 7 *G. W.*, 267; see also *ibid.*, 231, 238.
[79] *Ibid.*, 471 and *infra*, p. 465.
[80] 7 *G. W.*, 67, 77–78, 217, 267. If Charles Lee ever finds a biographer, the visit that
Morris paid him in March, 1777 (*Moore's Lee*, 103) may prove of importance.
[81] 7 *JCC.*, 204.

Pickering was to find the duties exacting and tedious [83] and even if he had been available in the winter of 1776–77, he did not then have the acquaintance in the Army that might have supplemented usefully the knowledge of the Commander-in-Chief in dealing with the shortage of general and field officers caused by sickness,[84] death, resignation and the increase in the number of Regiments. There sometimes had been a surplus of militia officers—six Companies of unarmed Maryland temporary troops, to a total of 101 men only, had fifty-six commissioned officers and nco's [85]—and the applicants for rank as junior officers soon exceeded vacancies and new positions; [86] but it was difficult, and always had been, to find competent field officers,[87] to establish a seniority system, to advance able men of energy, and to get rid of those who lacked courage or enterprise.[88] Because qualified Colonels were few, Congress had difficulty in finding ten whom conscientious Delegates could promote to Brigadier in partial fulfilment of Washington's request that the total number of officers of that rank be raised to thirty,[89] in order that there might be a Brigadier for every four Regiments.[90] Congress was

---

[82] 7 G. W., 336–37, 374, 471; 8 ibid., 114–15, 264; 1 LTW., 365, 368–70; 1 Pickering, 129, 131, 133–35. During the interval between Reed's withdrawal and Pickering's formal beginning as Adjutant General, June 18, George Weedon (7 G. W., 5), Isaac Budd Dunn, (ibid., 218) and Lt. Col. Morgan Connor (ibid., 375, 382), acted in the office.

[83] Cf. his letter of Oct. 13, 1777, to his wife: "Whenever we are not marching, I write incessantly from morning till night . . ." (1 Pickering, 173).

[84] The most conspicuous officer ill during the winter was Lord Stirling. He was sick in January and unable to perform duty. See Israel Putnam to Stirling, Jan. 9, 1777; 159 Papers Cont. Cong., 35, LC.

[85] Congress had thanked the men and then had discharged the Companies because of the disproportion of officers to men. Subsequently a limit was set by formal resolve on the number of officers the militia could have in continental service (7 JCC., 44–45, 190).

[86] Cf. R. H. Lee's hints to Patrick Henry on how to procure a commission for a friend (2 Burnett, 221). See also Washington's own discovery that George Baylor had filled all commissions in his Regiment of Light Horse and could not provide even cornets' positions for two namesakes (7 G. W., 154). Cf. Washington's earlier request that a troop be saved for a "gentleman, a friend of mine" (ibid., 24).

[87] Stirling, for example, noted in a letter of Feb. 26, 1777 to Washington that "Colonel" Wilson—evidently Lt. Col. George Wilson of the Eighth Pennsylvania—had died and that the Regiment's sole field officer was a Major who had gone on duty two days previously (42 Papers of G. W.,) 21, LC.

[88] See 7 G. W., 92–93 for evidence of his knowledge of his officers. Cf. the case of a Colonel considered morally good and physically courageous but not active (ibid., 134, 186). Washington's authorization to settle questions of rank appears in 7 JCC., 109–10. The method of employing this authority through boards of officers, as at Cambridge in 1775, is outlined in 7 G. W., 153. All commissions in the new Army were to bear the date of Jan. 1, 1777. The boards were then to fix relative rank on the basis of previous commissions (ibid., 157). For Washington's self-imposed rule of not interfering with the appointment by the state authorities of the officers of the earlier Battalions, see 7 G. W., 181–82. The major proceedings of 1777 for the determination of seniority, some of them both interesting and informative, appear in 7 G. W., 435; 8 ibid., 93, 164–65, 245, 418; 10 ibid., 34–35, 87, 210, 211; 8 JCC., 418–19, 450–51; 9 ibid., 896–97, 981.

[89] 7 G. W., 49; 7 JCC., 138.

[90] Three Brigades were to constitute a Division.

not believed to be disinclined to name additional Major Generals, but members shook their heads over Washington's appeal for three Lieutenant Generals from among the senior Major Generals.[91] Some of the officers who were charged with the care of Divisions were regarded by certain Congressmen—John Adams among them—as scarcely fitted for their exalted positions.[92] Other Delegates believed Washington could use his Major Generals for the duties he proposed to assign to some of them at higher rank.[93]

As for individuals, Washington now could recommend one only of the two men who had most distinguished themselves in leading Brigades during the Trenton-Princeton operations. Col. Daniel Hitchcock, who certainly would have been made Brigadier, had died of consumption after the Army reached the winter cantonments.[94] The other most distinguished senior officer of Brigade, John Cadwalader of Philadelphia, was particularly commended to Congress by Washington who said, also, that he would like to name Joseph Reed to lead the Light Horse. In a postscript, the Commander-in-Chief confessed he had forgotten that Benjamin Lincoln, whom he praised warmly, did not have already a continental commission but was in the service of Massachusetts.[95]

The response of Congress was a decision to elect five additional Major Generals as well as the ten Brigadiers. Stirling, Thomas Mifflin, Arthur St. Clair and Benjamin Lincoln were made Major Generals;[96] Enoch Poor, John Glover, John Paterson, Anthony Wayne, James M. Varnum, John P. DeHaas, George Weedon, Peter Muhlenberg, John Cadwalader and William Woodford, all of them Colonels, were promoted to brigade command;[97] but these choices disappointed more officers than they gratified.[98] Instead of getting relief, Washington had to spend hours

---

[91] 7 G. W., 49.
[92] John Adams to his wife, Feb. 21, 1777; *Adams, Fam. Let.*, 248; also in 2 *Burnett*, 269.
[93] William Whipple to Josiah Bartlett, Feb. 22, 1777; 2 *Burnett*, 271.
[94] 1 *Greene's Greene*, 312.
[95] 7 G. W., 49, 52. A memorandum of R. H. Harrison, for Washington's information, July 2, 1777, explains how State and Continental commissions had become confused (*L. W. Smith Cols.*).
[96] Feb. 19, 1777; 7 *JCC.*, 133. In his letter of acceptance, Stirling, who had been suffering from rheumatism (see his letter to unnamed correspondent, II Dreer *Coll. Letters of Rev. Generals*, 40, PHS), asked Congress, if consistent with public policy, to make good certain losses of property sustained while he was in service. He put at £500 the damage done when his quarters in New York (see *supra*, p. 181) were looted (Stirling to the President of Congress, Mch. 3, 1777; 162 *Papers Cont. Cong.*, pt. II, p. 523, LC). The application was declined (7 *JCC.*, 185).
[97] Feb. 20–21, 1777, *ibid.*, 138, 141.
[98] Nathanael Greene to John Adams, Mch. 3, 1777, 1 *Greene's Greene*, 339.

smoothing down Brigadiers Benedict Arnold and Andrew Lewis, who thought they should have been promoted.[99] More hours had to be devoted to prevailing on some of the others to accept.[100] In the end, Cadwalader declined,[101] John Armstrong[102] and Andrew Lewis[103] resigned, and John DeHaas was so slow in acknowledging his appointment as Brigadier that Washington wrote to inquire whether he still considered himself an officer of the Army.[104] Afterward, Washington had repeatedly to point out the needs of the troops[105] and what he termed "the chaos of confusion"[106] before he could prevail on Congress to name three additional Brigadiers—Edward Hand, Charles Scott and Ebenezer Learned[107]—to fill vacancies, and even then he felt a continuing lack of Generals of that rank.[108]

The whole experience was an unpleasant one. During the original debate of Feb. 19, 1777, over the choice of Major Generals, a motion to refer the names to the general officers of the Army was opposed by John Adams on the ground that some members of Congress were "disposed to idolize an image which their own hands have molden." The Massachusetts leader particularized: "I speak here of the superstitious veneration that is sometimes paid to General Washington. Although I honor him for his good qualities, yet in this house I feel myself his superior. In private life I shall always acknowledge that he is mine."[109] Besides this personal reproach, Washington had at the time the burden of the unhappiness of Heath over public criticism of his fiasco at Fort Independence. Sullivan was disgruntled because he was not given command at Ticonderoga; Arnold could not fail to resent the fact that Congress had advanced men whose records for hard fighting were not comparable to his.[110]

The one solace of this vexatious upstir of pride and ambition was the

99 7 G. W., 233–34, 235, 251–52, 352–53. Cf. 2 Burnett, 311.
100 7 G. W., 238–39, 239, 472.
101 7 JCC., 170; 78 Papers Cont. Cong., 79, LC.
102 Ibid., 220; 162 Papers Cont. Cong., II, p. 264, LC.
103 Ibid., 270.   104 Letter of June 15; 8 G. W., 244.
105 7 ibid., 206, 267, 287.   106 Ibid., 319.
107 7 JCC., 213, 218.
108 Cf. his recall of Wayne from Gates, May 7, 1777; 7 G. W., 486; 8 ibid., 24–25.
109 Benjamin Rush's Diary, quoted in 2 Burnett, 263. Adams was irritated by what he termed "this delicate point of honor, which is really one of the most putrid corruptions of absolute monarchy, I mean the honor of maintaining a rank superior to abler men." More specifically, "I mean the honor of preferring a single step of promotion to the service of the public." This "honor," he said, "must be bridled" because "it is incompatible with republican principles." He added: "I hope, for my own part, that Congress will elect annually all the general officers." (Letter of Mch. n.d., 1777 to Nathanael Greene, 2 Burnett, 300).
110 1 LTW., 336, 352, 355.

application of Artemas Ward for relief from command in Massachusetts. This permitted Washington to oblige Heath, who wished service
in his own State, and at the same time it made possible a change of commander in the Highlands.[111] Heath had been loyal. Few even of his
friends would have pronounced him enterprising. That, unhappily,
could be said of many officers. Washington wrote sadly: "It is next to
impossible, I find, to get either officers or men out of comfortable winter
quarters, issue what orders you will . . ." [112]

That word, "comfortable," explained the indifferent slowness of all
except a few of the officers. January and February, 1777, were the winter
of their content: once the troops ceased moving, good food was available daily and was ample for so small an army; if doors were not
opened too often by men tramping in and out with snow high on
their boots, the houses of Morristown were warm enough even for
Southerners. Why budge till Spring? So long as the British kept close
to Brunswick, why not postpone all bother about new officers and
recruits and plans? In a Jersey winter, Mars should exchange his helmet
for a nightcap. That was the state of mind. It angered Washington,
who wondered how any man who loved his liberty could indulge his
ease when the fate of America hung on the readiness of an adequate,
well-led and well-equipped army to march quickly in assured understanding of the British objective. The moment word came that the
redcoats were filing out of Brunswick, alarm guns should be fired at
Morristown; "to arms" should be sounded on every drum; [113] the men
should "fall in" at once. Then and always, the Commander-in-Chief
should be free to devote himself to the larger duties. Instead, "I do not
think," said the overburdened Washington, "that any officer since the
creation ever had such a variety of difficulties and perplexities to encounter as I have." [114]

Perhaps this accumulation of woes shook even the strong nervous
system of Washington, made him irritable,[115] and contributed to an illness that sent him to bed at the end of the first week in March. His staff
for several days kept from him all business that did not call for his
personal decision, but as Alexander Hamilton wrote, the General was

[111] 7 G. W., 231.
[112] Ibid., 322.
[113] General orders on this were issued January 20. See ibid., 41.
[114] Letter of Jan. 22, 1777 to John Parke Custis; ibid., 53.
[115] Hamilton to Alexander McDougall, Mch. 10, 1777; ibid., 268 n. Benedict Arnold, in
Rhode Island, heard that Washington had been "exceedingly ill" (1 LTW., 359).

"much pestered with things that [could] not be avoided." [116] By the 15th, when Washington was able once again to carry his full burden, Jersey "three-months' men," the militia of Cecil County, Maryland, and the Virginia volunteers began to stir in their quarters. In another fortnight they could be packing their belongings; on the 1st of April their time would expire.[117] The flow of incoming new soldiers had ceased temporarily; Robert Morris, the most regular of correspondents as Chairman of the Committee of Congress, had been unable to write because of an eye-ailment;[118] Washington, left in the dark, could not undertake to solve half-a-score or more of his puzzles of organization until he knew the will and the policy of the Delegates. Nathanael Greene, who had continued to develop the art of dealing with men, must go to Philadelphia, whither Congress now had returned from Baltimore,[119] and there he must report in detail on the condition of the Army.[120] Washington scarcely could afford to have the alert Rhode Islander absent even for a few days;[121] nor could Greene quickly disengage himself from the duties his little Division required of him; but by the 20th,[122] he made his bow to the Delegates.

During the time that Greene was in Philadelphia, Washington had bad news. Shortly before Heath left his post on the Hudson,[123] General Wooster withdrew his Connecticut militia from New Rochelle, because of a threatened attack, and he did not succeed in getting them to return. This provoked from Washington a rebuke and an order to advance toward King's Bridge and to do what he could to confine the British to New York Island.[124] Further intelligence from the Hudson led Washington to elaborate a review he had made in February of probable British operations from the headwaters and from the mouth of that strategic river.[125] His early conclusion had been that General Carleton would not attempt to pass the Lakes until spring, if then;[126] but Wash-

---

[116] William Smith quoted in his *Diary*, Mch. 3, 1777 (NYPL), an officer who had been with Washington at Morristown and had found the General testy and displeased.

[117] 7 *G. W.*, 319.   [118] 1 *LTW.*, 351.

[119] Adjournment in Baltimore was on February 27; the date set for reconvening in Philadelphia was March 5, but a quorum was not present until March 12. See 7 *JCC.*, 168–69. John Hancock's entry, p. 169, concerning adjournment is incorrect.

[120] 7 *G. W.*, 294–95; 1 *Greene's Greene*, 344.

[121] 7 *G. W.*, 295.   [122] 7 *JCC.*, 187.

[123] He went to Peekskill February 10 and started from that base the next day for Roxbury (*Heath*, 126).

[124] Letter of Mch. 11, 1777; 7 *G. W.*, 271. See also William Duer to Alexander McDougall, Feb. 25, 1777 (*McDougall Papers*, NYHS) and Wooster to Duer, Mch. 2, 1777, Rye Neck (*Henkel's Cat.*, No. 683).

[125] 7 *G. W.*, 28, 117, 118–19, 124.   [126] *Ibid.*, 196.

ington began to suspect in mid March that the British might be planning to move their Canadian forces by sea to join Howe in an overwhelming attack on Philadelphia. It then seemed best to the American commander to concentrate at Peekskill the New England part of the sixteen new Regiments,[127] the recruiting of which had been his supreme aim during the winter. These troops and any others that might be available for reenforcing the Brigades already in the Northern Department could be moved easily from Peekskill in any direction.

While Washington still was exerting himself to get this larger body of fighting men to that station,[128] he learned on the 25th of March [129] that a British force, with four light field pieces, had gone ashore there two days previously from a frigate and from a number of transports that remained in the river. Brigadier Alexander McDougall was at Peekskill, but his infantry were so few that he could do no more than burn some of his stores and evacuate the village.[130] This manifestly might be the first in a series of British expeditions to seize the forts and passes of the Hudson, the loss of which was regarded as almost certainly fatal to the American cause. At the very least, British success in such a movement would necessitate the evacuation of Fort Ticonderoga because it could not be victualed or supplied.[131] The situation appeared the more serious because several days passed without any report from General McDougall.[132] So long as uncertainty prevailed, Washington continued to plead for help from Governor Trumbull,[133] and he directed most insistently that Heath forward to Peekskill or to Ticonderoga the troops recruited in Massachusetts for the Continental Army.[134]

[127] *Ibid.*, 272–76. This is one of the most detailed examples of Washington's strategical reasoning.

[128] 7 *G. W.*, 317–18.

[129] Possibly in the early morning of the 26th. Cf. *ibid.*, 317 and 319.

[130] See McDougall's report to Washington Mch. 29, 1777 (43 *Papers of G. W.*, 102, LC), a basic document for any student of this operation. A list of stores captured and destroyed at Peekskill will be found in 47 *Gentleman's Mag.*, 241. A copy of Howe's congratulatory GOs, of a period missing from *Kemble*, appears under date of Mch. 30, 1777, in Glyn's Journal, *loc. cit.* These orders stated that no British loss of life was sustained. The first reports to Morristown headquarters probably did not contain the news of an attack on this landing party the next day, March 24, by men from the garrison of Fort Constitution under Lt. Col. Marinus Willett.

[131] 7 *G. W.*, 333–34.

[132] Cf. *ibid.*, 339. McDougall's report of March 29 reached Washington on or by April 2, and contained full evidence, as the Commander-in-Chief wrote Congress, that "every prudential step appears to have been taken by the General, and as good a disposition made, as his small number of men would admit of" (*ibid.*, 348).

[133] *Ibid.*, 333.

[134] *Ibid.*, 331–32. Previous calls on Heath for these Massachusetts Regiments and for continental troops had been written March 13 and 23 (*ibid.*, 282–83, 314–15).

It was in the course of this effort to strengthen the northern forces [135] that Washington received his second budget of bad news during the time Greene was in Philadelphia: Recruitment was progressing so slowly that it might be termed a failure, not to say a scandal. Gen. Samuel Parsons, for example, had sent his son to Morristown [136] to draw 400 small arms which were required, he said, for that number of recruits, already raised. When General Parsons on the 6th of March made an explicit return, three of these Connecticut Regiments had only eighty men each, one had 140, none had reached half its authorized strength.[137] From Massachusetts, James Warren wrote John Adams of the transfer of the Bay State command from Ward to Heath, but he either had forgotten the new Regiments or else did not think their numbers worth setting down. "What [Heath] is designed to command," said Warren, "I know not." He specified: "I neither see [n]or hear of any men. About 300 men only are here, besides Craft's, and their time expires in about ten days." [138] As Washington cited some of these figures in explaining why more troops had not reached Peekskill, he grew almost sarcastic: ". . . sorry I am to observe, the militia have got tired, and . . . the Colonels of the Continental Regiments have been greatly deceived themselves, have greatly deceived me, or the most unheard of desertions or most scandalous peculations have prevailed, among the officers who have been employed in recruiting; for Regiments, reported two or three months ago to be half completed are, upon the Colonels being called upon in positive terms for a just state of them, found to contain less than 100 men; and this is not the case of a single Regiment only, but of many." [139]

Because of these blasts and disappointments, there were black clouds in the spring sky when Greene returned from Philadelphia,[140] but some bright spots could be seen in the outlook of hopeful eyes. The brig *Sally* had arrived in the Delaware with 6800 muskets, 1500 gunlocks

---

[135] See also the letters to Generals Poor and Parsons, *ibid.*, 330–31.

[136] This was late in February or early in March, 1777.

[137] Washington to Gov. Jonathan Trumbull, Mch. 23, 1777; *ibid.*, 316.

[138] Letter of Mch. 23, 1777; 1 *Warren-Adams Letters*, 304. Warren misplaced his apostrophe in this quotation. The name was not Craft but Crafts.

[139] Letter of Mch. 26, 1777; 7 *G. W.*, 318.

[140] He was not at Morristown on the 28th, when Washington handled the correspondence of the day (7 *G. W.*, 327); but Greene was there on the 30th (1 *Greene's Greene*, 355). Washington's letter of March 29 (7 *G. W.*, 329), to the President of Congress, mentioned the receipt "last night" of papers from Philadelphia that may have been brought by Greene. For the reports of the Major General during his absence, see 1 *Greene's Greene*, 340 ff.

and other ordnance stores.[141] An express from the East, making good news better, brought word on the 29th [142] that the French ship *Mercury* had anchored safely on the 17th at Portsmouth, New Hampshire, with nearly 12,000 firelocks, 1000 barrels of powder, forty-eight bales of woolens and many scarce articles.[143] Washington breathed easy as he added 12,000 to 5000 and reflected, in the words of one of his letters to Governor Trumbull, "that we shall have no further complaints for the want" of arms.[144]

Other wants were not relieved by anything that Greene had been able to accomplish in Philadelphia, though many of the Army's problems had been explained to Delegates who were disposed to assist as best they could under their awkward system of administration by committee.[145] Various resolves on methods of handling the business of the

[141] *Ibid.*, 351–52; 2 *Burnett*, 310; *Penn. Gazette*, Mch. 26, 1777.   [142] 7 *G. W.*, 329–30.

[143] 7 *JCC.*, 211. Rumor found even more in the cargo of *Mercury*. Col. Henry Jackson wrote Henry Knox that the ship carried "a complete set of cannon for the frigate at Portsmouth" (letter of Mch. 20, 1777; *Knox Papers*, MHS).

[144] Letter of Mch. 29, 1777; 7 *G. W.*, 334. The desperate shortage of 1775 had been relieved before the end of 1776 (6 *G. W.*, 215), but had been renewed by failure to repair small arms that were damaged (7 *JCC.*, 55, 8 *ibid.*, 698, 1 *LTW.*, 430; 7 *G. W.*, 163; 9 *ibid.*, 19, 167; 10 *ibid*, 231) and, still more, by the carelessness of officers in allowing men to carry off arms when troops went home on the expiration of service (7 *ibid.*, 68, 208–09, 216; 8 *ibid.*, 388; 9 *ibid.*, 496–97). Washington believed the only way of preventing this sort of theft was to stamp "United States" on every movable part of public arms and to prevail on the States to declare the possession by any citizen of arms so marked a criminal offence (7 *JCC.*, 84–85, 151; 7 *G. W.*, 340–41; 10 *ibid.*, 153–54; 1 *LTW.*, 435–36). In addition, the States were urged to buy arms when and where they could, to lend to Congress or to other States any surplus they possessed, and to use their feeble manufacturing facilities to the utmost (7 *G. W.*, 55, 113, 370; 7 *JCC.*, 173). The new French arms were destined to disappear quickly and almost mysteriously by liberal continental issue, grant to the States, negligence and theft. (1 *LTW.*, 339; 7 *G. W.*, 390, 424; 8 *ibid.*, 334, 366, 417; 1 *Warren-Adams Letters*, 339.) See 7 *JCC.*, 324, 361, for the rejection of a proposal to manufacture repeating arms. The inventor, Joseph Belton, stated in a letter to the Continental Congress, Apr. 11, 1777, that with his "improvement . . . a common small arm may be made to discharge eight balls, one after another, in eight, five or three seconds of time and each one to do execution five and twenty or thirty yards and after so discharged to be loaded and fired with cartridge as usual . . ." When Congress asked Belton for his terms in altering "some hundred" muskets, he declined so petty an undertaking (Letter of May 7, 1777; 78 *Papers Cont. Cong.* II., 175, LC) but in a letter of May 8 he offered to prove to five experienced officers that his invention would make an American force equal to twice their number in battle. In that event he was to receive £500 for each State; and if he demonstrated that his invention was equal to a three-to-one superiority, he was to have £1000 per State. As nothing further was done, the probabilities are that his device was found to be of no practical use. See Belton's two letters in 41 *Papers Cont. Cong.*, I, 123 and 78 *ibid.*, II, 183, LC. Later in 1777, inspection was ordered as a means of ascertaining whether the arms of different organizations could be uniform. (9 *G. W.*, 363.) A GO as of Oct. 6, 1777 provided that buckshot were to be put in all cartridges (*ibid.*, 313). The same month, Joseph Reed wrote (1 *Reed*, 333) that he believed most of the militia left their arms at home in the hope they would get others of which "they will not render the most honorable account."

[145] Some of the numerous subjects discussed by Greene with a committee were sketched by Greene in a letter to Washington, Mch. n.d., 1777, in 1 *Greene's Greene*, 349. The committee that heard him was an enlargement (7 *JCC.*, 189), of one named, March 13, "to confer with General Gates upon the general state of affairs" (*ibid.*, 175).

Army had been adopted at Greene's instance.[146] Washington was assured carefully that the Congress never had intended he should be bound by a majority vote of a council of war when its recommendation was contrary to his judgment.[147] Along with these papers, Greene brought back much news of appointments, reproofs and suspension. General Schuyler had been reprimanded, in terms almost insulting, for saying he should have been acquainted with the reasons for the dismissal of the Director of Hospitals in the Northern Department.[148] Perhaps for the punishment of Schuyler, but more because of its admiration for Gates, Congress directed the former Adjutant General to proceed to Ticonderoga and to take command of the Army there[149]—instead of reopening his office, as Washington had hoped, at Morristown. In the same marked, if unusual spirit of decision, Congress on receipt of charges against the senior naval officer, Commodore Esek Hopkins, had suspended him from command.[150] Further, the position of commandant of the forts in the New York Highlands had been created and George Clinton had been named to it.[151]

Washington digested Greene's report and turned again to his own task of confining Howe, of clinging to restive militia, of trying vainly to expedite recruiting, and of arousing officers from their lassitude and laziness. In particular, Washington sought to improve his system of intelligence so that he could discover quickly and accurately the direction of the enemy's advance. The test was certain to come, he thought, long before the Army was large enough to meet it victoriously. A junior officer could say of Howe that "the *Conqueror* of America finds himself . . . in possession of a string of land, inhabited by half-starved Tories, of about fourteen miles in length and one and a half in width, and but one way to make his escape, and that . . . by way of Amboy." [152] Washington was not so complacent. He reasoned that the condition of the roads alone could be holding Howe at Brunswick,[153] and that this could not continue for many days. The spring seemed to

---

[146] 7 *JCC.,* 221.
[147] *Ibid.,* 196; *Adams, Fam. Let.,* 255.
[148] 7 *JCC.,* 180. For the action against the director, Dr. Samuel Stringer, see *supra,* p. 389.
[149] 7 *JCC.,* 202.
[150] *Ibid.,* 202, 204.
[151] *Ibid.,* 203.
[152] John Chilton to "Major Pickett," Mch. 19, 1777; 12 *T* 116.
[153] Washington to James Warren, Mch. 15, 1777; 1 *Warren-Adams Letters,* 298–99; George Johnston, Mch. 17, 1777, in 12 *T* 115. The hostile *N. Y. Gazette* unwittingly supplied intelligence on this score to the Americans when it reported Mch. 24, 1777, that a British force sent from Amboy to Spanktown in order to "surprise a party of rebels" had failed to bag them, even under the leadership of Colonel Mawhood, because of the badness of the roads.

be forward.[154] That raid of the 23rd–24th on Peekskill might mean that Howe was planning to ascend the Hudson.[155] Now, on the last day of March, an American Captain of a "tobacco ship" who had escaped from New York reported at headquarters. About 3000 troops, he stated, had embarked there and apparently were ready to sail. "It was generally said," Washington wrote after the examination of the Captain, "they had in contemplation an expedition to Chesapeake Bay, and to make a descent on the Eastern Shore." Further, "there were some who conjectured, they mean to go up the North River and to take the highland fortifications if possible." [156]

That was usually the way of it in this unequal contest: a numerically superior British Army had the help of that mighty fleet of armed vessels and transports, and could carry the war, swiftly and secretly, wherever its commander thought he could reach the vitals of America.

[154] 7 G. W., 317.   [155] Ibid., 333–34.
[156] Letter of Mch. 31, 1777, to George Clinton; ibid., 340.

CHAPTER XVI

Three Months' Labor Ends in Bad News

(April 1–July 10, 1777)

The first days of April brought no confirmation of the report by the escaped Captain that 3000 troops had gone aboard transports at New York,[1] but the news, whether correct or erroneous, heightened the pitch of the argument at Morristown over the perennial question, where would the British strike? The theories advanced in answer varied from day to day with the interpretation different officers put on changing intelligence reports. Washington's own opinion was that Howe's army was about to move up the Hudson or to Philadelphia, with the probability in favor of the Quaker City, but whether the southward advance would be by water or overland, he was as yet unable to ascertain.[2] Congress, for its part, was so nearly convinced the enemy was soon to descend on Philadelphia that it adopted such measures as it could devise to safeguard the approaches and to remove the more valuable stores.[3]

[1] 7 G. W., 348. Current intelligence reports were summarized in Putnam to John Hancock, from Princeton, Apr. 8, 1777; 159 Papers Cont. Cong., 57, LC. The collection of Dr. F. M. Dearborn, New York, includes a most interesting account of the organization of American espionage on New York Island. With Doctor Dearborn's consent, this is now printed as Appendix IV–2.

[2] Of twenty-four opinions recorded by Washington and the ablest and best informed of his general officers, Greene, Knox and Sullivan, thirteen were that Howe's objective was Philadelphia, eight were that the target was Philadelphia or the Hudson, and three that the British would try to subjugate New England. The expression of these opinions will be found in 7 G. W., 348, 361, 381, 385, 388, 425, 428–29, 437; 8 ibid., 39, 145, 146, 150–51, 157, 204, 232–33, 275, 341, 363, 366; 1 Greene's Greene, 361, 368; 9 A. Hamilton, 67; 1 Sullivan Papers, 387–88; Henry Knox to Mrs. Knox, Apr. 13, May 4, 1777; Knox Papers, MHS; Washington to unnamed correspondent, June 20, 1777, Washington MSS., Huntington Lib.; same to same, June 20, 1777, another text; Rutgers Univ. MSS. Samuel Adams believed the British would try to subdue New England and that region only in 1777. See 1 Warren-Adams Letters, 315. An account of what appears to have been an "invasion scare" in Massachusetts will be found in Lucy Knox's letter to her husband, May 8, 1777; Knox Papers, MHS.

[3] 7 JCC., 236 ff., 246–47, 250–51, 268–69, 271, 284; 2 Burnett, 322, 324; 7 G. W., 400–01; 8 ibid., 195–96. John Adams, on the other hand, told his wife as late as May 27, 1777, that no apprehension for the safety of the town was felt in Philadelphia. Said he: "Howe is unable to do anything except by stealth. Washington is strong enough to keep Howe where he is" (Adams, Fam. Let., 278). Earlier, on the basis of Washington's reference to an intelligence report of a possible attack in Chesapeake Bay, Congress ordered stores or powder removed from Baltimore and Annapolis (7 JCC., 219; 7 G. W., 380). Washington's continuing share (see supra, p. 385) in the discussion of the probable evacuation of Rhode Island by the British and of a possible offensive against the reduced force there may be traced in 7 G. W., 350–51, 434, 436; 8 ibid., 126–27; 7 JCC., 272–73.

The defence of the city by Washington had to be fitted, of course, into his broader strategical plan, which now, as in the past, was to avoid a general engagement with the entire British force and, at the same time, to prevent the severance of the New England States from those to the southward. General Carleton was expected to make the utmost of his advantage in controlling the whole of Lake Champlain. He or Gen. John Burgoyne would be able to invest, or at least to approach Ticonderoga without effective challenge. If Ticonderoga fell, the road to Albany would be open. In event the enemy simultaneously attacked from the South the defences of the Highlands and captured them, nothing could prevent the junction of a strong British column moving up the Hudson and of the forces descending from the North. Washington therefore considered it absolutely essential to hold Ticonderoga and the Highland passes if this were possible at any price short of removing his own Army from in front of Howe. The supreme difficulty was the elemental one of providing adequate strength on the line of the Hudson without weakening the line of the Delaware. All the while, too, Washington had to keep an eye on Rhode Island and, even more vigilantly, on the British fleet. Any evening an express might gallop into Morristown with the word that troops had been disembarked at some point where previously not even the shadow of a redcoat had fallen.

"In short," Washington wrote one of his Brigadiers on the 3rd of April, "the campaign is opening, and we have no men for the field." [4] It was incredible, but substantially true: By the middle of April, the weakness of the Army was even more ominous than it had been in the late winter. Because of the constant coming and going of militia, Washington scarcely knew what his numbers were.[5] In spite of repeated and urgent orders from headquarters for the utmost speed in the dispatch of recruits,[6] ease-loving officers [7] were so slow in forwarding detachments for the "additional" Regiments [8] that Washington had again to call on the Governors of nearby States to supply militia.[9] When April

---

[4] Letter to Brig. Gen. Samuel H. Parsons; 7 G. W., 354. See, also, Washington to Gov. Thomas Johnson, Apr. 11, 1777; ibid., 392, and to Edmund Pendleton, Apr. 12, 1777; ibid., 393.
[5] 7 G. W., 196.   [6] For example, ibid., 261, 264.
[7] Ibid., 361, 365, 372.
[8] H. Jackson to Henry Knox, Apr. 3, 1777, Knox Papers, MHS.
[9] 7 G. W., 203–04, 244–45, 254, 262, 263, 333, 359, 361, 363, 396; 7 JCC., 299. See 7 G. W., 319, for Washington's feeling that New Jersey militia were undependable, and see ibid., 400–01, for his request that the Pennsylvania militia be kept at a distance from the Continental Army because their lax discipline spread "the seeds of licentiousness among the Regulars . . ."

returns were made of new troops "present for duty, fit," the condition that had prevailed in March was duplicated: official figures rarely were anywhere near the totals recruiting officers had set down hopefully. On April 3, 1777, Washington wrote: "except for a few hundred from Jersey, Pennsylvania and Virginia, I have not yet received a man of the new continental levies." [10]

Even in that plight, he refused to fall back on the policy of short-term enlistment from which the Army had suffered almost fatally in 1775 and again in 1776.[11] He had to fight, he confessed, to "keep the life and soul of this Army together," [12] but he retained the confidence of most of his men [13] and he did not weaken in determination even for an hour. Three times in March he had been compelled to give warning that the débâcle might not be far distant unless the Army was recruited heavily and at once with dependable troops.[14] Early in April he renewed this,[15] and on the 12th painstakingly he set down, State by State, the pitiful results of the effort to fill the continental Regiments.[16] This he prefaced with the statement, "I wish I could see any prospect of an Army, fit to make proper opposition, formed anywhere," [17] and, when he reiterated this nearly two weeks later, he told Philip Schuyler that the Army already had "a much longer indulgence" at the hands of the enemy, than Americans "had any right to expect." [18] From every gain in numbers during the weeks the British idled, a constant subtraction went on among Washington's troops not only because men's terms of service ended,[19] with the resulting exposure of part of his front,[20] but also because desertion continued to an irritating, and in some commands, to a threatening extent.[21]

In February, Congress had called on the public to report deserters [22] and had modified the articles of war concerning appeals and execu-

---

[10] 7 G. W., 350.

[11] 1 LTW., 361; 7 G. W., 407–08, 439. In ibid., 450, are his regretful observations on Connecticut recruiting for brief service.

[12] Ibid., 225.

[13] See ibid., 436, for the unauthorized action of the Headquarters Guard in terming themselves "General Washington's Life Guard."

[14] Ibid., 223, 286, 317.   [15] Ibid., 354–55.

[16] Ibid., 396–97. On the 17th he wrote in another connection that the "remains" of the Virginia Regiments still with him amounted to approximately 1000 (ibid., 421).

[17] Ibid., 396.   [18] Ibid., 454.

[19] He had on one occasion to ask a Maryland Battalion to remain with him for as brief a time as eight days (7 G. W., 334–35).

[20] Ibid., 345.

[21] Compare Putnam to Council of Safety of Philadelphia, Jan. 21, 1777, Henkel's Cat. 683, no. 597, and George Weedon to John Page, Apr. 14, 1777; Chicago HS. MSS.

[22] 7 JCC., 115 ff, 154–55.

tions.[23] Deserters had been tried in the usual manner, sentenced and sometimes put to death,[24] though frequently, condemned renegades were reprieved [25] because Washington had come to doubt the disciplinary value of over-numerous hangings, even for this offence.[26] Sometimes the execution of one deserter was made the occasion of pardon for others.[27] On Apr. 6, 1777, Washington proclaimed the pardon of all deserters who would rejoin the Army by May 15,[28] but in cases of desertion where the penalty imposed by the court was flogging, he directed prompt infliction of penalty [29] and he did not forbid strange punishments.[30] The General pursued an unusual but practical policy, also toward soldiers not of American birth, who were tempted to desert, especially from the Light Horse,[31] in order to get the bounty General Howe offered those coming into British rank with their arms.[32] Many men were disaffected. The Eighth Pennsylvania Regiment, in particular, was in so ill a state of mind that Washington thought expediency dictated the pardon of ten of its members who had deserted.[33]

He believed the cure for military disorder was prompt pay, good provisions,[34] and the general improvement of discipline through the better choice, careful instruction and faithful individual study of his officers.[35] ". . . Nothing," he said, "can be more hurtful to the service than the neglect of discipline, for . . . discipline, more than numbers,

---

[23] *Ibid.*, 265.   [24] E.g., 7 *G. W.*, 163, 197, 351, 353.

[25] *Ibid.*, 183–84, 412; 8 *ibid.*, 59–60; 9 *ibid.*, 99.

[26] 7 *ibid.*, 459; 8 *ibid.*, 18–19, 50; 9 *ibid.*, 80–81.

[27] 8 *ibid.*, 214, 452; 9 *ibid.*, 30.   [28] 7 *ibid.*, 364.

[29] 7 *ibid.*, 183–84.

[30] Among them were these: one man was given 100 lashes for deserting one Regiment and fifty for leaving another command (8 *ibid.*, 343); several were lashed and then sentenced to serve on an American frigate for the duration of hostilities (e.g., *ibid.*, 268); a deserting horse-thief was to be led around the camp, with his coat turned and his head toward the animal's tail, after which he was to be discharged (9 *ibid.*, 99); still another deserter was to have the front of his head shaved, tarred and feathered, whereupon he was to run the gauntlet of his Company and then was to be sent to a frigate, there to remain until the end of the war (*ibid.*, 170).

[31] 8 *ibid.*, 136, 264.

[32] 8 *ibid.*, 8–9, 123. Howe's bounty was reported to be twenty-four dollars to those who "went over" and had their firelock or carbine (8 *ibid.*, 17); an offer Congress matched May 9 (7 *JCC.*, 340). Simultaneously some Americans were accused of enlisting, getting the twenty-dollar bounty given by Congress, deserting, reenlisting, and collecting the bounty a second time (8 *G. W.*, 111).

[33] 7 *ibid.*, 483–85. The reasons for the poor condition of the Regiment are sketched in *ibid.*, 484 n.

[34] 8 *ibid.*, 198, but as late as November, one Brigade, Poor's, had eleven months' pay due its men (10 *G. W.*, 41).

[35] Some exceedingly interesting examples of what he did in these directions on his own motion or at the instance of Congress will be found in 7 *ibid.*, 371; 8 *ibid.*, 127 ff, 308, 345 ff, 406, 412–13; 7 *JCC.*, 157.

gives one army the superiority over another." [36] Sound discipline of this sort was not inculcated easily. The long tedium of the spring had inevitably its demoralizing effect on some of the officers. Men who should have set an example were accused of drunkenness, of gambling and of loitering on journeys and around the hospitals in order to escape drab, routine duty.[37] Suspicion was raised, also, that some officers were holding out their men's pay or were collecting for fictitious soldiers carried on the payrolls as "absent, sick." [38] Washington dealt sternly with all such cases,[39] and though he believed that "the benefits arising from the moderate use of strong liquor have been experienced in all armies and are not to be disputed," [40] he maintained that "there cannot be a greater failure in a soldier than drunkenness." [41] When that condition was given as the explanation of misconduct, he regarded it as an aggravation of the offence.[42]

In spite of everything, Washington tried to hold each officer to the highest standard the individual could attain, and so long as men with commissions did not fall below the minimum requirements of their rank, he did not expect of the dullest and least lettered what he demanded of the ablest and best schooled.[43] He counselled all those he found within his reach and in need of admonition or of assistance; but in this hard labor of training soldiers to obey, he needed more help than he had. For reasons he did not understand, unless it was shortsighted economy in "saving" pay in winter,[44] Congress delayed the

[36] 8 G. W., 359.
[37] See 7 G. W., 481; 8 ibid., 8–9, 13, 14, 38, 123, 251.
[38] 8 G. W., 97; 7 JCC., 342. See 8 G. W., 45–46 for Washington's appeal to Congress for auditors to examine the accounts of officers.
[39] On occasion he frankly opposed the promotion by a State of men he deemed unworthy to serve as officers. For a typical case, see 7 ibid., 381–82.
[40] 9 G. W., 73. Cf. ibid., 105. For Washington's efforts to protect his men and the public against excessive prices for liquor, see 9 ibid., 119, 464; 10 ibid., 102, 225. See also his announcement of Feb. 11, 1777, 7 ibid., 140, that the issue of liquor as a part of the ration had to be suspended because of the scarcity and exorbitant price of the supply. John Adams wrote his wife from Philadelphia, Aug. 29, 1777 (Adams, Fam. Let., 301), "Whiskey is used here instead of rum and I don't see but it is just as good."
[41] 7 G. W., 335.   [42] Ibid.
[43] Typical, in the one category, are his admonition to five hot-headed Lieutenants (9 G. W., 68–69) and his tactful, sympathetic letter to an officer who was passed over in promotions because he had left the Northern Army in a manner "inconsistent with the character of an officer" and, in addition was charged with indulging "in a loose, unguarded way of talking which has often brought your own veracity in question . . ." (7 G. W., 309–10). In contrast were letters to Capt. Oliver Towles (ibid., 475) and to Col. Theodorick Bland (10 ibid., 26), who were admonished that men of their station must remain with the Army even to the neglect of pressing private affairs. In like spirit, when Elias Boudinot declined Washington's request that he take charge of the exchange of prisoners, the General told him that if men of character and influence did not come forward and help, all would be lost. (See Elias Boudinot, op. cit., 9.)   [44] See 7 G. W., 464.

election of the additional general officers he required. New Brigades, which should have the best and earliest direction, had none or were to have it late. In the Army, in Congress and in the attitude of hundreds of public officials and of citizens by the thousand, Washington observed with alarm this disposition to delay, to hope rather than to act, in a vague, passive sort of belief that the hard realities of war could be evaded. Said Washington, "a strange unaccountable languor seems but too generally to prevail at a time when the preservation of our rights and all that is dear calls loudly for the most vigorous and active exertions." [45] Henry Knox expressed the same thing from a different point of view when he wrote: "The people are supine; thank Heaven, the inability of our enemy seems proportionate to our exertion . . ." [46]

If "inability" was not the accurate word to describe British failure to take the field, "disinclination" was—and to the infinite gain of America. The snow disappeared from the hills around Morristown; spring came to the fields of New Jersey; the roads mysteriously seemed to find bottoms that had been lost in mud. Once only, in the whole of April, did the British attempt to do more than to protect their foraging parties. Word of this particular affair reached Washington on the 13th in a hasty and brief dispatch from Maj. Gen. Benjamin Lincoln, who was in command of the outpost at Bound Brook, seven miles upstream from Brunswick on the Raritan. Lincoln had with him the Eighth Pennsylvania, part of the Fourth Continental and some militia, a total of approximately 500 men. Early in the morning, through the negligence of the militiamen at the crossing of the river,[47] the British passed the stream easily and undertook to surround the outpost, but Lincoln learned of the advance in time to get most of his men out of the village before the flanking columns formed a junction in his rear. The artillery detachment and its trio of three-pounders were captured by British Light Horse; a number of Lincoln's men were wounded or captured, and a few were killed. Although the Americans could make no esti-

---

[45] Letter of Apr. 13, 1777, to Patrick Henry; 7 *G. W.*, 409. See also William Duer to Pres. N. Y. Conv., Apr. 17: ". . . notwithstanding the invasion which threatens this city, a languor prevails amongst the inhabitants of almost all ranks" (2 *Burnett*. 331).

[46] Letter of Apr. 13, 1777, to Mrs. Knox; *Knox Papers*, MHS. On April 6 he wrote his wife: ". . . were it not that I have the most enthusiastic assurance of mind that it is the will of heaven that America be great—she may not deserve it—her exertions have been small, her policy wretched, nay, her supineness in the past winter would, according to the common operations of things, mark her for destruction" (*Knox Papers*, loc. cit.).

[47] Except in freshets, the upper Raritan was passable almost anywhere, Timothy Pickering was told. See his Journal, 1 *Pickering*, 119.

mate of the British casualty list, they believed that the marksmen of the Pennsylvania Regiment had shot down many by their steady fire against the head of one of the enemy's columns.

The redcoats wasted little time after they found their quarry gone and Bound Brook almost without stores. As soon as the British satisfied themselves they could get no booty, they left the village and returned as they had come. Lincoln, reenforced by Greene, occupied the place and again took up the guarding of the river crossings.[48] In the course of an inquiry into the reasons for the surprise, suspicion was raised against a farmer of the neighborhood who was alleged to have learned the countersign and to have passed it on to the British; but Washington refused to arrest the man on so vague a charge. It would be enough, he said, to watch the farmer and, if any actual offence was discovered, to punish it.[49] No blame for the affair was attached to Lincoln or to any of his troops except the militia at the crossing of the Raritan, but the episode led Washington to reduce the number of posts, in order that the forces might be less exposed to surprise attacks and more readily assembled in event the enemy made the expected major thrust.[50]

The General had very soon to justify in the eyes of Connecticut the application of this same policy of maintaining the minimum number of posts. At 3 o'clock on the morning of April 28, Washington was awakened to receive a dispatch in which Brig. Gen. Alexander Mc-Dougall forwarded reports that a British force had landed on the coast of Connecticut and had started inland toward Danbury. That town had become an extensive base, both because it was supposed to be safe from raiders and also because it was conveniently situated in relation

[48] Washington's reports, all of them brief, are in 7 *G. W.*, 399, 411, 427. Somewhat fuller accounts will be found in Greene's letter of Apr. 13, 1777, to John Adams (1 *Greene's Greene*, 362). A few details, not in print, were given in Henry Knox to Nicholas Everleigh, May 5, 1777 (*Knox Papers*, MHS). Washington's estimate on Apr. 17 of thirty-five to forty casualties (7 *G. W.*, 427) was reduced by Knox, May 5 (*loc. cit.*), to "twenty or thirty prisoners and six killed." Kemble (*op. cit.*, I, 113) gave the number captured by the British as eighty. Glyn's Journal (*loc. cit.*, Apr. 12, 1777) included the British "after orders" for this affair. A distorted account of the episode will be found in Putnam to Hancock, Apr. 13, 1777 (159 *Papers Cont. Cong.*, 67, LC). The British official summary will be found in 47 *Gentleman's Mag.*, 289. "Colonel Butler," mentioned by Greene, was Lt. Col. Richard Butler in temporary command of the Eighth Pennsylvania Foot, which had passed on the death of Col. Eneas Mackay, Feb. 14, 1777, to Col. Daniel Broadhead, commissioned Mch. 12, 1777. See *Heitman*.

[49] *Boudinot*, 66.

[50] 7 *G. W.*, 416. See 8 *ibid.*, 120, on the disadvantages of overnumerous posts. In 12 *T* 122 appears an interesting letter from John Taylor to Edmund Pendleton on "these little cantonments . . . daily liable to surprise . . ." Washington's intelligence report of Mch. 28, 1777, with its estimate of 7800 British and Hessians, in and near Brunswick, will be found in 43 *Papers of G. W.*, 95, LC. Intelligence filed by Adam Stephen, Apr. 23, 1777, is in 152 *Papers Cont. Cong.*, IV, p. 103, LC.

to Peekskill, where provisions, quartermasters stores and ammunition were exposed to attack from the Hudson.[51] As Washington did not know of the presence nearby of any American force large enough to deal with the raiders, he feared that all public property at Danbury would be destroyed. The British might sack the town, devastate the country, and get back to the coast before troops could be marched from Peekskill to oppose them, but he thought the effort should be made to overtake them and he sent McDougall an order to start for Connecticut if such a move held any promise of success.[52]

No detailed intelligence concerning the raid reached Washington until the morning of the 30th, when he received a further report from McDougall: the British had reached Danbury unopposed, had burned all the stores and some private buildings besides; on their withdrawal, April 28, they had been assailed by a small body of men—militia, a few Continentals and some convalescents whom Gen. David Wooster had scraped together. Another column of the same sort was organized by Brig. Gen. Gold S. Silliman, who yielded command to Benedict Arnold when that officer arrived. Wooster assailed the British rear; Arnold threw his force across the road by which the King's men were retiring, and, when pushed aside, he continued to harass flank and rear. Wooster was mortally wounded, approximately twenty Americans were killed and about four times as many were wounded, but the redcoats had been met with so much powder and shot that natives thought again of Concord and Lexington. British casualties were variously estimated at figures as high as "500 or 600"[53] and in reality ran to the substantial total of about 154 killed and wounded.[54]

Materially, one loss was more serious than all the others combined. Tents to the number of almost 1700 had been sent from Peekskill to Danbury for safe-keeping and were destroyed there.[55] These were irre-

---

[51] The distance between the two points on a straight line is twenty-seven miles. By road in 1777, it was about thirty-five.

[52] 7 G. W., 487–88.

[53] Henry Knox to Nicholas Everleigh, May 5, 1777; *Knox Papers*, MHS.

[54] *A. Robertson's Diaries*, 130. In 1 *Kemble*, 115, the total is given as 161; in Glyn's Journal, *loc. cit.*, it was put at 123.

[55] 1 *Sullivan Papers*, 333, 334. McDougall's important MS reports of Apr. 27 and 29, 1777, are in 46 *Papers of G. W.*, 29, 55, LC. For the details of the Danbury raid, which is more definitely a part of the history of the Revolution than of the biography of Washington, see Jed. Huntington to McDougall, Apr. 23, 26 (two dispatches), 27, 1777; *ibid.*, 22, 23, 24, 34, LC; J. Field to McDougall, Apr. 27, 1772 (two dispatches), *ibid.*, 30, 33; J. Campbell to McDougall, Apr. 27, 1772 (two dispatches), *ibid.*, 31, 32; Benedict Arnold to McDougall, Apr. 26, 28, 1777; *ibid.*, 35, 50; 7 G. W., 487, 488, 490, 493–94, 8 *ibid.*, 1, 3, 4–5, 27; 1 *Greene's Greene*, 378; Henry Knox to Nicholas Everleigh, May 5, 1777; Ralph Isaacs to Mrs. Henry Knox, Apr. 30,

placeable, otherwise than by importation.[56] Another evil result of the raid was the development of an increasing reluctance on the part of Connecticut authorities to send their militia to Peekskill, lest another raid be made on their State,[57] though, in reality, the raid had shown that the Connecticut towns and the country immediately to the East of the Hudson were strategically one defensive area. McDougall started from Peekskill for Danbury as soon as practicable after he heard of the landing. He halted and turned back when informed that the British were re-embarking but, if the raid had been prolonged, he soon would have come within striking distance.[58] Washington did not believe the coast of Connecticut could be protected from landings and from raids that would carry troops one day's march inland. The provident course, he reasoned, was to move all valuable large stores farther northward, beyond the string of towns and villages the enemy would be apt to reach before the militia could be assembled. Congress ordered this done,[59] but it did not answer a question that might arise dangerously: Who was responsible for the protection and disposition of continental military stores in the States? [60] Should the Quartermaster or Commissary General say where these stores should be located and whither removed; or was that the duty of Washington and his representative, the senior officer of the nearest large body of continental troops? Had State authorities any rights or obligations concerning these stores?

The answer to these and to many other questions had to be deferred by Washington, who somehow endured the confinement of his work [61]

1777, *Knox Papers*, MHS. Several contemporary newspaper accounts appear in 1 *Moore*, 423 ff. Kemble's remarks (*op. cit.*, v. 1, p. 116–17) are familiar. Alexander Hamilton's comment, in a letter to Robert Morris, is interesting: "I congratulate you also on the Danbury expedition. The stores destroyed there have been purchased at a pretty high price to the enemy" (Letter of May 7, 1777; 9 *A. Hamilton*, 66). An admirable British account is that in *A. Robertson's Diaries*, 127 ff. Howe's report to Germaine, Apr. 24, 1777, is in 47 *Gentleman's Mag.*, 289.

[56] As it chanced, when Maj. Robert Troup, Gates's aide, wrote from Fishkill, May 2, and described the Danbury disaster, he told his chief that he had word of the arrival of 925 tents in the cargo of a ship that had reached Boston. Troup said he intended "to get these if possible" (*Gates Papers*, NYHS). Tents were in short supply among the American forces almost everywhere in 1777. See Mifflin to Washington, 43 *Papers of G. W.*, 41, LC; 8 *G. W.*, 423; 9 *ibid.*, 213; 10 *ibid.*, 214; 8 *JCC*, 481. For Washington's controversy with Gates over the apportionment of tents, after the Danbury raid, see 8 *G. W.*, 62, 65, 66, 87–88, 206, 319.

[57] Cf. 8 *G. W.*, 96–97.

[58] See Washington's commendation in 8 *G. W.*, 1.

[59] *Ibid.*, 1, 3, 4–5, 27; 7 *JCC.*, 314–15.   [60] See 8 *G. W.*, 3, 8.

[61] 7 *G. W.*, 322–23. This was a rebuke to George Weedon for over-long furloughs. General Weedon took it in good part. On Apr. 14, 1777, Weedon wrote John Page: ". . . no other man but our present General, who is the greatest that ever did or ever will adorn the earth, could have supported himself under the many disappointments and disgraces he was subjected to from this singular system of carrying on a war against the most formidable enemy in the world . . ." (*Chicago HS.* MSS).

and found time to protect Congress against unreasonable charges in accounts that passed over his desk,[62] to consider personal appeals for relief or for special consideration in cases of illness or death,[63] and to exercise vigilance in endorsing applications where any charge of nepotism might be made.[64] He managed, also, to see that proper uniforms were supplied his Headquarters Guards,[65] who now were recruited from the Virginia Regiments,[66] and that his stable was kept up.[67] To his private affairs, he could not set aside a single hour beyond those required for indispensable matters at Mount Vernon, where, unhappily, smallpox had developed.[68]

Thanks to his habit of early rising, Washington usually dispatched his routine army business by dinner time, when, if conditions permitted, the senior officers and Brigade Majors of the day were his guests.[69] Over the table, as a hostess, Martha herself now presided. She had come to Morristown in mid-March and was to remain until nearly the end of May, and around her, as always, she gathered ladies of established station who, in most instances, had come to camp to visit their husbands, officers at headquarters.[70] As far as possible, all of Washington's aides shared in the entertainment of these guests and brought to their duties a diversity of social talents. Mrs. Theodorick Bland, who saw them

[62] 7 G. W., 316, 488–89. In one instance, he directed General Heath to pay the account of an importunate minister, if there was "the least shadow of right" in the claim. Otherwise, said Washington, the clergyman "will write me and travel himself to death" (8 ibid., 439).

[63] Even for such hostile individuals as Gov. William Franklin (8 G. W., 474, 476, 498) and Joseph Galloway (10 ibid., 176). See also his letter to his brother Samuel, whose wife had died (9 G. W., 39) and his gift to the widow of a fallen officer for whose family Congress had made no provision (7 ibid., 482).

[64] Cf. 7 G. W., 321–22, 37 ibid., 539.

[65] 7 G. W., 452–53. He remarked in his letter to Caleb Gibbs that he himself wore buff and blue.

[66] 7 G. W., 494–95; 8 ibid., 178–79.

[67] For some of his horse trades and purchases in 1777, see G. W. Rev. Accts., 25; 8 G. W., 10–11, 10 ibid., 228–29. In a letter to Count Pulaski, Dec. 31, 1777, Washington said: "No pains should be spared to inspire the men with an affection for their horses . . ." This is the first instance observed in the present research of any expression by Washington of personal regard for horses, though there is no reason to doubt that he had cherished affection for his mounts. He did not attempt to use his phaeton in the opening campaigning of 1777. See 9 ibid., 232–33. During the year he lost two horses in an epidemic. G. W. Rev. Accts., loc. cit.

[68] 7 G. W., 181; 37 ibid., 539. For some of his problems on his home estate, see 7 ibid., 309; 9 ibid., 281; 10 ibid., 60–61. The last of these references is to Washington's participation with Lund Washington and George Baylor in a share John Parke Custis had in a privateer. Washington complained (7 G. W., 54), that the "badness" of his memory hampered him in managing his affairs at long range. At headquarters, his only relief, as a commander, was in the fact that he no longer had any responsibility for naval affairs (9 G. W., 117).

[69] The hour was 2 or 3 P.M. according to circumstance and season. Cf. two invitations to Knox, Feb. 11, Mch. 8, 1777 (Knox Papers, MHS), where the hour is 2; see also 8 G. W., 176; 10 ibid., 19. John Adams (Fam. Let., 304) observed approvingly in September, 1777, that Washington had banished wine from the table and was serving rum and water.

[70] 51 NIHSP., 150; 7 G. W., 361; 8 ibid., 223.

often in April and in May, prepared for her sister a register of some of the qualities of the men who drafted the General's letters, prepared his orders, delivered his verbal instructions and attended to a thousand matters of business for him: "his aid de camps . . . are Col. [John] Fitzgerald, an agreeable broad-shouldered Irishman—Col. [George] Johnston . . . who is exceedingly witty at everybody's expense but can't allow other people to be so at his own, though they often take the liberty—Col. [Alexander] Hamilton, a sensible, genteel, polite young fellow, a West Indian—Col. [Richard] Meade—Col. [Tench] Tilghman, a modest, worthy man who, from his attachment to the General lives in his family and acts in any capacity that is uppermost, without fee or reward [71]—Col. [Robert] Harrison, brother of Billy Harrison that kept store in Petersburg and as much like him as possible, a worthy man—Capt. [Caleb] Gibbs of the General's Guard, a good natured Yankee who makes a thousand blunders in the Yankee style and keeps the dinner table in constant laugh." [72] Mrs. Bland agreed that all these were "polite, sociable gentlemen who make the day pass with a great deal of satisfaction to the visitors," but she insisted that the great hour was that of the riding parties after dinner. The General usually went along when the day brought no report of calamity or new misery, and then, said the Colonel's lady, Washington "throws off the hero and takes on the chatty, agreeable companion—he can be downright impudent sometimes—such impudence, Fanny, as you and I like . . ." [73]

It was, of course, a relief to him to have these rides with interesting women; and it was a physical stimulation, when the afternoon was free of burdening duty, to go to a nearby field and to catch ball with some of his juniors. [74] Riding and sports were part of the life for which he yearned, the life he had in mind when he wrote his old-time counsellor, Edmund Pendleton, perhaps with more emotion than his formal

---

71 If anyone thinks this reference to Tench Tilghman as a "modest, worthy man" has a condescending tone, it must be attributed to Mrs. Bland's lack of familiarity with the connections of a gentleman who would himself have been the last to boast of a family that enjoyed an established position in two States. Washington had the highest opinion of Tilghman and, when he had opportunity of bestowing the most distinguished honor the war could bring a staff officer, he selected Tilghman to carry a certain dispatch dated Oct. 19, 1781.

72 Mrs. Bland's misspelling of several of the names has been corrected; her somewhat erratic punctuation has been conformed throughout to her own standard. This letter is one of the most interesting of the all-too-rare gossipy communications from Morristown during the time Washington had his headquarters there. The full text will be found in 51 *NJHSP.*, 150 ff.

73 *Ibid.*

74 Cf. Letters of François de Barbé-Marbois, edited by E. P. Chase, and published under the title, *Our Revolutionary Forefathers*, 114, cited in 3 *Hughes*, 328.

language released: "That the God of Armies may enable me to bring the present contest to a speedy and happy conclusion, thereby gratifying me in a retirement to the calm and sweet enjoyment of domestic happiness, is the fervent prayer and most ardent wish of my soul." [75] Except when he could hold himself to these hopes, or fix his thought on the pleasant companions at his side as he rode in the fair country around Morristown, the wretchedness of his Army, especially of the outposts, might have overwhelmed even his stout soul. As it chanced, the day after Washington wrote Pendleton, another Virginian, a young officer of 23, poured out the distress of himself and of his comrades at Princeton in a letter to the same attorney. "The desertions from our Army," John Taylor told Pendleton, "are to the last degree alarming, some Companies having lost thirty odd men, and by a desertion of theirs (an accident that rarely happens) we learn that thirty have come in with their arms in a day." Taylor gave the sombre details: "This misfortune is not likely to stop because its causes cannot be removed; the first that the northern troops are mostly composed of foreigners; the second that Congress has greatly deceived the men in their enlistments; explicit and frequent promises have been made of good and speedy clothing; but we ourselves, although we were amongst the foremost of the troops, were detained week after week and at last sent off with one-sixth of our men naked, and one-third without blankets; and what is most monstrous of all is that although the resolution of Congress ran in the same disjunctive, promising the men a suit of clothes or twenty dollars, yet they begin now to talk of making the men pay any additional price that they may cost over the twenty dollars, which will in my opinion cause a mutiny if it should take place. Indeed I find that soldiers here are sacrificed for the private emolument of the Commissaries, Quartermasters, Surgeons, Barrack Masters and Captains. The low pay of officers first led them to fraud, in order to support themselves and were it now to be raised they would not forego the habit they have acquired. The armies of the northern States are really mercenaries and being foreigners have no attachment to the country except what accrues from the emoluments of the service. The high price of commodities having made them contemptible, the defence of America must revert to its original safeguard, to wit: the yeomanry; and as very many of those of the middle States are Tories and the inhabitants of the middle

[75] Letter of Apr. 12, 1777; 7 *G. W.*, 394.

States mostly undisciplined, I augur ill of events at least until injury replete shall have put the match more generally to the hearts of our people. Hope for the best but the same time fear for the worst; I wish from my soul we had more Virginias than one but as we have not, the honor of preserving America must be acquired by one alone." [76] In other words, the feeble or venal administration of resources limited almost ruinously was complicated and hampered by the resentments and the sectional prejudices of many officers and men. Perhaps neither the soldiers nor their commander realized how the life of the Army and the success of the cause alike depended on the inflexibility of Washington's courage, determination and patience.

Of these three qualities, patience in the early spring of 1777 was the one most needed and most tested. From the day Washington had accepted command, there never had been a time when he could devote himself to the solution of a single military equation. Always his problems were as numerous as those the young John Taylor at Princeton had listed in his letter to Edmund Pendleton. Sometimes, too, the examination of a need disclosed a kindred want. Study of weakness at a particular fort made plain the lack of defences on the same range of hills or on the same river. It was so at the end of April. Had the British landed suddenly on the Connecticut shore? What was to prevent their appearance a week later at Peekskill? If Howe prolonged his winter's sleep into spring, was it safe to assume that Carleton in Canada would be content to yawn and not to move? Washington could not gamble on such idle conformity to ancestral vice. He sent Greene and Knox to Peekskill to study the Highland defences; [77] he read somewhat skeptically George Clinton's cheerful assurance that chains could be stretched across the Hudson and that the new defences would prevent the passage of that enterprising fleet of Lord Howe's; [78] Washington tried, likewise, to strike a balance between having so limited a supply of provisions at a given fort that the garrison might go hungry, and so large a store that the commissary would be crippled if the place were captured; [79] all the while the General had to try to set up a corps of observation at White Plains and to persuade Connecticut she could send troops to the Hudson with minimum risk that a new raid from Long Island Sound would penetrate far. [80]

[76] Letter of Apr. 13, 1777; 12 T 122, with the punctuation revised in several sentences.
[77] 8 G. W., 4–5, 26, 51.   [78] 7 ibid., 445; 8 ibid., 34–35; 1 LTW., 377.
[79] 8 G. W., 55, 161–62.   [80] Ibid., 103–04, 164.

In the same spirit, after Washington had sent Putnam to the vicinity of New York, in the command vacated by Heath,[81] the Commander-in-Chief had to spend time on letters designed to coax "old Put" into an attack on King's Bridge or, at the least, into a demonstration against that post.[82] Ticonderoga, the northern bastion of the Hudson, demanded like attention of the burdened mind of Washington. Some observers believed the fort was doomed;[83] others soon passed on reports that Carleton already was advancing;[84] Washington did his utmost to get the New England States to complete the recruiting of the additional Regiments and to hurry them to Ticonderoga,[85] where Gates was given the service of the alert Arthur St. Clair and was told he need not attempt to defend the entire perimeter of the old defences.[86] Schuyler, who had visited Washington's headquarters early in April,[87] had won vindication at the hands of Congress, had worked usefully for some weeks in Philadelphia,[88] and soon was to have again the command of a redefined Northern Department, in which Gates was to serve under him or else was to resume duty as Adjutant General.[89]

In May, as in every month after Gates had left headquarters, Washington could have used the experience and reasoning power of that officer, because perplexities continued to multiply. It was impossible for Washington to know all that was happening in his Army. He found it particularly difficult to get trustworthy estimates or prompt

81 Washington's first choice for the command was Benedict Arnold, but he did not think Arnold willingly would leave Philadelphia where the Connecticut officer was seeking restoration of seniority. For this see *infra*, p. 418, 424. From Watertown, in a letter of Mch. 4, 1777, to Mrs. Henry Knox (*Knox Papers*, MHS), Arnold had asked, with a verbal flourish, what she thought his prospects were with "the charming Mrs. Emery."

82 8 *G. W.*, 121, 144.

83 Cf. Henry Jackson to Henry Knox, Apr. 1, 1777; *Knox Papers*, MHS.

84 8 *G. W.*, 9, 17.

85 7 *ibid.*, 353–57, 358–59; 8 *ibid.*, 6–7, 9–10.

86 7 *JCC.*, 306–07, 307; 2 *Burnett*, 346, 351.

87 7 *G. W.*, 359.

88 7 *JCC.*, 273, 279, 298, 326–27, 333, 364; 2 *Burnett*, 337, 341–42, 357, 364, 370 ff, 375; 8 *G. W.*, 12.

89 7 *JCC.*, 364; 8 ibid., 375. Gates's letters of April and May, 1777, are full of interest. They show Gates in confidential correspondence with Joseph Trumbull (April 27; *Joseph Trumbull Papers*, Mil. and Gen. Corres., v. 1, p. 60 a; Conn. State Lib.) and with James Lovell (April 29, *Gates Papers*, NYHS) and suspicious of Washington's good will to him (*ibid.*, letter of May 25). Gates was outwardly deferential toward the Commander-in-Chief, though disposed to argue over the allotment of tents to his army—(*ibid.*, letters of Mch. 26, Apr. 19, May 9, 13, 24, 1777, and *supra*, p. 411, n. 55) and at the same time he was putting his needs directly before Congress (cf. Gates to Hancock, *ibid.*, letters of Apr. 22, May 24, 1777, and same to same May 2, 11; *154 Papers Cont. Cong.*, 161, 189, LC). Particularly informative of Gates's state of mind is a letter of May 23, 1777 to Brig. Gen. [John] Paterson, whose name Gates always spelled Patterson (*Gates Papers*, NYHS).

action from the Commissary General, who remained in New England, and from recruiting officers, scattered everywhere.

Some of Washington's subordinates, even among those close at hand, could not be trusted to make reports that told the truth, the whole truth and nothing but the truth. On the 10th of May, Adam Stephen once again sent troops on a mission of his own devising. Perhaps in a desire to show that he could execute a surprise as admirable as the one delivered on Lincoln at Bound Brook, Stephen assailed the camp of the 42nd Regiment at Piscataway.[90] He was repulsed and pursued toward his own cantonment, but when he was ready with his report it was a proud narrative of combat. "I can now with propriety congratulate your Excellency," he began, "on a certain and considerable advantage gained over the enemy's best troops by the continental troops of my Division." He proceeded to describe an action in which his adversary twice was driven from the field. Five British officers and thirty-nine men were left dead on the ground taken by the Americans. "I am convinced," Stephen went on, "the enemy have at least 200 killed and wounded," at small cost to America. The General concluded: "It was a bold enterprise. It was the time and rapidity of the attack that secured us the success we met with." [91]

On reading this, Washington became suspicious that Stephen was following an old habit of exaggerating successes,[92] and he called for the testimony of other officers. Their statements were so much at variance with Stephen's that the Commander-in-Chief wrote his lieutenant of the seventeen-fifties such a letter as he never had been called upon to address to a subordinate. It read thus:

DEAR SIR: Your account of the attempt upon the enemy at Piscataway is favorable, but I am sorry to add, widely different from those I have had from others, (officers of distinction) who were of the party. I cannot by them learn that there is the least certainty of the enemy's leaving half the slain upon the field, you speak of in your letter of this date; that instead of an orderly retreat, it was (with the greatest part of the detachment) a disorderly rout, and that the disadvantage was on our side, not the enemy's, who had notice of your coming and was prepared for it, as I expected.[93]

90 Approximately on the site of the present Greensand, between Brunswick and Amboy, almost opposite the mouth of South River.

91 Stephen, at Chatham, N. J., to Washington, May 12, 1777; 47 *Papers of G. W.*, 9, LC.

92 Washington's letter of May 12 to Congress (7 *G. W.*, 47) discloses his suspicion in his reference to the skirmish "as reported to me . . ."

93 8 *G. W.*, 53, with the difficult punctuation revised.

This came as close as a polite letter could come to telling a man that he was lying; but it did not shake Stephen. The Major General replied with the avowal that he told the truth: "Your Excellency has not seen an officer that was in the action Saturday night they were of the body; but to their staying at such a distance from the Scene of Action the Highlanders owe their existence . . . Time will disclose the loss of the enemy—a more accurate account than I had is seldom obtained. The troops who stayed a quarter or near half a mile in the rear must needs have run damned hard to retreat by the way the troops engaged did. But the fighting troops were killed a considerable time on a rising ground until they had an opportunity of coming off." [94]

A case of a different sort, not smelling of alcohol, but of larger possibilities of injustice, concerned Benedict Arnold and his dissatisfaction over the outcome of his political campaign to recover his "rights." A resolve of Congress made him a Major General but it did not restore him to the seniority he had enjoyed, low as it was, when he was among the Brigadiers.[95] Arnold came to headquarters on the 12th of May with the statement that he wished to go to Philadelphia for a settlement of his accounts and for an examination of charges he had heard some individuals had made against his integrity. In explaining this to Washington, the angry Arnold probably asked for a letter to the President of Congress in order to assure him a hearing. Washington wrote such a paper, in which he sketched the arguments Arnold had advanced, and he concluded: "These considerations are not without their weight, though I pretend not to judge what motives may have influenced the conduct of Congress upon this occasion. It is needless to say anything of this gentleman's military character. It is universally known that he has always distinguished himself as a judicious, brave officer of great activity, enterprise and perseverance." [96]

---

[94] Stephen, at Chatham, N. J., to Washington, May 14, 1777; 47 *Papers of G. W.*, 25, verbatim. British accounts of this affair were poles removed from the account of Stephen. In his Diary (v. 1, p. 118), Kemble wrote that the Americans killed eight but left twenty-seven on the field in addition to thirty-eight taken prisoner. Archibald Robertson, (*op. cit.*, 131), noted that Stephen's troops were pursued almost three miles to their camp on the heights near Metuchen. British losses Robertson put at nine killed and nineteen wounded. "The rebels," he recorded, "had missing one Major, two Captains and seventy privates." The incident made Washington increasingly critical of Adam Stephen's subsequent proposals for attacks on enemy posts. See 7 *G. W.*, 473; 8 *ibid.*, 80–81, 86–87. While Washington did not say so bluntly, he manifestly felt that Stephen was inclined to undertake small and sometimes dangerous forays, involving a vain loss of life, and that Stephen then would present each such affair as a slaughter of the enemy.

[95] 1 *LTW.*, 353, 360; 1 *Greene's Greene*, 359; 7 *JCC.*, 323; 8 *G. W.*, 16, 26.

[96] Letter of May 12, 1777; 8 *G. W.*, 47–48.

Off Arnold rode to demand that his wrongs be righted; back into
the rough groove of routine duty slipped Adam Stephen, still averring
that he had slain many foes at Piscataway; but the difficulties of Washington in dealing with officers took still another turn. In disgust, John
Adams soon was to write: "I am wearied to death with the wrangles
between military officers, high and low. They quarrel like cats and
dogs. They worry one another like mastiffs, scrambling for rank and
pay like apes for nuts." [97] Had Washington read this, he might have
told the Delegate from Massachusetts that a seat in Congress or a chair
in Philadelphia lodgings showed a man far less of the frailties of his
fellows than were to be observed from the desk of a commanding
General.

Nor would Washington have come justly under the imputation of
a provincial point of view if he had affirmed that of all the difficult
officers with whom he had to deal, the French were *sui generis.*
Through the early months of 1777 the policy of Congress had been to
discourage foreign officers from coming to America, but to phrase its
resolve in such a manner as not to discredit Silas Deane in Paris, or to
offend the Comte d'Argoud of Martinique, who was an enthusiastic
supporter of the American cause and the sponsor of numerous applicants for commission.[98] The feeling had been confirmed that most of
the foreign officers arriving in 1775–76 were adventurers who had been
given rank far beyond their military merits.[99] There was agreement,
also, that officers who did not understand English were of little use
and should not be advised to come, or commissioned if they arrived on
their own initiative; [100] but exceptions were frequent,[101] advances of
pay were made,[102] and sometimes volunteers who could not be employed by Congress were thanked and were given certificates of their
tender of service, and, more tangibly, funds to pay for passage home.[103]
On occasion, officers who importuned Congress were sent to Washington without recommendation.[104]

[97] *Adams, Fam. Let.,* 276, cited in 8 *G. W.,* 47 n.
[98] Cf. R. H. Lee to Washington, May 22, 1777; 1 *Ballagh, Lee Letters,* 293.
[99] Cf. 1 *St. Clair Papers,* 382; 7 *G. W.,* 169, 174; 8 *ibid.,* 71, 74–75; 7 *JCC.,* 131; 9
A. Hamilton, 63–65; 1 *Greene's Greene,* 417, 418, 419.
[100] 8 *G. W.,* 32; 7 *JCC.,* 174, 177; 1 *LTW.,* 357; 2 *Burnett,* 303, 304, 310–11, 361;
7 *Smyth's Franklin,* 38–40, 59, 65, 77, 80.
[101] 7 *JCC.,* 185, 189, 196, 210–11, 256, 346; 8 *ibid.,* 385; 7 *G. W.,* 363, 399–400, 441;
1 *LTW.,* 375–76.
[102] 7 *JCC.,* 269; 8 *ibid.,* 380; for more numerous later instances, see *infra,* p. 457, 538.
[103] 7 *JCC.,* 189, 258–59; 8 *ibid.,* 423.
[104] 7 *JCC.,* 65, 66, 156. See also R. Morris in 2 *Burnett,* 260. In February, Washington

Now, in May, the Commanding General had confidentially to ask Richard Henry Lee, "What Congress expects I am to do with the many foreigners they have, at different times, promoted to the rank of field officers?" [105] In detail, Washington explained: "These men have no attachment or ties to the country, further than interest binds them; they have no influence and are ignorant of the language they are to receive and give orders in; consequently great trouble or much confusion must follow; but this is not the worst. They have not the slightest chance to recruit others, and our officers think it exceedingly hard, after they have toiled in this service and probably sustained many losses, to have strangers put over them, whose merit, perhaps, is not equal to their own but whose effrontery will take no denial." Washington dwelt briefly on the manifestly mistaken policy that had prevailed and he continued: ". . . the man who was a Captain in France, finding another who was only a Subaltern there, or perhaps nothing, appointed to a majority with us, extends his views instantly to a Regiment. In like manner, the field officer can accept nothing less than a Brigade, and so on, by which means the man of real rank and merit must be excluded, or perhaps your whole military system disordered. In the meantime, I am haunted and teased to death by the importunity of some and dissatisfaction of others." [106]

The broad exception that Washington made in this declaration of policy concerned engineers and artillerists. He thought skilled foreigners of character who understood fortification or gunnery should be commissioned,[107] though he gave warning that even in these branches of military art, precautions had to be taken.[108] Congress had been of this mind, and as long previously as Dec. 2, 1775, had instructed the Committee of Correspondence "to find out and engage . . . skillful engineers not exceeding four . . . and that the said Committee be authorized to assure such able and skillful engineers as will engage in that service, that they shall receive such pay and appointments as shall be equal to what they have received in any former service." [109]

had complained to Gates that he had been compelled to give half his time for ten days to French applicants for commission (7 *G. W.*, 178).

[105] Letter of May 17, 1777; 8 *G. W.*, 74.

[106] *Ibid.*, 75–76. This passage has been repunctuated drastically. The long sentence has been broken after "is not the worst" and a new sentence, for clarity's sake, has been opened with "They have not the slightest" etc.

[107] 7 *G. W.*, 388; 8 *ibid.*, 76.

[108] ". . . We have at present in pay and high rank two (Frenchmen) who, in my judgment, know nothing of the duty of engineers." (*ibid.*; cf. 6 *G. W.*, 405).

[109] 3 *JCC.*, 400–01. See also Franklin to Dumas, Dec. 19, 1775; 2 *Wharton*, 66.

Long delay had been experienced in procuring qualified engineers of character, but while Washington was at Morristown foreign officers of other types began to descend in numbers that created problems almost as puzzling as some of those that had prompted the resolve of Congress for employment of engineers. As Henry Laurens said later, it seemed that Silas Deane in Paris "would not say nay to any French-man who called himself Count or Chevalier" and solicited a high com-mission in the American Army.[110] On the 8th of May, a French officer of approximately Washington's own age arrived at headquarters, and introduced himself in English as Col. Thomas Conway of the Army of His Most Christian Majesty. He had a letter of introduction from Silas Deane and he admitted that Deane had not contracted with him for services in America at any particular rank, but, Conway said suavely, it would be "mortifying to him to hold a rank under that of Monsieurs de Fermoy and de Borre, who were inferior officers in their own service and subject to his command." [111]—a familiar plaint that Washington must have groaned to hear once again from a newcomer. Conway ex-plained his name and his knowledge of English by saying that he was Irish-born, though educated in France. He spoke of some of the French officers who had come with him to America aboard a ship that brought a much-desired cargo of cannon,[112] but he may not have told of a con-troversy with an engineer who had tried to dismiss him before their ship left France.[113] Washington formed a good first opinion of Conway and sent him to Philadelphia with a letter more commendatory than the General usually wrote of a stranger.[114] Congress received the Frenchman enthusiastically, accepted at face value all that Deane said

[110] Letter of Aug. 12, 1777, to John Rutledge; 2 *Burnett*, 448; cf. the contract with Sieur de Montieu, June 6, 1777; 256 *Stevens' Facsimiles*. Washington had found it difficult in May to convince the Marquis François de Malmédy that Rhode Island's grant to him of a commission as Brigadier did not entitle him to the same rank in the Continental Army (8 *G. W.*, 68–70, 71). See also, Washington's letters written to induce Henry Emanuel Lutterloh to enter the Quartermaster's service in which that applicant had experience, though Lutterloh wanted to attempt to organize a corps of Light Infantry. Other vexing cases were those of Prudhomme de Borre (8 *G. W.*, 98; 9 *ibid.*, 6–7), Chrétien de Colerus (*ibid.*, 89, 179, 180), and, as previously, Fermoy (*ibid.*, 485).

[111] The quotation is from Washington's report of his conversation with Conway (8 *G. W.*, 30–31). According to *Biographie Universelle*, Conway was born in County Kerry, Ireland, Feb. 27, 1733, became a second Lieutenant in the Clare Regiment in 1747, lost his commission in 1754, won reinstatement in 1756, and rose by regular promotion to the rank of Colonel, November, 1772. His titular first commission at 14 was not unusual. Cf. *Lasseray*, 160–66.

[112] This was *Amphitrite*, for which see Dr. Gardner to Henry Knox, Apr. 24, 1777, *Knox Papers*, MHS.; 8 *G. W.*, 7, 15; 7 *JCC.*, 335, and a valuable note, with quotations from con-temporary newspapers, in 2 *Burnett*, 352–53. The vessel reached Portsmouth, N. H., Apr. 20 or 21, 1777.

[113] See Deane to Conway, Feb. 7, 1777; 1 *Deane Papers*, 468–87.

[114] 8 *G. W.*, 30–31.

of him,[115] and on the 13th of May elected him a Brigadier General.[116] Hearing of this, American Colonels of long service might have pondered alternatives: They themselves must be exceedingly poor officers or else this General Conway must be superlative.

Behind Conway came the man who had wished to get rid of him in advance, Philippe Charles Tronson du Coudray. This gentleman, the most extravagant acquisition of Silas Deane, had no less than eighteen other officers and ten Sergeants in attendance on him; [117] and with this entourage he had stopped May 14 in Boston where he had expressed much contempt for the British who let themselves be driven from so strong a position.[118] Then du Coudray journeyed southward and paused for a day at Morristown headquarters, enroute to Philadelphia. At 39 years of age, and a *Chef de Brigade,* though of recent appointment, he put the highest valuation on his professional standing, his connections and his writings on military subjects.[119] He did not tell Washington precisely what he expected to do, but he dropped hints to other officers that led to the belief he had a contract with Deane, under which he was to be vested with the chief command of the artillery.

Washington sat down forthwith and prepared a letter to the President of Congress in a determination to have the dangers of such an appointment plain when du Coudray presented his papers. "General Knox," wrote Washington, ". . . has deservedly acquired the character of one of the most valuable officers in the service, and . . . combatting the almost innumerable difficulties in the department he fills, has placed the artillery upon a footing that does him the greatest honor." Were he superseded, Knox "would not think himself at liberty to continue in the service." In that event, Washington gave warning, the artillery

---

[115] Deane to Committee of Secret Correspondence, Nov. 29, 1776; 2 *Wharton,* 202.

[116] 7 *JCC.,* 347–49. Washington notified him that the troops of this Brigade were not assembled (8 *G. W.,* 88).

[117] Deane had trouble with du Coudray before the party left Europe on the supply ship *Amphritrite.* See 1 Deane Papers, 351 ff, 377, 467–68, 469, cf. 486–87. See also Barbe de Bourg to "my dear Master" [Benjamin Franklin?], June 12, 1776 (26 *Papers of G. W.,* 26, LC).

[118] *Heath,* 129.

[119] Although the command of a Chef de Brigade in the French army at this period was a Regiment, that organization consisted of three Battalions, each of which was supposed to number 1000 men (William Duane, *op. cit.).* The command thus was considerably more extensive than that of an American Brigade. For du Coudray's previous career, professional papers, etc., see A. Lasseray, *Les Français sous les Treize Étoiles,* 444 ff. Du Coudray's own version of his services in France to advance American interests, with a full statement of his later "grievances," will be found in his undated memorial to Congress, 156 *Papers of Cont. Cong.,* 468 ff, LC. This was termed by Wharton a Memoir.

would be convulsed and unhinged. Would it not be possible to satisfy du Coudray by appointing him to some other position? Much address and delicacy might be required, but without any distrust of the French officer, it might be questioned "whether so important a command as that of the artillery should be vested in any but a native, or one attached by the ties of interest to these States." Washington asked that Congress excuse "the freedom he had taken" and, with another reference to the importance of the matter, he left the decision to the Delegates.[120]

Du Coudray hurried on to Philadelphia and presented to the amazed members of Congress articles of agreement entered into Sept. 11, 1776, between him and Deane. These carried a variety of financial guarantees for du Coudray, prefaced by the statement that he was to have the title of General of Artillery and Ordnance, with the rank of Major General. His was to be "the direction of whatever relates to the Artillery and Corps of Engineers, under the order and control only of the Congress of the United Colonies, their Committee of War, or the Commander-in-Chief for the time being."[121] It was common knowledge of all members who had been in Congress when Deane was commissioned that the American agent had no authority to make such a contract. Were it accepted, it would give du Coudray and his French artillerymen seniority over all American officers of like rank who had been recommissioned Jan. 1, 1777.[122] In a situation so manifestly dangerous, Washington asked himself whether it would be possible to put the French artillerists in a separate corps [123] and, if that was not feasible, whether American officers could not have their commissions antedated to give them seniority over the French.[124]

These vexations were among the worst that Washington had been called upon to endure in the endless task of finding intelligent officers, training those who gave promise, and putting incompetents where they could do the least harm if they could not be dismissed. His idlers were a continuing nuisance—no less. In dealing with them, Washington hit upon the expedient of ordering Heath to "dispatch an active, spirited officer, on whom you can depend, with orders to sweep every town between Boston and Peekskill" and to send loiterers to their posts. For

[120] Letter of May 31, 1777; 8 *G. W.*, 148–49.
[121] 2 *Force* (5), p. 283–84.   [122] 8 *G. W.*, 187–90, 194.
[123] Somewhat the same idea in the form of a proposal for a "corps of French cadets," had been advanced, Mch. 22, 1777, by Gates to Hancock, 154 *Papers Cont. Cong.*, pt. 1, p. 151, LC., but this apparently was for junior officers.
[124] See 8 *G. W.*, 189.

the future, officers who were moving troops were to be given a route and a specified time in which to reach their station. If they were delayed, they must explain the reason.[125] Lesser troubles with American officers were presented, solved, compromised or deferred;[126] the Frenchmen remained a continuing enigma at the time, of all times, when Washington should have been free to devote a mind otherwise untroubled to what might prove the decisive test of the year.

Howe manifestly was to move soon. That was apparent while Washington was engaged in the first stage of correspondence about du Coudray; but there was as much doubt as ever in Washington's mind regarding the objective of the enemy, except that it probably was one that required the use both of the transports and of the fleet.[127] The few skirmishes that occurred in May disclosed nothing unless perhaps it was the prospect that, as Washington had anticipated,[128] the British would have the armed support of numerous Loyalists.[129] All the probabilities and the few known facts led Washington to decide that he should move closer to Brunswick and into a strong position, whence he could follow quickly any British advance, whether toward the eastern States or toward Philadelphia.[130] The command at Princeton was passed to Sullivan when Putnam was sent to Peekskill; Benedict Arnold

---

[125] *Ibid.,* 38.

[126] See, for example, the instructions of Washington by Congress to investigate reports that officers were holding out their men's pay (7 *JCC.,* 342); Wilkinson's observations on "a very treacherous proportion of officers" (1 *Wilkinson,* 165); Washington's exhortation to Mifflin not to permit friendship to influence appointments (8 *G. W.,* 137); the case of Lieut. Christian Myers of the German Battalion (*ibid.,* 255); the plan for the use of the newly established Invalids' Corps as a military school (8 *JCC.,* 485); the remarkable court martial of Maj. Valentine Peers, whose commanding officer, Col. Alexander Spotswood, apologized for putting him under arrest (8 *G. W.,* 286–87); Washington's argument that the indiscriminate grant of commissions to men in the civil departments of the Army cheapened rank (*ibid.,* 442); certain officers' protest on the existing system of rations (9 *ibid.,* 38; 2 *Burnett,* 483); and John Adams' testy observation, "I think we shall never defend a post until we shoot a General" (2 *Burnett,* 455).

[127] See 8 *G. W.,* 39, 50, 136, 150–51, 157, 190. Washington's intelligence reports of May 10, concerning the movement of ships and small craft near Amboy, will be found in 46 *Papers of G. W.,* 133, LC. While doing all he could to ascertain what the enemy was planning, Washington was trying, more vigilantly than ever, to keep from the British all information about his own forces. Cf. Washington to Alex. McDougall, Mch. 15, 1777; *McDougall Papers,* NYHS (not in *G. W.*).

[128] 7 *G. W.,* 476; 9 *A. Hamilton,* 70.

[129] For the recruiting of Tories, see Howe's *Observations,* 52, in pagination with his *Narrative.* In the affair of May 13 at Paramus, Washington reported, the 300 men who raided the deserted post were "Tory levies" (8 *G. W.,* 72). Nathanael Greene dismissed all operations of this period as of small importance (see his letter of May 20, 1777, to Mrs. Greene; *Greene Papers,* Clements Lib.). A petty brush near Bound Brook on May 26 was described by Washington in a letter of the 28th (*ibid.,* 133). The General was much pleased with the news of a successful raid on Long Island, May 23–24, by a force under the command of Lt. Col. Return J. Meigs (8 *G. W.,* 139–40, 143).

[130] Cf. *ibid.,* 157.

later was given by Congress substantially the same command Gates had held at Philadelphia.[131]

With these Pennsylvania positions in good hands, Washington prepared to recall the Continentals from Newark and Elizabeth Town and to entrust the patrol of those places to the Jersey militia who already were guarding adjoining districts [132] in order to protect American supporters from Tory violence.[133] In Washington's ranks there was more than normal desertion,[134] and some feeling by Dr. Benjamin Rush that much of the danger of summer sickness among the men could be averted if they remained a few weeks longer in their barracks; [135] but Washington thought the change should be made as soon as the weather favored.[136] He selected as the most advantageous position a well-protected valley at Middle Brook,[137] on the left bank of the Raritan, seven miles Northwest of Brunswick, and he moved headquarters to the new encampment on the evening of May 28. The greater part of the Army followed on the 31st.[138]

In many hearts was a feeling of relief that winter quarters had been evacuated. From the new station, Adam Stephen, unabashed at Washington's rebuke, wrote John Sullivan: "We shall get languid here. The enemy are in possession of a fine country, well supplied with green lamb,[139] veal, beef, mutton and pretty girls." [140] In the eyes of Brig. Gen. George Weedon, who had been called back to the Army from a long leave of nonchalant absence,[141] the outlook was bright. As he described it to a fellow Virginian: "The whole of [the Army is] now encamped

---

[131] As of June 14, 1777. See 8 *JCC.*, 467. In addition, Congress presented him with a horse "properly caparisoned" and vindicated him of certain charges preferred by John Brown. 7 *ibid.*, 372; 8 *ibid.*, 382.

[132] 7 *G. W.*, 492–93.

[133] 8 *ibid.*, 118–19; a slightly different text is among the MSS of Rutgers Univ.

[134] See R. H. Harrison to unnamed correspondent, May 20, 1777; *L. W. Smith Coll.*

[135] 8 *G. W.*, 74.   [136] *Ibid.*   [137] *Ibid.*, 157.

[138] *Ibid.*, 139, 144, 152. It is interesting to note that Hall set May 31 as the date of the beginning of the campaign of 1777, because Brigadier James Agnew then crossed North River and encamped with the garrison of Amboy as Howe's second line (Hall, *Civil War in America*, 277). Some of the British officers credited Washington with skill in evading a general action after the Trenton-Princeton Campaign, though they did not realize how weak his Army still was. Lt. Col. William Harcourt wrote his father that same 31st of May: "America is never to be regained without making an absolute conquest of her; . . . great art in their leaders, and a perfect enthusiasm in their people have hitherto prevented any of the most distant overtures towards a peace, excepting upon a footing of independence; . . . their Army, though less numerous than the last year is certainly not less formidable . . ." (*The Evelyns in America*, 239).

[139] This is an interesting example of the use of the adjective "green" in a sense of "young and tender," now seldom applied to meat but probably implied in the term "green vegetables."

[140] Letter of June 1, 1777; 1 *Sullivan Papers*, 353.

[141] 7 *G. W.*, 322–23.

in comfortable tents on a valley covered in front and rear by ridges which affords [sic] us security; his Excellency, our good old General [142] has also spread his tent and lives amongst us. Every department of the Army is properly arranged and strictly attended to. As different is our situation in every respect to what it was last campaign that a friendly heart cannot help being greatly elated, our men all happily over the smallpox and remarkable healthy, well armed and well clothed, and from our Commander-in-Chief down to the private sentinel in the highest spirits. Was our deficiencies but completed and sent on, we would hang heavy on Sir William's hands . . ." [143]

Washington could not have subscribed to this optimistic appraisal. He would have admitted, in relief of spirit, that organization was better and he soon could write that only one case of smallpox was known to exist in the Army; [144] but he would not deceive himself concerning laxity of discipline, [145] the continuing poor quality of many officers, the numerical weakness of his Regiments, and the undependability of the militia whom he still had to employ. He knew that this applied to the troops at Ticonderoga and in the New York Highlands as surely as to his own men. He wrote Congress: "the shameful deficiency in all our Armies affords but too just grounds for disagreeable apprehensions. If the quotas assigned the different States are not immediately filled, we shall have everything to fear. We shall never be able to resist their force if the militia are to be relied on, nor do I know whether their aid, feeble and ineffectual as it is, is much to be expected. Can no expedient be devised to complete the Regiments and to rouse our unthinking countrymen from their lethargy? If there can, the situation of our affairs calls loudly for it." He did not dare commit to writing the dis-

---

[142] Actually, Weedon was as old as Washington or older. He is believed to have been born about 1730.

[143] Letter of May 31, 1777; *Chicago HS.* MSS. The original is a difficult document to read and is almost without punctuation, which is here inserted. Weedon was not alone in his optimism. Henry Knox's letters of Apr. 6, 13 and 20, 1777, to his wife, combined hope and defiance. In writing her on the 20th, he said, ". . . I assure you we by no means think ourselves despicable . . ." (*Knox Papers,* MHS).

[144] Letter of June 17, 1777 to Brig. Gen. Samuel H. Parsons; (8 *G. W.,* 259). This triumph had been won over a disease that Washington regarded as "more destructive to an Army in the natural way than the enemy's sword" (7 *G. W.,* 409). Success had been achieved by inoculating the entire force and then isolating and inoculating all recruits and reenforcements. See *ibid.,* 38, 44–45, 73, 75, 105, 128–29, 130–31, 153, 162–63, 219, 220, 228–29, 233, 237, 349–50, 423, 432; 8 *ibid.,* 85, 259; 10 *ibid.,* 165; 2 *Burnett,* 249; 1 *Bland Papers,* 55. For mismanagement of inoculation at Alexandria, Va., see 9 *JCC.,* 1016, 1039. Cf. 7 *ibid.,* 292. As concerned the civil population, Henry Knox had written his wife, Mch. 12, 1777: "The smallpox is spreading through Connecticut and will spread the influx to your place" (*Knox Papers,* MHS).   [145] Cf. 8 *G. W.,* 155.

heartening figures of such returns as his staff could collect—a total not in excess of 9200 men.[146] Nor did he report, if indeed he knew,[147] the extent to which, month after month, men had been slipping away and going home or joining the British. The enemy was boasting of this and was saying that during the first five months of the year, as many as 3000 deserters had come into the camps of the King in New Jersey and Pennsylvania.[148]

Doubtful but still resolute, Washington took advantage of warm weather and field encampment to discipline the men, to drill the officers in military etiquette,[149] and, of course, to watch the enemy. Prior to June 7, nothing of importance was reported to Washington concerning Howe's plans. It was known that troops, Hessian and British, had left Rhode Island,[150] but the destination of this force had not been established. Troops from New York had joined Howe.[151] On the 7th, word was received that "many vessels" at New York were being fitted out for horses.[152] Three uneventful days followed. Then, on the 10th of June, Col. David Forman reported that from a lookout on the coast he had seen much activity in shipping off Sandy Hook, Amboy and Prince's Bay. As well as he could make out, two-thirds of the tents at Amboy had been struck. At 5:30 A.M., three ships of war, eleven transports and three small vessels had weighed anchor and had stood out to sea.[153] In the belief the next express might bring news that would set every wheel turning, Washington ordered all baggage loaded, except the tents;[154] but Thursday, June 12, brought intelligence of the arrival of additional Regiments from Europe, of the ferrying of British troops from Staten Island to Amboy, and of the gathering of British shipping in Prince's Bay.[155]

What, then, was afoot? Was Howe about to proceed by land, by sea, or by both a voyage and a march along the coastal plain? Washington,

---

[146] This quotation is from Washington's letter of June 2, 1777; *ibid.*, 168. The returns of May 21 (Nat. Arc., *op. cit.*) are summed up at 8378, but the correct total of the items is 9129. Most probably, the difference represents some unexplained deduction.

[147] Cf. William Smith's Diary, *NYPL*, Mch. 3, 1777, with quotation from an officer who said he did not believe the Generals themselves knew the strength of the Army when militia always were coming and going.

[148] Col. Carl von Donop, quoted in Hans Huth, "The Letters of a Hessian Mercenary," 62 *Penn Mag.*, 497.

[149] 8 *G. W.*, 345 ff.

[150] Letter of May 26, 1777, to General Putnam, with report of express from Governor Trumbull; *ibid.*, 126–27.

[151] See *Hall*, loc. cit.   [152] 8 *G. W.*, 198.

[153] 48 *Papers of G. W.*, 121, LC.   [154] 8 *G. W.*, 214–15.

[155] 49 *Papers of G. W.*, 17, 18, LC.

weighing reports and probabilities, decided that the British were reenforcing Brunswick heavily and that they were aiming at the destruction of the American main Army or were preparing an expedition to
capture Philadelphia. The Hudson seemed the less probable objective.
A council of war was held that evening, to review the evidence and to
consider particularly the question suggested by the belief that Howe
was looking to the Delaware rather than to the Hudson: Should the
main Army be strengthened with part of the troops under Putnam at
Peekskill? The advice of the council was that all troops in excess of
1000 be called from that station.[156] Morristown was to be held lightly;
Sullivan should move from Princeton to Millstone River, where his
flank could not be turned by the enemy, though he would be free to
maneuver.[157]

Two days later, June 14, American headquarters learned that Howe
had started his movement: the British advance was at Somerset Court
House, reckoned as eight or nine miles from Brunswick. As far as the
Continentals could ascertain, the enemy was covering the road between
the two places and was occupying Brunswick still.[158] Washington was
ready. Thomas Mifflin had been directed to collect boats on the upper
Delaware;[159] Congress had ordered Arnold to proceed to Trenton and
to take command there;[160] Washington dispatched a call for the New
Jersey militia,[161] and at Middle Brook, he expected all day the news that
the enemy either had turned to the left and was headed for the Delaware, or else was forging its bolts for a general attack along the upper
Raritan.[162]

Howe did neither. He merely stayed where he was. The American
General waited in vain with tents struck, wagons loaded, and horses
harnessed and hitched to the vehicles.[163] So little happened that Washington found the hour in which to write a letter that restored full,
friendly relations with Joseph Reed, to whom he vainly had offered
command of the cavalry. With Charles Lee no longer talking freely

156 See also Putnam to Washington, June 13, 1777, *ibid.*, 28.
157 8 *G. W.*, 231-32, 232-33, 248-49; 1 *Sullivan Papers*, 383.
158 8 *G. W.*, 253. See *ibid.*, 314, for a later correction that placed the British rear at
Middlebush.
159 48 *Papers of G. W.*, 102; 49 *ibid.*, 4, LC.
160 Arnold to Hancock, June 13, 18, 1777; 162 *Papers Cont. Cong.*, I, 92 and II, 96, LC;
Arnold to Washington, June 16, 1777; 49 *Papers of G. W.*, 28, LC. Arnold's report on the
condition of the river crossings was enclosed in his letter of June 18 to the President of Congress.
161 Cf. Tench Tilghman to General Heard, June 14, 1777; 49 *Papers of G. W.*, 32, LC.
162 *Ibid.*　　　　163 8 *G. W.*, 249.

and writing carelessly from American headquarters, reconciliation was easy. The differences with Reed, in fact, had dwindled to unimportance as time had passed during Lee's captivity.[164] It would have been gratifying if at that very hour, Reed had been present to add his suggestions for ascertaining what the British were to do next and how they could be checkmated. American outposts were commanded to keep on the alert; Sullivan was told to get beyond the right flank of the redcoats by moving to Flemington.[165] Were he to remain on the left of the British he might be separated from the main Army.[166] To their surprise, both Washington and Sullivan received a steady flow of militia [167] and thereby they gained so much strength that the commanding General began to consider the possibility of an offensive when the troops from Peekskill arrived.[168] At the moment, he did not feel that he could assail the British in their strong position,[169] where one flank was covered by the Millstone, the other by Brunswick, and the front by the Raritan.[170] Across that stream, the British, too, remained

[164] See *supra*, p. 292 ff. Washington had continued to work with Reed from the time the General unintentionally read Lee's letter of Nov. 24, 1776, until Reed informally resigned as Adjutant General in January (cf. 7 G. W., 5, 190). Although Reed had felt that his chief was less confiding than before the exchange of letters, Washington had his regard for the soldierly qualities of Reed increased by the conduct of the Colonel during the Trenton-Princeton campaign, and he held more steadfastly than ever to his intention of giving Reed the command of all the cavalry of the Army as soon as Congress authorized. Before the Delegates acted on Washington's recommendation (cf. *ibid.*, 50, 190–91), Reed expressed the wish on Mch. 8, 1777, that he might have "one hour of private conversation" with Washington on the subject of Reed's letter to Lee that had brought from Lee the answer the Commander-in-Chief had seen (1 *Reed*, 259). No early opportunity for such a conversation was found, but Reed on the 4th of June wrote again in earnest, affectionate tone and asked for a restoration of their friendship (*ibid.*, 259–60). It was to this that Washington replied on the 14th with the assurance that he was "perfectly convinced of the sincerity" of Reed's "friendly and affectionate sentiments" (8 G. W., 247). Washington then explained why he had been hurt by the conclusion he drew from Lee's letter, as set forth already on p. 271. Reed's answer of the 18th (1 *LTW.*, 386 ff) was an avowal that his letter to Lee, of which he had no copy, was not intended as anything more than an expression of regret over the loss of Fort Washington and over the hesitation that contributed to that disaster. Washington was entirely satisfied with this statement. The one remaining distress was that Reed would not accept the cavalry command. His reasons were numerous. Among them, in particular, was resentment that Congress delayed so long his election as a Brigadier (1 *Reed*, 296 ff; 7 *JCC.*, 347; 8 *ibid.*, 428). The text of Reed's letter of Nov. 21, 1776, to Charles Lee, was never available to Washington, nor was it recovered by Reed, but it came to light later and appears in 1 *Reed*, 255.

[165] Twenty-two miles West of Brunswick, fifteen miles Northwest of Princeton and close to the right bank of the South Branch of the Raritan. Washington's references to right and left in these instructions to Sullivan will not be understood unless it is remembered that the American Commander-in-Chief assumed his adversary to be looking South. See 8 G. W., 248–49.   [166] *Ibid.*

[167] *Ibid.*, 251, 253, 258. Henry Knox to Mrs. Knox, June 21, 1777 (*Knox Papers*, MHS).
[168] 8 G. W., 254.
[169] See Lewis Willis to Charles Gates, June 19, 1776; 2 V 214.
[170] 8 G. W., 314. Washington wrote "front," but in the sense in which he described Howe's position the "front" actually was the rear of the British Army as it looked toward Philadelphia.

quiet on the 15th and again on the 16th, except that they began to construct a chain of redoubts.[171]

There was something mystifying about all this. Were the redcoats trying to maneuver the American Army out of its position? If they failed in that, they manifestly could not proceed to Philadelphia and disregard Washington on their flank or in their rear.[172] A blow at Washington's Army, a crippling blow, appeared to be an unavoidable preliminary of a safe overland advance on the town where Congress was sitting.[173] The 17th of June yielded no explanation of a "movement" that scarcely deserved the name because it had been halted so close to its starting point. Morgan's riflemen and other light troops did what they could to harass the British,[174] but the only other thing that happened, in the way of action, was the departure of Howe's wagons. Loaded with baggage, they headed back to Brunswick: was this part of the plan of a General who did not wish to be encumbered when he began to advance swiftly? Deserters said so, in effect.[175] Washington still could think of no more likely target than his own Army, prior to a rapid British advance on Philadelphia, and he consequently called to him 1000 of Sullivan's Continentals and a like number of that officer's militia.[176]

Another day came, the 18th. The British continued to work on their redoubts but made no move. Early the next morning, June 19, Washington had a report that puzzled him: The British were withdrawing to Brunswick. They had started during the night and as they had so short a march, they could not be overtaken or injured. What had happened? Why had they gone back without making even a single attack on the American positions? From the fact that the King's men had been working the previous day on their redoubts, Washington concluded that the decision to end the watch on the Raritan was reached suddenly. He assumed that the British had found it difficult to assault the advantageous ground the Americans had strengthened at Middle Brook, and he reasoned that Howe perhaps had been discouraged by the extent to which the militia had flocked to the American camp.[177]

---

171 Washington to unnamed correspondent, June 20, 1777; *Huntington Lib. MSS.*
172 Cf. Lewis Willis to Charles Gates, *supra*, n. 169.
173 8 *G. W.*, 243, 258, 259; 1 *Sullivan Papers*, 393.
174 8 *G. W.*, 291.   175 8 *G. W.*, 262–63.   176 *Ibid.*, 263.
177 *Ibid.*, 206, 269–70. One shot of Washington's surmise did not miss his mark far. Howe explained later that he sought a general engagement whenever, but only when, the circumstances were least hazardous to the royal army, "for even a victory," said he, "attended by a heavy loss on our part, would have given a fatal check to the progress of the war, and

Another British attempt to proceed overland to Philadelphia, said Washington, was not probable.[178]

What, then, was next? Had Howe let down his guard? In a knowledge that British numbers had not been reduced appreciably by the operation and that they had stout defensive positions, Washington did not yield to the temptation to strike. He followed the retreat of his adversary and he continued to prod but he did not attack immediately. His self-restraint and patience seemed to earn an easy reward. On the 21st of June, two days after the British returned to Brunswick, Washington heard that one Regiment after another was leaving town and was removing its baggage to Amboy.[179] Here, at last, was an opportunity. If militiamen familiar with that part of Jersey would conceal themselves along the bank of the Raritan, they might confuse this transfer of the royal army's belongings.[180] A demonstration by other American forces, close to the British lines, would disarrange plans and would multiply the troubles any large body of troops would encounter in getting its equipment downstream almost twenty miles, to a base on the opposite side of a wide river. Orders went out from American headquarters, late in the evening,[181] for Sullivan to advance his Division and to feint against Brunswick. General Maxwell with 1500 men[182] was to take position between Brunswick and Amboy, on the flank of the enemy.[183]

---

might have proved irreparable." The movement against Middle Brook was undertaken in the hope of tempting the Americans to leave their strong positions and to hasten to the Delaware to defend its crossings. When Howe found that the Americans showed no inclination to make the first move into the open, he did not think he should spend the time or take the risks involved in a wide turning movement at that hot season, and when he did not have sufficient men to keep up his lengthened communications (*Howe's Narrative*, 15–16). His conduct inspired some startling stories in England—one of them that Cornwallis had been captured and his men, 3000 in number, killed or captured. Washington was said to have forced Howe to retreat with great loss of ammunition and baggage (Auckland MSS., 260, *Stevens' Facsimiles*). A convenient text of Howe's report of operations, June 12–July 5, 1777, will be found in 1 *N. J. Arc.* (2), p. 476 ff.

178 8 *G. W.*, 275. Henry Knox's letters of June 21 to his wife and to J. Jackson (*Knox Papers*, MHS), most admirably supplement Washington's reports. The greatest surprise to Knox was the rally of the Jersey militia.

179 Cf. Henry Knox to Mrs. Knox, June 21, 1777: "I think in five days there will not be an enemy in the Jersies. But I fear they will go up North River where perhaps they may plague us more" (*Knox Papers*, MHS).

180 8 *G. W.*, 279–80; 1 *Sullivan Papers*, 395.

181 8 *G. W.*, 283.

182 His Brigade of Stirling's Division, consisted of the First, Second, Third and Fourth New Jersey Regiments (8 *G. W.*, 130).

183 1 *Sullivan Papers*, 395–96. Although it nowhere is stated explicitly, Maxwell's troops probably were employed in place of the militia Washington first planned to send down the Raritan. In fact, the Commander-in-Chief may have abandoned altogether the plan to attack the river shipping. Cf. Samuel H. Parsons to his wife, June 22, 1777; *Hall's Parsons*, 103.

While these preparations were being made, everything indicated what dawn of the 22nd confirmed—that Howe was evacuating Brunswick. As soon as this was established, Washington recast his plans and directed Greene to fall on the rear of the British as they proceeded down the northern bank [184] of the river toward Amboy; but this proved a task beyond the power of the Army to execute on short notice. Everything, so to say, went wrong. Sullivan's orders were not received soon enough for him to come up promptly; [185] mistakes were made in timing the march of the different Brigades; [186] delay was encountered in the delivery of instructions to James Varnum, a Brigadier who had arrived not long previously with troops from Connecticut and Rhode Island; [187] the messenger sent to General Maxwell disappeared—whether through capture, desertion or accident, Washington did not know.[188] The result of all these mishaps was a limping and ragged pursuit, during which Morgan's riflemen were the only American troops who got within range to inflict any damage,[189] and they did much less than was indicated in first reports.[190]

At the end of the day, Washington knew that the redcoats still were almost unscathed as a fighting force and were concentrated in Amboy. He resolved to move up at 6 o'clock the next morning, June 23, and to take a closer look at the British defences; [191] but after he did this, he so nearly abandoned all hope of an offensive that he released most of the Jersey militia on the 23rd with thanks and praise,[192] and he did not feel particular distress that rain prevented an advance that day.[193] When he sent his troops toward Amboy on the 24th, he felt distinct misgiving, because he suspected he might have to yield quickly the territory he took—"no small misfortune," he said, one that would lower the high spirits of his troops and revive a depressed adversary.[194]

[184] Washington called it the "east side" (8 G. W., 282).

[185] Ibid., 283.   [186] Ibid., 296.

[187] As far as existing GOs show, Varnum had not been assigned formally to any Division. For the miscarriage of orders to him, see 8 G. W., 296.

[188] Ibid., 299.

[189] Ibid., 291, 312. In noting that Wayne's Brigade was the only one of Greene's Division that reached the front in time to be of service on the 22nd, Washington said Wayne's men "behaved in a manner that does them great honor," but he did not specify any particular service other than that of joining Morgan in advancing to the British redoubts on the left bank of the Raritan (ibid., 282, 291).

[190] Cf. ibid., 308–09.   [191] Ibid., 283, 285.

[192] Ibid., 287. See also Washington's observations of July 1 and 4 to the same effect in ibid., 325, 341, and Samuel Adams to James Warren, June 23, 1777: "Great credit is due to the New Jersey Militia who have turned out with spirit and alacrity" (1 Warren-Adams Letters, 337).   [193] 8 G. W., 287–88, 296, 298.

[194] Letter of June 23, 1777, to Joseph Reed, ibid., 295.

Observation of the district in which Washington halted his troops that day did not ease his mind. Stirling's Division and some other Regiments encamped near Metuchen Meeting House, about five miles Northwest of Amboy,[195] but they were, in Washington's words, on "low and disadvantageous" ground, where water was scarce.[196] Ahead of them, the enemy's position appeared unassailable by such a force as Washington could throw against it. Howe's flanks rested on waterways; strong redoubts ran across the neck on which Amboy stood. Washington and his senior officers agreed that they would be taking profitless risk if they placed more men on Stirling's insecure front.[197] Army headquarters consequently were opened about five miles North of Brunswick, at Quibble Town,[198] where most of the troops not with Stirling were held.[199]

Their wait was short. In the face of reports that many of the British troops had been sent to Staten Island,[200] Washington was notified on the 26th of June [201] that the British had sallied from Amboy in greater strength than ever and were advancing several columns as if they intended to do one or more of three things—to cut off Stirling at Metuchen Meeting House, to bring the main Army to battle, or to occupy the high ground in the vicinity of Middle Brook. Moreover, the march of the British was said to be rapid, as if they hoped to overwhelm Stirling or to get to elevated positions before Washington could. This was not a fisherman's cast at which Washington would snap. His forces at Quibble Town he put on the march for Middle Brook, and he doubtless directed Stirling to disengage himself from troops who already were assailing the position at Metuchen. Both retreats were completed without heavy casualties, though Stirling's rearguard, which had to be left unsupported, lost three field guns.[202] The British columns pursued

---

195 Erskine's map put Metuchen (Matochin) Meeting House slightly North of the present compass bearing of the city of Metuchen in relation to Perth Amboy.

196 Letter of June 25, 1777, to the President of Congress; 8 G. W., 298.

197 Ibid. An amusing and satirical account of a futile demonstration by Col. Theodorick Bland with about 260 Light Horse, on the 25th, appears in Benjamin Talmadge to Jere. Wadsworth, July 9, 1777; Wadsworth Papers, CHS.

198 The present New Market, N. J.   199 8 G. W., 296, 298.

200 Ibid., 307.

201 Journal of Timothy Pickering, 1 Pickering, 145.

202 Stirling's withdrawal was via Westfield (8 G. W., 307 ff; 9 A. Hamilton, 77 ff). See an interesting account of this affair in a letter of Col. Lewis Willis to Charles Yates, July 10, 1777 (2 V 429). A British version appears in William Harcourt to his father, July 12, 1777 (Evelyns in America, 241). The court of inquiry on the loss of the three field pieces exonerated the officers (8 G. W., 370). The Army's cannon were so few at the time that Washington, on June 23, had to direct that two, and two only, should be allowed each Brigade (8 G. W., 290).

as far as Westfield and halted there, in a movement so nearly duplicating the advance of the 13th to the vicinity of Middle Brook that Sullivan, among others, suspected another offensive was developing.[203] Instead, the British fell back to Spanktown on the 27th,[204] and on the 28th returned to Amboy,[205] whereupon Washington advanced two Brigades, Scott's and Conway's, to observe and to harass, though he did not think they could do the enemy much harm from the distance at which they had to operate.[206] On the 1st of the new month the jubilant word brought to Middle Brook was that the enemy the previous day had evacuated Amboy completely and had reestablished themselves on Staten Island.[207]

It was true. The long operation that began November 20 when Cornwallis crossed the Hudson and moved against Fort Lee had now ended in the withdrawal from New Jersey of all large bodies of British. A revolutionary cause that had been close to complete ruin seven months previously was not yet assured of victory over a powerful adversary; but it had recovered to a vigor of effort justifiying John Hancock's statement that the British evacuation of Jersey "will be the most explicit declaration to the whole world that the conquest of America is not only a very distant but an unattainable object." [208] The good news reached Philadelphia in time to double the rejoicing on the first anniversary of the Declaration of Independence, when, significantly, the "Hessian band of music who were taken at Princeton performed very delightfully . . ." [209]

These Germans tooted and doubtless enjoyed the holiday, with little knowledge of what had happened around Amboy and perhaps with little regard for it, one way or the other, but many British were angered and humiliated. An officer of the Royal Engineers wrote in his diary: "I believe it was generally imagined upon our army's making the . . . move [to Middle Brook, Washington] would have quitted his strong-

---

[203] *Ibid.*, 309.

[204] *Ibid.*, 308. *A. Robertson's Diaries*, 139. Spanktown is the present Rahway.

[205] *Ibid.*   [206] 8 *G. W.*, 322.

[207] *Ibid.*, 318. In these maneuvers of June 19–30, Washington had not lost heavily. Captures by the British were reported to him as sixty-four (*ibid*, 310). He had no authoritative figures on his killed and wounded. Kemble, *op. cit.*, v. 1, p. 123, estimated them at 100, probably an exaggerated total.

[208] Letter of June 24, 1777; 1 *LTW.*, 390–91.

[209] Thomas Burke to Gov. Richard Caswell; July 5, 1777. Burke went on, "the pleasure being not a little heightened by the reflection they were hired by the British court for the purpose very different from those to which they were applied." The slip of Burke in placing the capture of the band at Princeton instead of Trenton was not unnatural (2 *Burnett*, 399).

hold and retreated towards the Delaware. However, it proved otherwise, he stood firm." [210] Another said tersely and with self-conscious philosophizing: "Find from the general tenor of officer's conversation that they are not well pleased with affairs, but they often speak without thought." [211] Still another British observer set down dark daily notes on the gloom of friends over the slow progress of the "cause of our King and country," of the fact that "all men appear dissatisfied," and of a whisper that Galloway, the loyalist, had a conference with "a person who gave up every hope of obtaining America by arms." [212]

Washington himself was not elated, for the reason that he knew the deficiencies of his Army and the immensity of the advantage Howe still enjoyed. "Our situation," Washington told Gov. John Rutledge, "is truly delicate and perplexing and makes us sensibly feel now, as we have often done before, the great advantage they derive from their Navy." [213] Always, too, Washington had to ask himself whether the scanty American forces were balanced strategically between New Jersey and the Hudson, or whether the danger of having Carleton and Burgoyne sever New England from the rest of the country was greater than the risk that Howe, if confronted with too few, might subdue the Middle States. The defensive had saved America. Patience, conservation of force and a courageous refusal to be goaded into battle with a superior adversary—these had been among the most powerful weapons with which Washington had kept the Army alive and had evaded or had held at bay the King's fine Regiments. It had not been pleasant to see the wisdom of this indispensable policy overlooked, and to hear it asserted that he should attack the British wherever he met them. During the attempt to drive Howe from Amboy without having to risk a general engagement, Washington had written Joseph Reed: "We have some among us, and I dare say Generals, who wish to make themselves popular at the expense of others; or who think the cause is not to be advanced otherwise than by fighting; [214] the peculiar circumstances under which it is to be done, and the consequences which may follow, are objects too trivial for their attention, but as I have one great

[210] *A. Robertson's Diaries,* 137; entry of June 13, 1777.

[211] 1 *Kemble,* 124; entry of July 4, 1777.

[212] The "person" is supposed to have been Lord Howe. See *Serle,* 238, cf. 235, 236.

[213] Letter of July 5, 1777; 8 *G. W.,* 356. A similar sentiment was expressed in a letter of July 6, 1777, from Alexander Hamilton to Gouverneur Morris, 9 *A. Hamilton,* 88.

[214] Cf. Samuel Adams to James Warren, June 18, 1777: "I confess I have always been so very wrong headed as not to be over well-pleased with what is called the Fabian War in America" (1 *Warren-Adams Letters,* 331).

end in view, I shall, maugre all the strokes of this kind, steadily pursue the means which, in my judgment, leads to the accomplishment of it, not doubting but that the candid part of Mankind, if they are convinced of my integrity, will make proper allowances for my inexperience, and Frailties. I will agree to be loaded with all the obloquy they can bestow; if I commit a wilful error." [215] Had Washington, when young, been called upon to write such a letter as this concerning any of his operations in the French and Indian War, he almost certainly would have coupled with it a threat to resign. Now it was the cause of America and not his own regard for "honor" and reputation that had to be put first.

Before Washington could measure the improvement in his military situation or even give himself rest from strain, his Army was involved anew in troubles as baffling as those he had to face in the winter of 1776–77. On the 3rd of July he withdrew his troops from Middle Brook to his former station at Morristown, whence he could move swiftly to the Hudson or to Philadelphia as Howe's next maneuver might require.[216] Washington had no convincing intelligence reports on British preparations [217] but the probabilities seemed to him decisively on the side of an advance by Howe to form a junction with Burgoyne when the latter assailed Ticonderoga,[218] which the American commander hoped the enemy never would be able to capture.[219]

A more immediate danger, as Washington saw it, was that of a surprise attack by Howe on the Highland defences. Putnam, in general command of the lower Hudson, was invoked to watch vigilantly for the coming of the enemy and, meantime, to keep his forces concentrated.[220] Gen. George Clinton was asked to cooperate and to call out the New York militia.[221] Sullivan's Division was moved to Pompton,[222] sixteen miles Northeast of Morristown and about twenty miles West

[215] Letter of June 23, 1777; 8 *G. W.*, 295. The capitalization and punctuation of this historic utterance are untouched, though the spelling of a word or two has been conformed to modern usage.

[216] *Ibid.*, 336.   [217] *Ibid.*, 315.

[218] *Ibid.*, 325, 326, 331, 335.

[219] This was postulated on the adequate provisioning of the garrison. See *ibid.*, 273, 332, 357; 1 *LTW.*, 383.

[220] For Washington's early exhortations see 8 *G. W.*, 205; for his instructions of June 22 and the fortnight thereafter, see *ibid.*, 284, 300, 310–11. Putnam's insistence on maintaining a post at White Plains, and Washington's reluctant permission for him to do so are recorded in *ibid.*, 321–22.

[221] *Ibid.*, 324–25.

[222] *Ibid.*, 340. Cf. *ibid.*, 358–59, for the transmission to Sullivan of a suggested plan of attack on the British post at Bergen.

of the Hudson. From that point, if necessary, Sullivan could hasten to the support of Putnam, in balking an attack on the forts of the Highlands, "the thing of all others," Washington wrote Schuyler, "most fatal to our interests," because "the possession of the Highlands [by the British] would effectually bar all mutual assistance of our two Armies."[223] Putnam previously had been told to make ready four Regiments to assist Schuyler in event the full weight of attack fell on Ticonderoga at a time when the Highlands were not threatened.[224]

Taken together, these dispositions seemed to Washington the best he could make in balancing his forces for a rapid concentration in any nearby district where Howe or Burgoyne, or both, might take the offensive. The one circumstance that suggested a possibility of attack elsewhere than in the Valley of the Hudson was the reported fitting out of some of Howe's ships for the conveyance of horses. Howe would not do this for operations close to New York.[225] The last report that Washington had received concerning the situation at Ticonderoga had reached him at Middle Brook on the 26th of June. Nothing that had arrived later from the Northern Department had brought even second-hand confirmation of reports that Burgoyne was on the march. It might well be, Washington thought, that the British were feinting at Ticonderoga in order to cover a stroke elsewhere.[226]

The burdened American Commander-in-Chief could not devote himself exclusively to this study of the defence of the Hudson. He had to give it his prime thought but he had to deliberate on other conditions that were exasperating in themselves and full of danger to the Army. One of these was the violent resentment Greene, Knox and Sullivan were showing because of the pretentions the Frenchman, du Coudray, was making. Doubtless Washington knew what these senior lieutenants of his had done, and he must have felt deep anxiety because of it, but he had not heard, as yet, what action Congress had taken on their communication.[227] Another cause of uneasiness was a murmur, now first audible, that Washington was devoting himself and the Army too much to the defence of the Hudson and was disregarding the danger of an attack on Pennsylvania, and, in particular, on Philadelphia. Quartermaster General Mifflin was among the first to voice com-

---

[223] Letter of July 2, 1777; *ibid.*, 332.   [224] *Ibid.*, 271–72.
[225] *Ibid.*, 364, 368.
[226] *Ibid.*, 363.
[227] See *infra*, p. 455.

plaint and he already was becoming progressively alienated on this account from Washington.[228]

A more acute concern was the plight of the commissary. As long previously as the beginning of February, Washington had felt that Carpenter Wharton, the Deputy Commissary General at headquarters, was utterly incompetent, and that Joseph Trumbull, head of the department, should come to Morristown and should remain there.[229] Trumbull was then in Connecticut, wrestling with his accounts, though in no better health, and he was not in accord with Washington's view that the balancing of his books was less important than personal supervision of the feeding of the main Army. Congress, for its part, was cognizant of Wharton's derelictions, and, in addition, was suffering at the time from what Richard Henry Lee termed "a rage of reformation." [230] Trumbull himself was harassed increasingly and was convinced that he never had received fair treatment; [231] some of his deputies had been accused not only of bidding one against another in the Middle States,[232] but also of putting up prices because their commissions were based on the gross amount of purchases; [233] the very air smelled of scandal. Trumbull first was urged [234] and then was commanded to come to Philadelphia and to set right the muddled affairs of his subordinates.[235] He arrived on the 22nd of April,[236] suspended the discredited deputy,[237] reassured Congress regarding provisions immediately available,[238] and then he dismissed Wharton; [239] but he did not silence other complaints [240] or satisfy Washington, who protested that

[228] No details of this developing estrangement have been found. The reality of it is not to be questioned, but it was not brought into the open until the events described *infra*, p. 559 ff.

[229] Jere. Wadsworth to Joseph Trumbull, Feb. 2, 1777; *Joseph Trumbull Papers*, Mil. and Gen. Corres., v. 5, p. 525 b, Conn. State Lib.

[230] 1 *Ballagh, Lee Letters*, 352.

[231] Cf. his letter of May 26, 1777, to Jere. Wadsworth (*Yale Univ. Lib.*), and that of June 19, 1776, to Horatio Gates: "I soon expect to enlist myself in your honorable corps of resigners. The treatment I have received from first to present time is too much to bear. Mr. Lovell can give you particulars. Let us retire to our fields and leave to our back door friends to bustle and squabble for pillage and plunder. Heaven will not suffer the cause to be lost, and pillage and plunder we despise" (*Gates Papers*, NYHS).

[232] See *supra*, p. 386.

[233] 7 *JCC.*, 70, 177; 7 *G. W.*, 185; 2 *Burnett*, 315, 334–35.

[234] 2 *Burnett*, loc. cit.; 7 *G. W.*, 160–61.   [235] *Ibid.*, 325.

[236] 2 *Burnett*, 340.

[237] Trumbull to Wharton, Apr. 26, 1777; *Joseph Trumbull Papers*, CHS.

[238] 7 *JCC.*, 293.

[239] 2 *Burnett*, 361; 8 *JCC.*, 499–500. A typical instance of Wharton's negligence in the specific matter of accepting poorly packed beef, will be found in William Graham to Trumbull, May 1, 1777 (*Joseph Trumbull Papers*, CHS).

[240] Cf. 2 *Burnett*, 38; 7 *JCC.*, 266–67; 8 *G. W.*, 54–55, 176. See 7 *JCC.*, 323, for the appointment of a Superintendent of Bakers and Director of Baking. In *ibid.*, 281, is reference

it had taken two months to get Trumbull to Philadelphia whence now the Commissary General could not be budged.[241]

A crisis came at the end of May, when Washington told Trumbull that he must visit Morristown and procure sufficient supplies or else see the Army disperse for lack of food.[242] The explanation was that when provisions had been removed to avoid the possibility they would fall into the hands of the enemy, the food left in the old magazines had been insufficient to sustain the Army until new supply-lines were opened.[243] All these circumstances and the loss at Danbury, Connecticut, prompted a detailed and inevitably prolonged debate in Congress, during the course of which some of Trumbull's assistants quit and some became demoralized.[244]

On June 10 Congress adopted new regulations for the commissariat,[245] and on the 18th fixed the pay and named the men to direct a complicated organization.[246] Washington had felt that the purchase and distribution of provisions had outgrown control by one man; [247] Trumbull had looked with some favor on the general plan of the new service, though he had felt that its success and his labor for it depended on the compensation allowed him, on the nature of the regulations, and on the character of the man in charge of the Department.[248] Congress was as careful as it knew how to be in a matter regarding which few of the Delegates had precise information, and its membership was insistent that one of the new chiefs of the Commissary keep his office in the city where it was sitting.[249]

The organization provided no longer for one inclusive category of commissaries, but for two classes, one to have charge of purchase and the other to control issue. Deputies were to be assigned to areas beyond

---

to the assignment of Brig. Gen. John Armstrong to examine Wharton's management, etc. See *ibid.*, 314, 395, 396, for the movement of supplies. Cf. *ibid.*, 203, for an apology by Washington for a mistake in the drafting of a letter, and *ibid.*, 433, for a report that the British were getting supplies indirectly from Philadelphia.

[241] 8 *G. W.*, 130. [242] *Ibid.*, 136.

[243] 8 *JCC.*, 405. Cf. Tench Tilghman to Trumbull, June 4, 1777 (*Joseph Trumbull Papers,* as cited, Conn. State Lib., v. 1, p. 119) against the placing of any large quantity of provisions at Trenton.

[244] Joseph Trumbull to Jere. Wadsworth, June 6, 1777 (*Wadsworth Papers,* Yale Univ. Lib.).

[245] 8 *JCC.*, 386, 406, 409, 410, 414–15, 433 ff.

[246] *Ibid.*, 469, 477, and 1 *LTW.*, 391. [247] 8 *G. W.*, 25.

[248] Letter of May 17–19, 1777, to Jere. Wadsworth (2 *Burnett,* 364 n); Joseph Trumbull to his father, June 6, 1777 (*Joseph Trumbull Papers,* as cited, Conn. State Lib., v. 6, p. 131 a); Joseph Trumbull to James Lovell, June 15, 1775 (*ibid.*, v. 5, p. 491); James Bate to Joseph Trumbull, May 4, 1777 (*Joseph Trumbull Papers,* CHS).

[249] 8 *JCC.*, 452.

which they were not to operate. Senior officers of either branch were to call on the Quartermaster General for transportation and in emergencies could hire wagons at prices authorized by Congress.[250] Branding of government cattle, elaborate record-keeping, the purchase of salt for curing meat, the making of casks and barrels, the establishment of vegetable gardens, and the recovery and tanning of hides were among the duties outlined in much detail by Delegates who seemed better to understand what should be than what could be done.[251]

From the standpoint of commissary officers, the most disturbing feature of the new system was that fixed pay and rations, rather than commissions, were to be allowed them. Trumbull had said he would not take office otherwise than on commission.[252] He now resigned his old post and agreed with much reluctance to act temporarily as Commissary General of Purchases, and while serving, to seek essential changes in the amended regulations.[253] His friends sympathized with him and assured him they would have endorsed his action in resigning if they had not felt that the life of the Army depended on his continued direction, with their fullest help, until the new system worked smoothly.[254] Some of Trumbull's assistants were less disposed to accept conditions they considered harmful to the Army and unjust to them. One Deputy Commisary, Capt. Matthew Irwin, declined outright;[255] eight others asked for permission to resign and, in doing so, pointed out what they considered the unfairness of the modified rules.[256] Trumbull himself struggled on, for some weeks, and with so few assistants that he had

[250] A case in point developed when Joseph White was engaged by the Board of War to procure "a temporary supply of vinegar, beer and vegetables" for the Army. Richard Peters had to write to Washington, August 6, to assist White in getting wagons because, as the contractor was not in the Commissary Department, there would be "some clashing" (53 *Papers of G. W.*, 51, LC).

[251] The text of the approved regulations occupies fifteen pages (433–448) in 8 *JCC*.

[252] Cf. his letter of May 17–19, 1777 (2 *Burnett*, 364 n): "I am determined to have my own terms or have nothing."

[253] See *ibid.*, 393 and n, 407. He and his deputies were requested to continue to serve, apparently in Trumbull's case on his old terms, until the new establishment was ready to take over the commissary (*ibid.*, 491). For Trumbull's resignation, which may not have been filed as dated, see Trumbull to John Hancock, two letters, June 15, 1777 (*Joseph Trumbull Papers*, as cited, Conn. State Lib.); Trumbull to Horatio Gates, June 19, 1777 (*Gates Papers*, NYHS); Trumbull to his father, June 29, 1777 (*Joseph Trumbull Papers* (MHS) Conn. Col. Office Papers, v. 6, p. 159 a; Conn. State Lib.).

[254] Eliphalet Dyer to Trumbull, June, n.d., 1777, July 15, 1777 (*Joseph Trumbull Papers*, CHS); James Lovell to Joseph Trumbull, June 30, 1777 (*ibid*).

[255] 2 *Burnett*, 506. Robert Hoops was named in his stead (*ibid.*, 517). See *ibid.*, 536, for an instance in which Congress was not certain whether a Deputy Commissary of Issue would undertake to discharge the duties.

[256] Application of July 1, 1777; *Wadsworth Papers*, CHS.

on occasion to stand in person at the scales to check the weight of provisions brought in.[257]

Washington had counted it a "peculiar mark of providence" that the British had evacuated Jersey before the standing grain was ripe enough to be set on fire.[258] The crop was saved and soon would be cut. When available, it would yield some of the flour the Army needed. Whence the greater part of the supply was to come, Washington did not know, nor could he have confidence in the ability of the Commissary to find it, buy it and transport it. At the moment, the question was not whether the troops could be fed in February, 1778, but whether they could be provisioned to the end of the month of July, 1777, or even to the close of the next week. Joseph Trumbull sent one of his deputies to Washington on the 9th of July with a letter in which he said that the bearer, Major Robert Hoops, had found it impossible to act because of the "difficulties arising from the strictness of Congress' new regulations." Trumbull wrote earnestly: "I really fear the Army will suffer if not be disbanded soon if some effectual measures for my relief are not taken." [259]

The proposal of Trumbull—he had confessed his patience exhausted—was that Congress be requested to send a committee to Morristown as soon as possible in order that members might see for themselves the existing danger and might recommend to their fellow Delegates corrective measures.[260] Washington immediately forwarded this to Congress with the warning that unless something was "done in aid of Mr. Trumbull immediately, this Army must be disbanded." He reiterated: "If the present difficulties continue, it is impossible it can exist." Washington went on to say that the Army might be obliged to move within a few hours and might have more to dread from the disorder of the Commissary than from the acts of the enemy.[261]

[257] James Lovell to Joseph Trumbull, June 30, 1777 (*Joseph Trumbull Papers,* CHS). Joseph Trumbull to his father, July 5, 1777 (*Trumbull Papers,* MHS., Conn. State Lib.) as cited n. *supra.* In the *Emmet Col.* NYPL., is a letter from Joseph Trumbull to Matthew Irvin—the name also is spelled Irwin and Irvine—June 22, 1777, on the acute shortage of provisions at "Camp Middlebrook." ". . . push on all the provisions you possibly can," said Trumbull, "with all possible dispatch or we shall starve."

[258] 8 *G. W.,* 341.

[259] 152 *Papers Cont. Cong.,* pt. IV, p. 335; 2 *Burnett,* 293 n.

[260] 50 *Papers of G. W.,* 117, LC.

[261] Letter of July 9, 1777; 8 *G. W.,* 373. Cf. Timothy Pickering to Joseph Trumbull, June 28, 1777: "His Excellency, the Commander-in-Chief, observes with extreme concern and regret that almost every expedition he forms is either frustrated or greatly impeded by the want of a regular supply of provisions, partly bread. But besides this mischief, another is daily growing in the camp. The bread made of the flour delivered the men is of the most unwholesome

This, then, was the situation: a ragged citizen Army far too small for the task assigned it and under dissatisfied officers, might be compelled to scatter and to plunder in order to keep from starvation at a time when every Regiment should be well fed and well shod and ready to move swiftly if it was to continue maneuver against a powerful professional force able to strike anywhere on deep water. Washington's greatest need of all was for a prolongation of quiet in order that provisions might be collected and distributed. Instead, (how that word and its companion "if" pursued the Army!) the express who arrived on the morning of July 10 brought a dispatch from General Schuyler, dated July 7 to this effect: a report had been forwarded by a responsible officer that General St. Clair had evacuated Ticonderoga; it was feared that the greater part of the garrison had been captured.[262]

---

kind, and from it diseases are constantly increasing. For these reasons his Excellency most earnestly desires the Commissary General ever to have in readiness a competency of provisions and especially of hard bread for every emergency that may arise and that the health of the troops may be preserved" (*Joseph Trumbull Papers*, Mil. and Gen. Corres., v. 3, p. 230; Conn. State Lib.). These instructions had a certain justification in a sadly humorous phrase in a letter Trumbull had written William Dean, May 2, 1777: All flour, said Trumbull, was to be marked in three grades—good, bad and very bad (*Joseph Trumbull Papers*, CHS).

[262] 8 *G. W.*, 376. Washington had heard on the 8th that Burgoyne had approached Ticonderoga and had taken position at Mount Hope, Northwest of the fort and close to it. On the strength of this, Washington had concluded that the Highlands would be assailed in a short time by Howe. Sullivan had been ordered to cross the Hudson but on the 9th he had been halted West of the river because no intelligence had been received of the embarkation of any of Howe's troops at New York (*ibid.*, 371, 373).

CHAPTER XVII

MANEUVER WEARS OUT MEN AND SHOES
(July 10–September 9, 1777)

WASHINGTON could not, would not believe it. Ticonderoga fallen? The enemy free to descend the Hudson and to join hands with Howe? It was too dark a disaster for Providence or fate to visit on the American cause, especially when Gates had felt confident the place could be held, and St. Clair had written cheerfully to Washington as late as July 3.[1] Although the Commander-in-Chief refused to accept the news in all its blackness, it created a gnawing suspense he did not attempt to conceal.[2] The movement he previously had dreaded—that of a British advance on Philadelphia—now appeared the lesser of evils,[3] and for this reason: If Howe's army were embarked, prompt notice of its departure for the Delaware would give Washington time to reach Philadelphia ahead of the foe; and if Howe took his men off ship and started southward overland toward Pennsylvania, the Americans assuredly could outstrip him.[4] Every consideration of strategy seemed to indicate that instead of doing either of these things, Howe would proceed up the Hudson to a junction with the northern army as soon as he confirmed the report that Burgoyne had reached Ticonderoga. On like grounds of military logic, Washington believed that Burgoyne would not proceed farther southward until he knew Howe's drums had sounded the advance up the river.[5] The three essential and immediate tasks, as Washington saw them, were to move the main Army closer to the Highlands of the Hudson; second, to assure the utmost vigilance at the posts the enemy would pass or assail in moving from New York to cooperate with Burgoyne,[6] and third, to prevail on the Eastern States

[1] 8 G. W., 395; Gates to unnamed correspondent, May 12, 1777 (Gates Papers, NYHS).

[2] 8 G. W., 375, 376, 379. Cf. Henry Knox to his wife, July 13, 1777: "We have received the most chagrining news of the evacuation of Ticonderoga, pregnant, in my opinion, with the most disagreeable consequences of anything during the war . . ." (Knox Papers, MHS).

[3] 9 A. Hamilton, 82 ff.   [4] 8 G. W., 378.

[5] 8 G. W., 384. Cf. Washington to William Sever, Aug. 10, 1777: ". . . I had no doubt in my own mind but that [General Howe] would have pushed up the North River, to cooperate with General Burgoyne . . ." (9 G. W., 54). See, also, ibid., 21.

[6] In instructions of July 13, Putnam was told the loss of his post "could not fail of consequences almost if not irremediable" (8 G. W., 383. See, also, ibid., 394).

to send their militia to strengthen Schuyler. Temporary troops assembled to resist the advance of the enemy from the New York Lakes should be placed under some aggressive man, Benedict Arnold, for example, whom they trusted;[7] orders must be prepared for the continental Brigades to start northward. Their unannounced objective was Pompton Plains, eighteen miles from Morristown.[8] Thence Washington intended to proceed through Smith's Clove to the vicinity of West Point,[9] and to await word of what was happening in the troubled area up the Hudson.

Neither the news nor the march was pleasant. En route to Pompton,[10] during the evening of July 11, which was the first day on the road, Washington received a dispatch that verified the report of the evacuation of Ticonderoga.[11] Although details were lacking, he had to accept the event, which he put "among the most unfortunate that could have befallen us." [12] The disaster might be worse than reported, because Washington did not yet know what had happened to St. Clair's garrison after it had abandoned Ticonderoga on the 6th of July.[13] As Washington wrote Schuyler, who became almost frantic in his demands for help,[14] "the whole affair is so mysterious that it even baffles conjecture." [15]

Washington pointed out that the one sure way of preventing the junction of Howe and Burgoyne, with its "most fatal consequences," was to recruit the Army to a "respectable footing" [16] but, at the moment,

[7] 8 G. W., 386. Arnold at this very time was tendering his resignation because some of his juniors had been promoted ahead of him. See Arnold to the President of Congress, July 11, 1777; 162 Papers Cont. Cong., I, p. 106.

[8] 8 G. W., 380.

[9] Ibid., 393. Apparently he had no good map of this district.

[10] Probably the best source of information on this march is the Diary of Capt. John Chilton of the Third Virginia in 12 T 283 ff.

[11] In a letter of Philip Schuyler's, July 7, 1777; 1 LTW., 393.

[12] Letter of July 12, 1777, to the President of Congress; 8 G. W., 384.

[13] St. Clair had deferred summoning militia reenforcement because, at the outset, he had so limited a supply of provisions that the addition of some thousands of mouths would have meant the quicker exhaustion of food. When he received more provisions, he called to him 900 militia but found them so poorly equipped that they could remain for a few days only. The principal of several reasons for abandoning the defences was the success of the British in scaling nearby Sugar Loaf Hill, to the top of which they carried several field guns. St. Clair maintained that if he had remained at the fort, his troops would have been surrounded and would have been forced into complete surrender. The story is told in 1 St. Clair Papers, 420–21, 447 ff, and in 1 Wilkinson, 165 ff. Of particular interest is St. Clair to James Wilson, July 14, 1777; Henkel's Cat. 683, No. 602. See also 1 John Jay, 140, 145, 146; 1 LTW., 391–92, 393, 395 ff; Journal of du Roi the Elder, 92–93, 96 ff, with a useful description of Ticonderoga and the bridge to Mt. Independence. Also worth consulting are Heath, 131, 1 Moore, 470 ff. Washingington's final judgment was that the disaster was due primarily to the delay in the recruiting of the New England Regiments intended for service at Ticonderoga. See 8 G. W., 483.

[14] 1 LTW., 393, 395 ff.   [15] 8 G. W., 392–93.   [16] Ibid., 428.

he marched in the darkest uncertainty concerning the fate of St. Clair, and he had to deal with endlessly conflicting reports of Howe's movements. In the face of discouraging wet weather,[17] Washington advanced most of his small Army to a point eleven miles in the Clove, Orange County, New York,[18] and there he halted on the 22nd until he could clarify reports he had received of the presence of British ships up the Sound, in North River, off Sandy Hook, and at sea on voyages to unascertained anchorage.[19] Until he discovered which of these tales was true, Washington did not know whether to send the two advanced Divisions, Sullivan's and Greene's, to the support of Putnam.[20] The fog of war seemed complete. Almost every clattering express contradicted the report the horseman ahead of him had brought.

On the 24th of the month, Washington felt sure the British fleet had left Sandy Hook.[21] Philadelphia seemed its most probable destination, and one that justified him in starting Stephen's and Lincoln's Divisions for the Delaware; but even then he had to admit the possibility that the descent of the King's ships might be on New England.[22] Once more he paid tribute to sea power when he said simply, "The amazing advantage the enemy derive from their ships and the command of the water keeps us in a state of constant perplexity and the most anxious conjecture." [23] Feeble though he was at the moment, hopeless as the attainment of his ideal appeared to be, the American commander saw clearly that his success depended, as always, on the fundamentals: he must have a better-clad, a better-equipped and a larger Army [24] which would shun all minor operations of doubtful value,[25] place less reliance on fixed positions,[26] and work steadfastly to destroy the British forces in America. It was the future that counted. As he wrote Robert Liv-

---

[17] *Ibid.*, 379, 405, 446.

[18] His successive advances and his various delays may be followed in Chilton's Diary, *loc. cit.*, and in 8 *G. W.*, 379, 380, 398, 405, 407, 409, 437–38, 446. One British intelligence report on this advance is in the *Clinton Papers*, loc. cit., and is summarized in Howe to Clinton, July 18, 1777.

[19] These constitute a most interesting example of the confusion that can be caused by conflicting intelligence reports. See 8 *G. W.*, 409, 437–38, 447, 449, 451, 453, 472.

[20] *Ibid.*, 414, 447, 452, 453; cf. 1 *Greene's Greene*, 400. The two Divisions crossed the Hudson (8 *G. W.*, 487) but apparently did not come under Putnam's command.

[21] David Forman, from Shrewsbury, N. J., July 23, 1777; 52 *Papers of G. W.*, 2, LC.

[22] 8 *G. W.*, 461, 462, 464, 466, 472–73, 483.   [23] *Ibid.*, 470.

[24] *Ibid.*, 475, 483. As concerns clothing and provisions, see *infra*, p. 451 ff.

[25] Cf. Washington's reference to the proposal, through Heath, of an operation against St. John's River, 8 *G. W.*, 482, 487.

[26] See Washington to Schuyler, July 22, 1777: "I begin to consider lines as a kind of trap, and not to answer the valuable purposes expected of them, unless they are passes that cannot be avoided by an enemy" (*ibid.*, 450).

ingston: ". . . we must look forward to more fortunate events. The evacuation of our posts on the Lakes has taken place and cannot be recalled." [27]

In the foreground was the imperative task of placing the continental Brigades where they would have the shortest distance to cover when, at last, the plan of the enemy was disclosed by the reappearance of the British squadrons. The Light Horse manifestly should proceed toward Philadelphia; [28] the best disposition of the main Army, Washington thought, probably would be at the crossings of the Delaware, on either side of Trenton, whence the march to Philadelphia or to North River would not put too heavy a strain on the legs of his men.[29] Sullivan's, the rear Division, was to proceed with the possibility in mind of a recall to Putnam in event Howe turned about and appeared in North River.[30] On the other hand, if Howe's main attack was to be on Philadelphia, Putnam could spare at least two Brigades to reenforce the defending Army. These troops should be moved immediately to the west side of the Hudson and held there [31] until the situation developed.

With these dispositions in prospect, Washington moved southward the larger part of his Army.[32] On the 27th of July, as he was approaching Flemington, eleven miles only from the nearest crossing of the Delaware, he received word that seventy sail of the British fleet had been sighted the previous day off Egg Harbor, a place not much more than thirty miles from the northern cape at the mouth of the Delaware. Washington felt it was more probable than ever that the destination of Howe was Philadelphia,[33] but he was not quite convinced. "Howe's in a manner abandoning General Burgoyne," he said, "is so unaccount-

[27] Letter of July 18, 1777; *ibid.*, 434.
[28] *Ibid.*, 488; Washington to Theodorick Bland, July 24, 1777; 52 *Papers of G. W.*, p. 22, LC (not in *G. W.*).
[29] Cf. 8 *G. W.*, 477, 478, 496. Washington's dispositions during the last week of July have to be pieced together from surviving orders to separate units. He did not put in writing any general plan of locating his troops strategically.
[30] Compare 8 *G. W.*, 497, with *ibid.*, 492.
[31] *Ibid.*, 484, 488. The diarist William Smith, entry of July 17, 1777, was of opinion that Washington had been outgeneraled and was on the wane. Smith's Diary, which is in *NYPL*, is a confusing and difficult MS to handle, but it is informative on operations along the Hudson and is worth studying by anyone who writes in detail of the campaigns in that area. A most interesting review is that of Samuel H. Parsons in a letter to Washington, July 30, 1777; *Hall's Parsons*, 106–07.
[32] His halts may be followed from the headings of his letters of July 24–28, in 8 *G. W.*, 464–86.
[33] 8 *G. W.*, 491. Cf. A. Hamilton to Gouverneur Morris, July 22, 1777: "I cannot conceive upon what principle of common sense or military propriety Howe can be running away from Burgoyne to the southward" (9 *A. Hamilton*, 90).

able a matter that till I am fully assured it is so, I cannot help casting my eyes continually behind me." [34] In that spirit he directed Putnam to make ready the two Brigades that were to be detached from the Highlands command,[35] and he remained confident his men would have time to take position around Philadelphia after the enemy reached the capes and was ascending the river and arranging to land.[36] Greene's Division was at Coryell's Ferry,[37] where it had arrived on the evening of the 28th; Stephen had his own and Lincoln's Division [38] at Howell's Ferry, four miles upstream from Coryell's; [39] Sullivan, some of whose men had been accused of plundering and horse-stealing,[40] was in the vicinity of Morristown.[41]

At 9:30 on the morning of July 31, an express from the President of Congress reached Washington with important news: The British fleet had appeared off the capes of Delaware Bay on the 30th,[42] and presumably was making ready to enter. In response, it was an easy matter to start a movement that had been anticipated. Orders were prepared and circulated; [43] instructions were sent Sullivan to march for Philadelphia by the shortest route; [44] Washington hoped his leading Division would reach the city, or at least camp close to it, on the evening of the 1st of August.[45] He would have been justified in feeling some pride over the ease with which he saw his orders executed and his little Army put in motion, while he hurried on in advance with his staff toward Philadelphia.

His first task, after his arrival,[46] was to ride through the environs of

---

[34] Letter of July 30, 1777, to Horatio Gates, 8 *G. W.*, 499.

[35] *Ibid.*, 491 and *supra*, n. 31. [36] 8 *G. W.*, 492–93.

[37] For this ferry and Washington's temporary headquarters there, see *NJHSP.*, new ser. v. 11, p. 160 ff. A most interesting brief history is Alfred G. Petrie, *Lambertville, New Jersey, from the Beginning as Coryell's Ferry.* The crossing was a "base point" in the reckoning of marches. In *Gates Papers*, NYHS, Oct. 30, 1777, is a table of distances from "General Washington's Camp at the 15-mile stone to Coryell's Ferry" and thence, stage by stage, to Albany. The distance from the ferry to Albany was reckoned at 220 miles.

[38] Lincoln had been ordered on the 24th to join Schuyler and to take command of the militia from the Eastern States (8 *G. W.*, 462–63. Cf. *ibid.*, 446, 459).

[39] *Ibid.*, 501–02. [40] 8 *G. W.*, 469.

[41] He had been directed, July 29, to halt at Morristown, "or upon good ground near the place where this shall meet you . . ." (8 *G. W.*, 497). On the 31st, Washington apparently did not know exactly where Sullivan was encamped (see *ibid.*, 504). One of the best statements of the position of the troops, as of July 29, is in Clement Biddle to James Wilson, *Cadwalader Papers*, PHS. [42] 8 *G. W.*, 505.

[43] *Ibid.*, 503. [44] *Ibid.*, 504.

[45] *Ibid.*, 504, 508. Washington decided, after reaching Philadelphia, "that if troops enter this city it will only tend to debauch them," and he consequently ordered them to proceed to Germantown (Tench Tilghman to Daniel Morgan, Aug. 1, 1777; 53 *Papers of G. W.*, 123, LC).

[46] He reached Philadelphia about 10 P.M. on the 31st of July. Pickering's Journal in 1 *Pickering*, 148.

the city in order to ascertain where the troops could be placed for the best strategic defence and, if compatible with that, for their comfort and convenience. Washington was at Chester on this mission and had settled himself for the night of August 1 when up from Cape May rode an express who was not a courier of calamity but a teller of riddles: The British fleet that had been riding off the entrance to Delaware Bay had sailed off at 8 A.M. on the 31st, had steered East, and had passed beyond the horizon three hours before the express left.[47] In the orders Washington soon began to draft, he spoke of this intelligence as "provoking" [48] but he might with equal candor have termed it mystifying also. Two hundred and twenty-eight sail had been counted off the capes [49]— manifestly the entire fleet. If its objective had not been Philadelphia, why had it entered those waters; and if Howe had designed to attack the city, what had deterred him? The feeble forts and the incomplete obstructions? Could he be engaged in some maneuver that would bring him back before many hours? Was the voyage to the mouth of the Delaware a feint to draw the continental Army to that region? Had the British slipped away to land in New England or to ascend North River while the American column toiled through New Jersey again? His men, Washington confessed, had "been more harassed by marching and counter-marching than by anything that had happened to them in the course of the campaign." [50] Was this now to be renewed, until the troops, as well as their shoes, were worn out? Young Henry Knox was not so philosophical when he wrote his wife: "The enemy have maneuvered us to this place [Philadelphia] and after all, left us in the lurch. They appeared within the capes—came to anchor, put out their buoys or guides and after all gave us the slip the very day that we came down here." [51]

Until something more was ascertained concerning the strange move-

---

[47] 9 G. W., 4, 5.　　　　[48] Ibid., 5.　　　　[49] Ibid., 15.

[50] Letter of Aug. 5, 1777 to his brother "Jack" (9 G. W., 20). Substantially the same statement of like date to John Tayloe will be found in 37 ibid., 540. Capt. John Chilton of the Third Virginia was with his men throughout these gruelling weeks and, in summarizing for his brother the dreary details, remarked, "We have made a complete tour of the Jerseys" (Letter of Aug. 17, 1777; 12 T 129).

[51] Letter of Aug. 2, 1777; Knox Papers, MHS. Equally interesting is a letter of July 30 (loc. cit.), in which he confessed "I own freely that I thought the campaign would have been pretty nearly decisive of Great Britain's interest but the affair at the northward may render it otherwise." See the similarly disgusted expressions of Joseph Trumbull (letter to his father, Aug. 3, 1777; Joseph Trumbull Papers, MHS Col. Official Papers, v. 7, pt. 1, p. 6 a, Conn. State Lib.), of S. H. Parsons (letter of Aug 4, 1777 to Thomas Munford, Pierpont Morgan Lib., Generals of Rev., 92), and of Walter Stewart (letter of Aug. 13, 1777 to Gates; Gates Papers, NYHS).

ments of the unpredictable Howes,[52] military common sense directed that Washington start his troops back to the middle ground of the Delaware Valley above Trenton, and that Sullivan and two Brigades that had been summoned from Putnam's Army proceed to Peekskill. Orders were issued accordingly and at once.[53] Two days later, reports came from Cape May that the enemy's fleet had been sighted again and might be tacking to reenter Delaware Bay. Washington was confused, of course, by these sudden changes and was frank to admit it. "They keep our imaginations constantly in the field of conjecture," he wrote and added: ". . . I wish we could but fix on their object. Their conduct really is so mysterious that you cannot reason upon it so as to form any certain conclusion." [54]

Enigma off Cape May, following disaster at Ticonderoga, had on him the usual effect of long-continued adversity: It aroused his deeper determination, one component of which was dogged cheer. "I trust," he wrote Governor Trumbull, ". . . though matters do appear somewhat gloomy at present, that a steady perseverance and our spirited exertions, will put things right again." [55] He remained in Philadelphia until the 5th and, in spite of military duties, found time to attend at least one dinner. It was an interesting affair because of the presence of a young Frenchman, not yet 20, to whom Congress on the 31st of July had voted the rank of Major General,[56] though with the implied understanding that the commission was to be honorary and without compensation. The resolve of Congress stated that this high distinction was given him because of "zeal, illustrious family and connections"; but as Washington had been taxed to find some accommodation between ambitious foreigners of excessive rank and American officers jealous of their high position in the Army, the Commander-in-Chief could have been pardoned some misgiving when the young man was introduced as Major General, the Marquis de Lafayette.[57]

---

[52] The explanation of the changed British strategy, as set forth in Howe to Clinton, July 30, 1777, *Clinton Papers*, Clements Lib., will be found *infra*, p. 460, n. 135.

[53] 9 *G. W.*, 2–6.

[54] Letter of Aug. 4, 1777, to John Langdon; 9 *G. W.*, 18, cf. *ibid.*, 15. As it chanced, nothing more was heard this time of the reappearance of the fleet. If it actually had been seen, as reported, it disappeared again. Residents of towns occupied by the British were as much puzzled as American leaders were by these maneuvers. See E. G. Schaukirk's diary, Aug. 31, 1777; 10 *Penn. Mag.*, 424: ". . . people begin to speak loudly that commanders don't do what they might, and seem to protract rather than make an end of these calamities." As was remarked in n. 5 of Chapter VIII, *Schaukirk* usually was spelled *Shewkirk* in records of the New York Moravian congregation.

[55] Letter of Aug. 4, 1777; 9 *G. W.*, 16.   [56] 8 *JCC.*, 592–93.

It was apparent immediately that this volunteer was not the impover-
ished, grasping seeker after honors that had tried the soul of Congress.
Lafayette appeared to be modest, tactful, admiring and not at all inclined to tell the Americans how to manage their affairs. If he was
ambitious, he was patient, also. He made a deliberate effort to win
immediately the goodwill of Washington and he showed so much social
skill in this that Washington invited him to visit the camp, and took the
enthusiastic young soldier with a party that made a careful examination
of the existing and proposed water defences of Philadelphia.[58] It did
not seem as if those defences would be tested in the near future because,
by the 7th, Washington was convinced that the British either were proceeding around Long Island to get into the Sound and to attack on that
coast, or were preparing a descent farther eastward,[59] and he started the
Army by slow and easy marches for Coryell's Ferry on the upper
Delaware.[60]

On the evening of August 10, intelligence reports took on still another
cast: From Sinapuxent Inlet, vaguely described as "about sixteen leagues
to the southward of the Capes of Delaware" [61] a large fleet had been
sighted on the 7th, though there was no information concerning the
number of vessels or the course they were following.[62] If this report
were true, what could it possibly forecast? Washington was convinced
already that the British would not land on the coast of Carolina or
Georgia at the season of ague, and for that reason he was well nigh

[57] Charlemagne Tower consistently spelled the name LaFayette, but *DAB* and Louis Gottschalk in his edition of *The Letters of Lafayette* wrote the name as one word with a lower
case f. In an earlier book on the Marquis's coming to America, Gottschalk pointed out, p. 153,
that Lafayette signed his name in such a way as to make it indeterminable whether he wrote
f or F; but his immediate ancestors always used Lafayette.

[58] For the conclusions from this survey of the obstructions and forts of the lower Delaware,
see 9 *G. W.*, 46 ff. The story of the introduction of Lafayette rests upon 5 *Sparks*, 454. Sparks
cited no authority, nor did Lafayette's "Memoirs of Myself" contain any mention of the incident other than (v. 1, p. 18) the editor's inclusion of a translated paragraph of Sparks, *loc. cit.*
Unsatisfactory as is this evidence, the dates and circumstances accord with Sparks's statement.
The edition of Lafayette's *Memoirs* cited hereafter, unless otherwise stated, is that published in
New York, 1837.

[59] 9 *G. W.*, 34–35.

[60] *Ibid.*, 36, 37, 40, 42, 44, 46. The last of these references is to a letter in which Washington explained that in the proposed camp at Coryell's the Army "will be near enough to
succor Philadelphia should the enemy, contrary to appearances, still make that the object of their
next operations; and will be so much more conveniently situated to proceed to the northward,
should the event of the present ambiguous and perplexing situation of things call them that
way. I was the most inclined to this step as the nearness of the Army to the city, besides other
disadvantages, afforded a temptation both to officers and men, to indulge themselves in licenses
inconsistent with discipline and order consequently of a very injurious tendency."

[61] 9 *G. W.*, 55; cf. *ibid.*, 57, and Knox to Mrs. Knox, Aug. 12, 1777; *Knox Papers*, MHS.

[62] 9 *G. W.*, 45, 55.

bewildered by the new information. Joint action by Burgoyne and Howe appeared to Washington to be, in his own words, "so probable and of such importance" that he would, he said, "with difficulty give into a contrary belief" until the evidence demanded it.[63] Pending that, he could do nothing else than halt the Army at a convenient place and wait.[64]

His choice of a campsite was one of the main crossroads of Bucks County, close to the Neshaminy River, about twenty miles North of Philadelphia and an equal distance West of Trenton.[65] Dangerous as a long halt might prove, while the enemy was moving with little effort, a rest was much needed for the Army and no less for Washington who had to treat half-a-score, more or less, of administrative ills. It always was so. If he was not preparing the Army for a maneuver, or trying to restore it after a reverse, he was grappling with one part or another of his greatest and most complicated task, that of keeping the Army alive.

Some of his problems in August, 1777, had been a torture from the time he had assumed command; others represented friction or weakness that had developed while the Army was on the march. The new organization of the commissary was ill. After a succession of shortages, when much confusion had been brought to light,[66] a committee of Congress had visited Washington [67] and had received a shocking statement of the wretched incompetence of some of the agents entrusted with the supply of the Army. "Our soldiers . . . ," said Washington, "have scarcely tasted any kind of vegetables, had but little salt" and did not receive sufficient vinegar, drink, or soap.[68] As many similar complaints of neglect and mismanagement had been made, Congress advertised for bids on the required small items of the ration [69] and adopted the greater part of the suggestions made somewhat tardily [70] by the committee that

[63] Letter of Aug. 11, 1777, to Artemas Ward, 9 G. W., 57–58.
[64] Ibid., 37, 38, 45. Cf. Henry Knox's proposal to Washington, Aug. 20, 1777, of an offensive against Burgoyne. See, also, a wise letter of Nathanael Greene's, Aug. 11, 1777; 1 Greene's Greene, 430. British intelligence reports of Aug. 6–10 in the Clinton Papers, Clements Lib., covering these operations, are quite full and approximately accurate. See William Shireff, Aug. 6 and 9, Skinner, Aug. 10 and 17, 1777.
[65] At the present-day Hartsville, Penn. (9 G. W., 56 n). Washington, his aides and his secretaries used no less than eight different names or phrases, with minor variants, from day to day, in giving the location (ibid., 45 ff). For a description of his headquarters in a stone dwelling "on the old York Road to Warwick Township, about twenty miles north of Philadelphia," see W. J. Buckin, 1 Penn. Mag., 275.
[66] 8 G. W., 373; 1 LTW., 319; 8 JCC., 504, 515, 524.
[67] It was chosen July 11. See 8 JCC., 546; 8 G. W., 415.
[68] 8 G. W., 441.   [69] Including "sour crout," 8 JCC., 580.
[70] Aug. 5, 1777; ibid., 609 ff.

had been to headquarters. Meantime, Joseph Trumbull had asked to
be released from the duties he was discharging unwillingly as Commissary General of Purchases.[71] He was relieved, and William Buchanan
was named Commissary General of Purchases.[72]

Clothing was another subject of inquiry by the committee of Congress. In humiliating contrast to their adversaries,[73] the men of the
American Army had been in tatters at the opening of spring.[74] Little
enough had been collected from civilians for the use of the troops,[75] but
the worst conditions had been those arising from the shortage of new
garments of almost every sort and from the seizure by the States or by
department commanders of uniforms and clothing intended for the
main Army.[76] In addition, there had been a mysterious shortage of
clothing for Massachusetts troops, who were supposed to be well clad.[77]
Suspicion had been raised that some officers were making requisition
both for the troops they had and for those they hoped to enlist.[78] Congress held, in theory, if not in application, to the principle that the men
were entitled to all the articles set forth in the original resolution on
clothing, even though the cost exceeded the twenty dollars originally

[71] *Ibid.*, 598. Some maneuvering followed in a vain effort by some of Trumbull's friends
to procure larger allowances for the commissaries (*ibid.*, 603). A motion to request Trumbull
and his deputies to prolong their service was defeated. So was one to authorize Washington
to discharge officers of the commissary (*ibid.*, 620). A small increase in the pay of these agents
was allowed (*ibid.*, 621). Trumbull agreed to remain in service until August 20, and when he
won dismissal then, he wrote his father: "I wish I could say I quit without fears for my
country and its cause therefrom but let the consequences be as they may, my duty and my
honor require that I should act the part I have . . . but I am sorry to see the department go
into the hands of men who never took an active part in the cause till now . . ." (Letters of
Aug. 3 *et post*, 1777, as cited *supra*, n. 51). The retiring Commissary General expected to be
compelled to spend most of the winter in getting his accounts in proper form for final settlement (Joseph Trumbull to Horatio Gates, Sept. 1, 1777, *Letters to Gates*, NYHS). The final
papers of *"Joseph Trumbull in account with the United States"* are in the files of CHS.
[72] Aug. 5, 1777; 8 *JCC.*, 607. For the resignation of various deputy commissaries and the
belated declination of one of those chosen in the Spring, see 8 *JCC.*, 601, 617, 627, 640, 744,
and Robert White to Congress, Sept. 15, 1777; 78 *Papers Cont. Cong.*, XXIII, p. 421. Several
officers entrusted with other tasks sent in their resignations at this time. Cf. as typical, *ibid.*,
583, 586. Regulation of the office of Superintendent of Bakers is outlined in *ibid.*, 639. Salt-
making from sea water was undertaken more widely during the summer (*Adams, Fam. Let.*,
301).
[73] For example, British GOs of the spring of 1777 had provided that when the Guards took
the field, Captains were to see to it that each soldier was supplied with two shirts, two pairs
of stockings, two pairs of shoes and a pair of soles and heels (Glyn's Journal, *loc. cit.*, entry
of Apr. 26, 1777).
[74] 7 *G. W.*, 421; 1 *Wilkinson*, 162.   [75] Cf. 2 *Burnett*, 221.
[76] 7 *G. W.*, 13, 64; 8 *ibid.*, 223, 472–73; 1 *Sullivan Papers*, 414. Many interesting and odd
occurrences are recorded in papers relating to clothing. See 1 *Wilkinson*, 162, for references
to shirts so poor in quality that the soldiers would not wear them. Washington's rebuke of
alleged reservation of scarce goods for officers will be found in 8 *G. W.*, 33. The troubles
apprehended from the manufacture of red uniforms and Washington's insistence that some of
these be dyed another color may be followed in *ibid.*, 55, 98.
[77] *Ibid.*, 95, 205–206, 207–208.   [78] *Ibid.*, 196–97.

promised.[79] Clothier General James Mease, whom Washington had continued in office,[80] apparently gave the fullest effort to the discharge of his duties.[81] The continuing demand simply was beyond the resources of a country that had a limited number of journeymen tailors and no organization for employing all those. In July Washington stated this to the committee and at the same time explained the place that decent clothing had in the health, cleanliness and self-respect of the soldier.[82]

The committee, agreeing heartily, included in its report several recommendations for ascertaining what clothing the Army would need during the winter. This was to be imported or was to be provided by each State for its own men at continental cost.[83] Needless to say, this arrangement disregarded the tightening of the British blockade,[84] the frequent inability of the Board of Treasury to provide even the depreciated continental currency,[85] and the general carelessness that seemed to be spreading to other bureaus from the loosely managed and often neglected office of the Quartermaster General. Early in the year, Washing had called on Mifflin to prepare the tents, implements and vehicles required for the campaign.[86] The spirit in which Mifflin carried out his instructions probably was exemplified in a letter to a dealer from one of the representatives of that officer: "Brigadier General Mifflin gave me an order to employ some proper person here to get him 5000 tents for the Army next spring . . . I should be obliged to you to endeavor to

[79] *JCC.*, 426. Cf. John Taylor to Edmund Pendleton, Apr. 13, 1777, *supra*, p. 414.
[80] 7 *G. W.*, 247. For his accounts see 7 *JCC.*, 221.
[81] 8 *G. W.*, 441.
[82] His words are worth quoting in full for the admonition of lawmakers who not unnaturally complain of the high cost of an Army's clothing: "It is a maxim which needs no illustration that nothing can be of more importance in an Army than the clothing and feeding it well; on these the health, comfort and spirits of soldiers essentially depend, and it is a melancholy fact that the American Army are miserably defective in both these respects. The distress most of them are in, for want of clothing, is painful to humanity, dispiriting to themselves, and discouraging to every officer. It makes every pretension to the preservation of cleanliness impossible, exposes them to a variety of disorders, and abates or destroys that military pride without which nothing can be expected from an Army" (Letter of July 19, 1777; 8 *G. W.*, 442, with considerable repunctuation).
[83] 8 *JCC.*, 611–12.
[84] Lord Howe's dispatch of Mch. 31, 1777, in *London Gazette*, May 6–10, 1777; *London Chronicle*, May 10, 1777, admirably illustrated the growing success of the British in capturing American merchantmen. See also Henry Laurens to John Rutledge, Sept. 10, 1777, 2 *Burnett*, 491. Laurens maintained that the sudden rise in prices was not due solely to the large issue of paper money. A more important factor, he thought, was the stoppage of imports. While he did not so state, this was of course the result, in some degree, of the blockade.
[85] A typical instance on a small scale is represented by Uriah Forrest, Major of the Third Maryland, to Charles Carroll, May 6, 1777, in 78 *Papers Cont. Cong.*, IX, p. 83, LC.
[86] Letter of Jan. 31, 1777; 7 *G. W.*, 83.

get the cloth proper for tents and get them well made into tents, each
to hold six men, and a proportion of marquees and send them on to
General Mifflin or order as soon as possible and draw on him for payment as you shall think proper" [87]—about as improper a method of
contracting as could have been devised.

Almost as vexatious as any of this to Washington, though by no
means so serious in its possible consequences, was a problem represented
by two words that had made some Americans flush with anger whenever they were uttered—"Foreign Officers." Washington's suggested
alternative solutions of dating back his own Generals' commissions, or
organizing a separate French artillery corps [88] had been complicated
by violent rivalries between du Coudray and French engineers who had
been employed by Deane in accordance with the instructions drafted by
the Committee of Correspondence, Dec. 2, 1775.[89] Three of these engineers, formally engaged Feb. 15, 1777,[90] had arrived in Philadelphia
during the last week of June and had let it be known at once that they
would not take orders from du Coudray.[91]

Perhaps with foreboding, while this dispute of the Frenchmen still
was in its first stage, Congress on the 8th of July commissioned the
senior French engineer, Louis le Bèque Duportail, a Colonel and gave
his two subordinates, Bailleul la Radière and Obry Gouvion, the agreed
rank of Lieutenant Colonel and Major respectively.[92] Two weeks later,
Congress settled some of the rivalries by voting that Duportail should
"take rank and command of all engineers previously appointed." [93]
Washington was disturbed, in some measure, by the prospect that
Duportail and du Coudray would clash again; but he was alarmed
deeply by the knowledge that Greene, Sullivan and Knox were angered
and humiliated by the thought that du Coudray would have seniority
over them. Knox, in particular, was wrathfully and recklessly outraged
by what he considered an inexcusable slight.[94] It would be proper,

---

[87] Unsigned letter in Henry Knox's autograph to Abraham Livingston, Mch. 1, 1777; *Knox Papers*, MHS, with some repunctuation.   [88] See *supra*, p. 423.

[89] See *supra*, p. 420.   [90] See their contract in 2 *Wharton*, 269.

[91] See Samuel Adams to Richard Henry Lee, June 26, 1777; 2 *Burnett*, 389, with a full note on the circumstances of the engagement, voyage, arrival and journey of the three engineers. See also 7 *JCC.*, 347–49; 8 *ibid.*, 532, 539. A fourth officer, J. B. J. Laumoy, did not land until the early autumn. The fullest contemporary account of the status of these engineers is that of James Lovell in 2 *Burnett*, 417; another text is in 1 *LTW.*, 408.

[92] 8 *JCC.*, 539. Congress declined the application of these engineers for compensation in excess of that stipulated in their contract with Deane (*ibid.*, 538, 539, 639).

[93] *Ibid.*, 571.

[94] 8 *G. W.*, 148–49, 159; Mrs. Henry Knox to her husband, May 30, 1777; *Knox Papers*, MHS.

Washington said—now as always in a practical spirit of adjustment—to make an agreement with du Coudray, but this should be so drawn that the American Generals would not resign.[95] As it chanced, du Coudray aroused the ready enthusiasm of John Adams[96] and the sharp-edged hostility of James Lovell, one of the few members of Congress, if not the only one in Franklin's absence, who could tell the Frenchmen in their own language precisely how shameful he thought their bargain was.[97] "The city," said William Williams, "swarms with Frenchmen"[98] and he would have been accurate had he reported that Congress buzzed with debate over them. On the 1st of July,[99] Greene, Sullivan and Knox addressed individual letters to the President of Congress to the same effect. Sullivan's read in this wise:

Camp at Middle Brook, July 1st, 1777
Dear Sir: I am informed that Monsieur du Coudray has lately been appointed by Congress a Major General of artillery with order that his rank shall take place from the first day of August last. If this report be true I shall be under the disagreeable necessity of quitting the service. I therefore beg the favor of a line from you informing whether the report has any foundation and if it has that you would please to enclose me a permit to retire.[100]

Washington may not have seen these letters until he received copies of them, about July 10, from the President of Congress. In transmitting the papers, Hancock told the Commander-in-Chief that the contents of the communications were "highly derogatory to the honor and justice of Congress" and "could not fail to be extremely displeasing."[101] Hancock wrote this as cover for an angry resolve the Delegates had passed July 7, whereby Washington was directed to let the three Generals know that Congress regarded their letters as "an attempt to influence its decision." The conditional resignations were accounted an "invasion of the liberties of the people" and indicated "a want of confidence in

95 *Ibid.*, 162. 96 2 *Burnett*, 386.
97 See *ibid.*, 394. 98 *Ibid.*, 400.
99 See *supra*, p. 437.
100 1 *Sullivan Papers*, 403, with some repunctuation and revision of capitalized letters. For Greene's letter, similar in purport but different in wording, see 1 *Greene's Greene*, 420. The original is in 151 *Papers Cont. Cong.*, I, p. 35, LC. On the satisfaction of Greene in his relations with Washington, see 1 *Greene's Greene*, 311, 458. The text of Knox's letter of resignation, which does not appear to have been printed, is in 155 *Papers Cont. Cong.*, I, p. 35, LC. A copy is among the *Knox Papers*, MHS.
101 Letter of July 8, 1777; 50 *Papers of G. W.*, 111, LC.

the justice of Congress." Suitable "acknowledgment" was expected by Congress "for an interference of so dangerous a tendency." If, finally, the officers were "unwilling to serve their country under the authority of Congress, they shall be at liberty to resign their commissions and retire." [102]

This letter of Hancock's had come to Washington when General and Army and country were stunned by the news of the evacuation of Ticonderoga. An irresolute man, a coward or even a strong leader of gloomy nature would have counted his calamities and perhaps would have despaired. The Army ill fed, some troops unable to serve in the field because of their nakedness,[103] Howe enjoying all the advantage of potential surprise that seapower gave him, Burgoyne past the great barrier at the head of Lake George, the sixteen new American Regiments not yet recruited to authorized strength, the continental currency steadily losing its value, desertion still frequent, that strange "languor" paralyzing the people,[104] divergent and sometimes reckless practices by the States in the choice of officers,[105] disaffection rearing its ugly head— to all these burdens and perplexities now was added this vehement rebuke of three of Washington's best officers, because they protested against the supposed grant of seniority to a French soldier who had not marched a mile in America or faced even one bullet in the battle for independence!

Washington acknowledged Hancock's letter, stated that he had transmitted the resolves of Congress to Greene, Knox and Sullivan—and, for the moment, said, no more,[106] but he immediately had to admonish du Coudray, as tactfully as possible, not to interfere with the artillery until Congress had determined who was to have authority over it.[107] The Delegates, almost as much embarrassed as Washington himself, at length voted to tell du Coudray that Deane had exceeded his commission in signing the agreement but that a committee was willing to

---

102 8 *JCC.*, 537. See also *ibid.*, 527, 531, 535. The outraged sensibilities of Congress are described in 2 *Burnett*, 403, 404, 405–06, 408.

103 Cf. Washington to Putnam, June 17, 1777: "If the troops can possibly be clothed, so that they can do duty, send them on . . ." (8 *G. W.*, 258).

104 "We now feel sensibly the fatal consequences arising from the deficiency in our Regiments, and that languor which has but too generally prevailed throughout the States." Washington to Governor Trumbull, Aug. 4, 1777 (9 *G. W.*, 16).

105 Cf. *ibid.*, 95.

106 8 *G. W.*, 387. Greene's "acknowledgment" of the resolves was, in reality, a justification of his action. See 1 *Greene's Greene*, 420. Apparently, neither Sullivan nor Knox made any formal answer to Congress.

107 Letter of July 13, 1777; 8 G. W., 399.

make proper compensation.[108] In these negotiations, du Coudray had a sharp exchange with James Lovell and then lost both his temper and his opportunity by memorializing Congress to dismiss Lovell from the committee that was acting for the larger body.[109]

In spite of this interference, Congress finally decided to give du Coudray staff, instead of line appointment, at the promised rank of Major General, and to make him Inspector General of Ordnance and Military Manufactories.[110] Allowances and expenses of travel were voted liberally,[111] in a compromise that proved acceptable to Greene, to Sullivan, and to Knox, the officer most directly concerned. Washington felt much relief, but he feared he would have to reconcile himself to the fortification of one bank of the Delaware near Philadelphia by du Coudray,[112] and of the other bank by Duportail, between whom unconcealed jealousy persisted.[113] Congress had among its correspondents another foreign officer, Brig. Gen. la Rochefermoy, usually styled General Fermoy, whom some of the members doubtless regarded as a nuisance. Horatio Gates had turned him back to Congress, with the statement that no brigade command was available to him,[114] after which occurrence Fermoy wrote directly to the President, as if he had a relationship different from that of other general officers. As Fermoy now was preparing to ask for a larger command,[115] the Delegates doubtless had a fellow-feeling when Washington remarked painfully that he was "exceedingly embarrassed how to dispose of the French officers." [116]

It was not altogether that way. Washington already had good opinion of one or two of the younger Frenchmen who had come to America,[117] and now, while he was waiting near Neshaminy River for news of Howe's movements, he welcomed to headquarters the young Marquis

---

[108] 8 JCC., 553, 554.

[109] The letter from du Coudray to Lovell, July 28, and Lovell's brief and brusque reply of the 29th are included in du Coudray's "memorial" of Aug. 5, 1777, which is in 41 Papers Cont. Cong., II, p. 19, LC. See also 8 JCC., 615; 2 Burnett, 444. Somewhat surprisingly, four States voted against a motion to reject the French officer's memorial. Lovell himself was unpopular; a considerable minority still thought it was desirable to placate du Coudray and, through him, the country whence he had come.

[110] This was voted Aug. 11, 1777; 8 JCC., 630.   [111] Ibid., 571, 606, 705.

[112] For du Coudray's report on the condition of the defences, see 24 Penn. Mag., 343.

[113] 8 G. W., 496–97.

[114] Gates to Hancock, Apr. 14, 1777; 78 Papers Cont. Cong., IX, p. 141, LC.

[115] "Had I the command of 4000 men under either General Washington or General Gates, it would be very acceptable to me as it would then be in my power to testify my love of this country by my works" (Fermoy to Hancock, Aug. 10, 1777; ibid., 113).

[116] Letter of July 19, 1777, to Committee of Congress; 8 G. W., 444.

[117] For example, Charles Tuffin Armand, Marquis de la Roueire. See ibid., 90–91, 224–25. The name was given by David M. Matteson, that invaluable indexer, as Armand-Tuffin.

of whom he had formed a favorable opinion in Philadelphia. Lafayette
had purchased horses, equipment, uniforms and all the "necessaries" of
a soldier's life in the field, and he doubtless appeared in shining contrast
to most of the members of Washington's staff. "It is somewhat embarrassing," said the General, "to show ourselves to an officer who has just
come from the French Army." Lafayette's answer was instant: "C'est
pour apprendre et non pour enseigner que je suis ici." [118] That was
the spirit of everything Lafayette did: he had come to learn, not to teach;
but it soon was apparent that he wished to share and not merely to
observe the Army's hardships, marches and battles. Washington had
to inquire of Benjamin Harrison whether he correctly had understood
Congressmen to say that Lafayette's commission was nominal only and
did not cover, even prospectively, the direction of troops at the rank
voted him. ". . . certain it is," Washington said, "if I understand *him*,
that he does not conceive his commission is merely honorary, but given
with a view to command a Division of this Army." Washington explained: "he has said that he is young and inexperienced, but at the
same time he has always accompanied it with a hint that so soon as *I*
shall think him fit for the command of a Division, he shall be ready to
enter upon the duties of it, and, in the meantime has offered his service
for a smaller command." [119] Harrison replied immediately that Congress had thought Lafayette's "chief motive in going into our service
was to be near you, to see service, and to give him an eclat at home,
where he expected he would soon return." The young Frenchman,
said Harrison, "could not have obtained the commission on any other
terms." [120]

That clarified the record but it did not dispose of Lafayette or stifle his
martial ambition. Nor was there any certainty concerning what Congress would feel itself compelled to do with an older, personable gentleman who had a knowledge of English and some physical resemblance
to the American Commander-in-Chief. [121] Although a previous tender
of service had been declined, [122] Johann Kalb, who styled himself Baron
de Kalb, had come to Philadelphia with one of Deane's contracts and
was demanding the rank of Major General or else money with which

[118] 1 *Memoirs*, 19.
[119] Letter of Aug. 19, 1777; 9 *G. W.*, 95.
[120] Letter of Aug. 20, 1777; 2 *Burnett*, 458–59.
[121] James Lovell to William Whipple, Sept. 17, 1777; 1 *PHS Buls.*, 44.
[122] 7 *JCC.*, 185.

to return to France where he proposed to sue the American agent for breach of covenant.[123]

Serious as might be the results of such advancement of foreigners, Washington at the moment could give little time to an attempt to adjust rank, because the maddening doubt with respect to Howe's objective once again absorbed his hours and shaped his action. In the absence of all news of the fleet, Washington guessed that the British commander was bound for Charleston, South Carolina.[124] Perhaps the British intended to block the harbors in that region, to garrison the important coastal towns, and then to come North again.[125]

As it manifestly was impossible to move overland and to confront Howe at so great a distance, Washington and his council decided on the 21st of August that the continental troops should break camp in Bucks County and should march against Burgoyne.[126] Execution of this involved, of course, the exposure of Philadelphia to possible attack, for which reason Washington thought he should ask Congress' approval of his proposed move. Colonel Hamilton was hurried off to Philadelphia with a statement of Washington's plans and with an inquiry concerning the control of operations in event Washington entered the Northern Department which, said the Commander-in-Chief, "has been all along considered as separate and in some measure distinct." [127] Congress had few who were disposed to maintain that Washington should not have full direction of affairs in the Northern Department; but as that might start a debate that ran to long hours and to many a dull excursus, the Delegates were content, for the day, to endorse the plan and to affirm that "General Washington was to act as circumstances may require." [128]

Within a few hours, the prospect of a long northward advance was forgotten. On the 21st of August, a messenger arrived at headquarters with a letter from John Page, member of the Council of Virginia, who announced that a British fleet had appeared off the entrance to Chesapeake Bay, August 14, and that it seemed to be standing in.[129] Similar intelligence came from Congress, also, during the afternoon,[130] but as none of the informers stated that the British ships actually had passed the Virginia Capes, Washington ordered the Army to remain where it

---

[123] Kalb to Congress, Aug. 1, 1777; *Kapp's Kalb,* 114–16, 119.
[124] 9 *G. W.,* 102–03.
[125] This was James Lovell's solution. See 2 *Burnett,* 461.
[126] Council proceedings, 9 *G. W.,* 109–10 and n.
[127] *Ibid.,* 109. [128] 8 *JCC.,* 663.
[129] 9 *G. W.,* 106. [130] *Ibid.,* 111.

was.[131] He scarcely could credit the reports. Had Howe intended to sail into Chesapeake Bay, he certainly would have arrived there, Washington reasoned, within the time that had elapsed after the fleet had left the mouth of the Delaware. Surely, Charleston was the mark of Howe's advance.[132]

The next day's developments refuted this reasoning: Indisputable reports, reaching camp at sunset, showed Howe far up Chesapeake Bay, above Swan Point.[133] The British General evidently was putting into operation a variant of a plan that had been credited to him during the winter and early spring.[134] Instead of attempting to capture Philadelphia by marching overland from the North or by battering down the forts and demolishing the obstructions in the lower Delaware, the British were to land at the northern end of Chesapeake Bay and were to proceed northward about fifty-five miles, as the roads ran, to the city that probably had been their objective all the while.[135] American marching orders were reversed; Regiments that had been bound for the upper Delaware must turn about in the road and must concentrate at Chester.[136] General Putnam must convince New England States that Howe could do them no harm and that they should put every musket in line to destroy Burgoyne.[137]

Washington felt relief both because the mystery at last was resolved and also because the British debarkation would be far enough from Philadelphia for him to interpose his Army between the redcoats and

---

131 *Ibid.*, 115. Cf. Washington to Nash, Aug. 21, 1777; 54 *Papers of G. W.*, 71, LC.

132 Cf. 9 *G. W.*, 111, 112–13.

133 1 *Sullivan Papers*, 436; 9 *G. W.*, 115; 1 *LTW.*, 429; 2 *Burnett*, 464. Swan Point (Lat. 39° 08', Long. 76° 17') is on the Eastern Shore of Maryland, opposite the mouth of Patapsco River and close to the town of Rock Hall, Kent County.

134 7 *JCC.*, 128; 2 *Burnett*, 259; 7 *G. W.*, 339–42, 348, 353, 380. The last of these references is to a letter of Apr. 9, 1777, in which Washington stated his disbelief "that the enemy intend an expedition of any great consequence in Chesapeake Bay . . ." Col. Carl von Donop was critical of the entire strategy of Howe at this time. See his letter of Sept. 2, 1777, 62 *Penn Mag.*, 499.

135 9 *G. W.*, 115 ff. His avowed reason for approaching Philadelphia from the South was that this was easier than reducing the forts and destroying the obstructions of the Delaware. In addition, Howe seems to have had the idea, at the time, that he could gain vastly by severing Washington's communications with the South. On the 30th of July, he wrote Clinton from *Eagle*, at the mouth of the Delaware: "Having fully considered all circumstances, and from the information of Washington's march to the Delaware, I have determined to proceed immediately to the Chesapeake Bay, in order to land at the head of it. Had our passage hither been more successful, we might [blank in MS] have landed in the Delaware, in time to get between the Susquehannah and Mr. Washington's Army, which would not now be the least prospect of." This final clause probably means, "of which there would not now be the least prospect" (*Clinton Papers*, Clements Lib.). Howe's official explanation is in his *Narrative*, 23–25. Details of the dull voyage to the Chesapeake will be found in *Montresor Journals*, 429–42.

136 9 *G. W.*, 115 ff and 124.   137 *Ibid.*, 115.

their goal. The prospect was brightened, too, by fine news from the North, received that same 22nd of August. A strong detachment of British and German troops had proceeded from Burgoyne's main army

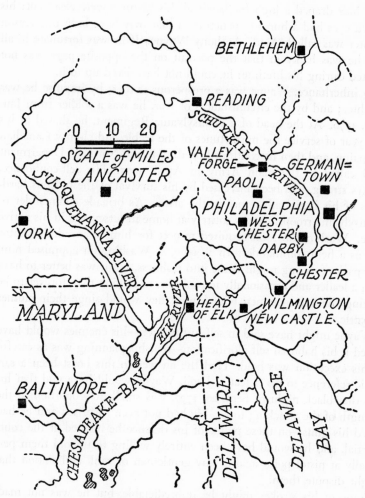

PHILADELPHIA VIA CHESAPEAKE BAY

Gen. Sir William Howe's unexpected choice of a line of advance in the late summer of 1777 was from Head of Elk, on the northernmost reach of Chesapeake Bay, to the Valley of the Schuylkill.

toward the village of Bennington, in the New Hampshire Grants, presumably to seize provisions and horses. The enemy had been met on the 16th by an American force of 2000, most of them militia, under

ANTHONY WAYNE, FIERY, NOT "MAD"

Anthony Wayne was a good soldier and a handsome gentleman. His dark hair draped a high forehead; all his features were clean cut; his brown eyes had a burning penetration that may have been one reason he later was called "Mad" Anthony Wayne. If he was fortunate in all this, he was lucky in that the portrait on the opposite page was not painted during his lifetime: he could not have lived up to it.

By inheritance, Wayne was a prosperous tanner; by impulse he was a fighter; and by the circumstances of war, he was a soldier from January, 1776. At the head of a Pennsylvania Regiment, he shared in his first year of service the misfortunes of the feeble and clumsy Canadian campaign, and then he continued on duty in the Northern Department until called to the main Army in April, 1777. His self-confidence, always strong, had been increased by his survival of the hideous hardships of his initial adventure in the army. As brigade commander of Pennsylvania troops, he was entirely at home in Jersey and in his native State. Washington soon acquired respect for him as an administrator and as a field commander. In Wayne, as Washington appraised him, the spark of daring might flame into rashness, but it was better to have such a leader and occasionally to cool him to caution than forever to be heating the valor of men who feared they would singe their plumes in battle.

Wayne might have said in self-justification—his enemies would have styled it his habitual self-glorification—that his planning was as careful as his execution was bold. Had the answer to this boast been a sarcastic reference to his defeat at Paoli, Wayne would have said that his loss that black night of Sept. 20, 1777, was small in proportion to the strength of the attacking force. He had not been surprised and he had saved his guns—on these points of his defence he insisted at the court martial, and he would have been entirely willing to uphold them personally at pistol point against any gentleman of rank and station that might dispute them.

Some of his strokes might be unpredictable, but he was not mad. "Fiery" was the word for him.

(After the portrait by Peter F. Rothermel, based on John Trumbull's study, in the gallery of The Historical Society of Pennsylvania.)

LAFAYETTE, WHO "CONQUERED" EASILY

A trick of history, a perverse trick, has denied Lafayette the place he deserves among the eminent men of his generation: Posterity has been more mindful of what he did not achieve in the French Revolution than of what he contributed to the success of the earlier Revolution in America. The disposition has been to regard his service in the United States as training for a rôle he did not play well in the great European upheaval of 1789–1815.

He deserves better estimation. In France, his great wealth and his shining marriage to an heiress of the de Noailles family had not compensated for an awkwardness that had provoked Marie Antoinette to laughter. Although he was the son of a Colonel of French Grenadiers, killed in the Battle of Minden, he himself was a garrison Captain in 1776 and had never heard a bullet whine in action. He came to America, moreover, when Washington and the Congress had been soured on all foreign soldiers by the importunate venality of some early volunteers whose self esteem was double par and their actual performance nil. Lafayette received so cold and casual a reception that he might have felt himself justified in walking from the door of Congress straight up the gangplank of the first vessel outward bound for his own country.

That was the 28th of July, 1777. Within three days, the Marquis was commissioned a Major General, though he was not then 20 years of age; in less than three months from the time of his landing in America, he had received a wound in battle; by Christmas, 1777, he was regarded by Washington with almost as much affection as the General could have shown a son of his own; when Lafayette seemed in danger of defeat and capture in an operation entrusted to his command in May, 1778, the whole Army was concerned for his safety.

Never during the Revolution was there so speedy and complete a conquest of the heart of Washington; never was the good will of jealously ambitious Generals, and the enthusiastic admiration of the younger officers bestowed in a measure so lavishly overflowing. The Marquis had aptitude for arms—all would admit that—but he had also, the rare quality of a personality that first disarmed and then captivated. How did he do it? History has no answer.

(After the original by C. W. Peale, Independence Hall, Philadelphia.)

John Stark, former Colonel of the Trenton campaign and now a Brigadier of New Hampshire. In confused fighting, the raiders had lost
thirty-two officers and staff and about 700 prisoners. British and Hessian
dead were reckoned at 200; American casualties were put at seventy or
eighty. Booty was considerable; included were four brass field pieces.
In General Orders, Washington announced this "signal victory" and
told the Army, "our troops behaved in a very brave and heroic
manner." [138]

While the soldiers were in the confident mood this news stimulated,
some of Washington's officers urged him to march his Brigades through
Philadelphia en route to Chesapeake Bay. They maintained that the
appearance of so many armed men might impress "Tory" sympathizers
and those who had been awed by reports of British superiority.[139] Washington agreed and, as his troops still lacked uniforms, he directed that
clothes be washed, that arms be burnished, and that every soldier's hat
be dressed with a "green sprig, emblem of hope." [140] Sunday morning,
August 24, had stern rain as its herald,[141] but by seven o'clock, the skies
relented, as if they would tolerate, though they would not give the sunshine of approval to the pageant.

The line of march was to be down Front Street and up Chestnut to
the Common. Each Brigade knew its place; all the wagons except a
few of those carrying ammunition were diverted by another road.
About a mile outside the town, the troops were halted and all the last-
minute adjustments were made. Then, at tap of drum, the Army
moved into the little Quaker City that providentially had become the
capital of this adventure in free government. Washington on his best
steed rode with his mounted aides near the head of the column.[142] A
proud subaltern led twelve members of the Light Horse. Behind them,

---

[138] The figures here given of casualties, prisoners, etc., are those sent Washington and by
him announced to the troops on the 22nd of August, 9 G. W., 122–23. Later totals were fourteen killed and forty-two wounded (Stark to Council of New Hampshire, Aug. 18, 1777; Gates
Papers, NYHS). Echoes of the subsequent controversy over Stark's relationship to the Continental Army may be heard in 2 Burnett, 463, 468. Washington's extreme care to be neutral in
the boundary dispute between Vermont and New York is shown in his letter of July 21, 1778,
to George Clinton, 12 G. W., 194.

[139] See Washington's letter of Aug. 23, 1777, to the President of Congress; 9 G. W., 127–28.

[140] See Chilton's Diary, 12 T 287; Lafayette's account is in 1 Memoirs, 20. Whitely in his
"Revolutionary Soldiers of Delaware" (Hist. and Biog. Papers of the Hist. Soc. of Delaware,
v. 2, p. 41) stated without citation of authority that this decoration of hats was suggested
in a "letter from a lady" not otherwise identified.

[141] Chilton's Diary, loc. cit.

[142] The order of march did not specify the position of the Commander-in-Chief. Cf. 9
G. W., 125–26.

at an interval of 200 yards, came an entire troop, and then the mounted Regiment of George Baylor and that of Theodorick Bland.

Precisely as if the Army were moving in a strange country, the cavalrymen who were to "find the road" were followed at a distance of 100 yards by a Company of pioneers, who had been told to see that their axes and other implements were in order. Another hundred yards of open space served to turn every spectator's eye down the street to Nathanael Greene and his staff, all mounted, behind whom came his first Brigade under Peter Muhlenberg. That Parson-General was said to have preached his final sermon to his congregation in a little Virginia town and then to have pushed back his gown and to have disclosed his uniform as he announced he was leaving to join General Washington. On the heels of the reverend Brigadier marched his leading Regiment, twelve abreast, and in their rear rumbled Muhlenberg's artillery, with the other Regiments in support, as it were, of their guns. Midway the Brigade were its massed drummers and fifers who had been enjoined to play "a tune for a quick step" but to do so, Washington had specified, "with such moderation that the men may step to it with ease, and without dancing along, or totally disregarding the music . . ."[143]

The other Brigades of Greene's Division followed—Weedon's, Woodford's and Scott's. Next in line were the men of Lincoln's Division and then those of Stirling's. To one of Stirling's Regiments was given the honor of guarding the rear, 150 yards behind the last of the Infantry. Similarly spaced were Sheldon's and Moylan's Horse. Not a woman was in the column.[144] If any soldier tried to slip out of ranks and into the throng on the sidewalk, he had notice in advance that he would be brought back and at the next halt would be given thirty-nine lashes.[145]

It was a gallant and, at the same time, a pathetic two-hour display[146] of what the troops were and were not.[147] John Adams wrote later in the day: "The Army . . . I find to be extremely well armed"—he exaggerated that—"pretty well clothed, and tolerably disciplined . . . Much remains yet to be done. Our soldiers have not yet quite the air

[143] GOs of Aug. 23, 1777; 9 G. W., 127.
[144] Washington had sought in GOs of Aug. 4, 1777, to reduce the "multitude of women, particularly those pregnant or having children with them" (9 G. W., 17).
[145] Ibid., 126.   [146] Adams, Fam. Let., 298.
[147] In leaving the town, the troops crossed the Schuylkill, on the floating bridge, marched down to the Darby Road and thence to Darby (Chilton's Diary, loc. cit.).

of soldiers. They don't step exactly in time. They don't hold up their heads quite erect, nor turn out their toes exactly as they ought. They don't all of them cock their hats; and such as do, don't all wear them the same way." [148] In the eyes of a Lieutenant who had been captured at Fort Washington, the men of the marching column "though indifferently dressed, held well burnished arms, and carried them like soldiers." [149]

Washington probably was satisfied with the showing his men made on their march through Philadelphia.[150] He believed in discipline as firmly as in the justice of his cause, but he knew that the real test went beyond the manner in which the soldiers turned out their toes and cocked their hats. America would survive or perish according to the willingness of all the people to contribute their effort through able leaders who would subordinate ambition and self-interest to winning their country's freedom. Now, as Washington marched southward to meet an advance from an unexpected quarter, he had more evidences of unsuccessful leadership than of unselfish spirit. John Sullivan had attempted to deliver a surprise attack on Staten Island, August 22—the very day that Washington had the good news of Stark's victory at Bennington—but the boatmen had failed or the plan had been defective in some particular not immediately observable to Washington. In withdrawing from the island, the Americans had lost perhaps 150 men and had a score wounded.[151]

Leadership had become involved almost simultaneously in another chapter of the rivalry between Gates and Schuyler. After Schuyler had been vindicated and restored to full command of the Northern Department,[152] Gates had spurred to Philadelphia and, on the 18th of June, had made his way to the floor of Congress on the plea that he had important information to give. He had proceeded then to defend himself and to assail all his critics, Delegates included, with a vehemence that brought members to their feet in angry demands that he withdraw.

---

[148] *Ibid.*   [149] *Graydon*, 291.

[150] Surprisingly little was written by members of Congress about this march. Articles in the newspapers were brief. Cf. 1 *Moore*, 486.

[151] The reserved comment of Washington, who awaited a full statement of the difficulties, will be found in 9 *G. W.*, 133–36. Sullivan's report is in 1 *Sullivan Papers*, 437 ff. The testimony and findings of the subsequent inquiry are in *ibid.*, 482 ff. Sullivan was exonerated. For newspaper accounts of the affair, see *N. J. Arc.*, ser. 2, v. 1, p. 461 ff and 1 *Moore*, 482 ff. See also 1 *Kemble*, 127 ff., with the report of Brig. Gen. Mungo Campbell. Cf. Benjamin Lincoln to Gates, Aug. 26, 1777; *Gates Papers*, NYHS.

[152] See *supra*, p. 416.

He shouted back furiously until at last his friends prevailed on him to leave the hall.[153] When Congress found the time and temper on July 8 for considering the proper employment of a man who manifestly had lost his head, it voted that he repair to headquarters "and follow the directions of General Washington."[154] The Commander-in-Chief decided, at length, that the best employment of a senior officer unwilling to resume his old duties of Adjutant General would be to assign him Lincoln's Division during the absence of that officer.[155]

Then came the evacuation of Ticonderoga which was blamed in part on Schuyler. Those Delegates who questioned his ability made common cause with those who felt he should be replaced because he did not have the good will of the New England militia. Gates's friends proclaimed anew his military excellencies.[156] The result of a long debate was a decision on August 1 to call Schuyler to headquarters and to direct Washington to name "such general officer as he shall think proper" in Schuyler's place [157]—a task from which the embarrassed friend of both men asked at once to be excused. For this request, he wrote, "many reasons might be mentioned, and which I am persuaded will occur to Congress upon reflection." He explained that the Northern Department always has been "considered as separate" and "more peculiarly" under the direction of Congress. "I have never interfered, further than merely to advise, and to give such aids as were in my power" on the requisition of the commanding officers.[158] Congress appreciated Washington's feelings and itself chose Gates as head of the Northern Department.[159] Washington forthwith issued the orders and wished his comrade success;[160] but the circumstances of this appointment were among the reasons why the Commander-in-Chief asked Congress on the 21st of August to define his responsibility for operations in the Department that included the upper Hudson and the adjacent Lakes.[161] The day after the march through Philadelphia, Washington was assured in a formal resolve "that Congress never intended by any commission heretofore granted by them, or by the

---

153 2 *Burnett*, 382–83, 384–85. The second of these references is to a particularly interesting letter from William Duer to Philip Schuyler.

154 8 *JCC.*, 540.　　　　　　　　　　155 8 *G. W.*, 491.

156 2 *Burnett*, 424 ff, 440, 465.

157 8 *JCC.*, 596; 2 *Burnett*, 441, 445, 465. For the judgment of Nathanael Greene on this, see 1 *Greene's Greene*, 435. John Adams's views were expressed in his letter of Aug. 11, 1777, to his wife. *Adams, Fam. Let.*, 289.

158 9 *G. W.*, 8–9.　　　　　　　　　159 8 *JCC.*, 604.

160 9 *G. W.*, 11–12.　　　　　　　161 See *supra*, p. 459, and 9 *G. W.*, 109.

establishment of any Department whatever to supersede or circum-
scribe the power of General Washington as Commander-in-Chief of
all the continental land forces within the United States." [162] This declaration might prove useful in any future controversy with Gates, who
had felt, at least once, that Washington had discriminated against the
Northern Department.[163] At the moment, the Gates-Schuyler controversy served to show how quickly Congress could change its mind [164]
and how desperate was the need of officers, sufficiently able and experienced to head even a small army.

It was because of this continuing shortage of skilled officers of brigade and divisional rank that Washington had particular satisfaction
in a report from Rhode Island in July. During the night of the 9th–
10th, a daring Lieutenant Colonel of state troops, William Barton, with
a party of forty men, had crossed waters commanded by British forts,
had gone ashore on Rhode Island, had seized Maj. Gen. Richard Prescott in his bed, and had carried that astonished officer and an aide into
the American lines.[165] The capture of General Prescott gave Washington a prisoner of Charles Lee's rank to offer for the strange man
snatched up by the British in December.[166] Lee would be an encum-

---

[162] 8 JCC., 668.

[163] This was with respect to the issue of tents. See 8 G. W., 87–88, and supra, p. 416, n. 89.

[164] Henry Laurens wrote, Sept. 9, 1777, that he had witnessed that day the submission of a
report by the Committee of the Whole, the entry of the item in the Journal and the supersession
of the entire proceeding by a new resolution without reference to the report. In another instance, said Laurens, who was a new member, a resolution was carried almost unanimously, was
entered, and half-an-hour later was reconsidered and expunged (2 Burnett, 482). "Congress,"
he wrote, "is not the respectable body I expected to have found . . . I have discovered parties
within parties . . ." (ibid., 476–77).

[165] See 8 Records of R. I., 290; 1 Mercy Warren, 380; 8 G. W., 415–16; 1 Moore, 467, with
an article from the Penn. Evening Post of Aug. 7, 1777. This narrative included the remarkable
statement that a brave Negro used his head, in a most literal sense, to break down the doors
of the General's quarters. In recording the major exploit, Captain Hall remarked (op. cit., 303)
that Colonel Barton was "by trade a hatter." The Captain did not make it plain whether he
regarded this as a slur or a compliment.

[166] Washington did his best to effect the exchange promptly but was unsuccessful (8 G. W.,
415–16, 417, 418–19, 422, 488–89; 8 JCC, 621) except in so far as discussion of this particular
exchange may have rendered negotiations for an inclusive cartel slightly less suspicious on both
sides. Congress authorized a general exchange on July 22, without regard to previous argument over men who died on the road (7 JCC., 371). Washington was given specific powers of
negotiation on the 12th of August (ibid., 621), but he could not reach accord until November
28 (10 G. W., 118–19) on an agreement which Congress proceeded to review critically because
of the distinction drawn between military and civilian prisoners (9 JCC., 1007, 1009–10,
1036). Before this could be settled, new differences arose over the medium to be employed
in purchases for the relief of prisoners (ibid., 1036–37). In all these transactions, Washington
was patient and was determined to show no favoritism (cf. the case of Baron de St. Ouary, a volunteer in British hands, whose exchange Washington was urged to seek out of the regular order,
9 JCC., 991; 10 G. W., 155. See also 9 ibid., 161). He was unwilling to raise any issue on
the basis of mistaken information (see 2 Burnett, 518–19, and Washington's answer in 9 G. W.,
382, compared with his vigorous pursuit of a valid complaint, as in 10 ibid., 64–65, 97),

brance rather than a valuable lieutenant, if he continued in the mood that had possessed him during the weeks that preceded his capture, but he might have been disciplined by his confinement.[167]

From the consideration of these tangled and troublesome duties of administering the affairs of his Army, Washington had now to turn again to operations. At the beginning of the last week in August, reports were that Howe soon would disembark at a place with the odd name, Head of Elk.[168] Thither Washington turned his horse in the belief that the enemy's objective was Philadelphia, though the route was "very strange." [169] The American Commander-in-Chief continued mindful of the imperative need of strengthening the water defences of Philadelphia,[170] and he did all he could to draw militia to him;[171] but he hurried on in person to Wilmington,[172] put his entire force on the alert,[173] reconnoitered with considerable risk and small success on the 26th,[174] and then moved up his Army[175] so that he could resist any effort Howe might make to clear the road to Philadelphia. Now, as

---

and was consistent in requiring that all routine exchanges be handled through the American commissioner, Elias Boudinot, while all large and basic questions of policy were referred to Congress (9 *ibid.*, 161, 482–83). Early in the labors of Boudinot, that devoted man reported that he could get no money for the relief of prisoners. The reply of Washington was to urge that Boudinot personally advance the funds; in the same breath the General offered to bear half of any loss Boudinot might sustain if Congress did not repay him (*Boudinot*, 10).

[167] For the discussion of Lee's imprisonment, exchange and personal affairs during 1777, and subsequent to the note *supra*, p. 380–81, see 7 *G. W.*, 154–55, 224, 343–44, 378; 8 *ibid.*, 337; 2 *Burnett*, 263, 264; 7 *JCC.*, 141, 207; 1 *Greene's Greene*, 337; 1 *LTW.*, 349–50; *Adams, Fam. Let.*, 256, and two letters not printed in *Lee Papers* but preserved in those of Sir Henry Clinton, *Clements Lib.*—Lee to Clinton, Aug. 22, 1777, Lee to Commodore William Hotham, later Admiral and first Baron Hotham. Both these concern small personal affairs of Lee. His main correspondence of this period is in 2 *Lee Papers*, 357 ff.

[168] Close to the present-day Elkton, Maryland, then the "head" of navigation on Elk River, the estuary of Chesapeake Bay that runs farthest to the Northeast, and stretches out as if it were seeking to reach Philadelphia, from which it is distant by air approximately forty miles.

[169] 9 *G. W.*, 115. The steps to this conclusion may be followed in Washington's letters of the 21st and 22nd.

[170] 8 *JCC.*, 630; 9 *G. W.*, 47–48, 57, 69, 128.

[171] *Ibid.*, 130 ff., 140–42, 142–43, 152, 174–75, 178. For some of the special difficulties encountered in Delaware, see *ibid.*, 202.

[172] Cf. 9 *G. W.*, 130 ff. George Forsyth's bill for the entertainment of Washington, the staff, servants and guests is in 55 *Papers of G. W.*, 13, LC.

[173] 9 *G. W.*, 139.

[174] *Ibid.*, 136–37; 1 Lafayette, *Memoirs*, 20, 21; 1 *Greene's Greene*, 443–44. He spent the night with Greene and Lafayette at a farmhouse where some of his admirers thought he might have been captured readily by a British raiding party of the sort that had taken Charles Lee. In a letter of Oct. 27, 1777, to Landon Carter, his long-time Virginia friend, Washington insisted he had not been "in the dangerous situation you have believed." He explained: "I was reconnoitring, but I had a strong party of Horse with me. I was (as I afterwards found) in a disaffected house . . . but I was equally guarded against friend and foe" (9 *G. W.*, 451–52). Fortunately for him, also, the day of the 26th and the night of the 26th–27th were rainy.

[175] The line of march was substantially that of the existing main line of the Pennsylvania Railroad from Chester to Iron Hill. The day-by-day camp sites are mentioned in Chilton's Diary, 12 *T* 287.

previously, Washington wished to avoid a general engagement unless the circumstances were particularly favorable. Fruitful as well as prudent strategy demanded, in his opinion, that he advance his most mobile forces, keep them close to the British, and harass the foe without exhausting his own men.[176] The main Army should remain perhaps as far as eight or ten miles from the enemy, but the American Light Horse and some of the small parties of Foot could drive off cattle and remove supplies and provisions from the reach of the enemy.[177]

In the southward movement the discipline of most of the Regiments had been good.[178] Now some of the troops under a French Colonel, Charles Armand-Tuffin, got so completely out of hand and plundered so defiantly that they had to be sent back to Wilmington.[179] Washington followed this with strict and repeated orders against unauthorized foraging and against the burning of fences.[180] Discipline had to be good to assure careful watch on the enemy but much of the galloping over the hills was unrewarded stir.

Although Washington's patrols took some prisoners in various skirmishes and received numerous deserters,[181] from the adversary, the British covered their front skillfully, kept inquisitive cavalry at a distance and contrived to mystify Washington almost as completely as when the royal army had been at sea. The American commander and everyone else now took it for granted that the enemy's objective was Philadelphia;[182] all agreed that the British undoubtedly had lost many of their horses during their long voyage, and that Howe would have to proceed slowly until he procured new mounts and fresh draft animals

---

[176] 9 G. W., 148, 155–56, 162, 173, 183 ff.   [177] Ibid., 153, 155–56.

[178] For about two months after the alleviation in June of conditions that had led to an increase in desertion and unrest (see supra, p. 426–27), Washington had no more than the normal degree of poor discipline. Too many officers, in the opinion of their Commander-in-Chief, had enjoyed long furloughs, some of which set no time limit (9 G. W., 90–91). Washington deplored this but in the case of Thomas Nelson, Jr., he relented even to the extent of permitting the Captain to resign in order to marry (ibid., 93 and n). Few of the disciplinary cases of this period were as simple as that of the private of the Ninth Virginia, who was charged with "damning the General and his orders" (8 ibid., 209). In August conditions grew worse. Fifteen of Moylan's Light Horse deserted and fell into American hands again. They were adjudged guilty and deserving the death-penalty, but at the time Washington considered it wiser to pardon them (9 ibid., 99).

[179] Ibid., 166–67.

[180] Ibid., 178–79, 199, 268. Among the interesting disciplinary efforts of the late autumn were an exhortation on the prompt execution of orders, with another comparison of a good army with a well-running clock (ibid., 348). Still another GO was an appeal for tidiness on the part of guards, who should wash their faces and comb their hair (10 ibid., 31). In December, Washington instituted the practice of sending back to previous campsites in order to pick up stragglers (ibid., 151).

[181] Ibid., 146, 160.   [182] Cf. ibid., 172–73, 181, 183.

for his wagons.[183] It did not seem impossible for him to make good his deficiencies, in a reasonable time, because after the British advanced eight or ten miles inland from Head of Elk on the way to Philadelphia, they would be in country inhabited largely by Quakers, who remained neutral, and by other farmers who were far from enthusiastic for American Independence.[184] At the beginning of September, Henry Knox wrote of the British, "if they will not come to us, we shall go to them," [185] but nothing of importance occurred until, on the 5th, the British appeared to be ready to start their offensive.[186] The fleet began to drop down the Chesapeake [187] and on the 8th was so far southward, according to reports, that Washington was convinced the ships of war were to be used against Philadelphia, via the Delaware. An assault by water was to be simultaneous with an advance by land. The British forces took the road toward Christiana, on the creek of the same name, which flowed into the Brandywine close to Wilmington.[188] "A little time," Washington wrote of his adversary, "must unfold his true designs, which I trust we shall be able to baffle . . ." [189] The American commander suspected that Howe, as usual, would attempt to turn the flank of the Continentals and to get between them and Philadelphia. To prevent this, Washington set his troops in motion at 2 o'clock on

[183] *Montresor Journals*, 444–47; A. Yates, Jr., to [Gates?], Sept. 7, 1777, *Letters to Gates*, NYHS; Major Baurmeister's letters of Aug. 31 and Oct. 17[?], 1777, to General von Jungkenn, 59 *Penn. Mag.*, 394 ff. Cf. A. Hamilton to Gouverneur Morris, Sept. 1, 1777 (9 *A. Hamilton*, 99–100); Hamilton to Gates, Aug. 29, 1777 (*Gates Papers*, NYHS). Hall (*op. cit.*, 307) recorded that "three days were spent in landing the ammunition, provisions and carriages with the few horses that were left, many having perished at sea for want of forage . . ." Knox's letter of Aug. 25, 1777, to Mrs. Knox (*Knox Papers*, MHS) is informative and interesting. Another chatty account of these days of waiting is in Benjamin Talmadge to Jere. Wadsworth, Aug. 29, 1777 (*Wadsworth Papers*, CHS). See also J. Cadwalader to Washington, Sept. 2, 1777 (55 *Papers of G. W.*, 74, LC) and John Morin Scott to Gates, Sept. 8, 1777 (*Gates Papers*, PHS).

[184] See *Adams, Fam. Let.*, 314–15, and Joseph Galloway's testimony before the House of Commons, 1779, quoted conveniently in 1 *Reed*, 304: "I don't believe that I saw in the whole route of the army, from thence to Philadelphia, consisting of at least seventy miles, above ten or at the most fifteen houses deserted . . . The inhabitants were found quietly at their homes, and to me there appeared every mark of pleasure at the [British] troops arriving in the Colony." Howe's "declaration" of Aug. 20, 1777, promising security to the unresisting appears in *London Gazette*, Oct. 28–Nov. 1, 1777; *London Chronicle*, Nov. 1–4, 1777.

[185] Letter to Mrs. Knox, Sept. 1, 1777; *Knox Papers*, MHS.

[186] Gen. Sir Henry Clinton was hoping that he simultaneously could make a diversion near Elizabeth Town, New Jersey. See his letter of Sept. 3, 1777, to Commodore Hotham; *Clinton Papers*, Clements Lib.

[187] 9 *G. W.*, 197.

[188] 1 *Greene's Greene*, 446; 9 *G. W.*, 196; 8 *JCC.*, 726; Matthew Visscher to Gates, Sept. 3, 1777 (*Letters to Gates*, NYHS); *Chilton's Diary*, Sept. 1–8, 1777; 12 *T* 288–89. Details of the British advance were given fully by Major Baurmeister in a letter to General von Jungkenn; 59 *Penn. Mag.*, 400–03, and, less verbosely, in *A. Robertson's Diaries*, 167.

[189] 9 *G. W.*, 197.

the morning of the 9th of September, put the Brandywine Creek between his men and Howe's,[190] and took position on the high ground near one of the principal crossings of that stream, Chad's Ford.[191] If Howe was advancing in full strength, Washington would attempt no more than a continuance of skirmishing and harassment; but he would have satisfaction, of a sort, when he knew precisely where the British were and what they were trying to do. For more than a fortnight he had been feeling for the enemy in the dark, with a pike of doubtful strength.

[190] Benjamin Harrison, viewing the scene from his Virginia plantation, thought that if available militia were as numerous as they were reported to be, they could form two armies and close on Howe from North and South. See Harrison to Theodorick Bland, Sept. 8, 1777; 12 T 132.

[191] 9 G. W., 197–98.

CHAPTER XVIII

THE INTELLIGENCE SERVICE GOES ASTRAY

(September 10–12, 1777)

BRANDYWINE CREEK flows from Northwest to Southeast into the Delaware on a course parallel to that of the Schuylkill and at a distance of fifteen to twenty miles from that stream. Wilmington then was entirely on the right bank of the Brandywine; the Schuylkill flanked the southern and southwestern section of Philadelphia. The area between the two streams consequently included the direct approaches to the Quaker City from Head of Elk. Unless the enemy were held on the Brandywine, he scarcely could be stopped until he reached the Schuylkill. Once on that stream, he might maneuver without great difficulty and throw his troops into Philadelphia.

As a defensive barrier, the Brandywine had no particular value other than that it was of sufficient depth to require troops to use the fords. It could be assumed that the British would have to pass at one or more of these established crossings; but, unfortunately, the fords were so numerous that the King's men had a wide choice. At and below the forks of the Brandywine which were seven or eight miles Northwest of Wilmington, there were no less than seven fords accessible to an army advancing from the Southwest on Philadelphia, to say nothing of others that might be employed by turning off a few miles, to right or to left, from the direct and generally used road. In this situation, a commander defending the Brandywine had to be vigilant and could not be certain where to concentrate most heavily, but the position taken by the Americans at Chad's Ford appeared to be about as good as any available nearby for an Army that wished to be free to maneuver and to avoid or to accept the enemy's attack as the contingencies of the hour might dictate. General Armstrong and the Pennsylvania militia were put at Pyle's Ford,[1] the one below Chad's, and probably the station least apt to be assailed on that front. Washington himself assumed the direction of the defence at Chad's. Maxwell's 800 light troops of

---

[1] 1 Reed, 307.

Lincoln's Division were placed on the southern bank of the creek, the side nearer the enemy.[2] On the opposite shore, Sullivan was entrusted with the right.[3] Greene's Division and Wayne's Brigade, which was Lincoln's other command, were placed close to the creek, directly below Chad's Ford, with Stephen in support. Stirling was stationed above that crossing, in a position corresponding to that of Stephen, but close enough to Sullivan to assist quickly any threatened point on the right.[4]

All indications early on the 10th of September were that the enemy was in what Washington termed a "tolerably compact body" at Kennett Square.[5] As that village was distant six miles only on a straight line from Chad's Ford, the American commander sent all his wagons to the rear, though he let the men keep their blankets,[6] and he had the alarm guns fired and the entire force put under arms.[7] Sullivan, who had not examined previously the ground on the right,[8] came to headquarters late in the day of the 10th and received orders to guard the fords above Chad's. The names of these were given Sullivan, but as they were new to him, they were not remembered by him in sequence. Sullivan thought the right was the flank most apt to be turned by the enemy[9] and he asked whether any fords existed above those under his care. In answer, he was informed that country people, presumably familiar with the creek, said there was none within twelve miles. Above that point was a crossing, but the approach to it was over a very bad road. All the Light Horse of the Army, Washington told Sullivan, were being shifted to the right to watch the enemy there.[10] An intelligent officer of Pennsylvania militia, Major Spear, was sent across the Brandywine, to reconnoitre in a district with which he was entirely familiar.[11]

[2] 9 *G. W.*, 206; Col. Elias Dayton in 9 *NJHSP* (1), p. 183.

[3] 9 *G. W.*, 207.

[4] Washington did not state in any of his letters precisely where these Divisions were encamped on the night of the 10th–11th, but George Weedon to John Page, Sept. 11, 1777 (cited hereafter in this chapter as *Weedon Letter*), Chicago HS. MSS, included a sketch of the order of battle.

[5] 9 *G. W.*, 203. The name is spelled with several variants. One favored form in the revolutionary years was Kennet's.

[6] *Ibid.*, 208.

[7] Capt. William Beatty's Journal, *His. Mag.* (new ser.), v. 1, no. 1, p. 81.

[8] 1 *Sullivan Papers*, 466.   [9] 1 *Sullivan Papers*, 549.

[10] Sullivan to Washington, Oct. 24, 1777, 5 *Sparks*, 458, and unfortunately omitted from the *Sullivan Papers*; Washington to Sullivan, same date, 9 *G. W.*, 425–26; Sullivan to Hancock, Oct. 25, 1777; 1 *Sullivan Papers*, 549. No denial of Sullivan's later assertions on these matters appears to have been made by Washington or by anyone else at headquarters.

[11] 1 *Sullivan Papers*, 476. Major Spear's given name has not been ascertained.

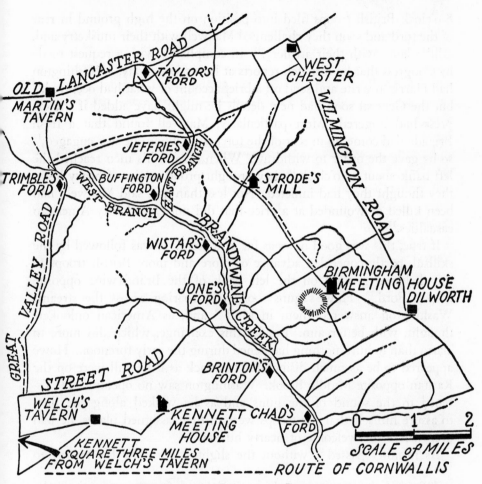

THE VALLEY AND FORDS OF THE BRANDYWINE

The scene of the battle of Sept. 11, 1777, was surveyed carefully in 1846 for the Historical Society of Pennsylvania; the resulting map was published in Vol. I of its *Bulletin,* and is reproduced acceptably on a smaller scale in Charlemagne Tower, *Marquis de Lafayette in the American Revolution,* v. 1, p. 222, from which this sketch is adapted. It will be observed from the reference to Welch's that the location of the tavern was beyond the left edge of the drawing.

Early next morning, September 11, word reached Washington that the enemy was advancing to Chad's Ford, whereupon everything was made ready for a defence. If Howe offered battle there and tried to cross the creek under fire, Washington scarcely could hope to engage his adversary in circumstances more advantageous, except for the fact a thick fog obscured everything for several hours after dawn. About

8 o'clock British troops filed into position on the high ground in rear of the ford and soon they challenged Maxwell with their musketry and, a little later, with their artillery.[12] In compliance with a request made by Congress that he dispatch reports at least twice a day,[13] Washington had Harrison write and send off a brief account of what had occurred,[14] but the General soon had new details he might have added if the express had lingered. Most particularly, Maxwell found that a fresh Brigade had come up in rear of the force with whom he was engaged,[15] so he gave the order to withdraw. When he and his men reached the left bank about 10 o'clock,[16] they brought proud stories of heavy losses they thought they had inflicted. Not less than 300, said Maxwell, had been killed or wounded at a price that did not exceed fifty American casualties.[17]

If true, this was good news as far as it went. It was followed by the skillful, partly concealed advance of more and more British troops to the sheltered ground on the left bank of the Brandywine opposite Chad's Ford.[18] Howe's guns soon were roaring across the stream; Washington answered them in kind[19] and, as American onlookers thought, with better aim. Besides this exchange, which did more to alarm than to hurt, nothing happened during the early forenoon. Howe appeared to be as much disinclined to attack as if he still were on the Raritan opposite Middle Brook. Washington saw no opening. He listened to the sound of the guns and as he walked along the lines to assure himself that the troops were in their assigned places, he had everywhere the welcome of hearty huzzas.[20]

As minutes passed[21] without the slightest effort by the enemy to

---

[12] For the fog, see *Montresor Journals*, 449. In his letter of September 11, *loc. cit.*, Weedon gave 8:30 as the time of the enemy's arrival on the high ground above the ford, and he made the assertion, accepted in the text, that the British took the initiative in the exchanges with Maxwell. A somewhat different view is presented in Harrison to Hancock, Sept. 11, 1777, 8 A.M., 6 *Ford*, 67 n; reprinted in 3 *Hughes*, 158. It should be noted that Hughes's research uncovered several sources not previously known. In the present study, the fullest, most grateful use has been made of some of this material.

[13] 8 *JCC.*, 726–27.   [14] Harrison to Hancock, as *supra*.

[15] Dayton, *op. cit.*, 184. A full and exceedingly dull account of Hessian activities throughout the day at Chad's Ford will be found in Baurmeister's letter of Oct. 17[?], 1777, to General von Jungkenn; 59 *Penn. Mag.*, 404–07.

[16] *Weedon Letter.*

[17] 8 *G. W.*, 206. Needless to say, Maxwell's figures were exaggerated.

[18] *Ibid.*   [19] *Ibid.*, and *Weedon Letter.*

[20] 1 Lafayette, *Memoirs*, 22.

[21] Unfortunately, Washington's note to Theodorick Bland, which might make possible an accurate timing of the day's intelligence reports, has the heading "20 minutes after   o'clock" (9 *G. W.*, 205).

cross the Brandywine, Washington and his officers began to suspect that Howe was trying to amuse them at Chad's Ford while he made his crossing elsewhere.[22] Washington consequently could not have been surprised when, about 11 o'clock, reports began to reach headquarters of a British column marching from Howe's left upstream, parallel to the Brandywine. Col. Moses Hazen, who was guarding Jones's Ford,[23] sent word, probably through General Sullivan, that these British were proceeding to the forks of the creek.[24] Washington immediately wrote Colonel Bland, who was with the Light Horse on the right, to send out an officer to reconnoitre and to ascertain the truth of the intelligence.[25] Then or shortly afterward, Washington directed Stirling and Stephen to move their Divisions to Birmingham Meeting House, three and a half miles from Chad's Ford and on a site that commanded the road over which the British were most apt to advance from the upper fords of the Brandywine. Obediently and promptly these two small Divisions started.[26] Confirmation of Hazen's report and of the wisdom of this shift of Stirling and Stephen was forthcoming almost immediately in a dispatch from Lt. Col. James Ross of the Eighth Pennsylvania, who with seventy men had been patrolling the so-called Great Valley Road on the right bank of the creek. Ross wrote at 11 A.M. and said that "from every account five thousand with sixteen or eighteen field pieces, marched along this road just now." Their route, said Ross, led "to Taylor's Ferry and Jeffrey's Ferry" on the Brandywine and also into the road from Lancaster to Philadelphia.[27]

Washington was not clear in his own mind concerning these various

---

[22] Journal of Timothy Pickering, 1 *Pickering*, 155.

[23] This ford was about two and a half miles above Chad's Ford, but was confused by some of the American officers with crossings higher up the Brandywine. For Hazen's presence there, see Sullivan in 5 *Sparks*, 458.

[24] Hazen's dispatch is not believed to be in existence. It certainly is not the one to Sullivan that appears in 1 *Sullivan Papers*, 555, but it may have been the message "by Major Morris," that Sullivan mentioned in his dispatch to Washington (*infra*, p. 476) concerning the report made later by Major Spear. Doubtless "Major Morris" was Lewis Morris, Jr., aide-de-camp to General Sullivan.

[25] 9 *G. W.*, 205.

[26] This new detail, of the movement of Stirling and Stephen, is set forth explicitly in the *Weedon Letter*, but nothing is said there of Washington's decision, a little later in the day, to undertake an attack on the British forces left opposite Chad's Ford. This omission on Weedon's part does not invalidate his statement concerning the movement of Stirling and Stephen but it leaves in doubt the time the two Divisions were ordered to their new position. The orders to move to Birmingham Meeting House seem best to fit into the sequence of events set forth in the text. That is the most that can be said.

[27] 5 *Sparks*, 459. It was assumed by Sparks and various other writers, not unnaturally, that Ross' letter was addressed to Sullivan and was forwarded to Washington through that General, but the copy in the *Papers of G. W.*, LC, is addressed directly to the Commander-in-Chief.

fords, but surely, if Howe had started 5000 men upstream, to turn the American flank or for any other purpose, comparatively few troops could have been left at the position first occupied that morning by the British. Washington's long-desired opportunity of striking with superior force might be at hand: The Continentals at Chad's Ford and at the one directly above it (Brinton's), where Sullivan had his station, must cross the Brandywine forthwith and attack and destroy the men left there by the departing column. Stirling and Stephen must proceed to Birmingham Meeting House [28] as already ordered; but Greene's, Lincoln's and Sullivan's Divisions must fight on the enemy's side of the creek. At Chad's the troops were prepared, almost, to plunge into the water when Sullivan forwarded this dispatch:

Brinton's Ford, 11 September

Since I sent you the message by Major Morris I saw some of the Militia who came in this morning from a tavern called Martins on the forks of the Brandywine. The one who told me, said he had come from thence to Welches Tavern and heard nothing of the Enemy above the forks of the Brandywine and is Confident that [sic] are not in that Quarters. So that Colonel Hazen's Information must be wrong. I have sent to that Quarter to know whether there is any foundation for the Report and shall be glad to give your Ex'y the earliest information.

I am, & c.

John Sullivan [29]

---

[28] Here again reservation has to be made concerning the precise time at which a different decision was reached, as presently will appear; but in his *Letter*, Weedon stated that Stephen's and Stirling's columns marched for about a mile and a half. That would conform roughly with the schedule the text assumes Washington to have followed.

[29] 56 *Papers of G. W.*, p. 21, LC. Here is an instance where Jared Sparks seems to have disdained historical accuracy. His text of Sullivan's dispatch (5 *Sparks*, 459) reads as follows: "Since I sent you the message by Major Moore, I saw Major Spear of the militia, who came this morning from a tavern called Martin's, at the fork of the Brandywine. He came from thence to Welch's Tavern, and heard nothing of the enemy about the forks of the Brandywine, and is confident they are not in that quarter; so that Colonel Hazen's information must be wrong. I have sent to that quarter, to know whether there is any foundation for the report, and shall give your Excellency the earliest information." The similarity between this text and the original in the Washington Papers is so close that they must be the edited and inedited versions of the same document. Sparks correctly identified "the one" who told Sullivan. He was Major Spear, but that identification was made verbally, and was not a part of the dispatch placed in Washington's hands. It is manifest, also, that Sullivan's reference to Martin's Tavern "on the forks of the Brandywine" is not correctly given by Sparks as "at the fork of the Brandywine." Further, Sullivan stated that the militia heard nothing of the enemy "above the forks of the Brandywine" but Sparks put this as "about the forks of the Brandywine," which is quite different. Two theories concerning this gross falsification in editing are possible: Sparks may simply have been careless in reference to the "forks" and may have thought he elucidated the dispatch when he interpolated the name of the militia officer. The other and less probable theory is that Sparks's determination to justify Washington in all things may have prompted the

Was Hazen mistaken? Was Ross, or were the militiamen correct? The individual who gave Sullivan the information in this new dispatch proved to be Major Spear, the militia officer sent out the previous day.[30] If Washington now questioned Spear, whom Sullivan had ordered to follow the express to headquarters,[31] the Commander-in-Chief concluded quickly that where there was an unresolved conflict of intelligence reports, it would be rash to assume the offensive. The enemy might be employing a strategem and might be waiting on the other side of the stream for just such an attack. Orders must be revoked; Stirling and Stephen must be halted where they were and should be held there until the situation was clarified;[32] American troops along the bank of the creek should be drawn back to the high ground so that they would not be exposed to the enemy's artillery, which did not slacken its cannonade [33] as midday passed.[34]

No sound of firing came from the right. If any additional intelligence reports reached Washington from Sullivan, they were confirmatory, in the main, of information that the enemy had not been seen within the forks of the Brandywine.[35] Washington accepted this as the correct interpretation of the contradictory reports, and in the belief the main British force still was in his front, he changed his tactics once again, and permitted Maxwell to cross the creek several times to skirmish with the enemy,[36] while the batteries continued their futile exchanges.

---

belief that the General's acceptance of this intelligence report would seem more reasonable if it were attributed to a Major who later was described as a man of "rank, reputation and knowledge" (9 *G. W.*, 425) than if it were on the authority of a militiaman of whom nothing was known or said.

[30] Cf. Washington to Sullivan, Oct. 24, 1777 (9 *G. W.*, 425) and 1 *Sullivan Papers*, 476.

[31] It is of record that Sullivan ordered Spear to proceed immediately to headquarters, and it probably is to be taken for granted that the Major arrived promptly but there is no positive proof of this. Washington subsequently (see *infra*, p. 485) spoke only of "the information of Major Spear, transmitted to me by you."

[32] The *Weedon Letter* states that this was done.

[33] Most of the accounts of this proposed counterstroke cite no source and sometimes refer to late secondary authorities, for which reason some skepticism appears to have been shown in dealing with the incident. It is authentic. In his letter of Oct. 6, 1777, to President Hancock (1 *Sullivan Papers*, 475–76), Sullivan wrote of it and stated that he was preparing to attack when Major Spear, the militiaman, came to him from the other side of the creek.

[34] All the timing of these events from 8 A.M. to about 2:30 P.M. is hypothetical or at best provisional; but the probabilities are that the hour was later with most of the incidents than has been assumed. Ross' dispatch, for example, could not have reached Washington before 12:30 P.M.

[35] Sullivan stated (1 *Sullivan Papers*, 476), that he sent out "a Sergeant Tucker of the Light Horse," who said he had found no enemy, though he had gone as far as the Lancaster Road, which was about nine miles from Sullivan's lines.

[36] *Weedon Letter.*

Early in the afternoon a farmer rode up to Washington's headquarters, which were at the house of Benjamin Ring, below Chad's Ford.[37] The stranger, a heavy man with dark skin and black eyes, said he had important news and must see the General at once. Staff officers could not silence or satisfy him; he had to speak to Washington. When admitted, he blurted out, in much excitement, that the Army must move immediately; otherwise it would be surrounded; the enemy was coming down the eastern side of the creek and already was near at hand. Washington could not believe it; his information, he said, was that all the British were on the other side of the Brandywine. The farmer insisted he was relating facts of his own observation, and he spoke with so much positiveness and concern that the General decided to see for himself whether the man possibly could be correct.[38] Washington probably had started for the right when, about 2 P.M., a messenger rode up with a dispatch from Colonel Bland of the Light Horse to Sullivan. This read:

¼ past one o'clock

Sir,

I have discovered a party of the enemy on the Heights just on the right of the two widows who live close together on the road called the forks road, about half a mile to the Right of the meeting-house. There is a higher hill in their front.

Theod^ck Bland [39]

Either the man who brought this dispatch, or a soldier galloping up behind him, delivered this further news:

Two o'clock, P.M.

Dear General,

Colonel Bland has this moment sent me word, that the enemy are in the rear of my right about two miles, coming down. There are, he says, about

---

[37] Townsend in 1 *PHS Buls.*, 19; W. W. MacElree in *Along the Western Brandywine*, 134, called it the Ring Tavern.

[38] This is about as much as can safely be accepted of the familiar traditoin that Squire Thomas Cheney saved the Army from destruction. The full story, with a sketch of Cheney, appears in 1 *PHS Buls.*, 10, 32. Included is the text of Cheney's alleged statement to Washington: "You are mistaken, General. My life for it, you are mistaken. By hell, it is so; put me under guard till you find my story true." Doubtless, Cheney's information was useful, but it could not have been received long before Bland's dispatch, mentioned in the text. Nor was the Army in immediate danger of being surrounded when Stirling and Stephen already were close to the road of the enemy's advance. Sullivan, too, could be employed, though this would involve a tactically troublesome change of front.

[39] 56 *Papers of G. W.*, 14, LC.

two brigades of them. He also says he saw a dust back in the country for above an hour. I am, &c.

John Sullivan [40]

The enemy in the rear—the same maneuver against the man who had been outflanked on Long Island a year previously! Militiamen from the right bank must have been frightfully in error; Ross and Hazen had been correct. No doubt, the British column had been moving from the left all morning; a great opportunity had been lost by not attacking the force that Howe had left behind him to hold Chad's Ford, to bluster and to distract. Sullivan must march at once to meet the column advancing on his rear. Stephen's and Stirling's Divisions must proceed at a trot [41] to their original objective, Birmingham Meeting House.[42] Sullivan, as senior Major General "of the right" wing, should direct the fighting.

Orders were sent immediately to the three division commanders, whose front, as yet, mercifully was silent. By swift movement and with good fortune, a numerically superior American force might hurl back and pursue those venturesome two Brigades before the arrival of the supports who had raised the dust cloud; and even if the British were more numerous than the estimated 2000 or 3000, the Continentals might find an opening.[43] Washington decided that he himself should remain with Greene at Chad's Ford, where he could keep his hand on all the troops. It was an unacceptable duty, because nothing was happening at Chad's other than casual artillery dispute and occasional skirmishing between Maxwell and the British [44] on the right bank.

The afternoon wore on. Sullivan was assumed to be moving farther to the right; Stirling and Stephen already were in line, or soon would be, on high ground that overlooked the road along which the enemy was apt to advance past the Birmingham Meeting House. At length, about 4:30,[45] straining ears at Chad's Ford heard the sound they had been dreading and expecting—the challenge of cannon-fire that swelled

---

[40] 5 Sparks, 460, verbatim.

[41] Simes, edition of 1776, did not include "quick time" or "quick step," but Duane, edition of 1810, recognized both and mentioned, also, "quickest time" or "quickest step," 120 steps of twenty-four inches each, per minute.

[42] Weedon Letter.

[43] Washington wrote later in the afternoon: "Generals Sullivan, Stirling and Stephen with their Divisions are gone in pursuit and to attack it, if they can, with any prospect of success" (9 G. W., 206).

[44] Actually Hessians, but it is not certain they had been identified as such by the Americans

[45] 9 G. W., 207.

to a salvo and dropped to a growl and rose again in wrath. Soon, too, the hateful stammer of uneven volleys was audible, and then the spiteful bark of rifles in the hands of men fighting in the Indian manner behind trees. It was difficult for Washington to restrain himself and to stay at headquarters while a battle of uncertain issue was raging within two miles; but he noticed that the artillery fire from across Chad's Ford was quickening, as if an infantry attack were in preparation, and, while he waited impatiently for the next move, he occupied himself by telling Colonel Harrison what to say in the second of the promised dispatches of the day to the President of Congress. A cheerful paper it was, as if it were the report of an observer, rather than of a commander. The final paragraph, though written to the echo of the cannon, read thus: "At half after four o'clock, the enemy attacked General Sullivan at the ford next above this, and the action has been very violent ever since. It still continues. A very severe cannonade has began [sic] here, too, and I suppose we shall have a very hot evening." [46]

He could fashion his words calmly, but he could not stifle the question that every man around him was asking: How was Sullivan faring? What was happening to Stirling whom the discerning young Marquis at headquarters was to describe as "plus brave que judicieux"? [47] Stephen, too, was in that battle: he of course would have a valiant tale to tell of windrows of British dead in front of his position, but, actually, would he succeed in holding his men to the blast of the bullets?

It was a cruel ordeal to remain passive while that steady drumbeat of doom rolled across the fields. The idler the hands, the faster was the gallop of the imagination. Soon Washington's concern got the better of his consideration for Sullivan's natural, pugnacious wish to fight an independent battle. The commander of the right wing must be facing more than two Brigades; he should have help. Greene still was in reserve. He must move at once to the right. Washington would go with him. Lincoln's Division must remain at Chad's Ford and must repulse any attempt of the enemy to cross there. When he gave orders to this effect, Washington probably did not observe on the part of General Maxwell any peculiarity of conduct that led some of that officer's subordinates to think that the Brigadier was incompetent or drunk. [48]

[46] 9 G. W., 206–07.   [47] 1 Lafayette, Memoirs, 19.
[48] See William Heth to Daniel Morgan, Sept. 30, 1777; 1 Winchester His. Soc. Papers, 31.

Off went Washington with his staff and with a guide who knew all the short paths across wide fields that leisurely roads skirted.[49] Behind the General, pushed to their utmost endeavor, Greene's men half ran, half walked toward the sound of the firing.[50] As Washington approached the engaged flank, he encountered the usual number of skulkers and many wounded men;[51] but he had not a minute in which to reproach the one or to assist the other, because he had to ascertain, if he could, what was happening as a result of a confused struggle around a plowed hill Southwest of the Birmingham Meeting House. Stirling and Stephen had reached that elevation after racing from the place where they had been halted by Washington's order. They had found the enemy approaching in much greater strength than earlier reports indicated, but they had occupied strong ground [52] and almost had completed their dispositions when Sullivan, who never had been on that part of the field before, suddenly found his advance guard an eighth of a mile from an oncoming British column. When Sullivan got his bearings, he perceived that he was to the left and almost half-a-mile in front of Stephen and Stirling. Hastily he ordered their Divisions to extend their lines to the right so as to give him space to form. The change was made though, in Stephen's command, it placed Scott's Brigade disadvantageously, compelled Woodford to retire 200 yards, and put in front of Colonel Marshall the timberland that officer previously had occupied.[53] Worse still, while Sullivan's men were being shifted awkwardly and painfully to the right, they were attacked and thrown into some confusion.[54] The fullest effort was made to hold off

[49] The tradition is that Washington kept urging this guide, Joseph Brown, to greater speed, with the cry, "Push along, old man," a remark that does not "sound like" Washington. The first appearance of the story appears to have been in a letter written Nov. 29, 1845, by William Darlington. He remarked: "This anecdote I had from my father, who was well acquainted with Brown, and had often heard him relate the adventure." (1 *PHS Buls.*, 59, a volume of puzzling pagination). The interval of time between the event and the narration is too long to make the story valid evidence in all its details.

[50] Weedon's Brigade by one road, Muhlenberg's by another (*Weedon Letter*).

[51] A caveat has to be entered here concerning the time of Washington's arrival on the right. If he did not leave Chad's Ford until shortly before 5 o'clock—the hour at which Harrison began the second dispatch to Congress—he could not have arrived at the scene of combat until 5:30 P.M. Weedon stated in his *Letter* that his Brigade reached at 6 o'clock the ground on which it formed. Sullivan noted that the enemy's advance was halted between sunset and dusk (1 *Sullivan Papers*, 465). Sunset was at approximately 6:16.

[52] Weedon particularized: ". . . they formed in an agreeable manner; Woodford's Brigade [of Stephen's Division] being to the right, he detached Col. Thomas Marshall with his Regiment (only 170 men) to a fine wood on the right to cover his field pieces and right flank . . ." *Weedon Letter*. For the fact that the hill was plowed, see *Montresor Journals*, 450.

[53] *Weedon Letter*.

[54] The fullest first-hand account of this phase of the battle is in Sullivan to Hancock, Sept. 27, 1777 (1 *Sullivan Papers*, 463–64), though Sullivan certainly did not minimize the part he

the enemy with artillery fire while these troops were being rallied. For a time, cannon balls and the steadiness of Stirling and Stephen on the right and of three Regiments [55] on Sullivan's left sufficed to hold off the enemy.

Now, at the moment of Washington's arrival, the left was beginning to break, and the whole of the line was sagging under pressure by the British. Marshall, fighting with furious tenacity, had to be ordered to quit his position because he was nearly surrounded. Woodford was compelled to leave the front because of a wound. His artillerists continued to serve their guns until most of the officers and half the men were shot down. Even then, leaders of the Brigade might have succeeded in hauling the guns away had not the horses been killed.[56] A rout of the Army's staunchest veterans appeared to be imminent when the leading Company of Weedon's Brigade of Greene's Division pushed forward. On Sullivan's order, and, doubtless with Washington's approval, these men spread out in a plowed field on the right [57] and prepared to halt the enemy's advance. Washington saw and admired but he did not attempt to take command in person as he had at Princeton. Instead, he, his aides and young Lafayette rode among the fugitives and sought to rally them. Lafayette got a bullet in the leg as his reward; [58] the Commander-in-Chief, as usual, was unscathed.

So long as mounted officers shouted and threatened close to the front, they were able to hold part of the line together. When they rode back from a position then within about 200 yards of the foe, many of the men ran off.[59] Weedon's Brigade opened ranks to permit the broken Regiments from the front to pass to the rear, and then it closed again and confronted the enemy.[60] A little later, in the confusion of the

and his men had in the action. Nowhere, for example, is there confirmation of his statement (*ibid.*, 465) that the Americans were driven from the hill five times and each time were able to recover position. Colonel Dayton (9 *NJHSP* (1), p. 184), doubted whether some of Sullivan's troops got into action at all.

55 Hazen's, Dayton's and Ogden's, 1 *Sullivan Papers*, 464.

56 *Weedon Letter.*

57 *Weedon Letter;* Col. C. C. Pinckney's statement of Sept. 24, 1777; 1 *Sullivan Papers*, 557.

58 1 Lafayette, *Memoirs*, 23. De Kalb wrote de Broglie the wound was in the left thigh (*Kapp's Kalb*, 125).

59 Clark in 7 *NJHSP* (1), p. 99.

60 Sullivan maintained that Weedon's Brigade was the only part of Greene's Division to be engaged (1 *Sullivan Papers*, 473); both Colonel Dayton (*op. cit.*, 187), and Joseph Clark (7 *NJHSP* (1), p. 99), spoke more broadly of what Greene's Division did to stop pursuit by the British. G. W. Greene (*op. cit.*, v. 1, p. 452–53) wrote of the engagement of Muhlenberg as well as of Weedon. In his *Letter*, Weedon said: "About 6, General Greene's Division arrived to cover the retreat. One of his Brigades (Weedon's) gave the enemy such as produced the desired effect. Nash's Brigade also marched but too late to be of any service." Nothing was said of Muhlenberg.

field, some badly led American troops mistook Weedon's Third Virginia Regiment for an adversary and fired into it. The result was fatal to many.[61]

In spite of this, the resistance and good handling of the Brigade in the last hour of daylight forced the weary British to abandon pursuit everywhere on the American right. Against the centre of the line at Chad's Ford the enemy had thrown himself vigorously after the departure of Washington. The troops of Wayne and of Maxwell, lacking the support of Greene, put up the best defence they could, but they had to retreat and, in doing so, lost their artillery,[62] while the militia on the left, unassailed, made an easy withdrawal. So tangled were the troops of the centre and the right, along the road to Chester, that Washington did not get them in order until nearly midnight.[63] He then was close to exhaustion, and, as he was dragging himself to bed, he said to his staff, "Congress must be written to, gentlemen, and one of you must do it, for I am too sleepy." Colonel Harrison, in much the same condition, prevailed on Adjutant General Pickering to undertake the drafting of the letter. When Pickering had finished it, he took it to Washington who read and bade the officer interpolate a word of hope that another day would yield a more favorable result.[64] The Colonel had written: "Notwithstanding the misfortune of the day, I am happy to find the troops in good spirits." He now added, "and I hope another time we shall compensate for the losses now sustained." [65]

First fears that casualties included many prisoners were relieved somewhat the next day by the emergence of men who had lost their way or had spent the night in the woods for fear of running into an enemy patrol if they went out to the road. The Seventh Virginia, which had suffered heavily, had been hidden by its wounded commander, Maj. John Cropper, until nearly daylight and then had been marched to the rear. Because the Ensign had fallen with the colors, Cropper had no flag, but he put a red bandanna handkerchief on a

---

[61] Joseph Clark's Diary, op. cit., 99. Casualties in this Regiment were thought by some observers to exceed those in any other.

[62] 9 G. W., 207. When Washington wrote the dispatch mentioned in the next paragraph of the text, he did not know precisely how many cannon had been lost, and he set down the number as "about seven or eight" (ibid., 208). The figures given in André's Journal (v. 1, p. 88, cited in 3 Hughes, 718), were "eleven pieces of ordnance, five French brass guns, three Hessian, and three American."

[63] Cf. the heading of his dispatch, 9 G. W., 208.

[64] 1 Pickering, 156; with some embellishment in 1 Greene's Greene, 156.

[65] 9 G. W., 208.

ramrod and, with the survivors of his Regiment, limped into Chester. When he went to headquarters to report, Washington congratulated him.[66]

Hundreds did not come back, though Washington did not set down any figures then or thereafter. American wounded had been left on the field where Howe was so little able to provide care that he invited Washington to send surgeons to attend them.[67] These bleeding men, together with the dead and the uninjured prisoners, were estimated by General Greene at 1200 or 1300.[68] Howe said of American casualties only this: thanks to the presence of a corps "that had not been engaged . . . the enemy's army escaped a total overthrow that must have been the consequence of an hour's more daylight." [69] The British losses, which Washington thought greater than his own, were in reality eighty-nine killed, 488 wounded and six missing, a total of 583.[70] Washington saved all his wagons but as his men had gone into action with their blankets on their backs, hundreds had thrown away covering they missed almost immediately because the nights already were cool.[71]

If, then, Washington had lost the field, the lives of hundreds of men, and a considerable part of his artillery, the reasons were plain. Besides the usual factor of unskilled leadership and ill discipline, there was on the part of the Americans a most discreditable ignorance of the ground. Little or no reconnaissance was undertaken on the 10th of September. Neither Washington nor any of his staff or division commanders or Colonels of cavalry appears to have known the correct names and location of the fords.[72] It is doubtful, indeed, if many of

[66] 11 *VHS Cols.*, new ser., 278–79.

[67] 9 *G. W.*, 217. Benjamin Rush was among those who entered the lines on this mission. "I was much struck," Rush wrote, "in observing the difference between the discipline and order of the British and Americans." He added: "I lamented this upon my return. It gave offense and was ascribed to fear and to lack of attachment to the cause of my country." (*Autobiography*, ed. Corner, 133). Rush did not abandon in the face of this criticism his efforts to improve the condition of the soldiers. See Rush to Gates, Apr. 9, 1778 (*Letters to Gates*, NHYS).

[68] 2 *Gordon*, ed. 1801, p. 226.

[69] Dispatch of Oct. 18, 1777; quoted in Belcher, the *First American Civil War*, v. 1, p. 248. *Montresor Journals*, 450, put American casualties at 450 and prisoners at 400.

[70] 1 *Kemble*, 135. A subsequently circulated list of casualties, running to 1976, must have been a forgery. See 3 *Hughes*, 718.

[71] 9 *G.W.*, 208; Timothy Pickering's Journal, 1 *Pickering,* 161.

[72] Cf. Timothy Pickering's Journal, Sept. 16, 1777, with two sentences thrown together: "To reconnoitre thoroughly . . . ought to be the first point attended to in taking a post. Before the Battle of Brandywine, we had time to have viewed all the ground several miles on our right, but did not do it . . . 'Tis of very great importance to have correct maps of the country which is the seat of war" (1 *Pickering*, 160). A full list of the fords appears in 1 *PHS Buls.*, "Sketch of the Battle of Brandywine," p. 7–8. After the Revolution, the names of some of

the responsible officers were aware of the existence of Jeffries Ford, over which the British crossed the East Branch of the Brandywine. If Col. Theodorick Bland had the duty of ascertaining where the creek could be forded, he performed it ill; and if it was a fact, as Henry Lee stated years later, that Bland was "never intended for the department of military intelligence," [73] Washington had others with aptitude for this essential art of war. As the Commander-in-Chief might readily have employed these men, he has to be charged with being less careful than usual in his dispositions on the Brandywine. He was tired or temporarily over-confident or else the instance was one, familiar if not frequent, in which an able man for some unascertainable reason fails to grasp the realities of a problem he normally would master without prolonged effort.

The other reason for the defeat on the Brandywine was an aspect of the poor reconnaissance and lack of knowledge of the ground. "A contrariety of intelligence, in a critical and important point," Washington wrote about a fortnight later, "contributed greatly, if it did not entirely bring on the misfortunes of that day." [74] His reference was more specific in one of his letters to Sullivan: ". . . I ascribed the misfortune which happened to us on the 11th of September principally to the information of Major Spear, transmitted to me by you . . ." but Washington did not permit himself to finish the sentence without making it plain that he did not blame Sullivan for "conveying that intelligence." The Commander-in-Chief went further: "On the contrary, considering from whom, and in what manner it came to you, I should have thought you culpable in concealing it. The Major's rank, reputation and knowledge of the country gave him a full claim to credit and attention." [75]

In actual fact, the importance of what Spear had to tell the commanders was misinterpreted by them because of their unfamiliarity with the region. Sullivan wrote, initially, it will be recalled, that "the one" who supplied the news had come "this morning from a tavern called Martin's on the forks of the Brandywine—he came from thence

the crossings were changed. In one instance a ford was given the name previously applied to one higher upstream.

[73] He was, in Lee's words, "noble, sensible, honorable and amiable." See Henry Lee, *Memoirs of the War in the Southern Department* . . . , ed. of 1869, cited hereafter as *Henry Lee*, p. 88.

[74] Letter of Sept. 27, 1777, to Brig. Gen. Thomas Nelson, Jr.; 9 *G. W.*, 272.

[75] Letter of Oct. 24, 1777, to Maj. Gen. John Sullivan; 9 *G. W.*, 425.

to Welches Tavern and heard nothing of the enemy above the forks of the Brandywine and is confident that they are not in that quarter . . ." [76] If Spear said Martin's Tavern was "on the forks of the Brandywine," it was natural that Sullivan should understand him to mean "at the forks," which might have been misleading; but if Spear said "in the forks" he spoke with absolute accuracy concerning both the location of the tavern and the fact that no British had passed there. Martin's hostelry was between the West and East Branches of the Brandywine, and was more than a mile North of the road along which Howe's column moved across the country between Trimble's Ford on the West Branch and Jeffries Ford on the East Branch. If the American commanders had examined the ground or had questioned Spear or any informed residents of the area around the East Branch, they could have learned that the absence of British on the road past Martin's Tavern was no guarantee the enemy was not moving to the right in the manner both Colonel Hazen and Colonel Ross reported.

Too little attention may have been paid to the element of time in appraising Major Spear's statement that he had gone from Martin's to Welch's Tavern. The establishment of Welch must have been known to Washington or to some of his officers who certainly had passed its door, a mile and a quarter by road West of Kennett Meeting House and three miles East of Kennett Square. Even if Major Spear was so familiar with the country that he rode straight across fields and fences, he had to cover seven miles from Martin's to Welch's. By the shortest lanes, the distance would be ten miles. He had begun his reconnaissance on the 10th: at what hour had he left Martin's and when had he been at Welch's? The time of his ride was all-important. Proceeding southward, he could have been at both places in the early morning of the 11th without encountering the British column, because—most distinctly—that column had not "filed off about 11 o'clock from their left," as Washington had thought. [77] Instead, these troops, who included the Guards and the Grenadiers, had broken camp near Kennett's Square and had marched northward at daylight; but as they had twelve or

---

[76] 1 *Sullivan Papers,* 451.

[77] Nor, incidentally, had it "later passed Brandywine at Jones's Ford, between five and six miles above Chads" (9 *G. W.,* 206). Jones's Ford was three miles above Chad's, not five or six, and was four miles below Jeffries, the ford actually used by Howe in crossing the East Branch.

fifteen miles of road to cover to the second crossing of the Brandywine, they doubtless had not reached either Trimble's or Jeffries Ford when Spear passed southward from Martin's to Welch's while the sun still was low in the East.

The second crossing of the British, that of Jeffries Ford, was at 2 P.M.[78] Colonel Ross' intelligence report of 11 o'clock was absolutely correct;[79] so, in all probability, was Colonel Hazen's;[80] Spear's information, to repeat, was not misleading; it merely was not given proper critical evaluation by Sullivan or by Washington. To repeat, neither of the Generals appears to have asked the essential question: at what hour did Spear make his reconnaissance? Failure to ascertain this was the more amazing and the more discreditable because circumstances nearly duplicated those existing on the eve of the Battle of Long Island the previous August. The danger of another flanking operation by Howe should have been in the mind of all the senior officers and should not have been put aside merely because the march across the two streams above the fork was said to be over circuitous, bad roads.

Sullivan, in particular, should have been superlatively careful to avoid a "second Long Island." He was said by Adam Stephen to have procured regularly "the best intelligence of any in the army." [81] and he was not believed to have been unduly excited on the day of battle.[82] Moreover, he insisted that he had expected the attack to be from the right,[83] that he executed orders to guard the fords all the way to Buffington's,[84] and that he inquired of Washington whether there were no fords higher up. To this, said Sullivan, "the persons who were then giving [Wash-

---

[78] Howe's report, *loc. cit.* Uncertainty regarding the time of crossing Trimble's Ford is due to (1) the equivocal language of Howe's report, which makes it doubtful whether he counted the distance twelve miles to Trimble's Ford or to Jeffries Ford, three miles farther than Trimble's, and, (2) the absence of any reference, one way or the other, to a halt for the mid-day meal. As sunrise was at 5:35, a march that started at "daybreak" found the men on the road by 5:00. They consequently did not reach Trimble's until 10 o'clock at earliest and more probably did not arrive there until 11 A.M., or perhaps later. The column, in short, was on the road eight or nine hours in covering twelve to fifteen miles. Montresor (*Journals*, 516) stated that the march to the point from which the attack was delivered on the plowed hill near the Meeting House was seventeen miles and that the halt—presumably before the assault—was for an hour only. The men went forward, he said, at 3:30 P.M. A familiar British account of the action is that in *André's Journal* (ed. 1930), p. 45–47.

[79] Ross resigned his commission Sept. 22, 1777. No papers concerning his reason for doing so have been brought to light.

[80] It will be remembered that no text of this has been found.

[81] Letter of Sept. 27, 1777 to Sullivan; 1 *Sullivan Papers*, 456.

[82] *Ibid.* and Pinckney's statement, *ibid.*, 557.   [83] *Ibid.*, 476, 549.

[84] He called it Buffenton.

ington] information of the country, replied there is none within twelve miles, the roads leading to and from which are almost inaccessible." [85] Sullivan defended himself by stating, in addition, that he had not taken post at Brinton's Ford until the evening before the action and that he had assurance from Washington "that all the Light Horse of the Army were ordered on the right wing to give information." Four Light Horsemen only, said Sullivan, were supplied him. Two of these he "kept at the upper fords to bring me intelligence, the others I kept to send intelligence to headquarters." [86] In his own report of the distance from one ford to another,[87] as far upstream as Buffington's,[88] Sullivan was not greatly in error; but he knew nothing and apparently made little effort to learn anything about the fords above the forks.[89]

Perhaps the strangest fact of all that Sullivan set down in his own behalf was his admission that he did not make and transmit to Washington any critique [90] of Spear's verbal report to him of conditions at Martin's and at Welch's Taverns. Sullivan wrote: "I considered that if my opinion or the intelligence I had sent the General had brought him into a plan of attacking the enemy on the advantageous heights they were possessed of, and a defeat should follow that I should be justly censured for withholding from him part of the intelligence I had received, and thereby brought on the defeat of our Army; I therefore set down and wrote Major Spear's account and forwarded it to his Excellency by a Light Horseman and ordered the Major to follow himself. I never made a comment or gave my opinion upon the matter." [91]

Opinion might and did vary concerning the responsibility of Sullivan for the defeat and for the misinterpretation of intelligence that contributed to the loss of the day, but the heaviest judgment that could be imposed on Sullivan would not exculpate his Commander-in-Chief. Washington conducted the Brandywine operation as if he had been in a daze. Three months later, a new aide remarked that he had never known Washington to err in passing judgment on military intelli-

---

85 1 *Sullivan Papers,* 549.
86 Sullivan to Hancock, Oct. 25, 1777; 1 *Sullivan Papers,* 549.
87 *Ibid.*
88 To avoid confusion it must be remembered that Buffington's later was known as Brinton's. The Brinton's of 1777 was nearly four miles downstream from Buffington's.
89 As far as the index to his *Papers* is a guide, the names of Jeffries and Taylor's Fords are not mentioned in his dispatches.
90 The correct professional term, needless to say, was "appreciation," but Washington apparently did not use the awkward word, though its definition as "deliberate judgment" was familiar at the time.
91 Letter to Hancock, Oct. 6, 1777; 1 *Sullivan Papers,* 475.

gence,[92] but it was not so that September day on the Brandywine. The General who always had stressed the necessity of procuring the fullest intelligence and of analyzing it correctly had failed to do either or to employ his Light Horse adequately [93] when the price of error might be the loss of Philadelphia.

[92] John Laurens, conveniently quoted in 10 *G. W.*, 157 n.

[93] The complete absence of all contemporary reports of the use of the American cavalry on the right flank makes it impossible to say how serious this error was, or to ascertain the truth of the tradition that the troopers who should have discovered and reported the advance of the British spent the forenoon with their cups at a tavern table. A general condemnation of Washington's use of his cavalry appears in C. F. Adams, *Studies, Military and Diplomatic*, 59.

CHAPTER XIX

GERMANTOWN—DEFEAT IN VICTORY

(September 13–October 12, 1777)

EXPLAIN THE Battle of the Brandywine as one might, it was a defeat that called for an immediate deep withdrawal. From Chester, Washington moved the greater part of his Army to the Schuylkill and over it to Germantown, where he had the stragglers collected and the lost detachments sent back to their Regiments. All the troops were given rest and such food as the feeble and disorganized commissary could provide.[1] In shaping his strategy anew, Washington's deep caution reasserted itself. As he saw it, the desertion and disorganization resulting from the long September marches, when added to the losses of the bloody action on the creek, made the speedy reenforcement of the Army essential if even the semblance of resistance to an advance on Philadelphia was to be maintained. Unhappily, trained men could come quickly in considerable number from one source only, Putnam's command. In full appreciation of the risks involved in reducing force on North River and the Highlands of New York, Washington decided first that he must draw to him 1500 men whom Congress had ordered Putnam to send to New Jersey, where an anticipated invasion proved to be merely a raid to collect cattle. Then, on a review of the force required to prevent the seizure by the enemy of the forts and passes of the Hudson, the Commander-in-Chief concluded that another 1000 men could be spared by "Old Put"—a total of 2500—without excessive risk.[2] As Washington explained later, ". . . such was the reduced state of our Continental Regiments . . . and such the sloth and difficulty of procuring reenforcements of militia from the southward that without the troops from Peekskill, we should scarcely have been able to have kept the field against General Howe." [3]

Washington's plan was to harass the British momentarily with such of his Regiments as still remained to the South of the Schuylkill, and

[1] 9 G. W., 209, 218.
[2] The details of "The Reconcentration in the Autumn of 1777" are discussed in Appendix IV–3 of this volume.
[3] Letter of Oct. 15, 1777, to George Clinton; 9 G. W., 373.

then, when the other Continentals had recovered from the shock of battle, he intended to leave the militia on guard at the fords toward which the British columns were heading. With the veteran organization, he would recross the Schuylkill and watch the enemy.[4] This maneuver was exacting but it was attended by no widespread demoralization of the troops or of American supporters in Philadelphia. The rally, as usual, was firmer and faster than Washington had thought it would be. If the Army had not yet learned how to win victories, it had developed a self-confidence that overcame its costly rebuff on the 11th of September. "Heaven frowned on us in a degree," said Henry Knox, but he prefaced that with assurance, "our people behaved well." [5] Almost everywhere, the result of the Battle of the Brandywine was accepted without flinching and in the usual hopeful belief that the enemy's losses exceeded those of Washington's Army.[6] The spirit of the aftermath on the American side was, "better next time." In London many doubtless were of the opinion subsequently printed in a review of the year's military operations: "[The victory] was not of that final and decisive character which the [British] people had expected as a certain consequence of such a meeting . . . The rebels were not disheartened; and Mr. Washington exerted himself with ability and diligence to repair his defeat." [7]

Although Pennsylvania Loyalists scarcely could conceal their delight over the success of the King's arms,[8] supporters of the Revolution did not blame either Washington or his troops for failure.[9] Members of Congress, who were about to move to Lancaster,[10] voted thirty hogs-

---

[4] *Ibid.*, 215.

[5] Letter of Sept. 13, 1777, to Mrs. Knox; *Knox Papers*, MHS.

[6] 9 *G. W.*, 211; Richard Henry Lee to Patrick Henry, 1 *Ballagh, Lee Letters*, 322; John Hancock to Washington, 1 *LTW.*, 433. Cf. John Adams in 2 *Burnett*, 504.

[7] *Dodsley's Annual Register for 1777*, p. 131.

[8] Cf. 1 *Deane Papers*, 248. Cf. also Timothy Pickering to his brother, Sept. 25, 1777. ". . . I feel in some degree reconciled to Howe's entering Pennsylvania and Philadelphia, that the unworthy inhabitants (of which 'tis apparent a majority of the State is composed) may experience the calamities of war, which nothing but their own supineness and unfriendliness to the American cause would have brought on them. Possibly Heaven permits it in vengeance for their defection, that their country should be the seat of war" (1 *Pickering*, 165).

[9] See the letters of Delegates to Congress in 2 *Burnett*, 520.

[10] 8 *JCC.*, 742. It could not reconvene until the 27th of September (*ibid.*, 755), and then after one day in Lancaster it transferred its sittings to York, where it reorganized, at length, October 1 (*ibid.*, 754, 755, 756, and 2 *Burnett*, 502–03). For the thinness of attendance, twenty-one or twenty-two members, see 2 *Burnett*, 523. Effort to improve administration by the establishment of a new Board of War, consisting of three persons not members of Congress (see 9 *JCC.*, 818, proceedings of Oct. 17, 1777), will be mentioned later. Attempts to procure larger representation were typified by the resolve of December 9, for which see *ibid.*, 1013.

heads of rum to the Army,[11] sent out vigorous calls for militia re-enforcement,[12] and renewed for sixty days, within seventy miles of headquarters, substantially the same broad powers Washington had exercised in the winter of 1776–77.[13]

Congress' sole openly voiced resentment, as respected the battle, was against John Sullivan, who was blamed by some for the loss of the field. Washington already had been directed to hold a court of inquiry on Sullivan's handling of the expedition against Staten Island,[14] and now the Commander-in-Chief was informed that Congress had re-called that unlucky officer from his command until the inquiry should be completed.[15] At Sullivan's instance, Washington attested that in all he had seen at Brandywine the accused General had behaved well, though he could not undertake to pass judgment, one way or the other, on what had happened that day prior to his arrival at the front near Birmingham Meeting House.[16] As for the suspension of the New Hampshire leader, Washington asked and Congress somewhat re-luctantly consented to let the Major General continue temporarily in service because Washington had so few officers of that rank.[17] In the Army itself there were mutterings against several other officers and a definite attempt on the part of some critics to procure the dismissal of Brig. Gen. William Maxwell.[18]

As always, Washington tried to prevail on grumblers to forget the lesser grievance in serving the larger cause, and he made every effort to speed the movement of the Army by reducing the number of wagons. As an example to his officers, he let it be known that for the time he would carry no baggage except his blankets.[19] On the 15th of Septem-ber, Washington called his still-weary soldiers to pass southward over

[11] 8 *ibid.*, 735–36.

[12] 2 *Burnett*, 492; 8 *JCC.*, 750–51, though it was realized that New Jersey and probably Delaware would need, or would think they needed, for service in their own territory, all the militia they could hope to put in the field. See 9 *G. W.*, 231; 10 *ibid.*, 106; 1 *LTW.*, 434, 443; 2 *ibid.*, 22 ff.

[13] 8 *JCC.*, 752; 9 *G. W.*, 237. Aside from making a few interim appointments, Washing-ton used these powers primarily and almost exclusively for the impressment of clothing. See 10 *G. W.*, 152.

[14] See *supra*, p. 464 and 8 *JCC.*, 700, proceedings of September 1.

[15] 2 *Burnett*, 496–97. Doubt of Sullivan's abilities as a commander were voiced openly (*cf. ibid.*, 517–18).

[16] 9 *G. W.*, 241–42.

[17] See *ibid.*, 227–28; 8 *JCC.*, 449–50; 9 *ibid.*, 253; 2 *Burnett*, 496–97, 514–15, 517; 1 *Sul-livan Papers*, 455, 457, 475, 476 ff. Sullivan was acquitted unanimously, October 16, 1777, of charges that he mishandled the attack of August 22, 1777, on Staten Island. See 9 *G. W.*, 380.

[18] See *infra*, p. 535. Maxwell meantime continued to act with vigor. Cf. his letter of Sept. 16, 1777, to Washington. 2 Dreer, *Coll. Letters Revol. Gens.*, 47, PHS.

[19] Weedon's *Valley Forge Orderly Book*, 46.

the Schuylkill once again in an effort to prevent the entry of the British into Philadelphia or, at least, to make them pay heavily in life for the town. On the 16th, reports indicated that swift maneuver might give the Americans an opportunity that seldom had been theirs—the opportunity of delivering a sudden blow against the enemy while his long, red column was in motion. Washington saw his opening near Warren Tavern on the road from Lancaster to Philadelphia and he prepared to strike. His prospect was of the fairest when, of a sudden, he encountered something he never before had faced on like scale. The weather had changed on the 12th; the wind had switched to the Northwest and had risen in violence; the lingering warmth of summer had been transformed into the cold of late Autumn.[20] Now on the afternoon of the 16th, the wind rose to a gale from the Northeast and brought a furious rain that did not relent for a second.[21] "It came down so hard," a Hessian officer recorded, "that in a few moments we were drenched and sank in mud up to our calves."[22] Washington's Continentals had learned to defy the worst Nor'easters that ever swept in from the tempestuous North Atlantic, but this time they were caught with forty rounds of ammunition in their cartridge boxes. Some of the men had boxes with an inside flap that covered the ammunition;[23] most of the troops had a box made of poplar, covered with poor leather, the flaps of which did not extend far down the sides and ends.[24] The better containers turned the rain; the others proved worthless against a long-continued, searching deluge. Before the day ended, Washington was told that tens of thousands of rounds had been ruined and that many Regiments could not fire a shot. It was the first time in his experience as Commander-in-Chief that "the whole safety of the Army," as Washington later wrote the Board of War, depended in action on the "goodness" of a simple and familiar accouterment.[25] "A most terrible stroke," Henry Knox termed it, one "owing entirely to the badness of

---

[20] *Montresor Journals*, 451.   [21] *Ibid.*, 453.
[22] Major Baurmeister to General von Jungkenn, Oct. 17, 1777; 59 *Penn. Mag.*, 410–11.
[23] 9 *G. W.*, 497.
[24] *Ibid.*, 366. This appears to have been a familiar fault. On Aug. 14, 1778, Gen. William Heath wrote Gov. William Greene of Rhode Island that part of Sullivan's loss of ammunition on Rhode Island was due to bad cartridge boxes, "the ill effects of which we have repeatedly experienced" (2 *Sullivan Papers*, 211).
[25] *Ibid.*, 415. Had American officers seen at the time the contemptuous letters General Kalb was writing Comte de Broglie, they would have been irritated by the manner in which he failed to make any allowance for the difference between the fine British equipment and that which the inexperienced Americans had been able to devise. In this instance, Kalb said that Washington did not think "the enemy's powder was in as bad condition as his own" (755 *Stevens' Facsimiles*, partially printed in *Kapp's Kalb*, 125–26). Actually, the British cartridge

of the cartouche boxes which had been provided for the Army." [26] There was no immediate hope—if indeed there was ultimate hope—of drying any of this ammunition, because the rain continued all night and most of the next day.[27] Washington's men had no shelter and little food;[28] no less than 1000 of them were barefooted.[29] On the flooded lowlands, and the heavy roads,[30] dripping and barefooted men had to shiver and splash; many of them lacked even the comfort of a blanket, because they could not replace those they had lost or thrown off in their retreat from the Brandywine.[31] Opposite the dripping, woebegone American columns, the British, moreover, maneuvered as if they intended to envelop both flanks[32] and they gained such definite superiority of position that on the 19th, though the day was lovely and the wind from the Northwest,[33] Washington again decided to recross the Schuylkill by way of Parker's Ford.[34] He left on the British side of the stream the Brigade of Smallwood and the Division of Anthony Wayne, who then were separated but were to make common cause in harassing the enemy's flank and rear, and especially in trying to cut off the British baggage.[35] Maxwell with the Light Infantry and Brig. Gen. James Potter with his Pennsylvania militia were to join Wayne if they could. The remainder of the Army would retire to a safe distance but would return to the right bank to challenge the enemy when and if the opportunity offered and the men could march.[36]

This possibility was reduced by black news. On the evening of Sep-

---

boxes protected the ammunition of Howe's men so well that comparatively little was lost. For Washington's efforts to improve the cartridge box, or to use a tin canister in its stead, see 9 *G. W.*, 252, 305, 361, 363, 366, 378, 404, 415.

[26] Letter of Sept. 24, 1777, to his wife, *Knox Papers*, MHS.

[27] *Montresor Journals*, 453.   [28] 9 *G. W.*, 231, 238.

[29] *Ibid.*, 259. In GOs of the 15th, Washington announced that the "Clothier General is in attendance with shoes &c; the officers commanding Regiments are to delay no time in getting their men supplied" (*ibid.*, 227), but the supply proved trifling in terms of needs.

[30] *Montresor Journals*, 453.   [31] 9 *G. W.*, 229; cf. *supra*, p. 474.

[32] 9 *G. W.*, 239 ff.   [33] *Montresor Journals*, 455.

[34] 9 *G. W.*, 237–38. Washington's fullest report of this marching and counter-marching is in his letter of Sept. 23, 1777 (*ibid.*, 257). A few details had been given in an earlier letter of the 19th (*ibid.*, 237). Probably the most informative brief narrative is in Timothy Pickering's Journal, 1 *Pickering*, 159–61. See also 1 *Reed*, 311 ff with important communications from Reed to Washington, and 1 *Greene's Greene*, 461 ff. The best British accounts of this maneuver are in *A. Robertson's Diaries*, 147, and in an anonymous "*Journal of the Proceedings of the Army under the Command of Sir William Howe in the year 1777,*" cited hereafter as *Anon. Proc. Howe*, and printed in *AASP.*, April, 1930, p. 80–81, after the original in the Harvard College Lib.   [35] 9 *G. W.*, 235, 240, 241.

[36] Washington to Wayne, Sept. 19[?], 1777; 9 *G. W.*, 235–36. This is undated but was bracketed by Fitzpatrick as of September 18. An almost identical letter to Smallwood (*ibid.*, 240) is dated September 19, which would seem to be the correct date. Wayne was then at Paoli, Smallwood near White Horse, Potter and Maxwell at Pott's Forge, and Washington with the main Army at Reading Furnace.

tember 20–21, Brigadier Anthony Wayne had encamped his small Division along the fringe of thick woods near Paoli, then about twelve miles from Philadelphia. During the night, three British Regiments made a swift and skillful approach, attacked furiously, confused the best of Wayne's troops, drove the less hardy to panic and, in a short time, scattered the entire Division. Those Continentals who thoughtlessly ran in front of the camp-fire were shot down; many who sought the shadows were bayonetted. Wayne succeeded, somewhat surprisingly, in getting his cannon beyond the reach of the enemy and he collected his survivors after daylight, but he had lost at least 150 killed, captured or wounded.[37] Washington made no formal report of this unhappy affair, because Congress was not then in session. Three weeks later, when danger to the Army was less acute, he approved a court of inquiry on the strength of complaints that Wayne had "timely notice" of the intentions of the British and failed to take soldierly precautions.[38]

The disaster to Wayne, coming when it did, not unnaturally cost the Army some experienced troops and accelerated the disappearance of militia who, as always, quickly yielded to fear. Washington felt that he must be wary of every move of the British.[39] With an increasing

[37] These are the figures on which most of the American senior officers agreed. Residents of the countryside who visited the scene of what became known immediately as the "Paoli Massacre," found fifty-three mangled dead (J. Smith Futhey, "The Massacre of Paoli," 1 Penn. Mag., 306). The British carried off seventy-one prisoners, of whom forty were so badly injured that they had to be left at houses by the roadside. (Gaine's N. Y. Mercury, quoted in 1 Moore, 499). Major Samuel Hay of the Seventh Pennsylvania, who helped on the 21st to succor the injured men, reported American casualties as 300 (Futhey, op. cit., 314). Archibald Robertson (Diaries, 149) put Wayne's loss between 400 and 500, a hearsay figure. In writing Gen. Sir Henry Clinton on October 8, General Howe maintained that the American casualties were 500. "Our loss," Howe said, "was Capt. Wolfe of the 40th killed, two or three officers slightly wounded, five privates killed, and about twenty wounded" (Clinton Papers, Clements Lib.). The attack was delivered by the 2nd Light Infantry and the 42nd and 44th Regiments. Futhey's article (loc. cit.) included various documents (p. 310–19), collected with much patience, and it gave the names applied in 1877 to the sites of the previous century. Other facts of interest will be found in André's Journal (ed. 1930), p. 49–51.

[38] 9 G. W., 352. The most vigorous accusant was Col. Richard Humpton of the Eleventh Pennsylvania, the man who had been responsible for the successful removal of boats from the mid stretches of the Delaware the previous December. See Wayne in Futhey, op. cit., 317. Charges were disproved before a subsequent courtmartial, convened at Wayne's instance (John Fitzgerald to Wayne, September 18; Wayne to Washington, September 21 and September 23; Tilghman to Wayne, Sept. 27, 1777, 4 Wayne Papers, 8, 10, 16, 17, PHS. He was acquitted "with the highest honor" (9 G. W., 491. Cf. ibid., 352, 361, 421, 422). Wayne felt that he had been vindicated but he was physically worn and was doubtful whether he would continue in the service. "There are certain Generals," he wrote, "as Lee, Gates, Mifflin, who will point out by their conduct the line which I shall follow next campaign" (Letter of Nov. 10, 1777, to Thomas Mifflin; Letters to Gates, NYHS).

[39] Kalb, loc. cit., stated that an Army of nearly 20,000 was reduced to 6000, but the upper figure probably had not been approached during the campaign. The minimum was not greatly in error. For the prospect on Sept. 28, 1777, see infra, p. 501.

number of his men barefooted, he was nearly baffled in a region where the hostile or apathetic natives gave him no information of the enemy's movements.[40] In the eyes of Nathanael Greene, the Commander-in-Chief seemed to be drifting back into the hesitation of mind that had plagued him before the fall of Fort Washington. One night, when Timothy Pickering and Greene stopped to water their horses at a ford, the new Adjutant General remarked, ". . . Before I came to the Army, I entertained an exalted opinion of General Washington's military talents, but I have since seen nothing to enhance it." Pickering did not confess what he actually thought—that Washington was a less able soldier than he had assumed. Greene answered immediately and pridefully, "Why, the General does want decision; for my part, I decide in a moment."[41] A newcomer, General Kalb, wrote more elaborately: "Washington is the most amiable, kind-hearted and upright of men; but as a General he is too slow, too indolent and far too weak; besides, he has a tinge of vanity in his composition, and overestimates himself. In my opinion, whatever success he may have will be owing to good luck and to the blunders of his adversaries, rather than to his abilities. I may even say that he does not know how to improve upon the grossest blunders of the enemy. He has not yet overcome his old prejudice against the French."[42]

The concern of Kalb and of Greene doubtless was shared by other ranking officers not quite so self-confident, but actually at this time Washington was almost as hopeful as he was cautious and apparently of doubtful mind. Crippled because his Army was illshod and illclothed, he believed that time would bring him reenforcements with which to meet the British, even if, in the end, the enemy occupied Philadelphia.[43] He successfully resisted the effort of Congress to take troops from him and to use them in expediting the construction of the defences on Delaware River.[44] Almost daily he sought to hasten the march of Mc-Dougall's Brigade,[45] the van of the 2500 men called from Putnam for service with the main Army.[46] Washington endeavored, also, to draw to him four other contingents—Philemon Dickinson and David Forman with their Jersey militia, similar temporary troops to the number

[40] 9 G. W., 257, 259.
[41] Pickering, quoted in 1 Greene's Greene, 468. The author of that work recorded his regret that his grandfather said this.
[42] Letter of Sept. 24, 1777, to Comte de Broglie; Kapp's Kalb, 127.
[43] 9 G. W., 239.   [44] Ibid., 215.
[45] Ibid., 239, 245 n, 246–47.   [46] Ibid., 253.

of perhaps 1000 from Virginia,[47] the Continental Regiments under Heath in Massachusetts,[48] and Morgan's riflemen who had been loaned Gates.[49]

As always—it was the vice of America no less than of the Army—the speed of fulfilment seldom equalled that of expectation. Scattered forces concentrated slowly. Until some, at least, of his reenforcements assembled, Washington could do no more than to keep vigilant, to render difficult the British passage of the nearby watercourses,[50] and to repair, as far as time permitted, the manifest weaknesses of his command.

The worst and most pressing of these was in the Light Horse. It was not Washington's nature to complain of evils he could not correct, for which reason, primarily, he seldom had written Congress regarding his cavalry. He had hoped that Joseph Reed would accept the command of the mounted arm, for which he thought his Adjutant General had shown aptitude during the Trenton-Princeton campaign; but after Reed had declined in June,[51] Washington had deferred action. None of the few Colonels of Light Horse was qualified for promotion; no Brigadier of Infantry was available because of the continuing scarcity of officers of that rank. Washington had reasoned, further, that as the cavalry Regiments usually were detached separately, they stood less in need of a general officer than if they had been foot soldiers.[52] Washington later became convinced that if the cavalry were brought together and employed as a unit, they might prove a powerful instrument.

This changed decision had been due, in considerable measure, to the insistence—it might have been termed the persistence—of Count de Pulaski, a Polish officer of about 29 years of age, who had come to headquarters with letters from the American Commissioners in France. Washington had found no employment for him, but when Pulaski had described how he had used cavalry in a Polish uprising, the American commander had concluded that the leadership of the American troopers might fit Pulaski' abilities and might make that officer "extremely useful." A letter to that effect had been written Congress in August.[53]

[47] Ibid., 223, 246, 260, 271–72, 273–74, 277; Washington to Col. William Edmunds of Fauquier, Sept. 24, 28, 1777; Richmond (Va.) Enquirer, semi-weekly ed., Oct. 6, 1857.
[48] 9 G. W., 219; Heath, 138, 139, 140.   [49] 9 G. W., 265.
[50] Ibid., 220, 221, 224, 237.   [51] 8 ibid., 117, 121 n, 141, 248, 293–94.
[52] 9 ibid., 143–44.
[53] Ibid. Pulaski's preliminary correspondence on his proposed service in America and some letters writen after his arrival are in the fine collection of Dr. F. M. Dearborn of New York City.

Pulaski most unwisely had been applying directly to that body and, after the manner of other ambitious foreigners, imperiously had sought rank subordinate only to that of Washington and of Lafayette. This had created against him a prejudice not readily overcome, but now, September 15th, Congress created the post of "Commander of the Horse," with rank of Brigadier, and elected Pulaski to it.[54] Washington announced the appointment in General Orders of the 21st,[55] but neither he nor Pulaski could be sure of the reception this would have, particularly by Col. Stephen Moylan, a gentleman with a mounted Regiment and ambitions of his own. If Pulaski succeeded in winning the good opinion and hearty support of Moylan and of the two Virginia cavalry Colonels, Theodorick Bland and George Baylor, the Light Horse might strike many a stout blow to aid the Infantry when—or did Washington again have to say "if"?—the footmen could find shoes for bad roads and warm clothing for wintry bivouacs.

That dark contingency was deepened almost immediately. The danger to Philadelphia had compelled Congress and the Commander-in-Chief to remove to magazines in less exposed towns all stores not immediately required in the city. Ten days after the Battle of the Brandywine, the Americans concluded not only that Howe had heard of this transfer, but also that he knew the particular value of supplies deposited in Reading. A march begun on the 21st of September, up the right bank of the Schuylkill, seemed to be directed straight at the irreplaceable new base.[56] Washington conformed and shifted his right in the same direction,[57] whereupon, overnight, the British reversed their march, slipped back down the river and crossed at Fatland and nearby fords. On the 26th, the enemy, unopposed, moved into Philadelphia, with the easy air of proprietorship.[58]

The American commander was out-maneuvered so easily that the sole immediate question became that of where he should place and how he should employ his troops now that he had lost the largest American city, in a manner more humiliating, if possible, than that of his forced abandonment of New York in September, 1776. Three days before

[54] 8 *JCC.*, 631, 673, 687, 698, 711, 745.   [55] 9 *G. W.*, 244.
[56] Cf. Washington to his brother, John Augustine, Oct. 18, 1777: ". . . the loss of [Reading] must have proved our ruin" (9 *G. W.*, 397).
[57] Cf. Washington to McDougall, Sept. 24, 1777; *McDougall Papers*, NYHS.
[58] 9 *G. W.*, 257, 258–59, 262–63, 397; 1 *Reed*, 315 n; 1 *Moore*, 500; *A. Robertson's Diaries*, 150; Diary of Robert Morton, 1 *Penn. Mag.*, 7; *C. Marshall's Diary*, 130; *Montresor Journals*, 456–57.

Howe raised the King's standard again in the town of the Quakers, Washington had asked his council of war whether he should attack the enemy at once or should await the arrival of reenforcements, a question to which there could be one answer only, unanimous advice to postpone the offensive.[59] Even after the British took the city where American Independence had been declared, Washington deferred a close approach to Philadelphia because Wayne and Smallwood had not rejoined.[60]

As he waited in camp about six miles North of Parker's Ford on the Schuylkill,[61] he and his senior officers had an astonishing experience: they found that British capture of the city meant little compared with what they had feared in the autumn of 1776 the fall of Philadelphia would involve. During the nightmare of Washington's vain pleading with Charles Lee to come to his assistance in mid-December, 1776, the Commander-in-Chief had said that the loss of the Quaker City "must prove of the most fatal consequences to the cause of America." [62] Now that the calamity had fallen, it was manifest that the course of the campaign had lessened enormously the industrial importance of Philadelphia. British obstruction of the Delaware, and the consequent southward turn of Howe's transports had given time for the removal of stores previously reduced in volume. The slowness of the voyage to the Head of Elk and delay in starting from that point had been another reprieve, so well employed by the Americans that the British found in Philadelphia virtually no public property of any service or value. The city was a shell and to some it might be a symbol: it no longer contained the living organism of independence. Besides, if the Continentals could continue to hold the water approaches, they could prevent the supply of Howe's army by the easy route of the Delaware.[63] He would be compelled to forage in the country around the city for all fresh provisions. If this were undertaken by small parties, they could be cut off. In event large forces were sent out, long marches in the mud would exhaust them.

Would the loss of the city prove to be serious in any moral sense?

[59] 9 *G. W.*, 263. [60] *Ibid.*, 258, 265.
[61] The two successive camps were around Fagleysville and Schwenkville, roughly six to twelve miles Northeast of Pottstown, where Washington had his temporary headquarters. The district was known loosely as Potts Grove. Washington computed that he was twenty-eight miles from Philadelphia. Cf. 9 *G. W.*, 249.
[62] See *supra*, p. 284 and 6 *G. W.*, 341.
[63] 9 *G. W.*, 255–56, 259, 283, 284.

Behind the instant answer of a vigorous "No," were two reasons: Washington's soldiers, from highest to humblest, had come by this time to regard the fall of Philadelphia as inevitable and they consequently did not permit it to dampen a spirit that was rising again now that tired men were rested.[64] The second and the weightier reason was the joyous certainty, plain to every eye, that the darkest cloud of the war was losing its blackness. The strategical danger that Washington had dreaded most was being dissipated. On the 19th of September, at Freeman's Farm, North of Albany,[65] Gates had worsted his opponent so thoroughly that the Commander-in-Chief felt the Americans could "count on the total ruin of Burgoyne." [66] Washington announced to the Army on September 28 the first exaggerated reports of the victory,[67] and for celebration he ordered all troops paraded that afternoon and a gill of rum presented each man. Thirteen guns were fired.[68] It was a great day in its effect on the good cheer of the men, and in its bearing on all future plans of major operations: unless there was an incredible reversal of fortune, the Hudson no longer would have to be shielded, hourly and vigilantly, as the jugular of America, the severance of which meant death.

Washington's Army was reenforced at the same time it was reanimated. McDougall's Brigade from Putnam arrived about the 27th,[69] though its 900 men were fewer than Washington had expected as first relief. Other troops were close at hand in numbers not known in every instance but estimated, with some caution, as sufficient, when all of them reported, to raise the total strength of the Army to 8000 Continentals and 3000 militia, rank and file.[70] "I am in hopes," Washington wrote Heath, "it will not be long before we are in a situation to repair the consequences of our late ill success . . ." [71] With that in view, he

---

[64] Ibid., 295.

[65] The action sometimes is styled the Battle of Bemis Heights and occasionally the Battle of Stillwater.

[66] Ibid., 285. Cf. ibid., 295 and the rhetorical GOs of Oct. 3, 1777, ibid., 305–06. See also 2 Burnett, 503.

[67] 9 G. W., 276–77.

[68] This is the first instance observed in the present research of that number of cannon fired in salute by formal order in Washington's Army.

[69] The date is not fixed with certainty. Washington wrote on the 26th that the Army was "advancing to form a junction with General McDougall" (9 G. W., 270) and on the 28th he told his council of war that McDougall had arrived (ibid., 278).

[70] Ibid., 278. John Adams had written his wife as long previously as August 29: "The Continental Army under Washington, Sullivan, and Nash, besides, is in my opinion more numerous by several thousands than Howe's whole force" (Adams, Fam. Let., 300, verbatim).

[71] Letter of Sept. 30, 1777; 9 G. W., 287.

again asked his council of war whether he should "make a general and vigorous attack upon the enemy" or mark time until more troops came from Putnam and from Virginia, whence 2000 poorly armed militia were believed to be on their way.[72] On this, the council was divided, ten to five, but the majority, including all the experienced seniors in the service, recommended that he move forward to a point within about twelve miles of the British and there await either an advantageous opening or the additional men of whom he spoke.[73]

Opportunity outmarched militia. At the beginning of the new month, October,[74] Washington received two intercepted letters which mentioned the detachment of a British force to proceed against Billingsport,[75] and to aid there in the attempt of the British navy to open Delaware River.[76] Other intelligence reports showed that the main army of Howe was encamped in a described order of battle at and near Germantown, a handsome, if sprawling village five miles Northwest of Philadelphia.[77] When Washington communicated this information to his general officers, they were unanimous in advising him to attack the camp at Germantown.[78] The Commander-in-Chief had moved the

[72] The minutes may appear to be slightly equivocal on this point but they almost certainly mean that Washington spoke of subsequent reenforcement and not of the arrival of those who would bring the total to 11,000. A few days previously, it will be recalled (see n. 47 *supra*), Washington had expected the Virginia militia reenforcement to number no more than 1000.

[73] *Ibid.*, 279.

[74] The exact date is not known, though it probably was the 1st.

[75] On the Delaware River, in Gloucester Co., New Jersey, close to the present-day Paulsboro.

[76] 9 *G. W.*, 308.

[77] In dispatches, no specific mention is made of supplementary intelligence reports, but Sullivan's letter of Oct. 25, 1777, mentions dispositions that scarcely could have been known otherwise than through some resident or spy who had given headquarters an occount of them. See 1 *Sullivan Papers*, 542. As the American Army previously had been posted for a short time around Germantown, Washington and his ranking officers had some familiarity with the place. The General's organized espionage may be glimpsed in his correspondence of 1777, but his care in protecting his spies led him, apparently, to destroy most of the secret reports and the detailed vouchers of agents for money paid them. An amusing incident of the spring had been the arrest of one of the American spies by Benjamin Lincoln who thought the man was collecting information for the enemy (Letter of Apr. 7, 1777; 7 *G. W.*, 368–69). Washington believed in employing numerous agents of espionage (cf. *ibid.*, 385), in paying them amply (8 *ibid.*, 2), and in straining every effort to procure their information as promptly as it possibly could be forwarded (7 *ibid.*, 371). Sometimes, as a reward of effort, he received or at least thought he received early news of the enemy's movements (cf. *ibid.*, 327–28). The men most active in directing Washington's intelligence service in 1777 were first Nathaniel Sackett (*ibid.*, 92, 101, 221 n) and then Maj. John Clark, Jr., who was given some difficult assignments (cf. 10 *ibid.*, 104, 115). Clarke's spies, who included at least one old woman (*Elias Boudinot*, 50) and some men supposed to be farmers or hucksters (10 *G. W.*, 183), were allowed on his pass to go where they pleased (*ibid.*, 169). Certain aspects of Washington's counter-espionage are mentioned in 8 *ibid.*, 67, 154, and 9 *JCC.*, 784–85.

[78] It has been assumed that a third council of war was held, but no minutes of it have been found. Washington's language in his letter of Oct. 5, 1777, fits the idea of individual conferences as readily as that of a council of war (9 *G. W.*, 308).

Army on September 29 from Pennypacker's Mill [79] to the crossing of Shippack Creek on the road of the same name.[80] Now, on the 2nd, Washington marched down this road into Worcester Township and made camp not far from the residence of Peter Wentz.[81]

According to Washington's maps and information, this advance put the Army twenty miles from Philadelphia [82] and therefore fifteen miles from Germantown—as close as he dared advance in daylight because he hoped to surprise the enemy [83] by attacking at dawn over roads that seemed to form an ideal stage for a surprise. The road from Reading and the Shippack Road [84] ran parallel to each other until they reached a point about four miles from the centre of Germantown. There they met at Chestnut Hill and ran southward together as the "Main Road" or the "Main Street." The course of the two roads, in short, would facilitate a deployment at Chestnut Hill or South of it. Moreover, Northeast of the Shippack Road was the Lime Kiln Road which came into Germantown from the East. Again, West and Southwest of the Main Street and connected easily with it was the so-called Manatawny Road,[85] which crossed Wissahickon Creek and a smaller stream in following the course of the Schuylkill. Thus Washington could push his Army down any of the highways, draw his lines, advance on three or even on four roads, and assail simultaneously the front and flanks of the British.

The greater part of Germantown was built along its main street, which was about two miles in length and was lined at intervals on both sides with houses. Some of these were humble shelters, and some of them stone structures almost strong enough to serve as small fortresses. Although there were no cross streets in the normal sense of the word, several lanes ran from the main highway to the parallel roads. Any of

---

[79] *Ibid.*, 285. Washington and his staff spelled the name Pennybacker, Pennybecker, Pennybaker and Pennibacker. A marker was placed Oct. 7, 1897 (21 *Penn. Mag.*, 498) on the site, which is close to the present Schwenkville. See N. D. Wright, "Itinerary of General Washington in Montgomery County, 1777–78." This is an annotated map and is the easiest guide to most of the movements of Washington and his Army in the fall of 1777.

[80] 9 *G. W.*, 286.

[81] *Ibid.*, 303. The locality is that of Centre Point.

[82] *Ibid.*, 300.

[83] See his letter of Oct. 8, 1777, to Governor Trumbull: "Having obtained information of the situation of the enemy, we determined to endeavor to do something by way of surprise" (9 *G. W.*, 330). It may be proper to note here that Washington somewhat underestimated distances in this operation. He probably was about two miles farther from the British than he thought he was. Cf. John Armstrong to Thomas Wharton, Oct. 12, 1777; *Reed Papers*, NYHS.

[84] Sometimes called the Bethlehem Road.

[85] Washington spelled it the Monatany Road.

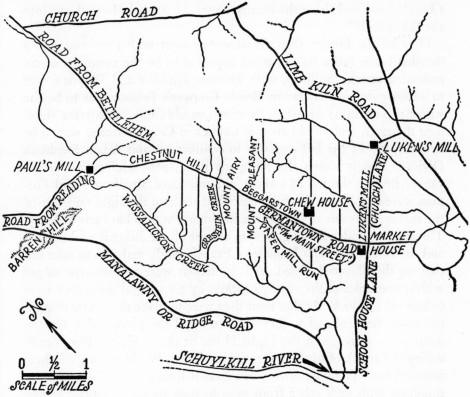

THE BATTLE OF GERMANTOWN, OCT. 4, 1777

The later phases of Washington's attempt at the simultaneous convergence of American columns at Germantown for an attack at dawn went awry, though the prime design was soldierly if not simple. This sketch is after the careful map of Spencer Bonsall, September, 1877, reproduced in 1 *Penn. Mag.*, 368.

these lanes, with its fences, would shelter a line and would check an advancing force. The best known of the byways had been drawn at right angles from the vicinity of the German Church and of the Market House, near the southern end of the town. To the eastward, the traveler was in the Church Lane; the western passage was styled the School House Lane. It was on or close to these two, the Americans were informed, that the greater part of the British had their camps, the principal objective of the attack.

Washington, in other words, was to approach a main street and two major lanes—the whole in the form of a cross—and he hoped to do this in such a way that he could break the front, hurl back the flank on the

Church Lane and drive the enemy down the School House Lane into the Schuylkill.[86]

Over all the known facts, Washington went with care, and into a detailed battle order he put what appeared to be the essentials of co-ordinated attack. Sullivan, with his own Division and Wayne's, was to advance down Manatawny Road. Conway's Brigade was to be the van of this column; Armstrong's militia would form the extreme right, next the river, and would cross Wissahickon Creek. Greene was to be in command of the left and was to conduct his and Adam Stephen's Division straight down the Shippack Road, with McDougall in advance. Beyond the left of Greene, the militia of Smallwood and Forman were to follow a carefully described route to the right and rear of the enemy, but none of the militia Regiments was to have any artillery. The reserve, under Stirling, was to consist of the Brigade of Maxwell and the North Carolina Brigade of Francis Nash, and was to take station on the Shippack Road. All the troops were to endeavor to get within two miles of the enemy's pickets by 2 A.M., and there they were to halt till 4 o'clock. At that hour they were to make their final dispositions; on the stroke of 5, they were to assail the pickets. No written instructions were given the Light Horse or the Artillery. For coordinating the attack of his four converging forces, Washington gave these instructions: "The columns of continental troops and militia to communicate with each other from time to time by Light Horse. Proper flanking parties to be kept out from each column."[87]

Once only in his three years and more of command of the Army had Washington drafted and executed a general order for offensive action by the whole of his Foot. That had been for the advance on Trenton, Dec. 25–26, 1776. This new, second order was more elaborate and perhaps bewildering to men unfamiliar with the ground, but the only omitted point of importance concerned the route by which Sullivan was to get to the Main Street if he found it to his advantage to use that highway. This was explained verbally and was not misunderstood.[88]

[86] This last feature of the plan is not mentioned in Washington's battle order, but Sullivan remarked it in explaining why the left wing of the Continental Army was stronger than the right (1 *Sullivan Papers*, 543).

[87] 9 *G. W.*, 307–08.

[88] Washington said in his GO of October 3: "The Divisions of Sullivan and Wayne are to march down the Monatany Road" (9 *G. W.*, 307); but in his letter of October 5 to the President of Congress he wrote: "The Divisions of Sullivan and Wayne . . . were to enter the town by Chestnut Hill, while General Armstrong with the Pennsylvania Militia should fall down the Monatawny Road . . ." (*ibid.*, 307). Sullivan's language would indicate that he came to the Main Street from the Shippack Road, at Chestnut Hill (1 *Sullivan Papers*, 543).

Reading these orders, critics in the Army who sometimes accused Washington of overcaution must have been silenced for the moment: Trained reenforcements had not begun to arrive until the 27th of September. One week later the "American Fabius" was to take the offensive.

The Army started its march at 7 o'clock [89] on the evening of October 3, though it was 9 P.M. when Sullivan's Division moved out of its camp on Metuchen Hill.[90] As some of the troops had been allotted little sleep on the night of October 2–3,[91] Washington had to reconcile himself to the prospect that the morning would find them weary, even before they went into action; but he had no remedy for this other than to conduct a careful march with proper intervals of rest. Probably to avert further criticism of Sullivan, the Commander-in-Chief decided to remain personally on the right with that officer, and to entrust the entire management of the left wing to Nathanael Greene. The longer road was Greene's by as much as four miles,[92] because a part of his route was circuitous.[93]

The night wore dismally on, as the night of every march does, with hours lengthened when legs grew weary, but by 3 A.M., on the 4th, Washington, riding near the head of Sullivan's column, was inside the area covered by the British patrols.[94] No alarm was audible; the troops continued quietly on their way toward the known picket posts of the enemy. Washington had given instructions that the pickets should be seized or bayonetted before they could make an outcry;[95] at the moment the orders seemed to have a good prospect of execution by the troops designated to "take off" these guards.[96] The weather during the night had not been unpromising. Some of the Regiments were to have a glimpse of the rising sun,[97] but as morning approached, the advance of

---

[89] 9 *G. W.*, 307. The troops were to be ready at 6 P.M. (*ibid.*, 307).

[90] 1 *Sullivan Papers*, 544.

[91] Asher Holmes in *NJHSP.*, 1922–23, p. 34–35, cited hereafter as *Asher Holmes*.

[92] 1 *Sullivan Papers*, 544.

[93] Timothy Pickering's letter of August 23, 1826, in *North American Review*, v. 23 (new ser., v. 14) p. 429–30. This is a late document to be accepted as a primary source, but as far as it can be verified, it seems accurate, and it does not deal with a subject on which Pickering could have had any reason for writing as a partisan. The paper is cited here as *Pickering's Letter*, with the page reference to *N.A. Review*. In preparing it, Pickering seems to have forgotten his letters and Journal of September–October, 1777, for which see 1 *Pickering*, 154–180, though actually his contemporary records contain less of an important nature on Germantown than did the paper written in his old age.

[94] Howe's report in 2 *Belcher*, 274.

[95] 9 *G. W.*, 308.   [96] *Ibid.*

[97] John E. Howard to Timothy Pickering, Jan. 29, 1827; 5 *Sparks*, 468. This letter, which is not important, is subject to the same criticism as Pickering's own, because of the date at which it was written, fifty years after the events.

the Army ran into fog, which limited vision, distorted the appearance of landmarks, and confused every sound.

A bad setting did not balk a good beginning. Unchallenged, Sullivan's men tramped down the main road; Conway's Brigade shifted toward the right across the fields. About dawn,[98] Washington heard the rattle of a few muskets, contrary to orders. Evidently the British pickets had been reached, but they had not been surprised altogether. After that, in less time than should have been required for these men to fall back on the first line, the roll of a British volley reached Washington's ears. The pickets, Sullivan explained later, "were suddenly reenforced by all their Light Infantry," [99] who seemed to be drawn up in an orchard,[100] unprotected by trenches or redoubts.[101] Conway had to halt his flank march and form his Brigade in line; [102] soon Washington learned that the enemy was advancing.[103]

Was this the first act of the familiar tragedy, all over again—a repulse and then a rout? Had Americans learned nothing since Long Island and Kip's Bay? If the question rose in any mind, the answer, even though the fog marred and muffled it, was reassuring for the moment: The British musketry was no nearer; the American line must be standing firm—but what a torture it was to be waiting there, in daylight, and not to be able to see! Perhaps that fog drowned the sound of Greene's advance. Nothing had come from him, neither a messenger nor the roll of a single volley: he might be succeeding so well that he did not have to use small arms, even though the battle on the American right had spread the alarm, but it was possible that Greene had lost his

[98] Reports of the time of the beginning of the action do not actually differ as greatly as they may appear on first reading to do. Walter Stewart, Colonel of what soon became the Thirteenth Pennsylvania, wrote that the attack opened "past 6 o'clock" but he was on the American left. (Stewart to Gates[?] Oct. 12, 1777; *Reed Papers*, NYHS). General Armstrong gave the time as about sunrise, which on October 4 was at 5:59 (See Armstrong to Wharton, Oct. 5, 1777, *ibid.*). General Howe wrote Gen. Sir Henry Clinton the attack came soon after day (Letter of Oct. 8, 1777; *Clinton Papers*, Clements Lib.). James Wallace gave the time as "before it was quite light" (Letter of Oct. 12, 1777, to Michael Wallace; 12 *T* 134).

[99] Sullivan's letter of Oct. 25, 1777, to Pres. Meshech Weare of New Hampshire; 1 *Sullivan Papers*, 544. This is the most detailed of the American accounts of action on the right during the Battle of Germantown. The troops who met this American advance were the 2nd Light Infantry and the 40th Infantry (Howe to Clinton, Oct. 8, 1777, *loc. cit.*).

[100] Howard, *op. cit.*, 468.

[101] Howe said later that he constructed no redoubts for the security of the camp or outpost, because works of this nature "are apt to induce an opinion of inferiority . . . I wished to create always the impression of superiority" (Howe's *Narrative*, 27).

[102] 1 *Sullivan Papers*, 544.

[103] *Ibid.* It is not possible to ascertain precisely when reports of the different developments in this battle reached Washington, but his subsequent correspondence indicates that he was familiar with most of the incidents on Sullivan's front. Cf. 9 *G. W.*, 310–11: "Sullivan and the whole right wing of the Army . . . acted immediately under my eye. . . ."

way or had met some overpowering obstacle. Why did Armstrong and his Pennsylvania militia on the extreme right withhold their fire? It looked as if Sullivan's Division might have to fight the battle alone. The New Hampshire General consequently ordered Wayne to form on his left where Greene's troops were to have taken position. With like prudence, Sullivan started two Regiments in the direction of Armstrong's advance and he dispatched Moylan's Light Horse to aid the Infantry.[104] By these dispositions, Sullivan sought to secure his flanks as well as possible, though he might be compelled to pull both of them back.[105]

About the time this was done, the sounds and the snatches of information that came back to Washington indicated that the attack of the British Light Infantry had been beaten off. The initiative had passed to Sullivan, whose men began to push forward again across heavy fields, planted in buckwheat.[106] Troops found this slow work and doubly dangerous, because they might encounter the enemy behind any fence or hedge and in the enclosure of any residence. To advance, Sullivan's Regiments had to tear down each of these fences, or climb over—a target for every courageous British soldier within range and sight.[107] Perhaps fortunately, in this part of the contest, range and sight were not as nearly equal as on other fields where Americans had faced British. Had it been possible, at the instant, for the redcoats to stand off 100 yards and fire at the Continentals on top the fences, Sullivan's attack would have ended in a slaughter. As it was, the fog, now thick with mingled smoke, made the Americans' pursuit a grope, but it blinded the British and at some points cut visibility to thirty yards.[108] So long

---

104 1 *Sullivan Papers*, 544.
105 That is to say, with both flanks "in the air," he might find it necessary to "refuse" them, but these terms do not seem to have been current in 1777. "Refused" soon was to find its place in the books. William Duane's *Military Dictionary*, ed. 1810, defined "refused" and devoted an interesting paragraph to the tactical development of "refusal" by Frederick the Great.
106 McMichael's Diary, 15 *Penn. Arc.* (2), p. 213.
107 1 *Sullivan Papers*, 545. In his Journal, Timothy Pickering discussed, after the battle, the advantage of throwing down a fence when this could be done, and he described how this often could be accomplished if a number of men would pull and push together until they loosened the posts and then could lift the fence out of the ground and throw it down. See 1 *Pickering*, 170–71.
108 Washington wrote that friends could not be distinguished from foes beyond thirty yards (9 *G. W.*, 397). An officer's letter of Oct. 10, 1777, in *Va. Gazette* of Oct. 17, 1777 (12 *T* 136) gave the distance as fifty yards. On the left, Brig. Gen. George Weedon recorded, one could not identify uniforms beyond sixty yards. See his letter to John Page, Oct. 5, 1777, wrongly dated October 4; *Chicago HS*. In the fine Weedon MSS of that collection is another letter of Oct. 8, 1777, to some Virginia official. These are cited hereafter as, respectively, the *First* and *Second Weedon Germantown Letters*.

as the left flank of Sullivan did not overlap the right of Greene, or drift too far off axis, the fog was more of a protection to the troops on Main Street than they or their officers realized. When the Continentals drove the enemy from one fence line, they did not hesitate to run to the next and then to the next. Soon the troops were far in front of the Commander-in-Chief and were firing furiously. Washington turned to Adjutant General Pickering: "I am afraid General Sullivan is throwing away his ammunition; ride forward and tell him to preserve it." [109] Farther the sound receded; heavier still were the fog and the smoke; [110] soon a messenger brought the Commander-in-Chief verbal confirmation from Sullivan of what the firing already had told: the enemy was giving way, Sullivan said; Wayne should push on. Washington agreed. What was more, he ordered Maxwell and Nash, the leaders of the two reserve Brigades, to put their troops on the flanks of the advancing line.[111]

As Maxwell's Brigade moved up to support Sullivan, in accordance with Washington's orders, it ran into a considerable fire of musketry from the windows of a large stone residence, Cliveden, which natives called the Chew House.[112] Evidently, some of the British Light Infantry had entered and had barricaded the dwelling and were using it as if it were a blockhouse. From the second-story windows, which had stout and heavy shutters, the redcoats delivered a sharp fire.[113] An American battery was brought up to throw its projectiles into the rooms and halls through the windows, but the cannon, six-pounders, were placed at an angle to the structure and struck mere glancing blows. Officers who were with Washington began to argue whether they should mask the Chew House and continue the advance, regardless of the fire and a possible sortie from the building,[114] or whether they should summon the garrison to yield and, on refusal, undertake to storm the place. Henry Knox was altogether for demanding that the

109 *Pickering's Letter*, 427.
110 *Asher Holmes*, loc. cit. Cf. Anthony Wayne, in 1 *Reed*, 320: "The fog, together with the smoke occasioned by our cannon and musketry, made it almost as dark as night."
111 1 *Sullivan Papers*, 545. Although Washington did not so state, it seems probable that these troops were in echelon. This, of course, would give both added weight and new security to the line. For this advance, see Lt. Col. Adam Hubley to Col. William Atlee, Oct. 9, 1777, Harrisburg (Penn.) *Democratic Union*, Sept. 5, 1845.
112 As the map on p. 503 shows, the residence stands back from the street, on the left hand (eastern) side of Main Street as the troops proceeded southward. See the delightful *Guide Book to Historic Germantown*, by Charles F. Jenkins, 113, 152.
113 Major Baurmeister to General von Jungkenn, Oct. 17, 1777; 59 *Penn. Mag.*, 416.
114 Anonymous account, 2 *Papers of George Clinton*, 369.

occupants lay down their arms; Pickering was equally positive in saying the troops should skirt the residence and go on. Washington sided with his Chief of Artillery and authorized the transmission, under flag, of a call for the surrender of the place. Lieutenant Colonel Smith, Deputy Adjutant General, volunteered to carry the summons and, for his gallantry, received a fatal wound in the leg.[115]

When the American reserve at length was instructed to keep out of range of the Chew House and otherwise to disregard it, half an hour had been lost,[116] but Sullivan apparently had not been hampered by the delay in the arrival of the reserve. His men were pressing gallantly on across the fields, among the camps of British outposts, over the fences, and through the blinding, choking smoke and fog. Wayne's troops were equally aggressive in their furious resolution to get revenge for the slaughter at Paoli. It was in vain that officers tried to protect the British wounded or the occasional redcoat who was captured unhurt. All these were bayonetted.[117] Washington was not told of this, but the sound of battle made his pulse beat high as it had that cold morning in January at Princeton. Discretion and the importance of keeping a fixed position on the field lost all meaning. He pressed so far to the front that Sullivan had to ask him to retire—a request he heeded for a few minutes but then forgot as his soldiers kept their pace. He could not stay in the rear if those banners of the young republic were sweeping onward.[118]

All this time there had been intense concern in Washington's mind over the lack of any news from Greene, but now his anxiety was relieved. Stephen's men appeared on the left of Wayne; from the countryside beyond Stephen came the bark of cannon and the rattle of small arms. Greene apparently was in position, and, no doubt, was driving the British.[119] Victory appeared to be that much closer: Defeat of Howe

---

[115] Pickering in 1 *Pickering*, 169, 173; *Pickering's Letter*, 428. Regrettably, the young officer who carried the flag cannot be identified from *Heitman*, but he may have been William Smith, former Lieutenant of the Fifteenth Virginia.

[116] *Pickering's Letter*, 428–29; 1 *Sullivan Papers*, 544–45. Wilkinson visited the Chew House not long prior to the publication of his *Memoirs* in 1816 and he included, (v. 1, p. 364–65), a brief account of the remaining scars of conflict. Lossing's description is in 2 *Field Book*, 314.

[117] Wayne to Mrs. Wayne, Oct. 6, 1777; 4 *Wayne Papers*, 31, PHS.

[118] 1 *Sullivan Papers*, 547. It is impossible to determine the exact stage of the advance at which this occurred.

[119] *G. W.*, 309–10. The elimination from Washington's report of the sentences reprinted in *ibid.*, 309 n. 47 raises some question regarding the sequence of events at this stage of the battle. Washington's reference to the beginning of the attack by Greene "about three quarters of an hour after that from the right" (*ibid.*, 310), would indicate that the sound of the action

when disaster was about to overwhelm Burgoyne might mean the end of the war! Washington summoned Armstrong to instruct him on the deployment and advance of the militia on the extreme right.[120] "The great cause," George Weedon said later, "was, in my opinion, in one quarter of an hour of being finally settled . . ."[121]

Washington was about to give the order for a general advance toward Philadelphia,[122] when something happened. On the left, where Wayne's men were extending Sullivan's line and were trying to keep up with the advance, there was confused firing. Shouts were heard and were answered from a greater distance. On Sullivan's front a loud volley shook the ground but provoked an uneven answer. The clatter of musketry soon was nearer and more nervous. Out of the fog men came back on the run, some frantic with fear, some able to gasp a few words—that the enemy was in the rear,[123] that the flank had been turned,[124] that friends had been mistaken for foes,[125] that orders to retreat had been shouted. Every man had a different tale, but none paused long to tell it. Nor could they be halted, even to snatch up the booty of the British camps they had overrun.[126] Presently the artillery galloped past and took the road to the rear.[127] Officers from the front, swinging their swords and swearing or pleading, tried to stop what in the course of a few minutes became a mad panic.[128] Washington, his staff and several mounted Colonels joined in the attempt to rally the troops. It was as if they had been shouting to the fog to dissipate itself.[129] Hundreds ran as if the Devil himself were lunging at them; the line was a mob; the road was jammed; the fields were crowded

---

was audible. Sullivan (1 *Papers*, 545) put the time half an hour later but he stated specifically that "firing from General Greene's [Division] was heard still farther to the left."

[120] Armstrong's letter of Oct. 5, 1777, in 1 *Reed*, 322. The Pennsylvania commander did not state the reason for the call but it doubtless concerned attack and pursuit. The message, said Armstrong, was received about 9 o'clock. (Letter of Oct. 5, 1777, to Pres. Thomas Wharton, *Reed Papers*, NYHS.)

[121] *Second Weedon Germantown Letter.*

[122] He so informed Thomas Paine later. See Paine to Benjamin Franklin, May 16, 1778; 1 *Writings of Thomas Paine*, 389.

[123] *Asher Holmes*, loc. cit.; 1 *Sullivan Papers*, 546.

[124] *First Weedon Germantown Letter.*

[125] Wayne in 1 *Reed*, 320; 12 *T* 136; 1 *Greene's Greene*, 478–79.

[126] Weedon, as *supra.*

[127] 1 *Sullivan Papers*, 547; *Va. Gazette* letter, 12 *T* 136.

[128] Cf. Washington to the President of Congress: "The troops began suddenly to retreat, and entirely left the field in spite of every effort that could be made to rally them" (9 *G. W.*, 310).

[129] "The utmost exertions to rally them again was [sic] in vain." *Second Weedon Germantown Letter.*

with fugitives. By 10 o'clock incredibly, the action was over.[130] Two hours and forty minutes had sufficed to see a victory won, as the Americans believed, and then thrown away. Most of the men halted before many minutes had passed, but Washington could do no less than order the retreat continued till pursuit was shaken off [131] and the maddest fugitive concluded that he was safe. With intervals of rest for the men who remained together, the backward march dragged for twenty miles and more, until the Army was again at Pennypacker's Mill.[132]

What had caused the panic? That was the question every one asked and none could answer to the satisfaction of his comrades. "I never could, and cannot now learn," said Thomas Paine months later, "and I believe no man can inform truly the cause of that day's miscarriage." [133] It was a fact that in the fog, some of Wayne's men and some of Stephen's mistook a dim and distant line for the enemy and exchanged fire several times, and that the retreat had continued for some distance before the identity of the troops who constituted Stephen's right flank was understood by Wayne's soldiers.[134] True it was, also, that about that time, farther to the left and front, the British had cut off the Ninth Virginia and thereby had disordered that wing.

The main cause of the retreat probably was that on the right, while the 2nd Light Infantry and the 40th Regiment were giving ground, the British had formed the 15th, the 17th, and the 44th, with the 4th Brigade in support,[135] and had advanced these troops with much vigor when Sullivan's men were extended, half exhausted, and almost without ammunition.[136] American commanders did not know that these were fresh troops. Washington, Sullivan and most of the others believed that the halt of Maxwell's Brigade at the Chew House, the

---

[130] Knox to Mrs. Knox, Oct. 6, 1777; *Knox Papers*, MHS. Wayne in 1 *Reed*, 321.

[131] Paine to Franklin, May 16, 1778, *loc. cit.*; Wayne to Washington, Oct. 4, 1777, 8 P.M.; 4 *Wayne Papers*, 30, PHS.

[132] 1 *Sullivan Papers*, 547, heading of Washington's report of Oct. 5, 1777, 9 *G. W.*, 308; Timothy Pickering to his brother, various dates in October, 1777, 1 *Pickering*, 171; McMichael's Diary, 15 *Penn. Arc.* (2), p. 213. Some of the incidents of the days immediately following the retreat are described in John Armstrong to Thomas Wharton, Oct. 8, 1777; *Reed Papers*, NYHS.

[133] Paine to Franklin, as *supra*, n. 122.

[134] See *infra*, p. 513, and Wayne to Mrs. Wayne, Oct. 6, 1777; 4 *Wayne Papers*, 31, PHS. Thomas Paine wrote Franklin, May 16, 1778, *loc. cit.*, that one reason for the confusion was that many of the Americans were in red uniforms, but no other mention of this has been observed. Tench Tilghman (*Memoir*, 161) wrote his father, Oct. 6, 1777, that, in his judgment, the fog was responsible for the failure of the Continentals to recognize their own comrades at the point of contact between Sullivan and Greene. Had the day been clear, said Tilghman, "everything was in our hands."

[135] Howe to Clinton, Oct. 8, 1777; *Clinton Papers*, Clements Lib.

[136] For the depletion of powder and ball, see 9 *G. W.*, 398.

exchange of fire on the left, and the confusion created by the fog had given the beaten British troops time to rally.[137] It could fairly have been said, therefore, that until the retreat became a rout, the realities were not nearly so disgraceful to the Americans on the right as the general officers thought.

Much was made of Greene's failure to attack at the time General Orders directed. Here, again, in most respects, the reason was misfortune, not misconduct. Greene's march was longer than had been reckoned; his troops had been formed at too great a distance from the enemy;[138] the advance in line of a part of the left wing was on a wide front, with Stephen's right out of contact with Wayne's left in country pockmarked with heavy land and wrinkled with fences.[139] Certain of the troops, moreover, had marching orders so complicated that even their guide lost his way.[140] In spite of this, some of Greene's men, including the Ninth Virginia, had pushed gallantly on, but had encountered unexpected resistance.[141] Howe had two Regiments in front position on his right and used these to slow the American attack. In support, were five other Regiments, while still two more were on the extreme right. Three of the Regiments in support were advanced at the time the counter-attack was made by the British against the American right. To Continentals so widely scattered, these British represented a superiority of force at the point of contact.[142] Greene's retreat consequently had about the same justification—whether it be deemed full or partial—that Sullivan's had on the American right. Apparently the most serious failure on the left was Stephen's. He was alleged by some to have given the order to retreat,[143] though he maintained he shouted

[137] 9 *G. W.*, 310; 1 *Sullivan Papers*, 547; *Second Weedon Germantown Letter*.

[138] Adam Stephen to Washington, Oct. 7, 1777, 58 *Papers of G. W.*, 16, LC. Part of the text of this letter is printed in 5 *Sparks*, 467–68, none too accurately, and with no indication whatsoever that sentences excoriating Brig. Gen. Charles Scott are not included in the text as printed.

[139] *Ibid.* and Wayne to Mrs. Wayne, Oct. 6, 1777, 4 *Wayne Papers*, 31, PHS.

[140] See *infra*, p. 515–16.

[141] Howard in 5 *Sparks*, 469; James Wallace's letter of Oct. 12, 1777, in 12 *T* 134; 3 Marshall's *Washington*, 182; 1 *Sullivan Papers*, 546; Adam Stephen's letter of Oct. 7, 1777, *loc. cit.*

[142] The troops who first met the American attack on the British right were the 1st Light Infantry and the 4th Regiment. The 5th and the 55th also were on that side of the village, according to Howe, but apparently they were not engaged until the counter-stroke. Still farther to the right, facing Greene's attack, were the Guards, and the 28th and 49th Regiments. In rear of the British right were the 27th and the Queen's American Rangers. These two commands were not employed. Howe to Clinton, Oct. 8, 1777, *Clinton Papers*, Clements Lib.; Howe to Germaine, 2 *Belcher*, 274–75. See also *André's Journal* (ed. 1930), p. 53–56.

[143] Cf. Walter Stewart: ". . . Everything appeared in our favor when the unfortunate retreat took place, which cannot yet be accounted for; it is left on General Stephen [he spelled it Stevens] who certainly gave the orders to the left wing . . ." (*Reed Papers*, NYHS).

to his men they were running away from victory.[144] To what extent he was responsible for the firing between his troops and Wayne's, his critics could not say. His own explanation was that Wayne's flankers shot at a body of British who were coming forward to surrender.[145] The principal charge against Stephen was that, if not actually drunk, he had been drinking so heavily for so long that he was not able to discharge his duty with sound judgment.[146]

When the Continentals had asked themselves what had caused the panic and what had detained the left wing, they had still another question: had the episode at the Chew House been responsible in whole or in part for the American defeat? Washington thought it had. He did not know how many constituted the party "thrown . . . into Mr. Chew's house," but these men, he said, "were in a situation not to be forced easily, and had it in their power, from the windows, to give us no small annoyance, and in a great measure to obstruct our advance." [147] Actually, the troops barricaded in the residence were six Companies of the 60th Regiment [148] and they had no arms but their muskets.[149] They were distinctly what Washington said they were, an "annoyance" that held up the advance of Maxwell for about thirty minutes. Sullivan made it plain that his Division had passed the Chew House before the British began to fire from it. The same thing may be said of Wayne's Division, because Sullivan noted that Wayne's com-

---

[144] Stephen, as *supra*, n. 138.

[145] *Ibid.* He did not admit the exchange with Wayne, but the Pennsylvanian described it in his letter of October 6 to his wife (4 *Wayne Papers*, 31, PHS), and Washington himself wrote that the fog "occasioned [the Americans] to mistake one another for the enemy, which, I believe, more than anything else, contributed to the misfortune that ensued" (9 G. W., 310). Tench Tilghman, writing his father, said nothing of any exchange of fire. He mentioned only a halt and then a retreat by each Division in the belief the other was the enemy (*Memoir Tench Tilghman*, 161).

[146] Three weeks were to pass before these charges were specific enough to be presented to a court of inquiry, which was to consider three occasions when Stephen was accused of "acting unlike an officer." The more general subject of inquiry was of "drunkenness, or drinking so much, as to act frequently in a manner, unworthy of the character of an officer" (9 G. W., 436). Cf. a letter of deep regret from Charles Carroll to Washington, Sept. 22, 1777, on drinking in the Army; 57 *Papers of G. W.*, 35, LC). The findings of the court of inquiry dictated a court martial which Washington on November 2 ordered. The minutes of the court have not been found and probably were destroyed, but if they still are in existence and ever are brought to light, they may add to present meagre knowledge of what happened on the American left at Germantown. For the verdict, see *infra*, p. 535. On charges of cowardice or misconduct at Germantown, four Virginians in addition to Stephen were among those brought before "infinite resulting courtmartials," as St. Clair termed them (1 *Wilkinson*, 357), but three of the four were acquitted (9 G. W., 438–39).

[147] 9 G. W., 309.

[148] Howe to Clinton, Oct. 8, 1777, *loc. cit.*

[149] Walter Stewart mistakenly wrote that the British had four field pieces in the building (Letter of Oct. 12, 1777; *Reed Papers*, NYHS).

mand came abreast of his at the residence and then "advanced far beyond." [150] Occupation of the stone dwelling, therefore, cannot be said to have affected the outcome materially, unless, in the first place, Sullivan was correct in saying that Wayne drew back and thereby exposed the left of Sullivan's Division because the Pennsylvanian heard the sound of firing in his rear and feared the British might be attacking there.[151] Again, the British defence of the Chew House may have been serious in its effect if, by delaying the advance of Maxwell, it kept that officer from reaching the front when the presence of his men there would have prevented panic. The answer to the question the Continentals asked regarding the Chew House thus seems to involve two insoluble "ifs"; but the affair was of interest because it demonstrated, once again, how a few men, well led and well placed, sometimes have it in their power to delay an advance.[152] A significant touch was added, also, by the contribution of Henry Knox to the argument whether it was better to mask or to attempt to storm the house. The artillerist had no personal experience with any such problem and he consequently cited a dubious historical principle that it would be unmilitary "to leave a castle in our rear." On difficult matters of tactics or strategy, so youthful an Army still had to get its guidance out of the books.[153]

A fourth question was asked in American camps after the Battle of Germantown: Had the British been surprised? Did the speedy appearance of the Light Infantry indicate that they were under arms when the attack began? Washington was of opinion that surprise was achieved "so far as reaching their guards before they had notice of our coming." [154] Armstrong believed a partial surprise had been effected.[155] Weedon thought the enemy had received warning.[156] At British headquarters where the facts were known, the German aide of the commanding General affirmed that because of fog and the quiet approach of the Americans, "we were not aware of them until they fell upon

---

[150] 1 *Sullivan Papers,* 545, 546.

[151] *Ibid.,* 546. Corroborative evidence of this statement of Sullivan's has not been found, but it will be remembered that in the anonymous account sent George Clinton, *supra,* n. 114, fear of a sally from the Chew House was mentioned.

[152] These men were under Lt. Col. Thomas Musgrave, aged 30, who subsequently became General and held two or three of the most honorable garrison posts in England. He is sketched in *British Military Panorama,* v. 2, p. 496, and in *DNB.*

[153] *Pickering's Letter,* 429–30   [154] 9 *G. W.,* 397.

[155] 1 *Wilkinson,* 353.

[156] See his *Second Germantown Letter.*

us." [157] General Howe insisted, on the other hand, that the only surprise was that of an attack by Washington so soon after the defeat in the Battle of the Brandywine.[158] Patrols had learned at 3 A.M. of the approach of the American columns, and had notified the British commander without letting the Continentals know their advance had been discovered. All the British Regiments then had been put under arms promptly,[159] but some of the senior officers had remained skeptical and had thought the alarm had been created by a mere "flying party." [160] In studying these lessons from loss, most of the Americans showed an open, and some of them an humble mind, though, of course, others minimized all failure and exaggerated each achievement, even to the extent of giving ear to the absurd tale that the Ninth Virginia had fought its way to the "Philadelphia commons" where it was surrounded and captured.[161]

Strangely, the details of the attempted simultaneous convergence of Washington's columns received little analysis by the Americans, though this was the most interesting as well as the most complicated single aspect of the operation. Washington scarcely could have demanded more of his officers than that they conduct their illshod troops in darkness over comparatively unfamiliar roads to distant positions, deploy and form them there, and have all of them ready to attack together at dawn. The American commander patiently studied the routes and timed the march of the separate columns by the condition of the various roads as well as by the distance to be covered; but he did not succeed in drafting orders that put every movement in simple, understandable language. Here, for example, were the instructions for the least-trained soldiers of the left wing, the militia of Smallwood and Forman. In the blackness of late night, they were expected "to pass down the road by a mill formerly Danl. Morris and Jacob Edges mill into White marsh road at the Sandy run: thence to white marsh Church, where take the left hand road, which leads to Jenkins tavern, on the old york road, below Armitages, beyond the seven mile stone half a mile from which turns off short to the right hand, fenced on both sides, which leads

---

[157] Journal of Capt. F. F. von Münchausen, 23 *Penn. Mag.*, 484.
[158] See his report in 2 *Belcher*, 274.
[159] *Ibid.*, and Howe to Clinton, Oct. 8, 1777, *Clinton Papers*, Clements **Lib.**
[160] *Hall*, 321–22.
[161] James Wallace's letter, 12 *T* 134.

through The enemys incampment to Germantown market houses." [162]
An interested student might try his hand at writing a travesty of instructions more nearly certain to confuse a column. The marvel is not
that the left elements were late because the guide lost his way,[163] but
that they reached their objective at all.

Washington said little about these or any other difficulties. When he
subsequently wrote the President of Congress and described the dis-
astrous effects of the fog, he mentioned among them the fact that the
thick air "served to keep our different parties in ignorance of each
other's movement and hindering their acting in concert." [164] Adjutant
General Pickering, a keen and systematic observer, was the one man at
headquarters, so far as known, to set down any detailed reflections on
the problems of simultaneous convergence. He thus expressed himself:
"This disposition appears to have been well made; but to execute such
a plan requires great exactness in the officers conducting the columns,
as well as punctuality in commencing the march, to bring the whole
to the point of action at once; and for this end it is absolutely necessary
that the length and quality of the roads be perfectly ascertained, the
time it will take to march them accurately calculated, and guides chosen
who are perfectly acquainted with the roads. It is also necessary to
assign proper halting places, if either column would arrive before the
appointed hour. All these points, I believe, were attended to in the
present case . . ." Then he went on to repeat the story that the guide
on the left had lost direction, and that the advance of the right wing
was halted for a time because of a false report that half a British
Battalion had been posted well in advance of the pickets.[165] That was
the most that anyone said of the convergence, instructive though it was.

The results—were they in keeping with the effort, or were they, too,
a frustration? Perhaps the answer was given unwittingly by a Germantown diarist who wrote on the 5th of October: "Great numbers came
out of town today to satisfy their curiosity as to the battle yesterday,
and everyone spoke as they affected." [166] That was it: each man's sympathy shaped his judgment. Washington's faith in the fundamental

162 9 G. W., 307, verbatim.   163 Supra, p. 512.
164 9 G. W., 310.
165 Timothy Pickering's Journal in 1 Pickering, 167.
166 This diarist was John Miller. His Journal is in the Reed Papers, NYHS; a few extracts
of it appear in Watson's Annals of Philadelphia, v. 2, p. 67–68.

rightness of his cause led him once again to assume the enemy's losses must be larger than his own, though, actually, his gross casualties, including prisoners, were close to 1100 and those of the British about half that total. The American commander shared, also, the general belief that the advance halted and the panic began when Howe was about to retreat across the Schuylkill, and perhaps even to Chester [167]—a belief for which there is not a shadow of justification in Howe's report to his government.

Heavy as were the losses, mistaken as was the Commander-in-Chief regarding the nearness of victory at the onset of panic, the undertone of army comment on the battle was even more optimistic than after the contest on the Brandywine. The struggle in the fog around Germantown yielded not a square acre of disputed ground to the Americans and imposed on the British no damage serious enough to hamper their efforts to open their line of supply up Delaware River, but in spirit, the losers were the gainers. George Weedon doubtless spoke for most of his companions in arms when he wrote, ". . . Though the enterprise miscarried, it was worth the undertaking." [168] Thomas Paine reported to Franklin that the troops appeared "to be sensible of a disappointment, not a defeat." [169] Washington was distinctly of that mind. The most he conceded to adversity was: "Upon the whole, it may be said the day was rather unfortunate than injurious." [170] Washington, moreover, was pleased to be able to report that Sullivan and the officers and men on the right wing, immediately under the eye of the Commander-in-Chief, "behaved with a degree of gallantry that did them the highest honor." [171]

That could have been said of nearly all the troops. They were learning their bloody business and tactically were by no means as inferior to

---

[167] 9 *G. W.*, 330, 374; *Asher Holmes; Second Weedon Germantown Letter.* Detailed British losses, as set down by Kemble, were as follows: Killed, seventy; wounded, 450; missing, fourteen; total, 534. Heaviest casualties were in the 2nd Light Infantry (seventy-three) and in the 4th Regiment of Foot (sixty-eight). See 1 *Kemble,* 137. Washington's return of his losses has disappeared (9 *G. W.*, 319 and n). On the authority of the "Board of War"—no more than that is cited in the note—Gordon reported American killed as 152, wounded as 521 and "upward of 400," including fifty-four officers, as prisoners or missing; a gross of more than 1073. See 2 *Gordon* (ed. 1801), p. 234.

[168] *Second Weedon Germantown Letter.*

[169] Letter to Benjamin Franklin, May 16, 1778, *loc. cit.*

[170] Letter of Oct. 5, 1777, to the President of Congress; 9 *G. W.*, 310. Two days later, on the receipt of the estimate of his casualties, he had to admit, "our loss . . . appears to have been much more considerable than I at first apprehended . . ." (*ibid.,* 319).

[171] 9 *G. W.*, 310–11.

the British as they had been a year previously. Many officers were increasing both in understanding and in appreciation of their seniors. If, simultaneously, there was even more jealousy of Greene, this was because the Rhode Islander again was alleged to have given Washington unwise counsel, though nobody said wherein.[172] Washington himself rose, rather than waned in esteem, as a result of the Battle of Germantown. His plan was not criticized; his boldness in attacking so soon after the defeat on the Brandywine was applauded. He and his Army received the thanks of a Congress which reminded itself that it never had provided the medal it had voted him after the occupation of Boston.[173] In making his acknowledgments, Washington looked, as always, to the future and voiced the hope that "under the smiles of Providence," his men would "merit by more substantial services the further applause of the country."[174] Less formally and in his old-time confusion of Providence and destiny or fortune, Washington wrote in a letter to Thomas Nelson: "It is vain to look back to our disappointment . . . at Germantown. We must endeavor to deserve better of Providence, and, I am persuaded, she will smile upon us."[175] He did not pause to explain why "Providence" was feminine.

His hope for the future was buttressed by the spirit of the Army. American soldiers had shown, Washington reminded them, that "the enemy are not proof against a vigorous attack, and may be put to flight when boldly pushed."[176] Another officer was more specific: ". . . the enemy have gained no advantage of any consequence over us. We have lost no baggage and no artillery, and the enemy are only on the same ground they were before. On the other hand, our men are now convinced they can drive the chosen troops of the enemy, their Light Infantry and Grenadiers, whenever they attack them with ardor, and are satisfied they would have been successful if their ammunition had not been expended and they had not mistaken their own men for the enemy. They are now in high spirits and appear to wish ardently for

172 1 *Wilkinson*, 352. In a somewhat obscure part of this reference, Wilkinson may have intended to say he later was told that Greene was responsible for giving Washington unsound advice on masking the Chew House, though Greene was not in the vicinity of the residence at any time during the action. Cf. James Duane in 2 *Burnett*, 512.

173 9 *JCC.*, 785; 2 *LTW.*, 1.

174 9 *G. W.*, 351–52.

175 Letter of November 8, 1777; 10 *ibid.*, 28.

176 9 *ibid.*, 312, Cf. *ibid.*, 337; 1 *Sullivan Papers*, 547; James Wallace's letter of Oct. 12, 1777, 12 *T* 134. See also *First Weedon Germantown Letter:* "[The troops] have no objection to another trial, which must take place soon."

another engagement." [177] In the eyes of a young Frenchman who had had his first view of Washington at this time, the Commander-in-Chief himself seemed a major reason for the spirit of his men: "Washington was intended for a great position—his appearance alone gave confidence to the timid and imposed respect on the bold." [178]

[177] Anonymous account, 2 *Papers of George Clinton,* 372, with minor repunctuation and change of capital letters.

[178] See R. B. Douglas, trans. and ed.: *Charles Albert, Comte de More, Chevalier de Pontgibaud, a French Volunteer of the War of Independence,* 42, cited hereafter as *Pontgibaud.* That interesting visitor added of Washington: "He possessed also those external advantages which a man born to command should have; tall stature, a noble face, gentleness in his glance, amenity in his language, simplicity in his gesture and expressions. A calm, firm bearing harmonized perfectly with these attributes."

CHAPTER XX

GATES ECLIPSES WASHINGTON

(October, 1777)

DURING THE NIGHT of the 12th–13th of October,[1] Washington had news that on the 6th, a British force had stormed successfully the two guardian defences of the Hudson, Fort Montgomery and Fort Clinton, on the west bank of the river, approximately four miles Northwest of Peekskill and consequently about forty-eight from New York harbor. Washington had said often that the loss of the passes of the Highlands would be well nigh fatal to the American cause in New York and the Eastern States. It was for this reason, among others, that he had regretted the necessity of calling on Putnam after the Battle of the Brandywine for 2500 troops.[2] When the order to that effect had reached him, Putnam had protested directly to President Hancock. Although "Old Put" was disinclined to take the offensive on his own account, he had maintained that Washington should do so. On September 16, the New Englander had written: "I hear that General Washington has retired with his Army over the Schuylkill. The assailants have infinitely the advantage of those who act upon the defensive only, and it is my opinion we shall always be beat, until we learn to begin the attack. This has been verified in our own experience in almost every instance."[3] Putnam's later warning had been that the British were organizing an expedition which probably was to be directed against Peekskill and Fort Montgomery. He continued: "The large detachments lately drawn from this post have reduced its strength to about 1000 effective continental troops and 400 militia, 200 of whom are from this State, one-half of them without arms and, what is worse, it would be damned unsafe to trust them. . . . This post, I am sensible, is of the last consequence to the continent, and I will exert myself for its defence, weakened as it is; but permit me to tell you, sir, that I will not be answerable

---

[1] 9 G. W., 364.
[2] See *supra*, p. 490 and Washington to George Clinton, Oct. 15, 1777; 9 G. W., 373.
[3] Letter of Sept. 16, 1777; 159 *Papers Cont. Cong.*, 95, LC.

for its safety, with the strength left me, against the force I am sensible the enemy are able and, I believe, will speedily send against it." [4]

Washington, cognizant of all this, had directed that the garrisons of all non-essential outposts be recalled. He had hoped, too, that Connecticut militia would replace the withdrawn Continentals [5] and, in the gamble of probability, he had thought it likely that if Sir Henry Clinton's British troops made any move from the vicinity of the city of New York, they would go into Jersey and would attempt an overland march to join Howe.[6] In this expectation, Washington now was proved in error. He took pains to make clear the circumstances in which he had felt himself compelled to recall troops from Putnam [7] and he did not blame that officer for the reverse.[8] Neither did he attempt to minimize the possible consequences of a misfortune for which both Congress and he were held by some to be responsible, in part, on the ground that they

---

[4] Letter of Sept. 29, 1777, to John Hancock, *loc. cit.*, 99. In this and in the preceding quotation, Putnam's punctuation has been revised and some of his capitalization conformed to modern usage.

[5] 9 *G. W.*, 373.   [6] *Ibid.*, 289–90.

[7] *Ibid.*, 349–50.

[8] 9 *G. W.*, 371, 372–73, 400–01. Perhaps because of what occurred during the fortnight that followed the loss of Fort Montgomery and Fort Clinton, no comprehensive study of that operation has been published. Source material on it is extensive. John Hills's excellent map is reproduced in 2 *Papers of George Clinton*, 380. Some of Putnam's letters to Washington are in 1 *LTW.*, 438–40, 441–42 and, as respects later developments, 2 *ibid.*, 5–6. See also the informative letters of Putnam to Hancock, Oct. 6 and 16, 1777, in 159 *Papers Cont. Cong.*, 103, 107, LC. Among contemporary accounts, that in 1 *Moore*, 506 ff and that in 1 *Kemble*, 134 are of value. In *Heath*, 141, is a brief but informative account of the defences. Washington's reports on the situation in the Highlands and on the detachment of troops from that area will be found in 9 *G. W.*, 323, 325, 339, 349–50, 364, 371, 401. Particularly to be commended to the student of this affair is the collection of documents in 1 *Webb*, 322–72. On Dec. 20, 1777, in accordance with Washington's request (10 *G. W.*, 136), Gen. George Clinton made a careful, confidential report on the "management" of the Highland defences. His opinion was that "we have either been very unfortunate or [the direction of affairs] has not been as wise as might be wished—prudent management of our small forces, in my humble opinion would have saved the forts, though perhaps with the far less important loss of the continental village . . ." (1 *Webb*, 406–07, with minor repunctuation). In other words, as Clinton saw it, Putnam mistakenly had sought to save Peekskill at the price of the forts. Putnam himself noted that when the British landed and took possession of Fort Independence, on a point of land directly across Peeks' Kill from the village of Peekskill, "one small cannon" only had been mounted there (Letter of Oct. 6, 1777, to John Hancock; 159 *Papers Cont. Cong.*, 103). Heath's description (*op. cit.*, 141), would indicate that, as far as he was informed, Fort Montgomery had not been completed on the inland side. Sir Henry Clinton's letter of Oct. 13–14, 1777, is an interesting account of his faint hopes of reaching Burgoyne and of his efforts to do so. See Sir Henry Clinton to McGlaghy, Sept. 29, 1777 and Tryon to Clinton, Oct. 8, 1777. All these are in the *Clinton Papers*, loc. cit. Clinton's report was printed in *London Gazette*, Dec. 2, 1777, and in *London Chronicle*, Dec. 2–4, 1777. The immediate aftermath of Gen. John Vaughan's destruction of Esopus, with various minor occurrences, is set forth in Vaughan to Clinton, Oct. 17, 18, 19, 26, 1777; *Clinton Papers*, Clements Lib. A strong American protest (H. B. Livingston and Gates to Henry Clinton, Oct. 31, 1777) is in *ibid*. Perhaps more informative than any of these sources is the correspondence of Alexander McDougall in NYHS archives. McDougall's papers and personal comments on the findings of the subsequent court of inquiry are indispensable.

had overestimated the numerical strength of Putnam's force.[9] So deep was the concern of Washington that, for a day or so, he almost forgot the confidence he had expressed after hearing of the defeat of Burgoyne at Freeman's Farm on the 19th of September.[10]

Then came another of those strange revivals of good fortune that would have justified any army Chaplain in taking as his text the assurance of the Psalmist: "I will say of the Lord, He is my refuge and my fortress: my God; in him will I trust, surely he shall deliver thee from the snare of the fowler . . ."[11] It was amazing: On the 6th of October, by their capture of Forts Montgomery and Clinton, the British unlocked the southern gate to the region in which Sir Henry Clinton and Gen. John Burgoyne were to meet; the very next day, Horatio Gates slammed the northern gate on the face of the British moving down from Canada. For a second time on Freeman's Farm, General Burgoyne offered battle, October 1, and advanced a column which the Americans repulsed and pursued in a savage action that continued till late evening. The result showed incontestably that Burgoyne could not hope to penetrate farther southward. If he was to save his Army, he must shorten his supply lines immediately. General Gates hoped that even retreat would not be possible.[12]

Incomplete news of this action reached Washington late on the 14th of October [13] and, of course, changed instantly the outlook on the Hudson. In writing to Putnam of the loss of the two Highland defences,

[9] James Duane, Nov. n.d., 1777, 2 *Burnett*, 566–67. For a review of the transfer of troops from Putnam in the fall of 1777, see Appendix IV–4.

[10] See *supra*, p. 500, and, in contrast, Washington to William Livingston, Oct. 8, 1777: "The success of the present attempt on Peekskill, may, in its consequences, entirely change the face of our Northern affair and throw them into a very disagreeable and unfavorable train" (9 *G. W.*, 340). Cf. Washington to Putnam, Oct. 15, 1777; *ibid.*, 371.

[11] Psalm XCI, 2–3.

[12] See Gates to John Hancock, Oct. 12, 1777. *Gates Papers*, NYHS. Needless to say Gates's correspondence contains many letters and other documents on the progress of the Saratoga campaign. The following have been found of particular interest: Gates to Washington, Aug. 22, 23, 28, Oct. 5, 1777; Gates to Benjamin Lincoln, Aug. 23, Sept. 15, 17, 22, 1777; Gates to John Hancock, Aug. 20, 1777; Gates to Joseph Trumbull, Sept. 10, 1777; Gates to Benedict Arnold, Sept. 23, 28, 1777; Gates to John Stark (two letters) Sept. 10, 1777; Gates to his wife, Sept. 22, 1777. In this last letter, Gates remarked: "a General of an American army must be everything, and that is being more than one man can long sustain. This campaign must end my military labors." Another item, highly instructive, is Benedict Arnold to Gates, Oct. 1, 1777, a vigorous complaint that Gates was not using his services.

[13] The information is not mentioned in Washington's few letters of October 14 (9 *G. W.*, 368–71) but is announced in GOs of October 15 (*ibid.*, 377) and is discussed at length in Lutterloh to Mifflin, Oct. 16, 1777 (161 *Papers Cont. Cong.*, I, p. 24, LC). It is possible, though scarcely probable, that the report was received at headquarters after midnight of the 14th–15th. No dispatch from Gates, concerning the Second Battle of Freeman's Farm, appears in the *Papers of Cont. Cong.* prior to that of October 12, cited *supra*. Gates did not inform Washington of the victory. See *infra*, p. 525, 546, n. 26.

the Commander-in-Chief said: "This stroke would have perhaps proved fatal to our northern affairs in its consequences, had not the defeat of General Burgoyne so providentially taken place upon the 7th . . . I can scarcely think that Sir Henry Clinton will pursue his route now the object of it is disappointed, I mean a junction with Burgoyne." [14] While Washington would not permit himself to predict to Congress the speedy surrender of Burgoyne, he did observe: "From the happy train in which things . . . were [on the 7th], I hope we shall soon hear of the most decisive advantages." [15] To Putnam he said: "Should providence be pleased to crown our arms in this campaign with one more fortunate stroke, I think we shall have no great cause for anxiety respecting the future designs of Britain. I trust all will be well in his good time." [16]

If Washington hoped the next "fortunate stroke" was to be on his own front, he was disappointed; but if he looked for another great achievement in the North, he had swift fulfilment. On the 17th of October, he opened a dispatch from Putnam that described in some detail recent operations on the Hudson and then buried this thrilling news in the middle of his narrative: "Yesterday, about forty sail passed up the river, crowded with troops, and are now at anchor above Poughkeepsie, the wind not favoring. We were on our march after them, when I met the agreeable intelligence of General Burgoyne and his army, as prisoners of war, a copy of which is enclosed; and thereupon I do most sincerely congratulate your Excellency." [17]

It was one of the three most shining American accomplishments of the war to that date, and it equaled in every respect the capture of Boston and the maneuvering of the British out of Jersey; but Washington prudently refrained from public announcement until this "most inter-

---

[14] Letter of Oct. 15, 1777; 9 *G. W.*, 371. Language almost identical, including the reference to Providence, appears in a letter of the same date to Gen. George Clinton, *ibid.*, 372.

[15] Letter of Oct. 16, 1777, to John Hancock; 9 *G. W.*, 382.

[16] *Ibid.*, 400–01, with the capitalization as in the original.

[17] Letter of Oct. 16, 1777; 2 *LTW.*, 5–6. This must have been hurried to Washington by successive expresses, in a most remarkable feat of riding; but there seems to be no doubt of the receipt of the news by Washington on the 17th. See 9 *G. W.*, 387 and n. Unfortunately Putnam's enclosure does not appear to have been preserved in the *Papers of G. W.*, LC. The same must be said regretfully of another copy of the enclosure mentioned by Putnam in his dispatch of Oct. 16, 1777, to John Hancock, 159 *Papers Cont. Cong.*, 107, LC. It is not unlikely that the missing paper, but not a subenclosure, is Gates to Putnam, Sept. [Oct.] 15, 1777; *Gates Papers*, NYHS. The important paragraph began in this manner: "Yesterday General Burgoyne proposed to surrender upon the enclosed terms. The capitulation I believe will be settled today when I shall have nothing but Genl. Clinton to think of . . ." Cf. Weedon to John Page [?], Oct. 18, 1777, with Clinton to Putnam, Oct. 15, 1777, copied in full. *Chicago HS.* MSS.

esting and happy intelligence," as he described it,[18] was confirmed by some other officer close to the scene and not apt to confuse hearsay with fact. Again fortune spared the General and his Army. On the 18th, Washington had not long finished a letter to his brother, John Augustine,[19] and was turning to other tasks when an express laid before him this dispatch from George Clinton:

> Albany, October 15, 1777
>
> Last night at 8 o'clock the capitulation, whereby General Burgoyne and the whole army surrendered themselves prisoners of war, was signed, and this morning they are to march out towards the river above Fishers Creek with the honors of war (and there ground their arms). They are from thence to be marched to Massachusetts Bay. We congratulate you on this happy event and remain, yours & ca.[20]

Washington's first written observation on Putnam's report of Gates's victory has been, "It remains for us to play a counterpart . . ." [21] Now that Clinton confirmed the news, great possibilities seemed to lie ahead —the Hudson no longer a possible boundary line between free and subjugated States, troops available to reenforce the thin Divisions that confronted Howe, the restoration of Pennsylvanians' and Jerseymen's faith in victory, and the rally of their militia to the cause of their country.[22] So great an event must be celebrated! On the afternoon of the 18th, at 5 o'clock, the various Chaplains delivered what Washington was careful to specify as "short discourses," after which, just before sunset, thirteen guns were fired, and a "feu-de-joy" was discharged by the Army drawn up in two lines.[23] Everywhere in the main Army, hopes built up at Germantown were raised still higher. As far as his modesty allowed, Washington was gratified personally as well as officially, because he felt he had done all that lay within his power to assist first Schuyler and St. Clair at Ticonderoga, and then Gates,[24]

---

18 9 G. W., 387.   19 Ibid., 399.
20 Copied at Washington's instance into his letter of Oct. 18, 1777, to Col. Christopher Greene; 9 G. W., 393.
21 Ibid., 387.   22 Ibid., 391 ff.
23 GOs of Oct. 18, 1777, ibid., 390–91; T. Pickering to his wife, Oct. 20, 1777; 1 Pickering, 177.
24 To continue the references on the Ticonderoga operation, given supra, p. 444, details of St. Clair's retreat will be found in 1 St. Clair Papers, 415 ff., 1 LTW., 397 ff. His report appears in ibid., 400–05. For Washington's reception of the news of the evacuation of Ticonderoga, and his efforts to encourage the commanders of the Northern Department, see 8 G. W., 406–07, 408, 447, 449–50; 9 ibid., 22, 102. His calls on New England to reenforce Schuyler may be traced in 8 ibid., 429–30, 433, 457, 458; 9 ibid., 114–15. The known antipathy of that

but he and many other persons were now to be much irritated. The capitulation did not occur until three days after the premature announcement of it had been circulated. Subsequently, though it was assumed everywhere that British arms had been stacked, Gates was guilty of incomprehensible tardiness in forwarding a detailed report and the text of the "convention." [25] When the triumph at length was confirmed in full, it was so "important and glorious," in Washington's own words [26] that he stifled the anger he felt because of the failure of Gates to send the dispatch through headquarters.[27] There was no undertone of jealousy in anything Washington said of the victor or the victory. Perhaps the closest approach to that feeling was in the observation that Gates was said to have had no less than 14,000 militia with him. Washington remarked of the New England States that mistakenly were supposed to have sent so many men to the Northern Department: "Had the same spirit pervaded the people of this and the neighboring States we might before this have had General Howe nearly in the situation of General Burgoyne, with this difference, that the former would never have been out of the reach of his ships, whilst the latter increased his danger every step he took having but one retreat in case of a disaster, and that blocked up by a respectable force." [28] Never for an hour, while operating close to deep water, could Washington forget seapower.

region for Schuyler appears, among many references, in 1 *LTW.*, 415–16, 419–20; 2 *Burnett*, 432, 433. The counsel of Washington on the reenforcement of Fort Schuyler and the assignment of Benedict Arnold to that post will be found in 8 *G. W.*, 458; 9 *ibid.*, 102, 151, 154. St. Leger's report on the Mohawk campaign is conveniently in 1 *Wilkinson*, 212–14. The widespread criticism of St. Clair, his recall and that of Schuyler, the appointment of Gates, and Washington's careful conduct with respect to all these proceedings appear in these basic references: 8 *G. W.*, 427, 438; *ibid.*, 23, 26, 29; 2 *Burnett*, 415, 440–41, 445, 452; 8 *JCC.*, 585, 590, 596, 599, 600–01, 653, 659, 669, 673, 681–86; 1 *Warren-Adams Letters*, 352; *Adams, Fam. Let.*, 293–94.

[25] Gates's interesting letter to his wife, Oct. 20, 1777, on his victory is in *Gates Papers*, NYHS. His dispatch of Oct. 18, 1777, to Hancock—"I have the satisfaction to present your Excellency with the convention," also is in *Gates Papers*, NYHS. The suspense of Congress, which did not receive the news officially until October 31 (9 *JCC.*, 851, 857–58), is set forth in *ibid.*, 824–25, 851, 857–58; 2 *Burnett*, 530, 531, 535, 538, 545; *Adams, Fam. Let.*, 319–20; 1 *Wilkinson*, 330–32; 9 *G. W.*, 440. As noted more particularly *infra*, p. 537, it was for his belated delivery of this news that James Wilkinson was given brevet rank of Brigadier General. A highly diverting entry on Burgoyne's surrender appears in *Anon. Proc. Howe* to this effect: "[October] 31st . . . An express arrived from General Burgoyne, with an account of his having been obliged, from untoward circumstances, after fighting the rebels twice at vast odds, to sign on the 20th of October a convention; by which himself and army, are not to serve against the Americans during the present contest" (*AASP.*, April, 1930, p. 90). In 1 *Webb*, 232, is an interesting expression of concern over the easy terms granted Burgoyne, followed by another, to the effect that Gates was not strong enough to impose stern conditions.

[26] 9 *G. W.*, 399.　　　　　　　　[27] *Ibid.*, 440, 465, 466 n.

[28] Letter of Nov. 13, 1777, to Patrick Henry; 9 *G. W.*, 51–52. Cf. letter of Oct. 27, 1777, to Samuel Washington, *ibid.*, 451.

As if in acknowledgment of the change in its prospect—a shift toward a defensive—the royal army evacuated Germantown on the night of October 18-19 and drew back to Philadelphia. Washington slowly conformed and soon moved his camp to White Marsh, but he could do no more than "hover" around the Quaker City.[29] Below that city, an effort was being made by the British on land and in Delaware River to drive off the Americans and to clear the way for the supply ships, without which Howe could not hope to hold the town against the Continentals.[30] Washington was responsible for manning the forts and for selecting the officers to command them. His it was to send reenforcements or to shift garrisons, but the defence on the water was in the hands of officers responsible to the Navy Board and working in cooperation with Commodore John Hazelwood, who had full power over the Pennsylvania Navy. In so clumsy an engine of war, loss of motion was unavoidable; friction was all too likely.[31] Two days before the Battle of the Brandywine, the British had occupied Billingsport on the Jersey shore of the Delaware [32] but they made no effort at that time to seize Red Bank, five miles above Billingsport.[33] On the opposite Pennsylvania shore, the nearest stretch of which they by that time commanded, the British were hoping to place batteries on what was known as Province Island, in reality a marshy part of the mainland cut off by small creeks. The Americans meanwhile worked steadily on the defences at Red Bank, styled Fort Mercer, and regarded as the more powerful of the two land works. The other principal American fortification consisted of four blockhouses and a battery of ten eighteen-pounders. These works were known as Fort Mifflin and were located in the stream on the treacherous ground of Port Island, at a distance of 1900 yards from Fort Mercer.[34] In knowledge that Fort Mifflin was

---

[29] For Howe's withdrawal, see 9 *G. W.*, 400. Washington's reference to "hovering" around the British "to distress and retard their operations as much as possible" was in a letter of Oct. 27, 1777, to Samuel Washington (*ibid.*, 451). Letters dated October 30 carry the heading "near White Marsh" (*ibid.*, 465); those of November 2 *et post* are marked "White Marsh" (*ibid.*, 493). See the map, *infra*, p. 531.

[30] Cf. Henry Knox to Mrs. Knox, Oct. 15, 1777: "If the enemy cannot get their shipping up, Philadelphia is one of the most ineligible places in the world for an army, surrounded by a river which is impassable, and an army above them . . ." (*Knox Papers*, MHS). See also Anthony Wayne to Mrs. Wayne, Oct. 18, 1777: "General Howe will soon meet the same fate [as Burgoyne] unless he immediately gets on board his vessels" (4 *Wayne Papers*, 33, PHS).

[31] Cf. Washington to Capt. Isaiah Robinson, Oct. 25, 1777; *ibid.*, 427–28. See also 1 *Reed*, 334–35.

[32] See *supra*, p. 467 ff. In relation to Philadelphia, the position at Billingsport was twelve miles below Cooper's Ferry, the present Camden, New Jersey.

[33] *Anon. Proc. Howe*, 86.

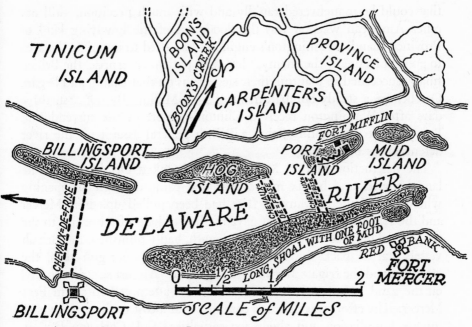

TINICUM ISLAND

BOON'S ISLAND CREEK

BOON'S ISLAND

PROVINCE ISLAND

CARPENTER'S ISLAND

FORT MIFFLIN

BILLINGSPORT ISLAND

HOG ISLAND

PORT ISLAND

MUD ISLAND

CHEVAUX=DE=FRISE

CHEVAUX DE FRISE

CHEVAUX DE FRISE

DELAWARE RIVER

LONG SHOAL WITH ONE FOOT OF MUD

RED BANK

FORT MERCER

BILLINGSPORT

0   ½   1   2

SCALE of MILES

AMERICAN DEFENCES OF THE DELAWARE BELOW PHILADELPHIA, NOVEMBER, 1777

A small squadron of galleys and a few frigates supported the fire of the forts and the obstacle of the submerged *chevaux de frise*, so called. This sketch is from the finely executed "Plan of the City and Environs of Philadelphia, Surveyed by N. Scull and G. Heap, Engraved by Willm. Faden, 1777," a copy of which is in the Library of Congress.

feeble, engineers were endeavoring to strengthen it as much as the nature of the ground and the scarcity of materials permitted.

Besides these forts, the defenders had fashioned a large number of heavy timber obstructions[35] which had been sunk across the channel. If the enemy tried to remove these chevaux de frise, as they were called, they could be swept by American artillery in the forts.[36] Above these barriers were the light continental craft, most of which were galleys

[34] Port Island often was confused in reports with Mud Island, a few hundred yards upstream. A map will be found in 5 *Sparks*, 156, but, unfortunately, it lacks a scale of miles. In 5 *Penn. Arc.* (1), p. 720 is a crude sketch of part of the river, adjacent to the fort. The ground plan of Fort Mifflin is sketched in W. S. Stryker, *The Forts on the Delaware in the Revolutionary War*, p. 6, after an original in LC. The best map of the river defences as a whole is that of N. Scull and G. Heap, published by William Faden in 1777 as "A Plan of the City and Environs of Philadelphia," used above.

[35] Timothy Pickering wrote his wife, Oct. 13, 1777, that these "ranges" of chevaux de frise were six in number (1 *Pickering*, 174).

[36] A full description of these sunken timbers will be found in the *Anon. Proc. Howe*, 84. The location of the "ranges" of these obstructions is in *ibid.*, 83; but is presented more clearly in two diagrams in 1 *Penn. Arc.* (2), 768, 770. Pages 749-73 of that volume are devoted to various proposals for obstructing the river, and to the execution in 1784 of a contract for removing obstacles that survived the war.

that could be maneuvered rapidly and with much precision. Still another American weapon was the floodgates of the low-lying land of Province Island. Washington's engineers had tried to inundate the area to prevent its use by the enemy,[37] but with patient enterprise, the British finally succeeded in planting their siege guns on that island, and began, October 10, a steady bombardment of Fort Mifflin. By the 21st, three days after Washington received Clinton's report of the surrender of Burgoyne, it was manifest that a British general assault on the river defences was impending.[38]

The destruction of Fort Mifflin was undertaken October 22 by the land batteries and by six men-of-war that came through an opening where two of the chevaux de frise had been pulled up. Fort Mercer and the American armed craft gave the hearty help of a hot fire to the well-served guns of Fort Mifflin. At length, badly punished, the British vessels started back down the river, but a sixty-four-gun ship, the *Augusta,* and the frigate *Merlin* [39] ran aground. Almost simultaneously, on the 22nd, a force of about 1200 Hessians attempted to storm Fort Mercer. The effort was defeated completely at a cost to the assailants of intense humiliation and about 400 casualties. Col. Carl von Donop, who led this expedition, was the officer who had been in command to the East of Trenton when Washington had surprised the Hessian garrison on the 26th of December, and to a singular degree, Donop had a fate that paralleled Rall's at Trenton. In the assault on Fort Mercer, Colonel Donop received a wound which prevented his escape and caused his early death while a prisoner of war. Before he succumbed, the final stroke of this successful phase of the defence came on the 23rd, when an explosion wrecked *Augusta,* and fire destroyed *Merlin.*[40]

This repulse, in Washington's judgment, was nothing more than a

[37] See "The Siege of Fort Mifflin" in 11 *Penn. Mag.,* 82, a reprint of an article in the *United States Magazine,* May, 1779.

[38] Washington's diversified efforts to anticipate the enemy's moves, to strengthen the defences, to provide reenforcements, and to assure the employment of sound tactics may be followed in 9 *G. W.,* 283, 284, 292–93, 299, 321, 326, 334, 343, 345, 356–58, 369, 375–76, 380, 392, 394–95; 2 *LTW.,* 3–4; 9 *JCC.,* 813. A rich documentary collection is W. C. Ford, "Defences of Philadelphia in 1777" which appeared serially in *Penn. Mag.* The dates covered by the various sections of this article are as follows: v. 18, p. 1–19 to Aug. 6, 1777; *ibid.,* p. 163–184, August 7–15; *ibid.,* 329–353, August 21–October 28; *ibid.,* 463–95, October 29–November 5–6–November 10; *ibid.,* 234–50; *ibid.,* 359–73; November 15–16; *ibid.,* 481–506, November 17–24; 20 *ibid.,* 87–115, November 24–26; *ibid.,* 213–247, November 25–December 1; *ibid.,* 391–408, December 1–3; *ibid.,* 520–551, December 4; 21 *ibid.,* 51–71, December 4.

[39] She was classed by the British as a sloop (*A. Robertson's Diaries,* 153).

[40] For these operations of October 22–23, the dates of which often are confused, see 9 *G. W.,* 392, 394–95, 400, 410, 411–12, 413, 416, 417, 419, 422, 424–25, 428–29; 2 *LTW.,* 12–13, 18–21; Henry Knox to Mrs. Knox, Oct. 29, 1777; *Knox Papers,* MHS; Jed. Huntington

respite,[41] but it was welcome both because it afforded time in which to strengthen the works and the garrison at Fort Mercer, and because it gave him a few more hours each day in which to meet, as far as he could, increasing needs of an enlarged Army. Winter was approaching; the requirements of the troops were changing with the season; the commissary still was demoralized by loss of men and by the manifest impracticability of regulations Congress had shaped unwisely. Quartermaster General Mifflin had neglected his duties for months, and he now reported himself in such ill health that he had to quit his office, with small apparent prospect of being able or willing to resume it.[42] A reassignment of duty soon was to be made for the full use in another sphere of Mifflin's abilities [43] but, in spite of hard work on the part of his principal deputy, the service continued to be disordered by the prospect that new men might employ different methods [44] to even less advantage.

Where the issue of shoes was concerned, the men in the ranks doubtless would have insisted that no change could be for the worse. Long and frequent marches had worn out leather soles faster than at any time, probably, in the life of the Army. Cool weather and stony roads brought calls for footgear from hundreds of men who had gone without shoes during the summer months. Washington and Congress had anticipated this in some measure [45] but, when demands multiplied

to Joseph Trumbull, Oct. 21, 1777; *Joseph Trumbull Papers* (MHS) Conn. Col. Office Papers, v. 7, pt. 2, p. 1270, Conn. State Lib.; Robert Morton's Diary in 1 *Penn. Mag.*, 22; Hazelwood to President Wharton, Oct. 29, 1777, 5 *Penn. Arc.* (1), p. 721–22; Stephen Olney, in Williams, *Biog. of Rev. Heroes*, 222 ff; Howe's *Narrative*, 28–29; *A. Robertson's Diaries*, 153. This last-named author had his chronology badly muddled.

[41] 9 *G. W.*, 431.

[42] Mifflin to Hancock, Oct. 8, 1777; 161 *Papers Cont. Cong.*, 16, LC; 9 *JCC.*, 792. General Mifflin paid tribute to his deputy, Henry E. Lutterlough or Lutterloh, whose name is spelled in almost as many ways as there are letters in it. After nearly a month's delay, Mifflin's resignation was accepted (*ibid.*, 874), but he was requested to act until a successor was named and meantime he was given full power (9 *JCC.*, 882). It developed that Mifflin objected only to serving as Quartermaster, and, when he found his health improving, he consented to remain a Major General of the Army (1 *Ballagh, Lee Letters*, 349–50). He had, moreover, a plan for the reorganization of the Quartermasters Department (*ibid.*, 350), and for the correction of defects in the regulations adopted the previous May 10, for which see 7 *JCC.*, 355. His guiding policy and that of Congress had been to order from France in large quantity all quartermaster stores that could not be had in the United States (8 *JCC.*, 488; 9 *ibid.*, 883). During September, the States, too, had been urged to import tents, arms, etc., with no arrangement of any sort to prevent competitive buying (8 *ibid.*, 708).

[43] See *infra*, p. 558.

[44] The year's end was to find Washington pleading that the office be filled (10 *G. W.*, 184).

[45] Early in June a committee of three had been named by Congress to devise ways and means of supplying the Army with shoes, shirts and hats (8 *JCC.*, 414). This Committee's detailed report, filed on the 20th, proposed that a Commissary of Hides be named to barter the hides of the Army's slaughtered cattle for leather and shoes. If necessary, the new official was to establish tanyards (*ibid.*, 487). A qualified man was named at once (*ibid.*, 487) because the Clothier General reported on July 8 that shoes were becoming very scarce (James

vastly,[46] no immediate relief could be suggested otherwise than through an appeal to the government and people of Pennsylvania.[47] The need of blankets was equally desperate and neither new [48] nor easily met. During the chill second week of November, Washington was to write: "There are now in this Army by a late return 4000 men wanting blankets, near 2000 of which have never had one, although some of them have been twelve months in service." [49]

When such figures as these were mentioned, the Army seemed large, but when its employment against the enemy was considered, it appeared to be dangerously small and to increase slowly because Washington faced all his familiar difficulties and some he had not experienced previously.[50] Repeatedly he had called on his officers to forward recruits, even in small parties, as rapidly as the men had been discharged by the surgeons who had inoculated them.[51] How many such reenforcements he might expect within a given time, Washington seldom could estimate because of the absence of returns.[52] Over certain periods, it had

Mease to Washington, 50 *Papers of G. W.*, 104, LC), but unfortunately the selected Commissary of Hides had to decline the duty. It was August 5 before another acceptable commissary could be found in the person of George Ewing (8 *JCC.*, 585–607). The second week in October had begun when his bureau was operating (9 *ibid.*, 794–95) and then without sufficient funds (George Ewing to the President of Congress, Oct. 18, 1777; 41 *Papers Cont. Cong.*, III, 13, LC). Washington had urged the large scale manufacture of shoes, had given notice that those arriving from France were worthless or too small (8 *G. W.*, 432–33), and now he had to advise Congress that he had a "great many men" unable to perform duty because of their lack of shoes (9 *G. W.*, 35).

[46] See, as typical, a call from headquarters to General Wayne, Sept. 27, 1777 (57 *Papers of G. W.*, 30, LC), to return 300 pairs of shoes because 200 pairs already had been obtained by him.

[47] 9 *JCC.*, 799.

[48] In March, 1777, the States had been asked to make assessment of blankets for their soldiers (7 *JCC.*, 172), and in July New York had been urged to supply 1500 blankets for the men at Ticonderoga, with the promise that the covering would be returned from the first importation (8 *ibid.*, 537). During September and thereafter, organized efforts were made to procure blankets in Jersey and in Pennsylvania, especially for the soldiers who had lost theirs at Brandywine (8 *JCC.*, 741–42, 748; 9 *G. W.*, 249, 269–70 and n). Officers were sent out with virtual powers of impressment and under instructions to be more considerate of patriotic than of loyalist households (8 *G. W.*, 318, 319; 9 *ibid.*, 273, 357–58), but so little success attended this search for easily concealed blankets that Washington had to pronounce the undertaking a failure. Larger importation was necessary; the States must aid; officers must not purloin blankets being transported through their districts (10 *G. W.*, 36–37, 39, 41, 79; 1 *St. Clair Papers*, 459). Immediate results were sadly meagre—one of many conditions that prompted Richard Peters to write: "The people seem to be sinking fast into avarice and its concomitant vices, and if a speedy stop is not put to their destructive propensities to serve themselves at the risk of the country, Providence will not look on them as worth saving . . ." (Letter of Oct. 11, 1777 to Anthony Wayne; 4 *Wayne Papers*, 32, PHS).

[49] 10 *G. W.*, 42.

[50] This resumé takes up the questions of reenforcement and recruiting where they were left off as of April 15, approximately, *supra*, p. 404 ff.

[51] 8 *G. W.*, 73, 84, 262; 8 *JCC.*, 538. On June 8 the proviso concerning inoculation prior to the march had been put aside for the season (8 *G. W.*, 258–59, 272–73).

[52] E.g., 7 *G. W.*, 479.

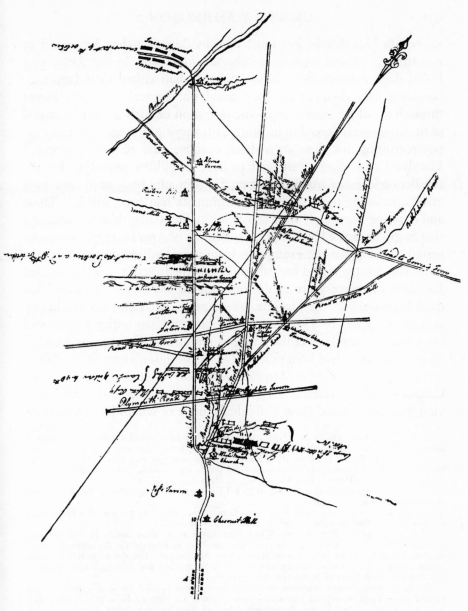

THE CAMPS OF OCTOBER–DECEMBER, 1777

Of this sketch, American officers probably could say only that it was better than nothing. In lieu of scale, it gave the location of the milestones on the Shippack Road. The best known of the various camps in this area were those of White Marsh, in the southern and southeastern quarters of this sketch, which is a reproduction of the original in the Library of the Historical Society of Pennsylvania.

531

seemed to him that he lost more men by desertion than he gained by enlistment.[53] Some who were exhorted to remain in the Army professed their willingness to do so after they had visited their families,[54] but once they disappeared, they could not be reached again except through a call for militia or by the operation of such a draft as several of the States were forced to institute with varying success.[55] Some States put recruiting for their own defence above that of the continent.[56] Maryland and others were said to have forbidden recruiting for the Artillery and other troops raised on a continental basis until their own State quotas for the sixteen new Regiments had been filled.[57] These and other perplexities[58] were less serious, potentially, than the situation that might be created by Congress' resolution of Apr. 14, 1777, which suggested to the States the exemption from active militia duty of any two men who jointly would furnish an able-bodied recruit to a continental Battalion for three years or the duration of the war.[59] This had led quickly to abuses.[60] In Virginia, for example, two rich men would pay as much as £100, or £50 each for a substitute,[61] an outlay which, said one Cornet, "puts it out of the power of recruiting officers to get men."[62] Another inequity had been practiced in Washington's own State. When recruiting officers had failed to get men by any other device in the upper Counties and in Midland Virginia, they had gone to indentured convicts and had enlisted these individuals, most of whom had come from

[53] 8 *ibid.*, 160–61. On Oct. 17, 1777, Congress was to recommend a new proclamation of pardon for deserters who would return to duty (9 *JCC.*, 816). This was issued by the Commander-in-Chief October 24; 9 *G. W.*, 426–27. For the course of desertion in the Army during the summer and autumn of 1777, see 8 *G. W.*, 128, 482; 9 *ibid.*, 362, 406, 412–13.

[54] H. Jackson to Henry Knox, May 12, 1777; *Knox Papers*, MHS.

[55] 7 *G. W.*, 78–79; 81 n; 9 *G. W.*, 165; 1 *LTW.*, 431. The last two of these references are to the experience of Virginia.

[56] 8 *G. W.*, 101–03, 124–25; 8 *JCC.*, 549. Concern was raised by a report that Connecticut troops did not intend to fight beyond the borders of their State.

[57] 8 *G. W.*, 431; 9 *ibid.*, 84–85. When Washington wrote these letters, he had not seen the text of the law. If it was, as seems probable, the "Act to Promote the Recruiting Service," of Mch. 31, 1777, its terms were misrepresented to Washington. The statute merely extended certain exemptions from arrest to men who enlisted in the artillery and infantry forces (*Recorded Laws of Maryland*, Liber G A No. 1, f. 16, 1777–78).

[58] Cf. the Pennsylvania Regiment that maintained it was paroled (8 *G. W.*, 169–70); the various problems of inoculation and recruitment in North Carolina (7 *JCC.*, 317; 8 *ibid.*, 475; 8 *G. W.*, 12–13, 242–43); and the strange record of Georgia in enlisting outside her own borders (*ibid.*, 168–69) and in sending blank continental commissions to Europe for engineers (9 *JCC.*, 821), to say nothing of the riotous behavior of Georgia troops in Maryland (*ibid.*, 792–93).

[59] The exemption was valid only for the term of the substitute's service (7 *JCC.*, 262).

[60] *Ibid.*, 343.   [61] 1 *Bland Papers*, 69.

[62] *Ibid.* Washington reported Nov. 1, 1777, that substitutes were being paid forty dollars for two months' service with the militia, compared with a continental bounty of only half that amount for three years in an active command (9 *G. W.*, 487).

the British Isles within a few years and under criminal sentence. Part of the bargain with convict recruits was that money would be taken from their pay to recompense the masters who previously had bought "the time" of the culprits. When Washington learned of this, his comment was: ". . . I shall have no reliance upon such troops, nor shall I ever be without apprehensions of their deserting with their arms." [63]

Fortunately, this bad example of Virginia was not duplicated elsewhere at the time to any dangerous extent, but if there was no general substitution or recruiting of convicts, some other device on the part of a State usually hampered enlistment. On occasion, when slowly organized Companies at length were brought together as Regiments, and the Regiments were assembled as a Brigade and marched to the front, the total number would fall so far short of authorized strength that army commanders despaired. Schuyler had written Washington in July: "General Nixon arrived the night before last with his Brigade. From the slowness with which they moved from Albany to this [Fort Edward], being four days marching forty-six miles, I was led to conclude that they were a formidable body; but to my great mortification, I find the whole to consist of 575, rank and file, fit for duty, and eleven sick. Several of these are Negroes, and many of them young, small and feeble boys." [64] Of some other commands, Colonel Harrison had said in August: "The deficiency—from desertion and other causes is almost incredible . . . in the instance of the two independent Companies, they are returned sixty and when they first joined they were about 140 strong." [65]

In spite of these and similar disappointments, Washington held to the conviction that if the Regiments were filled, the Army would be, as he said, "on a more permanent footing" [66] of long-term enlistment. For a time he had seemed in a fair way of achieving a considerable fraction of what he sought. In May, the troops of the main Army had reached once again an effective strength above 8000,[67] a low but a fairly stable figure. There had been temporary encouragements also—a better

---

[63] 8 G. W., 56. His suggestion was that Congress discharge these recruits or else pay the former masters the sums that were to be taken from the soldiers' pay (*ibid*). Congress voted to make no deduction from the men's pay and to leave to future consideration whether the money given the holders of the indentures should be charged against the State or should be assumed by the continent (7 *JCC.*, 369).

[64] Letter of July 14, 1777; 1 *LTW.*, 397–98.

[65] R. H. Harrison to unnamed correspondent, Aug. 20, 1777; *L. W. Smith Coll.*

[66] 8 G. W., 46. Cf. *ibid.*, 487.

[67] Specifically 8188, according to the return of May 21, 1777 (8 G. W., 99 n).

response by the New Jersey militia,[68] the organization of Morgan's corps of rangers,[69] the transfer of some Pennsylvania State troops to the continental establishment [70] and, in general, the anxious if passing zeal that usually developed when men had thought the enemy's next move might bring him to their doors.[71] Most promising of all, certainly in future possibilities, had been the decision of Washington, which Congress approved, to shift to the States the burden of enlisting recruits and of apprehending deserters.[72] One of the immediate gains from this new policy, if executed with vigor, would be the return to the Army of recruiting officers who were acquiring "idle habits," in Washington's words, while professing to be on the search for men.[73]

Now that the forests around the camps were flying the red and yellow warnings of autumn, the Army began to dissolve. Besides losing the militia, Washington soon would have to say farewell to some and perhaps all the troops of the first nine Virginia Regiments, because their time was expiring.[74] In their place, if for a short period only, Washington must get Pennsylvania militia, but how to procure them, he did not know. ". . . this State acts most infamously," he confided to his brother, "the people of it I mean as we derive little or no assistance from them." [75] There was one other area from which men might be drawn, trained men at that: Since Burgoyne had been beaten and his Army captured, the line of the Hudson no longer would need as many troops as were with Gates and with Putnam. Many could be sent southward to Pennsylvania, but in this, as in much besides, the gulf between *could* and *would* was as wide as that between caution and cooperation.[76]

In attempting to fill his shivering ranks and to keep his ill-clad Army

---

[68] After the Army had moved nearer the town of Newark (8 *G. W.*, 163–64), but this force was threatened with collapse in October (9 *ibid.*, 313, 383, 477, 485).

[69] On June 13, 1777, in sending instructions to Colonel Morgan, the Commander-in-Chief spoke of it as "the Corps of Rangers, newly formed . . ." (8 *G. W.*, 236).

[70] 8 *JCC.*, 482.

[71] Cf. the calls for militia June 10, *ibid.*, 432, July 31, *ibid.*, 592, and of August 21, 9 *G. W.*, 113. Congress' authorization, July 12, of calls on New England will be found in 8 *JCC.*, 549.

[72] 8 *G. W.*, 440; Congress' endorsement, July 31, is in 8 *JCC.*, 593; Washington's circular to the States, Aug. 4, 1777, appears in 9 *G. W.*, 11.

[73] 8 *Ibid.*, 440. See his refusal to commission officers for Regiments he did not believe it possible to organize, 9 *G. W.*, 233.

[74] *Ibid.*, 480–81.   [75] *Ibid.*, 399, verbatim.

[76] In November, Alexander Hamilton was sent to New York to arrange for the transfer of troops that were subject, in theory, altogether to Washington's orders. As represented in Gates to Washington, Nov. 7, 1777 (*Gates Papers*, NYHS), and in 2 *LTW.*, 24–26, 26–30, 39, 41–42, 549, 9 *A. Hamilton*, 106 ff, and 10 *G. W.*, 83, the letters that passed between Hamilton and Washington on one side and Gates on the other read almost as if Hamilton had been an agent sent to a foreign court to solicit an alliance of doubtful value to the country whose representative he was addressing.

from freezing or starving or both, Washington did not have the uniform support of able lieutenants who understood his perplexities and intelligently endeavored to relieve them. On the contrary, though he had some senior officers like Greene, Lincoln and Knox, who were developing steadily, he had found at Brandywine and at Germantown that several lacked, or were suspected of lacking, the essential qualities of leadership.[77] The Army had been operating for weeks without a sufficient number of Generals and now it had lost Francis Nash, a promising young North Carolina Brigadier, who had died of wounds.[78] In addition, five general officers of experience faced charges—Prudhomme de Borre for mismanagement or worse at Brandywine,[79] Sullivan for the affair on Staten Island as well as for the action of September 11, Wayne for the attack on his troops near Paoli, Stephen for misconduct and excessive drinking, and William Maxwell for substantially the same charges. Sullivan was acquitted unanimously and was given by Congress an approving vote that was an apology to him in all but explicit words;[80] Wayne, too, was said by the court to deserve "highest honor"[81] after he had insisted that certain questions brought to light before a court of inquiry be examined by a court martial.[82] Maxwell was given something of a Scotch verdict,[83] but Adam Stephen was not that fortunate. Although Stephen had enjoyed prestige as Washington's former second in command, one of the officers who had been at Fort Necessity,[84] he now was convicted of "unofficerlike behavior" and of "drunkenness" and was recommended for dismissal. Washington approved the sentence in six words;[85] Stephen tried vainly to keep his place by telling what he professed to have done in getting men to reenlist,[86] and then he

---

[77] Cf. 10 G. W., 99–100.   [78] 9 Ibid., 332, 336, 342.

[79] See infra, p. 539.

[80] 9 G. W., 347, 367–68, 379–80; 9 JCC., 808, 809, 822–23; 2 Burnett, 514–15, 517, 530. The opinion of the court was delivered to Washington October 12, was forwarded to Congress on the 13th, and was made public in GOs of October 16.

[81] 9 G. W., 491.

[82] Ibid., 352, 354, 361, 421, 422; Wayne to Washington, Oct. 11, 22, 1777; 4 Wayne Papers, 18, 22, PHS. The verdict of the court was published in GOs of November 1.

[83] Nov. 4, 1777. For his case see 9 G. W., 379, 438, 470; 10 ibid., 3–4, 20, 99. His chief accuser appears to have been Maj. William Heth, who wrote Daniel Morgan: ". . . since the enemy's landing at Head of Elk Maxwell's corps 'twas expected would do great things—we had opportunities and anybody but an old woman would availed themselves of them—He is to be sure a damned bitch of a General . . ." Letter of Oct. 2, 1777; 1 Winchester His. Soc. Papers, 33; cf. ibid., 31. Heth himself was not without critics. See John Chilton in 12 T 129. Lafayette thought the American courtmartial system defective, because in this and similar cases it left an officer with a stigma, though it could not find sufficient reason to dismiss him from the service (Lafayette to Washington, c. Jan. 13, 1778; Louis Gottschalk, ed., The Letters of Lafayette to Washington, 1777–1779, cited hereafter as LOLTW, 23).

[84] See Vol. I., p. 409 ff.   [85] Nov. 20, 1777.   [86] Cf. ibid., 208.

appealed to Congress with the countercharge, "It has been my misfortune to become the object of hatred of a person of high rank for no other reason that I know, but for delivering my sentiments on the measures pursued this campaign with that candor which an old officer of experience who has the interests of America at heart." [87] He aroused no sympathy. Elbridge Gerry doubtless echoed the finality of Delegates' judgment when he informed Joseph Trumbull, "General Stevens [Stephen] is broke for drunkenness"—that and no more. [88]

These results of the courtmartial proceedings eased any possible apprehension in Washington's mind that he might lose Sullivan, Wayne and Maxwell. While the Commander-in-Chief did not say so in any published word, he undoubtedly was glad to be rid of Stephen, and he felt the Army would gain by the substitution of a competent, alert and cooperative man in Stephen's place; but the need of additional officers of brigade and divisional rank remained. [89] Too much of important service had to be imposed on too few men. Colonels temporarily in command were hampered. In the case of Brig. Gen. Alexander McDougall, promotion had been denied improperly; outside the Army remained John Cadwalader, whose unusual abilities Washington coveted for the continental cause. Nothing could be done in the autumn of 1777 to overcome Cadwalader's reluctance to accept commission; [90] but it was possible, Washington thought, to advance McDougall. Immediately after the Battle of Germantown, Washington wrote to Congress regarding the New Yorker: "This gentleman, from the time of his appointment as Brigadier, from his abilities, military knowledge and approved bravery, has every claim to promotion." [91] Congress acted as Washington asked and, October 20, named McDougall a Major General. By the same resolve, it gave like rank to Robert Howe, a North Carolina Brigadier, [92] whom Washington did not know. When the Commander-in-Chief next had occasion to write Howe he made it plain, politely but positively, that he had no hand in lifting Howe a step higher on the roster of the Army. [93]

[87] Here the unfinished sentence ended. Stephen to Pres. Henry Laurens, 162 *Papers Cont. Cong.*, 235, LC.

[88] 2 *Burnett*, 572.

[89] Washington described the situation in a letter of Oct. 7, 1777, to the President of Congress, 9 *G. W.*, 321–22.

[90] See Cadwalader to Washington, Apr. 27, 1778; 2 *LTW.*, 109–10.

[91] 9 *G. W.*, 322. McDougall was regarded everywhere as a New Yorker, though actually he was born in the Hebrides.

[92] 9 *JCC.*, 823.   [93] 10 *G. W.*, 301.

Among the numerous ill effects of this shortage of senior officers was a dangerous lack of discipline among ambitious, place-hunting Colonels, several of whom were hot-headed and in a double sense intemperate.[94] Other regimental commanders—some of them patriotic men of character—were discouraged by the low purchasing power of their pay [95] and by the promotion over them of "foreigners" and of staff officers who were regarded as the pets of powerful Generals. The main Army was outraged, in particular, by the compliance of Congress with the request of General Gates that Lt. Col. James Wilkinson be given brevet as Brigadier for bringing the news of Burgoyne's surrender.[96] These men would not have been satisfied, either, had they read the explanation of one Delegate, who said: "I was glad Gates asked no more at this time, for assured I am that if he had it would have been granted while they were rejoicing for the goodness of God in delivering our enemies into our hands." [97] Along with this there was, as always, the canker of jealous controversy over seniority.[98] Washington soon was to write Congress in weariness of spirit, "My feelings are every day wounded by the discontent, complaints and jarring of officers, not to add resignations." [99] He did not need to explain that, per contra, he always was glad to receive the resignation of incompetent or unworthy men.[100]

[94] Cf. the court martial of Col. Stephen Moylan for "disobedience to the orders of General Pulaski, a cowardly and ungentlemanly action in striking Mr. Zielinski, a gentleman and officer in the Polish service, when disarmed; and putting him under guard; and giving irritating language to General Pulaski." Moylan was acquitted but was increasingly the furious, personal enemy of Pulaski, who was himself a difficult officer with whom to work in harmony. Zielinski later had more trouble with Moylan. See 10 *G. W.*, 419.

[95] Cf. 9 *G. W.*, 97–98; Surgeon A. Waldo's Diary in 21 *Penn. Mag.*, 314.

[96] Gates to John Hancock, Oct. 18, 1777, *Gates Papers*, NYHS; 9 *JCC.*, 870; 10 *G. W.*, 116; 1 *Sullivan Papers*, 606–08; 2 *Burnett*, 560. Of particular interest are the observations of John Laurens in a letter to his father. See *John Laurens*, 83. So far as Gates himself was concerned, Congress took the edge off its expression of thanks to him and its vote of a medal of honor, by including in the congratulatory resolve the names of three officers of lower rank who had distinguished themselves in the defence of the Delaware River below Philadelphia (9 *JCC.*, 861–62).

[97] Nathaniel Folsom to Josiah Bartlett, Jan. 2, 1778; 3 *Burnett*, 4.

[98] Cf. 10 *G. W.*, 186: "When rank is once given . . . the party in possession of it in most cases is unwilling to give it up. . . ."

[99] Dec. 22, 1777; 10 *G. W.*, 185.

[100] Cf. his observations of Dec. 25, 1777, in a letter to Gov. Richard Caswell of North Carolina: "A spirit of resigning their commissions . . . has been too prevalent in the Army of late. I have discountenanced it as much as possible, especially where the applications were of men of merit and in some such instances have peremptorily refused to grant them. The practice is of a pernicious tendency and must have an unhappy influence on the service. At the same time, it is to be observed, where officers wish to resign whose characters are exceptionable or do not stand in a favorable point of view, their commissions should be received, as their continuance would not promote the public interest and might prevent the promotion of better men" (10 *G. W.*, 201–02). In GOs of December 27 Washington was to order an inquiry by all the regular and acting Brigadiers into the reasons for absences and he was to direct that

Washington would have said this, *mutatis mutandis,* of foreigners whose applications for positions of high rank in the American service had continued in spite of appeals by Congress and by him to the Commissioners in France.[101] Those representatives of the American revolutionary government were themselves embarrassed by what Silas Deane styled the "rage" among Frenchmen for this adventure.[102] The agents in Paris were told firmly that the decision of Congress to refuse commissions to foreigners who did not understand the English language must not be construed to mean that all those who had knowledge of that tongue would be employed.[103] General Heath, still commanding in Boston, was asked by Washington not to assist any foreigners in coming to headquarters unless they had contracts with the American spokesmen in France.[104] Occasionally, when applicants arrived without such agreements, the Delegates in Congress declined as tactfully as possible the tender of service.[105] Other officers were told they would have a step upward when they gave proof of their right to it by the service they rendered, but that, until this was done, they could expect no pay above that of a Captain.[106] Meantime—and for months to come—Congress begrudgingly advanced money to those of the French officers who either were extravagant or were without funds of their own. Somewhat reluctantly, too, and scarcely knowing why, the Delegates made Johann Kalb a Major General and voted him 1200 dollars besides.[107] In the most embarrassing case of all, that of du Coudray, accident served where diplomacy had failed. On the 15th of September, this ambitious officer had insisted on remaining astride his horse when he was going aboard the Schuylkill ferry. The animal had taken fright, had run to the other side of the ferryboat and had plunged into the river. Du Coudray was drowned—a "dispensation," said John Adams, "that will save us much

---

those who had not been granted leave or had overstayed it were to be notified to "return to camp without delay on pain of being suspended or cashiered" (*ibid.,* 215). Military leaders interested in the training of officers may wish to read Washington's undated "General Instructions [of 1777] for the Colonels and Commanding Officers of Regiments in the Continental Service" (*ibid.,* 238).

101 Cf. 9 *G. W.,* 85.

102 1 *Deane Papers,* 342.

103 2 *Burnett,* 398.

104 8 *G. W.,* 482.

105 Cf. 9 *JCC.,* 837, 930.

106 8 *ibid.,* 562.

107 See 8 *JCC.,* 574, 588, 618, 651, 679, 697, 702, 728, 765; 9 *ibid.,* 1018, 1049. Some of these officers looked to Congress to provide them with horses and servants (9 *G. W.,* 83). For the promotion of Kalb, who became a frequent petitioner and correspondent of Congress, see 8 *JCC.,* 743, 746.

altercation," [108] or, as another observer put it, death had "relieved the Congress from a very troublesome malcontent." The same writer stated: "Of all the French officers I have seen among us, he could have done the greatest injury if France should at any time [have] formed ambitious schemes against us." [109] Congress subsequently voted that the other members of du Coudray's party [110] could remain in the American Army at the rank they severally had in French service; [111] but Congress' unwillingness to conform to Deane's agreement with these men, said Richard Henry Lee, "disgusted them greatly." [112] Another French officer who quit in the same state of mind but for a different reason was Brig. Gen. Prudhomme de Borre. When he learned that a court of inquiry was to be held on his conduct at the Battle of the Brandywine,[113] he indignantly tendered his resignation, which Congress willingly accepted. He subsequently maintained that he had been condemned before he had been heard and that he should be made a Major General. The reply of Congress was that he no longer was in American service and would not be elected to the rank he sought.[114] Still another French officer to resign in pique at this time was Col. Mottin de la Balme, Inspector General of Cavalry, who had been recommended warmly by Deane.[115] Singular persistence marked the effort of General Fermoy, the Martinique volunteer, to procure the rank and emolument of a division commander, but he directed his campaign to Congress, not to Washington, and was not a nuisance at headquarters, whence Fermoy's departure for the Northern Army must have been welcome in

108 Diary of John Adams, 2 *John Adams*, 438, also in 2 *Burnett*, 497. Du Coudray two days previously had asked Congress to grant him and his companions brevet commissions at low rank so that if they were captured by the British they could be exchanged (8 *JCC.*, 740). These commissions were allowed the day du Coudray lost his life (*ibid.*, 745). The *Gates Papers*, NYHS, show du Coudray to have been an admirer of the commander of the Northern Department (see particularly his letter of Aug. 27, 1777). Had du Coudray lived, he might have become a member of the Conway cabal.

109 William Clajon to Gates, Sept. 29, 1777; *Gates Papers*, NYHS.

110 Seven of them did not arrive in Pennsylvania until the end of September, or early October, 1777. See Charles Louis Lebrun to Congress, Oct. 2, 1777; 78 *Papers Cont. Cong.*, 275, LC.

111 9 *JCC.*, 799. For the burial arrangements of du Coudray, the financial settlement and the return of most of these officers and men to their own country, see 8 *JCC.*, 751; 9 *ibid.*, 799, 845, 875, 879, 885–86, 902, 904–05; 1 *Ballagh, Lee Letters*, 326, 348–49, 364, 367; 2 *Burnett*, 549, 558.

112 1 *Ballagh, Lee Letters*, 364.   113 See *supra*, p. 535.

114 8 *JCC.*, 739, 740, 760, 763; 9 *G. W.*, 216.

115 1 *Deane Papers*, 328; 9 *JCC.*, 797. His resignation of Oct. 3, 1777, is in 41 *Papers Cont. Cong.*, 144, LC. He continued to importune Congress for months, though told in February, 1778, that nine hundred and ten dollars then paid him were in full for all claims, and that Congress had "no further occasion for his services" (10 *JCC.*, 157). Cf. *ibid.*, 43, 92, and 11 *ibid.*, 809. See also 41 *Papers Cont. Cong.*, 150, LC.

March, 1777.[116] Thanks to the example set by Lafayette, Duportail and a few others somewhat less conspicuous, Washington was undergoing a change of mind concerning qualified foreign officers,[117] but at this time, most of them added to burdens which soon were to lead Nathanael Greene to say: "I think I never saw the Army so near dissolving since I have belonged to it." [118] Apparent disintegration had been a continuing process, the worst of which manifestly had not been realized yet; but this time it had not brought Washington as low in spirit as he had been at the beginning of winter in 1776, when he had written his brother, "If every nerve is not strained to recruit the New Army with all possible expedition, I think the game is pretty near up . . ." [119] Now, ten months later, to the day, when he sketched for the same brother's eye the perplexities he faced—the lack of clothing, the thinning of the ranks, and the efforts of the British to destroy the water defences of the lower Delaware—Washington said: "I am doing all I can in my present situation to save them; God only knows which will succeed." [120]

[116] For his departure at that time, see 7 *JCC.*, 211. His recall and his importunity to the date of the settlement with him in February, 1778, may be traced in 8 *G. W.*, 485, 8 *JCC.*, 596, 602, 681, 700, 958, 9 *ibid.*, 978, 1048, 1069, 10 *ibid.*, 105, 151, 174 and in 78 *Papers Cont. Cong.* 95, 99, 107, 129, 133, 149, LC. His birth in Martinique is mentioned in *Les Combattants Français de la Guerre Américaine*, 1778–87. It may be in order to repeat that his family name was Rochedefermoy or de Rochefermoy. His signature to the autograph letters cited *supra* is derochefermoj.

[117] 10 *G. W.*, 35.

[118] Letter of Nov. 17, 1777, to Henry Marchant; 1 *Greene's Greene*, 411.

[119] Letter of Dec. 18, 1776, to John Augustine Washington, *supra*, p. 295, and 6 *G. W.*, 398.

[120] 9 *G. W.*, 399, with some repunctuation.

CHAPTER XXI

To a Place Called Valley Forge
(November–December, 1777)

A SHOCKING incident on the 15th of October would have justified Washington in saying of the morale fibre of Americans substantially what he had written of their war for independence: God alone knew whether it would outwear adversity. A devout woman of culture and of some literary attainments, Mrs. Elizabeth Graeme Ferguson, came to headquarters that day and asked to see the General. Washington knew her not only by her own reputation, but also as the daughter of a distinguished Philadelphian, Dr. Thomas Graeme, who had died five years previously; and the Commander-in-Chief had full faith in her, despite the fact that her husband, Henry Ferguson, had been among the civilian attendants of General Howe when the British marched into Philadelphia.

Business was put aside; Mrs. Ferguson was to be ushered in. She entered—a woman of 40—and, after some preliminaries, handed Washington a bulky package of fourteen folio pages.[1] It proved to be a letter to Washington from a man he admired, Rev. Jacob Duché, the Philadelphia clergyman whose eloquence had stirred the heart of every Delegate to Congress in 1774.[2] Because of the General's respect for Duché, it was a blow in the face to read long, fervent paragraphs in which the minister urged that Washington call on Congress to rescind the Declaration of Independence and to open negotiations for peace with Britain. Duché was confident that such a move would meet with favor in America. "If it should not," the former Chaplain of Congress said, without abashment, "you have an infallible recourse still left; negotiate for your country at the head of your Army."[3]

Washington was as much concerned as he was surprised:[4] what had happened to Duché? Was the cleric the victim of selfish fears, which made him seek favor at the hands of the British, or had he been made

---

[1] They still are in 152 *Papers Cont. Cong.*, V, p. 119, LC. A sketch of Elizabeth Graeme Ferguson, with ample bibliography, will be found in *DAB*.
[2] See *supra*, Vol. III, p. 375.　　　　　[3] Letter of Oct. 8, 1777; 1 *LTW.*, 458.
[4] 10 *G. W.*, 92.

the tool of others? Washington reflected immediately that if he had
been given even an inkling of the contents of the letter he would have
returned the paper unopened. As he could not do that now, he would
transmit it to Congress lest it be found among his records in event they
were stolen or he was killed or made prisoner. Were it discovered in his
files, he might be accused of conspiracy with Duché against the freedom
of America.[5] As for the delivery of such a document, Washington told
Mrs. Ferguson that he disapproved her participation in the affair and
that he would expect her to make no such mistake for the future.[6] With
that, he bowed her out of the room. The next day he forwarded Duché's
letter to Congress,[7] which body shared his amazement and, somewhat
contrary to his expectations,[8] decided to make the paper public.[9] Delegates, attachés and Pennsylvanians by the thousands talked of the incident for days with a zest little below that of their discussion of Burgoyne's surrender.[10]

Washington dismissed the incident from mind when he laid Duché's
paper before Congress, and he wrote no more about it at the time otherwise than to explain the circumstances to Francis Hopkinson, the
clergyman's brother-in-law, who tried to send Duché, through Washington's hands, a plea to renounce disloyalty to America.[11] Washington
never referred, so far as is known, to the statement Duché made concerning the Army in his letter: "The whole world knows that its only
existence depends upon you; that your death or captivity disperses it in a
moment, and that there is not a man on that side the question, in America, capable of succeeding you. As to the Army itself, what have you to
expect from them? Have they not frequently abandoned you yourself,
in the hour of extremity? Can you have the least confidence in a set of
undisciplined men and officers, many of whom have been taken from
the lowest of the people, without principle, without courage? Take
away them that surround your own person, how very few are there you
can ask to sit at your table!"[12]

[5] This is another of the instances, lamentably few, in which Washington left a record of
his thoughts at the time of an important incident. See his letter of Nov. 21, 1777, to Francis
Hopkinson, 10 *G. W.*, 92.

[6] 9 *G. W.*, 383.   [7] *Ibid.*, 382.   [8] 10 *G. W.*, 92.

[9] The receipt of Washington's communication is noted 9 *JCC.*, 822, though the entry does
not record any vote to print.   [10] Cf. 2 *Burnett*, 526–27.

[11] 10 *G. W.*, 92–93. The greater part of Hopkinson's letter to Duché, Nov. 14, 1777, will
be found in G. E. Hastings, *Life and Work of Francis Hopkinson*, 271 ff.

[12] 1 *LTW.*, 453. Cf. Lafayette to Washington, Dec. 30, 1777: ". . . if you were lost for
America, there is nobody who could keep the Army and the Revolution for six months"
(*LOLTW.*, 14).

The taste and the truth of parts of this were disputable, of course, but it was significant that Duché held the "existence" of the Army so manifestly dependent on Washington that the minister did not think argument on that point was necessary. As Duché saw them, "cause" and "commander" were almost synonyms. He believed this was the opinion of "the whole world" and he set in contrast to the rise of Washington the decline of Congress. Said Duché: "Take an impartial view of the present Congress, and what can you expect from them? . . . These are not the men you engaged to serve; these are not the men that America has chosen to represent her. Most of them were chosen by a little, low faction, and the few gentlemen that are among them now are well known to lie on the balance, and looking up to your hand alone to turn the beam. 'Tis you, sir, and you only that support the present Congress; of this you must be fully sensible." [13]

Had Washington been disposed to discuss the composition of Congress with a man who seemed to him to have been enticed into the British camp, the Commander-in-Chief would of course have insisted that Duché erred in generalizing, but he would have been compelled to admit that Congress no longer represented America's best. Nearly all the members of that body who had voted unanimously in June, 1775, to put their Virginia colleague at the head of the Army had died, had terminated their service, or had taken long leave, with or without the consent of their colleagues.[14] Six only remained—John Adams, Samuel Adams and John Hancock of the Massachusetts delegation, Eliphalet Dyer of Connecticut, James Duane of New York, Samuel Chase of Maryland, and Richard Henry Lee of Virginia.[15] Of these six, Samuel Chase was saying his farewells, and the three senior members from Massachusetts were preparing to leave York.[16] Before December arrived, Dyer and Duane were to be the only Delegates[17] in a shrunken body of twenty-one or twenty-two who had seen Washington in uniform when Congress had filled the seats during the late spring of 1775, and a majority still had hoped for reunion with England. Newcomers were acquainted, of course, with Washington's high reputation;

[13] Ibid.

[14] Cf. Washington to Robert Morris, Mch. 2, 1777: ". . . your observation on the want of many capital characters in that Senate are but too just" (7 G. W., 225).

[15] It will be understood that numbers of others who had served with Washington still were on the roster but were not in regular attendance. Some of these men did not sit in Congress during the whole of 1777.

[16] See the roster in 2 Burnett, xlvi–xlvii, li.

[17] Richard Henry Lee was still a Delegate but was not in attendance (3 Burnett, lxii).

most of them had never seen him in committee or council of war and did not know the quality of his judgment.

Duché wrote that Washington alone supported Congress, but the question in reality was, would Congress continue to support Washington? His good name was at the mercy of strangers, some of whom were divided by sectional jealousies [18] and were dazzled by Gates's easy success in the Northern Department. Gates always had been a favorite in New England, where Schuyler never had been popular. Now Gates appeared to have demonstrated his superiority [19] not over Schuyler only but over Washington also. Inexperienced Delegates did not realize that Washington had to do much more than to maneuver an Army. When these men compared Gates's decisive victory near Saratoga with Washington's defeats on the Brandywine and at Germantown, they naturally would reason that Gates was the better General. He had captured an entire army. While he was achieving that, what had been Washington's next accomplishment? The loss of Philadalphia—so members of Congress might be disposed to answer. In doing so, they failed to perceive the vast difference between Gates's task and Washington's. In contest with Burgoyne's army, Gates knew that every mile of British advance was an added mile of long and tenuous lines of communication up rivers, through narrow lakes, and over rocky forest road. Wash-

[18] Washington for a long time had been ashamed of this ill-feeling, especially when it was exhibited by his own people. Months previously, he had written Custis: "It is painful to me to hear of such illiberal reflections upon the Eastern States as you say prevails in Virginia. I always have and always shall say that I do not believe any of the States produce better men, or persons capable of making better soldiers, but it is to be acknowledged that they are (generally speaking) most wretchedly officered. To this, and this only, is to be attributed their demerits. The policy of those States has been to level men as much as possible to one standard . . . [At this point in the manuscript several words in successive clauses have been scratched out, so that it is impossible to follow a part of Washington's argument] we have found that wherever a Regiment is well officered, their men have behaved well—when otherwise, ill—the misconduct or cowardly behavior always originating with the officers who have set the example. Equal injustice is done them, in depriving them of merit in other respects; for no people fly to arms readier than they do, or come better equipped, or with more regularity into the field than they" (Letter of Jan. 22, 1777, 7 G. W., 53–54). On this declaration Washington stood, and with equal care he tried to avoid every act that might seem to indicate any partiality for men of his own State (See, for example, his reference to the equitable distribution of blankets, 8 G. W., 288; his unwillingness to enlarge the command of Charles Mynn Thruston, 7 G. W., 201–02, his refusal to approve the commission in Baylor's Light Horse of two Virginians of high social station who had left the Army without permission, ibid., 215, and his observation on clothing for the Southern Regiments, ibid., 206). Among the interesting references to sectionalism in the Army during 1776–77 are: John Chilton's letter of Sept. 17, 1776, in 12 T 92, George Johnston's postscript in ibid., 111; Washington's own remarks on the Northern Army, 7 G. W., 124; Sullivan's denunciatory "Southern valor appears to be a composition of boasting and conceit," 1 Sullivan Papers, 319, and John Adams's remarks, 1 John Adams, 258, and Adams, Fam. Let., 322–23.

[19] Cf. Eliphalet Dyer to Gates, Nov. 5, 1777, and James Lovell to Gates, same date, 2 Burnett, 546.

ington faced an adversary who could disembark troops almost anywhere and could supply them easily by waterlines Britain controlled.

Even some of those Delegates who were familiar with this decisive difference and were cognizant of Washington's perplexing and long-continued labors had become impatient of what appeared to be a policy of delay, if not of actual avoidance of attack. They did not admit the necessity of a continuing defensive. John Adams and perhaps others had still another complaint—that Washington was being deified. Among the reasons for a day of thanksgiving on account of the victory over Burgoyne, the Massachusetts Delegate wrote his wife, was the fact that turning the tide of arms was "not immediately due to the Commander-in-Chief nor to the Southern troops." Adams sharpened the line: "If it had been, idolatry and adulation would have been unbounded; so excessive as to endanger our liberties, for what I know. Now, we can allow a certain citizen to be wise, virtuous and good without thinking him a deity or a savior." [20]

Horatio Gates made the utmost of the praise he received and of the flattering comparisons in letters swollen with enough of laudation to turn any except the steadiest of heads.[21] One immediate effect on Gates was an abrupt change of attitude toward Washington. Most of the careful deference to "Your Excellency" disappeared from his communications, which became less and less frequent. Even after many days, no report on Burgoyne's surrender was made directly to Washington, who wished to reshape his plans in the light of what had been achieved so splendidly at Saratoga.[22] Indeed, Washington had waited so long for authentic news that at one time he had begun to doubt whether the report of a great victory was not unfounded.[23] When young Colonel Wilkinson at last reached headquarters with the dispatches, which were addressed to the President of Congress, not to Washington, the aide observed the surprise over Gates's disregard of "channels of command," and he wrote back to his chief in partisan spirit: "The dissensions, the jealousies, calumnies and detractions which pervade a certain quarter must be reserved for some other opportunity. I am often asked the cause of your not writing to General Washington, so that this omission has been noticed publicly." [24] Gates continued to communicate directly

[20] Letter of Oct. 26, 1777; *Adams, Fam. Let.*, 322–23.

[21] Many such letters will be found in *Gates Papers*, NYHS. Congratulations were received by him as late as March, 1778.

[22] 37 *G. W.*, 543.   [23] 9 *ibid.*, 440; 37 *ibid.*, 543–44.

[24] Letter of Nov. 4, 1777; 1 *Wilkinson*, 337–38.

with Congress and later forwarded to the President the news of the British evacuation of Ticonderoga,[25] though by that time he had received Washington's congratulations and a mild reprimand for failing to send official notice to headquarters.[26] To this, Gates's reply was casual, in a letter of November 2, that dealt primarily with the return to the main Army of Morgan's Regiment. "Congress having been requested immediately to transmit copies of all my dispatches to them, I am confident your Excellency has long ago received all the good news from this quarter"; [27] but he was not prompted by this exchange to report, as formerly, to the Commander-in-Chief. On the contrary, in a somewhat stiff letter to Washington, acknowledging suggestions about the port of embarkation for Burgoyne's men, Gates spoke of another communication to Congress and added in what might have been regarded as a deliberate parenthesis "(a copy of which I conclude your excellency has received)." [28] During the entire month of November, Gates wrote to the Commander-in-Chief three times and no more. On two of these occasions he merely was answering letters.[29]

Washington did not build a grudge on this disregard of his position as Commander-in-Chief; but he could not fail to observe how promptly some officers now became his critics and Gates's avowed supporters. In the foreground, rather because of arrogance than of eminence, was Thomas Conway, a French officer who had signed a contract with Deane, had won the commissioner's good will,[30] and after coming to America on the *Amphitrite*,[31] had made a somewhat favorable impression on Washington. Congress had elected Conway a Brigadier,[32] May 13, 1777, whereupon headquarters had assigned him Regiments

25 Gates to Laurens, Nov. 25, 1777; 154 *Papers Cont. Cong.*, I, 300, LC.

26 Washington to Gates, Oct. 30, 1777: ". . . I cannot but regret that a matter of such magnitude and so interesting to our general operations should have reached me by report only, or through the channel of letters, not bearing that authenticity which the importance of it required, and which it would have received by a line under your signature, stating the simple fact" (9 *G. W.*, 465). Privately, Washington was much more outspoken about Gates's failure to notify him. In a letter of Oct. 28, 1777 he told Richard Henry Lee: "[I] cannot help complaining, most bitterly, of General Gates's neglect in not giving me the earliest authentic advice of [Burgoyne's surrender]; as an affair of that magnitude might, and indeed did give an important turn to our operations in this quarter, at least in our designs, but which for want of confirmation we began to doubt the propriety of . . ." (37 *G. W.*, 543).

27 9 *G. W.*, 466 n.

28 Gates to Washington, Nov. 23, 1777; 154 *Papers Cont. Cong.*, I, 306, LC.

29 There is, of course, the possibility, though it is remote, that letters passed of which neither drafts nor originals remain.

30 1 *Deane*, 380–81, 487, Deane to Washington, Nov. 30, 1776; 152 *Papers Cont. Cong.*, IV, p. 163, LC.

31 2 *Burnett*, 353 n.   32 7 *JCC.*, 349.

in Sullivan's Division. At Brandywine, Conway had won the admiring praise of his immediate superior and, by the time he had completed his part of the fighting and marching around Germantown, he had created in the mind of Sullivan a respect that amounted almost to awe. The New Hampshire General wrote of Conway: "His regulations in his Brigade are much better than any in the Army, and his knowledge of military matters in general far exceeds any officer we have." [33]

That was Conway's own opinion, freely admitted to other officers and, as occasion offered, to Congress. Two weeks after Brandywine, he addressed to President Hancock a letter that began: "It is with infinite concern that I find myself slighted and forgot when you have offered rank to officers who cost you a great deal of money and have never rendered you the least service. Baron de Kalb to whom you have offered the rank of Major General after having given him large sums of money is my inferior in France." Then, in a tone half boastful, half scolding, Conway set down in sequence seven reasons why he thought he should be made a Major General, and he ended with more of a bark than a bow: "Your very speedy and categorical answer will very much oblige him who is with respect . . ." [34]

This letter greatly offended Congress but it by no means included all that Conway had to say. He visited widely and discussed personalities without restraint. "No man," said he, "was more a gentleman than General Washington, or appeared to more advantage at his table, or in the usual intercourse of life; but as to his talents for the command of an Army"—and he shrugged as he spoke—"they were miserable indeed." [35] Washington ignored such of this disparagement as may have come to his ears. Although, under the skin, he was scarcely less sensitive than he had been, he did not have the time, and he would not pilfer it from his crowded duties, to notice every man who disliked or disparaged him. Nor, in this instance, was he inclined to put a high estimation on Conway's abilities or judgment. [36]

[33] Letter of Nov. 10, 1777, to John Adams; 1 *Sullivan Papers,* 577. Cf. Conway to "Board of War of Pennsylvania" Aug. 15, 1777, Pierpont Morgan Lib., *Gens. of the Rev.,* 10; Conway to the Executive Council of Pennsylvania, Aug. 17, 1777; 2 Dreer Coll. *Letters of Rev. Gens.,* p. 71, PHS. These two letters cover appeals to strengthen his command.

[34] Conway to Hancock, Sept. 25, 1777; 159 *Papers Cont. Cong.,* 453, LC.

[35] *Graydon,* 299–300. This may have been said by Conway somewhat later—Graydon did not attempt to date it—but there is no reason to doubt it was Conway's opinion earlier.

[36] In the *William Alexander Papers,* NYHS, is an unsigned, undated draft, apparently in Lord Stirling's autograph, of a complaint to Washington that Conway was insubordinate and had given orders to a Brigade Major not to heed any orders from division headquarters unless Conway himself approved them.

Conway kept up his campaign of importunity and criticism and, after Saratoga, he found that what he had been saying in dispraise of Washington fitted perfectly into the arguments advanced by those who were trying to exalt Gates. Some members of Congress who previously had been incensed by Conway's arrogance now were willing to listen, to accept his own estimate of himself and to ask whether, after all, it might not be in the country's interest to use his much applauded military knowledge by giving him the rank he sought. One report reached Washington that this had been done, or soon would be voted, and it both aroused his fears and outraged his sense of justice. The Army was suffering already from a downpour of resignations. Within less than a week approximately a score of officers had dampened spirits by asking permission to leave the service. As Washington understood their reasons, most of these men considered their duties so difficult and were themselves so tired that their obligation to their country no longer had first place in their minds.[37] Besides, the lower purchasing power of their pay in depreciated currency left them little or nothing for their families.[38] All twenty-three of the American Brigadiers[39] were Conway's seniors in date of commission. If now a boastful self seeker, a "foreigner" at that, and the most recently created Brigadier were promoted over these men, they would have a grievance that would seem to them to justify what some were anxious to do anyway. The best method of preventing this seemed to be for Washington himself to protest to Congress against the elevation of Conway.

Had this consideration of necessity not applied, justice itself would have demanded the same action by Washington in behalf of men who already had given more than two years to military service at the sacrifice of family and property. As Benjamin Harrison, his former spokesman, had left Congress, Washington addressed his appeal to Richard Henry Lee, the only member of the Virginia Delegation of 1777 with whom he had served. In plainest words he told Lee the appointment of Conway would be "as unfortunate a measure as ever was adopted" and, he said, "I may add (and I think with truth) that it will give a

---

37 9 G. W., 388–89.

38 See infra, p. 579–80, 614. This was progressive. Soon, Jed. Huntington was to predict that "more than half our officers will leave the Army" (Letter of Nov. 10, 1777 to "Colonel Williams," 2 Dreer Coll. Letters of Rev. Gens., 26).

39 Their seniority is given in Heitman (ed. of 1914), p. 10. Fermoy's commission antedated Conway's by eight months, but as Fermoy was not esteemed highly, his "rights" would not have been regarded as an obstacle to the advancement of Conway.

fatal blow to the existence of the Army." Forthrightly he explained:
"General Conway's merit . . . as an officer, and his importance in this
Army, exists more in his imagination than in reality: For it is a maxim
with him to leave no service of his untold, nor to want anything that is
to be had by importunity." Conway did not possess the "conspicuous
merit" that would justify his advancement over the Army's other Brigadiers, or dispose them to fight under him. Washington then told of
the desire of many officers to leave the Army. "Do not, therefore," he
exhorted Lee, "afford them good pretexts for retiring." After brief
elaboration of this, he wrote: "I have been a slave to the service: I have
undergone more than most men are aware of, to harmonize so many
discordant parts; but it will be impossible for me to be of any further
service if such insuperable obstacles are thrown in my way." [40]

Lee's reply was reassuring and at the same time alarming. Conway
had not been elected Major General and would not be, Lee predicted,
"whilst it is likely to produce the evil consequences you suggest." The
Virginia Delegate then proceeded somewhat coldly [41] to discuss the
reorganization of the Board of War and the identity of three individuals
who were to take the place of Congressmen and were to constitute the
entire membership. Washingon doubtless needed all his self control
as he read what some members of Congress favored: they wanted to
put on the board, Joseph Reed, Timothy Pickering, who was Washington's Adjutant General, and Robert H. Harrison, the indispensable
headquarters Secretary, and they talked of electing General Conway—
of all possible choices!—to be Pickering's successor as Adjutant General. Lee had the grace to say that he did not think Congress would
elect Harrison "without first knowing whether you could spare him"; [42]
but the hint was enough to stagger Washington. At a time when he
was seeking to hold the forts of the Delaware, and to supervise the

[40] Letter of Oct. 17, 1777; 9 *G. W.*, 387. That final antithesis could be interpreted readily
as a threat to resign; indeed, that might appear to be the obvious meaning of it. Washington
did not so intend it. See his letter of Feb. 15, 1778, to William Gordon: ". . . I can assure
you that no person ever heard me drop an expression that had a tendency to resignation"
(10 *G. W.*, 462–63).

[41] Lee had been under fire in Virginia for alleged (1) oppression of his tenants, (2) partiality to New England, and (3) opposition to laying the proceedings of the Secret Committee
before Congress because he wished to conceal "peculations." Absurd as were the charges, they
rendered him temporarily so unpopular in Virginia that he was dropped for a month from the
Virginia delegation to Congress (1 *Ballagh, Lee Letters*, 297, 303–04 and n). William Duer,
a warm supporter of Washington's, regretted the return of Lee because of what he termed the
Virginian's "smooth discourse and art of cabal." (2 *Burnett*, 410 and n.)

[42] 1 *Ballagh, Lee Letters*, 337–39.

labor of recruiting, clothing and feeding the Army, he was threatened with the loss of his Adjutant General and of his Secretary, and with the prospect of having Conway sent to headquarters to hector and to boast! Did Congress wish to make life intolerable for the Commander-in-Chief? In answering Lee's letter, Washington did not put this question directly, but he canvassed with some care the qualifications of Conway for the clerical duties the Adjutant General had to discharge, and he spoke of recommendations made in behalf of another man. As for the appointment of Reed, Pickering and Harrison, the General admitted them "equal to any you could make choice of," and, though doubtless with regret, he said that if Harrison and Pickering "should incline to accept the appointment, it will meet with my hearty concurrence." [43]

This was the situation when, during the evening of the 8th of November, a messenger brought Washington a letter written by Lord Stirling at Reading on the 3rd. It was a report on numerous small affairs—the rope ferries across the Schuylkill, the military outlook at Red Bank, the return of malingerers and the recovery of Stirling from illness. At the end of the last paragraph was this sentence: "The enclosed was communicated by Col. Wilkinson to Major McWilliams"—Stirling's aide— "such wicked duplicity of conduct I shall always think it my duty to detect." [44] The enclosure itself consisted merely of this: "In a letter from Genl. Conway to Genl. Gates he says—'Heaven has been determined to save your country; or a weak General and bad Councellors would have ruined it.' " [45]

Conway in correspondence with Gates—that, and not the Frenchman's sarcastic reference to Washington, struck home. How far had Conway gone in trying to undermine and discredit the Commander-in-Chief? Had he and Gates made common cause against their senior officer? This was a possible conclusion from the scrap Stirling had forwarded, but Washington's amiability led him to conclude that young Wilkinson had communicated the message at the instance of Gates and as a means of warning him.[46] Nothing could be done about the matter, of course, and nothing should be attempted; but it might be

[43] Letter of Oct. 28, 1777; 37 *G. W.*, 543.

[44] 69 *Papers of G. W.*, 111, LC.

[45] 10 *G. W.*, 30. The original is not among the *Papers of G. W.*, LC.

[46] Cf. Washington to Gates, Jan. 4, 1778: ". . . I considered the information as coming from yourself; and given with a friendly view to forewarn and consequently forearm me against a secret enemy; or, in other words, a dangerous incendiary . . ." (10 *G. W.*, 265).

worth while to let General Conway know that his contemptuous criticism had been reported. So, the next day, November 9, Washington sat down to draft a note to Conway, and with few erasures—for he was quite sure what he wanted to say—he signed and sent this:

Sir: A Letter which I received last Night, containd the following paragraph.

In a letter from Genl. Conway to Genl. Gates he says: "Heaven has determind to save your Country; or a weak General and bad Councellors would have ruined it."

I am Sir Yr. Hble Servt [47]

Washington knew that members of his military family would see this note, and he talked with them confidentially about Conway's apparent effort to stir up strife, but even in that circle, little time or thought could be given the incident because every officer was busy with one phase or another of the preparations being made to meet the enemy's anticipated final attacks on the river defences of Philadelphia. From the top of the Chew House at Germantown when the firing was heaviest, Washington sometimes could look down to the river and could see the smoke and the masts of tall ships; [48] but to observe and not to be able to stop the enemy epitomized the story of the battle. Washington strained and pleaded and did his absolute utmost to reenforce Fort Mifflin and Red Bank, [49] to eliminate bickering, [50] to employ and then to preserve the armed craft, [51] and to try every tactical device that ingenuity could suggest and common sense approve; [52] but the task was almost hopeless. Howe's fleet had been able from the beginning of operations to supply the army by using at night the shallow channel between Fort Mifflin and the right bank of the Delaware. At length Washington undertook to have Anthony Wayne's and Daniel Morgan's troops deliver a surprise attack and spike the British guns on Province Island, but the last hour was striking. [53] The end of a gallantly stubborn defence was the evacuation of the ruins of Fort Mifflin on the night of November 15–16 and of Fort Mercer on the night of the 20th-

[47] Verbatim; 10 G. W., 29, with a reproduction of the draft in Washington's autograph.
[48] John Laurens, 63.
[49] 9 G. W., 443–47, 455, 460, 465, 469, 473, 477, 489, 494; 10 ibid., 24, 29, 73, 89–90, 91, 95, 96.
[50] 2 LTW., 18–21; 9 G. W., 458, 459, 460, 489.
[51] 9 JCC., 863, 864; 10 G. W., 33, 86–87 n, 100, 121.
[52] 9 ibid., 475, 478, 489; 10 ibid., 5, 6, 8–9.
[53] John Laurens, 62; Wayne to Richard Peters, Nov. 18, 1777, 4 Wayne Papers, 39, PHS.

21st before Cornwallis could deliver an intended assault.[54] The great river now would be open to the British as soon as they removed a few more of the chevaux de frise. On the 22nd the first of their light-draft vessels reached Philadelphia.[55] Howe once again could maintain at all hours easy lines of supply by water. Washington had met his third defeat around the country's largest city, though neither the burden nor the honors of an admirable defence had been the Army's alone.

What next? As of the last week in November, the situation was this: In accordance with Washington's orders, Nathanael Greene and his Division had crossed the Delaware near Bristol on the 21st in order to deal with Cornwallis in event that officer attempted a sweep through Jersey after finding Fort Mercer abandoned. Glover's Brigade, moving from Gates's command through Putnam's, had been diverted to Greene;[56] the Jersey militia who had been under arms in the area around the fort were being exhorted to remain in service and to increase their numbers, though with small chance that either would be done.[57] Many of the best continental Regiments were almost unable to move any considerable distance at a reasonable rate of march because their shoes were worn out.[58] Unless some ruinous danger threat-

---

[54] 1 *Webb*, 387; 1 *Greene's Greene*, 513 ff; 1 *Ballagh, Lee Letters*, 359; 10 *G. W.*, 30, 33, 86–87 n, 100, 121; *Montresor Journals*, 476–78; *Anon. Proc. Howe*, AASP., April, 1930, p. 91–92; Lord Howe in 47 *Gent. Mag.*, 639; *A. Robertson's Diaries*, 155–56; 1 *Moore*, 520–22; Knox to Mrs. Knox, Nov. 17, 1777, *Knox Papers*, MHS; J. Mifflin to Gates, Nov. 14, 15, 17, 1777, *Gates Papers*, NYHS. A brief but informative account of what was known at headquarters day by day of the fighting on the river will be found in *John Laurens*, 69–70 and 75–78. Nearly all minor documents appear in Ford's collection, mentioned *supra*, Chap. XX, n. 38.

[55] Robert Morton's Diary in 1 *Penn. Mag.*, 31, though the *Montresor Journals*, 478, state that two barges from the ships came up the 21st. Morton noted on the 3rd of December that none of the large ships had docked, but Washington's chief of intelligence reported, November 26, that "this day upwards of thirty sail of transports came up the river; above one hundred now lie opposite the city . . ." (1 *PHS. Bul.*, Clark Letters, No. 9, p. 19). All these may have been of shallow draft.

[56] 9 *G. W.*, 464–65, 468.

[57] Cf. Nathanael Greene to Washington, Nov. 24, 1777; 1 *Greene's Greene*, 519.

[58] When the prospect was for a clash between Greene and Cornwallis, Morgan's Riflemen, who had returned from Gates's Army, were ordered to the scene of threatened action but 170 of these marksmen were all who had footgear stout enough for use on roads that already were hard and might be covered overnight with ice (See Washington to Greene, Nov. 22, 1777; 10 *G. W.*, 95). Washington on the 24th of October had to report to Congress his fear that within a few days two-thirds of his small Army would be unable to operate because of lack of shoes (9 *G. W.*, 424). For the effort to devise some substitute from raw hides, see 10 *ibid.*, 94, and for an attempt to procure leather and deerskins in North Carolina, see 9 *JCC.*, 965. The situation was to become so bad before the end of November that Washington had to ask through GOs for information concerning shoes, stockings and leather breeches in any quantity (10 *G. W.*, 105). Sullivan's Division, through the activities of Col. Moses Hazen, appeared to have a fair prospect of getting shoes for all its men (1 *Sullivan Papers*, 592). A most interesting German comment on the shortage of footgear was made by Capt. Johann Heinrichs, Jan. 18, 1778, to "The Chancellor of the Court." Heinrichs wrote: "[American troops] have

ened, the main Army could not be employed offensively at a distance from the good position [59] it had taken at White Marsh, twelve miles NNW of Philadelphia.

That was one controlling fact. Another was the weakness of the trained forces at Washington's command. Four councils of war, including one as late as November 24, had considered the possibility of attacking Howe, and in every instance had concluded that the Army was not strong enough to make the attempt.[60] Washington knew that he would be criticized for this decision.[61] "Our situation . . ." he told Nathanael Greene, "is distressing from a variety of irremediable causes, but more especially from the impracticability of answering the expectations of the world without running hazards which no military principles can justify, and which, in case of failure, might prove the ruin of our cause; patience and a steady perseverance in such measures as appear warranted by sound reason and policy must support us under the censure of the one, and dictate a proper line of conduct for the attainment of the other; that is the great object in view." [62]

More specifically, he would recall Greene from lower Jersey,[63] would put his Army in winterquarters close to Philadelphia, and would try to keep his barefooted men from starving or freezing. Smallwood might take Sullivan's Division to Wilmington.[64] The more vigilant part of the Light Horse and such Infantry as could move swiftly with decent shoes and satisfied stomachs, Washington would employ to guard against surprise, to discourage raids by Howe's forces, and to prevent the movement of supplies into Philadelphia from the nearby counties. If Washington saw an opening, he would try to make the most of it; in general, he would remain on the defensive.

The struggle for the forts on the lower Delaware and the reconcentration that followed the loss of those defences so occupied Washington during November that he had little time to study a bright event of that

---

neither shoes nor stockings; for the shoemaker is either a soldier or a Loyalist" (22 *Penn. Mag.*, 139).

[59] Covered by two commanding hills and secured by a very strong advanced post (*John Laurens*, 62). See also Elias Boudinot to his brother, Dec. 9, 1777, for another description of the position and of a brief demonstration in front of it (*Henkel's Cat.* 683, no. 162). For the move to White Marsh, see Chapter XX, n. 29.

[60] Council of October 27, 9 *G. W.*, 461 ff; council of November 8, 10 *ibid.*, 23–24; council of November 12, 10 *ibid.*, 48 n; council of November 24, 10 *ibid.*, 103 n, 106; 1 *Sullivan Papers*, 584; 1 *Greene's Greene*, 525.

[61] 10 *G. W.*, 106.

[62] *Ibid*, 106–07.

[63] *Ibid.*, 17–18, 120.

[64] *Ibid.*, 171, 174.

dark month—the completion by Congress of the Articles of Confederation and the dispatch on the 17th of the text to the States for ratification.[65] In Washington's eyes, the close cooperation of the States had been and still was the first essential of success in the attainment of independence, but not one line had he, the soldier, written of the compact Congress had been discussing at intervals since July 12, 1776.[66] The perfection of those articles, as far as it was attainable at all, was the work of the civil arm of government. He who held the sword must not use its point as a pen.

In another event of that absorbing month of November, 1777, Washington had a part he took pains to subordinate to the direction of Congress. The "convention" that covered the surrender of Burgoyne's Army had stipulated that the prisoners were to proceed to Boston whence they were to sail for Great Britain under parole not to perform any military duty again in North America during the war.[67] There was no restriction on continued active service by these troops in any other part of the world. His Majesty's government would not be violating the letter of the agreement if, for example, they ordered these troops to home stations and sent to America the garrisons thus relieved.[68] This had not been contemplated by Gates, of course, when he granted the terms of surrender, but there the loophole was, clear for even the clumsiest legal marksman. Washington did not dispute for a moment the validity of the argument the British might apply. The substitution of British troops could be made: his fear was that it might be completed quickly. Fresh troops might arrive on American shores in time to participate in the campaign of 1778.

If strict construction of the terms made this possible, would equally rigid interpretation of some other part of the convention offset the advantage? One phrase only could be found that might serve this end—the words "port of Boston" as the point of embarkation for the

[65] 9 JCC., 907 ff, 923 ff. The story of the drafting is well told in Merrill Jensen, Articles of Confederation. Antagonisms and clashes of interest are explained in Charles A. Beard, Economic Interpretation of the Constitution, and in Robert L. Brunhouse, Counter-revolution in Pennsylvania.

[66] 5 JCC., 546.

[67] The precise language of Article II was: "A free passage to be granted the Army under Lieutenant General Burgoyne to Great Britain, on condition of not serving again in North America, during the present contest; and the port of Boston is assigned for the entry of transports to receive the troops, whenever General Howe shall so order" (Dodsley's Annual Register for 1777, p. 301).

[68] It was recognized in America that the treaties for German mercenaries forbade the employment of those soldiers in Great Britain.

troops. Boston was no easy haven to reach when the winter began to bite from beyond Cape Anne. Weeks would be required to assemble British transports there for Burgoyne's men; en route to that Massachusetts port, vessels might be delayed and might be blown off their course or destroyed, even. Later in the season, as Washington knew from his observations in the winter of 1775–76, ice might close the harbor or render navigation so hazardous that Burgoyne's men might not be able to leave until it would be too late for garrison troops from England and Ireland to reach America and to share in the operations of 1778. The American commanders, therefore, must insist upon literal compliance with this part of the convention, must refuse to let the British embark from any port more accessible than Boston, and must decline to facilitate in any way the victualing of the transports. When Washington decided this was the course to take, he cautioned Heath,[69] and he advised Congress against any moderation of terms—counsel that accorded with conclusions the Delegates already had reached and now applied.[70] Small courtesies could be shown Burgoyne and his officers. They might, indeed, be allowed to leave America ahead of the troops and from some other port than Boston. The British Regiments captured at Saratoga must—absolutely must—be held in Boston till winter was past.[71]

Washington had been confident that Congress was of one mind with him on this, but on some disquieting questions of his own command, he no longer was altogether sure he would receive sympathetic support. Opposition to him was being fomented by a few critics who alleged that events around Philadelphia in late November and early December rendered still more humiliating the contrast to Gates's clean-cut, decisive performance in upper New York. Washington did not know, as yet, how far these men would go in opposition to him, and personally he did not care greatly, but in an official way, the outlook was discouraging, humiliating, disheartening even.

Conway had made immediate reply to the blunt note of November 9 in which Washington had enclosed him the text of the Frenchman's observation in his letter to Gates that Heaven "has been determined to save your country; or a weak General and bad Councellors would have ruined it." [72] The Frenchman began by explaining that on the 9th or 10th of October, through the courtesy of Gates's aide, Lt. Col. Robert

[69] 10 G. W., 57.   [70] Ibid., 110–111; 9 JCC., 982.
[71] Cf. 10 G. W., 154, 157–58, 165, 177; 10 JCC., 1032.
[72] Supra, p. 550.

Troup, he had sent his written congratulations to the General on the success of the campaign, and had thanked the victor for the "anxiety he shewed to my brother in law." [73] Conway went on: "I gave [General Gates] an account of the operations of this Army. I spoke my mind freely and found fault with several measures pursued in this Army; but I will venture to say that in my whole letter the paragraph of which you are pleased to send me a copy cannot be found. My opinion of you, sir, without flattery or envy is as follows: You are a brave man, an honest man, a patriot and a man of good sense. Your modesty is such that although your advice is commonly sound and proper you have often been influenced by men who were not equal to you in point of experience, knowledge or judgment."

Then Conway began a new paragraph and came to the point: "These are my sentiments; I have expressed them in private conversation with some general officers, and in particular to General Mifflin at Reading, before Dr. Craik.[74] Think they will be found such in my letter to General Gates. I believe I can assert that the expression *Weak General* has not slipped from my pen; however, if it has, this Weakness by my very letter cannot be explained otherwise even by the most malicious people than an excess of modesty on your side and a confidence in men who are much inferior to you in point of judgment and knowledge. I defy the most keen and penetrating detractor to make it appear that I leveled at your bravery, honesty, patriotism or judgment, of which I have the highest sense."

This much asserted, Conway wrote of the manner in which general officers of all armies were encouraged to correspond because from this "something useful might arise." He proceeded: "Although this inquisition in letters from particular to particular will be a proceeding of this country of which there are few instances in despotic and tyrannical governments, still, in order that the least suspicion should not remain in your Excellency's mind about my way of thinking, I am willing that my original letter to General Gates should be handed to you. This, I trust, will convince you of my way of thinking. I know, sir, that several unfavorable hints have been reported by some of your aide de camps as the author of some discourse which I never uttered. These advices never gave me the least uneasiness because I was conscious I never said

[73] The brother-in-law apparently was in Burgoyne's Army.
[74] He spelled the name Craig, but evidently meant Washington's old friend, Dr. James Craik.

anything but what I could mention to yourself. I have an account to give of my conduct in France, where I am the only Colonel continent [75] in actual service. I mean to write an account of the operations which I saw during this campaign. This account will be such that I am sure you will acknowledge to be true and I pledge my word of a gentleman and of an officer that I will write nothing in that account but what I will impart to you before I leave this continent." [76]

This letter could be regarded, of course, either as candid or as cunning. At headquarters, Washington's opinion probably was echoed some weeks later by John Laurens, a most intelligent aide, who said of the Frenchman, "the perplexity of his style, the evident insincerity of his compliments, betray his real sentiments and expose his guilt." [77] Washington did not think Conway's explanation called for a reply and he probably felt some satisfaction when he learned that in a long letter of November 14 to the President of Congress, the French officer had submitted his resignation. Conway complained of the criticism he had received for asking promotion, but he made the election of Johann Kalb as Major General the reason for his own action. "If I patiently bore such wrongs," he said, "it might be concluded in France that I misbehaved and, indeed, the Congress, instead of looking on me as an officer who enjoyed some esteem and reputation in the French infantry, must take me for a vagabond who fled here to get bread." [78] This paper was followed by a written request to Washington from Conway for a leave of absence in which to collect his scattered effects. In making this application, Conway said nothing of the affront he alleged

[75] "Continent" is added above the line. He evidently intended to distinguish rank on the continent of Europe from French colonial rank.

[76] 60 *Papers of G. W.*, 7, LC. The letter is misdated November 5, but must have been written about November 9 or 10. As here printed, its punctuation has been revised to make Conway's meaning clear. Capitalization has been standardized. Sentences or clauses subject to two interpretations are verbatim.

[77] John Laurens to his father, Jan. 3, 1778; *op. cit.*, 101.

[78] 159 *Papers Cont. Congress*, 461, LC. In a letter of Nov. 15, 1777 (2 Dreer Coll., *Letters of Rev. Gens.*, 72, PHS), Conway returned his commission. His resignation was not laid before Congress until Nov. 24, 1777. See 9 *JCC.*, 958. Washington was unaware Conway had written Gates on the 9th of November that he had sent his resignation to Congress that day. "I could no longer Brook the contemptible manner," Conway said, "in Which I yesterday learn that some members have spoke concerning me the French gentlemen wondered how I remained so long I did it out of a principle honour which made me Determine to finish the Campaign I now look upon the campaign as being at an end at least it appears to me that nothing can be undertaken with any reasonable prospect of success." He added: "I shall Wait upon you before I leave the continent General Stephens trial which was not over yet will Delay me a few days I hope no longer than three or four Whatever Dissatisfactions I might have I will ever cherish the cause in Which General Mifflin is engaged and shall be happy to serve it as far as I can with propriety" (*Gates Papers*, NYHS; verbatim). The nature of the "cause" engaging Gen. Thomas Mifflin is discussed p. 529, n. 48, and p. 607, n. 105.

he had received through the election of Kalb as a Major General. His only statement was: ". . . I am in actual service in France . . . a longer stay in this country will endanger my hopes of promotion in France, Congress is not a stranger to my generous way of acting with Mr. Deane and I am pretty sure will have no objection to my departure."

The request was granted through Colonel Harrison the same evening it was received.[79] Washington himself signed a letter in which he explained that acceptance of the resignation of Conway was the prerogative of Congress. If Delegates agreed, said the Commander-in-Chief, "I shall not object to your departure, since it is your inclination." Then Washington added: "I thank you very much for your wishes for the liberty of America, and the success of our arms, and have only to add that in case you are permitted to return by Congress, you will have my hopes for a favorable passage and a happy meeting with your family and friends."[80]

Washington soon found that he was not to be rid of Conway by a polite farewell on the smooth road of retirement. When the Frenchman's resignation was presented to Congress, there was no motion to accept it, but, instead, an order to refer it to the Board of War,[81] on which, at this stage of the reorganization,[82] the most powerful member, the best informed and the most persuasive, was Thomas Mifflin. He had consented on November 18[83] to serve and was entering on the discharge of his duties. Timothy Pickering, too, had agreed to become a member,[84] though as yet he could not leave headquarters in the absence of anyone who was qualified to be the Adjutant General. As

[79] Conway to Washington, Nov. 16, 1777, with appended draft of Harrison's reply of the same date. 61 *Papers of G. W.*, 5, LC.

[80] Letter of Nov. 16, 1777, 10 *G. W.*, 71–72. The draft, in the *Papers of G. W.*, LC, is in the handwriting of Tench Tilghman.

[81] Nov. 24, 1774, 9 *JCC.*, 958.

[82] Careless use of the term "Board of War" is apt to confuse the student. As first designed, the "new" Board was to consist of three persons not members of Congress (See *supra*, p. 549) but this Board was so slow in organizing that Congress on the 21st of November authorized two members of the former congressional Board of War to sit with the member or members of the elected Board who then were in York (9 *JCC.*, 946). Before this could be made effective, Congress changed its mind and decided that the "old" Board would act on its own account until the "new" Board was prepared to begin its labors (*ibid.*, 953). Two days later the decision was to increase the "new" Board by two members (*loc. cit.*; see also 2 *Burnett*, 572–74). On the 24th of November, the Board of non-members having still been unable to organize, Congress amended its previous resolve and authorized the "old" Board to act "until such time as a quorum of the commissioners of the War Office shall attend" (9 *JCC.*, 960).

[83] *Ibid.*, 936.

[84] *Ibid.*, 955; proceedings of November 21.

Colonel Harrison had declined,[85] Congress filled out the membership of five by electing Gates, Joseph Trumbull, and Richard Peters, who had been Secretary of the "old" Board.[86] Delegates voted that Gates should be President,[87] should retain his military rank, and should "officiate at the Board, or in the field, as occasion may require." [88] With this personnel, Congress felt that it would assemble a most unique combination of experience. Gates and Pickering were former Adjutants General, one of them a highly successful field commander; Mifflin and Trumbull were the two men most familiar with quartermaster and commissary service; Peters had complete knowledge of the records and methods of the "old" Board. From the viewpoint of the Delegates, the one flaw immediately apparent in the new organization was that Mifflin and Peters were the only members at hand to share in work that should be undertaken forthwith.

Washington, for his part, was not sure Gates would accept,[89] but he probably was aware by this time that Mifflin, though cautious and adroit in approach, was regarded already as head of the movement to make the largest use of the abilities of Gates.[90] That was the best face to put on the activities of Mifflin, who two years previously had been among the most useful and active of Washington's supporters and had so continued until, in the early summer of 1777, he had been alienated by the refusal of the Commander-in-Chief to disregard the possibility of a British attack based on New York. Mifflin had wanted all the American forces employed to save Philadelphia.[91] Increasingly now his name was being associated with those of men who sometimes spoke mysteriously of their unwillingness to pay homage to "the image." [92]

So far as Conway and his resignation were entangled in these matters of personality, the Board of War did not report to Congress one way or the other on his resignation, but some leaders in York began to sup-

---

[85] *Ibid.*
[86] Mifflin to Joseph Trumbull, Nov. 30, 1777; *Joseph Trumbull Papers,* CHS. Peters was named at the instance of Mifflin (9 *JCC.,* 959).
[87] *Ibid.,* 971; 2 *Burnett,* 571, 573–75. Cf. Gates to Henry Laurens, Dec. 11, 1777, and Gates to Col. John Greaton, Dec. 28, 1777; *Gates Papers,* NYHS.
[88] 9 *JCC.,* 972.   [89] 10 *G. W.,* 136.
[90] This statement, as of Nov. 16, 1777, cannot be verified by specific citation, but is plainly to be inferred from events that followed immediately.
[91] 2 *Greene's Greene,* 30, and *supra,* p. 437–38.
[92] Cf. letter of an anonymous writer at Reading, Nov. 17, 1777, to General Gates: "Repeated slights and unjustifiable arrogance combined with other causes to drive from the Army those who would not worship the image and pay undeserved tribute of praise and flattery to the great and powerful" (5 *Sparks,* 484).

port a proposal for which Conway took the credit, that Congress name an Inspector General who would instruct the troops, apprehend deserters, and see that public property had careful custody. When the Board of War asked the opinion of the Commander-in-Chief on what such an inspector might do to prevent the theft of public arms by departing militia, Washington already had received from Colonel d'Arendt a plan for a system of inspection [93] and he confined his answer to the specific question concerning arms. Deserters, he said, were responsible for most of the stealing; unless "an Inspector General could prevent desertion, he would do nothing." [94] Congress did not wait on Washington's views, this expression of which was delayed until December 14 by his preoccupation with field duties.[95] On the 13th, the Delegates adopted a long resolve on the establishment of a system of inspection. Conway forthwith was elected Inspector General and was made a Major General.[96]

Doubtless some members of Congress would have defended this as action necessary for the improvement of the Army, and they would have justified their disregard of Washington's warning concerning the effect that the advancement of Conway might have on Brigadiers whose commissions antedated his by many months. Delegates would have pointed out that Conway's promotion was "on the staff," not "in the line." He would have no command over American general officers who had been at the head of Brigades before he even came to the United States.

Washington might have put a different interpretation on the resolves, might, indeed, have regarded them as a carefully planned affront. Had such an incident occurred while he had been a Virginia Colonel in the French and Indian War, he would have resigned wrathfully and at once. Now it was different. When liberty was at stake, pride and personalities dwindled in perspective. He would see to it that official dealings with Conway were in every way correct,[97] though personally he would not pretend to like a man he distrusted. Moreover, if Congress wished to administer army affairs and to decide questions that previously had come to his desk, he would tell correspondents to communi-

---

[93] See *infra,* p. 592.

[94] Doubtless Washington meant that an Inspector General could "do nothing" in this particular, but, as used, the language was subject to a different interpretation (10 *G. W.,* 154).

[95] *Ibid.*   [96] 9 *JCC.,* 1023–26.

[97] John Laurens to his father, Jan. 3, 1778, *John Laurens,* 101.

cate directly with that body.[98] Was there dissatisfaction with him as Commander-in-Chief? Did Congress think Gates a superior General? Washington would make no defence of what he felt had been the best he could do; if another were preferred in command, let the gentleman have the sash, the epaulettes, and the daily, devouring duties! All that Washington desired, then or thereafter, was to perform the task to which he had set his hand, until he was relieved of it—not at the instance of a rival or through the shabby maneuvers of a cabal but by the deliberate voice of the people he had undertaken to serve, in a cause that commanded both his heart and his mind.

Doubts and resentments in Congress, strangely enough, now created for Washington an opportunity of showing members some depressing realities it had not been prudent to set down even in a letter read behind closed doors. Already a committee of Delegates had been named to consider means for conducting a winter campaign.[99] On the day of Conway's promotion, Congress had voted to scrutinize the "causes of the evacuation of Fort Mercer" and had followed that with orders for like investigation of the loss of Fort Montgomery and Fort Clinton. The failure of the Rhode Island expedition also was to be investigated. This, in turn, had been fortified with bristling assurance that whenever an operation failed or a post fell to the enemy, Congress would seek to establish the reason by inquiry conducted "in such manner as [it] shall deem best adapted for the investigation of truth in the respective cases." [100]

To what extent all this was intended to be critical of him, and in what degree it merely reflected the anxiety of honest men, Washington did not know, but he did know, experientially, how readily the Delegates responded if he unfolded to them the problems of the Army on the scene—in the smoke of campfires and to the sound of drumbeat. When the new committee came to White Marsh, Washington told the members how nearly naked and how ill-shod his troops were. As was his practice, he had collected in advance, for his own guidance, the written opinions of his senior officers, and when the committee inquired if a large body of militia could not be called out to give him added strength for an attack on Philadelphia, he asked his Generals for their views, with full assurance of what their answers would be.

---

[98] See, as typical, his letter of Dec. 17, 1777, to Gen. William Heath; 10 *G. W.,* 165–67.
[99] Nov. 28, 1777; 9 *JCC.,* 972.   [100] 9 *JCC.,* 976.

The commanders pointed out, of course, that the season was too far advanced to summon militia from distant States and that, even if the men reached the camp, it was doubtful "whether they could be furnished with provisions and forage, and brought to act in concert with the regular Army."

Committeemen questioned and consulted and, before returning to York, they drafted a report, the substance of which they sent Washington on December 10.[101] Six days later they informed Congress that, in their opinion, a winter offensive was "ineligible." [102] The Army should take up winterquarters where it would "be most likely to overawe the enemy," to protect the country, and to find provisions and shelter. In like understanding of unhappy realities and long disregarded needs, the committee endorsed Washington's proposals for improving the corps of officers and for assuring the continued service of leaders qualified to "introduce that order and discipline amongst the troops so essential to the military character." [103]

Congress was not content to accept the committee's findings without the papers on which the report was based. By resolves of December 19, the Delegates called for these documents, which were forthcoming immediately.[104] The facts presented there might not satisfy the element critical of Washington but they were a final answer to those who looked at the actual condition of the continental Army vis-a-vis Howe's. Congress did not have to rely on Washington's interpretation only. The testimony of all the senior officers was the same: strategical mistakes and tactical blunders had been made through ignorance, poor judgment or lack of experience, but none of these probably meant as much as the fundamental inferiority of the Army in almost every material thing fighting men required. At bottom, the issue was not that of supplanting Washington but that of supplying him, where he and his officers decided they would post the Army.

Warm argument and sharp division arose over the selection of these winterquarters, because the extent of the area open to British depreda-

---

101 2 *Burnett*, 585.   102 9 *JCC.*, 1029–31.

103 Committee's letter of Dec. 10, 1777, to Washington; 2 *Burnett*, 585. As the proposals of the committee are similar to some of those Washington submitted to the next Committee of Congress, Jan. 29, 1778, 10 *G. W.*, 362 ff, they are epitomized *infra*, p. 583. Sullivan's letters to Washington, Dec. 1, 4, 26, 1777, 1 *Sullivan Papers*, 593, 597 ff, 602, appear to be the only complete set, in print, of the answers made by the general officers to the questions the Commander-in-Chief addressed them but MS replies by nearly all the others are in the *Papers of G. W.*, LC.

104 9 *JCC.*, 1035.

tion might depend on the distance of the American camp from Phil-adelphia.[105] If Washington's Divisions were placed close to the city, they would be exposed to surprise, which would be an excessive price to pay for reducing by a few square miles the district exposed to British pillaging. Conversely, if the Army were remote, it would not be able to deal with parties that might improve British rations and the health of the troops by stripping bare a wide and prosperous countryside. A related subject of discussion was whether the forces should or could requisition quarters in nearby towns and villages, which already were overcrowded with refugees from Philadelphia. On both these subjects the Council and Assembly of Pennsylvania sent Congress a vigorous remonstrance, in which they pointed out nervously the danger of expos-ing to the enemy lower Jersey and that part of Pennsylvania East of the Schuylkill. The Pennsylvanians maintained, also, that many fami-lies had fled from Philadelphia and had so crowded nearby towns that soldiers could not be quartered there. Before this paper reached Con-gress or came to Washington's hand, the choice of a campsite had been made [106]—a wooded region on the south side of the Schuylkill,[107] eighteen miles Northwest of the occupied city, at a place called the Valley Forge.

[105] 10 G. W., 133 and n; John Laurens, 91.

[106] The course of the river, on this particular reach, is from West to East, but, in general, contemporary references were to positions as East and West of the stream.

[107] The remonstrance, undated, is in 6 Penn. Arc. (1), p. 104. What appears to be a preliminary draft is in 5 ibid., 307. In its final form, this was laid before Congress Dec. 17, 1777 and on the 18th and 19th was considered. The resulting resolution was that the remon-strance be forwarded to Washington, with the request that he inform Congress whether he had decided to canton the Army and, if so, where he intended to place the troops. Protection of the exposed areas was enjoined on him (9 JCC., 1033, 1034, 1036. Cf. 2 Burnett, 591 and n, 592, 595). Washington by that date had moved the Army to Valley Forge whence, on the afternoon of December 22, he acknowledged receipt of the paper adopted on the 19th (10 G. W., 186). His reference of the 23rd to drawing "remonstrances in a comfortable room by a good fire" is quoted infra, p. 568 from 10 G. W., 196. Nothing in the remonstrance justifies the statement often made that Pennsylvania threatened to withdraw her forces from the Army and her support from the American cause unless the eastern part of the State was protected by the continental Army.

CHAPTER XXII

THE ARMY FACES THREE MORTAL FOES

(Early Winter of 1777–78)

THE AREA into which the Army was to move a week before Christmas, 1777,[1] formed a crude right-angle triangle that covered the Fatland Ford, about four and a half miles North and slightly East of the scene of the "Paoli Massacre." Valley Creek, rising North of Paoli and twisting often, flowed generally with the meridian, and fell into the Schuylkill. The eastward course of the river made it the longer side of the right angle formed with the North-and-South creek. A rambling succession of hills, running Northeast from Valley Creek to the Schuylkill, formed the hypotenuse of the triangle. Both the watercourses were scarped by bluffs for the greater part of their sweep around the camp. A few redoubts and a line of entrenchments would consolidate the hills and high ground into a strong defensive position. Thick woods would offer fuel and logs for the construction of quarters. The streams would supply water conveniently and in abundance. Iron works of considerable output had been located on part of the site,[2] a saw mill had operated on the creek, and a part of the Army's reserve flour, shot and iron utensils had been kept in the vicinity for some months prior to the third week in September, when the British, in maneuvering along the river bank, had destroyed almost everything.[3]

[1] The Army began its movement from White Marsh Dec. 11, 1777 (10 *G. W.*, 148), but it had a chance meeting with a British column that was foraging in the country on the right bank of the Schuylkill near Matson's Ford at "the Gulph," now West Conshohocken, Penn. This delayed the advance on the 11th and forced the troops who had crossed the river to return temporarily to the left bank (*ibid.*, 156; *John Laurens*, 93, 95 ff). If any student is interested in these operations, which do not seem of sufficient importance to be treated here, the background circumstances will be found in John Armstrong to Thomas Wharton, Dec. 7, 1777; (*Reed Papers*, NYHS). Details are given in Reed to unnamed correspondent, December 10, and to Thomas Wharton, Dec. 13, 1777 (*ibid*), in Kalb to Comte de Broglie, Dec. 12, 1777 (*Kapp's Kalb*, 133–34), and in Major Baurmeister to General von Jungkenn, Dec. 16, 1777 (60 *Penn. Mag.*, 41–45). When the Army moved to the right bank on the 13th, it had to wait at the Gulph until the 19th and then it proceeded to Valley Forge (John Laurens, *loc. cit.*).

[2] For the early history of the forge, the ownership of that property and the conveyance of other nearby real estate and buildings, see Howard M. Jenkins, "The Old Iron Forge—'Valley Forge'" in 17 *Penn. Mag.*, 430 ff. This was the maneuver to cover the advance on Philadelphia.

[3] *Anon. Proc. Howe*, 82. Montresor noted, Sept. 18, 1777, that the British found at Valley Forge 3800 barrels of flour, twenty-five barrels of horseshoes, several thousand tomahawks, kettles, etc. (*Journal*, 454–55).

A few scattered dwellings and farm buildings were the sole man-made facilities of which the Army could avail itself. Everything else had to be provided after the troops arrived.

Some of the officers, Johann Kalb in particular, regarded this choice of a campsite as hopelessly bad. Valley Forge must have been selected, Kalb wrote his patron, at the instance of a speculator, or on the advice of a traitor, or by a council of ignoramuses.[4] Washington and the majority of his subordinates saw the defects, but they knew that the camp area could be held against any other foe than one so powerful he could command all the roads leading to the triangle, and could starve the Army into submission. Carefully, in General Orders of the 17th of December, Washington explained why he intended to establish the Army at Valley Forge, and why, as he put it, the General "persuades himself that the officers and soldiers, with one heart, and one mind, will resolve to surmount every difficulty with a fortitude and a patience, becoming their profession, and the sacred cause in which we are engaged." Then the assurance was added that Washington would "share in the hardship and partake of every inconvenience."[5]

The preliminaries of the march to winterquarters scarcely accorded with Washington's high words. "This is Thanksgiving Day . . . ," Lt. Col. Henry Dearborn wrote in his Diary on the 18th of December, six miles from the new camp. Then he reflected: "but God knows we have very little to keep it with, this being the third day we have been without flour or bread, and are living on a high, uncultivated hill, in huts and tents, lying on the cold ground. Upon the whole I think all we have to be thankful for is that we are alive and not in the grave with many of our friends."[6] Sergeant Ebenezer Wild grumbled as he remembered his "poor thanksgiving—nothing but fresh beef and flour to eat, without any salt, and but very scant of that."[7] It was, in a word, with doubtful mind and empty or protesting stomachs that officers and men marched into a district as naked as themselves. If the attractive name, Valley Forge, made any student-soldier anticipate such a place

[4] *Kapp's Kalb*, 137.

[5] 10 *G. W.*, 168, verbatim. On the larger question of strategic location of the camp, see John Cadwalader to unnamed correspondent [Joseph Reed?], Nov. 30, 1777 (*Reed Papers*, NYHS). General Sullivan's recommendation of cantonment at Germantown and his arguments against other positions for the winter will be found in 1 *Sullivan Papers*, 593, 597 ff.

[6] Journal of Henry Dearborn, *MHSP*, 1886–87, p. 112. Some revision of orthography and punctuation has seemed desirable. In the later and larger Brown-Peckham edition (1939) of the *Revolutionary War Journals of Henry Dearborn*, this entry is p. 118.

[7] Journal of Ebenezer Wild, *MHSP*, 1890–91, p. 105.

of pleasantness as Nol Goldsmith, recently dead, had described in his lines about "Sweet Auburn, loveliest village of the plain," the new-comer must have been staggered. There was no village, no plain, and little valley. Most of the precinct where the engineers were staking out the quarters was windy and forbidding hillside.[8] On that bleak and comfortless soil, the troops were told, they must camp in their tattered tents until axemen went into the woods, felled trees and brought in logs that must be raised and roofed and made into cabins which the soldiers themselves were to fit with hearths and chimneys.

This was something the Army never had undertaken on such a scale before, but it was work that made a certain appeal to young men who were not many years beyond the age at which, in play, they had built themselves tiny houses. Erection of the new "city" doubtless would have been taken in hand briskly as soon as the engineers gave the word[9] if all the troops had received their usual rations after arrival. As it was, the shortage of provisions continued and rapidly became worse. Some Brigades had a small amount of salt pork issued them on the 21st[10] from a commissary that was in the last stages of collapse. Then provisions gave out entirely. Many soldiers got nothing and, in the violence of their mounting misery, made loud complaint. Soon Washington had news of open mutiny in the Army. It did not take the form of violence. A sombre chant was repeated endlessly in the tents of one Regiment after another, till the long hillsides rang with the wail, "No meat, no meat." Along with this came the simulated hoot of the angry owl and the "caw, caw" of the quarrelsome crow.[11] Although officers were able promptly to put an end to this defiance of discipline, they warned headquarters they might have more trouble unless the men were fed.

[8] The only contemporary map of trustworthy precision is that of Duportail reproduced on p. 567. Most of the later "maps" in guidebooks and travel works represent more of surmise than of survey. Lossing's familiar sketch (op. cit., v. 1, p. 334), is not accurate in detail. Students who wish to take the contours into account may consult the Norristown Quadrangle of the United States Geological Survey.

[9] Cf. Journal of Ebenezer Wild, Dec. 24, 1777; MHSP, 1890–91, p. 106. Col. Henry B. Livingston stressed a shortage often disregarded in narratives of events at Valley Forge: ". . . we . . . are now building huts for our winterquarters without nails or tools so that I suppose we may possibly render ourselves very comfortable by the time winter is over" (Letter of Dec. 24, 1777, to R. R. Livingston; R. R. Livingston Papers, NYPL). This lack of nails and of tools may have been one of the reasons some of the huts were half-underground, damp and unhealthy (13 G. W., 395).   [10] Ibid.

[11] Although this part of the incident was not recorded by Washington, nor was mutiny mentioned by Doctor Waldo, to whom posterity owes the preservation of this story (see his Diary in 21 Penn. Mag., 308), there can be little doubt the two men were writing of the same occurrence. Doctor Waldo specifically dated it "before Christmas."

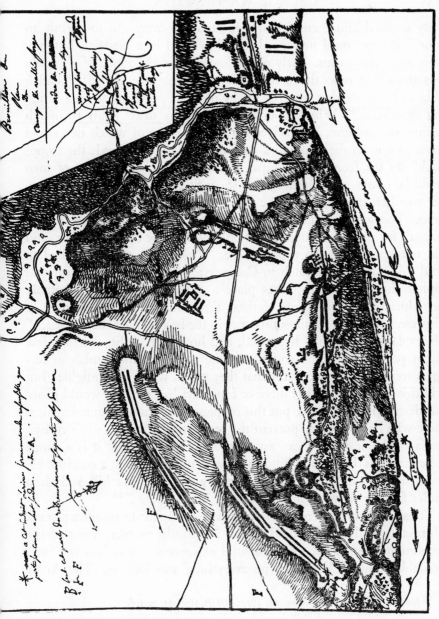

Duportail's Map of the Valley Forge Defences

So far as is known, the Chief Engineer of the Army, Brig. Gen. Louis Le Bèque Duportail never completed this sketch of the camp and he entered his notes upside down, but he left a clear idea of where he thought the defences should be located. The original belongs to the Historical Society of Pennsylvania.

567

By strained effort, enough was brought up overnight to permit an issue,[12] but not until new need had developed in a situation immediately more dangerous. Early on the morning of the 22nd, Washington was aroused by news that a British force of some size had left Philadelphia and was moving towards Derby on what appeared to be a foraging expedition.[13] When he ordered the Army made ready to march against this column, he received a report the like of which never had come to him in the two and a half years of his command: the troops could not stir from their camps. Even if a sufficient number of men could be found with clothing and shoes fit for outdoor use in December weather, they could not be provisioned for even brief field operations. The sole commissary officer in camp reported that he had no animals for slaughter, could count only twenty-five barrels of flour, and did not knew when to expect more. Washington was compelled to send this alarming dispatch to Congress: ". . . unless some great and capital change suddenly takes place . . . this Army must inevitably be reduced to one or other of these three things. Starve, dissolve or disperse, in order to obtain subsistence in the best manner they can . . ." He explained what had happened, and how he had dispatched a few "light parties" to watch and harass the enemy, while American foragers were sent out to collect what they could, where they might: "But will this answer? No, sir: three or four days bad weather would prove our destruction." [14] As he put this on paper his wrath mounted against those who had sought to prevent the occupation of quarters in Pennsylvania towns nearby: "I can assure those gentlemen that it is a much easier and less distressing thing to draw remonstrances in a comfortable room by a good fireside than to occupy a cold, bleak hill and sleep under frost or snow without clothes or blankets . . ." [15]

Those last words were not written as a metaphor to round a phrase. Murderous reality lay behind them. Previously, at every twist of the revolutionary struggle, some essential of successful war had not been available; now at Valley Forge everything was lacking. The Army

[12] Journal of Ebenezer Wild, Dec. 22, 1777; *MHSP*, 1890–91, p. 106.

[13] 10 *G. W.*, 184 and 183–84 n.

[14] Letter of Dec. 23, 1777, 10 *G. W.*, 193, verbatim. See *ibid.*, 205, for Washington's order to farmers to thresh at least half their wheat by Feb. 1, 1778. In *ibid.*, 217, is his plea for the accumulation of thirty days' supply of provisions, or more, as a safeguard against delayed deliveries when bad weather blocked roads. See also *John Laurens*, 97.

[15] 10 *G. W.*, 196. See *ibid.*, 225–26, 233, on the suffering of military prisoners and of men in the hospitals.

might freeze before it starved; and if it found shelter and food, the shortage of clothing and footgear would keep it from taking the field. These were heartbreaking conditions that optimism could not soften or patience endure and they were not conditions due to bad choice of a campsite. Like hardship would have been encountered, except perhaps as to quarters, almost anywhere the Army might have encamped. The fault was not with the place but with equipment and supplies. In a knowledge that troop movement in winter depended on clothing, shoes and blankets as surely as on food,[16] Congress had relied on the delivery of uniforms ordered in France[17] but meantime had adopted new regulations[18] and had looked to the States to replace what was worn out.

Little actually had been accomplished either by Congress or by most of the States until the approach of cold weather spurred efforts to collect garments from those who gave willingly, and to impress from those who hoarded.[19] Even then, the yield had been small in terms of need that foreshadowed ruin.[20] Congress and the Commander-in-Chief had been compelled to say in plain words to the Governors that the Clothier General could not meet the requirements of shivering thousands; but the States that responded at all to this renewed appeal[21] followed different methods and had varying success in finding warm garments for their continental Regiments.[22] So dark was the outlook that Washington already had warned the Governor of Virginia: "Our importations from abroad are so uncertain from the number of the enemy's cruisers that infest our coasts that we can scarcely count upon any supplies through that channel, and the stock of goods that were upon hand are so nearly consumed that I look with the greatest concern upon the sufferings of the soldiers for the remainder of this year; and as for the next I view them as naked, except some measures can be fallen upon

---

[16] 10 G. W., 14–15.   [17] 9 JCC., 905.

[18] 8 JCC., 690; cf. ibid., 716–18. See ibid., 699, for increase in the monetary allowance for deputy clothiers, and ibid., 761, for secrecy concerning all that related to supplies and clothing.

[19] 9 G. W., 374–75, 487; 10 ibid., 125; 9 JCC., 809, 905, 906.

[20] See 10 G. W., 14–15, 20–21, for the dispatch of officers to collect clothing in Maryland and Delaware. In ibid., 45, and in 9 JCC., 1043, 1071–73, are echoes of blasts against dealers who would not sell and against contractors who would not deliver.

[21] 9 G. W., 487; 9 JCC., 809.

[22] For Massachusetts, see 9 JCC., 893; Virginia, 10 G. W., 55, 172–73; 1 Ballagh, Lee Letters, 362–63; 2 LTW., 52–53; New Jersey, 10 G. W., 102; Pennsylvania, 9 JCC., 1011–12; 10 G. W., 195–96; Connecticut, ibid., 161. Needless to say, State archives and published records include much material, not directly relating to Washington and his Army, on this subject of clothing.

to collect from the inhabitants of the different States part of their stock of clothing, which I fear is but scanty." [23]

This had been as close to despair as Washington ever had come, and it had been followed by a pessimistic committee report to Congress on what might be expected from importation.[24] New inquiry into the competence of the Clothier General's management,[25] a summons of that harassed individual to headquarters, the assurance that officers would join him in trying to find new supplies,[26] the dispatch of still other representatives to Boston [27]—these were four only of the numerous desperate moves of December. John Sullivan probably was speaking from sympathetic observation when he told his chief: "The situation of your Army will be scarcely tolerable if placed in the warmest houses during the winter. The whole of them without watch coats, one half without blankets, and more than one third without shoes, stockings or breeches, and many of them without jackets. Indeed, there are some without coats and not a few without shirts. Even the officers in sundry instances are destitute of proper clothing, some of them being almost naked." [28] Sullivan in another letter disclosed the humiliating fact that "many officers who have behaved with credit have petitioned me for leave to retire for a season or to resign their commissions and assigned as a reason for not waiting on me that they were so naked they were ashamed to be seen." [29]

Reenlistment, like resignation, was involved when torn breeches could not be mended again, and threadbare coats were no better than rags held together by long association only. So low was the stock of clothing near the end of the year that after some of the veterans of the nine original Virginia Regiments offered to continue in service if the bounty was doubled and the promised clothing was allowed them, Congress had to tender money instead of garments.[30] From "Head

[23] Letter of Nov. 13, 1777, to Patrick Henry; 10 *G. W.*, 55.

[24] Nov. 26, 1777; 9 *JCC.*, 968–69.   [25] *Ibid.*, 966.

[26] 10 *G. W.*, 124.   [27] *Ibid.*, 229.

[28] Letter of Dec. 1, 1777; 1 *Sullivan Papers*, 595, somewhat drastically repunctuated. Washington himself noted that when clothing for officers was available at all, it usually was at a price beyond their reach (10 *G. W.*, 126).

[29] Letter of Dec. 4, 1777, to Washington; 1 *Sullivan Papers*, 598–99. Cf. Col. Henry B. Livingston to R. R. Livingston, Dec. 24, 1777: "All my men except eighteen are unfit for duty for want of shoes, stockings and shirts, breeches and coats. Hats they can do without, though it's disagreeable, and to add to this miserable tale, we are becoming exceedingly lousy; I am not myself exempted from this misfortune; the few shirts I had with me are quite worn out—what I shall do for a new stock I am at a loss to find out" (*R. R. Livingston Papers*, NYPL).

[30] Resolve of Dec. 20, 1777; 9 *JCC.*, 1038–39. The desperate state of army recruiting in the winter of 1777–78 is illustrated by Congress' willingness to have the bounty doubled when

Quarters, Valley Forge" on the last day of a dreadful year, Washington compassed the misery of thousands in a single exclamation: "Our sick naked, our well naked, our unfortunate men in captivity naked!" [31]

Thus, at the beginning of 1778, the Army was witnessing one of the strangest of races, a contest between the axes of the men building huts and the harsh wear-and-tear of the remaining garments of those who still had sufficient clothing to permit them to perform outdoor duty. "We are busy in forming a new city at this place," Anthony Wayne wrote from Valley Forge. "My people will be covered in a few days, I mean as to huts, but naked as to clothing—they are in that respect in a worse condition than Falstaff's recruits for they have not one whole shirt to a Brigade." [32] Either the huts had to be finished speedily for all the troops, or else nakedness would be fatal to the Army. That was the only word for it—nakedness. "The want of clothing," Washington said in mid-January, "added to the rigor of the season, has occasioned [the men] to suffer such hardships as will not be credited but by those who have been spectators." [33] Sickness increased with exposure. Although the hospital huts were built early and in what was believed to be sufficient number, they soon were overcrowded with miserable men who died fast or, if they survived, received little attention and had so few medicines that they were not cured of the itch, even.[34]

Would shelter be provided before the strongest soldiers went down as weaker individuals already had? An observer, no less a person than Thomas Paine, thought an affirmative answer would be given by the men. ". . . They appeared to me like a family of beavers; everyone busy, some carrying logs, others mud, and the rest fastening them together." [35] To encourage the troops, Congress authorized an extra month's pay [36] for zeal in building huts—a bounty that caused as much contention as content [37]—but progress was slow.[38] Washington made one

Virginia had agreed to pay the second twenty dollars, a proceeding that had been deplored, not to say denounced, early in the year when it had been adopted in New England.

[31] Letter of Dec. 31, 1777, to Gov. William Livingston; 10 *G. W.*, 233.

[32] Wayne to unnamed correspondent, Dec. 30, 1777; 4 *Wayne Papers*, 61, PHS.

[33] 10 *G. W.*, 301–02. Cf. an unsigned, unaddressed letter, dated at Valley Forge, Jan. 7, 1778: "Twenty-six in one York Regiment have been three weeks without a shirt; one-fourth of our men now barefoot without blankets or breeches, now lying uncovered in the field—and believe me this is real" (*Joseph Reed Papers*, NYHS).

[34] 10 *G. W.*, 297, 300, 405, 432, 499; *Kapp's Kalb*, 139. For the principles on which the hospitals were to be reorganized, see 11 *G. W.*, 125, 10 *JCC.*, 128–29.

[35] Letter of May 16, 1778, to Benjamin Franklin; 1 *Writings of Thomas Paine*, ed. Conway, 392.

[36] 9 *JCC.*, 1067–68; 10 *ibid.*, 8.   [37] 10 *G. W.*, 266, 286, 288, 462.

[38] *Ibid.*, 301. Standard inside dimensions—fourteen by sixteen feet, with side walls of six

DU PORTAIL, PREMIER OF ENGINEERS

No Army, no general officers, no staff—that was, strictly speaking, the order of adversity the American Colonies had to overcome in 1775. It was easier to enlist thousands of men than it was to find twenty competent general officers; and even when the Regiments had been organized and had been given at least the form of command, quartermasters and commissaries and ordnance officers were merchants or ironmongers whose zeal was no substitute for training. Engineer was the dignified name given a surveyor who might or might not have an eye for ground that could readily be fortified. Congress and the Commander-in-Chief made the best of such talents as Richard Gridley and Rufus Putnam and a few others possessed, but amateurs and beginners usually laid out much larger works than could be finished, or, if completed, successfully defended. The need of professional military engineers became more and more pressing until du Portail, la Radière and de Gouvion reached Philadelphia in July, 1777 and went to work. The three were officers of engineers in the French army and were employed by Benjamin Franklin and Silas Deane at the instance of Congress. Louis le Bèque de Presle du Portail, then 34 years of age, was the senior of these officers and had been given temporary rank as Lieutenant Colonel before he left France. In the United States he was commissioned Colonel, then Brigadier General and, subsequent to the events described in this volume, Major General. His steady promotion reflected the admiration the continentals had for him. Washington's patience was worn thin in 1777 by the importunity of foreign officers who were no more than greedy adventurers of doubtful competence, but always he would have excepted from his condemnation Lafayette, Steuben and "the engineers." At the outset du Portail aroused many jealousies and had a clash with du Coudray that might have made trouble for Washington if the imperious and impatient du Coudray had not lost his life in September, 1777. After that, du Portail had no rival among the engineers. All the Generals and Colonels who took the pains to observe his work realized that he possessed the soldier's needful combination of brains, energy, devotion and professional knowledge.

(After the original by C. W. Peale, Independence Hall, Philadelphia.)

Head Quarters Valley forge Feb:
1778.

Sir,

       I was duly favoured with your
Letter of the 23d. of last Month; to which I sh.
have replied sooner, had I not been delayed
by business that required my more immediate attention.

       It is my wish to give implicit
credit to the assurances of every Gentleman,
but in the subject of our present correspondence
I am sorry to confess, there happen to be some
unlucky circumstances, which involuntarily
compel me to consider the discovery you mention
not so satisfactory & conclusive as you seem
to think it. —

       I am so unhappy as to find
no small difficulty in reconciling the spirit
and import of your different Letters, and
sometimes of the different parts of the same
Letter with each other. — It is not unreasonable to presume, that your first information
of my having notice of General Conway's
Letter came from himself; there were so
few in the secret, and it is natural to suppose
that he being immediately concerned, would

he

THE LETTER THAT WRECKED THE CABAL

The great surprise of the "Conway Cabal" to discredit Washington as a military commander was not that it occurred and not that it collapsed so quickly but that it showed Washington to be what nobody appears to have thought he was—a most vigorous controversialist.

This was not a part he played with zest in the drama of the Revolution. Amiability, not contention, was his most marked social quality. He always undertook to prevent division among those whose full, united effort was required if America was to be an independent nation. If differences did develop, he sought to keep them within the Army and to adjust them in friendly spirit. Besides, he knew too well the exactions of his post to covet a continuance of power. The greatest ambition of his heart was to win the war and then to return to the peace of his own plantation. Whenever a responsible majority in Congress lost confidence in his leadership, or concluded that some other man could head the Army with more success, Washington joyfully would turn over to that officer the headquarters papers and would head his horse toward the Potomac.

So clear in his mind were these rules of conduct that he thought it scarcely worthwhile to explain them; but his obligations were altogether different when, in his judgment, unworthy men were sowing selfishly the tares of quick-growing dissension. To refute their slanders was, in a personal way, to maintain his self-respect and to preserve his integrity: the larger, imperative reason for facing and defeating them was to keep the Army and the country united in the hard battle for freedom. That was why Washington denounced the Irish-born Frenchman, Thomas Conway, Major General in the American service, as an "incendiary"; and it was because of General Horatio Gates's association with Conway that Washington addressed to the victor of Saratoga the letter of Feb. 9, 1778, the front page of which is reproduced on the facing page. The argument in this famous document was that of Washington, the draft perhaps was the brilliant work of Alexander Hamilton, the autograph is that of the Commander-in-Chief—and the result? Devastating!

of the first cabins his headquarters,[39] and he did his utmost to hasten the completion of the camp, to relieve the special distresses of military prisoners,[40] and to give decency to the quarters by having offal and dead horses buried or removed.[41] In spite of all exertion, it was about the middle of January when the last of the troops were under roof.[42] Even then they did not always have straw with which to take the chill from the earthen floor of their huts.[43] Thousands of them had no bed covering. The shortage of blankets, which had been serious for months, now had become so critical that when Virginia troops reached the end of their term of enlistment, Washington had to order the Quartermaster to take from these men the blankets, belonging to the Army, that would have made their bivouacs endurable on the long road home.[44]

Part of the blame for the cruel suffering from cold at Valley Forge rested on the shoulders of Quartermaster General Thomas Mifflin, who, it was said, had not maintained his office at headquarters from the time the Army had entered Pennsylvania.[45] Washington had himself tried to give a measure of supervision to the department Mifflin was charged with neglecting,[46] but the Commander-in-Chief had not been able to

---

feet, six inches—are given in *ibid.*, 171. The huts were built "in three lines, each line four deep, five yards asunder . . ." (*George Ewing's Journal*, 25). Probably the most accurate account of the construction of the camp is in the Diary of Dr. A. Waldo, 21 *Penn. Mag.*, 308 ff. See also letter of William Gifford in 59 *NJHSP.*, 53, and Nathanael Greene to his brother, Jan. 3, 1778, 1 *Greene's Greene*, 543.

[39] *John Laurens*, 93–94. As Martha explained in a letter of Mch. 7, 1778, to Mercy Warren (2 *Warren-Adams Letters*, 6) the General later added a "cabin . . . to dine in." After the entire Army was "hutted," he moved his headquarters to the home of Deborah Hewes, later known as the Isaac Potts house, for which see 1 *Lossing*, 332, 333–34; and Mabel L. Ives, *Washington's Headquarters*, 172. As Isaac Potts's name is associated with most of the stories that Washington often prayed on his knees in a thicket near this dwelling, it is proper to state that no contemporary evidence of any sort has ever been adduced in support of this tradition. The various contradictory versions of the story are printed and dissected in 3 *Hughes*, 270 ff.

[40] 10 *G. W.*, 307, 461.   [41] *Ibid.*, 273.

[42] A precise statement of the terminal date cannot be made, primarily because of the vagueness of the Diaries and the paucity of reports. George Ewing, for example, wrote only: "About the 10th of this month [January, 1778] we got into our huts" (*op. cit.*, 26). Washington told Robert Howe, Jan. 13, 1778, "the men are scarcely now covered in log huts" (10 *G. W.*, 301), after he had indicated in General Orders of Jan. 4, 1778, that part of the Army still was under canvas and was in process of moving into cabins (*ibid.*, 262). On the other hand, it is possible to interpret a letter of Feb. 8, 1778, to Thomas Nelson, Jr. (*ibid.*, 432), as indicating that some of the troops had not then gone into huts, though the more probable meaning is that the entire Army was then in small houses, the greater number of which were tolerably good.

[43] 10 *G. W.*, 307; report of committee of Congress, 2 *Greene's Greene*, 44.

[44] 10 *G. W.*, 332.

[45] 1 *Greene's Greene*, 543. As is mentioned *supra*, p. 438 and p. 559, Nathanael Greene believed that Mifflin's antagonism to Washington originated in the refusal of the Commander-in-Chief to abandon the line of the Hudson and to employ all the continental forces in Pennsylvania during the summer of 1777 before it was clear to the General that the enemy's objective was Philadelphia (Nathanael Greene to Jacob Greene, Feb. 7, 1778; 2 *Greene's Greene*, 30).

[46] Cf. Greene to Washington, n.d., 1778: ". . . your Excellency's declaration to the Committee of Congress that you would stand Quartermaster no longer . . ." (*ibid*, 50).

devote to the task the time required to get the best performance from Mifflin's deputies. Weeks previously, Washington should have disregarded sensibilities and should have called on Congress to replace Mifflin or to insist that the Quartermaster General discharge the duties of the office. Instead, Washington's amiability had led him to hope against hope for some betterment until, in this respect, he was unjust to his own troops.

Much of the wretchedness at Valley Forge was merely the aggravation of miseries the men in the ranks had learned to expect and to endure. They had ceased long previously to be ashamed of tatters, and they had shared the harsh companionship of surly winter until they were inured to all except its most wrathful assaults. The one snow that fell during the first weeks at Valley Forge had a depth of no more than four inches.[47] Rain was most persistent but was defied by humor-loving young men who made it the subject of this, the most familiar exchange of their camp:

"Good morning, brother soldier, how are you?"

"All wet, thank'e; hope you are so." [48]

Men of that temper were not driven readily either to desertion or to mutiny. As always, they differed vastly from Regiment to Regiment, according to the quality of their commanders; but as individuals, the stronger of them could survive, somehow, despite nakedness and lack of blankets and the cruelly cold earth of their unfloored cabins, provided they had enough to eat. Food, of course, was the absolute, the unescapable, the daily essential—and food, more than even clothing or blankets or straw, was lacking at Valley Forge.

Joseph Trumbull, the Commissary General, was an able and a diligent man, but he had been sick for months and had been absent in far-off New England, with the result that his department, like that of the Quartermaster General, did not have the daily supervision of an experienced and competent head. Demoralized by resignation, by

---

[47] This snow came on December 25–26, though Captain Montresor dated it (*Montresor Journals*, 480) December 28. See Timothy Pickering to his wife, Dec. 30, 1777, 1 *Pickering,* 200. There had been a light snow that did not "stick" in the Philadelphia area on December 3 (*Montresor Journals*, 479) and another, slightly heavier, at camp on the 10th of December (Journal of Ebenezer Wild, MHSP., 1890–91, p. 105) but this was before the Army reached Valley Forge. While it is possible there were other snowfalls of which no record has been observed in the Diaries consulted, comments on the severity of the weather are so rare that they seem negligible compared with those written from the vicinity of Boston during the winter of 1775–76.

[48] Dr. A. Waldo's Diary, 21 *Penn. Mag.*, 308.

criticism and by incomplete reorganization, the commissary was in a condition so tangled that Washington did not attempt to assess blame for the scarcity of provisions, though this now was approaching famine.[49] Judgment of responsibility must wait till meat could be provided to supplement the "fire cakes"[50] that frequently were all the half-naked men had to eat in their overcrowded, smoky huts.

Little relief could be given by Washington himself at the scene of his men's suffering. Parties were sent out to thresh wheat;[51] all available wagons were collected and used to haul provisions and forage;[52] officers were besought to accept money in place of their extra rations;[53] the desperation of the Army was explained in full to the senior commissaries;[54] an especially humiliating penalty was devised for an officer of that department who had been found guilty of theft;[55] all agents were reminded that a resolve of Congress, long on the Journal, made them subject to courtmartial and military penalties.[56] An increase of bread, with a corresponding reduction of the meat in the daily ration, was considered;[57] farmers were urged to establish a market in camp;[58] some of the best young officers of the Army were given mounted detachments and were sent to collect cattle at points as far off as Head of Elk;[59] authorities in States that might be able to supply more meat were exhorted to fatten their cattle;[60] the plan to get pork from North Carolina was pushed,[61] and was coupled with a plea that the State limit the provisions purchasable by the masters of outward bound vessels who might sell to the enemy;[62] Pennsylvania was encouraged to buy flour for the continental commissary, though the arrangement soon was voided.[63]

All these devices failed to improve the organization or to uncover any new source of supply. Early in the New Year, most of the Regiments

---

[49] For the background of the collapse of the Commissary in 1777–78, see Appendix IV–3, *infra*, p. 639 ff.

[50] Dr. A. Waldo's Diary, Dec. 21, 1777; 21 *Penn. Mag.*, 309.

[51] 10 *G. W.*, 268.   [52] 10 *ibid.*, 313; 1 *Greene's Greene*, 553–55.

[53] 10 *G. W.*, 259, 421.   [54] *Ibid.*, 424, 425, 427, 463.

[55] *Ibid.*, 266–67.

[56] *Ibid.*, 415. The resolve was that of June 10, 1777, for which see *ibid.*, and 8 *JCC.*, 440–41. This resolve was one of the new regulations for the department.

[57] 10 *G. W.*, 433.   [58] *Ibid.*, 436.

[59] *Ibid.*, 467, 491, 513, 524; 2 *LTW.*, 76–78; Wayne to Washington, Feb. 25, 1778, 4 *Wayne Papers*, 92; *PHS*; Nathanael Greene to Colonel Hollingsworth, Apr. 7, 1778, *Reed Papers*, NYHS; Frank H. Stewart, "Foraging for Valley Forge . . ." in *NJHSP.*, new ser., v. 14, p. 144.

[60] 10 *G. W.*, 480–81.   [61] 10 *JCC.*, 62–63.

[62] 10 *JCC.*, 156.

[63] 10 *JCC.*, 151–53, 166, 176, 189; 1 *Pickering*, 206; 3 *Burnett*, 94–95, 99.

had to be told the commissary could issue no provisions because it had none, none whatsoever.[64] After this second period of fasting had become almost intolerable, some flour and a few cattle reached camp. For several days there then was a hand-to-mouth distribution, with little certainty that even bread would be had beyond the morrow, if on the morrow. Meagrely after that, a half-allowance of meat or of bread was issued daily, until about the beginning of the second week in February,[65] when winter fired all its siege guns. A thieving Lieutenant was to have had his sword broken over his head on the morning of the 9th; the extreme penalty of 250 lashes was to have been imposed on men found guilty of smuggling supplies into Philadelphia;[66] but the bombardment by the gray skies was so overwhelming that Washington had to suspend the outdoor infliction of punishment. During this storm, no teams could reach a camp where all reserve provisions of the general commissary were exhausted—to the last thin cow and the bottom slab of pork in the one remaining barrel. A few provident commissaries of Brigade could furnish a little meat with which to grease the passage of dry and sooty "fire cakes" to empty stomachs, but from the 11th of February onward, few troops had anything besides flour delivered them.[67] A week and more passed before any flesh was available for the men in the ranks. As Washington, intensely anxious, walked through the camp during that dreadful week, he heard an ominous chant—"no pay, no clothes, no provisions, no rum." [68]

"This is the second time in the course of the present year," the General wrote Governor Livingston, "that we have been on the point of dissolution, and I know not whether the melancholy event may not take place." [69] As Gouverneur Morris put it, "The skeleton of an Army

---

[64] The date is not known, because no more specific record has been found than Washington's observation, Feb. 14, 1778, that the Army's prolonged fast at that time was the second of the year (10 *G. W.*, 459; cf. Gouverneur Morris to Lewis Morris, Feb. 17, 1777; Emmet Col., *NYPL*). It is entirely possible that some of the reports of long continued scant rations at Valley Forge deal with exceptional hardship in particular outlying commands and not a general suspension of issue for all troops. Something must have depended on the frugality and enterprise of the brigade commissaries. Otherwise it would be difficult to account for the complete silence of some diarists on the subject of food at times when certain troops are known to have been entirely without provisions. For example, in the brief entries of Ebenezer Wild's Journal for January–February, 1778, there is no mention of any shortage of food at Valley Forge (*MHSP*, 1890–91, p. 106).

[65] Probably but not certainly on the 9th. See 2 *Greene's Greene*, 46, and *Thacher*, 128.

[66] 10 *G. W.*, 434, 436, 442. For Washington's efforts to break up trade with the British in Philadelphia, see *ibid.*, 413, 420, 421, 435, 453, 454, 478, 523. Cf. 1 *Reed*, 358–60. An abortive scheme to harass the enemy with long-range fire on shipping in waters close to the city is mentioned in 10 *G. W.*, 509, 524, 529.

[67] *Ibid.*, 469.   [68] *Ibid.* and *Thacher*, 128 n.   [69] 10 *G. W.*, 459.

presents itself to our eyes in a naked, starving condition, out of health, out of spirits." [70] Washington expected the disintegration of his forces or open mutiny and desertion en masse [71]—alternatives so ruinous that they frightened even those members of Congress who had appeared skeptical concerning the breakdown of the Commissary.[72] The last and most stubborn-minded Delegates were shaken from their persistent confidence in the dual system of purchase and supply they had set up in 1777.[73] Fundamental changes were projected. If possible, Congress must have again the services of Joseph Trumbull,[74] from the date of whose departure, Washington himself said, the Army had lived precariously.[75] Time would not wait on deliberation. "The evil [of shortage], great as it is," one of the Committees wrote Governor Johnson of Maryland, "seems rather to increase than diminish." Commissaries were quoted as saying they had great difficulty in buying and could not forward what they purchased. On the speedy transportation of provisions available in Maryland, the Governor was told, "the very existence of our Army depends." [76]

These were the reflections of desperate hours, when some of the stoutest hearts at Valley Forge faltered. "God grant we may never be brought to such a wretched condition again," said Nathanael Greene.[77] In words even more emotional, General Varnum wrote: "The situation of the camp is such that in all human probability the Army must soon dissolve . . . the love of freedom, which once animated the breasts of those born in the country is controlled [78] by hunger, the keenest of necessities." [79] Washington continued to watch and to warn. "A prospect now opens," he said February 17, "of absolute want such as will

[70] Letter of Feb. 1, 1778, to John Jay; 1 Sparks's *Morris*, 153–54.

[71] 10 *G. W.*, 117, 469, 474; Alexander Scammell to Timothy Pickering, Feb. 6, 1778, 1 *Pickering*, 204; Eliphalet Dyer to Joseph Trumbull, Feb. 8, 1778, 3 *Burnett*, 78; John Henry, Jr. to the Governor of Maryland, Thomas Johnson, Feb. 14, 1778, *ibid.*, 85.

[72] James Lovell, Jan. 22, 1778, *ibid.*, 45; Henry Laurens, Jan. 26, 1778; *ibid.*, 51. Cf. Nathanael Greene to Henry Knox, Feb. 26, 1778: "A mystical darkness has spread over the councils of America and prevents her councillors from seeing her true interest" (1 *Greene's Greene*, 562).

[73] Cf. Timothy Pickering to Alexander Scammell, Feb. 17, 1778: "What a fatal change was that of Commissary General last summer! Congress, too late, are convinced of their error" (1 *Pickering*, 206).

[74] Cf. Gouverneur Morris to John Jay, Feb. 1, 1778, 1 *John Jay*, 174; J. B. Smith, Jan. 5, 1778, in 3 *Burnett*, 15; Henry Laurens, Jan. 5, 1778, *ibid.*, 14; John Henry., Jr., Jan. 27, 1778; *ibid.*, 55; 1 *St. Clair Papers*, 103.

[75] 10 *G. W.*, 459 and Appendix IV–3, *infra*, p. 639 ff.

[76] Letter of Feb. 16, 1778, 3 *Burnett*, 86.

[77] Letter of Feb. 16, 1778; 1 *Greene's Green*, 557.

[78] The original reads "controlling."

[79] Letter of Feb. 12, 1778; 10 *G. W.*, 470 n.

make it impossible to keep the Army much longer from dissolution unless the most vigorous and effectual measures are pursued to prevent it." [80] He had been inclined for a day or two to suspect that mutiny was near; [81] thereafter it looked as if the alternative would prevail—that the Army simply would fall apart as the men left their huts and scattered in quest of food. They would have to walk because, even if they were disposed to steal the horses, the animals that had survived the lack of forage were too few and too feeble to carry them far.[82]

The men exceeded the faith of their officers in them. They neither mutinied nor marched defiantly away as the Connecticut militia had in the summer of 1776.[83] Desertion, which never had been worse than in the first few days of February,[84] actually diminished when the shortage of provisions was most depressing. The troops had confidence in Washington [85] and they deserved everything that John Laurens implied when he spoke of "those dear, ragged Continentals whose patience will be the admiration of future ages . . ." [86] In different temper, General Kalb wrote: "How sad that troops of such excellence, and so much zeal, should be so little spared and so badly led!" [87] Nathanael Greene was privileged to pay tribute and to relate the climax of the story as it concerned part of his command: "Such patience and moderation as they manifested under their sufferings does the highest honor to the magnanimity of the American soldiers. The seventh day [without rations] they came before their superior officers and told their sufferings in as respectful terms as if they had been humble petitioners for special favors; they added that it would be impossible to continue in camp any longer without support." [88]

[80] *Ibid.*, 474.   [81] *Ibid.*, 461.

[82] See report of Committee of Congress, 1 *Reed*, 360 ff. Cf. Tench Tilghman to Clement Biddle, Feb. 15, 1778: ". . . . if some [forage] is not got in soon, it will be too late as I fear we shall not have a horse left alive to eat it" (*Biddle Papers*, PHS). Desperate as was this need, Washington previously had been compelled to caution his men against taking too large a part of the forage of nearby farmers (10 *G. W.*, 342). On the starvation of horses, see 1 *Greene's Greene*, 563. In 68 *Papers of G. W.*, p. 34, LC, is a letter of Biddle's, March 5, that may be a reply to Tilghman's of February 15. It contains much information on the procurement and transport of forage.

[83] See *supra*, p. 180.   [84] 10 *G. W.*, 427.

[85] Cf. Dr. A. Waldo's avowal in his Diary, Dec. 26, 1777; 21 *Penn. Mag.*, 312–13.

[86] Letter of Mch. 9, 1778; *John Laurens*, 136.

[87] *Kapp's Kalb*, 142–43.

[88] Letter of Feb. 26, 1778, to Henry Knox, 1 *Greene's Greene*, 563. Greene's statement may be taken to indicate that these men came as the spokesmen of the entire Army, but this could not have been the case. The men in the ranks were not then nor were they thereafter organized in such a manner that they had a committee to act for all of them. Besides, if such a committee had been set up, some mention certainly would have been made elsewhere of so extraordinary an occurrence.

Mercifully, some of the detachments sent out earlier by Washington were returning at the very time with cattle that sufficed, though barely, to relieve the immediate hunger of the half-starved troops.[89] The third breakdown of the commissary was repaired—for how few or how many days, none could say—but as some of the officers of the department were beginning to learn more about the performance of their duties, hope, though frail and feeble, began to show itself. Perhaps the Army would be held together—if the men's clothing could be.

On the day of suspense when Washington heard the cry, "no pay, no clothes, no provisions, no rum," he saw pathetic evidence of the unbelievable extent to which the few garments left to the troops were being worn out. While the General was passing through a company street, a soldier emerged from one hut and dashed to another to pay a visit. Around him was a blanket, but beneath it Washington saw the man's bare body and legs. Except for that blanket the veteran was naked—in February.[90] By the middle of that month, close to 4000 men lacked the simplest apparel,[91] and many of the troops, by their commander's own admission, were unable to leave their quarters.[92] Seizure of private belongings was not to be permitted again, unless everything else failed, because forced requisition yielded little and angered many.[93] There was no recourse other than to the loom, the shop and the peg from which the citizen willingly would take down his extra coat for a shivering soldier. The States must emulate Connecticut, which had procured and forwarded sufficient clothing for all its troops. Where States could do no better, they must gather cloth and must dispatch this to the camp. Tailors in the Army then would turn it quickly into uniforms or undergarments.[94] In addition, agents must be sent to promising markets, Boston, for example, to get what was offered there;[95] shipments intended for the Army must be protected en route from plunderers, military and civilian.

[89] *Ibid.*, 563, 564. This must have been about the 20th of February because approximately as of that date, the tone of Washington's letters became less alarming with reference to provisions. Washington himself is one authority for the statement that the Army was six days without meat. See 11 *G. W.*, 117.

[90] *Thacher*, 128 n.   [91] 10 *G. W.*, 334.

[92] *Ibid.*, 453.   [93] *Ibid.*, 247.

[94] *Ibid.*, 243, 251, 252, 331, 345, 358, 495, 501–02. For the appeal in Pennsylvania, a State that seemed to Washington completely able to care for its troops, see *ibid.*, 318, 444, 448, 482; 2 *LTW.*, 69–71; Stirling to Wayne, Jan. 26, 1778, 4 *Wayne Papers*, 69, PHS; Wayne to Richard Peters, Feb. 8, 1778, *ibid.*, 78; Wayne to Stirling, Feb. 11, 1778, *ibid.*, 70. Connecticut's care of its men is mentioned in Colonel Shepard's letter, cited *infra*, p. 579.

[95] 10 *G. W.*, 256, 486.

Some shoes, though far from enough, were being procured through the barter of hides with cobblers in nearby towns.[96] There was no inclusive means of improving a situation so desperate that clothing of the dead was appraised and reissued,[97] and soldiers were found to have cut up the tents they were quitting, in order to use the coarse fabric for clothing or for cover.[98] Col. William Shepard of the Fourth Massachusetts wrote in mingled wrath and anguish of spirit: "The State has not supported the troops with one single article for more than three months past. I do assure you that there is at least 400 men in the Brigade which I belong to that have not a shoe nor a stocking to put on and more than that number have not half a shirt apiece . . . I have seen the soldiers turned out to do their duty in such poor condition that notwithstanding all the hard heartedness I am naturally possessed of, I could not refrain from tears. It would melt the heart of a savage to see the state we are in." [99]

Officers' plight was almost as humiliating as that of the men.[100] A few of those who held commissions made a jest of their tatters, as, for example, when they arranged a dinner to which they admitted nobody who had a whole pair of breeches; [101] but other officers found in the condition of their clothing a further reason for sending in resignations they already had been tempted to submit because their pay left nothing for their families when their own expenses were met.[102] The candid Colonel of the Fourth Massachusetts described how the troops, "almost naked," were "going into the snow and frost to defend the rights of those very men that are contriving every way to distress the poor soldiers now in service, by putting their specie at such exorbitant price and undervaluing the currency." Then the Colonel became sternly particu-

---

[96] *Ibid.*, 311, 320, 331, 343, 488.　　　　[97] *Ibid.*, 527.
[98] *Ibid.*, 262. For the "indecent" nakedness of Washington's own man servant, see *infra*, p. 620.
[99] Letter of Jan. 25, 1778, to Capt. David Mosely; 174 *Mass. Council Papers*, (2) Mass. Arc. Some less dramatic examples of wholesale nakedness of troops are cited, without reference to the sources, in William S. Stryker, *The Battle of Monmouth*, edited by William Starr Myers (cited hereafter as *Stryker-Myers, Monmouth*), p. 5.
[100] 10 *JCC.*, 11; Wayne to Richard Peters, Jan. 26, 1778, 4 *Wayne Papers*, PHS. Aboard the brig *Symetry*, which was seized near Wilmington, late in December, was clothing for four Regiments and much baggage of officers. The appropriation of this by the captors or its division and sale among all officers (2 *Sullivan Papers*, 4) was the subject of a prolonged and intense correspondence, shared actively by Washington (10 *G. W.*, 245, 260, 295, 302). For a diverting yarn concerning the richness of this cargo, see Dr. A. Waldo's Diary, in 21 *Penn. Mag.*, 322.
[101] Duponceau in *Chinard*, 15.
[102] See Shepard's letter, as *supra*, n. 99; 2 *LTW.*, 73, and Dr. A. Waldo's Diary, Dec. 27, 1777, *loc. cit.*

lar in his indictment: "The soldiers' wages are stated at a certain price which is out of their power to alter and they cannot take any advantage by trafficking or trading. The soldier last spring when he engaged in the service . . . could purchase a pair of shoes for eight shillings that now he is obliged to give eight dollars for, and other specie has risen in like proportion . . . The people at home are destroying the Army by their conduct much faster than Howe and all his army can possibly do by fighting us. By this means many of the best of our officers are leaving the Army daily which if not prevented will ruin the Army very soon." [103]

"Ruin the Army"—had it actually come to that?

[103] Letter to Capt. David Mosely, *loc. cit.*, with some revision of punctuation and spelling.

CHAPTER XXIII

THE DEMIGOD SHOWS HIMSELF HUMAN

(Late Winter of 1777–78)

THROUGH THE worst of the ordeal, even in the dreadful third week of February, 1778, Washington had retained outwardly his unshaken composure, "his calm and firm behavior," as one officer styled it;[1] and he did not lose that self mastery as the days of late winter dragged by, and the hour-by-hour uncertainty and concern over provisions was aggravated by a hundred vexations in the problems of things material and in the management of men. His was the task of planning for the victorious long life of an Army that might die of starvation the very next week. Washington had, fortunately, the companionship of Martha[2] who lighted the long evenings and directed the spartan entertainment at headquarters, where, on occasion, she had the assistance of Mrs. Nathanael Greene,[3] Lady Stirling, Lady Kitty Stirling and others. Simple as were the diversions in officers' quarters,[4] they represented some unhappy hours because they were in heartrending contrast to the life of the soldiers. Washington made the best of what he could not change, and as his duties multiplied, he used increasingly the service of a staff he now was free to augment as he saw fit[5] though actually he added no members.[6] Col. Alexander Scammell, the new Adjutant General, proved competent and highly diverting as a humorist but he had to confess that his duties were intolerably heavy.[7]

[1] Pontgibaud in *Chinard*, 30. Cf. Duponceau (*ibid.*, 14), as of Feb. 23, 1778: "I could not keep my eyes from that imposing countenance, grave yet not severe; affable, without familiarity. Its predominant expression was calm dignity, through which you could trace the strong feelings of the patriot, and discern the father, as well as the commander of his soldiers. I have never seen a picture that represents him to me as I saw him at Valley Forge."

[2] She arrived between Feb. 1 (10 *G. W.*, 414) and Feb. 9 (*LOLTW.*, 25), 1778.

[3] Duponceau (*Chinard*, 16) described Mrs. Greene as a "handsome, elegant and accomplished woman" though Henry Knox and his wife, in their private letters, had gossiped that all was not well between Greene and his lady. Cf. Knox to Mrs. Knox, Dec. 2, 1777; *Knox Papers*, MHS.

[4] Cf. 3 *Hughes*, 324–25.   [5] 10 *JCC.*, 15.

[6] Besides Henry Lee (see *infra*, p. 616) he considered but did not appoint Maj. Peter Scull of Pennsylvania, later secretary of the Board of War (11 *G. W.*, 242).

[7] For his election, see 10 *JCC.*, 21. His first experiences are recorded in Timothy Pickering to Mrs. Pickering, Jan. 5 et post, 1778, 1 *Pickering*, 201–02, 203. For his humor, see the authorities cited in 3 *Hughes*, 737, n 10.

Had Scammell, Washington, Robert Harrison and Alexander Hamilton jointly found the time, they might have been able to solve part of the chief mystery of the late winter, the authorship of a series of forged personal letters of Washington that apparently had been published in England and were reprinted in loyalist newspapers. One aim of these letters obviously was to discredit Washington's leadership by making him appear averse to independence as late as the summer of 1776 and critical of those who favored separation from England. The forgery was the somewhat skillful work of a person who knew the main facts concerning Washington's family and way of living but erred amusingly on the smaller, more intimate details of Washington's life during the months the contest was developing. The General suspected that the man responsible for this falsification was the former Attorney General of Virginia, John Randolph, who had fled to England. There was little or no embarrassment in the publication, because Washington had said time and time again, and still was saying publicly what the forgery alleged—that he had not been an early advocate of independence.[8]

Washington had full assurance that his way of living was proof against all such falsification and, besides, he had no time to waste on personal affairs. While laboring to prevent the starvation of his men, he was busy with the hard, anxious administration of the Army and with plans for making it better able to face its foe. His reforms were advanced through a committee of Congress that had been named at his instance to discuss with him and to recommend to other Delegates such changes in organization, fundamental or otherwise, as its judgment and the counsel of officers suggested.[9] Originally, the proposal had been for a committee of three from Congress and three from the "new" Board of War, which by this time was beginning to perform its duties, though as late as January 20, only General Gates and Richard Peters were in attendance.[10] For several reasons, Gates wished to avoid

---

[8] See *supra*, Vol. III, p. 366; Tench Tilghman to his father, Apr. 24, 1778; *Memoir Tench Tilghman*, 166; 11 *G. W.*, 5, 276, 450, 495, 500; 1 *Ballagh, Lee Letters*, 371. Students who wish to examine the history of this forgery will find the entries in the index to *G. W.* under the heading Spurious letters. Nothing material is to be added to Worthington C. Ford's findings, set forth as long ago as 1889 in *The Spurious Letters Attributed to Washington* (Brooklyn; privately printed).

[9] Resolve of Jan. 10, 1778. On the scope of the committee's powers, see Henry Laurens, Jan. 13 et post, 1778, 3 *Burnett*, 36; cf. *ibid.*, 61.

[10] See Peters to Robert Morris, Jan. 21, 1778, *ibid.*, 45, and 1 *Pickering*, 183, 189. For the slow organization and varied perplexities of the board during the winter and early spring, consult 3 *Burnett*, 54, 61 n; Gates to Joseph Trumbull, Jan. 20, 1778 (*Joseph Trumbull Papers*, as cited, v. 1, p. 59a, Conn. State Lib.); Jed. Huntington to Joseph Trumbull, Jan. 31, 1778,

this assignment and he succeeded in begging off with the result that the committee was enlarged to five, all of them Delegates.[11] Most of these committeemen came to camp and remained there during part of the period of hardship [12]—a most fortunate circumstance because it gave them an understanding of what Washington had to endure. For the use of the committee, he took time, burdened though he was, to prepare a detailed review of the Army, in all its activities and deficiencies.[13] The four supreme needs, as Washington saw them, were the strengthening of the officers' corps, the assurance of recruits for the continental infantry, the improvement of the cavalry, and the better organization of the Quartermasters, the Commissary and the other weak departments; but in explaining these essentials, Washington did not neglect any of the others.

If good officers were to be retained, they should have the guarantee of half pay when honorably retired or discharged and the pledge of pensions for their widows in event of their death. Congress agreed immediately to allowances for these war widows,[14] but it challenged, disputed and deferred the measure for half-pay.[15] Washington held to his argument and, with equal conviction, to the view that recruiting for the continental Army had to be on a changed basis. "Voluntary enlistments seem to be entirely out of the question . . ." he told the committee, because "the country has been already pretty well drained of that class of men whose tempers, attachments and circumstances disposed them to enter permanently, or for a length of time, into the Army . . ." No way of filling the Regiments existed other than that of drafts from the militia. Able-bodied men in sufficient number should be drawn annually, for twelve months' service, to begin the 1st of January. On or before October 1, an effort should be made to reenlist these

---

ibid., v. 3, p. 231a. See also in 1 *Pickering*, 213, the statement of Pickering, Apr. 26, 1778, that most of the work of the board had fallen to him, a possibility James Lovell professed Congress had in mind when it named the Adjutant General to membership (3 *Burnett*, 54).

[11] 10 *JCC.*, 66–67. Cf. James Lovell to Samuel Adams, Jan. 22, 1778; 3 *Burnett*, 45. Pickering was with the committee, January 13–20, 1 *Pickering*, 183, but not officially a member.

[12] 1 *Greene's Greene*, 563.

[13] 10 *G. W.*, 362–403; dated in *G. W.* Jan. 29, 1778. Fitzpatrick noted, *ibid.*, 362, that the meetings of the committee considering this report were held "at Moore Hall, the house of William Moore, about two and a half miles North of the Valley Forge headquarters."

[14] 10 *JCC.*, 19–20, on the basis of recommendations by the previous committee that had visited the Army at White Marsh. Congress in the same spirit promptly corrected an oversight concerning rations and pay for imprisoned or paroled officers (*ibid.*, 61).

[15] 2 *LTW.*, 66–68; 3 *Burnett*, 31–32, 34. James Lovell, the principal opponent, insisted that in America, where land was cheap and opportunity large, an officer easily could start again and without permanent loss.

one-year soldiers for another term of like duration. Twenty-five dollars should be offered for reenlistment, but no bounty was to be given men when drafted.[16]

Washington's argument for his third major reform, an increase in the size of the cavalry Regiments, showed a firmer grasp than previously of the tactical value of mounted troops, especially in defensive war of the sort he had to conduct.[17] The plea for a reorganization of the Quartermaster's Department included the assertion that the principal post should be filled by a man of military training. Purchase should be primarily by contract; an active, careful Wagonmaster General "would be a great saving to the public." His assistants "should be plain, sober, diligent men, acquainted with the management of horses and wagons, and untainted with absurd fancies of gentility, [men] who would understand the end and design of their appointment, and not consider the means of making themselves useful as a degredation of their imaginary dignity."[18] In this, needless to say, the Virginia planter and the colonial officer who had scaled the defiant ridges on the way to Fort DuQuesne was seconding the recommendations of the man who had watched the mismanagement and neglect of wagons on the roads to Valley Forge.

The General was less precise, less sure of himself, in what he had to say about the reform of the commissary. In the spirit of the letters he had written during the crisis of February, he did not attempt to fix blame for failure; he merely gave warning that "unless ample magazines are laid up in the course of this winter and the approaching spring, nothing favorable is to be looked for, from the operations of the coming campaign . . ." On the contrary, "our arms, enfeebled by the embarrassing and fluctuating supplies of provisions, will reap no other fruits than disgrace and disappointment." Able men should be employed; the sites of magazines should be chosen with care; responsibility for transporting commissary stores should be fixed; the content of the ration and of the issue of liquor, if any, should be determined. That was all he had to say,[19] in virtual admission that he had found the problem too difficult to solve—at least in the time he could give to it.

The committee of Delegates felt as Washington did concerning the necessity of finding able men to bring back the Quartermasters and Commissary Departments to a decent standard and to operate them

---

[16] 10 G. W., 366.   [17] Ibid., 368.
[18] Ibid., 390–91, with the punctuation somewhat revised.
[19] Ibid., 392–94.

with vigor, sound sense and daily attention. Reports and parliamentary maneuvering of the usual sort delayed action [20] but ended in the conclusion that Philip Schuyler would not be acceptable as Quartermaster General,[21] and that Thomas Mifflin was unwilling to resume the duties. Mifflin, in fact, had left his post on the Board of War and had quit York in a huff because he affirmed he was falsely accused of seeking to displace Washington.[22] The ablest man available for the post appeared to be Nathanael Greene, who was most reluctant to accept, but at length was prevailed upon to do so, on the condition he imposed—that he have two assistants of his own choosing. Greene made reservation, also, of his rank so that, if he resigned as Quartermaster General, he still would retain his seniority in the continental Army. In all this, Greene maintained later, the persuasive influence was that of Washington himself.[23]

Election of Greene was a blow and at the same time a comfort to Washington, a blow in that it partially deprived him of the counsel of the lieutenant he esteemed most, but a reassurance in that it certainly would mean diligent, conscientious and intelligent direction of the department. No similar man was procurable immediately for Commissary General. Joseph Trumbull's letters showed him to be unhappy, in continuing ill health and almost under the delusion that he had been persecuted.[24] His deputy of Purchases, Jere. Wadsworth of Massachusetts, a former sea captain, aged 34, was the man who seemed most likely to succeed,[25] but election was delayed. The minor new positions in both services were left by Congress to be filled at the discretion of the committee and of Washington.[26]

The draft of militia for twelve months, as recommended by the General and approved by the Committee, involved politics and public sensibilities that frightened every time-server in Congress, but it was endorsed in its essentials. Because two months of the year had passed when the Delegates voted, they decided that needs for 1778 would be

---

[20] 10 *JCC.*, 102–03, 104, 126–27, 138.

[21] He had been favored early (3 *Burnett*, 62), but later was eliminated (*ibid.*, 99 and 1 *Reed*, 363).

[22] 1 *Pickering*, 206–07. For his recall, see 10 *JCC.*, 182.

[23] He was elected Mch. 2, 1778; 10 *JCC.*, 210; 1 *Reed*, 363; 2 *Greene's Greene*, 42 ff. For Washington's understanding of Greene's reservation, see 16 *G. W.*, 223.

[24] Joseph Trumbull to Henry Laurens, Nov. 2, 1777 and Jan. 12, 1778, wrongly dated 1777, *Joseph Trumbull Papers*, CHS.

[25] 1 *Reed*, 363. See *infra*, p. 620.

[26] 10 *JCC.*, 185, 186.

met if the draft were effective for nine months from the time the recruits reached the prescribed rendezvous. In determining the respective State quotas, hostile occupation was taken into account. New York and New Jersey together were asked for no more men than North Carolina was called upon to furnish. Discretion was allowed for the employment of other methods than those of a draft in raising the required force, provided the troops were forthcoming. A man enlisted for three years was to be counted as equivalent to three men drafted successively for one year each.[27] The design for the organization of larger cavalry Regiments was not questioned but was postponed temporarily, along with other details of the "Establishment of the American Army."[28] Efforts were to be made meantime, under the terms of a somewhat bombastic resolve, to have "the young gentlemen of property and spirit" form volunteer Troops of Light Horse to serve to the end of 1778.[29]

This partial reorganization was effected, and the miseries of Valley Forge were endured while Washington was having an extraordinary adventure in command. General Thomas Conway had returned to camp late in December, 1777, from York, where he had spoken, to quote Lafayette, "as a man sent by heaven for the liberty and happiness of America." The young Marquis observed, half humorously, "he told so to them and they are fools enough to believe it"[30]—and, Lafayette might have added, to swallow a score of other absurdities. At York and everywhere else that politicians gathered, they still were talking of the difference between Washington's apparent failure and Gates's manifest success, and they were willing to listen to self-assured critics who maintained that Washington had wasted his numerical superiority.[31] Jonathan Sergeant, former Delegate from New Jersey and now Attorney General of Pennsylvania, was saying privately that Washington had been guilty of "such blunders as might have disgraced a soldier of

27 Proceedings of Feb. 26, 1778; 10 JCC., 199 ff.

28 11 ibid., 538 ff. The table of cavalry organization (ibid., 540) was that recommended by Washington (10 G. W., 369), except for a few minor staff positions.

29 10 JCC., 213–15. The MS of this report and of a related "essay" in 60 Papers Cont. Cong. is in the autograph of William Duer, the New York Delegate who had served for a time in India as aide to Lord Clive.

30 Lafayette to Washington, Jan. 5, 1778; LOLTW., 20.

31 James Craik to Washington, Jan. 6, 1778; 64 Papers of G. W., 137, LC. Nothing in 5 Sparks, 493–94, indicates the omissions in the text of this letter as there presented. It is an instance of Sparks at his worst. Cf. James Lovell to Gates, Nov. 27, 1777: "Depend upon it for every ten soldiers placed under the command of our Fabius, five recruits will be wanted annually during the war" (2 Greene's Greene, 7). This sentence is not in that part of the letter printed in 2 Burnett, 570.

three months' standing." [32] A further complaint was that Washington had been under the domination of Greene and Knox; [33] still another allegation was that the Commander-in-Chief had lost numerous opportunities. [34] His early resignation was predicted; Gates, Conway, Mifflin or Charles Lee, on release, were put forward as his successor. [35] For a time, Washington stood so low in the esteem of some Delegates that even his recommendation for the reform of the Quartermasters Department had been "treated with . . . much indecent freedom and levity." [36] The Marquis Lafayette, who had expected to find America a patriotic Utopia, was shocked to observe the dissension in Congress and to hear—as he wrote Washington—that "stupid men who without knowing a single word about war, undertake to judge you, to make ridiculous comparisons . . ." As Lafayette saw it: ". . . they are infatuated with Gates without thinking of the different circumstances, and believe that attacking is the only thing necessary to conquer." [37]

Washington read these words in a mood that combined resolution, philosophy and restraint. In answer to the young Frenchman he said simply: ". . . it is much to be lamented that things are not now as they formerly were; but we must not, in so great a contest, expect to meet with nothing but sunshine." [38] He explained his difficulties to Lafayette and, while the Committeemen of Congress were in camp, he disclosed to them all the conditions that were paralyzing the Army. John Harvie, a Virginia member of the Committee, waited until he was alone with Washington and then he said earnestly, "My dear General, if you had given some explanation, all these rumors would have been silenced a long time ago."

Washington's answer was a question: "How could I exculpate myself without doing harm to the public cause?" [39] He did not ask this in vain of Harvie or of some other intelligent and discerning members of Congress. They understood. Henry Laurens wrote his son, the General's aide: "In [Washington's ruin] would be involved the ruin of our

[32] Letter of Nov. 20, 1777, to James Lovell; *Samuel Adams Papers*, NYPL, as cited in 2 *Burnett*, 570 n.
[33] 2 *Greene's Greene*, 33.
[34] E. Blaine to R. H. Harrison, Jan. 18, 1778; 65 *Papers of G. W.*, 131, LC.
[35] Nathanael Greene to Alexander McDougall, Feb. 5, 1778; *McDougall Papers*, NYHS. In listing these four men, Thacher (*op. cit.*, 129) remarked, "Mifflin has no claim and it is believed, no desire, to be elevated to this responsible position."
[36] Henry Laurens to John Laurens, Jan. 10, 1778; 3 *Burnett*, 24.
[37] Letter of Dec. 30, 1777; *LOLTW.*, 14.
[38] Letter of Dec. 31, 1778; 10 *G. W.*, 237.
[39] Philip Mazzei, quoted in *Chinard*, 84; cf. 10 *G. W.*, 411; 11 *ibid.*, 164.

cause. On the other hand his magnanimity, his patience will save his country and confound his enemies." [40]

Laurens did not overvalue Washington's patience but it was a virtue that had limits which already had been passed with Thomas Conway. The Commander-in-Chief had concluded that ambitious pretentions and incredible self-esteem made the Irish-born Frenchman an "incendiary," who would not hesitate to stir up dangerous contention and to set comrades against one another. The rank and the office of the new Inspector General were to be regarded. Further, about the time of Conway's return to camp, Washington learned that his Brigadiers intended to make formal protest to Congress against the promotion of a comparative newcomer over their heads,[41] but he urged them to be cool in their attitude [42] and he did not associate himself directly with their effort. Election and promotion of general officers were in the hands of Congress. Washington would work as best he could with those men Congress assigned him. Personal relations were another matter. In these there would be no deference, no pretense. It was both futile and unbecoming, Washington thought, to employ diplomacy or to make personal appeals to such a detestable individual. Conway was not to be moderated, conciliated or converted. He was a personal enemy and must be faced. Seldom, if ever, had Washington taken that stand with any man. Of no person, since his answer to George Muse's letter on the allotment of soldiers' land,[43] had he put on paper what now he was prepared to write of Conway.

This was the situation when Conway called at headquarters to pay his respects. He was received with flawless, cold courtesy, the "ceremonious civility," which Washington had described two years previously as tantamount to incivility.[44] Conway came again and had precisely the same treatment, such a reception, he protested later, "as I never met with before from any General during the course of thirty years in a very respectable Army." [45] As if to avoid unnecessary personal contact, Washington next sent Lt. Col. John Fitzgerald to inquire

---

[40] Letter of Jan. 8, 1778; 3 *Burnett*, 22. Cf. Lafayette to Washington, Dec. 30, 1777: "You shall see very plainly that if you were lost for America, there is nobody who could keep the Army and the Revolution for six months" (*LOLTW.*, 14).

[41] 10 *G. W.*, 227.   [42] *Ibid.*, 237.

[43] See Vol. III, p. 342.

[44] See letter of Dec. 15, 1775, to Joseph Reed; 4 *G. W.*, 165.

[45] Conway to Washington, Jan. 27, 1775; 5 *Sparks*, 503. Cf. 10 *G. W.*, 249. The fact that Conway made two calls is mentioned in Conway to Washington, Jan. 10, 1778 (65 *Papers of G. W.*, 35, LC).

what methods Conway proposed to employ in the new office of Inspector General. The Frenchman replied, December 29, with an explanation of his plan to prepare models, together with printed rules and regulations and, meantime, to begin the verbal instruction of officers and nco's from each Regiment. This was followed, in Conway's communication, by a flourish on his experience in this work, and that, in turn, by the statement that the rank of Major General was "absolutely requisite" for the discharge of the duties. Conway went on: ". . . if my appointment is productive of any inconvenience or anyways disagreeable to your excellency, as I neither applied nor solicited for this plan, I am very ready to return to France where I have pressing business, and this I will do with the more satisfaction that [sic] I expect even there to be useful to the cause." [46]

The offer in those final clauses might be accepted as arrogantly defiant or as patriotically subordinate. Washington was not concerned over alternative interpretations, but he was resolved, in the cool spirit he urged on his officers, to write the Frenchman a letter that would represent the issue as one of justice to American brigade commanders, whom the Inspector General now outranked.[47] Conway could not misunderstand how these officers felt about his promotion, because he, though the junior of all the Brigadiers, had been the most vehement in his protests when Kalb had been made a Major General.

In words as calm and as formal as those of his personal reception of the ambitious Inspector General, Washington disposed of the essential matters of business and then he proceeded to assure Conway, "Your appointment of Inspector-General to the Army, I believe, has not given the least uneasiness to any officer in it." Washington continued: "By consulting your own feelings upon the appointment of Baron de Kalb you may judge what must be the sensations of those Brigadiers who by your promotion are superseded. I am told they are determined to remonstrate against it; for my own part, I have nothing to do in the appointment of general officers and shall always afford every countenance and due respect to those appointed by Congress, taking it for granted that, prior to any resolve of that nature, they take a dispas-

[46] 64 *Papers of G. W.*, 10, LC., with some revision of punctuation and spelling. Part of this letter is printed in 10 *G. W.*, 226–27 n.

[47] Washington used the word "supersede," which was good usage early in the eighteenth century but apparently was not employed long because the meaning might be confused. Duane in his edition of 1810 defined "to be superseded" strictly: "to be deprived of rank and pay for some offence and to have others put in one's stead."

sionate view of the merits of the officer to be promoted, and consider every consequence that can result from such a procedure; nor have I any other wish on that head but that good attentive officers may be chosen, and no extraordinary promotion take place but where the merit of the officer is so generally acknowledged as to obviate every reasonable cause of dissatisfaction thereat." [48]

At this point, the exchange might have ended, with tacit assumption by Conway that he possessed the special merit to justify his advancement; but he apparently was as confident of his finesse in debate as of his skill in war, and he replied at once with observations on the necessity of a prompt beginning of inspection. He maintained, next, that he was warranted in his demand for the rank of Major General because this, or even higher place, was allowed Inspectors General in European armies. As for Kalb, a commission at least of equality with that officer was necessary, Conway argued, because he had outranked Kalb in France. Thereupon, in his letter, Conway availed himself of the opening Washington had left: "you are perfectly right in taking for granted that the honorable Congress has taken a dispassionate view of the matter before having appointed me. You may also take it for granted and be very certain that I have made use of neither art nor interest to extort or steal this appointment from Congress." [49]

Here, again, Conway might have halted with the honors of controversy not uneven, but he could not forbear rushing into this:

What you are pleased to call an extraordinary promotion is a very plain one. There is nothing extraordinary in it, only that such a place was not thought of sooner. The general and universal merit which you wish every promoted officer might be endowed with is a rare gift. We see but a few men of merit so generally acknowledged. We know but the great Frederick in Europe and the great Washington in this continent. I certainly never was so rash as to pretend to such a prodigious height. Neither do I pretend to any superiority in personal quality over my brother Brigadiers for whom I feel much regard; but you, sir, and the great Frederick know perfectly well that this trade is not learned in a few months. I have served steadily thirty years, that is, before some of my comrades, Brigadiers, were born; therefore I do not think that it will be found marvelous and incredible if I command here a number of men which falls much short of what I have commanded these

[48] Letter of Dec. 30, 1777; 10 *G. W.*, 226–28.
[49] Conway to Washington, Dec. 31, 1777; 64 *Papers of G. W.*, 41, LC. Part of this letter, not including this quotation, appears in 10 *G. W.*, 228 n.

many years in an old army. However, sir, by the complexion of your letter
and by the reception you have honored me with since my arrival, I perceive
that I have not the happiness of being agreeable to your Excellency and that
I can expect no support in fulfilling the laborious duty of an Inspector General. I do not mean to give you or any other officer the least uneasiness.
Therefore I am very ready to return to France and to the army where I hope
I will meet with no frowns.[50]

Four things in this angered Washington—the manifest insincerity of
linking his name with Frederick's, the insinuation that Conway had not
been received properly at headquarters, the assumption that nobody in
the Army had thought previously of creating a system of inspection,
and finally the statement that Conway could "expect no support" in the
discharge of his official duties, because of the Commander-in-Chief's
dislike for him personally. Washington's aide, John Laurens, who had
been schooled at Geneva, explained afterwards that Conway's association of the American commander with Frederick was "a most insolent
attempt at what the French called persiflage, or humoring a man." Conway, said Laurens, would not have dared to employ such a device if he
had not known that Washington's position made "revenge in a private
way impossible." [51] John's father, the President of Congress, remarked
subsequently that if Conway pretended sincerity in the parallel, he was
"guilty of the blackest hypocrisy," and that if the Frenchman was indulging "unprovoked sarcasm," it was "unpardonable." [52]

Washington's decision was instant and sharp: If, improbably, Congress so desired, it could make its choice between him and the Frenchman.[53] For his own part, he was in no mood to calculate risks. As a
soldier and a gentleman, his immediate concern was to denounce the
intimation that he would fail to support Conway—or anyone else for
that matter—in the performance of duties assigned by Congress. On
the 2nd of January, Washington transmitted to the Delegates in York
his correspondence with Conway and in the plainest words he could
put on paper, he told Congress precisely how he felt: "If General Conway means, by cool receptions . . . that I did not receive him in the

---

[50] A postscript read, "Beg leave to wish your Excellency a happy New Year and a glorious
campaign" (64 *Papers of G. W.*, 41, LC, with the addition of punctuation that is lacking in
the original).

[51] *John Laurens*, 100–01.

[52] Letter of Feb. 3, 1778, to John Laurens, 3 *Burnett*, 69.

[53] *John Laurens*, loc. cit.

language of a warm and cordial friend, I readily confess the charge. I did not, nor shall I ever, till I am capable of the arts of dissimulation. These I despise, and my feelings will not permit me to make professions of friendship to a man I deem my enemy, and whose system of conduct forbids it. At the same time, Truth authorizes me to say that he was received and treated with proper respect to his official character, and that he has had no cause to justify the assertion that he could not expect any support for fulfilling the duties of his appointment."

Washington wrote the usual conclusion of "I have the honor, etc." and then he added as a postscript: "The enclosed extract from the proceedings of a council of general officers will show the office of Inspector General was a matter not of such modern date as General Conway mentions it to be, and that it was one of the regulations in view for the reform of the Army. The foreign officers who had commissions and no commands and were of ability were intended to be recommended to execute it, particularly the Baron d'Arendt with whom the idea originated and whose capacity seemed to be well admitted." [54]

Before this paper was read in Congress,[55] Washington received an excited communication of December 8 from Horatio Gates[56] who had heard by that time of Washington's first letter to Conway, with the quotation Lord Stirling had sent.[57] Gates was much disturbed: Conway's letters to him had been "stealingly copied," he said, "but which of them, when, and by whom, is to me as yet an unfathomable secret." He could not find justification for suspecting any of his staff, and he believed it was in Washington's "power to do me and the United States a very important service, by detecting a wretch who may betray me, and capitally injure the very operations" under the direction of the Commander-in-Chief. The "crime" was "important"; a loss of time

---

[54] 10 G. W., 249–50. The punctuation of the quoted passage has been modernized, but the somewhat unusual capitalization of "Truth" has been preserved. The enclosed "extract" from council proceedings of Oct. 29, 1777, has disappeared from the records but it doubtless corresponded to the text printed in 9 G. W., 442 n. Washington on the 26th of October had addressed to his general officers a circular in which, among other things, he had asked: "Will the office of Inspector General, for the purpose, principally, of establishing one uniform set of maneuvers and manual be advisable, as the time of the Adjutant General seems to be totally engaged with other business?" The advice of council was: "Such an officer is advisable. The manual maneuvers, or any regulations to be established, previously to be settled or agreed to by the Commander-in-Chief or a board of officers appointed by him for that purpose" (9 G. W., 441–42).

[55] Jan. 7, 1778; 10 JCC., 27.

[56] Washington's answer of Jan. 4, 1778, stated that Gates's "letter of the 8th ulto. came to my hands a few days ago" (10 G. W., 263).

[57] See *supra*, p. 550.

was serious; whether Washington had the information from an officer or from a member of Congress was unknown to Gates. For these reasons, he said, he was sending the President a copy of the letter.[58]

Washington was astonished. He strangely overlooked the fact that he had laid his exchanges with Conway before the Delegates; and instead of conceding a similar right to the head of the semi-independent Northern Department, he asked himself why Gates was reporting to Congress a matter that concerned the custody of records, the honor of a staff, and the intimacy of relations with a long-time friend and senior officer? The first assumption of Washington had been that Gates had intended to inform him of what Conway had been saying: was it possible that gossip was well founded in linking Gates's name with Conway's in an alleged conspiracy to have the command of the Army vested in the victor of Saratoga? Gates's letter contained no denial of the accuracy of the quotation that "Heaven has been determined to save your country, or a weak General and bad counsellors would have ruined it." Moreover, Gates twice mentioned "letters" from Conway in the plural, as if they might have been sufficiently numerous to make it difficult to determine from which of them the extract might have been taken. Gates wrote, also, of the possibility that the letter containing the offensive words might have been shown Washington by a member of Congress: did this mean that correspondence of Conway and Gates, critical of Washington, was being circulated among Delegates?

In one sense, as always had been the case, Washington did not care, because more than ever he now would be glad to lay his burdens down; but he was ready with a stern, inflexible "No," by way of answer, if a conspiring, selfish faction sought to force him out.[59] He faced the same sort of challenge he had read in Conway's persiflage, a challenge of his integrity, because there was, he thought, an intimation in Gates's letter that he had received in some discreditable manner an extract from a paper "stealingly copied" at Gates's headquarters. Previously, Washington would have written directly to Gates about this; but now that the commander of the Northern Department had laid the indirect accusation before Congress, Washington decided to send through the same

---

[58] 5 *Sparks,* 487.
[59] Cf. Washington to William Gordon, Feb. 15, 1778: ". . . while the public are satisfied with my endeavors I mean not to shrink in the cause; but, the moment her [sic] voice, not that of faction, calls upon me to resign, I shall do it with as much pleasure as ever the weary traveller retired to rest" (10 *G. W.,* 463, verbatim).

tribunal a letter in which, as he believed, his statement of the facts would be his sufficient denial. In doing this, Washington could see no impropriety in saying that Gates's own aide, James Wilkinson, had talked of Conway's letter while on the way to York with Gates's victory dispatch. Nothing in the circumstances, as far as they were known to Washington, indicated that Wilkinson's disclosure was in any way confidential.

As it happened, perhaps fortuitously, and certainly without any suggestion by the Commander-in-Chief, both Conway and Wilkinson now became objects of attack. The Brigadiers of the main Army had determined to protest against the promotion of Conway to the rank of Major General; the Colonels were preparing to direct a similar paper against Wilkinson who overnight was given the brevet of a Brigadier for bringing a paper from Saratoga to York, though many Colonels who had shared courageously in all Washington's campaigns had tacitly been denied advancement. Nine of the Brigadiers joined in the "memorial" to Congress regarding the promotion of Conway, and they forwarded their paper to Washington, through Sullivan, with the request that it be transmitted to the Delegates at York as soon as convenient.[60] It was a somewhat overwrought complaint, in the usual fervent style, but it contained one sentence that bore out everything Washington had written about the insignificant military accomplishments of Conway: "We have commanded [with?] him in the field and are totally unacquainted with any superior act of mind which could entitle him to rise above us." The memorial described how the Generals felt themselves "disgraced by their representatives . . . without the least imputation of demerit . . ." At the end was an assurance to this effect: "We wish not to depart from our duty but in pursuance thereof, choose rather to point out than resent our grievances, in doing which we doubtless shall receive the approbation and relief of Congress."[61]

What the expected "relief" was to be, the signers did not specify, but they were men of influence from seven States,[62] and they had asked Sullivan to assure Washington and the members of Congress that their

[60] Sullivan to Washington, Jan. 2, 1778; 64 *Papers of G. W.*, 94, LC; cf. Sullivan to Washington, Dec. 30, 1777, *ibid.*, 33.

[61] 162 *Papers Cont. Cong.* 276, LC.

[62] Jed. Huntington was from Connecticut, Lachlan McIntosh from Georgia, Henry Knox and John Paterson from Massachusetts, Enoch Poor from New Hampshire, William Maxwell from New Jersey, James Varnum from Rhode Island, and Charles Scott and George Weedon from Virginia.

paper expressed the views of the absent Generals as fully as their own.[63] Nathanael Greene added a personal protest, deferential and at the same time firm in its warning that if regular promotion were denied, "a sense of injury [would] mean a lessening of military service." Art and cabal would succeed; "low intrigue" would be the "characteristic and genius of the Army." [64] Sullivan somewhat tardily took the same general position in a yes-and-no letter that combined sympathy for the officers with avowed admiration for Conway.[65]

Congress received the memorial of the nine Brigadiers and the communication of Greene, and defiantly laid them on the table.[66] Members doubtless affirmed they would not permit soldiers to dictate to them; but as a matter of practical politics, they did not disdain the protest. Nor could they overlook the fact that most of the senior American officers disliked, if they did not actually distrust Conway.[67] Said Henry Laurens, "a particular friend of General Conway has lamented to me that all the French officers hated him, and I learned from others that none of the English officers (except a little party) love him." [68] Some of the juniors who had served under Conway, and some even who merely had come in contact with him, vehemently resented his contemptuous attitude toward them. On occasion he would ask one of them peevishly, "Did Congress see you before they appointed you?" [69] Alexander Hamilton probably bespoke the sentiments of these officers, along with his own, when he denounced Conway as "one of the vermin bred in the entrails of his chimera dire, and there does not exist a more villainous calumniator and incendiary." [70]

Manifestly, Washington did not have to fight alone against whatever forces there were, feeble or strong, clumsy or cunning, that sought to displace him. Without soliciting it, he had the support of most of his officers, men whom Congress could not afford to dismiss or even to dis-

---

[63] Sullivan to Washington, Jan. 2, 1778, as *supra*.
[64] 155 *Papers Cont. Cong.*, I, p. 51, LC; 1 *Greene's Greene*, 547–48.
[65] Sullivan to Henry Laurens, Jan. 20, 1778; 2 *Sullivan Papers*, 14 ff.
[66] 10 *JCC.*, 63; 3 *Burnett*, 63, 64.
[67] Cf. McDougall to Greene, Feb. 14, 1778: "If [Conway] has seen service equal to his years, his proficiency in arms is but very moderate . . . The men who pass him off to the public as one of the greatest Generals of his age must be very ignorant themselves or very wicked men, and I trust their ambitious machinations will be frustrated" (*McDougall Papers*, NYHS).
[68] Letter of Jan. 26, 1778, to Isaac Motte; 3 *Burnett*, 53.
[69] *Graydon*, 314.
[70] Letter of Feb. 13, 1778, to George Clinton; 9 *A. Hamilton*, 127. The line from "Paradise Lost" (Book II; line 628) reads: "Gorgons and Hydras and Chimæras dire."

regard. Something of this changed feeling of Delegates was to be observed, perhaps, between the lines of a letter written a few days later by Abraham Clark, one of the New Jersey members, who had been critical of Washington in February, 1777. Conway, said Clark, had been credited with much ability: that was all he ever had heard of the new Inspector General whose correspondence with Gates was not known when Conway was promoted. Were the thing "now to be done," Clark wrote, "Congress probably would act otherwise." [71]

It was, then, to some Delegates of shifting mind as well as to his stout supporters in Congress that Washington dispatched a copy of his reply of January 4 to Gates's letter of the 8th of December. The Commander-in-Chief apologized for adding anything to the burdens of Congress, but, he said, circumstance made this necessary: "What could induce General Gates to communicate a copy of his letter to me to that honorable body," he expostulated, "is beyond the depth of my comprehension upon any fair ground." The enclosed answer to Gates was an explicit denial of any possible charge that Washington had "practiced some indirect means to come at the contents of the confidential letters between you and General Conway." After relating precisely how the quotation from Conway reached him, Washington explained that he thought at first it had come through Wilkinson from Gates himself, "with a friendly view to forewarn, and consequently forearm me against a secret foe, or, in other words, a dangerous incendiary; in which character, sooner or later, this country will know General Conway." To these plain words Washington added only, in the letter he sent Gates: "But, in this, as in other matters of late, I have found myself mistaken." [72]

There Washington left the issue. Gates might answer, if he saw fit, and, meantime, might settle accounts with James Wilkinson. The Colonels' protest against the promotion of that young gentleman to the rank of Brigadier had not yet been received by Congress, but the rumble of their dissatisfaction already had been audible. "A plan is laid by sundry members of Congress, which I believe will be carried out, to remove him by the way of appointing him Secretary to the Board of War or by sending him to Georgia." [73] Such had been the reflection of the Delegate who had expressed his relief that Gates had asked no more

---

[71] Letter of Jan. 15, 1778, to Lord Stirling; 3 *Burnett*, 40.
[72] 10 *G. W.*, 263–65. See *supra*, p. 550.
[73] Nathaniel Folsom to Josiah Bartlett, Jan. 2, 1778, with the spelling drastically and the punctuation moderately revised (3 *Burnett*, 4). See *supra*, p. 537.

than a brevet as Brigadier for Wilkinson. Appointment by the Board of War was made immediately without waiting to ascertain whether it would please Wilkinson or placate the Colonels over whom he had stepped.[74]

Conway, for his part, did not wait on Congress or on Gates or on anyone else. He informed John Sullivan: "I depend upon my military promotion in rank for to increase my fortune and that of my family. I freely own to you it was partly with a view of obtaining sooner the rank of Brigadier in the French army that I have joined this." [75] In that unabashed pursuit of fortune, he again wrote Washington and, half reproachfully, asked if the Commander-in-Chief of an Army "raised for the defence of liberty" intended to order an inquisition because an officer wrote such a letter of criticism as any subaltern in Europe might indite without having the least notice taken of it by his superiors. Conway proceeded:

I cannot believe, nor does any officer in your Army believe, that the objection to my appointment originates with anybody living but from you, for since three French officers, who did not serve here or elsewhere as long as I did, have been promoted without difficulty, I have, and everyone has reason to consider that my promotion would have been as acceptable, had you seemed to give it the least countenance. But the two receptions you honored me with when I paid my respects [and] the dissatisfaction you testified as [with?] the resolves of Congress, were more than sufficient to incense the officers and encourage them to an opposition. Your dispositions towards me, sir, have been clear, and the behaviour of some gentlemen of your family did not permit me or anyone else to entertain the least doubt of them.

I have told you, sir, and have the honor to repeat to you that I do not wish to give you or any officer in the Army the least uneasiness. Since you will not accept of my services, since you cannot bear the sight of me in your camp, I am ready to go wherever Congress thinks proper and even to France; and I solemnly declare that far from resenting the undeserved rebuke I met with from you, I shall do everything in my power to serve this cause.[76]

[74] Jan. 6, 1778; 10 *JCC.*, 24. Wilkinson had been alarmed from the first by the opposition to his advancement and he had called on Anthony Wayne to "assist me by unmasking to me the assassins who dare traduce me" (Letter of Nov. 26, 1777; 4 *Wayne Papers*, p. 46, PHS).

[75] Letter of Jan. 3, 1778; 2 *Sullivan Papers*, 2.

[76] Conway to Washington, Jan. 10, 1778, "at Benjamin Bartholomew's"; 65 *Papers of G. W.*, 35, LC. The original is almost unpunctuated and consequently may appear to be confused, but repunctuation is in no way difficult and raises no question of Conway's meaning. There is no evidence, one way or the other, that some other hand more experienced than Conway's shaped the argument. The letter throughout is in the autograph of the Frenchman.

Washington had decided to answer no more of Conway's communications and he did not waste time in analyzing this letter. From reports brought Washington, it was manifest that if Conway could have neither a conspicuous post with the main Army nor a separate command in the South,[77] he wished to get a place in an expedition the Board of War was hoping to organize for an irruption into Canada.[78] Washington did not believe this enterprise feasible but he felt that he should not intervene or oppose because it was the first venture the new Board had made in strategy.[79] He was the more reserved in passing judgment on the project because he was not taken promptly into the confidence of the Board concerning it, and he was restrained, also, because titular command was to be vested in his trusted young friend, Lafayette.[80]

Before the Canadian adventure took form, Conway had or thought he had, on the 19th of January, the most powerful possible reenforcement. Horatio Gates arrived in York that day [81] and brought with him the original of Conway's letter, alleged to include the reference to a "weak General" and "bad counsellors." Gates showed this paper to Conway and to several other friends [82] and satisfied them it did not contain the sentence Stirling had quoted. Conway was triumphant and was anxious, he said, to have it printed, but he was discouraged by Henry Laurens [83] to whom he spoke of the text, though he did not offer to let the President see it. Laurens read a copy that had been confided to other hands and he wrote a friend that some of the contents were "ten times worse in every way" than the alleged original.[84] In a short time it became generally known that the letter was primarily a display

[77] LOLTW., 18, 20.

[78] Ibid., 10, and 3 Burnett, 60. For the conception of this affair as a raid on the shipping at Fort St. John, consult 3 Burnett, 129. See also ibid., 50, 64; 10 JCC., 84–85, 87, 107, 172, 190–91; 1 Tower, 270, 275; LOLTW., 24–25, 26–27; McDougall to Lafayette, Feb. 18, 1778; McDougall Papers, NYHS; Lafayette to Conway, Feb. 19, 1778; Conway to Gates, Feb. 24, Feb. 25, 1778, Gates Papers, NYHS; Robert Troup to Gates, Feb. 23, Mch. 9, 1778, ibid.

[79] 10 G. W., 433.

[80] Ibid., 355–56; Gates to Washington, Jan. 26, 1778; Gates Papers, NYHS. Washington thought it of importance quietly but clearly to record the fact that prior to approximately Jan. 27, 1778, he had not been made acquainted with the "extent of the objects in view" for the Canadian expedition, "nor the means to be employed to effect them" (Letter of Jan. 27, 1778, to the Board of War, 10 G. W., 355–56). Cf. his observation of Feb. 8, 1778, to Thomas Nelson, Jr.: "An expedition is also on foot against (rather into) Canada, which I am well persuaded is the child of folly, and must be productive of capital ill, circumstanced as our affairs are at present, but as it is the first fruit of our new board of war, I did not incline to say anything against it" (ibid., 432–33).

[81] See Diary of George Neisser, 16 Penn. Mag., 433; cited in 3 Burnett, 42 n.

[82] See Conway to Washington, Jan. 27, 1778; 5 Sparks, 502.

[83] Ibid.

[84] Henry Laurens to Isaac Motte, Jan. 26, 1778; 3 Burnett, 52.

of Conway's military wisdom, in a critique of the Battle of the Brandy-wine, for the loss of which the Frenchman assigned no less than thirteen reasons.[85]

Not until the 22nd of January did Gates receive Washington's reply of the 4th, in which the Commander-in-Chief had explained how he learned of Conway's alleged remark. The next day, January 23, Gates wrote a long answer that reached Washington about the time the short-age of food was beginning to threaten starvation to the tattered men in the huts of Valley Forge. Gates undertook this time to describe the communication, which he pronounced "harmless," and he said of Con-way: "The reasons which, in his judgment, deprived us of the success we could reasonably expect, were methodically explained by him; but neither the 'weakness' of any of our Generals, nor 'bad counsellors' were mentioned." Then Gates proceeded to assert that in spite of the innocuous nature of the letter, "anxiety and jealousy would arise in the breast of every respectable officer, who rendered sensible of faults which inexperience, and that alone, may have led them into, would be un-necessarily disgusted, if they perceived a probability of such errors being recorded." He consequently was returning the letter to Conway, but he repeated, "the paragraph conveyed to your Excellency as a genuine part of it, was in words as well as in substance a wicked forgery."

Then, in self-justification, Gates said that concern over possible delay in tracing a spy who might be transmitting secret documents to the enemy had led him to send to Congress a copy of his communication to Washington. The next paragraph told how Wilkinson had hinted that Robert Troup of Gates's staff might have shown Conway's letter to Alexander Hamilton when that officer had visited Albany to arrange for the transfer of troops to the main Army.[86] "I did not listen," said Gates, "to this insinuation against your aid-de-camp and mine." The

---

[85] 1 *Wilkinson*, 330. To this period belongs the episode of the discovery of a mysterious document on the stairway of the temporary hall of Congress in York. Numerous folios were covered with a lengthy attack on Washington for alleged awkward strategy and shortsighted administration of the Army. An incomplete, "edited" text of this is in 5 *Sparks*, 497–99; the original is in *Papers of G. W.*, LC. Henry Laurens somewhat apologetically on Jan. 27, 1778 forwarded the composition to Washington (3 *Burnett*, 56), who urged that it be laid before Congress and that the Delegates be informed he "would not desire in the least degree to sup-press a free inquiry into any part of my conduct that even faction itself may deem reprehensible" (10 *G. W.*, 410). Nothing was done, both because the charges were anonymous and because they included nothing more than gossip that doubtless had been heard, discussed and dismissed in the taverns of York.

[86] See *supra*, p. 599, n. 76. Troup's account of the affair was not written until 1827 and is primarily an exposé of Wilkinson. The original is in the *Sparks Papers*, Harvard Col. Lib.

communication closed with some words of regret that Washington had predicted—in a letter "which came to me unsealed through the channel of Congress"—that Conway would be proven an "incendiary." Said Gates, "I hope always to find that gentleman a firm and constant friend to America." [87] Nowhere, among all Gates's assurances of the "harmless" character of Conway's critique, was there a single quotation from that paper, or the vaguest hint of an offer to let Washington have a copy of it.

Gates's letter was followed by one in which Conway made similar assertions and averred that only the arguments of Laurens and others had deterred him from publishing what he originally had written Gates. "Therefore, sir," Conway said to Washington, "I must depend upon your justice, candor and generosity, for putting an end to this forgery"; but he, too, failed to send a copy of the critique to prove the truth of what he affirmed.[88] Washington had no intention of resuming any sort of personal relations with Conway and, for that reason, he ignored both the appeal and the omission. The case with Gates was different. As Washington saw it, the commander of the Northern Department was proclaiming himself solicitous for the feelings of the officers and the reputation of the Army when, in reality, he was attempting to conceal an embarrassing and unsoldierly correspondence with a man who would not hesitate to employ any device of self-glorification or selfish advancement. Conway was imposing on Gates, perhaps, but Gates must not be permitted to impose on Congress and the Army. It was of small importance to know what was in the critical letter, but it was a matter of public duty and personal honor to expose the duplicity that attended the circulation and then the suppression of it.

On February 9, approximately the date when the supply of meat failed at Valley Forge, an answer to Gates's defence of January 23 was completed,[89] an answer that wisely was hung on a few brief questions: If the letter of Conway was so "harmless," why was it not made public? Did not Gates insist that "particular actions rather than persons

---

[87] 5 *Sparks*, 500–02.   [88] *Ibid*, 502–03.

[89] The verb is passive because it is not certain Washington drafted this letter, which is one of the most carefully written papers that ever appeared over his signature. The ideas and basic argument undoubtedly were his, but the style has a balance, a smoothness and a regard for the fine points of logical presentation that suggest the hand of a skilled lawyer, rather than of Washington himself. Remarkable as he was for ability to concentrate, even when all the dogs of disaster were howling, it scarcely seems possible that he who carried the woes of an Army on his shoulders could have had mind and hand free for the preparation of so finished a document.

were blamed"? What reason was there, then, for assuming "officers could have been unreasonable enough to take offence at a performance so perfectly inoffensive"?

When the variations on this theme had been played, and the contradictions of Gates's letters exposed, Washington's reply echoed an unusual note of satire on Conway's pretensions:

It is greatly to be lamented, that this adept in Military science did not employ his abilities in the progress of the Campaign, in pointing out those wise measures, which were calculated to give us 'that degree of success we might reasonably expect.' The United States have lost much from that unseasonable diffidence, which prevented his embracing the numerous opportunities he had in Council, of displaying those rich treasures of knowledge and experience he has since so freely laid open to you. I will not do him the injustice to impute the penurious reserve which ever appeared in him upon such occasions to any other cause than an excess of modesty; Neither will I suppose he possesses no other merit than of that after kind of sagacity, which qualifies a Man better for profound discoveries of errors, that have been committed, and advantages that have been lost, than for the exercise of that foresight and provident discernment which enable him to avoid the one and anticipate the other. But, willing as I am to subscribe to all his pretentions, and to believe that his remarks on the operations of the Campaign were very judicious, and that he has sagaciously descanted on many things that might have been done, I cannot help being a little sceptical as to his ability to have found out the means of accomplishing them, or to prove the sufficiency of those in our possession. These Minutiae, I suspect, he did not think worth his attention, particularly, as they might not be within the compass of *his views*.

Sarcasm sometimes may dignify. For that reason, probably, Washington did not permit the letter to end in terms that might indicate he merely differed with Conway on a question of strategy or tactics concerning which there could be two opinions. The issue was one of sincerity or its equivalent, military *bona fides*. Washington was determined to make that clear and he consequently added this:

Notwithstanding the hopeful presages, you are pleased to figure to yourself of General Conway's firm and constant friendship to America, I cannot persuade myself to retract the prediction concerning him; which you so emphatically wish had not been inserted in my Last. A better acquaintance with him, than I have reason to think you have had, from what you say, and a concurrence of circumstances oblige me to give him but little credit for the qualifications of his heart; of which, at least, I beg leave to assume the privilege of being a tolerable judge. Were it necessary, more instances than one might be adduced, from his behaviour and conversation, to manifest, that he is capable of all the malignity of detraction, and all the meanness of intrigue, to gratify the absurd resentment of disappointed vanity, or to answer the purposes of personal aggrandizement, and promote the interests of faction. [90]

Before this was dispatched and probably before it was written, Henry Laurens informed his son at army headquarters that he thought Gates desired a reconciliation with Washington. The President of Congress reported that he had told Gates of Conway's letter concerning the "parallel" between Washington and Frederick. Previously, said Laurens, Gates had not heard of this paper, which he disapproved. When Laurens went on to say in Gates's presence that Conway either had written hypocritically or with unprovoked sarcasm, "the General," Laurens reported, "perfectly acquiesced in that sentiment and added such hints as convinced me he thought lightly of Conway." The South Carolinian then asked his son: "Shall such a man separate friends or keep them asunder? It must not be." [91]

The younger Laurens showed part of this letter to Washington, who remarked, in effect, that Gates was merely the instrument of dangerous men.[92] Nathanael Greene was not precisely of that mind. He thought Thomas Mifflin was at the head of the opposition to Washington and he suspected that Gates was party to it. One circumstance that induced Greene to keep a doubting eye on the commander of the Northern army was the private circulation of Gates's long letter to Washington in a form that put on young Wilkinson the principal blame for the misunderstanding of what Conway had written [93]—an "artifice," said Greene, "too barefaced to deceive anybody." [94] Whoever the men might be that supported Conway in his cabal against Washington,

---

[90] 10 G. W., 440–41, verbatim; inaccurately printed in 5 Sparks, 504–07.
[91] Letter of Feb. 3, 1778; 3 Burnett, 70–71.
[92] John Laurens to his father, Feb. 9, 1778; 3 Burnett, 70 n.
[93] The changed paragraphs, at the end of the letter, are printed in 5 Sparks, 502 n. If the MS of this in the Gates Papers, NYHS, represents the original form of the communication, the slurs on Hamilton and Wilkinson were stricken from the text of the letter sent Washington. The supposition usually has been that these charges were added to the copy retained by Gates after the paper was dispatched to Washington.
[94] Greene to Knox, about Feb. 7, 1778; 2 Greene's Greene, 31.

they were, Greene thought, in great discredit and were "prodigiously frightened." [95]

Washington himself scarcely cared whether they were aggressive or disheartened. He would scotch Conway; for the rest, he wished all friends of America, and particularly all soldiers, to work amicably together. In this state of mind he received on the 23rd of February Gates's acknowledgment of his letter of the 9th, which apparently had not reached York until the 18th. Gates said:

. . . [I] earnestly hope no more of that time, so precious to the public, may be lost upon the subject of General Conway's letter. Whether that gentleman does or does not deserve the suspicions you express, would be entirely indifferent to me, did he not possess an office of high rank in the Army of the United States; for that reason solely I wish he may answer all the expectations of Congress. As to the gentleman, I have no personal connection with him, nor have I any correspondence, previous to his writing the letter which has given offence; nor have I since written to him, save to certify what I know to be the contents of the letter. He therefore must be responsible; as I heartily dislike controversy, even upon my own account, and much more in a matter in which I was only accidentally concerned. In regard to the parts of your Excellency's letter addressed particularly to me, I solemnly declare that I am of no faction; and if any of my letters taken aggregately or by paragraphs convey any meaning, which in any construction is offensive to your Excellency, that was by no means the intention of the writer. After this, I cannot believe your Excellency will either suffer your suspicions or the prejudices of others to induce you to spend another moment upon this subject.[96]

Washington replied the next day:

I am as averse to controversy, as any Man and had I not been forced into it, you never would have had occasion to impute to me, even the shadow of a disposition towards it. Your repeatedly and Solemnly disclaiming any offensive views, in those matters that have been the subject of our past correspondence, makes me willing to close with the desire, you express, of burying them hereafter in silence, and, as far as future events will permit, oblivion. My temper leads me to peace and harmony with all Men; and it is peculiarly my wish, to avoid any personal feuds with those, who are embarked in the same great National interest with myself, as every difference of this kind must in its consequences be very injurious.[97]

[95] Ibid.   [96] 5 Sparks, 512.
[97] Letter of Feb. 24, 1778; 10 G. W., 508–09, verbatim.

Washington prudently made reservation in the words "as far as future events will permit." He had particular reason for doing this because of a letter from Patrick Henry, who enclosed an anonymous missive that repeated most of the complaints against Washington. Written in York, this paper asserted: "The northern army has shown us what Americans are capable of doing, with a General at their head. The spirit of the southern army is no way inferior to the spirit of the northern. A Gates, a Lee, or a Conway would in a few weeks render them an irresistible body of men." Not once was the name of Washington used, but the innuendo was that of his incompetence in command. The author took good pains in writing Henry to say that if his handwriting gave a hint of his identity, the name must not be mentioned. "Even the letter," one anxious sentence ran, "must be thrown in the fire." [98] To Washington's astonishment, the autograph unquestionably was that of Dr. Benjamin Rush, who, Washington wrote Henry, "has been elaborate and studied in his professions of regard for me, and long since the letter to you." [99] Nothing was to be gained by raising an issue over this, but it was enough to keep Washington on the alert. To a certain extent, the same thing was true of the hot dispute, involving the threat of duels with Gates and Stirling, that James Wilkinson pursued to vindicate himself from the accusation that he betrayed Gates's confidence and had his own betrayed in turn by Stirling. It seemed to Washington that Wilkinson was entitled to see the correspondence that involved him. With Stirling's consent the papers were shown the young officer and the relevant facts were explained.[100] What Wilkinson did thereafter seemed to the Commander-in-Chief a personal matter.

[98] Letter from York, Jan. 12, 1778; 5 *Sparks*, 495–97.
[99] 11 *G. W.*, 164.
[100] *Ibid.*, 125; cf. 1 *Wilkinson*, 395. Wilkinson stated that he twice declined invitations to headquarters but was prevailed upon at length to go. In the end, Wilkinson was the heaviest direct loser through the controversy. It was reported that Gates refused to accept him as Secretary of the Board of War (Nathanael Greene to Henry Knox, c. Feb. 8, 1778, 2 *Greene's Greene*, 31), but in reality, after a temporary patch-up of their differences, Wilkinson served until Mch. 29, 1778, when he resigned indignantly (1 *Wilkinson*, 409–10) in a letter so abusive of Gates that Congress refused to permit the paper to remain among the records (10 *JCC.*, 297). Meantime, it would appear, a protest by a few regimental commanders (3 *Burnett*, 64) had been enlarged or was alleged to have been extended, to the signature of forty-seven Colonels (1 *Wilkinson*, 389) who complained of Wilkinson's election as brevet Brigadier. Wilkinson, in response, offered his resignation from the Army, which Congress accepted, Mch. 6, 1778 (10 *JCC.*, 226). His *Memoirs* (v. 1, 330 ff) give his version of his part in the discovery and defeat of the cabal. Gates's accusation of Wilkinson was in a note of Feb. 23, 1778, evidently written in answer to a demand for an explanation. Tersely Gates prefaced in these words an extract from the letter of Washington to him, Jan. 4, 1778 (10 *G. W.*, 263: "[This] will show

Whether or not rivalry and backbiting were renewed, Washington thus far had profited doubly by what now had come to be known as "Conway's cabal." If any ambitious officer or politician had been under the impression that amiability and politeness covered an unresentful, compliant nature readily dominated by less able and more positive minds, they discovered in the exchange with Gates that the head of the Army could be a vigorous, unflinching adversary—a man best left alone or treated with the deference he showed to others. He might not be invincible in controversy but, with the resources he commanded, personally and through his friends, he was not to be assailed by any who took their task lightly. That was one gain from the dispute. The other was the evidence from many sources that the nature of Washington's burden and the integrity of his command were understood by men of station and judgment. An illustrative tale came down from the North: Gates was reported to have informed Col. Daniel Morgan of the rangers that the principal officers of the Army intended to resign unless Washington was replaced. Morgan was said to have answered, "I have one favor to ask of you, sir, which is never to mention that detestable subject to me again; for under no other man than Washington as Commander-in-Chief would I ever serve." [101] Joseph Jones, retiring as a Virginia member of Congress, had written Washington in January, concerning Mifflin and Gates: ". . . Whatever may be the design of these men, and however artfully conducted, I have no doubt that in the end it will redound to their own disgrace. You stand too high in the public opinion to be easily reached by their attempts and the same equal and disinterested conduct, the same labor and attention, which you have mani-

---

how your honor has been called in question, which is all the explanation necessary upon that matter—any other satisfaction you may command." To the quotation from Washington's letter, Gates added: "After reading the whole of the above extract I am astonished if you really gave Major McWilliams such information. How could you intimate to me that it was possible Colonel Troup had conversed with Colonel Hamilton on the subject of General Conway's letter" (*Gates Papers*, NYHS). Numerous other relevant documents, some of them unpublished, are included in the same *Papers*. Among them are Wilkinson's challenge of Gates, Feb. 24, 1778; Benjamin Stoddard's appeal to Gates, Mch. 1, 1778, for a reconciliation with the repudiated aide; William Gordon to Gates, Mch. 16, 1778; Wilkinson's demand on Stirling, Mch. 18, 1778, for a statement that the disclosure of Conway's alleged remarks on Washington was made "in a convivial hour"; and Robert Troup to Gates, Mch. 26, 1778, on the fortunate outcome of the threatened duel. In 70 *Papers of G. W.*, 119, LC, is Wilkinson's memorandum, Mch. 28, 1778, of his conversation with Gates that day. Col. Walter Stewart's efforts to make peace between Gates and Wilkinson are recorded in appeals of Feb. 4 and 8, 1778, to Gates (*Letters to Gates*, NYHS).

[101] James Graham, *Life of Daniel Morgan*, 173, cited in 2 *Greene's Greene*, 15. When Morgan returned to the main Army, he was so vehement in his support of Washington that Richard Peters accused him of trying to pick a quarrel. See Peters to Joseph Reed, Jan. 29, 1778; 4 *Wayne Papers*, 72, and Robert Troup to Gates, Apr. 8, 1778, *Gates Papers*, NYHS.

fested in the public service from the first of the contest, will shield and protect you from the shafts of envy and malevolence." [102]

Perhaps the most discerning letter that came to Washington was from Patrick Henry, who wrote again soon after he sent Washington the anonymous attack by Benjamin Rush. Said Henry, with something of the wrath that had echoed in his greatest speeches: "While you face the armed enemies of our liberty in the field, and by the favor of God have been kept unhurt, I trust your country will never harbor in her bosom the miscreant, who would ruin her best supporter. I wish not to flatter; but when arts, unworthy honest men, are used to defame and traduce you, I think it not amiss but a duty to assure you of that estimation in which the public hold you . . ." [103] Briefer and more dramatic was Mercy Warren's report to her husband: "The toast among the soldiers, Washington or no Army." [104]

In none of these letters was there any expression of doubt concerning the reality of the cabal against him, nor did Washington's friends in camp or at York have difficulty in identifying some of the men involved in the attempt to oust the Commander-in-Chief. All the supporters of Washington felt sure that Conway arrogantly conspired against him— and probably hoped for larger pay and greater influence under another, a new head of the Army; but few could believe the Frenchman had either the finesse or the knowledge of America required to lead so complicated an enterprise as that of getting rid of a leader whose popularity still was greater than that of any other soldier or any Delegate.

Who, then, was prompting Conway or using him as a mouthpiece? Horatio Gates and Thomas Mifflin were the two men most widely suspected, and they were thought by some to have given indisputable proof of their purpose to supplant Washington, but there was more than one opinion of the precise extent to which the Northern commander and the former Quartermaster General had committed themselves. Their ambitious wish was taken for granted: their hostile acts could not be specified to the satisfaction of all of Washington's supporters. Alexander McDougall wrote Nathanael Greene, for example, "I have heard much of the machinations of a certain junta to intrigue our Chief out

---

[102] 3 Burnett, 44. Cf. Jonathan Bayard Smith to Joseph Reed, Feb. 21, 1778: "The General's conduct on occasions truly affecting to a man's honor, evinces how much more infinitely he prefers the good of his country to any personal considerations" (ibid., 93).

[103] Henry to Washington, Mch. 5, 1778; 5 Sparks, 513–14.

[104] Letter of Mch. 10, 1778; 2 Warren-Adams Letters, 7. Cf. Memoir of Samuel Shaw, 45.

of command, but I want such proof of it as will bear the public eye." [105]
In the particular case of Mifflin, even those champions of Washington
most convinced of the Pennsylvanian's leadership in the cabal were well
nigh baffled in their attempts to draw a moral indictment of a man who
fast was acquiring the arts of political equivocation.[106] Mifflin himself
"solemnly disavowed" that he was aiming to remove the Commander-
in-Chief.[107]

Gates was put by Washington's supporters in a category different
from that of Conway and Mifflin. The victor of Saratoga was believed
to be anxious to succeed Washington and was proved, by his own
words, to have corresponded with Conway. If Wilkinson was to be
believed, Gates had been much pleased with Conway's critique of the
failure on the Brandywine and had "read it in triumph." [108] The undertone of Gates's letters to those who congratulated him on his military success was expectant and cordial; his disregard of the channels of
command through Washington was deliberate and must have been designed to establish entirely independent relations with Congress. In the
same way, his early acts as President of the Board of War were not
those of an official disposed to cooperate with the Commander-in-

---

[105] Letter of Feb. 25, 1778; *McDougall Papers*, NYHS.

[106] 3 *Burnett*, 21, 44, 93; George Lux to Nathanael Greene, Apr. 28, 1778, F. R. Kirkland,
ed., *Letters on the American Revolution in the Library at Karolfred*, 51–53, quoted in small
part in 2 *Greene's Greene*, 37; same to same, May 20, 1778, *Greene Papers*, Clements Lib.
Even after 150 years, it is exceedingly difficult to appraise the full extent of Mifflin's participation in the cabal, primarily for the reason that no large collection of his letters is known to
remain in existence. Scattered papers bearing his signature are found in various collections,
but none of those uncovered in the present study has yielded any firm proof of his active direction of the campaign to displace Washington. One of the suggestive items has been known for
many years. In a letter of Nov. 28, 1777, Mifflin wrote to Gates of Conway's "just sentiments,"
presumably those expressed in the critical review of the Brandywine (5 *Sparks*, 485). Another
possible hint mistakenly has been thought to lie in a letter Conway addressed to Gates, Nov. 9,
1777, when the Frenchman was planning to return to France, in disgust over the refusal of
Congress at that time to give him the rank of Major General. Conway said: "I will ever
cherish the cause in which General Mifflin is engaged and shall be happy to serve it as far as
I can with propriety." This almost certainly referred to Mifflin's plans for importing supplies
and equipment from France, as set forth, *supra*, p. 529, n. 42. Mifflin's few surviving letters to
Gates indicate that the two men corresponded frequently. The absence of most of these papers
from Gates's carefully kept files may mean the letters were so sharply critical that Gates destroyed them.

[107] See Timothy Pickering to Alexander Scammell, Feb. 17, 1778; 1 *Pickering*, 206, quoted
in 3 *Burnett*, 79 n. Significant, also, is a passage to this effect in a letter of introduction Mifflin
gave the Chevalier de Crenis, Apr. 17, 1778, when the Frenchman was going to wait on
Gates. It was Mifflin's opinion that de Crenis could instruct young officers most usefully, but
Mifflin wrote: "For my part I am determined to be cautious [in] what I propose lest I should
from the infamous treatment I have met with and the wicked suspicions of some great men be
considered as scheming for revenge or making establishments for sinister purposes" (*Letters
to Gates*, NYHS).

[108] 1 *Wilkinson*, 408.

Chief.[109] Washington believed Gates to be hostile and he probably did not underestimate the great increase in that officer's reputation after the events of September and October, 1777; but from the time Gates was caught in the inconsistencies of refusal to make Conway's letter public, Washington apparently felt that Gates would not again associate with the Frenchman or make another effort at an early date to win first place in army command. Even so, Washington kept up his guard.

To what extent did the participants in the cabal, identified or suspected, have support in Washington's Army and in Gates's? It would have been miraculous if every influential officer at Valley Forge had remained uncritical of Washington throughout the hardships and hunger, the crowding and the shivering of the weeks'-long torture in the wintry camp. Complainants may have been numerous; active sharers in the move to displace Washington were few.[110] Although John Sullivan's love of popularity had led him to seek the good will of all parties to the controversy,[111] in the pinch he almost certainly would have supported Washington and his own subordinates who were resentful of the promotion of Conway and of Wilkinson. In Gates's army the situation was substantially the same. Among his officers must have been some ambitious individuals who hoped for their rise through his, but of these men and their machinations Washington heard nothing. Instead, at the end of May he was to write a long-time friend in Virginia: "I have very sufficient reasons for thinking that no officers in the Army are more attached to me than those from the northward, and of those none more so than the gentlemen who were under the immediate command of G—s last campaign." [112] Washington's statement was inclusive. When the immediate exchange of correspondence and gossip had ended, he wrote: "That there was a scheme of this sort on foot, last fall, admits of no doubt; but it originated in another quar-

---

109 This was shown particularly in his reticence concerning the "irruption" into Canada. See *supra*, p. 598, n. 80.

110 If any man of prominence at headquarters joined hands with the open foes of Washington, he perhaps was the former Judge Advocate General, Lt. Col. William Tudor. As will appear in the narrative of 1779, Tudor was avowedly a critic of Washington's in the spring of that year, but the current research has brought to light no reference of his name in connection with the cabal during the winter of 1777–78. Outside the Army, Rev. William Gordon could not have been accounted a member of the cabal and he doubtless would have denied most earnestly that he had anything short of the greatest veneration for Washington, but a sympathetic and almost tearful letter to Gates, May 14, 1778 (*Letters to Gates*, NYHS) shows him most anxious "neither you nor Mifflin nor any other officer will be sacrificed to a junto."

111 Cf. *supra*, p. 547, and 2 *Sullivan Papers*, 14–16.

112 Letter of May 30, 1778, to Landon Carter; 11 *G. W.*, 493.

ter . . . with three men who wanted to aggrandize themselves; but, finding no support, on the contrary that their conduct and views, when seen into, were likely to undergo severe reprehension, they slunk back, disavowed the measure, and professed themselves my warmest admirers. Thus stands the matter at present. Whether any members of Congress were privy to this scheme and inclined to aid and abet it, I shall not take upon me to say, but am well informed that no whisper of the kind was ever heard in Congress." [113]

Although Washington did not name the individuals who told him of the attitude of Congress, those who gave him assurance included, among others, President Henry Laurens and Charles Carroll of Maryland. As early as Jan. 12, 1778, Laurens had written Lafayette: "I think the friends of our brave and virtuous General may rest assured that he is out of the reach of his enemies, if he has an enemy, a fact of which I am in doubt of [sic] . . . All men acknowledge General Washington's virtue, his personal bravery, nor do I ever hear his military abilities questioned but comparatively, with the fortunate event you allude to," Burgoyne's surrender.[114] Two months after Laurens penned this, Col. John Fitzgerald of Washington's staff rode southward and, en route, talked with Charles Carroll, then one of the members of the Maryland delegation in Congress. Fitzgerald wrote his chief: "Mr. C—ll . . . was very uneasy at a report having prevailed that a combination was formed in Congress against you and gave me the strongest assurance that he never heard a member of the House utter a word which could be construed in the least disrespect for you except once and then a gentleman was so warmly replied to from different quarters that he has since been silent on that head." [115] Carroll should have excepted specifically James Duane of New York and James Lovell of Massachusetts, a school-

---

[113] *Ibid.*, 493–94. In this quotation and the one preceding, the punctuation has been conformed to modern usage.

[114] 3 *Burnett*, 29.

[115] Fitzgerald to Washington, from Alexandria, Va., Mch. 17, 1778; 69 *Papers of G. W.*, 115, LC. Colonel Fitzgerald added: "I thought it too delicate a point to ask who this was but have some reason to believe it was your friend from this State whose good intentions you have for some time suspected." He doubtless was referring to Richard Henry Lee, whose coolness to Washington at this time may be inferred from the letters the Virginia Delegate occasionally wrote the Commander-in-Chief. There are no direct criticisms of Washington in Lee's correspondence, and one reference only that may be construed as a hint that Lee was associated with a movement that might possibly have been directed against Washington. This was in a long letter of Nov. 23, 1777 to Samuel Adams, as follows: "General Mifflin has been here, and he urges strongly the necessity of having General Gates to be President of the new Board of War. He thinks the military knowledge and the authority of Gates necessary to procure the indispensable changes in our Army. I believe he is right" (1 *Ballagh, Lee Letters*, 358).

master turned Delegate. Duane was believed by some of Washington's close associates to be active in the cabal; [116] Lovell, a man of the greatest assiduity in his work, possessed high admiration for Gates, with whom he carried on a correspondence that contained numerous slurs on the Commander-in-Chief and some sarcasms at Washington's expense.[117]

At strongest, the hostile, the disaffected and the unacquainted in Congress [118] and in the Army showed themselves so feeble when challenged that this question rises: Should Washington have given attention to the cabal? Did he invest it with distinction and lose a certain measure of dignity on his own account, when he made so much of Conway's criticism? Could the three assumed leaders in the movement against him do what Washington's friends feared the trio might—put so many obstacles in his way through the activities of the new Board of War, dominated by Gates and Mifflin, that Washington would resign in disgust or frustration? [119]

Washington made no effort to answer these questions while the maneuvers against him were in progress, and later when the cabal manifestly had become powerless, he had more important concerns. His observations, at one time or another, show that he had mixed motives for giving serious attention to the affair: he confessed to Henry Laurens, ". . . conscious as I am of having ever done all in my power to answer the important purposes of the trust reposed in me," knowledge that a "malignant faction" had been operating to his hurt "could

[116] See Nathanael Greene to Alexander McDougall, Apr. 16, 1778: "I am well informed there is one of your New York members extreme inimical to the Commander-in-Chief. He says it is folly to have any considerable force, that the General does not know how to manage considerable large bodies of men. He is a great friend to the Irish hero and is closely connected with the junto" (*McDougall Papers*, NYHS). By elimination from the New York delegation then in Congress, Duane alone fitted this description.

[117] See 3 *Burnett*, 42, 477, 493. The sketch of Lovell in *DAB* is by the late E. C. Burnett and is believed to be a just appraisal of the man. As Burnett stated, it is impossible to say to what extent Lovell sponsored or furthered the Conway cabal but there can be no doubt, from the evidence, that he sympathized with it and had a sharp dislike to Washington or, at the least, a jealous resentment of what he considered the semi-deification of the Commander-in-Chief.

[118] The facts set forth in the text are a sufficient refutation of the story in Dunlop's *History of New York*, v. 2, p. 133, that Congress was almost evenly divided over a proposed resolve to "arrest" Washington as a means of supplanting him as Commander-in-Chief. As the tale ran, Washington's friends learned in advance of the scheme and, though outnumbered by one on the day set for the passage of the resolve, managed to get Gouverneur Morris to the floor in time to prevent any action. William Duer was said to have been exceedingly ill but was alleged to have asserted he would be carried on his bed into the hall, so that he could vote against the resolve, even if it cost him his life. No basis for this fabrication exists. It probably had its origin in the anticipated closeness of the vote on the "half-pay" resolves, for which see 3 *Burnett*, 164–65, 173.

[119] Cf. James Craik to Washington, Jan. 6, 1778; 64 *Papers of G. W.*, 137, a part of which is printed in 5 *Sparks*, 493–94.

not but give me some pain on a personal account . . ." That was one consideration. The second and "chief concern," he told the same friend, arose "from an apprehension of the dangerous consequences which intestine dissensions may produce to the common cause." [120] As he explained to the Marquis de Lafayette, the cabal involved the "fatal tendency of disunion." [121] For that reason he was convinced that it should be resisted to the utmost, regardless of its strength or weakness; and he doubtless shared the feeling of Nathanael Greene that it was defeated easily because it was challenged promptly.[122] Washington took the action he did, in the third place, because he regarded Conway as a treacherous personal foe. The Frenchman's malignancy and, later, Gates's evasion violated Washington's sense of honor, aroused his wrath and made him resolve that he would not permit a self-seeking faction— "three men who wanted to aggrandize themselves" [123]—to drive him from his post of duty, of service and of honor.

His enemies sneeringly styled him "demigod" [124] but he was in nothing more completely human than in dealing with the Conway cabal.

[120] Letter of Jan. 31, 1778; 10 *G. W.*, 410.

[121] Letter of Dec. 31, 1777; *ibid.*, 237.

[122] Cf. Greene to McDougall: Feb. 5, 1778: ". . . the poor and shallow politicians unmasked their batteries before they were ready to attempt any execution . . ." (*McDougall Papers*, NYHS).

[123] Letter of May 30, 1778, to Landon Carter; 11 *G. W.*, 493–94.

[124] Cf. Lovell to Samuel Adams, Jan. 20, 1778: "You could not expect more smartness in a resolve which was meant to rap a Demi G— over the knuckles . . ." (3 *Burnett*, 42).

CHAPTER XXIV

Spring Comes to America

(March 15–April 30, 1778)

Resolute as Washington proved to be in facing the Conway cabal and in trying to hold the Army together in the winter of 1777–78, he could not say until after the end of April that he had defeated Conway finally and irrevocably. While the Frenchman was at Albany preparing for the Canadian "irruption," he had been deep in discontent and particularly so after the coming of Kalb.[1] By the beginning of April Conway was fuming over an "unaccountable way of boxing me about" and he was outraged that another man now had the place he had desired as Inspector General. Once again he professed his willingness to resign,[2] and injudiciously did so, in tones promptly described as "taunting."[3] Congress accepted the resignation on the 28th—with two of the four votes against that action cast by Delegates from Washington's own State[4]—and it refused to reconsider when Conway expostulated that he had not meant his letter to be more than a private communication to President Laurens.[5] During the course of this vain maneuver to repeat his success of 1777 in gaining promotion by threatening to go home, Conway wrote Washington what the Commander-in-Chief called "another impertinent letter," in which he "demanded" that he be assigned a Division in the continental Army.[6] When Washington ignored this, and Congress no longer paid any attention to Conway, that officer's strange influence was at an end.

Washington could not write that word "end" at the bottom of the story of Valley Forge on March 15 or on April 1. Even when the mud dried in the roads and green appeared in the fields, he had no assur-

---

[1] Conway to Gates, Feb. 25, 1778; *Gates Papers*, NYHS; Kalb to Comte de Broglie, Apr. 10, 1778; 830 *Stevens Facsimiles*.

[2] Conway to Gates, Apr. 3 [or 2?], 1778; *ibid.*

[3] 3 *Burnett*, 211.

[4] Francis Lightfoot Lee and John Banister, 10 *JCC.*, 399. The resignation was dated April 22nd.

[5] 3 *Burnett*, 211, 212, 260, 273, 276, 277.

[6] 11 *G. W.*, 414. The letter is not in the *Papers of G. W.*, LC.

ance his troops would get sufficient meat every day.[7] There was emergence, not deliverance, from the miseries of Valley Forge. Every gain might be lost through the accidents of nature or the negligence of man. If, by good fortune, the pens at camp were crowded temporarily with bullocks for slaughter, and Washington consequently did not have to fear that his men would be half-starved before a week was out, he always had an accumulated burden of business, the most galling part of which was put on his shoulders by men who wished to leave the Army.

No particular regret was recorded when Joseph Spencer resigned the Rhode Island command and his commission as Major General, but as neither Israel Putnam nor William Heath was considered acceptable in his stead, Washington had to send John Sullivan and with no guarantee that Congress would elect an additional officer of divisional rank.[8] At the time the command in Rhode Island was being discussed, it was manifest that a change would be necessary in New York also. A great name had lost its resonance there; the frail nag, reputation, no longer would carry an obese rider. On the 16th of March, Alexander McDougall was named to relieve "Old Put," whose standing as a commander was alleged to have been destroyed by indolence, ignorance and patent incompetence.[9] The veteran of Bunker Hill was given the task, more important than honorific, of hurrying forward the recruits from New England, an assignment that made him agitate for more active duty.[10] Meantime he posted himself, so to say, on the list of the dissatisfied higher elements in the Army—the three Virginia Brigadiers, who were quarreling over their relative rank,[11] and the other Generals

---

[7] An excellent review of the difficulties the Commissary General of Purchases had to endure because of distance, lack of able assistants and, above all, private speculation will be found in William Buchanan to the Board of War, Mch. 4, 1778, with explanatory note of the same date to Washington in 68 *Papers of G. W.*, 105, 106, LC. Buchanan had been sick and wished to retire as soon as he cleared himself of charges implied in Congress' resolve that inquiry be made into the conduct of his department (Buchanan to the President of Congress, Mch. 20, 1778, 78 *Papers Cont. Cong.*, 114, LC).

[8] 10 *JCC.*, 47, 94, 188; 3 *Burnett*, 91, 103, 111; 11 *G. W.*, 1, 31, 56; 2 *Webb*, 14 n. Sullivan was very unhappy at this time and twice applied for leave in which to attend to his distressed personal affairs. See 2 *Sullivan Papers*, 17–19, 20. His early difficulties in Rhode Island are reported in *ibid.*, 44, 47, 50, 57, 83.

[9] 11 *G. W.*, 68, 69, 90–91, 95–97, 100, 101–02, 103. The harshest, most inclusive indictment of Putnam will be found in George Clinton to Alexander McDougall, Nov. 7, 1778; *McDougall Papers*, NYHS. Cf. R. R. Livingston to Washington, Apr. 12, 1778 (*R. R. Livingston Papers*, NYPL).

[10] Cf. 11 *G. W.*, 319.

[11] 10 *JCC.*, 269. This clash of jealous and ambitious men, Peter Muhlenberg, William Woodford and George Weedon, may be traced through the index of 11 *G. W.*, and 12 *JCC.* See also George Weedon to the President of Congress, Dec. 26, 1777 (11 *Weedon Papers*, APS, Philadelphia) and Anthony Wayne to Washington, Dec. 29, 1777 (4 *Wayne Papers*, p. 60,

who thought themselves affronted by the promotion of Conway and Wilkinson.[12] Among field and company officers, the "rash of resignation" had become a disease that menaced and might prove mortal. It was especially severe in the cavalry [13] and in the Virginia Regiments,[14] but was so nearly pandemic that Washington estimated the number of resignations at more than 200 within eight months.[15] Every day he had applications from two or three officers who wished to leave the service.[16] Congress reserved to itself the right to pass on these requests of field and general officers; [17] where he felt authorized to act, Washington said "No," particularly to officers of his own State, and he deferred some applications he knew he would be compelled to grant later,[18] for the reason often and anxiously advanced the previous winter, namely, the financial distress of the applicants.

Even when officers could provide for their families, some of them found that military service was destroying their opportunities of accumulating anything for the future. As Washington studied the needs of these men and the requirements of the Army, he saw three alternatives, three only: Congress must make the requested provision for retirement pay, or the number of qualified leaders would "moulder to nothing," or, again, in his own plain words, the officers corps would "be composed of low and illiterate men void of capacity for this, or any other business." [19] Although Washington went so far as to say, "I do most religiously believe the salvation of the cause depends upon" the grant of retirement pay,[20] he found persistent opposition in Congress, even among men as devoted to him as President Laurens was.[21] Until this was overcome, and the "half-pay establishment" was set up, the resignation of desirable officers and the resulting threat to the intelli-

---

PHS). A later but scarcely less wrathful review by Weedon of his "degredation" in being declared the junior of Woodford appears in Weedon to Greene, Sept. 20, 1779 (*Greene Papers*, Clements Lib.).

[12] James Varnum to McDougall, Feb. 7, 1778; McDougall to Varnum, Feb. 26, 1778; *McDougall Papers*, NYHS.

[13] 11 *G. W.*, 244–45.

[14] Washington wrote, Apr. 21, 1778, that ninety officers of Virginia troops had presented him their resignations. *Ibid.*, 285.

[15] *Ibid.*, 139.   [16] *Ibid.*, 237.

[17] *Ibid.*, 50. See, for example, the acceptance of General Learned's resignation, 10 *JCC.*, 281.

[18] 11 *G. W.*, 210 ff.

[19] Letter of Apr. 10, 1778, to the President of Congress; 11 *G. W.*, 237; cf. *ibid.*, 285, 327, 332.

[20] *Ibid.*

[21] 10 *JCC.*, 285, 359, 362, 373–74, 393, 394 ff; 3 *Burnett*, 154, 162–63, 163–64, 169, 173, 174, 176, 181 ff., 191, 210, 213, 214, 221. James Lovell was sarcastic concerning Washington's choice of words in advocating half pay, *ibid.*, 173.

gent leadership of the troops could not be ended. That remained Washington's conviction. While Congress doubted and debated, he had to soothe as many of the officers as he could and, at the same time, to deny furloughs which some of his Generals had been allowing with excessive freedom during the winter.[22] He was obliged to refuse those who sought to comfort their wives or to repair their finances, to say nothing of those who wanted to visit their sweethearts. Capt. Benjamin Walker presented as best he could the usual arguments for a furlough during which he might console his affianced. When the General shook his head, Walker broke out—

"If I don't go, she will die."

"Oh, no; women do not die for such trifles."

"But, General, what shall I do?"

"What will you do? Why, write to her to add another leaf to the book of sufferings." [23]

The officers who heard of this exchange smiled at it, but there was no smiling at headquarters over the thinness of the corps of native officers, and none over the sensitiveness of some of the foreigners. Fermoy and a few others continued vainly to plead for more money or higher rank;[24] a number of good men were commissioned;[25] the claims or pretensions of others were compromised at the same time that applicants were discouraged;[26] the Count Pulaski and the Marquis de Lafayette became problems.

Pulaski spoke no English, did not understand Americans, and soon found himself in so much difficulty that he resigned the general command of the cavalry and successfully solicited permission to organize an independent corps, in which he was authorized by Congress to enlist deserters if Washington approved.[27] Washington had no intention of allowing this, because experience had shown that deserters often ran away from the service they had adopted, and especially from the Light Horse, in order to get the bounty the British allowed those who brought in a mount and its furnishings. The Commander-in-Chief consequently was surprised and provoked to learn, a little later, that Pulaski

[22] 11 G. W., 226. [23] Duponceau in Chinard, 18.

[24] Cf. Fermoy to Gates, Jan. 21, 1778; Gates Papers, NYHS; 10 JCC., 174.

[25] For example, du Coudray's Sergeants (10 JCC., 118–19).

[26] Ibid., 122, 138, 138–39, 155, 157, 177.

[27] 11 G. W., 81, 230; John Laurens, 141; 10 JCC., 291, 312. In applying for permission to organize this corps, Pulaski stated that he had been "Commander-in-Chief of the Army of Poland," 2 LTW., 87. This, in reality, was the revolutionary force raised by his father, Count Joseph Pulaski, under the Confederation of Bar.

had been recruiting among prisoners of war.[28] It was in part because
of Pulaski's mishandling that Washington saw little prospect of having
the cavalry take the field in the spring, well trained and adequately
mounted,[29] though there was reason to hope for good performance by
young Harry Lee who was promoted Major and was entrusted with
recruiting and directing independently two Companies of Light Dragoons.[30]

Lafayette was a problem of a different sort. He was able, diligent,
appreciative and almost embarrassingly affectionate. At the same time,
he was ambitious to such a degree and was so insistent on the avoidance
of any impairment of what he already considered a high reputation that
after the ludicrous failure of the attempt at an "irruption" into Canada,
he had to be nursed and coddled by Congress and by Washington.[31]
The youthful Marquis was lovable in spite of his vanity; but in the
behavior of numerous other officers, native and foreign, who quarrelled
and complained about rank and everything else, there was much to irk
and to perplex Washington.

When all the whims and frailties and derelictions of malcontents
were added to the doubts of the campaign, Washington still found hope
for America in the performance of two men that spring, one a newcomer and the other an old lieutenant with a changed assignment. On
February 23 an attractive German soldier, aged 47, had come to Valley
Forge with letters from President Laurens, who introduced him as
"Baron Stüben" and explained that after a conference between a committee and this "illustrious stranger," Congress had voted its thanks
for the gentleman's tender of service as a volunteer and had directed
him to report to Washington.[32] This was procedure unhappily familiar
to the busy General at headquarters. He had been compelled to listen
endlessly as foreign soldiers had told him through an interpreter what
great men they were and what priceless service they could give America
if . . . Only as that "if" had been specified in terms of rank and pay
had there been substantial difference among the adventurers from

---

[28] 11 *G. W.*, 337.
[29] *Ibid.*, 275; Cf. 9 V 60–61. Col. Stephen Moylan temporarily succeeded to the command
of the four Regiments, 11 *G. W.*, 114–15.
[30] Washington had invited Lee to serve on his staff, but the young officer preferred field
service, 11 *G. W.*, 198. For his promotion and authority to enlist and equip a "separate corps,"
see *ibid.*, 205–06, 251; 10 *JCC.*, 314–15, 401; 3 *Burnett*, 158, 197. The reason for raising
Lee's rank is given *infra*, p. 627.
[31] *LOLTW.*, 35; 11 *G. W.*, 59, 60, 113, 240; 10 *JCC.*, 217, 254.
[32] 10 *JCC.*, 50; 3 *Burnett*, 91.

across the Atlantic. Steuben had a new approach. With John Laurens to put his acquired French into English,[33] the visitor said he would prefer to remain for a time at camp and to become acquainted before he undertook any specific task, lest hasty appointment give offence. Washington's questions elicited the admission that Steuben, who said he had been a Lieutenant General in the service of Frederick the Great, was interested in the training of troops and would be glad to receive the rank and pay of a Major General, though he did not desire the command of a Division.[34]

The apparent candor, the asserted rank under a renowned King, and the delightful personality of Steuben prompted Washington to approve a temporary arrangement which soon created confidence in the character, the equipment and the zeal of the Prussian. Within little more than a fortnight, Washington detached 100 men as a supplementary Headquarters Guard and assigned them to Steuben for training in drill and maneuver.[35] By the end of another week, Washington was writing of Steuben as a "gentleman of high military rank, profound knowledge and great experience in his profession," who was to be "at the head" of a "department of inspection." [36] This was followed immediately by an extraordinary honor: Washington announced that Steuben "[had] obligingly undertaken to exercise the office of Inspector General" and that, until the pleasure of Congress was known, Steuben was to be obeyed and respected in that position and was to have "every aid" other officers could give.[37] Congress soon approved Steuben's system of maneuver and made him a Major General [38] in which position he aroused enthusiastic interest and at the outset stirred few antagonisms.[39]

No other foreign soldier, except Lafayette and perhaps the engineer Duportail, so quickly won a place in the esteem of the Army.[40] As Henry Laurens reported to an absent member of Congress, Steuben "has hit the taste of the officers, gives universal satisfaction and I am assured has made an amazing improvement in discipline." [41] Adjutant

---

[33] *John Laurens*, 131–32. [34] *Ibid.*
[35] 11 *G. W.*, 98.
[36] Letter of Mch. 24, 1778, to Francis Barber; 11 *G. W.*, 136.
[37] GOs of Mch. 28, 1778; 11 *G. W.*, 163.
[38] May 4, 1778; 11 *JCC*, 465.
[39] Cf. Steuben to Gates, Mch. 21, 1778: "I have met with the most favorable reception from all the Generals, General Washington in particular" (*Gates Papers*, NYHS).
[40] For the progress of Steuben, see *John Laurens*, 146–47, 152, 160; 11 *G. W.*, 108, 119, 132, 136, 174, 329–30, 346.
[41] Letter of Apr. 7, 1778, to James Duane; 3 *Burnett*, 153–54.

STEUBEN, TEACHER OF AN ARMY

Friedrich Wilhelm Ludolf Gerhard Augustin, Baron von Steuben, came honestly by the "von," to the extent at least that his grandfather had inserted it in the family name about 1708, twenty-two years before Friedrich was born in the fortress of Magdeburg, son of a Lieutenant of Prussian Engineers. The younger soldier earned the title of Frei-herr, which was considered the equivalent of Baron, though the honor was conferred by the prince of the petty state of Hohenzollern-Hechingen.

Be that as it might be, he was Baron von Steuben at home as well as in America, without any stretching of the verities. It was different with his military title. Steuben represented himself as a former "Lieu-tenant General in the King of Prussia's service," though in reality, he was a retired Captain of the General Staff who had been on duty, at the headquarters of Frederick the Great, as one of the King's titular aides.

This falsification of the record was excused by the parties to it on the ground that Steuben would not have been given an opportunity if he had come to Congress simply as one more Captain who wanted money and a higher commission. On the ethics of this, there might of course be two opinions, but the lasting importance of the incident, so far as it relates to the history of the American Army, is that Steuben scarcely could have been more useful if he had held the rank he alleged to have been his. It was not possible for him to engraft all the branches of the General Staff on the rough stem of a feebly officered and hungry Army; but he made a sound system of drill and inspection a part of the organism of the armed forces and he contributed in a dozen other ways to the fighting power of Washington's troops. If Washington rightly is venerated as the father of the American Army, Steuben was its first teacher. "The Baron" was extravagant and he never had for any length of time the extensive line command that probably repre-sented his heart's deepest desire. He had, as he deserved, almost every-thing else that the affection and gratitude of the American people could bestow.

(After the original by C. W. Peale, Independence Hall, Philadelphia.)

MC DOUGALL OF "THE STORMY HEBRIDES"

"Rebels" was a sufficiently inclusive term of damnation to satisfy most of the British for their description of their American adversaries. Had the King's supporters been more precise, they might have denounced the revolutionaries as sons of rebels, refugees, European adventurers, wanderers, and creatures from the farthest cabins and corners of the Kingdom. All these derogatory epithets would have been proclaimed badges of honor. To any list of wastrels and rascals, as the angry servants of King George might have termed them, the Americans would have added the names of still others from remote lands, as proof that America's cause was that of mankind.

Alexander McDougall, for example, had been born at Islay, the southernmost of the Inner Hebrides, and was brought to America in 1738, when he was six years old. His father belonged to Lachlan Campbell's party that intended to settle South of Lake George, but when this enterprise failed, Ronald McDougall had to content himself with laboring as a milkman in New York. Young Alex had too much vigor and ambition to remain in humble station. By the time he was 24 he was commanding a privateer in the war against France, and when he was 31, the end of hostilities found him financially able to stock a store in New York and, while profiting as a merchant, to advance himself as a scholar. When the controversy with Great Britain developed, he was by impulse and by conviction altogether on the side of the Colonies. For his zeal in an alleged libel of the General Assembly, he spent more than a year in jail, February, 1770–March, 1771, but punishment did not tame his spirit. In the front rank of New York supporters of colonial rights, he was Colonel of the First New York Regiment on its organization and, in August, 1776, became a continental Brigadier. Promotion to divisional command, as a Major General, was his in October, 1777. Washington rated him high for sound sense, energy and military judgment. A slight impediment of speech did not interfere greatly with McDougall's public utterance. If his letters were too numerous and too long, they never were lacking in reason or staunchness. Had the health of McDougall been better, his place among American commanders might have been near the top.

(Reproduced by courtesy of Sons of the Revolution in the State of New York, from the portrait in its headquarters, Fraunces Tavern, New York City.)

General Scammell admiringly wrote his friend John Sullivan: ". . . to see a gentleman dismissed with a Lieutenant General's commission [42] from the great Prussian monarch, condescend with a grace peculiar to himself, to take under his direction a squad of ten or twelve men in capacity of a drill Sergeant induce the officers and men to admire him and improve exceeding fast under his instructions." [43] An Ensign wrote enthusiastically in his Diary that his Brigade had gone through the maneuvers under Steuben: "The step is about half way betwixt slow and quick time, an easy and a natural step, and I think much better than the former. The manual also is altered by his direction. There are but ten words of command . . ." [44]

While Steuben was introducing uniform and expeditious maneuver, Washington saw that better equipment and transportation would be made available to the Army through the skillful, industrious and military approach of Nathanael Greene to his new duties as Quartermaster General. After his election,[45] which was received by officers with much satisfaction,[46] Greene was not able immediately to take over his duties,[47] but he already was familiar with the negligence and wastage that had progressed without check during the later months of Mifflin's maladministration. The committee that had spent weeks at the camp had reported to Congress: "We find the property of the continent dispersed over the whole country; not an encampment, route of the Army, or considerable road but abounds with wagons, left to the mercy of the weather and the will of the inhabitants; large quantities of entrenching tools have in like manner been left in various hands, under no other security, that we can learn, than the honesty of those who have them in possession. Not less than 3000 spades and shovels, and a like number of tomahawks have been lately discovered and collected in the vicinity of the camp by an order from one of the general officers. In

---

[42] Steuben actually had no higher rank in Prussia than that of Captain and had been dropped from Frederick's service fourteen years prior to arrival in America. With the connivance and aid of friends, Benjamin Franklin among them, the ex-Captain exalted his rank and prevaricated most extravagantly in order to get military employment in the United States. It will be remembered that the rank of a German Lieutenant General corresponded to that of an American Brigadier.

[43] Apr. 8, 1778; 2 *Sullivan Papers*, 32–33.

[44] *George Ewing's Journal*, 34; entry of Apr. 7, 1778.

[45] For his election, Mch. 2, 1778, see *supra*, p. 585 and 10 *JCC.*, 210.

[46] Cf. Lafayette to Washington, Mch. 25, 1778, *LOLTW.*, 38: "It is very interesting to have [in that office] an honest man and a friend of yours."

[47] 11 *G. W.*, 111. For the financial arrangements with his assistants, see Charles Pettit to Joseph Reed, Mch. 5, 1778; *Reed Papers*, NYHS.

the same way a quantity of tents and tent-cloth, after having laid a whole summer in a farmer's barn, and unknown to the officer of the department, was lately discovered and brought to the camp by a special order from the General. From these instances, we presume there may be many other stores yet unknown and uncollected, which require immediate care and attention." [48]

Where chaos thus prevailed, it perhaps was futile for Congress to instruct Mifflin to acquaint Greene with what was available and what had been ordered for the campaign of 1778,[49] though Washington was pressing for supplies.[50] Hampered as Greene was by the resignation of Mifflin's deputy,[51] he proceeded with much vigor to employ to advantage the business experience of his able new assistants,[52] to make acquaintances that would be useful,[53] to reduce the wagons employed in nonessential service,[54] to select sites for his magazines,[55] to improve the roads [56] and, in general, to devote all his energies to what he knew to be a task of great complexity that called for the service of the most competent aides he could engage.[57]

Training under von Steuben and the improvement of the Quartermasters service by Greene soon could be left by Washington to the men in charge. He himself had to wrestle with the perplexities of provisions and shoes, of recruits and inoculation, of trade with the enemy and the exchange of prisoners. Sound methods were solving a few of the difficulties that had baffled his previous attempts. The arrangement by which hides were bartered for shoes worked out surprisingly well and, by the end of April, had supplied footgear for most of those in painful need.[58] Nakedness was not yet covered. The Clothier General was regarded by some officers as arbitrary and inefficient and was increasingly unpopular. Cases of individual distress were almost unbelievable.

[48] Report of Feb. 12, 1778; 2 *Greene's Greene*, 43–44.
[49] 10 *JCC.*, 211. A better start had been made in procuring some supplies and equipment than Congress realized. Anthony Butler's reports of Mch. 9, 1777, to Washington list many articles in process of manufacture and several orders completed and delivered. See 69 *Papers of G. W.*, 26, 27, LC.
[50] Cf. 11 *G. W.*, 33.
[51] *Ibid.*, 102; H. E. Lutterloh to Washington, Mch. 22, 1778; 70 *Papers of G. W.*, 44, LC.
[52] Joseph Cox and Charles Pettit, both of Philadelphia. For their equipment, contract and connections, see 2 *Greene's Greene*, 50, and Greene to Joseph Reed, Mch. 9, 1778, *Reed Papers*, NYHS.
[53] Cf. 11 *G. W.*, 154–55.
[54] *Ibid.*, 161, 175. Cf. T. C. Wharton to Washington, Mch. 10, 1778; 2 *LTW.*, 82–83.
[55] 11 *G. W.*, 177.
[56] Greene to Charles Pettit, Apr. 11, 1778; *Reed Papers*, NYHS.
[57] Greene to the President of the Board of War, May 27, 1778; *ibid.*
[58] 11 *G. W.*, 35, 274, 318; 10 *JCC.*, 371.

Washington himself had to confess that the man who attended his table and acted as his body servant was "indecently and most shamefully naked." [59] The one note of cheer—on this theme—was a report, none too well authenticated, that garments still could be procured from New England.[60]

As for provisions, Washington was able on the 1st of March to thank the Army for the patience it had shown during the days of shortage, which commissary officers appeared temporarily to have overcome, and he did not have to dwell heavily on the probable return of scarcity from time to time.[61] A week later he had some assurance of a continuing supply of cattle, though he was apprehensive that a small amount of meat only might be salted for the Army.[62]

Congress now was nervously concerned over the failure of the commissary and no longer was disposed to defend the system disastrously adopted in 1777.[63] A report by the committee that visited the camp during the winter became the subject of scrutiny and of a series of enactments designed to facilitate purchase and to hold out the prospect of decent compensation to qualified agents.[64] This course was entirely in accord with Washington's view that conditions during the winter had not been attributable to the exhaustion of provisions in America but to the incompetence, abusive methods and small number of the men engaged in the commissary service.[65] Jeremiah Wadsworth was prevailed upon to become head of the purchasing division under the amended regulations, which were said to leave him unfettered.[66] Soon the word from the more optimistic officers was, "we fare much better than heretofore," [67] though it was undeniable that life in the camp still was meagre, uncertain and dirty.[68] When Washington wrote John Cadwalader in some detail of the situation as it existed on March

---

[59] Apr. 17, 1778; 11 G. W., 270. For the deficiencies of Clothier General Mease, who was said to have been at one time the butler of the Duke of Bolton (John Jay to Gouverneur Morris, Apr. 29, 1778, 1 John Jay, 181), see infra, Vol. V. Daniel Kemper's report of Mch. 26, 1778, to Washington (70 Papers of G. W., 94, LC) showed some improvement of supply.

[60] Penn. Gazette, Jan. 10, 1778; 11 G. W., 240.

[61] 11 G. W., 10.

[62] Ibid., 54–55. In the early spring, a storm and a very high tide on the coast of New Jersey wrecked many of the small establishments where salt was being recovered from seawater. (Penn. Gazette, Apr. 18, 1778).

[63] 3 Burnett, 121.   [64] 10 JCC., 236–37, 248–49, 250 ff, 274.

[65] See 11 G. W., 165, 267.

[66] 10 JCC., 293, 305, 324, 327, 328, 345, 353, 356–57. See also 3 Burnett, 166, 175 and supra, Chapter XXIII, n. 25.

[67] James M. Varnum to John Sullivan, Apr. 28, 1778; 2 Sullivan Papers, 41.

[68] 11 G. W., 260, 274–75.

20, he could not then substitute a flat and final "was" for a continuing "has been," but he could present a cheerful antithesis at the end:

By death and desertion, we have lost a good many men since we came to this ground, and have encountered every species of hardship that cold, wet, and hunger and want of clothes were capable of producing; notwithstanding and contrary to my expectations we have been able to keep the soldiers from mutiny or dispersion, although, in the single article of provisions, they have encountered enough to have occasioned one or the other of these in most other armies; as there have been (two or three times), days together, without provisions; and once six days without any of the meat kind; could the poor horses tell their tale, it would be in a strain still more lamentable, as numbers have actually died from pure want; but, as our prospects begin to brighten, my complaint shall cease.[69]

He could "cease complaint" but he could not forget. A little later in the spring, evidence of jealousy of the Army on the part of a certain element in Congress led him to protest. Into a long letter simply but eloquently drafted by Colonel Harrison at headquarters, Washington himself put this paragraph:

. . . without arrogance or the smallest deviation from truth it may be said that no history, now extant, can furnish an instance of an Army's suffering such uncommon hardships as ours have done, and bearing them with the same patience and fortitude. To see men without clothes to cover their nakedness, without blankets to lay on, without shoes, by which their marches might be traced by the blood from their feet, and almost as often without provisions as with; marching through frost and snow, and at Christmas taking up their winter quarters within a day's march of the enemy, without a house or hut to cover them till they could be built, and submitting to it without a murmur, is a mark of patience and obedience which in my opinion can scarce be paralleled.[70]

Perhaps it was not unnatural that some Delegates felt the jealousy of which Washington sought to make them ashamed by recounting the misery his men had endured. A Congress of few members, and most of them undistinguished, was laboring long hours and was expending far too much of its time in passing on financial accounts it tried to

[69] 11 *G. W.*, 117, with a minimum of revision in the unusual punctuation. Cf. Clement Biddle to unnamed officer of Washington's staff, Mch. 5, 1778; 68 *Papers of G. W.*, p. 34, LC.
[70] Letter of Apr. 21, 1778, to John Banister; 11 *G. W.*, 291–92.

discharge with a currency that continued to depreciate;[71] but a majority of the members held firmly to their views on such questions as militia and the exchange of prisoners, concerning which Washington was of different mind and of conviction no less tenacious. As the spring of 1778 approached, there was no occasion for disagreement over the employment of temporary State troops, because it was manifest that if the British undertook a vigorous offensive, Washington would be compelled to use some or all of the 5000 militia Congress had authorized him to call out.[72]

In the painful matter of the long delayed, long disputed cartel for the exchange of prisoners, some hurts were inflicted where Washington was sensitive. He followed four rules of conduct in all that related to men who fell into the hands of enemy or surrendered to the American forces: Initially and fundamentally, a general exchange of prisoners was to be arranged with absolute honesty as soon as practicable; second, pending such a broad cartel, special exchanges of officers of any rank were to be made only in the order in which the men were captured— first in, first out; third, mercy was to be shown to and demanded for all prisoners, with an absolute minimum of reprisal; fourth, officers of the enemy were to be treated as gentlemen, whether in prison or in permissible dealings as individuals. It had been in this spirit that Washington had acted during the winter when a lost sporting dog came to headquarters with a collar that bore General Howe's name. By the next flag of truce, Washington returned the animal to the British commander.[73]

Members of Congress did not subscribe in every instance to this code. Most of the Delegates felt themselves justified in resolving to hold the survivors of Burgoyne's Army in America until the Saratoga convention was ratified by the government of Great Britain.[74] On this repudiation of an essential part of the terms Gates had allowed, Alexander

---

[71] For Congress' thin attendance and the attempts to adjust its hours to its duties, see 10 *JCC.*, 282, 405; 3 *Burnett*, 108, 153, 165, 166, 210.

[72] Returns of effective strength for the early months of 1778 seem to have disappeared from the records. From July onward, the returns of effective infantry strength month by month, including all forces in New England, on the Hudson and elsewhere in New York, were as follows: July, 14,487; August, 14,719; September, 18,472; October, 16,779; November, 16,489; December, 17,343. The artillery, when reported for four of these months, ranged from 1403 to 1918; the cavalry was returned twice only and then had a strength of 506 in August and 382 in October (*War Dept. Coll. Rev. War Records*; National Archives).

[73] *Pontgibaud*, 47.

[74] The course of the action and the resulting protests may be traced in 10 *JCC.*, 13–14, 16–17, 29 ff, 44–45, 74 ff, 184–85, 196 ff; 3 *Burnett*, 5 ff, 18 ff; *Heath*, 156–58.

Hamilton was not expressing the opinion of Washington when he said, "there was . . . a strong temptation for this, and it may be excused, though I cannot say the measure is to my taste." [75] In subsequent new instructions to Washington on the negotiation of a general cartel of exchange, Congress insisted that no British soldiers be released until all bills for the expense of maintaining these men in captivity had been settled between the two governments. Washington regarded this and various lesser requirements of a new sort as violating preliminary agreements to which he had committed his personal honor in his correspondence with the British authorities, and he protested to the Delegates.

They acquiesced so far as costs of caring for prisoners were involved,[73] but they would not recede from their order that all Loyalists taken in arms, after voluntary enlistment with the British, be confined closely in jail and then be turned over to the States for punishment in accordance with a resolve of Dec. 30, 1777.[77] The exchange of Gen. Charles Lee for Gen. Richard Prescott was reasserted as a *sine qua non*.[78] Viewed in its various parts, the overzealous attitude of Congress created at headquarters some doubt of the willingness of the Delegates to assent to any inclusive cartel, though refusal to effect agreement might mean continued hopeless incarceration for American soldiers in British hands—a price far too high to pay for the detention of those English, Scots and Hessians whose release to General Howe would reenforce his Regiments.[79] An unhappy situation might have developed between Washington and Congress had not the negotiations for a cartel collapsed speedily because General Howe could give no more than a personal guarantee of British adherence to an accord.[80]

Partial compensation for this failure seemed to be given the Army in

[75] Letter of Mch. 12, 1778, to George Clinton; 9 *A. Hamilton*, 129. See *supra*, p. 554.

[76] 10 *G. W.*, 428 and n. 78, 444; 10 *JCC.*, 194, 197–98, 262, 266; For instructions to Washington, Feb. 27, 1778, to limit strictly the size of British flag-of-truce parties, "on pain, if taken, of being treated as marauders and punished with death," see 10 *JCC.*, 205. The improper seizure at Lancaster, Penn., of British with supplies and clothing for prisoners is described briefly in 9 *A. Hamilton*, 129. See also 10 *JCC.*, 258, 344.

[77] 9 *JCC.*, 1069. For Washington's protest of Apr. 4, 1778, see 11 *G. W.*, 216 ff; the conciliatory answer of Congress, discussed on the floor, is in 10 *JCC.*, 329 ff, 333, 334, 336, 339, 370–71. Cf. 3 *Burnett*, 161–62, 163.

[78] 10 *JCC.*, 295, 333.

[79] The letter of Hamilton to George Clinton, Mch. 12, 1778, *loc. cit.*, probably was written on his own initiative.

[80] 11 *G. W.*, 276; 3 *Burnett*, 179, 180, 203. Vexatious quibbling over a meeting place is set forth in 11 *G. W.*, 173, 176, 209, 212, 213–14. For the credentials of the American commissioners, see *ibid.*, 212.

the successful termination of the long bargaining over the special exchange of Lee and Prescott. During the last stages of this negotiation, Washington had instructed Elias Boudinot, the Commissary-General of Prisoners, not to permit trifles to stand in the way because, said Washington, he never had needed Lee more.[81] When final arrangements were made for the parole of Lee within the American lines, as a preliminary of his full exchange,[82] the Commander-in-Chief fashioned for his senior lieutenant such a reception as would have been accorded the victor in a campaign that had liberated Philadelphia or New York. An escort of horse under a member of Washington's staff awaited the paroled General at the British picket on the 5th of April.[83] The Commander-in-Chief and most of his senior officers went out to meet Lee at the lines and escorted him to camp, where troops were drawn up to salute. Fifes screamed; the drummers outdid themselves; a band blared a welcome; at headquarters, Mrs. Washington was hostess to Lee and to those who came to do him honor.[84]

He proved to be the same self-confident individualist. If any change had occurred it was of the sort that disposes a prisoner or an invalid to be autocratic and to covet more power than usual because he has been exercising less. Even before Lee's parole ended in complete freedom of action,[85] he forwarded Washington a new "Plan for the Formation of the American Army in the least Expensive Manner Possible . . ." with the statement, not altogether jocular: "I have taken it into my head that I understand it better than almost any man living."[86] Reluctant to be matched with the inconspicuous Prescott, he proposed that he be exchanged for Burgoyne. Said Lee to President Laurens: ". . . to speak plainly and perhaps vainly I am really convinced as things are circumstanced, I am of more consequence to you than General Burgoyne is to the other party . . . I am well and hope always shall be well with

---

[81] *Elias Boudinot,* 77.

[82] 11 *G. W.,* 218–19. See also 3 *Burnett,* 161, 170.

[83] 11 *G. W.,* 214; Josiah Loring to Elias Boudinot, Apr. 3, 1778; *Henkel's Cat.* 694, p. 267.

[84] Elijah Parker's Diary in *Godfrey,* 275. Elias Boudinot, *op. cit.,* 77, gave a more elaborate account of the return of Lee, but he wrote late and included some incidents that are rendered dubious by the tests of internal evidence. Boudinot, who was exceedingly hostile to Lee, stated that the General brought from Philadelphia the wife of a British Sergeant and on his first night at Valley Forge had her with him in his quarters, which adjoined Mrs. Washington's sitting room. Capt. John Montresor noted in his Diary that Lee had an interview with Gen. Sir William Howe on the 3rd of April (*Montresor Journals,* 484). It is not known whether Lee informed his American friends of this visit. A note of his to General Sir Henry Clinton, expressing good will and dated June 4, 1778, is in the *Clinton Papers,* Clements Lib.

[85] His later paroles will be found in 2 *Lee Papers,* 381–82.

[86] *Ibid.,* 383.

General Washington—and to speak again vainly I am persuaded (considering how he is surrounded) that he cannot do without me." [87] Although it may have bruised the conceit of Lee, he was traded for Prescott, not for the loser at Saratoga, and back on duty, he soon was trying to prevail on Congress to give him the rank of Lieutenant General. This he insisted would have been his by 1778 in the Polish, Portuguese or Russian service, had he not thrown in his fortunes with America's. [88]

Whether Lee would justify by his counsel and leadership this conception of his self-importance, or whether he would repeat the part he had played in the dark drama of the late autumn of 1776, Washington required all the sound counsel the Army could get, because, as April advanced, the American cause had to face the possibility of a double, perhaps of a triple British offensive. One prong of the coming attack was to be political. Word had reached America that Lord North had introduced two "reconciliation bills," one to set forth the intentions of Parliament concerning the exercise of the right to tax the Colonies, and the other to appoint Commissioners to "treat, consult, and agree upon the means of quieting the disorders subsisting in certain of the Colonies, Plantations and Provinces of North America." [89] When copies of these measures first appeared in America, Washington, who admitted himself distrustful of British proposals, [90] thought forgery was being perpetrated, [91] but he soon changed his mind and concluded the King and Lord North were seeking to divide and then to enslave an America they hoped they first could lull into belief that peace would be easy and honorable.

Increased, and not diminished effort was necessary. [92] Washington wrote Henry Laurens:

"The enemy are determined to try us by force, and by fraud; and while they are exerting their utmost powers in the first instance, I do not doubt but that they will employ men in the second, versed in the arts of dissimulation, of temporizing, negotiating genius's.

"It appears to me that nothing short of independence can possibly do. The

[87] Letter of Apr. 17, 1778; 2 *Lee Papers*, 387–88.
[88] Letter of May 13, 1778; *ibid.*, 292–93.
[89] For the acts, as passed, see 32 *Statutes at Large*, 4 ff, and for the opening debate in the Commons, see 19 *Proceedings of Parliament*, 762. The summary in *Dodsley's Annual Register for 1778*, p. 131 ff, is admirable.
[90] 11 G. W., 4.   [91] *Ibid.*, 27.
[92] *Ibid.*, 281, 290, 296, 301.

injuries we have received from Britain can never be forgotten, and a peace upon other terms would be the source of perpetual feuds and animosities. Besides, should Britain from her love of tyranny and lawless domination attempt again to bend our necks to the yoke of slavery, and there is no doubt but that she would, for her pride and ambition are unconquerable, no nation would credit our professions, nor grant us aid. At any rate, their favors would be obtained upon the most advantageous and dishonorable terms." [93]

All the Delegates were of this mind and promptly adopted resolutions designed to convince the people that the British proposals were nothing more than a snare for unwary feet. ". . . these United States," said Congress, "cannot, with propriety, hold any conference or treaty with any commissioners on the part of Great Britain, unless they shall, as a preliminary thereto, either withdraw their fleets and armies, or else, in positive and express terms, acknowledge the independence of the said States." [94] When Governor Tryon sent copies to Washington of North's two bills, ostensibly in order that the people might know how anxious the King was to make peace, the American commander acknowledged the documents and said they would have a "free currency" among his soldiers, "in whose fidelity" to the United States, Washington assured the former Governor, "I have the most perfect confidence." As a return of compliment, Washington forwarded several prints of a resolve of April 23, in which Congress recommended that the States offer pardon to those citizens who had joined or had aided the British forces in America.[95] Tryon was asked to distribute this paper. "The benevolent purpose it is intended to answer will, I persuade myself," Washington blandly wrote, "sufficiently recommend it to your candor." [96]

The first of the British offensives, the offer of peace, thus was blunted before it was delivered. Would there be one other, or two, a campaign

[93] Letter of Apr. 30, 1778; 11 *G. W.*, 326–27, an awkward text, heavily repunctuated here. A new sentence is begun with the words "At any rate," in front of which there is no mark at all in the text.

[94] Proceedings of Apr. 22, 1778; 10 *JCC.*, 379; 3 *Burnett*, 178–79. For Henry Laurens's urgent counsel that the ablest leaders of the country be named to deal with the British commissioners, see *ibid.*, 192, and for the commission issued by the King to the three men sent to negotiate with America, see *Dodsley's Annual Register for 1778*, p. 323 ff.

[95] 10 *JCC.*, 381–82.

[96] 11 *G. W.*, 309. In compliance with what must have been instructions to all British senior commanders in America, Gen. Robert Pigot at Newport, Rhode Island, forwarded copies of the British bills to Gen. John Sullivan, who wrote a vigorous answer (2 *Sullivan Papers*, 37–38, 39). This he dispatched by the hand of Col. William Barton, who had captured General Prescott (1 *Mackenzie*, 271–72).

by Howe from Philadelphia and one by Sir Henry Clinton, based on New York City? Washington was not sure. He had expected that Howe would make an early start in operations [97] which during the winter had brought no attack on the strong position at Valley Forge.[98] Nothing more serious had happened anywhere than some brushes of foraging parties,[99] and a fine defence by Capt. Henry Lee of the Spread Eagle Tavern,[100] where he and seven companions on the 20th of January, 1778, beat off an attack by a strong British patrol.[101] In anticipation now of active combat, involving all the American forces, Washington recalled absent general officers [102] and studied as closely as practicable the confusing movement of ships to and from Philadelphia and New York; but he could ascertain nothing tangible. Reports of heavy reenforcement of Howe's army in Philadelphia seemed to be unfounded;[103] there was no evidence at the moment to justify Charles Lee's theory that a replacement of British troops in Rhode Island was underway.[104] At the suggestion of Benjamin Lincoln,[105] who was recovering from a wound, Washington considered the possibility of an attack on New York,[106] and sought on this the particular counsel of Alexander McDougall.[107] That officer had relieved Israel Putnam of command [108] and in circumstances of some perplexity [109] was display-

[97] 11 G. W., 138. Washington's intelligence reports had included news of embarkation at New York and of large-scale movement of vessels on the lower Delaware. See Silas Seely, Elizabeth Town, to Washington, Mch. 20, 1777 (*Washington Papers*, Huntington Lib.) and William Smallwood, Wilmington, Del., to Washington, Mch. 17, 1778 (152 *Papers Cont. Cong.*, pt. v, p. 409, LC).

[98] Cf. *Howe's Narrative*, 30: The presence of the Americans at Valley Forge did not "occasion any difficulties so pressing as to justify an attack on that strong position during the severe weather." See also *Henry Lee*, 106: Valley Forge "possessed every advantage which strength of ground or salubrity of climate could bestow."

[99] Anthony Wayne to Washington, Mch. 4, 14, 1778; 4 *Wayne Papers*, 99, 104, PHS.

[100] The tavern was about five miles South and slightly East of Valley Forge on the road from Lancaster to Philadelphia.

[101] See the introduction to *Henry Lee*, 16–17, with a quotation by the editor, Gen. R. E. Lee, from Weedon to R. H. Lee, Feb. 1, 1778. See also *John Laurens*, 111; N. J. *Gazette*, Jan. 28, 1778, in 2 *Moore*, 10; William Gifford to Benjamin Helm, MS, *NJHS.*, RE 49–53. Washington commended Lee and his comrades in GOs of Jan. 20, 1778, and in a letter of that date, 10 G. W., 322. This exploit was the immediate occasion of Lee's promotion and authorization, noted *supra*, to raise two Companies of unattached Light Dragoons.

[102] 11 G. W., 87, 87–88, 113, 250–51.   [103] *Ibid.*, 146, 172–73, 227.
[104] *Ibid.*, 227.   [105] 2 *LTW.*, 85.
[106] 11 G. W., 188. Lincoln's wound had been received in the last phase of Gates's campaign against Burgoyne.

[107] 11 G. W., 178.

[108] 11 G. W., 90–91, 96–97, 100, 101–02, 103.

[109] Cf. the controversy between Col. Thaddeus Kosciuszko and Lt. Col. Lewis de La Radière (*Ibid.*, 119, 222, 298). The complaint against La Radière, as set forth in S. H. Parsons to McDougall, Mch. 28, 1778, *McDougall Papers*, NYHS, was the vague one of "an attachment to his opinion in his profession and some other matters." Kosciuszko was much beloved by the officers along Hudson River.

ing skill in the collection of intelligence,[110] the movement of troops,[111] the study of the strategical problem,[112] the accumulation of supplies [113] and, for a short time, the employment of General Conway without the usual scheming and agitation.[114] On the subject McDougall was to study, Congress had opinions of its own. Its members had been thought negligent in not providing for the better defence of the Hudson [115] but at length they ordered the demolition of what remained of Forts Independence and Ticonderoga,[116] and on the 15th of April, they directed Gates to resume command of the Northern Department and to have special regard for the maintenance of communication with the Eastern States.[117]

During the preliminaries of this decision, there had been whispers of a plan to make Gates independent of Washington and answerable to Congress only,[118] but the final resolution naming Gates was silent on that point. As a result, McDougall could come back to the main Army, where he would be most welcome; [119] Gates would be free to make his own plans which he might or might not communicate in advance to Washington. Nothing was done by Congress to reduce the authority of the Commander-in-Chief; nothing was said openly of any restriction of Gates's command within his department.[120] If this appeared to be the political trimming of men still grateful to Gates for his victory but disgusted with his part in the Conway cabal, two further resolves quietly made it plain that Washington remained in fact what

---

110 McDougall to Washington, Apr. 3, May 21, 1778; *McDougall Papers*, NYHS.

111 Cf. Conway to McDougall, Apr. 6, 1778, *loc. cit.*

112 For example, McDougall to the Convention of New York, Apr. 21, 1778; McDougall to Brig. Gen. William Winds, Apr. 25, 1778, *loc. cit.*

113 McDougall to Brig. Gen. G. S. Silliman, Apr. 14, 1778, *loc. cit.*

114 10 *JCC.*, 280; Conway to McDougall, Mch. 31, Apr. 6, 1778, *loc. cit.*, Conway to George Clinton, Apr. 11, 1778, *Clinton Papers*, NYHS. Cf. Varnum to McDougall, Apr. 10, 1778: "We hear [Conway] is appointed to your command. I hope it is not true, as I know it will give you pain to form a balance between an order of Congress and the absurdity of it"; *McDougall Papers*, NYHS. Cf. John Jay to Gouverneur Morris, Apr. 29, 1778; 1 *John Jay*, 181. Conway had not relinquished command at this time and, of course, did not know, as yet, that his resignation had been accepted on the 28th. See *supra*, p. 612.

115 3 *Burnett*, 155.   116 10 *JCC.*, 287.

117 *Ibid.*, 354.

118 Henry Laurens to Lafayette, Mch. 24, 1778; 3 *Burnett*, 142.

119 11 *G. W.*, 298.

120 This assignment of Gates to field duty left the work of the Board of War almost entirely in the hands of Timothy Pickering and Richard Peters. Illness, which soon proved fatal, had detained Joseph Trumbull in Connecticut and led him to resign (10 *JCC.*, 363; resignation accepted April 18); Thomas Mifflin was considering the assumption of the command of the Pennsylvania militia (1 *Pickering*, 213) and, on May 21, was to take the action set forth in Chapter I of Volume V. Washington had word from Gouverneur Morris, April 18, that another effort might be made to put Col. R. H. Harrison of the General's staff on the Board of War. See *Sparks's Morris*, v. 1, p. 165.

he was in title. His authority to seize property and to confine persons in the area around Philadelphia had expired on the 10th of April, probably through inadvertence, but it now was renewed and made effective to August 10.[121] By another vote, Washington was "authorized and directed" on April 18 forthwith to convene a council of war and, with its advice, "to form such a plan for the general operations of the campaign as he shall deem consistent with the general welfare of these States." To this unusual instruction, a few amendatory lines were added of a nature that may have seemed perfunctory—"that Major Generals Gates and Mifflin, members of the Board of War, have leave to attend the said council." [122] The real purpose of this language was unmistakable: As Major Generals, these two critics of the Commander-in-Chief were subject to his summons and under his orders. Congress gave them leave from the Board of War in order that they might answer the call of their superior officer.[123]

On his own account, Washington had intended to take counsel with Gates,[124] and now he wrote not only Gates and Mifflin but also John Armstrong, Pennsylvania Major General, and invited all of them to the council.[125] The letter to Mifflin was stiff but unexceptional.[126] Gates could not leave York as soon as he had hoped,[127] for which reason the council had to be deferred; but the delay might not be immediately of serious consequence, and for this most interesting reason: By the 23rd it was reported unofficially in camp that Gen. Sir William Howe had been recalled to England and that Gen. Sir Henry Clinton was to succeed him in the American command.[128] Washington credited the

---

[121] Resolve of Apr. 23, 1778; 10 *JCC.*, 384. The previous resolutions were those of Sept. 17, 1777, 8 *ibid.*, 751; Oct. 8, 1777, 9 *ibid.*, 784; and Nov. 14, 1777, 9 *ibid.*, 905.

[122] 10 *JCC.*, 364.

[123] Gouverneur Morris became somewhat confused when he undertook to disclose to Washington the inwardness of what had occurred. The New Yorker said: "We have determined to send Gates to Hudson River, where he is to command very largely. But he is to receive instructions, which shall be proper. You are directed to call a council of *Major* Generals, in which the Chief Engineer is *officially* to be a member, and to which, by a subsequent resolution, Generals Gates and Mifflin were ordered to repair. As these gentlemen ought not to receive orders *immediately* from Congress, they are, as you will see, permitted to leave the board of war upon *your* order. This *amendment* was therefore acquiesced in unanimously" (Letter of Apr. 18, 1778; 1 Sparks's *Morris*, 164).

[124] 11 *G. W.*, 302.   [125] 11 *G. W.*, 303–05.

[126] *Ibid.*, 304. The original, bearing marks of carefully corrected composition, is in the autograph of Alexander Hamilton, 72 *Papers of G. W.*, 107, LC.

[127] He wrote McDougall Apr. 21, 1778: "I shall set out in a day or two to wait on General Washington . . ." (*McDougall Papers*, NYHS). On the 26th, Gates wrote Washington from York that he was awaiting the return of Lee to that town and, on the arrival of that officer, would set out immediately in Lee's company for headquarters (*Gates Papers*, NYHS).

[128] 11 *G. W.*, 302.

news [129] and, while he suspected that Howe might try to strike a parting blow, he doubtless reasoned also that some weeks might elapse before the new commander would have a plan ready to put into execution.[130]

Washington and his senior officers meantime could consider the three alternatives he already had formulated and had submitted to the criticism of his Generals—an offensive against Philadelphia, an attack on New York, or a continued defensive.[131] If Gates or Mifflin or anyone else could demonstrate the superiority of one plan over the others, Washington wished it done. The larger relation of Gates to the plans of the Commander-in-Chief, and of Washington to administration on the upper Hudson, was clarified, tactfully and cautiously, by Congress on April 21 when the instructions to the head of the Northern Department were adopted. Gates was not to stop supplies sent to the main Army from New England; when called on to do so, he must dispatch continental troops to reenforce Washington, while privileged to ask for help from the Divisions in the Middle States. Gates was to conform, also, as far as practicable, to the plan adopted at the council of war Washington was to assemble.[132]

In anticipation of that council, the general officers at camp were replying promptly to a circular sent out by Washington, and were expressing a diversity of opinion.[133] Most of them favored an offensive but all

[129] It was true. On the 14th of April, *Andromache* reached New York with dispatches, among which was one from Lord George Germaine to General Clinton which announced that the King had acquiesced in Sir William Howe's desire to come home and that Clinton was to "take the command of the army with the rank of General." (Germaine to Clinton, Feb. 4, 1778; *Clinton Papers,* Clements Lib. The arrival of *Andromache* is noted in 1 *Kemble,* 149). Clinton had been unhappy under Howe, who did not show him always the consideration he thought his due, and, though he regarded the second position in America as honorable, he had preferred the Canadian command and the previous year had planned to return to England, probably to solicit that post (Henry Clinton to Benjamin Carpenter, Jan. 18, 1777; *Clinton Papers,* Clements Lib.).

[130] As a matter of fact, Howe confessed later that after receiving his orders he "became cautious of hazarding exploits which might have reduced the army of [his] successor." He made one attempt only, to be described later. This, he thought, was acceptance of a good opportunity (Howe's *Narrative,* 31).

[131] 11 *G. W.,* 282–83 and n. The circular to the Generals bore date of April 20 and had been prepared before receipt of the resolves of the 18th, which reached camp on the evening of the 22nd (*ibid.,* 302). It is almost certain, too, that the detailed "Thoughts upon a Plan of Operations . . ." (*ibid.,* 185 ff), were written prior to the drafting of the "circular"; but as there is a possibility, though dim, that the "Thoughts" were elaborated from the "circular," a doubt has to be noted concerning the date on which the detailed plan was drafted. This scarcely can be termed a material doubt.

[132] 10 *JCC.,* 368–69.

[133] Most of the answers that have survived the years are in 72 *Papers of G. W.,* 71, 84, 86, 87, 100, LC. Another copy of Wayne's is in 4 *Wayne Papers,* 17, PHS. Greene favored the confinement of Howe to Philadelphia by Lee and an attempt on New York by Washington

of them took into account the difficulties that compelled the Commander-in-Chief to list as the third alternative: "remaining quiet in a secure, fortified camp, disciplining and arranging the Army, till the enemy begin their operations, and then to govern ourselves accordingly."[134] Recruits were not being forwarded in numbers needed to fill the Regiments. Virginia[135] was enlisting for six months only, and other States might pursue the same temporizing policy; in Massachusetts, men were hiring deserters from Burgoyne's army as substitutes;[136] the Maryland Legislature was expected to show reluctance in ordering a draft;[137] British officers, prisoners of war, were believed to have deepened disaffection in Pennsylvania, and to have converted many ignorant persons;[138] a forged resolve of Congress was being circulated to the effect that all men on short enlistment were to be held in the Army till the war was concluded.[139]

Besides all this, a gross blunder had been made in underestimating the percentage of men who would have to be inoculated for smallpox. Between 3000 and 4000 were being treated at the end of March; 2000 others did not possess sufficient clothing to take the field.[140] This meant a reduction in the superiority of numbers Washington had hoped to have as a means of offsetting the better training and leadership of the British. The King's soldiers were to be tempted to desert by the promise of large grants of land and domestic animals;[141] but there was no reason to anticipate early gain, if there ultimately was any, from this appeal. Manifestly and in spite of all previous hopes that the draft of militia from the States would remove the necessity for levies en masse,[142] Washington would be compelled to call on the "Long Faces" to help him. Authorization for bringing 5000 into the field from New Jersey, Pennsylvania and Maryland consequently was voted by the Delegates on the 4th of April, with the stipulation that the States were to arm

---

(2 *Greene's Greene*, 68–69). Knox thought an offensive most desirable but difficult, whether directed against New York or against Philadelphia, though he inclined toward an attack on the forces at the mouth of the Hudson; Wayne's argument for an offensive was somewhat too theoretical to be of much value; Enoch Poor advocated an operation against New York; John Paterson favored the maintenance of a fortified camp for training and disciplining the Army, which later would assume an unspecified offensive.

[134] 3 *G. W.*, 282. This was elaborated in the "Thoughts upon a Plan of Operations . . .", *ibid.*, p. 185.

[135] 11 *G. W.*, 34.   [136] *Ibid.*, 98–99.

[137] 3 *Burnett*, 110.   [138] *Ibid.*, 159.

[139] *Ibid.*, 299, 301.

[140] *Ibid.*, 182. For typical orders on the inoculation of recruits, see *ibid.*, 238. Cf. 15 *V* 285.

[141] Resolve of Apr. 29, 1778; 10 *JCC.*, 405.

[142] Cf. 11 *G. W.*, 248.

and accoutre these men.[143] In his correspondence with the Governors,[144] the Commander-in-Chief had to give the strictest attention to the equipment of these forces in advance by the States, because the work of the armorers had been so poorly performed that the Army had no surplus muskets and, indeed, a paltry store even of cartridges.[145]

These shortages, exceedingly dangerous in themselves, showed ominously that besides the commissary and the quartermasters' service, almost everything else in the Army had suffered direly from neglect, or despair or incompetent direction during that frightful winter at Valley Forge. ". . . at no period of the war," Washington had to write Congress, "have I felt more painful sensations on account of delay than at present . . ." [146] Richard Henry Lee was to be more outspoken in a letter he soon was to write Thomas Jefferson: "For God's sake, for the love of our country, my dear friend, let more vigorous measures be quickly adopted for reenforcing the Army. The last draft will fall greatly short of the requisite number." [147]

It was now the end of April, blessed in memory because it was the season when all the gardens were blooming on the Potomac, and the fresh, vivid greens of spring had not been deepened or seared by the summer sun. Five years previously that 30th of April Washington had been rejoicing in the fine hauls of fish his servants had made off Sheridan's Point; in 1774, he saw the last twilight of the first spring month from the portico of Mount Vernon on a quiet day when not one guest sat down at table with him and Martha; the year after that he had witnessed the approach of May while busy with the Alexandria volunteers and with preparations to leave home for the second Continental Congress.[148] When he reflected now on spring in three years that had followed—1776, 1777 and 1778—what brightness had there been in any of them, what but a mockery of everything that ought to rejoice the heart and mind of man? Washington had been called to face the threat of Howe's descent on New York with European veterans and a mighty fleet in the year of the Declaration of Independence; in '77 he had struggled with the baffling uncertainty of British movement

---

[143] 10 *JCC.*, 310.   [144] 11 *G. W.*, 311.

[145] *Ibid.*, 315, 317, 339.

[146] Letter of Apr. 10, 1778, to the President of Congress; 11 *G. W.*, 239.

[147] Letter of May 2, 1778, *Ballagh, Lee Letters*, v. 1, p. 395. He added optimistically that America's enemies were sore pressed and that "wisdom and vigor now will presently compel Great Britain, proud as she is, to acknowledge our independency."

[148] 2 *Diaries*, 109, 150, 193.

from the Raritan; 1778 thus far had been a nightmare of cabal and intrigue in command, and of pallor, hunger, tatters and foul odors at Valley Forge.

For what besides this torture of spirit must Washington now steel his soul? Would there be another summer of mad running from the Delaware to Head of Elk? Were there to be more months of vain defensive while Congress fumed and asked why Washington could not do as Gates had done? Must the Commander-in-Chief reconcile himself to the certainty that belated inoculation and reluctant militia and small-minded members of State Legislatures once again would leave him with nothing more than the shadow of an Army? That very morning of the 30th of April, he had written Henry Laurens a renewed appeal for the half-pay bill, and had admitted that "while this matter is held in suspense, everything is at a stand and the most fatal consequences may result from it." Then, almost despairingly he had said:

I do not to this hour know whether (putting half-pay out of the question) the old or new establishment of the Regiments is to take place; how to dispose of the officers in consequence; whether the instituting of the several other corps, as agreed to by the committee, and referred by them to Congress, is adopted or not; in a word, I have no ground to form a single arrangement upon; nor do I know whether the augmentation of the Cavalry is to take place, or was rejected, in order that I may govern myself thereby . . . In short, our present situation (now the first of May) is beyond description irksome and dangerous . . ." [149]

There had been other letters to answer that morning, and at length, as the day wore on, there came two more by express, one from Alexander McDougall and the other from Simeon Deane, a stranger. Washington opened and read: Deane had left Brest on the 8th of March, aboard the fast French frigate *La Sensible,* and after a swift voyage had reached Falmouth, Casco Bay, April 13. He had hurried to Boston [150] and then had proceeded on the road to York with utmost speed in order to deliver to Congress five packets. [151]

One of them contained the text of a treaty, signed February 6, at Versailles, [152] by which France recognized the independence of the United States. [153]

[149] 11 *G. W.,* 327–28.
[150] He arrived there April 19; 2 *Sullivan Papers,* 36; *Heath,* 174; C. *Marshall's Diary,* 178.
[151] 2 *Wharton,* 490–91, 495–97, 567. [152] Text in 11 *JCC.,* 448–53.
[153] 11 *G. W.,* 324.

APPENDIX IV-1

Washington's Headquarters in New York City, 1776

REMARKABLY little is known concerning Washington's residence in New York City during 1776. He arrived from New England on the 13th of April [1] and according to the Loyalist, Judge Thomas Jones, went to William Smith's house, directly opposite a dwelling Governor Tryon had hired on Broadway.[2] Four days later, Mrs. Washington reached the city, after a leisured journey from Cambridge, and established herself at the fine mansion of Abraham Mortier,[3] long the Paymaster General of British forces in America. This property, later known as Richmond Hill, was on what now is Varick Street, at the corner of Charlton,[4] in "Lispenard's Meadows," [5] and at a distance of two and a half miles from the fort at the tip of New York Island.[6] Washington doubtless moved his belongings to Mortier's before or by the time Martha came to New York. She accompanied him on his visit to Philadelphia, May 21–June 6,[7] and in that city, she underwent inoculation.[8] Whether she returned to New York after her recovery is doubtful. She certainly had left the island [9] before July 1 and as late as July 22, she was said in one of her husband's letters to be in Philadelphia.[10]

Even if Martha's stay in New York was from April 17 to May 21 and no longer, Washington undoubtedly resided with her during that time at Mortier's. No evidence of any sort indicates that he subsequently left that pleasant residence and went back to spend his nights in the town during the hot summer months. He was absent at intervals, of course, as for example during the unhappy period of operations on Long Island, but Mortier's almost certainly was his formal place of residence from approximately April 17 to about the 14th of September. This demonstrably was the situation on June 10 [11]. Moreover, Charles Carroll waited on him there the previous day after

[1] N. Y. Mercury and Gazette, Apr. 16, 1776.
[2] 1 Jones, History N. Y., 58, 85.
[3] N. Y. Mercury and Gazette, Apr. 22, 1776.
[4] J. F. Watson, Annals of New York, 341; WPA Guide to New York City, 143.
[5] J. W. Francis, "Old New York" in 3 His. Mag. (3), p. 16.
[6] According to Thomas Kitchin's Map of New York Island, 1778.
[7] 5 G. W., 76, 78n, 101. These dates include time on the road.
[8] Ibid., 93.
[9] Joseph Reed to Mrs. Reed, July 1, 1776: "Mrs. Washington and the other ladies are gone from here" (Reed Papers, NYHS).
[10] 5 G. W., 327. He said, in addition, she "has thoughts of returning to Virginia as there is little or no prospect of her being with me any part of this summer."
[11] See note 14, infra.

returning from Canada.[12] The Morris House, later the Jumel Mansion, which was used by Washington in the second half of September, is the best known New York structure associated with his revolutionary career.[13]

So much for Washington's residence in New York during the spring and summer of 1776. What of his office? Where was that located? From the date of his return to New York from Philadelphia, June 6, it is almost certain that he transacted his official business at Mortier's.[14] No evidence has been adduced to prove that he had headquarters "downtown" during this period, though doubtless he held conferences at the offices of one or another of his subordinates.

The question, therefore, narrows itself to this time bracket: Where did Washington attend to army affairs from the time he left William Smith's to May 21, the date of his departure for Philadelphia? Traditionally, the greater part, if not the whole of this period was spent on Bayard's "Hill" or "Mount," [15] near Grand and Mott Streets, or, more generally, the vicinity of Chatham Square, but confusion or vagueness seems to have existed for a long time regarding the alleged location of these headquarters. In a recent guide book, Washington's office is said to have been on Pearl Street across from Hanover Square; Lossing was told by an old resident that part of the original house was preserved in the building numbered 180 Pearl Street, which was opposite Cedar Street. This site is about 300 yards from Hanover Square. On the other hand, Chatham Square is about three-quarters of a mile from Hanover Square.[16]

It is entirely possible that some truth lies behind one or another of these traditions, but none of the various orderly books or contemporary records of other sorts gives even a hint of the location of the General's office anywhere in the vicinity of Bayard's Hill. If confirmation ever is found, it probably will be a casual reference in some Diary or letter.

Positive evidence is limited to these two established facts: First, headquarters, as of May 19, 1776, were in a building on so elevated a site that the roof of it was used as a signal station.[17] Second, on May 22, mention was

[12] 1 *Rowland's Carroll*, 172. [13] See *supra*, p. 190.

[14] Cf. McDougall's Orderly Book, NYHS, June 10, 1776, notice that the Paymaster General has removed his office to Leonard Lespinard's house, to be "near his Excellency, General Washington." The same notice appears in Captain Hyatt's Orderly Book, LC, and in the transcript of Gen. John Glover's Orderly Book, Columbia Univ. Lib. Glover stated under date of May 24 that the "removal of General Washington from his headquarters in town" had caused changes in the detail of guards. This somewhat ambiguous language may indicate headquarters were moved during the General's absence.

[15] For contemporary reference to a fortification on this elevation, temporarily called Montgomery's Mount, see 5 *His. Mag.*, pt. 2, p. 203. The works were to be "superior to any" the writer "could ever conceive."

[16] WPA *Guide to New York City*, 89; 2 *Lossing*, 800.

[17] Glover explained that the raising of the flag in daytime and of lanterns at night, "on the top of General Washington's headquarters" would be one of the two general alarms. (Transcript of Glover's Orderly Book, *loc. cit.*)

made of the "Oyster Battery," behind General Washington's headquarters. The exact location of the "Oyster Battery" is not known, but that careful student of New York topography, Prof. H. P. Johnston, thought it probably was in the vicinity of the present Morris and Greenwich Streets.[18]

Lossing[19] stated that after returning from Philadelphia, Washington "went to the Kennedy House, No. 1 Broadway,[20] where he remained until the evacuation in September." This is certainly erroneous. Numerous references show that the Kennedy House was the residence of Col. Henry Knox and that Washington went there July 21 to receive the Adjutant General of the British Army. Nothing in these accounts suggests even the possibility that Washington had his headquarters in the Kennedy House at that time.[21] Washington may have had an office there later, but no reference to it has been found. The tradition that Washington moved his headquarters to the City Hall, not long before July 9, rests solely on the reference in the *Kentish Gazette,* Canterbury, England,[22] to the effect that this was done "upon the discovery of a design to seize and deliver [Washington] to Governor Tryon."

In summary, then, the evidence justifies this only: On his arrival in New York, Apr. 13, 1776, Washington went to the residence of William Smith, on Broadway, opposite the temporary abode of Governor Tryon, but Washington moved by the 17th to Mortier's, later called Richmond Hill, on the present Varick Street at the corner of Charlton, and there he had his sleeping quarters until about September 14. Then he went to Harlem Heights and established himself at the Morris House, 161st Street. From an undetermined date in April, subsequent to the 13th, until June 6, Washington doubtless maintained a headquarters office somewhere "downtown" in New York, but all that has been established definitely to this time about the location is that it was on a conspicuous elevation and was near the so-called Oyster Battery. After June 6 he almost certainly had his office as well as his residence at Mortier's.

---

[18] Transcript of Glover's Orderly Book, *loc. cit.*; 3 *LIHS Mem.,* 86.

[19] *Loc. cit.*

[20] For a detailed statement of the traditional splendor of this structure, see Martha J. Lamb, *Historic Homes and Landmarks,* 66.

[21] 1 *Webb,* 156; Gaine's *N. Y. Mercury,* July 22, 1776, *Penn. Gazette,* July 24, 1777. Knox's own language, in a letter of the 22nd to Mrs. Knox is conclusive: The British Adjutant General [Lt. Col. James Patterson] "met the General at our house" (*Knox Papers,* MHS). In Gaine's account (*loc. cit.*), the reference is to "the dwelling of Colonel Knox in this city, where his Excellency, General Washington, accompanied by his bodyguard, awaited [Patterson's] arrival." As of June 1, Colonel Glover gave orders for sentries to parade "at the Bowling Green, before Colonel Knox's door" (Transcript of Glover's Orderly Book, *loc. cit.*).

[22] Quoted in 5 Stokes, *Iconography,* under date of July 9, 1776.

APPENDIX IV-2

Organization of American Espionage in New York Area, 1777

(After the Original in the Collection of Dr. F. M. Dearborn
of New York City)

May it Please your Excellency:

Emediately upon my appointment I Repaired to the State of New York where I entered on the business assigned me, but as it was of a secret nature and knowing that if either the business or any Circumstance attending it have a tendency to that would give a clue to the Enemy, and render the whole abortive made the Execution of it Exceeding Difficult and found myself under a necessity of placing confidence in some particular gentleman tho' never opened the business to any except Wm Duer, Esqr. without first administering the oath of secrecy to them. After spending a fortnight in the Business I almost despaired of success, but fortunately a Gentleman that I had engaged to secure me a proper person for to go into the city of New York, sent me one who he recommended to be well educated and a good siveyer [surveyor] and every way calculated for the Business. On the night of the 7th March I got him thro' our Lines at the English Neighborhood on his way to the City. His business was to get what Intelligence he could—hire a room in the City and get a license to carry on a secret trade for poltry to enable him to convey our intelligence once or twice a week. He has not yet returned, neither have I heard from him since. Enclosed your Excellency the copy of the Oath he took before he went off, but think imprudent therefore must beg to be excused until a Personal Interview. Immediately on my return, I fortunately received two other Gentlemen of well known attainments to our Camp, who are honest, sensible and intriguing and have undertaken to go into the Enemy and seat themselves down in their camps. I propose one of them for Brunswick and the other for Amboy. One did sit out on the Business, and to enable him to go in under proper circumstances to get the best intelligence, has for some time past associated with the first rate Torys in these parts and carried matters so far as to get a written invitation from Wm. Bayard now in the City. His son is a Col. in the British service and will go in recommended to Col. Buskirk and Major Tenpenny in their service. This gentleman has not had the small pox, a circumstance he did not mention to me untill every needful preparation was made for his entering upon the Business. I immediately ordered him to return home and be Enoculated. He set off last Friday, intended to take the Infection yesterday, and will return as soon as he is able to go in to establish his Character with the enemy and remove every suspicion. I have given him Liberty to enlist 8 or 10 men to take in with him as an evidence of his sincerity, other gentlemen was enoculated and returned to me from the Small Pox day before yesterday, and is now among the Principal Torys near the enemies Lines—in order to get Letters of Recommendation to some Principle Gentlemen in the enemeies service. I expect him back tomorrow with Proper credentials to enable him to enter their camp with credit. I have also imployed a Hessian who has lived in the country for near 40 years. He is either to go in himself, or get one of that nation that may be relied on to go in. He is to meet me here next Thursday and he gives it as his opinion that he can use such arguments with them as will prevail with great numbers to desert. He will make use of the Deserters as pipes to convey Intelligence. I could wish that your Excellency would point out the most proper place for the last mentioned man. Week before Last I sent in a woman—the wife of a man gone over to the enemy. Our people has taken her Grain for our use. She made a very heavy complaint. I advised her to go to New York and complain to Lord Howe. She was pleased with the advice and set off to his Lordship and to request the time that she might expect relief. She left the city last Friday week, and says that she despairs of any relief soon; that there is a large number of flat bottomed boats in the harbour of New York which are intended for an Expedition against Philadelphia and that the British army is going to subdue that city; and that the poor Tory sufferers will not be relieved until that Expedition is over. She says that provisions of every kind in New York is very dear; that when a cow calves, they let the calf suck until it is fit to kill, and then kill both cow and calf together and eat them; that the beef of such cows sells from 18 to 2/ per Pound; that flower is 28/ per hundred wt and everything in proportion and she fears very much that the Kings army will not be able to subdue the Rebels, in less than two or three years. I also enclosed your Excellency a copy of the examination taken from two dissenters yesterday. I have no further intelligence. . . . etc., etc. [Last seven lines missing.]

TO: GEORGE WASHINGTON, Esq., Apl. 7, 1777. [Unsigned]

APPENDIX IV-3

THE COLLAPSE OF THE COMMISSARY IN 1777-78

AT DIFFERENT times and in varying degree, numerous minor difficulties of the usual sort beset the commissary of Washington's Army during the early months of 1777. Poor cooperage and lack of barrels and of salt threatened

several times to ruin considerable stores of meat;[1] during the winter of
1776–77 there had been a lack of funds, even for the essential purchase of
provisions;[2] first and last, a good deal of energy must have been given to
the purchase of non-essentials for officers;[3] both transportation and trouble
were involved in getting beer, rum and whiskey, of which the Army consumed all the Congress and the Commander-in-Chief would authorize and
provide.[4] In general, transportation sufficed, if narrowly, during the summer
of 1777, but by September broken-down wagons probably were being abandoned and then neglected in a manner certain to create a shortage when
winter came and all forage, as well as the provisions and bed-straw for the
troops, had to be hauled.[5] The handling of wagons was negligent and lacked
competence in almost every particular.[6]

Another threat to the Army's commissary was represented by the approaching exhaustion of the supply of meat within the reach of officers who, in
many instances, were losing their zeal. At the end of 1776, agents of the
Commissary General still were convinced that food could be supplied in
needed quantity,[7] and at least one of Trumbull's subordinates questioned, as
late as February, 1777, whether the troops would need all the wheat that was
being offered.[8] By May, optimism had vanished; the shortage was upon the
Army.[9] It was manifest that Connecticut could supply few more than 1000
cattle and that the forces could not hope to sustain themselves even temporarily on what was available in and near the valley of the Raritan.[10] Re-

---

[1] James Bate to Joseph Trumbull, Apr. 23, 1777; William Graham to Joseph Trumbull,
May 1, 1777; H. Hollingsworth to Joseph Trumbull, May 5, 1777; T. Lowry to Joseph Trumbull, July 8, 1777. All these are references to the *Joseph Trumbull Papers,* CHS. Cf. Joseph
Trumbull to J. Wadsworth, Aug. 13, 1777; MS, *Yale Univ. Lib.* In contrast, Joseph Trumbull
wrote his father, Jan. 5, 1777: ". . . I am convinced that the scarcity of salt is artificial more
than real."

[2] David Trumbull to Joseph Trumbull, Dec. 9, 1776; Daniel Grey to Joseph Trumbull,
same date; James Bate to Joseph Trumbull, Dec. 28, 1776; H. Hollingsworth to Joseph Trumbull, May 5, 1777; *Trumbull Papers,* loc. cit. By this shorter title the *Joseph Trumbull Papers*
will be cited hereafter in this appendix.

[3] Cf. Joshua Land's report on the loss of stores in the Peekskill raid of Mch. 23, 1777, and
Trumbull's accounts of purchases of wines, liquors, etc., for Washington and other officers
as of Aug. 7, 1776, all in the *Trumbull Papers,* loc. cit.

[4] Account of David Trumbull for malt, n.d., 1776–77; Thomas Russell's account of Apr.
n.d., 1777 against Joseph Trumbull for thirty pipes of Madeira and 10,800 gallons of brandy
and other spirits. Leonard Lispenard, by June 30, 1776, had extended credit to the continent
for £826, odd money, to cover 1600 barrels of beer. In an invoice of July 9, 1777, for sundries
delivered Commissary General Trumbull at Middle Brook, rum outweighed nearly all the
other products. To the envy of the remainder of the Army, artillerists in February, 1777, received two gills of rum daily per man, as compared with a regular ration of one gill. See
Mathew Irwin's report of Feb. 8, 1777; *Trumbull Papers,* loc. cit.

[5] See the report of the committee of Congress that visited the camp in January–February,
1778; 2 *Greene's Greene,* 44.

[6] This is mentioned in Washington's general review of the service, January, 1778, 10 *G. W.,*
390 ff.

[7] See David Grey to Joseph Trumbull, Dec. 9, 1776; *Trumbull Papers,* loc. cit.

[8] Jonathan Warner to Joseph Trumbull, Feb. 1, 1777, *ibid.*

[9] See the letters of James Bate to Joseph Trumbull, May 1, 23, 1777; *loc. cit.*

[10] *Ibid.*

quirements of 10,000 head for the period from June 21 to the end of the year 1777 would exceed greatly all that could be purchased in New Jersey, in Pennsylvania, in Maryland and in Virginia combined. Arrangements must be made forthwith to get a supply of pork from North Carolina.[11]

Among the results of this shortage were a sharp increase in prices,[12] the marketing of poor cattle,[13] and costly competition between private dealers and army contractors, few of whom were active at any great distance from camp.[14] "Butchers from Philadelphia," complained an agent of Trumbull's in Easton, "push up everything, fat and poor alike." [15] The manifest incompetence of several functionaries [16] aggravated the shortage and aroused resentments which, in turn, prompted Congress to adopt the plan of dual commissaries. Thereby the Delegates created uncertainty throughout the department, inspired new resignations and provoked threats of retirement.[17] Committeemen went to camp to "inquire into the state of the Army," but the report they filed on Aug. 5, 1777, was a disappointing document.

Advocates of the division of the commissary into separate bureaux of purchase and of issue felt in the early autumn that sufficient time had not elapsed for the merits of the system to be plain; adversaries of the new organization pronounced it a menacing failure,[18] though Congress sought, of course, to keep secret a situation that manifestly might prompt General Howe to strike.[19] Congressmen on Oct. 2, 1777, added to the commissary's burden that of supplying food and provender, at cost, to them and to specified officials of the several boards.[20] As late as the second week in November, the organi-

[11] Matthew Irwin's estimate of Apr. 4, 1777; *ibid.* Virginia apparently supplied more than 2000 barrels of pork in June and immediately thereafter (William Aylett's report of June 13, 1777; *ibid.*), though by July 3, New England magazines contained only 853 barrels of pork and eighty-four of beef (Daniel Grey to J. Wadsworth, July 3, 1777; *Wadsworth Papers,* CHS).

[12] H. Hollingsworth to Joseph Trumbull, May 5, 1777. James Bate reported from Morristown on the 16th of May, 1777, that twenty-seven cattle, purchased recently, had cost 12 d per pound (*Trumbull Papers,* loc. cit.).

[13] James Bate to Joseph Trumbull, Mch. 27, May 15, 1777; *ibid.*

[14] Bate, as *supra,* Mch. 27, 1777. Joseph Trumbull to M. Irwin, Mch. 5, 1777, *Joseph Trumbull Papers,* Mil. and Gen. Corres., Vol. V, p. 489a, Conn. State. Lib.

[15] Richard Backhouse, to Joseph Trumbull, July 6, 1777. James Bate had reported to Trumbull, May 3, 1777, that a herd, intended for the Army, had been driven into Philadelphia (*Ibid.*).

[16] M. Irwin to Joseph Trumbull, Jan. 15, 1777, concerning Washington's dissatisfaction with some of these officers, Carpenter Wharton in particular; William Hoskins to Joseph Trumbull, Feb. 4, 1777, in denunciation of commissaries "big with art" and "unacquainted with the conduct" of the office (*Ibid.*).

[17] James Bate to Joseph Trumbull, May 3, 1777; *ibid.,* Joseph Trumbull to J. Wadsworth, June 6, 1777, *Yale Univ. Lib.;* Seven deputy Commissaries to Congress, July 1, 1777; *Wadsworth Papers,* CHS; Eliphalet Dyer to Joseph Trumbull, July 15, 1777, *Trumbull Papers,* loc. cit. Benjamin Talmadge to J. Wadsworth, Aug. 14, 1777, *Wadsworth Papers,* CHS.

[18] Putnam to Washington, Oct. 2, 1777, 1 *Webb,* 321; E. Gerry to Joseph Trumbull, Oct. 2, 1777, and Nov. 27, 1777, 2 *Burnett,* 506, 571; William Williams to Joseph Trumbull, Nov. 28, 1777, *ibid.,* 573; R. H. Lee to Washington, Nov. 20, 1777, 1 *Ballagh, Lee Letters,* 352.

[19] 9 *JCC.,* 761.

[20] 8 *JCC.,* 760. For a tangle at Peekskill and farther up-state in the Northern Department, see 9 *JCC.,* 766, 858–59 and 9 *G. W.,* 488. Various other woes and perplexities of the com-

zation was not complete;[21] on the 24th Congressmen realized through a letter from Commissary General William Buchanan that old problems were recurring and new perplexities arising—that the supply of flour was exceedingly low, that Pennsylvania farmers had refrained from threshing wheat because they feared the grain would be taken from them, that sufficient barrels were not being coopered, that it was uncertain whether needed salt was being sent from New England, that teams were not available for hauling all provisions the Army required—that, in short, the commissary was close to ruin.[22] This stirred Congress, first, to seek in Pennsylvania some of the required supplies,[23] and, second, to make the demand already noted, that every farmer thresh at least one-half of his wheat by February 20.[24] Salt was to be moved forthwith;[25] reforms were to be instituted. Activity that followed this alarm accomplished relatively little. If Joseph Trumbull had kept his health, had left his accounts to the keeping of honest clerks, and had used diligently his experience, he probably could have foreseen the shortage and would have sent his agents to Carolina and to the remoter counties in time to get cattle or to have salt meat prepared for winter. As noted in the text, Washington thought this personal consideration perhaps the most important of all. Later, when the Army had passed through the "starving time" at Valley Forge, Washington insisted, "our difficulties and distresses, in this instance, have not arisen from a scarcity of provisions, but from improper persons, or rather none at all, being employed."[26]

In summary, then, the removal of the main Army to Valley Forge was made when a small staff of commissary officers, including some who were inexperienced and some who were incompetent—to say nothing of those possessing both deficiencies—was operating under new regulations in a country of depleted resources. The keen, competitive bidding for the cattle and hogs by Philadelphia butchers had ceased outwardly, but there was clandestine trade. Disaffection or the hope of higher prices held back some dealers; British raiders captured many animals; drovers were indifferent, roads were bad. Almost every interest seemed to conspire against the supply of provisions for the men in the camp on the Schuylkill. Instead of one reason for the failure of the commissary, there were half a score.

---

missary in the fall of 1777, together with some plans of reform, will be found in 9 *JCC.*, 748, 766–67, 768, 805, 829; 2 *Burnett*, 542–43, 544; 9 *G. W.*, 204–05; 10 *ibid.*, 38, 91.

[21] 9 *JCC.*, 871, 890.   [22] *Ibid.*, 961.

[23] *Ibid.*, 962, 976, 977, 1014–16, 10 *G. W.*, 162.

[24] 10 *G. W.*, 175.   [25] 9 *JCC.*, 977.

[26] Letter of Mch. 28, 1778; 11 *G. W.*, 165. Cf. *ibid.*, 267.

APPENDIX IV-4

Reconcentration in the Autumn of 1777

On the 7th of September, 1777, Gov. William Livingston of New Jersey wrote Congress, from Philadelphia, that he had information of an impending descent of a British force on East Jersey from Staten Island.[1] His call for 1400 militiamen of his own constituency had been answered by 400 only; it was imperative that 1500 Continentals from Peekskill be dispatched to New Jersey.[2] Congress responded the next day with a resolution that directed General Putnam to hold 1500 men in readiness to cross the Hudson into Jersey when Washington so ordered.[3] Instructions were forwarded accordingly by the Commander-in-Chief,[4] with this counsel of Washington to Putnam: "I think you should call in all your parties upon out commands, and that you should keep your force pretty well drawn together."[5] Initial requisition on Putnam thus did not originate with Washington and did not represent any direct effort to strengthen the main Army at the expense of the defenders of the Highlands of New York, but the transfer was one that Washington approved.

The day after these orders were dispatched to Putnam, the adverse outcome of the Battle of the Brandywine exposed Philadelphia to early and easy British occupation. An alarmed Congress sent for all the militia it could hope to muster, and it required, most particularly, that Putnam forward to Washington the 1500 troops who were to have been made ready for the defence of East Jersey.[6] On the 14th, Washington received a report that two columns, to a total of about 2000 British, had entered New Jersey from Staten Island and New York—a dangerous move by every test. If the situation became desperate, the 1500 troops presumably en route from the Hudson to the main Army might be returned toward their original objective in East Jersey. Could other soldiers from Putnam be sent there, to build up a stronger defence, if need be, or to replace the 1500 in event the thrust did not appear formidable? In answering his own question, Washington could use as one basis of calculation a return Putnam had made, apparently with some difficulty,[7] about the 5th of September.[8] This showed that with his Sergeants

[1] For preliminary British discussion of this raid, see George Clinton to Commodore William Hotham, Sept. 3, 1777; *Clinton Papers*, Clements Lib.
[2] 68 *Papers Cont. Cong.*, 277, LC.   [3] 8 *JCC.*, 720.
[4] 2 *Burnett*, 487–88; 9 *G. W.*, 201, 203.   [5] 9 *G. W.*, 201.
[6] 8 *JCC.*, 736.
[7] Cf. Putnam to Washington, Aug. 30, 1777. Included is a statement that orders had been given repeatedly for a return of the artillery but that none had been procurable and none would be unless "steps were taken" (55 *Papers of G. W.*, 35, LC).
[8] Enclosed in Putnam to Washington; *ibid.*, 113.

included, Putnam had Continentals and militia to a total of 5108—or 3608 after the deduction of the 1500 already ordered from the Hudson.[9]

Washington had never visited the upper part of the district occupied by Putnam's command and he had no first-hand information concerning the strength of the forts. He therefore asked those of his nearby senior officers who were familiar with the region, how many men would suffice to hold the defences and the Highland passes. The consensus was that 2000 should be able to repel any force that probably would be sent against Putnam.[10] On this assurance, Washington decided that an additonal 1000 men could proceed from Putnam's district into Jersey for use there or for the stiffening of the line of the Schuylkill.[11] In ordering Putnam to detach this second body, Washington urged him to call immediately on Governor Trumbull of Connecticut for 2000 militia "to secure the posts in the Highlands and to enable [Putnam] to make further detachments, if circumstances should render it necessary." Washington went on to particularize: "You will garrison Fort Montgomery and the other fortifications about it with some of your best troops and secure the passes into the Highlands with the remainder of the continental troops and militia. As it is not improbable the enemy may make a diversion up the North River, by way of amusing you and to take advantages, as circumstances may favor their design, you cannot be too vigilant." He reiterated: "You will write in the most pressing terms, to Governor Trumbull to hasten in the militia." [12]

If Washington had felt any misgiving over the reasonableness of his calls on Putnam in the dual emergency of an advance on Philadelphia and a probable invasion of New Jersey, his mind would have been set at ease by the arrival, within a week,[13] of a most optimistic dispatch from Putnam, who wrote of the good news from Gates's front and proceeded to say: "I have for some time been meditating an expedition towards New York and expect to be able to attack the enemy at Staten Island, Powles Hook, York Island and Long Island at one time. I have information from one quarter and another and I have gained knowledge of their strength very nearly at their different posts and that an enterprise of that kind might be undertaken with good prospects of success. Enclosed I send a return of the troops under my com-

[9] 9 G. W., 218.   [10] Ibid., 325–26.
[11] It is to be noted that Washington's order to Putnam (ibid., 218–19) reads as if these troops were intended primarily for the defence of Jersey, but Washington's later reference to this call for reenforcement (ibid., 372–73), shows that he expected to draw Putnam's contingent to the main Army if the men were not needed to resist what appeared on September 14 to be an invasion of Jersey.
[12] 9 G. W., 219.
[13] The original of Putnam's letter bears no endorsement to show when it reached headquarters, but as Washington on October 1 acknowledged the receipt of letters of September 27 and 28 from Putnam (ibid., 289), it is safe to say that a dispatch from Putnam, written September 13, came to Washington's hands by the 20th and certainly by the 23rd which is the important date in the correspondence on this subject.

mand at this and adjacent posts in case I should go on the proposed expedition Governor Trumbull [14] has assured me a large reenforcement from Connecticut which together with the reenforcement of the Continental troops here and what assistance I can get from this State and the Jersies, I imagine I shall have a sufficiency of men." [15] If Putnam had men enough for an offensive, he assuredly was sufficiently strong to maintain a defensive after the detachment of 1000 to supplement the 1500 ordered into Jersey and then to the Schuylkill.

There was nothing whatever in Putnam's next letter, which was dated September 14, that showed apprehension on his part. He mentioned a rumor that a British force estimated all the way from 1000 to five times that number had crossed the Hudson opposite Fort Lee and had marched to Hackensack, but he explained: "I sent this morning General McDougall with about 1200 men and two field pieces over after them—shall attend the advice and direction in your letters." [16] The only disappointing detail in this was the remark that McDougall had about 1200 men instead of the 1500 ordered from Putnam in the first contingent. In another communication, written on the 16th, Putnam said that McDougall had crossed with approximately 1500 and he asked, somewhat anxiously, whether Congress meant that this force should proceed to Pennsylvania regardless of the situation in Jersey or the danger to the Hudson, "especially," he said, "as I am well informed that a considerable force has arrived at New York." [17]

The reenforcement moving southward under McDougall [18] turned out to number not 1500 or even 1200 but a meagre 911 only, of whom nearly 200 were militia.[19] Consequently, on the 23rd of September, when Washington had to deal with an adversary who had crossed the Schuylkill, a new order had to be hurried to Putnam: The total detachment must be brought up to the required figure, 2500; the second contingent must move to the main Army by way of Morristown and Coryell's Ferry. Washington wrote: "I must urge you, by every motive, to send on this detachment with the least possible delay. No considerations are to prevent it. It is our first object to defeat, if possible, the Army now opposed to us here. That the passes in the

---

[14] These clauses are verbatim because the lack of punctuation makes it uncertain whether Putnam intended to end the sentence with "posts" or with "expedition," a difference that affects the meaning.

[15] Putnam to Washington, Sept. 13, 1777; 56 *Papers of G. W.*, 41, LC. The tone of the Putnam-McDougall correspondence in the *McDougall Papers*, NYHS, is one of cooperation and encouragement of the part of Putnam.

[16] 56 *Papers of G. W.*, 63, LC.

[17] *Ibid.*, 85. Putnam gave the same figure, 1500, in his letter of Sept. 16, 1777, to Hancock (159 *Papers Cont. Cong.*, 95, LC).

[18] It crossed the Hudson Sept. 14–15, 1777; McDougall to Washington, Sept. 17, 1777; 56 *Papers of G. W.*, 104, LC; Putnam to McDougall, Sept. 15, 1777; *McDougall Papers*, NYHS.

[19] 56 *Papers of G. W.*, 104, LC. There is a difference of twenty in the reports of the size of this force.

Highlands may be perfectly secure, you will immediately call in all your forces now on command at outposts. You must not think of covering a whole country by dividing them; and when they are ordered in and drawn together, they will be fully competent to repel any attempt that can be made by the enemy from below in their present situation . . . That you may not hesitate about complying with this order, you are to consider it peremptory and not to be dispensed with." [20]

The threat against New Jersey proved by September 18 to be nothing more than a cattle raid,[21] but Washington continued to feel the need of reenforcement in Pennsylvania. About the 27th of September, it will be recalled, on his order, McDougall joined the main Army with approximately 900, or 600 less than Putnam had been ordered to send. McDougall brought from Putnam no explanation of this deficiency of numbers, nor was there word of any troops on the road McDougall had covered. Washington consequently reiterated his call for other detachments on the basis of Putnam's return of September 5, which indicated that 1800 men would be left on the Hudson if Putnam sent the whole of the specified 2500.[22] Within three days, there came letters in which Putnam gave assurance that these reenforcements were in what Washington described as "forwardness." [23] In acknowledging these communications Washington expressed the belief that reported accessions of British strength in New York were exaggerated. Further, said the Commander-in-Chief, if Burgoyne were defeated the Hudson would "be no object for the enemy." Washington added: "I rather think, if General Clinton moves at all, it will be through Jersey to form a junction with General Howe." [24] Conspicuously, in a postscript, Washington told Putnam to call on Governor Trumbull of Connecticut "in the most pressing manner" to replace with militia the continental troops ordered to the main Army.[25]

Putnam, for his part, said no more about his plan to attack the enemy in the district around New York City. In a mood entirely different, he proceeded to make it clear that he felt he was weakening his forces dangerously in complying with Washington's requisitions for men. This was why he wrote directly to Congress on the 29th of September that, depleted as his troops were, he would "not be answerable for its safety." [26] At that time he reported his force as "about 1000 effective continental troops and 400 militia, 200 of whom are from this State, one half of them without arms and, what is worse, it would be damned unsafe to trust them." [27] To this, Washington replied: ". . . by your return of the 5th of September, you would have 1800

[20] 9 G. W., 254.
[21] McDougall to Putnam; Putnam to McDougall, Sept. 18, 1777; McDougall Papers, NYHS.
[22] 9 G. W., 280, 326.   [23] Ibid., 289.
[24] Ibid., 290.   [25] Ibid.
[26] Quoted in the text, supra, p. 521.   [27] 9 G. W., 290.

effective rank and file left . . . ; besides these, the noncommissioned ought to be counted upon, and some of the invalids, for in the defence of stationary posts, every man that can lift a musket must do his duty." [28]

That was the last exchange of letters before the successful British attack of October 6 on Fort Montgomery and Fort Clinton. After their fall, Putnam wrote Washington that on the day of the disaster he had "not more than 1200 continental troops and 300 militia." His principal complaint was in this language: "I have repeatedly informed your Excellency of the enemy's design against this post; but, from some motive or other, you always differed with me in opinion." [29] Washington, in turn, told George Clinton: "Nothing but the absolute necessity could have induced me to have withdrawn any further part of the troops alloted for the defence of the posts up North River; but such was the reduced state of our continental Regiments, after the Battle of Brandywine, and such was the sloath and difficulty of procuring reenforcements of militia from the southward, that without the troops from Peekskill, we should scarcely have been able to have kept the field against General Howe. I had the greatest hopes that General Putnam would have drawn in as many Connecticut militia as would have replaced the continental troops, and I make no doubt that he did all in his power to obtain them in time." [30]

This was generous in its disregard of all the preliminaries that concerned the threatened invasion of New Jersey by the British. Washington spoke only of the ultimate employment of the troops from Putnam as if that, from the first, had been the reason for his call. The question, therefore, is whether the withdrawal of these troops from the line of the Hudson was necessary and was responsible for the loss of the forts. Washington had weakened himself previously in order to strengthen the Northern Department and the Highlands, and while he never proposed for an instant to cripple Gates in the face of Burgoyne, it was natural that the commander of the so-called "main Army," confronting the Howe brothers, should wish to make good the losses of Brandywine and of the long summer campaign of march and counter march. If desired reenforcement could come from Putnam, without excessive risk, Washington was entitled to it. Putnam was notoriously careless about making returns [31] and was suspected increasingly of a lack of energy and competence. In the general decline of his administrative qualities, Putnam might be husbanding men and might be far better able to spare the second detachment of 1500 men than he professed to be. If this was in

[28] Letter of Oct. 7, 1777; *ibid.,* 326.

[29] Letter of Oct. 8, 1777; 1 *LTW.,* 439, 440.

[30] Letter of Oct. 15, 1777; 9 *G. W.,* 372–73. His report of Oct. 10, 1777, to the President of Congress, had been to the same effect (*ibid.,* 349).

[31] Cf. Richard Peters to Washington, July 23, 1777, 52 *Papers of G. W.,* 4, LC., with the intimation that Putnam did not send returns to Washington, though he declined to submit them to the Board of War.

the mind of Washington, he scarcely was to be blamed for doubting whether he was receiving accurate information from Putnam.

So much must be said in Washington's proper defence; but beyond this, existing records do not show the condition of his Army to have been as serious as he thought it was. He rightly was cautious always in challenging the British, because the destruction of his Army would have ruined the American cause, but in this instance, when he justified his transfer of men from Putnam on the ground that he scarcely could have kept the field without them, he seems to have been overcautious, unless desertions were far more numerous than the records show. It is manifest, also, that he was dismally and surprisingly mistaken in his guess of General Sir Henry Clinton's next move. This may have been due in part to the fact that most, if not all the intelligence reports from New York City were going to the commanders at White Plains and at Peekskill, instead of to the headquarters of the main Army. Had Washington been correctly informed of British dispositions and preliminary movements, he probably would not have withdrawn any troops from that area, and almost certainly not those of Alexander Mc-Dougall. That officer and his well disciplined men might have been invaluable on the day of the attack. To this basic critique the sole reasonable objection may be the usual one—that it is wisdom after the event.

Did Washington have such a response from Putnam as that officer should have given? Putnam manifestly did not comply fully with orders by sending 900 men only in McDougall's column when Washington had called for 1500 rank and file; but it may be that the error was due to Putnam's negligent ignorance of the numbers he commanded. On the second call, he probably sent the full contingent demanded of him, and sent it promptly.[32] At the subsequent court of inquiry, he testified that about 1100 Continentals and approximately 400 militia were left him. In addition he had the artillery, whose strength he did not state, though he spoke of 125 men of that arm without saying whether they were all he had.[33] As of September 28, he had 876 men at Fort Montgomery,[34] and on the 8th of October, immediately after the attack, he wrote that he had 1200 to 1300 Continentals.[35] The lowest total of these figures was 175 under the 1800 shown in the return mentioned by Washington; the highest estimate by Putnam put his effective strength at less than 2000. The evidence does not show to what extent he displayed good

[32] That is to say, if he moved fewer than the required total, no protest or reprimand by Washington has been found. Little is known of the march of these troops, who consisted principally of Varnum's and Huntington's Brigades and perhaps of a few unattached continental Regiments. Christopher Greene's and Israel Angell's Rhode Islanders constituted the van. They and about half the others were committed forthwith to the defence of Red Bank (Fort Mercer). For the advance of these forces and their subsequent organization as a Division under McDougall, see 9 *G. W.*, 326, 327, 333, 335, 343, 344, 380.
[33] *McDougall Papers*, NYHS.   [34] *Ibid.*
[35] *Letters to Gates*, NYHS.

judgment in conforming to Washington's insistent warning that he recall men from useless outposts.

In any event it had been necessary that he supplement his garrison, as the Commander-in-Chief had directed, with more militia. Putnam frequently had received short-term reenforcement of this sort. In August, he had three New York Regiments from Gov. George Clinton [36] and then, on Washington's appeal, three more.[37] Fort Montgomery was supplied directly with still other New York militia. Most of these men remained a short time only. In September, six Regiments of temporary troops reported to Putnam. At the time, Governor Clinton could not state how large or small these Regiments were, and when at length he got figures, he had to admit that not more than 300 from these commands actually had reported to Putnam.[38] Additional rank and file might arrive later, but no other Regiments could be expected, the Governor explained, because all the able-bodied of the remaining counties had been ordered to General Gates.[39] Calls, therefore, had to be addressed to Connecticut, whence Governor Trumbull had stated on the 21st of August he had ordered 3000 to Peekskill.[40] Many, said Trumbull, already had reached that post but, like the New Yorkers, they must have stayed a short time only.

Putnam had not held the few whom he could have kept under martial law when, as it later proved, their presence might have been necessary to prevent a junction between the British on North River and those above Albany. In August, Putnam on his own account had bargained with some of the militia to employ part of them only at any one time.[41] Later, even when reports were circulating that the British in New York were reenforced and were contemplating an attack on Peekskill, there was much murmuring on the part of the militia ordered to Putnam. They had not sown their winter grain; they saw no evidence of impending attack. As Governor Clinton reported later: "They solicited General Putnam for leave to return, and many of them went home without his permission. Urged by these considerations he thought proper to dismiss part of them." [42] By so doing he weakened himself, but to what extent, the records once again do not show, because they contain no statement of the gross number of militia with Putnam prior to the order whereby some of them were dismissed.

In the hour of immediate danger, it was futile for Putnam to attempt to recall these New York militia. If any help was forthcoming it had to be

---

[36] *Public Papers of George Clinton,* v. 2, p. 183–84.
[37] *Ibid.*   [38] *Ibid.,* 322–23, 323–24, 349.
[39] George Clinton to Putnam, Sept. 28, 1777; *ibid.,* 347.
[40] *Letters to Gates,* NYHS.
[41] Dirck Brinckerhoff to George Clinton, Sept. 4, 1777; 2 *Public Papers of George Clinton,* 280.
[42] Governor Clinton to Washington, Oct. 9, 1777; *ibid.,* 390.

from Connecticut, but in seeking this, Putnam delayed too long. General Parsons sent him warning on September 26 that the enemy was planning a sweep as far as the Croton River,[43] and the next day Parsons forwarded a report that 3000 British reenforcements had reached New York City.[44] Putnam probably had written Trumbull already for militia to replace the Continentals sent to Washington,[45] but even after receipt of these dispatches from Parsons, expresses were not dispatched until the enemy appeared in the Hudson on the 2nd of October. Not a militiaman from Connecticut put in an appearance in time to help defend the forts. While this alleged tardiness caused some grumbling on the part of commanders,[46] it was much to the credit of Connecticut that 1200 militia, most of them mounted, reached the Hudson on the 7th.[47] The next day, Putnam was all optimism for the future. ". . . he is confident," George Clinton wrote, "that he soon will have 10,000 with him; in which case he will keep up posts as far as Poughkeepsie and Rynbeck to head the enemy, should they push up the river." [48]

Such is the evidence concerning the transfer of troops from Putnam to Washington and the responsibility of Washington, if any, for the loss of Forts Montgomery and Clinton. These five conclusions seem justified:

1. Washington probably was overcautious in recalling as many as 2500 men from the Hudson to Schuylkill after the Battle of Brandywine, though this seemed the natural thing to do when troops had been detached from Putnam to cope with a New Jersey invasion that proved to be merely a raid.

2. The Commander-in-Chief entirely misjudged the plans Sir Henry Clinton was making for the troops in New York.

3. Putnam probably did not intend to deceive Washington in dispatching McDougall with fewer than 1500 men, but Putnam's negligent record-keeping and the endless coming and going of short-term militia in his scattered command denied him, in all likelihood, the requisite knowledge of the number of troops actually available at a given time. The error was circumstantial, rather than deliberate, the expression of administrative incompetence and not of disobedience.

4. In the occupation of Dorchester Heights and in the campaign of Trenton and Princeton, Washington had employed militia precisely as he expected Putnam to do if an emergency developed on the Hudson after the 2500 Continentals were transferred to the front near Philadelphia. Where manpower nearly always was inadequate, the defence of a desperate cause made this use of militia unavoidable. Washington specifically directed Putnam to appeal to

---

[43] Parsons to Putnam; *ibid.*, 345.
[44] Parsons's testimony at Putnam court of inquiry; *McDougall Papers*, NYHS.
[45] *Ibid.*   [46] *Ibid.*
[47] *Ibid.*, but without any remark on the excellence of the accomplishment. Parsons, on the contrary, thought the men very slow.
[48] Clinton to the Legislature, Oct. 8, 1777; 2 *Papers of George Clinton*, 387.

Governor Trumbull for help, and doubtless the Commander-in-Chief remembered that in extreme cases the Colonels of Connecticut militia Regiments could call out their men without waiting for orders from the Governor
at Lebanon.[49] Putnam's orders from Washington thus were not impossible
of execution in normal conditions, nor, indeed, were they unusual.

5. It is not necessary, for present purposes, to attempt to say whether Putnam's failure on the day of battle was due to lack of troops or to tactical
blunder. He manifestly should have been able to fight better if he had been
able to employ the Continentals who had been sent away; but if he lost
the two forts solely because he did not have men enough to defend them,
these four circumstances have to be considered: First, the number of militia
who could be ordered to him was restricted by similar calls for temporary
troops to reenforce Gates in the final contest with Burgoyne; second, Putnam
yielded too readily to the men who wanted to go home for the fall sowing;
third, Putnam may not have concentrated wisely the detachments at his
various small outposts, though the lack of evidence on this subject must not
be regarded as necessarily adverse to him; fourth, he delayed in urging that
Connecticut militia be dispatched him in utmost haste. Had he sent for the
border Regiments forty-eight hours earlier, he would have had 1200 of these
men with him when the enemy landed. Insistence on the performance of
duty by the whole of the New York militia Regiments at his disposal would
not have assured him so large a reenforcement as he might have had from
Connecticut, but a disciplined policy would have given him considerably
more men than had been considered necessary, under good leadership, for
the successful defence of the forts and the Highland passes.

In summary, Washington made the wrong guess of the enemy's plans and
to that extent was to blame for what happened in the Highlands. The calls
he made on Putnam for men were not unusual and, in Washington's opinion, were not excessive, according to the best information he could get.
Tactics apart, Putnam erred in not calling sooner for help from Connecticut;
he may or may not have concentrated wisely at the points of danger;
he certainly showed himself dangerously indulgent of the militia.

[49] By the most direct route, Lebanon was more than 100 miles from Peekskill.

GENERAL BIBLIOGRAPHICAL NOTE

GENERAL BIBLIOGRAPHICAL NOTE

With few exceptions of no large importance, the source materials of the first fifteen chapters of Volume III of this work are those described in the bibliographical note printed on pages 413–21 of Volume II. For the period of Washington's service in the Continental Congress of 1774, and for the six and a half months between his return home, Oct. 20, 1774, and his departure for Philadelphia May 4, 1775, additional witnesses appear. After Washington became Commander-in-Chief, the historical testimony, which is described summarily in the Introduction to Vol. III, p. xxxi–xxxvi, increases vastly in bulk and in diversity. The present note merely elaborates what already has been said of materials that lend themselves to classification as (1) documents of official bodies, (2) diaries and letters, (3) contemporary newspapers and fugitive publications, (4) dispatches and reports on military affairs, and (5) miscellaneous contributions, deliberate or otherwise, to the record of the times.

Three of the indispensable publications, the *Journals of the Continental Congress*, Fitzpatrick's edition of *The Writings of George Washington,* and Burnett's *Letters of Members of the Continental Congress* are available in large editions, are printed on paper that will survive hundreds of years of use, and are a constant satisfaction. In most other works on those events of June, 1775–April, 1778, that relate directly to George Washington, a student meets with many pleasant surprises and with disappointments as numerous. Some modest memorials of men who were not of great eminence—the letters of Col. Leven Powell, for example— occasionally include material not found elsewhere. Side by side with these useful volumes may be books, ambitiously labelled, that are in nothing so notable as in their omissions. Perhaps the labor best rewarded for the investigator is that spent in turning, article by article, if not page by page, the publications of the various State governments and of certain State historical societies. Pennsylvania is in this respect almost a model. The full resources of the Pennsylvania Archives and of the Pennsylvania Magazine of History and Biography have by no means been exhausted, even yet, by scholars.

Among the early biographies of men of the Revolution, Austin's *Gerry,* Sparks' *Gouverneur Morris,* William B. Reed's *Joseph Reed* and G. W. Greene's *Nathanael Greene* are highly creditable works when one takes into account the small number of related collections of source material available to the authors. As for biographies of recent years, several volumes, and in particular, Louis Gottschalk's studies of Lafayette, are highly distinguished. Numerous *Lives* of revolutionary leaders meet essential requirements, but many gaps remain. The most serious of these is the lack of a comprehensive portrayal of Henry Knox who probably is regarded by most military writers as third only to Washington and to Greene among American soldiers of the Revolution.

Once again it has to be said that the greatest disappointment in the historical materials of the period is presented by the diaries. This is not because they are few—scores are listed in William Matthews' fine bibliography—but because most of those that do not run in narrow, personal channels soon disappear in the sands of dull days. Apparently a considerable number of junior officers and enlisted men resolved, when they entered the Army, to keep a record of their experiences.

Not many of them possessed the combination of resourcefulness and industry required for the task when ink was scarce and chill fingers weary. Those diarists who persevered to the end are among the benefactors of military history. Praise might be still higher if some of them, Surgeon James Thacher in particular, had not "touched up" long after the war their simple contemporary tale of marches and fasts and fights. For two campaigns, and two only, Arnold's Canadian expedition of 1775–76 and Sullivan's operations on the New York-Pennsylvania frontier in 1779, the diaries supply almost everything a student could ask. Kenneth Roberts' *March to Quebec* is one of the most remarkable and inclusive collections of soldiers' journals ever brought together concerning a single operation. Those on Sullivan's march are scarcely less diverse. Comprehensive diaries for the encampments, the marches and the battles of the main Army in 1777–78, simply do not exist in corresponding number. A writer consequently feels a deep gratitude to such a man as Deacon Nathan Beers, of whose diary Peter Force preserved what appears to be a full transcript. In like spirit, a student bids a mournful farewell to a chatty diarist when he reaches the last entry in some worthy's informative journal.

Newspapers of the years 1759–1778, it may be repeated, are invaluable on many phases of life in the Colonies and in the struggling young States, but they are of small assistance in writing the life of Washington for this period. Occasionally they show in what estimation he was held, and often they help to frame the background of his acts, but of the man himself during the Revolution they say little and that, more often than not, in an admiringly casual manner. Editors, like Congressmen, soon formed the habit of taking Washington for granted.

Maps have been discussed briefly in the Introduction to Volume III. For the military operations of 1775–77, chief reliance has to be on the British maps. By the time the consummation of the French alliance was announced, Robert Erskine's surveys for Washington were being extended and his maps were being improved. Many of his later drafts, now preserved in the New-York Historical Society, are entirely trustworthy. Of other materials on the movement of men and supplies, the most useful papers are the "Tables of Distances" found in some of the collections of manuscripts.

In summary, then, it may be said that when the long-needed revision of the history of the American Revolution is taken in hand by individual students and by the seminar of some American university, investigators will be relieved or distressed, as personal feeling may dictate, to discover how large a part of the general source material is in book form and is accessible in most of the great libraries of the country. This is true not only of legislative proceedings and related executive documents but also of the correspondence of leaders. Lacunae are encountered in the papers of nearly all the great revolutionaries but these are not numerour or serious for the years covered by these volumes. One may wish that Alexander Hamilton had left copies of more of his personal letters from army headquarters, precisely as one may regret that Joseph Reed and Alexander McDougall were not proficient in the art of condensation. These and kindred complaints apart, long handling of these sources never quite prepares one for the volume and variety of what one finds in print. To be sure, the files of libraries and of historical societies often include long lists of "unpublished manuscripts" but these seldom illuminate the career of Washington or the great story of the Revolution. Many reams of these papers, in fact, should be classified as relics, rather than as records. While a careful student will reject no manuscripts without examining them at least cursorily, he may be assured that so far as the present research has gone it has shown that the greater part of the unpublished material on Washington's career during 1775–77 is in his own papers, in those of the Continental Congress and in those of the nine persons mentioned on p. xxxiv of the Introduction to Volume III. These are Horatio Gates, Nathanael Greene, Henry Knox, Alexander McDougall, Joseph Reed, Joseph Trumbull, Jeremiah Wadsworth, Anthony Wayne and George Weedon.

The appended list was prepared, in large part, by Dr. Gertrude R. B. Richards, the author's principal research assistant, who has examined personally all the collections here cited. Four limitations have been set. First, manuscripts included in the Bibliographical Note, Vol. II, p. 413–21, and used also in Volumes III and IV, are not entered again unless—as in the Custis and the Washington Papers—documents not previously analyzed in this work are involved. Second, it has been thought convenient to the reader to defer the promised note on French sources (see Vol. II, p. 415) to the volume in which the active participation of the French in the American campaigns is described. Third, single documents, cited in the footnotes, with specific reference to the depositories, are not included here. Fourth, this list is not burdened with references to the manuscripts of revolutionaries, other than Washington himself, whose writings have been collected and edited by experienced scholars. This applies, for example, to Richard Henry Lee. Many of his papers are owned by the Virginia Historical Society, and even more are the property of the American Philosophical Society; but as James Custis Ballagh combed these and all other depositories, it has not seemed necessary, save in a few instances, to charge a student's memory with references to original documents that are available everywhere in trustworthy printed form. Finally, the names of some men are missing altogether—Thomas Mifflin's in particular—because no substantial store of their papers has been found outside the files of letters received by other persons.

PRINCIPAL MANUSCRIPT SOURCES

ADAMS, SAMUEL. See Bancroft Collection.

ADAMS, RICHARD and THOMAS. Papers. VHS. This small store of interesting mercantile and personal papers helps to explain the viewpoint of Virginia shippers during the preliminaries of the Revolution. Included are the amusing and despairing letters of George Mercer while in England, desperately in love and frantically embarrassed for money.

ALEXANDER, MAJ. GEN. WILLIAM. See Stirling, Lord.

ANONYMOUS NEW YORK DIARY, 1775–1776. LC. A very good account of the first appearance of the British fleet in New York harbor and of its progress up the Hudson.

ARMY RETURNS. Nat. Archives, etc. Army returns for 1775–76 frequently are summarized in *Force,* and, for those years and a somewhat later period, in *Sparks.* A number of returns not found in one or the other of these sources are in the Papers of George Washington or in 152 Papers of the Continental Congress, LC. Still others are in the National Archives; War Records Branch: War Department.

BALDWIN PAPERS. Har. Col. Lib. and Clements Lib. Loammi Baldwin was an intelligence officer during the first years of the war and later served as regimental commander until ill health forced his resignation. His papers in the Harvard College Library are of no small value for what they tell of enemy movements and of refugees. In his letters to his wife he gives a vital and human account of informal aspects of military life. A few of his reports, from the vicinity of Boston, are also in the Washington volumes of the Papers of the Continental Congress. Col. Loammi Baldwin is not to be confused with his cousin Jeduthan Baldwin, Colonel of Engineers and Colonel of the Artillery Artificer Regiment. Jeduthan Baldwin's *Military Journal, 1775–79* was published in a small edition (Bangor, Maine, 1906) and is quite rare.

BANCROFT COLLECTION. NYPL. The two hundred and more volumes in this collection are promiscuously assembled. Original letters, pages of printed volumes, parts of newspapers, and transcripts are saved from utter confusion by an excellent card index. Information is included on almost every aspect of American history, drawn from sources on either side of the Atlantic. Among the original papers which deal with the Revolution are letters to Samuel Adams from his more prominent contemporaries; papers of the Boston Committee of Correspondence, and various documents and narratives regarding the German troops serving in the British armies.

BEERS, NATHAN. Diary. LC. Deacon Beers' journal, covering the years of his service in Connecticut and along the Hudson, has disappeared. This Force transcript of seventy-eight pages bears evidence of being a faithful copy of an important document.

BOUCHER, JONATHAN. Journal. Lib. U. S. Naval Academy, Annapolis. This diary has been incorporated in *Reminiscences of an American Loyalist, 1758–80,* but it is listed here because the original MS shows the excision of eight folios that has aroused the curiosity of students. (See Vol. III, p. 286, n. 103.) The sheets are gone, completely gone.

CADWALLADER PAPERS. PHS. Although the Cadwallader Papers, taken as a whole, form one of the most important collections of the Pennsylvania Historical Society, there is little of importance in the meagre lot belonging to General John Cadwallader, compared with those of General Thomas Cadwallader. Nearly all the John Cadwallader papers have been published. Scattered letters in other revolutionary sources contain much more valuable material on John Cadwallader than the few in Philadelphia.

CLINTON, SIR HENRY. Papers. Clements Lib. Needless to say, the Papers of Gen. Sir Henry Clinton at Ann Arbor form one of the notable historical collections in America. For information concerning the British Army, they are unrivalled; for the life of Washington, their value is sporadic rather than constant. Intelligence reports from spies form one important contribution to any review of the general conditions of the American armies, because these documents usefully supplement the fragmentary reports by continental officers.

COMMISSARY DEPARTMENT. Papers. LC, PHS, CHS, Conn. State Lib. The Library of Congress has Commissary Gen. Ephraim Blaine's Papers, his Letter Books of 1777–78 and his accounts of 1777–83. In that depository are, also, the letters of Samuel Gray, 1776–80, and Force transcripts of the Papers of Charles Stewart, 1777–82, the originals of which are in CHS. Among the papers of Robert Morris, LC, are many that concern provisions and other commissary affairs. The following volumes of the Papers of the Continental Congress contain commissary manuscripts:

XXIX: Reports of Committees
CXXXVII: Morris, Robert: Letters
CXXXIX: Revolutionary accounts
CXLVII: Board of War Papers: Commissary

In PHS are the Chaloner and White Papers, the Morris-Hollingsworth Correspondence and the Papers of Levi and Henry Hollingworth. Joseph Trumbull's Papers and those of Jeremiah Wadsworth are separately reviewed under their respective names.

CONTINENTAL CONGRESS. Papers. LC. The correspondence, reports, journals and documents in this collection make it rank with the Papers of Washington in their importance as a superlative source for the progress of the war. Of particular value are:

Vol. I: Original Journal of Continental Congress, 1774–1789. 39 v. (Vol. 15, Mch. 19–May 2, 1778, missing)
III: Secret domestic Journal of Congress, 1775–1787
XIII: Official Letterbooks of Henry Laurens. 2 v.
XV: Letters of Samuel Huntington, 1778–1780
LI: Intercepted letters from Loyalists, 1775–1781
LXXVIII: Letters to the Presidents of Congress, 1775–1779. 24 v. arranged chronologically
CLII: Letters of Washington, 1775–1781. These include many important letters addressed to Washington.
CLIII: Letters from Philip Schuyler to Congress, 1775–83. 3 v.
CLIV: Letters of Gates, 1776–1782. 2 v. which duplicate the letters in the NYHS. The whole supplements that larger collection.
CLV: Letters of Nathanael Greene, 1776–1782. 3 v.
CLVI: Letters of Lafayette and of du Coudray, 1777–78. This volume includes letters from other French officers in the American service.
CLIX: Letters of I. Putnam, Hugh Mercer . . . and Weedon
CLXI: Letters of Thomas Mifflin, A. McDougall . . .
CLXII: Letters of B. Arnold, Adam Stephen . . . and Stirling
CLXIV: Letters of Pulaski, von Steuben, DeKalb, Du Portail . . . and Comte d'Estaing
CLXXII: Letters of Nathanael Greene with papers relative to the QM's Department, 1777–1784. Included are several Joseph Trumbull letters.

CUSTIS, DANIEL PARKE. Estate Papers. VHS, Washington and Lee Univ., LC. A note on the Custis Papers appeared in Vol. II, p. 417. For the period 1759–1777, the only necessary bibliographical addendum is that the two badly damaged Custis Account Books in VHS have been restored and now are usable, though not completely legible. Some odd sheets of Custis accounts of widely varying dates are in the Treasurer's Office of Washington and Lee University.

DEARBORN, DR. F. M. Collection. Private hands, New York City. This is fundamentally a collection of autographs, but it includes: (1) the originals of the *Correspondence de Casimir Pulaski avec Claude de Rulhière, 1774–78*, edited by François Pulaski, (2) sixteen important letters of Nathanael Greene, chiefly to Henry Lee, June 25–Sept. 25, 1781, and (3) the review of the proposed system of espionage in New York, reproduced as Appendix IV-2.

DISMAL SWAMP COMPANY. Minutes and Papers. LC and Duke Univ. Lib. These papers include some of the minutes, financial accounts and miscellaneous records of a company in which Washington invested more hopefully than profitably.

DREER COLLECTION. PHS. Over 40,000 manuscripts, collected for their autographs rather than for their contents. This collection has occasional papers of interest, often of value. Perhaps the most interesting single item, bibliographically, is the extant part of the manuscript of Marshall's *Washington,* vols. 4 and 5. The earlier sections were burned when the publishing house was destroyed in 1804.

DUANE, JAMES. Papers. NYHS. The papers and letters of James Duane cover the years 1767–1795. They relate, for the most part, to family matters, to his development of Duanesboro, and to his relations with the Indians. A few only have any bearing on the Revolution. Such letters usually are duplicated in the Papers of Continental Congress and in the files of the individuals to whom they are addressed. There are several gaps in the correspondence between May, 1776, and March, 1778.

DUNMORE, LORD. Miscellaneous Papers. LC, College of William and Mary, etc. Scattered papers of Lord Dunmore, chiefly transcripts of P.R.O., C.O. 5: 1355, are in the Library of Congress. William and Mary has several Washington letters to Dunmore, all of which have been printed. A collection of Dunmore's letters and dispatches would make an interesting volume.

EMMET COLLECTION. NYPL. Dr. Thomas Addis Emmet's treasury includes over 10,000 autograph letters from practically every distinguished soldier or civil official of the Revolutionary period. The more important of these have been printed, but in the minor papers may be found odd items of interest.

FAIRFAX FAMILY. Papers. Huntington Lib. This omnium gatherum of the Fairfax family, running to hundreds of items, includes survey warrants and grants, rent rolls, bills of sale, lists of voters, etc., from 1721 to 1799. In the collection are a number of surveys signed by Washington while he was working as a young engineer for Lord Fairfax.

FEBIGER, CHRISTIAN. Papers. In private hands. The papers, orderly books and correspondence of Christian Febiger. VSL has microfilms of the originals owned by William S. Febiger, Boston. Included is an informative letter on the action at Stony Point, quoted in Vol. V.

FORD, ALLYN K. Collection. In private hands, Minneapolis. A large and interesting store of autographs, particularly rich in documents relating to the Virginia campaign of 1781.

GATES, HORATIO. Papers of. NYHS. This important collection includes over thirty boxes of letters and public papers covering the years 1750–1803. As few of these have been published, they constitute one of the outstanding sources of new material on the conduct of the Revolution, especially Gates' correspondence with his fellow officers during critical periods of the war. The letters to Gates are cited in the present work as *Letters to Gates;* those from him, *Gates Papers.*

GLYN JOURNAL. Princeton Univ. Lib. A manuscript Journal in the field, 1776–

1777 (55 p.), kept by a British Ensign, Thomas Glyn. Included is a description of the Battle of Princeton. In the Journal are reproduced many of the General Orders of William Howe, missing from *Kemble*.

GREENE, NATHANAEL. Papers. Clements Lib. This is the largest single collection of Greene Papers. It consists of seventy volumes and covers the entire period of Greene's life. The most interesting letters are those written to his fellow officers and to his aides; the most important are those relating to his campaigns in the Southern Department, 1780–81.

HONEYMAN, DR. ROBERT. Diary. LC. This remarkably accurate account of events during the entire period of the Revolution was kept by Dr. Honeyman, in Hanover County, Virginia. Distance did not prevent his getting information from a wide variety of sources. While he notes whatever he hears, he is careful to comment on the accuracy of his news and to check it by later intelligence.

HUNTER, ANDREW. Diaries. Princeton Univ. Lib. Hunter was Chaplain of the Third New Jersey Regiment during the greater part of the New York–Jersey campaign of 1776, and he served also during Sullivan's expedition of 1778. Although extracts from the Diaries have been printed, they contain much useful, unpublished material.

KNOX, HENRY. Papers. MHS. Along with many unique military papers, this highly valuable correspondence of Gen. Henry Knox includes letters to Mrs. Knox, to his brother William, to Henry Jackson of Boston, and to fellow officers. For the period covered by Vols. III and IV of this work, these Knox Papers are certainly among the half-dozen most important collections that deal with the career of Washington as a soldier.

LAMB, JOHN. Papers. NYPL. A small collection, chronologically arranged, of miscellaneous papers more interesting for their association with a picturesque artillerist than for their connection with Washington.

LIVINGSTON, R. R. Letters. NYPL. These letters from the elder Robert Livingston to his sons belong to the opening years of the Revolution and deal with the Northern Department and with affairs in New York. They are bound separately from the miscellaneous materials in the Bancroft Collection.

McDOUGALL, ALEXANDER. Papers. NYHS. The four thousand and more papers in this collection form a highly valuable and diversified source for Revolutionary history. Included are many reports, army returns, courtmartial records and other military material. McDougall's letters are detailed, and disclose much of the strategical argument that preceded or attended some of the campaigns.

MERCER, GEORGE. See Adams, Thomas.

MOFFATT, DR. THOMAS. Diary. LC. Dr. Thomas Moffatt, a physician, served as Comptroller of His Majesty's Customs, New London, Conn., from July, 1775, to October, 1777. Later he went to London to confer with Lord North. This diary records the events of that trip and also the position and state of the fleet before New York.

MOUNT VERNON PAPERS. Miscellaneous. Manuscripts and printed items are being added constantly to the records accumulated by the Mount Vernon Ladies Association. While the more important letters donated in recent years deal with Washington and his home subsequent to the Revolution, all students of Washington's career should examine the annual reports of the

Association and, if possible, should visit Mount Vernon often to examine the accessions. The Edward Ambler Armstrong Collection, purchased in 1947, is a notable supplement to treasures that include the Powel and Thom Papers.

NELSON, WILLIAM, AND SONS. Letter Book. VSL. This Letter Book, covering 1760–1772, contains a part of William Nelson's correspondence to his death in 1772. It deals primarily with business but it has many references to public affairs in Virginia and a few to occurrences in other Colonies. Nelson's heirs, Hugh and Thomas, used the Letter Book for approximately two years after the demise of their father. Some of the letters include the only known references to some of the later phases of the Dunbar case.

ORDERLY BOOKS. BPL, PHS, NYHS, LC, etc. Nearly all the large depositories of revolutionary material contain some orderly books for commands that range, in different libraries, from Companies to field Divisions. These often are of importance for operations by particular forces but, since the publication of virtually all of Washington's GO's in Fitzpatrick's edition of the *Writings*, the orderly books of small organizations seldom are of use in his biography. Among the most comprehensive and best preserved orderly books are those of Brig. Gen. John Glover in the Essex Institute and those of Lt. Col. Thomas Grosvenor in BPL. The collection of similar books in NYHS and that in PHS is opulent.

REED, JOSEPH. Papers. NYHS. William Bradford Reed's life of Joseph Reed contains many of the letters now in the twelve volumes of Reed Papers. They cover the period 1750–1784. Perhaps half of the papers have no particular value for the biography of Washington, dealing as they do with Reed's personal affairs, with the years when he was President of the Supreme Executive Council of Philadelphia, and his post-war years in Europe; but the other half of the collection, so to speak, has much that is usable. This is especially true of the incoming letters.

SCHUYLER, PHILIP. Papers. NYPL. The Schuyler Papers include letters to Gen. Philip Schuyler from military officers, members of the Continental Congress and private individuals, and deal for the most part with the war in the Northern Department, 1775–1777. Schuyler's Letter Book contains copies of letters and instructions from General Washington and Congress, 1775–1778. In the orderly books are copies of letters from General Schuyler to his aides, as well as GO's of 1776–1777.

SMITH, L. W. Collected Papers. In private hands, Madison, N. J. This remarkable collection, described in Vol. II, p. 414, is even richer for the revolutionary period than for the earlier years of Washington's life. Many of its pamphlets and other fugitive publications are almost unique.

SMITH, WILLIAM. Diaries. NYPL. The eleven volumes of William Smith's Diaries, as yet unpublished, are perhaps the most comprehensive memoir of the period 1753–1783. At times Smith devoted himself so entirely to his own affairs and personal problems, that months pass with no entry of importance. Then will come passage after passage of comment, intelligence and records of conversations held with military leaders, that are of unique value. He was a Tory but he had patriot associations. Consequently he has as much to set down of public opinion concerning Washington as he had to write of Sir Henry Clinton.

STEPHEN, ADAM. Papers. LC. The greater part of the letters by and to Gen. Adam Stephen have been transferred to the Papers of the Continental Congress; the hundred and more found here deal with his private affairs. Occasionally they give details of importance not in the more formal correspondence. See also Vol. II, p. 419.

STEUBEN, FRIEDRICH VON. Papers. NYHS. This rich major collection of the papers of the Inspector General contains much on the Revolution in general, but "the Baron's" vigorous letters to the Commander-in-Chief are perhaps more readily accessible to the average student in the Washington Papers, LC. Most of the other large stores of personal papers contain some by Steuben. A careful selection from these would make a most interesting and an almost continuous narrative of the later years of the Revolution as seen through the eyes of a professional soldier.

STIRLING, LORD. Papers. NYPL, and LC. Those Stirling Papers in NYPL cover 1750–83 and relate primarily to the development of his estate at Baskinridge, N. J., and to the iron works nearby. The revolutionary material includes a number of returns and a few letters, none of them as important as those which may be found in the correspondence of his contemporaries and in the Papers of the Continental Congress. As for the Stirling Papers in the Force Transcripts, LC, the originals of most of these are found in other collections, but some are copies of documents that no longer exist. They are for the most part letters addressed to Lord Stirling and they deal principally with the state of troops in New Jersey. In reviewing Stirling's correspondence, it may be worth a student's time to check the list in 7 *NJHSP* (1) p. 138. Many of his letters are lost altogether.

THOMAS, JOHN. Papers. MHS. The brevity of General Thomas' military career is evidenced by the small number of papers belonging to his years of service. Several of them are of outstanding importance, especially those addressed to his wife. Few of his letters are to be found in other collections of revolutionary correspondence.

TOMLINSON COLLECTION. (Disposition Unknown) Originally in the Mercantile Library of the City of New York, these papers were deposited for many years in the New York Public Library. In 1947 they were removed and offered for sale. So far as is known, no record of purchasers was kept; the whereabouts of the individual papers is a matter of speculation. Some of them were printed in the Parke-Bernet catalogue for 1947. Others were used in a volume edited by Henry B. Dawson, *New York City During the Revolution* (New York, 1861).

TRUMBULL, JOSEPH. Papers. CHS, Conn. State Lib., Yale Univ. Lib., LC. In the Connecticut Historical Society and the Connecticut State Library, are boxes of loose papers belonging to the time when Trumbull was Commissary General. The Connecticut State Library has, in addition, several bound volumes formerly in the possession of the Massachusetts Historical Society. The few Joseph Trumbull Papers in the Library of Congress, and two or three at Yale, give official information but throw little light on the personal aspects of his service and of his relations with Washington.

VIRGINIA, COLONY OF. County Records. The note in Vol. II, p. 419, applies to the records of certain Virginia Counties for the fifteen years preceding the Revolution. As concerns Washington, much the most important are the

Order Books of Fairfax County, which contained numerous references to his affairs, especially in 1772–74.

VIRGINIA, COLONY OF. Council, Executive Journal. Additional extracts from lost Journals of the Council of Virginia are being found at intervals in the British Public Record Office, but as yet (1951) they do not include sufficient items to add a sixth volume to those that have been printed.

WADSWORTH, JEREMIAH. Papers. CHS, Conn. State Lib. The Connecticut Historical Society's collection of the papers of Jeremiah Wadsworth consists of sixteen boxes of loose correspondence, three of accounts, miscellaneous papers, bills and account books that cover his years as Deputy Commissary, Commissary General and Commissary for the French troops. The papers in the Connecticut State Library include his correspondence from 1775–1798.

WARD, ARTEMAS. Papers. MHS. Most of the papers of the General who commanded in front of Boston before the arrival of Washington in July, 1775, have been lost or scattered. Those that remain in the Massachusetts Historical Society are pathetic memorials of limited historical value.

WARREN, MERCY. Papers. MHS. These papers include some of the letters of the able woman who is represented by many communications in the Warren-Adams Letters. The remainder are quoted a few times but those still unpublished are of small bearing on the career of Washington.

WASHINGTON, GEORGE. Papers. LC. Five hundred and more volumes of original papers of Washington in this collection are classified according to material: letters, diaries, account books, etc. Each group is arranged chronologically. To supplement the originals are the Varick Transcripts, 44 volumes, begun under Washington's direction in 1781. As many of the original letters were destroyed in a warehouse fire in Alexandria, Varick's volumes often take the place of lost originals. The papers begin with Washington's exercise books, kept during his early childhood, and continue through the whole of his career. Much of this material has been published; practically all of it has been calendared; the description in 1 *G.W.*, explains the history and, for the purposes of this work, the unapproachable value of this collection. Scores of other depositories include one or more Washington letters among their treasures, but all these were searched for Fitzpatrick's edition of the *Writings*. Some of the two-way Washington correspondence—as, for example, that with Alexander McDougall (Huntington Lib.)—is of importance.

WASHINGTON, GEORGE. Pocket Day Books. LC and Huntington Lib. These are as follows:

391 Papers of G. W. (LC), Pocket Day Book: Aug. 9, 1772–May 27, 1773. A small leather covered note book with jottings of all moneys spent or received or promised, for the period covered. These were later transferred to Ledger B.

394 Papers of G. W. (LC), Pocket Day Book: May 29, 1773–Mch. 22, 1774. Similar in every way to 391.

395 Papers of G. W. (LC), Pocket Day Book: Oct. 26, 1774–May 3, 1775. Similar in every way to 391 and 394.

396 Papers of G. W. (LC), Pocket Day Book, May 3, 1775–Jan. 7, 1776, and from Sept. 20, 1783, to Dec. 2, 1784. Similar in format to 391, 394 and 395. For 1775–76, there is only a page of entries, all of which are copied in the facsimile of Washington's army accounts.

Besides these, Washington's Pocket Day Book Mch. 25–Oct. 4, 1774, is in the Huntington Library.

WAYNE, ANTHONY. Papers. PHS. Practically all the surviving papers of General Anthony Wayne are in the Pennsylvania Historical Society—forty-seven volumes of correspondence with army and civil leaders; three volumes of courtmartial proceedings, three of military records and eighteen orderly books for 1781. Some of the more important letters of this superb storehouse were used in Stillé's *Major General Anthony Wayne and the Pennsylvania Line in the Continental Army.*

WEEDON, GEORGE. Papers. Chicago HS, Am. Phil. Soc. The score and a half Weedon letters in the Chicago Historical Society are, with three exceptions, all concerned with the campaigns of 1777 and are of very high value. The collection in the American Philosophical Society is inclusive but relates primarily to matters of military administration. These two files of the Papers of Weedon, who was a good correspondent, are supplemented by occasional odd letters in other collections, particularly (1) the Gates Papers for the Southern campaign, and (2) the Allyn K. Ford autographs.

SHORT-TITLE INDEX

SHORT-TITLE INDEX

The appended Short-Title Index includes those manuscripts, serial publications and separate printed works cited frequently in Volumes III and IV and not always sufficiently identified by the titles used in the footnotes. Books mentioned once only, or at long intervals in the text, are not listed here. Works cited in previous volumes and used again in Volumes III and IV are included. Other short titles for years prior to 1759 are eliminated. All references are to the first letters of the short titles. For example, *Adam Stephen* is under *Adam,* not under *Stephen.* As a further device for quick reference, quotation marks are not used for manuscript collections or for serial publications still current. Quotation marks are employed for completed serial publications, as well as for individual works, regardless of the number of volumes. Further details of the principal manuscript collections in this Short-Title Index will be found in the Bibliographical Note on the Principal Manuscript Sources.

AASP. Proceedings of the American Antiquarian Society.
Abbott, New York in the Revolution. WILBUR C. ABBOTT. "New York in the American Revolution."
Abernethy. T. P. ABERNETHY. "Western Lands and the American Revolution."
Adam Stephen Papers. Papers of Maj. Gen. Adam Stephen. LC.
Adams, Fam. Let. CHARLES FRANCIS ADAMS, ed. "Familiar Letters of John Adams and his Wife Abigail . . ."
A. Hamilton. H. C. LODGE, ed. "The Works of Alexander Hamilton." 12 v.
A.H.R. American Historical Review.
Alexander Papers. Papers of the Alexander (Lord Stirling) Family. NYPL.
Andrew Hunter Diary. Diary of Andrew Hunter. Princeton Univ. Lib.
Anon. Proc. Howe. "Journal of the Proceedings of the Army under . . . Sir William Howe," *AASP.,* April, 1930.
A. Robertson's Diaries. H. M. LYDENBERG, ed. "Archibald Robertson . . . His Diaries and Sketches, 1762–1780."
Asher Holmes. Letter on the Battle of Germantown, *NJHSP.,* 1922–23, p. 34–35.
Austin's Gerry. J. T. AUSTIN. "Life of Elbridge Gerry." 2 v.
Baldwin Papers. Papers of Col. Loammi Baldwin. Harvard Univ. Lib.
Ballagh, Lee Letters. J. C. BALLAGH, ed. "The Letters of Richard Henry Lee." 2 v.
Barker's Diary. ELIZABETH E. DANA, ed. "The British in Boston. Being the Diary of Lieutenant John Barker . . ."
Bigelow's Franklin. JOHN BIGELOW, ed. "The Works of Benjamin Franklin." 12 v.
Birch Cat. 663. "Catalogue (No. 663) of the Final Sale of the Relics of General Washington, Compiled for Thomas Birch by S. V. Henkels."
Blanton. W. B. BLANTON. "Medicine in Virginia in the Eighteenth Century."
Bolton. C. K. BOLTON. "The Private Soldier under Washington."
Boudinot. See ELIAS BOUDINOT.

Brydon, Mother Church. G. MacL. BRYDON. "Virginia's Mother Church . . ."
Burnaby. ANDREW BURNABY. "Travel Through the Middle States."
Burk. JOHN DALY BURK. "History of Virginia." 3 v.
Burnett. E. C. BURNETT. "Letters of Members of the Continental Congress."
  8 v.
Cadwalader Papers. Papers of Brig. Gen. John Cadwalader. PHS.
Campbell, History of Virginia. CHARLES CAMPBELL. "History of the Colony
  and Ancient Dominion of Virginia."
Carter, Letters to a Friend. WILLIAM CARTER. "A Genuine Detail of the Sev-
  eral Engagements . . . in . . . Letters to a Friend."
Chinard. GILBERT CHINARD. "George Washington as the French Knew Him."
Clap's Diary. CALEB CLAP. "Diary of Ensign . . ." in "Hist. Mag.," 3rd ser.,
  v. 3.
CHS. Cols. Connecticut Historical Society Collections.
Clinton Papers. Papers of Gen. Sir Henry Clinton, Clements Library.
C. Marshall's Diary. WILLIAM DUANE, ed. "Extracts from the Diary of Chris-
  topher Marshall."
Col. Docs. N.Y. "Documents Relating to the Colonial History of New York."
  11 v.
Conway's Barons. MONCURE D. CONWAY. "Barons of the Potomac and Rappa-
  hannock."
Cresswell. [SAMUEL THORNELY, ed.] "Journal of Nicholas Cresswell, 1774-77."
Custis Papers. Papers of the Custis Family. VHS.
DAB. Dictionary of American Biography.
Deane Papers. "The Silas Deane Papers," NYHS. Collections, 1886 *et post.* 5 v.
Diaries. JOHN C. FITZPATRICK, ed. "The Dairies of George Washington." 4 v.
Dreer Collection. Dreer Collection of Autograph Letters, etc. PHS.
Eben. Huntington's Letters. [C. F. HEARTMAN, compiler]. "Letters Written by
  Ebenezer Huntington during the American Revolution."
E.J. H. R. MCILWAINE and (later) W. L. HALL, ed. "The Executive Journals
  of the Council of Colonial Virginia." 5 v.
Elias Boudinot. ELIAS BOUDINOT. "Journal or Historical Recollections . . ."
Emmet Collection. Manuscript Collection of Thomas A. Emmet. NYPL.
First Weedon Germantown Letter. George Weedon to John Page, Oct. 5, 1777.
  Chicago HS. MSS.
Fithian. PHILIP V. FITHIAN. "Journal, 1775-1776."
Force. PETER FORCE. "American Archives." Fourth Series, 5 v; Fifth Series,
  3 v.
Ford. WORTHINGTON C. FORD, ed. "The Writings of George Washington."
  14 v.
French's First Year. ALLEN FRENCH. "The First Year of the American Revolu-
  tion."
French Visitor's Diary. [ANON.] "Journal of a French Traveller in the Colonies,
  1765." 26 and 27 *A.H.R.*
Frothingham's Siege. RICHARD FROTHINGHAM. "History of the Siege of Boston."
Gage. C. F. CARTER, ed. "The Correspondence of General Gage with the Secre-
  taries of State, 1763-1775." 2 v.
Gates Papers. Papers of Maj. Gen. Horatio Gates. NYHS.
George Ewing's Journal. THOMAS EWING, ed. "George Ewing, Gentleman, a
  Soldier of Valley Forge."

George Washington Atlas. LAWRENCE MARTIN, ed. "The George Washington Atlas."

Gipson. LAWRENCE H. GIPSON. "The British Empire before the American Revolution." 7 v. to date.

Glyn Journal. Journal and Orderly Book of Thomas Glyn, April, 1776–August, 1777. Princeton Univ. Lib.

Godfrey. CARLOS E. GODFREY. "The Commander-in-Chief's Guard, Revolutionary War."

Gordon. WILLIAM GORDON. "History of the Rise, Progress and Establishment of the Independence of the United States of America." 4 v.

Graydon. LITTELL, J. S., ed. "Memoirs of His Own Time by Alexander Graydon."

Greene Papers. Papers of Maj. Gen. Nathanael Greene. Clements Lib.

Greene's Greene. G. W. GREENE. "The Life of Nathanael Greene." 3 v.

G. W. JOHN C. FITZPATRICK, ed. "The Writings of George Washington . . ." 39 v.

G. W. P. Custis. GEORGE WASHINGTON PARKE CUSTIS. "Recollections and Private Memoirs of Washington."

G. W. Rev. Accts. PETER FORCE, ed. "Monuments of Washington's Patriotism: Containing a Facsimile of his Public Accounts Kept during the Revolutionary War."

H. W. W. HENING, ed. "[Virginia] Statutes at Large." 13 v.

Hall's Parsons. CHARLES S. HALL. "Life and Letters of Samuel Holden Parsons."

Hamilton. S. M. HAMILTON, ed. "Letters to Washington, 1755–1775." 5 v.

Hayden. HORACE E. HAYDEN. "Virginia Genealogies."

Heath. R. R. WILSON, ed. "[William] Heath's Memoirs of the American War."

Heitman. F. B. HEITMAN. "Historical Register of Officers of the Continental Army during the War of the Revolution" (ed. 1914).

Henry Lee. HENRY LEE. "Memoirs of War in the Southern Department" (ed. 1869).

Howe's Narrative. LT. GEN. SIR WILLIAM HOWE. "The Narrative of . . . in a Committee of the House of Commons, on the 29th of April, 1779 . . . to which Are Added Some Observations upon a Pamphlet entitled, Letters to a Nobleman . . ."

Howe's Observations. See next preceding title. The "Observations" are p. 35–110 of the "Narrative."

Hughes. RUPERT HUGHES. "George Washington" 3 v. (Ends with the Victory at Yorktown).

JCC. WORTHINGTON C. FORD [and his successors, eds.] "Journals of the Continental Congress," 34 v.

Jefferson. A. E. BERGH, man. ed. "The Writings of Thomas Jefferson." 20 v. (Soon to be superseded completely by JULIAN P. BOYD, ed. "The Papers of Thomas Jefferson.")

John Adams. CHARLES FRANCIS ADAMS, ed. "The Life and Works of John Adams." 10 v.

John Howland. E. M. STONE. "Life and Recollections of John Howland."

John Jay. H. P. JOHNSTON, ed. "The Correspondence and Public Papers of John Jay . . ." 4 v.

John Laurens. W. G. SIMMS. "The Army Correspondence of Col. John Laurens in the Year 1777–78, with a Memoir . . ."

Mrs. Richard Montgomery's Notes. LOUISA L. HUNT, ed. "Biographical Notes Concerning General Richard Montgomery."

N. H. Prov. Rec. "New Hampshire Provincial Records." 38 v.

N. J. Col. Rec. "New Jersey Colonial Records." 10 v.

NJHSP. New Jersey Historical Society Proceedings. 69 v.

Papers Cont. Cong. Papers of the Continental Congress. LC.

Papers of George Clinton. [HUGH HASTINGS, ed.] "Public Papers of George Clinton." 10 v.

Papers of G. W. Papers of George Washington. LC.

Penn. Arc. "Pennsylvania Archives." Nine series.

Percy Letters. C. K. BOLTON, ed. "Letters of Hugh Early Percy from Boston and New York, 1774–1776."

Pickering. O. PICKERING and C. W. UPHAM. "Life of Timothy Pickering." 4 v.

Pickering's Letter. TIMOTHY PICKERING, Aug. 23, 1826, in *North American Review,* v. 23, p. 425–30.

Pitt. GERTRUDE S. KIMBALL, ed. "William Pitt, Lord Chatham, Correspondence." 2 v.

Pontgibaud. R. B. DOUGLAS, trans. and ed. "Charles Albert, Comte de More, Chevalier de Pontgibaud."

Pubs. RIHS. Publications of the Rhode Island Historical Society.

Reed. WILLIAM B. REED. "Life and Correspondence of Joseph Reed." 2 v.

Returns of Army. Returns of the Revolutionary Army, National Archives.

R. Hist. MSS. Comm. Royal Historical Commission Reports.

Rowland, Carroll. KATE MASON ROWLAND. "Life and Correspondence of Charles Carroll of Carrollton." 2 v.

Rowland, Mason. KATE MASON ROWLAND. "The Life of George Mason." 2 v.

R. R. Livingston MSS. Manuscripts of R. R. Livingston. NYPL.

Samuel Adams. H. A. CUSHING, ed. "The Writings of Samuel Adams." 4 v.

Samuel Haws's Diary. Diary of Samuel Haws in "The Military Journals of Two Private Soldiers, 1758–1775."

Samuel Shaw. See "Memoir of Samuel Shaw."

Schuyler Papers. Papers of Philip Schuyler. NYPL.

Second Weedon Germantown Letter. George Weedon to unnamed correspondent, Oct. 8, 1777. Chicago HS. MSS.

Serle. EDWARD H. TATUM, ed. "The American Journal of Ambrose Serle."

Smyth. J. F. D. SMYTH. "A Tour in the United States of America."

Smyth's Franklin. A. H. SMYTH, ed. "The Writings of Benjamin Franklin." 10 v.

Snowden, Historic Landmarks. W. H. SNOWDEN. "Some Historic Landmarks of Virginia and Maryland."

Solomon Nash's Diary. C. I. BUSHNELL, ed. "Journal of Solomon Nash."

Sparks. JARED SPARKS, ed. "The Writings of George Washington." 10 v.

Sparks Papers. Papers of Jared Sparks. Harvard Univ. Lib.

Sparks's Morris. JARED SPARKS. "The Life of Gouverneur Morris." 3 v.

St. Clair Papers. W. H. SMITH, ed. "The St. Clair Papers. The Life and Public Services of Arthur St. Clair." 2 v.

Stevens Facsimiles. B. F. STEVENS, ed. "Facsimiles of Manuscripts in European Archives relating to America, 1773–1783." 24 portfolios.

Stiles's Lit. Diary. EZRA STILES. "Literary Diary." 3 v.

Stobo. [ANON.] "Memoirs of Major Robert Stobo."

Stokes, Iconography. I. N. P. STOKES. "The Iconography of Manhattan Island." 6 v.

Stryker. WILLIAM S. STRYKER. "The Battles of Trenton and Princeton."

Stryker-Myers, Monmouth. WILLIAM STARR MYERS, ed. W. S. STRYKER, "The Battle of Monmouth."

Sullivan Papers. OTIS G. HAMMOND, ed. "Letters and Papers of Major-General John Sullivan, Continental Army." 3 v.

Swem. E. G. SWEM, ed. "Virginia Historical Index." 2 v.

Tench Tilghman. SAMUEL ALEXANDER HARRISON, compiler. "Memoir of Lt. Col. Tench Tilghman."

Thacher. JAMES THACHER. "Military Journal of the American Revolution."

Thom Collection. The Thom MSS. Mount Vernon, Virginia.

Thomas MSS. Papers of Maj. Gen. John Thomas. MHS.

Tomlinson MSS. The Tomlinson Papers. NYPL.

V. Virginia Magazine of History and Biography. 55 v.

Va. Land Grants. FAIRFAX HARRISON. "Virginia Land Grants."

W. William and Mary Quarterly. Three series.

Wadsworth Papers. Papers of Jeremiah Wadsworth. Conn. SL.

Ward Papers. Papers of Maj. Gen. Artemas Ward. MHS.

Warren-Adams Letters. "Warren-Adams Letters, Being Chiefly a Correspondence among John Adams, Samuel Adams and James Warren." 2 v.

Washington Papers, Huntington Lib. Papers of George Washington. Huntington Lib.

Wayne Papers. Papers of Maj. Gen. Anthony Wayne. PHS.

Webb. WORTHINGTON C. FORD, ed. "Correspondence and Journals of Samuel Blachley Webb." 2 v.

Weedon Letter. Letter of George Weedon to John Page, Sept. 11, 1777. Chicago HS. MSS.

Weedon Papers. Papers of Brig. Gen. George Weedon. American Phil. Soc. and Chicago HS.

Wertenbaker. T. J. WERTENBAKER. "The Battle of Princeton" in "The Princeton Battle Monument."

Wharton. FRANCIS WHARTON. "The Revolutionary Diplomatic Correspondence of the United States." 6 v.

Wilkinson. JAMES WILKINSON. "Memoirs of My Own Times." 3 v.

Willard. MARGARET WHEELER WILLARD. "Letters on the American Revolution, 1774–76."

William Smith Diary. MS. Diary of William Smith. NYPL.

W. S. Baker. W. S. BAKER. "Itinerary of General Washington, 1775–1787."

W. W. Henry. W. W. HENRY. "Patrick Henry, Life Correspondence and Speeches." 3 v.

INDEX

INDEX

Compiled by Bernice Kenyon Gilkyson